Lecture Notes in Artificial Intelligence 2718
Edited by J. G. Carbonell and J. Siekmann

Subseries of Lecture Notes in Computer Science

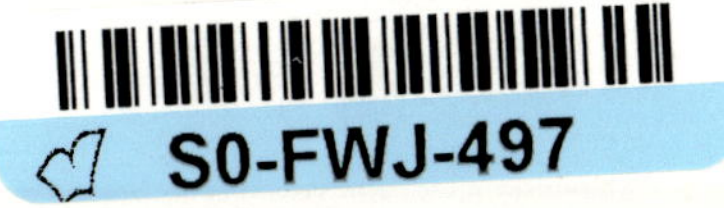

Springer
*Berlin*
*Heidelberg*
*New York*
*Hong Kong*
*London*
*Milan*
*Paris*
*Tokyo*

Paul W. H. Chung   Chris Hinde
Moonis Ali (Eds.)

# Developments in Applied Artificial Intelligence

16th International Conference on
Industrial and Engineering Applications of
Artificial Intelligence and Expert Systems, IEA/AIE 2003
Loughborough, UK, June 23-26, 2003
Proceedings

Series Editors

Jaime G. Carbonell, Carnegie Mellon University, Pittsburgh, PA, USA
Jörg Siekmann, University of Saarland, Saarbrücken, Germany

Volume Editors

Paul W. H. Chung
Chris Hinde
Loughborough University, Dept. of Computer Science
Loughborough, LE11 3TU, England
E-mail: {p.w.h.chung/C.J.Hinde}@lboro.ac.uk

Moonis Ali
Southwest Texas State University, Dept. of Computer Science
601 University Drive, San Marcos, TX 78666, USA

Cataloging-in-Publication Data applied for

A catalog record for this book is available from the Library of Congress.

Bibliographic information published by Die Deutsche Bibliothek.
Die Deutsche Bibliothek lists this publication in the Deutsche Nationalbibliografie; detailed bibliographic data is available in the Internet at <http://dnb.ddb.de>.

CR Subject Classification (1998): I.2, F.1, F.2, I.5, F.4.1, D.2

ISSN 0302-9743
ISBN 3-540-40455-4 Springer-Verlag Berlin Heidelberg New York



Springer-Verlag Berlin Heidelberg New York,
a member of BertelsmannSpringer Science+Business Media GmbH

http://www.springer.de


Printed in Germany

Typesetting: Camera-ready by author, data conversion by Steingräber Satztechnik GmbH
Printed on acid-free paper SPIN: 10928929 06/3142 5 4 3 2 1 0

# Preface

The Recent focus on developing and applying intelligent systems to real-world applications is the theme of the papers presented in this volume. Papers in soft computing cover modeling of noisy data in industrial processes, network applications, inter-city traffic, predictions, fuzzy cognitive mapping, damage assessment, and diagnosis. Knowledge representation papers include knowledge fusion, engineering skill acquisition, skill inheritance and integration, and modeling for knowledge management. Autonomous reasoning papers address VHDL designs, diagnosing systems, configuration of traffic messages, and retrieval of assumptions from process models. Machine learning papers encompass information extraction from HTML, similarity assessment for XML documents, textual knowledge extraction, generation of similarity measures, and supervised clustering. Planning and scheduling papers focus on solving manufacturing and production scheduling problems, discrete simulator control, urban traffic controls, simulation of engineering systems, high-performance production systems, and optimization of disassembly sequences. Papers in evolutionary computing focus on dynamic trait expressions, time-series forecasting, layout of irregular shape objects, and course scheduling. Vision papers concentrate on fault detection of circuit boards and PCB inspection. There are many other papers covering a wide range of real-life applications in the areas of software engineering, intelligent manufacturing systems, autonomous agents, intelligent controls, robotics, data mining, speech recognition, searching, design, tutoring, distributed problem solving, intelligent financial analysis and advising, and development of expert systems for specific domain applications.

We received over 140 papers from 33 different countries. Each paper was sent to at least two referees for review. Only 81 papers were selected for presentation and publication in the proceedings. We would like to express our sincere thanks to the Program Committee and all the reviewers for their hard work. This year's submissions were of a very high quality. Six papers were nominated for the best paper award by the reviewers. The ranking of these papers was decided by the votes cast by the conference delegates during the conference.

We would also like to thank Ms. Cheryl Morriss for her efficiency in dealing with the registration and management issues. There are many other participants, as well as all the authors, who are critically important in the organization of this conference. The conference would not have been possible without their valuable support.

Moonis Ali
Paul Chung
Chris Hinde

## Program Committee

Moonis Ali
Chimay Anumba
Ruth Aylett
Senen Barro
Fevzi Belli
Ivan Bratko
Edmund Burke
CW Chan
Kai Chang
Paul Chung
Christian Dawson
Roberto Desimone
Gino Dini
Tadeusz Dobrowiecki
Graham Forsyth
Christian Freksa
Perttu Heino
Tim Hendtlass
Chris Hinde
Mohamed Jmaiel
Catholijn Jonker
Mark Lee
Andras Markus
Steve McCoy
Laszlo Monostori
Derek Partridge
Don Potter
Henri Prade
Chris Price
David Robertson
Pedro Sanz
Michael Schroeder
Fabrizio Sebastiani
Flavio Correa da Silva
Kazuhiko Suzuki
Liansheng Tan
Takushi Tanaka
Spyros Tzafestas
Sunil Vadera
Xuezhong Wang
Shuanghua Yang
Xin Yao

## External Reviewers

Eduardo Alonso
Henri Avancini
Jorge Badenas
Maher Ben Jemaa
Tibor Bosse
Jan Broersen
Alberto Bugarin
W. Amos Confer
John Connolly
Jason Cooper
Edwin de Jong
Gino Dini
Gerry Dozier
Eran Edirisinghe
Bilel Gargouri
Daniela Giorgetti
Perry Groot
Guoqiang Hu
Zhisheng Huang
Alexander Klippel
Alex Kozlenkov
Fred Labrosse
Raúl Marín
Manuel Mucientes Molina
Fesil Mushtaq
Matthew Newton
Sara Passone
Robert Patching
Iain Phillips
Jesus Maria Rodriguez Presedo
Kai-Florian Richter
Jose M. Sanchiz
Amelia Simó
Ondrej Sykora
Allard Tamminga
V. Javier Traver
David Lopez Vilarino
Jan Oliver Wallgrün
Mark Withall
Diedrich Wolter

# Table of Contents

## Session 1a: System Integration



## Session 1b: Genetic Algorithms



## Session 1c: Vision and Signal Analysis



## Session 2a: Intelligent Systems

## Session 2b: Learning



## Session 2c: Data Mining



## Session 3a: Knowledge Management



## Session 3b: Modelling

## Session 3c: Vision



## Session 4a: Neural Networks

## Session 4b: Knowledge Based System



## Session 4c: Reasoning



## Session 5a: Agent Based Systems



## Session 5b: Machine Learning

## Session 5c: Intelligent Systems



## Session 6a: Neural Networks



## Session 6b: Data Mining

## Session 6c: Heuristic Search



## Session 7a: Genetic Algorithms



## Session 7b: Robotics

## Session 7c: Problem Solving



## Session 8a: Speech



## Session 8b: Genetic Algorithms



## Session 8c: GIS Systems

# Intelligent Operational Management and the Concept of Integration

Yvonne Power and Parisa A. Bahri[1]

School of Engineering and
A.J. Parker Center for Hydrometallurgy
Murdoch University (Rockingham Campus), Murdoch WA, Australia
{yvonne, parisa}@eng.murdoch.edu.au

**Abstract:** Current data acquisition systems provide the user with hundreds and even thousands of variables which need to be monitored and processed. These variables need to be organized within an expert control architecture encompassing tasks such as regulatory control, data reconciliation, process monitoring, fault detection and diagnosis, supervisory control, planning and scheduling. Task integration involves the integration of techniques in a continuously changing environment. This paper presents a new integration framework known as the Knowledge Management Method using hierarchical timed place Petri nets. Applicability of the proposed framework is demonstrated through the integration of the data reconciliation and supervisory control modules.

**Keywords:** Autonomous agents, expert systems, intelligent systems, knowledge management, system integration, Petri nets.

## 1 Introduction

Until recently the concept of an integrated framework for coordinating operational tasks in industrial plants has not been possible due to technological limitations. As a result of increased computing power and powerful memory systems, a fully computer integrated system is now possible. Integration of functions within an integrated expert architecture would result in improved plant performance, safety and an increase in production. However, achieving an integrated framework for operational tasks is quite complex. Integration frameworks proposed in the past include the functional hierarchy, which is limited by its inability to allow for transfer of information flow between all modules, and so is no longer considered sufficient. Problems of task integration include not only information flow and timing for a continuously changing environment, but the integration of various problem-solving methodologies. A new approach to accommodate the changing dynamics of a plant's operation is thus necessary.

This paper will begin with a description of the components, which need to be integrated to encompass intelligent process operation. It will then go on to examine various integration frameworks. Petri nets including place/transition nets, timed place

[1] Author to whom all correspondence should be addressed.

P.W.H. Chung, C.J. Hinde, M. Ali (Eds.): IEA/AIE 2003, LNAI 2718, pp. 1–10, 2003.

and hierarchical Petri nets are introduced as a method for task integration and the proposed Coordinated Knowledge Management Method framework based on the use of hierarchical timed place Petri nets is presented. The data reconciliation and supervisory control sub-nets are used to illustrate this method of task integration.

## 2 Operational Levels

The need for an integrated framework encompassing intelligent process operation stems from the growing complexity of current systems, as well as from the traditional expense, time constraints and limited availability of human expertise (Tzafestas and Verbruggen, 1995). The benefits resulting from implementation of an integrated knowledge based expert system include improved plant performance, improved environmental aspects of the plant, reduction in plant running costs and minimization of labor intensive tasks allowing the operator to make more frequent and better informed decisions.

The functional tasks which computer aided process operations encompass can be partitioned into seven plant operational tasks. The components which need to be integrated include (i) data acquisition, (ii) data reconciliation, (iii) regulatory control, (iv) fault detection and diagnosis (v) supervisory control, (vi) planning and (vii) scheduling. These tasks are categorized as low, mid and high-level tasks. In the following sections these tasks will be outlined starting from the low-level tasks followed by the mid- and high-level tasks.

### 2.1 Low Level Tasks

**Data Acquisition.** The basic component is data acquisition. Process data is acquired from the plant through sensors attached to the plant. Transducers convert the data to a form recognizable by a computer. The data is then used as a foundation either directly or indirectly for every other task.

**Data Reconciliation.** On-line process measurements are corrupted by errors during measurement and transmission of data. Before plant data can be usefully used, it is necessary to reconcile this data into meaningful values. This is the objective of the data reconciliation module.

**Regulatory Control.** Regulatory control occurs when the control system functions to counteract the effect of disturbances in order to maintain the output at its desired set-point (Ogunnaike and Ray, 1994). The most common regulatory controller used in industry is the PID controller.

### 2.2 Mid Level Tasks

**Fault Detection and Diagnosis.** Fault detection and diagnosis involves the tracking of process execution, detection of departures from normal operation and identification of cause (Reklaitis and Koppel, 1995). Fault detection uses data in order to detect abnormal situations and isolate faults. Methods used to solve the fault detection and diagnosis problem include knowledge-based, model-based and pattern recognition based methods.

**Supervisory Control.** Supervisory control involves the on-line calculation of set-points (SP) allowing the unit or plant to achieve maximum profits while satisfying operation constraints. Process and economic models of the plant are used to optimize plant operation by maximizing daily profit, yields or production rate (Seborg, 1989).

### 2.2 High Level Tasks

**Planning and Scheduling.** Planning is the allocation of production resources and assignment of production targets for the plant averaged over a suitable time scale. The time scale for planning is long term, typically in the range of weeks, months or years. Scheduling is the determination of the timing and sequence in the execution of manufacturing tasks so as to achieve production targets in an optimal fashion (Reklaitis and Koppel, 1995). The time frame in this case is usually days to weeks. Planning and scheduling will not be discussed in this paper, as they are application specific.

## 3 Integration of Tasks

Past research has focused on individual task implementation. This has led to many different techniques being developed in order to implement tasks in each level of the hierarchy. However, with the goal of improving plant performance, increasing production and reducing plant variability, research is leading towards the integration of these tasks.

To date no known integration of low-level (data acquisition, data reconciliation and regulatory control), mid-level (supervisory control, monitoring and diagnosis) and high-level tasks (planning and scheduling) has been developed and implemented in processing plants. This paper presents a new method of task integration based on timed place Petri nets.

Previous structures proposed for integration include the functional hierarchy and the blackboard model. In the functional hierarchy, tasks are isolated from each other and executed in a hierarchical manner with upper level decisions imposed on lower levels with limited feedback up the chain (Reklaitis and Koppel, 1995). Plant complexity and uncertainty can upset this hierarchy and there is also no relation to timing of tasks. The structure does not take into account situations in which the flow of information may be upset and information flow needs to be changed which makes it necessary to find a more adaptive framework.

The blackboard metaphor involves a group of generic problem solvers (experts) looking at the same blackboard recording individual states of the ongoing problem solving process. Each expert takes appropriate action based on the information presented on the blackboard. A key feature of this structure is that the problem solving states are made available in the form of global data structures while maintaining the isolation of each of the modules (Albayrak and Krallmann, 1995). The large volume of data sent to the blackboard must be hierarchically structured and an external control mechanism is used to coordinate modules. A disadvantage of blackboard architecture is that performing a search through the masses of information is inefficient.

With the Coordinated Knowledge Management Method, hierarchy is present but is not as rigidly structured as in the functional hierarchy. The method takes into account information flow and timing of the modules by using Petri nets as the coordination mechanism. Running the modules can be translated into events and operator input and data flow can be translated into conditions. These suitably map into a Petri net description for the co-ordination mechanism, where events are modeled by transitions and conditions by places (Peterson, 1981). The output of each transition represents the current state of the system. Timing is incorporated into the Petri net by using a timed place Petri net. Simple hierarchy is introduced in order to break down the large scale Petri net into simpler sub-nets using hierarchical Petri nets. A description of these nets is provided in the following sections.

## 4 The Coordinated Knowledge Management Method

The proposed Coordinated Knowledge Management Method framework is presented in Fig. 1. The blackboard in the traditional blackboard model has been replaced by hierarchical timed place Petri nets, which are timed place Petri nets organized in a tree structure. (For further information on Petri nets refer to Appendix 1.) Each individual module (regulatory control, process monitoring, data reconciliation, supervisory control, fault detection and diagnosis) contains information (including rules, procedures, Petri nets, optimization and neural networks) which enables each module to operate autonomously similar to the blackboard structure. However, the hierarchical timed place Integration Petri nets co-ordinate the information flow and timing between modules. Each module (apart from regulatory control) is developed in G2 (a commercial programming environment for real-time systems). Data is transferred between G2 and the monitoring system via a bridge. Communication with the operator is achieved through the operator interface developed in G2.

By examining the Integration Petri nets in Fig. 1 we see that there is an inherent hierarchy between modules. The supervisory control (SC) module uses data from the data reconciliation (DR) module and thus calls the DR module before it can continue running.

Hence the DR integration Petri net is a subsystem of the SC integration Petri net and so is placed in a hierarchically represented net. The fault detection module (FDD) is continuously running, however, when the SC module introduces a SP change, the FDD module FDD must stop running until the process has reached its new steady state. Hence, a SP change would cause the FDD module to pause and wait until the process monitoring module indicates that the process has reached its new steady state. Similarly, if a fault is detected in the process, the SC and DR modules should not be run until the fault is corrected.

The techniques used in each individual module are not important, as long as the correct data is made available to the integration Petri nets. The Integration Petri nets are generic enough to be applied to any plant for integration using existing modules already in use.

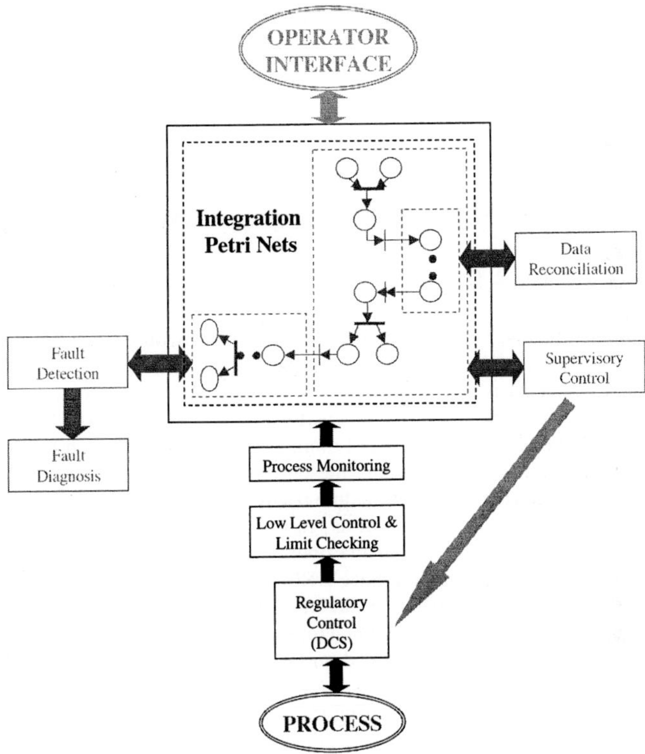


**Fig. 1.** The Coordinated Knowledge Management Method for Task Integration

### 4.1 Data Reconciliation Integration Petri Net

The application of a Petri net to DR task integration is illustrated in Fig. 2. Operator inputs and module requests can be converted into conditions relating to event occurrences. These conditions translate to places in a Petri net. A description of places is presented in Table 1.

*Operator inputs* to the Petri net are represented by tokens located on places DR0, DR11 and DR12. For example, a token located on place DR0 represents the operator's request to run the DR module. Similarly, the plant or another module requesting to run the DR module is indicated by a token on DR1. Once this request has been made, then in order for the DR module to run, the plant must be at steady state, which is indicated by a token located on PM2.

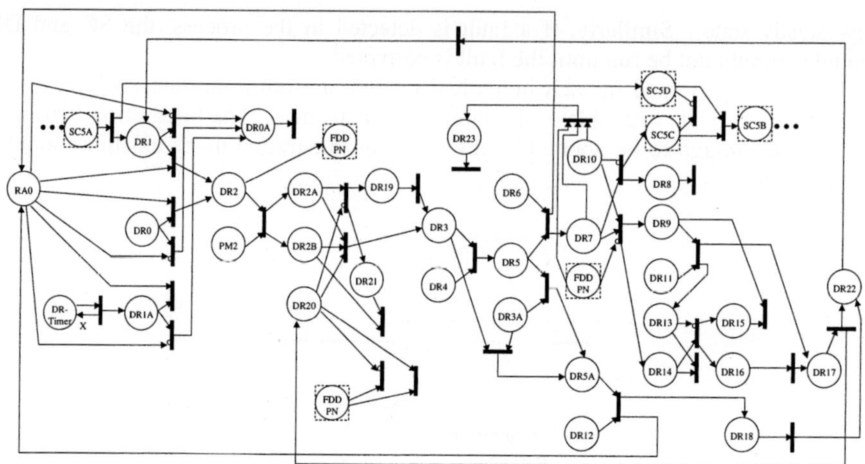


**Fig. 2.** Data Reconciliation Integration Petri Net

*DR module inputs*, that is, requests that are sent to the DR module, are represented by tokens located on places DR2, DR3, DR16 and DR19. For example, whenever a token arrives at DR3, a rule is activated which starts the DR module. *DR module outputs* that is, data which comes from the DR module, are represented by tokens located on places DR3A, DR4, DR6, DR10. For example, when there is an error in the DR module, a token is created on DR3A.

The *output* of each transition represents the current state of the system. For example, a token located on DR5 means that the DR module is currently running.

The place labeled RA0 can be thought of as "resource allocation" and prevents the build-up of tokens on place DR2. For example, if the operator sends a request to run the DR module which is indicated by a token located on place DR0, and the DR module is not already running (indicated by a token located on RA0), then the transition attached to DR0, RA0 and DR2 fires removing a token from DR0, RA0 and adding a token to DR2. If then a request comes from the plant to run the DR module, a token is placed on DR1. Now, at this point, no token is located on RA0 and so the transition connected to RA0 (through the inhibitor arc) and DR1 fires, removing the token from DR1, thus preventing tokens building up on this place. The token on RA0 is replaced when the DR module can be run again.

The places labeled SC5A, SC5B, SC5C and SC5D form part of the SC integration Petri net and are described in the next section. Similarly, places labeled FDD form part of the FDD integration Petri net. The fault detection and diagnosis integration Petri net has been developed, but has not been included in this paper.

## 4.2 Supervisory Control Integration Petri Net

The application of a Petri net to SC task integration is illustrated in Fig. 3. A description of places is presented in Table 2. Place descriptions are similar to those described for the DR Integration Petri net.

As described in the previous section, in order for the SC module to run, the DR module must be run first. Thus the DR Integration Petri net forms part of the SC Integration PN and is indicated by the boxed area in Fig. 3, which encapsulates the places labeled DR1 and SC5C. In other words, when there is a request to run the SC module (indicated by a token located on SC5), the transition connecting SC5 to SC5D and DR1 fires, removing a token from SC5 and creating tokens on SC5D and DR1.

**Table 1.** Place Descriptions for Data Reconcilaiton Integration Petri net

| Place Name | Description |
|---|---|
| *Petri Net Inputs* | |
| DR-Timer | Frequency (entered by operator) at which DR module should be run. |
| DR0 | Operator input - request running DR. |
| DR1 | Plant requests running DR module. |
| DR1A | Automatic request to run DR module. |
| PM2 | Process is at steady state. |
| DR3A | DR module error. |
| DR4 | DR module running. |
| DR6 | DR module finished/not running. |
| DR10 | Sensor drift detected. |
| DR11 | Operator input – confirm/fix sensor drift. |
| DR12 | Operator input – confirm/fix DR module error. |
| *Petri Net Output Places* | |
| DR0A | Inform operator – Request to run DR module aborted. |
| DR23 | Inform operator – DR aborted because of sensor drift & fault detected by FDD module. |
| *Requests to DR Module* | |
| DR2 | Waiting for process to be at steady state. |
| DR3 | Send request to run DR module. |
| DR16 | Use nominal sensor values for sensors in drift. |
| DR19 | Use raw sensor values for all sensors. |
| *Petri Net State Places* | |
| DR5 | DR module running. |
| DR5A | Error in DR module. |
| DR7 | DR module finished running. |
| DR8 | DR OK! |
| DR9 | Sensor drift detected. |
| *Intermediate Places* | |
| RA0 | Resource allocation. |
| DR2A | Use raw values in DR (pathway). |
| DR2B | Use both raw and nominal values in DR (pathway). |
| DR13 | Holding place. |
| DR14 | Sensor drift detected (holding place). |
| DR15 | Holding place for token removal DR9. |
| DR17 | Ready to request DR running (intermediate place – using both nominal & raw sensor values in the reconciliation). |
| DR18 | Ready to request DR (using only raw sensor values in the reconciliation). |
| DR20 | Bypass place DR19. |
| DR21 | Holding place for token removal DR2B. |
| DR22 | Intermediate place – request to run DR. |

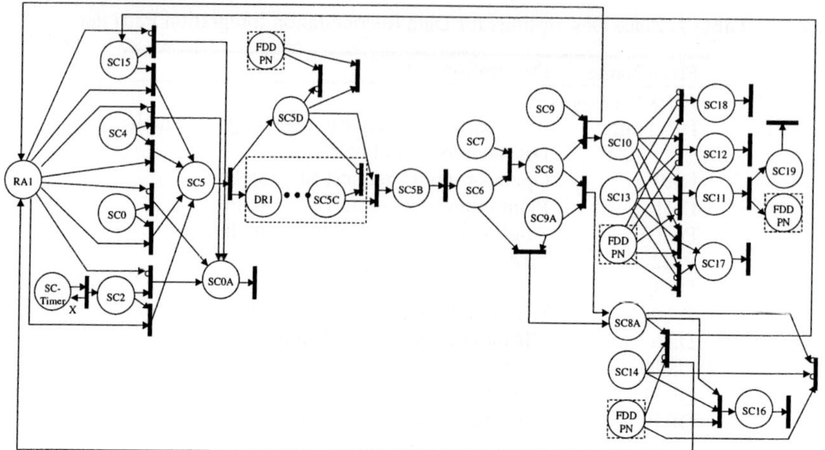


**Fig. 3.** Supervisory Control Integration Petri Net

The place labeled DR1 requests that the DR module is run. The place labeled SC5D is used to indicate that the request for the DR module to run comes from the SC module and not some other module. Once the DR module has successfully run, SC can continue.

The arrival of tokens on input places labeled SC7, SC9, SC9A and SC13 are governed by rules attached to the SC control module. For example, when the SC module has finished running a rule fires which creates a token on SC9. If the SC module has finished running and there is no SP change, a token is placed on SC12, indicating that the plant is ok and that there is no SP change. A SP change would be indicated by a token on place SC11 which then stops the FDD module.

## 5 Conclusion

This paper describes the need for task integration encompassing intelligent process operation, with a description of tasks which need to be integrated. The paper then explores the limitations of integrated frameworks proposed in the past. It presents a coordination mechanism, which makes use of hierarchical timed place Petri nets in order to organize modules, information flow and timing. The Coordinated Knowledge Management framework with its hierarchically structured Petri nets and autonomous modules is presented as a method of overcoming past problems of task integration. The technique is demonstrated by applying the method to the integration of the data reconciliation and supervisory control modules.

**Table 2.** Place Descriptions for Supervisory Control Integration Petri net

| Place Name | Description |
|---|---|
| *Petri Net Inputs* | |
| SC-Timer | Frequency (entered by operator) at which SC module should be run. |
| SC0 | Operator input - operator requests running SC module. |
| SC2 | Automatic request to run SC module. |
| SC4 | Request running SC module (water temperature change). |
| SC15 | Plant requests running SC module. |
| SC7 | SC module running. |
| SC9 | SC module finished/not running. |
| SC9A | SC module fault. |
| SC13 | SP change. |
| SC14 | Operator input – Confirm/fix SC module error. |
| *Petri Net Output Places* | |
| SC0A | Inform operator – Request to run SC module aborted. |
| SC16 | Inform operator – SC aborted because of error in SC module and fault detected by FDD module. |
| SC17 | Inform operator - SP's not written as fault detected by FDD module. |
| SC18 | Remove tokens FDD12K. |
| *Petri Net State Places* | |
| SC5B | DR module finished running and DR OK! |
| SC8 | SC module running. |
| SC8A | Error in SC module. |
| SC10 | SC module finished/not running. |
| SC11 | SC OK & SP change. |
| SC12 | No SP change and SC successfully run. |
| *Requests to SC (DR or FDD) Module* | |
| SC5 | Initial request to run SC module. |
| SC6 | Send request to run SC module. |
| FDD7 | Request to stop running FDD module. |
| *Intermediate Places* | |
| RA1 | Resource allocation. |
| SC5D | Request for DR module to run has come from SC module. |
| SC5C | DR module has finished running from request from SC module. |

## References

1. Albayrak, S. and H. Krallmann (1995). "Distributed Artificial Intelligence in Manufacturing Control (Chapter 9)", Artificial Intelligence in Industrial Decision Making, Control and Automation, p. 247 – 294, Tzafestas, S.G. and Verbruggen, H.B. (ed.), Kluwer Academic Publishers, The Netherlands.

2. Dittrich, G. (1995). "Modeling of Complex Systems Using Hierarchical Petri Nets (Chapter 6)", Codesign Computer-Aided Software/Hardware Engineering, p. 128 – 144, Rozenblitz, J. and Buchenrieder, K. (ed.), IEEE Press, New York.
3. Gu, T. and P. Bahri (2002). A Survey of Petri Net Applications in Batch Processes, Computers in Industry, 47, p. 99 – 111.
4. Nissanke, N. (1997). Realtime Systems, Prentice Hall, London.
5. Ogunnaike, R. A. and W.H. Ray (1994). Process Dynamics, Modeling and Control, p. 46 – 47, Oxford University Press, New York.
6. Peterson, J.L. (1981). Petri Net Theory and Modeling of Systems, Prentice-Hall Inc., New Jersey.
7. Reklaitis R. G. V. and L.B. Koppel (1995). "Role and Prospects for Intelligent Systems in Integrated Process Operations", AIChE Symposium, International Conference on Intelligent Systems in Process Engineering, Snowmass, Colorado, p. 71 – 84, July 9-14.
8. Seborg, D.E., T.F. Edgar, and D.A. Mellichamp (1989). Process Dynamics and Control, John Wiley and Sons, New York.
9. Tzafestas, S., and H. Verbruggen (1995). "Artificial Intelligence in Industrial Decision Making, Control, and Automation: An Introduction (Chapter 1)", Artificial Intelligence in Industrial Decision Making, Control and Automation, p. 1 – 39, Tzafestas, S.G. and Verbruggen, H.B. (ed.), Kluwer Academic Publishers, The Netherlands.
10. Wang, J. (1998). Timed Petri Nets Theory and Application, Kluwer Academic Publishers, Boston.

## Appendix 1: Petri Nets

A Petri net is a bipartite graph consisting of two sets of nodes (places and transitions) and a set of arcs between pairs of nodes (Nissanke, 1997). Pictorially places are depicted as circles and transitions as bars or boxes. Each place may potentially hold either none or a positive number of tokens, pictorially represented by small solid circles. The distribution of these tokens in places is referred as the marking and a Petri net containing tokens is called a marked Petri net. In a marked Petri net, transitions may be enabled and fired. The transitions firing renders tokens being redistributed, and result in a new marking (Gu and Bahri, 2002).

Timing can be incorporated into a Petri net by considering a timed place, transition or arc Petri net (Wang, 1998). In a timed place Petri net, a token deposited in a place becomes available only after a certain time period of time (time delay). Only available tokens can enable transitions.

Hierarchically structured Petri nets are useful when splitting the whole description of a system using a well-structured set of comprehensive descriptions using nets that are organized in a tree (Dittrich, 1995). This is particularly useful in the case of large-scale systems where a large net can be split into sub-nets rather than using one large Petri net.

# Ontology-Based Knowledge Fusion Framework Using Graph Partitioning

Tsung-Ting Kuo, Shian-Shyong Tseng, and Yao-Tsung Lin

Department of Computer and Information Science, National Chiao Tung University, Hsinchu 300, Taiwan, R.O.C.
{ttkuo, sstseng, gis88801}@cis.nctu.edu.tw

**Abstract.** For a variety of knowledge sources and time-critical tasks, knowledge fusion seems to be a proper concern. In this paper, we proposed a reconstruction concept and a three-phase knowledge fusion framework which utilizes the shared vocabulary ontology and addresses the problem of meta-knowledge construction. In the framework, we also proposed relationship graph, an intermediate knowledge representation, and two criteria for the fusion process. An evaluation of the implementation of our proposed knowledge fusion framework in the intrusion detection systems domain is also given.

## 1 Introduction

Knowledge fusion is to combine knowledge from multiple, distributed, heterogeneous knowledge sources in a highly dynamic way [14]. It is evolved from the issue of schema integration in database systems and the interoperability problem in software engineering. Knowledge fusion has the following advantages [14][24]: knowledge reuse, knowledge validity, knowledge coverage, the ability to solve more complex problems, and faster and cheaper way to build knowledge-based systems. Generally speaking, knowledge fusion is the major concern of the following two issues of building knowledge-based systems: (1) the meta-knowledge of different knowledge sources may vary dramatically (such as computer-aided learning systems), and (2) the response time of the knowledge-based systems is critical (such as emergency expert systems). As we may know, two main difficulties about knowledge fusion are the structural heterogeneity and the semantic heterogeneity [22]. In this paper, we provide both structural and semantic knowledge fusion.

The basic knowledge fusion concept we proposed is *reconstruction*. Firstly, knowledge bases are transformed to *relationship graphs*, the intermediate knowledge representation we proposed. The relationship graph is then partitioned into multiple subgraphs by our proposed two criteria, the *structural succinctness criterion* and the *semantic clustering criterion*. Finally, the partitioned relationship graph is utilized to reconstruct the meta-knowledge of the fused knowledge base.

We proposed a three-phase knowledge fusion framework based on the reconstruction concept mentioned above. The first phase (preprocessing phase) is to integrate all rules in all knowledge bases to a flat knowledge base and construct the corresponding relationship graph. The second phase (partitioning phase) is to partition

P.W.H. Chung, C.J. Hinde, M. Ali (Eds.): IEA/AIE 2003, LNAI 2718, pp. 11–20, 2003.

the relationship graph to multiple inter-relative sub-graphs, which represents the classes of the knowledge objects [21], by the two criteria we proposed. The third phase (meta-knowledge construction phase) is to construct the new meta-knowledge of the flat knowledge base according to the partitioned relationship graph, and the new meta-knowledge along with the flat knowledge base form a new fused knowledge base. An evaluation of the implementation of our proposed knowledge fusion framework is also provided.

## 2 Related Work

Recently, many researches focus on knowledge fusion [7][13][14][24]. Two main difficulties about knowledge fusion are the structural heterogeneity and the semantic heterogeneity [22]. Some approaches provide structural fusion, such as COBWEB [4]. Some other approaches provide both structural and semantic fusion, such as the common subgraph method mentioned in [13]. In this paper, we provide both structure and semantic knowledge fusion.

Two main categories of approaches are applied to the knowledge fusion problem: the hierarchical approaches and the non-hierarchical approaches. Hierarchical approaches include COBWEB [4], CLASSIT [5], AutoClass [20], SUBDUE [10], and so on. These approaches generate only hierarchical meta-knowledge, which are usually not appropriate for the actual application of the knowledge-based systems. Non-hierarchical approaches include the common subgraph approach [13] and the concept lattice approach [7]. However, the assumption of common subgraph approach that all knowledge objects being clustered shares similar syntactical forms is usually not true in the real world, and the concept lattice approach deals only binary relations. Therefore, both approaches have some limitation on the knowledge bases being fused.

## 3 Problem Definition and Goals

In this paper, we try to provide structure and semantic knowledge fusion, represented by rules, using ontologies by hybrid approach. We can thus define our problem in more detail: Given a shared vocabulary ontology and a set of rule-based knowledge bases from different systems with different meta-knowledge, fuse all the knowledge bases to one with new meta-knowledge, optimizing the structural and the semantic meanings of the original knowledge bases.

Our goals are as follows: (1) Fuse multiple rule-based knowledge bases. The output of our proposed approaches should be a new knowledge base and a new meta-knowledge. (2) Optimize the structural and the semantic meanings. (3) Use only shared vocabulary ontology for facilitating the fusion process.

## 4 Relationship Graph and Partitioning Criteria

In this section, the intermediate knowledge representation relationship graph is introduced. The criteria to partition the relationship graph are also discussed in detail.

## 4.1 Definitions

We propose a representation, relationship graph, for expressing the structural and the semantic meanings of the rule bases. First-order logical rules [17][18] are used as the knowledge representation of the rule bases. Before describing the relationship graph, we firstly give some basic definition, partly referencing the syntax of first-order logic [17][18]. Assume that a first-order logical rule base contains $n$ variables, $m$ rules which are classified into $t$ classes.

•*TRUE* = the logical constant representing "always true".
•*FALSE* = the logical constant representing "always false".
•*EMPTY* = the logical constant representing "empty".
•$v_i$ = a first-order logical variable of the rule base, $1 \square i \square n$.
•$V = \{v_1, v_2, \ldots, v_n\}$ is the set of all first-order logical variables in the rule base.
•$s$ = a first-order logical sentence, composed by variables and logical connectives.
•$VAR(s) = \{v_i \mid s \text{ contains } v_i\}$.
•$LHS_i$ = left-hand side (condition) sentence of a rule, $1 \square i \square m$;
•$RHS_i$ = left-hand side (action) sentence of a rule, $1 \square i \square m$;
•$r_i$ = a rule of 2-tuple $(LHS_i, RHS_i)$, $1 \square i \square m$;
•$R = \{r_1, r_2, \ldots, r_m\}$ is the set of all rules of the rule base.
•$c_i$ = a rule class, which is a subset of $R$, $\bigcup_{1 \le i \le t} c_i = R$, $c_j \bullet c_k =$ , $j \neq k$.
•$C = \{c_1, c_2, \ldots, c_t\}$ is the set of all rule classes of the rule base.
•$B$ = a first-order logical rule base of 3-tuple $(V, R, C)$.

Now we give the definitions about relationship graph. Assume that there is $u$ links in the relationship graph.

•$l_i$ = a link of 3-tuple $(V_i, CAUSE\_RULE_i, EFFECT\_RULE_i)$, $V_i \subseteq V$, $1 \square i \square u$,
$CAUSE\_RULE_i = r_j$, $1 \square j \square m$, $V_i \subseteq VAR(LHS_j)$,
$EFFECT\_RULE_i = r_k$, $1 \square k \square m$, $V_i \subseteq VAR(RHS_k)$.
•$L = \{l_1, l_2, \ldots, l_t\}$ is the set of links of the relationship graph.
•$p_i$ = a partition, which is a subset of $R$, $\bigcup_{1 \le i \le t} p_i = R$, $p_j \bullet p_k =$ , $j \neq k$.
•$P = \{p_1, p_2, \ldots, p_t\}$ is the set of all rule classes of the rule base.
•$IN(p_i) = \{ l_j \mid l_j \in L, CAUSE\_RULE_j \notin p_i, EFFECT\_RULE_j \in p_i\}$ is the set of incoming links of a partition $p_i$.
•$OUT(p_i) = \{ l_j \mid l_j \in L, CAUSE\_RULE_j \in p_i, EFFECT\_RULE_j \notin p_i\}$ is the set of outgoing links of a partition $p_i$.
•$I$=incoming variables of a relationship graph, $I \subseteq V$, $I = \bigcup_i VAR(LHS_i)$, $1 \square i \square m$.

•$O$=outgoing variables of a relationship graph, $O \subseteq V$, $O = \bigcup_i VAR(RHS_i)$, $1 \square i \square m$.

•$G$ = a relationship graph of 6-tuple $(V, R, P, L, I, O)$.

A rule base has one-to-one mapping to a relationship graph. A rule class of a rule base has one-to-one mapping to a partition of a relationship graph. A rule $r_i$ is *connected* to a partition $p_j$ if there exists an incoming link or an outgoing link between $r_i$ and $p_p$, *1□i□m, 1□i□t.* For each rule class in the rule base, there is exactly one mapping partition in the relationship graph. Note that the logical meaning of the rules is eliminated, because the relationship graph is used for an intermediate representation for partitioning (which is introduced in the Section 4.2), not for logical inference.

## 4.2 Criteria of Relationship Graph Partitioning

As discussed before, the partitions of relationship graphs represent exactly the rule classes of rule bases. Therefore, "good relationship graph partitioning" means "good rule class classification". We define two criteria for "good partitioning" according to our second goal, optimizing the structural and the semantic meanings, respectively.

The first criterion is to optimize the structural meanings of a relationship graph, or minimize the links cut by the partitioning if possible [11]. That is, for a relationship graph, the average inter-partition links (incoming links and outgoing links) should be minimized. Assume that a relationship graph $G$ contains $t$ partitions, $\{p_1, p_2, \ldots, p_t\}$, each partition $p_i$ contains $|IN(p_i)|$ incoming links and $|OUT(p_i)|$ outgoing links. Let $L_p(p_i)$ be the total number of the incoming and outgoing links of $p_i$; that is, $L_p(p_i) = |IN(p_i)| + |OUT(p_i)|$. Let $L_G(G)$ be the average number of the incoming and outgoing links of $G$; that is,

$$L_G(G) = \sum_{1 \le i \le t} L_p(p_i)/t \qquad (1)$$

Therefore, the *Structural Succinctness Criterion* is defined as follows:

**Criterion 1.** For a relationship graph G, minimize $L_G(G)$ if possible.

The second criterion is to optimize the semantic meanings of a relationship graph, or minimize the intra-partition semantic heterogeneity. Ontologies are often used for content explication or as common dictionary [1][23]. Shared vocabulary ontologies [23] contain the basic terms for the local ontologies and provide a basis for the fusion of the ontologies. Semantic distances [3] are utilized to measure the semantic heterogeneity. For two variables $v$, $v'$, the semantic distance is given by $S_v(v, v')$ = "the number of links from $v$ to $v'$ in the shared vocabulary ontology" + 0.5 * "the number of changes of directions" (this definition will be explained in Section 5.2.1). For a partition $p_i$ with $u$ variables, the average semantic distance is given by

$$S_p(p_i) = \sum_{1 \le j,k \le u, j \ne k} S_p(v_j, v_k) \; / C(u, 2) \qquad (2)$$

Let $S_G(G)$ be the average semantic distance of $G$; that is,

$$S_G(G) = \sum_{1 \le i \le t} S_p(p_i)/t \qquad (3)$$

Therefore, the *Semantic Clustering Criterion* is defined as follows:

**Criterion 2.** For a relationship graph G, minimize $S_G(G)$ if possible.

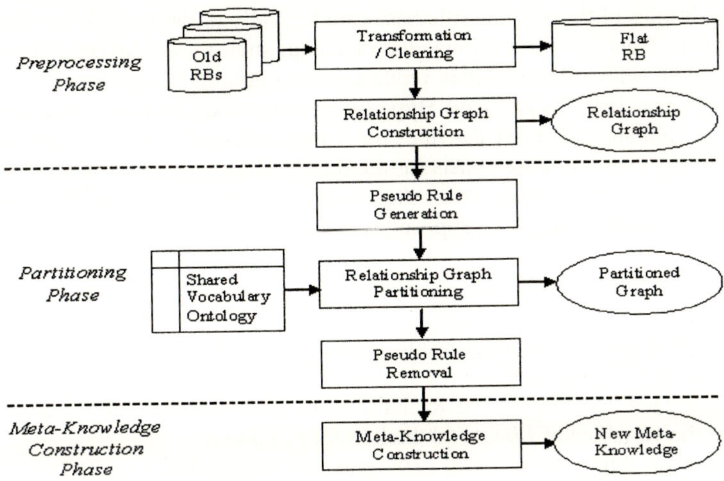


**Fig. 1.** The knowledge fusion framework

These two criteria are used later in our partitioning algorithm for optimizing the structural and the semantic meanings.

## 5 Knowledge Fusion Framework

The framework consists of three phases: the preprocessing phase, the partitioning phase, and the meta-knowledge construction phase. The whole process is illustrated in Figure 1. Firstly, the preprocessing phase deals with syntactic problems such as format transformation and rule base cleaning, and construct the relationship graph according to the cleaned, transformed flat rule base. Secondly, the relationship graph is partitioned according to *Criterion 1* and *Criterion 2* in the partitioning phase. Finally, the new meta-knowledge of the flat rule base is constructed using the partitioned relationship graph in the meta-knowledge construction phase. The three phases can be described in detail in the rest of this section.

### 5.1 Preprocessing Phase

The preprocessing phase consists of format transformation, rule base cleaning, and relationship graph construction. The format transformation of the source rule bases consists of two steps: one is to transform the rules to first-order logic, and the other is to remove the meta-knowledge of the rule bases. In this paper, we assume that the syntactic heterogeneity is solved by ODBC, HTML, XML, and any other technologies [22]. After preprocessing, the rules from all rule bases are then stored into a flat rule base. There is currently no meta-knowledge about the flat rule base. The meta-knowledge will be built in the relationship graph partitioning phase.

After all rules of the original rule bases are logically preprocessed, we should put all rules together and perform knowledge cleaning, such as validation and verification. The problem with rules includes redundancy, contradiction/conflict, circularity and incompleteness [6][17]. Directed Hypergraph Adjacency Matrix Representation [15] is used to validate and verify the rules for completeness, correctness, and consistency. This cleaning step provides a basis for the relationship graph construction.

After cleaning the flat rule base, the construction of the relationship graph can be performed. The algorithm we proposed is as follows:

**Algorithm 1.** Relationship Graph Construction Algorithm
Input: A rule base $B = (V_B, R_B, C_B)$
Output: An un-partitioned relationship graph $G = (V_G, R_G, P, L, I, O)$
Step 1. Set $V_G = V_B$, $R_G$ =s $R_B$.
Step 2. For each two rules $r_1, r_2 \in R_G$, let $S$ be the intersection of the variables of $RHS_1$ and the variables of $LHS_2$, add the link $(S, r_1, r_2)$ to $L$.
Step 3. Set $I$ as the variables of all $LHS$ sentences of all rules.
Step 4. Set $O$ as the variables of all $RHS$ sentences of all rules.

## 5.2 Partitioning Phase

Before introducing our proposed algorithm, we take a brief discussion about shared vocabulary ontology, semantic distance function, and pseudo rules in the following Sections.

### 5.2.1 Shared Vocabulary Ontology and Semantic Distance Function

The shared vocabulary ontology can be constructed either by domain experts or by the general lexical reference system, such as WordNet [12]. If the knowledge sources to fuse are in the same or related domains, the customized shared vocabulary ontology for the domains is more proper than general one. The semantic distance function we use, based on the Hirst and St-Onge's semantic relatedness measure [9], is as follows:

$$S_v(v_1, v_2) = path\_length + c * d,\ v_1, v_2 \in V \tag{4}$$

Where path_length is the length from $v_1$ to $v_2$ in the shared vocabulary ontology, $d$ is the number of changes of direction in the path, and $c$ is constant. If the path does not exist, the function returns "*infinity*". $S_v(v_1, v_2) = 0$ if and only if $v_1 = v_2$.

### 5.2.2 Pseudo Rules

Before partitioning the relationship graph, we should firstly transform the incoming variables and outgoing variables of a relationship graph into two set of pseudo rules, Pseudo Incoming Rule Set and Pseudo Outgoing Rule Set, respectively. These pseudo rules add connections among rules and help for dealing with shallow knowledge, of which the connected rules may be too few for generating partitions. Each of the incoming variables is transformed to a Pseudo Incoming / Outgoing Rule by the following format, respectively:

**If** *TRUE* **Then** <An_Incoming_Variable>

**If** <An_Outgoing_Variable> **Then** *EMPTY*

The pseudo rules should be eliminated after partitioning the relationship graph. The removal of the pseudo rules is to simply discard all pseudo rules of all rule classes. If a rule class is empty after the removal, remove the rule class too.

### 5.2.3 The Partitioning Algorithm

After the un-partitioned relationship graph (including pseudo rules) is constructed, the partitioning process can be performed. Combining *Criterion 1* and *Criterion 2*, the following function for a partition $p_i$ is used for the partitioning process:

$$F_p(p_i) = L_p(p_i) + k * S_p(p_i) \tag{5}$$

Where k is a constant, represents the ratio of the importance of two criteria. The algorithm we proposed based on the greedy growth concept is as follows.

**Algorithm 2.** Relationship Graph Partitioning Algorithm
Input: An un-partitioned relationship graph *G*, pseudo rules added.
Output: A partitioned relationship graph *G'*, pseudo rules not removed yet
Step 1. Randomly select a rule from rules of *G*, and add it to a new partition p.
Step 2. Select rule *r* from *G* which is connected to *p*, $p'=p+\{r\}$, with minimal $F_p(p')$.
Step 3. If $F_p(p')$ □ $F_p(p)$, $p = p'$.
Step 4. If there is any rule that is connected to *p*, go Step 2.
Step 5. Add *p* to *G'*.
Step 6. If there is any rule in *G*, go to Step 1.

## 5.3 Meta-knowledge Construction Phase

The final phase of our proposed framework is to construct meta-knowledge according to the partitioned relationship graph. Two important aspects of meta-knowledge are discussed in our work: classes and relationships. The classes and relationships of the generated meta-knowledge are summarized in Table 1.

**Table 1.** The classes and relationships of the generated meta-knowledge

| Class | Relationships (Properties) | | |
|---|---|---|---|
| | Property | Type | Description |
| Variable | Name | Unique Text | The name |
| Rule | Name | Unique Text | The name of a rule |
| | Rule Class | Rule Class Name | The rule class belonged |
| | Ante. Var. | Set of Variable | The LHS variables |
| | Cons. Var. | Set of Variable | The RHS variables |
| Rule-Class | Name | Unique Text | The name |
| | Rules | Set of Rule Name | The rules contained |
| | Key. Var | Set of Variable | The key variable |
| | In. Var. | Set of Variable | The incoming variables |
| | Out. Var. | Set of Variable | The outgoing variables |

# 6 Experiment

In this section, we describe our implementation of the proposed knowledge fusion framework in the domain of network intrusion detection system, of which the meta-knowledge vary dramatically and the real-time responses are required. The implementation is realized in Java (jdk1.3.1) on Intel Celeron 1G with 512MB RAM.

We use the knowledge bases of two network intrusion detection system: Snort 1.8.1 [16] and Pakemon 0.3.1 [19]. In our experiment, we utilize only the intersection parts of rules of two intrusion detection systems. The categories and numbers of rules are shown in Table 2. We unify the format of the rules of Snort and Pakemon as follows:

**If** *<protocol> <src_port> <dst_port> <content>* **Then** *<intru_type> <intru_name>*

The shared vocabulary ontology about network intrusion detection system is created by domain experts, and is illustrated in Figure 2. This shared vocabulary ontology is quite simple, but is enough for the partitioning work. The constant $c = 0.5$. Three experiments are made, of which the constant k = 1.0, 1.65, and 2.0.

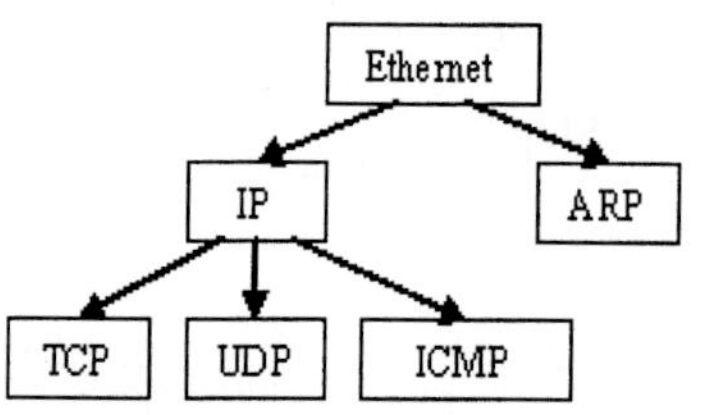


**Fig. 2.** The shared vocabulary ontology built by the domain expert

**Table 2.** Original categories and number of rules of two intrusion detection systems

| | Snort | Pakemon | Total |
|---|---|---|---|
| CGI | 99 | 55 | 154 |
| DOS | 16 | 7 | 23 |
| DNS | 18 | 2 | 20 |
| FTP | 30 | 4 | 34 |
| IIS | 82 | 8 | 90 |
| RPC | 32 | 1 | 33 |
| SMTP | 19 | 14 | 33 |
| Total | 296 | 91 | 387 |

For *k*= 1.0, the structural criterion dominates the results, therefore only 2 partitions are generated but the rules are not cleanly classified into the partitions. For *k*=2.0, the semantic criterion dominates the results, therefore the classification of each partition is clean but many 1-rule partitions are generated. For *k*=1.65 (Table 3), the classification of each partition is considerably clean, and only 7 partitions totally generated. For lower k values, the partitions are fewer, but may be uncleaner. For higher k values, the partitions are cleaner, but may be too more. A proper k value is important to the partitioning result.

**Table 3.** The partitions and rules (*k*=1.65, the major category is shown in bolder form)

| Rules | Partitions | Rule composition in each partition |
|---|---|---|
| 225 | 1 | **CGI***153, IIS*33, DNS*18, RPC*7, DOS*6, SMTP*4, FTP*2 |
| 110 | 1 | **IIS***65, FTP*27, SMTP*10, DOS*5, DNS*1, CGI*1, RPC*1 |
| 29 | 1 | **RPC***21, FTP*5, DOS*3 |
| 22 | 1 | **SMTP***19, DNS*2, RPC*1 |
| 4 | 2 | **DOS***2, IIS*2 / **RPC***3, DOS*1 |
| 3 | 1 | **DOS***3 |

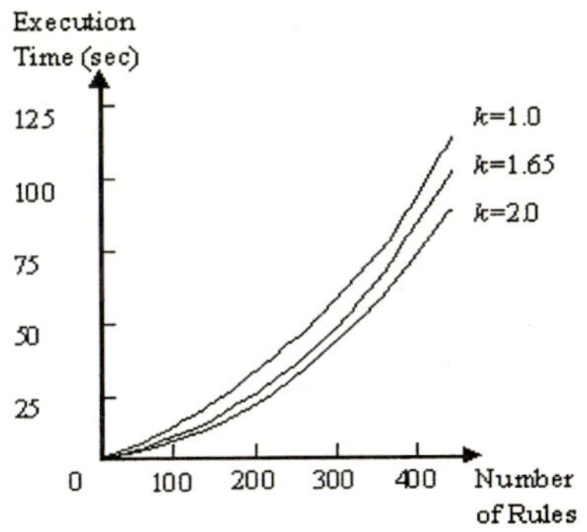


**Fig. 3.** The execution time of the algorithms

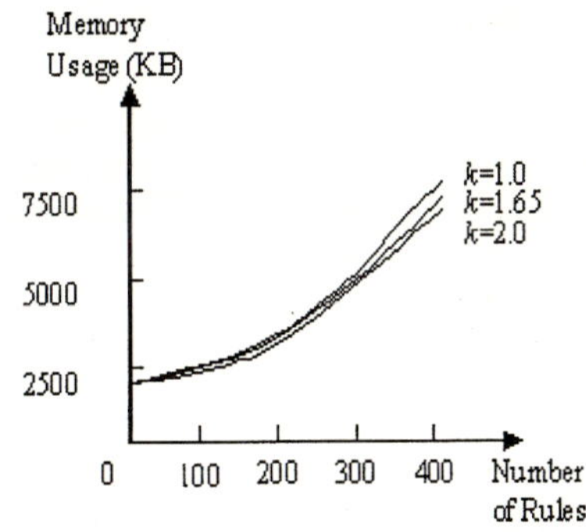


**Fig. 4.** The memory usage of the algorithms

The execution time and memory usage are illustrated in Figure 3 and Figure 4, respectively. For lower k values, each partition is bigger, therefore more time and space is needed to compute $L_G(G)$ and $S_G(G)$. For higher k values, each partition is smaller, and less time and space is needed.

## 7 Conclusion

In this paper, we proposed a knowledge reconstruction concept and a three-phase framework, and our goals are achieved as follows: (1) fusing multiple rule-based knowledge bases by utilizing the relationship graph, to build the meta-knowledge-various or time-critical knowledge-based system and its new meta-knowledge, (2) optimizing the structural and the semantic meanings by partitioning by the structural and the semantic criteria, and (3) using only shared vocabulary ontology for facilitating the fusion process.

Although we have proposed algorithms for knowledge fusion, the time and space complexity are still high. Now, we are trying to improve the performance of the algorithms. It is difficult to decide the threshold of the structural and the semantic criteria (the *k* constant), but the threshold may be derived from analyzing the characteristics of the knowledge. Besides, although the construction of shared vocabulary ontology is easier than that of domain ontology, it may still be a difficult task for the domain experts. The construction of shared vocabulary ontology, or the use of general vocabulary ontology such as WordNet, is still an open problem.

**Acknowledgement**

This work was partially supported by MOE Program for Promoting Academic Excellence of Universities under grant number 89-E-FA04-1-4, High Confidence Information Systems.

## References


1. W Behrendt, E Hutchinson, KG Jeffrey, CA Macnee, MD Wilson, "Using an Intelligent Agent to Mediate Multibase Information Access", CKBS-SIG, Keele, September 1993
2. H. Boley, S. Tabet, and G. Wagner, “Design Rationale of RuleML: A Markup Language for Semantic Web Rules”, Proc. SWWS'01, Stanford, July/August 2001.
3. A. Budanitsky, G. Hirst, “Semantic distance in WordNet: An experimental, application-oriented evaluation of five measures”, Workshop on WordNet and Other Lexical Resources, Pittsburgh, June 2001
4. D. Fisher, "Knowledge Acquisition via Incremental Conceptual Clustering", Machine Learning, 2, 139-172, 1987.
5. J.H. Gennari, P. Langley, and D. Fisher, "Models of Incremental Concept Formation", J. Carbonell, Ed., Machine Learning: Paradigms and Methods, Amsterdam, The Netherlands: MIT Press, 11-62, 1990.
6. J. Giarratano and G. Riley, Expert Systems-Principles and Programming, PWS-KENT Publishing Company, 1989.
7. R. Godin, R. Missaoui, H. Alaoui, “Incremental concept formation algorithms based on Galois (concept) lattices”, Computational Intelligence, 11(2), 246-267, 1995
8. F. van Harmelen, P. F. Patel-Schneider and I. Horrocks (editors), “The DAML+OIL language”, http://www.daml.org/2001/03/reference.html
9. G. Hirst and D. St-Onge, Lexical chains as representations of context for the detection and correction of malapropisms, pp. 305–332, Fellbaum, 1998.
10. I. Jonyer, L.B. Holder, D.J. Cook, “Graph-Based Hierarchical Conceptual Clustering”, International Journal on Artificial Intelligence Tools, 2000
11. G. Karypis and V. Kumar. “Multilevel Algorithms for Multi-constraint Graph Partitioning”, Proceedings of Supercomputing '98, 1998
12. G.A. Miller, R. Beckwith, C. Fellbaum, D. Gross, and K. Miller, “Introduction to WordNet: An On-line Lexical Database”, Journal of Lexicography, 1990
13. G.W. Mineau, R. Godin, “Automatic Structuring of Knowledge Bases by Conceptual Clustering”, IEEE TKDE, 7(5), 824-828, 1995.
14. A. Preece, K. Hui, A. Gray, P. Marti, T. Bench-Capon, Z. Cui, & D. Jones. “KRAFT: An Agent Architecture for Knowledge Fusion”, International Journal of Cooperative Information Systems, 10, 171-195, 2001
15. M. Ramaswamy, S. Sarkar, Member and Y.S. Chen, “Using Directed Hypergraphs to Verify Rule-Based Expert Systems”, IEEE TKDE, Vol.9, No.2, Mar-Apr, pp.221-237, 1997
16. M. Roesch, “Snort - Lightweight Intrusion Detection for Networks”, Proceedings of the USENIX LISA '99 Conference, Nov. 1999.
17. S.J. Russell, P. Norvig, Artificial Intelligence: Modern Approach, Prentice Hall, 185-216, 1995.
18. J.F. Sowa, Knowledge Representation: Logical, Philosophical, and Computational Foundations, Brooks Cole Publishing Co., Pacific Grove, CA, 2000
19. K. Takeda, Packet Monster, http://web.sfc.keio.ac.jp/~keiji/backup/ids/pakemon/index.html
20. K. Thompson and P. Langley, “Concept formation in structured domains”, In D. H. Fisher and M. Pazzani (Eds.), Concept Formation: Knowledge and Experience in Unsupervised Learning, Chap. 5. Morgan Kaufmann Publishers, Inc. 127-161, 1991.
21. C.F. Tsai, Design and Implementation of New Object-Oriented Rule Base Management System, Master Thesis, Department of Computer and Information Science, NCTU, 2002
22. U. Visser, H. Stuckenschmidt, T. Vögele and H. Wache, “Enabling Technologies for Interoperability”, Transactions in GIS, 2001.
23. H. Wache, T. Vgele, U. Visser, H. Stuckenschmidt, G. Schuster, H. Neumann, and S. Hbner. “Ontology-based integration of information - a survey of existing approaches”, Proceedings of the Workshop Ontologies and Information Sharing, IJCAI, 2001
24. C.H. Wong, GA-Based Knowledge Integration, Ph. D. Dissertation, Department of Computer and Information Science, National Chiao Tung University, 1998

# Deductive and Inductive Reasoning for Processing the Claims of Unsatisfied Customers

Boris Galitsky and Rajesh Pampapathi

School of Computer Science and Information Systems
Birkbeck College, University of London
Malet Street, London WC1E 7HX, UK
\{galitsky,rajesh}@dcs.bbk.ac.uk
http://www.dcs.bbk.ac.uk/~galitsky/complaints.htm

**Abstract.** We report on the novel approach to modeling a dynamic domain with limited knowledge. A domain may include participating agents such that we are uncertain about motivations and decision-making principles of some of these agents. Our reasoning setting for such domains includes deductive and inductive components. The former component is based on situation calculus and describes the behavior of agents with complete information. The latter, machine learning-based inductive component (with the elements of abductive and analogous reasoning) involves the previous experience with the agent, whose actions are uncertain to the system. Suggested reasoning machinery is applied to the problem of processing the claims of unsatisfied customers. The task is to predict the future actions of a participating agent (the company that has upset the customer) to determine the required course of actions to settle down the claim. We believe our framework reflects the general situation of reasoning in dynamic domains in the conditions of uncertainty, merging analytical and analogy-based reasoning.

## 1 Introduction

In the last decade, such artificial intelligence techniques as information extraction from text and inductive learning programming have found a variety of emergent and sophisticated applications. Also, disciplines such as reasoning about action and reasoning about mental attributes have become promising from the standpoint of applications.

In this study we focus on the quite specific problem domain of processing the textual claims of unsatisfied customers. The software is intended to help consumer advocacy companies to handle the claims automatically or to semi-automatically generate advice or suggest courses of actions to help the customer. As such, the task requires advanced text analysis and understanding, extensive reasoning about actions of conflicting agents, simulation of multiagent behavior and prediction of the opponent agent's actions.

P.W.H. Chung, C.J. Hinde, M. Ali (Eds.): IEA/AIE 2003, LNAI 2718, pp. 21–30, 2003.

We choose an information extraction technique that is based on full-scale syntactic natural language (NL) processing and a logic programming approach to knowledge representation in order to extract the parameters of conflicting multiagent behavior from text. To model the mental states of participating agents in the complex cases (a customer, a company, a customer's partner who conducts his business via this company, etc.), we deploy the natural language multiagent mental simulator NL_MAMS, described in [3]. It is capable of yielding the consecutive mental states, given the current ones, taking into account such complex forms of behavior as deceiving, pretending, explaining, reconciling, etc. In this paper, we will not describe NL and NL_MAMS components, rather focusing on their role in the overall claim processing system (Fig.1).

Concerning the reasoning about action, a series of formalisms, developed in the logic programming environment, have been suggested for robotics applications. Particularly, the system for dynamic domains, GOLOG, suggested by [4], has been extended by multiple authors for a variety of fields (e.g. [6,9]). Involvement of sensory information in building the plan of multiagent interaction has significantly increased the applicability of GOLOG. However, GOLOG is still not well suited to handle the multiagent scenarios with lack of information concerning the actions of opponent agents, when it is impossible to sense them.

At the same time, the methodology of obtaining a formal description for a set of facts in the form of inductive reasoning in the wide sense has found a series of applications, including bio-chemistry, protein engineering, drug design, natural language processing, finite element mesh design, satellite diagnosis, text classification, medicine, games, planning, software engineering, software agents, information retrieval, ecology, traffic analysis and network management [7].

In this paper, we target the domain that cannot be solved with classical attribute value learning system. A knowledge discovery system that is based on inductive logic programming or similar approaches [5] is insufficient, taken alone, because it is incapable of performing necessary reasoning about actions and knowledge in accordance to heuristics available from domain experts. Neglecting this knowledge would dramatically decrease the extents of possible predictions. Also, a generic knowledge discovery system is not oriented to handle dynamic kinds of data. Therefore, we intend to merge reasoning about action-based and learning based systems to form the environment to handle dynamic domains with incomplete information.

## 2 The System Architecture

We choose the GOLOG [4] and JSM [2] environments for reasoning about action and inductive machine learning respectively because of their flexibility and powerfulness. Using the above approaches to illustrate our methodology, we keep in mind that our architecture of merging deductive and inductive components is independent of the choice of particular formalism and better models real-world domains than these approaches taken separately.

A generic environment for reasoning about actions is not well suited for handling essentially incomplete data, where neither totality of procedures, nor actions preconditions nor successor state constraints are available. Evidently, situation calculus by itself does not have predictive power and needs to be augmented by a learning system capable of operating in the dynamic language. Abstraction of reasoning about action in the way of GOLOG assumes that action preconditions, successor state expressions and expressions for complex actions are known.

Incomplete knowledge about the world is reflected as an expression for non-deterministic choice of the order in which to perform actions, non-deterministic choice of argument value, and non-deterministic repetition. These settings are adequate for the selected robotics application, where the designer uses a particular approximation of the external world. In a general setting, an agent that performs reasoning about actions is expected to learn from the situations, where the actual course of actions has been forced by the environment to deviate from the obtained plan, using the current world model.

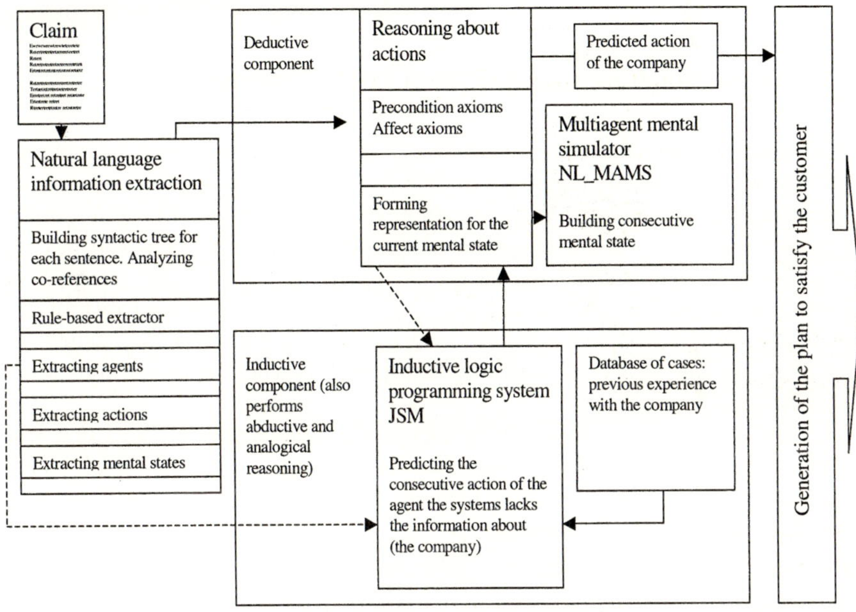


**Fig. 1.** Architecture of the claim processing system. The natural language information extraction unit (on the left) provides the deductive component (on the top right) with the extracted actions. If the *reasoning about action* component determines a lack of information on the opponent agent, the *inductive component* (on the bottom right) is initiated. The *inductive* component loads the set of accumulated claims for the given company (its name is extracted by NL component) and predicts the following action given the state, obtained by the *reasoning about action* component. If the multiagent scenario is rather complex, the simulation by means of NL_MAMS is required to predict the following mental state

There are two basic kinds of methodologies for deriving the future action or set of possible actions:

1) By means of reasoning about actions. Its framework specifies a set of available basic and combined actions with conditions, given a current situation, described via a

set of fluents. These fluents in turn have additional constraints and obey certain conditions, given a set of previous actions. Action possibilities, pre-conditions and successor state axioms are formulated *manually*, analyzing the past experience. This methodology can fully solve the problem if full formal prerequisites for reasoning about action are available.

2) By means of learning the future action from the set of examples. Given a set of examples with a sequence of actions and fluents in each, a prediction engine generates hypotheses of how they are linked to future actions. Resultant hypotheses are then applied to predict the future action. Such kinds of learning requires enumeration of actions and fluents; learning itself is performed automatically. This methodology is worth applying in a stand-alone manner if neither explicit possibilities for actions nor their pre-conditions are available.

The application domain of the current study demonstrates that the above methodologies are complementary.

# 3 Inductive Machine Learning as a Logic Program

In this paper we implement both the GOLOG and JSM environments in logic program. We will only briefly comment on GOLOG in the following section because it has been thoroughly presented in the literature. The JSM approach [2] was inspired by the plausible similarity-based reasoning of the philosopher J.S. Mill who has suggested a set of five canons by means of which to analyze and interpret our observations for the purpose of drawing conclusions about the causal relationships they exhibit. In this study we build the JSM system as a logic program, called JaSMine http://www.dcs.bbk.ac.uk/~galitsky/JaSMine/, following the formal frameworks of [1, 10].

The JSM environment consists of features, objects and targets. Within a first-order language, objects are individ constants, features and targets are terms which include these constants. For a target (feature), there are four groups of objects with respect to the evidence they provide for this target:

*Positive – Negative – Inconsistent - Unknown.*

An inference to obtain a target feature (satisfied or not) can be represented as one in a respective four-valued logic. The predictive machinery is based on building hypotheses, $target(X)\text{:-}\, features_1(X, \ldots), \ldots, feature_n(X, \ldots)$, that separate examples, where *target* is an effect, and $features_1, \ldots, feature_n \in features$ are the causes; $X$ ranges over objects.

Desired separation is based on the *similarity* of objects in terms of features they satisfy. Usually, such similarity is domain-dependent. However, building the general framework of inductive-based prediction, we use the anti-unification of formulas that express the totality of features of the given and other objects (our futures do not have to be unary predicates and are expressed by arbitrary first-order terms).

Our starting example of JSM settings for unary predicate is as follows (from now on we use the conventional PROLOG notations for variables and constants):

```
features([a,b,c,d,e]). objects([o1, o2, o3, o4, o5, o6, o7]).
targets([v1]).
a(o1). b(o1). c(o1).                a(o2). b(o2). c(o2). e(o2).
a(o3). d(o3).                       a(o4). c(o4). d(o4).
a(o5). b(o5). e(o5). a(o6). d(o6).
a(o7). b(o7). c(o7). e(o7).         v1(o1). v1(o2). v1(o5).
unknown(v1(o7)).unknown(v1(o6)).
```

Starting with the positive and negative examples, *jPos(X, V)* and *jNeg(X, V)*, for the target *V*, we form the totality of intersections for these examples ( positive ones, *U*, that satisfy *iPos(U,V)* and negative ones, *W*, that satisfy *iNeg(W,V)*, not shown ):

*iPos(U, V):- jPos(X1, V), jPos(X2, V), X1\=X2, similar(X1, X2, U), U\=[ ].*
*iPos(U, V):- iPos(U1, V), jPos(X1, V), similar(X1, U1, U), U\=[ ].*

Above are the recursive definitions of the hypothesis. As the logic program clauses that actually form the totality of intersection of examples, we derive the following (the negative case is analogous):

*iPos(U, V):- iPos(U, V, _).*
*iPos(U, V, Accums):- jPos(X1, V), jPos(X2, V), X1\=X2, similar(X1, X2, U), Accums=[X1, X2], U\=[ ].*
*iPos(U, V, AccumsX1):- iPos(U1, V, Accums), !, jPos(X1, V), not member(X1, Accums), similar(X1, U1, U), U\=[ ], append(Accums, [X1], AccumsX1).*

To obtain the actual positive and negative hypotheses from the respective intersections, we filter out the hypotheses that are satisfied by both positive and negative examples *j0Hyp(U, V)*:

*j0Hyp(U, V):- iPos(U, V), iNeg(U, V).*
*jPosHyp(U, V):-iPos(U, V), not j0Hyp(U, V).*
*jNegHyp(U, V):-iNeg(U, V), not j0Hyp(U, V).*

The following clauses deliver the background for (enumeration of objects that cause) positive, negative and inconsistent hypotheses:

*ePos(X, V):- jPos(X, V), jPosHyp(U, V), similar(X, U, U).*
*eNeg(X, V):- jNeg(X, V), jNegHyp(U, V), similar(X, U, U).*
*j01(X, V):-jT0(X,V), jPosHyp(U1, V), jNegHyp(U2, V), similar(X, U1, U1), similar(X, U2, U2).*

Finally, we approach the clauses for prediction. For the objects with unknown targets, the system predicts that they either satisfy that targets, do not satisfy these targets, or that the fact of satisfaction is inconsistent with the input facts (examples):

***jPos1(X,V):- jT0(X, V), jPosHyp(U, V), similar(X, U,U), not j01(X, V).***
*jNeg1(X,V):- jT0(X, V), jNegHyp(U, V), similar(X, U,U), not j01(X, V).*
*jT1(X,V):- jT0(X,V), not jPos1(X, V), not jNeg1(X, V), not j01(X, V).*

Indeed, the first clause above will serve as an entry point to predict (choose) an action from the explicit list of available actions that can be obtained for the current state, given the precondition axioms. Also, if there is no positively predicted action, we settle for an inconsistent prediction (assuming it is better to select and commit to some action rather than do nothing at all).

*predict_action_by_learning(ActionToBePredicted,S):-*
*findAllPossibleActionsAtThisState(S, As), loadRequiredSamples(As),*
*member(ActionToBePredicted, As), jPos1(X, ActionToBePredicted), !, X\=[ ].*

For example, for the knowledge base above, we have the following results:

```
  Intersections    for    positive,    negative    and    unassigned    exam-
ples[[a(_E0C),b(_E1C),c(_E2C)],[a(_DDC),b(
  _DEC)],[a(_D9C),b(_DAC),e(_DBC)]]
  [[a(_E84),d(_E94)]]
  [[a(o7),b(o7),c(o7),e(o7)],[a(o6),d(o6)]]
  Positive,    negative    and    contradiction    hypotheses:
[[a(_FDC),b(_FEC),c(_FFC)],[a(_
  FAC),b(_FBC)],[a(_F6C),b(_F7C),e(_F8C)]] , [[a(_1054),d(_1064)]] , []
  Background   for   positive,   negative   and   inconsistent   hypotheses:
[[a(o1),b(o1),c(o
  1)],[a(o2),b(o2),c(o2),e(o2)],[a(o5),b(o5),e(o5)]]                    ,
[[a(o3),d(o3)],[a(o4),c(o4)
  ,d(o4)]] , []
  Prediction   for   positive,   negative   and   inconsistent   results:
([[a(o7),b(o7),c(o7),e(o7)]] , [[a(o6),d(o6)]] , [])
```

## 4 Merging Deductive and Inductive Reasoning about Action

Based on the motivations, which were presented in the Introduction, we have the following methodology to predict an action of an agent in an environment where we do not have complete information on this agent. If we are unable to derive the actions of this agent given the preconditions of his actions and successor state axioms to sufficiently characterize his current state, learning-based prediction needs to come into play. Instead of just taking the current state into account, as reasoning about action would do, learning-based prediction takes into account the totality of previous actions and states. It is required because there is a lack of knowledge about which previous actions and situations affect the current choice of action.

Situation calculus is formulated in a first-order language with certain second-order features[8]. A possible world history that is a result of a sequence of *actions* is called *situation*. The expression, *do(a,s)*, denotes the successor situation to *s* after action *a* is applied. For example, *do(complain(Customer, do(harm(Company),$S_0$))*, is a situation expressing the world history that is based on the sequence of actions \{ *complain(Customer), harm(Company)*}, where *Customer* and *Company* are variables (with explicit meanings). We refer the reader to [4] for the further details on the implementation of situation calculus. Also, situations involve the *fluents,* whose values vary from situation to situation and denote them by predicates with the latter arguments ranging over the situations, for example,

*upset(Customer, do(harm(Company),$S_0$)).*

Actions have *preconditions* – the constraints on actions:

*poss(complain(Customer), s)* ≡ *upset(Customer, s).*

*Effect axioms* (post-conditions) describe the effect of a given action on the fluents:

*poss(complain(Customer), s) & responsive(Company ) ⊃*
*settle_down(Customer, do(complain(Customer), s)).*

Effect axioms express the causal links between the domain entities.

As we see, the methodology of situation calculus is building a sequence of actions given their pre- and post-conditions. To choose an action, we verify that the preconditions are dependent on the current fluents. After an action is performed, it affects these fluents, which in turn determine the consecutive action, and so forth.

The *frame problem* [4] comes into play to reduce the number of effect axioms that do not change (the common sense law of inertia). The successor state axiom resolves the frame problem:

$poss(a,s) \supset [\, f(\hat{y}, do(a,s)) \equiv \gamma_f^+(\hat{y}, a,s) \vee (\, f(\hat{y},s) \,\&\, \neg\gamma_f^-(\hat{y}, a,s)\,)\,]$,

where $\gamma_f^+(\hat{y}, a,s)$ ( $\gamma_f^-(\hat{y}, a,s)$ ) is a formula describing under what conditions doing action $a$ in situation $s$ makes fluent $f$ become true (false, respectively) in the successor situation $do(a,s)$.

GOLOG extends the situation calculus with complex actions, involving, in particular, *if-then* and *while* constructions. Macros $do(\delta, s, s')$ denotes the fact that situation s' is a terminating situation of an execution of complex action $\delta$ starting in situation $s$. If $a_1,\ldots, a_n$ are actions, then

- $[a_1{:}\ldots{:}\, a_n]$ is a deterministic sequence of actions;
- $[a_1\#\ldots\#\, a_n]$ is a non-deterministic sequence of actions;
- *ifCond(p)* is checking a condition expressed by *p*;
- *star(a)*, nondeterministic repetition;
- $if(p, a_1, a_2)$, if-then-else conditional;
- $while(p, a_1, a_2)$, iteration.

We suggest the reader to consult [4] for more details, and proceed to the GOLOG interpreter. Below the last line is added to the conventional GOLOG interpreter to suggest an alternative choice of action by means of learning by example, if the other options for the following action are exhausted (see the Section above).

```
do(A1 : A2,S,S1) :- do(A1,S,S2), do(A2,S2,S1).
do(ifCond(P),S,S) :- holds(P,S).
do(A1 # A2,S,S1) :- do(A1,S,S1) ; do(A2,S,S1).
do(if(P,A1,A2),S,S1) :- do((call(P) : A1) # (call( not P) : A2),S,S1).
do(star(A),S,S1) :- S1 = S ; do(A : star(A),S,S1).
do(while(P,A),S,S1):- do(star(call(P) : A) : call( not P),S,S1).
do(pi(V,A),S,S1) :- sub(V,_,A,A1), do(A1,S,S1).
do(A,S,S1) :- proc(A,A1), do(A1,S,S1).
do(A,S,do(A,S)) :- primitive_action(A), poss(A,S).
do(A, S, do(A, S)):- predict_action_by_learning(A, S).
```

## 5 Modeling the Claims of Unsatisfied Customers

To suggest an extensive illustration of reasoning about actions in the conditions of uncertainty, we consider a real-life problem of automation of customers' claim. This problem requires a logical component that is capable of modeling the process of interaction between a customer and a company. This logic component is expected to exhibit predictive power: given the initial circumstances of a conflict, it needs to suggest a set of procedures that would likely lead to customer satisfaction by a company or a third party.

Our problem domain is based on the experience of a series of consumer advocacy companies that try to help the customers, unsatisfied by particular products, services, or, especially, customer support. We base our model on publicly available database of complaints. In our considerations, we skip the natural language component that extracts actions, fluents and their parameters; we refer to quite extensive literature on information extraction or to our particular approach, based on logic programming [3]. The task of the written claim processing can be formulated as relating a claim to a class that requires a certain set of reactions (directly contacting a producer or retailer, clarifiying the situation to a consumer, bringing a case to court, addressing a particular consumer advocacy firm etc.). Performing such kinds of tasks allows us to automate the claim processing, significantly accelerating the results and reducing the cost of operations for a consumer advocacy firm (Fig.2).

Clearly, the application of statistical machine learning would skip too many details to adequately relate a natural language claim to a reaction class. If the determination of such a class deploys keyword-based information extraction methods, peculiarities of both natural language representation and the dispute process itself are ignored. The reader should take into account that similar claims with slightly distinguishing mental states of agents may frequently belong to totally different classes of reaction in accordance to the willingness of a company to satisfy its customer (so that he or she drops his/her claim).

Hence, we reveal a set of actions and fluents for each claim. The claim scenario includes two main agents: a customer and a company (for simplicity, we consider multiple representatives of a company as a conventional agent). The behavioral patterns for these two agents are quite different with respect to uncertainty: a customer is assumed to be with us (the consumer advocacy company), and her intentions and motivations are clear. Conversely, we can observe the actions of a company, but we can only build beliefs on its intentions and motivations: we are uncertain about the causal relations between the company's actions and its strategy.

Our current approach to modeling the claims is based on reasoning about actions and respective data mining; here we do not model mental states of involved agents in details, using a special machinery of reasoning about mental states, developed elsewhere [3,11]. As we said in the introduction, we perform this step of approximation (ignoring the peculiarities of the mental world) to focus on merging reasoning about action with deductive data mining. Also, in this domain we did not use default reasoning to describe typical and abnormal situations.

Processing a database of claims, we can reveal the typical action patterns for both customers and companies. What we have discovered (and may be natural for the reader) is that the set of possible strategies for both companies and customers is limited. The claim databases we use allow a statistically significant analysis of a variety of claims for a given company.

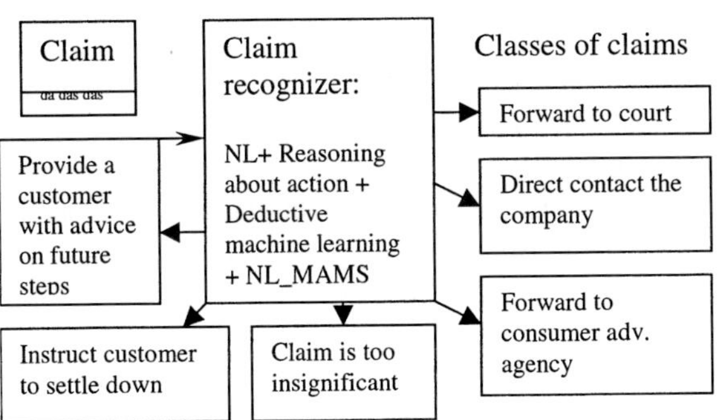


**Fig. 2.** The problem domain for our hybrid approach: recognizing the class of a claim

In the complaints, the customers explicitly mention their actions and most of the fluents expressing their mental states. Ambiguity in representation of actions for the customers may be caused by the errors in natural language processing and inadequate writing by the customer. As to the company, we obtain a description of its actions and incomplete plot of its fluents in accordance to the customer's viewpoint. This data is insufficient to perform the prediction of the company's planning given only current scenario. On the other hand, using pure predictive machinery without actually modeling the company's sequence of action in the deductive way does not allow obtaining the latter in sufficient details to relate a given claim to a class.

The customer component includes complete knowledge of the precondition for primitive actions, successor state axioms and constraints on fluents. The customer's component is ready for modeling its sequence of actions. However, the company's component is incomplete: we don't fully know preconditions for primitive actions; also, our knowledge on successor state axioms and constraints on fluents is incomplete.

Note that we cannot conduct a supervised learning for our system in a usual sense because no company would ever disclose its customer support policy to eliminate uncertainty in our representation for the company's fluents. We form the learning dataset using the past claims, where we may get information about the claim results and manually assign the class of reaction. At the same time we would never get information on the company's side.

Indeed, recognition of a claim is determining the following action of an opponent. A usual claim is the description of the process of interaction between two conflicting agents, a customer and a company. The fragment of the claim database with the claim classification criteria (the column names) can be found at http://www.dcs.bbk.ac.uk/~galitsky/CLAIMS/AnalyzedClaims.htm

## 6 Conclusions

In this paper, we merged deductive reasoning about action with logic and combinatorial predictive machinery that implements inductive, abductive and analogical reasoning. This resulted in a hybrid reasoning system, involving multiagent simulation, which is a major component of the overall claim processing system.

The merged formalisms were found adequate in terms of modeling the agent interaction during the automated processing of claims. Our model includes about ten consecutive actions, including deterministic and non-deterministic ones. For a particular claim, given an initial sequence of actions, the system provides predictions of consecutive actions, which are expected to follow from each of the opposing agents. The predictions are then the basis of decisions concerning the plan of action for a customer to resolve the conflict: as a result, the claim is assigned a class of reactions. Our initial testing showed that the proper decisions are carried out in more than 82% of cases if the NL component is eliminated (required information is extracted manually). The testing environment included 50 claims for inductive learning and 50 claims for testing. The claims were in the banking services sector and were taken from PlanetFeedback.com, a consumer advocacy portal aimed at a general audience.

The NL component requires a much larger corpus of claims for training and evaluation of action extraction rules. Such a required collection of claims in this specific, narrow domain is not yet available. In our further studies we plan to conduct a joint verification of the four suggested components for a sufficiently large, classified database of claims (www.dcs.bbk.ac.uk/~galitsky/complaints.htm).

## References

1. Anshakov, O.M., Finn, V.K., Skvortsov, D.P.: On axiomatization of many-valued logics associated with formalization of plausible reasoning, *Studia Logica v42 N4*(1989) 423-447.
2. Finn, V.K.: On the synthesis of cognitive procedures and the problem of induction NTI Series 2 N1-2 (1999) 8-45.
3. Galitsky, B.: Using mental simulator for emotional rehabilitation of autistic patients. *FLAIRS – 03,* May 12-14, St. Augustine, FL (2003).
4. Levesque, H.J., Reiter, R., Lesperance, Y., Lin, F., Scherl, R.B.: GOLOG: A logic programming language for dynamic domains. *Journal of Logic Programming* v31, 59-84 (1997).
5. Muggleton, S. (ed.): Inductive Logic Programming, Academic Press (1992).
6. Lakemeyer, G.: On sensing in GOLOG. in Levesque, H.J., Pirri, F., (eds). *Logical foundations for cognitive agents*, Springer (1999).
7. De Raedt, L.: A perspective on Inductive Logic Programming. In Apt, K.R, Marek, V.W., Truszczynski, M., Warren, D. Eds. *The Logic Programming Paradigm* Springer (1999).
8. Shanahan, M. Solving the frame problem. MIT Press (1997).
9. Souchansky, M.: On-line Decision-Theoretic GOLOG Interpreter. *IJCAI*-01 (2001).
10. Vinogradov, D.V.: Logic programs for quasi-axiomatic theories NTI Series 2 *N1-2* (1999) 61-64.
11. Wooldridge, M.: Reasoning about Rational Agents. The MIT Press Cambridge MA London England (2002).

# Preserving Diversity in Particle Swarm Optimisation

Tim Hendtlass

Centre for Intelligent Systems and Complex Processes,
Swinburne University of Technology,
Melbourne, Australia.
thendtlass@swin.edu.au

**Abstract.** Particle Swarm Optimisation (PSO) is an optimisation algorithm that shows promise. However its performance on complex problems with multiple minima falls short of that of the Ant Colony Optimisation (ACO) algorithm when both algorithms are applied to travelling salesperson type problems (TSP). Unlike ACO, PSO can be easily applied to a wider range of problems than TSP. This paper shows that by adding a memory capacity to each particle in a PSO algorithm performance can be significantly improved to a competitive level to ACO on the smaller TSP problems.

## 1 Introduction

Few real life optimisation problems have only a single minimum[1], normally a host of sub optimal minima also exist. The challenge in applying optimisation algorithms is to maximize the possibility of finding the global minimum. Greedy algorithms that optimise each individual step, for example gradient descent or differential evolution, have the advantage of speed but the disadvantage of a higher probability of becoming trapped in a local minimum. Alternate techniques, for example evolutionary algorithms, maintain a finite spectrum of moves in case these become advantageous later. This reduces the probability of becoming trapped in a sub optimal minimum but such techniques are slower owing to the need to maintain a population of moves. It is obviously important to make as efficient use of the population as possible.

For evolutionary algorithms it is possible to store historical information about good and poor points in problem space in a neural network and use this to minimize (but not eliminate) the number of individuals in the population that are close to points in problem space that have previously been investigated. [Podlena and Hendtlass 98] Limiting the number of offspring allowed close to known points has the effect of reducing the tendency for the population to bunch up around the current optimum and thus maintain diversity.

Even with this evolutionary algorithms are slow to converge as considerable information is lost as successive generations die out. The use of elites can minimize but not eliminate the loss of good solutions. In the past few years, algorithms have be-

[1] Optimization problems can involve looking for either a minimum or maximum, depending on the problem. For simplicity the term 'minimum' will be used in this paper on the understanding, unless clearly stated otherwise, that the word 'maximum' may be substituted if the problem so requires.

P.W.H. Chung, C.J. Hinde, M. Ali (Eds.): IEA/AIE 2003, LNAI 2718, pp. 31–40, 2003.

come popular in which individuals do not die but rather continually move through the problem space themselves. The two best-known examples are Ant Colony Optimisation (ACO) and Particle Swarm Optimisation (PSO).

Ant Colony Optimisation is an algorithm that is traditionally used to find solutions to travelling salesperson problems or any other problem that can be cast as a path minimization / set order problem. In ACO artificial ants leave pheromone trails after they have explored a possible path, the pheromone being laid along the path they have just completed with a concentration proportional to the path quality. When constructing a new path an ant is influenced by local conditions (such as relative magnitudes of the possible next valid path elements) together with the pheromone concentration along each of these path elements. The pheromone provides a historical record of where the ants have gone previously that acts as a counter balance to the greedy local condition influence. The pheromone diminishes with time to remove old information that has not been reinforced so that the collective effect of the pheromone trails reflects the collective optimal path wisdom of the colony.

Particle Swarm Optimization is an algorithm in which particles move through problem space under a number of influences. These include their momentum (the tendency to continue moving as they were), a tendency to move towards the currently best known results obtained by the swarm and a tendency to move towards the best current result amongst that particles neighbours. The latter two influences are both of a greedy nature as they will tend to cause the particle to move in the direction of known good solutions; the first influence partly compensates for this by preventing any thing from happening too fast. As a result PSO algorithms are fast but may readily become trapped in local minima. As the position of the particles is calculated at discreet times, it is possible that particles may have crossed positions of good fitness between evaluations. The speed of the particles is therefore important and needs to be managed to obtain a good balance between aggressive exploration and detailed search. Various PSO algorithms are described in more detail below.

This paper considers an addition to the PSO algorithm that adds a memory influence conceptually derived from the pheromone trails of the ACO algorithm. It will be shown that this reduces the tendency of the PSO to find local minima. PSO results on a TSP type problem will be shown to be significantly improved by the addition of this memory and will be shown to be similar to those produced by ant colony optimisation. This is important as PSO, unlike ACO, can be applied to problems that cannot readily be turned in TSR form.

## 2 The Particle Swarm Optimisation Algorithm

The Particle Swarm Algorithm [Eberhart and Kennedy 95, Eberhart and Shi 95. Eberhart, Dobbins and Simpson 1996, Kennedy 97, Eberhart and Shi 00] is a population-based algorithm in which the individuals move through a problem space with a velocity that is regularly updated as a consequence of the performance of all the individuals in the swarm. The updated velocity is a combination of the previous velocity $V_T$, a component towards the best position $B$ found by any individual in the swarm so far, and a component towards a position $S$ derived from comparing the relative performance of this individual with the performances of a number of other swarm members.

The new velocity ($V_{T+t}$) is:

$$V_{T+t} = \chi(MV_T + (1-M)(rand * P(\frac{X-B}{t}) + rand * G(\frac{X-S}{t})) + VC) \quad (1)$$

where $M$ is the momentum, $X$ is the current position of the individual, *rand* returns a random number in the range from 0 to 1,and $P$ and $G$ set the relative attention to be placed on the positions $B$ and $S$. Both $M$ and $G$ are bounded to the range from 0 to 1. The recently introduced factors  and $VC$ are defined below,  may be taken to be unity and $VC$ zero for the traditional algorithm. If $M$ is large, the $B$ and $S$ positions have little effect; if $G$ is large $B$ has more influence than $S$. The parameter $t$ is the time between updates and is required for dimensional consistency. It is usually taken to be unity.

Without the component towards $S$, the swarm tends to rush towards the first minimum found. An appropriately chosen $S$ will cause the swarm to spread out and explore the problem space more thoroughly. The position $S$ is derived in an effective but computationally modest way in [Hendtlass 2001]. All other swarm members influence all other individuals but the magnitude of the influence decreases with both fitness and distance for a minimization problem. (For a maximization problem it would increase with fitness but decrease with distance.) Individuals within a nominated threshold distance are considered to be exploring the same region of space and make no contribution. An individual $j$ is attracted to the position $S_j$ whose components $S_{ji}$ are calculated from $D_{ni}$, the distance along the i$^{th}$ axis from this individual to some other individual $n$ in the swarm together with $F_n$, the fitness of individual $n$. The position $S$ for individual $j$ is defined by:

$$S_{ji} = \sum_{n=1}^{N} W_{ji} \quad (2)$$

$$where \quad W_{ji} = \frac{1}{D_{ni}^2(1+F_n)} \quad if \; D_{ni} \geq threshold,$$
$$= 0 \; otherwise$$

The allowable velocity is often bounded by a relationship such as

$$v_{id} = \begin{cases} -v_{max} & , v_{id} < -v_{max} \\ v_{max} & , v_{id} > v_{max} \end{cases} \quad (3)$$

A further enhancement introduced by Clerc involves a 'constriction factor' in which the entire right side of the formula is weighted by a coefficient [Clerc 98, Clerc 99]. Clerc's generalised particle swarm model allows an infinite number of ways in which the balance between exploration and convergence can be controlled. The simplest of these is called Type 1 PSO (T1PSO), and recent work by Eberhart and Shi [Eberhart and Shi 2000] showed that placing bounds on the maximum velocity of a particle in T1PSO "*provides performance on the benchmark functions superior to any other published results known by the authors*".

The equations defining the constriction factor are:

$$\chi = \frac{2\kappa}{\left|2-\phi-\sqrt{\phi^2-4\phi}\right|} \tag{4}$$

where $\varphi = (P+G) > 4$, *and* $\kappa \in [0,1]$

In general, each particle will have a unique position *S* to which it is attracted giving the swarm good spreading characteristics. In the swarm algorithm particles continuously search the problem space under the influence of both the entire swarm's current performance and prior history. The momentum component ensures that individuals are less likely to get trapped in a local minimum. In time, all swarm individuals will circle around one or a few points in problem space.

Knowledge of how a swarm is travelling can be used to influence how extended the swarm should be. When the swarm is centred upon a good solution, the particles will move with little common velocity component between members. In this case it is desirable for the swarm to converge. However, if the swarm is travelling as a structured entity in which all particles have a significant common velocity component, then the swarm should be made to spread out in the search space. This is achieved by an additional coherence velocity term *VC* is defined as follows.

The coherence of the swarm's movement (*CSM*) can be defined by:

$$CSM = \frac{speed\_swarm\_centre}{average\_particle\_speed}$$

where: $$speed\_swarms\_centre = \left\| \frac{\sum_{i=1}^{\#particles} \vec{v}}{\#\,particles} \right\|$$

This *CSM* term is used as the basis with which to calculate a new velocity term known as the coherence velocity (*vc*) to be included in equation 1 . The desired effect of this term is that a swarm on the move will tend to be spread out, and when it encounters a local minimum, the 'momentum' term of the PSO will carry the swarm a small distance past the minimum. If the swarm has encountered the true minimum it will converge back on this point. If it has only encountered a local minimum the combination of the momentum and increased spread of the swarm is far more likely to cause the swarm to explore other surrounding minima, thus allow the swarm to move on to the global minimum.

The coherence velocity for the $i^{th}$ particle in dimension *d* is given by:

$$vc_{id} = sh*Step(CSM, so) * average\_particle\_speed_d * CauchyDist() \tag{5}$$

where *sh* is a multiplier and *so* an 'offset' and $Step(CSM, so) = \begin{cases} 0 & CSM <= so \\ 1 & CSM > so \end{cases}$

The Cauchy distribution random number is included to prevent the coherence velocity causing the swarm to accelerate in its current direction, without spreading out significantly. Because the random number can have either positive or negative values, the effect is to make the swarm to spread out around its current position. The average particle speed is included to scale the coherence velocity to the same order of magnitude as the velocity of particles within the swarm.

## 3 Expanding PSO: Adding Memory to Each Particle

The purpose of the added memory feature is to maintained spread and therefore diversity by providing individual specific alternate target points to be used at times instead of the current local best position. To optimise this effect each particle in the swarm maintains its own memory. The maximum size of the memory and the probability that one of the points it contains will be used instead of the current local optimal point are user specified parameters. The local optimum point will be added to the memory if the fitness of this point is better than the least fit stored point. It may also be required to differ by at least a specified amount from any point already in the memory. The new memory point replaces the least fit point if the memory is full. There is a certain probability that a point from the memory will be used instead of the position $S$ in equation 1 above. When a point from a particles memory is to be used the point may be chosen randomly or the probability of selection may be fitness based (with better fitness producing a higher probability of selection).

## 4 The Test Problem

The test problem used was the Burma 14 TSP data set. This data set consists of the longitude and latitude of 14 cities in Burma and the aim is to find the shortest path that visits each city one and only once. This is only a modest size problem of this class. Since neither the starting point of the path nor the direction of travel is specified, there are 13!/2 individual paths (just over $3*10^9$) producing a total of 5704 different path lengths. The lengths of these paths are distributed as shown in Fig. 1,.Fig. 2 and Fig. 3 show more detail of shorter subsets of these paths.

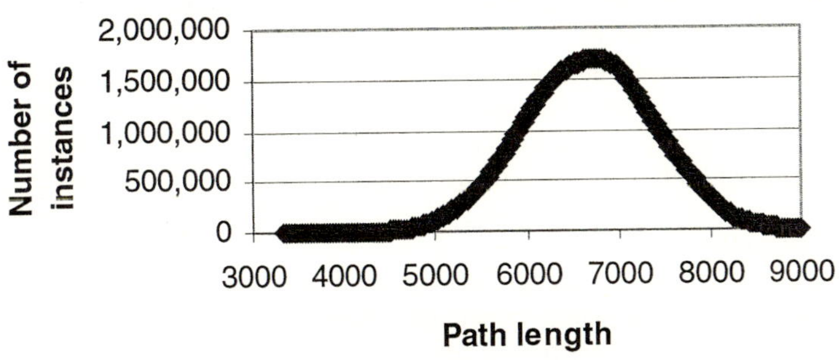


**Fig. 1.** The number of instances of all solution lengths less than 9000.

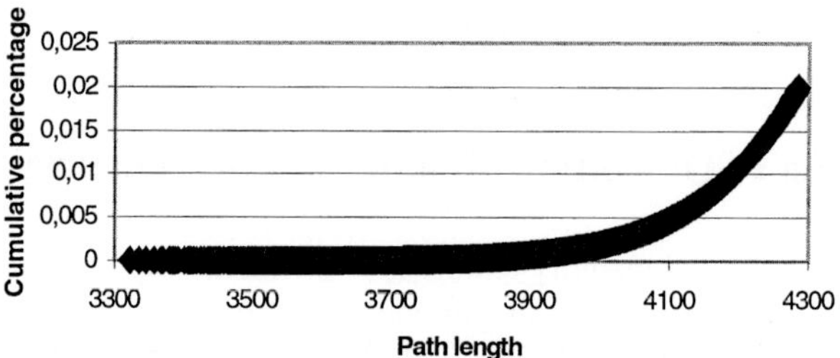


**Fig. 2.** Instances of solution lengths less than 4300 as a percentage of the total number of paths.

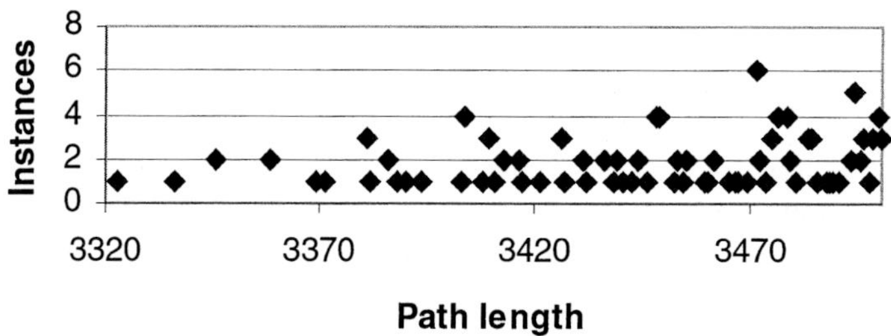


**Fig. 3.** The number of instances of all solutions less than 3500for the Burma 14 TSP data set

## 5 Methodology

The addition of a memory gives another option from which to select point *S* in equation 1 but has no bearing on the need to manage the speeds of the particles. A simple PSO algorithm without speed management was used to more clearly demonstrate the effect of adding the memory.

A variety of list sizes and use probabilities were considered. The memory-filling algorithm described above was used both with and without the requirement for a minimum difference to any point already on the list. The points to be used from the list were selected both randomly and also using a rank based selection scheme.

Each of the results quoted below is derived from 250 independent repeats (unless otherwise stated).

The position of a particle in 14 dimensional space was mapped to an order by sorting the dimensional component values into order of deceasing value. As each dimension was associated with a particular city the sorted order is the city order.

A number of measures of the solutions produced by a particular set of parameters are used. The minimum possible path length is 3323 km so that any path longer than this is non optimal. The first two figures of merit are the number of times the optimal path was found, and the average excess path length. However for many purposes, for example scheduling, solutions that are close to optimal are also useful. Hence for this problem the percentage of paths less than 3417km (in the top $10^{-6}$% of all paths) and 3510km (in the top $5*10^{-6}$% of all paths) are also suitable to use as performance figures when comparing sets of parameters. Finally the average number of iterations to find the best solution for a particular parameter set is of obvious importance.

## 6 Results

The results shown below were all obtained using a common population size of thirty and the normal local point of influence was derived from the ten closest neighbours, (values that prior experimentation had shown to be suitable for this test set). For similar reasons the three parameters $M$, $P$ and $G$ from equation one were set to 0.97, 0.04 and 0.96 respectively. The values that were varied were the depth of the memory (0-20), the probability of using a memory point rather than the current local point (0 – 20%), whether the memory point to be used was based on the rank order of performance (rank) or just randomly selected (random) and the minimum difference (D) required between a potential memory point and all the points already in the memory before the potential memory point would be considered for storage. In each of tables 1 to 4 one of these variables was altered, with the other three being held constant. The constant values will be found in each table caption. The performance of the swarm algorithm without the particles having a memory is also shown in each table for easy reference.

**Table 1.** Performance variation with memory depth. 10% probability, rank, D=0.

| Memory depth | % ideal result | % in top $1*10^{-6}$% | % in top $5*10^{-6}$% | Average excess path length |
|---|---|---|---|---|
| No memory | 2 | 9.1 | 24 | 390 |
| 5 | 3.2 | 11.6 | 28 | 353 |
| 10 | 4.8 | 17.2 | 32 | 313 |
| 20 | 6 | 20.4 | 38 | 296 |

**Table 2.** Variation with memory probability. Deep = 10, rank, D=0.

| Memory use probability | % ideal result | % in top $1*10^{-6}$% | % in top $5*10^{-6}$% | Average excess path length |
|---|---|---|---|---|
| No memory | 2 | 9.1 | 24 | 390 |
| 5 | 3.2 | 15.6 | 31.2 | 351 |
| 10 | 4.8 | 17.2 | 32 | 313 |
| 15 | 4.4 | 13.6 | 30.4 | 338 |
| 20 | 5.2 | 13.2 | 29.2 | 315 |

**Table 3.** Variation with memory choice. Depth as noted, probability 10%, D=0.

| Memory choice | % ideal result | % in top $1*10^{-6}$% | % in top $5*10^{-6}$% | Average excess path length |
|---|---|---|---|---|
| No memory | 2 | 9.1 | 24 | 390 |
| 10 deep rank | 4.8 | 17.2 | 32 | 313 |
| 10 deep random | 2 | 11. 6 | 21.6 | 352 |
| 20 deep rank | 5.2 | 13.2 | 29.2 | 314 |
| 20 deep random | 2.8 | 13.6 | 29.6 | 340 |

**Table 4.** Variation with minimum separation. Depth =10, 10% probability, rank.

| Minimum difference (D) | % ideal result | % in top $1*10^{-6}$% | % in top $5*10^{-6}$% | Average excess path length |
|---|---|---|---|---|
| No memory | 2 | 9.1 | 24 | 390 |
| 0 | 4.8 | 17.2 | 32 | 313 |
| 50 | 10 | 22.4 | 44.4 | 224 |
| 100 | 16 | 29.6 | 47.6 | 214 |
| 150 | 19.6 | 38 | 50.8 | 198 |
| 200 | 10.8 | 25.6 | 43.2 | 242 |

From tables 1 to 4 it can be seen that, as might be expected, performance increases with memory depth. Too much use of the memory contents appears to be counter-productive and for this problem a probability of 10% gives the best result. It seems clear that when choosing which location is to be taken from the memory a bias towards the better performing memory locations via rank selection outperformed random selection in almost every case (only two of which are shown in table 3). The final table, table 4 shows that it is desirable that the locations stored in the memory are unique as repeats decrease the effective memory size and also alters the selection process. However, insisting on too large a difference can become counter productive as the memory may not actually fill. For the Burma 14 problem a difference of 100 to 150 seems to have been most suitable.

Fig. 4 shows a plot of the average iterations taken by the algorithm, for particular sets of parameters, to find the final solution plotted against the number of times that parameter set resulted in the optimum solution being found. As might be expected the improved performance comes at the cost of the number of iterations needed.

Table 5 shows the top performing parameter sets for each performance measure sorted into order with the performance without using particle memories shown for comparison. The order of merit is remarkably consistent, no matter which performance measure is used. The parameter set found by combining the individual best values from tables one to four is actually only the second best performing of the parameter sets tried, possibly suggesting the parameters are not fully independent. The improvement obtained by using either of the top two-parameter sets is clearly significant compared to a swarm of memory less particles. The result obtained using Ant Colony optimization (ACO) are also shown, these were taken from [Hendtlass and Angus 02]. While a detailed comparison would need to take into account the value of parameters uses, they are included to show that the results obtained by both algorithms are comparable.

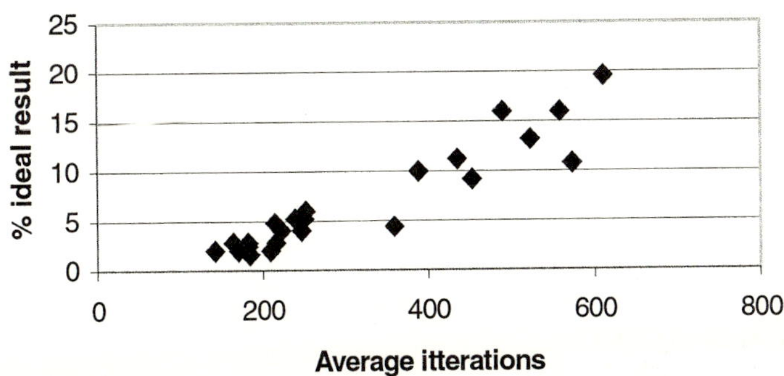


**Fig. 4.** The percentage of times that the ideal result was found versus the average iterations required to find the best result.

**Table 5.** The top performing parameter sets for each performance measure sorted into order. Each parameter set is identified by memory depth/probability/selection method/minimum difference. Again the performance without using particle memories is shown for comparison. Also shown are result obtained using ant colony optimization (ACO) for comparison.

| Sorted by % ideal solution | | Sorted by % in top 0.000001% | | Sorted by top 0.000005% | |
|---|---|---|---|---|---|
| 10/10/rank/150 | 19.6 | 10/10/rank/150 | 38 | 10/10/rank/150 | 50.8 |
| 20/15/rank/100 | 18.8 | 20/15/rank/100 | 35.2 | 20/15/rank/100 | 48.8 |
| 10/10/rank/100 | 16 | 10/10/rank/100 | 29.6 | 10/10/rank/100 | 47.6 |
| 10/10/random/200 | 16 | 10/10/random/150 | 27.6 | 10/10/rank/50 | 44.4 |
| 10/10/random/150 | 13.2 | 10/10/random/200 | 27.2 | 10/10/rank/200 | 43.2 |
| 10/10/rank/200 | 10.8 | 10/10/rank/200 | 25.6 | 10/10/random/150 | 41.6 |
| 10/10/rank/50 | 10 | 10/10/rank/50 | 22.4 | 10/10/random/200 | 40 |
| 10/10/random/100 | 9.2 | 10/10/random/100 | 22.4 | 20/10/rank/0 | 38 |
| 20/10/rank/0 | 6 | 20/20/rank/0 | 21.2 | 10/10/random/100 | 37.2 |
| No memory | 2 | No memory | 9.1 | No memory | 24 |
| ACO | 2 | ACO | 49 | ACO | 67 |

## 7 Conclusion

Providing a memory to each of the particles in a particle swarm algorithm clearly improves the performance of the PSO algorithm on the Burma 14 data set. It comes at the cost of introducing four new parameters and increasing the time taken to converge to a solution. None of the parameter values appear overly critical and the number of iterations increased by no more than a factor of three. The magnitude of improvement suggests that the reward is well worth the cost. Experience with other problems with many local minima shows this conclusion to be also valid for them.

For the Burma 14 data set the performance of Particle Swarm Algorithm with Memory is comparable to that obtained suing Any Colony Optimisation. However, Any Colony Optimisation appears to scale better as the dimensionality of the problem further increases. More work is needed to understand why and see how it may be corrected.

**Acknowledgements**

Helpful discussions with Clinton Woodward, Marcus Randall and Daniel Angus are gratefully-acknowledged.

## References

Eberhart, R., Dobbins, R. and Simpson, P. (1996) Computational Intelligence PC Tools, Boston, USA, Academic Press.

Eberhart, R. and Kennedy, J. (1995)``A New Optimizer Using Particles Swarm Theory", Proceedings of the 6th International Symposium on Micro Machine and Human Science, Nagoya, Japan, pp. 39-43.

Eberhart, R. and Shi, Y. (1995) ``Evolving Artificial Neural Networks". In Proceedings of the International Conference On Neural Networks and Brain. Beijing, P.R.China.

Eberhart, R. and Shi, Y. ``Comparing Inertia Weights and Constriction Factors in Particle Swarm Optimisation". Proceedings of the 2000 Congress on Evolutionary Computation, pp. 84-88, 2000.

Hendtlass, T and Angus, D. (2002) *"Ant Colony Optimisation Applied to a Dynamically Changing Problem*" Lecture Notes in Artificial Intelligence, Vol 2358 pages 618-627, Springer-Verlag, Berlin.

Kennedy, J. (1997) ``The Particle Swarm: Social Adaptation of Knowledge", Proceedings of the IEEE International Conference on Evolutionary Computation, Indianapolis, Indiana, USA, pp. 303-308.

Podlena, J and Hendtlass, T (1998) *An Accelerated Genetic Algorithm*, Applied Intelligence, Kluwer Academic Publishers. Volume 8, Number 2.

# A Genetic Algorithm for 1,5 Dimensional Assortment Problems with Multiple Objectives

Tuğba Saraç and Müjgan Sağır Özdemir

Osmangazi University, Department of Industrial Engineering
26030, Bademlik Eskisehir, Turkey
{tsarac, mujgano}@ogu.edu.tr

**Abstract.** In most studies on cutting stock problems, it is assumed that the sizes of stock materials are known and the problem is to find the best cutting pattern combinations. However, the solution efficiency of the problem depends strongly on the size of stock materials. In this study, a two-step approach is developed for a 1,5 dimensional assortment problem with multiple objectives. Cutting patterns are derived by implicit enumeration in the first step. The second step is used to determine the optimum sizes of stock materials by applying a genetic algorithm. The object is to find stock material sizes that minimize the total trim loss and also the variety of stock materials. Specialized crossover operator is developed to maintain the feasibility of the chromosomes. A real-life problem with 41 alternative stock materials, 289 order pieces and 1001 patterns is solved.

## 1 Introduction

The cutting stock problem is one of the earliest problems in the literature of operational research (Goulimis, 1990). Different size stock materials are cut in order to produce different order pieces in a variety of industries. There are many studies related to cutting stock problems in the literature. Of these, 69 papers written between 1985-2000 were considered and classified with respect to their dimensions, solution methods and objective functions as shown in Tables 1, 2 and 3 respectively.

**Table 1.** Papers According to Their Dimensions

| | |
|---|---|
| **1 Dimensional** | 12,20,29,43,48,65,69,72,76. |
| **1,5 Dimensional** | 2,10,62. |
| **2 Dimensional** | 1,3,4,6,7,9,11,17,18,19,24,25,26,27,29,31,35,36,37,38,39,40,41,44,45, 46,47,49,50,51,52,53,54,55,56,58,59,60,61,63,69,74,75,77. |
| **3 Dimensional** | 14,42,46. |

The main characteristic of a cutting stock problem is its dimension. As can be seen in Table 1, most of the studies are two dimensional. *One dimensional problems* are to be found in lines of production where stocks of bar or rolls are cut into smaller pieces of the same size cross section. *Two dimensional* problems exist in situations where flat material is divided into products of smaller square measures (Dyckhoff, 1990). *1,5 dimensional* cutting problems is a particular case of the two-dimensional problem

P.W.H. Chung, C.J. Hinde, M. Ali (Eds.): IEA/AIE 2003, LNAI 2718, pp. 41–51, 2003.

in which the length of a sheet is infinite. This kind of problem applies when rectangular pieces are laid out on a very long roll of material (Chauny et al., 1991). Although rectangular blanks are cut, it is not a two-dimensional problem because trim loss along the length of the stock material is not a dimensional issue. The problem is more complex than a one-dimensional problem because of the desire to match up orders both across the width and along the length dimensions (Haessler and Sweeney, 1991). As we can see from Table 1, most of the studies are two dimensional. 1,5 dimensional problem has been discussed rarely.

**Table 2.** Papers According to Their Solution Methods

| | | |
|---|---|---|
| **Artificial Intelligence** | **Genetic Algorithms** | 3, 16, 41, 60. |
| | **Simulated Annealing** | 8, 12, 24, 28, 36. |
| | **Neural Networks** | 35, 36. |
| **Other Heuristic Methods** | | 7, 12, 29, 56, 59, 74, 78. |
| **Exact Solution Methods** | | 1, 25, 37, 39, 40, 44, 54, 62, 64, 72. |
| **Hybrid Approaches** | | 6, 10, 11, 23, 27, 31, 38, 43, 45, 51, 69, 77. |

As we can see from Table 2, most of the researchers have preferred heuristic or hybrid methods instead of the exact solution methods.

**Table3.** Papers According to their Objective Function

| | |
|---|---|
| **Minimum Waste Cost** | 7,10,11,17,19,29,37,42,43,46,51,58,62,63,65,72,73,74,78. |
| **Minimum Total Cost** | 1,6,12,20,31,45,56,59,64,77. |
| **Multi Objective** | 51,65,66. |

As seen in Table 3, relatively few problems have been considered with multi objectives.

In most of these studies, it is assumed that the sizes of stock materials are known and the problem is to find the best cutting pattern combinations in a way to minimize the total trim loss. On the other hand the solution efficiency of a problem depends strongly on the size of stock materials so that the same cutting pattern may result in different assortments of trim losses. In spite of its importance, relatively little work has been published on the assortment problem ( 6, 26, 29, 31, 59, 74, 78 ).

In this paper we deal with assortment problems and introduce a new method based on genetic algorithms that has not been considered as a solution technique by previous studies. The object is to minimize both total trim loss and the variety of stock materials. The method is applied to a real life company where the first author has worked for 3 years.

## 2 Assortment Problem and the Developed Mathematical Model

The assortment problem may be defined as follows: Given a set of sizes of qualities of some product and their demands. Because of storage or manufacturing limitations, economies of scale in production or storage, or the costs associated with holding different size in stock, a subset of sizes will be stocked (Pentico, 1988).

Beasley (1985) gave a heuristic algorithm for two-dimensional guillotine cutting assortment problem based upon a sophisticated cutting pattern generation procedure, a linear program and interchange procedure. The discrete two dimensional version of the problem has been examined by Pentico (1988). In this study objective was to determine the stock material size for minimizing the combined stocking and substitution costs. Gochet and Vandebroek (1989) developed a heuristic algorithms based on dynamic programming for solving two dimensional assortment problems. Gemmill and Sanders (1990) considered one and two dimensional portfolio problem to minimize material wastage. Farley (1990) analyzed selection of stock plate characteristics and cutting style for two dimensional cutting stock situations that a range of stock size is available. Yanasse et al. (1991) discussed two dimensional problem its objective was to minimize wastage. A heuristic algorithm for both generating cutting patterns and selecting the stock material size has been developed by them.

None of these works have solved that problem by using exact solution methods. Most approaches are based on heuristics. As different from previous studies, in this study 1,5 dimensional assortment problem with multiple objectives are considered. A mathematical model was developed for the problem.

$m$ : the number of different stock materials

$b$ : the maximum number of different stock materials will be selected among $m$ different stock materials.

$n$ : the number of different order pieces

$p$ : the number of different patterns

$W_i$ : wide of stock material $i$ [cm] $\quad i = 1,..,m$

$d_j$ : the demand for order piece $j$ [unit] $\quad j = 1,..,n$

$a_{jk}$ : the amount of order piece $j$ in cutting pattern k [unit/m] $\quad j = 1,..,n;\ k = 1,..,p$

$f_{ik}$ : the amount of trim loss $i$ for the combination of stock material $i$ and cutting pattern $k$ [$cm^2$/m] $\quad i = 1,..,m;\ k = 1,..,p$

$y_i$ $\begin{cases} 1, & \text{if the stock material } i \text{ is used} \\ 0, & \text{o.w.} \end{cases}$ $\quad i = 1,..,m$

$x_k$ : the amount of cutting pattern $k$ will be used [m] $\quad k = 1,..,p$

$z_{ik}$ $\begin{cases} 1, & \text{if cutting pattern } k \text{ is cut by using stock materials } i \\ 0, & \text{o.w.} \end{cases}$ $\quad i = 1,..,m;\ k = 1,..,p$

$\alpha$ : the weight of the trim loss ratio in objective function [0,1]

$$\min x_o = \alpha[(\sum_i \sum_k f_{ik} z_{ik} x_k) / (\sum_i \sum_k W_i z_{ik} x_k)] + (1-\alpha)[(\sum_i y_i) / m]$$

subject to

$$\sum_k a_{jk} x_k = d_j \qquad \forall j \qquad j=1,..,n$$

$$\sum_k z_{ik} \le y_i p \qquad \forall i \qquad i=1,..,m$$

$$\sum_i z_{ik} \le 1 \qquad \forall k \qquad k=1,..,p$$

$$\sum_i y_i \le b$$

$x_k \ge 0$ $\quad y_i$ and $z_{ik}$ : $0$ - $1$ integer

The objective is to find the optimum sizes of stock materials in a way to minimize both total trim loss and the variety of stock materials used. Having many different sizes of materials in stock reduces the trim loss but it also increases the material and holding costs. Our objective function consists of two parts. The first term refers to the trim loss ratio which is obtained by the ratio of total trim loss to the total amount of stock materials used. The second term is obtained by dividing the number of different stock materials selected to use in production by the total number of different stock materials. Since both terms are fractional, the coefficients of the objective function which represent the weight of each term become usable in an efficient way that would be made clear in the development of the application.

## 3 Genetic Algorithms

Cutting stock and assortment problems that are combinatorial optimization problems belong to NP-hard type problems. An efficient search heuristic will be useful for tackling such a problem. In this study a heuristic search approach using genetic algorithms is chosen to find the optimal or near optimal size of stock materials. Genetic Algorithms are powerful and broadly applicable in stochastic search and optimization techniques based on principles from evolution theory (Gen and Cheng, 1997). Genetic algorithms are different from normal optimization and search procedures in four ways (Goldberg, 1989):

- GAs work with a coding of the parameter set, not the parameters themselves.
- GAs search from population of points, not a single point.
- GAs use payoff (objective function) information, not derivatives or other auxiliary knowledge.
- GAs use probabilistic transition rules, not deterministic rules.

### 3.1 Representation

A chromosome which is defined for this problem has two parts. The first part consists of *(b-1)* genes used to determine the stock materials to be selected. Each of the rest of the genes which are in second part represents the amount of each cutting pattern that is going to be used. The selected cutting patterns are assigned to the stock materials in a way to obtain the minimum trim loss. In order to guarantee a feasible solution, one of the stock material sizes is obtained according to the following formula:

$$pwide_{max} + nw$$

$nw$ : minimum trim loss
$pwide_{max}$ : selected cutting patterns that has maximum wide

A gene has a value between 0 and 0.99. In order to obtain the corresponding stock material size (*sms*), the following formula is used:

$$sms \begin{cases} sms_{min} + \lfloor gv / (1 / pwide_{max} - pwide_{min} - nw) \rfloor & pwide_{max} > sms_{min} - nw \\ sms_{min} & pwide_{max} \leq sms_{min} - nw \end{cases}$$

$pwide_{min}$ : selected cutting patterns that has minimum wide
$sms_{min}$ : minimum stock metarial size
$gv$ : value of gene between 0 and 0.99.

### 3.2 Handling Constraints

The central question in applying genetic algorithms to the constrained optimization is how to handle constraints because the genetic operators used to manipulate the chromosomes often yield infeasible offspring. The existing techniques can be roughly classified as rejecting strategy, repairing strategy, modifying genetic operators strategy and penalizing strategy. In this study a modified genetic operators strategy is chosen to generate feasible solutions.

**Initial Population.** Since without having feasible initial solutions using modified genetic operators would be useless, a procedure is used to generate a feasible initial population. The first (*b-1*) gene is generated randomly between 0 and 0.99. The following procedure is used to generate the remaining genes:

```
Initialization Procedure.
begin
repeat
        select a random k
        assingn available maximum amount of units to x_k
        x_k ← min {d_n / a_nk ;d_m / a_mk }
        update data
        d_n ← d_n - ( x_k a_nk), d_m ← d_m - ( x_k a_mk)
until all di=0
end
```

$d_n$ *and* $d_m$ : the amount of demand for the order pieces n and m respectively.

### 3.3 Genetic Operators

The feasibility of the chromosomes that are generated by the initialization procedure must be satisfied while they are being processed by the genetic operators. A crossover operator is introduced to prevent us from having this infeasibility as explained below.

**Reproduction.** A normalization technique for one kind of dynamic scaling given by Gen and Cheng, (1997) is used.

$$p_{s(k)} = (f_{max} - f_k + \gamma) / (f_{max} - f_{min} + \gamma)$$

where *fmax* and *fmin* are the best and the worst raw fitnesses in the current population, respectively and $\gamma$ is a small positive real number that is usually restricted within the open interval (0,1). The purpose of using such transformation is twofold; to prevent the equation from zero division and to make it possible to adjust the selection behaviour from fitness-proportional to pure random selection.

**Crossover.** A specialized crossover operator is developed to maintain the feasibility of chromosomes. Randomly selected two parents chromosomes are used to generate an offspring. Each gene of the first chromosome is added to the corresponding gene that is placed in the same order of the second chromosome and divided by two to obtain the new chromosome. It is seen that the new chromosome satisfies problem constraints.

```
Crossover Procedure.
begin
krg(i,j) ←kr(i,j)
t ← 1
repeat
        rs ← random number from [0,1] for chromosome t
        if rs < p_c then;
                select a random chromosome r
                rs ← random number from [0,1]
                r ← rs*(nkr-1)+1
                kr(t,j) ← [ krg(t,j) + kr(r,j) ] / 2
                t ← t + 1
until t = nkr
end
```

**Immigration.** Instead of a mutation operator, we use an immigration operator proposed by Bean (1994). This operator replaces a randomly selected chromosome by the chromosome that is generated by an initialization procedure.

The algorithm to determine the standard stock material size is given as follows:

```
begin
t ← 1
initalization
calculate the fitness values
repeat
        reproduction
        crossover
        immigration
        calculate the fitness values
until t = number of generations
end
```

## 4 An Industrial Case Study

The firm, in which this study was developed, produces 4.000 different types of corrugated carton boxes by using different sizes paper rolls. Corrugated paper is produced and cut certain sizes rectangularly by a corrugator. Amount of corrugator side trim in container plants is a significant number because, in the majority of cases, it is the second largest item in the controllable waste. If a plant cuts up 40.000 tons of roll stock annually, 2,5% side trim is equal to 1.000 tons and the minimum cost of US$ 325.000 per year (Cloud, 1994). It is our aim to decide the minimum number of different sizes paper rolls that would provide the minimum trim loss.

The constraints which depend on technical ability of the corrugator are as follows:

- Only two different types of order pieces can be produced at the same time.
- Maximum strip number can be eight.
- Minimum trim loss is 3cm.

In addition to corrugator constraints, two different type order pieces which have different order date can not be located in the same cutting pattern so only 45 types of order pieces that have higher and continuous demand were allowed to be in the same pattern with the others. These constraints must be considered for generating cutting patterns.

In classifying the data 289 types of order pieces were determined. 1001 cutting patterns that satisfy the constraints were generated by implicit enumeration. There are 41 different sizes stock materials, paper rolls, between 210cm. and 250cm that can be selected. The maximum number of different stock materials selected is 5.

### 4.1 Genetic Parameters

In order to determine the population size, the crossover rate and the generation number forty tests were performed. They are found to be 15, 0.9 and 100 respectively. As the number of iterations increases, the solution time also increases. It is concluded by examining the fitness values that reasonable solutions can be obtained in about 100 iterations. Therefore the number of iterations was set at 100. On the other hand, it is proposed to work with a larger number of iterations when there is no time limitation since it can increase the accuracy of the solution. When these parameters are used the average solution time is approximately 20 minutes.

By considering the reality that the paper cost is about the % 40 of the total cost in this sector, so it is not suggested to work with a low weight of the first term of the objective function and it is determined as 0.9.

### 4.2 Solution and Discussion

By using the parameters defined in the previous section, the problem was solved and the sizes 210, 220, 226, 244 and 250 were obtained for the optimum paper rolls. Table 4 summarizes the result.

**Table 4.** The result and the comparison with the current system parameters

| | First Term | Second Term | Objective Value |
|---|---|---|---|
| **Proposed Solution** | 0,05250477 | 0,12195122 | 0,05944941 |
| **Current Situation** | 0,06281390 | 0,12195122 | 0,06872763 |

The annual demand for this firm is approximately 33.000.000m$^2$. It should be noted that the difference between the trim loss ratios of the proposed solution and the current situation is about 0,01. This corresponds to 330.000m$^2$ stock materials in a year that would be saved.

## 5 Conclusions

In this study, a two-step approach was developed for 1,5 dimensional assortment problem with multiple objectives. The objectives are to minimize the total trim loss and to minimize the variety of stock materials. In the first step, cutting patterns were generated by implicit enumeration and the sizes of stock materials were determined by using genetic algorithms. Followed by generating a feasible initial population, a specialized crossover operator was developed to maintain the feasibility of the chromosomes. Instead of the mutation operator, an immigration operator proposed by Bean (1994) is used. The method used gives solutions in reasonable time. In GA, the effectiveness of the solutions depends on the problem parameters. It is recommended that an experimental design to decide on the best values of the model parameters be made, which is one of the ideas for further research on this subject.

## References


1. Abd EA, Reda MS, (1994), "An Interactive technique for the cutting stock problem with multiple objectives", *European Journal Of Operational Research,* 78, (3) 304-317.
2. Abel D, Gal T, (1985), "Trim loss and related problems", *International Journal of Management Science,* 13, (1) 59-72.
3. Anand S, McCord C, Sharma R, Balachander T, (1999), "An integrated machine vision based system for solving the nonconvex cutting stock problem using genetic algorithms", *Journal Of Manufacturing Systems,* 18, (6) 396-415.
4. Antunez HJ, Kleiber M, (1996), "Sensitivity analysis of metal forming processes involving frictional contact in steady state", *Journal Of Materials Processing Technology,* 60, (1-4) 485-491.
5. Bean JC, (1994), "Genetic algorithms and random keys for sequencing and optimization", *ORSA Journal on Computing*, 6, (2), 154-160.
6. Beasley JE, (1985), "An algorithm for the two dimensional assortment problem", *European Journal Of Operational Research,* 19, 253-261.
7. Benati S, (1997), "An algorithm for a cutting stock problem on a strip", *Journal of The Operational Research Society,* 48, (3) 288-294.
8. Bennell JA, Dowsland KA, (1999), "A tabu thresholding implementation for the irregular stock cutting problem", *International Journal Of Production Research,* 37 (18) 4259-4275.
9. Carnieri C, Mendoza GA, Gavinho LG, (1994), "Solution procedures for cutting lumber into furniture parts", *European Journal Of Operational Research,* 73, (3) 495-501.
10. Chauny F, Loulou R, Sadones S, Soumis F, (1987), "A Two-phase heuristic for strip packing algorithm and probabilistic analysis.", *Operations Research Letters,* 6, (1) 25-33.
11. Chauny F, Loulou R, Sadones S, Soumis F, (1991), "A Two-phase heuristic for the two-dimensional cutting-stock problem.", *Journal of The Operational Research Society,* 42, (1) 39-47.
12. Chen CLS, Hart SM, Tham WM, (1996), "A simulated annealing heuristic for the one-dimensional cutting stock problem", *European Journal Of Operational Research,* 93, (3) 522-535.
13. Cheng CH, Feiring BR, Cheng TCE, (1994), "The cutting stock problem - A survey", *International Journal of Production Economics,* 36, 291-305.
14. Chien CF, Wu WT, (1998), "A recursive computational procedure for container loading", *Computers & Industrial Engineering,* 35, (1-2) 319-322.
15. Cloud FH, (1994), "Analysis of corrugator side trim", *Tappi Journal,* 77, (4) 199-205.
16. Cook DF, Wolfe ML, (1991), "Genetic algorithm approach to a lumber cutting optimization problem.", *Cybern. Syst.,* 22, (3) 357-365.
17. Dagli CH, Tatoglu MY, (1987), "Approach to two dimensional cutting stock problems", *International Journal Of Production Research,* 25, (2) 175-190.

18. Dagli CH, Poshyanonda P, (1997), "New approaches to nesting rectangular patterns", *Journal of Intelligent Manufacturing, 8, (3) 177-190.*
19. Daniels JJ, Ghandforoush P, (1990), "An improved algorithm for the non-guillotine-constrained cutting stock problem", *Journal of The Operational Research Society,* 41, (2)141-149.
20. Decarvalho JMV, Rodrigues AJG, (1994), A computer based interactive approach to a 2 stage cutting stock problem", *Infor,* 32, (4) 243-252.
21. Dyckhoff H, (1990), "A typology of cutting and packing problems", *European Journal Of Operational Research,* 44,145-159.
22. Dyckhoff H, Kruse HJ, Abel D, Gal T, (1985), "Trim Loss and Related Problems", *OMEGA The International Journal of Management Science,* 13, (1), 59-72.
23. Faggioli E, Bentivoglio CA, (1998), "Heuristic and exact methods for the cutting sequencing problem", *European Journal Of Operational Research,* 110, (3) 564-575.
24. Faina L, (1999), "Application of simulated annealing to the cutting stock problem", *European Journal Of Operational Research,* 114, (3) 542-556.
25. Fan Z, Ma J, Tian P, (1997), "Algorithm for the special two-dimensional cutting problem", *Proceedings of the IEEE International Conference on Systems, Man and Cybernetics,* 1, 404-409.
26. Farley AA, (1990), "Selection of stock plate characteristics and cutting style for two dimensional cutting stock situations", *European Journal Of Operational Research,* 44, 239-246.
27. Fayard D, Hifi M, Zissimopoulos V, (1998), "Efficient approach for large-scale two-dimensional guillotine cutting stock problems", *Journal of The Operational Research Society,* 49, (12) 1270-1277.
28. Foerster H, Waescher G, (1998), "Simulated annealing for order spread minimization in sequencing cutting patterns", *European Journal Of Operational Research,* 110, (2) 272-281.
29. Gemmill DD, Sanders JL, (1990), "Approximate solutions for the cutting stock 'portfolio' problem", *European Journal Of Operational Research,* 44,167-174.
30. Gen M, Cheng R, (1997), *Genetic Algorithms and Engineering Design,* John Wiley&Sons, NY.
31. Gochet W, Vandebroek M, (1989), "A dynamic programming based heuristic for industrial buying of cardboard", *European Journal Of Operational Research,* 38, 104-112.
32. Goldberg DE, (1989), *Genetic Algorithms in Search, Optimization, and Machine Learning*, Addison-Wesley, USA.
33. Goulimis C, (1990), "Optimal solutions for the cutting stock problem", *European Journal Of Operational Research,* 44, 197-208.
34. Haessler RW, Sweeney PE, (1991), "Cutting stock problems and solution procedures.", *European Journal Of Operational Research,*54, (2) 141-150.
35. Han GC, Na SJ, (1994), "Multi-stage solution for nesting in two-dimensional cutting problems using neural networks", *Welding in the World, Le Soudage Dans Le Monde,* 34, 409-410.
36. Han GC, Na SJ, (1996), "Two-stage approach for nesting in two-dimensional cutting problems using neural network and simulated annealing", *Proceedings of the Institution of Mechanical Engineers, Part B: Journal of Engineering Manufacture,* 210, (B6) 509-519.
37. Hifi M, (1997a), "An improvement of Viswanathan and Bagchi's exact algorithm for constrained two-dimensional cutting stock", *Computers & Operations Research,* 24, (8) 727-736.
38. Hifi M, (1997b), "The DH/KD algorithm: A hybrid approach for unconstrained two-dimensional cutting problems", *European Journal Of Operational Research,* 97, (1) 41-52.
39. Hifi M, Ouafi R, (1997), "Best-first search and dynamic programming methods for cutting problems: The cases of one or more stock plates", *Computers & Industrial Engineering,* 32, (1) 187-205.

40. Hifi M; Zissimopoulos V, (1996), "Recursive exact algorithm for weighted two-dimensional cutting", *European Journal Of Operational Research,* 91, (3) 553-564.
41. Ismail HS, Hon KKB, (1995), "Nesting of two-dimensional shapes using genetic algorithms", *Proceedings of the Institution of Mechanical Engineers, Part-B: Journal of Engineering Manufacture,* 209, (B2) 115-124.
42. John AG, (1992), "A method for solving container packing for a single size of box", *Journal of the Operational Research Society,* 43, (4) 307-312.
43. Johnson MP, Rennick C, Zak E, (1997), "Skiving addition to the cutting stock problem in the paper industry", *Siam Review,* 39, (3) 472-483.
44. Klempous R, Kotowski J, Szlachcic E, (1996), "Interactive procedures in large-scale two-dimensional cutting stock problems", *Journal Of Computational And Applied Mathematics,* 66, (1-2) 323-331.
45. Krichagina EV, Rubio R, Taksar MI, Wein LM, (1998), "A dynamic stochastic stock-cutting problem", *Operations Research,* 46, (5) 690-701.
46. Lai KK, Chan JWM, (1997a), "Developing a simulated annealing algorithm for the cutting stock problem", *Computers & Industrial Engineering,* 32, (1) 115-127.
47. Lai KK, Chan WM, (1997b), "An evolutionary algorithm for the rectangular cutting stock problem", *International Journal of Industrial Engineering-Applications And Practice,* 4, (2) 130-139.
48. Lefrancois P, Gascon A, (1995), "Solving a one dimensional cutting stock problem in a small manufacturing firm-A case study", *IIE Transactions,* 27, (4) 483-496.
49. Li S, (1996), "Multi-job cutting stock problem with due dates and release dates", *Journal of The Operational Research Society,* 47, (4) 490-510.
50. MacLeod B, Moll R, Girkar M, Hanifi N, (1993), "An algorithm for the 2D guillotine cutting stock problem", *European Journal Of Operational Research,* 68, (3) 400-412.
51. Madsen OBG, (1988), "Application of travelling salesman routinesto solve pattern allocation problems in the glass industry", *Journal of The Operational Research Society,* 39, (3) 249-256.
52. Morabito R, Arenales MN, (1995), Performance of 2 heuristics for solving large scale 2 dimensional guillotine cutting problems", *Infor,* 33, (2) 145-155.
53. Morabito R, Arenales MN, (1996), "Staged and constrained two-dimensional guillotine cutting problems: An AND/OR-graph approach", *European Journal Of Operational Research,* 94, (3) 548-560.
54. Morabito R, Garcia V, (1998), "The cutting stock problem in a hardboard industry: A case study", *Computers & Operations Research,* 25, (6) 469-485.
55. Morabito RN, Arenales MN, Arcaro VF, (1992), "And-or-graph approach for two-dimensional cutting problems.", *European Journal Of Operational Research,* 58, (2) 263-271.
56. Noans SL, Thortenson A, (2000), "A combined cutting stock and lot sizing problem", *European Journal Of Operational Research,* 120, (2) 327-342.
57. Olovsson L, Nilsson L, Simonsson K, (1999), "An ALE formulation for the solution of two-dimensional metal cutting problems", *Computers & Structures,* 72, (4-5) 497-507.
58. Parada V, Sepulveda M, Solar M, Gomes A, (1998), "Solution for the constrained guillotine cutting problem by simulated annealing", *Computers & Operations Research,* 25, (1) 37-47.
59. Pentico DW, (1988), "The discrete two dimensional assortment problem", *Operations Research,* 36, (2) 324-332.
60. Rahmani AT, Ono N, (1995), "Evolutionary approach to two-dimensional guillotine cutting problem", *Proceedings of the IEEE Conference on Evolutionary Computation,* 1.
61. Rinnooy KAHG, De Wit JR, Wijmenga RTh, (1987), "Nonorthogonal two dimensional cutting patterns", *Management Sci.,* 33, (5) 670-681.
62. Savsar M, Cogun C, (1994), "Analysis and modeling of a production line in a corrigated box factory", *International Journal Of Production Research,* 32, (7) 1571-1589.

63. Scheithauer G, Sommerweiss U, (1998), "4-block heuristic for the rectangle packing problem", *European Journal Of Operational Research,* 108, (3) 509-526.
64. Schultz TA, (1995), "Application of linear programming in a Gauze splitting operation", *Operations Research,* 43, (5) 752-757.
65. Sinuanystern Z, Weiner I, (1994), The one dimensional cutting stock problem using 2 objectives", *Journal of The Operational Research Society,* 45, (2) 231-236.
66. Sumichrast RT, (1986), "New cutting stock heuristic for scheduling production", *Computers & Operations Research,* 13, (4) 403-410.
67. Sweeney PE, Paternoster ER, (1992), "Cutting and packing problems: A categorized, application-orientated research bibliography", *Journal of the Operational Research Society,* 43, (7) 691-706.
68. Vahrenkamp R, (1996), "Random search in the one-dimensional cutting stock problem", *European Journal Of Operational Research,* 95, (1) 191-200.
69. Van DWA, (1995), "UGC: an algorithm for two-stage unconstrained guillotine cutting", *European Journal Of Operational Research,* 84, (2) 494-498.
70. Vance PH, (1998), "Branch and price algorithms for the one-dimensional cutting stock problem", *Computational Optimization And Applications,* 9, (3) 211-228.
71. Vasko FJ, (1989), "A computational improvement to Wang's Two-dimensional cutting stock algorithm", *Computers & Industrial Engineering,* 16, (1) 109-115.
72. Vasko FJ, Cregger ML, Newhart DD, Stott KL, (1993), "A Real time one dimensional cutting stock algorithm for balanced cutting patterns", *Operations Research Letters,* 14, (5) 275-282.
73. Vasko FJ, Wolf FE, (1989), "Practical solution to a fuzzy two-dimensional cutting stock problem.", *Fuzzy Sets Syst.,* 29, (3) 259-275.
74. Vasko FJ, Wolf FE, Stott KL, (1994), "A Pratical Approach for Determining Rectangular stock size", *Journal of The Operational Research Society,* 45, (3) 281-286.
75. Viswanathan KV, Bagchi A, (1993), "Best-first search methods for constrained two-dimensional cutting stock problems", *Operations Research,* 41, (4) 768-776.
76. Wascher G, Gau T, (1996), "Heuristics for the integer one-dimensional cutting stock problem: A computational study", *Or Spektrum,* 18, (3) 131-144.
77. Westerlund T, Isaksson J, Harjunkoski L, (1998), "Solving a two-dimensional trim-loss problem with MILP", *European Journal Of Operational Research,* 104, (3) 572-581.
78. Yanasse HH, Zinober ASI, Harris RG, (1991), "Two-dimensional Cutting Stock with Multiple Stock Size", Journal of The Operational Research Society, 42, (8) 673-683.

# How to Create Priorities in Genetics

Müjgan Sagır Özdemir

Osmangazi University Industrial Engineering Department
Bademlik Campus 26030 Eskisehir Turkey

**Abstract.** We draw the reader's attention to a different way of thinking at genetic combinations. It is the use of prioritization in genetics. Since we can control those not yet born who are the result of genetic mixing, we would be able to control the outcome by using the most essential inputs to obtain a desired outcome. Because the characteristics to perform a task are not equally important, we prioritize them to see which contributes more. The question is how to establish priorities for the desired attributes in the child? We introduce1 two decision theories: The Analytic Hierarchy Process (AHP), an approach to obtain priorities for a set of criteria, and the Analytic Network Process (ANP) involving dependence and feedback. We relate these approaches and genetics by using the networks to define the relations among characteristics. The result of this discrimination process is a vector of priorities of the elements with respect to each property.

## 1 Introduction

Genetics has developed as an experimental science during the twentieth century, following the discovery in 1900 of the work of the father of genetics, Gregory Mendel [1]. The genes lie at the base of all we are, and so have been of great interest to science. The study of genes is the science of genetics, and it is one of the most misrepresented of the life sciences. Many people know that it is terribly complicated, or that it is all about evaluation, or that it may be something to do with eugenics. Like other academic subjects, genetics has accumulated a jargon which enables its practitioners to talk to each other precisely, but which forms a dense jungle of terms which can take the student years to penetrate and which most people do not have time to master [2].

By combining parts of two genes, biology is able to produce a new gene and the properties of this new gene strongly depend on its parent genes. The method of genetic algorithms imitates and applies the logic of this organic process to problem solving in a striking way. It basically takes two solutions, combines them to get a new solution by using special operators called genetic operators. Since the new solution, the child, depends on the parent "solutions", it is important to know well what one has at the start. Actually this process has a dynamic structure, so that until one has an acceptable solution, one repeats this process by using genetic operators to obtain new children and by using those children as aaaaaaaanew parents to generate new children in the next iteration. A function called fitness function evaluates both the feasibility and the desirability of the newly generated solutions.

P.W.H. Chung, C.J. Hinde, M. Ali (Eds.): IEA/AIE 2003, LNAI 2718, pp. 52–61, 2003.

In this work, we would like to draw the reader's attention to a different consideration. It is the use of prioritization in genetics. Since we can control those not yet born who are the result of genetic mixing, we would be able to control the outcome by using the most essential inputs to obtain a certain desired outcome. The question is how do we know which necessary inputs are needed to accomplish a specific task and how important are these inputs? For instance let us assume that the goal is to create a champion chess player. There are several characteristics known in the literature [3] and investigated in depth, that appear to be necessary to become a chess grand master: Intelligence, experience, good health, imagination, intuition, memory, preparation, relative youth, technique, ego, gamesmanship, personality. Because these characteristics are not all equally important, we can identify and prioritize them to see which ones the expert think contribute more to be a winner at chess. We would then be better able to link scientifically the extent to which we want these characteristics to appear in the child to the kind and degree of mixing in the parents. Admittedly this may be a difficult task but nevertheless important for establishing the connection between what we have and what we want in genetics. The question is how to establish priorities for the desired attributes in the child? The next section introduces a decision theory that is a powerful approach to obtain priorities for a set of criteria.

## 2 Paired Comparisons and Weighting

The youngest, and mathematically most general and robust decision theory that applies paired comparisons to tangibles and intangibles equally is the Analytic Hierarchy Process (AHP) developed by Thomas L. Saaty. The AHP depends on the values and judgments of individuals and groups. Decision makers who use the AHP first structure the problem into a hierarchy, highest level is the overall objective, the lowest includes the final actions, or alternative plans, that would contribute positively or negatively to the main objective through their impact on the intermediate criteria.

Relative Measurement: Choosing the Best House. The following example although not in genetics illustrates the process of prioritization adequately. A family of average income wants to purchase a house. They must choose from three alternatives. The family identifies eight factors to look for in a house. These factors fall into three categories: economic, geographic, and physical. Although one might begin by examining the relative importance of these categories, the family feels they want to prioritize the relative importance of all the factors without working with the categories to which they belong.

The problem is to select one of three candidate houses. In applying the AHP, the first step is decomposition, or the structuring of the problem into a hierarchy (see Figure 1). On the first (or top) level is the overall goal of Satisfaction with House. On the second level are the eight factors or criteria that contribute to the goal, and on the third (or bottom) level are the three candidate houses that are to be evaluated in terms of the criteria on the second level. The definitions of the factor and the pictorial representation of the hierarchy follow.

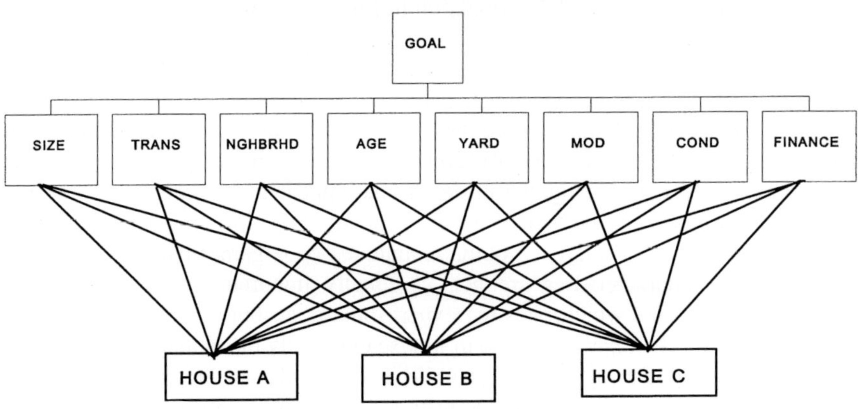


**Fig. 1.** Decomposition of the problem into a hierarchy

The criteria or factors important to the family are:

1. Size of House: Storage space; size of rooms; number of rooms; total area of house.
2. Transportation: Convenience and proximity of bus service.
3. Neighborhood: Degree of traffic, security, taxes, physical condition of surrounding buildings.
4. Age of House: Self-explanatory.
5. Yard Space: Includes front, back, and side space, and space shared with neighbors.
6. Modern Facilities: Dishwasher, garbage disposal, air conditioning, alarm system, and other such items.
7. General Condition: Extent to which repairs are needed; condition of walls, carpet, drapes, wiring; cleanliness.
8. Financing: Availability of assumable mortgage, seller financing, or bank financing.
9.

The next step is comparative judgment. The elements on the second level are arranged into a matrix and the family buying the house makes judgments about the relative importance of the elements with respect to the overall goal, Satisfaction with House. The questions to ask when comparing two criteria are of the following kind: of the two alternatives being compared, which is considered more important by the family and how much more important is it with respect to family satisfaction with the house, which is the overall goal? The matrix of pairwise comparisons of the criteria given by the home buyers in this case is shown in Table 2, along with the resulting vector of priorities. The judgments are entered using the Fundamental Scale as shown in Table 1 first verbally as indicated in the scale and then associating the corresponding number. The vector of priorities is the principal eigenvector of the matrix. This vector gives the relative priority of the criteria measured on a ratio scale. That is, these priorities are unique to within multiplication by a positive constant. However, if one ensures that they sum to one they are then unique. In this case financing has the highest priority, with 33 percent of the influence.

**Table 1** Fundamental scale

| | |
|---|---|
| 1 | Equal importance |
| 3 | Moderate importance of one over another |
| 5 | Strong or essential importance |
| 7 | Very strong or demonstrated importance |
| 9 | Extreme importance |
| 2,4,6,8 | Intermediate values |
| Use reciprocals for inverse comparisons | |

Associated with the weights is an inconsistency. The consistency index of a matrix is given by $C.I. = (\lambda_{max} - n)/(n-1)$. The consistency ratio (C.R.) is obtained by forming the ratio of C.I. and the appropriate one of the following set of numbers as shown in Table 2, each of which is an average random consistency index computed for $n \leq 7$ for very large samples. They create randomly generated reciprocal matrices using the scale 1/9, 1/8, 1,..., 8, 9 and calculate the average of their eigenvalues. This average is used to form the Random Consistency Index R.I.

**Table 2.** Random index

| Order | 1 | 2 | 3 | 4 | 5 | 6 | 7 | 8 | 9 | 10 |
|---|---|---|---|---|---|---|---|---|---|---|
| R.I. | 0 | 0 | 0.52 | 0.89 | 1.11 | 1.25 | 1.35 | 1.40 | 1.45 | 1.49 |

It is recommended that C.R. should be less than or equal to .10. Inconsistency may be thought of as an adjustment needed to improve the consistency of the comparisons. But the adjustment should not be as large as the judgment itself, nor small that using it is of no consequence. Thus inconsistency should be just one order of magnitude smaller. On a scale from zero to one, the overall inconsistency should be around 10 %. The requirement of 10% cannot be made smaller such as 1% or .1% without trivializing the impact of inconsistency. But inconsistency itself is important because without it, new knowledge that changes preference cannot be admitted [4]. In Table 3, instead of naming the criteria, we use the number previously associated with each. Note for example that in comparing Size of House on the left with Size of House on top, a value of equal is assigned. However, when comparing it with Transportation it is strongly preferred and a 5 is entered in the (1,2) or first row, second column position. The reciprocal value 1/5 is automatically entered in the (2,1) position. Again when Size of House in the first row is compared with General Condition in the seventh column, it is not preferred but is moderately dominated by General Condition and a 1/3 value is entered in the (1,7) position. A 3 is then automatically entered in the (7,1) position.

The consistency ratio C.R. is equal to 0.169 and one needs to explore the inconsistencies in the matrix with the help of Expert Choice to locate the most inconsistent one and attempt to improve it if there is flexibility in the judgment. Otherwise, one looks at the second most inconsistent judgment and attempts to improve it and so on.

**Table 3.** Pairwise comparison matrix for level 1

| | 1 | 2 | 3 | 4 | 5 | 6 | 7 | 8 | Priority Vector |
|---|---|---|---|---|---|---|---|---|---|
| 1 | 1 | 5 | 3 | 7 | 6 | 6 | 1/3 | 1/4 | 0.173 |
| 2 | 1/5 | 1 | 1/3 | 5 | 3 | 3 | 1/5 | 1/7 | 0.054 |
| 3 | 1/3 | 3 | 1 | 6 | 3 | 4 | 6 | 1/5 | 0.188 |
| 4 | 1/7 | 1/5 | 1/6 | 1 | 1/3 | 1/4 | 1/7 | 1/8 | 0.018 |
| 5 | 1/6 | 1/3 | 1/3 | 3 | 1 | 1/2 | 1/5 | 1/6 | 0.031 |
| 6 | 1/6 | 1/3 | 1/4 | 4 | 2 | 1 | 1/5 | 1/6 | 0.036 |
| 7 | 3 | 5 | 1/6 | 7 | 5 | 5 | 1 | 1/2 | 0.167 |
| 8 | 4 | 7 | 5 | 8 | 6 | 6 | 2 | 1 | 0.333 |

C.R. = 0.169

We now move to the pairwise comparisons of the houses on the bottom level, comparing them pairwise with respect to how much better one is than the other in satisfying each criterion on the second level. Thus there are eight 3 × 3 matrices of judgments since there are eight elements on level two, and three houses to be pairwise compared for each element. Table 4 gives the matrices of the houses and their local priorities with respect to the elements in level two.

In Table 5 both ordinary (distributive) and idealized priority vectors of the three houses are given for each of the criteria. The idealized priority vector is obtained by dividing each element of the distributive priority vector by its largest element. The composite priority vector for the houses is obtained by multiplying each priority vector by the priority of the corresponding criterion, adding across all the criteria for each house and then normalizing. When we use the (ordinary)distributive priority vectors, this method of synthesis is known as the distributive mode and yields A=0.346, B=0.369, and C=0.285. Thus house B is preferred to houses A and C in the ratios: 0.369/ 0.346 and 0.369/0.285, respectively.

When we use the idealized priority vector the synthesis is called the ideal mode. It is the one we need here for hierarchies. This yields A=0.315, B=0.383, C= 0.302 and B is again the most preferred house. The two ways of synthesizing are shown in Table 5.

Figure 2 shows an illustration of how this scale of judgments when applied to real life problems that have measurements gives back relative values that are close to the measurements in normalized form and then give the matrix.

The Analytic Network Process (ANP) for making decisions involving dependence and feedback is a generalization of the AHP. Its feedback approach replaces hierarchies of the AHP with networks. When we use networks (ANP), a more realistic way to deal with complex problems, it is essential to consider all influences among the criteria, sub-criteria and the alternatives. We put our alternatives under networks with all their related influences on the others. After developing the structure, the planners establish the relationships between elements in pairs. These relationships represent the relative impact of the elements in a network. The result of this discrimination process is a vector of priorities or of relative importance, of the elements with respect to each property. This paired comparison is repeated for all the elements [5].

**Table 4.** Pairwise comparison matrices for the alternative houses

| Size Of House | A | B | C | Distributive Priorities | Idealized Priorities |
|---|---|---|---|---|---|
| A | 1 | 5 | 9 | 0.743 | 1.000 |
| B | 1/5 | 1 | 4 | 0.194 | 0.261 |
| C | 1/9 | 1/4 | 1 | 0.063 | 0.085 |
| | | | | C.R. =0 .07 | |

| Yard Space | A | B | C | Distributive Priorities | Idealized Priorities |
|---|---|---|---|---|---|
| A | 1 | 6 | 4 | 0.691 | 1.000 |
| B | 1/6 | 1 | 1/3 | 0.091 | 0.132 |
| C | 1/4 | 3 | 1 | 0.218 | 0.315 |
| | | | | C.R. = 0.05 | |

| Transportation | A | B | C | Distributive Priorities | Idealized Priorities |
|---|---|---|---|---|---|
| A | 1 | 4 | 1/5 | 0.194 | 0.261 |
| B | 1/4 | 1 | 1/9 | 0.063 | 0.085 |
| C | 5 | 9 | 1 | 0.743 | 1.000 |
| | | | | C.R. =0 .07 | |

| Modern Facilities | A | B | C | Distributive Priorities | Idealized Priorities |
|---|---|---|---|---|---|
| A | 1 | 9 | 6 | 0.770 | 1.000 |
| B | 1/9 | 1 | 1/3 | 0.068 | 0.088 |
| C | 1/6 | 3 | 1 | 0.162 | 0.210 |
| | | | | C.R. =0 .05 | |

| Neighborhood | A | B | C | Distributive Priorities | Idealized Priorities |
|---|---|---|---|---|---|
| A | 1 | 9 | 4 | 0.717 | 1.000 |
| B | 1/9 | 1 | 1/4 | 0.066 | 0.092 |
| C | 1/4 | 4 | 1 | 0.217 | 0.303 |
| | | | | C.R. =0 .04 | |

| General Condition | A | B | C | Distributive Priorities | Idealized Priorities |
|---|---|---|---|---|---|
| A | 1 | 1/2 | 1/2 | 0.200 | 0.500 |
| B | 2 | 1 | 1 | 0.400 | 1.000 |
| C | 2 | 1 | 1 | 0.400 | 1.000 |
| | | | | C.R. =0 .00 | |

| Age of House | A | B | C | Distributive Priorities | Idealized Priorities |
|---|---|---|---|---|---|
| A | 1 | 1 | 1 | 0.333 | 1.000 |
| B | 1 | 1 | 1 | 0.333 | 1.000 |
| C | 1 | 1 | 1 | 0.333 | 1.000 |
| | | | | C.R. = 0.00 | |

| Financing | A | B | C | Distributive Priorities | Idealized Priorities |
|---|---|---|---|---|---|
| A | 1 | 1/7 | 1/5 | 0.072 | 0.111 |
| B | 7 | 1 | 3 | 0.650 | 1.000 |
| C | 5 | 1/3 | 1 | 0.278 | 0.430 |
| | | | | C.R. =0 .06 | |

We now relate our network approach and genetics in a sense we mentioned previously. Our aim is to obtain a desired outcome and we propose to decide on the most important characteristics of the outcome by first prioritizing them. Since these characteristics may have influences on each other, we use networks to define the relations among those characteristics.

In selective breeding of plants or animals for example, offsprings are sought that have certain desirable characteristics- characteristics are determined at the genetic level by the way the parents' chromosomes combine. In a similar way, in seeking better solutions to complex problems, we often intuitively combine pieces of existing solutions. In the context of most obvious relevance to Operations Research, that of finding the optimal solution to a large combinatorial problem, a genetic algorithm works by maintaining a population of M chromosomes- potential parents- whose fitness values have been calculated [3]. Each chromosome encodes a solution to the problem, and its fitness value is related to the value of the objective function for that solution.

**Table 5.** Distributive and ideal synthesis

| | Size (0.175) | Trans (0.062) | Nghbd (0.103) | Age (0.019) | Yard (0.034) | Modrn ( 0.041) | Cond (0.221) | Financ (0.345) | Composite priority vector |
|---|---|---|---|---|---|---|---|---|---|
| | | | | | | | | | Dist. Mode |
| A | 0.743 | 0.194 | 0.717 | 0.333 | 0.691 | 0.770 | 0.200 | 0.072 | 0.346 |
| B | 0.194 | 0.063 | 0.066 | 0.333 | 0.091 | 0.068 | 0.400 | 0.649 | 0.369 |
| C | 0.063 | 0.743 | 0.217 | 0.333 | 0.218 | 0.162 | 0.400 | 0.279 | 0.285 |
| | | | | | | | | | Ideal Mode |
| A | 1.00 | 0.261 | 1.00 | 1.00 | 1.00 | 1.00 | 0.500 | 0.111 | 0.315 |
| B | 0.261 | 0.085 | 0.092 | 1.00 | 0.132 | 0.088 | 1.00 | 1.00 | 0.383 |
| C | 0.085 | 1.00 | 0.303 | 1.00 | 0.315 | 0.210 | 1.00 | 0.430 | 0.302 |

**Which Drink is Consumed More in the U.S.?**
**An Example of Estimation Using Judgments**

| **Drink Consumption in the U.S.** | **Coffee** | **Wine** | **Tea** | **Beer** | **Sodas** | **Milk** | **Water** |
|---|---|---|---|---|---|---|---|
| **Coffee** | 1 | 9 | 5 | 2 | 1 | 1 | 1/2 |
| **Wine** | 1/9 | 1 | 1/3 | 1/9 | 1/9 | 1/9 | 1/9 |
| **Tea** | 1/5 | 2 | 1 | 1/3 | 1/4 | 1/3 | 1/9 |
| **Beer** | 1/2 | 9 | 3 | 1 | 1/2 | 1 | 1/3 |
| **Sodas** | 1 | 9 | 4 | 2 | 1 | 2 | 1/2 |
| **Milk** | 1 | 9 | 3 | 1 | 1/2 | 1 | 1/3 |
| **Water** | 2 | 9 | 9 | 3 | 2 | 3 | 1 |

The derived scale based on the judgments in the matrix is:

| Coffee | Wine | Tea | Beer | Sodas | Milk | Water |
|---|---|---|---|---|---|---|
| .177 | .019 | .042 | .116 | .190 | .129 | .327 |

with a consistency ratio of .022.

The actual consumption (from statistical sources) is:

| .180 | .010 | .040 | .120 | .180 | .140 | .330 |
|---|---|---|---|---|---|---|

**Fig. 2.** Estimating drink consumption

Here we propose using the logic of this organic process in a more efficient way by first deciding on what are the most important characteristics and then arranging our inputs in a way that the inputs will have those desired characteristics so we will guarantee having the desired outcomes as a result of our mixing process. This approach can be considered as a backward process in which we decide a desired outcome first and then mixing and directing our present inputs to obtain that desired outcome in the future.

## 3 What Are the Priorities of the Criteria to Make an Original and Creative Contribution to a Field of Research?

We will deal with characteristics and their importance priorities needed to make an original and creative contribution to a field of research. The characteristics are divided into two main groups as intrinsic and extrinsic resources with related sub-criteria under each shown in Figure 3.

In our problem the criteria affect each other, so we need to consider all such dependencies to obtain good estimates in the prioritization process. We can do this by applying the ANP process that requires giving details of influences that determine how that decision may come out. As it can be seen from Figure 4, all influences have been represented by connections between elements that are related to each other. A criterion may influence another while it may also be influenced by that criterion. So the connections can be made in two ways.

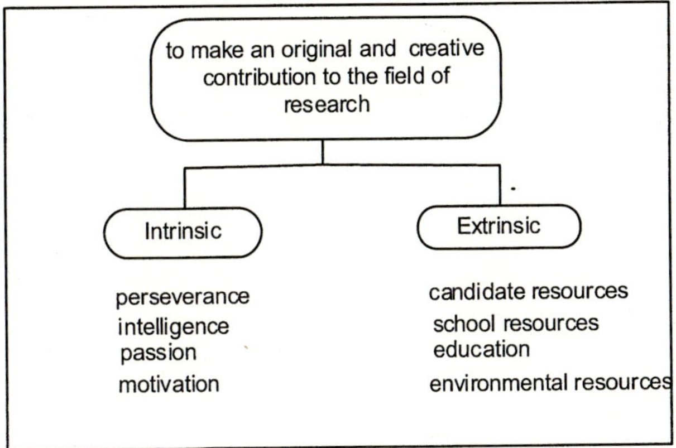


**Fig. 3.** The criteria

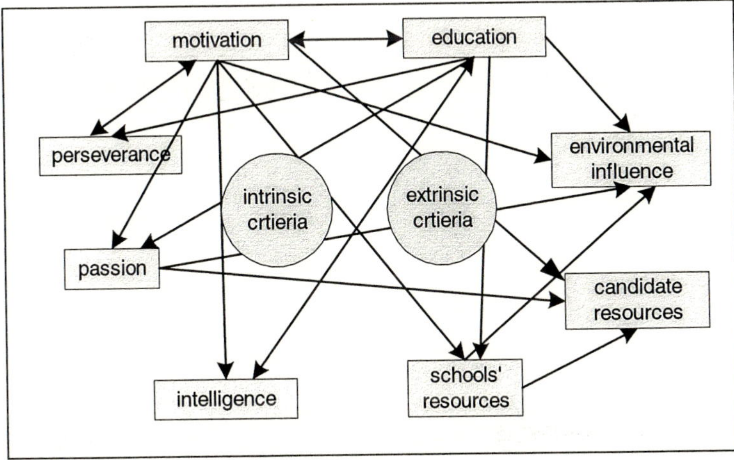


**Fig. 4.** The network structure of the problem

We perform paired comparisons on the criteria within the groups themselves according to their influence on each element in another group to which they are connected or on criteria in their own group. In making comparisons, we must always have a criterion in mind. We provide judgments by answering the question as to which a criterion influences a given criterion more and how much more strongly than another criterion with which it is compared in doing this we have an overriding control criterion or sub-criterion in mind such as intellectual, psychological, social, political, or economic influence. For example we compare the intrinsic criteria with respect to their effect on the goal as shown in Table 6 and get the priorities of each criterion.

We then compare perseverance, passion, intelligence, school resources, candidate resources and environmental resources criteria in pairs with respect to their effects on motivation. Since motivation is connected to these criteria, in this case we should ask for example, which criterion has more influence on motivation: passion or candidate resources. A criterion gets an overall priority by synthesizing all its paired comparisons. Table 7 shows the local and global priorities of the criteria.

**Table 6.** Paired comparisons matrix for intrinsic criteria with respect to making an original and creative contribution to the field of research

| Criteria | Intelligence | Passion | Perseverance | Motivation |
|---|---|---|---|---|
| Intelligence | 1 | 4 | 1 | 3 |
| Passion | 1/4 | 1 | 1/6 | 2 |
| Perseverance | 1 | 6 | 1 | 4 |
| Motivation | 1/3 | 1/2 | 1/4 | 1 |
| C.R. = 0.057 | | | | |

**Table 7.** The Local and the global priorities of each criterion

| Intrinsic Criteria | Local Priorities | Global Priorities | Extrinsic Criteria | Local Priorities | Global Priorities |
|---|---|---|---|---|---|
| Intelligence | 0.244 | 0.123 | Candidate Resources | 0.250 | 0.124 |
| Passion | 0.184 | 0.092 | Environmental Influence | 0.187 | 0.092 |
| Perseverance | 0.376 | 0.190 | School Resources | 0.283 | 0.140 |
| Motivation | 0.194 | 0.098 | Education | 0.278 | 0.137 |

It is interesting that in order to make an original and creative contribution to a field of research one should have perseverance followed by resources provided by the school and then by education. The latter are important because without support by the school and having a good education, being intelligent and motivated are not enough.

## 4 Conclusion

Genetics imply behavioral and physical characteristics. These characteristics determine performance of tasks. If we know the main characteristics that one needs to have to perform a certain task, this tells us what genes (characteristics) to mix to get greater abilities to perform that task and then the priorities of those characteristics help us to distinguish the most important ones. As the level of the most important gene in our mixture increases, we know in advance that the desirability of our outcome increases. So there is a link between genetics and decision making. We can control those not born yet who are made by mixing. This kind of analysis gives us a hold on arranging our inputs in a way to get the desired outcome. This study is intended as a proposal about how to improve genetic selection through prioritization.

Contrary to classical GA applications in which children's chromosomes are simply generated by their parent's chromosomes and these new chromosomes are subsequently evaluated according to their fitness or feasibility, this analysis directs us to determine normative importance values for the criteria that an outcome (e.g. a child) can have to attain an improved proficiency and perhaps also creativity at becoming an achiever at certain desired tasks by applying GA. It appears that these ideas may not have been considered concretely before, and point to new horizons in our thinking and planning process in applying GA.

## References


1. Elseth, G., Baumgardner, K. D., Principles of Modern Genetics, West Publishing Company, St. Paul (1995)
2. Bains. W., Genetic Engineering for Almost Everybody, Penguin Books, Harmondsworth, Middlesex, England (1987)
3. Saaty. T.L., The Analytic Hierarchy Process Series Vol.VIII, The Logic of Priorities, Applications of the Analytic Hierarchy Process in Business, Energy, Health and Transportation, RWS Publications, Pittsburgh (2000)
4. Saaty. T.L., Fundamentals of Decision Making and Priority Theory with the Analytic Hierarchy Process, RWS Publications, Pittsburgh (1991)
5. Saaty, T.L., Decision Making wih Dependence and Feedback The Analytic Network Process, RWS Publications, Pittsburgh (2001)

virtual database images. This paper presents a framework that maps a virtual object in a virtual database to an image of real view. In an automated system, four steps may be involved in registering imageries of two different camera views: feature extraction, finding the correspondence between the two imageries using the selected features, extracting corresponding points from matched image features, and finally, computation of the intrinsic and extrinsic parameters between the two camera coordinate systems, virtual and real view in our application, using a reliable set of corresponding points. This paper concentrates on selecting a reliable set of control points used in the calculation of intrinsic and extrinsic parameters of a camera model. The computational procedure used to calculate the intrinsic and extrinsic parameters of a camera system is called camera calibration[1,2,3,4,5,6]. A camera calibration procedure calculates transformation matrices(extrinsic parameters) and camera parameters(intrinsic parameters) based on a set of corresponding points. The accuracy of the camera calibration very much depends on the accuracy of the corresponding points[7]. Once we obtain the intrinsic and extrinsic parameters of the camera model, we can place a virtual object, visible or occluded, accurately in the real scene.

## 2 A Framework for Mapping Virtual Objects to Real Scene

Figure 1 illustrates the proposed framework for mapping a virtual object to a video image. There are two components in the framework. The first component shown in Figure 1 (a) attempts to calculate the camera calibration parameters necessary to transform virtual objects into the real view scene. In our application, a video camera is mounted on a moving vehicle and the location of the vehicle, therefore the location of the camera on the vehicle, can be determined using a GPS devise. If the GPS reading is accurate, the virtual database image at the view point that matches the GPS reading should exactly match the current video image frame. Due to the limited of accuracy of the GPS systems, the virtual image retrieved based on a GPS reading often does not accurately match the video image. However the estimated location of the video camera can be used to retrieve virtual images that have the viewpoints similar to the location of the video camera. Then two images of different views can be registered using the framework shown in Figure 1(a). This framework assumes that image features used for matching virtual and video have been defined and the virtual images have these features marked in the database. Research has shown that sharp edge points, corner points and intersection points are important features for image registering[8]. Figure 1 (b) shows that the location of a virtual object in a real scene can be found based on the calibrated intrinsic and extrinsic parameters of the virtual camera model. There are a number of existing camera calibration techniques[1,2,3,4,5] that can be used to determine both the intrinsic and extrinsic parameters for a given set of control points. For coplanar cases $n \geq 5$, for non-coplanar cases, $n \geq 7$. We have chosen to implement the camera calibration procedure presented by Roger Tsai[1].

*Our focus of research is to obtain a set of reliable control points to be used in a camera calibration model.* The accuracy of the constructed intrinsic and extrinsic parameters very much depends on the accuracy of the control points $\Sigma$ used in the camera calibration procedure. Research work has shown that all camera calibration

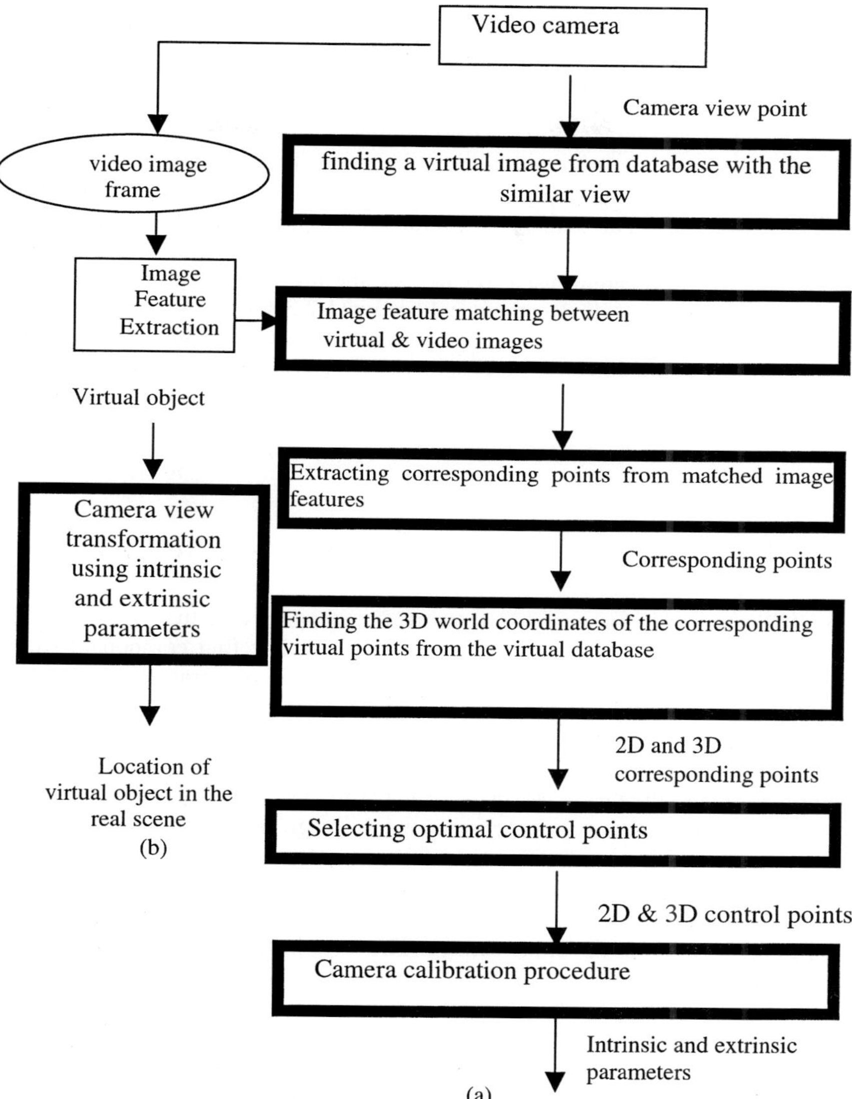


**Fig 1.** The framework of virtual and real view image registration

techniques are very susceptible to noise in image coordinates[4,5,6]. Haralick et al. showed that when the noise level exceeds a knee level, many camera calibration methods became extremely unstable and the errors could be outrageously large[7]. Therefore it is extremely important to find a reliable set of control points to construct the intrinsic and extrinsic parameters. The next section addresses this issue.

# 3 Selecting Reliable Control Points for Camera Parameters Construction

As we showed in section 2, in order to obtain accurate and stable camera parameters, it is critical to provide the system with a set of representative and accurate control points. There are two issues involved, representative and accuracy. The reconstructed camera parameters are representative if points anywhere in the virtual image can be mapped to the real image with the same accuracy. The reconstructed camera parameters are accurate if the points in the virtual image can be accurately mapped to the real image plane. In order to address these two issues, we developed the following principles to guide our algorithm development. Let a control point be represented by a triplet, $[(X_v, Y_v, Z_v), (x_v, y_v), (x_r, y_r)]$, where $(X_v, Y_v, Z_v)$ is the 3D coordinates of a point in the virtual database, $(x_v, y_v)$ is the corresponding coordinates in the virtual image, and $(x_r, y_r)$ is the corresponding coordinates in the real view image.

We developed a two-stage approach guided by the above principles. At the first stage we developed an algorithm that selects a set of corresponding points from the virtual and real images from the matched image features. At the second stage, we use an optimization algorithm to select a more reliable and stable set of control points from the corresponding points. To select reliable corresponding points from matched image features, we propose the following steps. First we select the junction points of matched image features, which are more stable and reliable than other features. If more corresponding points, we use the junction points to align the corresponding image features, and then extract the corresponding points scattered over the matched image features. As we mentioned in section 2 that in theory, we need at least seven corresponding pairs of points to construct a set of camera parameters. However it is has been shown 7 points are not sufficient for reliable results[1,5,9]. At the first stage of this algorithm, we recommend to extract at least 30 corresponding points from the matched image features. Figure 2 (a) and (b) show the corresponding feature points selected by the above algorithm. A Linear Structure Feature based corresponding points extraction algorithm can be found in [8].

(a) (b)

**Fig. 2.** Selected corresponding points in a pair of virtual and real images

At the second stage, we attempt to select an optimal set of control points for camera calibration from the corresponding points. Many researchers [1,9] believe that more points used in the construction of transformation matrices give better accuracy. However we found in[10] that better performance is possible when we used only a subset of the corresponding points. The problem of selecting an optimal control point set is non-trivial and remains to be explored. The most common framework to the problem is to define criteria for measuring the goodness of a set of control points, and then use a search algorithm to find an optimal or quasi-optimal set of control points in a larger point space based on the criteria. We formulate the problem as follows. Let $\Omega = \{p_1, p_2, \ldots, p_n\}$ be a set of corresponding points generated at the first stage and $n > 7$. We explore the problem based on the following two principles.

**Principle 1.** Let $F(\Omega_\alpha) = \langle I\_P_\alpha, E\_P_\alpha \rangle$ be a procedure that generates the intrinsic and extrinsic parameters, $I\_P_\alpha$, $E\_P_\alpha$, using control points in $\Omega_\alpha$. We attempt to find $\Omega_{op} \subseteq \Omega$ and $|\Omega_{op}| \geq 7$ such that the mapping function $F(\Omega_{op}) = \langle I\_P_{op}, E\_P_{op} \rangle$ along with $I\_P_{op}$ and $E\_P_{op}$ give the best possible performance on the mapping of unseen data points of a virtual objects to the corresponding video image points. This is different from a general optimization technique that evaluates the performance on the control points.

**Principle 2.** The distribution of control points should spread over all the different planes. In general, we should be selecting the control points distributed broadly across the field of view. The determination of two points on the same plane can be made based on their depth values which can be obtained in a stereo vision system or motion in for a monocular video camera system.

We developed the following three algorithms based on the above two principles for selecting a set of control points $\Omega_{op}$ for the construction of $I\_P_{op}$ and $E\_P_{op}$. For each algorithm we use a training set

$\Omega = \{[(X_v^1, Y_v^1, Z_v^1), (x_v^1, y_v^1), (x_r^1, y_r^1)], \ldots, [(X_v^n, Y_v^n, Z_v^n), (x_v^n, y_v^n), (x_r^n, y_r^n)]\}$, $n \geq 7$.

We refer $[(X_v^1, Y_v^1, Z_v^1), (x_v^1, y_v^1), (x_r^1, y_r^1)]$ to as a triplet.

### *Alg1. K-fold Cross Validation Method*

This method employs a variant of cross-validation known as *k-fold cross validation* used in training an intelligent system. The method has the following computational steps.

[step 1] Data set $\Omega$ of n examples is divided into k subsets of approximately equal size, $\Omega_1, \ldots, \Omega_k$. If n is not divisible by k, then the remaining elements are distributed among the k subsets such that no subset should have more than one extra data element compared to the other subsets. If a prior knowledge of points of different planes is available, each subset should contain points of different planes.

[step 2] Construct the intrinsic and extrinsic parameters on the k-1 subsets and validated on the *i*th subset for $i = \{1, 2, 3, \ldots, k\}$.

[step 3] Set $I\_P_{op} = I\_P_j$ and $E\_P_{op} = E\_P_j$ such that the intrinsic and extrinsic parameters generated at the $j$th step that give the least overall errors on the validated subset only for all $i$, $i = \{1, 2, 3, \ldots, k\}$ and $\Omega_{op} = \Omega_j$.

A generalization performance measure can be obtained by averaging the validation errors of the $k$ validation sets.

### *Alg2. Best One First In*

The second algorithm starts on constructing a set of I_P and E_P using the entire set of the corresponding points $\Phi$. Then it selects 11 points to construct a set of I_P and E_Ps that give the minimum projection errors. It evaluates the projection error over all the data and selects the best point to add into the control point set at a time until it reaches the whole set of available data. A set of control points is the subset of $\Phi$ that generates the I_P and E_P that gives the minimum project errors. Specifically it has the following computational steps.

[step 1] Construct the intrinsic and extrinsic parameters denoted as I_P and E_P using all points in $\Phi$.

[step 2] Calculate projection error of every triplet in $\Phi$.

[step 3] Put 11 triplets in $\Sigma$ that give the minimum projection errors, and set i = 1.

[step 4] Construct the intrinsic and extrinsic parameters denoted as $I\_P^i$ and $E\_P^i$ using all points in $\Sigma$.

[step 5] Calculate the projection error on every triplet in $\Sigma$ and ($\Phi$ - $\Sigma$) using $I\_P^i$ and $E\_P^i$ and the average errors on ($\Phi$ - $\Sigma$), $Ave\_error\_validation^i$.

[step 6] If $|\Sigma| < |\Phi|$, then $\Sigma = \Sigma \cup \{\text{triplet} \mid \text{triplet} \in \Phi - \Sigma$ that has the minimum error$\}$ and go to step 5.

[step 7] Stop the process and return the $I\_P^j$ and $E\_P^j$ that give the minimum $Ave\_error\_validation^j$.

### *Alg. 3 Worst One First Out*

The third algorithm starts on constructing I_P and E_P using the entire set of the corresponding points $\Phi$. It then evaluates the projection errors and throw out the worst point one at each iteration. At the end the algorithm selects the intrinsic and extrinsic parameters that give the best performance on the entire training data. Specifically the algorithm has the following computational steps.

[step 1] $\Sigma = \Phi$, i = 1.

[step 2] Construct the intrinsic and extrinsic parameters denoted as $I\_P^i$ and $E\_P^i$ using all points in $\Sigma$

[step 3] Calculate the projection error of every triplet in $\Sigma$ using $I\_P^i$ and $E\_P^i$ and the average error on $\Phi$, $Ave\_error\_train^i$.

[step 4] If $|\Sigma| > 11$, then $\Sigma = \Sigma - \{\text{triplet with the largest error}\}$ and go to step 2.

[step 5] Stop the process and return the $I\_P^j$ and $E\_P^j$ that gave the minimum $Ave\_error\_train^j$.

All three algorithms use the following procedure to calculate the projection error at each step. For a given set of points, $\Psi = \{[(X_v^1, Y_v^1, Z_v^1), (x_v^1, y_v^1), (x_r^1, y_r^1)], \ldots,$

$[(X_v^n, Y_v^n, Z_v^n), (x_v^n, y_v^n), (x_r^n, y_r^n)]\}$, we calculate $(x_{dj}^i, y_{dj}^i)$ following the system of equations given in (2) for i = 1, …, n, using the intrinsic and extrinsic parameters, $I\_P^j$ and $E\_P^j$ obtained at step j in each algorithm. The average error on $\Psi$ at step j is calculated as follows:

$$E_\Psi^j = \frac{1}{n}\sum_i \sqrt{\left(x_{dj}^i - x_r^i\right)^2 + \left(y_{dj}^i - y_r^i\right)^2} \text{ and}$$

the projection error of *i*th point is $E_i^j = \sqrt{\left(x_{dj}^i - x_r^i\right)^2 + \left(y_{dj}^i - y_r^i\right)^2}$.

We have conducted a few experiments to evaluate the above three algorithms. The intrinsic and extrinsic parameters are tested on the test set. The error on the test set gives a realistic measure of the system performance on the future unseen data set.

Figure 3 shows the one pair of the images used in our experiments. In this experiment, we used two virtual database images of two different camera views. We obtained 49 corresponding points. The dataset was divided into two subsets: training and blind test set. The blind test data contains 11 points. Each algorithm used the training data to select an optimal set of control points.

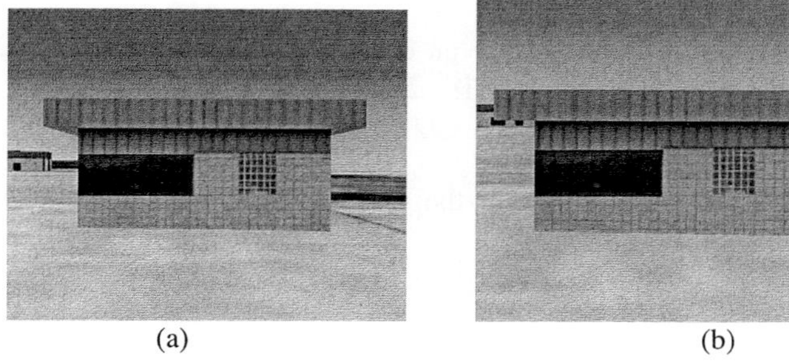

(a) (b)

**Fig. 3.** A pair of images used in optimal control point selection experiments

The graphs in Figure 4 show the performance of the intrinsic and extrinsic parameters generated by the data points selected at each step of each algorithm on the images shown in Figure 3. The x-axis indicates each iteration step in each algorithm, different color curves represent different performance parameters as indicated in each graph. Note the algorithm 1 represents the K-fold Cross Validation algorithm, algorithm 2 represents the Best One First, and algorithm 3 the Worst One Out First. Each graph illustrates the average error calculated on different data set data in different colors when a control point set was selected at each algorithm step, the navy blue curve indicates the average error on the training, the yellow curve the test set, the magenta the validation set, and the light blue indicates the error margin on the test set. Figure 4 shows that the k-fold Cross Validation algorithm selected the parameters generated at the second step since the validation error was minimum, which generated not the minimum test error but still very small test error. More important it generated very small error margin. The Worst One Out First selected the set of control points that gives the minimum error on the training data which was at the step 15. The

# Mapping Virtual Objects into Real Scene

Yi L. Murphey[1], Hongbin Jia[1], and Michael Del Rose[2]

[1] Department of Electrical and Computer Engineering
The University of Michigan-Dearborn
[2] U. S. Army TACOM-TARDEC
Vetronics Technology Center

**Abstract.** This paper presents a computer vision based framework for mapping virtual objects into a real scene captured by a video camera. Virtual objects are objects contained in a virtual scene stored in a virtual database. This technology has a number of applications including visually-guided robotic navigation, surveillance, military training and operation. The fundamental problem involves several challenging research issues including finding corresponding points between the virtual and the real scene and camera calibration. This paper focuses on our research in selecting reliable control points for the construction of intrinsic and extrinsic camera parameters, which is a vital portion for mapping virtual objects into a real scene.

## 1 Introduction

Video imagery is rapidly emerging as a low cost sensor in a variety of applications including target detection and tracking, robot navigation, surveillance, and military training and operation. In order to achieve high accuracy in real time operations, many of these applications generate a virtual database of the scene and combine it with video imagery to get more accurate operational information. A virtual database contains 3D models of the objects and the environment of interests. There are a number of reasons for the need of this type of technologies. The virtual database of a simulated environment can be generated artificially using 3D computer graphics and/or a virtual reality software. Some objects may not be generated as accurately as others due to both the large demand on labor and the difficulty in attaining accurate measurements. In addition, the virtual database can never include any dynamic objects, such as a car parked on the street, road construction, etc. Visible and infrared(IR) video cameras are increasingly deployed on moving vehicles, both manned and unmanned, to provide observers with a real time view of activity and terrain. However, video imagery does not provide sufficient information for detecting occluded objects, camouflaged objects. In particular video imagery does not provide much detectable information in bad weather, smoke, etc. A virtual database should be able to provide such information in all conditions. Therefore the best solution is to combine both imagery to extract information of interest.

The mapping of virtual objects to a real time video imagery requires a full registration of at least one video image frame with a virtual image. The registration results can be used to simplify the mapping between the subsequent image frames and

P.W.H. Chung, C.J. Hinde, M. Ali (Eds.): IEA/AIE 2003, LNAI 2718, pp. 62–71, 2003.

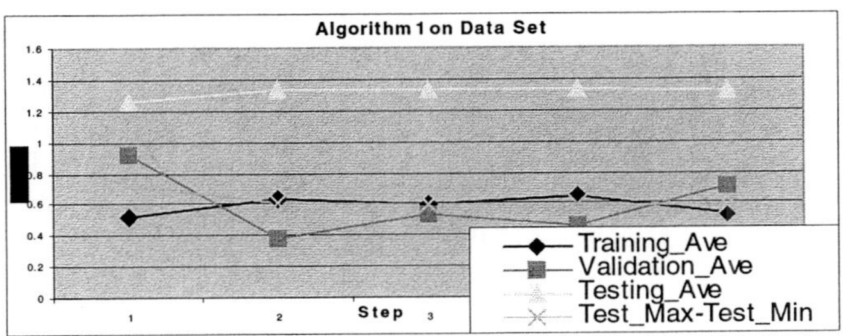


(a) performance of K-fold Cross Validation method

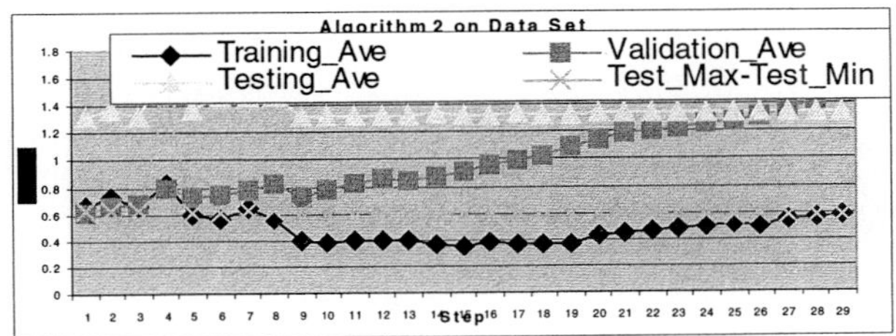


(b) performance curve of Best One First algorithm

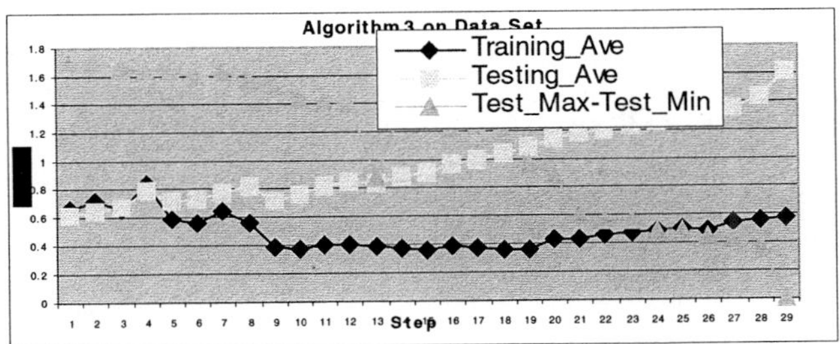


(c) The performance of the Worst One First Out algorithm

**Fig 4.** Performance of three optimal control point selecting algorithms

training error curve was sturdily low, and for the most part the test curve was low as well in comparison to the other two algorithms. However the error it generated at this point on the test set was higher in comparison to others and the error margin was relatively large as well. In summary the K-fold Cross Validation algorithm gave very good and stable performance on both sets of experiments.

## 4 An Application Case

We have applied the proposed system illustrated in Figure 1 to place virtual objects, which could be difficult to identify in the video image or hidden from the video camera view, accurately in a real scene. We used the pair of virtual database image and a video image to shown Figure 2 to register the virtual and real scene. Figure 2 also showed 30 corresponding points extracted from both the virtual and real images. We used the K-fold cross validation algorithm to select a set of 24 control points and implemented Tsai's camera calibration model [5] to construct the intrinsic, extrinsic, and the lens distortion parameters from the selected 24 control points. Figure 5 shows the results of mapping the object points in blue color in a virtual image to the real view image shown in red color using the intrinsic and extrinsic parameters generated by our system. Figure 6 shows the results of mapping the points of a virtual object(shown in RED) that is not visible in the real scene to a real scene image using the same intrinsic and extrinsic parameters. All these results are very satisfactory.

(a) (b)

**Fig. 5.** An example of mapping virtual objects to an image of real scene. (a) shows the virtual image containing the control points and three virtual objects. (b) shows a real view image with mapped virtual objects shown in "RED."

**Fig. 6.** An example of mapping a hidden virtual object to a real scene image

## 5 Conclusion

We have presented a framework that can place virtual objects accurately in a real scene through image registration and three algorithms, K-fold Cross Validation, Best One First and Worst One Out First, for selecting an optimal set of control points in registering virtual and real scenes. Through experiments we showed the k-fold Cross Validation algorithm is capable of selecting an optimal set of control points from a larger set of corresponding points that can be used to construct the intrinsic and extrinsic parameters that give minimum mapping error on unseen points. We showed in this paper that the intrinsic and extrinsic parameters generated by less number of control points can give better performance and have better generalization. The algorithms that select optimal control points are applicable to general image registration problems beyond virtual and real imageries.

**Acknowledgment**

The research project is supported in part by a contract from U.S. Army TACOM-TARDEC, Vetronics Technology Center.

## References

[1] R. Tsai, "A Versatile Camera Calibration Technique for High-Accuracy 3D Machine Vision Metrology Using Off-the-Shelf TV Cameras and Lenses," *IEEE Trans. on of Robotics and Automation*, Vol. RA-3, No. 4, pp. 323-344, 1987.

[2] Robert J. Valkenburg, *Classification of Camera Calibration Techniques*, Machine Vision, In *Image and Vision Computing New Zealand*, Lincoln, August 1995, pp 43-48.

[3] Ravi Samtaney, *A Method to Solve Interior and Exterior Camera Calibration Parameters for Image Resection,* Nas-99-003, April 1999

[4] Qiang Ji, Yongmian Zhang, *Camera Calibration with Genetic Algorithms*, IEEE Transactions on Systems, Man, And Cybernetics, VOL. 31, No. 2, March 2001

[5] J. Weng, P. Cohen, and M. Herniou, "Camera calibration with distortion models and accuracy evaluation," IEEE Trans. Pattern Analysis and Machine Intelligence, Vol. 10, pp. 965-980, 1992

[6] X. Wang and G. Xu, "Camera parameters estimation and evaluation in active vision system," Pattern Recognition, vol. 29, no. 3, pp. 439-447, 1996.

[7] R. M. Haralick, H. Joo, C. Lee, X. Zhang, Vaidya, and M. Kim, "Pose estimation from corresponding point data," IEEE Transaction on syst., Man, Cybern., Vol. 19, pp. 1426-1446, June, 1989

[8] Yi Lu Murphey, Hongbin Jia, and Michael Del Rose, "Registering Real and Virtual Imagery," submitted to Journal of Pattern Recognition, June 2002

[9] Yi L. Murphey, Jianxin Zhang and Michael DelRose, "Registering Video With Virtual Imagery Using Robust Image Features," International Conference on Visualization, Imaging and Image Processing, Spain, September, 2001

# Color Image Segmentation in Color and Spatial Domain

Tie Qi Chen[1], Yi L. Murphey[1], Robert Karlsen[2], and Grant Gerhart[2]

[1] VisiTek, Inc. 1409 Harbrooke Ann Arbor, Michigan 48103, Yilu@umich.edu
[2] U. S. TACOM, AMSTA-TR-R/263, Warren, MI 48397-5000
Department of Electrical and Computer Engineering
The University of Michigan-Dearborn
Dearborn Michigan 48128-1491, U.S.A.
Voice: 313-593-5028, Fax: 313-593-9967
yilu@umich.edu

**Abstract.** In this paper we describe a color image segmentation system that performs color clustering in a color space followed by a color region segmentation algorithm in the image domain. In color space, we describe two different algorithms that clusters similar colors using different measuring criteria and present our evaluation results on these two algorithms in comparison with three well-known color segmentation algorithms. The region segmentation algorithm merges clusters in the image domain based on color similarity and spatial adjacency. We developed three different methods for merging regions in the image domain. The proposed clustering algorithms are applicable to color image indexing and retrieval, object segmentation using color feature and color image mining. The color image segmentation system has been implemented and tested on a variety of color images including satellite images, moving car images and etc. The system has shown to be both effective and efficient.

## 1 Introduction

In the past decade, color imaging has become popular in many applications including object classification and recognition, video surveillance, image indexing and retrieval in image databases and video databases, feature based video compression, data mining, etc. [1,2]. In some applications, image contents can be better described in terms of color features combined with spatial relations such as enclosure and adjacency due to the irregularity of object shapes in images. This paper describes our research in color image segmentation, which is often a necessary computational process for color-based image retrieval and object recognition[2].

Image segmentation is a process of partitioning image pixels based on selected image features. The pixels that belong to the same region must be spatially connected and have the similar image features. If the selected segmentation feature is color, an image segmentation process would separate pixels that have distinct color feature into different regions, and, simultaneously, group pixels that are spatially connected and have the similar color into the same region. In color imagery, image pixels can be

P.W.H. Chung, C.J. Hinde, M. Ali (Eds.): IEA/AIE 2003, LNAI 2718, pp. 72–82, 2003.

represented in a number of different color spaces e.g. RGB, XYZ, or LUV[3, 4]. One major concern in color image segmentation is that the computational complexity, which has increased significantly in comparison with gray scale image segmentation. The process of image segmentation can be considered as an unsupervised clustering, if a priori knowledge about the *number and type of regions* present in the image is not available [5]. Image clustering procedures often use the individual image pixels as units and compare each pixel value with every other neighboring pixel value, which require excessively long computation times for images of high resolutions. A high quality representation of a color requires 8 bits using PCM (Pulse Code Modulation) quantization for each of the three color-components, Red(R), Green(G), Blue(B). For each image pixel, 24 bits of amplitude quantization is required, allowing specification of $2^{24}$ = 16,777,216 distinguishable colors. This leads to high computational cost in image clustering.

In this paper we describe an efficient color image segmentation system shown in Figure 1. The color image segmentation system consists of two stages of computation. At the first stage, we use a color clustering algorithm to generate clusters of similar colors in the color histogram space of an image. The histogram of a color image in a selected color space is a three dimensional(3D) discrete feature space that provides the color distribution of the image. The output of the color clustering algorithm is a set of non-overlapping color clusters, $CL_1$. Each cluster in $CL_1$ contains similar colors and all colors in the same cluster are assigned with the same color label. The labeling of the clusters in $CL_1$ results in image domain a multithresholded image in which pixels of the same region have the same color label and are spatially connected. These regions form the second cluster set $CL_2$ to be used in the second stage. At the second stage, a region segmentation algorithm agglomerates the initial clusters in $CL_2$ based on the spatial connection and the color distances between the adjacent regions. The second stage only merges the selected adjacent regions, it does not split any regions. Therefore the first design criterion for the fuzzy clustering algorithm is that different color regions should be in different clusters in $CL_1$. However, we should prevent from generating a too large set of clusters: for one extreme is that each cluster in CL1 contains one color only, which certainly satisfies the first criterion but misses the purpose of the histogram based clustering. Therefore, the second design criterion is that $CL_1$ must be compact. These two criteria have been used to guide the development of clustering algorithms.

The second set of clusters, $CL_2$, is obtained by labeling image pixels with the corresponding color clusters in $CL_1$. Because there is no spatial information used at the first stage, the pixels in the same cluster in $CL_1$ can be scattered over the entire image resulting, in many cases, $|CL_2| >> |CL_1|$. The segmentation algorithm at the second stage iteratively merges the regions in $CL_2$ based on the color distances between the neighboring regions, region sizes and the maximum number of clusters in $CL_3$, the system output that contains the meaningful color regions with respect to objects in the image.

This paper is organized as follows. Section 2 will describe two different algorithms that perform clustering computation in a color space and their performance evaluation. Section 3 will present a region segmentation algorithm that groups clusters in the image domain based on color similarity and spatial adjacency. Section 4 presents our experiment results and the performance analysis of each algorithm in the segmentation system.

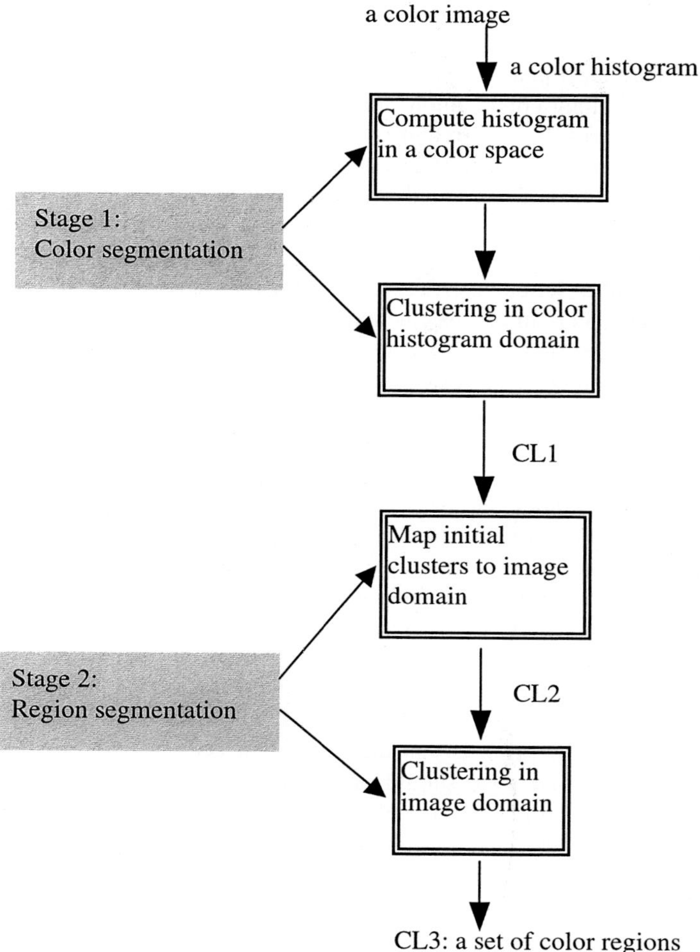


**Fig. 1.** An overview of the color image segmentation system

## 2 Clustering in Color Space

Color is the most popular feature used in image retrieval and object recognition within color imagery. Color is often described by terms of intensity, luminance, lightness, hue and saturation. Intensity is a measure over some interval of the electromagnetic spectrum of the flow of power that is radiated from, or incident on, a surface. There are a number of color spaces been defined based on different criteria of applications and most of those are three dimensional[2]. In general for a given color space, we can calculate a color historgram function $F(C_i)$ from a color image $I$, where $C_i$ is a color in the color space and $F(C_i)$ denotes the number of pixels in $I$ that have color C. The dimensions of a color histogram are determined by the color space used to represent the image. For example, in the L*u*v* space, $C_i$ is represented by a vector (l, u, v) and $F(C_i)$ is the number of pixels that have L*u*v* values equal to (l,u,v); in RGB color space, $C_i$ is represented by a vector (r, g, b) and $F(C_i)$ is the number of pixels in $I$ that have color equal to (r, g, b). Considering the uncertainty nature of classifying similar colors into clusters, we developed two color clustering algorithms, Max Quantization Error, and Optimal-Cut.

**Max Quantization Error(MQE)**

This is a greedy algorithm that aggressively reduces the global color quantization error by creating new clusters at the place where the maximum quantization error is. This algorithm has the following steps:

1. $CL1=\{\}$ *and* $j=0$.
2. Find the color bin in the histogram with the maximum color frequency, and create a color cluster centered in that bin. Mathematically, we are trying to find a color, $C_{cluster}$, such that $F(C_{cluster}) \geq F(C_i)$ for all color $C_i$ in the image domain. $C_j = C_{cluster}$, *and* $CL1=CL1 \cup \{C_j\}$.
3. Calculate color quantization error for every bin in the histogram using the following equation: $E_i = F(C_i)\|C_i - C_j\|^2$.
4. Find $C_{cluster}$, such that $E_{cluster} = F(C_{cluster})\|C_{cluster} - C_j\|^2 \geq E_i$ for all i. set j=j+1, $C_j = C_{cluster}$, and $CL1=CL1 \cup \{C_j\}$.
5. Recalculate the color quantization error for every color $C_i$ in the histogram using the following equation: $E_i = F(C_i)\|C_i - C_{nearest\_cluster}\|^2$, where $C_{nearest\_cluster} \in CL1$ is the cluster that is closest to $C_i$.
6. Find the color, $C_{cluster}$ with the maximum color quantization error defined in step 4, set j=j+1, $C_j = C_{cluster}$, and $CL1=CL1 \cup \{C_j\}$
7. Repeat steps 5 to 6 until one of the following conditions is met, go to step 8:
   a. $|CL1| = M$, M is the desired number of clusters set by the user
   b. the maximum quantization error, $E_{cluster}$ is below a threshold.
8. At the end the loop we have $CL1=\{C_j | i=0, 1, \ldots, M-1\}$, *which* is a set of colors representing M cluster centers. For every color C in the image, C is assigned a color label p $0 \leq p \leq M-1$, if

$$D_{color}(C, C_p) = \|C - C_p\|^2 \leq D_{color}(C, C_j) = \|C - C_j\|^2,$$ for all j such that $0 \leq j \leq M-1$.

**Optimal-Cut(OpC)**

The *optimal-cut* algorithm adopts a splitting process that generates a number of color cubes in a color space that minimize the global color quantization error. The algorithm is based on the searching of 3D boxes, i.e. a right rectangular prisms, in the color space that give minimized global color quantization error.

We define the quantization error function $E_{box}$ within a 3D box in the color space as follows: $E_{box} = \sum_{i \in box} F(c_i) \| c_i - \bar{c}_{box} \|^2$, where $c_i$ is the 3-dimensional *ith* color vector within *box*, $F(c_i)$ is the color frequency (or the number of pixels that have the color) of $c_i$, and $\bar{c}_{box}$ is the central color of the *box* calculated as follows:

$$\bar{c}_{bax} = \frac{\sum_{c_i \in box} F(c_i) c_i}{\sum_{c_i \in box} F(c_i)}.$$

The optimal-cut algorithm has the following steps

1. Define a minimum 3D box, i.e. a right rectangular prism, $box_0$ =($C_1$, $C_2$, $C_3$, $C_4$, $C_5$, $C_6$, $C_7$, $C_8$) in the color space that encompasses all the colors in the image *I*, where $C_i$, i = 1, 2, ..., 8 are the 3D coordinates of the eight vertices that uniquely define the color box. Add it to the cluster list CL1 = { $box_0$ }.
2. For each color box in CL1, search along each of the three coordinate axes in the color space to find a split point that can partition the box into two sub boxes and the reduction of the quantization error is maximum in comparison to all the other possible splits within all current color boxes. Assume a color box has coordinates box={($x_1$, $y_1$, $z_1$), ($x_2$, $y_1$, $z_1$), ($x_1$, $y_1$, $z_2$), ($x_2$, $y_1$, $z_2$), ($x_1$, $y_2$, $z_1$), ($x_2$, $y_2$, $z_1$),( $x_1$, $y_2$, $z_2$), ($x_2$, $y_2$, $z_2$)}. If a split occurred along the x-axis at point x*, where $x_1 < x^* < x_2$, then the two sub-boxes have coordinates, sub-box1={($x_1$, $y_1$, $z_1$), ($x_2$, $y_1$, $z_1$), ($x_1$, $y_1$, $z_2$), (x*, $y_1$, $z_2$), ($x_1$, $y_2$, $z_1$), (x*, $y_2$, $z_1$),( $x_1$, $y_2$, $z_2$), (x*, $y_2$, $z_2$)}, and sub-box2 = {(x*, $y_1$, $z_1$), ($x_2$, $y_1$, $z_1$), (x*, $y_1$, $z_2$), ($x_2$, $y_1$, $z_2$), (x*, $y_2$, $z_1$), ($x_2$, $y_2$, $z_1$), ( x*, $y_2$, $z_2$), ($x_2$, $y_2$, $z_2$)}. A split along y-axis and z-axis can be similarly calculated. The reduction of quantization error resulted from the split is calculated as follows:

   $$E_{box} - E_{sub-box1} - E_{sub-box2}.$$

   Based on the definition of the quantization error given above, it can be easily shown that $E_{box} > (E_{sub\text{-}box1} + E_{sub\text{-}box2})$
3. Readjust the two sub-boxes so that there are no empty color bins along their boundaries and then add them to the color cluster set CL1.
4. Repeat steps 2 and 3 until the desired number of color clusters is obtained, or the maximum quantization error is under a threshold.

We evaluated the two color clustering algorithms introduced above with three other algorithms published in literature, Pair-wised clustering, median-cut and Octree[6, 7, 8]. Figure 2. shows the experiment results on three different images generated by the proposed two methods as well as the other three. All algorithms were set to generate 16 different color clusters. From the resulting images we can see that the proposed

OpC and MQE generated better results than the other three algorithms on all three example images. We further evaluated the five algorithms by measuring the quantization errors on the resulting images. Table 1 shows the quantization error generated by the five color clustering algorithms on the three images shown in Figure 2.

Both the MQE and OpC algorithms gave much better performance in terms of minimizing quantization error on all three images in the experiments than the other three algorithms. Both algorithms gave similar performance in reducing the global color quantization error for image 1 and image 3. However MQE algorithm had much better lead on image 2 than OpC.

According to [6] the pairwised clustering algorithm should produce less quantization error than other algorithms such as *uniform*, *popularity*, *median-cut*, *local K-means*, *variance-based*, and *octree*. However, the pairwised algorithm needs to maintain a quantization error matrix that can be overwhelmingly large. For example, for a 24-bit color image, every color component has 256 levels. If we use 32 levels to generate the histogram (as most algorithms do), we will have $32^3$ = 32,768 bins. Therefore, initially, the quantization error matrix can have $32{,}768^2$ = 1,073,741,824 elements. In these experiments, we used clustering level 16, the pairwised clustering algorithm took significantly longer time than the other four algorithms but did not give better performance.

**Table 1.** Evaluation of quantization errors of five color clustering algorithms

| | OpC | MQE | Median-cut | Octree | Pariwised clustering |
|---|---|---|---|---|---|
| image 1 | 14.8643 | 14.9825 | 26.1717 | 36.369 | 37.9375 |
| image 2 | 31.0813 | 15.7932 | 31.8167 | 37.485 | 46.3871 |
| image 3 | 15.4799 | 15.3994 | 33.8684 | 32.870 | 43.9668 |

## 3 Region Segmentation in Image Domain

Region segmentation is implemented by a spatial clustering algorithm that groups the clusters generated by the color clustering algorithms mentioned in the previous section using various measurements. When mapping the color clusters in $CL_1$ to the image domain, we obtain a color cluster set $CL_2$, in which each cluster contains image pixels that are both spatially connected and within the same color cluster in $CL_1$. In general, one cluster in $CL_1$ can be decomposed into more than one cluster in $CL_2$, and therefore $CL_2$ is much larger than $CL_1$. This is evidenced by the color clustered images shown in Figure 2. Pixels of the same color can scatter all over the image domain, which results in many different clusters in $CL_2$. In general, $|CL_1| \ll |CL_2|$. The image segmentation algorithm in the image domain is an agglomerative process that uses the following three parameters:

- color distances among neighboring clusters in the spatial domain,
- cluster sizes and
- maximum number of clusters in $CL_3$.

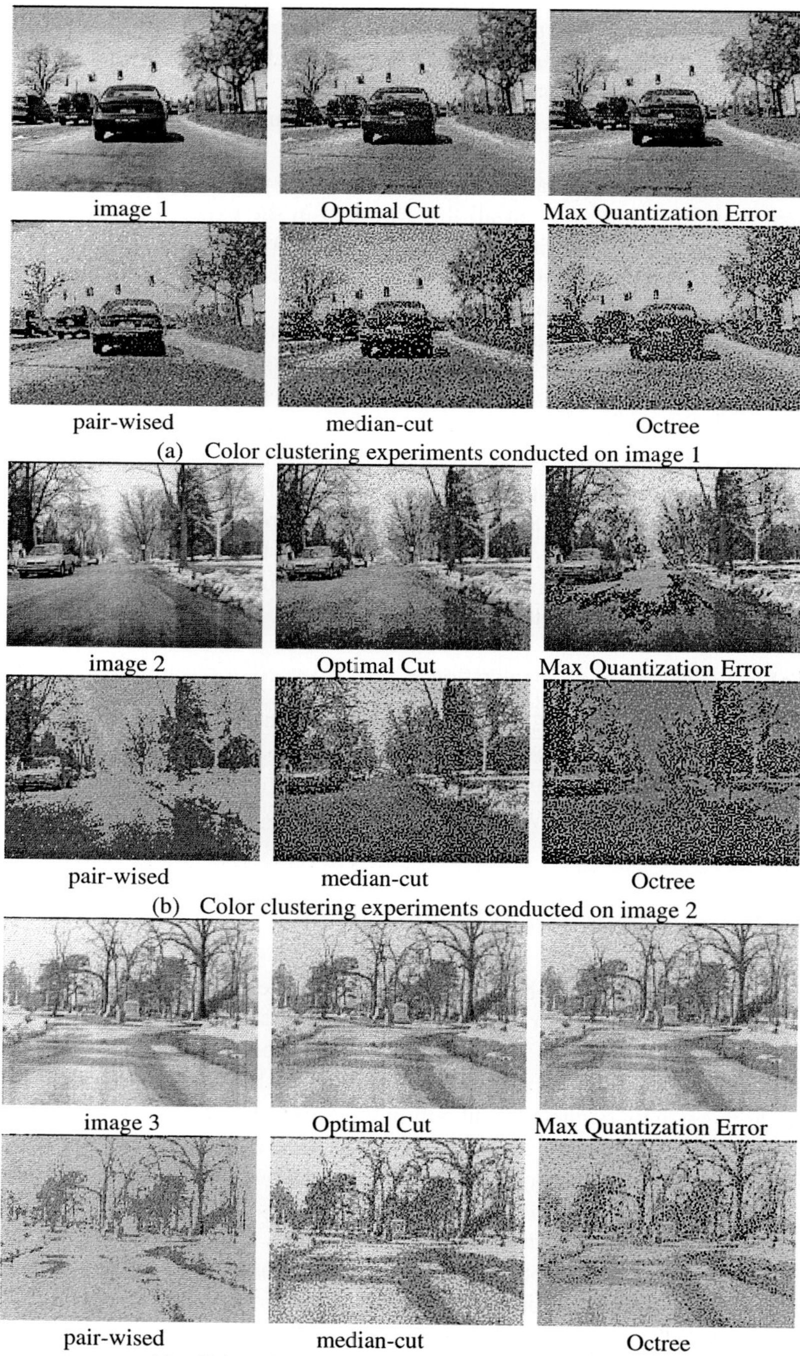


(a) Color clustering experiments conducted on image 1

(b) Color clustering experiments conducted on image 2

(c) Color clustering experiments conducted on image 3

**Fig. 2**. Experimental evaluation of various color clustering algorithms.

After every merge of two clusters, the center of the new cluster is calculated, and the size and the neighbors of the merged cluster are updated. We define the distance between two clusters as the color distance between the centers of the two clusters. During the sequential merging process, an important issue is the order of merging clusters, which can significantly affect the region segmentation result. We have investigated three clustering merging methods. All of the three methods use a common parameter, *max_cls,* to control the maximum number of clusters in $CL_3$. The three methods differ in the priority of selecting clusters to merge at each iterative step. The priorities of merge used in the three methods are set to meet the requirement of various applications. Method 1 attempts to merge the adjacent clusters that are similar in colors. In implementation, we use a control parameter, *cl_diff_th* to denote color difference threshold. At the first step, the algorithm attempts to merge the neighboring clusters whose color distances are below cl_diff_th. If the number of clusters at the end of the first step is greater than *max_cls*, then the algorithm begins the second step. At the second step, the algorithm selects the smallest cluster and merges the cluster with one of its neighbors to which it has the smallest color distance. This merging process repeats until the number of clusters in $CL_3$ is no more than *max_cls*. Method 2 considers the size of clusters as the only selection criterion. It selects the smallest cluster and merges it with one of its neighbors to which it has the smallest color distance. The process is repeated until the number of clusters in $CL_3$ is no more than *max_cls*.

Method 3 considers the color distance as the most important criterion in cluster merging in the image domain. However, the computation required in finding the minimum color distance between two adjacent clusters is quite time consuming if the number of clusters in $CL_2$ is large. To alleviate the computational burden, the algorithm consists of three passes of merging. At the first pass, it repeatedly merges the **smallest clusters** with their neighbors that have the closest color distance until the total number of clusters is reduced to a reasonable number. At the second pass, the algorithm selects a pair of two adjacent clusters that has the smallest color distance within the entire image to merge. This process repeats until the top max_cls clusters in size contain a large percentage of the image pixels. Since the largest max_cl clusters already cover the majority of the entire image pixels, the small clusters below the top max_cl should not affect too much the final segmentation result. Therefore at the third pass, the algorithm repeatedly merges the smallest cluster with its closest neighbor in color distance until the total number of clusters in $CL_3$ is no more than max_cls.

From the computational point of view, Method 1 and 2 are more efficient than Method 3. However, in many cases, Method 3 generates better results than the other two methods.

## 4 Implementation, Experiments and Conclusion

We have tested the segmentation system on a large number of images from video images taken from a moving vehicle. Due to the limited space, we use one image example to illustrate the performance of the proposed clustering system. Figure 3 experiments conducted on an image taken in a city street scene by a video camera mounted on a moving vehicle. The objects of interests in this application are vehicles in front of the primary vehicle. In these experiments, we used both Max Quantization Error and Optimal-Cut in the color space clustering and Method 3 in region segmentation. It appears that Optimal-Cut gave better segmentation results in the color space. The results from region segmentation that follow both Max Quantization Error and Optimal-Cut separated the vehicles from their surrounding objects such as road, trees, etc. However, the Optimal-Cut appeared to give better details. Figure 4 shows the region segmentation results when different number of clusters were specified. In comparison to the results shown in Figure 3, where cluster number 50 was used, we can conclude that when the number of clusters increases, more details are shown but more region fragments may result. In general Optimal-Cut followed by region segmentation gives effective object segmentation using color features.

(a) Color clusters generated by OpC

(b) Color clusters generated by MQE

(c) Image segmentation generated by OpC with 50 clusters

(d) Image segmentation generated by MQE with 50 clusters

**Fig 3.** Image segmentation using optimal-cut and max quantization error on image

In summary the clustering algorithms we presented in this paper are very effective in color image segmentation. In particular the optimal-cut followed by spatial clustering using cluster distances showed very promising results. The color image segmentation system has been implemented and tested on a variety of color images including satellite images, car and face images and has shown to be both effective and efficient.

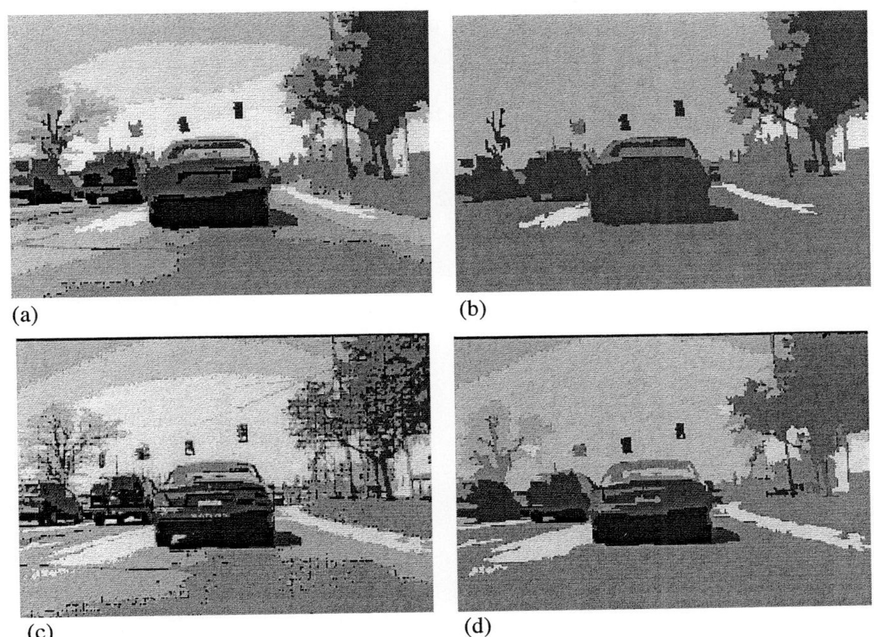

**Fig. 4.** Image segmentation results generated by MQE (a) followed by region segmentation with cluster number 100(b) and by OpC (c) followed by region segmentation with cluster number 100(d)

## Acknowledgment

This work is support in part by a SBIR contract from the U. S. Army TACOM.

## References


[1] J. Hafner, H. S. Sawhney, W. Equitz, M. Flickner and W. Niblack, "Efficient Color Histogram Indexing for Quadratic Form Distance Functions," IEEE Trans. on Pattern Analysis and Machine Intelligence, Vol. 17, No. 7, PP. 729-736, July 1995.

[2] Yi Lu Murphey "Image Search and Retrieval Strategies" a chapter in Encyclopedia of Imaging Science and Technology, edited by Dr. Joseph P. Hornak to be published by John Wiley & sons, Inc. 2002

[3] C. L. Novak and S. A. Shafer, "Color Vision," *Physics-Based Vision COLOR,* pp. 1-10, Jones an Bartlett, 1992

[4] G. D. Finlayson, "Color in Perspective," IEEE Trans. on Pattern Analysis and Machine Intelligence, Vol. 18, No. 10, PP. 1034-1035, October, 1996.

[5] Jean-Michel Jolion, Peter Meer, and Samira Bataouche, "Robust Clustering with Applications in Computer Vision," *IEEE Transactions on Pattern Analysis and Machine Intelligence,* pp 791-802, August, 1991.

[6] Velho, L.; Gomes, J.; Sobreiro, M.V.R. , "Color image quantization by pairwise clustering " X Brazilian Symposium on Computer Graphics and Image Processing, 1997, Page(s): 203 -210, 233

[7] P. Heckbert, "Color image quantization for frame buffer display," Computer Graphics, 16(3), pp297-307, July, 1982.

[8] M. Gervautz and W. Purgathofer, "A simple method for color quantization: octree quantization," Proceedings of CGI 88, pp219-231, 1988.

# Multiple Signal Fault Detection Using Fuzzy Logic

Yi Lu Murphey, Jacob Crossman, and ZhiHang Chen

Department of Electrical and Computer Engineering
The University of Michigan-Dearborn
Dearborn Michigan 48128-1491, U.S.A.
Voice: 313-593-5028, Fax: 313-593-9967
yilu@umich.edu

**Abstract.** In this paper, we describe a multiple Signal Fault Detection system that employs fuzzy logic at two levels of detection: signal segment fault and signal fault. The system involves signal segmentation, feature extraction and fuzzy logic based segment fault detection and signal fault detection. At the signal segment level, we developed a fuzzy learning algorithm that learns from good vehicle signals only. The system has been implemented and tested extensively of vehicle signals. The experiments using vehicle engine Electronic Control Unit(ECU) signals are presented and discussed in the paper.

## 1 Introduction

As electronic control systems become more advanced and sophisticated in recent years, malfunctions in many products such as automobiles have been increasingly more complicated. The complexity of engineering diagnostics lies in the fact that a sophisticated electronic instrument or device usually involves an abundance of signals. Some of these signals are primary, others are secondary; some are causal, others are symptomatic; taken together, they provide context. Therefore signal fault detection plays a critical role in engineering diagnosis. Often complicated systems experience faults that are manifested as *wrong combinations* of behaviors of multiple signals, but the individual behaviors of each signal may appear normal. Figure 1 gives an example of multi signal faults in a vehicle system. In this example the BAD MAF(Mass Air Flow) signal was generated by partially disconnecting the air intake manifold from the engine. This caused MAF sensor to

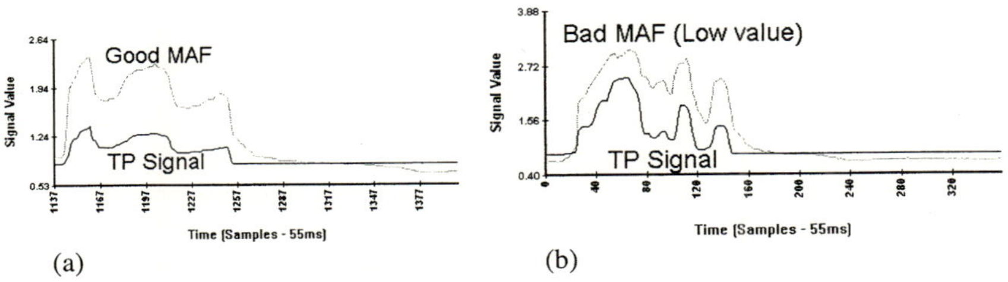


**Fig. 1.** An example of vehicle fault that demonstrates the need for multiple signal analysis. (a) and (b) show an two examples of GOOD and BAD MAF combining with TP signals.

P.W.H. Chung, C.J. Hinde, M. Ali (Eds.): IEA/AIE 2003, LNAI 2718, pp. 83–92, 2003.

read low because some air is bypassing the MAF sensor located near the air filter. This fault was generated to simulate a vacuum leak, which is a difficult fault to detect. However, looking at MAF by only it is impossible to detect the fault as MAF is behaving rather normally. But if we examine TP(Throttle Position) along with MAF we see that MAF was not rising as high as it should on acceleration. Because of the dependencies of the components and sensors in the system and the device operation itself, very few signals act independently from others. The interactions between signals are complex but nevertheless are important for many engineering diagnostic problems.

In this paper we present a multi-signal fault diagnostic systems that employs fuzzy logic for signal segment fault and signal fault detection. At the signal segment level we trained a fuzzy system using GOOD data examples only, and the resulting knowledge base is used to detect GOOD and BAD signals. At the signal level, a second fuzzy knowledge base was built based on segment faults detected by the first fuzzy system. Both fuzzy systems have been implemented in the applications of various vehicle signal fault diagnosis and the experiments of detecting Electronic Control Unit(ECU) signals in an automobile[1] are presented and discussed in the paper.

## 2 A Multi-signal Fault Diagnostic System

Figure 2 illustrates the major computational steps in the proposed multi-signal fault diagnostic system. The input signals, $S_1$, $S_2$, …, $S_m$, should be related, i.e. these signals interacted to each other, some are causal and others are symptomatic. The determination of related signals is not an easy task. It requires the knowledge of the physical system, the actual connections of physical components, and the momentum in the device under diagnosis. In this system this knowledge is assumed to be available. From a primary signal is selected among the input signals and all other signals are called reference signals. A primary signal should be the key signal that represents a physical event.

Most sensor signals are irregular, non-periodic, composed mainly of sharp transients (often in the form of edges) and periods of relative stability[2]. Most of the transients and stable sections of the signal have some physical significance and are related to the vehicle's behavior over time[3]. Therefore, vehicle signals, which contain both periodic and transient features, are best analyzed segment-by-segment using variable window sizes, where each signal segment within a window contains an event. The purpose of a signal segmentation process is to partition a signal into regions of consistent behavior. The primary signal is first segmented a sequence of segments, each of which is labeled by a vehicle state corresponding to a meaningful physical event that is labeled by a operational state corresponding to a meaningful physical event. For example, in vehicle signals we segment signals in response to three events, acceleration, cruise and deceleration[4]. Since all reference signals were recorded simultaneously with the primary signal, the segment boundaries of the primary signal can be mapped to every reference signal to obtain the corresponding segment, and a segment in a reference signal is labeled by the same state as the corresponding segment in the primary signal. From the signal segments, important features are extracted to best represent the corresponding physical events.

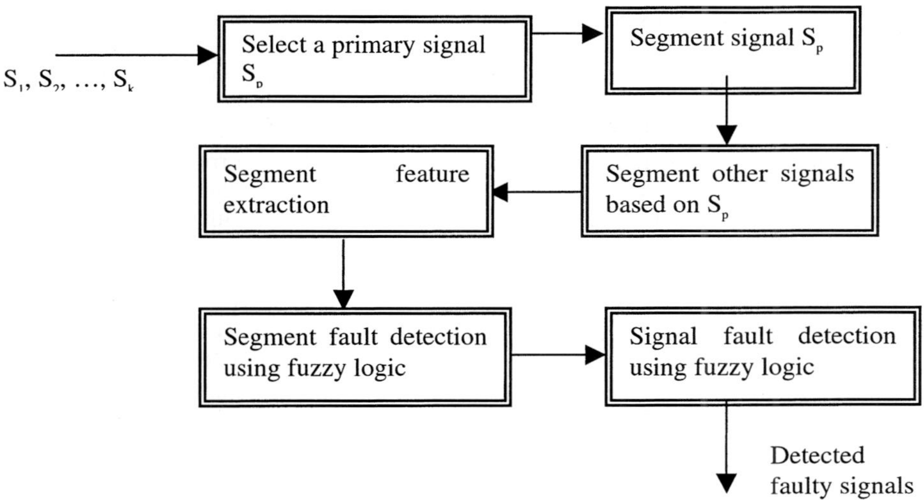


**Fig. 2.** A multi-signal fault detection system

The focus of this paper is to present our results for the last two processes in Figure 2, segment fault detection and signal fault detection using fuzzy logic.

## 3 Signal Segment Fault Diagnosis Using Fuzzy Logic

Segment fault detection is the analysis of signals segment-by-segment for any possible faulty behavior, which is very similar to the techniques used by trained technicians and engineers use to analyze signal faults. This process uses only local features within each segment.

After signal segmentation process described above, we obtain a sequence of segments, $\{ s_1^p, s_2^p, \ldots, s_k^p \}$, to represent the primary signal, and a sequence of segments to represent each reference signal i, $\{ s_1^{r_i}, s_2^{r_i}, \ldots, s_k^{r_i} \}$. Each segment, $s_j^q$, q = $r_i$ or p, is represented by a feature vector calculated based on the features selected by a feature selection process. The feature vectors of each primary signal segment and its corresponding reference segments are sent to a fuzzy intelligent system to detect segment faults.

Let a feature vector be $\Lambda = \{x_1, x_2, \ldots, x_m\}$, which combines the feature vector of a primary signal segment and its corresponding reference signal segments. In fuzzy logic we model the feature parameters as fuzzy control variables and one solution variable y to represents whether a segment is G/B/U, where G represents Good, B for Bad and U for Unknown. Each control variable is associated with a set of fuzzy terms, which can be collectively defined by a set of *critical parameters* that uniquely describe the characteristics of the membership functions, and the characteristic of an inference engine is largely affected by these critical parameters. The possible values of these critical parameters form a hyperspace and the system response to the control parameters form a control surface. In this paper we use triangular functions to model fuzzy membership functions.

For any machine learning system, its performance relies very much on the quality of its training data. The quality of training data can be described in two perspectives: reliability and representative. Within the scope of vehicle fault diagnosis, the reliability means that the training data have low noise and are correctly labeled (e.g. GOOD or BAD in this case), and the representative means that the data collectively represent most of the faulty behavior of vehicles. In our project with the support from the Ford Motor Company, we have made a tremendous effort to collect fault vehicle data from field cases reported by technicians at various auto dealer shops and from manually generated faults.

However the labeling of GOOD and BAD signal segments is usually a manual process, and it is not a trivial task since in many cases GOOD or BAD segments are subjective to individual engineers. Our solution to this difficult quandary is to train a fuzzy fault detection system with only GOOD data samples. This has several advantages: good data is relatively easy to collect and relatively reliable. However, to develop a fuzzy learning algorithm that learns knowledge from only GOOD examples poses two major challenging issues.

1. A fuzzy learning algorithm usually makes fuzzy membership functions cover the entire input domain based on the training data. But in the case of learning from GOOD class data only, this input domain is only the domain for good data. This results in fuzzy rules that will incorrectly classify most out-of-bounds fault data as good.
2. The fuzzy system can never output "segment is BAD."

We dealt these two issues by modifying the fuzzy rule generation process and the use of the UNKNOWN output. If we consider a single fuzzy variable with three fuzzy terms, LOW, MEDIUM and HIGH. The LOW and HIGH terms have shoulders that stretch out to infinity, thus covering all possible input values outside of the domain of the training data. This means that data that is well outside the window shown here may be called Low when it is actually "very low" and high when it is actually "very high." However, the "very low" and "very high" terms are not known to the fuzzy system because it never saw bad data. Now assume we generated the following fuzzy rule:

***IF*** *MAF_MIN is LOW* ***THEN*** *segment_is_good is HIGH*

If there were a bad MAF signal that had a MAF_MIN value of 0. It is clear that the given minimum is too low because engineering knowledge tells us that MAF should never be 0, in fact it should always be above about 0.75 Volts at all times when the car is running. But looking at the rule above, if we run the fuzzy inference on this bad data sample, the system will output segment_is_good is TRUE! Why? Because the fuzzy system assumed during training that it was looking at a representative sample of the data, all LOW values it saw were GOOD. It did not know there was such a class as BAD that might take up part of the input domain. Though the fuzzy system is working correctly, it has made a mistake: it has called an obviously bad segment GOOD. Our experience with vehicle diagnostics show that bad cases often show such out-of-bounds features.

The solution to this particular problem is to limit the coverage of the fuzzy terms to the input space inhabited by GOOD data. Any part of the domain that is not covered by GOOD data is assumed to hold another, unknown, class of data that the fuzzy system does not know the details about. Obviously, if no fuzzy term covers a region of the input domain, no fuzzy rule can cover this part of the input domain either, thus no data from an obviously different class than training data will be misclassified. Therefore after the fuzzy learning from data samples of "GOOD" class only using the algorithms described in[5], we add in the following post process to solve the end point misclassification problem:

1. For each of the left and right end shoulder term, replace it with a new term called such as LEFT_OUT_OF_BOUNDS or RIGHT_OUT_OF_BOUNDS respectively.
2. The boundary of these new terms should not overlap the domain of the GOOD data so as not to cause unnecessary false alarms.
3. For each of the new terms, generate the following new rule:

   **IF** fuzzy_variable is NEW_TERM **THEN** segment_is_good is LOW where either LEFT_OUT_OF_BOUNDS or RIGHT_OUT_OF_BOUNDS can be substituted for NEW_TERM.

These changes are illustrated in Figure 3. Notice that the careful placement of the new fuzzy terms means that no data from the training set will be misclassified. Also notice that the original boundary terms still extend beyond the range of the training data. This means if a data is close to the good boundary it will still be classified as GOOD.

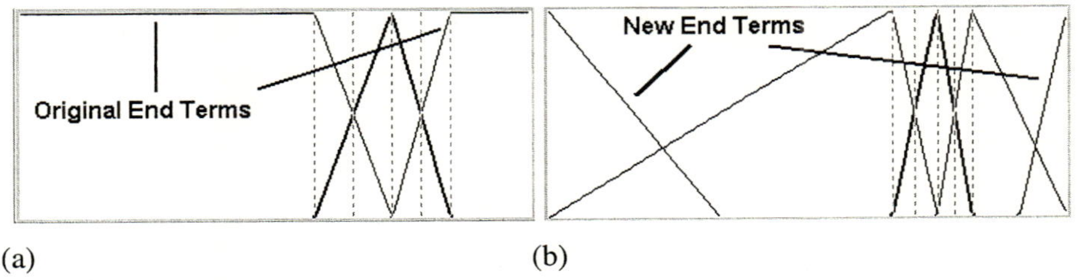


(a) (b)

**Fig. 3.** illustrating the fuzzy end term modification process. (a) shows the fuzzy end terms(shoulders) normally generated by a fuzzy learning algorithm using data samples from good class only and (b) shows the modified end terms as well as the new end terms that are used to define rules with a consequence segment_is_good is low.

With these changes in fuzzy membership functions and rule generation data outside the fuzzy term boundaries is no longer misclassified. However, we want to point out that caution should be made during the generation of new boundary terms on fuzzy variables. Some types of features, such as wavelet energy, may only require a boundary in one direction (it can never go below 0, and 0 is a valid value)[6]; or they may not require new boundaries at all (discrete valued features such as segment state are a good example of this case). *Therefore we should apply engineering knowledge about signals and vehicle systems, and scientific knowledge to segment features to in terms of generating new fuzzy terms as appropriate.*

The second issue is caused by the fact that fuzzy learning from only good data results in a set of fuzzy rules with the same consequence: segment_is_good is HIGH, except those modified by the step above. Based on the theory of fuzzy learning, though the fuzzy variables in the system cover the whole input domain, the fuzzy rules may not cover all possible scenarios of input data due to the fuzzy rule pruning for efficiency[5], and the areas in the multi-dimensional feature space that are not represented by the input data will not be covered by fuzzy rules. We use Figure 4 to illustrate this concept. For simplicity, the horizontal and vertical lines indicate the boundaries of fuzzy terms, although in most applications the boundaries are curved. The fuzzy rules cover only clusters (shaded blocks) containing good data (indicated by Xs). Any input data that falls in the blank areas does not fire any rules. Therefore the output for such data input can be labeled as UNKNOWN (indicated by *U*s). These unknown data samples are very likely to be extracted from bad segments, if the training data is representative enough of typical good behavior. In this implementation, if an input signal segment feature vector does not fire any fuzzy rule, the fuzzy system should interpret it as possibly a bad segment, i.e. segment_is_good = LOW.

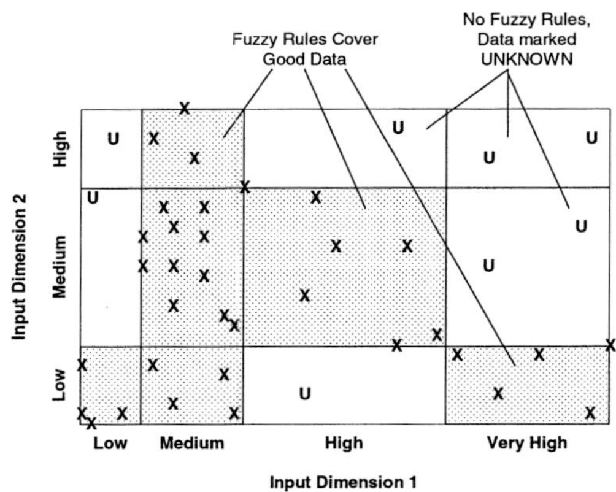


**Fig 4.** Illustration of fuzzy rule generation using a two-dimensional case

To summarize the above discussion, we present the following fuzzy learning algorithm from GOOD training examples only.
Step 1: Use a supervised fuzzy learning algorithm to generate a fuzzy rule knowledge base that contains a set of fuzzy rules, fuzzy variables and fuzzy membership functions.
Step 2: For each control variable, generate at most two new end fuzzy terms as appropriate as described above.
Step 3: For each new fuzzy term NEW_TERM, add fuzzy rules:
**IF** fuzzy_variable is NEW_TERM **THEN** segment_is_good is LOW
Step 4: For those combinations of fuzzy control variables and fuzzy terms that do not occur in the antecedence of any fuzzy rules, add new fuzzy rules that use these combinations as antecedence and use consequence such as segment_is_good is LOW or segment_is_good is UNCERTAIN.

The above fuzzy learning from 'GOOD" data only algorithm can be applied to any existing fuzzy knowledge base as a post process.

## 4 Signal Fault Detection Using Fuzzy Logic

One approach for diagnosing the fault of a signal is simply based on the individual segmentation fault detection: if one signal segment is detected as a fault, then the entire signal is abnormal. However, there is a possibility of misclassifications of individual signal segments due to a number of reasons: segment labeling process is prone error, and only local features are used in segment fault detection. Our experiments constantly show that 80% of BAD segments reported by the signal segment fault diagnostic system are actually bad and almost 100% of GOOD segments are actually good. This means about 20% of classified BAD segments are false alarms. The goal of signal fault diagnostics is to reduce false alarm by analyzing all BAD segment candidates produced at the signal segment fault diagnostic level.

By analyzing the results of signal segment fault diagnosis, we found the following interesting facts.

1. *Bad segments tend to have a low average belief value.* The belief value indicates how sure the fuzzy system is that the data sample in question fits the fuzzy rule(s) that fired. Bad segments tend to have lower belief values on average when they fire GOOD rules than the good segments.
2. *Bad segments tend to be far from good rules.* Bad signals tend to have a few segments that are VERY abnormal. These segments will be very distant (in the Euclidean sense) from the fuzzy rules classifying good segments, while segments from good recordings are usually much closer.
3. *Bad signals tend to contain "clusters" of segments classified as BAD or UNKNOWN.* Often signal faults occur in a section of contiguous BAD segments. If several adjacent or nearly adjacent segments of the signals are being marked as "BAD" or "UNKNOWN" that is a good indication that the signal is bad. On the other hand, the segments labeled as BAD or UNKNOWN in good recordings tend to be isolated rather than clustered together.
4. *Bad signals tend to have a relatively large number of bad clusters.* A large number of bad segment clusters in a signal is another good indication of a faulty signal. This is different from property 3. For example, if a signal contains 5 *Bad* segments that are not adjacent to each other, the signal cannot be detected by property 3 but can be detected by this property. This measure is especially valuable for bad signals with a small number of segments.

Based on these properties, we developed the following features for signal fault detection.

1. *Average Bad Belief* (**Avg Bad Bel**) and *Average Good Belief* (**Avg Good Bel**) Let $bb_i$ be the belief for segment i being BAD, be the belief for segment i being GOOD and N be the total number of segments in the signal,

$$AvgBadBel = \frac{\sum_{i=1}^{N} bb_i}{N}, \quad AvgGoodBel = \frac{\sum_{i=1}^{N} bg_i}{N}$$

2. *Average Distance to Good* (**Avg Dist To Good**): This is the average distance of **BAD or UNKNOWN** segments to GOOD rules (e.g. rules with a consequence of "segment_is_good = TRUE"). Let BUS be the set of all segments that were

labeled either BAD or UNKNOWN by the segment fault detection system, and $dg_i$ be the distance of segment i, to its nearest GOOD rule. The Average Distance to Good is defined as:

$$AvgDistToGood = \frac{\sum_{i \in BUS} dg_i}{|BUS|}.$$

The next three measurements are derived from the concept of Bad Segment Cluster. We define a Bad Segment Cluster within a signal as: *A contiguous sequence of segments, beginning and ending with either a BAD or UNKNOWN segment, with, at most, one GOOD segment separating each BAD or UNKNOWN segment from another BAD or UNKNOWN segment.*

3. *Maximum BAD Segment Cluster Size* (**Max Clust**).
4. *Number of Bad Segment Clusters* (**Num Clust**).

The following feature is related to the percentage of a signal that was labeled as GOOD, BAD or UNKNOWN (rather than the percentage of segments).

5. *Percentage of Bad or Unknown Samples* (**Bad %**):

$$Bad\% = \frac{\sum_{i \in BUS} len(b_i)}{L},$$ where $len(b_i)$ is the length of a segment in BUS, and L is the length of the entire signal (in samples).

These features are used together to predict whether a vehicle signal is normal. Figure 5 illustrates the hierarchical decision structure used in the multi-signal fault diagnostic system. At the lowest levels are the segment feature vectors of a signal. These segment feature vectors are processed using the signal segment fault detection system based on a segment fault knowledge base generated at an off-line training. The results of the segment fault detection are passed on to the Signal Feature Extraction process that generates the *Signal Feature Vector* described above. The *Signal Feature Vector* is processed by the Signal Fault Detection System that employs a global fuzzy knowledge base representing signal faults. Finally the system reports whether the signal is Good (G), Bad (B) or Unknown (U).

The proposed signal level fault diagnostics has one major advantage. It is usually much easier to mark a signal as GOOD or BAD, even if we don't know precisely what segments bear the faults. Consequently, the fuzzy detection system for signal fault can be trained on reliably labeled data for both classes: good and bad signal data. A fuzzy diagnostic system trained on populations of both classes has higher accuracy in fault diagnosis and less false alarms.

## 5 Experiments and Conclusion

We implemented the above two fuzzy systems in the application of vehicle signal fault diagnosis. Four groups of signals are tested, IAC, RPM, TP and MAF. The IAC group has IAC(Idle Air Control) as a primary signal and TP(Throttle Position) and MAF(Mass Air Flow) as reference signals, the RPM group has RPM as the primary signal and MAF, FUELPW, SPARKADV as reference signals, the TP group has TP

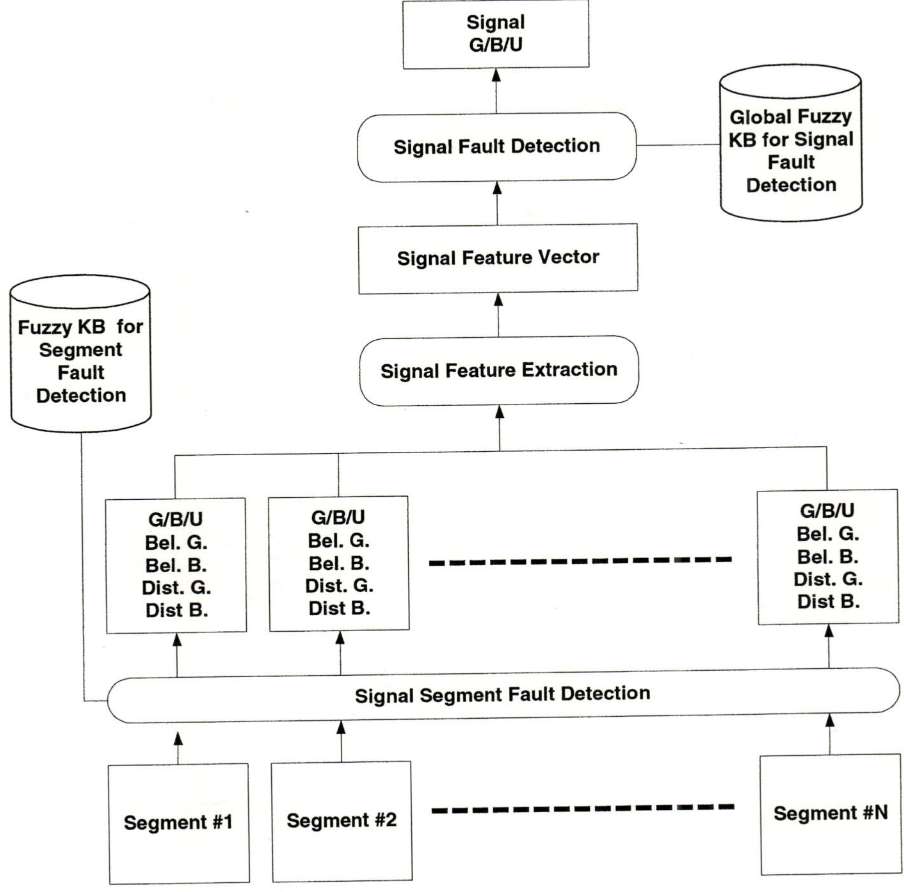


**Fig. 5.** Decision hierarchy in multi-signal fault detection using fuzzy logic

as the primary signal and TPCT(Throttle Position Closed Throttle) as the reference signal, and the MAF group has MAF as the primary signal and TP, RPM and IAC as reference signals.

Each multi-signal group was trained on its own training data at the segment level using the fuzzy learning algorithm described in Section 3. Table 1 lists the performance of all multi-signal groups on their respective training sets, test data and the test set of entire signals. As we can see all of the signal segments in the training data was correctly classified. On the test data of signal segments, the TP group performed extremely well on both GOOD and BAD segments, the MAF group performed well on GOOD segments but not as well on BAD segments, and the IAC and RPM did not have good detection rate on either GOOD or BAD segments. The misclassification of segments is due to a number of reasons including data mislabeling problem as we discussed earlier. It is clear that segment-by-segment analysis alone is not good enough to detect signal faults. However, the segment fault detection results can be effectively used in the signal fault detection as shown in the

**Table 1.** Segment Fault Detection results

| **Multi-signal group** | Performance on training data | Performance on GOOD segments in test data | Performance on BAD segments in test data | **Performance on entire signals** |
|---|---|---|---|---|
| IAC(M) | **100%** | **32.28%** | **36.21%** | **75%** |
| MAF(M) | **100%** | **91.19%** | **36.52%** | **100%** |
| RPM(M) | **100%** | **0%** | **56.97%** | **100%** |
| TP(M) | **100%** | **100%** | **100%** | **90%** |

last column, which presents the signal fault diagnostic results obtained on the signal test set. We separate signals into three categories, GOOD, BAD and UNCERTAIN. All four multi signal groups performed well: MAF(M), RPM(M) obtained 100% accuracy, TP(M) 90% and IAC 75%.

We have presented a system for multi-signal fault detection and described two fuzzy learning algorithms, one used at the signal segment level and another one used at the signal level. The fuzzy learning algorithm at the segment level can learn fuzzy knowledge from training data of a single class. This fuzzy learning from GOOD examples only algorithm provides a solution to the problems such as ambiguous and mislabeled signal segments. Our experiment results show these fuzzy learning algorithms can give good performance on signal segment based detection, and together with the analysis of all segments in a signal, signal faults can be detected quite accurately in both classes GOOD and BAD signals.

## Acknowledgements

The work presented in this paper was supported by a grant from NSF DMI-0090061 and a research contract from Ford Motor Company. I would like to thank Mr. Jacob Crossman, Dr. JianXin Zhang for their experimental work used in this paper.

# References

[1] Eric Chowanietz, Automobile electronics, Butterworth-Heinemann, 1995
[2] Hong Guo, Jacob A. Crossman, Yi Lu Murphey, and Mark Coleman, "Automotive Signal Diagnostics Using Wavelets and Machine Learning," IEEE Transaction on Vehicular, November, 2000.
[3] Feldkamp, L.A., Puskorius, G.V. "A Signal Processing Framework Based on Dynamic Neural Networks with Application to Problems in Adaption, Filtering and Classification," Proceedings of the IEEE. Vol. 86:11. pp. 2259-2277. Nov 1998.
[4] Jacob A. Crossman, Hong Guo, Yi Lu Murphey and John Cardillo, "Automotive Signal Fault Diagnostics: Part I: signal fault analysis, signal segmentation, feature extraction and quasi optimal feature selection," to appear in IEEE Transaction on Vehicular, 2002.
[5] Yi Lu, Tie Qi Chen, and Brennan Hamilton, "A Fuzzy System for Automotive Fault Diagnosis: -- Fast Rule Generation and Self-Tuning," IEEE Transaction on Vehicular, Vol. 49, No. 1, January 2000.
[6] Daubechies,I. *Ten Lectures on Wavelets*. Capital City Press. Montpelier,VT. 1992.

# Clustering On-Line Dynamically Constructed Handwritten Music Notation with the Self-organising Feature Map

Susan E. George

School of Computer and Information Science, University of South Australia, Mawson Lakes Campus, SA 5095, Australia
susan.george@unisa.edu.au
http://www.cis.unisa.edu.au/

**Abstract.** In this paper we consider the problem of recognising handwritten music notation in the context of a pen-based interface. The motivation for the paper stems from current pen-based input technologies that do not achieve true recognition of unconstrained handwritten music. The practical applications of music notation recognition in education, composing, music search tasks and other are obvious, warranting investigation of the problem. This paper explores the self-organising feature map (SOM) as a coarse classifier to categorise pen-down movements used by people when writing music notation, so creating a set of person specific 'primitives' based on pen strokes. Three different pre-processing methods are used to scale pendown movements and a 5 by 5 SOM is used to cluster the strokes. The stroke clusters form the basis of categories with which a multi-layer perceptron (MLP) could be trained for stroke recognition of pen-movements that comprise handwritten music notation.

## 1 Introduction

The Music notation information is most often entered onto the computer using (a) the computer keyboard, (b) computer mouse, (c) piano keyboard (or some other electronic instrument) attached to the computer, or (d) scanning device for a sheet of printed music with off-line recognition of printed symbols. With a few exceptions, there is a noticeable absence of research into the pen-based recognition of handwritten music symbols. One common paradigm of pen-based music recognition is simply using the pen as a stylus to select music symbols from a menu bar [1].We can also identify gesture based input where the user must learn a special sequence of movements to input a given music symbol [2], [3] and finally, the most desirable situation, where the user can naturally write conventional music notation symbols and have these interpreted on-line [4].

There are many different application reasons why we might want to input music notation into a computer. These range from editing, composing and transposition tasks, to more educational applications of teaching music theory – where part of the task is to learn the correct construction of music notation. If there is a way of entering a music fragment then sophisticated searches of music archives can be made and musicologists can analyse the style of a collection. Copyright enforcers may be

P.W.H. Chung, C.J. Hinde, M. Ali (Eds.): IEA/AIE 2003, LNAI 2718, pp. 93–103, 2003.

interested in detecting legal infringements and search for a fragment (and its arrangements) within a suitable electronic representation. There is also the theoretical question of whether and how simple recognition of music handwriting can be achieved. Other application areas have investigated pen-based input in fields as diverse as signature verification and character recognition, mathematical notations and postcodes. The omission of recognising handwritten pen-based music notation is obvious. This paper discusses some of the difficulties of recognising on-line handwritten music notation, beginning with the problem of the dynamic construction of music symbols – where there is an unlimited set of symbols, an absence of a set of primitive strokes, and an unconstrained method of writing these symbols are among the complexities of a dynamic editing environment. We continue outlining the basic approach to solve these difficulties where the pen-down movements of each person are identified and these used as the basis for recognition of the higher level constructs. Experiments are described where the primitive strokes are examined and used as the basis for recognition.

## 2 Problems of the Dynamic Construction of Music Notation

### 2.1 An Unlimited Set of Symbols

At first it may appear that music notation has a well defined set of primitive symbols. The 20 symbols of Figure 1 may in some ways be considered primary to modern day common music notation since they contain the basic elements that can be used to define pitch (a to e), rhythm (f to j, l to o) and pauses (k, p to t). While there are many other music symbols that we might include we may be deceived into thinking that these are somehow primary and fundamental in any notation recognition task. However, the set of notation symbols are really unlimited : a single quaver (i or n) may be combined to form a pair, a pair may be combined into a triplet, and the group of three may be extended further and so on. While we have demonstrated that a multilayer perceptron can learn these basic isolated symbols and recognise the isolated dynamically written symbol with good accuracy [4] the challenge remains to (a) recognise music notation in context and not just a subset of isolated symbols and (b) do so under dynamic construction.

### 2.2 Absence of Primitive Music Strokes

One of the first challenges we encounter in moving from recognising an isolated symbol instance to recognising symbols in context is the question of what are the primitives. Other handwriting recognition problems have a set of primitives – even cursive Roman script is composed of a basic set of letters and numerals and punctuation, and Chinese has a primitive set of strokes that are used to make up the characters. However, the basic units of Fig. 1 dramatically change their form when composed in various ways. While we might find an individual quaver note (i or n) we can also find many variations when this is combined with other symbols. Reducing the symbol to a notehead, stem and a beam (at some angle) may be the most accurate description of the symbol – and these may be the features that are sought in the off-line recognition of handwritten music – but they will remain arbitrary and essentially an approximation of a larger symbol that has a meaning in its own right.

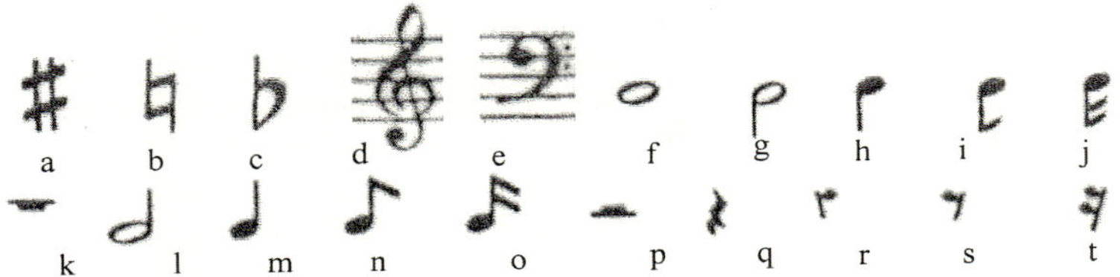


**Fig. 1 .** Some symbols of Common Music Notation in isolation

## 2.3 Variation in Dynamic Construction

If the set of music notation symbols are themselves unlimited and combined in many novel ways the actual dynamic construction of these symbols is similarly an open ended problem. People differ in how music notation is written. Just as there are no primitive strokes, there are no rules about order in which symbols are constructed stems may be written before note heads or after, they may be composed of a single pen movement or many and they may be modified in various ways after a valid symbol has been created. The cues from pen strokes, that may assist recognition in other contexts such as on-line Chinese writing, are not available with music. For example, Fig. 2a illustrates two beamed notes consisting of two note heads, two stems and a joining beam. Fig. 2b illustrates the variation in construction that may be found with three different methods of producing the symbol. These represent just some of the options possible in making the symbol. A different number of pen-up/down movements is required for the methods and we do not know whether the quaver pair is complete – it can still be modified in various ways: other notes could be added to the pair (forming a chord), the pair may contribute to an even larger collection added later, there may be timing modifications (dots or lines) added to the group or pitch variations (with accidentals placed before the note heads).

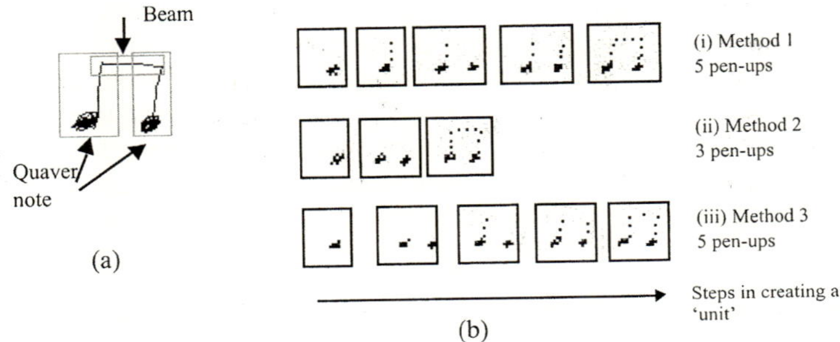


**Fig. 2 .** Variation in primitive pen strokes to construct music symbols

### 2.4 Symbol Completion

Related to the unlimited set of symbols and variation that is possible with dynamic construction is the question of when the symbol is complete. There are no rules about spatio-temporal construction to constrain the order in which components are added. Many post-hoc modifications, such as adding a 'sharp' accidental to a given note to change its pitch 'meaning', may be made, and new groups of notation symbols may be started before an existing one is completed. Some dynamic symbol recognition problems, such as recognition of on-line handwritten Chinese writing, often impose a time constraint upon the time to complete a character. While this would be possible with music notation, it may be useful to explicitly indicate that the symbols of a given page, or line, are complete.

## 3 Exploration of On-Line Dynamically Constructed Handwritten Music

### 3.1 Comparison with Handwriting Recognition

Despite the added complexities and challenges of recognising handwritten music, there are similarities with other handwriting recognition tasks such as cursive writing recognition. In both the on-line and off-line case of cursive writing recognition, the segmentation approach may be used – where the word is first segmented into letters, and then the letters are then recognised individually and matched up against particular words. Alternatively there is the global approach where the whole word is recognised by the use of identifying features. This is particularly useful if a particular keyword (or signature) is sought that can be differentiated from other writing. While there has been much success in recent years with on-line handwriting recognition Vuurpijl and Schomaker discuss the used a hierarchical clustering method for the categorisation of allographs or character shapes [5] They are concerned about capturing stylistic differences between writers that they believe has been ignored compared to the great interest there has been in various machine readable printed fonts. Ignoring the stylistic differences leads to less than optimal results. Thus a systematic naming scheme for the allographs in Western handwriting was sought in order to identify the 'primitives' with which handwriting recognition must be concerned. They deal with a database of over 500,000 handwritten characters believing this is highly representative of the variations that may be found among writers. The data is re-sampled to obtain spatially equi-distant points before clustering. They are specifically looking for a hierarchical clustering in order to name allographs and suggest an n-ary hierarchical clustering method as a modification of a binary agglomerative hierarchical clustering.

### 3.2 Clustering to Identify 'Primitives' of Handwritten Music Notation

Such a categorisation of 'primitive' strokes is of interest in the case of handwritten music, since the series of pen-up/down movements provide a natural record of how people went about writing a given music fragment. We may use these primitives to begin interpreting dynamically written music, and will find that they provide the natural basis for a segmentation approach in off-line recognition. Thus the approach taken by this paper is one which seeks to start to explore the basic pen-up/down movements made by people when copying a fragment of music. We choose to use an artificial neural network clustering approach known as the self-organising feature map (SOM). For the original description of the SOM and its clustering properties see [6], descriptions of its use in visualisation can be found [7] as well as analysis that has considered the well-formedness of such maps [8], [9]. The SOM has proved useful in many different application areas as a technique that is able to utilise the spatial information within data, in a way that enables a visualisation of the data and a greater understanding of its properties. It also conveniently acts as a coarse classifier clustering the data into groups so that a more sensitive classifier can then be applied to the examples within the clusters so that a finer distinction can be made between the examples of given characteristics. We use the SOM to group the pen-down strokes according to their spatial information, and propose that a multi-layer perceptron, or some other classifier can then make distinctions between the data within the basic groups of penmovements.

### 3.3 Data Collection

The Wacom PL-400 digitising tablet (screen resolution *1024 x 768*) connected to a computer, with the UP 811E pressure sensitive pen (256 pressure levels). Writers write directly onto the LCD display surface and have an image of pen-movements echoed as they write. While untested, writing directly on the LCD display is deemed more satisfactory than a pen-tablet removed from a display. A program recorded pen location and pressure at a sampling rate of 20 samples per second (sampling period of 50ms). A faster sampling rate would improve the amount of data available, since there would be more data points per symbol. Additionally, the more pressure exerted with the pen the more 'ink' was deposited on the display. For someone using heavy pressure colouring in an area such as a notehead would require less pen-down time, however, for someone exerting a lighter pressure they would need to make more movements in order to cover in the notehead with 'ink'. A zero pressure value indicated that the pen was not in contact with the tablet (ie there was a pen-up movement at that point). Some 25 volunteers were recruited to take part in a short exercise (10 minutes data collection) where they supplied some samples of music symbols (clefs, notes, etc.) and they also copied a music fragment. Approximately half of these people had some familiarity with music notation and the remaining were unfamiliar. Some12 people copied the music fragment, and were largely those with more musical experience.

The fragment of music that volunteers were asked to copy appears in Fig. 3. The example was designed to include examples of the various symbols that appear in Fig. 1, however they occur in context rather than isolation. Fig. 4 illustrates the fragments written by two of the 12 people. Nobody completed copying the whole fragment. The data from each person was isolated into basic pen-up/down movements. There were some 1222 pen down movements in the data set.

**Fig. 3.** Music Fragment from "Joseph's Amazing Technicolour Dreamcoat", Andrew Lloyd Weber, published by Novello and Co., Kent, UK 1969.

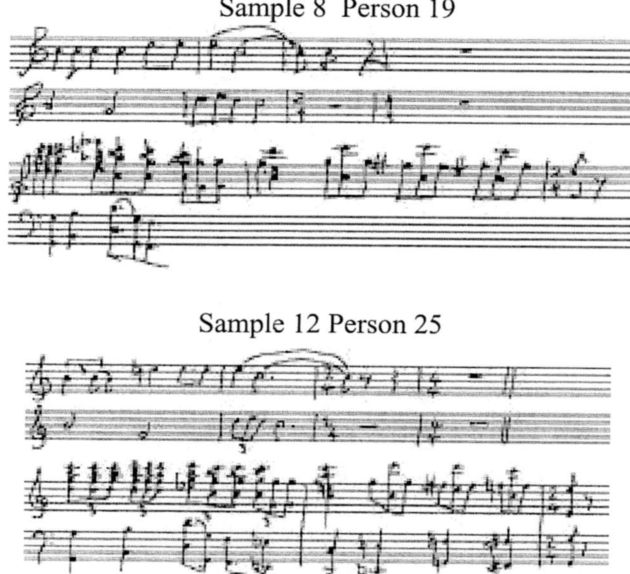


**Fig. 4** . Sample of handwritten copy of the music fragment

### 3.4 Informal Data Tagging of Pen Movements

The pen movements were inspected by plotting each 1222 pen-down movement and informally tagging the movement. A summary of some of the tagging information is provided in Fig. 5 where almost 60 different types of penstrokes were noted. These categories were informally delimited and based on spatial information alone. They include filled-in notehead (no. 12), empty note-head (no. 15), note stem (no. 13), bar line (no. 22), beam (no.23 and no.52), stem and upward notehead (no. 46) and so on. Naturally some of these manually tagged categories are difficult to differentiate. For example, the bar line (no. 22), the stem (no.13) and the fragment of a natural sign (no.

32) are virtually identical in their features (being a vertical line!).The most common category was a filled in note head (277 occurrences), followed by a stem (143 occurrences) and a bar line (91 occurrences). There were some interesting combinations that appeared within more than one person such as a stem, beam, stem and notehead (no. 14); this was a combination used to complete an already written notehead.

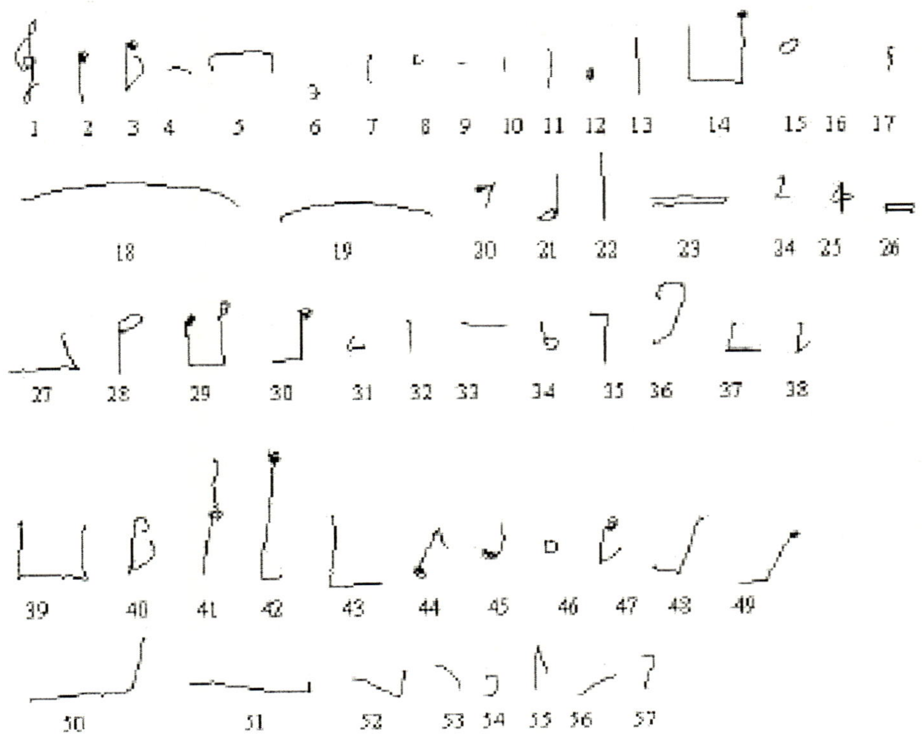


**Fig. 5 .** Summary of some of the types of pen-down movements

The exercise also revealed that some notes from the music fragments in Fig. 4 were actually constructed from many pen movements; sometimes the notehead would be coloured in after the outline was written, occasionally the stems were altered in length and old 'ink' revisited even though the symbol looks as if it was completed in one pen-down movement. Also some people required extra pen-down time to complete a notehead – this was related to the amount of pressure they were using on the pen since heavy pressure would deposit more 'ink' and give the appearance of a filled in notehead more easily than lighter pressure which would require more scribbling to shade the area. Thus there would be more data points for some similar fragments than others.

The difficulties in manually tagging the data set include (a) accurately distinguishing when a pen movement is similar to another. The variation demonstrated by some of the treble clef symbols in Figure 4 illustrates this difficulty since no two clefs are exactly the same as others even when written by the same person; but it would be useful to include them in the same class for recognition purposes. Also it is hard to (b) identify when a new category should be created. For example the beams/stems in

Fig. 5 (no. 50., no 51., no. 52 and no. 27) contain much similarity but are different. Should they be separate classes, or is there sufficiently similarity to include them in one class. And what variation could be permitted; can the length or angle of beam or stem be varied? Finally there is the problem that (c) very similar symbols mean very different things. As already mentioned the stem (no. 13) and bar line (no. 22) are virtually identical. They can be tagged differently when high level interpretation of their context is manually imposed – but based upon features alone there is little to differentiate them.

### 3.5 Pre-processing the Pen Movements

Crucial to the categories that any clustering mechanism would create is the representation of the data. It is usual to normalise the data - so removing any signal introduced purely by where the pen movement was made on the page. It is also usual to scale the data so that it is within a standard range. Whether a linear or non-linear scaling is used is an important question, since it affects whether the aspect ratio is maintained, or certain areas of the spatial region emphasised. We explored three different scaling methods as illustrated in Fig. 6. Each pen down movement was scaled to be within a 100 by 100 pixel square. Thus the value of high is 99 and low is 0. The max and min values are the maximum and minimum values within the pen down movement to be scaled. Clearly, scale method (1) does not utilise the whole square area, while the logarithmic method (3) stretches out the data points, importantly shifting some to new areas of the square compared with linear scaling method (2) that preserves the basic horizontal and vertical alignment of the points, while stretching them to fill the square area.

$$scalefactor = \frac{high - low}{\max - \min}, \quad offset = \min \qquad (1)$$
$$newvalue = (oldvalue - offset) * scalefactor$$

$$scalefactor = \frac{high - low}{\max - \min}, offset = \frac{(\max * low - \min * high)}{(\max - \min)} \qquad (2)$$
$$newvalue = (oldvalue * scalefactor) + offset$$

$$newvalue = high * \frac{\log(oldvalue) - \log(\min)}{\log(\max) - \log(\min)} \qquad (3)$$

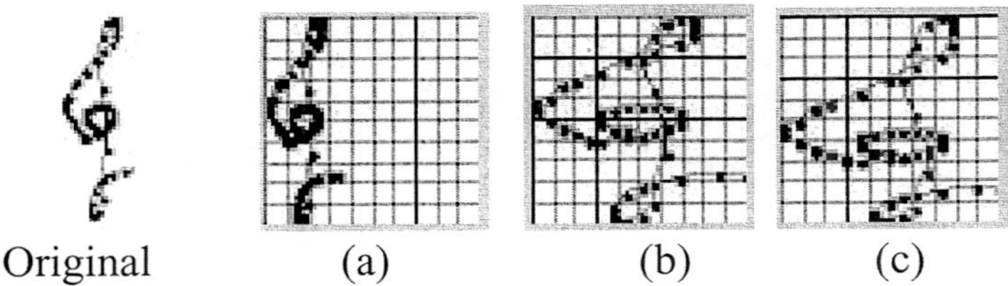


**Fig. 6 .** Illustration of Scaling

Fig. 6 also illustrates, with a blob, the points at which data was retrieved from the tablet. The bigger the distance between the blob points the more swiftly the pen moved. To utilise the spatial information of the pen down movement fully, it is necessary to interpolate and re-sample the original data to achieve an equal spacing between the points. This provides a more accurate representation of where the pen moved, rather than the amount of time spent at a particular point within the symbol being drawn. The pixel square of Figure 6 was divided into 100 different regions taking x coordinate values from 1 to 10, 11 to 20, 21 to 30 etc. and y over the same range. The number of scaled data values within a particular square were counted, importantly removing values with non-zero pressure (since these represented times when the pen was not in contact with the tablet). For each of the 100 regions on the pixel grid the percentage frequency of points in that space was computed. These 100 percentage frequencies were used as input to the network, and were scaled to a value between 0 and 1.

### 3.6 Clustering Pen Movements with the SOM

The focus of this research is simply to determine (a) that pen down movements can be clustered, (b) the relationships between the clusters visualised and then (c) to categorise the pen-down movements actually made by people in terms of the SOM classes. To demonstrate aims (a) and (b) the neural network toolkit of MatLab [10] was used to train each network for 3000 iterations and then test with the training data scaled according to methods (a), (b) and (c) respectively. Fig. 7 illustrates the visual representation of the 5 by 5 SOM output layer for each scaling method (a, b and c)

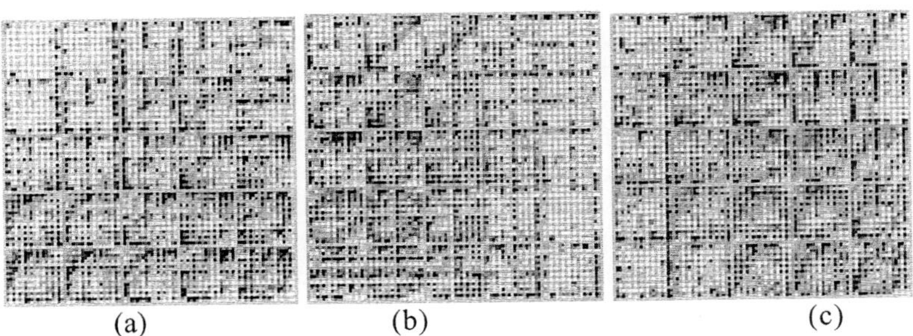


**Fig. 7 .** Representation of the SOM output maps for data scaled according to scaling methods (1), (2) and (3)

with each of the 25 SOM classes represented by the100 regions of the pixel square to which the data was scaled. A dot in each region represents the amount of 'ink' that can be expected for pen-down movements that are located in that SOM class.

Each pen-down movement fragment was classified on the SOM and the clusters involved in drawing the music notation were examined for each person to determine the difference between consecutive pen strokes. This measure was used as a way of quantifying how the SOM clustering was representing the writing of each person. Table 1 summarises how the SOM clustering for the different scaling methods represents the pen-down movement data. The results reveal that on average there are 7.8 class changes between consecutive pen-movements for each person with scaling method (a) and 7 with scaling method (b). This means that all scaling methods are locating approximately the same number of similar consecutive strokes in each person. The biggest difference in the scaling methods is found with person 6, where method (a) locates 15 similar strokes and method (c) locates only 7 similar consecutive strokes giving a difference of 8.Scaling methods (a) and (b) appear most similar with the average difference between number of consecutive classes being 2, while methods (a) and (c) have a difference of 2.67 and methods (b) and (c) have a difference of 2.17.

**Table 1.** Summary of consecutive classifications for pen-down movements

| Person | Method (1) | Method (2) | Method (3) | Person | Method (1) | Method (2) | Method (3) |
|---|---|---|---|---|---|---|---|
| **2** | 7 | 4 | 6 | **17** | 1 | 3 | 1 |
| **4** | 5 | 3 | 5 | **19** | 15 | 16 | 13 |
| **6** | 15 | 10 | 7 | **20** | 3 | 5 | 6 |
| **11** | 7 | 7 | 5 | **21** | 3 | 2 | 2 |
| **15** | 4 | 5 | 3 | **23** | 5 | 4 | 10 |
| **16** | 10 | 11 | 13 | **25** | 19 | 14 | 13 |

# 4 Conclusion

This paper has demonstrated that the SOM can be used to cluster the pen-down movements that individual people utilise in writing a fragment of music notation. The pen-down movements for each person can be pre-processed and scaled and clustered by the SOM. The SOM clusterings obtained by the 5 by 5 SOM for the different scaling methods are supportive in that similar results are obtained in the categorisation of consecutive strokes, although linear scaling methods demonstrate more similarity in the classifications made for consecutive strokes than does a logarithmic method. These results provide the basis of using the SOM as a coarse classifier to categorise pendown movements used within dynamically constructed music notation. Once the rough type of stroke has been identified more specific recognition methods (for example a multi-layer perceptron) can seek to identify features that will isolate the stroke into a more specific type; the slur, phrase mark and tie symbols are all similar and while these can be distinguished from other symbols by the SOM clustering, more specific methods can look at other features of the symbol to determine the precise type of stroke. It is anticipated that each person will have a unique set of primitives although there will be much overlap in the more common music notation symbols and pen movements needed to construct these. Future work will continue to examine the SOM clusterings of strokes and subsequent classification methods that will enable recognition of music notation symbols dynamically written in combination.

## References


1. Silberger, Putting Composers in Control, IBM Think Research, Vol 34, No4, 1996 ( http://domino.research.ibm.com/comm/wwwr_thinkresearch.nsf/pages/musiceditor496.html, last accessed 13th February 2002).
2. Anstice, Bell, Cockburn, Setchell, The design of a pen-based musical input system. In Proceedings of the Sixth Australian Conference on Computer-Human Interaction, , Los Alamitos, California, IEEE computer society, (1996), 260-267.
3. Forsberg,A. S., Dieterich, M. K., and Zeleznik, R.C., "The Music Notepad", Proceedings of UIST '98, ACM SIGGRAPH (1998).
4. George SE, Pen-Based On-line Input for Handwritten Music Notation. (to appear) in Visual Perception of Music Notation: On-line and Off-Line Recognition, Idea Group Publishing, USA, 2003.
5. Vuurpijl Louis, Schomaker Lambert, Finding Structure in Diversity : A Hierarchical Clustering method for the categorisation of allographs in handwriting, IEEE, ICDAR, (1997) 387-393.
6. Kohonen, T. “Self-organized formation of topologically correct feature maps”, Biological Cybernetics 43, (1982), 59 – 69.
7. Versanto J, SOM-Based Data Visualisation Methods, Intelligent Data Analysis, Vol 3, (1999) pg 111-26.
8. Kaski S. and K. Lagus. “Comparing self-organizing maps”, ICANN ‘ 96, Lectures Notes in Computer Science, Vol 11 / 2, Springer, Berlin, (1996), 809 - 814.
9. Varfis A., and C. Versino “Selecting reliable Kohonen maps for data analysis”, Artificial Neural Networks 2, I. Aleksander and J. Taylor (editors), (1992) , 1583 - 1586. 10. MATLAB Reference Guide. The MathWorks Inc., 1994.

# Cellular Automata Cryptography Using Reconfigurable Computing

David F.J. George and Susan E. George

School of Computer and Information Science
University of Western Australia, Australia

**Abstract.** Cryptography is an important and vital application in security, defence, medical, business and many other application areas. The effective measure of a cryptosystem, is how long it can be used to encrypt and decrypt messages without the 'key' being broken. A class of cellular automata (CA) based encryption algorithms presents a particular promising approach to cryptography, since the initial state of the CA is the key to the encryption, evolving a complex chaotic system from this 'initial state' which cannot be predicted. However, software implementations of CA cryptography have the disadvantage that special purpose hardware canbe applied to break the code. Thus implementation in hardware is desirable to ensure that this evolutionary approach to computing is done in real time.This short paper has demonstrated CA cryptography can be implemented on a reconfigurable computing architecture (SPACE-2). The algorithm was described and verified in the Circal process algebra, and demonstrated on the reconfigurable computer.

## 1 Introduction

### 1.1 Background to Cryptography

Cryptography is the art, or science, of keeping messages secret. Encoding the contents of a plain text message in such a way that hides its contents from outsiders is called encryption; retrieving the plain text from the cipher text is called decryption. A system that performs encryption and decryption is called a cryptosystem. The effective measure of the quality of a cryptosystem remains in practice what it has always been, the longer a cryptosystem is in wide use without being broken, the better it is. Up until the mid 1970's, cryptography was an arcane science practised largely by government and military security experts. That situation changed dramatically following the development of public key cryptography by Hellman and Diffie [1]. This development solved a major problem experienced by cryptosystems which was to do with the use and exchange of a 'key' that controls encryption and decryption.

There are two classes of key-based cryptography algorithms, symmetric (or secret-key) and asymmetric (or public-key) algorithms. The difference is that symmetric algorithms use the same key for encryption and decryption (or the decryption key is

P.W.H. Chung, C.J. Hinde, M. Ali (Eds.): IEA/AIE 2003, LNAI 2718, pp. 104–111, 2003.

easily derived from the encryption key), whereas asymmetric algorithms use a different key for encryption and decryption, and the decryption key cannot be derived from the encryption key. Generally, symmetric algorithms are much faster to execute on a computer than asymmetric ones. In most applications, cryptography is done in computer software although some cryptographic algorithms are designed to be executed by computers or specialized hardware devices. A well-known cryptosystem is DES (Data Encryption Standard), developed in the 1970s, and made a standard by the US government (Cryptographic Algorithms, http://www.ssh.fi/tech/crypto/algorithms.html). The security of the DES has recently been seriously challenged especially when used with special-purpose hardware.

## 1.2 Cryptograph and Complex Systems

Gutowitz linked complex chaotic systems with cryptology (Cryptography with Dynamical Systems, http://www.santafe.edu/~hag/crypto/crypto.html.).A complex system is one whose component parts interact with sufficient intricacy that they cannot be predicted by standard linear equations; so many variables are at work in the system that its overall behaviour can only be understood as an emergent consequence of the holistic sum of all the behaviours embedded within. As a complex system progresses deterministically in time it its initial state is "forgotten", that is the new state, after enough time has passed, has no resemblance to the initial state. However, the future state of a (chaotic) dynamic system does depend on its initial state and a complex dynamic system is unpredictable without access to the initial state. Gutowitx observed that a complex system may be used for encryption and decryption by making the key of the cryptosystem the initial state of a complex system. The message is encrypted by continually combining it with an information stream generated by forward iteration of the system. The message could then be decrypted by combining the cipher text with an information stream generated by forward iteration of the system. The evolution of the system over time bears little evident connection with the equations that define them, and anyone who does not know secret initial condition would not be able to recreate the development of the complex system.

Cryptography with complex systems can make use of reversible dynamic systems which may be run forward and backward. The system can be run forward in time to produce the cipher text. To decrypt the cipher text, the system is inverse iterated the same number of time steps. Reversible dynamic systems contrast with systems that only forward iterate. No longer is the key the initial condition of a fixed system (and the equations that define the dynamic system fixed) but the key for such a system is the equation(s) that define the dynamic system itself. Thus the 'key' operates directly on the message to encrypt and decrypt it. One system that uses reversible dynamic systems for cryptography is that by Guan [2]. The Guan uses a non-homogeneous cellular automata in which the rule that updates a site's value depends on the site. It essentially relies on the difficulty of inverting a complicated system of polynomial equations.

## 1.3 Cellular Automata

Cellular automata (CA) were invented in the 1940's by the mathematicians John von Neumann and Stanislaw Ulam, while they were working at the Los Alamos National Laboratory in northern central New Mexico [3], [4]. Ulam was working on cellular games where each pattern was composed of a square (or triangular or hexagonal) cell on a chessboard like surface. The fate of a given cell, at the next time step, depended only on the current state of the cell and the states of its neighbouring cells. All growth and change of patterns on the chessboard took place in discrete jumps. Ulam discovered many patterns grew almost as if they were alive. A CA is a lattice, or grid, of cells where each cell is a form of Finite State Machine (FSM), that can easily be expressed using a state transition diagram. The behaviour of a CA is often illustrated using space-time diagrams where the configuration of states in the lattice is plotted as a function of time. Observing system evolution means that it is particularly important to be able to model CA systems in real time, or faster. CA automata evolution may also be viewed as computation and this poses interesting theoretical questions about computability and decidability. No simple theory or formula has been found to describe the overall behaviour of such systems, and the consequences of their evolution cannot be simply predicted, but can only be found by direct simulation and observation.

When using a CA to model physical systems the physical space of a problem is divided up into many small, generally identical cells, each of which would be in one of a finite number of states. The state of a cell represents the current state of its part of the physical system (e.g. it may represent whether a gas particle is present or not). The state of the cell evolves according to a rule that is both local (involves only the cell itself and nearby cells) and universal (all cells are updated simultaneously using the same rule). CAs have particularly been applied to the simulation of complex systems [5].

Conventional computers are ill suited to run the inherently uniform and parallel CA models and so discourage their development mainly due to performance problems. In the 1960s a new trend in computing design began with the construction of cellular logic machines. These machines emulated the cellular automaton by using a single high-speed processing element to operate sequentially on an array of binary data. The Cellscan machine was built in the United States in the 1960's [6] and was followed by GLOPR used for basic image processing tasks. Cellular logic was performed by means of a lookup table, where the rule for the cells is stored as a table in memory, mapping each set of input values to an output value.

## 1.4 Reconfigurable Computing

Reconfigurable computing refers to a combination of hardware and software, where the software configures the functionality of the hardware to perform a particular task (or tasks) at runtime. The software can then interact with the hardware by sending and receiving data to and from the reconfigurable hardware for processing. The software is also able to modify and control the hardware while it is running, for example the software could change the speed of one of the clocks that run the hardware, or it could change the behaviour of one of the hardware functions. This means that the software is able to reconfigure 'on-the-fly' to meet the needs of the target application. Applications which have been found to be suitable for reconfigurable computing range from 'number crunching' and computing algorithms, to user interfaces. The Field Programmable Gate Array (FPGA), invented by Xilinx, Inc. in 1984, is the basis of the reconfigurable computer. In reconfigurable computing the FPGA may be configured differently for each problem, and possibly changed depending on the data input to the problem. A reconfigurable computing machine therefore consists of an array of logic gates (FPGAs) that can be reconfigured (programmed) to perform different functions. Specifically the logical function of each gate, and the interconnection between the gates can be configured.

A number of reconfigurable computing machines have been built including MORRPH and Splash 2 [7]. The Scalable Parallel Architecture for Concurrency Experiments (SPACE) Machine is an experimental platform for developing reconfigurable computing applications. The basic SPACE architecture is a highly regular, scalable array of logic function cells. SPACE was developed at the University of Strathclyde, Glasgow, Scotland starting in 1989 [8], [9], [10]. The SPACE processing board uses 16 CAL1024 FPGAs, whose boundary's are connected in a two-dimensional mesh to achieve genuine continuity in cell-to-cell communications across the board. Its successor, SPACE-2, has been developed at the University of South Australia, and was brought into production in the late 1990s where clock frequency can be programmed.

## 1.5 Cellular Automata and Reconfigurable Computing

The 2-dimensional uniform surface of programmable logic cells makes SPACE and SPACE-2, ideal for implementing CAs since it facilitates the direct representation of CA models on the hardware due to its regular 2 dimensional structure. The ability to directly access the hardware on the space machine allows the concurrent nature of CAs to be mapped directly onto the naturally concurrent hardware. To model and implement CAs it is desirable to specify the behaviour of the cells in a format that can be interpreted by a computer. Seceral specific programming languages have been developed for describing and modelling CA including CAM Forth [11],Cellang was developed as a CA programming language and defined by J.D. Eckart [12] and the process algebra Circal. Circal program specifications may be constructed from truth tables. When the program is run using the Circal System processes, it performs the behaviour described by the truth tables. Circal has been shown to be useful for modelling complex systems, but using a process algebra specification is a very different approach to the conventional CA models, which are generally described using matrices of cells and operations on these matrices. A process algebra leads to an elegant approach for simulating such systems while specifying and verifying the implementation the system.

# 2 Cryptography with Cellular Automata

## 2.1 Cellular Automata Rules for Encryption

Gutowitz describes the CA rules in the encryption algorithm as having a 'toggle' property. The 'toggle' rules can be either 'right toggle', or 'left toggle' or both. This means that, for a one dimensional CA, changing the value of the extreme (left of right) neighbourhood site always changes the result of the function state at the next iteration. Toggle rules are important as they allow a pre-image (a state of the CA which would lead to the current state at the next step) for the current state to be rapidly constructed. Fig. 1 illustrates an example of a rule that is left toggle, since changing the state of the left most bit (extreme left neighbour) will change the state of the cell at the next iteration (S(t+1)). The state of each cell is binary with its setting represented by '1' or '0'.

| Transition Rules for a 1-dimensional Left Toggle CA | | | |
|---|---|---|---|
| Neighbourhood & State S(t) | Cell State S(t+1) | Neighbourhood & State S(t) | Cell State S(t+1) |
| 1 0 0 | 1 | 0 0 0 | 0 |
| 1 0 1 | 0 | 0 0 1 | 1 |
| 1 1 0 | 0 | 0 1 0 | 1 |
| 1 1 1 | 0 | 0 1 1 | 1 |

**Fig. 1.** Illustration of a Left Toggle CA

The encryption algorithm proposed by Gutowitz takes the plain text as the initial state of the 1-dimensional CA. A pre-image is then found. This is a CA state whose next state is this pre-image state. To find a pre-image, each cell is updated in sequence, starting at the right of the CA (assuming a left toggle rule is used). Firstly additional CA cells are added to the right of the CA. The number of CA cells that are added is 2 times the CA rules radius. These cells can be set to a random state. For example, the rule shown in Fig. 1 has a radius of 1 (one neighbour on either side), and two cells would be added. Next, the state of the cell next to the added cells (e.g. the right most cell of the plain text for a left toggle rule) can be updated by applying the CA rule to the state of this cell with the added cells. This is then repeated, working left one cell at a time, until all the cells have had the rule applied to them. Each time a random bit is added to the right. To decrypt the message the CA rule is repeatedly applied the correct number of times to the cipher text.

An example the encryption and decryption sequences is shown in Fig. 2. Time progresses down the table row by row and the CA rule described in Fig. 1 is used. The lightly shaded top and bottom rows are the plain text (before encryption and after decryption); the darker shaded middle row is the cipher text containing the added cells.

| Encrypt | Added Cells |
|---|---|
| 1 1 1 1 1 0 0 0 0 0 1 0 0 1 1 0 0 1 0 1 0 0 0 0 0 0 0 1 0 | |
| 0 0 1 0 0 1 1 1 1 1 1 0 0 0 0 1 1 0 1 0 1 1 1 1 1 1 1 1 0 | 0 0 |
| 1 1 1 0 0 0 0 1 0 0 1 0 0 0 0 0 0 1 0 1 1 0 0 1 0 0 1 0 0 1 | 1 1 0 1 |
| 1 0 0 1 1 1 1 0 1 1 0 1 1 1 1 1 1 1 0 0 0 1 1 0 1 1 1 0 0 0 | 0 1 0 0 0 1 |
| 0 1 1 1 0 0 1 0 0 0 1 1 0 0 1 0 0 1 0 0 0 0 0 1 1 0 0 1 1 1 | 1 0 1 1 1 0 1 0 |
| 1 1 0 0 1 1 1 0 0 0 0 0 1 1 0 1 1 1 0 0 0 0 0 0 0 1 1 0 1 0 | 0 1 1 0 0 1 0 1 1 0 |
| Decrypt | |
| 0 1 1 1 0 0 1 0 0 0 1 1 0 0 1 0 0 1 0 0 0 0 0 1 1 0 0 1 1 1 | 1 0 1 1 1 0 1 0 1 0 |
| 1 0 0 1 1 1 1 0 1 1 0 1 1 1 1 1 1 1 0 0 0 1 1 0 1 1 1 0 0 0 | 0 1 0 0 0 1 0 1 1 0 |
| 1 1 1 0 0 0 0 1 0 0 1 0 0 0 0 0 0 1 0 1 1 0 0 1 0 0 1 0 0 1 | 1 1 0 1 1 0 1 0 1 0 |
| 0 0 1 0 0 1 1 1 1 1 1 0 0 0 0 1 1 0 1 0 1 1 1 1 1 1 1 1 0 | 0 0 1 0 0 1 0 1 1 0 |
| 1 1 1 1 1 0 0 0 0 0 1 0 0 1 1 0 0 1 0 1 0 0 0 0 0 0 0 1 0 | 1 1 1 1 1 0 1 0 1 0 |

**Fig. 2.** Example Encryption and Decryption

## 2.2 Cellular Automata Encryption on a Reconfigurable Computer

The crypto system was implemented on the SPACE 2 platform. The skeleton for the system consisted of the basic algorithm described above, which was implemented for each iteration of the decryption and encryption algorithms. Circal was used to model and verify the behaviour of the system, showing that the system could encrypt and decrypt data. This was done by composing the encrypt and decrypt processes together and then clocking some test data through the system. A Circal model for a toggle rule suitable for performing encryption is shown below.

```
Process LeftToggleRule1 (Bool Left, Middle, Right,
Currentstate) {

  static Bool nextstate,currentstate,left,middle,right
  static Process C

  C <- (left.0 middle.0 right.0 nextstate.0) C +
       (left.0 middle.0 right.1 nextstate.1) C +
       (left.0 middle.1 right.0 nextstate.1) C +
       (left.0 middle.1 right.1 nextstate.1) C +
       (left.1 middle.0 right.0 nextstate.1) C +
       (left.1 middle.0 right.1 nextstate.0) C +
       (left.1 middle.1 right.0 nextstate.0) C +
       (left.1 middle.1 right.1 nextstate.0) C

  return ((C * Time(nextstate,currentstate))
                      [Left/left, Middle/middle,
              Right/right, Currentstate/currentstate] -
nextstate)
```

As can be seen, the first, middle and last sections of the encryption model are basically the same, the primary difference being that the first and last sections connect the first and last rows of the model to the plain and encrypted data, whereas the middle section only connects to internal states. The decryption model is simply a number of single dimension CAs connected together to form a two dimensional CA. The key for the crypto system is the toggle rule at each site, plus the interconnections between iterations. The key for decryption is the same as the key for encryption.

## 3 Conclusion and Future Work

Cryptography is an important and vital application in security, defence, business, medical and many other application areas. As already observed, the effective measure of a cryptosystem, is how long it can be used without being broken. Special purpose hardware applied to software based public key encryption systems makes it possible to break the code, find the 'key' and hence decrypt private messages. Thus there is the need to ensure there are public key based coding methods that are secure.

A class of CA based encryption algorithms presents a particular promising approach to cryptography, since the initial state of the CA is the key to the encryption, evolving a complex system which cannot be predicted. The CA model of computing, originating in the 1950s, benefits from a direct hardware implementation. Being able to change the rule at each cell in real time as the code is generated, makes decrypting (even with special purpose hardware) extremely difficult to do. Hence there is potentially a secure public key based coding method that has potential to outperform software simulations.

This paper has demonstrated CA cryptography can be implemented using a reconfigurable computing architecture. The algorithm was described and verified in the Circal process algebra, and demonstrated on the SPACE-2 reconfigurable computer. Directions for future work would be (a) to explore alternative CA paradigms (including non-homogeneous CA systems and reversible/irreversible CAs) and their implementation on reconfigurable platforms, as well as (b) exploiting the run-time dynamic reconfigurability that is possible to change the CA rules dynamically during the encryption process.

## References


1. Diffie W., M. Hellman "New Directions in Cryptography," *IEEE Transactions on Information Theory* (1976).
2. Guan P., "Cellular Automaton Public-Key Cryptosystems," *Complex Systems* Vol. 1, 1987.
3. Von Neumann J., "Theory of Self-Reproducing Automata," edited and completed by A.W. Burks, Urbana, IL: University of Illinois Press, 1966.
4. Burks A. W., "Essays on Cellular Automata. Urbana," University of Illinois Press, 1970.
5. Wolfram S. "Cellular Automata as models of complexity," *Nature* Vol 311, pp 419-424 October 1984.

6. Preston K, M. Duff, "Modern Cellular Automata : Theory and Applications," Plenum Press, New York, 1985.
7. Buell D., J. Arnold, W. Kleinfelder editors, "Splash 2: FPGAs in a Custom Computing Machine," IEEE Computer Society Press, May 1996.
8. Cockshott P, P. Shaw, P. Barrie, G. Milne "Scalable cellular array architecture," *IEE Computing & Control Engineering Journal*, vol 3, no5, September 1992
9. Milne G., P. Cockshott, G. McCaskill, P. Barrie. "Realising massively concurrent systems on the SPACE machine," in *Proc IEEE Workshop on FPGAs for Custom Computing Machines*, pp. 26-32, 1993 and University of Strathclyde Research Report HDV-29-93.
10. Milne G., P. Shaw. "A highly parrallel FPGA-based machine and its formal verification," *Lecture Notes in Computer Science*, No705. Springer-Verlag 1993.
11. Margolus N, M. Toffoli, "STEP: A space time event processor. Software Reference," MIT Laboratory for Computer Science, Cambridge, MA 02139, 1995.
12. Eckart JD "Cellang: Language Reference Manual," Radford University, Radford, VA, April 1995.

# Pitch-Dependent Musical Instrument Identification and Its Application to Musical Sound Ontology*

Tetsuro Kitahara[1], Masataka Goto[2], and Hiroshi G. Okuno[1]

[1] Graduate School of Informatics, Kyoto University, Kyoto 606-8501, Japan,
kitahara@kuis.kyoto-u.ac.jp, okuno@i.kyoto-u.ac.jp,
http://winnie.kuis.kyoto-u.ac.jp/~{kitahara,okuno}/

[2] "Information and Human Activity", PRESTO, JST / National Institute of Advanced Industrial Science and Technology,
m.goto@aist.go.jp, http://staff.aist.go.jp/m.goto/

**Abstract.** To augment communication channels of human-computer interaction, various kinds of sound recognition are required. In particular, musical instrument indentification is one of the primitive functions in obtaining auditory information. The *pitch dependency* of timbres has not been fully exploited in musical instrument identification. In this paper, we present a method using an *F0-dependent multivariate normal distribution* of which mean is represented by a cubic polynomial of fundamental frequency (F0). This F0-dependent mean function represents the pitch dependency of each feature, while the F0-normalized covariance represents its non-pitch dependency. Musical instrument sounds are first analyzed by the F0-dependent multivariate normal distribution, and then identified by using the discriminant function based on the Bayes decision rule. Experimental results of identifying 6,247 solo tones of 19 musical instruments by 10-fold cross validation showed that the proposed method improved the recognition rate at individual-instrument level from 75.73% to 79.73%, and the recognition rate at category level from 88.20% to 90.65%. Based on these results, systematic generation of musical sound ontology is investigated by using the C5.0 decision tree program.

## 1 Introduction

Usually people use a wide range of auditory information in communication or to recognize and understand auditory and visual events. In order to augment communication channels in designing and developing sophisticated human-computer interface, this auditory and visual scene analysis is one of key techniques [12]. Auditory scene analysis includes non-speech sound recognition/identification, speaker identification, understand auditory events or environmental sounds, and musical scene analysis. Besides automatic music transcription, musical instrument indentification is also important in integrating visual processing. For example, musical instrument indentification may lead to visual search for musical instruments, and visual musical instrument recognition may improve the performance of musical instrument indentification.

* This research was partially supported by the Ministry of Education, Culture, Sports, Science and Technology, Grant-in-Aid for Scientific Research (B), No.12480090, and Informatics Research Center for Development of Knowledge Society Infrastructure (COE program of MEXT, Japan)

P.W.H. Chung, C.J. Hinde, M. Ali (Eds.): IEA/AIE 2003, LNAI 2718, pp. 112–122, 2003.

Musical instrument identification is an important subtask for many applications including auditory scene analysis and multimedia retrieval as well as for reducing ambiguities in automatic music transcription. The difficulties in musical instrument identification reside in the fact that some features depend on pitch and individual instruments. In particular, timbres of musical instruments are obviously affected by the pitch due to their wide range of pitch. For example, the pitch range of the piano covers over seven octaves.

To attain high performance of musical instrument identification, it is indispensable to cope with this *pitch dependency* of timbre. Most studies on musical instrument identification, however, have not dealt with the pitch dependency [2–4, 7, 8]. Martin used 31 features including spectral and temporal features with hierarchical classification and attained about 70% of identification by the benchmark of 1,023 solo tones played by 14 instruments. He pointed out the importance of the pitch dependency, but left it as future work [8]. Eronen *et al.* used spectral and temporal features as well as cepstral coefficients used by Brown [2] and attained about 80% of identification by the benchmark of 1,498 solo tones played by 30 instruments [3]. They treated the pitch as one element of feature vectors, but did not cope with the pitch dependency. Kashino *et al.* also treated the pitch similarly in their automatic music transpcription system [7]. They also coped with the difference of individual instruments, but did not deal with the pitch dependency [6].

In this paper, to take into consideration the pitch dependency of timbre in musical instrument indentification, each feature or basic vector of features is represented by an *F0-dependent multivariate normal distribution* of which mean is represented by a function of fundamental frequency (F0). This *F0-dependent mean function* represents the pitch dependency of each feature, while the *F0-normalized covariance* represents the non-pitch dependency. Musical instrument indentification is performed both at individual-insturment level and at non-tree category level by a discriminant function based on the Bayes decision rule.

Hierarchical representation of musical instruments can be generalized to *musical sound ontology* [8, 9], but its systematic generation has not been reported yet. We use the F0-based features to generate musical sound ontology by the C5.0 decision tree program [11].

The rest of this paper is organized as follows: Section 2 proposes the F0-dependent multivariate normal distribution, and Section 3 describes a discriminant function based on the Bayes decision rule. Sections 4 and 5 report the experimental results. Section 6 applies the results to generate musical sound ontology by using the C5.0 decision tree program, and finally Section 7 concludes this paper.

## 2 F0-Dependent Multivariate of Normal Distribution

### 2.1 Pitch and Non-pitch Dependencies

The distribution of tone features in the feature space is represented by an *F0-dependent multivariate normal distribution* with two parameters: the *F0-dependent mean function* and *F0-normalized covariance*. The reason why the mean of the distribution is approximated as a function of F0, that is an F0-dependent mean function, is that tone features at different pitches have different positions (means) of distributions in the feature space. In this paper, the F0-dependent mean function for each musical instrument $\omega_i$, $\boldsymbol{\mu}_i(f)$,

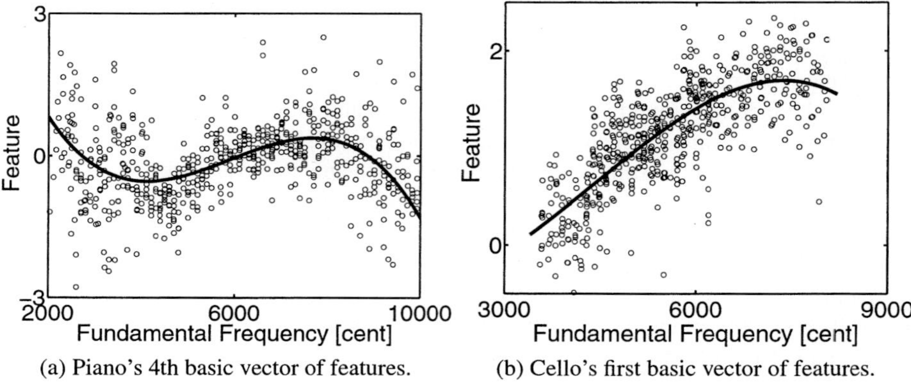


(a) Piano's 4th basic vector of features. (b) Cello's first basic vector of features.

**Fig. 1.** Examples of F0-dependent mean functions.

is approximated as a cubic polynomial by using the least squares method. For example, piano's fourth basic vector of features and cello's first basic vector are depicted in Figure 1 (a) and (b), respectively.

On the other hand, the non-pitch dependency of each feature is represented by the *F0-normalized covariance*. Since the F0-dependent mean function represents the mean of features, the covariance obtained by subtracting the mean from each feature eliminates the pitch dependency of features. For each musical instrument $\omega_i$, the F0-normalized covariance $\Sigma_i$ is defined as follows:

$$\Sigma_i = \frac{1}{n_i} \sum_{\boldsymbol{x} \in \chi_i} (\boldsymbol{x} - \boldsymbol{\mu}_i(f\boldsymbol{x}))(\boldsymbol{x} - \boldsymbol{\mu}_i(f\boldsymbol{x}))',$$

where $'$ is the transposition operator, $\chi_i$ and $n_i$ are the set of the training data of the instrument $\omega_i$ and its total number, respectively. $f_{\boldsymbol{x}}$ denotes the F0 of the data $\boldsymbol{x}$.

## 2.2 Features for Musical Instrument Identification

We used spectral, temporal, and modulation features as well as non-harmonic component feature resulting in 129 features in total listed in Table 1. The features except the non-harmonic component features are determined by consulting the literatures [8, 3, 7]. The non-harmonic component features are original and have not been used in the literature. We incorporated features as many as possible, since the feature space is transformed to a lower-dimensional space.

Each musical instrument sound sampled by 44.1 kHz with 16 bits are first analyzed by STFT (short-time Fourier transform) with Hanning windows (4096 points) for every 10 ms, and spectral peaks are extracted from the power spectrum. Then, the harmonic structure and F0 is obtained from these peaks.

The number of dimensions of the feature space is reduced by principal component analysis (PCA): the 129-dimensional space is reduced to a 79-dimensional space with the proportion value of 99%. It is further reduced to the minimum dimension by linear

**Table 1.** Overview of 129 features.

| | |
|---|---|
| (1) **Spectral features** (40 features) | *e.g.*, Spectral centroid, Relative power of the fundamental component, Relative power in odd and even components |
| (2) **Temporal features** (35 features) | *e.g.*, Gradient of a straight line approximating power envelope, Average differential of power envelope during onset, Ratio of the maximum power and the power of 0.20 sec after onset |
| (3) **Modulation features** (32 features) | *e.g.*, Amplitude and frequency of AM, FM, modulation of spectral centroid and modulation of MFCC |
| (4) **Non-harmonic component features** (22 features) | *e.g.*, Temporal mean of kurtosis of spectral peaks of each harmonic component (Their values become lower as sounds contain more non-harmonic components.) |

discriminant analysis (LDA). In this paper, the space is reduced to an 18-dimensional space, since we deal with 19 instruments.

## 3 A Discriminant Function Based on the Bayes Decision Rule

Once pitch and non-pitch dependencies of feature vectors are represented, the Bayes decision rule is applied to identify the name or category of musical instruments. The discriminant function $g_i(\boldsymbol{x}; f)$ for the musical instrument $\omega_i$ is defined by

$$g_i(\boldsymbol{x}; f) = \log p(\boldsymbol{x}|\omega_i; f) + \log p(\omega_i; f), \tag{1}$$

where $\boldsymbol{x}$ is an input data, $p(\boldsymbol{x}|\omega_i; f)$ is a probability density function (PDF) of this distribution and $p(\omega_i; f)$ is a priori probability of the instrument $\omega_i$.

The PDF of this distribution is defined by

$$p(\boldsymbol{x}|\omega_i; f) = \frac{1}{(2\pi)^{d/2}|\Sigma_i|^{1/2}} \exp\left\{-\frac{1}{2}D^2(\boldsymbol{x}, \boldsymbol{\mu}_i(f))\right\}, \tag{2}$$

where $d$ is the number of dimensions of the feature space and $D^2$ is the squared Mahalanobis distance defined by

$$D^2(\boldsymbol{x}, \boldsymbol{\mu}_i(f)) = (\boldsymbol{x} - \boldsymbol{\mu}_i(f))' \Sigma_i^{-1} (\boldsymbol{x} - \boldsymbol{\mu}_i(f)).$$

Substituting equation (2) into equation (1), thus, generates the discriminant function $g_i(\boldsymbol{x}; f)$ as follows:

$$g_i(\boldsymbol{x}; f) = -\frac{1}{2}D^2(\boldsymbol{x}, \boldsymbol{\mu}_i(f)) - \frac{1}{2}\log|\Sigma_i| - \frac{d}{2}\log 2\pi + \log p(\omega_i; f).$$

The name of the instrument that maximizes this function, that is $\omega_k$ satisfying $k = \operatorname{argmax}_i g_i(\boldsymbol{x}; f)$, is determined as the result of musical instrument identification.

The a priori probability $p(\omega_i; f)$ represents whether the pitch range of the instrument $\omega_i$ includes $f$, that is,

$$p(\omega_i; f) = \begin{cases} 1/c & (\text{if } f \in R_i) \\ 0 & (\text{if } f \notin R_i) \end{cases}$$

where $R_i$ is the pitch range of the instrument $\omega_i$, and $c$ is the normalizing factor to satisfy $\sum_i p(\omega_i; f) = 1$.

# 4 Experiments and Results

## 4.1 Experimental Conditions

Musical instrument indentification is performed not only at individual-instrument level but also at category level to evaluate the improvement of recognition rates by the proposed method based on the F0-dependent multivariate normal distribution. The recognition rate was obtained by 10-fold cross validation. We compared the results by the method using usual multivariate normal distribution (called *baseline*) with those by the method using the proposed F0-dependent multivariate normal distribution (called *proposed*).

The benchmark used for evaluation is a subset of the large musical instrument sound database RWC-MDB-I-2001 developed by Goto *et al.* [5]. This subset summarized in Table 2 was selected by the quality of recorded sounds and consists of 6,247 solo tones of 19 orchestral instruments. All data are sampled by 44.1 kHz with 16 bits.

The categories of musical insturuments summarized in Table 3 are determined based on the sounding mechanism of instruments and existing studies [8, 3]. The category of instruments is useful for some applications. For example, when a user wants to find a piece of piano solo on a music retrieval system, the system can reject pieces containing instruments of different categories, which can be judged without identifying individual instrument names.

## 4.2 Results of Musical Instrument Identification

Table 4 summarizes the recognition rates by both the *baseline* and *proposed* methods. The proposed F0-dependent method improved the recognition rates at individual-instrument level from 75.73% to 79.73% and at category level from 88.20% to 90.65% in average. It also reduced recognition errors by 16.48% and 20.67% in average at individual-instrument and category levels, respectively. The observation of these experimental results is summarlized below:

**Improvement by the Pitch Dependency**
The recognition rates of six instruments (Piano (PF), Trumpet (TR), Trombone (TB), Soprano Sax (SS), Baritone Sax (BS), and Faggoto (FG)) were improved by more than 7%. In particular, the recognition rate for pianos was improved by 9.06%, and its recognition errors were reduced by 35.13%. This big improvement was attained, since their pitch dependency is salient due to their wide range of pitch.

**Difference between Accuracy at Two Levels**
The recognition rates for the four types of saxophones at individual-instrument level (47–73%) were lower than those at category level (77–92%). This is because sounds

**Table 2.** Contents of the database used in this paper.

<table>
<tr><th>Instrument name</th><th>Abbrev.</th><th>pitch range</th><th># of tones</th><th># of individuals</th><th>Intensity</th><th>Articulation</th></tr>
<tr><td>Piano</td><td>PF</td><td>A0–C8</td><td>508</td><td rowspan="7">3</td><td rowspan="19">Forte, normal, & piano</td><td rowspan="19">normal only</td></tr>
<tr><td>Classical Guitar</td><td>CG</td><td>E2–E5</td><td>696</td></tr>
<tr><td>Ukulele</td><td>UK</td><td>F3–A5</td><td>295</td></tr>
<tr><td>Acoustic Guitar</td><td>AG</td><td>E2–E5</td><td>666</td></tr>
<tr><td>Violin</td><td>VN</td><td>G3–E7</td><td>528</td></tr>
<tr><td>Viola</td><td>VL</td><td>C3–F6</td><td>472</td></tr>
<tr><td>Cello</td><td>VC</td><td>C2–F5</td><td>558</td></tr>
<tr><td>Trumpet</td><td>TR</td><td>E3–A♯6</td><td>151</td><td>2</td></tr>
<tr><td>Trombone</td><td>TB</td><td>A♯1–F♯5</td><td>262</td><td rowspan="5">3</td></tr>
<tr><td>Soprano Sax</td><td>SS</td><td>G♯3–E6</td><td>169</td></tr>
<tr><td>Alto Sax</td><td>AS</td><td>C♯3–A5</td><td>282</td></tr>
<tr><td>Tenor Sax</td><td>TS</td><td>G♯2–E5</td><td>153</td></tr>
<tr><td>Baritone Sax</td><td>BS</td><td>C2–A4</td><td>215</td></tr>
<tr><td>Oboe</td><td>OB</td><td>A♯3–G6</td><td>151</td><td>2</td></tr>
<tr><td>Faggoto</td><td>FG</td><td>A♯1–D♯5</td><td>312</td><td rowspan="3">3</td></tr>
<tr><td>Clarinet</td><td>CL</td><td>D3–F6</td><td>263</td></tr>
<tr><td>Piccolo</td><td>PC</td><td>D5–C8</td><td>245</td></tr>
<tr><td>Flute</td><td>FL</td><td>C4–C7</td><td>134</td><td>2</td></tr>
<tr><td>Recorder</td><td>RC</td><td>C4–B6</td><td>160</td><td>3</td></tr>
</table>

**Table 3.** Categorization of 19 instruments.

| Category | Instruments (abbreviation) |
|---|---|
| Piano | Piano (PF) |
| Guitars | Classical Guitar (CG), Ukulele (UK), Acoustic Guitar (AG) |
| Strings | Violin (VN), Viola (VL), Cello (VC) |
| Brasses | Trumpet (TR), Trombone (TB) |
| Saxophones | Soprano Sax (SS), Alto Sax (AS), Tenor Sax (TS), Baritone Sax (BS) |
| Double Reeds | Oboe (OB), Faggoto (FG) |
| Clarinet | Clarinet (CL) |
| Air Reeds | Piccolo (PC), Flute (FL), Recorder (RC) |

of these saxophones were quite similar. In fact, Martin reported that sounds of various saxophones are very difficult for the human to discriminate [8].

**Instrument-Dependent Difficulty of Identification**

Since we adopt the flat (non-hierarchical) categrization, the recognition rates at category level depend on the category. The recognition rates of Guitars and Strings at category level were more than 94%, while those of Brasses, Saxophones, Double Reeds, Clarinet and Air Reeds were about 70–90%. This is because instruments of these categories have similar sounding mechanism: these categories are subcategories of "wind instruments" in conventional hierarchical categorization.

**Table 4.** Accuracy by usual distribution (baseline) and F0-dependent distribution (proposed).

| | | Individual-instrument level | | | Category level | | |
|---|---|---|---|---|---|---|---|
| | | *Baseline* | *Proposed* | Improvement | *Baseline* | *Proposed* | Improvement |
| Piano | (PF) | 74.21% | 83.27% | +9.06% | 74.21% | 83.27% | +9.06% |
| Classical Guitar | (CG) | 90.23% | 90.23% | ±0.00% | 97.27% | 97.13% | −0.14% |
| Ukulele | (UK) | 97.97% | 97.97% | ±0.00% | 97.97% | 98.31% | +0.34% |
| Acoustic Guitar | (AG) | 81.23% | 83.93% | +2.70% | 94.89% | 95.65% | +0.76% |
| Violin | (VN) | 69.70% | 73.67% | +3.97% | 98.86% | 99.05% | +0.19% |
| Viola | (VL) | 73.94% | 76.27% | +2.33% | 93.22% | 94.92% | +1.70% |
| Cello | (VC) | 73.48% | 78.67% | +5.19% | 95.16% | 96.24% | +1.08% |
| Trumpet | (TR) | 73.51% | 82.12% | +8.61% | 76.82% | 85.43% | +8.61% |
| Trombone | (TB) | 76.72% | 84.35% | +7.63% | 85.50% | 89.69% | +4.19% |
| Soprano Sax | (SS) | 56.80% | 65.89% | +9.09% | 73.96% | 80.47% | +6.51% |
| Alto Sax | (AS) | 41.49% | 47.87% | +6.38% | 73.76% | 77.66% | +3.90% |
| Tenor Sax | (TS) | 64.71% | 66.01% | +1.30% | 90.20% | 92.16% | +1.96% |
| Baritone Sax | (BS) | 66.05% | 73.95% | +7.90% | 81.40% | 86.05% | +4.65% |
| Oboe | (OB) | 71.52% | 72.19% | +0.67% | 75.50% | 74.83% | −0.67% |
| Faggoto | (FG) | 59.61% | 68.59% | +8.98% | 64.74% | 71.15% | +6.41% |
| Clarinet | (CL) | 90.69% | 92.07% | +1.38% | 90.69% | 92.07% | +1.38% |
| Piccolo | (PC) | 77.56% | 81.63% | +4.07% | 89.39% | 90.20% | +0.81% |
| Flute | (FL) | 81.34% | 85.07% | +3.73% | 82.09% | 85.82% | +3.73% |
| Recorder | (RC) | 91.88% | 91.25% | −0.63% | 92.50% | 91.25% | −1.25% |
| Average | | 75.73% | 79.73% | +4.00% | 88.20% | 90.65% | +2.45% |

*Baseline*: Usual (F0-independent) distribution
*Proposed*: F0-dependent distribution

## 5 Evaluation of the Bayes Decision Rule

The effect of the Bayes decision rule in musical instrument identificaton was evaluated by comparing with the $k$-NN rule ($k$-nearest neighbor rule; $k = 3$ in this paper) with/without LDA. Three variations of the dimensionality reduction are examined:

(a) Reduction to 79 dimension by PCA,
(b) reduction to 18 dimension by PCA, and
(c) reduction to 18 dimension by PCA and LDA.

The last one is adopted in the proposed system.

The experimental results listed in Table 5 showed that the proposed Bayes decision rule performed better in average than the 3-NN rule. Some observations are as follows:

(1) The Bayes decision rule with 79-dimension showed poor performance for Acoustic Guitar (AG), Trumpet (TR), Soprano Sax (SS), Tenor Sax (TS), Oboe (OB), and Flute (FL), since the number of thier training data is not enough for estimating parameters of a 79-dimensional normal distribution. For small training sets with 79-dimension, $k$-NN is superior to the Bayes decision rule.

**Table 5.** Accuracy by $k$-NN rule and the Bayes decision rule.

| | $k$-NN rule ($k = 3$) | | | Bayes decision rule | | |
|---|---|---|---|---|---|---|
| | (a) | (b) | (c) | (a) | (b) | (c) |
| | 79-Dim. | 18-Dim. | | 79-Dim. | 18-Dim. | |
| | PCA | | PCA&LDA | PCA | | PCA&LDA |
| Piano (PF) | 53.94% | 46.46% | 63.39% | 55.91% | 59.06% | 83.27% |
| Classical Guitar (CG) | 79.74% | 77.16% | 75.72% | 98.28% | 97.27% | 90.23% |
| Ukulele (UK) | 94.58% | 92.54% | 97.63% | 67.12% | 80.00% | 97.97% |
| Acoustic Guitar (AG) | 95.05% | 92.79% | 97.00% | 19.97% | 44.14% | 83.93% |
| Violin (VN) | 47.73% | 46.02% | 45.83% | 89.58% | 84.47% | 73.67% |
| Viola (VL) | 55.93% | 54.24% | 61.86% | 71.19% | 79.24% | 76.27% |
| Cello (VC) | 86.20% | 85.84% | 84.23% | 45.16% | 30.82% | 78.67% |
| Trumpet (TR) | 36.42% | 38.41% | 47.02% | 41.72% | 72.85% | 82.12% |
| Trombone (TB) | 70.99% | 54.58% | 77.86% | 75.19% | 78.24% | 84.35% |
| Soprano Sax (SS) | 23.08% | 14.20% | 24.85% | 48.52% | 66.86% | 65.89% |
| Alto Sax (AS) | 37.59% | 29.79% | 40.43% | 72.70% | 41.84% | 47.84% |
| Tenor Sax (TS) | 62.09% | 66.01% | 68.63% | 30.07% | 61.44% | 66.01% |
| Baritone Sax (BS) | 68.84% | 67.91% | 66.98% | 55.35% | 54.42% | 73.95% |
| Oboe (OB) | 47.68% | 48.34% | 49.01% | 43.71% | 81.46% | 72.19% |
| Faggoto (FG) | 64.10% | 65.06% | 74.36% | 40.38% | 30.12% | 68.59% |
| Clarinet (CL) | 93.45% | 87.93% | 93.10% | 95.51% | 93.45% | 92.07% |
| Piccolo (PC) | 84.08% | 84.90% | 84.08% | 63.27% | 58.37% | 81.63% |
| Flute (FL) | 88.06% | 72.39% | 94.03% | 35.82% | 84.33% | 85.07% |
| Recorder (RC) | 97.50% | 93.75% | 97.50% | 85.00% | 96.25% | 91.25% |
| Average | 70.27% | 66.98% | 72.53% | 62.11% | 66.50% | 79.73% |

(a) Dimensionality reduction to 79 dim. using PCA only
(b) Dimensionality reduction to 18 dim. using PCA only
(c) Dimensionality reduction to 18 dim. using both PCA and LDA

(2) LDA with the Bayes decision rule improved the accuracy of musical instrument identification from 66.50% to 79.73% in average. Although it seemed that PCA with 79-dimension performed better than LDA for Classical Guitar (CG), Violin (VN), and Alto Sax (AS), the cumulative performance of LDA for the categories of strings and saxophones is better than that of PCA.

## 6 Musical Sound Ontology

Usually, musical sound ontology are borrowed from the classification of musical instruments specified in musical literature, and has not been generated systematically [8,9]. In this section, we use the pitch-dependent features to generate musical sound ontology by using the C5.0 decision tree program, a successor of C4.5 program [11].

From the naive decision tree obtained by applying the C5.0 to all the notes listed in Table 2, the hierarchy of Figure 2 is formed. The details of the decision tree obtained by rule-level pruning is summarized in Figure 3.

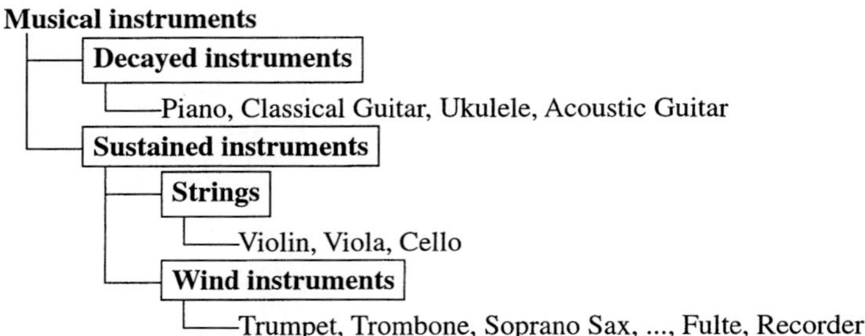


**Fig. 2.** Top-level category of musical sound ontology obtained by C5.0 decision tree program.

```
.....[74] > 5.621357
 :     :...[61] > -4.37589
 :     :     :...-1.35449 < [41] <= -0.666931 and [78] > 0.746687
 :     :     :     => Decayed(0)  Strings(150)  Winds(48)
 :     :     :...else
 :     :           => Decayed(46)  Strings(157)  Winds(2131)
 :     :...[61] <= -4.37589
 :           :...[82] > 1.521393
 :           :     => Decayed(0)  Strings(2)  Winds(59)
 :           :...[82] <= 1.521393
 :                 => Decayed(10)  Strings(1156)  Winds(139)
 :...[74] <= -5.621357
       :...[41] <= -0.625842 and [78] > 0.936492
       :     => Decayed(2)  Strings(55)  Winds(5)
       :...[41] <= -0.625842 and [78] <= 0.936492 and [82] > 0.91987
       :     => Decayed(0)  Strings(3)  Winds(26)
       :...else
             => Decayed(1913)  Strings(141)  Winds(53)
```

Where the features of sounds specified by a pair of bracket are summarized below:

| | |
|---|---|
| [41] | Gradient of a straight line approximating power envelope by LSM |
| [61] | Ratio of the maximum power and the power of 0.20 sec after onset. |
| [74] | Ratio of the maximum power and the power of 0.90 sec after onset. |
| [78] | Amplitude of AM (Amplitude Modulation) |
| [82] | Amplitude of the first coefficent of MFCC modulation |

**Fig. 3.** Top-level category of musical sound ontology

The top-level category of musical sound ontology consists of **Decayed instruments** and **Sustained instruments** and the latter consists of **Strings** and **Wind instruments**. This categorization is reasonable because it matches that of musical instrument classification. However, the lower-level catagories are not the case. For example, the classification of **Winds** consists of nine subcategories based on the features of the gradient of a straight line approximating power envelope by LSM ([41]) and amplitude of Amplitude Modulation (AM) ([78]), which is shown in Table 4.

The observations of the systematic generation of musical sound ontology by the C5.0 decision tree program with the proposed F0-dependent features are summarized below:

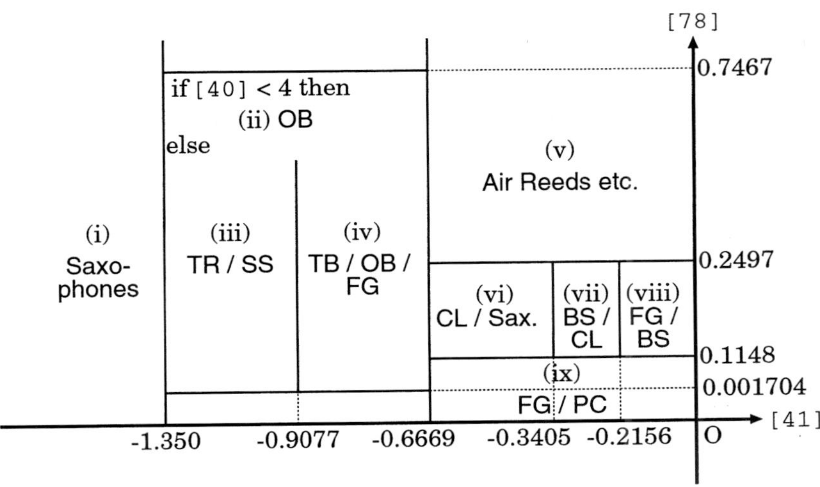


Nine categories are defined by each corresponding rule. For example, rule (i) specifies **Saxophones**, while rule (ii) checks whether the instrument is **Oboe** or not.

**Fig. 4.** Details of classification of **Wind instruments** except **Recorder**

(a) **Wind instruments** can be classified **Recorder** and **Non-Recorder**. This discrimination matches the known fact that **Recorder** is different from other wind instruments.
(b) The categorization of **Wind instruments** except **Recorder** differs from that of musical literature. In particular, **Trombone**, **Tenor Sax** and **Faggoto** are classified in the same category due to the pitch range, although their sounding mechanisms are different.
(c) Musical sound ontology needs plural aspects of sound features, in particular, sounding mechanism and pitch.

## 7 Conclusions

In this paper, we presented the method for musical instrument identification using the *F0-dependent multivariate normal distribution* which takes into consideration the pitch dependency of timbre. The method improved the recognition rates at individual-instrument level from 75.73% to 79.73%, and at category level from 88.20% to 90.65% in average, respectively. The Bayes decision rule with dimensionality reduction by PCA and LDA also performed better than the 3-NN method.

We also reported the systematic generation of musical sound ontology and showed that top-level categrization matches the conventional hierarchy of musical instruments. However, the categrization of wind instruments differs much from the conventional one. The musical instrument indentification by using the musical sound ontology is under investigation and its results will be reported by a separate paper.

Since MPEG-7 which is proposed to describe contents of audio-visual data does not specify how to design and what to use audio-tags, musical sound ontology is expected to play an important role in designing audio-tags [1, 10]. In addition, such sound onotologies should be defined with meta ontologies in order to alleivate efforts to develop automatic conversion between various sound ontologies.

Additional future works include evaluation of the method with different styles of playing, evaluation of the robustness of each feature against mixture of sounds, and automatic music transcription.

**Acknowledgments**

We thank everyone who has contributed to building and distributing the RWC Music Database (Musical Instrument Sound: RWC-MDB-I-2001) [5]. We also thank Kazuhiro Nakadai and Hideki Asoh for their valuable comments.

## References

1. Amatriain, X., and Herrera, P. Audio content transmission. In *Proceedings of the COST G-6 Conference on Digital Audio Effects (DAFx01)* (Dec. 2001), pp. 71–76.
2. Brown, J. C. Computer identification of musical instruments using pattern recognition with cepstral coefficients as features. *Journal of Acoustic Society of America 103*, 3 (1999), 1933–1941.
3. Eronen, A., and Klapuri, A. Musical instrument recognition using cepstral coefficients and temporal features. In *Proceedings of 2000 International Conference on Acoustics, Speech and Signal Processing (ICASSP-2000)* (2000), IEEE, pp. 753–756.
4. Fujinaga, I., and MacMillan, K. Realtime recognition of orchestral instruments. In *Proceedings of International Computer Music Conference (ICMC)* (2000).
5. Goto, M., Hashiguchi, H., Nishimura, T., and Oka, R. Rwc music database: Music genre database and musical instrument sound database *(in japanese)*. In *IPSJ SIG Notes* (2002), vol. 2002-MUS-45, pp. 19–26.
6. Kashino, K., and Murase, H. A sound source identification system for ensemble music based on template adaptation and music stream extraction. *Speech Communication 27*, 3-4 (1999), 337–349.
7. Kashino, K., Nakadai, K., Kinoshita, T., and Tanaka, H. Application of the bayesian probability network to music scene analysis. In *Computational Auditory Scene Analysis* (1998), D. Rosenthal and H. G. Okuno, Eds., Lawrence Erlbaum Associates, pp. 115–137.
8. Martin, K. D. *Sound-Source Recognition: A Theory and Computational Model.* MIT, 1999.
9. Nakatani, T., and Okuno, H. G. Sound ontology for computational auditory scene analysis. In *Proceedings of 15th National Conference on Artificial Intelligence (AAAI-98)* (1998), AAAI, pp. 1004–1010.
10. Peeters, G., McAdams, S., and Herrera, P. Instrument description in the context of mpeg-7. In *Proceedings of the International Computer Music Conference* (2000), pp. 166–169.
11. Quinlan, J. R. *C4.5 Programs for Machine Learning.* Morgan Kaufmann, 1993.
12. Rosenthal, D., and Okuno, H. G., Eds. *Computational Auditory Scene Analysis.* Lawrence Erlbaum Associates, Mahwah, New Jersey, 1998.

# Automated Case Base Creation and Management

Chunsheng Yang, Robert Orchard, Benoit Farley, and Marvin Zaluski

National Research Council of Canada, Ottawa, Ontario, Canada
{Chunsheng.Yang,Bob.Orchard,Benoit.Farley,Marvin.Zaluski}@nrc.ca

**Abstract.** In this paper, we report on a scheme for automated case base creation and management. The scheme aims at reducing the difficulty and human effort required for case creation. This paper provides an overview of the proposed scheme and outlines its technical implementation as an automated case creation system for the Integrated Diagnostic System. Some experimental results for testing the scheme and an interactive tool for evaluating the constructed case base are presented.

**Keywords**: case-based reasoning, case base maintenance, automated case creation, natural language processing

## 1 Introduction

Case base creation and management in case-based reasoning (CBR) systems have been recognized as the bottleneck issues that can determine whether a CBR system will be successful or not. To date a great deal of research effort has been devoted to case base maintenance [3][4][5][6][7][9] in CBR systems. This research has focused on a number of crucial issues such as the case life cycle [1], the optimization of the case indices [2] and so on. Some of the earliest case base maintenance works [4] [5] look at the development of maintenance strategies for deleting/adding cases from/to existing case bases. For example, in [4], a class of competence-guided deletion policies for estimating the competence of an individual case and deleting the case from a case base is presented. This technique has been further developed for adding a case to an existing case base [5]. Redundancy and inconsistency detection for case base management in CBR systems has also attracted a lot of attention from researchers [6]. In recent years, some new approaches based on automatic case base management strategies have been published. M.A. Ferrario and B. Smyth [8], introduced a distributed maintenance strategy, called collaborative maintenance (CM), which provides an intelligent framework to support long-term case collection and authoring. To automatically maintain the case base, L. Portinal et al [7] proposed a strategy, called LEF (Learning by Failure with Forgetting [9]), for automatic case base maintenance.

It is perhaps surprising that these works almost exclusively focus on maintaining case bases for runtime CBR systems and collecting cases from the on-line problem-solving procedures. Relatively little work has focused on automated case creation at an earlier stage, using existing historic maintenance experience that can be collected from past maintenance operational data. In fact, a

P.W.H. Chung, C.J. Hinde, M. Ali (Eds.): IEA/AIE 2003, LNAI 2718, pp. 123–133, 2003.

useful CBR system should provide the ability for a user to automatically create case bases from the recorded historic experience database at the initial stage and to automatically collect or author the cases at the on-line runtime stage. In order to reduce the effort required for case creation and overcome the difficulty of effective creation of high-quality cases, we propose a scheme for automated case creation and case base management that applies natural language processing (NLP) [11] and knowledge discovery technologies. The proposed scheme is presented in detail along with its technical implementation. Some experimental results from testing the effectiveness of the method and a case base evaluation tool are also discussed. The paper is organized as follows. Section 2 presents background information for automated case base creation; Section 3 describes the proposed scheme; Section 4 discusses the technical implementation of the scheme; Section 5 provides details on the tool developed for case base evaluation; and the final section discusses the conclusions.

## 2 Background Information

CBR is one component of the Integrated Diagnostic System (IDS[1]) [10], which was developed at the National Research Council of Canada. It is used to help refine solutions for aircraft maintenance by retrieving solutions to similar situations from the mechanic's historic experiences that have been stored in a case base. One important piece of data is the snag[2] message. A snag is a transcript of the hand-written notes describing a problem (reported by pilots, other crew or maintenance technicians) and the repair actions carried out to fix the problem. It is composed of well defined, fixed fields describing the date, the location, a unique snag identifier, etc. as well as unstructured free-text describing the problem symptoms, the pieces of equipment involved in the repair and the actions performed on them. Table 1 shows an example of a raw snag message. We can obtain a *clean* snag message (shown in Table 2) by preprocessing the raw message. This clean snag message contains the useful information for case creation. It is possible for someone to create a potential case (shown in Table 3) for the case base by combining the information in the cleaned snag message with information in the Fault Event Object (FEO) database. FEOs are created in the IDS runtime system that monitors the status of the aircraft. Onboard diagnostic systems record possible problems in the form of failure (FLR) and warning (WRN) messages that are delivered in real-time to the IDS system. These messages along with messages generated by the pilots are grouped according to the time they arrive and their relationship to each other (as determined by the aircraft troubleshooting manual) to form an FEO. This grouping of messages represents a set of symptoms that describe a potential or real problem. By matching a snag message to an FEO one can craft a case that describes the problem, identifies the symptoms present for this problem and shows the repair

[1] IDS is an applied artificial intelligent system that supports the decision-making process in aircraft fleet maintenance.

[2] A snag is a common term for an equipment problem in the aviation area. It is a record of the problem and the repair action.

action that was taken to fix the problem. By monitoring the aircraft after the fix is applied one can then determine whether the fix was successful or not (i.e. did the problem recur or not).

**Table 1.** An example of the raw maintenance data record

| |
|---|
| ACFT_MI_SEC:UNNNNNNNNNNNNNNNNNNNNNNYYYYYYYYYYYYYNYNNNNNNNNYYNN 6615 437820001N**M1003286** 2312 2312ACA01058P28Q0CL6**YUL** ACA0646RT **RMA 27-93-2127 AVAIL. REPEAT E/W "F/CTL ELAC 1 FAU LT" "ELAC 1 OR INPUT OF CAPT ROLL CTL SSTU 4CE1". R 7.** I2000-09-23NNDEFN 0000000000000 0000000000000 0000000000000 00000000000000 40227AC 74577LNNS ORDER AC74577 **1998-01-22 14:07:00**6650 |
| ACFT_MI_ACTN_SEC : INNNNNNNNNNNNNNNNNNNNNYYYYYYNN 615437820002000 6889450001Y **REPLACED CAPTAINS SIDE STICK AND TESTED AS PER AMM 27-92-41-501** 42000-09-2506.36.00FIX**YWG** 26525AC 26525NNNNNN 000000000000 AC26525 **1998-01-30 16:00:00**.898990 |
| ACFT_PART_RMVL_SEC:NNNNNNNNNNNNNNNNNNNNNNNN6615437820002000688945000100010 001Y0000000010000NNNAC002FD 9W19XFEA 15000000042983622-9852-003 4V792 111AC26525 **1998-01-30 16:00:00**.89916023-80-0100 Y |
| ACFT_PART_INST_SEC:NNNNNNNNNNNNNNYNYYNYNN6615437820002000 688945000 100010001 Y0000000010000NN AC002EA 150000000042983 1467 AC26525 **1998-01-30 16:00:00**.89921023-80-0100 Y |

**Table 2.** A clean snag message obtained from the Table 1

| Event Date & Time | *1998-01-22 14:07:00* |
|---|---|
| Report Station | *YUL* |
| Snag Number | *M1003286* |
| Problem Description | *RMA 27-93-2127 AVAIL REPEAT F/CTL ELAC 1 FAULT ELAC 1 INPUT CAPT ROLL CTL SSTU 4CE1* |
| Fin Number | *222* |
| Repar Station | *YWG* |
| Repair Date | *1998-01-30 16:00:00* |
| Repair Action | *REPLACED CAPTAINS SIDE STICK AND TESTED AS PER AMM 27-92-41-501* |

**Table 3.** A potential case created from Table 2 and FEO database

| Case ID | *Case-1* |
|---|---|
| Case creation date | *2002-04-05* |
| Event date time | *1998-01-22 14:07:00* |
| Snag number | *M1003286* |
| Case quality | *Success* |
| Success times | *1* |
| Failure times | *0* |
| Symptoms | *WRN321 FLR1188 WRN320 WRN340* |
| Problem description | *RMA 27-93-2127 AVAIL REPEAT F/CTL ELAC 1 FAULT ELAC 1 INPUT CAPT ROLL CTL SSTU 4CE1* |
| Fin number | *222* |
| Repar station | *YWG* |
| Repair date | *1998-01-30 16:00:00* |
| Repair actions | *Remove/Install (replace)* |
| Equipment (No) | *27-92-41-501* |

## 3 A Scheme for Automated Case Base Creation

To alleviate the considerable human effort required in CBR applications such as IDS, we propose a scheme for automated case base creation and maintenance. The aim is to extract useful maintenance information for a solution to a problem and related symptoms from the historic maintenance databases, and to create the cases that document these historical relationships by applying NLP, CBR and free-text matching technologies. To describe the proposed scheme, we use the following notations. Let $c$ denote a *case* and $CB$ denotes a case base, then $CB \supseteq (c_1, c_2 ......, c_i, ..., c_n)$. A case $c$ is defined as $c = ((p),(s),(m))$ where *(p)*, *(s)* and *(m)* denote problem attributes (called symptoms), solution attributes to the problem and information for case base management respectively. *(m)* contains all attributes related to case base maintenance including redundancy, inconsistency, positive actions, and negative action. *(p)* could be single symptom or multiple symptoms, and *(s)* could be single action or multiple actions for fixing the problem *(p)*. If $SB$ and $FB$ denote the historic snag maintenance database and the FEO database respectively, then $SB \supseteq (snag_1, snag_2, ...snag_k)$ and $FB \supseteq (f_1, f_2, ...f_l)$. Our task is to create $CB$ from $SB$ and $FB$.

The scheme, shown as pseudo-code in Figure 1, automates the procedures for case base creation as three main processes:

- Preprocessing snag messages,
- Creating a potential case,
- Maintaining the case base.

The proposed scheme is expected to be suitable for maintenance domains other than aviation as long as they provide historic diagnostic maintenance records in a well-defined data format. We use dynamic attribute definitions for the number and type of attributes in the case. This will make it easier to apply the scheme to other domains. The step in which we preprocess snag message will likely need some adjustment to handle the raw data format for different application domains but the approach remains the same. Following are the details for the aircraft maintenance application domain.

### 3.1 Preprocessing Snag Messages

The raw snag messages like the one shown in Table 1 are processed to give the clean message as shown in Table 2. The parse is a simple since the various fields of the raw message are in a predetermined order of the fixed size. We extract the date, the place where the fix was done, a unique snag identifier, etc, as well as unstructured free-text describing the problem symptoms and the repair actions. The free-text contains many unnecessary symbols or words. To deal with this, we filter the unnecessary characters (such as '#', '.', '*' and so on) and using a list of "poor single" words, we remove some words as well. The list of poor single words are constructed by analyzing a large set of snag messages to see which ones were not helpful in matching the unstructured text FLR and WRN messages. For example, the free-text of problem description obtained from the raw snag message, *RMA 27-93-2127 AVAIL. REPEAT E/W "F/CTL ELAC 1 FAULT" "ELAC 1 OR INPUT OF CAPT ROLL CTL SSTU 4CE1". R 7.* after processing, results in *RMA 27-93-2127 AVAIL REPEAT F/CTL ELAC 1 FAULT ELAC 1 INPUT CAPT ROLL CTL SSTU 4CE1*, as shown in Table 2.

The free-text of the "repair action" field will be processed using NLP techniques discussed in the next section.

```
SchemeForAutomatedCaseCreationAndManagement (CB, SB, FB)
BEGIN
      FOR each snag_i in SB DO
      BEGIN
               // Preprocess the raw snag message
               Get-snag-data (snag_i );
               Filter-and-clean-free-text(snag_i);
               // starting to create a potential case from snag message
               IF not Identify-symptoms(input=FB, snag_i; output =(p));
               THEN continue;
               ELSE
                  IF not NLP-identfy-solutions(input=snag_i, output=(s));
                  THEN continue;
                  ELSE
                          Create-potential-case(input=(p),(s); output = c_tmp);
                          IF not check-positive-case(input=FB; output=c_tmp);
                          THEN negative-case(c_tmp);
                          ELSE positive-case(c_tmp);
                          ENDIF
                  EENDIF
               ENDIF
               // starting case base management process
               FOR each case_j in CB DO
               BEGIN
                          IF not Detect-Redundancy-Inconsistency(c_j, c_tmp);
                          THEN add-new-case(CB,c_tmp);
                          ELSE maintain-case-bases(c_j, c_tmp );
                          ENDIF
               ENDFOR
      ENDFOR
END
```

**Fig. 1.** Figure 1: The scheme for automated case base creation and management

## 3.2 Creating a Potential Case

This part of the scheme requires four main steps. The first step, symptom identification, is to identify the symptoms for the problem *(p)*; the 2nd step, repair action identification, is to find the solution information *(s)*; the 3rd step, case template creation, is to create a potential case $C_{tmp}$; and the 4th step, case quality identification, is to determine if the case is positive (a successful solution) or negative (an unsuccessful solution) by checking to see if the symptoms disappeared after the solution *(s)* is applied to the problem *(p)*. If the symptoms disappeared we say the case is positive, otherwise the case is negative. In CBR applications, both positive and negative cases are useful for decision-making support. It is as important to know what will not fix a problem as to know what will fix it.

The symptom identification module finds a set of symptoms in the FEO database that match the problem described in the snag message. Identifying the symptoms for the problem is done using a free-text matching approach because the content of FLR and WRN message is described in formal (predetermined) text while the problem description in the snag message is unstructured free text. To match such free text to the formal text of the diagnostic messages, we use an N-gram algorithm. N-gram matching refers to a fragment of N consecutive letters of a text phase. For a given text phase of length ***L***, there are $L-N+1$ N-grams. Such matching algorithm helps to reduce the impact of misspelling, abbreviations and acronyms. After considering the trade-off between the algorithm performance and matching accuracy, we selected N to be 3 (tri-gram matching). For example, in the tri-gram matching algorithm, the text word "***diagnose***" could be disassembled into 6 tri-grams: $\{dia, iag, agn, gno, nos, ose\}$. If a text phase, "***diagnose***" is matched to the misspelled one, "***diagnoes***", the tri-gram will match them as two similar text phases.

The repair action identification module, called *NLP-identify-solutions* in the pseudo-code of Figure 1, extracts repair action and equipment information from the snag message using NLP techniques [11] [12]. In general, the free text of the repair action description of the snag message contains one or more "sentences" with extensive use of acronyms and abbreviations, omission of certain types of words (such as the definite article), and numerous misspellings and typographic errors. Extracting the required specific information, namely the pieces of equipment involved in the repair, the actions performed on the equipment (replace, reset, repair, etc.), and the results of those actions, from this free text is a typical natural language understanding procedure, consisting of the following main steps:

- dictionary and acronyms database creation,
- preprocessing of the free text message and morphological analysis,
- grammar and parsing , and
- semantic interpretation.

To carry out the NLP process for understanding the free-text maintenance messages, we have to build up a lexicon, which contains the words, acronyms and abbreviations used in the particular domain, and we have to create a knowledge base for interpreting these messages. For aircraft fleet maintenance, the lexicon and knowledge base were built from information in the snag databases [12]. The quality of the lexicon and knowledge base will directly affect of the ability to create good cases from the historic maintenance data.

In the natural language understanding procedure, the unstructured free text that describes the repair action is first preprocessed to determine the nature and properties of each word and token against the dictionary and acronyms database. Then the sequence of morphologically analyzed items is syntactically analyzed with a parser and checked against a grammar that describes the patterns of valid propositions. Finally the result of the syntactic parsing is semantically interpreted to generate the class of repair action and the equipment on which the action is performed. For example, the free-text that describes the repair action in the snag message, "*#1 EIU replaced*", is analyzed as follows: (1) If the part name is not found in the Airbus Illustrated Parts Catalog (IPC), part name is ***EIU #1*** and repair action is ***REPLACE.*** (2) If the part name is found in the IPC[3], the following values are assigned to the potential case, i.e. part name is ***EIU,*** part number is ***3957900612***, repair action is ***REPLACE,*** and part series number is ***3-25-8-2-40D*** (detailed in [12]).

A new potential case is created by the case template creation module using the symptoms and repair actions extracted from the previous modules. Then the case quality identification module checks this case to determine if the symptoms related to the problem have disappeared or not during a period of time (window size) after the repair actions were taken. The window size is set by aircraft fleet maintenance requirements. We assume that if the symptoms of the problem disappear for the specified period (window size) that the repair was successful and the case is labeled as a positive case, otherwise it is labeled as a negative one.

### 3.3 Maintaining the Case Base

The case base maintenance process implements the basic functions for case base management. The first set of functionality includes detecting any redundancy or inconsistency for the potential case against the existing case base. In effect we determine whether this case is similar to cases within existing case bases or not. The inconsistency detection function also helps to detect historic data that may contain conflicting information for the same problem over time. The second set of functionality involves adding a new case to the case base, updating an existing case in the case base, deleting a case and merging multiple cases into a new case. If a potential case is new, it will be added to the case base and the case base management information will be refreshed. If it is similar to an existing case, we have to modify the existing case by updating the case management information $(m)$ or merge them into a new case. For example, if we detected a similar case ($c_i$) in the existing case base against the potential case $c_{tmp}$, i.e. $(p)_i \cong (p)_{tmp}$ and $(s)_i \cong (s)_{tmp}$, then $(m)_i$ will is updated to reflect the effect of the repair action applied to the problem. If $c_{tmp}$ is a positive case, then we increase the count of successful repair actions of $(m)_i$ otherwise we increase the count of unsuccessful repair actions of $(m)_i$.

## 4 Implementation and Experimental Results

The proposed scheme has been applied to the IDS project to create the cases from the aircraft fleet maintenance historic data (snag database) and the FEO database. We developed a Java-based CBR engine, and an automated case creation system (ACCS) which incorporates the CBR engine, natural language processing, free-text matching, and database technologies. The goal of the ACCS tool is to

[3] IPC is a catalog of all the parts of the particular type of aircrafts. It describes the component makeup of an airplane with a list of all the part number and a keyword designating the part.

demonstrate that we can create an set of cases in an automated way that will enhance the decision making process of the maintenance technicians.

The ACCS, as shown in Figure 2, identifies the three main components: snag message preprocessing, potential case creation, and case base maintenance. The potential case creation component contains the four modules: symptom identification, repair action identification, case template creation and case quality identification. The case base maintenance component is supported by the Java-based CBR engine and the redundancy and inconsistency detection modules. We have used JDK2.0, Oracle7.0, and Prolog as development environments.

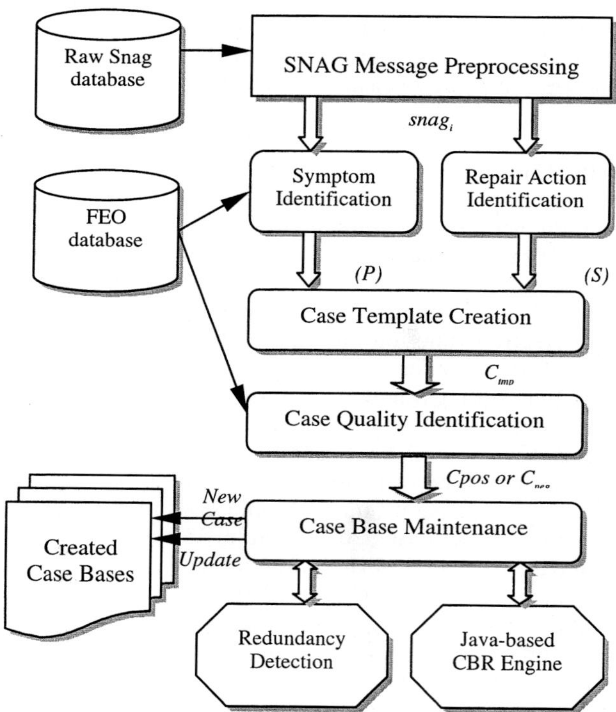


**Fig. 2.** ACCS system implementation

To test the effectiveness of our automated case creation, experiments were carried out using the ACCS with the aircraft fleet maintenance database from Air Canada and the FEO database created by our own IDS system. We used ACCS to create the cases from the 359 clean snag messages that were formed from January 1, 1998 to January 31, 1998 and the FEO database. The ACCS created 35 cases in 2 minutes. It is interesting that not each clean snag message contains the fully useful information for creating a potential case because ether the symptoms are not found from the FEO datable, or the fix does not exist the snag message. In the 35 constructed cases, 21 cases are created from single snag message and consist of positive case or negative case; 14 cases are linked to multiple snag messages, which recorded similar resolutions for similar problems or the same problem, and they contain information on the successful or failed repair action by the attributes of case base management $(m)$. From the statistic result, 45 snag messages from 359 snag messages were linked to those 14 cases. Totally, 66 clean snag messages among 359 snag messages were useful for creating the cases.

## 5 Case Base Evaluation

Before the cases that have been automatically created are incorporated into CBR applications such as IDS, they must be validated by either a knowledge-based system or domain experts. The validation of cases by a knowledge-based system is a very difficult task and requires rich domain knowledge from experts. Therefore, we are providing the domain experts with a supporting tool to help them validate the case base. This interactive environment allows the user to browse the constructed case base and evaluate cases one by one, checking the original snag message, problem symptoms, problem description, repair action and so on. It also provides the basic support for the user to do case base maintenance operations such as modifying a case, deleting a case and merging multiple cases. Figure 3 shows the main window of the validation tool.

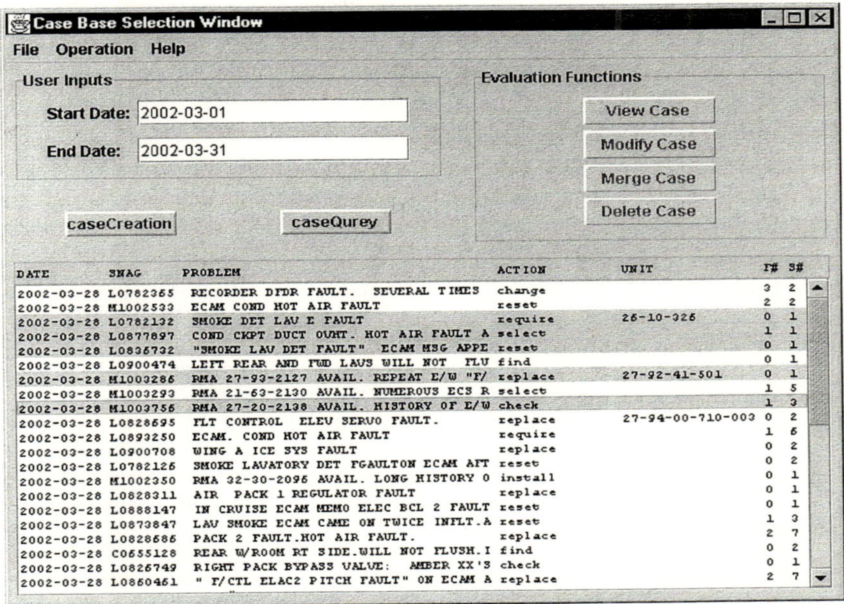


**Fig. 3.** The main window of the case base evaluation tool

## 6 Conclusions

In this paper, we first presented the proposed scheme for automated case base creation and management in CBR systems, then we briefly described the system implementation, an automated case creation system for IDS (an application in the aircraft maintenance domain) and discussed the experimental results. We also presented an interactive tool for domain experts to evaluate the case base. From the experimental results, it can be pointed out that the proposed scheme is feasible and effective for automated case base creation and management in CBR systems and it can significantly reduce the human effort required for case creation. Currently the ACCS system is creating case bases off-line. The constructed case base will be incorporated into IDS to provide the CBR support for aircraft fleet maintenance. The proposed scheme can be applied to other maintenance application domains by implementing specific preprocessing of snag messages and setting up a special lexicon and knowledge base corresponding to those application domains. Future work would be to integrate the system into IDS as an on-line component. This will be beneficial in providing a system for collecting and authoring the cases from real-time maintenance procedures.

### Acknowledgements

Many people at NRC have been involved this project. Special thanks go to the following for their support, discussion and valuable suggestions: M. Halasz, R. Wylie, and F. Dube. We are also grateful to Air Canada for providing us the aircraft fleet maintenance data.

## References

1. M. Minor and A. Hanft, *The Life Cycle of Test cases in a CBR System,* In Proceedings of Advances in case-based Reasoning: 5th European Workshop, EWCBR 2000, Trento, Italy, Setp. 2000, pp.455-466
2. D.W. Aha and L.A. Breslow, *Refining Conversational Case Libraies*, In Proceedings of Int'l Conference of Case-based Reasoning, RI, USA, 1997, pp.267-278
3. B. Smyth, *Case-Based Maintenance*, In Proceedings of the 11th Intl. Conference on Industry and Engineering Applications of AI and Expert Systems, Castellon, Spain, 1998.
4. B. Smyth, *Remembering to Forget: A Competence Persevering Deletion Policy for Case-Based Reasoning Systems*, In Proceedings of the 14th Intl. Joint Conference on AI, Morgan-Kaufmann, 1995, pp.377-382
5. J. Zhu and Q. Yang, *Remembering to Add: Competence Persevering Case-Addition Policy for Case-Base Maintenance*, In Proceedings of the 16th Intl. Joint Conference on AI, Stockholm, Sweden, 1999, pp.234-239
6. K. Racine and Q. Yang, *On the Consistency Management for Large Case Bases: The Case for Validation*, In Proceedings of AAAI-96 Workshop on Knowledge Base Validation, August 1996
7. L. Portinale and P. Torasso, *Automated Case Base Management in a Multi-model Reasoning System,* In Proceedings of Advances in case-based Reasoning: 5th European Workshop, EWCBR 2000, Trento, Italy, Setp. 2000, pp.234-246

8. M. A. Ferrario and B. Smyth, *Collaborative Maintenance—A Distributed, Interactive Case-based Maintenance Strategy,* In Proceedings of Advances in case-based Reasoning: 5th European Workshop, EWCBR 2000, Trento, Italy, Setp. 2000, pp.393—405
9. L. Portinale, P. Torasso, and P. Tavano *Speed-up, Quality and Competence in Multi-model Case-based Reasoning,* In Proceedings of 3rd ICCBR, LNAI 1650, Springer Verlag, 1999, pp. 303-317
10. R. Wylie, R. Orchard, M. Halasz and F. Dubé, *IDS: Improving Aircraft fleet Maintenance*, In Proceedings of the 14th National Conference on Artificial Intelligence, Calif, USA, 1997, pp.1078-1085
11. B. Farley, *From free-text repair action messages to automatic case generation*, In Proceedings of AAAI Spring Symposium: AI in Equipment Maintenance Service & Support, Technical Report SS-99-04, Menlo Park, CA,: AAAI Press, 1999, pp.109-118
12. B.Farley, *Extracting information from free-text aircraft repair notes,* Artificial Intelligence for Engineering Design, Analysis and Manufacture, Cambridge University Press 0890-0604/01, 2001, I5, pp.295-305

# The Study on Algorithm $AE_{11}$ of Learning from Examples

HaiYi Zhang[1], JianDong Bi[2], and Barbro Back[3]

[1] Jodrey School of Computer Science, Acadia University
Wolfville, Nova Scotia
Canada B4P 2R6
[2] Department of computer Science, Harbin Institute of Technology,
HeilongJiang, 150001,China
Turku Centre for Computer Science TUCS
[3] Department of Information Systems, Abo Akademi University,
Lemminkäinengatan 14 B, Fin-20520 Turku, Finland

**Abstract** We first put forwards the idea of positive extension matrix (PEM) in the paper. And then an algorithm $AE_{11}$ was built with the aid of PEM. Finally we made the comparisons of our experimental results. The result is fairly satisfied.

## 1 Introduction

Learning from examples is a main research direction of machine learning. Because it can be used in automatic construction of knowledge base of an expert system it is most widely studied [12]. Learning algorithms are the key aim of study. Development of high-quality algorithms will promote the growth of machine learning. For recent years, some international famous experts such as Feigenbaum criticized research on machine learning because it has not been used in the real-world [1]. So in present, the research on machine learning gives its attention to development of practical systems.

The subject of this paper is about the research on the algorithm and practical techniques of learning from examples. The idea of positive extension matrix (PEM) and an algorithm $AE_{11}$ based on PEM are put forwards.

The learning from examples is the core of the machine learning. It is widely used in creating knowledge base. Normally it is difficult for an expert to provide the knowledge to solve a problem, but it is easy to provide the examples of the decisions. Sometimes there exist some examples in some kind of works, for instance, oil exploring, at the beginning dig some check-wells [11]. In the digging, we obtain some data, which form examples. The examples represent a relationship between the data and the type of wells. Such examples are original examples. They are more accurate than the expert decision. Learning from those examples is more accurate.

The efficiency of learning algorithm and the accuracy of the predicating are main points for researching. The efficiency is related to training speed and classifying

P.W.H. Chung, C.J. Hinde, M. Ali (Eds.): IEA/AIE 2003, LNAI 2718, pp. 134–147, 2003.

speed. The predicating accuracy is related to the classifying correct ratio of the new data for the obtaining the conceptual description. In our days, people think that the simple conceptual description is powerful for summary and it possesses the high predicating accuracy. The famous algorithms are $ID_3$ and $AQ_{15}$ in the algorithms of learning from examples. $ID_3$ belongs to the Splitting algorithm [8,9], inducing the conceptual descriptions with the decision tree represented. The speed of an $ID_3$ algorithm is fast but its predicating accuracy is not high. If a value of some attribute in an example is wrong, it can cause the mistake of the classifying. In additional the knowledge representation with a decision tree is not powerful. The form of the knowledge representation is not easy to comprehensible. It is not suitable to use in an expert system. Although there are some new versions that try to convert a decision tree to rules, they cannot avoid the loss of accuracy on the decision tree. So, ID3 is mainly used as a classifier.

$AQ_{15}$ belongs to agglomerative algorithm [8, 9]. Inducing conceptual descriptions are presented with rules. A rule is a "condition – action" pair { C=>A}, normally it is presented with disjunction normal formula (DNF), that is, a conjunction form of a formula. Here, A is a class, that is, a positive example or a negative example, it stands for that the example satisfying the condition belongs to the positive example set (when A stands for a positive) or negative example set (When A stands for negative example). It is easy for people to understand the form of the rule. It is widely used in the expert systems. But the rules are quite similar to a linea list. It needs to check one by one when the new data are classified, the speed of classifying is slower. But the rule predicating accuracy of inducing with $AQ_{15}$ is higher. The extension matrix is one kind of learning from examples. The basic idea of the method is that it tries to convert obtaining rules into seeking the path in the extension matrix. The extension matrix is proposed with JiaRong Hong in 1985 [4], and it is proved that three optimal problems (MCV, MCOMP and OPL) are NP hard in the learning from examples using it. The extension matrix method is that at first, we find the distinguishing between the positive examples and negative examples. The extension matrix is used to represent those distinguishes, and then according to those distinguishes, the examples are induced so that the proper assertions are obtained. The extension matrix clearly reflects the distinguishing between positive examples and negative examples. It is easy to find the heuristic of a problem relying on it. Nowadays there are $AE_1$, $AE_5$ and $AE_9$ algorithms that are created by relying on the extension matrix [5,6]. All those algorithms are creating the heuristics starting from the nature of the path. In the algorithms, a rule is simplest with $AE_9$, and it obtains the simpler rule than the $AQ_{15}$. The algorithm $AE_{11}$ we proposed in the paper also belongs to the extension matrix. It is based on the positive extension matrix (PEM). It also creates heuristics to induce starting from the nature of the path. In the inducing the algorithm prior selects the required elements (The path must pass though the elements).

The algorithm prior selects the elements in the smallest line (it includes the non-dead elements in the extension matrix) to form selectors. The experimental results show that the rules obtained by $AE_{11}$ are simpler than $AE_9$ and $AQ_{15}$.

In the paper we first introduce the extension matrix, and then we describe the positive extension matrix and the algorithm $AE_{11}$ based on the extension matrix.

## 2 Positive Extension Matrix

First we recover the basic concepts for learning from examples.

Let E $=D_1$ x $D_2$ x … x $D_n$ be n dimensional infinitive vector space, here, $D_j$ is infinitive discrete symbol set; the element e = $(V_1, V_2, \ldots, V_n)$ in E simply written as $<v_j>$ named an example, $V_j \in D_j$.

Let PE and NE stand for two subsets in E, they are respectively called a positive example set and a negative example set.

**Definition 1**. A selector is a relation statement, its form is $[X_j = A_j]$, here, $X_j$ is a $J^{th}$ attribute, $A_j \subset D_j$, a formula (or item) is the conjunction form of the selectors, that is, $\wedge \lfloor x_j = A_j \rfloor$, here, J $\subseteq$ {1,2, ..,n}, A rule is the disjunction form of a formula, that is, $\vee L_i$, here $L_i$ is a formula. An example e = $<V_1, \ldots, V_n>$ satisfies a selector $[x_j = A_j]$ if and only if $V_j$ is an element of $A_j$, that is, $V_j \in A_j$, e satisfies a rule if and only if e satisfies at least one formula in the rule, An example satisfies a selector (formula, rule), it is also called that the selector (formula, rule) covers the example.

**Definition 2**. A selector (formula, rule) covers a positive example $e^+$ in the background of a negative example e- if only if it covers the positive example but it does not cover the negative example. A selector (formula, rule) covers a positive example in the background of NE set if and only if it covers the positive example in the background of every negative example in NE, A rule is called a cover of positive example set PE in the background set NE if and only if any positive example in the PE in the background of the negative set is covered by a formula in the rule.

### 2.1 The Description of the Extension Matrix Method

The extension matrix is one kind of methods learning from examples. It can be obtained by comparing the positive examples and the negative examples. Taking a positive example and comparing it with all the negative examples, if the value of the positive example is equal to the value of a negative example, then the element is a "dead element". It stands for "*". If the value of the positive example is not equal to the value of a negative example, then the element is the value of the negative example. In this way we get an extension matrix in which the row is same as the number of negative examples. A positive example has an n extension matrix. The Table 1 shows several weather cases, in which some cases are suitable for the game and some others are not.

By observing the Table 1, we can obtain the following rules:

The weather suitable for the game is:

[ humidity$\neq$ high] [ wind power$\neq$ big] [weather$\neq$ fine] [ Temperature $\neq$ cold $\vee$ warm]

**Table 1.** An Example Set

| Items | Weather | Sunny or not | Temperature | Humidity | Wind power |
|---|---|---|---|---|---|
| Suitable for the game | 1 | Cloudy | Hot | High | Small |
| | 2 | Rain | Hot | High | Big |
| | 3 | Rain | Hot | Low | Big |
| | 4 | Cloudy | Hot | High | Small |
| | 5 | Sunny | Cold | Low | Small |
| Not suitable for the game | 1 | Sunny | Hot | High | Small |
| | 2 | Sunny | Cold | Low | Big |
| | 3 | Rain | Warm | Low | Big |
| | 4 | Rain | Cold | High | Small |

The inducing process from the example set to rules may rely on the extension matrix to realize. The Table 1 shows five positive examples. Therefore there are five positive extension matrixes shown as the table 2. The path composed of the elements circled in the table 2 is corresponding to the rules above. Every element in the path is exclusives one negative example. In the forming an extension matrix the values of attribute of the negative example is kept. The rule form relying on an extension matrix is $[X_i \neq R_i]$. The relation operator in the intermedia is not equal ($\neq$). The positive extension matrix is different from an extension matrix. By forming a positive extension matrix the value of attribute of the positive examples is kept. So the form of a selector is $[X_i = R_i]$ when the rule is formed with the positive extension matrix, and the intermeddle relation operator is equal (=). In additional, the non-dead elements are same at the same column in the positive extension matrix, and after a selector is picked up, the negative examples, which the row including non-dead element at same column is corresponding to, are exclusive. This feature makes the generating algorithm easy to find the solutions of optimisation.

## 2.2 Extension Matrix

In the following discussion, we view matrix forms of the positive and negative example sets as equivalence: an example is corresponding to a row in the matrix.

**Definition 3**. Given $e^+ = <v_1^+, \ldots, v_n^+>$ and negative example matrix NE, For every $j \in N$, $N = \{1,2,\ldots, n\}$, Substituting with the dead element "*" to all the appearances of $v_j^+$ at $J^{th}$ column in NE. We obtain a matrix called the extension matrix in the background of a negative example set NE,. let $EM(e^+)$ stand for it.

Figure 1 shows an example set, in which there are 6 positive examples and 6 negative examples. They are respectively represented with a positive example matrix and a negative example matrix. And the extension matrixes of six positive examples in PE are shown in table 3.

**Table 2.** The Extension Matrix

$$\begin{vmatrix} * & hot & high & * \\ * & cold & * & big \\ rain & * & * & big \\ rain & cold & high & * \end{vmatrix} \quad \begin{vmatrix} sunny & * & * & small \\ sunny & cold & low & * \\ rain & warm & low & * \\ rain & cold & * & small \end{vmatrix}$$

$$\begin{vmatrix} sunny & * & high & * \\ sunny & cold & * & big \\ * & warm & * & big \\ * & cold & high & * \end{vmatrix} \quad \begin{vmatrix} sunny & * & * & * \\ sunny & cold & low & big \\ rain & warm & low & big \\ rain & cold & * & * \end{vmatrix}$$

$$\begin{vmatrix} * & hot & high & * \\ * & * & * & big \\ rain & warm & * & big \\ rain & * & high & * \end{vmatrix}$$

$$PE = \begin{vmatrix} e_1^+ \\ e_2^+ \\ e_3^+ \\ e_4^+ \\ e_5^+ \\ e_6^+ \end{vmatrix} = \begin{vmatrix} 0 & 0 & 0 & 0 \\ 0 & 0 & 2 & 0 \\ 0 & 2 & 0 & 1 \\ 1 & 1 & 1 & 1 \\ 1 & 2 & 1 & 1 \\ 0 & 2 & 1 & 0 \end{vmatrix} \qquad NE = \begin{vmatrix} e_1^+ \\ e_2^+ \\ e_3^+ \\ e_4^+ \\ e_5^+ \\ e_6^+ \end{vmatrix} = \begin{vmatrix} 0 & 2 & 1 & 1 \\ 0 & 0 & 3 & 0 \\ 1 & 2 & 0 & 0 \\ 1 & 1 & 1 & 0 \\ 1 & 0 & 2 & 1 \\ 1 & 2 & 3 & 0 \end{vmatrix}$$

**Fig. 1.** The Matrix of Positive Examples, Negative Examples

**Definition 4**. The connections of m non-dead elements respectively from the different rows in an extension matrix compose of one path; the common elements of extension matrixes are called if the matrixes possess none dead elements of same value in the two or more extension matrixes. A common path is called if the path only consists of common elements;

Two extension matrixes are intersected if they have a common path. Otherwise they are not intersected.

$EM_1$, $EM_2$ and $EM_3$ are intersected in the extension matrixes shown in the table 3. They have the common paths $\{L_{13}, L_{23}, L_{31}, L_{41}, L_{51}, L_{61}\}$, here the subscripts stand the row and column in the matrix. $EM_3$ and $EM_6$ are not intersected. They do not have a common path. $EM_5$ and $EM_6$ are not intersected.

**Table 3.** The Extension Matrix

$$EM(e_1^+) = \begin{vmatrix} * & 2 & 1 & 1 \\ * & * & 3 & * \\ 1 & 2 & * & * \\ 1 & 1 & 1 & * \\ 1 & * & 2 & 1 \\ 1 & 2 & 3 & * \end{vmatrix} \quad EM(e_2^+) = \begin{vmatrix} * & 2 & 1 & 1 \\ * & * & 3 & * \\ 1 & 2 & 0 & * \\ 1 & 1 & 1 & * \\ 1 & * & * & 1 \\ 1 & 2 & 3 & * \end{vmatrix} \quad EM(e_3^+) = \begin{vmatrix} * & * & 1 & * \\ * & 0 & 3 & * \\ 1 & * & * & 0 \\ 1 & 1 & 1 & 0 \\ 1 & 0 & 2 & * \\ 1 & * & 3 & 0 \end{vmatrix}$$

$$EM(e_4^+) = \begin{vmatrix} * & 2 & * & * \\ 0 & 0 & 3 & 0 \\ * & 2 & 0 & 0 \\ * & * & * & 0 \\ * & 0 & 2 & * \\ * & 2 & 3 & 0 \end{vmatrix} \quad EM(e_5^+) = \begin{vmatrix} 0 & * & * & * \\ 0 & 0 & 3 & 0 \\ * & * & 0 & 0 \\ * & 1 & * & 0 \\ * & 0 & 2 & * \\ * & * & 3 & 0 \end{vmatrix} \quad EM(e_6^+) = \begin{vmatrix} * & * & * & 1 \\ * & 0 & 3 & * \\ 1 & * & 0 & * \\ 1 & 1 & * & * \\ 1 & 0 & 2 & 1 \\ 1 & * & 3 & 1 \end{vmatrix}$$

In fact, obtaining rules of learning from examples is converted to seek the common paths in each extension matrix. From view of intuitive, the position of a dead element in the extension matrix is just the place in which the positive example and a negative example are same. A non-dead element is the difference between a positive example and a negative example. The algorithm finds out the difference and forms a formula that covers positive examples and exclusive negative examples. Since one row in the extension matrix is corresponding to a negative example, taking a non dead element from a row and put it to a selector whose relation operator is "≠" , the negative example is exclusive. Taking a non dead element from every row in the extension matrix and order them to form a path (or a rule), all the elements in this path compose a formula covering positive examples and negative examples, that is, the path can distinguish from examples of two classes. The table 3 shows a such extension matrix $EM(e_4^+)$, the element in the $1^{th}$ row and $1^{th}$ column is a non dead element. It stands for that the attribute value of the $4^{th}$ positive example is not equal to the attribute value of the $1^{th}$ negative example. So, the $1^{th}$ negative example is exclusive with a selector $[X_1 \neq 0]$. Following the same principle we can respectively select a non-dead element in the $2^{th}$ to $6^{th}$ raw to exclusive the $2^{th}$ to $6^{th}$ negative example. The path in the $EM(e_4^+)$ is quite like a formula which covers the positive example $e_4^+$ and exclusive all the negative examples. The common path is quite like a formula that covers more positive examples and exclusives all the negative examples. The task of seeking a simpler rule is equal to seek a common path in every extension matrix. The more paths we found, the less number of paths for all extension matrixes, and less number of formulas that cover all the positive examples and exclusive all the negative examples. Finally the rules we obtain are simple (The formulas are less).

An extension matrix possesses properties following:

Let $EM(e^+)$ be an extension matrix for a positive example $e^+$ in the background NE, and $EM(e^+) = [r_{ij}]$, $NE = [V_y^-]$,

(1)

$r_{ij} = v_{ij}^-$, if $v_j^+ \neq v_{ij}^-$

$r_{ij} = *$, if $V_j^+ = v_{ij}^-$

(2) If $e^+$ is not a element of NE, then there is at lest one non dead element at every row in the $EM(e^+)$. Therefore, there is at lest one path.

(3) If there is an appearance of an element in a position in the $EM(e^+)$, for a negative matrix, then any other element, that is at same column of the element and possesses same value, must have an appearance at same place in the $EM(e^+)$. Such element is called as similar element.

(4) A path in the extension matrix $EM(e^+)$ is corresponding to a formula for $e^+$ in the background NE.

Suppose two positive examples $e_k^+ = <v_{kj}^+>$ and $e_l^+ = <v_{lj}^+>$, then

(5) The element $v_{ij}^-$ in NE is a common element of $EM(e_k^+)$ and $EM(e_l^+)$ if and only if $V_{ij}^- \neq v_{kj}^+$ and $v_{ij}^- \neq v_{ij}^+$

(6) Two extension matrixes $EM(e_k^+)$ and $EM(e_l^+)$ are not intersected if only if there is at lest one row, let it i, $V_{ij}^- =$ or $v_{ij}^- = v_{ij}^+$ for every column $j \in \{1,\ldots, n\}$

## 2.3 Positive Extension Matrix

Based on the extension matrix theory, the algorithms $AE_1$, $AE_5$ and $AE_9$ are realized [4,5,6,9,10]. These algorithms are relying on seeking a common path in the extension matrix to obtain rules covered positive examples and exclusive negative examples. Since the extension matrix keeps the attribute value as an element, the forms of selectors in the algorithms are $[x_j \neq A_j]$, which is not easy for people to understand in the practice. Normally people are used to see that an attribute equals to something but it does not equal to something. In the paper, we propose the positive extension matrix to solve this problem. While forming the positive matrix, we compare positive examples to negative examples. The corresponding element in the extension matrix is a dead element * if the attributes of two examples are equal. If they are not equal, we keep the attribute value of the positive example as an element of the extension matrix. $AE_{11}$ is an algorithm based on the positive extension matrix, which relies on seeking a path in the positive extension matrix to induce a formula that covers the positive example and is exclusive the negative example. Since an element in the positive extension matrix is an attribute value of a positive example, in the induced rules a form of a selector is $[x_i = A_j]$, here intermediate relation operator is " = ". In additional, they all rely on the approximation solutions that are given a heuristic to get most optima ion cover problem (MCV) or most simple formula problem (MCOMP) [2,3]. The non-dead elements at same column are same in the positive extension matrix. When a none-dead element is used to form a selector, not only the negative example corresponding to the element is exclusive, but also the negative examples corresponding to all the none-dead elements at the column will be exclusive. This feature is similar to a heuristic of most simple formula problem

(MCOMP). From this point of view, we can say that MCOMP heuristic is hidden behind of the positive extension matrix. We adopt MCV problem heuristic in the $AE_{11}$ algorithm. The elements covering more the positive extension matrix are prior selected to form selectors. From this point of view, $AE_{11}$ Algorithm is an algorithm seeking approximation solutions of most optimising example problem (OPL) [7]. It is connivent for us to realize the algorithm with the positive extension matrix and it is more understandable.

**Definition 5**. Suppose that we have a positive example $e^+ = <v_1^+, v_2^+, \ldots, v_n^+>$ and a negative matrix NE. Let NE be m × n matrix, $r_{ij}^-$ be an element at $i^{th}$ row and $j^{th}$ column of the NE, $I \in \{1\ldots m\}$, $j \in \{1\ldots n\}$, then a positive extension matrix PEM($e^+$) of $e^+$ is also m × n matrix, the elements are:

$$R_{ij} = v_j^+, \text{ if } v_j^+ \neq r_{ij}^-$$
$$R_{ij} = *, \text{ if } v_j^+ = r_{ij}^-$$

We will simply write PEM to represent a positive extension matrix in this paper. The Figure 2 shows a matrix of examples. They have five positive examples and four negative examples. The positive extension matrixes of the five positive examples are shown in Table 4.

$$PE = \begin{vmatrix} e_1^+ \\ e_2^+ \\ e_3^+ \\ e_4^+ \\ e_5^+ \end{vmatrix} = \begin{vmatrix} 1 & 0 & 2 \\ 1 & 1 & 2 \\ 1 & 2 & 2 \\ 0 & 0 & 1 \\ 0 & 1 & 1 \end{vmatrix} \qquad NE = \begin{vmatrix} e_1^+ \\ e_2^+ \\ e_3^+ \\ e_4^+ \end{vmatrix} = \begin{vmatrix} 1 & 0 & 1 \\ 1 & 2 & 1 \\ 0 & 1 & 2 \\ 0 & 2 & 2 \end{vmatrix}$$

**Fig. 2.** The Matrices of Positive, Negative Examples

**Definition 6**. Let PEM($e^+$) be a positive extension matrix, an element is named as a required-select element if there is only one non-dead element in some row of the PEM($e^+$) .

**Definition 7**. M none-dead elements, respectively coming from the different rows in an extension matrix, link and compose of a path. A none-dead element, being at same position (row and column) in two or more positive matrix, is named as a common element. A common path is named if the path composes of common elements. Two positive extension matrixes are intersected if they possess a common path, other wise they are not intersected.

**Definition 8**. In a positive extension matrix a set of common elements is named as a common set, the position most appearing none dead elements in the positive extension matrix is called as a maximum position. The maximum position of a common element set is named as a maximum common element set. An element of maximum position is called a maximum common element.

**Table 4.** The Positive Extension Matrix

$$PEM(e_1^+) = \begin{vmatrix} * & * & 2 \\ * & 0 & 2 \\ 1 & 0 & * \\ 1 & 0 & * \end{vmatrix} \quad PEM(e_2^+) = \begin{vmatrix} * & 1 & 2 \\ * & 1 & 2 \\ 1 & * & * \\ 1 & 1 & * \end{vmatrix} \quad PEM(e_3^+) = \begin{vmatrix} * & 2 & 2 \\ * & * & 2 \\ 1 & 2 & * \\ 1 & * & * \end{vmatrix}$$

$$PEM(e_4^+) = \begin{vmatrix} 0 & * & * \\ 0 & 0 & * \\ * & 0 & 1 \\ * & 0 & 1 \end{vmatrix} \quad PEM(e_5^+) = \begin{vmatrix} 0 & 1 & * \\ 0 & 1 & * \\ * & * & 1 \\ * & 1 & 1 \end{vmatrix}$$

**Definition 9**. let a attribute value $v_j \in D_j$, a positive extension matrix PEM $(e^+) = [r_{ij}]$ if $\exists p$ , $v_j = r_{pj}$, then $v_j$ covers $p^{th}$ row of PEM($e^+$), Let $[x_t = R_t]$ be a selector, $R_t$ is a common element set, then a intersect set of rows, covering respectively in the PEM, all the elements in $R_t$ is named as a covered row $[x_t = R_t]$.

**Definition 10** In all rows of the positive extension matrix, the row, in which the number of non-dead elements is smallest, is named as the smallest row.

Suppose an example $e^+ = <V_1,\ldots, V_n>$, and negative example matrix NE = $[v_{ij}^-]$. The positive extension matrix has following features:

(1) $r_{ij} = v_j,\ v_j \neq v_{ij}^-$

$r_{ij} = *,\ v_j = v_{ij}^-$

(2) If $e^+$ is not an element of NE, then there is at least one none dead element in every row of PEM($e^+$), so there is at least one path.

(3) The elements at the same column, if they are not dead elements, in a positive extension matrix, then those elements are same and it is an attribute of e+ in the position.

## 3 Positive Extension Matrix Algorithm $AE_{11}$

### 3.1 Algorithm $AE_{11}$

Given a positive example set PE, and negative example set NE

1 rule $\leftarrow \varnothing$; PEMS $\leftarrow$ PEM of all the positive examples in PE,

2 RS $\leftarrow$ PEMS,

3 Complex $\leftarrow \varnothing$,

4 Seeking an element, which must be selective from a row excepting for the marked rows for the PEM in RS, (at beginning there is no row marked), If there is such an element, we take the maximum common element from thus required

select elements, and put its common element set $R_j$ to complex, that is complex $\leftarrow$ complex $\wedge$ $[x_j = R_j]$; if there is no such element, Seeking an the minimum maximum element set $R_j$, which must be selective from a row excepting for the marked rows for the PEM in RS, and put it to complex, that is, is complex $\leftarrow$ complex $\wedge$ $[x_j = R_j]$;

5 RS $\leftarrow \varnothing$,

6 Putting PEM related to Complex into set RS; marking the rows of PEM which is covered by Complex in RS,

7 Checking if each row in each positive extension matrix in RS is marked, if no, goto step 4; if yes, deleting the positive examples covered by Complex from PE, and deleting PEM covered Complex from PEMS, if PE is empty, then terminal the algorithm; if PE is not empty, then rule $\leftarrow$rule $\vee$ Complex, goto step 2.

In the algorithm above, that the row in PEM is marked means that the corresponding negative examples are excluded, that is, an element in the row is put into a path. If all the rows in PEM are marked, then it means that a path or a formula is already found and the path or the formula will cover the positive example and exclude all negative examples. RS is a set of PEM related the current formula. It is a PEM set of positive examples covered by the current formula. As the current formula does not exclude all negative examples, those PEM must be put into RS to continue seeking a path according to PEM specialization.

$AE_{11}$ algorithm possesses its rationalization from the extension matrix path to form nature and to select an element.

(1) A required-select element is a unique no-dead element in some row of PEM. In order to exclude negative examples corresponding to the row, we can only relay on the element. This is a reason why it is a path that we must pass, that is, it must be selected. $AE_{11}$ first forms a path with it.

(2) When there is no required-selective element, $AE_{11}$ will select a minimum maximum common set to form a path. A minimum row includes less non-dead elements. When the path passes the row, it only can select these non-dead elements. Thus $AE_{11}$ may reduce a range of selecting an element.

(3) $AE_{11}$ is a MCV heuristic algorithm. Because of its nature (3), that is, non-dead elements in the same column in PEM are same. As soon as a selector is formed all rows that include non-dead elements in the column are covered. This means that every formula obtained has lest selectors (MCOMP algorithm). From this point of view $AE_{11}$ is a heuristic algorithm seeking OPL solutions.

### 3.2 Experimental Results and Comparison

The data from two domains are tested for $AE_{11}$, $AE_9$ and $AQ_{15}$. Here is the comparison of the results.

The first group data is the data of six-stage sleep of human being. We divide sleeping states in to six stages. Each stage is a class.

The data possess 11 attributes. The value of every attribute is from 0 –11. There are total 1236 examples here. The number of examples of every stage in sleeping is shown in Table 5:

**Table 5.** The number of examples of every stages in sleeping

| 1 | 2 | 3 | 4 | 5 | 6 |
|---|---|---|---|---|---|
| 115 | 103 | 688 | 158 | 58 | 134 |

**Table 6.** The number of rules produced by $AE_{11}$, $AE_9$ and $AQ_{15}$ on sleeping data

| Systems | Stages | | | | | |
|---|---|---|---|---|---|---|
| | 1 | 2 | 3 | 4 | 5 | 6 | Total |
| $AE_{11}$ | 7 | 8 | 11 | 9 | 7 | 4 | 46 |
| $AE_9$ | 8 | 10 | 13 | 10 | 8 | 4 | 53 |
| $AQ_{15}$ | 10 | 11 | 15 | 13 | 9 | 5 | 63 |

**Table 7.** The number of rules produced by $AE_{11}$, $AE_9$ and $AQ_{15}$ run on the data of handwritten number recognition sleep data

| Systems | Digitals | | | | | | | | | | |
|---|---|---|---|---|---|---|---|---|---|---|---|
| | 0 | 1 | 2 | 3 | 4 | 5 | 6 | 7 | 8 | 9 | Total |
| $AE_{11}$ | 4 | 4 | 10 | 6 | 16 | 13 | 4 | 10 | 8 | 12 | 87 |
| $AE_9$ | 4 | 5 | 10 | 8 | 17 | 14 | 5 | 11 | 9 | 13 | 96 |
| $AQ_{15}$ | 5 | 6 | 13 | 11 | 23 | 16 | 5 | 13 | 9 | 16 | 117 |

The algorithm $AE_{11}$, $AE_9$ and $AQ_{15}$ respectively run on the data. The total number of rules obtained by $AE_{11}$, $AE_9$ and $AQ_{15}$ is shown in Table 6. From this Table we know $AE_{11}$ obtained fewer rules than $AE_9$ and $AQ_{15}$. So the ability of inducing of $AE_{11}$ is most powerful.

The second group data is from the handwritten number recognition. The handwritten number recognition has 29 features. As there are 9 digits (0 – 9), so the examples are divided into 10 classes. We take handwritten numbers from 6000 persons and respectively abstracted rules with $AE_{11}$, $AQ_{15}$ and $AE_9$. The numbers of rules is shown in Table 7. The tested rules said that the rules obtained with $AE_{11}$ are simpler than $AE_9$ and $AQ_{15}$.

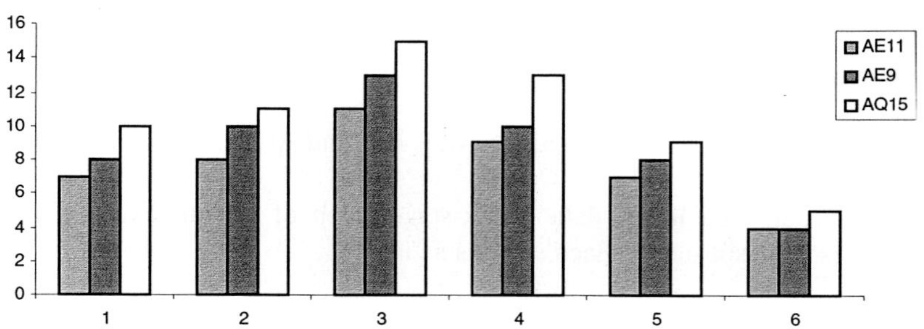


**Fig. 3.** The Comparison of the number of rules produced by $AE_{11}$, $AE_9$ and $AQ_{15}$

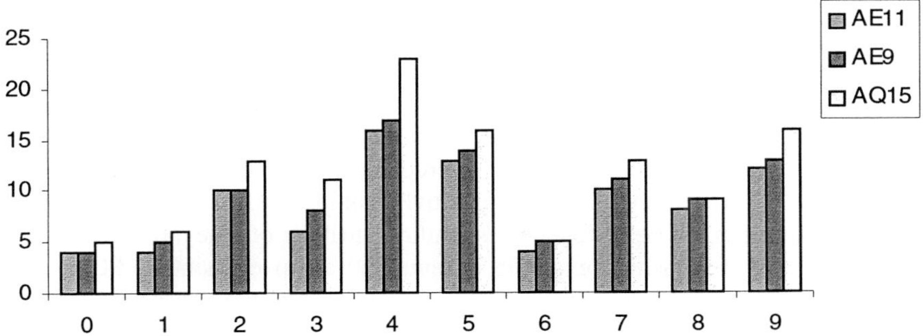


**Fig. 4.** The Comparison of the number of rules produced by $AE_{11}$, $AE_9$ and $AQ_{15}$

### 3.3 The Time Complexity Analysis for $AE_{11}$ Algorithm

The time complexity of $AE_{11}$ is related to the number of positive examples, the number of negative examples, the number of attributes and the situation for seeking the common paths. At the beginning of running the algorithm, in EPE (temporary positive example set) it includes all the positive examples, the number of examples is EPE-num, and in ENE (temporary negative example set) it includes all the negative examples, the number of examples is ENE-num. The time complexity in step 4 of the algorithm is a multiply of EPE-num, ENE-num and attr-num. As the algorithm is running normally the examples in EPE and ENE are becoming less and less so that when the step 4 is executed again, the time complexity is less than the beginning. If the number of the examples is no change or change a little while running the algorithm, then it means that there exist the common paths among all or most of positive extension matrices. In these cases EPE-number is big a little but the number of the common paths that need to seek by the algorithm is less. So some loops, for example step 4-7 , are executed less time, generally speaking, EPE-number is slowly getting small. The time complexity caused by loop in the algorithm is getting less. The time complexity in step 6 of the algorithm is almost same as the time complexity in step 4 of the algorithm. When finding a position of the common element in the algorithm, as it is for the particular negative example and the particular attribute, the time complexity is O(EPE-num).

## 4 Summary

The achievements of this paper are included:

1. The idea of positive extension matrix (PEM) is put forwards. Extension matrix (EM) is put forwards by Jiarong Hong in 1985 and used in solving some problems such as demonstration of most optima ion cover problem (MCV), most simple formula problem (MCOMP), most optimising example problem (OPL) to be NP-hard, seeking low-boundary of MCV. An element in EM is a "dead-element*" or an

attribute value of a negative example. When an attribute value of a positive example is not equal to corresponding attribute value of a negative example, the latter is remained as an element of extension matrix. So the form of rules gotten by extension matrix is $[X_i \; A_i]$ . The relation character in formula is "unequal ($\neq$ )" which is not convenient in the real-world because people are accustomed to "equal (=)" and not to "unequal ($\neq$)". Positive Extension Matrix overcomes this shortcoming. Its element is a "dead-element *" or attribute value of a positive example. When an attribute value of a positive example is not equal to a corresponding attribute of a negative example, the attribute value of the positive example is remained as an element of PEM. So the form of rules gotten by PEM is $[X_i = A_i]$. Moreover, in PEM the non-dead elements in the same rank are all equal. So the algorithm $AE_{11}$ developed based on PEM is approximately an algorithm of OPL. At the same time PEM makes implementation of algorithms more convenient and easier than EM.

2. An algorithm $AE_{11}$ is built with the aid of PEM. So far three algorithms have been developed on the basis of an extension matrix. They are $AE_1$, $AE_5$ and $AE_9$ respectively. Among them, $AE_1$ is fundamental. $AE_5$ was achieved by adding incremental learning and constructive learning functions to $AE_1$. $AE_9$ was built with the aid of generalized extension matrix, which is an extension matrix of formula (An extension matrix is an extension matrix of an example). $AE_{11}$ is built with the aid of PEM. In forming complexes "essential elements" and "mini-max elements" enjoy priority in order to make rules induced simpler.

**Acknowledgements**

The authors would like to thank Mr. Francisco Augusto Alcaraz Carcia, of the Abo Academy University in Finland, for his kindly help to complete the paper and some useful ideas for this project,

## References

1. E.A., Feigenbaum. Expert systems in the 1980s. In A. Bond(ED.), State of the art report on machine intelligence. Maidenhead: Perdamon-Infotech. 1981.
2. B. Hayes-Roth. The architecture for adaptive intelligent systems. Artificial Intelligence, 72:329-365, 1995.
3. B. Hayes-Roth, K. Pfleger, P. Lalanda, P. Morignot, and M. Balabanovic. A domain-specific software architecture for adaptive intelligent systems. IEEE Transactions on Software Engineering, 21(4):288-301,1995.
4. Jiarong Hong "AE1: An extension Matrix Approximate Method for the general Covering Problem", International Journal of Computer and Information Science, Vol. 14, No. 6, 1985.
5. Jiarong Hong "The theory of the extension matrix for the learning from examples", The Journal of Computer, (China), No. 6, 1991, p401-410.
6. Jiarong Hong "The learning from examples and Multi-functions learning algorithm AE5" The Journal of Computer, (China), No. 12, 1989.

7. A. K Jain., R. C Duber. "Algorithms for clustering data." Englewood Cliffs. NJ: Prentice-Hall. P42-59, 1988.
8. J.E. Laird and P.S. Rosenbloom "Toward Chunking as a General learning Mechanism", Proceedings of AAAI-84, Austin, Tex., 1984:p188-192.
9. RP. Lippman An introduction to computing with neural nets. IEEE ASSP Magazine April, 4-22 (1987).
10. R. S. Michalski and Jiarong Hong, "The Multi-purpose Incremental Learning System AQ15 and its Testing Application to Three medical domains", Proc. AAAI Vol. 2, August 1986, p1041-1045.
11. B.D. Ripley "Neural Networks and related methods for classification." Journal of the Royal. Stat. Society. 56(3):409-437, 1994.
12. Hugh J. Watson and Robert I. Mann. Expert System: Past, Present, and Future. Journal of International System management. 1998, Vol. 5, No. 4:39-46.

# Applying Semantic Links for Classifying Web Pages*

Ben Choi and Qing Guo

Computer Science, College of Engineering and Science
Louisiana Tech University, Ruston, LA 71272, USA
pro@BenChoi.org

**Abstract.** Automatic hypertext classification is an essential technique for organizing vast amount of Internet Web pages or HTML documents. One the of problems in classifying Web pages is that Web pages are usually short and contain insufficient text to clearly identify its category. Text classification mechanisms, by analyzing only the contents of the document itself, are relatively ineffective in classifying short Web pages. This paper proposes a new hypertext classification mechanism to address the problem by analyzing not only the Web page itself but also its linked Web pages referred by the URLs contained within the page. The URLs are treated as semantic links. The hypothesis is that the linked Web pages contain related information to help identifying the category of the Web page. Experimental results show that the proposed approach could increase the accuracy by 35% over the approach of analyzing only the Web page itself.

## 1 Introduction

Automatic hypertext categorization is an important technique for organizing vast amount of information available on the Internet and Intranet. However, Web pages or HTML documents tend to be short and usually contain insufficient text to clearly identify its category.

Many text classification mechanisms, by analyzing only the contents of the document itself, are relatively ineffective in classifying short Web pages. Rocchio [15], for instance, is a classification mechanism where a training set of documents are used to construct a prototype vector for each category, and category ranking given for a document is based on a similarity comparison between the document vector and the category vectors. Vector Space Model [1] [2] is a relatively new approach introduced by Vapnik in 1995 for solving two-class pattern recognition problems. The methods is defined over a vector space where the problem is to find a decision surface that best separates the data points in two classes. Bayes Rule [5] categorization comes from ideas in probability and information theory. A growing number of machine learning methods include LLSF [6]-a regression model, kNN [7]-a nearest neighbor classifier, RIPPER [8] and Charade-rule learning algorithms [9], Swap-1 [10], Widrow-Hoff [11], EG [12], and Experts [13]-inductive learning algorithms. Other techniques include fuzzy retrieval [3], neural network approaches [4], and so on.

---

* This research was supported in part by Center for Entrepreneurship and Information Technology (CEnIT), Louisiana Tech University, Grant iCSe 200123.

P.W.H. Chung, C.J. Hinde, M. Ali (Eds.): IEA/AIE 2003, LNAI 2718, pp. 148–153, 2003.

This paper proposes a new hypertext classification mechanism to address the problem by analyzing not only the Web page itself but also its linked Web pages referred by the URLs containing within the page (see Fig. 1). The URLs are treated as semantic links. The semantic relationship between a Web page and its linked pages can be generalization ("is-a"), association ("use"), aggregation ("has"), and composition ("part-of"). The hypothesis is that the linked Web pages (page 1 to n) contain information related to Web page 0. The related information is used to facilitate the identification of the category of Web page 0. If a Web page does not contain any URL, then a standard classifier is used.

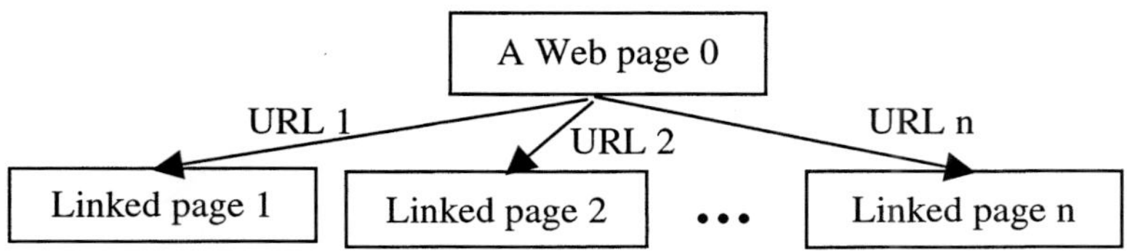


**Fig. 1.** Relation of a Web page and its linked pages

## 2 Proposed Page and Linked Pages (PLP) Classification

### 2.1 Architecture

Our proposed Page and Linked Pages (PLP) classification method consists of extracting surrounding information of a Web page by analyzing its linked Web pages. The overall architecture of the PLP classification is described in Fig. 2.

The Web page categorization process begins by using a standard text classifier to classify the Web page. For each URL contained within the Web page, the process retrieves and classifies the linked Web page. The process, then, computes the similarity between the resulting page category and each resulting linked page category, and assigned the similarity as a weight to each linked page. It groups linked pages that belongs to a same category and computes the weight of the group as the sum of the weights of its members. It selects the group having the highest weight and compares the highest weight with a given threshold. If the highest weight is larger than the threshold, then the process changes the page category to the category of the group that has the highest weight, otherwise it keeps the original category of the page.

### 2.2 Algorithm

We constructed the text classifier (see Fig. 2) based on term weighing approach [14]. In general the approach takes a document and builds a dictionary of its words (also called terms). It eliminates common words (also called stop words) such as pronouns, articles, and prepositions. For each word in the dictionary, it counts the number of occurrences in the document. The number is normalized to become a percentage. In

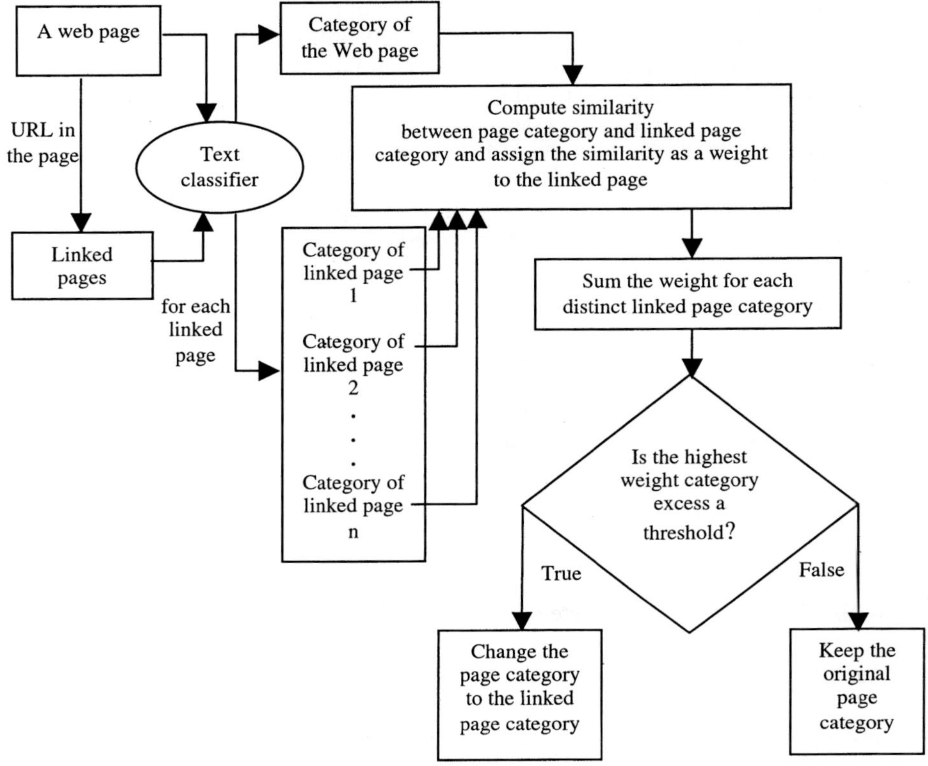


**Fig. 2.** Structure of PLP Classification

short, a document $D$ is represented by a set of ordered pair of a term $t$ and its corresponding weight $v$ (as shown in equation below).

$$D = \{(t_1, v_1), (t_2, v_2), \cdots, (t_m, v_m)\}$$

Similarly, a category $C$ is also represented by a set of ordered pair of term $s$ and its corresponding weight $u$ as shown below:

$$C = \{(s_1, u_1), (s_2, u_2), \cdots, (s_n, u_n)\}$$

To compute the similarity between a document $D$ and a category $C$, first obtain the intersection $E$ of the set of terms for $D$ and the set of terms for $C$, that is,

$$E = \{t_1, t_2, \cdots, t_n\} \cap \{s_1, s_2, \cdots, s_m\}$$

For each term in $E$ computes the product of its corresponding weights $v$ and $u$. The summation of all the products is a measure of similarity. This number is usually normalized to maximum similarity as 1.

We used the same process to compute the similarity between the page category $P$ and a linked page category $L$ (Fig. 2). The resulting similarity is then assigned as a weight to the linked page. Some of the linked pages may belong to the same category. We compute the sum of weight for each group of linked pages that belong to a category, says *G*. For each category of linked pages, we calculate the weight for it by using equation below.

$$w_l = \sum_{j=1}^{q} Similarity(P, L_j) \cdot \eta$$

Where $w_l$ is total weight of category *G*, *Lj* is the category of linked page *j* in list of linked pages, *q* is total number of linked pages, and $\eta = \begin{cases} 0 & \text{if } Lj \bullet G \\ 1 & \text{if } Lj = G \end{cases}$

$$W_k = \max(w_1, w_2, \cdots, w_q)$$

where $W_k$ is the highest weight in category list, let that category be *K*. The final category *C* for the page are decided by equation below:

$$C = \begin{cases} K & \text{if } W_k \geq \tau \\ P & \text{if } W_k < \tau \end{cases}$$

where *K* is the category having the highest weight in category list, and *P* is the page category. The $\tau$ is a threshold that determines how much influence the linked information will affect the page category. It is obtained empirically based on results of category similarity matrix (Table 1).

## 3 Experiments and Performance

### 3.1 Experiments

We experiment using 18 categories (Table 2) and a pre-classified training set of 2000 pages selected from top-level Yahoo. Using these pages we build a term frequency vector to represent each of the categories. To categorize a new Web page and its

**Table 1.** Category Similarity Matrix

| | A | B | C | D | E | F | G | H | I | J | K | L | M | N | O | P | Q | R |
|---|---|---|---|---|---|---|---|---|---|---|---|---|---|---|---|---|---|---|
| **A** | 1 | .58 | .85 | .30 | .44 | .49 | .41 | .33 | .27 | .21 | .47 | .66 | .73 | .30 | .55 | .30 | .61 | .39 |
| **B** | .58 | 1 | .60 | .19 | .30 | .39 | .29 | .32 | .28 | .19 | .35 | .62 | .36 | .19 | .57 | .29 | .49 | .24 |
| **C** | .85 | .60 | 1 | .61 | .49 | .74 | .62 | .47 | .24 | .23 | .58 | .70 | .80 | .41 | .82 | .62 | .76 | .46 |
| **D** | .30 | .19 | .61 | 1 | .33 | .52 | .49 | .28 | .03 | 0 | .25 | .35 | .48 | .31 | .65 | .65 | .53 | .24 |
| **E** | .44 | .30 | .49 | .33 | 1 | .43 | .33 | .53 | .37 | .36 | .37 | .65 | .50 | .34 | .53 | .42 | .61 | .45 |
| **F** | .49 | .39 | .74 | .52 | .43 | 1 | .58 | .60 | .28 | .18 | .71 | .64 | .73 | .42 | .71 | .61 | .81 | .44 |
| **G** | .41 | .29 | .62 | .49 | .33 | .58 | 1 | .47 | .16 | .10 | .38 | .52 | .54 | .38 | .69 | .54 | .72 | .29 |
| **H** | .33 | .32 | .47 | .28 | .53 | .60 | .47 | 1 | .55 | .42 | .62 | .83 | .45 | .59 | .56 | .52 | .80 | .46 |
| **I** | .27 | .28 | .24 | .03 | .37 | .28 | .16 | .55 | 1 | .48 | .39 | .74 | .24 | .30 | .34 | .15 | .51 | .40 |
| **J** | .21 | .19 | .23 | 0 | .36 | .18 | .10 | .42 | .48 | 1 | .37 | .60 | .19 | .27 | .25 | .11 | .42 | .31 |
| **K** | .47 | .35 | .58 | .25 | .37 | .71 | .38 | .62 | .39 | .37 | 1 | .71 | .50 | .40 | .46 | .35 | .70 | .48 |
| **L** | .66 | .62 | .70 | .35 | .65 | .64 | .52 | .83 | .74 | .60 | .71 | 1 | .68 | .56 | .70 | .47 | .87 | .79 |
| **M** | .73 | .36 | .80 | .48 | .50 | .73 | .54 | .45 | .24 | .19 | .50 | .68 | 1 | .39 | .67 | .46 | .73 | .46 |
| **N** | .30 | .19 | .41 | .31 | .34 | .42 | .38 | .59 | .30 | .27 | .40 | .56 | .39 | 1 | .40 | .34 | 63 | .32 |
| **O** | .55 | .57 | .82 | .65 | .53 | .71 | .69 | .56 | .34 | .25 | .46 | .70 | .67 | .40 | 1 | .77 | .74 | .48 |
| **P** | .30 | .29 | .62 | .65 | .42 | .61 | .54 | .52 | .15 | .11 | .35 | .47 | .46 | .34 | .77 | 1 | .66 | .36 |
| **Q** | .61 | .49 | .76 | .53 | .61 | .81 | .72 | .80 | .51 | .42 | .70 | .87 | .73 | .63 | .74 | .66 | 1 | .56 |
| **R** | .39 | .24 | .46 | .24 | .45 | .44 | .29 | .46 | .40 | .31 | .48 | .79 | .46 | .32 | .48 | .36 | .56 | 1 |

**Table 2.** Top 18 Categories

| Letter | Category | Letter | Category | Letter | Category |
|---|---|---|---|---|---|
| A | Companies | G | Health | M | Regional |
| B | Computers | H | Humanities | N | Religion |
| C | Economy | I | Movies TV | O | Science |
| D | Education | J | Music | P | Social Science |
| E | Fine Arts | K | News and Media | Q | Society & Culture |
| F | Government | L | Recreation | R | Sports |

linked pages we stripped the HTML tags, compute the word frequency vector of the pages, and calculate the similarities of the page and the categories. In order to speed up the classification process, we pre-calculated the similarities of the top 18 categories and save them in a category similarity table (Table 1). The threshold we use in the experiment is 0.65.

### 3.2 Performance

We randomly selected 32 Web pages from Yahoo top-level categories. These pages contain total 195 linked pages, average 6.1 links per web page. All 227 pages were classified by page classifier and the PLP classifier. In addition, we tested a large number of pages as part of our personal Web search filter project reported elsewhere.

Chart 1 shows the results of correct category numbers against Yahoo document categories by using page only classification and by using PLP classification. Chart 2 shows the correct percentage rate by using page only classification and by using PLP classification.

By using page only classifier to classify a web page, the correct percentage rate against Yahoo is 56%. Using the proposed PLP classifier, the correct percentage rate increase 35%. In this way, the correct percentage rate against Yahoo is 91%. These results show that the proposed PLP classifier could significantly increase the accuracy of automatic Web page classification. We anticipate if the proposed PLP classifier is used in conjunction with better page only classifier, the overall accuracy will improve further.

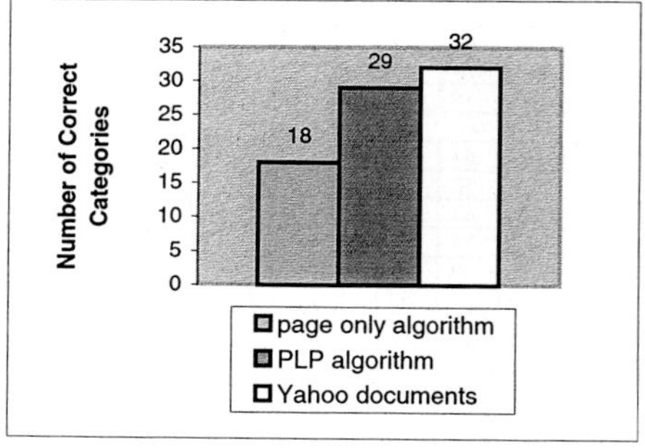


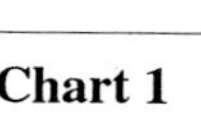

Chart 1

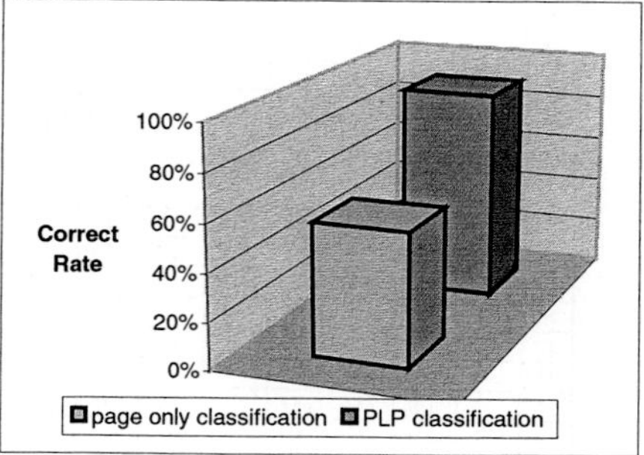


Chart 2

## 4 Conclusion

We described a new approach to automatically classify hypertext documents. The proposed approach exploits surrounding information extracted from analyzing linked documents. Our experimental results show that the proposed classifier could increase the overall accuracy of the classification by 35%. Much future research could be conducted on exploiting additional semantic information included in HTML documents.

## References


1. G. Salton, A. Wong, and C.S. Yang, A Vector Space Model for Automatic Indexing, *Communications of the ACM*, 18, pp. 613–620, 1975
2. D. D. Lewis, R. E. Schapire, J. P. Callan, and R. Papka, Training Algorithms for Linear Text Classifiers, In SIGIR '96, Proceedings of the 19th Annual International ACM SIGIR Conference on Research and Development in Information Retrieval, pp. 298-306, 1996
3. A. Bookstein and W.S. Cooper, A General Mathematical Model for Information Retrieval Systems, Library Quarterly, 46, pp. 153–167, 1976
4. E. Wiener, J.O. Pedersen, and A.S. Weigend, A Neural Network Approach to Topic Spotting, In Proceedings of the Fourth Annual Symposium on Document Analysis and Information Retrieval (SDAIR'95), 1995.
5. Joachims Thorsten, A Probabilistic Analysis of the Rocchio Algorithm with TFIDF for Text Categorization, Proceedings of International Conference on Machine Learning (ICML), 1997.
6. Y Yang and C. G. Chute, An Example-based Mapping Method for Text Categorization and Retrieval, *ACM Transaction on Information Systems* (TOIS), 12(3), pp.252-277, 1996.
7. Bulur v. Dasarathy, Nearest Neighbor (NN) Norms: NN pattern Classification Techniques, McGraw-Hill Computer Science Series. IEEE Computer society Press, Las Alamitos, California, 1991.
8. William W. Cohen and Yoram Singer, Context-sensitive learning methods for text categorization, In SIGIR 96: Proceedings of the 19th annual International ACM SIGIR Conference on Research and Development in Information Retrieval, pp.307-315, 1996
9. J. G. Ganascia, Deriving the Learning Bias from Rule Prosperities, *Machine Intelligence* 12, pp. 151-167, Clarendon Press, Oxford, 1991.
10. C. Apte, F. Damerau, and S. M. Weiss, Automated Learning of Decision Rules for Text Categorization, *ACM Transactions on Information Systems*, 1994
11. B. Widrow and S. D. Stearns, *Information Retrieval*, Butterworths, London, Second edition, 1996
12. J. Kivinen and M. K. Kivinen, Worst-case Loss Bounds for Single Neurons, In Advances in Neural Information Processing System, In SIGIR'94, pp.192-201
13. William W. Cohen and Yoram Singer, Context-sensitive learning methods for text categorization, In SIGIR 96: Proceedings of the 19th annual International ACM SIGIR Conference on Research and Development in Information Retrieval, 1996, 307-315
14. G Salton and C. Buckley, Term weighting approach in automatic text retrieval, *Information Processing and Management*, 24(5), pp. 513-523, 1988
15. Joachims Thorsten, A Probabilistic Analysis of the Rocchio Algorithm with TFIDF for Text Categorization, Proceedings of International Conference on Machine Learning (ICML), 1997.

# Learning Joint Coordinated Plans in Multi-agent Systems

Walid E. Gomaa[1], Amani A. Saad[2], and Mohamed A. Ismail[2]

[1] Department of Computer Science
University of Maryland College Park
College Park, MD, 20742
USA
walid@cs.umd.edu
[2] Department of Computer Science
Alexandria University
Alexandria, 21544
Egypt

**Abstract.** One important class of problems in Multi-Agent Systems (MASs) is planning, that is constructing an optimal policy for each agent with the objective of reaching some terminal goal state. The key aspect of multi-agent planning is coordinating the actions of the individual agents. This coordination may be done through communication, learning, or conventions imposed at design time. In this paper we present a new taxonomy of MASs that is based on the notions of optimality and rationality. A framework that describes the interactions between the agents and their environment is given, along with a reinforcement learning-based algorithm (Q-learning) for learning a joint optimal plan. Finally, we give some experimental results on grid games that show the convergence of this algorithm.

## 1 Introduction

Multi-Agent Systems is the branch of Artificial Intelligence that views the emergence of intelligence as a result of the interactions between multiple autonomous independent agents. One major problem in MASs is that of planning.

The key aspect of multi-agent planning is coordinating the actions of the individual agents. Coordination can be achieved by communication, conventions imposed by the system designer, or learning through repeated interaction.

Planning in single-agent systems has been addressed through Q-learning. One basic assumption for the convergence of this algorithm is that the agent-environment interaction can be modeled as a stationary Markov Decision Process (MDP). In this paper it is shown that this assumption can not be maintained in MASs because of the existence of other agents who cause unpredictable evolution of the environment.

So far in practice, most people still use single-agent Q-learning for learning in MASs [3]. However, during the past few years some multi-agent Q-learning algorithms have been proposed. For example, [4] extends Q-learning to zero-sum MASs. [2] further extends the work of [4] to the case of general-sum MASs that have certain restrictions. [5] uses single-agent Q-learning in the multi-agent setting giving the agents the facility to communicate. The purpose of communication is to share sensation, experience, and learned knowledge. [1] conjectures that single-agent Q-learning

P.W.H. Chung, C.J. Hinde, M. Ali (Eds.): IEA/AIE 2003, LNAI 2718, pp. 154–165, 2003.

will lead to equilibrium strategies in the fully cooperative MASs. The research done in this paper represents another attempt to extend the Q-learning algorithm to the multi-agent setting.

Section 2 addresses the planning problem in single-agent systems. In Section 3, we propose a new MASs taxonomy based on two basic notions: rationality and optimality. In Section 4, we extend the MDP model to cooperative MASs along with an algorithm to solve it. In Section 5 we show the experimental results along with a further extension to the learning algorithm. Section 6 concludes the paper.

## 2 Single-Agent Planning

### 2.1 Markov Decision Process

*Definition 1: Markov Decision Process:* MDP = (S,A,T,R) where

1. S is a discrete finite state space.
2. A is the agent's action space.
3. T is the state transition function T: S x A x S → [0,1]. It defines a probability distribution over next states as a function of the current state and the agent's action.
4. R is a bounded reward function R: S x A → $\Re$ ($\Re$ is the set of real numbers). It defines the expected immediate reward received when selecting an action from the given state.

An MDP has two basic properties: (1) it is Markovian, that is the state at time t+1 is completely specified by the state and action at time t and (2) it is stationary, that is T and R (the dynamics of the system) do not change over time.

Solving MDPs consists of finding a stationary optimal policy or plan, $\pi^*$: S→A, by which the agent can reach his goal. This leads to the definition of the *optimal action-value function* $Q^*(s,a)$ as follows:

$$Q^*(s,a) = R(s,a) + \gamma \sum_{s' \in S} \left[ T(s,a,s') V^*(s') \right], \quad V^*(s') = \max_{a' \in A} Q^*(s',a') \tag{1}$$

where $\gamma \in [0,1)$ is the *discount factor*. By solving Equation (1) for $Q^*(s,a)$ (given T,R are known), the task of finding an optimal policy becomes trivial:

$$\pi^*(s) = \arg\max_{a \in A} Q^*(s,a) \tag{2}$$

### 2.2 Q-Learning

In this algorithm learning is done directly from raw experience without a model of the environment's dynamics (the functions T and R). It is defined by the following update rule:

$$Q_{t+1}(s_t, a_t) \leftarrow Q_t(s_t, a_t) + \alpha_t \left( r_{t+1} + \gamma \max_{a \in A} Q_t(s_{t+1}, a) - Q_t(s_t, a_t) \right) \quad \textbf{(3)}$$

where $\alpha_t \in [0,1]$ is the learning rate. Q-learning is very well suited to solve the planning problem in single-agent systems and it is a good starting point for multi-agent planning due to the following reasons:

- □ It is a learning technique for multi-stage (delayed reward) tasks.
- □ It does not require a knowledge of the environment's model. Unknown model is often the case in real systems.
- □ Due to its incremental nature, it is efficient in terms of both time and storage.

## 3 A Taxonomy of Multi-agent Systems

Here we classify MASs according to the notions of rationality and optimality. An agent is rational if he always follows an optimal policy given the stationary joint policy of the other agents. The ideal optimal value of an agent is the possible maximum payoff the agent can gain. The real optimal value of an agent is the minimum level of expected payoff the agent guarantees given that all agents are rational.

Given these notions, MASs can be classified as follows:

- □ *Cooperative MASs (CMASs):* all agents can together achieve ideal optimality if and only if they are rational by following a stationary joint deterministic policy.
  - □ *Strongly Cooperative MASs (SCMASs):* SCMASs are CMASs which have the following property: if at least one agent is not rational, then none of the agents in the system can achieve his ideal optimality.
  - □ *Weakly Cooperative MASs (WCMASs):* WCMASs are CMASs which have the following property: there exists at least one joint policy by which some agents can achieve their ideal optimality while the others can not.
- □ *Competitive MASs (CTMASs):* given all agents are rational one or more agents can not achieve their ideal optimality. They can only achieve real optimality.
  - □ *Strongly Competitive MASs (SCTMASs):* SCTMASs are CTMASs where the agents can only follow a stationary non-deterministic joint policy.
  - □ *Weakly Competitive MASs (WCTMASs):* WCTMASs are CTMASs where the agents can follow a stationary deterministic joint policy.

## 4 Multi-agent Planning

Multi-agent planning consists of multiple single-agent planning problems, however, each agent must also consider the constraints imposed by the existence of other agents (activities, commitments, unpredictable evolution). Given this additional constraint the single-agent Q-learning based on the MDP model will not converge (the Q-function will actually oscillate due to the non-stationarity of the environment).

To recover stationarity, each agent must be aware of the others. We propose four levels of awareness where each level includes all the preceding ones plus an additional feature of its own. These levels are as follows:

- □ Level-1: Each agent considers the other agents as part of the environment state. For example, the environment state will consist of all agents' positions within the environment instead of a single agent's position.
- □ Level-2: Each agent considers the payoff functions of the other agents. This implies that each agent considers joint actions with other agents.
- □ Level-3: Each agent models the behavior of the other agents. This means that each agent tries to model or predict the learned plans of the others.
- □ Level-4: Each agent tries to model the internal state of the other agents.

Given that all agents are rational and are using the same learning algorithm, we assume only level-2 of awareness. This leads to the extension of the MDP model to:

*Definition 2: Multi-Agent Markov Decision Process (MMDP):* MMDP = (n, S, A, T, R), where n is the number of agents, S is the joint state space, A is the joint action space, T: S x A x S → [0,1] is the transition probability function, and R: S x A → $\Re^n$ is the joint reward function.

Solution to the MMDP planning problem combines ideas from two fields:

- □ Reinforcement Learning (Q-learning): where the multi-agent planning problem is a multi-step model-free problem so incremental experience-based learning is required.
- □ Game Theory: where the concept of matrix games is used to reformulate the multi-agent planning problem and to provide a new meaning to the Q-function.

## 4.1 Matrix Games

*Definition 3: Matrix Game (MG):* MG = (n, A, $P_{1..n}$), where n is the number of agents, A is the joint action space, and $P_i$: A → $\Re$ is the payoff function of agent i.

The ideal optimal value of agent i is defined as follows:

$$P_i^* = \max_{\overline{a} \in A} P_i(\overline{a}) \quad \textbf{(4)}$$

MGs can be viewed as single-state MMDPs, so the taxonomy of MASs can be applied to them. Figure 1 shows the coin matching game where each of two agents has two available actions: Head and Tail. If both agents take the same action, the row agent wins a dollar from the column one, otherwise he loses a dollar to him.

| | H | T |
|---|---|---|
| H | (1,-1) | (-1,1) |
| T | (-1,1) | (1,-1) |

**Fig. 1.** the coin matching game

Solution of MGs is based on the Nash equilibrium concept. In a Nash equilibrium, each agent's strategy is the best response to other agents' strategies, so no agent can do better by changing his strategy given that the other agents continue to follow the equilibrium strategy. What makes the notion of equilibrium compelling is that all matrix games have a Nash equilibrium, although there may be more than one.

In cooperative games there may exist multiple equilibria and hence arises the problem of which one should the agents choose for coordination given that they are not communicating. We solved this problem by assuming the pre-imposed lexicographic convention as follows:

- □ The set of agents is ordered.
- □ The set of actions available to each agent is ordered.
- □ These orderings are known by all agents.

Given this information, a cooperative MG can be solved as follows: Each agent i extracts all joint ideal optimal deterministic equilibrium strategy profiles. In each of these profiles the actions of the low order agents come first. Then agent i sorts these profiles lexicographically, that is, starting from the actions of the low order agents, the profiles with the low order actions come first. Finally, agent i adopts the $i^{th}$ component of the first profile as his action.

### 4.2 Cooperative Multi-agent Markov Decision Process (CMMDP)

It is mentioned above that a MG can be modeled as a single-state MMDP. This idea can be reversed, that is a state in an MMDP can be modeled as a MG. So an MMDP can be redefined as a set of interdependent MGs. This new view of an MMDP is formalized for *cooperative* MASs as follows.

*Definition 4: Cooperative Multi-Agent Markov Decision Process (CMMDP):* A Cooperative Multi-Agent Markov Decision Process (CMMDP) is a 5-tuple (n, G, A, T, R) where

1. n is the number of agents.
2. $G = \{M_i : 1 \le i \le m\}$, is a set of interdependent cooperative MGs (m corresponds to the number of states, that is |S|).
3. A is the agents joint action space, $A = A_1 \times A_2 \times \ldots \times A_n$ , where $A_j$ is the set of actions available to agent j.
4. T is the probability transition function between the MGs, T: G x A x G → [0,1]. It defines a probability distribution over next MGs to be played as a function of the current MG and the agents' joint action.
5. R is the joint reward function, R: G x A → $\Re^n$. It defines a vector of expected immediate rewards for all agents when they take a particular joint action in a particular matrix game.

Each matrix game $M_i \in G$ is a 3-tuple (n, $A_{1\ldots n}$ , $P^i_{1\cdots n}$), where

1. $A_j$ is the action space of agent j.
2. $P^i_j$ is agent j's payoff function in MG $M_i$, $P^i_j$ : A → $\Re$ . It is defined as follows:

$$P_j^i(\overline{a}) = R_j(M_i, \overline{a}) + \gamma \sum_{k=1}^{m} \left[ T(M_i, \overline{a}, M_k) O_j(M_k) \right] \quad (5)$$

$$O_j(M_k) = \max_{\overline{a} \in A} P_j^k(\overline{a}) \quad (6)$$

Equation 6 defines the ideal optimal value of agent j in matrix game $M_k$.

Solving a CMMDP means finding a *global* joint policy that is ideal optimal for all agents. The proposed solution exploits the previous definition of CMMDP as follows: *the global task of finding a joint ideal optimal policy can be decomposed into finding ideal optimal solutions to the individual local cooperative MGs that comprise the CMMDP*. The formal algorithm, Extended-Q, for agent i can be outlined as follwos:

```
For every agent j initialize Qj(s,ā) arbitrarily (ā is
ordered according to Assumption 1 in the lexicographic
convention)

Repeat

Given the current state s, decide an action ai either by
solving the corresponding cooperative MG using the cur-
rent estimation of the Q-functions or by exploring a
random action.

Take action ai. Observe agents' actions aj's, next state
s', and agents' rewards rj's.

Update the Q-functions of all agents based on this ex-
perience as follows:
```

$$\forall j \; Q_j(s,\overline{a}) \leftarrow Q_j(s,\overline{a}) + \alpha \left( r_j + \gamma V_j(s') - Q_j(s,\overline{a}) \right) \quad (7)$$

$$V_j(s') = \max_{\overline{a}' \in A} Q_j(s', \overline{a}') \quad (8)$$

```
Vj(s') represents the ideal optimal value of agent j in
the cooperative MG that corresponds to state s'.

s ← s'

Until termination
```

## 5 Experiments

### 5.1 Grid Game 1

In grid game 1, there are two agents B and R who start from their initial cells as shown in Figure 2 and try to reach their goals at the top right and top left cells respectively. A game ends when an agent reaches his goal cell.

There are two settings of the game: (1) the strong cooperative setting where each agent receives a reward of 100 if and only if both agents reach their goal cells simultaneously and (2) the weak cooperative setting where the first agent reaching his goal cell will receive a reward of 100 regardless of the status of the other agent. A collision occurs if both agents try to occupy the same cell; they are bounced back to their original cells and each is penalized -1. Each agent gets 0 if reaching other cells without colliding.

The lexicographic convention is imposed as follows:

- ☐ Agents: (B, R).
- ☐ Actions: (East, West, North, South).
- ☐ The above orderings are known by both agents.

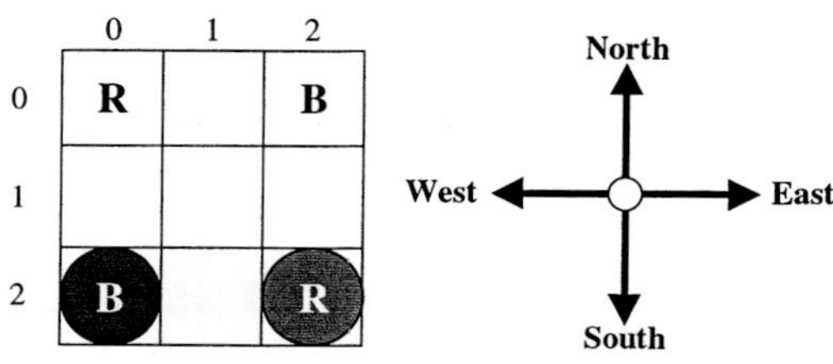


**Fig. 2.** Grid game 1

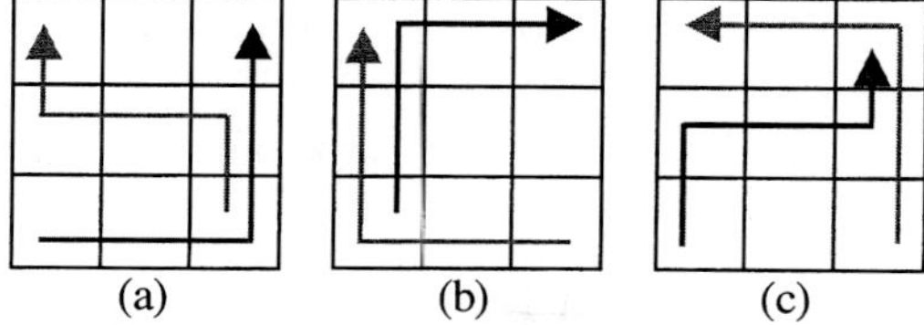


**Fig. 3.** Some solutions to grid game 1

**5.1.1 Game Solution.** Some of the solutions that are applicable to both settings of grid game 1 are shown in Figure 3.

Figure 4 shows the MG that corresponds to the initial state in the strong cooperative setting (with discount factor $\gamma = 0.999$).

| Blue/Red | E | W | N | S |
|---|---|---|---|---|
| E | (99.6,99.6) | (98.6,98.6) | * (99.7,99.7) | (99.6,99.6) |
| W | (99.6,99.6) | (99.6,99.6) | (99.6,99.6) | (99.6,99.6) |
| N | (99.6,99.6) | (99.7,99.7) | (99.7,99.7) | (99.6,99.6) |
| S | (99.6,99.6) | (99.6,99.6) | (99.6,99.6) | (99.6,99.6) |

**Fig. 4.** Initial state payoff matrix (strong cooperation setting)

All the rectangled profiles are pure (deterministic) equilibria, only three of them are ideal optimal for both agents namely: (E,N), (N,W), and (N,N). Due to the lexicographic convention both agents coordinate on (E,N). Since both agents have the same ideal optimal profiles, this MG is strongly cooperative. On the other hand, Figure 5 shows the counterpart MG in the weak cooperative setting. It has the same ideal optimal equilibria as in the strong setting. Due to the lexicographic convention, both agents coordinate on the profile (E,N).

We can see that some profiles in this MG are ideal optimal for one and only one agent, examples are: (E,E), (N,E), (W,W), and (W,N). This indicates that this MG is weakly cooperative.

| Blue/Red | E | W | N | S |
|---|---|---|---|---|
| E | (99.7,99.6) | (98.6,98.6) | * (99.7,99.7) | (99.7,99.6) |
| W | (99.6,99.6) | (99.6,99.7) | (99.6,99.7) | (99.6,99.6) |
| N | (99.7,99.6) | (99.7,99.7) | (99.7,99.7) | (99.7,99.6) |
| S | (99.6,99.6) | (99.6,99.7) | (99.6,99.7) | (99.6,99.6) |

**Fig. 5.** Initial state payoff matrix (weak cooperation setting)

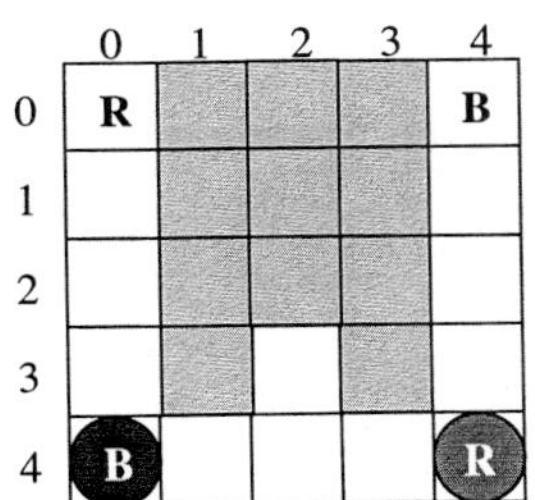


**Fig. 6.** Grid game 2

## 5.2 Grid Game 2

Grid game 2 is depicted in Figure 6. It is the same as grid game 1 except: (1) it is 5x5 board, (2) the agents can not move into the gray cells, and (3) a collision also occurs when both agents are trying to switch their cells.

In the strong cooperative setting both agents act as one team, that is each gains 100 only when they reach their goal cells simultaneously. In this case both agents succeeded to reach the joint plan shown in Figure 7.

**5.2.1 Weak Competition.** In this setting, any agent gains his positive reward only when he reaches his goal cell regardless of the status of the other agent. Clearly, the only possible solution to this game is that one agent x moves up to cell (2,3) to allow the other agent y to pass through. But agent x who makes this voluntary move becomes one step behind y who, given that he is rational, has no motivation to wait (unlike the strong cooperation setting where both agents act as a team) and so he moves straight to his goal cell winning the game while the other agent gains nothing. This implies that both agents can not win together so this game is competitive.

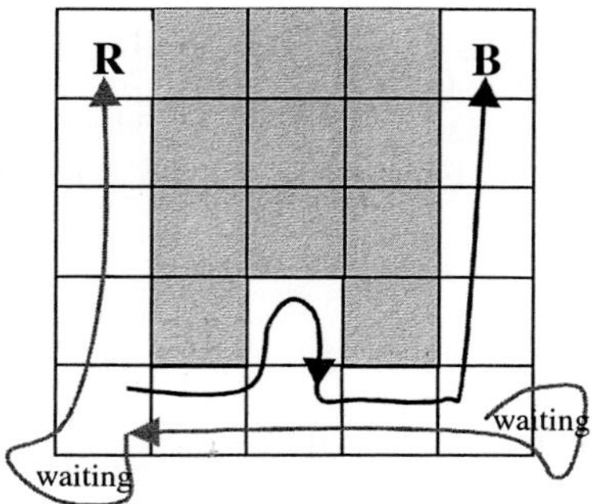


**Fig. 7.** Successful joint plan in grid game 2 (strong cooperation setting)

| Blue/Red | E | W | N | S |
|---|---|---|---|---|
| E | (99.1,99.2) | (98.2,98.2) | (99.2,99.3) | (99.2,99.3) |
| W | (99.1,99.1) | (99.2,99.1) | (99.2,99.1) | (99.2,99.1) |
| N | (99.1,99.2) | (99.3,99.2) | (99.2,99.2)* | (99.2,99.2) |
| S | (99.1,99.2) | (99.3,99.2) | (99.2,99.2) | (99.2,99.2) |

**Fig. 8.** Payoff matrix at state ((1,4),(3,4))

After each training phase it was observed that both agents adopt the initial joint action (E,W) moving to the critical state ((1,4),(3,4)) where a conflict arises between the two agents. Figure 8 shows the MG at this state.

This MG has many pure Nash equilibria which implies that the whole game has a pure equilibrium solution (it is the only state where the agents compete; other states comprise cooperative MGs). Hence grid game 2 in its second setting represents a weakly competitive MAS. These pure equilibria can be divided into three categories:

- The first group includes profiles: (E,N), (E,S), (N,W), and (S,W). In this group one agent x moves to cell (2,4) while the other agent y remains still in his cell. This ultimatley leads to agent y wins and x loses. Agent x is said to volunteer.
- The second group includes profiles: (W,E), (N,N), (N,S), (S,N), and (S,S). In this group neither agent volunteers and the game ends in draw.
- The third group includes profiles: (W,N), (W,S), (N,E), and (S,E). It was observed that the agent who remains still will ultimately lose the game.

From the discussion above the pure equilibria at state ((1,4),(3,4)) lead to one of the following:

- 100% of the games end in draw (the second group). This result is favored by the agents because of the domination of actions (north and south) that leads to a draw.

□ 100% of the games end in win for one and the same agent while the other agent gets nothing (the first and third groups).

By solving the MG in Figure 8 for mixed equilibria, we found that the resulting solutions to belong to the second group mentioned above, that is 100% of the games end in draw. So in searching for a better solution the non-equilibrium mixed profile ((0.5,0.0,0.5,0.0), (0.0,0.5,0.5,0.0)) is investigated. In this profile each agent volunteers 50% of the time and does not volunteer 50% of the time.

Given that the maximum game length k is sufficiently large, Table 1 compares between the equilibrium profile (N,N) and the non-equilibrium mixed profile (these results are obtained analytically and confirmed empirically).

**Table 1.** Performance comparison between the equilibrium and non-equilibrium profiles

| Equilibrium Joint Profile | Non-equilibrium Joint Profile |
|---|---|
| □ 100% of the games end in draw | □ 100% of the games end in win |
| □ Each agent has 0% chance of winning | □ Each agent has 50% chance of winning |
| □ The expected game length is k >> 10 | □ The expected game length is 10 |
| □ Probability of collision occurrence is 0 | □ Probability of collision occurrence is 1/3 |
| □ Expected number of collisions is 0 | □ Expected number of collisions is 0.5 |
| □ Expected payoff for each agent is 0.0 | □ Expected payoff for each agent is 49.5 |

From Table 1 it is clear that the non-equilibrium mixed strategy profile ((0.5,0.0,0.5,0.0), (0.0,0.5,0.5,0.0)) at the critical state ((1,4),(3,4)) outperforms the dominating pure equilibrium profile (N,N) at the same state. It is important to note that this conclusion is drawn given the framework of CMMDP.

We were motivated by the above result to develop a second version of the Extended-Q algorithm (for two agents) to handle WCTMASs as well as CMASs. First of all, the set of interdependent MGs of CMMDP may now be weakly competitive as well as cooperative. This is the only change to CMMDP.

The solution of a MG now goes as follows in version 2 of Extended-Q (the remaining steps are the same as in version 1):

```
Using the current learned estimation of the optimal
joint Q-function, find all pure Nash equilibrium strat-
egy profiles and sort them lexicographically. Let L be
the ordered list of these profiles.

Let I_j be the ideal optimal value of agent j, I_k be the
ideal optimal value of agent k.

Find the first profile ā_jk∈L: P_j(ā_jk) = I_j and P_k(ā_jk) = I_k

Find the first profile ā_j∈L: P_j(ā_j) = I_j, find the first
profile ā_k∈L: P_k(ā_k) = I_k.
```

```
Do one of the following:
If L = Φ, then it is a strongly competitive MG; exit.
If ā_jk ≠ nil, then it is a cooperative MG; play ā_jk; exit.
If exactly one of ā_j or ā_k is nil, then it is a weakly
competitive MG; play the non-nil profile; exit.
If (ā_j≠nil) and (ā_k≠nil) and (ā_j≠ā_k), then it is a weakly
competitive MG; play each profile of them with prob-
ability 0.5; exit.
```

Note that this version of the algorithm handles the following cases of weakly competitive MGs:

- The ideal optimal profiles of both agents are pure equilibria (play each with probability 0.5 to achieve fairness and avoid irresolvable draws).
- The ideal optimal profile of one agent exists while the other's does not. It is clear why the former profile should be played (the second agent (being rational) has no other choice since this profile is equilibrium).

So the only remaining case that is not handled by this algorithm is when both ideal optimal profiles are not equilibria.

## 6 Conclusion

The major points of this paper are:

- A new taxonomy of MASs is proposed. This taxonomy is based on two notions: rationality and optimality (both ideal and real). There are two main classes: cooperative MASs and competitive MASs. Within each class there are two subclasses: weak and strong.
- Single-agent Q-learning is shown to lack convergence guarantee when used in the multi-agent setting. The key aspect of successful planning in MASs is that each agent is aware of the existence of other agents. Four degrees of awareness are proposed. The research done assumes level-2.
- CMMDP (Cooperative Multi-Agent Markov Decision Process) is defined. It is a mathematical formulation of the planning problem in CMASs that greatly facilitates the task of finding a global joint optimal plan. CMMDP is based on the decomposition of the global planning problem into local MGs planning problems.
- A learning algorithm, called Extended-Q, is proposed to solve the planning problem in CMASs. Each MG is solved using the Nash equilibrium concept.
- A second version of this algorithm is proposed (with minor changes in the CMMDP framework) to solve the planning problem in most cases of WCMASs as well as CMASs.
- Experiments are performed on some grid games, as examples of MASs, these experiments show: (1) the convergence of Extended-Q to an ideal optimal joint plan in cooperative MASs and (2) the weakness of the Nash equilibrium solution concept in some weakly competitive MASs.

## References


1. Boutilier C., "Planning, Learning and Coordination in Multiagent Decision Processes," In Proceedings of the Sixth Conference on Theoretical Aspects of Rationality and Knowledge, pp. 195-210, Amsterdam, 1996.
2. Hu J. and Wellman M. P., "Multiagent Reinforcement Learning: Theoretical Framework and an Algorithm," In Proceedings of the Fifteenth International Conference on Machine Learning, pp. 242-250, San Francisco, CA, 1998.
3. Hu J. and Wellman M. P., "Experimental Results on Q-Learning for General-Sum Stochastic Games," In Proceedings of the $17^{th}$ International Conference on Machine Learning, pp. 407-414, 2000.
4. Littman M. L., "Markov games as a framework for multi-agent reinforcement learning," In Proceedings of the Eleventh International Conference on Machine Learning, pp. 157-163, New Brunswick, NJ, 1994.
5. Tan M., "Multi-Agent Reinforcement Learning: Independent vs. Cooperative Agents," In Proceedings of the Tenth International Conference on Machine Learning, pp. 330-337, 1993.

# Extracting Causal Nets from Databases

Chris J. Hinde

Department of Computer Science,
Loughborough University,
Loughborough,
Leicestershire,
LE11 3TU,
UK

**Abstract.** Causal nets (Pearl 1986) are an elegant way of representing the structure and relationships of a set of data. The propagation of changes through the net has been examined and reported on in many works (Pearl 1986, Lauritzen & Speigelhalter 1988, Neapolitan 1990). Causal nets are defined by the properties of conditional independence, and so the structure of the net may be obtained by discovering conditional independences. Many of the examples in the literature test for complete equality. However, the presence of noise and the unreliability of comparing two real numbers means that equality is taken to mean equality within a particular tolerance. Where a set of data contains a number of representative subsets this tolerance can be almost zero. If there is an incomplete subset in the data and conjoint events then the tolerance cannot be zero. The paper presents a method for estimating the size of the partial cohort, the size of the representative cohorts and thus provides a robust test for conditional independence.

**Keywords:** Reasoning Under Uncertainty, Machine Learning, Data Mining

## Introduction

The arguments given by Pearl and Neapolitan that a Causal Net represents the data more succinctly than an inference network are well made but do not compare causal nets with a full predicate calculus based representation. If the relationships embodied in a system are modelled without reference to any pre-defined conclusion the two representations are equivalent. The method of extracting relationships based on conditional independence results in useful knowledge about the structure of the data for many forms of representation. Kowalski (1980) shows that Horn clause formulation is inadequate to represent general predicate calculus problems and Clocksin & Mellish's conversion process between predicate calculus (Clocksin & Mellish 1981) amply reinforces this.

Poole (1993) shows how Horn Clauses are related to Causal Nets and points out the need for an exponentially large number of inference rules to model any discrete valued causal net. However Poole solves the equations by moving along the direction of the implication. If the relationships embodied in a system are modelled without reference to any pre-defined conclusion the two representations are equivalent,

P.W.H. Chung, C.J. Hinde, M. Ali (Eds.): IEA/AIE 2003, LNAI 2718, pp. 166–175, 2003.

however the propagation of belief becomes a central issue and the definition of implication based on the semantics of probability becomes that of a conditional probability. These conditional probabilities may be calculated from the joint probability table, however these tables become increasingly large as the number of variables increases and also as the number of values these variables may take increases. As any variable may depend on any other variable it is crucial that links between variables and propositions that carry no mutual influence are exploited to reduce the computation involved. Dubois et al (1997) and later Ben Amor (2000) explore various aspects of relevance, irrelevance and independence. Their qualitative independence measure is derived from an ordering induced by a possibility measure. The central theme though is based on formulae very close to the test for independence in probability, namely:

$C$ is independent of $A$ iff $Prob(C|A) = Prob(C)$.

This equality is central to independence and is also central to this paper.

## Burglar Alarm Problem

Throughout this paper the problem to be used as an illustration, as stated in Neapolitan (1990), and taken from Pearl (1986) is:

"Suppose that in the past few years, Mr Holmes has noticed that frequently earthquakes have caused his burglar alarm to sound. At present, he is sitting in his office, and his wife calls, informing him that the burglar alarm has sounded. He then rushes home, assuming that there is a good chance that his residence has been burglarized. On the way home, however, he hears on the radio that there is an earthquake. He now relaxes substantially, assuming that there is a good chance that the earthquake triggered his alarm."

Let the events be:

$A$ The burglar alarm sounds.

$E$ There is a earthquake.

$B$ The residence is burgled.

Figure 1 "tells it like it is". It is declarative and also represents a causal net. Although Pearl (1986) and Neapolitan (1990) use this example to show the complexity of a logic based representation, the logic statements that would be derived from Figure 1 are:

$$E \to A$$

$$B \to A$$

i.e.

$$E \vee B \to A$$

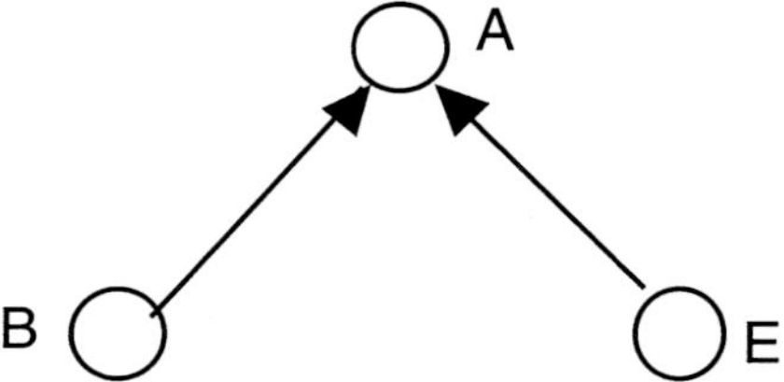


**Fig. 1**. The logic diagram showing that if there is a burglar ($B$) then the alarm sounds (event $A$) and if there is an earthquake (event $E$) then the alarm sounds (event $A$).

The causal net so derived, and also the logic statements are equivalent and are also equally succinct. However, by adding A to the logic statements we are unable to prove anything because the implications are in the wrong direction. All we are able to deduce is that the alarm has sounded and that it could be due to any one or more of a number of factors. Poole (1993) constructs an exponentially large set of implication rules to solve the problem, and furthermore requires independence between the rules. However, if we make the closed world assumption, that there are no other possible causes of event A (Reiter 1981), then this allows us to deduce the rule:

$$A \rightarrow E \vee B$$

and hence, from the new fact $A$, the statement:

$$E \vee B$$

By adding $\neg E$, $B$ may be deduced. The reason the alarm sounds is because of the burglar. This formulation is not required at the specification level and the deduction could be made by the system based on the closed world assumption.

The object of the preceding argument is to separate the specification from the implementation. All that is needed to represent the situation is the logical expression:

$$E \vee B \rightarrow A$$

Which is the equivalent of the causal net drawn in Figure 1

The implication rules have been treated as logical statements and so the problem can be solved naturally after making the closed world assumption.

In any useful representation of this scenario some measure of uncertainty is needed so we are able to take action based on the most likely outcome. The overall specification of the problem is identical in both cases. Specifying $B \rightarrow A$, we capture the essence of the situation for both causal nets and for logic systems. In this we are interpreting the $\rightarrow$ sign as meaning "influences".

We have so far shown that by treating rules as logical statements about the world they may be solved if the closed world assumption is made. In this treatment it is clear that the declarative nature of the statements enables situations to be represented clearly.

The use of the joint probability distribution in causal nets enables the direction of inference to be decided at execution time. Resolution of the rules and propagation of uncertainty may also be left until execution time.

The logic rules are:

$E \rightarrow A$

$B \rightarrow A$

Let the probabilities for the two links be as shown in Figure 2. These values have been calculated from a collection of fictitious data but are sufficient to illustrate the points. It is important to note that the original set of fictitious data is based on a set of events that are assigned to random sets based on the frame of discernment {f,t}, false {f}, true {t}, or undetermined {f,t}. From this set of events commitment to {f}, {t} and {f,t} may be calculated. From these values measures of possibility may be derived from {t} + {f,t}. The maximum likelihood probability of an event may be determined by assigning the uncommitted mass equally to {f} and {t}, {t} + {f,t}*0.5. This set of data will be explored later when evidence is extracted from a database is explored. The probabilities so derived are shown in figure 2.

| | | | |
|---|---|---|---|
| $P(B) =$ | 0.25 | $P(E) =$ | 0.2 |
| $P(A \mid B \wedge E) =$ | 1.0 | $P(A \mid B \wedge \neg E) =$ | 0.75 |
| $P(A \mid \neg B \wedge E) =$ | 1.0 | $P(A \mid \neg B \wedge \neg E) =$ | 0.25 |

**Fig. 2.** The minimal probabilities necessary for propagation.

Before Mr. Holmes knows his alarm has sounded he has a probability of being burgled is 0.25 on any given day; this is a very bad area for burglaries and earthquakes, and after he has been told his alarm has sounded the probability changes to:

$P(B \mid A) = 0.4$

If Mr. Holmes knows that an earthquake has not happened then he would be even more concerned. The causal net solution to this problem is given by $P(B \mid A \wedge \neg E)$ and results in:

$P(B \mid A \wedge \neg E) = 0.5$

However, if he knows an earthquake has happened

$P(B \mid A \wedge E) = 0.25$

He will relax as this is the prior probability of a burglary.

## Databases

The joint probability distribution may be calculated from records in a database which satisfy the propositions or predicates that are to be deduced. There are aspects of qualitative independence (Dubois et al. 1997, Ben Amor et al. 2000) that may be determined from the structure of the data base but probabilistic dependencies exist between propositions that would be deemed independent from the relational structure of the data base.

There are further problems when the conditional dependencies are tested. Given a set of three attributes in a database which may be causally related then given they are as above, $A,B$ and $E$, the conditional independences dictate the structure. We are interested in removing any links which have no effect on other propositions.

Definition (from Neapolitan 1990) Let $V$ be a finite set of finite propositional variables defined on the same probability space, let $(\Omega,F,P)$ be their joint probability distribution, and let $G = (V,E)$ be a directed acyclic graph. For each $v \in V$, let $c(v)$ 1 $V$ be the set of all parents of $v$ and $d(v)$ be the set of all descendants of $v$. Furthermore, for $v \in V$, let $a(v)$ be $V\text{-}(d(v) \cup \{v\})$, that is, the set of propositional variables in $V$ excluding $v$ and $v$'s descendants. Suppose for every subset $W$ 1 $a(v)$, $W$ and $v$ are conditionally independent given $c(v)$; that is, if $P(c(v)) > 0$, then

$$P(v \mid c(v)) = 0 \text{ or } P(W \mid c(v)) = 0 \text{ or } P(v \mid W \cup c(v)) = P(v \mid c(v)).$$

Then $C = (V,E,P)$ is a causal network. The set $c(v)$ is the set of causes (parents) of $v$. The set $a(v)$ is the set of vertices which are independent of $v$.

In the net above the variables $B$ and $E$ have no parents and so c($B$) and c($E$) are empty. $a(B) = \{E\}$ and for $a(E) = \{B\}$, $c(A) = \{B,E\}$. We are only interested in the third condition: $P(v \mid W \cup c(v)) = P(v \mid c(v))$ in this analysis as the others offer no interesting properties. In fact we will use the simple case where $P(v \mid W) = P(v)$. The analysis is conducted using the notation of the burglar alarm problem. However it is a simple matter to generalise the analysis. The net so far has possible links, or dependences between any two of $A,B$ and $E$. We are interested in establishing the $a$ set as this will simplify the computations. So the conditional independences required to establish the causal net as above are:

$$P(B \mid E) = P(B)$$

because $a(B) = \{E\}$

In general we have to explore all links and there are various methods for systematically checking these. Following the above notation this would be

$P(v \mid W \cup c(v)) = P(v \mid c(v))$. Where $v = B$, $c(v) = \{\}$. $W = \{E\}$. The simpler concrete notation is used for clarity and brevity.

$$P(B \mid E) = \frac{P(B \wedge E)}{P(E)}$$

All the probabilities are taken from the same probability space so the relation for conditional independence can be restated as:

$$\frac{N(B \wedge E)}{N(E)} = \frac{N(B)}{N}$$

Where $N$ is the size of the complete sample and $N(X)$ is the size of the set of records satisfying $X$. $N(B)$ is the number of burglaries.

### *Update Anomalies*

Let there be an update to the database. If a burglary occurs on its own without an earthquake, which is consistent with our underlying model, then

$N'(B \wedge E) = N(B \wedge E),$

$N'(E) = N(E),$

and

$N'(B) = N(B)+1.$

For conditional independence to hold after an update of a single burglary to the database:

$$\frac{N'(B \wedge E)}{N'(E)} = \frac{N'(B)}{N'}$$

i.e.

$$\frac{N(B \wedge E)}{N(E)} = \frac{N(B)+1}{N+1}$$

This is only true for $N(B) = N$ and so the strict test for conditional independence between $B$ and $E$ fails; albeit only marginally for large $N$. If there are more updates then the problem is worse.

Similarly for an earthquake happening on its own.

If both occur together then:

$N'(B \wedge E) = N(B \wedge E)+1,$

$N'(E) = N(E)+1,$

$N'(B) = N(B)+1$

and

$N' = N+1$

and as before

$$\frac{N'(B \wedge E)}{N'(E)} = \frac{N'(B)}{N'}$$

i.e.

$$\frac{N(B \wedge E)+1}{N(E)+1} = \frac{N(B)+1}{N+1}$$

Clearly this cannot hold, so unless partial events can be defined in a very precise manner, strict conditional independence cannot survive a single update to the database. Let alone several.

If a tolerance is applied to the test, then the test can be restated as:

$P(B \mid E) = P(B)+ \delta(B)$

and

$P(E \mid B) = P(E) + \delta(E)$

Where $\delta(E)$ is the tolerance on the probabilities of E.

However a simple tolerance is not useful for a variety of reasons. The most obvious one is that each database will have a varying number of items and generally its own structure, so the impact of an incomplete set of entries will vary and so will the tolerance required.

If we start with the assumption that there is a base database that is representative of the overall population and the conditional probabilities hold strictly. Then the following is true:

$$P(B \mid E) = P(B)$$

and so

$$\frac{N(B \wedge E)}{N(E)} = \frac{N(B)}{N}$$

let the changes in the numbers of the population after a partial update be represented by $\Delta(B \wedge E)$, $\Delta(B)$ and $\Delta(E)$. Let the tolerance on the conditional probability of $B$ be defined as:

$$P'(B \mid E) = P'(B) + \delta(B)$$

Similarly for E

Then

$$\frac{N(B \wedge E)}{N(E)} = \frac{N(B)}{N}$$

and

$$\frac{N'(B \wedge E)}{N'(E)} = \frac{N'(B)}{N'} + \delta(B)$$

so

$$\frac{N(B \wedge E) + \Delta(B \wedge E)}{N(E) + \Delta(E)} = \frac{N(B) + \Delta(B)}{N + \Delta(N)} + \delta(B)$$

Solving for $\delta(B)$

$$\delta(B) = \frac{N(B \wedge E) + \Delta(B \wedge E)}{N(E) + \Delta(E)} - \frac{N(B) + \Delta(B)}{N + \Delta(N)}$$

If conditional independence holds between the elements and the sample is at least representative, then if it doesn't hold for the whole set then it will hold for a subset such that:

$$\frac{N(B \wedge E)}{N(E)} = \frac{N(B)}{N}$$

and

$$\frac{N(B \wedge E)}{N(B)} = \frac{N(E)}{N}$$

If this is the largest such subset then:

$$\Delta(B \wedge E) \in \{0,1\}$$

because if $\Delta(B \wedge E) > 1$ then there is a larger subset as there will be another whole cohort.

If $\Delta(B \wedge E) = 0$ then $\delta(B) < 0$,

and if $\Delta(B \wedge E) = 1$ then $\delta(B) > 0$

So it is possible to determine $\Delta(B \wedge E)$ from $\delta$(B).

$$\delta(B) = \frac{(N(B \wedge E) + \Delta(B \wedge E)) * (N + \Delta(N)) - (N(B) + \Delta(B)) * (N(E) + \Delta(E))}{(N(E) + \Delta(E)) * (N + \Delta(N))}$$

Similarly for $\delta(E)$

$N+\Delta(N)$ is known, as is $N(B)+\Delta(B)$ , $N(E)+\Delta(E)$, $N(B \wedge E) + \Delta(B \wedge E)$, and because $\Delta(B \wedge E)$ can be deduced then also $N(B \wedge E)$ . What is not known is the value of $\Delta N$, $\Delta(B)$ and $\Delta(E)$. However, the values of any subset will be an estimate of the values of the whole set. $\Delta N$ and $\Delta(B)$ are related such that:

$$P(B) = \frac{\Delta(B)}{\Delta(N)}$$

The maximum likelihood estimate of $P(B)$ may be derived directly from:

$$P(B) = \frac{N(B) + \Delta(B)}{N + \Delta(N)}$$

and so given $\Delta(N)$ it is possible to estimate $\Delta(B)$ and $\Delta(E)$ as a function of $\Delta(N)$. What we are looking for is a solution to the set of equations:

$$\frac{N(B \wedge E) * N - N(B) * N(E)}{N(E) * N} = 0,\ \Delta(B) = \frac{N(B) * \Delta(N)}{N},\ \Delta(E) = \frac{N(E) * \Delta(N)}{N}$$

It is possible to solve these equations and determine a value for $N$ and hence $\Delta(N)$, $\Delta(B)$ and $\Delta(E)$. If the set is representative and conditional independence holds then there will be a set of cohorts which together have size $N$ and a partial cohort of size _$N$. The average size of the cohorts will be equal to $\frac{N}{N(B \wedge E)}$ and so if $\Delta(N)$ is less than this cohort size then conditional independence holds. The tolerance of the values between the conditional probability and the ground probability will decrease with $N$ whereas the values of $N$ and $\Delta(N)$ and the cohort size depend on the data alone. Typically each subset of attributes of a set of data will have a different cohort size. This represents a more robust test of conditional independence. Given particular values of $N$ and $\Delta(N)$, it is possible to calculate the probability that conditional independence holds in any given database. If $\Delta(B \wedge E) = 0$ then it is relatively straightforward to calculate the probability that the conjoint event has not happened in the event space size of $\Delta(N)$. A similar calculation can be performed for $\Delta(B \wedge E) = 1$.

$$P(B) = 0.24,\ P(E) = 0.2, N(B)+\Delta(B) = 22,$$

$$N(E)+\Delta(E) = 18,\ N+\Delta(N) = 90,\ N(B \wedge E) + \Delta(B \wedge E) = 4.$$

**Fig. 3.** The values taken from the 90 record database.

**Example**

Let there be a data set containing 4 identical sets of 20 records and a partial set of 10 records. Each set of 20 records supports conditional independence between *B* and *E* and dependence between *A* and *B* and *A* and *E*. The extra 10 records are arbitrarily selected from the 20 record set and so extend the data set consistently.

The statistics from the 90 records are given in Figure 4:

The solution to the equations which corresponds to the values in Figure 4 is $\Delta N = 8.3$. The actual value of $\Delta(N)$ built into the data set is 10 so the figure is quite close and well within the estimated cohort size of $\frac{N}{N(B \wedge E)} = 81.7/4 = 20.4$. There is no solution for $\Delta(N)$ for *A* and *B* and *A* and *E*. The standard conditional test on the 90 record set between *A* and *B* results in a difference of 0.13, compared with the difference between B and E of 0.02.

$$P(B) = 0.23,\ P(E) = 0.2, N(B)+\Delta(B) = 7,$$

$$N(E)+\Delta(E) = 6,\ N+\Delta(N) = 30,\ N(B \wedge E) + \Delta(B \wedge E) = 1.$$

**Fig. 4.** The values taken from the 30 record database.

Repeating the test with a data set of 30 records, as shown in figure 4, results in an estimated value for $\Delta(N)$ of 8.7 giving a cohort size of 30-8.7 = 21.3. The value for *A* and *E* in this case is 0.07 which compares with the value for *A* and *B* of 0.1, which is equivocal. There is no solution to the equations above for *A* and *B* or *A* and *E*.

## Conclusion

The paper has shown that extracting relationships from a database in order to learn the underlying structure requires more than just calculating the conditional probabilities and comparing them with the ground probabilities. The calculations described above based on cohort sizes reliably discover independence and dependence between data attributes with much smaller data sets than the standard test requires. The probabilities were derived from a set of mass assignments and thus give rise to probability and possibility distributions. It has been shown that these distributions necessarily vary with updates and a technique introduced for determining independence more reliably. The induced possibility distributions also vary and measures derived from an arbitrary point in the history of the data base are likely to be as unreliable as ones shown in this paper. In particular the pre-ordering induced from the possibility distributions is likely to change as the data base obtains more records. In the case that the data base contains a large number of records then as the size increases then estimates of the probability and possibility improve.

## References

Baldwin, J.F., Martin, T.P. & Pilsworth B.W., 1995, Fril-Fuzzy and Evidential Reasoning, Research Studies Press, Wiley.

Ben Amor, N., Benferhat, S., Dubois, D., Geffner, H. & Prade, H., 2000, Independence in qualitative uncertainty frameworks, Proc. KR2000 pp. 235-246.

Clocksin, W.F. & Mellish, C.S., 1981, Programming in PROLOG, Springer-Verlag.

Dubois, D. Farinas del Cerro, L., Herzig, A. and Prade, H.,1997, Qualitative Relevance and Independence: A Roadmap, in Proc. IJCAI pp. 62-67.

Kowalski, R.A., 1980, Logic for Problem solving, North-Holland.

Lauritzen, S.L. & Speigelhalter, D.J., 1988, Local Computation with probabilities in Graphical Structures and Their Applications to Expert Systems, Journal of the Royal Statistical Society B, Vol 50, No. 2.

Lauritzen, S.L. (1996). Graphical models. Oxford University Press, London. ISBN 0-19-852219-3

Neapolitan, R.E., 1990, Probabilistic Reasoning in Expert Systems:Theory and Algorithms, Wiley .

Pearl, J., 1986, Fusion, Propagation and structuring in Belief Networks, Artificial Intelligence 29 pp. 217-222.

Poole, D., 1993,Probabilistic Horn abduction and Bayesian networks, Artificial Intelligence 64 pp. 81-130.

Reiter, R. 1978, On closed world databases, in ed Gallaire, H. & Minker, J. Logic and Data Bases, Plenum Press New York, pp 55-76.

# Extraction of Meaningful Tables from the Internet Using Decision Trees *

Sung-Won Jung[1], Won-Hee Lee[1], Sang-Kyu Park[2], and Hyuk-Chul Kwon[1]

[1] AI Lab. Dept. of Computer Science, Pusan National University, San 30, Jang-geon Dong, 609-735, Busan, Korea
{swjung, whlee, hckwon}@pusan.ac.kr
[2] Electronic and Telecommunications Research Institute, 161 Gajeong Dong, Yuseong Gu, 305-350, Daejeon, Korea,
parksk@etri.re.kr

**Abstract.** The information retrieval system currently in use fails to consider the structural information of documents but uses extracted indexes from documents instead. Structural information such as the font face, font size, indentation, tables, and etc. demonstrate the author's meaning and is clearly the prime means of documentation. This paper pays special attention to tables because tables are commonly used within many documents to make the meanings clear, which are well recognized because web documents use tags for additional information. On the Internet, tables are used for the purpose of the structure of knowledge and also the design of documents. This report will propose a method of extracting meaningful tables using a decision tree and to construct a dictionary of table indexes in order to apply an information retrieval system and thus enhance the accuracy.

## 1 Introduction

The ultimate goal of an information retrieval system is to offer the most suitable information to its users. Performance is measured by its ability to find documents with useful information for the user. The related works have, therefore, focused mainly on the method of improving recall and precision. Special attention was given to web documents where an increasingly large number of users produce un-verified documents. An efficient retrieval method is required to improve the accuracy of such systems.

To make a high precision system, we must analyze the semantics of html documents. However, it is very difficult with present technology to apply semantics to an internet retrieval system. Another method, by which we grasp the author's intention, is to analyze the structural information of html documents. For example, when an author creates a document, s/he appends the titles, make paragraphs and use indentations, numbers and symbols before the titles and tables.

* This work was partially supported by Korean Science and Engineering Foundation (Contract Number: R01 - 2000 - 00275) and National Research Laboratory Program (Contract Number: M10203000028-02J0000-01510 ) of KISTEP.

P.W.H. Chung, C.J. Hinde, M. Ali (Eds.): IEA/AIE 2003, LNAI 2718, pp. 176–186, 2003.

This paper examines tables in several informational structures in html documents. The table form is more obvious than the plane text form, because we use a structured table in documents to convey our subject clearly. A performance improvement of an information retrieval system can be expected through the analysis of the tables because it is easy to find the tables and easy to extract the meanings in the web documents. This method can also be applied on the ranking models of current information retrieval systems like the vector space model, the P-norm model [1,2,3,4,5] etc.

## 2 The Challenge

Current information retrieval systems rank related documents based on similarities between documents and the users' query [1,2]. Such systems place great importance on index words and have the following limitations.

Firstly, current systems do not draw the meaning from html documents. To retrieve information more accurately, semantics of html documents should be considered. These information retrieval systems measure the similarity between html documents and the users query based on the 'term frequency' and 'document frequency'. Furthermore, these systems accept the assumption that documents are related to the index word in proportion to the 'term frequency' of the documents. However, this assumption is only of limited validity.

Secondly, current systems do not distinguish relatively weighted indexes or keywords from general indexes in html documents. Because there can be more important keywords - even in the document, people tend to remember the important part when they read a certain document. If all keywords in a document are given the same weight, it is difficult to retrieve exactly what the users want. The systems consider the 'term frequency' and 'document frequency' of the indexes by an alternative method but it does not increase the matching accuracy sufficiently enough to satisfy all users.

Lastly, the current systems do not reflect structural information in html documents. We can grasp the writer's intention to some degree if we consider the structural information of the documents. As the writer uses titles for each paragraph, indentations and tabular forms to convey his intention clearly, they have significance in a document. These information retrieval systems, however, ignore the structural information when they extract index words from these documents.

In addressing these limitations the devised system aims to analyze and process tabular forms. For an author writing a document it may be more effective, therefore, to represent the document with a tabular form rather than to describe it in the usual methods. Related works [9, 10, 11, 12, 13] that study the extraction of table information handle a special tabular form, and extract information using abstraction rules. Similarities exist with this and our previous work [8]. The defect of such methods, however, is that it is difficult to apply them to various web document formats. In order to address this problem a method of extracting meaningful tables using decision trees and applying their results to an information retrieval system has been developed.

# 3 Implementation

To extract information in a table it is necessary to define a table that becomes the target of the extraction and understand the characteristic of the table. More features must also be added to those that were presented in previous work. The devised system does not apply features in a linear way as in our previous work but uses a decision tree. The method improves the accuracy of classification, and is robust to 'noise'. Thus, the extracted table becomes a data structure, which is suitable to be processed by our information retrieval system.

Following Figure 1 is the representation of some terms used in the paper:

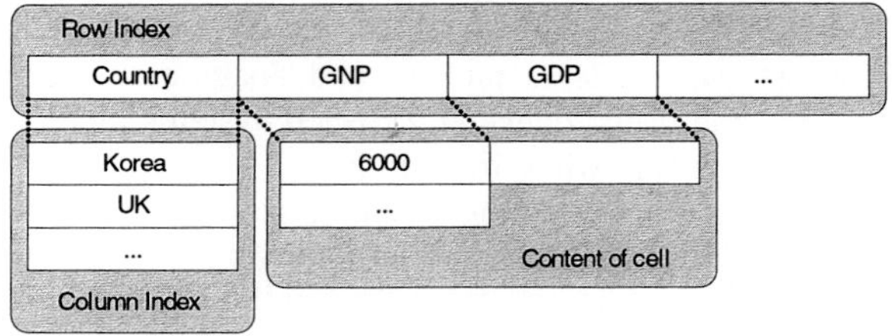


**Fig. 1.** Define terms: row index, column index and content of cell

## 3.1 The Classification of Tables on the Internet

Various kinds of tables exist on the Internet. In general, a table is a printed or written collection of figures, facts, or information, arranged in orderly rows across and down the page which conveys an author's meaning more clearly. The <table> tag is supported in HTML for use on the web in a table. However, tables on the web are used not only for the purpose of the original goal but also to make the information clearer by lining it up. The task of deciding which tables are meaningful on the web is necessary before the information in a table can be extracted. To achieve this, the tables on the web have been classified into two types:

First, it is important to know which tables can be processed by the information retrieval system from amongst the meaningful tables on the web to extract the required table information. Figure 2.a is a web page from the Busan Convention and Visitor Bureau [7]. In this paper this kind of table is called the 'meaningful table', which can be defined as having the following criteria:

- The index of the table is located in the first row and the first column.
- The contents of a cell extracted by a combination of rows and columns have specific information.
- The term and document frequency cannot represent a relation between row index, column index and the content of a cell in a table.

Besides the tables having the above characteristics, we can often usually see a web page like the one in Figure 2.b. The <table> tags are used all over the HTML source of this document. However, the tables of Figure 2.b are not illustrating the owners' meaning but are offering a well-arranged display to the users. This kind of table is defined as the 'decorative table' and the following criteria:

- The table does not have table indexes in the first row and the first column.
- The table has no repeatability of cell form, and is not structural.
- The contents of the table have complex contents such as long sentence, image, etc.

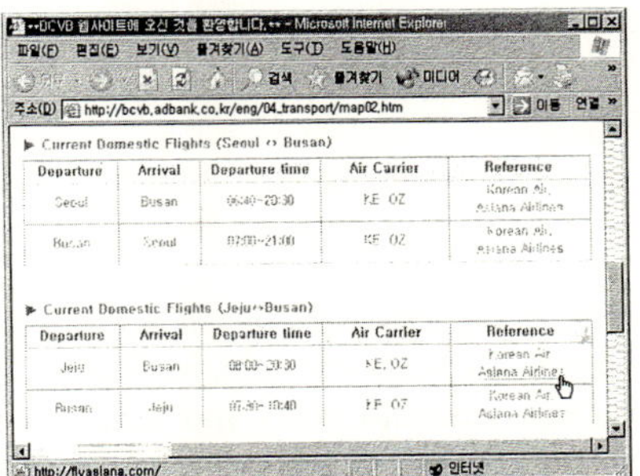


a. Meaningful table

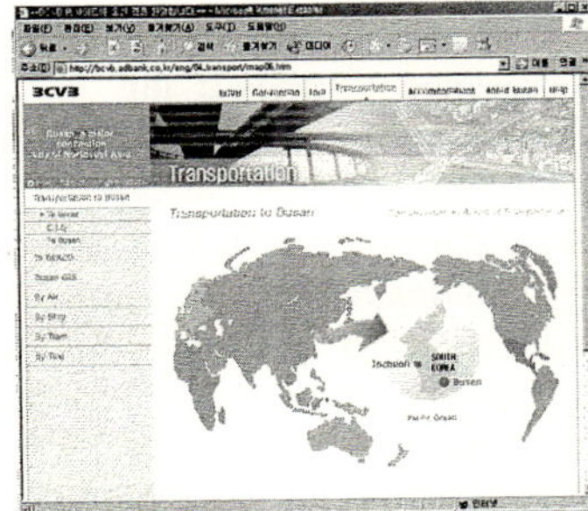


b. decorative table

**Fig. 2.** The types of table on the Internet

The statistics of the tables were researched manually on the web in relation to their classification. The results of the research may be seen in Table 1. The percentage of documents which include the <table> tags is about 77.78% - in total 86,475 documents. The <table> tags are used as frequently as was thought. The percentage of all investigated documents which included meaningful tables is 1.16%, which is less than was thought, and is about 1.5% if we consider only the documents which include tables. It is acknowledge that the tables on the web are used more often for the design of the document than for our original goal.

**Table 1.** The statistic of the tables on the Internet

| Item | Count |
|---|---|
| Total document number | 86475 |
| Number of documents with table | 67259 |
| Number of documents with meaningful table | 1009 |
| Rate of document including table in total documents ( B/A ) | 77.78% |
| Rate of document including meaningful table in total documents ( C/A ) | 1.167% |
| Rate of document including meaningful table in documents including table ( C/B ) | 1.500% |

## 3.2 Institution of Table Features

It is unusual to encounter a document which includes meaningful tables on the web - as the results show in table 1. Nevertheless, the meaningful tables should be extracted from amongst the others for effective information retrieval; however, it is impossible to extract them manually due to the large number of internet documents. Therefore, the tables should be defined automatically, to identify if they are meaningful or not on the basis of the characteristics which were obtained previously by analyzing meaningful tables in the training data. For example, several characteristics could be acquired from Figure 2: presence of pictures, presence of background colors and the table size.

The whole features used in the devised system are as follows:

1. The presence of <caption> tag
2. The presence of <th> tag
3. The presence of <thead> tag
4. The classification of the cells on the first rows
5. The difference of the background color option between the row with the index and the next row, or the difference of the background color option between the column with the index and next column
6. The difference of the font color option between the row with the index and next, or the difference of the font color option between column with index and next column
7. The difference of the font face between the row with the index and next row, or the difference of the font face between column with the index and the next column
8. The presence of the border option
9. The ratio of empty cells
10. The ratio of cells including <a href> tag
12. The ratio of cells consisting of text only
13. The presence of rows or columns consisting of numeric data only
14. The ratio of cells consisting of only symbols
15. The presence of other tables in the table
16. The table size
17. The number of sentences with more than 40 characters in a cell
18. The type of table shape
19. The difference of the font size between the row with index and next row, or the difference of the font size between the column with the index and the next column
20. The index word type

### 3.3 Application of the Decision Tree

Although features can be a criteria in deciding which are meaningful tables, the sequence of processing them is also important. The sequence of acquired features was implemented using the decision tree. ID3 algorithm [6] is used in the decision tree. The ID3 algorithm is demonstrated by the features which maximize information gain. These features are selected steps by step.

$$InformationGain(S,A) = Entropy(S) - \sum_{v \in Values(A)} \frac{|S_v|}{|S|} Entropy(S_v)$$

The information gain of A feature in S example set can be calculated through the above formula where V is the difference between the entropy of S and the sum of the entropy of each features' value as one of the features' value of A feature. If the entropy value of each feature decreases, that is, if the classification improves, this in turn improves the feature. Hence, it is better when the information increases.

**Table 2.** Features and feature values

| No | Value |
|---|---|
| 1 | 0 : null 1 : exist |
| 2 | 0 : null 1 : exist |
| 3 | 0 : null 1 : exist |
| 4 | 0 : null 1 : word 2 : sentence 3 : number<br>4 : image 5 : symbol 6 : composition |
| 5 | 0 : null 1 : row 2: column 3 : row and column |
| 6 | 0 : null 1 : row 2: column 3 : row and column |
| 7 | 0 : null 1 : row 2: column 3 : row and column |
| 8 | 0 : null 1 : exist |
| 9 | 10 sections divided by percentage |
| 10 | 10 sections divided by percentage |
| 11 | 10 sections divided by percentage |
| 12 | 10 sections divided by percentage |
| 13 | 0 : null 1 : exist |
| 14 | 10 sections divided by percentage |
| 15 | 0 : null 1 : exist |
| 16 | 0 : 1*n, m*1 1 : m*n < 10 2 : 10 ≤ m*n < 30 3 : other<br>( n : number of column , m : number of row ) |
| 17 | The number of sentence(n) ( if n > 10, than n = 10 ) |
| 18 | 0 : none 1 : index row span 2 : index column span<br>3 : index row and column span 4 : index row and bottom column span<br>5 : index column and bottom column span<br>6 : index row and column span and bottom column span<br>7 : other |
| 19 | 0 : null 1 : row 3: column 4 : row and column |
| 20 | 0 : none 1 : meaningless word ( ex) Num. number … )<br>2 : meaningful word ( ex) tel. name … ) |

### 3.4 Extraction of Table Information

The system extracts the table information from the meaningful tables after filtering the tables on the web pages. For this, it is necessary to separate the table indexes and the contents of cells. It is not a simple problem to extract indexes from a table because tables on the Internet appear in various forms. The system converts an applied feature into a vector. For example, the vector (2, 0, 0, 0, 0) means that the table has a background color in the first column. We distinguish different table forms based on these vectors. Table 3 shows the result.

**Table 3.** The criteria of the index extraction

| Type | Example vector |
|---|---|
| The row or column with index is obtained by feature 5, background color. | (1, 0, 0, 0, 0), (2, 0, 0, 0, 2) |
| The row or column with index is obtained by feature 6, font color. | (0, 2, 0, 0, 0), (0, 1, 0, 0, 1) |
| The row or column with index is obtained by feature 7, font face. | (0, 0, 3, 0, 0), (0, 0, 2, 0, 2) |
| The row or column with index is obtained by feature 16. font size | (0, 0, 0, 2, 0), (0, 0, 3, 0, 1) |
| The row or column with index is obtained by feature 18, table shape. | (0, 0, 0, 0, 1) |
| The row or column with index is obtained by reason of, the first row and the first column | (0, 0, 0, 0, 0) |

Our system converts the extracted indexes and contents of a cell into a suitable data structure. The data structure type produces three pairs of values; row index, column index, and contents of the cell, as shown in Figure 3. The row indexes and the column indexes are sorted for search.

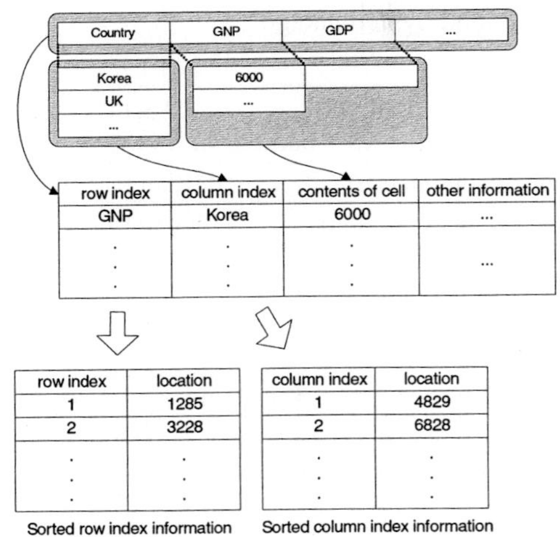


**Fig. 3.** The data structure for the table information

### 3.5 Applying on Information Retrieval

Our system uses mainly two methods in order to apply table information to an information retrieval system. The first method, which has been described in previous work[8], is obtained by application of the weight formula used in a general information retrieval system as follows:

if a document(*Doc*) includes table index such as query(*Query*),

$$Sim(Query, Doc) = Sim(\text{by Vector Space Mode}) + c \log_2 (N_{index})$$

else

$$Sim(Query, Doc) = Sim(\text{by Vector Space Mode})$$

where

$N_{index}$ = the number of table indexes in a document

c = 0.1 ( a correction constant )

The second method enhances the accuracy of the retrieval result by using the data structure mentioned in the previous chapter. For example, if a user input the query, 'the 1996's GNP of Korea', our system extracts index words from the query and gets results per each index. These results are merged and obtained as a final result.

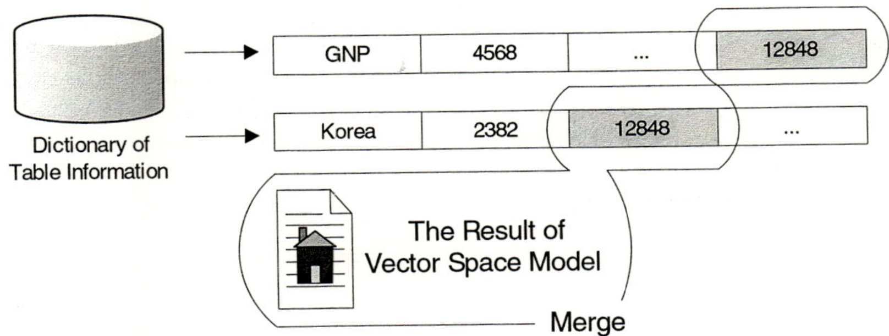


**Fig. 4.** Getting a result using dictionary of table information

### 3.6 The System Implementation

Figure 5 is a system implementation procedure. The whole procedure of the task is summarized as follows. Firstly, the sample data to be analyzed is collected and is then classified by tables and the others by hand. We investigate 100,000 documents to establish the sample data for this system. Secondly, we implement the system which extracts the features of each table automatically after the table information is extracted from the parsing of HTML documents. The sample data is generated from the merging of the former and latter results. Using this sample data, our system implements the decision tree and creates a table information dictionary. Finally, the system uses this dictionary for the information retrieval system.

## 4 Experimental Result

We implemented the system with an Intel Pentium IV that has a 2GHz CPU and 256 MBytes main memory. Sample data was extracted in about 100,000 internet documents and test data was chosen from about 5 millions internet documents that were collected in Artificial Intelligence Laboratory in Pusan National University.

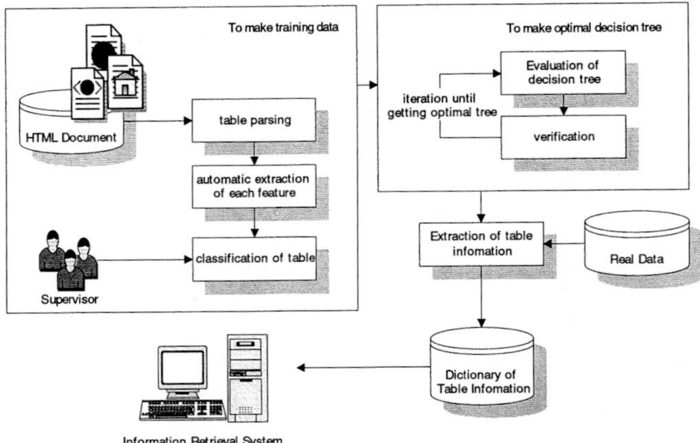


**Fig. 5** The process of the system implementation

Figure 6 is an experiment about the accuracy of the decision tree. When each feature is added to our system one by one, the degree of misclassification gradually decreases. If other features are added and feature values are adjusted improved results are expected.

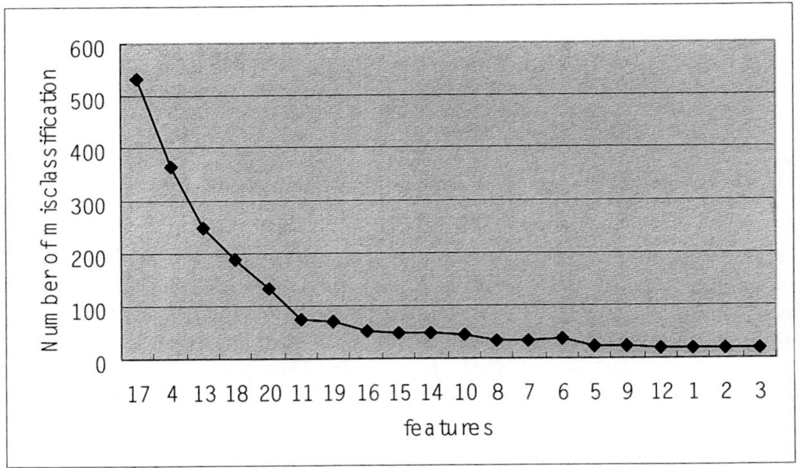


**Fig. 6.** The accuracy of the decision tree

Table 4 is a result from the application of the decision tree to test data. The data is 10,000 web documents collected on the Internet. For the results a recall of 83.7% and a precision of 78,5% were obtained. If additional features or classification methods are applied to the system, the accuracy may improve further.

**Table 4.** The application of the decision tree

| Number of Experiment | Number of table | A | B | C | Recall | Precision |
|---|---|---|---|---|---|---|
| 1 | 4203 | 246 | 252 | 212 | 0.841 | 0.862 |
| 2 | 11213 | 183 | 160 | 133 | 0.831 | 0.727 |
| 3 | 5448 | 223 | 236 | 208 | 0.881 | 0.933 |
| 4 | 15432 | 290 | 284 | 263 | 0.926 | 0.906 |
| 5 | 14991 | 80 | 82 | 62 | 0.756 | 0.775 |
| 6 | 14219 | 186 | 123 | 104 | 0.845 | 0.559 |
| 7 | 15084 | 163 | 145 | 135 | 0.931 | 0.730 |
| 8 | 9602 | 210 | 187 | 180 | 0.963 | 0.857 |
| 9 | 8024 | 123 | 129 | 91 | 0.705 | 0.739 |
| Total | 98216 | 1704 | 1598 | 1338 | 0.837 | 0.785 |

A: the number of extracted result with our system
B: the number of real meaningful table
C: $A \cap B$
Recall : C/B
Precision : C/A

Finally, the system implemented to weight the table form information with established Vector Space Model. Because the documents with valid tables were only about 1.5% of all documents, the accuracy of retrieval seldom improved.

**Table 5.** Accuracy improvement

| Criteria | Current System | First Method | Second Method |
|---|---|---|---|
| Retrieval accuracy | 81.5% | 81.5% | 82.3% |

* We describe the first and second methods in chapter 3.5

The retrieval accuracy of our current system is about 81.5% and it slightly increases up to 82.3%. However, if a query is answered only by meaningful tables, the results are much improved.

## 5 Conclusions and Future Work

The devised information retrieval system requires making estimates to show correct information to the user. For the system to extract information from a table, it must classify whether it is a meaningful table or a decorative table. If a meaningful table is extracted, it is easy to process the information in the table to other data forms. For example, when a user inputs a query such as the "Temperature of Busan", the system should output the correct result using abstracted table information. This work can process data of a general information retrieval system or a specific domain that has many tables. The work needs a more accurate algorithm for classifying and learning a table thereafter.

Future work will seek to identify the correlation between documents and tables. The rationale behind this work will research the link between tables and documents i.e. if a table can supply the contents of a document, how relevant tables can affect the importance of a document.

## References

1. Kobayashi, M., Takeda, K. : Information Retrieval on the Web. ACM Computing Surveys (2000) 144-173
2. Salton, G., McGill, M. J. : Introduction to Modern Information Retrieval, McGraw-Hill, New York (1983)
3. Fox, E. A. : Extending the Boolean and Vector Space Models of Information Retrieval with P-norm Queries and Multiple Concept Types, Dissertation Cornell University (1983)
4. Smith, M. E. : Aspects of the P-norm Model of Information Retrieval : Syntactic Query Generation, Efficiency, and Theoretical Properties, Dissertation Cornell University, (1990)
5. Salton, G., Fox, E. A., Wu, H. : Extended Boolean Information Retrieval, ncstrl.cornel, (1982) 82-511
6. Mitchell, T. M. : Machine Learning, McGraw-Hill (1997), 53-79
7. http://www.busancvb.org/eng/home.html
8. Jung, S.W., Sung, K.H., Park, T.W., Kwon, H.C. : Effective Retrieval of Information in Tables on the Internet, IEA/AIE June (2002) 493-501
9. Hammer, J., Garcia-Molina, H., Cho, J., Aranha, R., and A. Crespo. : Extracting Semistructured Information from the Web, SIGMOD Record, 26(2) (1997) 18-25
10. Huang Y., Qi G.Z., Zhang F.Y. : Constructing Semistructed information extractor from the Web document, Journal of Software 11(1) (2000) 73-75
11. Ashish., N., Knoblock, C. : Wrapper Generation for Semi-structed Internet Sources, SIGMOD Record, 26(4) (1997) 8-15
12. Smith, D., Lopez M. : Information Extraction for Semi-structed Documents, In Proceedings of the Workshop on Management of Semistructed Data, in conjunction with PODS/SIGMOD, Tucson, AZ, USA, May, 12 (1997)
13. Ning, G., Guowen, W., Xiaoyuan, W., Baile, S. : Extracting Web table information in cooperative learning activites based on abstract semantic model, Computer Supported Cooperative Work in Design, The Sixth International Conference on 2001 (2001) 492-497

# Theory and Algorithm for Rule Base Refinement[1]

Hai Zhuge[1], Yunchuan Sun[2], and Weiyu Guo[1]

[1] Knowledge Grid Research Group, Key Lab of Intelligent Information Processing, Institute of Computing Technology, Chinese Academy of Science, 100080, Beijing, China
zhuge@ict.ac.cn
Http://kg.ict.ac.cn
[2] Department of Computer Science, College of Information Science, Beijing Normal University, 100875, Beijing, China
Sun88@mail.bnu.edu.cn

**Abstract.** Rule base refinement plays an important role in enhancing the efficacy and efficiency of utilizing a rule base. A rule base concerns three types of redundancies: implication-rule redundancy, abstraction-rule redundancy and dead-end-condition redundancy. This paper proposes two approaches: one is to remove implication redundant rules by using the closure of literal set and the other is to remove abstraction redundant rules by using rule-abstraction. We have developed a software tool to support the first approach. Experiments show that the tool can work correctly and efficiently. The proposed approach can be applied to more application fields.

## 1 Introduction

Rule base refinement plays an important role in enhancing the efficacy and efficiency of utilizing a rule base. Many approaches and tools have been proposed for detecting and eliminating redundant and inconsistent rules. The static rule checking utility was proposed to check inconsistencies and incompleteness [16]. The system CHECK was developed to verify the consistency and completeness of knowledge base. Its operations are based on the construction of a dependency chart, which shows the dependencies among rules and between rules and classes [12, 13]. The EVA project aimed to build an integrated set of tools to check the redundancy, consistency, completeness, and correctness of any KBS written by any KBS language, but it only achieved its goal in a limited manner. Redundancy was checked in EVA by theorem proving [3, 4]. The Expert System Checker checks the completeness and consistency of a knowledge base through decision-tables [5]. The system KB-Reducer was developed for knowledge base reduction. It can also check inconsistency and redundancy in rule base [6]. The system COVER can carry out seven checking: redundancy, conflict, subsumption, unsatisfiable conditions, dead-end rules, circularity and missing rules [8, 14, 15]. Two general-purpose verification systems VSE and VSE II were developed based on the core of an interactive inductive theorem prover [9]. Applying the classical methods to detect some anomalies in non-monotonic knowledge base has been discussed in [7]. The issue of analysis and

[1] This Work was supported by National Science Foundation of China.

P.W.H. Chung, C.J. Hinde, M. Ali (Eds.): IEA/AIE 2003, LNAI 2718, pp. 187–196, 2003.

verification of selected properties of rule-based systems and a tabular form of single-level rule-based systems was studied [11]. A methodology for the validation of rule-based expert systems proposed in [10]. A partial instantiation schema that exports local search to first-order knowledge bases is proposed in [2], and it can handle the forms of depth-limited consistency and inconsistency. Zhuge presented a theory about object and object-abstraction and theories about rule-order and rule-mapping formalism, and also established an analogical reasoning model OAM [18]. Based on our previous work, this paper proposes the notion of abstraction rule redundancy and then develops a method for rule base refinement that uses object abstraction. We suppose that each rule in the rule base takes the form of Horn-clause for the convenience. Actually, any rule can be translated into one or several rule(s) with the form of Horn-clause, which is (are) equivalent to the original rule.

## 2 Implication Redundancy

### 2.1 Basics

If a rule r can be deduced through logical reasoning by some rules in a rule base R, we say r is implied by R, denoted as $R \models r$. If each rule of a rule set S is implied by R, we say S is implied by R, denoted as $R \models S$. A rule is called trivial, if it takes the form of $p_1 \wedge p_2 \wedge \ldots \wedge p_m \rightarrow p_i$, $1 \leqslant i \leqslant m$, i.e., the result of the rule appears in the preconditions. It is obviously that a trivial rule always holds.

Let R be a rule base, and r is a rule in R. If $R-\{r\} \models r$, we call r an implication redundancy rule for R, i.e., R's function is equivalent to that of R-{r}, for r can be replaced by some other rule(s) in R-{r}. Hence, r can be removed from R.

Implication redundancy can be caused by many factors such as equivalency, transitivity and subsumption, which have been studied by many researchers [1, 3, 4, 6, 8, 12-16]. Complicated implication redundancy also exists, for instance, if $p \rightarrow q_1$, $p \rightarrow q_2$, $q_1 \wedge q_2 \rightarrow w$, $p \rightarrow w$ are four rules in a rule base, then $p \rightarrow w$ is a redundant rule.

All implication redundant rules we discuss above are due to the logical implication relationship among rules. In order to decide whether a rule r is redundant or not for a rule base R, we should determine whether r could be derived from R-{r} or not.

### 2.2 Equivalence among Rule Bases and Minimal Cover of a Rule Base

The set of all rules implied by a rule base R is called the closure of R, denoted $R^+=\{r \mid R \models r\}$. Obviously, $R^+$ is unique for a given rule base R.

We say a rule base R is equivalent to another one S if $R^+=S^+$. In this case, R can be replaced with S. It is obvious that the equivalence among rule bases is reflexive, symmetric, and transitive.

**Lemma 1.** A rule base R is equivalent to S if and only if $R \subseteq S^+$ *and* $S \subseteq R^+$.

**Proof:** If R is equivalent to S, then $R^+=S^+$, $R\subseteq R^+$, $S\subseteq S^+$. So $R\subseteq S^+$ and $S\subseteq R^+$ hold. For any rule r in $S^+$, we can get S|=r, and $S\subseteq R^+$, so $R^+$ |=r, that is r is in $R^+$, of course $S^+\subseteq R^+$. Also we have $R^+\subseteq S^+$. So $R^+=S^+$ holds. □

During a rule base refinement, it is the primary requirement to keep the equivalence of the rule base. Here we give a definition for the minimal cover of a rule base. Essentially, the minimal cover of a rule base is a minimal rule base whose function is equal to the initial one. In other words, the minimal cover has no implication redundant rule.

**Definition 1.** The rule base M is the minimal cover of a rule base R, if: $M^+=R^+$ and no rule r exists in M such that $\{M-r\}^+=M^+$ holds.

Clearly, if a rule base does not have any redundant rule, it is a minimal cover of itself. And if there are some redundancies in a rue base, we can get a minimal cover by removing the redundant rules. Thus we get the following proposition.

**Proposition.** Any rule base has a minimal cover.
A rule base may have more than one minimal cover, which is relevant to the process of refinement. But, they are equivalent to each other. So *the rule base refinement is the process of finding a minimal cover.*

## 2.3 Closure for a Literal Set

**Definition 2.** Let $W=\{p_1, p_2, \ldots, p_n\}$ be a set of literals and R be a rule base, the closure C for W with respect to R, denoted $C_R(W)$, can be constructed as follows:

- Include $p_1, p_2, \ldots, p_n$ in C;
- If $q_1, q_2, \cdots, q_m$ are included in C and there exists a rule $q_1\wedge q_2\wedge\ldots\wedge q_m \rightarrow q$ in $R^+$, then include q in C.

**Lemma 2.** $C_R(W)= C_{R+}(W)$.

The proposition can be trivially derived from the definition 2.2.

**Lemma 3.** A rule r is implied by a rule base R if and only if the closure $C_R(P)$ includes the conclusion of r, where P is the set constructed with all literals in the precondition of r.

**Proof:** Assume that r is the form of $p_1\wedge p_2\wedge\ldots\wedge p_m\rightarrow q$, $P=\{p_1, p_2, \ldots, p_m\}$.

1. If r is implied by R, that is R|=r, then r can be derived from some rules in R. $r\in R^+$, $p_1, p_2, \ldots, p_m$ are included in $C_R(P)$ by definition 2, so $q\in C_R(P)$.
2. If the closure $C_R(P)$ includes q, now we should verify that R |=r.

By definition 2, the construct process for $C_R(P)$ can be described as follows. Initially, $P_0$ =P, that is $P_0=\{ p_1, p_2, \ldots, p_m \}$. If $P_0$ is $C_R(P)$ then there must exists some $p_i = q$ $(1\leqslant i\leqslant m)$ , i.e. q is included in P, the result is obvious. Otherwise, $P_0$ is not $C_R(P)$. In this case, there must be some rules, at least one rule, which satisfies: a) the preconditions of the rule are all included in $P_0$; b) the result of the rule is not included in $P_0$; and, c) the rule is in $R^+$. We take anyone of these rules, denoted as $r_1$, and assume its result is $q_1$. Since the preconditions of $r_1$ is all included in $P_0$, $P_0\rightarrow q_1$.

Now we set $P_1=P_0 \cup \{q_1\}$, $P_0 \rightarrow P_1$, then for $P_1$, we can do the same as for $P_0$, and the rest may be deduced by analogy. At last we get a literal set sequence $P_0$, $P_1$, …, $P_k$ and a rule sequence $r_1$, $r_2$, …, $r_{k-1}$, where $C_R(P)= P_k$, $P_{i-1} \rightarrow P_i$, all $r_i$ are included in $R^+$, the preconditions of $r_i$ are included in $P_{i-1}$, and $P_i$ is the union of $P_{i-1}$ and the result of $r_{i-1}$ ($1 \leqslant i \leqslant k$). So $C_R(P)=\{p_1, p_2, \ldots, p_m, q_1, q_2, \ldots, q_{k-1}\}$.

Since q is in $C_R(P)$, q is in $\{ p_1, p_2, \ldots, p_m, q_1, q_2, \ldots, q_k\}$.

For the first case, the result is obvious. For the second one, we can assume that q is some $q_j$ ($1 \leqslant j \leqslant k$). Since $P_0 \rightarrow P_1$, $P_1 \rightarrow P_2$ ,…,$P_{j-1} \rightarrow P_j$, and $P_j \rightarrow q_j$ , we get $P_0 \rightarrow q_j$, i.e., $P \rightarrow q$. All the rules $P_0 \rightarrow P_1$, $P_1 \rightarrow P_2$,…, $P_{j-1} \rightarrow P_j$, and $P_j \rightarrow q_j$ are in $R^+$, so $P \rightarrow q$ can be deduced from the closure of R, i.e., R|=r. □

Lemma 3 provides an algorithm to determine whether a rule is an implication redundancy in a rule base. In the following we give the detail of the algorithm.

### 2.4 Algorithms for Determining and Eliminating Implication Redundant Rules from a Rule Base

Implication redundant rules can be determined and eliminated by the following algorithms. Algorithm 1 aims to compute the minimal cover of a rule base, i.e., it can remove all the implication redundant rules. In order to determine if a rule is redundant, algorithm 1 uses the function *imply(r:rule, R:rulebase)* that is described in algorithm 2. Algorithm 3 computes the closure of a literal set used in algorithm 2.

In the following algorithms we use two functions: *precondition(r:rule),* which get the precondition of a rule r; and, *result(r:rule),* which get the result of a rule *r*.

**Algorithm 1.** Eliminating implication redundant rules from a rule base

```
Input: A rule base R={r(1),r(2),…,r(n)}.
Output: The minimal cover of R.
FUNCTION mini_cover(R)
  R(0)=R
  FOR i=1 to n DO
     IF imply(r(i),R(i-1)-r(i))THEN
       R(i)=R(i-1)-r(i)
     ELSE R(i)=R(i-1)
  RETURN R(n)
END.
```

**Algorithm 2.** Determining whether a rule is redundant for rule base

```
Input: A rule r and a rule base R.
Output: the logical value whether r is implied by R.
FUNCTION imply(r, R)
    P=precondition(r)
    q=result(r)
    C=closure(P,R)
    IF q ∈ C THEN RETURN true ELSE  RETURN false
END.
```

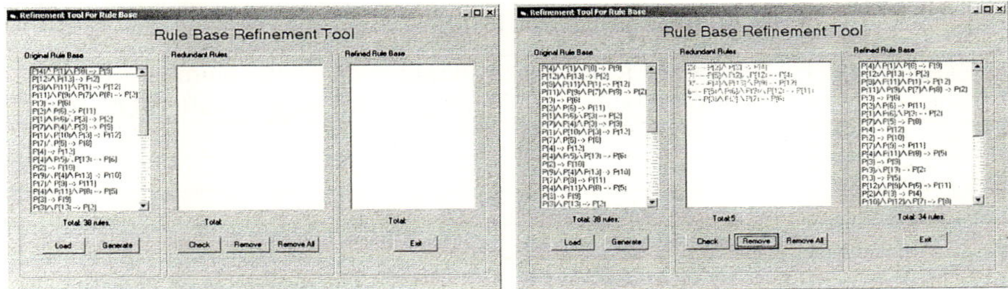


**Fig.1.** Interfaces of rule refinement tool.

**Algorithm 3.** Computing the closure for a literal set with respect to a rule base.

```
Input: A literal set W and a rule base R.
Output: the closure C for W with respect to R.
FUNCTION closure (W, R)
BEGIN
  i =0; C(0) =W; C(1)=φ
  WHILE NOT (C(i+1)=C(i)) DO
        S=φ
        FOR ALL r ∈R
         IF C(i) includes precondition(r) THEN
               S=S∪result(r)
        C(i+1)=C(i)∪S
        i = i +1
  ENDWHILE
  C= C(i)
  RETURN C
END.
```

### 2.5 Tool

Based on the algorithms in section 2.4, we developed a tool to refine rule base, which can determine and eliminate all the implication-redundant rules. Using this tool, we can select an existed rule base to refine, or generate a random one for test purpose. All the redundancies will be listed and the user can select some to remove or remove all. Fig.1 shows two interfaces of the tool, which is available at http://kg.ict.ac.cn.

We have generated 5 rule-bases as the experimental data. The results are listed in table 1. The results show that all the implication-redundancy rules can be checked and removed from the rule base.

## 3 Redundancy at Abstraction Level

### 3.1 Object Abstraction and Rule Abstraction

Some objects with a number of identical properties $O_1$, $O_2$, …, $O_n$ could be abstracted to a new object O, and O has the common properties of $O_1$, $O_2$, … , $O_n$, however, may

**Table 1.** Experimental data for rule base refinement tool.

| Experiment times | Number of Rules (before refinery) | Number of Redundant Rules | Number of Rules (after refinery) |
|---|---|---|---|
| 1 | 30 | 11 | 19 |
| 2 | 32 | 14 | 18 |
| 3 | 39 | 16 | 23 |
| 4 | 48 | 17 | 31 |
| 5 | 75 | 28 | 47 |

do not have the individual properties of each object. We say O is the abstraction of $O_1, O_2, \ldots, O_n$, denoted as $O_i \prec O$ [18].

Maybe there have some rules in a rule base that each predicate involved in each rule are identical correspondingly, but the objects involved in the predicates are different. In this case, these rules can be replaced with only one rule through objects abstraction, and then the rule base can be compacted. For example, there are two rules r: p(A)→q and s: p(X)→q, and the object X is an abstraction of the object A, then the rule r is redundant because its function is implied by s.

In another case, we suppose there is a group of rules that have the identical precondition predicates and identical conclusion predicate correspondingly, and the objects involved in each rule are different, but there are no abstract and instance relations among the objects. For example, p(A)→q, p(X)→q, where A is different from X, and there is no abstraction relationship between A and X. We can sum up these two rules as one rule: p(O)→q, and O is an abstraction of X and A.

If there are many rule-sets with above properties, the repetitions of predicates in different rules can be viewed as a kind of redundancy. We call it abstraction-rule-redundancy.

### 3.2 Rule Similarity

An atomic predicate may involve one or more terms. For instance, the atomic predicate, "X is larger than Y", involves two terms (object): X and Y.

**Definition 3.** If two literals are both positive or both negative, and their predicates agree, but the objects in the corresponding positions may be different, we call the two literals are similar to each other.

For example, $p(A_1,A_2,\ldots,A_n)$ and $p(B_1,B_2,\ldots,B_n)$ are similar, denoted $p(A_1, A_2,\ldots,A_n) \approx p(B_1,B_2,\ldots,B_n)$.

The similarity relation among literals is reflexive, symmetric, and transitive.

**Definition 4.** If two rules r and r' take the following forms:

$r : p_1(a_{11},\ldots,A_{1n(1)}) \wedge p_2(A_{21},\ldots,A_{2n(2)}) \wedge \ldots \wedge p_s(A_{s1},\ldots,A_{s\,n(s)}) \rightarrow q(A_{t1},\ldots,A_{tn})$, and

$r': p_1(B_{11},\ldots,B_{1n(1)}) \wedge p_2(B_{21},\ldots,B_{2n(2)}) \wedge \ldots \wedge p_s(B_{s1},\ldots,B_{sn(s)}) \rightarrow q(B_{t1},\ldots,B_{tn})$, where $p_i(A_{i1},\ldots,A_{i\,n(i)}) \approx p_i(B_{i1},\ldots,B_{in(i)})$, $(1 \leqslant i \leqslant s)$, and $q(A_{t1},\ldots,A_{tn})q(B_{t1},\ldots,B_{tn})$. We say r is similar to r', denoted as $r \approx r'$.

For example: p(A)∧q(B)→w(C) is similar to p(X)∧q(Y)→w(Z); p(A)→w is similar to p(C)→w.

The rule-similarity relation among rules in a rule base is reflexive, symmetric, and transitive.

### 3.3 Rule Abstraction Based on Rule Similarity

As a matter of fact, a similarity relation among rules is a classifier for a rule base, and each rule-similarity equivalent class can be replaced by only one rule with a two-dimensional table. Each row of the table is the list of objects involved a rule.

Suppose $G=\{r_1, r_2, \ldots, r_n\}$ be a rule-similarity equivalence class in a rule base, where the rules take the forms:

$r_1$: $p_1(A^1_{11}, A^1_{12},\ldots, A^1_{1k(1)})\wedge\ldots\wedge p_s(A^1_{s1}, A^1_{s2},\ldots, A^1_{sk(s)})\rightarrow q(A^1_{t1}, A^1_{t2}, \ldots, A^1_{tm})$,

$r_2$: $p_1(A^2_{11}, A^2_{12},\ldots, A^2_{1k(1)})\wedge\ldots\wedge p_s(A^2_{s1}, A^2_{s2},\ldots, A^2_{sk(s)})\rightarrow q(A^2_{t2}, A^2_{t2},\ldots, A^2_{tm})$,

… … … …

$r_n$: $p_1(A^n_{11},A^n_{12},\ldots,A^n_{1k(1)})\wedge\ldots\wedge p_s(A^n_{s1},A^n_{s2},\ldots,A^n_{sk(s)})\rightarrow q(A^n_{t2}, A^n_{t2},\ldots, A^n_{tm})$,

then G could be abstracted as one rule $r$:$p_1\wedge p_2\wedge\ldots\wedge p_s\rightarrow q$ with a two-dimensional object-table as follows:

$r_1$: $A^1_{11}, A^1_{12}, \ldots, A^1_{1k(1)}, \ldots, A^1_{s1}, A^1_{s2}, \ldots, A^1_{sk(s)}, A^1_{t1}, A^1_{t2}, \ldots, A^1_{tm}$;
$r_2$: $A^2_{11}, A^2_{12}, \ldots, A^2_{1k(1)}, \ldots, A^2_{s1}, A^2_{s2}, \ldots, A^2_{sk(s)}, A^2_{t1}, A^2_{t2}, \ldots, A^2_{tm}$;
… … … … …
$r_n$: $A^n_{11}, A^n_{12}, \ldots, A^n_{1k(1)}, \ldots, A^n_{s1}, A^n_{s2}, \ldots, A^n_{sk(s)}, A^n_{t1}, A^n_{t2}, \ldots, A^n_{tm}$.

Now, let us study some special cases about the above abstraction process.

1. If the preconditions of $u$ ($1\leqslant u\leqslant n$) rules in G are identical, and the conjunction of the conclusions of them is completeness, i.e., the logic value of $q(A^1_{t1},A^1_{t2},\ldots, A^1_{tm})\vee\ldots\vee q(A^n_{t1},\ldots,A^n_{tm})$ is always true, then these rules can be removed from the rule base and the precondition can be added into the fact base.
2. If $u$ ($1\leqslant u\leqslant n$) rules in G satisfy the following conditions:

– all literals of the preconditions of $u$ rules in G are identical except for one literal (supposing $p_s$), denoted as $P=p_1\wedge p_2\wedge\ldots\wedge p_{s-1}$,

– the conclusions of the $u$ rules are identical, i.e., the $u$ rules are of the form: $r_1$: $P \wedge p_s(A^1_{s1},A^1_{s2},\ldots,A^1_{s\,k(s)})\rightarrow q$, $r_2$: $P \wedge p_s(A^2_{s1},A^2_{s2},\ldots,A^2_{s\,k(s)})\rightarrow q$, … , $r_u$:$P\wedge p_s(A^u_{s1},A^u_{s2},\ldots,A^u_{s\,k(s)})\rightarrow q$,

– $p_s(A^1_{s1},A^1_{s2},\ldots,A^1_{s\,k(s)})\vee p_s(A^2_{s1},A^2_{s2},\ldots,A^2_{s\,k(s)})\vee\ldots\vee p_s(A^u_{s1},A^u_{s2},\ldots,A^u_{s\,k(s)})$ is always true.

Then the $u$ rules can be reduced to only one rule $P\rightarrow q$.

3. If each object involved in rule $r_i$ in G is an abstraction of the object located in corresponding position of rule $r_j$, that is:
$A^j_{11} \prec A^i_{11}, A^j_{12} \prec A^i_{12}, \ldots, A^j_{1k(1)} \prec A^i_{1k(1)}, \ldots, A^j_{s1} \prec A^i_{s1}, A^j_{s2} \prec A^i_{s2}, \ldots, A^j_{sk(s)} \prec A^i_{s\,k(s)}, A^j_{t1} \prec A^i_{t1}, A^j_{t2} \prec A^i_{t2}, \ldots, A^j_{tm} \prec A^i_{tm}$.
Then $r_j$ is an instance of $r_i$, and should be removed from the rule base.

4. Supposed that u rules in G are of the following forms:

   $r_1$: $p_1(A_{11},\ldots,O_1,\ldots,A_{1k(1)})\wedge\ldots\wedge p_s(A_{s1},\ldots,O_1,\ldots,A_{sk(s)})\wedge P\rightarrow q(A_{t1},\ldots,O_1,\ldots,A_{tm})$

   $r_2$: $p_1(A_{11},\ldots,O_2,\ldots,A_{1k(1)})\wedge\ldots\wedge p_s(A_{s1},\ldots,O_2,\ldots,A_{sk(s)})\wedge P\rightarrow q(A_{t1},\ldots,O_2,\ldots,A_{tm})$

   … … … …

   $r_u$:$p_1(A_{11},\ldots,O_u,\ldots,A_{1k(1)})\wedge\ldots\wedge p_s(A_{s1},\ldots,O_u,\ldots,A_{sk(s)})\wedge P\rightarrow q(A_{t1},\ldots,O_u,\ldots,A_{tm})$

   We can deal with this case in the following two steps.

- If the object $O_i$ involved in some rule $r_i$ is the abstraction of another object $O_j$ of some other rule $r_j$, then remove $r_j$. Repeat this process until there is no such a rule.
- If any object $O_i$ is not the abstraction of any other object $O_j$, then the objects $O_1$, $O_2,\ldots,O_n$ can be abstracted to an object O with an object-abstract set $O(O_1,O_2,\ldots, O_n)$, and all the rules can be abstracted as a rule:r: $p_1(A_{11},\ldots, O, \ldots, A_{1k(1)})\wedge\ldots\wedge p_s(A_{s1}, \ldots, O, \ldots, A_{sk(s)})\wedge P\rightarrow q(A_{t1}, \ldots, O,\ldots, A_{tm})$.

In this case object O is called abstract object of $O_1$, $O_2$, …, $O_n$ based on similar rule, and rule r is called abstract rule of $r_1, r_2,\ldots, r_n$. That is, a similar equivalent class of rules can be replaced with an abstract rule and a corresponding object-abstract set, e.g., $p(A_1)\wedge q(A_1)\rightarrow w(A_1)$, $p(A_2)\wedge q(A_2)\rightarrow w(A_2)$, and $p(A_3)\wedge q(A_3)\rightarrow w(A_3)$ can be abstracted to a rule $p(A)\wedge q(A)\rightarrow w(A)$ and an object-abstract set $A\{A_1, A_2, A_3\}$.

Some abstracted rules can be further abstracted, for example: $r_1$: $p(A_1)\wedge q(B_1)\rightarrow w(A_1, B_1)$, $r_2$: $p(A_2)\wedge q(B_1)\rightarrow w(A_2, B_1)$, $r_3$: $p(A_1)\wedge q(B_2)\rightarrow w(A_1, B_2)$, and $r_4$: $p(A_2)\wedge q(B_2)\rightarrow w(A2, B_2)$. The first two rules $r_1$ and $r_2$ can be abstracted as: $r_{12}$: $p(A)\wedge q(B_1)\rightarrow w(A, B_1)$, $A(A_1,A_2)$. The last two rules $r_3$ and $r_4$ can be abstracted as: $r_{34}$: $p(A)\wedge q(B_2)\rightarrow w(A, B_2)$, $A(A_1,A_2)$. Obviously, $r_{12}$ is similar to $r_{34}$ and they can be further abstracted, then we get the following rule: $r_{1234}$: $p(A)\wedge q(B)\rightarrow w(A,B),A(A_1,A_2)$, $B(B_1,B_2)$.

### 3.4 Algorithm for Rule Abstract Based on Rule-Similarity and Object Abstraction

**Algorithm 4.** Rule base refinement through abstraction.
**Input**: a rule base $R=\{r_1, r_2,\ldots, r_n\}$.
**Output**: a rule base $R_A$ without any similar rules.

- Classify the rule base R with the equivalence relation about rule similarity;
- Abstract all rules to a rule with a two-dimensional table about the involved objects for each equivalent class $R_i$;
- Study each table about objects after abstraction, if there are some rules satisfied the conditions of the special issues discussed in section 3.3 then the corresponding operations should be executed.

Sometimes, the last result for the abstraction refinement depends on the process, i.e., the result may not be unique. For example, we have $r_1$: $p(A_1)\wedge q(B_1)\rightarrow w(A_1, B_1)$, $r_2$: $p(A_2)\wedge q(B_1)\rightarrow w(A_2, B_1)$, and $r_3$: $p(A_1)\wedge q(B_2)\rightarrow w(A_1, B_2)$. Abstraction based on rules $r_1$ and $r_2$ is different from that based on $r_1$ and $r_3$.

## 4 Discussions and Application Prospect

- **Dead-end condition redundancy.** The third type of redundancy is dead-end condition redundancy whose precondition would never be satisfied, i.e., these rules would not be fired forever. The dead-end condition rules can be classified into following two types:
- The precondition conflicts itself, for instance, $p \wedge \sim p \rightarrow q$. In general, this kind of redundancy can be automatically checked by the system, and should be removed from the rule base.
- The precondition does not conflict itself, but it cannot be satisfied by the system forever. This kind of redundancies cannot be automatically checked by the system. According to the historical system log, we can find all rules that would have not been fired, so domain experts are required in case.
- **Applications.** Besides the traditional expert systems, the refinery for rule base can be applied in some new fields.

Mining association rules is an important task in data mining. Redundant rules may exist in the association rules mined from databases or data warehouses. So the association rule base needs to be refined. For instance, given a large database of transactions, where each transaction consists of a set of items and the taxonomy on the items, we can find associations between items at any level of the taxonomy [17]. For example, the following two association rules are mined from a supermarket sales database:

Buy a desktop computer→Buy a b/w printer [support=8%, confidence=70%], and
Buy an IBM desktop computer →Buy b/w printer [support=2%, confidence=72%].

We find that the second one is redundant for its confidence and support are almost near the expectation of the first. So we can refine them based on the proposed approach.

The proposed approach can be used in analyzing web structure. If we regard the web pages as literals and the hyperlinks among web pages as particular kind of rules, then all the hyperlinks on Internet can be regarded as a huge rule base. So the propose refinement approach can be used to simplify and generalize this huge rule base. It is especially useful when hyperlinks are extended to a kind of semantic link relationship [21]. The approach can also be used to refine inheritance rules between components [19] and to refine rules in Knowledge Grid [20].

## 5 Conclusions

This paper proposes the algorithms and a tool for refining rule base. The presented algorithms for detecting and eliminating implication redundancy are based on the closure of literal set. The refinement approach for eliminating abstraction-redundancy is proposed for the first time. Applications of the proposed approach have been presented.

## References


1. Andert, E.P.: Integrated Knowledge-based System Design and Validation for Solving Problem in Uncertain Environments, Int. J. Man-Mach Stud, 36, pp.357-373, 1992.
2. Brisoux, L. et al: Checking Depth-limited Consistency and Inconsistency in Knowledge-Based Systems, International Journal of Intelligence Systems, 16, pp.319-331, 2001.
3. Chang, C.L. et al: A report on the Expert Systems Validation Associate (EVA), Expert Systems with Applications, 1(3), pp.217–230, 1990.
4. Childress R.L. and Valtorta, M.: EVA and the Verification of Expert Systems Written in OPS5. In O'Leary, D. E. (edit), AAAI-91 Workshop on Verification and Validation of Knowledge Based Systems, AAAI, 1999.
5. Cragun, B.J. and Steudel, H.J.: A Decision-table-based Processor for Checking Completeness and Consistency in Rule-based Expert Systems. International Journal of Man-Machine Studies, 26, pp.633-648, 1987.
6. Ginsberg, A.: Knowledge-base Reduction: A New Approach to Checking Knowledge Bases for Inconsistency and Redundancy. In Proceedings, Seventh Annual National Conference on Artificial Intelligence, pp.585-589, 1988
7. Grigoris, A.: Integrity and Rule Checking in Non-monotonic Knowledge Bases, Knowledge-based Systems, 9 (5), pp.301-306, 1996.
8. Grogono, P.D. et al: 1993, A Review of Expert Systems Evaluation Techniques. In Working Notes, AAAI-93 Workshop on Validation and Verification of Knowledge-Based Systems, Washington, D.C., pp.120-125, 1993.
9. Hutter, D. et al: Formal Software Development in Verification Support Environment, Journal of Experimental and Theoretical AI, this issue, 2000.
10. Knauf, R. et al: Towards Validation and Refinement of Rule-based Systems. Journal of Experiment & Theoretical Artificial Intelligence, 12, pp.421-431, 2001.
11. Ligeza, A.: Toward Logical Analysis of Tabular Rule-based Systems, International Journal of Intelligence Systems, 16, pp.333-360, 2001.
12. Nguyen, T.A.: Checking an Expert Systems Knowledge Base for Consistency and Completeness, Proc. IJCAI'85, pp.375-379, 1985.
13. Nguyen, T.A. et al: Knowledge Base Verification. AI Magazine, 8 (2), pp.69-75, 1987.
14. Preece, A.D.: Verification of Rule-based Expert Systems in Wide Domains. In Research and Development in Expert Systems VI, Proceedings of Expert Systems '89, London, pp. 66-77, 1989.
15. Preece, A.D. and Shinghal, R.: Analysis of Verification Methods for Expert Systems. In Working Notes, AAAI-92 Workshop on Validation and Verification of Knowledge-Based Systems, San Jose, CA, 1992.
16. Suwa,M. et al: An Approach to Verifying Completeness and Consistency in Rule-based Expert Systems. AI Magazine, 3 (4), pp.16-21, 1982.
17. Srikant, R. and Agrawal, R.: Mining Generalized Association Rules, In Proc, 1995 int. Conf. Very Large Data Bases, pp.407-419, 1995.
18. Zhuge, H.: Research on Object Analogical Reasoning, Journal of Software, 6, pp.52-60, 1995.
19. Zhuge, H.: Inheritance Rules for Flexible Model Retrieval, Decision Support Systems, 22, pp.379-390, 1998.
20. Zhuge, H.: A Knowledge Grid Model and Platform for Global Knowledge Sharing, Expert Systems with Applications, 22, pp.313-320, 2002.
21. Zhuge, H.: Active Document Framework ADF: Concept and Method, in Proceedings of the 5th Asia Pacific Web Conference (LNCS), Xian, China, April, 2003.

# Developing Constraint-Based Applications with Spreadsheets

Alexander Felfernig, Gerhard Friedrich, Dietmar Jannach, Christian Russ, and Markus Zanker

Computer Science and Manufacturing, Universität Klagenfurt,
A-9020 Klagenfurt, Austria,
{felfernig,friedrich,jannach,russ,zanker}@ifit.uni-klu.ac.at

**Abstract.** Spreadsheets are in wide-spread industrial use for light-weight business applications, whereby the broad acceptance is both founded on the underlying intuitive interaction style with immediate feedback and a "programming model" comprehensible for non-programmers. In this paper we show how the spreadsheet development paradigm can be extended to model and solve a special class of search and optimization problems that occur in many application domains and would otherwise require the involvement of specialized knowledge engineers.

## 1 Introduction

Spreadsheet applications are in wide-spread industrial use for supporting several business processes like, e.g., back-office data analysis or cost estimation and quotation in the sales process. The broad acceptance of these systems is founded on two main pillars: First, the intuitive (tabular) spreadsheet user interface paradigm allows the user to directly manipulate the data. In addition, immediate user feedback is given in a way that the user is capable of detecting the effects of inputs and changes such that different scenarios can be easily analyzed. In fact, because many users are already accustomed to this specific interaction style, a spreadsheet-like interface can be used as mere front-end for more complex applications that would otherwise require more technical knowledge by the domain-expert [10, 12]. On the other hand, from the software development point of view, spreadsheets are a valuable tool that allow non-programmers to develop their own, small applications that support them in their work without requiring classical programming skills: The spreadsheet development model does (in principle) not require that the user understands concepts like *variables* or *program flow* in the first place. Moreover, the test and debugging process is alleviated for these applications as the user can immediately see the effects of changes in his/her program, i.e., the formulae. However, the main restriction of pure spreadsheet applications is their limited functionality, i.e., the main concepts are cells containing values and a set of predefined (mostly arithmetic) functions that contain references to other cells or areas. For these cases where complex business

P.W.H. Chung, C.J. Hinde, M. Ali (Eds.): IEA/AIE 2003, LNAI 2718, pp. 197–207, 2003.

logic is required, industrial-strength spreadsheets environments like Microsoft Excel offer the possibility to use an imperative (scripting) language for extending the application's functionality. Such extensions, however, require classical programming skills. Thus, the idea of having the domain expert as software engineer who develops his small software system based on his requirements is no longer possible.

Although classical Knowledge-based Systems (KBS) support the strict separation from processing logic and domain knowledge that is encoded as rules or constraints in a declarative way, there are several obstacles that prohibit non-programmers from encoding this knowledge without a knowledge engineer: First, existing systems have specific underlying conceptual models, e.g., some sort of Logic Programming, which is in many cases hard to comprehend even for programmers and require a paradigmatic shift in the way people are thinking of software systems and the problems to be solved. In addition, in many cases a problem arises also in terms of notation and syntax, i.e., given a certain lack of high-level modeling tools, the knowledge has to be encoded in a tedious, non-intuitive notation. Finally, these tools are often implemented using more or less academic languages and programming environments which makes the integration into the company's surrounding software infrastructure problematic.

Within this paper we present an approach to develop a special class of business application systems based on the extension of the functionality of standard spreadsheet environments; our goal is to narrow the gap between classical KBS development and standard software engineering processes using a interface that smoothly integrates the advanced reasoning capabilities into the spreadsheet interface paradigm. Our work is driven by real-world requirements and application scenario from the domain of intelligent product configuration outlined in Section 2. In Section 3 we describe the architecture of the CsSolver (Constraint Satisfaction Solver) system consisting of a domain-independent object-oriented constraint solver and its integration into the *Microsoft Excel* spreadsheet system. In the final sections, we discuss related work in the field and give our conclusions based on first evaluations of the prototype system.

## 2 Application Domain / Example Problem

Product configuration[1] deals with tailoring a configurable artifact (product or service) according to specific customer needs. The market demand for such systems is driven by the business model of *mass customization* [8] : nowadays, the variety of customizable goods and services ranges from personal computers, cars, or clothing to complex technical systems like telecommunication switches [4].

The result of an interactive configuration process is a customer-specific variant of the product, whereby this product constellation conforms all given business rules or technical constraints and is good or optimal with respect to some

[1] Note, that product or sales configuration must not be confused with Software Configuration Management.

objective function. Over the last decades, several AI-techniques have been successfully applied to configuration problems [13]. In particular, Constraint Satisfaction techniques [14] have shown to be specifically suited for these problems due to the simple, declarative knowledge representation paradigm and efficient solving algorithms. Informally speaking, a Constraint Satisfaction Problem (CSP) consists of a set of problem variables, each one assigned a finite domain of atomic values, and a set of constraints describing legal combinations of value assignments to the variables. A solution to a CSP is a value assignment to each problem variable such that no constraint is violated.

Let us consider a simplified example that shows the correspondence of CSPs to configuration problems from the domain of sales configuration of private telecommunication switches. In this business scenario, the sales engineer together with the customer tailor the telecommunication switch by selecting values from a set of features like *max. number of subscriber lines* or *Voice-over-IP* support.

In the CSP representation, the variables with their domains correspond to the different options, e.g.,

$$OperatingSystem = \{NT4.0, W2000\}, BasicModel = \{T200, T300, T330\},$$
$$voiceIP = \{yes, no\}, price = \{20000...50000\}$$
$$Manuals = \{English, German, French, Italian\}$$

The example constraints in our example are:

*The T300 is always delivered with voiceIP option.*
*No voiceIP available for the T200 model.*
*Manuals for T330 are English and German only.*

Let us further assume that the price is determined by some function based on the individual user choices and other pricing rules. Amongst others, the key requirements of an actual implementation are typically as follows:

- the user should not be forced to specify values for all choices, i.e., the system should be able to compute fitting values,
- the system should give immediate feedback on incompatible choices or remove choices that are no longer available due to prior selections,
- the system should be able to compute a good/optimal solution with respect to some objective function.

The mapping of this simplified application problem to a CSP is quite straightforward. However, due to the shortcomings of currently available systems the development of such an application typically requires significant coding efforts and highly-specialized development staff. Moreover, the transformation of the domain knowledge to the expert system's representation requires a possibly error-prone knowledge engineering process.

In order to overcome these problems, we developed the CsSolver system as an extension to standard spreadsheets environments; the major design goals were to fit our extensions to the interaction and development paradigm for spreadsheets as much as possible while hiding the technical details of the underlying reasoning process. Figure 1 shows, how the example problem described above can be solved using our system.

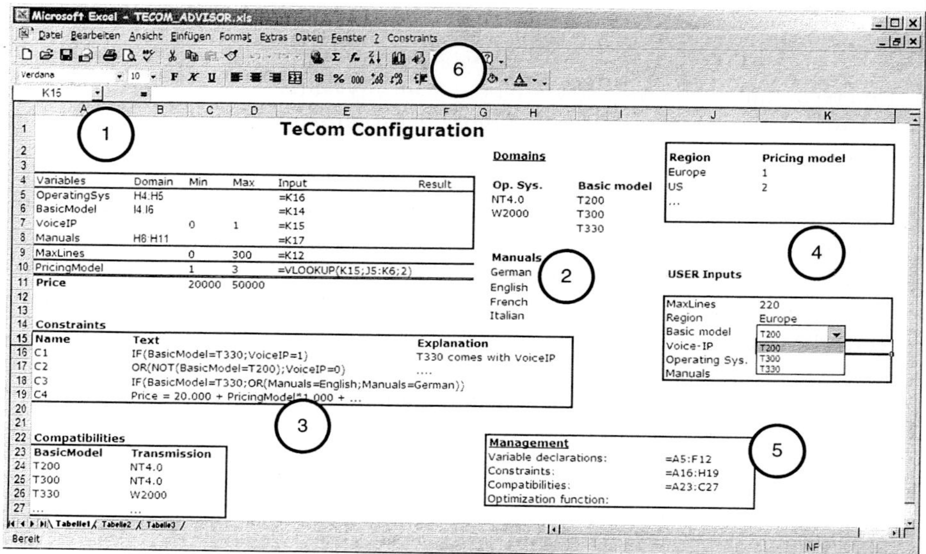


**Fig. 1.** Application screenshot for telecommunication switch configuration

In the first step (1) the user defines the named problem variables with their domain. This domain can either be an integer interval or an enumeration of symbolic values in a specified area (2). In addition, the developer can specify what the (user) inputs for the problem variables are, by referencing to other parts of the spreadsheet (4). Note that all the standard functionality of the spreadsheet system can be used for computing the input from e.g., some static data from the application domain. In our case, for instance, the input for the field "pricing model" is computed by looking up the pricing model in (4) that corresponds to the input from K13 (the customer's geographic location). The placement and layout of the fields for the user input can be arbitrarily chosen by the developer. In addition, within modern spreadsheet environments, it is also possible to integrate external data sources smoothly into the application, for instance via an ODBC (Open Database Connectivity) interface. This is a key requirement in our application domain of product configuration where product data is already stored in an e.g., underlying Enterprise Resource Planning system; moreover the results of the configuration process have to be transferred back to this system for order generation and invocation of other business processes.

In the next step (3) the developer defines the problem constraints: This can be done in two ways. In many domains, compatible value tuples for individual variables are naturally given in compatibility tables, i.e., the constraint is defined in *explicit* form by enumerating all allowed constellations. As a second choice, the user can state the constraints by using a constraint language having the same syntax as the standard "language" in our spreadsheet environment. For example, a conditional statement of type $if < cond > then < val1 > else < val2 >$

is expressed in Microsoft Excel as `IF(cond;val1;val2)`. Currently our constraint language supports standard arithmetic, relational, and logic operators ($=, +, -, *, /, >, <, NOT, OR, IF...$) for integer variables. In addition, some constraints that can typically be found in Constraint Satisfaction problems like *AllDifferent* - meaning that all variables of a given set of variables must take a different value - where introduced although there is no direct correspondence to a similar standard spreadsheet function. Note that the developer of the spreadsheet application has to be aware of the fact that formulated restrictions are *declarative* constraints rather than *functions*, which he can use in ordinary spreadsheet applications.

The developer states the constraints as plain text which is then parsed online, immediately translated into the internal representation of the underlying constraint solver, and dynamically added to the problem space. The individual constraints can be annotated with a name and an explanatory text. The constraint name and the parse errors are prompted in cases where the constraint parser detects syntactic or semantic errors, e.g., a reference to an undefined variable name or a type error. The explanatory text will be used if - during the propagation process of the user inputs - the solver detects a constraint violation. In these cases, the user will be prompted the information which of his/her selections caused a constraint violation and which value selections have to be undone or changed. Note however that the frequency of such situations is small because the underlying constraint propagator is capable of inferring the set of still consistent (allowed) values for the remaining variables after each user input.

All the information of the constraint problem is simply entered at arbitrary places in the spreadsheet application[2]. In the *Management* area (5) we define which areas contain the actual constraint satisfaction problem which allows us to arbitrarily design the layout of the application.

The standard spreadsheet environment is extended with a menu (6) that allows the developer to initiate the search or optimization process. If the constraint solver finds a consistent assignment the result is displayed in the output area of (1). In the example from Figure 1, the solver can derive fitting values for the operating system, the basic model and so forth. These computed values can then be referenced from within other parts of the spreadsheet application. During the interaction process where the user sequentially enters the input values, the solver can immediately propagate the effects of the new input and remove inconsistent values from the domains of the remaining variables. At any stage, the user can initiate the search process such that the constraint engine computes values for the remaining problem variables where no user input was given. As a net result for the developer, the trial and error interactive development style of spreadsheet applications without (lengthy) compilation, test, and debug runs is preserved. On the other hand - when *using* the application - high interactivity with immediate feedback is possible such that the user of the system can explore different solution variants and scenarios.

---

[2] Typically, the constraint problem is only a part of a larger application that e.g., includes reports or diagrams.

## 3 The CsSsolver System

**Architecture of the CsSolver System:** In Figure 2, we sketch the different components that make up the CsSolver system. The core of the system is formed by a small object-oriented finite-domain constraint solving library that is built in the tradition of the first approach from [9] that combines Constraint Programming and Object-Orientation using C++, i.e., variables, constraints as well as search goals are classes of the framework. The main advantages of such an approach that can also be found in commercial constraint solvers like ILOG Solver[3] are twofold: First, constraint solving functionality can be easily incorporated in an (object-oriented) application without needing a bridge to some e.g., Logic Programming environment. Second, the inherent extensibility of object-oriented systems can be exploited: The components of the framework can be subclassed for the given application domain, e.g., by introducing a specific type of constraint of new search heuristics. The library implements a forward-checking and backtracking search algorithm and a variant of the *AC-3* [14] algorithm for maintaining arc-consistency and reducing the search space.

The library was developed in *C#*, a programming language from Microsoft's *.Net Framework*[4]. *C#* is an object-oriented language that is syntactically and semantically similar to *Java* and introduces only a few novel language concepts. The most interesting feature from our perspective is interoperability between applications written in different programming languages which is made possible by compilation of the source code to an intermediate language. Consequently the developed constraint library can be easily included in other applications, which is a key requirement for broad acceptance of knowledge-based systems in industrial environments. Within the CsSolver system, communication between the spreadsheet environment and the core solver is based on a *COM* (Component Object Model) interface. While the standard behavior of the solver that can be accessed via the spreadsheet interface is limited in order to preserve simplicity, the solver's API allows programmers to access the full functionality of the underlying solver engine; thus, specific search heuristics or complex functions can be incorporated by the library developers.

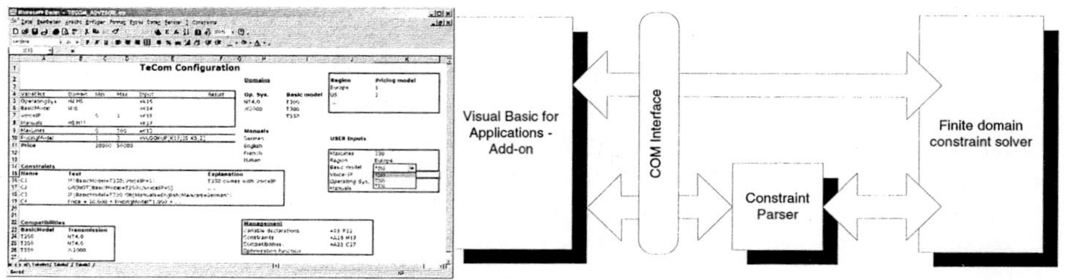


**Fig. 2.** Architecture overview.

[3] http://www.ilog.com

[4] http://www.microsoft.com/net

The other components of the CsSolver system are a small add-on program written in the scripting language of the spreadsheet environment that catches the events triggered by the user (e.g., definition of variables or initiation of the search process) and appropriately forwards data to the back-end constraint solver. When the user defines his/her constraint problem using the spreadsheet interface, the application-dependent constraints have to be transformed to the internal representation of the solver which is accomplished by a compiler that parses the expressions and issues calls to the solver library accordingly.

**Constraint Satisfaction and Object Orientation:** In [9], a C++ library (ILOG Solver) was presented that for the first time combined object-oriented programming with concepts from Constraint Logic Programming (CLP) like variables, constraints and backtracking search. Later on also other systems like CHIP[5], that were originally based on Prolog, were available as libraries for imperative languages (C and C++). For the CsSolver system we adopted a similar approach using the *C#* language, whereby at the moment only a subset of the functionality of commercial software packages is available, e.g., no floating-point arithmetic.

A fragment of how to use the constraint library is sketched below:

```
1: CsSolver s = new CsSolver();
2: CsVar a = s.createIntVar(0,3,"a");
3: CsVar b = s.createIntVar(0,3,"b");
4: s.addConstraint(a != b);
5: s.addGoal(new CsInstantiate(s,a));
6: s.addGoal(new CsInstantiate(s,b));
7: if (s.solve())
8:  Console.WriteLine("Found Solution");
```

After initialization of a new solver object that manages the constraint networks (1) two constrained variables with a finite domain [0..3] are declared. In line (4) a constraint is declared that in a consistent solution these two variables must have a different value. Note that we can utilize the *operator overloading* feature of the *C#* language such that an intuitive representation of the constraints is possible. In the following lines, the search goals (instantiation of variables) are declared and finally the solution search is initiated.

The important benefits of such an implementation are as follows (see also [9]): Since all the CSP related concepts are implemented as classes, the framework is intrinsically extensible for specific application domains that require e.g., special sorts of constraints, heuristics, or actions to be taken during the search process. For these cases, the particular behaviour for the application domain can be implemented by subclassing the framework's classes. On the other hand, the classes of the framework can certainly be members of other application-specific classes such that the constraint variables are instantiated for each application specific object.

[5] see http://www.cosytec.fr

### 3.1 Evaluation

The business scenarios addressed with the CsSolver system comprise e.g., on-site sales configuration and quotation, i.e., the users of the spreadsheet application are sales representatives that - possibly together with a customer - interactively tailor the solution to the customer's needs. Our experiences show that for these cases, companies tend to equip their sales representatives with sales force automation tools that are developed for the given application domain. These tools are typically implemented by incorporating an intelligent reasoning system like a rule engine, a Logic Programming environment, or a constraint reasoner. Within rule-based systems, the knowledge is encoded in terms of *if-then* rules which are on the one hand easy to understand for non-programmers (in cases where there is an intuitive notation) but on the other hand have shown to cause severe maintenance problems [1]. Moreover, these systems are limited in their expressiveness, optimization is only based on heuristics, and they are limited with regard to explanation both in cases where no solution can be found as well as in cases where the customer wants to know the reasons why the system came up with a particular solution. Logic Programming systems like *Eclipse*[6] offer a complete programming environment including constraint solving capabilities; constraint-based optimization tools like ILOG Solver provide a whole suite of different algorithms for complex, large-scale optimization problems. In principle, the latter two classes of systems can theoretically be used as a back-end for our CsSolver environment. However, when using Logic Programming environments, specialized programming staff and skilled knowledge engineers are required; in addition, the user interface is typically developed using a traditional programming language which can lead to integration problems if there are several development teams involved. On the other hand, commercial optimization tools are in many cases heavy-weight libraries that exceed the functionality that is required in our targeted application domains. Finally, given the small fraction of utilized functionality, the typically high license costs for these advanced systems may also hamper the wide-spread application of these systems.

In many cases we encountered limited acceptance for these sales-force automation tools by the sales personnel because of proprietary user interfaces: The terminology used in the interface is related to the underlying reasoning technology and therefore not understandable for the domain expert. In addition the problem solving process in many cases requires complex interactions where the user has to jump back and forward through different input screens. In fact, we encountered cases where the sales personnel did not use the provided sales-force automation tools but rather built small stand-alone systems based on spreadsheets by themselves.

Another method of solving optimization problems which is supported by some spreadsheet applications are *Operations Research* techniques like linear optimization. In fact there are many problems that can be more efficiently modeled and solved using different variants of classical mathematical algorithms like

[6] http://www.icparc.ic.ac.uk/eclipse.

the Simplex method. We see our work as complementary as these methods require a certain amount of mathematical background knowledge from the users that model the problem; moreover, the expressiveness is in many cases limited to equations and inequalities. The Constraint Satisfaction approach in contrast has its advantages as it relies on a very simple basic model and the relations among the variables can be intuitively modeled using a constraint language. While mathematical methods in many cases are able to compute *one* optimal solution, the search method used in our approach gives the user the possibility to compute multiple alternative solutions for cases where the optimization criterion cannot be expressed as purely mathematical function as the (more or less vague) user preferences have to be taken into account. Finally, the AI-based CSP approach enables the system to generate explanations, why a certain solution was found or no solution was found, which is an important factor in interactive applications.

## 4 Related Work

In [10], Renschler describes a practical application for the configuration of radio base stations using a spreadsheet-like interface. From the end user's perspective, this approach is similar to ours regarding the application domain of product configuration: the end user can interactively select the desired features and gets immediate feedback on incompatible choices whereby this computation is based on the integration of an underlying *Constraint Logic Programming* environment and a finite domain constraint solver. There are, however, several important differences when we compare their work with ours: First, although the interaction style is called "Configuration spreadsheet", in our opinion, the actual implementation resembles the main characteristics of spreadsheet only in the sense that the user interface elements are arranged in tabular form, no hard-coded sequence of interaction is required, and immediate feedback is given. The user of the system can not, however, insert any formulae or use additional input or output fields. Moreover, the user interface is extended with domain and search-specific input controls which are unknown in standard spreadsheet applications and therefore require a certain amount of knowledge on the reasoning mechanism by the system's user. Their approach addresses the aforementioned paradigm mismatch of easy-to-use spreadsheets and constraint programming only from the end user's perspective (using the spreadsheet as mere frontend) but does not solve the problem of program development for the knowledge base.

The *Knowledgesheet* approach presented in [5] is the most similar work compared with our CsSolver system: it relies on an extension of the function-based spreadsheet paradigm with predicates or constraints that are evaluated by an underlying Constraint Programming system. Likewise, with their system, a certain class of constraint problems can be modeled and solved requiring only a limited knowledge of declarative constraint programming concepts like variables or constraints. The main difference compared to our approach is the integration aspect into state-of-the-art spreadsheet environments: while their approach was validated by building a Java-based prototype that interacts with a fully-fledged Constraint Logic Programming (CLP) environment (Eclipse), the CsSolver system is completely integrated into the widespread Microsoft Excel spreadsheet environment and only requires a light-weight object-oriented constraint solver. Moreover, communication between the front-end and the solver in *Knowledgesheet* requires a specific file-based data exchange protocol whereas the CsSolver environment provides a modular API for communication and a flexible way of extending the functionality of the constraint solver. Finally, the constraint language in *Knowledgesheet* follows the notation of the underlying CLP system, whereas we wanted to have a notation for constraints that is as similar as possible to the ordinary spreadsheet functions in the spreadsheet environment. In our opinion, this basically syntactical difference is an important one because in typical applications, the search/optimization problem is always part of a larger (spreadsheet) problem where the standard spreadsheet functionality will be utilized (which is not supported in *Knowledgesheet*).

An even earlier approach to combine the power of interactive software development with spreadsheets and Logic Programming is described in [12]: Based on the idea of Programming-by-Example, the authors propose a spreadsheet-like programming environment (PERPLEX - System) for end users of logic programs. The tabular representation is used to overcome the usability limitations of classical line-oriented interfaces to logic programs: Using a spreadsheet interface, the end-user of the logic program can both incrementally extend the program by posting additional predicates as well as query the contents which are then displayed in tabular form. Compared with our approach, their work only uses the spreadsheet as extended interface for a given logic program, the program itself (i.e., the rules and facts) is still encoded in some logic programming language, like Prolog. Another limitating factor of the system is that the predicates and queries that can be interactively posted have to be expressed in the Logic Programming language of the underlying system.

Despite their wide-spread use in various application domains, e.g., Management Information or Decision Support, many facets of spreadsheet programs and spreadsheet development are still unexplored. The main research efforts in that direction aim at applying established software engineering practices to the spreadsheet development, see e.g., [6] or [11]. The significant demand for adequate development support is driven by the fact that most spreadsheet programs are developed by people who are not IT-professionals, which results is error-prone systems and severe maintenance problems. Complementary, current research efforts exist, that try to apply the intuitive spreadsheet interaction paradigm for general software development based on Visual Programming, see, e.g., [2].

## 5 Conclusions and Future Work

Our first experiences with the developed CsSolver framework showed the applicability of the approach for a wider range of search and optimization problems that can be modeled as Constraint Satisfaction Problems like product configuration or time-tabling. The first feedback received from potential end-users of the spreadsheet interface for modeling and solving such problems shows that only a small amount of additional background on Constraint Satisfaction concepts have to be learned in order to be able to design and use the system.

Our future work will be focused on improving the understandability of the reasoning process for the end-user. This includes both *explanation* of a solution or explanation of a failure [7] and repair support [3].

## References


1. V.E. Barker, D.E. O'Connor, J.D. Bachant, and E. Soloway. Expert systems for configuration at Digital: XCON and beyond. *Communications of the ACM*, 32, 3:298–318, 1989.
2. M. Burnett, J. Atwood, R. W. Djang, J. Reichwein, H. Gottfried, and S. Yang. Forms/3: A first-order visual language to explore the boundaries of the spreadsheet paradigm. *Journal of Functional Programming*, 11(2):155–206, 2001.
3. A. Felfernig, G. Friedrich, D. Jannach, and M. Stumptner. Consistency-based diagnosis of configurator knowledge bases. In $14^{th}$ *European Conference on Artificial Intelligence (ECAI2000)*, Berlin, Germany, 2000. IOS Press.
4. G. Fleischanderl, G. Friedrich, A. Haselböck, H. Schreiner, and M. Stumptner. Configuring Large Systems Using Generative Constraint Satisfaction. In B. Faltings and E. Freuder, editors, *IEEE Intelligent Systems, Special Issue on Configuration*, volume 13,4, pages 59–68. IEEE, 1998.
5. G. Gupta and S.H. Akhter. Knowledgesheet: A graphical spreadsheet interface for interactively developing a class of constraint programs. In *Practical Aspects of Declarative Languages, Lecture Notes in Computer Science 1753*, pages 308–323. Springer Verlag, 2000.
6. T. Isakowitz, S. Schocken, and H. C. Jr. Lucas. Toward a logical/physical theory of spreadsheet modeling. *ACM Transactions on Information Systems*, 13(1):1–37, 1995.
7. U. Junker. Quickxplain: Conflict detection for arbitrary constraint propagation algorithms. In *IJCAI'01 Workshop on Modelling and Solving problems with constraints*, Seattle, WA, 2001.
8. B.J. Pine, S. Davis, and B.J. Pine II. *Mass Customization : The New Frontier in Business Competition.* Harvard Business School Press, 1999.
9. J. F. Puget. A C++ implementation of CLP. In *Proceedings of the Second Singapore International Conference on Intelligent Systems*, Singapore, 1994.
10. A. Renschler. Configuration spreadsheet for interactive constraint problem solving. In *Practical Applications of Constraint Technology, PACT98*, 1998.
11. B. Ronen, M. A. Palley, and Henry C. Luca. Spreadsheet analysis and design. *Communications of the ACM*, 32(1):84–93, 1989.
12. M. Spenke and C. Beilken. A spreadsheet interface for logic programming. In *Proc. Computer-Human Interaction, CHI98*, 1998.
13. M. Stumptner. An overview of knowledge-based configuration. *AI Communications*, 10(2), June, 1997.
14. E. Tsang. *Foundations of Constraint Satisfaction.* Academic Press, 1993.

# Diagnosis of Dynamic Systems: A Knowledge Model That Allows Tracking the System during the Diagnosis Process*

Carlos J. Alonso, César Llamas, Jose A. Maestro, and Belarmino Pulido

GSI, Dept. de Informática, Universidad de Valladolid, Spain,
{calonso|cllamas|jose|belar}@infor.uva.es

**Abstract.** A knowledge-based model for on-line diagnosis of complex dynamic systems is proposed. Domain knowledge is modelled via causal networks which consider temporal relationships among symptoms and causes. Inference and task knowledge is described using the CommonKADS methodology. The main feature of the proposal is that the diagnosis task is able to track the evolution of the system incorporating new symptoms to the diagnosis process. Diagnosis is conceived as a task to be carried out by a supervisory system, which could select the suitable causal network to perform diagnosis, depending on the current system configuration and operation point.

**Keywords**: Knowledge model, Knowledge based diagnosis, Diagnosis of dynamic systems, Supervision

## 1 Introduction

Although diagnosis of dynamic systems has been approached in several ways and with different degree of success, [1–4], it is still an open problem and knowledge-based systems are a reasonable alternative [1], specially when facing complex systems for which a certain body of expert knowledge may be available.

Price in [5], gives a good and up to date synthesis of knowledge-based methods for the task of diagnosing dynamic systems. Eventually, he puts forward one of the motivations of this work: the majority of knowledge-based systems eludes the dynamic aspects of the problem, performing diagnosis at the request of the user and analyzing only the available data up to the moment when the request was originated.

Nevertheless, systems like industrial plants, [5, 6], require a continuous monitoring facility that may automatically launch a diagnosis process when an abnormal situation is detected and, possibly, watching system evolution from detection time. Though there are some proposal of knowledge-based systems with these kind of capabilities, like SIDIA, MUDIA [7] or MIDAS [8], to the best of

* This work has been funded by grants CICyT TAP99-0344 and MCyT DPI2002-01809 from Spanish government.

P.W.H. Chung, C.J. Hinde, M. Ali (Eds.): IEA/AIE 2003, LNAI 2718, pp. 208–218, 2003.

our knowledge these systems did not reach the production stage. Notable exceptions are the systems based on "Chronicles" [9, 10] or the approach taken on the OLID[1] generation [11, 12]. Both systems are able to integrate new information in an ongoing diagnosis task exploiting simple temporal models. The knowledge model presented in this paper is inspired in the OLID generation and could be considered as a generalization and formalization of the work presented in [12].

Before introducing the model, it must be said that in this work the diagnosis task is considered as an integral part of a supervisory system, as stated in [6], where eight basic supervisory task are proposed. Of these eight tasks, four of them are specially relevant in this context: State Assessment, Monitoring, Operation Mode and Diagnosis. State Assessment identifies the Operation Protocol currently in use to manage the plant; Monitoring tracks predefined signals; Operation Mode takes care of external faults, that is, deviations form the Operation Protocol. Consequently the diagnosis task only considers physical —internal— faults and can be adapted to the current Operation Protocol. The proposed model has been designed to work on this context, specifying a generic diagnosis strategy via COMMONKADS inference and task layers [13]. Domain specific knowledge is modelled with causal networks extended with basic temporal information, and the diagnosis task may be invoked with the casual network appropriate to the current Operation Protocol.

The rest of the paper is organized as follows. Next section defines the extended casual network used to model the domain knowledge. Section 3 briefly describes the knowledge model for the diagnosis task. Due to space limitations, this section has been reduced to a minimum, presenting detailed models only for the most innovative subtask: delayed-diagnosis, which is responsible for integrating new symptoms on the diagnosis process. A simple example to illustrate some of the main ideas and a short discussion will finish this work.

## 2 Domain Knowledge Schema

The necessary domain knowledge to carry out the diagnosis task is represented by means of a causal network. This causal network has been designed keeping in mind that diagnosis starts when the monitoring task assesses a significant deviation in a monitored variable. Each monitored variable will have an associated node in the net, that will act as the input node when diagnosis is invoked for this monitored variable.

### 2.1 Separable Causal Network

This section introduces the basic structure of the causal network (CN) (Figure 1), which has been designed to isolate the causes that could be identified with information available at detection time from causes whose discrimination requires new symptoms after the detection stage. The causal network contains

[1] OLID stands for *On-Line Industrial Diagnoser*

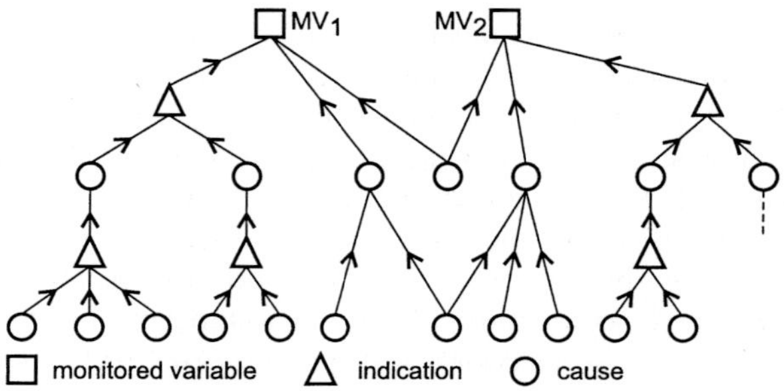


**Fig. 1.** Generic causal-effect graph.

three kinds of nodes: monitored variables ($MV$), indications ($I$) and causes ($C$). Let $N$ be the set of nodes and $A$ the set of arcs in the graph $\text{CN} = \langle N, A \rangle$, the causal network can be defined accurately as:

**Definition 1 (Causal network, CN).** *A finite, directed acyclic graph* $\text{CN} = \langle N, A \rangle$*, where* $N = MV \cup I \cup C$ *and constrained to*

*a)* $MV \cap I = MV \cap C = I \cap C = \varnothing$*,*

*b) the underlying undirected graph is connected*

*is a* causal network *if the following conditions are fulfilled:*

1. $\forall v \in MV$:
   (a) $father(v) = \{\varnothing\}$*, and* $leaf(v) = false$.
   (b) $v$ *is a root of a directed tree* $T_v$. $T_v = \langle N_v, A_v \rangle$*, such that* $N_v \subseteq N$*,* $A_v \subseteq A$ *and* $\forall k \in N_v$ *such that* $\exists(k, j, \ldots, v)$*, path from* $k$ *to* $v$*, the nodes* $k, j \in N_v$ *and the* $arc(k, j) \in A_v$.
2. $\forall i \in I$: $father(i) \in MV \cup C$, $leaf(i) = false$*, and* $\forall c\ child(i, c), c \in C$.
3. $\forall c \in C$: $father(c) \in MV \cup I$.

Each $T_v$ groups first hand information to diagnose $v$. Each $c \in C$ represents a cause that may explain a deviation of MV. Each $i \in I$ stands for a set of suspicious causes depending on some already observed *effects*, but further discrimination of one of these causes would rely on future additional *effects*. Another condition is imposed over the tree branches that contains indication nodes.

**Definition 2 (Separation condition).** *Let* CN *be a causal network and* $P = (n_1, \ldots, n_m, v)$ *a path in* CN *where* $n_1 \in C$ *is a leaf node,* $v \in MV$ *and at least exists a node* $n_j \in I$*. The path* $P$ *satisfies the* separation condition *iff every arc* $(n_j, n_{j+1})$ *in the path verify,*

$n_j \in C$ *and* $n_{j+1} \in I$*, or*

$n_j \in I$ *and* $n_{j+1} \in C$.

*except for the last arc* $(n_m, v)$ *where* $n_m \in I$.

**Definition 3 (Separable causal network, SCN).** *A causal network SCN is* separable *iff all the paths which contain indication nodes comply with the separation condition.*

The separation condition ensures that every path from a leaf to the root containing indication nodes is restricted to the form $(c_1, i_1, \ldots, c_{n_I}, i_{n_I}, v)$ where $c_i \in C$, $i_j \in I$ for $j = 1, 2, \ldots, n_I$ and $v \in MV$.

Figure 1 shows, as an example, some possibilities for a separable causal network. This figure shows a kind of forest, but in this case, trees can share some leafs. This makes sense for an efficient computing.

**Proposition 1.** *Let $SCG = \langle N, A \rangle$ be a separable causal network and $v \in MV$. Let $T_v = \langle N_v, A_v \rangle$ be the tree associated with $v$. Then $T_v$ permits a unique decomposition into two sub-trees, $T_{v,f} = \langle N_{v,f}, A_{v,f} \rangle$ and $T_{v,s} = \langle N_{v,s}, A_{v,s} \rangle$ such that $T_{v,f}$ contains only paths that do not include indication nodes and $T_{v,s}$ paths with indication nodes.*

From the Proposition 1 follows that $T_{v,f}$ and $T_{v,s}$ verify the properties:

- $T_v = T_{v,f} \cup T_{v,s}$ and, $T_{v,f} \cap T_{v,s} = \langle \{v\}, \varnothing \rangle$
- $N_{v,f} \cap I = \varnothing$ and $N_{v,s} \cap I \neq \varnothing$

## 2.2 An Extended Causal-Effect Network

The causal network allows us to model cause-effect relationships for each MV. However, causal networks could also be employed to include information related to symptoms and source causes that induce them: relationships of necessity, contingency, etc. Additionally, we will extend the representation in the temporal dimension since temporal location of causes and effects provides interesting information for diagnosing [14].

To include temporal information we will assume a linear, discrete time model, and resort to the classical McDermott proposal distinguishing between type proposition, without temporal location, and token proposition, which situates the proposition in an absolute time, to be determined at execution time.

**Definition 4 (Token node).** *A* token node *is a pair $(n, t_a)$ where $n \in N$ and $t_a$ is an absolute temporal reference.*

If $n \in MV$ then $t_a$ is the discrepancy detection time, fixed by the monitoring task. Otherwise, $t_a$ is stated by the diagnosis task.

**Definition 5 (Type effect).** *An* effect *is an expression that contains relations about the values of attributes of some objects.*

An example of *effect* could be $\Delta$LT1.value $\approx 0$. It states that the value of $\Delta$LT1 is close to 0.

**Definition 6 (Relative token effect).** *A* relative token effect *is a pair $(e, j)$ where $e$ is an effect and $j \in R^+ \cup \{0\}$ states the amount of time units, to the past regarding to an absolute reference, the effect had to be verified.*

For instance, ($\Delta$LT1.value $\approx$ 0, 13) represents the fact that $\Delta$LT1.value $\approx 0$ was true 13 time units before some absolute temporal reference.

**Definition 7 (Token effect).** *A* token effect *is a pair $(e, t_a)$ where $e$ is an effect and $t_a$ is an absolute temporal reference.*

**Definition 8 (Symptom).** *Let* CN $= \langle N, A\rangle$ *be a causal network. A* symptom *is a tuple* $\langle a, Er, k\rangle$ *such that,* $a \in A$*,* $Er$ *is a set of relative token effects and* $k \in R^+ \cup \{0\}$ *is a relative time reference.*

The concept of *symptom* formalizes the notion of set of effects needed to assess a cause, although its precise meaning depends on the relative time reference $k$.

Because of the dynamic nature of the process, the necessary effects to assess a cause could exhibit rather different dynamics. For effects appearing before the detection by the monitoring task, it is enough to log past values in order to query them at the detection instant. However, if a symptom only arises after the detection time, it will be necessary to keep watching the system evolution previous to confirm or reject its existence. This feature allow us to distinguish between two kinds of symptoms: symptoms already present at the detection instant —*fast* symptoms— and symptoms not yet present —*slow* symptoms.

**Definition 9 (Fast & slow symptoms).** $\langle a, Er, k\rangle$ *is a* fast symptom *if* $k = 0$*, otherwise* ($k \in R^+$) *is a* slow symptom.

If there exists a token cause $(c_1, t_a)$ and $a = (c_1, c_2)$ is an arc with origin at $c_1$ a fast symptom $\langle a, Er, 0\rangle$ means that to establish $c_2$ at time $t_a$ it is necessary to observe all the token effects $(e, t_a - j)$, with $(e, j) \in Er$. However, a slow symptom $\langle a, Er, k\rangle$ means that to establish $c_2$ at time $t_a$ it is necessary to observe all the token effects $(e, t_a - j + l)$ for some $l \in (0, k]$ and $(e, j) \in Er$. In sort, if $k = 0$, a cause is established if the effects are already present at the detection time. If $k > 0$, the diagnostician may wait for $k$ time units after detection time to observe the effects.

**Definition 10 (Separable symptom family, SSF).** *Let SCN be a separable causal network and* $S = \{(a, Er(a), k(a)), a \in A\}$ *a symptom family, with* $k : A \to R^+ \cup \{0\}$ *and* $Er : A \to \mathcal{P}(ER)$ *functions.* $ER$ *is the finite set of all relative effects in the system and* $\mathcal{P}(ER)$ *the power set of* $ER$*.* $S$ *is a* Separable symptom family *iff the next constraints are fulfilled:*

1. $\forall a \in A, \exists (a, Er(a), k(a)) \in S,$
2. $k(a) > 0$ *iff* $a = (i, c)$ *with* $c \in C$ *and* $i \in I$.

The key property of a *separable symptom family* stems in that all the symptoms are fast but (necessarily) those assigned to arcs leaving from indication nodes.

**Definition 11 (Extended causal network).** *Let SCN be a separable causal network and S a separable symptom family to SCN. An* Extended causal network *is the pair* $\langle RCS, S\rangle$.

According to Proposition 1, for every node $v \in MV$ of an Extended causal network, there is a tree $T_v = T_{v,f} \cup T_{v,s}$. The requirement on the symptoms to be separable warranties that $T_{v,f}$ may be used to diagnose with present and past data. On the contrary, $T_{v,s}$ will be use to diagnose with data to be collected after detection time.

## 3 A Knowledge Model for Dynamic Diagnosis

Inputs to the diagnosis task are *complaint* and *protocol*. The role *complaint* can only be instantiated by a node Monitored Variable, while the role *protocol* describes the current Operation Protocol. The static role that supports the task, *causal-temporal model*, is instantiated to the set of Extended casual networks available. The output of the task is a *causal explanation*, that is, a sequence of causes form a leaf cause to a node Monitored Variable.

The diagnosis task is decomposed into tree subtask: previous diagnosis, instant diagnosis and delayed diagnosis. These subtasks are sequentially invoked until one of them is able to find out a *causal explanation*. If this is not the case, the output of the task is UNKNOWN.

The previous diagnosis task has been designed to reduce to a minimum the number of considered causes. Basically, it searches, among the set of current active causes, for a path from one of them to the current *complaint*. In this situation the same cause is also considered as responsible for that new complaint.

The instant diagnosis task tries to find out a causal explanation for a complaint using only the observations available up to the detection time. The method proposed to perform the task is a plain alternative to the causal covering method in Schreiber et al. [13]. The search starts form the node Monitorized Variable that instantiate the complaint and is restricted to its associated fast tree, $T_{v,f}$.

The delayed diagnosis task was designed to wait for new symptoms to appear before yielding a diagnostic. It also starts searching form the node Monitorized Variable but the search is now limited to its associated slow tree, $T_{v,s}$. Its inference structure is given in Figure 2, and includes the following inferences:

**cover** *complaint*: that generates the nodes indication children of the complaint.

**immediate test** *indication*: tests the presence of the fast symptoms

**sort** *delayed hypotheses*: the hypotheses are ordered by the maximum waiting time for their associated effects, that is, the relative temporal reference that defines their symptoms.

**delayed test** *ordered hypotheses*: it checks the presence of the slow symptoms, rejecting those hypotheses whose maximum waiting time have already elapsed.

**generate** *causal explanation*: creates a causal explanation traversing the casual network from the current hypothesis, if it was established as a leaf cause.

This task, completely described in Figure 2, is able to discriminate among causes with common fast symptoms waiting for their slow symptoms.

## 4 An Example (Pieces of Domain Knowledge)

The proposed diagnosis model evolves from the OLID generation and it is being tested on a pilot plant at laboratory scale. A Real-time expert system shell is used for software development and the interface of the application is shown in Figure 3, including a plant sketch. The plant includes thermo/hydraulic processes and, hence, it is possible the manifestation of phenomena with very different

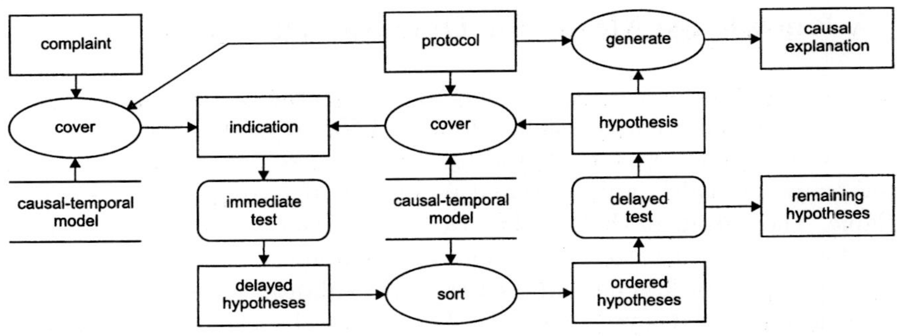


```
TASK delayed-diagnosis ;
  GOAL : "Finding a causal explanation for a complaint" ;
  ROLES : INPUT : complaint : "Observed discrepancy" ;
                  protocol : "Active operation protocol" ;
          OUTPUT :
                  causal-explanation : "Causal path from a cause to the complaint" ;
  SPECIFICATION : "Finding a causal path such that the complaint can be explained,
      in a consistent way with observations up to the present and in the future" ;
END TASK
TASK-METHOD simple-temporal-covering ;
  REALIZES : delayed-diagnosis ;
  DECOMPOSITION : INFERENCES : cover, sort, generate ;
                  TASKS : immediate-test, delayed-test ;
  ROLES : INTERMEDIATE :
    hypothesis : "A fulfilled cause for a complaint";
    delayed-hypotheses :"Set of hypotheses to be confirmed with future findings" ;
    ordered-hypotheses : "Set of hypotheses, in ascending bound time order" ;
    remaining-hypotheses : "Hypotheses to be confirmed with future findings" ;
    indications : "Entities that let us suspect from some causes" ;
  CONTROL-STRUCTURE :
    cover (complaint + protocol → indications) ;
    IF indications != ∅ THEN
      DO
        immediate-test (indications → delayed-hypotheses) ;
        delayed-hypotheses = delayed-hypotheses ADD remaining-hypotheses ;
        sort (delayed-hypotheses → ordered-hypotheses) ;
        delayed-test (ordered-hypotheses → hypothesis + remaining-hypotheses) ;
        IF hypothesis THEN
          cover (hypothesis + protocol → indications) ;
        END IF
      UNTIL SIZE remaining-hypotheses < 1 OR "ending cause instantiated" ;
      IF "an ending cause has been instantiated" THEN
        generate (hypothesis + protocol → causal-explanation) ;
      END IF
    END IF
END TASK-METHOD
```

**Fig. 2.** Inference structure, specification and method for the *delayed diagnosis* task.

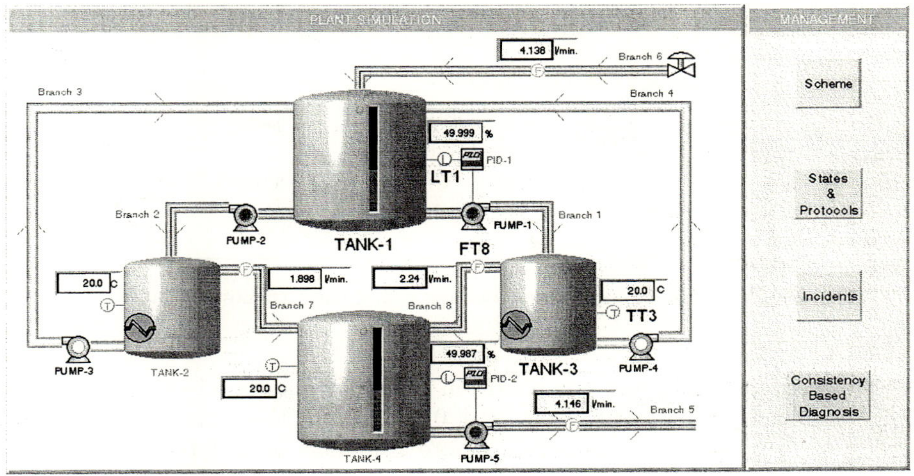


**Fig. 3.** Interface of the application for the laboratory plant.

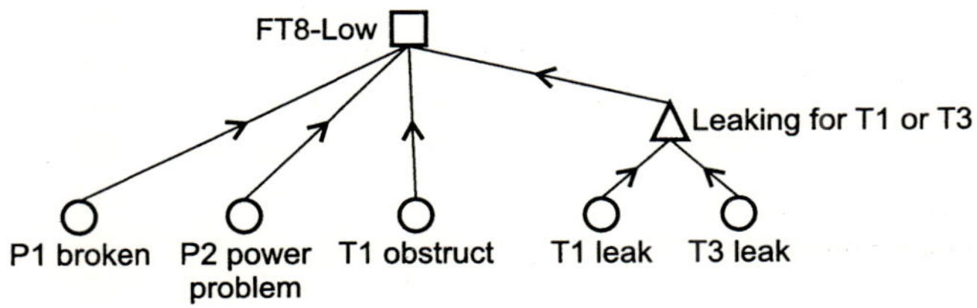


**Fig. 4.** Causal tree associated to FT8-Low monitored variable.

dynamic behavior. The plant admits different configurations, just changing the recirculation paths.

Figure 4 shows the tree associated to the FT8-Low Monitored Variable node. It includes three causes in its fast subtree and two additional causes in its slow subtree. In the COMMONKADS methodology that structure must be textually described. The symptoms that conform the Extended causal network are represented by rules with certain temporal quality: the relative temporal reference to the symptom. Figure 5 shows the symptoms associated to the arcs of the right most path of the tree shown in Figure 4, using a COMMONKADS alike notation.

With the notation introduced in Section 2, the first rule could be rewritten as the fast symptom ((FT8-Low, Leaking-for-T1-or-T3), $\{(\Delta$LT1.value $\approx 0$, $0)\}$, 0) where (FT8-Low, Leaking-for-T1-or-T3) is an arc of the network and ($\Delta$LT1.value $\approx 0$, 0) is a relative token effect. The variable NOW, in the rules, will be instantiated to the detection time by the diagnosis task. It is included in the rules state the relative nature of the temporal references.

```
FT8-Low == CRITICAL AND ΔLT1.value(NOW) ≈ 0
  ESTABLISHES
Leaking-for-T1-or-T3 = TRUE

Leaking-for-T1-or-T3 == TRUE AND
SOMETIME t IN [NOW, NOW + 2 min] :
    (ΔTT3.value(t - 1 min) ≈ 0 AND ΔTT3.value(t) > 0)
  ESTABLISHES
T3-Leak = TRUE
```

**Fig. 5.** Some example rules for diagnosing the FT8-Low variable.

The second rule could be rewritten as ((Leaking-for-T1-or-T3, T3.leak), $\{(\Delta$TT3.value $\approx 0$, 1), ($\Delta$TT3.value $> 0$, 0)}, 2). Now, there are two relative token effects, that have to be observed before 2 minutes after detection time.

## 5 Discussion

A knowledge model for the diagnosis task of dynamic systems has been presented. The main feature of the proposal is the division of the diagnosis task in three subtasks: previous, instant and delayed diagnosis. The articulation of these three tasks allows the diagnostician to watch the evolution of a continuous process in order to discriminate among competing hypotheses. Nevertheless, it is still feasible to obtain a diagnosis with the data available at detection time, if possible.

The main contribution of this work is the formalization of the knowledge model. This formalization includes a detailed description of the Extended causal network to represent the domain knowledge together with the specification of the Inference and Task knowledge, partially included in Section 3. The formalization tries to generalize the last model used by the OLID generation of industrial diagnosticians, and it is currently being tested on a pilot plant.

An important feature of the model is its relative simplicity, which is a consequence of the structure of the causal network used to represent the causal/temporal knowledge of the domain. The Extended causal network forces a separation of symptoms into fast and slow symptoms, w.r.t. the detection time. This property allows us to factorize the diagnosis task along this time dimension. Naturally, the price to be paid is a limited capability to represent temporal information. Thus, there are systems, like DIAPO [2], that permits a very rich temporal description of the domain knowledge, that certainly allows it to describe several temporal relationships of the domain: Reactor Coolant Pump Sets of Pressurized Water Nuclear Power Plants. It relies on advanced research in abductive and temporal reasoning [15]. Nevertheless, DIAPO is invoked at the request by the user, not automatically, by a monitoring subsystem, and only works with current and past data.

Summarizing, considering the industrial field experience with systems that relied on preliminary versions of the model presented in this paper [11, 12], we could assert that this model proposes a reasonable trade off between expressiveness and costs, both computationally and from the knowledge engineering point of view —that is, development and maintenance of the system.

## References


[1] Balakrishnan, K., Honavar, V.: Intelligent diagnosis systems. Journal of Intelligent Systems **8** (1998) 239–290

[2] Cauvin, S., Cordier, M.O., Dousson, C., Laborie, P., Lévy, F., Montmain, J., Porcheron, M., Servet, I., Travé-Massuyès, L.: Monitoring and Alarm Interpretation in Industrial Environments. AI Communications **11** (1998) 139–173

[3] Chen, J., Patton, R.: Robust model based fault diagnosis for dynamic systems. Kluwer Academic Publisher (1999)

[4] Dressler, O., Struss, P.: The consistency based approach to automated diagnosis of devices. In: Principles of knowledge representation. CSLI publications, Stanford (1996) 269–314

[5] Price, C.: Computer-based diagnostic systems. Springer (1999)

[6] Acosta, G., Alonso, C., Pulido, B.: Basic Tasks for Knowledge Based Supervision in Process Control. Engineering Applications of Artificial Intelligence **14** (2002) 441–455

[7] Guckenbiehl, T., Schäfer-Richter, G.: Readings in model based diagnosis. Morgan-Kauffman Pub., San Mateo (1992) 309–317

[8] Oyeleye, O., Finch, F., Kramer, M.: Qualitative modeling and fault diagnosis of dynamic processes by MIDAS. Chemical Engineering Communications **96** (1990) 205–228

[9] Cordier, M., Krivine, J., Laboire, P., Thiébaux, S.: Alarm processing and reconfiguration in power distribution systems. In: Proceedings of the 11th International Conference on Industrial and Engineering Applications of Artificial Intelligence and Expert Systems IEA/AIE-98. LNAI. Volume 1416., Springer-Verlag (1998) 230–241

[10] Dousson, C., Gaborit, P., Ghallab, M.: Situation recognition: representation and algorithms. In: Proceedings of the 13th International Joint Conference on Artificial Intelligence IJCAI'93. (1993) 166–172

[11] Alonso, C., Pulido, B., Acosta, G.: On Line Industrial Diagnosis: an attempt to apply Artificial Intelligence techniques to process control. In: 11th International Conference on Industrial and Engineering Applications of Artificial Intelligence and Expert Systems, IEA/AIE-98. LNAI. Volume 1415., Springer-Verlag (1998) 804–813

[12] Alonso, C., Pulido, B., Acosta, G., Llamas, C.: On-line Industrial supervision and diagnosis, knowledge level description and experimental results. Expert Systems with Applications **20** (2001) 117–132

[13] Schreiber, G., Akkermans, H., Anjewierden, A., de Hoog, R., Shadbolt, N., Van de Velde, W., Wielinga, B.: Knowledge Engineering and Management, The CommonKADS Methodology. The MIT Press (1999)

[14] Console, L., Torasso, P.: On the co-operation between abductive and temporal reasoning in medical diagnosis. Artificial Intelligence in Medicine **3** (1991) 291–311
[15] Console, L., Dupré, D.T.: On the dimensions of temporal model-based diagnosis. In: Proceedings of the DX'98. 9th Int. Workshop on Principles of Diagnosis. (1998) 16–23

# A Rigorous Approach to Knowledge Base Maintenance

John Debenham

University of Technology, Sydney
debenham@it.uts.edu.au

**Abstract.** A knowledge base is maintained by modifying its conceptual model and by using those modifications to specify changes to its implementation. The maintenance problem is to determine which parts of that model should be checked for correctness in response a change in the application. The maintenance problem is not computable for first-order knowledge bases. Two things in the conceptual model are joined by a maintenance link if a modification to one of them means that the other must be checked for correctness, and so possibly modified, if consistency of the model is to be preserved. In a unified conceptual model for first-order knowledge bases the data and knowledge are modelled formally in a uniform way. A characterisation is given of four different kinds of maintenance links in a unified conceptual model. Two of these four kinds of maintenance links can be removed by transforming the conceptual model. In this way the maintenance problem is simplified.

**Keywords:** KBS methodology, expert systems, intelligent systems

## 1 Introduction

The conceptual model of a knowledge base specifies what should be in an implementation of that knowledge base, but not what the implementation will be required to do. So the conceptual model may be used to drive the maintenance process. The maintenance problem is to determine which parts of that model should be checked for correctness in response a change in the application. The maintenance problem is not computable for first-order knowledge bases. Maintenance links join two things in the conceptual model if a modification to one of them means that the other must be checked for correctness, and so possibly modified, if consistency of that model is to be preserved. If that other thing requires modification then the links from it to yet other things must be followed, and so on until things are reached that do not require modification. If node A is linked to node B which is linked to node C then nodes A and C are *indirectly* linked. In a *coherent* knowledge base everything is indirectly linked to everything else. A good conceptual model for maintenance will have a low density of maintenance links [1]. The set of maintenance links should be *minimal* in than none may be removed.

Informally, one conceptual model is "better" than another if it leads to less checking for correctness. The aim of this work is to generate a good conceptual model. A classification into four classes is given here of the maintenance links for conceptual models expressed in the unified [2] knowledge representation. Methods

P.W.H. Chung, C.J. Hinde, M. Ali (Eds.): IEA/AIE 2003, LNAI 2718, pp. 219–228, 2003.

are given for removing two of these classes of link so reducing the density of maintenance links.

Approaches to the maintenance of knowledge bases are principally of two types [3]. First, approaches that take the knowledge base as presented and then try to *control* the maintenance process [4]. Second, approaches that *engineer* a model of the knowledge base so that it is in a form that is inherently easy to maintain [5] [6]. The approach described here is of the second type because maintenance is driven by a maintenance link structure that is simplified by transforming the conceptual model.

The majority of conceptual models treat the "rule base" component separately from the "database" component. This enables well established design methodologies to be employed, but the use of two separate models means that the interrelationship between the things in these two models cannot be represented, integrated and manipulated naturally within the model [2]. Neither of these two separate models is able to address completely the validity of the whole knowledge base.

The terms data, information and knowledge are used here in the following sense. The *data* things in an application are the fundamental, indivisible things. Data things can be represented as simple constants or variables. If an association between things *cannot* be defined as a succinct, computable rule then it is an *implicit* association. Otherwise it is an *explicit* association. An *information* thing in an application is an implicit association between data things. Information things can be represented as tuples or relations. A *knowledge* thing in an application is an explicit association between information and/or data things. Knowledge can be represented either as programs in an imperative language or as rules in a declarative language.

## 2 Conceptual Model

Items are a formalism for describing all data, information and knowledge things in an application [2]. Items incorporate two powerful classes of constraints, and a single rule of decomposition is specified for items. The key to this unified representation is the way in which the "meaning" of an item, called its *semantics*, is specified. The semantics of an item is a function that *recognises* the members of the "value set" of that item. The value set of an item will change in time $\tau$, but the item's semantics should remain constant. The value set of a data item at a certain time $\tau$ is the set of labels that are associated with a population that implements that item at that time. The value set of an information item at a certain time $\tau$ is the set of tuples that are associated with a relational implementation of that item at that time. Knowledge items have value sets too. Consider the rule "the sale price of parts is the cost price marked up by a universal mark-up factor"; this rule is represented by the item named *[part/sale-price, part/cost-price, mark-up]* with a value set of corresponding quintuples. The idea of defining the semantics of items as recognising functions for the members of their value set extends to complex, recursive knowledge items too.

An *item* is a named triple $A[S_A, V_A, C_A]$ with *item name* $A$, $S_A$ is called the *item semantics* of $A$, $V_A$ is called the *item value constraints* of $A$ and $C_A$ is called the *item set constraints* of $A$. The item semantics, $S_A$, is a $\lambda$-calculus expression that recognises the members of the value set of item A. The expression for an item's semantics may contain the semantics of other items $\{A_1, \ldots, A_n\}$ called that item's *components*:

$$\lambda y^1_1 \ldots y^i_{m_i} \ldots y^n_{m_n} \bullet [\, S_{A_1}(y^1_1, \ldots, y^1_{m_1}) \wedge \ldots\ldots \wedge$$

$$S_{A_n}(y^n_1, \ldots, y^n_{m_n}) \wedge J(y^1_1, \ldots, y^1_{m_1}, \ldots, y^n_{m_n})\,]\bullet$$

The item value constraints, $V_A$, is a λ-calculus expression:

$$\lambda y^1_1 \ldots y^1_{m_1} \ldots y^n_{m_n} \bullet [\, V_{A_1}(y^1_1, \ldots, y^1_{m_1}) \wedge \ldots\ldots \wedge$$

$$V_{A_n}(y^n_1, \ldots, y^n_{m_n}) \wedge K(y^1_1, \ldots, y^1_{m_1}, \ldots, y^n_{m_n})\,]\bullet$$

that should be satisfied by the members of the value set of item A as they change in time; so if a tuple satisfies $S_A$ then it should satisfy $V_A$ [8]. The expression for an item's value constraints contains the value constraints of that item's *components*. The item set constraints, $C_A$, is an expression of the form:

$$C_{A_1} \wedge C_{A_2} \wedge \ldots \wedge C_{A_n} \wedge (L)_A$$

where L is a logical combination of:

- Card lies in some numerical range;
- Uni($A_i$) for some i, $1 \leq i \leq n$, and
- Can($A_i$, X) for some i, $1 \leq i \leq n$, where X is a non-empty subset of $\{A_1, \ldots, A_n\} - \{A_i\}$;

subscripted with the name of the item *A*, "Uni(*a*)" means that "all members of the value set of item *a* must be in this association". "Can(*b*, A)" means that "the value set of the set of items A functionally determines the value set of item *b*". "Card" means "the number of things in the value set". The subscripts indicate the item's components to which that set constraint applies.

For example, each *part* may be associated with a *cost-price* subject to the "value constraint" that parts whose part-number is less that 1,999 should be associated with a cost price of no more than \$300. A set constraint specifies that every part must be in this association, and that each part is associated with a unique cost-price. The information item named *part/cost-price* then is:

*part/cost-price*[ $\lambda xy \bullet [\, S_{part}(x) \wedge S_{cost\text{-}price}(y) \wedge \text{costs}(x, y)\,]\bullet$,
$\lambda xy \bullet [\, V_{part}(x) \wedge V_{cost\text{-}price}(y) \wedge ((x < 1999) \rightarrow (y \bullet 300))\,]\bullet$,
$C_{part} \wedge C_{cost\text{-}price} \wedge (\text{Uni}(part) \wedge \text{Can}(cost\text{-}price, \{part\}))_{part/cost\text{-}price}$ ]

Rules, or knowledge, can also be defined as items, although it is neater to define knowledge items using "objects". "Objects" are item building operators. The knowledge item *[part/sale-price, part/cost-price, mark-up]* which means "the sale price of parts is the cost price marked up by a uniform markup factor" is:

$$
\begin{aligned}
&[\textit{part/sale-price, part/cost-price, mark-up}][\\
&\quad \lambda x_1x_2y_1y_2z\bullet[(\ S_{\textit{part/sale-price}}(x_1, x_2) \wedge S_{\textit{part/cost-price}}(y_1, y_2) \wedge\\
&\qquad\qquad S_{\textit{mark-up}}(z)\ ) \wedge ((x_1 = y_1) \rightarrow (x_2 = z \_\ y_2))]\bullet,\\
&\quad \lambda x_1x_2y_1y_2z\bullet[\ V_{\textit{part/sale-price}}(x_1, x_2) \wedge V_{\textit{part/cost-price}}(y_1, y_2) \wedge\\
&\qquad\qquad V_{\textit{mark-up}}(z)\ ) \wedge ((\ x_1 = y_1\ ) \rightarrow (\ x_2 > y_2\ ))]\bullet,\\
&\quad C_{[\textit{part/sale-price, part/cost-price, mark-up}]}\ ]
\end{aligned}
$$

Two different items can share common knowledge and so can lead to a profusion of maintenance links. This problem can be avoided by using objects. An n-adic *object* is an operator that maps n given items into another item for some value of n. Further, the definition of each object will presume that the set of items to which that object may be applied are of a specific "type". The *type* of an m-adic item is determined both by whether it is a data item, an information item or a knowledge item and by the value of m. The type is denoted respectively by $\mathbf{D}^m$, $\mathbf{I}^m$ and $\mathbf{K}^m$. Items may also have unspecified, or free, type which is denoted by $\mathbf{X}^m$. The formal definition of an object is similar to that of an item. An *object* named ***A*** is a typed triple ***A***[E,F,G] where E is a typed expression called the *semantics* of ***A***, F is a typed expression called the *value constraints* of ***A*** and G is a typed expression called the *set constraints* of ***A***. For example, the *part/cost-price* item can be built from the items *part* and *cost-price* using the ***costs*** operator:

$$
\begin{aligned}
&\textit{part/cost-price} = \textbf{\textit{costs}}(\textit{part, cost-price})\\
&\textbf{\textit{costs}}[\lambda P{:}\mathbf{X}^1 Q{:}\mathbf{X}^1\bullet\lambda xy\bullet[\ S_P(x) \wedge S_Q(y) \wedge \text{costs}(x,y)\ ]\bullet\bullet,\\
&\qquad \lambda P{:}\mathbf{X}^1 Q{:}\mathbf{X}^1\bullet\lambda xy\bullet[V_P(x) \wedge V_Q(y) \wedge ((1000 < x < 1999) \rightarrow (y \le 300))\ ]\bullet\bullet,\\
&\qquad \lambda P{:}\mathbf{X}^1 Q{:}\mathbf{X}^1\bullet[\ C_P \wedge C_Q \wedge (\text{Uni}(P) \wedge \text{Can}(Q, \{P\}))_{n(\textbf{\textit{costs}},P,Q)}\ ]\bullet]
\end{aligned}
$$

where n(***costs***, P, Q) is the name of the item ***costs***(P, Q).

Data objects provide a representation of sub-typing. Rules are quite clumsy when represented as items; objects provide a far more compact representation. For example, consider the *[part/sale-price, part/cost-price, mark-up]* knowledge item which represents the rule "parts are marked-up by a universal mark-up factor". This item can be built by applying a knowledge object ***mark-up-rule*** of argument type $(\mathbf{I}^2, \mathbf{I}^2, \mathbf{D}^1)$ to the items *part/sale-price*, *part/cost-price* and *mark-up*. That is:

*[part/sale-price, part/cost-price, mark-up]* =
***mark-up-rule***(*part/sale-price*, *part/cost-price*, *mark-up*)

Objects also represent value constraints and set constraints in a uniform way. A decomposition operation for objects is defined in [7].

A *conceptual model* consists of a set of items and a set of maintenance links. The items are constructed by applying a set of object operators to a set of fundamental items called the *basis*. The *maintenance links* join two items if modification to one of them necessarily means that the other item has at least to be checked for correctness if consistency is to be preserved. Item join provides the basis for item decomposition.

Given items $A$ and $B$, the item with name $A \otimes_E B$ is called the *join* of $A$ and $B$ on E, where E is a set of components common to both $A$ and $B$. Using the rule of composition $\otimes$, knowledge items, information items and data items may be joined with one another regardless of type. For example, the knowledge item:

$$[\textit{cost-price, tax}]\ [\lambda xy\bullet[S_{\textit{cost-price}}(x) \wedge S_{\textit{tax}}(y) \wedge x = y \times 0.05]\bullet,$$
$$\lambda xy\bullet[V_{\textit{cost-price}}(x) \wedge V_{\textit{tax}}(y) \wedge x < y]\bullet,\ C_{[\textit{cost-price, tax}]}]$$

can be joined with the information item *part/cost-price* on the set {*cost-price*} to give the information item *part/cost-price/tax*. In other words:

$$[\textit{cost-price, tax}] \otimes_{\{\textit{cost-price}\}} \textit{part/cost-price} =$$
$$\textit{part/cost-price/tax}[\ \lambda xyz\bullet[\ S_{\textit{part}}(x) \wedge S_{\textit{cost-price}}(x) \wedge$$
$$S_{\textit{tax}}(y) \wedge \text{costs}(x,y) \wedge z = y \times 0.05\ ]\bullet,$$
$$\lambda xyz\bullet[\ V_{\textit{part}}(x) \wedge V_{\textit{cost-price}}(x) \wedge V_{\textit{tax}}(y) \wedge$$
$$((1000<x<1999) \rightarrow (0<y\leq 300)) \wedge (z<y)\ ]\bullet,$$
$$C_{\textit{part/cost-price/tax}}\ ]$$

In this way items may be joined together to form more complex items. The $\otimes$ operator also forms the basis of a theory of decomposition in which each item is replaced by a set of simpler items. An item $I$ is *decomposable* into the set of items $D = \{I_1, I_2,..., I_n\}$ if: $I_i$ has non-trivial semantics for all i, $I = I_1 \otimes I_2 \otimes ... \otimes I_n$, where each join is *monotonic*; that is, each term in this composition contributes at least one component to $I$. If item $I$ is decomposable then it will not necessarily have a unique decomposition. The $\otimes$ operator is applied to objects in a similar way [7]. The rule of decomposition is: "Given a conceptual model discard any items and objects which are decomposable". For example, this rule requires that the item *part/cost-price/tax* should be discarded in favour of the two items *[cost-price, tax]* and *part/cost-price*.

## 3 Maintenance Links

A *maintenance link* joins two items in the conceptual model if modification of one item means that the other item must be checked for correctness, and maybe modified, if the consistency of the conceptual model is to be preserved [9]. The number of maintenance links can be very large. So maintenance links can only form the basis of a practical approach to knowledge base maintenance if there is some way of reducing their density on the conceptual model.

For example, given two items $A$ and $B$, where both are n-adic items with semantics $S_A$ and $S_B$ respectively, if $\pi$ is permutation such that:

$$(\forall x_1 x_2 ... x_n)[\ S_A(x_1,x_2,...,x_n) \leftarrow S_B(\pi(x_1,x_2,...,x_n))\ ]$$

then item $B$ is a *sub-item* of item $A$. These two items should be joined with a maintenance link. If $A$ and $B$ are both data items then $B$ is a *sub-type* of $A$. Suppose that:

$$X = \mathbf{E}\, D; \text{ where } D = \mathbf{C}\, A\, B \tag{1}$$

for items $X$, $D$, $A$ and $B$ and objects $\mathbf{E}$ and $\mathbf{C}$. Item $X$ is a sub-item of item $D$. Object $\mathbf{E}$ has the effect of extracting a sub-set of the value set of item $D$ to form the value set of item $X$. Item $D$ is formed from items $A$ and $B$ using object $\mathbf{C}$. Introduce two new objects $\mathbf{F}$ and $\mathbf{J}$. Suppose that object $\mathbf{F}$ when applied to item $A$ extracts the same subset of item $A$'s value set as $\mathbf{E}$ extracted from the "left-side" (ie. the "$A$-side") of $D$. Likewise $\mathbf{J}$ extracts the same subset of $B$'s value set as $\mathbf{E}$ extracted from $D$. Then:

$$X = \mathbf{C}\, G\, K; \text{ where } G = \mathbf{F}\, A \text{ and } K = \mathbf{J}\, B \tag{2}$$

so $G$ is a sub-item of $A$, and $K$ is a sub-item of $B$. The form (2) differs from (1) in that the sub-item maintenance links have been moved one layer closer to the data item layer, and object C has moved one layer away from the data item layer. This is illustrated in Fig. 1. Using this method repeatedly sub-item maintenance links between non-data items are reduced to sub-type links between data items.

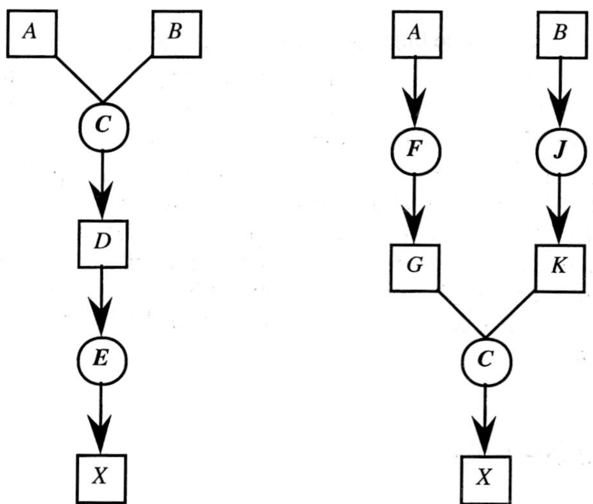


**Fig. 1.** Reducing sub-item relationships

It is shown now that there are four kinds of maintenance link in a conceptual model built using the unified knowledge representation. Consider two items $A$ and $B$, and suppose that their semantics $S_A$ and $S_B$ have the form:

$$S_A = \lambda y^1_1 \ldots y^1_{m_1} \ldots y^p_{m_p} \bullet [S_{A_1}(y^1_1, \ldots, y^1_{m_1}) \wedge \ldots\ldots \wedge$$

$$S_{A_p}(y_1^p,...,y_{m_p}^p) \wedge J(y_1^1,...,y_{m_1}^1,...,y_{m_p}^p)]\bullet$$

$$S_B = \lambda y_1^1...y_{n_1}^1...y_{n_q}^q \bullet[S_{B_1}(y_1^1,...,y_{n_1}^1) \wedge ...... \wedge$$

$$S_{B_q}(y_1^q,...,y_{n_q}^q) \wedge K(y_1^1,...,y_{n_1}^1,...,y_{n_q}^q)]\bullet$$

$S_A$ contains (p + 1) terms and $S_B$ contains (q + 1) terms. Let μ be a maximal sub-expression of $S_{A \otimes B}$ such that:

*both* $S_A \rightarrow \mu$ *and* $S_B \rightarrow \mu$ (a)

where μ has the form:

$$\lambda y_1^1...y_{d_1}^1...y_{d_r}^r \bullet[S_{C_1}(y_1^1,...,y_{d_1}^1) \wedge ... \wedge S_{C_r}(y_1^r,...,y_{d_r}^r) \wedge L(y_1^1,...,y_d^1,...,y_{d_r}^r)]\bullet$$

If μ is empty, ie. 'false', then the semantics of *A* and *B* are independent. If μ is non-empty then the semantics of *A* and *B* have something in common and *A* and *B* should be joined with a maintenance link.

Now examine μ to see *why A* and *B* should be joined. If μ is non-empty and if both *A* and *B* are items in the basis then:

*A* and *B* are a pair of basis items with logically dependent semantics (b)

If μ is non-empty and if *A* is *not* in the basis then there are three cases. First, if:

$S_A \leftrightarrow S_B \leftrightarrow \mu$ (c)

then items *A* and *B* are equivalent and should be joined with an *equivalence link*. Second if (c) does not hold and:

*either* $S_A \leftrightarrow \mu$ *or* $S_B \leftrightarrow \mu$ (d)

then either *A* is a sub-item of *B*, or *B* is a sub-item of *A* and these two items should be joined with a *sub-item link*. Third, if (c) and (d) do not hold then if • is a minimal sub-expression of $S_A$ such that $\Delta \rightarrow \mu$. Then:

*either* $S_{A_j}(y_1^j,...,y_{m_j}^j) \in \Delta$, for some j (e)

*or* $J(y_1^1,...,y_{m_j}^1,...,y_{m_p}^p) \in \Delta$ (f)

Both (e) and (f) may hold. If (e) holds then items *A* and *B* share one or more component items to which they should each be joined with a *component link*. If (f) holds then items *A* and *B* may be constructed with two object operators whose respective semantics are logically dependent. Suppose that item *A* was constructed by object operator ***C*** then the semantics of ***C*** will imply:

$$\Phi = \lambda Q_1{:}\mathbf{X}^{i_1}_{1}\, Q_2{:}\mathbf{X}^{i_2}_{2} \ldots Q_j{:}\mathbf{X}^{i_j}_{j} \bullet \lambda y^1_1 \ldots y^1_{d_1} \ldots y^r_{d_r} \bullet [$$

$$S_{P_1}(y^1_1, \ldots, y^1_{d_1}) \wedge \ldots\ldots S_{P_r}(y^r_1, \ldots, y^r_{d_r}) \wedge L(y^1_1, \ldots, y^1_{d_1}, \ldots, y^r_{d_r})] \bullet$$

where the $Q_i$'s take care of any possible duplication in the $P_j$'s. Let ***E*** be the object ***E***[ **Φ**, **T**, ∅] then ***C*** is a sub-object of ***E***; that is, there exists a non-tautological object ***F*** such that:

$$\boldsymbol{C} \simeq_W \boldsymbol{E} \otimes_M \boldsymbol{F} \qquad \text{(g)}$$

for some set M and where the join is not necessarily monotonic. Items *A* and *B* are *weakly equivalent*, written $A \simeq_W B$, if there exists a permutation π such that:

$$(\forall x_1 x_2 \ldots x_n)[S_A(x_1, x_2, \ldots, x_n) \leftrightarrow S_B(\pi(x_1, x_2, \ldots, x_n))]$$

where the $x_i$ are the $n_i$ variables associated with the i'th component of *A*. If *A* is a sub-item of *B* and if *B* is a sub-item of *A* then items *A* and *B* are weakly equivalent.

If (g) holds then the maintenance links are of three different kinds. If the join in (g) *is* monotonic then (g) states that ***C*** may be decomposed into ***E*** and ***F***. If the join in (g) is *not* monotonic then (g) states that either $\boldsymbol{C} \simeq_W \boldsymbol{E}$ or $\boldsymbol{C} \simeq_W \boldsymbol{F}$. So, if the join in (g) is not monotonic then *either* ***E*** will be weakly equivalent to ***C***, *or* ***C*** will be a sub-object of ***E***.

It has been shown above that sub-item links between non-data items may be reduced to sub-type links between data items. So if:

- the semantics of the items in the basis are all logically independent;
- all equivalent items and objects have been removed by re-naming, and
- sub-item links between non-data items have been reduced to sub-type links between data items

then the maintenance links will be between nodes marked with:

- a data item that is a sub-type of the data item marked on another node, these are called the *sub-type links*;
- an item and the nodes marked with that item's components, these are called the *component links*, and
- an item constructed by a decomposable object and nodes constructed with that object's decomposition, these are called the *duplicate links*.

If the objects employed to construct the conceptual model have been decomposed then the only maintenance links remaining will be the sub-type links and the component links. The sub-type links and the component links cannot be removed from the conceptual model.

Unfortunately, decomposable objects, and so too duplicate links, are hard to detect. Suppose that objects ***A*** and ***B*** are decomposable as follows:

$$\boldsymbol{A} \simeq_W \boldsymbol{E} \otimes_M \boldsymbol{F}$$
$$\boldsymbol{B} \simeq_W \boldsymbol{E} \otimes_M \boldsymbol{G}$$

Then objects ***A*** and ***B*** should both be linked to object ***E***. If the decompositions of ***A*** and ***B*** have not been identified then object ***E*** may not have been identified and the implicit link between objects ***A*** and ***B*** may not be identified.

## 4 Constraints

The *conceptual model* consists of a representation of each thing as an item. Both items and objects contain two classes of constraint. These two classes are the value constraints and the set constraints. Constraints play a significant role in knowledge base maintenance. They are employed for two distinct purposes:

- constraints protect the validity of the knowledge base during maintenance [10] (these are called pragmatic constraints), and
- constraints contribute to the efficiency of the maintenance procedure (these are called referential constraints).

Pragmatic constraints are an integral part of every item and object in the conceptual model. Pragmatic constraints apply equally to knowledge, information and data. A taxonomy of pragmatic constraints is:

- constraints which are attached to each item (these are called the *item constraints*), these are:
  - the item *value constraints* which are constraints on the individual members of an item's value set, and
  - the item *set constraints* which are constraints on the structure of an item's value set. Set constraints include:
    - *cardinality constraints*, denoted by "Card", which constrain the size of the value set;
    - *universal constraints*, denoted by "Uni", which generalise database universal constraints, and
    - *candidate constraints*, denoted by "Can", which constrain the functional dependencies in an item and generalise database key constraints.
- constraints which are attached to the conceptual model itself (these are called the *model constraints*).

The need to follow component links may be restricted by applying "referential constraints" to items. *Referential constraints* state that a particular component link need not be followed during the complete execution of a maintenance operation. They improve the efficiency of the maintenance procedure, but they complicate the maintenance of the item to which they are applied and so they should only be applied to items of low volatility. Model constraints are constraints on the conceptual model. They are used in database technology. The rule "the selling price of parts is always greater than the cost price of parts" is an example of a chunk of knowledge that could be a constraint on the information in a database. The information in the database is constrained to be consistent with this particular chunk of knowledge. Such a constraint is a *knowledge model constraint*. They may be used for knowledge-based systems. For knowledge-based systems the inverse of this idea can be used. In knowledge-based systems a chunk of information can be used as a constraint on the knowledge in the conceptual model. Such a constraint is an *information model constraint*. Hand-coded, simple but non-trivial information models can provide powerful information model constraints. Information model constraints are simple, powerful and effective constraints on the knowledge in the conceptual model. They may be useful in applications where the knowledge is subject to a high rate of change and the information is comparatively stable.

## 5 Conclusion

Maintenance links are used to maintain the validity of first-order knowledge bases. Maintenance links join two items in the conceptual model if modification of one of these items could require that the other item should be checked for correctness if the validity of the conceptual model is to be preserved. The efficiency of maintenance procedures depends on a method for reducing the density of the maintenance links in the conceptual model. One kind of maintenance link is removed by applying the rule of knowledge decomposition [7]. Another is removed by reducing sub-item relationships to sub-type relationships [2]. And another is removed by re-naming.

## References

[1] Mayol, E. and Teniente, E. (1999). "Addressing Efficiency Issues During the Process of Integrity Maintenance" *in proceedings Tenth International Conference DEXA99*, Florence, September 1999, pp270-281.
[2] Debenham, J.K. (1998). "*Knowledge Engineering*", Springer-Verlag, 1998.
[3] Katsuno, H. and Mendelzon, A.O. (1991). "On the Difference between Updating a Knowledge Base and Revising It", in *proceedings Second International Conference on Principles of Knowledge Representation and Reasoning, KR'91*, Morgan Kaufmann, 1991.
[4] Barr, V. (1999). "Applying Reliability Engineering to Expert Systems" in *proceedings 12th International FLAIRS Conference*, Florida, May 1999, pp494-498.
[5] Jantke, K.P. and Herrmann, J. (1999). "Lattices of Knowledge in Intelligent Systems Validation" in *proceedings 12th International FLAIRS Conference*, Florida, May 1999, pp499-505.
[6] Darwiche, A. (1999). "Compiling Knowledge into Decomposable Negation Normal Form" in *proceedings International Joint Conference on Artificial Intelligence, IJCAI'99*, Stockholm, Sweden, August 1999, pp 284-289.
[7] Debenham, J.K. (1999). "Knowledge Object Decomposition" in *proceedings 12th International FLAIRS Conference*, Florida, May 1999, pp203-207.
[8] Johnson, G. and Santos, E. (2000). "Generalizing Knowledge Representation Rules for Acquiring and Validating Uncertain Knowledge" in *proceedings 13th International FLAIRS Conference*, Florida, May 2000, pp186-2191.
[9] Ramirez, J. and de Antonio, A. (2000). "Semantic Verification of Rule-Based Systems with Arithmetic Constraints" in *proceedings 11th International Conference DEXA2000*, London, September 2000, pp437-446.
[10] Debenham, J.K. "The Degradation of Knowledge Base Integrity", in *proceedings 13th International FLAIRS Conference FLAIRS-2000*, Orlando, Florida, May 2000, pp113-117.

# Evaluation of Intelligent Systems for the Utilisation of HAZOP Analysis Results

Perttu Heino[1], Kati Kupila[1], Kazuhiko Suzuki[2], Shintaro Shinohara[1,2], and Jari Schabel[1]

[1] VTT Industrial Systems, Reliability and Risk Management
P.O. Box 1306, FIN-33101 Tampere, Finland
http://www.vtt.fi/tuo/

[2] Okayama University, Department of Systems Engineering
Okayama 700-8530, Japan
http://www.eng.okayama-u.ac.jp/

**Abstract.** In every industry sector, companies need to find ways to operate profitably and safely. Risk management offers a way of combining profitability and responsibility. However, no industrial company can afford to spend extensive amounts of time and money on safety and reliability studies – the collection of data and the preparation of the relevant documents. Advanced information technology is needed to make the necessary information acquisitions and processing activities more efficient – and includes data collection systems, and model-based simulation and safety analysis systems. As described in this paper, part of the study focused on the evaluation of both an intelligent HAZOP system and a dynamic process simulator in order to know how the systems could support hazard studies.

## 1 Introduction

In the process industry, qualitative safety and reliability studies are standard practise. Those studies enable the companies to recognise the causes and consequences of hazards, failures and disturbances in a plant in order to improve its performance. Nowadays, studies are still often done manually without any computerised support, and the results are then often available only as a paper documents.

Intelligent systems to support qualitative safety analyses have recently been developed, and at the same time, many advanced features have also been added to process simulators. However, to our knowledge, little information is available on the utilisation of either today's dynamic simulators or intelligent HAZOP systems for supporting hazard studies. Also, the use of advanced decision support systems for abnormal situation management (ASM) is not yet commonplace in the chemical process industry.

The purpose of this study was to determine whether either an intelligent HAZOP System, or the use of a dynamic simulator, could support safety studies in the process industry. This paper also reports on the development of an operator decision support system that enables rapid access to relevant safety and reliability information.

P.W.H. Chung, C.J. Hinde, M. Ali (Eds.): IEA/AIE 2003, LNAI 2718, pp. 229–243, 2003.

## 2 Definition of the Problem

Industrial companies operate under difficult circumstances. International competition in every industry sector means that they must cut costs and avoid losses in their effort to identify ways of operating profitably. At the same time, companies are required to take responsibility for their employees and the surrounding environment, and this often extends to a responsibility of the society's well-being in general.

Risk management offers a solution to the problem of resolving the often conflicting aspects of profitability and responsibility by supplying corporate management a means to improve their understanding of all the undesirable events which could cause significant damage to their business. With this understanding, they can make arrangements to mitigate such events – some of which relate to loss off profits, while others may pose a risk to society. Safety and reliability related considerations are an important part of this risk management activity and Figure 1 illustrates their relationship within an advanced information technology framework in the business environment of an industrial company.

The existence of an organisational culture which supports safety and reliability is necessary for the introduction of the advanced information technology associated with improving the management of safety and reliability. Such a culture would encourage people to generate new up-to-date information and utilise information from all existing sources.

No industrial company can afford to spend extensive amounts of time and money in safety and reliability studies – the collection of data and the preparation of documents. Advanced information technology purports to make the necessary information acquisitions and processing activities more efficient – and data collection systems, and model-based simulation and safety analysis systems are examples of this.

Easy access to the information resulting from the data collection activities and the various studies is imperative. Both designers and operators need rapid access to the relevant safety and reliability information to support their decision-making. Furthermore, all the existing data and knowledge needs to be managed – a structured data repository which allows the information to be also used for other purposes, such as training and focused reporting would be ideal.

This paper focuses mainly on two areas that have recently shown promise for increasing risk awareness: intelligent support for HAZOP studies, and the use of simulation to support safety studies.

## 3 Approach

The intention of the work carried out and presented in this paper was to evaluate the potential associated with advanced software to improve the hazard studies of chemical processes. Powerful software for processing and managing safety and reliability information have been developed by R&D laboratories. It has been suggested that the use of such software needs to be linked to the design and operation of industrial plants as a matter of standard practice.

The automated generation of HAZOP studies has already been a topic for research worldwide since the early 1980's. A prototype HAZOP expert system has recently been developed by Okayama University and this was applied to an example process and its performance was evaluated by comparing the results to the results of a human expert team. A similar comparison carried out in an earlier research project using another HAZOP expert system showed that 35% of relevant hazards can be identified automatically [1].

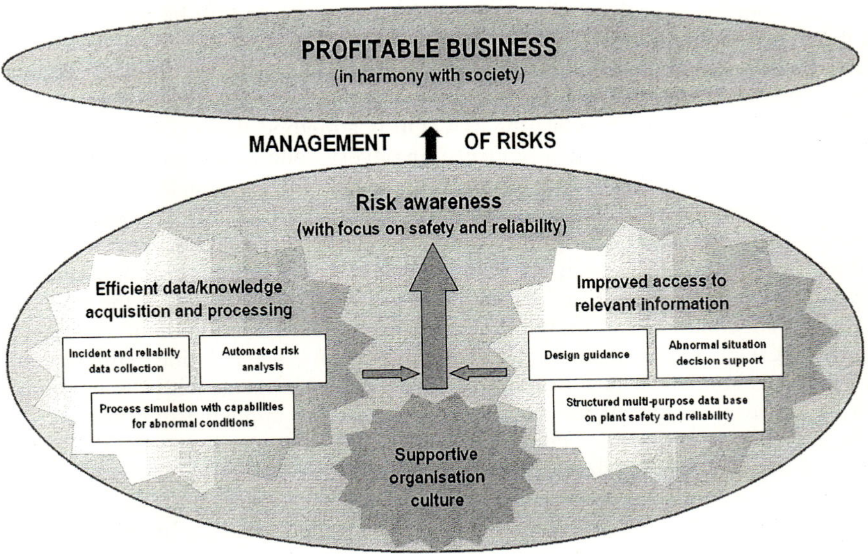


**Fig. 1.** Safety and reliability within an advanced information technology framework in the business environment can improve risk awareness.

Process simulation has established its role in industrial engineering, however, the simulations presently do not have any clear link to safety and reliability studies. In this project, the Visual Modeler simulation software (Omega Simulation Co., Ltd) was used for obtaining quantified information about the hazard scenarios identified by a team of human experts. The feasibility of the simulator software for that specific purpose was evaluated and requirements were then specified in relation to the industrial use of process simulation as a means to support safety and reliability studies.

When more information becomes available about the safety and reliability of a process, it is important that efficient ways to find the relevant information from a large repository of data are provided. As a parallel activity, the EU-supported CHEM project [1] aims to develop new ways to define the applicability of the data and then locate the relevant data in order to support decision making during abnormal situations.

[1] The CHEM Project is funded by the European Community under the Competitive and Sustainable Growth programme of the Fifth RTD Framework Programme (1998-2002) under contract G1RD-CT-2001-00466.

### 3.1 HAZOP System

A safety analysis involves the systematic examination of the structure and functions of a system. Its aim is to identify all factors having the potential to contribute to accidents, to evaluate the risk associated with these hazards, and to identify ways to minimise these risks. Both qualitative and quantitative studies are included in a typical safety analysis of a chemical process system.

The purpose of a Hazard and Operability (HAZOP) study is to identify all possible deviations from the way the design is expected to operate and all hazards associated with these deviations [2].

The HAZOP technique originated in the late 1960s and developed during the early 1970s – predominately at ICI in the UK – as a practical method for problem identification in the process industries. HAZOP is a method that examines the safety of chemical plants by systematically identifying every conceivable process deviation. The objective is to identify deviations from design intent, and subsequently the causes, the consequences, and the remedies, if known. The tools for the study are a set of abstract concepts known as guidewords. The guidewords are applied to process variables and parameters, such as flow rate and temperature. For example, the application of the guideword 'no' to the process variable 'flow rate' is the deviation 'no flow'. To conduct the study, the team examines the equipment model (for example, P&IDs). Each model is divided into sections, usually lines (piping), and each section is studied in turn to identify what could go wrong with the equipment (plant or process). Once all the possible deviations are applied to all the sections (lines), the study is complete. The results of the study are recorded as the deviations, causes and consequences of the deviations, and the remedies [3, 4].

HAZOP has established itself as common practice in chemical process safety. This technique requires the involvement of an experienced, interdisciplinary team, and hence it is desirable to reduce the time and engineering cost associated with HAZOP. One way of doing this would be to incorporate the knowledge used by human experts into an intelligent computer system – an expert system.

Automated HAZOPs could yield significant benefits – potentially:

- Less human effort is required to perform a HAZOP study,
- The HAZOP process becomes standardised,
- Alternative solutions can be assessed quickly with respect to hazards,
- A corporate memory on process hazards is created.

The basic architecture of the Okayama University HAZOP System (developed using the expert system shell G2) is shown in Figure 1. The HAZOP System consists of a HAZOP Inference Engine, a HAZOP Knowledge Base, and the graphical user interface. The HAZOP Knowledge Base consists of Generic Knowledge Base (GKB) and a Specific Knowledge Base (SKB).

The GKB consists of the model library and information about fault propagation. In the model library, there are generic unit models like pipe, heat exchanger, reactor, etc. and each unit model has a Fault Propagation Basic Model and Internal Situation Model. The Fault Propagation Basic Model shows the route of fault propagation as a result of the deviations, and the Internal Situation Model shows what effects result from the deviations. The system can infer from both models the effects of a particular deviation, and also how the deviations affect a unit. The knowledge is developed in a process independent manner and is applicable to a wide variety of process flow sheets.

The SKB consists of information about the materials, the reactions, and the plant structure (i.e. P&IDs). The plant specific knowledge varies from plant to plant and has to be provided by the user.

The user chooses the type of deviation to be considered by clicking on a guideword in the window of the HAZOP System. Then Inference Engine gets information regarding the interconnectivity of units from the SKB. The information on the causal relationship of the deviations is described in the Fault Propagation Models and Internal Situation Models of the GKB. The Inference Engine firstly searches through the Fault Propagation Models to identify where the deviations have an effect, and then through the Internal Situation Models to identify what effects result from the deviation. The HAZOP reasoning proceeds by repeating these procedures.

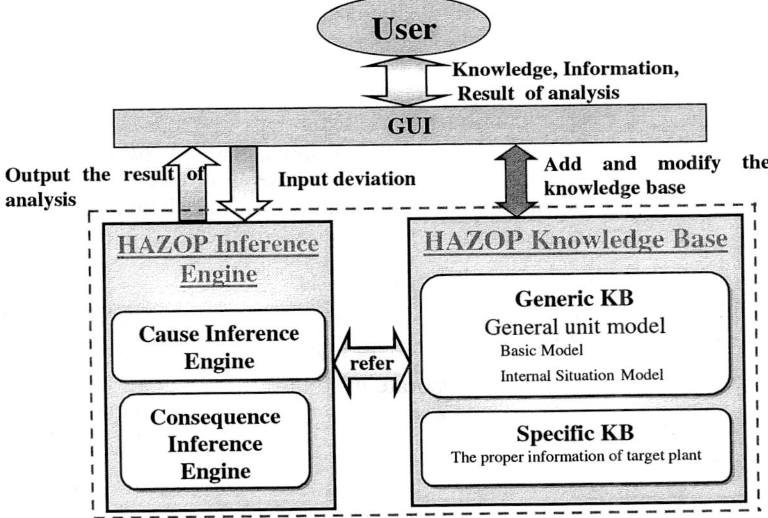


**Fig. 2.** Architecture of the HAZOP System.

## 3.2 Simulation

In recent times, the petroleum and chemical industries have also had to address environmental issues and ensure plant-safety and resource-efficiency in all phases of product development and over the entire life cycle of the plant. To assess these issues in advance, dynamic simulators have been heralded as a solution [5].

Usually, dynamic process simulators are used to train operators – to satisfactorily operate their processes, and to diagnose and correct operational problems or instrument malfunctions. With the aid of a simulator, the training can be done away from the process unit – without causing problems on the actual process unit.

This project aimed to identify how to better utilise HAZOP results. One way to accomplish this may be by using an advanced information technology like model-based simulation. Although many advanced features have been developed and added to the process simulators recently, there is little information available on the utilisation of today's dynamic simulators to support hazard studies. In this study, one aim was to identify how the process simulators of today handle the hazards and deviations associated with process plants.

The most interesting issue to be considered in this project was to determine whether the simulator could reliably recognise the correct consequences for a certain deviation. One objective of this research was also to find preliminary signs of whether or not it would be reasonable to utilise simulators to support HAZOP analyses, and would it even be possible for them to replace HAZOP meetings, where a group of specialists determine hazards.

A HAZOP study is a qualitative analysis made by a group of specialists to determine what would happen if the component were to operate outside its normal design mode. The HAZOP study results look at each parameter in turn and use guidewords to list the possible off-normal behaviour such as 'more', 'less', 'high', 'low', or 'no'. One interesting issue would be to study whether it would be possible to define quantitative deviations from qualitative deviations with the aid of the process simulators.

The dynamic process simulator, Visual Modeler, was used in this study. The software package offers an integrated environment for creating and executing a dynamic simulator for handling various forms of fluids and powders in chemical plants and oil refining facilities [6]. Visual Modeler includes a model editing function so a plant simulator can be constructed by combining various mathematical models of processes and instrument units, and an execute function to implement and test the constructed simulator [6]. Other functions help the process or control engineer of the plant build a customised model for use in a specific task [6].

The plant models can be used as an operating training simulator by incorporating them into a different computer system's environment, and also as commonly used tools to achieve optimal operations in online systems [7].

Visual Modeler offers flexibility, accuracy and calculation efficiency because it is capable of using any combination of the calculation methods simultaneously in one model [7]. Large processes, even with 10000–20000 units, can be simulated. To ease model building, different types of unit models have been registered in the Visual Modeler library [7]. The units are applicable and contain measures against abnormal conditions and malfunction occurrences [6]. In addition, the user can also add new unit models to the library if needed.

In Visual Modeler, simulation enables execution in real time and interactive responses per second. This is useful in situations where the engineers use the simulator for analytical purposes and desire a sense of reality [7]. When utilising simulators in a HAZOP analysis, it is important to get, for example, the consequences of the certain deviation in real time in order to know the realisation time. This enables one to estimate the critical time for safe operation. For large-scale plants, which require a substantial amount of time to reach, for example, the final state after a certain deviation, Visual Modeler also enables accelerated simulation as a necessary function.

### 3.3 Applicability Profile Problem

As part of the European part of the international CHEM project, an information system to support risk management is being developed. The aim is to develop a tool to support the processing and storage of the safety and reliability analysis results in such a form that they can be more easily utilised. The tool will also make reliability and safety analysis results available to engineering and operations personnel and provide a facility for reporting actual disturbances. The intention is to make reliability and safety considerations a part of daily routines in an industrial company [8].

The available reliability and safety information is considered to be decision support advice for ASM. An applicability profile will be attached to every piece of ASM advice. The applicability profile is defined as a combination of the values describing the process state. These values can be quantitative measurement values or their qualitative interpretations. A piece of advice is assumed to be relevant when it fulfils the conditions specified in the applicability profile. Careful definition of the applicability profiles is required in order to achieve a powerful disturbance analysis capability [9].

## 4 Results

To investigate how well the HAZOP system and simulation software can handle deviations compared to the manual HAZOP study, a standard vacuum gas oil hydrodesulfurisation (HDS) process was used as a case study. A HDS unit is designed to process 2,6 wt % sulfur contained vacuum gas oil at the rate of 166 kl/d (25000 BPSD) [10]. The following products are generated:

- Wild Naphtha
- Desulfurised Light Gas Oil (DSLGO)
- Desulfurised Vacuum Gas Oil (DSVGO)

In the study, three parts of the HDS process were chosen for more specific examination. All the results have been presented in the final report of the project [11]. In this paper, only the results of the reactor effluent part of the HDS process are described. In the reactor effluent part of the process, the fresh feed is routed through the reactor effluent heat exchanger to the reactor charge heater and further to the reactor. While passing through the heat exchangers, the reactor effluent cools. At the hot separator it is separated into liquid and vapour. The heat of the fraction feed, reactor feed and recycle gas is recovered through those heat exchangers. The vapour separated in the hot separator is routed to the cold separator. The liquid hydrocarbon is depressurised by a level control valve and sent to the hot flash drum. Another liquid and vapour is produced in the hot flash drum, and the vapour is sent to the hot flash vapour condenser and then on to the cold flash drum. The liquid from the hot flash drum is routed through the heat exchanger to the fractionator. The process part is illustrated in Figure 3.

A small group of experts in the areas of chemical engineering and hazard studies completed the HAZOP study for the process part. About 40 deviations with realistic causes and consequences were recognised.

In the research, the results of the manual HAZOP were compared to the results of the HAZOP System and the simulation. Those results are explained in the next two sections. In addition, the development of the abnormal situation decision support system is introduced.

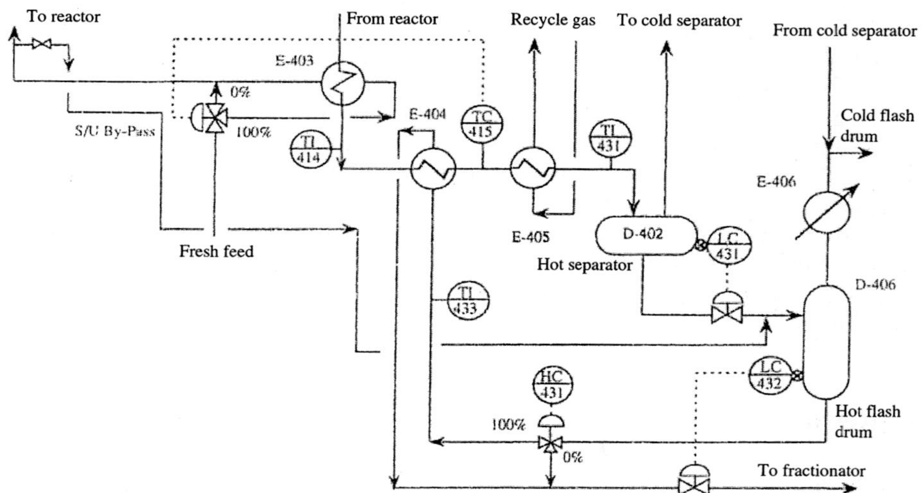


**Fig. 3.** HDS process part chosen for evaluation purposes.

## 4.1 The HAZOP System

For the HAZOP System, the same part of the HDS process, as presented in Figure 3, was analysed. The process part consists of 3 general-purpose heat exchangers, a hot separator, a hot flush drum and various pipelines. The process part modelled in the HAZOP System is illustrated in Figure 4. In this section, the result analysed by the HAZOP System is compared to the expert group's results.

In Table 1, the HAZOP analysis result for 'no flow' in the pipe between E405 and D402 is presented, while Table 2 shows the corresponding HAZOP System result. The HAZOP System shows the associated causes as: 'no flow' from reactor R401 and reactor effluent 'no flow' in E403, E404 and E405. The expert group noted slightly different causes. The differences are related to the fact that the HAZOP System infers causes and consequences in all areas (extensively and exhaustively) which are modelled in the system, and the expert group focuses more on the immediate vicinity of the unit concerned with the original deviation. The HAZOP System may consequently output quite a large amount of information.

Table 3 shows the HAZOP analysis result of 'more flow' in the pipe between D402 and D406, and the corresponding HAZOP System results are displayed in Table 4. The expert group identifies the increase of outflowing gas and liquid flow from D406 as a consequence, but a similar consequence is not noted by the HAZOP System. This is due to the fact that the expert group considered more specific information like the material balance. In other words, the expert group can consider chemical characteristics during the analysis, while the HAZOP system is based on highly generalised knowledge of the behaviour of process equipment and can not perform advanced reasoning on the special characteristics of the chemical process.

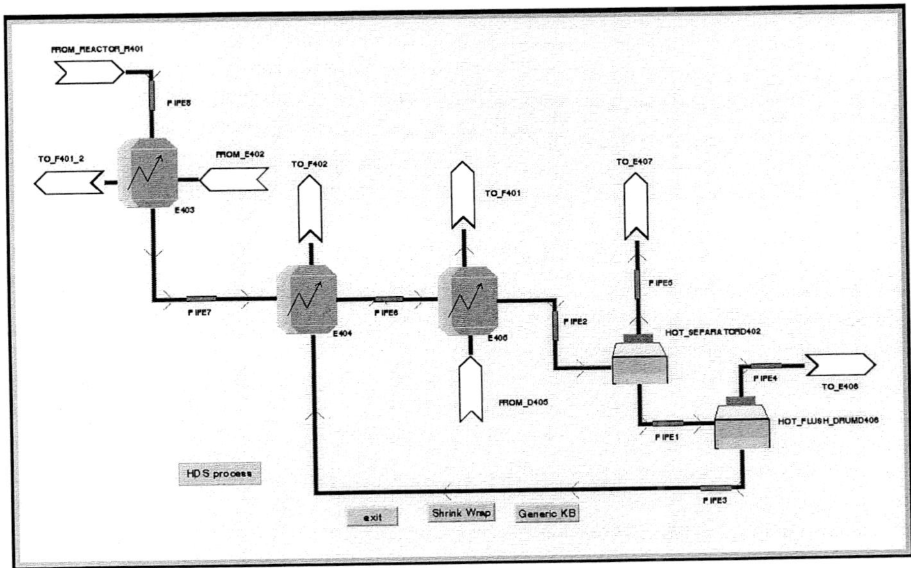


**Fig. 4.** HDS process part modelled in the HAZOP System.

**Table 1.** The HAZOP analysis result for 'no flow' in the pipe between E405 and D402.

| Deviation | Causes | Consequences |
|---|---|---|
| 'No flow' in pipe between E405 and D402 | • Blockage in pipe<br>• Pipe broken<br>• Big leak in previous heat exchanger E405 | • Leak to environment (fire, environmental damage)<br>• Level in reactor increases<br>• Level in D402 decreases<br>• Outflowing gas from D402 decreases<br>• If level increases, valve opens and thus liquid flow decreases |

This case study showed that the HAZOP System can analyse extensively and exhaustively in all areas modelled in the system, but the system could not identify any more specific causes and consequences than the expert group. Two ways of utilising the HAZOP System to support a safety analysis can be considered:

1) the HAZOP System is used to conduct a preliminary analysis which is then followed by a more extensive HAZOP study by a group of experts (this may enable the group of experts to reduce the human effort needed to perform the HAZOP analysis and still get an exhaustive list of causes and consequences),

**Table 2.** The HAZOP System result for 'no flow' in the pipe between E405 and D402.

| Deviation | Causes | Consequences |
|---|---|---|
| 'No flow' in pipe between E405 and D402 | • Blockage in previous pipes<br>• Breakage in previous pipes<br>• Leakage in previous pipes<br>• 'No flow' from reactor R401<br>• In E403, E404 and E405, reactor effluent 'no flow' | • Leakage in pipe<br>• D402 is empty<br>• D406 is empty<br>• From D406, liquid 'no flow'<br>• To E407, off gas 'no flow'<br>• To E406, off gas 'no flow'<br>• In E404, liquid 'no flow' and reactor effluent 'more temperature' |

**Table 3.** The HAZOP analysis result for 'more flow' in the pipe between D402 and D406.

| Deviation | Causes | Consequences |
|---|---|---|
| 'More flow' in pipe between D402 and D406 | • D402 doesn't work correctly, feeds only liquid<br>• Valve 431 doesn't work, stays open<br>• Level measure doesn't work<br>• Control parameters have been wrongly set | • Level in tank D406 increases<br>• Pressure in tank D406 increases<br>• Outflowing gas from D406 increases<br>• If level increases, valve opens and thus liquid flow increases<br>If the cause is that the valve stays open, level measure is not working<br>• Level of tank D402 decreases<br>• Pressure in tank D402 decreases<br>• Gas flow decreases |

**Table 4.** The HAZOP System result for 'more flow' in the pipe between D402 and D406.

| Deviation | Causes | Consequences |
|---|---|---|
| 'More flow' in pipe between D402 and D406 | • In D402, internal level more,<br>• In E405, reactor effluent 'more flow'<br>• In E404, reactor effluent 'more flow'<br>• In E403, reactor effluent 'more flow'<br>• From_reactor_R401, reactor effluent 'more flow' | • In D406, internal level more and vaporisation proceeds |

2) the comparison of the HAZOP System's result with the actual HAZOP analysis could eventually be analysed independently by the expert group, and an even greater level of detail may be obtained.

The generic fault propagation models defined for different process equipment are the most important elements of an intelligent HAZOP system. This makes it difficult to evaluate the performance of such systems and their potential for industrial applications. The obtained results depend heavily on the effort put into the comprehensive fault propagation considerations during the definition of the generic models. Since promising results can be obtained already after quite limited model development effort, it is suggested that more extensive modelling and evaluation exercises should be carried out in order to show the value of intelligent HAZOP systems in industrial applications.

### 4.2 Simulation

In this study, the HDS model created in Visual Modeler was utilised. A HDS unit simulator was designed to help a process operator get a better insight and knowledge of the behaviour of the actual unit in the plant for which he was responsible [10]. All unit models are based on the first principle physical phenomena, that is, the unsteady state heat and mass balance with thermodynamic properties [10].

The deviations (and their causes) as identified in the previous HAZOP analysis were simulated in the HDS unit simulator built up in Visual Modeler in order to identify its corresponding consequences. The evaluation helped to determine the extent to which the potential problems identified by the process simulator correspond to those recognised by a conventional HAZOP analysis team.

The findings roughly indicate that the dynamic simulator was able to generate the same kind, as identified by the HAZOP analysis, of consequences from certain deviations. In practice, problems also arose with certain deviations as they were impossible to simulate. These included, for example, pipe leak to environment or inside a heat exchanger, external warming (e.g. fire), or particular reverse flows which can not be created or presented concretely without making radical changes to the process model. These kinds of problems are still typical for most simulators, but can differ from one simulator to another.

If some deviations could not be created in the "right" place, they were instead generated as the consequence of some other deviation. Consequently, it was sometimes difficult to see whether the changes in the process were due to the real deviation, or if they were the consequence of that "generated" deviation. Also, in some cases, it was difficult to create only one deviation and see its effect; e.g. flow rate change in a cooling liquid also caused a temperature decrease.

In this study, the HAZOP team did not consist of any real HDS process experts. A lack in expertise on flowing materials and the process conditions caused some degree of ambiguity when analysing some of the cause-consequence chains. The biggest difficulties between the HAZOP analysis and the simulation results were due to pressure and temperature changes in the hot separator and hot flash drums.

One of the main findings was that the dynamic process simulator calculates larger entities than a group of experts may think of or handle in a HAZOP analysis meeting. For example, in the HDS case, the process handled in the HAZOP analysis was a part of a larger process. The deviations analysed were focused only on the adjoining equipment. All the consequences caused by, for example, the recycle line were not observed intentionally, or unintentionally. The simulation model, however, included the whole process model, and thus, in the simulation many deviations had effects outside the process section selected for the HAZOP purposes. The changes resulted in different kinds of consequences than were recognised in the HAZOP study (Table 5). The HDS process consists of many feedback connections, and this is the reason for the difficult and complicated cause-consequence chains identified by the HAZOP analysis. The simulator makes it possible to follow the process behaviour during the failure (Table 5).

**Table 5.** One of the cause-consequence chains for 'more pressure' in the hot separator (D402) and the corresponding simulation results.

| Deviation | Cause | Consequence | Result in simulation |
|---|---|---|---|
| 'More pressure' in D402 | No outflowing gas | Liquid level increases, valve is opening, and liquid flow increases | Deviation: Blockage in gas pipe.<br>Consequence: Pressure increased. Level decreased in D402, valve was shutting off, liquid flow decreased because the decreased gas flow ends up in the feed of the process and thus the incoming flow to D402 was decreased. Disturbance in E404 as cooling flow is affected. |

The simulator enables one to perform a dynamic and quantitative analysis instead of qualitative analysis usually associated with the HAZOP method. It appeared that different or even contradictory results could be obtained by using different values for certain deviations. For example, a small temperature increase in hot separator did not cause any consequences, but the larger change caused very dramatic changes in the pressure and the amount of outflowing gas and liquid. Table 6 shows the HAZOP analysis result for 'more temperature' in the hot separator, and Table 7 shows the simulation results with respect to different temperature increases in the hot separator. High temperature values (over 1000°C) are not realistic in chemical processes, however, the simulation software reacts to the temperature change in D402 just after 1500°C. From the simulation time, it is possible to see the time taken from initiation of the deviation to its consequences.

When using dynamic process simulators to support a HAZOP study, it is important to remember that the calculations may be valid only for a certain calculation range. A certain deviation may cause extremely large changes in the process and the corresponding calculation results after the deviation may not even be realistic.

Although the dynamic simulator was able to recognise relevant cause-consequence chains for certain deviations quite well, building the process model for the simulator and tuning it is very time-consuming, and extensive expertise on the process and the process simulator used is needed. However, process simulators are nowadays quite often used in the design phase. The process model should be built up to consider a future HAZOP analysis so that as many deviations as possible could be carried out during the simulation. If the process model is used in the design phase, it would be sensible to use the simulator as a support for the HAZOP analysis.

**Table 6.** The HAZOP analysis result of 'more temperature' in the hot separator (D402).

| Deviation | Causes | Consequences |
|---|---|---|
| 'More temperature' in D402 | • Income flow to tank is warmer<br>• External warming (fire, etc.)<br>• Sudden vaporisation | • Greater part is outflowing as gas (gas flow increases, liquid flow decreases)<br>• Finally, liquid level can disappear as all liquid has changed to gas<br>• Pressure increases<br>• Effects on process balance and product distribution<br>• Sudden pressure increase may result from sudden vaporisation |

**Table 7.** Simulation results of different temperature changes in hot separator, D402.

| Temp [°C] | Time in simulator [hh:mm:ss] | Pressure [kPa] | Liquid flow [kmol/h] | Gas flow [kmol/h] | Level [m] | Valve position [-] |
|---|---|---|---|---|---|---|
| **273 (initial state)** | **24:41:11** | **4 845,68** | **432,569** | **1418,58** | **1** | **0,4** |
| 500 | infinite | 4 845,68 | 432,569 | 1418,58 | 1 | 0,4 |
| 1000 | infinite | 4 845,68 | 432,569 | 1418,58 | 1 | 0,4 |
| 1500 | 24:46:59 | 4 853,41 | 423,948 | 1429,26 | 0,9955 | 0,3929 |
| | 24:49:00 | 4 849,69 | 421,652 | 1428,07 | 0,9961 | 0,3909 |
| | 28:00:43 | 4 848,37 | 423,375 | 1422,93 | 1 | 0,3937 |
| 1600 | 24:42:53 | 4 900,74 | 409,452 | 1472,37 | 0,9806 | 0,3776 |
| | 24:46:00 | 4 871,29 | 381,922 | 1458,18 | 0,9759 | 0,3505 |
| | 28:00:34 | 4 860,98 | 395,319 | 1423,73 | 1 | 0,3647 |
| 2000 | 24:42:53 | 5 985,54 | 446,573 | 5419,31 | 0,9463 | 0,35202 |
| | 24:46:02 | 16 820,7 | 178,887 | 23501,3 | 0,8211 | 0,0461 |
| | 24:50:51 | 32 707,8 | 0 | 55023,6 | 0,8596 | 0 |

### 4.3 Applicability Profile

As part of the European part of the international CHEM project, an information system to support risk management is to be developed over the next two years. The system will be developed such as to be able to interface with commercial plant database and process control software. The developed methodology will be tested and validated, both offline with real process data and online in a paper manufacturing process. More information about the CHEM project can be found from Internet: http://www.chem-dss.org/.

## 5 Conclusions

In this research, the intelligent HAZOP System and a dynamic process simulator were evaluated in order to determine how the systems could support hazard studies.

The findings indicate that the HAZOP System can analyse extensively and exhaustively in all the areas modelled in the system. However, the system will generally not identify more specific causes and consequences than an expert group. The HAZOP System may therefore be used as a preliminary analysis for a HAZOP study proceeded by an expert group. This may help the expert group reduce the human effort needed to perform the HAZOP analysis and result in a more exhaustive list of causes and consequences.

More extensive modelling and evaluation exercises should still, however, be carried out in order to show the value of intelligent HAZOP systems in industrial applications.

In the simulation part of the study, the findings indicated that the simulator was able to identify the same kinds of consequences from a certain deviation as was raised in the HAZOP analysis – in most of the cases. However, some deviations proved to be impossible to simulate, and in a few cases it was difficult to induce only one deviation at a time. The simulator turned out to provide good support when a defining quantitative deviation instead of a qualitative one. Creating the process model in the simulator, and then tuning it, was however very time-consuming and demanding, but if the process model has been already created as part of the design phase, it could easily also be utilised to support the HAZOP study.

As part of the European part of the international CHEM project, an information system to support risk management is being developed. The aim is to develop a tool to support the processing and storage of a company's safety and reliability analysis results in such a form that they can be more easily utilised. An information system is to be developed over the next two years. This could be especially useful for the operator's decision-making support during abnormal situations.

**Acknowledgements**

This project was supported by the National Technology Agency of Finland (TEKES), VTT Industrial Systems (Finland), and Okayama University (Japan). The simulation program Visual Modeler (Omega Simulation Co., Ltd) and the HAZOP system (developed by Okayama University) were used during this project. The authors wish to thank the numerous individuals at the participating organisations for their support and fruitful discussions during the project.

## References

[1] Heino, P. Fluid property reasoning in knowledge-based hazard identification. *VTT Publications*; 393. Espoo, VTT, 1999. 170p. + app. 44p. ISBN 951-38-5395-0; 951-38-5396-9

[2] Heino, P., Suzuki, K., and Chung, P.W.H. Challenge in the field of HAZOP information processing and utilization.

[3] Suzuki, K., Shimada, Y., Sayama, H. and Nojiri, I. 1997. Application of Knowledge Engineering to Automated HAZOP. *Proceedings of ECCE1*, Vol.1, 1997, pp.787-790.

[4] Suzuki, K., Shimada, Y. and Nojiri, I. An Object-oriented Approach for Computer-aided HAZOP for Batch Plants. *Proceedings of The European Conference on Safety and Reliability, ESREL'98*, 1998, pp.1335-1342.

[5] Takatsu, H., Nozaki, T., and Okada, K. Application of Virtual Simulation Environment to the Crude Distillation Unit Control. ISA2001. *The Instrumentation, Systems, and Automation Society (ISA).* 10-12 September 2001. Houston, Texas, USA.

[6] Visual Modeler User's Manual. Omega Simulation Co., Ltd. *VM-ML-4101-1E.* 1st Edition. December 2001, Tokyo.

[7] Visual Modeler. Dynamic Simulator of the New Era. http://www.omegasim.co.jp/contents_e/contents/products_e/index_e4.html. 9.4.2002.

[8] Heino, P., Valkokari, P., Rönkkö, K., Kotikunnas, E., and Lamberg, S. Operator support for abnormal situations using safety and reliability knowledge. *15th Triennial World Congress of the International Federation of Automatic Control.* Final Program. Book of Abstracts. International Federation of Automatic Control (IFAC). 2002. p.84.

[9] Heino, P., Karvonen, I., Pettersen, T., Wennersten, R., and Andersen, T. Monitoring and analysis of hazards using HAZOP-based plant safety model. *Reliability Engineering and System Safety*, 44, 1994, pp.335-343.
[10] VGO Hydrosulfurization Unit, Training Manual. *PJDocNo. JCCP-SIM_50-H-S-401*.
[11] Heino, P., Kupila, K., Shinohara, S., Schabel, J., Yamamoto, H., and Suzuki, K. Evaluation of an automated HAZOP System and a dynamic process simulator for the better utilisation of HAZOP analysis results. Research report BTUO: 42-031113. Tampere, 2003. VTT Industrial Systems. 37p.

# State-Based Modelling in Hazard Identification

Stephen McCoy, Dingfeng Zhou, and Paul W.H. Chung

Modelling and Reasoning Research Group, Department of Computer Science,
Loughborough University, Loughborough, Leics., LE11 3TU, UK,
s.a.mccoy@lboro.ac.uk

**Abstract.** The signed directed graph (SDG) is the most commonly used type of model for automated hazard identification in chemical plants. Although SDG models are efficient in simulating the plant, they have some weaknesses, which are discussed here in relation to typical process industry examples. Ways to tackle these problems are suggested, and the view is taken that a state-based formalism is needed, to take account of the discrete components in the system, their connection together, and their behaviour over time. A strong representation for operations and actions is also needed, to make the models appropriate for modelling batch processes.

**Keywords:** Model-Based Reasoning, Qualitative Modelling, Simulation.

## 1 Introduction

Chemical process plants are very complex systems, and computers have been used for many years now, to aid their detailed design and operation. Most applications have applied computer power to graphics or numerical calculations in this domain, such as mass and energy balances, computer-aided design, numerical simulation, etc.

In addition to these numerical applications, computers have also been applied to dynamic modelling of plant behaviour using qualitative approaches. Typical applications of techniques such as expert systems and qualitative reasoning have included:

- The analysis (and grouping) of alarms during plant operation, to diagnose causes of plant upsets and help the operators of the plant.
- Evaluation of design plans, to find potential sources of operability problems or hazards in the plant when built.

The latter application has been worked on extensively by the authors and coworkers [1, 2], in work on developing a software tool for emulating HAZOP studies on chemical plant, and by other research groups in their own work [3, 4].

The approach used is to build models of equipment types (units), which are capable of predicting the dynamic behaviour of the equipment items, in normal operation and under deviations from normal plant operation. Such models have most often been based around a simulation of the important state variables in the equipment item, together with a range of information to capture the possible failures of the equipment, and the susceptibility of the equipment to deviations propagated from elsewhere. The equipment models are connected together to form plant models, within which the effects of deviations can be assessed by propagation of the disturbances modelled.

P.W.H. Chung, C.J. Hinde, M. Ali (Eds.): IEA/AIE 2003, LNAI 2718, pp. 244–253, 2003.

A very important decision in building such models is the knowledge representation to be used. If a highly complex representation is chosen, it may allow a wide range of phenomena to be modelled, but will incur penalties in the shape of the extra work required to build models and the computational costs of driving simulations. If a simpler representation is used, the models will be easier to understand and to build, and will execute more efficiently but may not be as expressive as the more complex representation. There is therefore a trade-off between the expressive power of the formalism chosen and the complexity of building models and driving simulations using it.

In much of the work done historically, a simple graphical representation, the signed directed graph (SDG), has been used. This has the advantages of being simple to understand and also very efficient in dynamic simulation of the plant – the SDG of the plant is just searched for paths between remote locations to find all fault propagation scenarios predicting hazards. However, work with SDGs in modelling plants for hazard identification has revealed a number of disadvantages of choosing this formalism:

- The SDG only readily supports two deviations of a process variable ("more" and "less"), whereas there can often be a need for more values.
- The SDG doesn't include any information about the state of the equipment. Thus, it uses the same model of a healthy unit, even when the unit may have malfunctioned, meaning that its behaviour might be quite different from the healthy model.
- Sequences of events (and so-called "enabling" faults, which cause a condition in which the plant is susceptible to other failures) are not modelled well by the SDG, which can only handle single linear chains of events.
- Ambiguity – It can sometimes be impossible to tell which of a number of scenarios is actually possible and which impossible, using the SDG model, because the graph does not capture the constraints operating in the real world closely enough.
- Over-reporting hazards – Because the models do not include all that is known about a unit (the SDG will not support all this information), hazards are over-reported. Over-reporting is preferable to missing scenarios, but places a burden on the user of checking all the predictions to see which ones are realistic and which are not.

Our view is that the weakness of the SDG representation is the cause of most of these problems – important features of the real process are missing from SDG models. The question then becomes: How can the process be better modelled?

In this paper, two cases are examined where the current system is clearly weak. We hope that by taking this approach of analysing the weaknesses, some indication of how to improve the knowledge representation can be given.

## 2 Level Control Example

The scenario shown in Figure 1 is a very common one – the level of liquid in the tank is regulated by varying the output flow using feedback control.

Liquid flows into the tank at a certain flowrate Q1 and flows out of it at flowrate Q2. The level of liquid in the tank is L. This level is measured by a level transmitter instrument (LT), and transmitted to a "level indicating controller" (LIC), which compares the level to a setpoint level (and also provides an indication in the control room of what the level is). Depending on whether the level of liquid is higher or lower than the setpoint, the

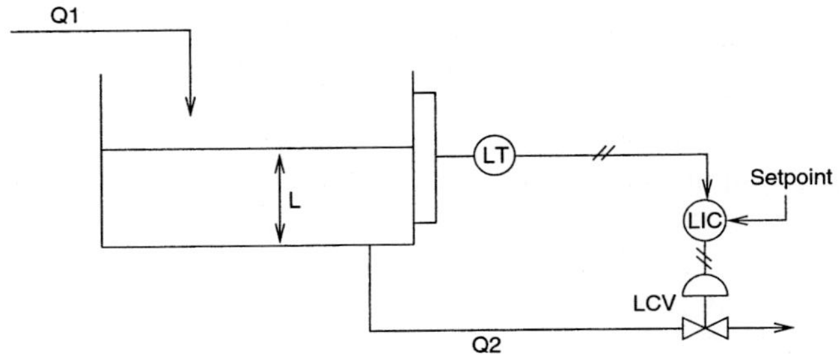


**Fig. 1.** Level control example plant

controller then instructs a level control valve (LCV) to open or close, thereby affecting the output flow, Q2. The LIC seeks to maintain the level in the tank at the specified setpoint value, despite changes in the input flow, Q1.

The simplest possible causal model of the tank ignores the presence of the control loop entirely (i.e. it is an "open loop" model). Here it is in SDG notation:

The two relevant hazards, from the point of view of the tank, are overflow and emptying. These are linked directly to the level node in the model, but could be caused by deviations in either flow, Q1 or Q2. Note that an additional arc could be added to this "open loop" plant-only model:

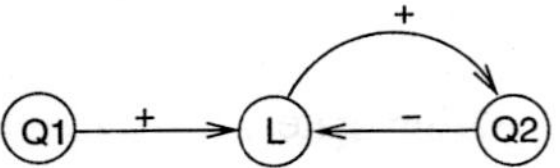


The $L \rightarrow Q2$ arc models the effect of changes in the level of liquid in the tank on output flow induced by the "static head" pressure in the output pipe.[1] The validity of this link very much depends on the conditions in the outlet line from the tank – if there are control valves, pumps, etc., these may tend to override the "passive" behaviour of the tank + valve + liquid system. Therefore, the "static head" link will be ignored in this example.

The behaviour of the control loop can be examined by breaking it down into its component parts, each of which corresponds to a common item of process equipment. By building models of each item and connecting them together, the whole plant behaviour can be predicted. The components of the control loop shown in Figure 1 are:

- Level Transmitter (LT)
- Signal Line from LT to LIC
- Level Controller (LIC)
- Signal Line from LIC to LCV
- Level Control Valve (LCV)

[1] The static head is the pressure generated by the weight of a depth of liquid – the pressure increases for increased depth of liquid, which might have an effect on the flow out of the tank.

This breakdown doesn't show very much detail – other equipment items could have been included if a more refined model was needed, but the high level model serves to cover the overall structure and function of the loop.

## 2.1 Level Transmitter (LT)

At a very abstract level, the LT is a device which converts the value of a process variable (here, the level of the liquid in the tank) into a signal representing that value (electrically or pneumatically). Therefore, we could represent it as a single connection:

The validity of this link really depends on whether the transmitter is operational – the presence of malfunctions will affect the value transferred to $L_{sens}$.

To identify more accurately what the failure modes could mean for this transmitter, we need to look at its components and consider *their* characteristic failure modes. For the example of a level transmitter, the equipment involved might include a float gauge with a transducer for converting the float position into an electrical signal. Possible failures here include the case where the float is "stuck", for some reason, meaning that variations in level are not measured and transmitted. Alternatively, the transmitter unit may be inoperative due to it being switched off intentionally, or due to power failure. All these would result in a loss of function for the LT unit as a whole.

So, the successful production of a signal by the LT depends on the state of that device being "on_line" (or some other label representing the normal operational state). In other states, a different $L_{sens}$ is propagated to the signal line and thence to the LIC.

If we accept the need for modelling states, some of the relevant state values for the transmitter might include:

**on_line.** Transmitter in normal operational state, receiving power and transmitting a value which accurately represents the level in the equipment item it is attached to.

**power_failed.** Loss of electrical power (for an electrical transmitter), meaning that the output of the transmitter does not represent the level accurately.

**air_failed.** Instrument air failure (for a pneumatic transmitter), having similar effects to power_failed.

**off_line.** Transmitter turned off.

**float_stuck.** The level sensing element (here a float inside the vessel) is stuck, meaning that the transmitter output doesn't accurately reflect changes in the level of liquid in the vessel.

## 2.2 Transmission Lines

The signal transmission lines from the LT to LIC, and from the LIC to the LCV, are also prone to various modes of failure. These depend on whether the signal (and transmission line) is electrical or pneumatic.

Some of the states appropriate for electrical signal transmission lines include:

**ok.** The signal line is in its normal operational state and capable of conveying electrical signals accurately.
**power_failed.** The power supply needed to transmit the signal has failed.
**severed.** The cable has been cut or severed at some point, meaning that no signal transmission is possible.

Some of the states appropriate for pneumatic signal lines include:

**ok.** The line is operating normally, transmitting the required signal pressure accurately.
**instrument_air_failed.** The air supply needed to transmit pneumatic signals has failed.
**leaking.** The line is punctured or severed at some point.
**overpressurised.** The line is being supplied with air at too high a pressure.
**obstructed.** The line is blocked or partially blocked somewhere.

## 2.3 Level Controller (LIC)

The types of failure appropriate for the level indicating controller (LIC) will depend on the particular controller used in a given case. A number of the states to be expected for a controller device in general could include:

**on_line.** Automatically regulating output based on controlling the level to a requested setpoint.
**manual.** Controller output is a constant which may be set by the operator.
**off_line.** The controller is switched off and is not providing an output signal.

## 2.4 Level Control Valve

The control valve itself is composed of an actuator assembly, attached to a valve body. The valve body has an input and output process connection, carrying the process fluid whose flow is to be regulated. The actuator has two inputs, one from the power supply (electrical power or pressurised air) and one delivering the signal from the controller to the valve (which again may be electrical or pneumatic in nature).

The actuator may have a default intended behaviour upon power failure, which could be to open the valve, close the valve or keep the valve steady at the last good value. Possible states for the control valve might include:

**on_line.** On-line and accepting commands from the signal input.
**failed_open, failed_closed or failed_stuck.** Valve failure modes (each of which may be the default mode or not).
**blocked.** Process side of the valve is obstructed, restricting or preventing the flow of fluid through the valve body.
**valve_air_failed.** The air supply used to move the valve stem has failed (if pneumatically actuated).
**valve_power_failed.** The power supply used to move the valve stem has failed (if electrically actuated).

# 3 Batch Reactor Example

This example deals with the situation when modelling batch plants, where the plant operation moves through a number of stages, rather than each equipment item remaining in a "steady state" indefinitely, as is normal for continuously operating plants. The changes in equipment state over time mean that batch processes are more difficult to model accurately than continuous processes.

Figure 2 shows the reactor section of a plant in which product $P$ is produced from two reactants $A$ and $B$, using the simple chemical reaction $A + B \rightarrow P$. An excess of reactant $B$ is used so that reactant $A$ is completely consumed in the reactor.

To safely produce the product, a sequence of operating instructions is followed by the human operators of the plant. A simplified example of such a sequence might be:

1. Charge the reactor with reactant $A$.
2. Turn on the agitator and the cooling water flow through the cooling jacket.
3. Gradually add a sufficient excess of reactant $B$ to the vessel.
4. Continue mixing reactor contents for a while, to allow reaction to complete.
5. Pump the product mixture away for separation.
6. When reactor is empty, switch off mixer, product transfer pump and cooling water.
7. Wash reactor internals thoroughly with water.

In order to reason about what could possibly go wrong with such a plant, it is essential that operating procedures such as this one can be represented. Not only is a knowledge representation needed, for the actions and quantities involved, but also some means of representing the (typically) implicit assumptions associated with each step.

For instance, the above procedure assumes that the reactor is clean and empty at the start of the batch. If, however, an operator had not adequately washed the reactor, or (worse still) had not pumped away the product mixture after the last batch had finished, adding reactant $A$ to the reactor in such a state could have potentially hazardous consequences (such as a premature reaction with reactant $B$ present from the last batch).

Predicting such consequences is possible if some way of representing the sequence of actions in the procedure is available, as well as a way of expressing the assumed state

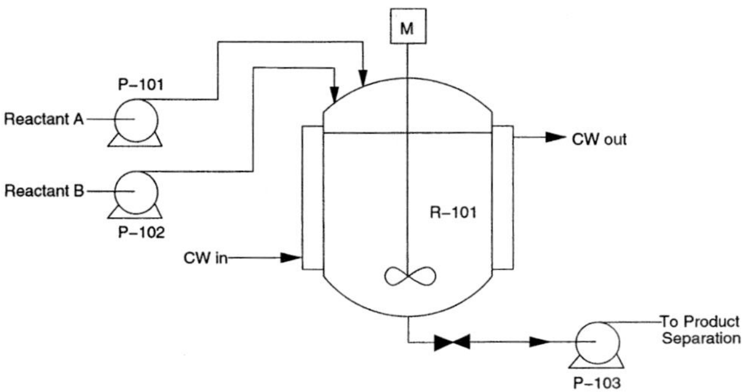


**Fig. 2.** Batch reactor example plant

of the plant items before and after each of the steps. A combination of human error analysis and process modelling can be used to detect these situations and to suggest redesign of the plant to eliminate such dangers.

The points raised in this section point towards enhancing the models used to simulate plant behaviour by adding, not only equipment states, but also the notion of sequence and (by implication) time, into the system. These are typically not tackled in any SDG based modelling system.

In addition to these, it is clearly important to model the actions of operators, as events which should take place in the operation of a batch plant. The various details of actions, such as quantity of material to transfer, duration to wait, etc., have an important but lesser role in identifying hazards, than modelling the presence or absence of the actions in the required sequence.

## 4 A "Domain Theory" for Plant Systems

As a means of capturing knowledge representation issues, a domain theory (or "ontology") for chemical plant systems should distinguish between the different sorts of information to be modelled, and should allow an integration of these different sources.

### 4.1 Classification of Objects

The first thing to do is to draw up a taxonomy of the objects to be modelled, covering all the types of information needed to predict plant behaviour. We can start to draw some of the higher level types in the hierarchy as a tree (see Figure 3). The placement of objects within this tree is tentative at this stage and potentially open to modification; nevertheless, it is a good first framework for the relevant objects in this domain.

The first level distinguishes between "physical objects", corresponding to tangible entities in the world, and "abstract objects", which are the intangible elements which are essential to know how the plant is operated and how its behaviour is modelled in terms of variables whose values change over time.

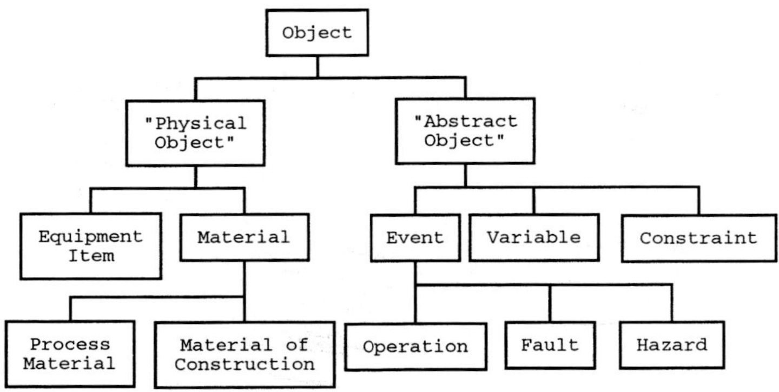


**Fig. 3.** Top Levels of a Taxonomic Tree for objects of interest in modelling Chemical Plants

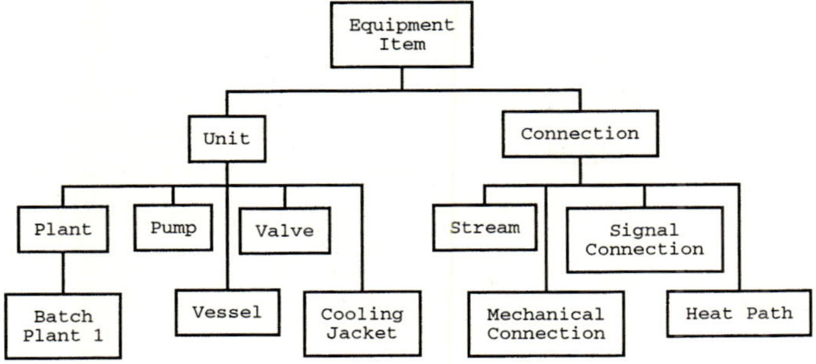


**Fig. 4.** Top levels of a possible equipment hierarchy

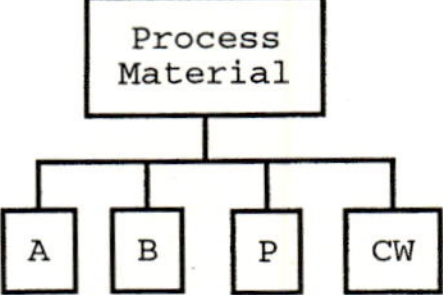


**Fig. 5.** Possible process materials hierarchy for batch plant example

An equipment item is a countable physical object which forms part of the plant. A partial hierarchy of equipment items, showing the distinction between units and connections between units, is shown as Figure 4.

Materials are "liquid-like" in the knowledge representation sense of being mass-noun entities with particular properties, but are not discretely countable. A distinction is made between the materials processed by the plant (solid, liquid and gaseous chemicals) and the materials from which the plant is constructed (steel, glass, plastic, etc.). Some possible process materials, for the earlier batch plant example, are shown in Figure 5.

The abstract part of the hierarchy in Figure 3 governs all the non-physical entities which determine the plant behaviour. Events are things which may cause or be associated with changes in physical state of equipment or materials in the plant – three sub-types are given so far. Operations define the operating instructions of the plant, and can be highly structured. Faults are spontaneous failures and Hazards are potentially dangerous events which occur due to Faults or other plant disturbances. A Variable is a plant item property such as a flow, temperature, pressure, etc. Variables will typically be modelled using a Quantity whose value type is qualitative, rather than numerical. The Constraint class allows a range of functional relationships to be modelled, so that causal (or non-causal) constraints between variables or events can be captured.

## 4.2 Structure in the Plant

The physical plant itself is modelled as an equipment item – albeit one with a complex structure and many components. Each component is an instance of an equipment model. A similar breakdown is possible at any level for any equipment model – a Unit or a Connection can be composed of a number of Units, connected together by Connections. Using a standard breakdown structure like this allows models to be built of equipment sub-components, such as agitators, motors, cooling jackets, etc. The sub-components can then be reused in many different models without change.

This compositional modelling approach can also be applied to other parts of the plant modelling problem – to model the interconnection of instrument systems (using signal connections) or the relation between operating instructions in a plan (using precedence constraints).

## 5 Discussion

The example scenarios above have shown some problem areas for the SDG-based modelling approach. Such an analysis is most useful in pointing the way to further improvements in the representation used for modelling the plant.

One thing that is clearly right about the SDG-based approach used to date is the decomposition of the plant into unit models corresponding to equipment items on the plant. This feature of the formalism must remain – structural decomposition in this way makes sense from the point of view of handling complexity and is also the way engineers tend to think about the plant and its design. Keeping this approach also means that the topology of the model will superficially resemble that of the plant itself, which may aid understanding.

However, as mentioned above, the decomposition process must be taken further, to allow components and sub-components to be defined within the equipment models. In previous work [1, 2], the unit models contained a large number of the "atomic" components in the system (SDG arcs), which added to their complexity. The task of modelling the unit behaviour can be simplified by defining components which are smaller than equipment units, but larger than the "basic unit" of the model system (whatever that might be in the chosen formalism). From the level control loop example, a level transmitter was composed of a float gauge component connected to a transducer component.

Most important, for the modelling of malfunctioning units, is the concept of defining the state of the units (not possible in the SDG approach). Equipment items most often behave according to the default "healthy" model, but may have different behavioural modes, corresponding to "off-normal" states (e.g. if the unit is switched off, or not connected to needed information or power sources). State-based models can support reasoning about "common mode" failures, which can arise due to power or utility failures across the whole plant. Common mode failures are difficult to model using the SDG because of the inability to envisage the parallel development of scenarios in different parts of the plant at the same time.

For batch processes, the SDG is particularly poor in capturing the actions needed to operate the plant and the changes in state which occur during normal operation. To support this area, the representation must include the idea of a sequence of operating instructions, which are operator actions which should be performed in order. Ideally, each action should also be associated with a set of assumptions about the state of the plant and an expectation of what the results of the action should be. Incorporating these fields will allow the intended function of the plant to be compared with the simulation of what will actually happen in "normal operation". Furthermore, by formalising the actions that take place in the batch plant, we can start to look at the most likely human failure modes which could lead to hazards in the plant (in contrast to the process-initiated ones).

Despite the points made above about state dependent models, the most usual mode of operation for units in the plant will correspond to the same type of model previously used when modelling using the SDG. Therefore, the models may behave in a very similar way, most of the time. As was seen in the level control example, the connectivity of the loop is only broken when one of the failure modes takes over in an equipment item.

These improvements are the basis of a representation system currently under development, to allow more accurate process system modelling. While the field of application is currently based around the identification of hazardous scenarios in chemical plants, the techniques being developed are directed at the general problem of qualitative physical systems modelling. Therefore, it is expected that the tools currently being developed should find applications in other areas (analysis of electrical circuits is one possibility that springs to mind, as it is a problem with a similar connectivity metaphor).

## 6 Conclusion

This paper has discussed some of the knowledge representation issues of particular importance to the field of hazard identification in chemical plants. It has examined two typical examples, pointing out where the most commonly used qualitative models, based on the signed directed graph, have had difficulties. We have made some suggestions for how a range of these problems can be tackled, in connection with the on-going research programme at Loughborough University, to further develop representations for modelling and simulating complex systems such as process plants efficiently.

Some techniques for coping with the complexity of process systems have already been proven and will be extended further (e.g. the definition of generic models of equipment and their inter-connection). Modelling the state of a plant and its component units appears to be the most important unsolved problem in this domain, and will form the focus of the next phase of our research here. This work will include not only the state-based evolution of behaviour from physical units in the plant, but also a study of how to model the possible operations (and operational errors) in batch plants.

## References

1. S.A. McCoy, S.J. Wakeman, F.D. Larkin, M.L. Jefferson, P.W.H. Chung, A.G. Rushton, F.P. Lees, and P.M. Heino. HAZID, a computer aid for hazard identification. *Trans IChemE, Part B (Process Safety and Environmental Protection)*, 77:317–353, November 1999. (Papers 1 to 3 in a series of 5).
2. S.A. McCoy, S.J. Wakeman, F.D. Larkin, P.W.H. Chung, A.G. Rushton, and F.P. Lees. HAZID, a computer aid for hazard identification. *Trans IChemE, Part B (Process Safety and Environmental Protection)*, 78:91–142, March 2000. (Papers 4 and 5 in a series of 5).
3. R. Vaidhyanathan, V. Venkatasubramanian, and F.T. Dyke. HAZOPExpert: An expert system for automating HAZOP analysis. *Process Safety Progress*, 15(2):80–88, 1996.
4. C.A. Catino and L.H. Ungar. Model based approach to automated hazard identification of chemical plants. *AIChE Journal*, 41(1):97–109, 1995.

# Deriving Consensus for Conflict Data in Web-Based Systems

Ngoc Thanh Nguyen and Czeslaw Danilowicz

Department of Information Systems, Wroclaw University of Technology, Poland
thanh@pwr.wroc.pl, danilowicz@zsi.pwr.wroc.pl

**Abstract.** Reconciling of conflict data is needed when there exists a data conflict situation in a distributed system, particularly in a Web-based system. A conflict situation takes place when some system sites generate and store different versions of data, which refer to the same subject. In purpose to solve this problem one final version for the data should be determined. This final data version is called a consensus of given versions. In this paper we propose to solve conflict situations by determining consensus functions. We present a consensus system, the postulates for consensus choice functions, their analysis and an algorithm for consensus determining.

## 1 Introduction

The ability of reconciling of conflict data in purpose to make use of them should be one of the features of intelligent Web-based distributed information systems. Distributed intelligent systems consist of autonomous sites and the autonomous feature is the resource of such kind of conflicts that the information generated by the sites on some matter is inconsistent. Such information may include results of retrieval processes made by independent agents for the same user query, or solutions of the same task whose solving is entrusted to different agents. The problem is how to determine the final version of the inconsistent results for given query or different solutions of given task. Generally, this kind of situations is related with preserving of data consistency. It often happens that the environments occupied by distributed system sites overlap. The reason of this phenomenon is resulted from the needs of mutual verification and data replication in purpose to increase the computation efficiency and to relieve the Web. For example, the information about all borrowers is replicated in each site of the distributed system of the bank, or the regions occupied by different meteorological stations overlap. Thus we can assume that in different sites of a Web-based distributed system there may be stored and processed data referring to the same part of the real world. Because each site makes the data processing in an independent way [3], particularly if the data are uncertain and incomplete (which for example come from observations), it is very likely that in these sites there is stored different information for the same subject [4]. We call such a situation a conflict because if these data are collected in a view for the user, they should be inconsistent.

P.W.H. Chung, C.J. Hinde, M. Ali (Eds.): IEA/AIE 2003, LNAI 2718, pp. 254–263, 2003.

Generally, such kind of situations can take place when the system sites realize a common task, or solve a common problem or gather information about a common environment.

In this work we propose a tool for solving this kind of conflict in distributed systems. This tool consists of methods for consensus choice. We should show that the version which is the consensus of given versions of data, should be the most credible one. In general, consensus choice is sensible if it is not possible to generate the final version on the basis of certain and complete data.

Consensus methods, firstly used in social and sociological science, are a very good tool for data reconciling and working out an agreement in solving conflicts [9]. These methods are particularly useful for these systems in which uncertainty of information is assumed but the decision making process is required. For conflicts in distributed systems (particularly in multiagent systems [6]) consensus methods are useful for their solving [1], [7], [10], [13]. In Section 2 we present the notion of conflict and the way to define it, Section 3 gives the elements of so called *consensus system* and Section 4 includes a general algorithm for consensus choice.

## 2 Conflicts in Distributed Systems

What is conflict? The simplest conflict takes place when two bodies have different opinions referring to the same subject. In work [12] Pawlak specifies the following elements of a conflict: a set of agents, a set of issues, and a set of opinions of these agents about these issues. The agents and the issues are related with one another in some social or political context. Each agent for each issue has 3 possibilities for presenting his opinion: (+) - yes, (–) - no, and (0) - neutral. We say that a conflict should take place if there exist at least two agents whose opinions on the same issue differ from each other.

Generally, one can distinguish the following 3 constrains of a conflict:

- *Conflict body*: specifies the participants of the conflict.
- *Conflict subject*: specifies to whom (or what) the conflict refers and its topic.
- *Conflict content*: specifies the opinions of the participants on the conflict topic.

In Pawlak's approach the body of conflict is a set of agents, the subject is a set of contentious issues and the content is a collection of tuples representing the participants' opinions.

We define conflicts in distributed systems in the similar way. However, we will define a tool which can include more than one conflict, and within a conflict the attributes representing the agents' opinions have variables which more precisely describe these opinions. Besides, in our approach the conflict content is partitioned into three groups. The first group should include opinions of type "*Yes, the event should take place*", the second should include opinions of type "*No, the event should not take place*", and to the last group contains the opinions of type "*I do not know if the event should take place or not*". For example, making the forecast of rainfall for tomorrow a meteorological agent can present its opinion as "(*Certainly*) *it will rain between* 9*a.m.* *and* 12*a.m. and will not rain from* 3*p.m. to* 6*p.m.*", that means during the rest of the day the agent does not know if rain will fall or not. These types of information should take place because the set of possible states of the real world in which a system site is placed, is large and an agent having limited possibilities, is not assumed to "know everything".

The information about conflicts will be used for consensus determining. Consensus theory has a root in the era of ancient Greek City states. *Consensus has been understood as a general agreement in matters of opinion or testimony and is a powerful tool for solving many problems for which the solvers are in conflict* [5]. A *general agreement* is understood as a product resulting from the agents' opinions, which in general satisfies these agents. It means that this product may be simultaneously consistent with opinions of several agents and inconsistent with some others. However, the word "general" suggests the consistency with the majority of agents' opinions. Consensus methods have many applications in computer science [5], for which an extensive review has been made in works [6], [11].

# 3 Consensus System

This section includes the basic notions of so called *consensus system*, the definition of consensus and its properties.

## 3.1 Basis Notions

Assume that some real world is described by means of a finite set of attributes $A$ and a set $V$ of attribute *elementary values*, where $V=\bigcup_{a\in A}V_a$ ($V_a$ is the domain of attribute $a$). Let $\Pi(V_a)$ be the powerset of set $V_a$ and let $\Pi(V_B)=\bigcup_{b\in B}\Pi(V_b)$. We assume that for each attribute $a$ its value is a set of elementary values from $V_a$, thus it is an element of set $\Pi(V_a)$. By an elementary value we mean that one which is not divisible in the system. Thus it is a relative notion, for example, one can assume the following values to be elementary: time chronons, numbers, partitions of a set etc.

We define the following notions: Let $B\subseteq A$, a tuple of type $B$ is a function $r: B \rightarrow \Pi(V_B)$ where $(\forall b\in B)(r(b)\subseteq V_b)$. Instead of $r(b)$ we will write $r_b$ and a tuple of type $B$ will be written as $r_B$. A tuple is elementary if all attribute values are empty sets or 1-element sets. Empty tuple, whose values are empty sets, is denoted by symbol $\varepsilon$. Partly empty tuple, whose at least one value is empty, is denoted by symbol $\theta$. The set of all tuples of type $B$ is denoted by $TYPE(B)$. A nonempty set $R$ of tuples of type $B$ is called a relation of type $B$, thus $R\subseteq TYPE(B)$. A sum $\oplus$ of 2 tuples $r$ and $r'$ of type $B$ is a tuple $r''$ of type $B$ ($r'' = r\oplus r'$) such that $\forall b\in B)(r''_b = r_b\cup r'_b)$. A product $\otimes$ of 2 tuples $r$ and $r'$ of type $B$ is also a tuple $r''$ of type $B$ ($r'' = r\otimes r'$) such that $(\forall b\in B)(r''_b = r_b\cap r'_b)$. Let $r,r \in TYPE(B)$, we say that tuple $r$ is included in tuple $r'$ (that is $r\prec r'$), iff $(\forall b\in B)(r_b\subseteq r'_b)$.

### 3.2 Definition of Consensus System

We assume that some real world is commonly considered by agents which are placed in different sites of a Web-based system. The subjects of agents' interest consist of events which occur (or have to occur) in the world. The task of the agents is based on determining the values of event attributes (an event is described by a tuple of some type). The system defined below should include this information.

**Definition 1.** *By a consensus system we call the following triple:*

$$Consensus\_Sys = (\boldsymbol{A},\boldsymbol{X},\boldsymbol{P})$$

*where:*

- $\boldsymbol{A}$ – *a finite set of attributes, which includes a special attribute Agent; each attribute* $a\in\boldsymbol{A}$ *has a domain* $V_a$ *(a finite set of elementary values) such that its values are subsets of* $V_a$*; values of attribute Agent are 1-element sets, which identify the agents.*
- $\boldsymbol{X}$ – *a finite set of consensus carriers;* $\boldsymbol{X} = \{\Pi(V_a): a\in\boldsymbol{A}\}$
- $\boldsymbol{P}$ – *a finite set of relations on carriers from* $\boldsymbol{X}$*, each relation is of some type A (for* $A\subseteq\boldsymbol{A}$ *and* $Agent\in A$*).*

The purpose of Definition 1 is relied on representing of two kinds of information: the first consists of information about conflicts in the distributed system, which require solving, and the second includes the information needed for consensus determining. The following example should more clearly explain the above notions.

Consider a meteorological distributed system in which the sites are meteorological stations placed in different regions of a country. Each station uses an agent whose task relies on monitoring the weather phenomena occurring in its regions and determining the weather forecast for next day. Assume that the forecasts refer to the degrees and timestamps of occurrence of such phenomena as rainfall, snow, sunshine, temperature and wind. The elements of *Consensus_Sys* are the following:

- $\boldsymbol{A}=\{Agent, Region, Wind\_Speed, Time, Temperature\}$,
- $\boldsymbol{X}=\{\Pi(V_{Agent}), \Pi(V_{Region}), \Pi(V_{Time}), \Pi(V_{Temperature}), \Pi(V_{Wind\_Speed})\}$,

where $V_{Agent} = \{a_1,a_2\}$; $V_{Region} = \{r_1,r_2,r_3,r_4\}$; $V_{Time}$ = set of time chronons, for example 2000–10–28:5a.m., or 5a.m. if the day is known, because the subject of the forecast is the next day, then $V_{Time}$ = [0a.m.–12p.m.]; $V_{Temperature}$ = set of integers representing Celsius degrees; $V_{Wind\_Speed}$=set of integers representing speeds of wind measured in unit *m/s*.

- $\boldsymbol{P}=\{Rain^+, Rain^-, Sunshine^+, Sunshine^-, Temp^+, Temp^-, Wind^+\}$, where
  $Rain^+, Rain^-, Sunshine^+, Sunshine^- \subseteq \Pi(V_{Agent}) \times \Pi(V_{Region}) \times \Pi(V_{Time})$,
  $Temp^+, Temp^- \subseteq \Pi(V_{Agent}) \times \Pi(V_{Region}) \times \Pi(V_{Time}) \times \Pi(V_{Temperature})$ and
  $Wind^+ \subseteq \Pi(V_{Agent}) \times \Pi(V_{Region}) \times \Pi(V_{Time}) \times \Pi(V_{Wind\_Speed})$.

We accept the following assumptions:

- Let $R\in\boldsymbol{P}$ be a relation of type $A$ and $r\in R$, tuple $r_B$ where $B=A\backslash\{Agent\}$ represents a set of events described by elementary tuples $r'$ of type $B$ where $r' \prec r_B$ (for each $b\in B$ $r'_b=\emptyset$ iff $r_b=\emptyset$).
- Relations belonging to set $\boldsymbol{P}$ are classified in such way that each of them includes relations representing similar events. For identifying relations belonging to given group the symbols "+" and "−" should be used as the upper index. If $P$ is the name of a

group, then relation $P^+$ is called a positive relation (contains positive knowledge) and $P^-$ – negative relation (contains negative knowledge).

• If $r \in P^+ \subseteq TYPE(A)$ then we have the following interpretation: In the opinion of agent $r_{Agent}$ one or more events included in $r_A$ should take place.

• If $r \in P^- \subseteq TYPE(A)$ then we say that in the opinion of agent $r_{Agent}$ none of the events included in $r_A$ should take place.

• The same agent cannot simultaneously state that the same event should take place and should not take place. It means that the same event cannot be classified by the same agent into positive and negative relations simultaneously.

**Definition 2.** *Let R and R' be relations of type A ($A \subseteq \mathbf{A}$, $Agent \in A$) and $B,B' \subseteq A$ where $B \cap B' = \emptyset$, we say that relations R and R' are (B,B')–disjoint iff*

$$(\forall r \in R)(\forall r' \in R')[((r_{Agent} = r'_{Agent}) \wedge (r_B \otimes r_B \neq \varepsilon)) \Rightarrow (r_{B'} \otimes r_{B'} = \theta)].$$

From the example of meteorological system it implies that relations $Sunshine^+$ and $Sunshine^-$ are $(\{Region\},\{Time\})$–disjoint. It means that the same agent cannot assign to the same region 2 contradictory events. Similarly the relations $Wind^+, Wind^-$ should be $(\{Region\},\{Time, Win\_Speed\})$–disjoint.

### 3.3 Structures of Consensus Carriers

In this section we define the structures of the consensus carriers. Because it is assumed that values of an attribute $a$ are not elementary values but subsets of non-empty set $V_a$, as the structure of a carrier we will define distance functions between sets of elementary values. We present 2 general distance functions, namely δ and ρ. These functions are the general forms of defined in the literature distance functions for such structures as $n$-trees [5], semillatices [2], [8].

**Function δ:**

The general idea of this function is relied on determining the distance between two sets as the minimal cost needed for transformation of one set into the other. For the need of the definition of this function we define the following cost functions:

- Function $d$: $V_a \rightarrow (0,+\infty)$: specifies the cost for adding (or removing) of an elementary value to (or from) a set.

- Function $t$: $V_a \times V_a \rightarrow [0,+\infty)$: specifies the cost for transformation of one elementary value into another.

For functions $d$ and $t$ we accept the following assumptions:

a) Function $t$ is a metric, i.e. for any $x,y,z \in V_a$ the following conditions are held:

$$t(x,x)=0,\ t(x,y)=t(y,x) \text{ and } t(x,y)+t(y,z) \geq t(x,z).$$

b) $(\forall x,y \in V_a)(|d(x) - d(y)| \leq t(x,y) \leq d(x)+d(y))$.

Let $D_a = \sum_{x \in V_a} d(x)$, we define distance function $\delta_a$ between subsets of set $V_a$ as follows:

**Definition 3.** *Distance function* $\delta$: $\Pi(V_a)\times\Pi(V_a) \rightarrow [0,1]$ *for a pair of sets* $X,Y\subseteq V_a$ *assigns a number* $\delta(X,Y) = \frac{T_{X,Y}}{D_a}$ *where* $T_{X,Y}$ *is the minimal cost needed for transforming set X into set Y.*

Such defined distance function should be a metric.

**Function ρ:**

The idea of this kind of functions is based on determining the value of participation of elements of set $V_a$ in the distance between 2 subsets of this set. For example, if one wants to determine the difference between 2 time intervals (as 2 sets of time chronons), then undoubtedly the chronons which belong to only one interval, should have participation greater than 0 and the chronons which belong to both intervals, should have participation equal 0. Of course, the participation of the elementary values depends on the sets, between which the distance is measured.

Let $a\in A\setminus\{Agent\}$, we define following 3-argument participation function:

$$Part: \Pi(V_a)\times\Pi(V_a)\times V_a \rightarrow [0,+\infty)$$

which determine the participation of given elementary value in the distance between 2 sets. We take the following assumptions for function *Part*: For any $X,Y,Z\subseteq V_a$:

- $(\forall z\in X\div Y)(Part(X,Y,z) = 1)$
- $(\forall z\in X\cap Y)(Part(X,Y,z) = 0)$
- $(\forall z\in V_a\setminus(X\cup Y))(Part(X,Y,z)=0 \vee Part(X,Y,z) = \alpha)$ where $\alpha$ is a constant
- $(\forall z\in V_a)((X=Y) \Rightarrow Part(X,Y,z)=0)$
- $(\forall z\in V_a)(Part(X,Y,z) = Part(Y,X,z))$
- $(\forall z\in V_a)(Part(X,Y,z) + Part(Y,Z,z) \geq Part(X,Z,z))$

The first 3 conditions state that the participation of value $z$ belonging to only one of sets $X$ i $Y$ is equal 1; if $z$ belong to both sets then the participation is 0 and for $z$ being outside sets $X$ and $Y$ the participation is equal 0 or $\alpha$. The next 3 conditions impose on function *Part* reflexivity, symmetry and transitivity referring to its first 2 arguments. It is worth to note that above conditions are not inconsistent, that means there always exists a function *Part* fulfilling all of them.

The distance between 2 sets should now be defined as the participation sum of elementary values referring these sets, by means of the following function:

$$\rho: \Pi(V_a) \times \Pi(V_a) \rightarrow [0,1].$$

**Definition 4.**: *For any sets* $X,Y\subseteq V_a$ *their distance* $\rho(X,Y)$ *is equal to*

$$\rho(X,Y)=\frac{1}{2card(V_a)-1}\sum_{z\in V_a} Part(X,Y,z)\ .$$

Function ρ is also a metric.

On the basis of distance functions between sets of elementary values one can define the distance function between tuples of the same type.

**Definition 5.** *For 2 tuples r and r' of type A the distance function* $\varphi$ *assigns a number* $\varphi(r,r')=\frac{1}{card(A)}\sum_{a\in A}\partial(r_a,r'_a)$ *where* $\partial\in\{\rho,\delta\}$.

### 3.4 Consensus Definition and Postulates

**Definition 6.** *A consensus situation is a pair* $<\{P^+,P^-\}, A\rightarrow B>$ *where* $A,B\subseteq E$, $A\cap B=\emptyset$ *and for every 2 tuples* $r\in P^+$ *and* $r'\in P^-$ *there should be held* $r_A\neq\theta$ *and* $r'_A\neq\theta$.

The first element of a consensus situation includes the domain from which the consensus should be chosen, and the second element includes the subject of the consensus. Interpretation of the consensus subject is that in the consensus for one tuple of type *A* there should be assigned only one tuple of type *B*. For example, a consensus situations may be: $<\{Rain^+,Rain^-\}, Region\rightarrow Time>$, or $<\{Wind^+\}, Region\rightarrow\{Time, Wind\_Speed\}>$.

For given relations $P^+$ and $P^-$ let us define relation $P^\pm$ (uncertain relation) as

$$P^\pm=\{e\in TYPE(E): (\forall r\in P^+)(e\otimes r=\theta)\wedge(\forall r'\in P^-)(e\otimes r'=\theta)\}.$$

Relation $P^\pm$ is called *complementary* to relations $P^+$ and $P^-$. Notice that relation $P^\pm$ contains all possible events which do not occur in relations $P^+$ and $P^-$. These events, therefore, should be treated as uncertainty of agents. For each subject $e\in Subject(s)$ let us determine relations $profile(e)^+$ and $profile(e)^-$ of type *B* which include the positive and negative opinions of agents on subject *e*, as follows:

- $profile(e)^+=\{r_{B\cup\{Agent\}}: r\in P^+ \text{ and } e\prec r_A\}$,
- $profile(e)^-=\{r_{B\cup\{Agent\}}: r\in P^- \text{ and } e\prec r_A\}$.

Relations $profile(e)^+$ and $profile(e)^-$ are called *conflict profiles.*

Let *A* and *B* be sets of attributes where $A\cap B=\emptyset$.

**Definition 7.** *For situation* $s=<\{P^+,P^-\}, A\rightarrow B>$ *a pair* $(C(s)^+,C(s)^-)$ *where* $C(s)^+,C(s)^-\subseteq TYPE(A\cup B)$, *is called a consensus if the following conditions are fulfilled:*

*a) For any* $r,r'\in C(s)^+$ *tuples* $r_A$ *and* $r'_A$ *are elementary and if* $r_A=r'_A$ *then* $r_B=r'_B$,

*b) For any* $r,r'\in C(s)^-$ *tuples* $r_A$ *and* $r'_A$ *are elementary and if* $r_A=r'_A$ *then* $r_B=r'_B$,

*c) Relations* $C(s)^+$ *and* $C(s)^-$ *are (A,B)-disjoint*

Let relation $C(s)^\pm$ be complementary to relations $C(s)^+$ and $C(s)^-$.

Relation $C(s)^+$ is called the positive component, relation $C(s)^-$ – negative component and relation $C(s)^\pm$ – uncertain component of the consensus.

Below we present 6 postulates for consensus, their formal forms and comments are presented in work [11]:

- P1. *Closure of knowledge*: The positive component of consensus should be included in the sum of positive elements of the consensus basis and the negative component of consensus should be included in the sum of negative elements of the consensus basis.
- P2. *Consistency of knowledge*:

a) The common part of positive elements of consensus basis should be included in positive component and should not be included in negative component of the consensus,

b) The common part of negative elements of consensus basis should be included in negative component and should not be included in positive component of the consensus

- P3. *Consistency of uncertainty*: The common part of uncertain elements of consensus basis should be included in uncertain component of the consensus

• P4. *Superiority of knowledge*: If for given subject $e$ only one agent generates opinion (positive or negative) and other agents do not, then the opinion of this agent should be in consensus for subject $e$.
• P5. *Impasse solving:* For any $e \in Subject(s)$ and $r \in E\text{-}TYPE(B)$ where $r \neq \varepsilon$, if the number of tuples including $r$ in $profile(e)^+$ is equal to the number of tuples including $r$ in $profile(e)^-$, then $r \prec C(s,e)^{\pm}$.
• P6. *Maximal similarity*: The distance between consensus $C(s) = (C(s)^+, C(s)^-)$ and the basis $\{P^+, P^-\}$ should be minimal.

### 3.5 Analysis of Postulates

Each of postulates P1, P2,... and P6 is a characteristic property of consensus functions and may be treated as a logical condition for candidates for consensus. We use postulates' names as the names of logical formulas and create new formulas using logic conjunctions. The semantics of these formulas includes consensuses of situations in all consensus systems.

**Theorem 1.** *For any situation and its consensus the following dependencies are true*:

1. P3 $\Rightarrow$ P1
2. P6 $\Rightarrow$ (P1$\wedge$P2$\wedge$P3$\wedge$P5).

**Theorem 2.** *There exists a situation for which the consensus satisfying any of the following formulas does not exist*

1. P2$\wedge$P4
2. P4$\wedge$P5
3. P1$\wedge$P2$\wedge$P3$\wedge$P4$\wedge$P5$\wedge$P6.

The above theorems should enable the choice of this criterion for consensus choice, which is most suitable for given conflict situation. Namely they inform about the possibilities (or the lack of possibility) for determining consensus, which should satisfy established postulates. The proofs are given in work [11].

## 4 A General Algorithm for Consensus Determining

Notice that postulate P6 plays an important role in consensus choice. Satisfying of this postulate implies also satisfying of the major of other postulates (Theorem 1). Therefore in this section we present an algorithm for determining consensus satisfying this postulate.

For determining the minimal distance between a tuple $e \in C(s)^+$ and tuples $r$ from $P^+$ such that $e_A \otimes r_A \neq \theta$ it is needed to determine a set $e$-profile$^+(b)$ (Procedure 1) of sets of values of attribute $b$, which are a part of agents' opinion on subject $e$. Next for each attribute $b \in B$ we determine the consensus ingredient for its values in $e$-profile$^+(b)$ (Procedure 2). At last the final consensus should consist of determined ingredients. The similar way should be used for $P^-$.

**Procedure 1:** Determining $e$-profile$^+(b)$
BEGIN

1. Determine the set of agents which have opinions on subject $e$:
   $e\text{-agent}^+=\{a\in V_{Agent}:(\exists r\in P^+)(e\prec r_A \wedge r_{Agent}=\{a\})\}$;
2. For agent $a$ determine the set of values of attribute $b$, which are a part of his opinion on subject $e$
   $e\text{-profile}^+(a,b) = (\bigcup_{r\in P^+,\, r_{Agent}=\{a\},\, e\prec r_A} r_b)$ for $a\in e$-agent$^+$;
3. Determine the set (with repetitions) of values of attribute $b$ such that
   $e\text{-profile}^+(b) = \{e\text{-profile}^+(a,b): a\in e\text{-agent}^+\}$

END.

**Procedure 2:** Determining consensus ingredient $c_b^+$ satisfying postulate P6 for $e$-profile$^+(b)$ and $\partial\in\{\rho,\delta\}$.
BEGIN

1. Let $c_b^+=\varnothing$; $S=\sum_{y\in e-\text{profile}^+(b)}\partial(c_b^+,y)$;
2. Select from $V_b\backslash c_b^+$ an element $x$ such that $\sum_{y\in e-\text{profile}^+(b)}\partial(\{x\}\cup c_b^+,y)$ is minimal;
3. If $S > \sum_{y\in e-\text{profile}^+(b)}\partial(\{x\}\cup c_b^+,y)$ then
   Begin
   $S:=\sum_{y\in e-\text{profile}^+(b)}\partial(\{x\}\cup c_b^+,y)$;
   $c_b^+:=\{x\}\cup c_b^+$; GOTO 2
   End

END.

**Algorithm:** Determining consensus for situation $s=<\{P^+,P^-\}, A\rightarrow B>$ satisfying postulate P6 using distance function $\partial\in\{\rho,\delta\}$.
BEGIN

1. For each $e\in TYPE(A)$ do
   Begin
   For each $b\in B$ do
   Begin
   Determine $e$-profile$^+(b)$ using Procedure 1;
   Determine ingredient $c_b^+$ using Procedure 2;
   End;
   Create tuple $C(s,e)^+$ of type $B$ on the basis of ingredients $c_b^+$;
   End;
2. Create positive component $C(s)^+$ of consensus as the set of tuples $C(s,e)^+$;
3. Create negative component $C(s)^-$ of consensus in the similar way;
4. Create consensus $C(s) = (C(s)^+,C(s)^-)$;

END.

## 5 Conclusions

In this work we present a consensus system which enables to store information about conflicts in Web-based distributed systems, and to solve these conflicts by determining consensus. The future works should concern the investigation of criteria, which allow to state if the chosen consensus is sensible for given situation, in other words, if this conflict situation consensus-oriented or not.

## References


1. Badache, N., Hurfin, M., Madeco, R.: Solving the Consensus Problem in a Mobile Environment. In: Proceedings of IEEE International Performance, Computing and Communications Conference. IEEE Piscataway NJ (1999) 29-35
2. Barthelemy, J.P., Janowitz, M.F.: A Formal Theory of Consensus. SIAM J. Discrete Math. 4 (1991) 305-322
3. Coulouris, G., Dollimore, J., Kindberg, T.: Distributed Systems, Concepts and Design. Addison-Wesley (1996)
4. Daniłowicz, C., Nguyen, N.T.: Consensus Methods for Solving Inconsistency of Replicated Data in Distributed Systems. Distributed and Parallel Databases **14** (2003) 53-69
5. Day, W.H.E.: Consensus Methods as Tools for Data Analysis. In: Bock, H.H. (ed.): Classification and Related Methods for Data Analysis. North-Holland (1988) 312-324
6. Ephrati, E., Rosenschein, J.S: Deriving Consensus in Multiagent Systems. Artificial Intelligence **87** (1998) 21-74
7. Hurfin, M., Mostefaoui, A., Raynal, M.: Consensus in Asynchronous Systems where Processes Can Crash and Recover. In: Proceedings of Seventeenth IEEE Symposium on Reliable Distributed Systems. IEEE Comput. Soc. Los Alamitos CA (1998) 325-335
8. McMorris, F.R., Powers, R.C.: The Median Procedure in a Formal Theory of Consensus, SIAM J. Discrete Math. 14 (1995) 507-516
9. Nguyen, N.T.: Consensus systems for conflict solving in distributed systems. Journal of Information Sciences **147** (2002) 91-122
10. Nguyen, N.T.: Representation Choice Methods as the Tool for Solving Uncertainty in Distributed Temporal Database Systems with Indeterminate Valid Time. In: Proceedings of IEA/AIE-2001. Lecture Notes in Artificial Intelligence **2070** (2001) 445–454
11. Nguyen, N.T.: Consensus Methods and their Application to Solving Conflicts in Distributed Systems. Wroclaw University of Technology Press (2002) (in Polish)
12. Pawlak, Z.: An Inquiry into Anatomy of Conflicts. Journal of Information Sciences **108** (1998) 65-78
13. Sobecki, J.: Interface Model in Adaptive Web-based Systems. In W. Cellary, A. Iyengar (eds): Internet Technologies, Applications and Societal Impact. Kluwer Academic Publishers (2002) 93-104

# Knowledge Based Support for the Authoring and Checking of Operating Procedures

Paul W.H. Chung[1], Qingying Wen[1], John H. Connolly[1], Jerry S. Busby[2], and Steve McCoy[1]

[1] Department of Computer Science, Modelling and Reasoning Group
Loughborough University, Loughborough, United Kingdom

[2] Department of Mechanical Engineering, University of Bath
Bath, United Kingdom

**Abstract.** This paper presents a system, named CAPTOP, for authoring and checking operating procedures for plant operations. It consists of a knowledge base of plant unit operations that can be linked to a graphical front end for inputting operating instructions. The system then builds a formal model of the instruction set as an interlingua and then uses it to output multilingual operating procedures. It avoids the problems of natural language understanding that make machine translation so difficult. Furthermore, the system could also generate output in a formal syntax that can be used as input to another knowledge based component, CHECKOP, for checking the procedure for operability and safety problems.

## 1 Introduction

Writing operating procedures for the operation of a process plant is an unavoidable tedious task. Some research work has been done with the aim of fully automating the task using AI planning techniques [1,3,9,11], yet none of the systems developed so far can solve realistic applications. The problem is that operating procedure authoring is a knowledge-intensive task. It requires knowledge about the process plant, i.e. its components, their connectivity and the properties of the material for processing. It also requires knowledge about unit operations and how a set of operations could be combined to achieve an overall objectivity, such as moving material from two different sources into a single tank and then mixing them up. Safety checks will also have to be carried out to ensure that the generated procedure is safe, i.e. it will not cause any hazardous situations such as causing an unintended flow of material. Furthermore, with processing plants being designed in one country and being built and operated in other countries, operating procedures will need to be translated into different languages too. In this paper we consider a novel approach to creating operating procedures. Instead of a fully automated system, we advocate a computer-assisted approach that removes the chore from the task of specifying procedures.

P.W.H. Chung, C.J. Hinde, M. Ali (Eds.): IEA/AIE 2003, LNAI 2718, pp. 264–270, 2003.

The unique feature of CAPTOP is the facility for an engineer to interact with a process plant design diagram to build a formal operating instruction set. In this way, AI planning is substituted by human decision-making but without the tedium of having to type in the details of every instruction. Operating instructions are sometimes required in different languages. Human and machine translation with human post-editing are resource consuming, and the current trends are shifting from post-hoc translation to in-process multilingual authoring [7]. One of the greatest difficulties with machine translation lies in the analysis, or understanding, of the source language text. Yet in the CAPTOP authoring system, this step is removed because the multilingual output is directly generated from a common interlingua. CAPTOP can be regarded as a natural language generation system without planning, and a machine translation system without analysis.

## 2 System Design

CAPTOP is a component that can be attached or plugged in to a diagramming software application such as Microsoft Visio®. It is composed of several sub-components that fall into six groups each of which represents a component or package of the system model. The first client component acts as an interface to diagramming applications and is driven by user mouse events. The capture component receives the captured object and elicits applicable constraints from the knowledge base and finally presents a simple natural language description of the operation involved through the transfer component. The knowledge base component is responsible for the knowledge elicitation and organisation into a formal representation and feedback for the next layer. The transfer component initiates the user selected natural language modules to complete the translation from the internal representation to the natural language. An animator component is used for multimedia output, which is not covered in this paper. Finally the formatter component renders the presentation in different specified document formats such as XML/HTML or Microsoft® Word.

The Capture component is used to grab what the user selected from the plant design diagram and to present the user with appropriate operating options and constraints to specify a complete instruction. Considering the extendibility to support more natural languages, the transfer component uses a single engine to do the transfer from the interlingua to different natural languages. As the system is implemented following the object-oriented paradigm, an instance of an output generator class can be attached with a suite of the dictionary and grammar of a particular language. Thus, each instance will work independently with its own attached language resources without knowing about the language itself. The output from the transfer component is sent to the formatting component to produce the final document in different formats like HTML.

## 3 Authoring Instructions

The task of authoring an operating procedure involves specifying the devices that need to be operated on, the operation that needs to be carried out, the constraints on these devices and operations, and the sequence of these operations. Being a collaborative system, CAPTOP is different from a standalone system like DRAFTER [10] that provides its own user interface for interactive planning. Therefore, it is not a stand-alone application that supports its own proprietary data source. It makes use of existing tools that plant designers use such as CAD systems for drawing and specifying plant component details. A plant diagram and the associated database carries information about the components, their connections, and operating conditions.

Figure 1 is a Visio® diagram showing a plant design, each icon on the drawing represents an instance of a component in the process plant. The instance belongs to a class of component that has certain attributes associated with it. Device connectivity is shown in the diagram itself.

An object refers to an entity in the design diagram which is usually a component installed in the system. It can also be a part of a composite object, e.g., an indicator on a device. Each type of object is shown as a different shape on the diagram (see Figure 1). To specify an instruction related to a particular component, CAPTOP is activated by a click on the toolbar button in the Visio® window followed by a click on the plant component on the diagram. The selected object with a default operation is immediately appended to the list of operations in the CAPTOP window. As can be seen, the displayed instruction in the list is not just the name of the selected object, but an operation associated with the component, "open valve", in this example. A list of possible operations for the object also appears as options in the CAPTOP window so that the user can select an alternative operation to overwrite the default.

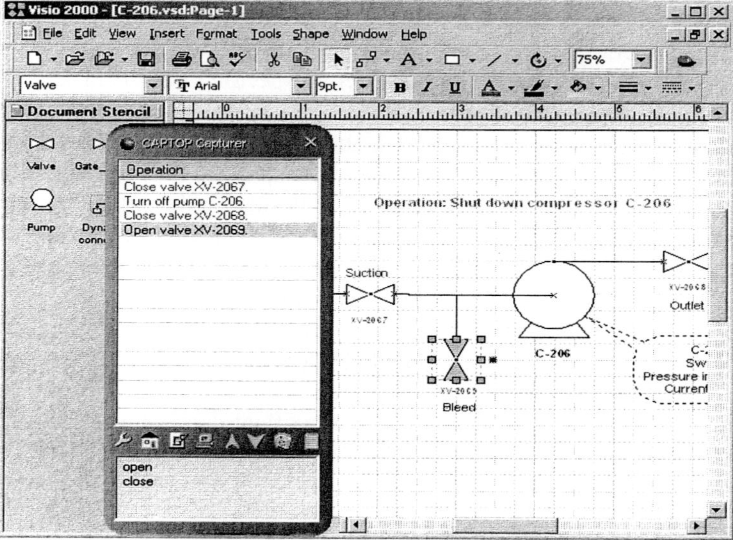


**Fig. 1.** Capturing an instruction from a Visio diagram

As more and more instructions are specified through interacting with the diagram, a sequence is formed showing the order of operations in the whole operating procedure. In the process, the user might have made some mistakes. Therefore, a facility is provided for the user to delete or correct a particular instruction or to modify the order of the operating steps. As shown in figure 1, the order of an instruction listed in the CAPTOP window can be changed by highlighting it first and then clicking the up or down arrow accordingly.

## 4 Knowledge Bases

In CAPTOP, the knowledge base contains domain-specific knowledge about different types of components, e.g. the operations and constraints associated with them. The knowledge is used both at the design and the operating procedure authoring stage. Another important knowledge source is the linguistic resource including a dictionary and a grammar for each supported natural language.

Knowledge related to plant components is stored in the knowledge base in the form of an ontology. In the domain of process plant design, individual plant components can be categorised by their functionalities. For example, a ball valve and a gate valve all belong to the group of valves. This generalisation of components into types makes it possible to collect enough knowledge for a wide range of similar components. Apart from building a taxonomic hierarchy, the equipment modelling also includes operations associated with the components on different abstract levels with an inheritance nature. Constraints are also available for different operations. All these pieces of information form the basis of the ontology.

A complex piece of equipment may contain several parts that entail separate operations. This requires the representation of a whole-part relationship in the ontology. The whole-part relationship is represented in the knowledge base as an XML [13] fragment.

To output multilingual text without resorting to machine translation, it is important that the ontology be represented in a neutral language as a pivot that can easily be mapped to other natural languages. In other words, it should be built upon an interlingua. The CAPTOP system uses controlled English language as the interlingua. For example, a valve is stored as VALVE in the taxonomy, and the operation 'open' is based on its basic meaning and named as OPEN-1 representing a sense of the word. A sense is tagged by a lexical unit without linguistic ambiguity so that a one-to-one correspondence can be established in different languages. Interlingua reflects semantics only without language-specific syntax involved. The semantic functions in Functional Grammar [5], such as agent, goal, recipient, time, location, etc., are used to describe the roles and relations of the objects of interest.

Linguistic resources are indispensable to the CAPTOP authoring system. For each supported language, a dictionary and a grammar are needed. The transfer component consults the dictionary for all the sense tags in an operating step message passed over from the capture component, and then searches the grammar templates for an appropriate sentence structure. When all the chunks of the message are determined, the remaining task is to fill the slots in the templates with the matched terms in the dictionary.

The dictionary is bilingual in nature with the interlingua as the source language. A dictionary entry is a pair of corresponding terms with an interlingual sense tag and a target language equivalent word. As the words in the interlingua represent fine-granular senses, no duplicated entry should exist in the dictionary. It is possible to have more equivalents for one sense tag accompanied by usage or context. But this functionality is not implemented in the current system.

Grammar is target language-specific. Different languages may have different grammatical categories. For example, there are gender and case inflections with German nouns but not in English or Chinese. Grammar rules are represented using templates that are directly parsed and instantiated by the transfer engine. They are organised hierarchically so that different groups of templates are selected for different linguistic constituents. For example, there are lexical, phrasal, sentential and inter-sentential templates.

Formalisation is a process carried out by the knowledge base component to convert the operating step into a semantic network structure showing the concepts and the relations between them. Such an internal structure is then used by the transfer component as a data input formalism. Formalisation is a mechanism to isolate the transfer component from the domain data so that the natural language package is domain-independent.

## 5 Natural Language Generation

From the point of view of natural language generation, the CAPTOP transfer mechanism corresponds to surface realisation. Available feature-based realisation systems like KPML [2] and FUF/SURGE [6] are not used because of their complexity and the difficulty of integrating them into CAPTOP. A template-based approach is adopted for its simplicity and efficiency [4]. The transfer component works with the specified predication structure, starting from top to bottom, and recursively realises all the child nodes.

In CAPTOP, a template is defined as a frame structure that contains an *n*-ary tuple with *n* slots as its attributes. Templates are either query-oriented or order-oriented. The query-oriented templates are used for pattern matching, defined as (*cond1,cond2,..., conclusion*) where *cond* is a condition and *conclusion* is the return value for the query. And the order-oriented templates specify the order of the constituents represented by slots, each of which can contain a constant or variable. The Basic operation on order-oriented templates is the instantiation of these slots. A constant is copied to the output instance while a variable needs further evaluation. For example, "close the valve" is represented by the order template (*Verb, Obj*) in English, while in German, the template is (*Verb, 'Sie', Obj*) where "Sie" is a constant. The instantiated output is "Schließen Sie das Ventil". In this example, query-oriented templates are used to determine the article, specifically, when the noun is neuter in gender, singular in number, and accusative in case, the article is "das".

Templates are also categorised by their functionality and scope of application. One template may be used for modification while another for coordination, and the scope may be word, phrase, sentence or paragraph. Such a classification avoids a thorough traversal of all the templates, and makes maintenance easier.

Realisation is a process to transfer an interlingual message in the predication structure into a target language sentence. Single words are looked up in the bilingual dictionary and then transformed according to the grammar rules in the query-oriented templates. The result is an instantiated predication structure.

Linearisation is concerned with the ordering of the words for a constituent. A template applicable to the current constituent is selected by first following the types and groups of the template classification and then matching the slots. The best matched template is normally selected, or a generic template when nothing has been found.

## 6 Checking Instructions

As mentioned previously, CAPTOP can also generate operating instructions in a formal syntax that can be used as input to another component which checks the instructions for operability and safety problems. Currently, the CHECKOP component is written in CLIPS using objects and rules [12]. Given the initial state of a plant, the effect of executing a given instruction set is simulated operation by operation. If the plant is in an undesirable state after the execution of an instruction, one of the rules in the CHECKOP rule base will be activated and an appropriate message is printed. Deliberate mistakes can be introduced into the instruction set to mimic situations where human operators may make mistakes by not following the procedure properly. The system will inform the user of any possible undesirable consequences.

CHECKOP in a limited way mimics and automates the established methodology of the Hazard and Operability Study (HAZOP) [8] for identifying hazards and operability problems in process plants.

## 7 Conclusion and Future Work

In this paper we have investigated the advantage of computer-aided authoring and checking of operating procedures. Based on the system design, an interactive modelling mechanism is devised which produces a formal structure applicable to multilingual generation. There are, however, still limitations that need to be overcome before a fully practical system can be built. One problem with CAPTOP is that the instruction templates are too limited. In many real life situations it is not sufficient to specify an instruction just in terms of the object and action. There is other information that needs to be included in the instruction, particularly operating conditions like temperature, time, flow rate, etc. The graphical user interface will need to be extended to capture a wider range of information. Another limitation with the current version of CAPTOP is that the linguistic knowledge cannot be learned or captured automatically and all supported languages will have to be updated whenever the domain knowledge is expanded. CHECKOP is limited in terms of its simulation capability. However, the prototypes that have been built showed that the proposed approach is potentially very powerful, making the tasks of authoring and checking operating instructions much easier.

Our current research effort is focused on understanding how operating instructions should be organised and creating a representation that can capture the richness of information that is associated with operating instructions. Once the required information is identified and categorised then the appropriate interfaces and knowledge bases can be built based on the proposed approach outlined in this paper.

## References


1. Aylett, R. S., Petley, G. J., Chung, P. W. H., Chen, B., Edwards, D. W. (2000). AI Planning: Solutions for Real World Problems. Knowledge-Based Systems, vol. 13, pp61-69.
2. Bateman, J. A. (1995). KPML: The KOMET-Penman (Multilingual) Development Environment. Technical Report, Institut für Integrierte Publikations- und Informationssysteme (IPSI), GMD, Darmstadt, July 1995.
3. Castillo, L., Fdez-Olivares, J. and Gonzalez, A. (2000). Automatic generation of control sequences of manufacturing systems based on partial order planning techniques. Artificial Intelligence in Engineering, vol.4, n.1, pp15-30, 2000.
4. Channarukul, S. (1999). YAG: A Template-Based Natural Language Generator for Real-Time Systems. Technical Report NLKRRG-2000-01. Natural Language and Knowledge Representation Research Group, Department of Electrical Engineering and Computer Science, The University of Wisconsin-Milwaukee.
5. Connolly, J. H. & Dik, S. C. (eds.) (1989). Functional Grammar and the Computer. Dordrecht: Foris.
6. Elhadad, M. and Robin, J. (1999). SURGE: a Comprehensive Plug-in Syntactic Realisation Component for Text Generation. Technical Report. Department of Computer Science, Ben Gurion University, Beer Sheva, Israel.
7. Hartley, A. and Paris, C. (1997). Multilingual document production: from support for translating to support for authoring. Machine Translation, Special Issue on New Tools for Human Translators, pp109-128.
8. Kletz, T. (1999). HAZOP and HAZAN (4th Edition), Institution of Chemical Engineers.
9. Lakshmanan, R. & Stephanopoulos, G. (1988). Synthesis of Operating Procedures for Complete Chemical Plants – II. A Nonlinear Planning Methodology. Computers in Chemical Engineering, Vol 12, pp1003-1021.
10. Paris, C. and Linden, K. V. (1996). DRAFTER: An interactive support tool for writing multilingual instructions. IEEE Computer, pp49-56, July 1996.
11. Soutter, J. (1997). An integrated architecture for operating procedure synthesis, PhD thesis, Loughborough University.
12. STB (1993). CLIPS Reference Manual, Software Technology Branch, Lyndon B. Johnson Space Centre.
13. W3.org. http://www.w3.org/XML

# A Concept of Modeling PVC Batch Plant in Object Oriented Approach for Safety Analysis

Datu Rizal Asral and Kazuhiko Suzuki

System Analysis Laboratory, Department of Systems Engineering, Okayama University
3-1-1, Tsushima-Naka, Okayama, 700-8530, Japan
rizal@syslab.sys.okayama-u.ac.jp, kazu@sys.okayama-u.ac.jp

**Abstract.** This paper proposes model for *Polyvinyl Chloride* (PVC) batch plant including structure, process, and behavior in integrated system. The design follows S88 standard for batch control system. The novel approach in this model is introducing the fault diagnosis during plant processes that important for safety analysis. The model is implemented by using object-oriented methodology that depicts of the systems integration between static and dynamic relationship. This proposed system is developed based on UML (Unified Modeling Language) as modeling standard language for computer based application design.

## 1 Introduction

Recently, chemical industries have to ensure their plant and process running safely and reduce the environmental impact. Safety aspects become important due to worldwide attention to the chemical industries brought on by several accidents including explosion, gas releases and environmental incidents, especially in PVC production which using *vinyl chloride monomer* (VCM). VCM is a flammable, explosive, produces toxic combustion products and carcinogen. Therefore, risk management and batch standard becomes important factor in control system design and operation.

ANSI/ISA-S88.01-1995 (S88) provides references in design the batch control model that based on the standard will overcome communication barrier among models in batch plant.

Model is built for existing system as a way to better understanding the system or to propose the improvement of the system. There are many strategies and technique for performing system analysis such as modern structure analysis, information engineering, prototyping and object oriented analysis. Object oriented analysis is the best suited that can implement systems using emerging technologies to construct, manage, and assemble the systems under computer aided system engineering tools. A model is used for describing the system, and to achieve the goal of the system, usually model is a mapping result of systems and its contain. Besides the model thinking framework, there is system thinking framework, as explained by E.C Martinez (2000), a system is an entity that exists and functions as whole through the interaction of its parts whilst exhibiting an emergent behavior that is unique to its internal structure and degree of complexity. Considering about the connection between inlet (pre-condition that cause to object), internal (condition that happen to object) and outlet (post-condition that consequence to object) is required to formulate safety analysis.

P.W.H. Chung, C.J. Hinde, M. Ali (Eds.): IEA/AIE 2003, LNAI 2718, pp. 271–276, 2003.

## 2 Plant Modeling in S88

There are several models that describing batch control system in S88. This paper intends to implement some of models to related work in development of batch modeling for safety analysis. Physical model, process model and Procedural Control model are used to describe plant in normal operation, as shown in the left side of Fig.1. The models are important to understand the application of batch processes. Physical model describes the asset of an enterprises/industries about their plant.

Meanwhile process model depicts sequence of activities, from beginning (raw material) into finishing (final product). Procedural control model is the link between physical model and process model. Procedural control directs the physical equipment to carry out the process task. The difference between Procedural Control and Process model is Procedural Control contain a strategy for carrying out the processing activities, however Process Model contain a set of processing activities.

In S88 overview, the model can be seen as three main modeling as physical, process and procedural control model. The relationship between three models is each part of procedural control model combine with individual equipment provides processing functionality to carry out a process model. Besides that, S88 describes recipe model that contain minimum set of information of manufacturing requirements for a specific product. Recipe model provide a way to describe products and how those products are produced.

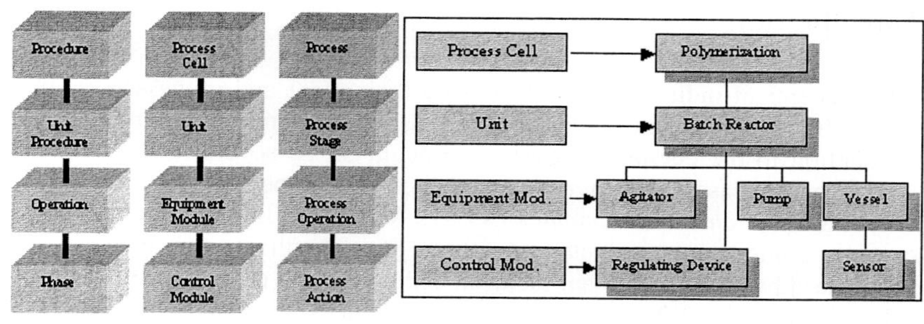


**Fig. 1.** Batch Model in ISA S.88 & Example Mapping to Batch structure

Recipes consist of information about batch process including header, formula, equipment requirement, procedure and other necessary information. Header may include identification, version number, the issue date and other administrative information. Formula consists of process input (information about raw material), process variable (temperature, pressure, flow that is pertinent to product) and process output (identification or material expected to result, including impact, quantity, etc.). Recipe procedure defines strategy for carrying out a process. The functionality of this procedure corresponds to the analogous level in Process Model and Procedural Control Model. Recipe model introduces the safety parameter including process variable, information about raw material, output and its impact to environment. It can be used to analyze batch plant under abnormal or emergency condition.

The right side of Fig.1 shows the example of S88 mapping to P&ID model. Process cell is mapping to Polymerization cell. Batch Reactor is representation of Unit in S88. There are some equipment include in batch plant such as part of the unit (agitator) or stand alone equipment grouping within a process cell (pump, vessel, etc.) and the last is control module (regulating device, sensor, etc.).

## 3 Knowledge Model Frameworks

The construction of model framework is started from development of knowledge model. Action model (implementation phase) can be built from the knowledge model (KM). KM of the system is divided into three categories: (1) logical subsystem, represents flow of the process, set of operation, (2) physical system, describes topology of physical subsystem in large system and their interconnections, (3) decisional subsystem, contains management/control of system and rules (Hill, 1996). This decomposition has correlation with S88 model. Physical model represents physical subsystem, process model represents logical subsystem and both of procedural control and recipe model represents decisional subsystem. The KM framework for batch plant can be seen in Fig.2.

In this framework, structure model describes physical model (S88) or physical subsystem (KM) that contains batch unit and its equipment. Structure model consists of equipment (e.g. valves, sensors, controllers, reactor, etc.) in batch unit. The Operational model describes process model (S88) or logical subsystem (KM) that explain about plant lifecycle and its condition with step-by-step operation in batch, how the process is beginning, operating and ending. The behavior model describes procedural control and recipe (S88) or decisional model (KM). Behavior model contains process variable, safety parameter, cause and consequence database system.

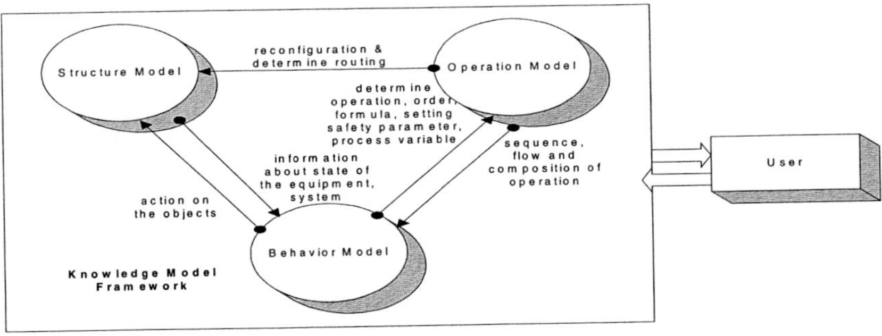


**Fig. 2.** Model Framework

Control activities of the batch plant are centralized at behavior model. In normal condition, behavior model provides normal procedural control to execute batch process. As behavior change dynamically, process variable monitoring is needed to achieve safety analysis and manage batch process in undesired condition. When monitoring activities detect process variable deviation, exception-handling system is working to start fault diagnostic and recovery system.

# 4 Modeling Based on Object Oriented Analysis (OOA)

Fig.3 shows simplified PVC batch plant P&ID in a process cell to produce PVC from VCM. When using OOA for plant model, plant system will be improved with integrating fault diagnosis in the plant existing model and perform safety analysis and generate accident scenario to handle process variable deviation and abnormal situation such as Total Shutdown, Partial Shutdown, etc.

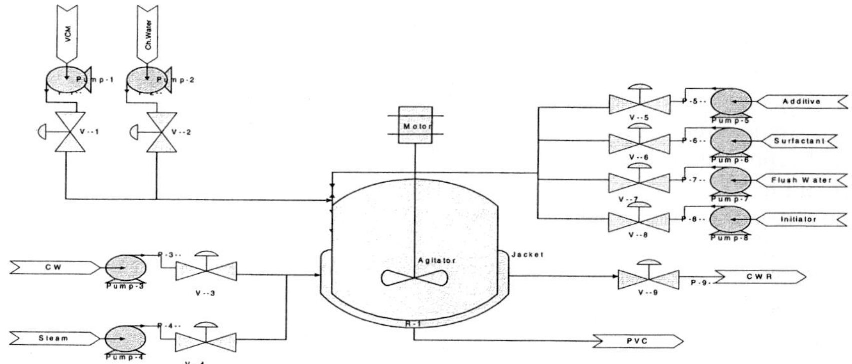


**Fig. 3.** Simplified flow diagram of the PVC Batch Plant

This paper agrees with UML diagram that offers OOA environment. Different diagrams are used to implement knowledge model framework. Class diagram describes structure model that shows the existence of classes and their relationships in the logical design of a system (plant structure). A class diagram represents all or part of the class structure of a system. A class is a set of objects that share a common structure and common behavior (the same attributes, operation). A class represents of real world items (e.g. valve, tank, reactor, etc.) as shown in Fig. 4. The structural model gives the static relationship between equipment (object) and does not describe how the process to be done. Interaction and behavior during plant operation is shown in Fig.5, also the process work in time sequence for exception handling system is shown in Fig.6.

Fig.5 describes behavior model for batch control system in doing batch task. In one task, for example "charging VCM", control system implements several subtasks before moving to "heating" step. When finds abnormalities like "high pressure" of VCM that could cause "high temperature" and tend to explosion, system sends "msgFailure" message and requests Exception Handling System working to reduce the risk into the lowest level.

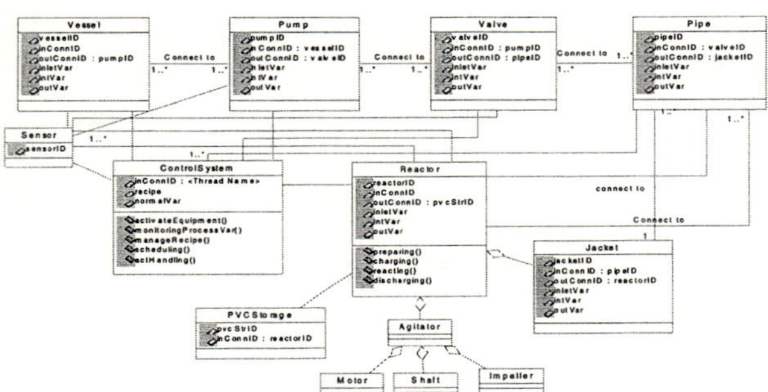


**Fig. 4.** Structure Model Using Class Diagram

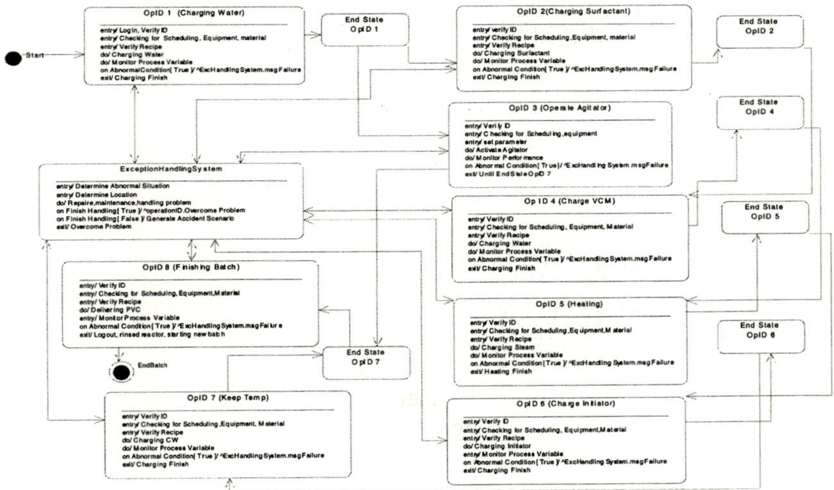


**Fig. 5.** Behavior Model of Batch Control System Using State Chart Diagram

For example, how safety analysis can be implemented is shown in Fig.6. In case of internal pump failure when charging phase, it will generate fault propagation and this condition affects states of components (pump, valve, filter, etc.) that connected in the pipeline. For the pump failure, "no power" and "motor failure" could cause "no flow" in the outlet side of pump. Deviations of "flow no" and "flow less" could cause "pump cavitations" and "pump over heat". Due to exothermic reaction, deviations of "flow no" and "flow less" in the cooling unit could result "temp high", "pressure high", "abnormal reaction inside reactor" and "fire". The information regarding to safety analysis is described in operation model. All of information appears in Graphical User Interface (GUI) which part of control system. GUI can serve as useful aid to operator in batch process and help operator to make appropriate decision during abnormal condition.

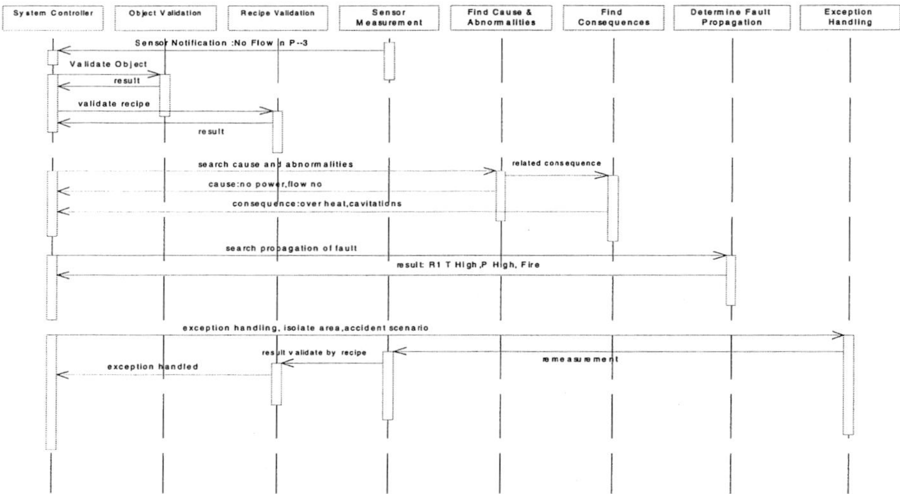


**Fig. 6.** Example of Operation Model for Exception Handling

# 5 Summary

In this paper, we have proposed the framework of PVC batch plant modeling in object oriented approach for safety analysis purpose and implemented by UML diagram. The UML diagrams integrate static relationship (structure) and dynamic relationship (operation & behavior) as well as fault diagnostic in plant modeling. The model presented in this paper is part of system improvement towards future development of safety application in computer-aided environment for batch plant.

# References


[1] ANSI/ISA-88.01.1995 Batch Control Part 1:Models and Terminology

[2] Hill David R.C., Object Oriented Analysis and Simulation, Addison-Wesley, 1996

[3] Kang, Suh, Wakakura, Yoon, Multi-modeling Approach for Automated Hazard Analysis of Batch Process Plants, Journal of Chemical Engineering of Japan, Vol.34, No.6, pp.802-809, 2001

[4] Martinez, E.C, Systems Thinking and Functional Modeling of Batch Process Management Using Projects, Journal Of Computer and Chemical Engineering, Vol. 24, pp.1657-1663, Elsevier, 2000

[5] Siemensen J., Johnsson C., Arzen K.E., A Multiple-View Batch Plant Information Model, Journal of Computers and Chemical Engineering, Vol.21, suppl.pp.S1209-S.1214, Elsevier, 1997

[6] Suzuki, K., Shimada Y., Nojiri I., An Object Oriented Approach for Computer-aided HAZOP for Batch Plant, Department of Systems Engineering, Okayama University, Japan

# Automatic Visual Inspection of Wooden Pallets

Miguel Ángel Patricio[1] and Darío Maravall[2]

[1] Departamento de Informática, Universidad Carlos III de Madrid, Spain,
mpatrici@inf.uc3m.es

[2] Departamento de Inteligencia Artificial, Universidad Politécnica de Madrid, Spain,
dmaravall@fi.upm.es

**Abstract.** We present an automatic visual measurement and inspection system, currently operating at several European inspection plants. The main objective of the system is to automate the inspection of used wooden pallets. The paper begins with a brief description of the system, including some comments on the electromechanical handling of the inspected objects and the illumination set-up. Then, the paper presents the segmentation method used to extract the pallet elements, as an initial step for pallet measurements and the detection of possible defects. This method consists of an initial threshold on the histogram based on a Bayesian statistical classifier, followed by an iterative, heuristic search of the optimum threshold of the histogram. Finally, the paper introduces the application of the histogram of connected elements to the detection of very thin cracks, one of the hardest problems involved in the visual inspection of used pallets.

## 1 Introduction

The paper describes some functionalities of an automatic computer vision-based inspection system of used pallets, currently in full operation at several industrial plants in a number of European countries. The objective of the automatic inspection of pallets is to gradually substitute manual inspection, which, apart from being a hard and painstaking job, is prone to errors, both false alarms - i.e., ready-for-use pallets classified as defective- and false negatives. After several years of R+D efforts, the ratios currently achieved by the inspection system are comparable to those of qualified human operators. Concerning operating times, automation inspection has surpassed manual operation by almost one order of magnitude: 3 seconds versus 20 seconds on average, respectively.

The pallets arrive at the visual inspection plants after a period of several months of use. This mean that inspection can be really complex as many potential defects may be present: splinters, cracks, fissures, broken elements, lack of volume in several elements of the object, etc. Figure 1 shows some instances of typical defects. To make things worse, the surface of wooden pallets is often stained with different kinds of remains, such as grease, mud, paint and so on. As an extra difficulty for the automation of visual inspection of used pallets, we should mention that the automatic visual inspection of wooden materials, [1],

P.W.H. Chung, C.J. Hinde, M. Ali (Eds.): IEA/AIE 2003, LNAI 2718, pp. 277–286, 2003.

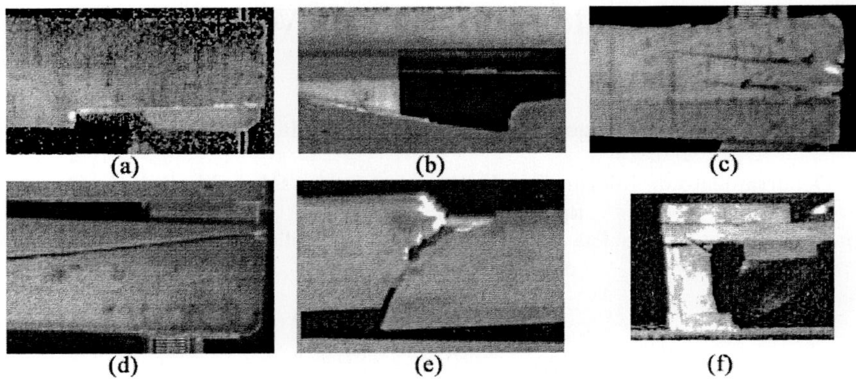


**Fig. 1.** Some instances of possible defects: (a) outer splinter; (b) inner splinter; (c) fissures; (d) cracks; (e) broken board and (f) lack of volume in block.

has a shorter tradition than other machine vision applications, [2]. The paper focuses on one of the hardest problems in the automatic inspection of textured materials [3], namely, the detection of very thin cracks -in the 1 mm range-. The main difficulty in classifying thin cracks does not lie in actual detection -which can be successfully performed when applying appropriate segmentation techniques and provided that there is enough resolution in the digital images- but in the numerous false alarms generated by wood veins, paint remains, shadows induced by the lighting system, etc. Roughly speaking, the better the detection ratio of thin cracks is, the higher the false alarm ratio is, which means that a very delicate balance between both ratios has to be struck.

Curiously enough and partly as a consequence of our work on this hard classification problem, we have recently introduced a novel idea for the segmentation of textured images, namely, the frequency histogram of connected elements (FHCE), [4] and [5]. Being, as it is, a conventional unidimensional histogram, the FHCE incorporates all the computational advantages, in terms of both simplicity and speed, inherent to the histogram-based segmentation methods. Simultaneously, it includes information about the spatial distribution of the specific discriminant feature in the digital image, as bidimensional histograms also do. The FHCE concept has an additional advantage over bidimensional histograms, as it is based on a much more powerful spatial function than the simple two-point relationships, typical of bidimensional histograms and co-occurrence matrices, which is the concept of structuring element or spatial predicate, which is somewhat, though not entirely, related to the structuring element concept used in morphological image processing [6]. Furthermore, there is still another interesting advantage of the FHCE, as compared with the conventional unidimensional histogram, which is its flexibility in regard to the range of values of the discriminant variable -which in conventional unidimensional histograms is absolutely rigid- and affords an interesting degree of freedom, what we have called the connectivity level, for texture analysis and recognition.

The paper has been organized in three parts. In the first one, the general structure of the system, known as the Visual Inspection Machine (VIM), is presented. Afterwards, the module for the automatic measurement of the elements of the pallet is very briefly described. Finally, we introduce the application of the FHCE to crack detection and recognition.

## 2 General Structure of the Visual Inspection Machine

The VIM has the following elements: (1) mechanical object handling; (2) illumination system; (3) eight video-cameras; (4) two digitizer cards, each controlling four video-cameras with a resolution of 768 x 576 pixels and 256 gray levels; (5) PC-based multiprocessor system with a customized real-time operating system and the machine vision software for the automatic measurement and inspection of pallets and (6) the PLC controlling the mechanical and electrical components of VIM. Figure 2 shows the general lay-out of the visual inspection system.

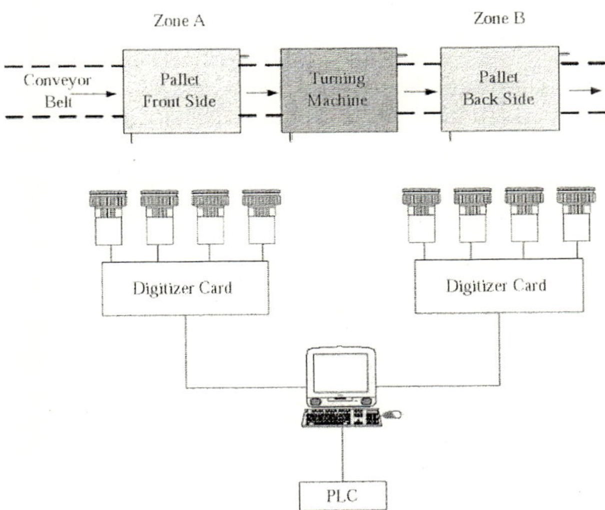


**Fig. 2.** General structure of the VIM. Note the two zones A and B for visual inspection of pallets on the conveyor belt.

There are some aspects of the illumination set-up that are worthwhile mentioning. Indeed, illumination is vital for human vision and for machine vision as well, so a very carefully designed illumination set-up has been implemented, as shown in Figure 3a. First of all, an external booth was built for the VIM and installed to guarantee complete control of the illumination.The internal walls and the ceiling are painted in dull black to eliminate reflections. Several types of floodlights have been used. A series of reflectors, diffusers, and filters are used

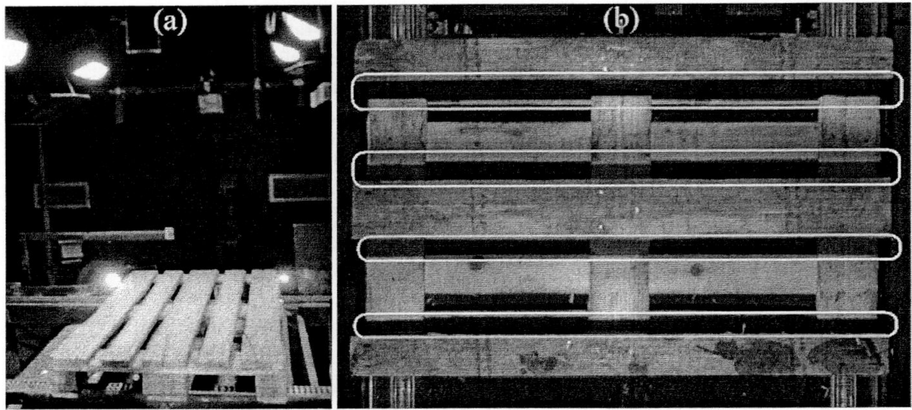


**Fig. 3.** General view of the illumination set up (a) and an image taken from zone B to illustrate the special shadow generated for baseboard segmentation (b).

for proper defect exploitation. For instance, in zone B, where the pallet has been turned upside down, two special floodlights with optical lenses are utilized for the optical segmentation of the baseboards, which are by far the hardest elements to inspect in a wooden pallet. Figure 3b displays an instance of how a well-designed illumination set-up can solve problems that otherwise would be very hard for the machine vision software to cope with.

## 3 Automatic Visual Measurement of Pallets

Each individual pallet consists of 20 elements and over 40 measurements are to be taken. The total computation time for this task, including all the housekeeping and PLC-VIM communication is less than one second, using only one of the two processors available in the computer system. The automatic visual measurement is implemented by means of three modules: (1) calibration, (2) segmentation, and (3) measurement.

### 3.1 Calibration Module

The purpose of the calibration module is to obtain an accurate correspondence between the distances of the pixels in the digital image and the physical distances in the corresponding scene. To this end, we use what we call a 'virtual pallet', see Figure 4a, made of very light and manageable material and with the exact same dimensions as the real pallet. Printed on the virtual pallet are special patterns used to compute the correspondence between the image dimensions and the physical dimensions of the pallet. Using well-known numerical methods, the accuracy of the calibration module is submillimetric, far above the required accuracy.

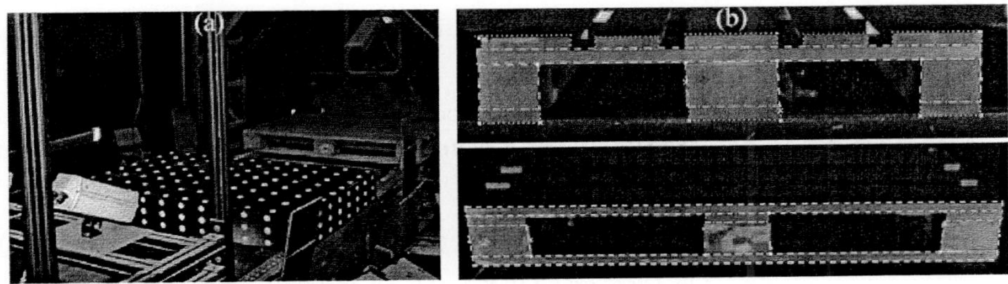


**Fig. 4.** A snapshot of the virtual pallet in (a) and segmentation of two lateral views in (b).

### 3.2 Segmentation Module

The goal of this module is to obtain the contour and to individualize each of the 20 elements of a pallet, as a first step towards the computation of the measurements. In this application, the segmentation task is, essentially, a typical pattern recognition problem, as each pixel must be classified either as belonging to the pallet or to the background. The digital images of the wooden pallets generally present a quasi bimodal distribution, one of the modes corresponding to the pallet and the other one to the background. Thus,using the grayscale intensity as a single discriminant variable, the segmentation process can be modelled as a conventional statistical classification problem

$$p(\alpha_1)p(x/\alpha_1) \lessgtr p(\alpha_2)p(x/\alpha_2) \tag{1}$$

where $p(\alpha_1)$ and $p(\alpha_2)$ are the a priori probabilities of the existing two classes and $p(x/\alpha_1)$ and $p(x/\alpha_2)$ are the respective probability density functions, with $x$ being the grayscale intensity. For our segmentation problem, $\alpha_1$ and $\alpha_2$ are the pallet class and the background class, respectively.

For our application, however, both statistical distributions are very seldom perfectly Gaussian and, furthermore, they vary from one image to another. For this reason, we have applied an adaptive Bayesian method, which, after a few iterations converges to a stable segmentation threshold. With an additional ad hoc process for edge extraction and line fitting, the pallet elements are successfully segmented. Finally, by making use of the information obtained from the calibration module, all the pallet measurements are taken. Figure 4b shows the results of the segmentation process for just two lateral views of a pallet.

## 4 Crack Detection Using the FHCE

Figure 1 shows several potential defects in pallets. In the sequel, we will concentrate on the application of the FHCE to the problem of detecting very thin cracks -in the range of 1 mm width- in wooden boards of used pallets. As discussed above, a difficult balance between the crack detection and the false alarm ratios must be struck. Let us start with a brief description of the theoretical foundation of the FHCE.

**Definition 1 (The Neighborhood Concept).** *Let* $\{I(i,j)\}_{NxM}$ *be a digital image. If we denote the coordinates of a generic pixel as* $(i,j)$*, the neighborhood of this pixel,* $\mathcal{N}$*, is defined as follows*

$$\mathcal{N} \triangleq \{\varphi_{i,j} \subset \{I(i,j)\}_{NxM}\} \quad (2)$$
$$\varphi_{i,j} = \{\forall(k,l) \;/\; D[(k,l),(i,j)] \; is \; true\}$$

*where* $D$ *is a predicate defined by a distance-based condition. For instance, a valid definition of the neighborhood of a pixel* $I(i,j)$ *can be given by the set*

$$\varphi_{i,j}^{r,s} = \{\forall(k,l) \;/\; ||k-i|| \leq r \; and \; ||l-j|| \leq s\} \; ; \; r,s \in \mathrm{N} \quad (3)$$

*which indicates that the neighborhood of the pixel is formed by a set of pixels, whose distances are not greater than two integer values* $r$ *and* $s$*, respectively.*

**Definition 2 (The Connected Element Concept).** *We mean by a connected element*

$$C_{i,j}(T) \triangleq \varphi_{i,j}^{r,s} \;\; / \;\; I(k,l) \subset [T-\varepsilon, T+\varepsilon] \;\; , \; \forall(k,l) \in \varphi_{i,j}^{r,s} \quad (4)$$

*where* $I$ *is the grayscale intensity or brightness of pixel* $(k,l)$*. In other words, a connected element is any neighborhood unit, such that its pixels have a grayscale level close to a given grayscale level* $T$*.*

**Definition 3 (The Frequency Histogram of Connected Elements).** *The frequency histogram of connected elements (FHCE) is defined as*

$$H(T) = \sum_{\forall(i,j)\in\{I\}} C_{i,j}(T)$$
$$0 \;\leq\; T \;\leq\; I_{max} - 1 \quad (5)$$

*That is to say,* $H(T)$ *approximates a density function for a random event occurring in a digital image* $\{I(i,j)\}_{NxM}$*. This event is related to the idea of connected element, which in turn is related to the pseudo-random structure of the grayscale intensity distribution of a particular texture. Our main purpose here is to demonstrate that this novel concept is an ideal tool for the automatic analysis of the textures appearing in a variety of digital images. We can understand the information conveyed by the function* $H(T)$ *intuitively: high values of* $H(T)$ *indicate that there is a sizeable number of connected elements in the image whose grayscale levels are homogeneous and close to level* $T$*.*

Obviously, there is no universal connected element valid for any domain application. In the design leading to the FHCE, there is a critical and domain-dependent step, which is responsible for the selection of the parameters defining the optimum, connected element. Such parameters are: (1) the morphological structure and (2) the connectivity level.

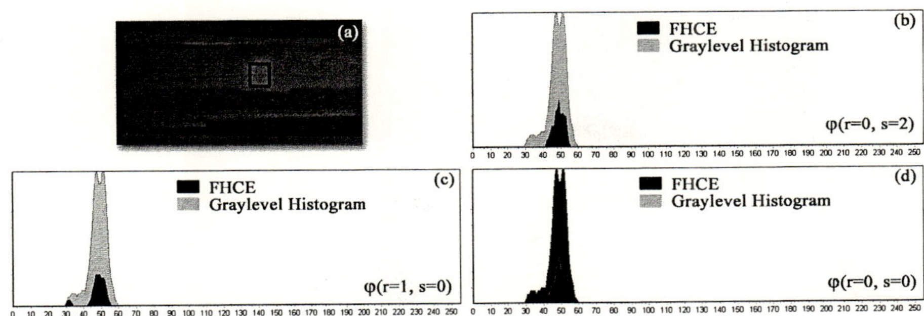


**Fig. 5.** Portion of a thin crack in wood and several FHCEs obtained using different morphological structure.

### 4.1 Morphological Structure

The morphological structure determines the shape of the connected elements; i.e., what we have called neighborhood. Obviously, this parameter is very dependent on the application domain, and final system efficiency will rely on the correct selection of the morphological structure. The selection of the suitable morphological structure for a particular application is not an easy task, and it requires a thorough empirical analysis. Even if specialized algorithms are used to choose the optimum morphological structure, the special feature of the computer vision application at hand will determine the results. Thus, any knowledge we have about the application domain is crucial for the correct selection of the morphological structure. As an illustration of this fact, just take a look at Figure 5, where different FHCEs have been computed and compared. In Fig. 5a we have selected a region of interest, denoted by a square, in order to illustrate the methodology for designing the morphological structure.

From the FHCE shapes, it is apparent that the correct choice of the morphological structure is vital for successfuly solving the problem of detecting thin cracks in wooden images. For $r = 0$ and $s = 0$, Fig. 5d, the neighborhood of each individual pixel is composed of itself alone and, thus, every pixel of the region holds the connected element restriction given by expression (3). Thus, we show that the conventional grayscale level histogram is a particular case of the FHCE. Clearly, the case of Fig. 5c ($r = 1$; $s = 0$) is the optimal choice, as it perfectly discriminates the connected elements belonging to the crack -the distribution on the left side of the FHCE- from those belonging to the sound wood. On the contrary, the morphological structure of Fig. 5b ($r = 0$; $s = 2$) do not provide any information at all about this discrimination.

### 4.2 Connectivity Level

The connectivity level of a FHCE depends on the value $\varepsilon$ that appears in the definition of connected element given by equation (4) and determines the restrictions that every pixel in a neighborhood must meet in order to form a connected

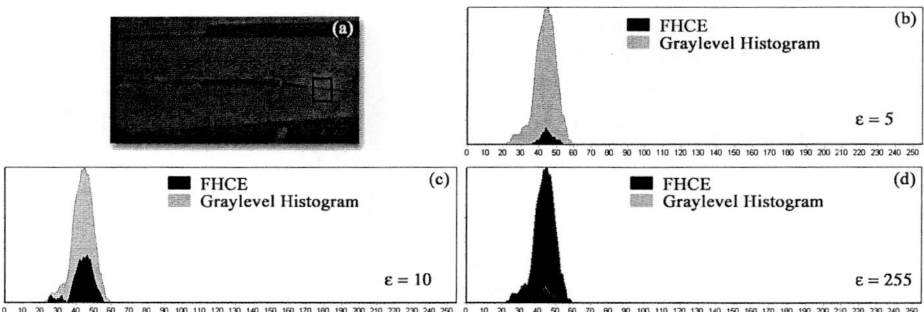


**Fig. 6.** Wooden image with a thin crack and several FHCEs obtained with different levels of connectivity, decreasing from (b) to (d).

element. As is the case for morphological structure, the connectivity level is highly dependent on the application domain, and its correct choice is a matter of thorough experimentation. To illustrate this, let us compute several FHCEs with different connectivity levels. As before, we shall use an image of a piece of wood with a thin crack -see Figure 6-.

The connectivity level decreases from highest connectivity in Figure 6b to null connectivity in Figure 6d. Null connectivity means that every neighborhood defined by a morphological structure is considered as a connected element, which in fact leads to the conventional grayscale level histogram. Looking at the different FHCEs in Figure 6, it is clear that the choice of an optimum connectivity level is of vital importance. Thus, a clear bimodal distribution appears in Figure 6c, where the first distribution –on the left-hand side- represents the connected elements formed by the crack and the other distribution corresponds to the sound wood.

### 4.3 FHCE Parameters for Crack Detection

As for any other contextual segmentation procedure aimed at exploiting the local or spatial information of the image under analysis, the key issue when applying the FHCE concept is a correct selection of the scanning window's size. In textured images, as is well known, the basic idea is to apply a window whose size is big enough to capture the essential structure of any texture present in the image. In our particular application of detecting thin cracks, we have found that a window of 40x30 pixels seems to be optimum in most cases.

After exhaustive experimentation with a plethora of digital images of sound and defective wooden boards, we have selected a 5x3 window as the neighborhood or morphological structure. Note that the number of horizontal pixels is higher than the vertical pixels, which is owing to the a priori knowledge available about the problem at hand. In fact, there is empirical evidence that cracks in a piece of wood tend to appear in the same direction as the wood grain. As the computer vision inspection is performed horizontally from the wooden boards standpoint, the shape of the selected neighborhood function is easily deduced.

To conclude the selection of the FHCE parameters, the connectivity level that a particular neighborhood should possess to be considered as such must be selected. The FHCE is computed for each image portion by moving a window of the same 5x3 shape than the neighborhood across all the pixels . This scanning process is performed by means of a top-bottom and left-right movement and by computing, at each pixel, the maximum and the minimum gray level within its neighborhood. Each pixel's neighborhood is classified as a connected element if and only if the difference between the maximum and the minimum values is small as compared with the dynamic range of the histogram in the whole window. After experimental work, we have chosen a 10% ratio, which is a good compromise between wooden portions in good and bad conditions. Therefore, for a neighborhood to be labeled as a connected element the following condition has to hold: $((i_{max} - i_{min})/(I_{max} - I_{min})) \leq 0.1$ ,where $I_{min}$ and $I_{max}$ are the maximum and minimum values of the window –i.e. the dynamic range of the window's histogram-, and $i_{min}$ and $i_{max}$ are the maximum and minimum grayscale intensities of the neighborhood. Therefore, if a particular neighborhood possesses a gray-level variability of less than ten percent of the dynamic range of the global window, the respective pixel is a connected element and the FHCE will compute a new event with value $\mathrm{T} = (\mathrm{i}_{min} + \mathrm{i}_{max})/2$. Fig. 7 shows the results obtained with the FHCE method for several thin cracks. Note the efficiency in segmenting the cracks appearing in all the wooden boards.

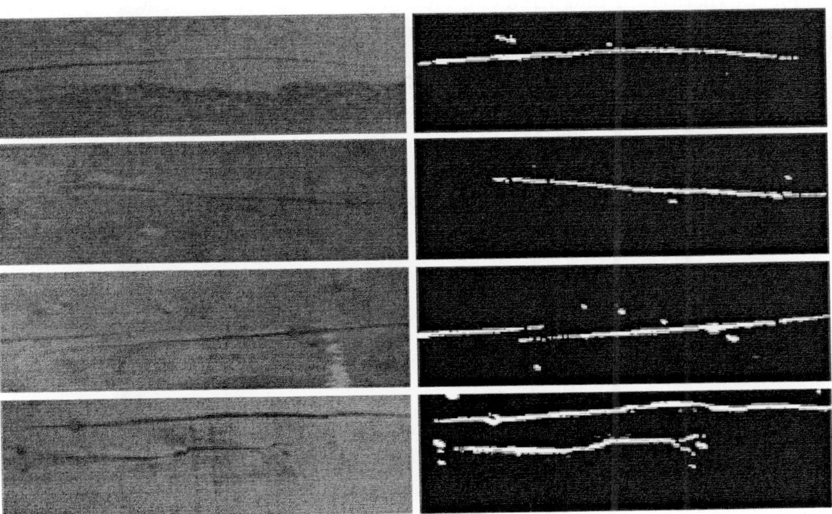

**Fig. 7.** Results of the segmentation process by applying the FHCE concept to several cracks.

## 5 Conclusions

We have presented an automatic visual measurement and inspection system that is fully operative in several European inspection stations. An important element of the system is the segmentation module, consisting of two steps: (1) an initial histogram thresholding using a Bayesian statistical classifier and (2) an iterative, heuristic optimum threshold search procedure. This segmentation method and a strict calibration module have been decisive for the pallet element measurement and classification results, whose resolution is submillimetric. Finally, an application of the histogram of connected elements to the detection of very thin cracks -in the range of 1 mm width- in wooden boards of used pallets has been presented. The experimental results have demonstrated that the FHCE method performs excellently and can be considered an attractive and versatile novel instrument for the analysis and recognition of textured images.

## References

1. Silven, O., Kanppinen., H.: Recent Developments in Wood Inspection. Int. Journal Pattern Recognition and Artificial Intelligence 10, (1996) 83–95.
2. Rosandich, R.G.: Intelligent Visual Inspection. Chapman Hall, London, (1997).
3. Kumar, A., Pang, G.K.H.: Defect Detection in Textured Materials Using Optimized Filters. IEEE Trans. Systems, Man, and Cybernetics-Part B, vol. 32, 5, (2002) 553–570.
4. Patricio, M.A., Maravall, D.: Wood Texture Analysis by Combining the Connected Elements Histogram and Artificial Neural Networks. In J. Mira, A. Prieto (Eds). Bio-inspired Applications of Connectionism, LNCS 2085, Springer, Berlin, (2001) 160–167.
5. Maravall, D., Patricio, M.A.: Image Segmentation and Pattern Recognition: A Novel Concept, the Histogram of Connected Elements. In D. Chen and X. Cheng (Eds). Pattern Recognition and String Matching, Kluwer Academic Publishers, (2002) 399–452.
6. Soille, P.: Morphological Image Analysis. Springer, Berlin, (1999).

# Feature Extraction for Classification of Caenorhabditis Elegans Behavioural Phenotypes

Won Nah, Seung-Beom Hong, and Joong-Hwan Baek

School of Electronics, Telecommunication & Computer Engineering
Hankuk Aviation University, Koyang City , South Korea
{nahwon, sbhong, jhbaek}@mail.hangkong.ac.kr

**Abstract**. Caenorhabditis (C.) elegans is often used in genetic analysis in neuroscience because it has simple model organisms; an adult hermaphrodite contains only 302 neurons. We use an automated tracking system, which makes it possible to measure the rate and direction of movement for each worm and to compute the frequency of reversals in direction. In this paper, we propose new preprocessing method using hole detection, and then we describe how to extract features that are very useful for classification of C. elegans behavioural phenotypes. We use 3 kinds of features (Large-scale movement, body size, and body posture). For the experiments, we classify 9 mutant types of worms and analyze their behavioural characteristics.

## 1 Introduction

C. elegans is about as primitive an organism that exists which nonetheless shares many of the essential biological characteristics that are central problems of human biology. The result of genome project, C. elegans gene is similar to human gene about 40% and 75% of 5,000 known human gene is shared. In this reason, the worm is often used to study of cancer, Alzheimer disease, aging, etc. So, understanding the relationship between genes and the behaviour of C. elegans is a fundamental problem in neuroscience. An experienced observer was previously able to subjectively distinguish worm types, but requirements for objective classification are now increasing. For this reason, automated classification systems using machine vision appeared for the purpose of objective classification.

In the previous works [1], [2], classification was automated using the patterns from reliable egg-laying event timing data. In the previous work [3], a closing morphological operation was used to remove noise. However, this method causes some problems on binarization. That is, holes are filled up when the worm is coiled tightly with a small sized hole. Thus, it is difficult to get reliable features from the binary image obtained using the closing operation. In this paper, we propose a new binarization method, which recognizes the event of holes occurring and preserves the hole until the binarization is finished. Contrary to the previous work, we perform the thresholding and median filtering first, and then detect the holes using the worm's thickness. Finally, we remove unwanted holes, leaving the actual holes.

P.W.H. Chung, C.J. Hinde, M. Ali (Eds.): IEA/AIE 2003, LNAI 2718, pp. 287–295, 2003.

In [3], wild type and its five mutant types (goa-1, nic-1, unc-36, unc-38, and egl-19) were classified using 94 features. In this paper, nine mutant types (unc-2, unc-29, and tph-1 mutant types are added) are classified using 117 features.

## 2 Proposed Preprocessing Method

Binarization and preprocessing are the most important factors for the successful classification and analysis of C. elegans. In this paper, we propose a new preprocessing method using hole detection. The method is performed with the following 2 procedures.

### 2.1 Binarization

First, we should find the background intensity level before the threshold decision. The background intensity of the snapped image has a constant intensity value, because light intensity is constant. It is highly unlikely that the four corner points of the image are parts of the worm's body. So we use the maximum value of the four corner points as a background intensity value. To decide upon the threshold, a 5×5 moving window is used for scanning over the experimental image, and the mean and standard deviation of the 25 pixels inside the window are computed at every pixel position.

$$
\begin{aligned}
m(x,y) &= \frac{1}{5\times 5}\sum_{i=-2}^{2}\sum_{j=-2}^{2} f(x+i,y+j) \\
\sigma(x,y) &= \left[\frac{1}{5\times 5}\sum_{i=-2}^{2}\sum_{j=-2}^{2}\left[f(x+i,y+j)-m(x,y)\right]^2\right]^{1/2}
\end{aligned} \tag{1}
$$

The pixel is estimated experimentally to be on the worm's body when the intensity value of the pixel is less than 70% of the background intensity. Note that the background intensity level is higher than that of the worm's body. Also, pixels on the worm's body tend to have a larger variance in their intensity values than pixels on the background. So when the standard deviation of the pixels within the window is over 30% of the mean, we consider the pixel as a part of the worm's body. Now, the binary image can be obtained by the following equation:

$$
g(x,y) = \begin{cases} 0 & \text{if } f(x,y) < Th_1 \text{ or } \sigma(x,y) > Th_2 \\ 255 & \text{else} \end{cases} \tag{2}
$$

where

$$
\begin{aligned}
Th_1 &= 0.7 \times Background\_GrayLevel \\
Th_2 &= 0.3 \times m(x,y)
\end{aligned} \tag{3}
$$

After binarization, median filtering is performed. A median filter has a superior effect for removing impulse noise [4]. Median filtering can preserve small sized holes and remove impulse noise, which is caused by reflecting on the worm's body. In this paper, we use a 9×9 window for median filtering to remove impulse noise in the binary worm image.

## 2.2 Hole Detection

Even after applying the median filter to the binary worm image, some noise occasionally remains on the worm's body. To remove the remaining noise, we propose a method that can distinguish between hole and noise.

A hole is created when the worm loops or touches itself, while noise is located on the worm's body. Therefore, we can determine whether the region is a hole or noise by measuring the total thickness of the body enclosing the region. In order to measure the thickness, we define 16 vectors. We traverse and count the number of pixels from the centroid of a region, ($C_x$, $C_y$), in each vector direction until we reach the background. The total thickness is the sum of two opposite direction thickness. If the minimum is less than 25, the region is considered as noise, because the thickness of the worms used in this work is not larger than 25. If a region is determined as noise, we fill the region with body pixels. Otherwise, we preserve the region as a hole.

After detecting holes, we remove the remaining noise using a closing morphological operation. However, even though the closing operation is performed, it is possible that other objects could exist, apart from the worm body and hole. A worm's crawling tracks or eggs could cause the unwanted object. In order to remove the object, we perform labeling [5] and take only the largest object to be the worm's body, while we remove the other labeled objects. After removing the isolated objects, we then restore the hole region onto the worm's body. Fig. 1 shows the results of previous binarization method and newly proposed method including hole detection method.

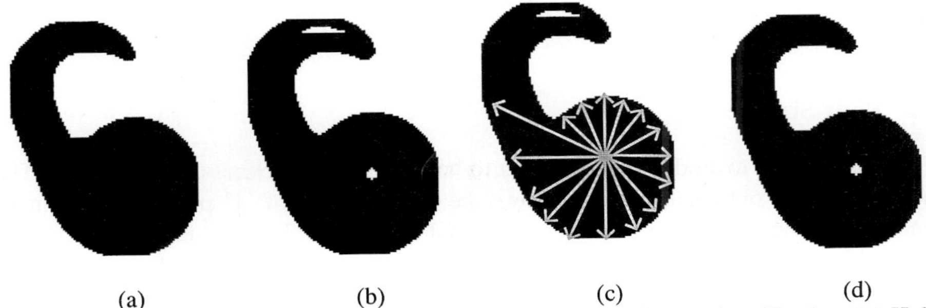

(a) (b) (c) (d)

**Fig. 1.** (a) After closing operation using previous method. (b) After median filtering. (c) Hole detection methods. (d) After removing noise.

# 3 Feature Extraction

After binarization and preprocessing such as skeletoning, feature extraction is performed. In this paper, 3 kinds of features are extracted: Large-scale movement, body size, and body posture. However several more features such as centroid movement, omega shape, frequency of omega shape change, etc. are added comparing to [3].

**Fig. 2.** Directional change detection method.

### 3.1 Large-Scale Movement

Features for the large-scale movement are global moving distance and reversal frequencies during some intervals. To measure moving distance, the centroid position data are computed at every frame (In this paper, the frame rate is 2Hz). And to measure reversal, the trajectory of the worm's centroid (black solid line in Fig. 2) is sampled at intervals of 30 pixels, which is about one-tenth of the normal worm length. The directional change position (mark with a star) is found by computing the angle deviation at every vertex of the polygon (gray line). If the angle (θ) is greater than 120°, then the position is considered to be a reversal.

We also compute the moving distance of worm's normalized centroid (CNTMV). The coordinates of the worm's centroid, $(C_w, C_h)$, are normalized with the MER (Minimum Enclosing Rectangle) width and height. Normalization and moving distance are computed with the following equation:

$$CNTMV = \left|\mathbf{C}_{n,t} - \mathbf{C}_{n,t-1}\right|, \text{ where } \mathbf{C}_n = \left(\frac{C_w}{width}, \frac{C_h}{height}\right), \quad \mathbf{C} = (C_w, C_h) \tag{4}$$

### 3.2 Body Size

Features related to body size are worm's area, length, thickness, and fatness. The worm's area is obtained by determining the total number of '1' pixels in the binary image. And the worm's length can be obtained by determining the number of pixels in the image skeleton. The worm thickness is measured at the center and head/tail positions of the worm skeleton. Fig. 3(a) shows thickness measuring method.

### 3.3 Body Posture

Several other parameters that correlated with both body size and body posture could be obtained by finding the best fit ellipse to the binary shape, and then using the length of the major and minor axes of the ellipse as shape features (Fig. 3(b)). An eccentricity variable is then computed as the ratio of the distance between the foci of the ellipse and its major axis length; this value (which is between 0 for a circle and 1 for a line) provides a measure of the elongation of the worm. By rotating the image according to the orientation of the best-fit ellipse's major axis (Fig, we can also obtain the MER of the shape. Features related to body posture are eccentricity, height and width of the MER (Fig. 3(c)), amplitude, and angle change rate. Then, combined features such as minimum, maximum, and average of each feature are computed. A total of 94 features are used in [3].

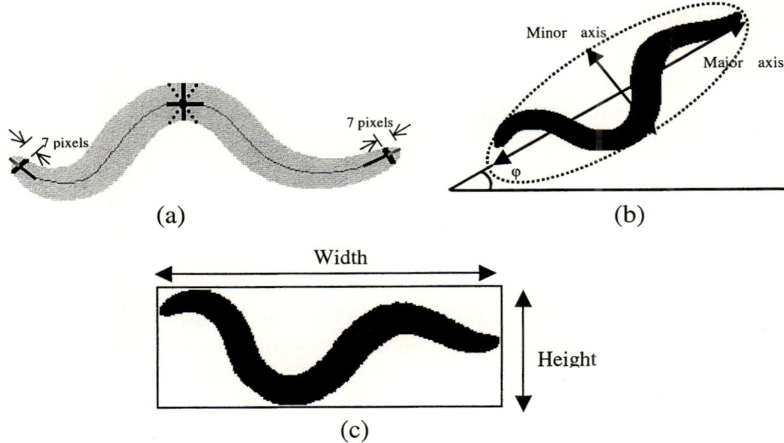


**Fig. 3.** (a) Thickness measuring method. (b) Best fit ellipse. (c) MER (Minimum Enclosing Rectangle).

Adding to the 94 features, we compute the ratio of worm length and MER width (LNWDR). This measurement provides information on the worm's straightness or waviness. We also use the number of frames with omega shape (NUMOMEGA) and the number of times the worm changes from non-omega shape to omega shape (OMEGACHG). These measurements give information about the regularity of the worm's skeleton wave. Omega shape can be detected by the amplitude ratio, $A_r$. If $A_r$ is 0, then we can decide that the worm's posture is omega shaped. The amplitude ratio is evaluated by the following equation:

$$A_r = \frac{\min(A,B)}{\max(A,B)} \quad \mathbf{(5)}$$

Where *A* and *B* are maximal distances in both sides of the straight line connecting two end points of the worm skeleton. The sum of *A* and *B* is considered to be the amplitude of the skeleton. Skeleton's amplitude and an example of an omega shaped worm are shown in Fig. 4.

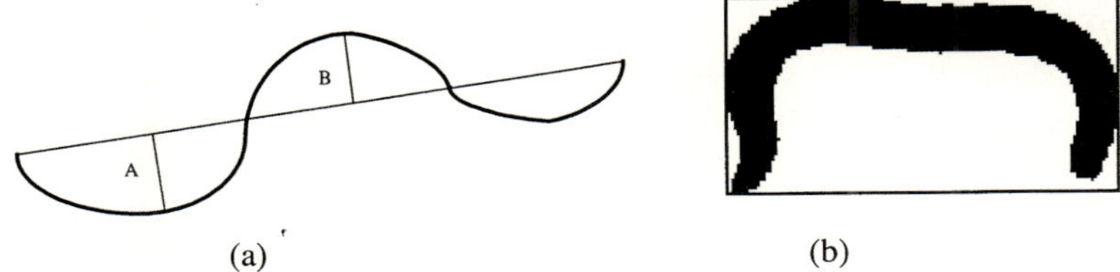


**Fig. 4**. (a) Skeleton's amplitude. (b) Omega shaped worm.

We also subdivide the interval for measuring the reversals. The number of reversals is measured during 10, 20, 30, 40, 50, and 60 sec. Including the combined features of the new feature set, a total of 23 new features are added to the 94 previous features. The total number of features extracted in this paper is now 117.

## 4 Classification Using the CART

The CART (Classification and Regression Tree) makes a binary classification tree using a learning sample [6]. The root node of the tree contains all the training cases; the worm types are equally mixed together in this node. The goal of the CART is to successively subdivide the training set using binary splits in such a way that the data associated with the terminal nodes of the tree do not have a mix of worm types; rather, each node should be as pure as possible. In order to measure the impurity of a data set, the Gini index of diversity is applied. A simple rule is to assign the most popular class to each terminal node.

To estimate the classification rate, the CART uses 10-fold cross-validation. To perform the 10-fold cross-validation, it splits the learning sample into ten equal parts. Nine tenths of the learning sample is used to create the tree and the remaining tenth is used to estimate the error rate of selected sub-trees. This procedure is performed until all the subsets are tested.

## 5 Experimental Results

C. elegans locomotion is tracked with a stereomicroscope mounted with a CCD camera. A computer-controlled tracker is used to put the worms in the center of the optical field of the stereomicroscope during observation. To record the locomotion of a worm, an image frame is snapped every 0.5 seconds for 5 minutes. So the video clip of each worm consists of 600 frames. All of the software for binarization and feature extraction is coded in C++ and implemented on a PC with a 1.7GHz CPU.

In this experiment, we use 9 different worm types (wild, goa-1, nic-1, unc-36, unc-38, egl-19, unc-29, unc-2, tph-1). Each worm type has 100 worms, except tph-1 which has 60 worms. So a total of 860 worms are used in this experiment. Primary features are extracted from each frame after binarization and preprocessing. Then, 117 features for a worm are computed from the primary features of 600 frames. Finally, the 860×117 variable set is fed into the CART for analysis and classification. The CART creates a maximal tree and then prunes it back to obtain an optimal one. For our case, the optimal tree has 42 terminal nodes. To reduce the complexity of the tree, we set the complexity parameter to 0.007. The resulting classification tree has 13 terminal nodes [7].

Table 1 shows the cross-validation classification probability. The success rates are listed along the shaded diagonal, while the off-diagonal entries represent the misclassification error rates. From this, we can see that wild, goa-1, nic-1 and egl-19 types have relatively high success classification rates compared to unc (uncoordinated mutants) types. This is due to the fact that unc-36, unc-38, unc-2, unc-29, and tph-1 have similar behavioural characteristics.

Fig. 5 shows characterization of mutant phenotypes using features used in the classification tree. In the plots, top of the box indicates the mean, and the lower and upper bar indicate the one standard deviation interval. From Fig. 5 (h), (i), (j), and (k), we can see that nic-1 is most sluggish while wild or goa-1 is most active. Fig. 5 (a) and (g) reveal that unc-2 is most kinky or loopy. Also, from Fig. 5 (b), (c), (e), and (f), we can see that nic-1 is shortest and thickest, while egl-19 is longest and thinnest.

These characterizations are exactly same as what experienced observers have obtained. Thus we can conclude that our vision system can be used for automatic classification and analysis of C. Elegans.

**Table 1**. Cross-validation classification probability table

| Actual \ Predicted | wild | goa-1 | nic-1 | unc-36 | unc-38 | egl-19 | unc-2 | unc-29 | tph-1 |
|---|---|---|---|---|---|---|---|---|---|
| wild | 0.950 | 0.000 | 0.000 | 0.000 | 0.000 | 0.020 | 0.030 | 0.000 | 0.000 |
| goa-1 | 0.010 | 0.930 | 0.000 | 0.020 | 0.010 | 0.000 | 0.020 | 0.000 | 0.010 |
| nic-1 | 0.000 | 0.000 | 0.880 | 0.000 | 0.060 | 0.000 | 0.000 | 0.040 | 0.020 |
| unc-36 | 0.000 | 0.000 | 0.000 | 0.760 | 0.050 | 0.020 | 0.000 | 0.120 | 0.050 |
| unc-38 | 0.000 | 0.000 | 0.000 | 0.040 | 0.730 | 0.000 | 0.050 | 0.070 | 0.110 |
| egl-19 | 0.000 | 0.000 | 0.000 | 0.020 | 0.000 | 0.930 | 0.000 | 0.020 | 0.030 |
| unc-2 | 0.033 | 0.067 | 0.017 | 0.017 | 0.083 | 0.000 | 0.717 | 0.000 | 0.067 |
| unc-29 | 0.000 | 0.000 | 0.000 | 0.160 | 0.020 | 0.010 | 0.010 | 0.760 | 0.040 |
| tph-1 | 0.000 | 0.010 | 0.020 | 0.100 | 0.210 | 0.010 | 0.040 | 0.060 | 0.550 |

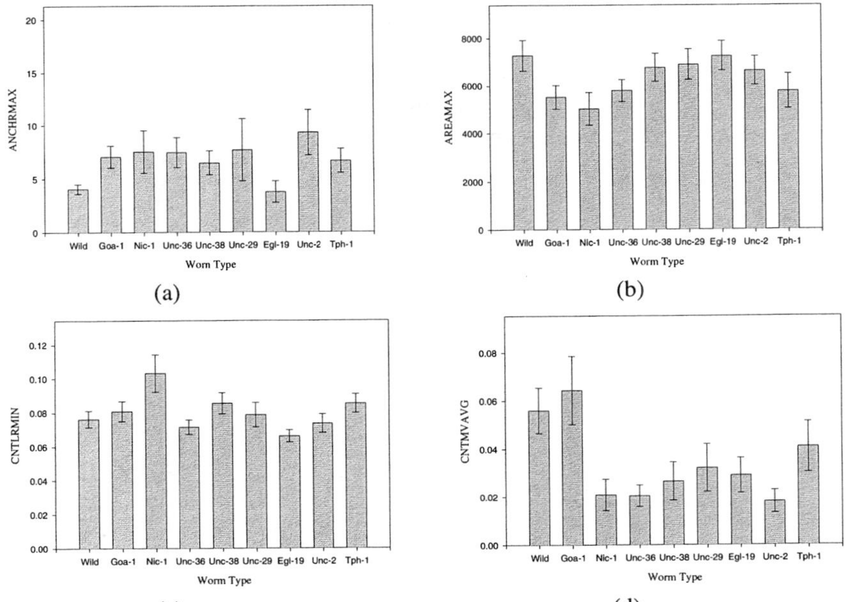


**Fig. 5.** Characterization of mutant phenotypes using features used in the classification tree. (a) Maximum angle change rate. (b) Maximum area of the worm. (c) Minimum ratio of center thickness to length. (d) Average of normalized centroid movement. (e) Average ratio of worm length to MER fill..

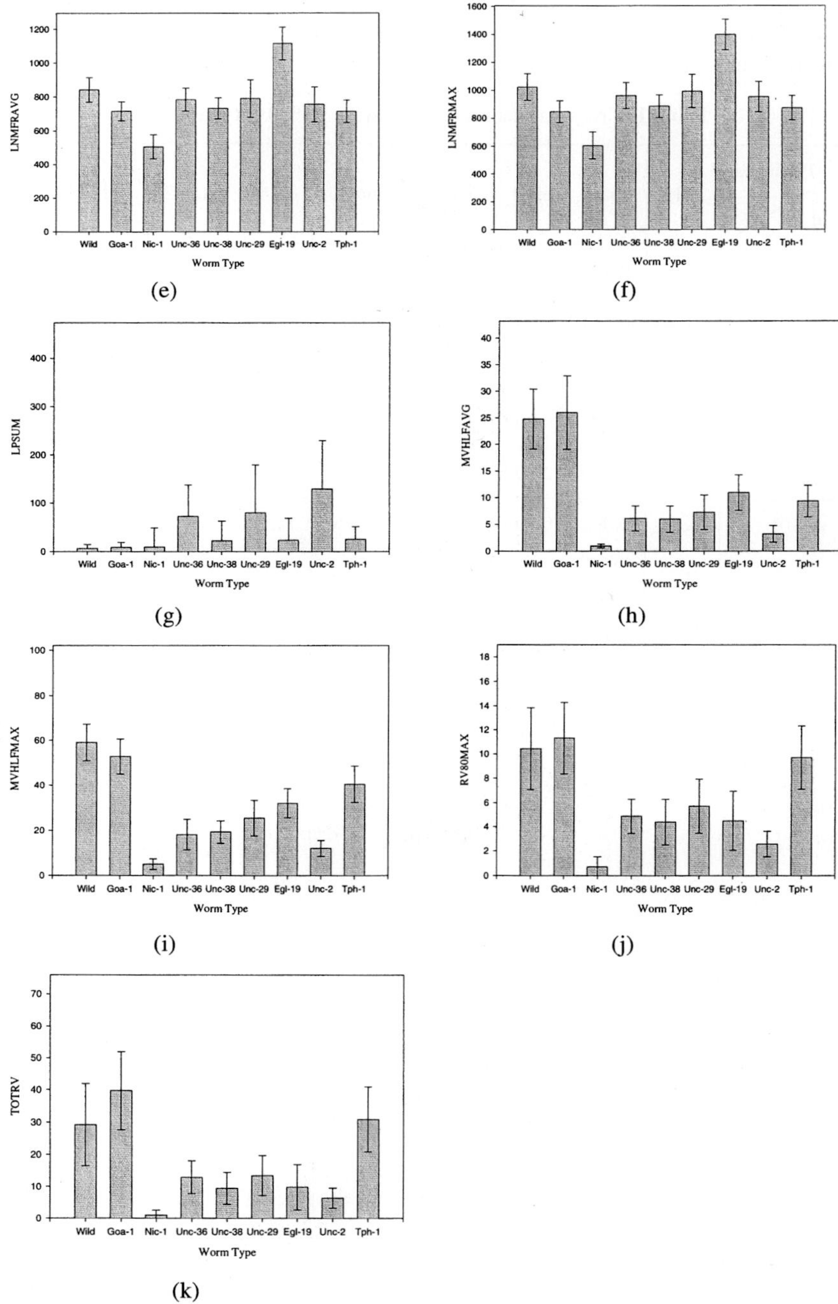


**Fig. 5**. (cont.) (f) Maximum ratio of worm length to MER fill. (g) Total number of frames in which the worm is looped. (h) Average distance moved in 0.5 sec. (i) Maximum distance moved in 0.5 sec. (j) Maximum number of reversals in 40 sec. (k) Total number of reversals in 5 min.

## 6 Conclusions

Using our proposed preprocessing and feature extraction methods, we can obtain precise features that can be used for automatic classification and analysis of C. Elegans. From the CART results, we can see that wild, goa-1, nic-1 and egl-19 types have relatively high success classification rates, but unc types and tph-1 have a low classification probability, which is due to the fact that unc types have very similar behaviours. For further work, more significant features for unc types and tph-1 are to be extracted.

**Acknowledgements**

The authors are grateful to Prof. Pamela Cosman and Prof. William Schafer in University of California, San Diego, for their invaluable advice.

## References

1. Waggoner, L., et al.: Control of behavioral states by serotonin in Caenorhabditis elegans. Neuron (1998) 203-214
2. Zhou, G.T., Schafer, W.R., Schafer, R.W.: A three-state biological point process model and its parameter estimation. IEEE Trans On Signal Processing (1998) 2698-2707
3. Baek, J.H., et al.: Using machine vision to analyze and classify Caenorhabditis elegans behavioral phenotypes quantitatively. Journal of Neuroscience Methods, Vol. 118. (2002) 9-21
4. Gonzalez, R.C., Woods, R.E.: Digital Image Processing. Prentice Hall Inc., New Jersey (2002)
5. Jain, R., Kasturi, R., Schunck, B.G.: Machine Vision. McGraw-Hill Inc., New York (1995)
6. Breiman, L., Friedman, J.H., Olshen, R.A., Stone, C.J.: Classification and regression trees. Chapman & Hall Inc., New York (1984)
7. Nah, W. and Baek, J. H.: Classification of Caenorhabditis Elegans Behavioral Phenotypes Using an Improved Binarization Method. To be appeared in LNCS (2003)

# Measurement System of Traffic Flow Using Real-Time Processing of Moving Pictures

Hyeong-Taek Park[1], Tae-Seung Lee[1], Sung-Won Choi[1], Sang-Seok Lim[1], Syng-Yup Ohn[1], Seung-Hoe Choi[2], and Byong-Won Hwang[1]

[1] Hankuk Aviation University, School of Electronics, Telecommunication and Computer Engineering, Seoul, Korea
[2] Hankuk Aviation University, General Studies, Seoul, Korea
{htpark, tslee, swchoi, sslim, syohn, shchoi, bwhwang}@mail.hangkong.ac.kr

**Abstract.** In this paper, an automatic traffic flow measuring system and a real-time image processing algorithm have been developed. The pictures of moving vehicles taken by an industrial television (ITV) camera are digitized into sample points in odd ITV frames and the points are processed in even ITV frames by a personal computer. We detect the presence of vehicles by comparing the brightness of the sample points of vehicle with that of the road. After eliminating noises contained in the digitized sample points by appropriate smoothing techniques, we obtain a contour of each vehicle. Using the contour, the number of passing vehicles is effectively measured by counting the number of sample points of each vehicle. Also the type of a vehicle is easily figured out by counting the number of sample points corresponding to the width of vehicle's contour. The performance of the proposed algorithm is demonstrated by actual implementation. From the experimental results 1~2% measuring error was observed.

## 1 Introduction

Recent development on road traffic surveillance and control system using computers gives rise to the necessity of gathering large quantity of traffic information in real time basis. Information on special traffic parameters such as the length of queue and the grade of congestion and also information on unusual traffic incident are requested in particular.

Real time processing of moving pictures of traffic flow is considered to be useful for obtaining various types of special traffic parameters. It is also expected to reduce time and work required in traffic investigation.

So far, vehicle detection and tracking system [1], [2], [3], [4], road surveillance system [5], [6], [7], [8] and traffic analysis for control [9], [10], [11] have been developed. However, many of those systems are difficult to implement for the real-time processing in the field.

The previous works in this field can be broadly divided into two groups [15]. One group utilizes vision sensors to take the traffic image. The video image is processed by image processing algorithm to extract traffic data.

P.W.H. Chung, C.J. Hinde, M. Ali (Eds.): IEA/AIE 2003, LNAI 2718, pp. 296–305, 2003.

The other group's approaches are based on the magnetic loop, infrared or ultrasonic sensors. These are weather-independent, applicable in the night or under poor visibility conditions, costly, limited to single lane coverage, hard to maintain, and difficult to relocate. The vision sensor based methods are cost effective, easy to maintain, easy to relocate, low detection error rated, but fails to use in poor visibility condition.

Microwave radar based system [16] is also recently employed and is capable of multi-lane, weather-independent, roadside mountable, but its performance is limited by blockage of small size vehicles by neighboring larger ones. Both approaches have widely used in traffic control systems yet their performances were somewhat limited.

A traffic flow measuring system using industrial television (ITV) camera [12], [13] and charge coupled device (CCD) camera [14] was developed by Hwang et al. In [14], they designed and made a special device called Video Information Sampler and Converter (VISC) for real time image processing. In this system, real time measurement was made possible by dealing with only the information on brightness at the relatively few number of sample points on the picture instead of dealing with all of the picture elements. Although the VISC achieved a notable improvement in the real-time processing of the traffic image, the performance was not quite satisfactory.

Recently a new system using ITV or CCD camera and an efficient real-time processing algorithm have been developed by the authors. It enables *real-time measurement* of traffic flow in the field while the performance is more improved. Further, the new system has much flexibility compared with the previous VISC system.

The paper is organized as follows. Section 2 describes the new system using ITV or CCD camera. The traffic flow measuring algorithm based on real-time image processing is presented in section 3. The results from experimental implementation are analyzed in section 4.

## 2 The Image Processing System

The structure of the traffic image processing system is illustrated in Fig. 1. Pictures taken by the ITV or CCD camera in the field are recorded and played back in our laboratory to be processed by the proposed automatic image processing algorithm. After the algorithm is developed, the ITV or CCD camera is connected directly to the image processing system that is capable of processing in real time.

In this system, we use the Frame Grabber instead of VISC mentioned above. VISC samples a video signal at maximum 64 points from 256*256 points in the picture. In VISC the brightness of a sample point is digitized into 16 discrete levels (0~15) using 4-bits.

The Frame Grabber can sample a video signal at 640 points (maximum) on one scan line. The brightness of each sample point is digitized into 256 discrete levels using 8-bits. In our experiment, we choose only 160 sample points (equally separated) out of 640 sample points per scan line and the brightness of a sample point is digitized into 16 discrete levels (0~15) using 4-bits by the image processing algorithm.

The operation of the whole system consists of two cycles alternatively running. The first cycle is a process of taking pictures of vehicles by camera and digitizing the picture in odd ITV frames. The second cycle is a process of extracting the measurement from the digital image in even ITV frames.

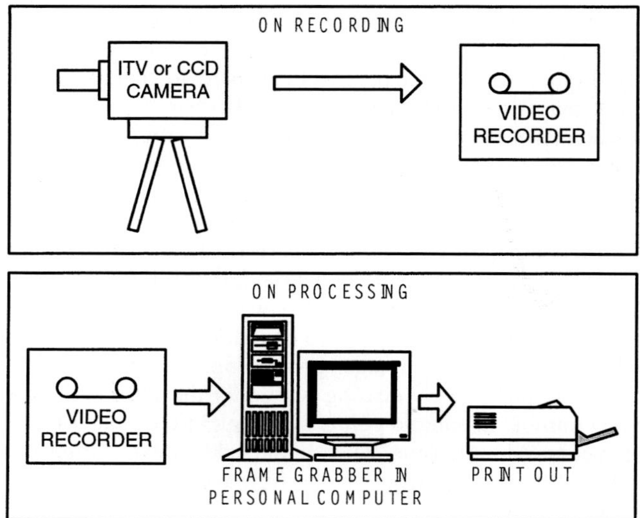


**Fig. 1.** The structure of the image processing system

# 3 The Measuring Algorithm

## 3.1 The Objective and Method

In this paper, an automatic measuring system and real-time image processing algorithm for measuring traffic-flow have been developed. In the sequel, "traffic flow data" means the number of passing vehicles per lane, the total number of passing vehicles and the types of vehicles. The sample points are set across the lanes at the 15m distance from the footprint of the camera. Sample points of moving pictures taken by an ITV or CCD camera are digitized in odd ITV frames and the points are processed in even ITV frames by a personal computer. We can detect presence of vehicles by comparing the brightness of the sample points of vehicle image and that of the road (background).

Optical and electrical noises are eliminated by smoothing along the time axis (Y axis) and the spatial axis (sample points line, i.e. X axis). Finally, we can extract contours of the vehicles and determine the center point of each contour. The number of passing vehicles through the sample points line is measured by counting the number of center points.

The relationship between the position of the camera and the sample points line are illustrated in Fig. 2. The sample points on the line are established at the same interval of 8cm across the moving direction of vehicles. The type of a vehicle is also measured by counting the number of sample points belonging to the width of the contour.

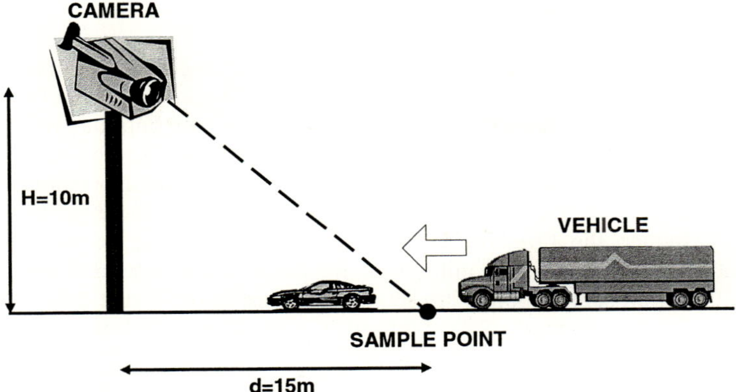


**Fig. 2.** The relationship between the position of the camera and the sample point

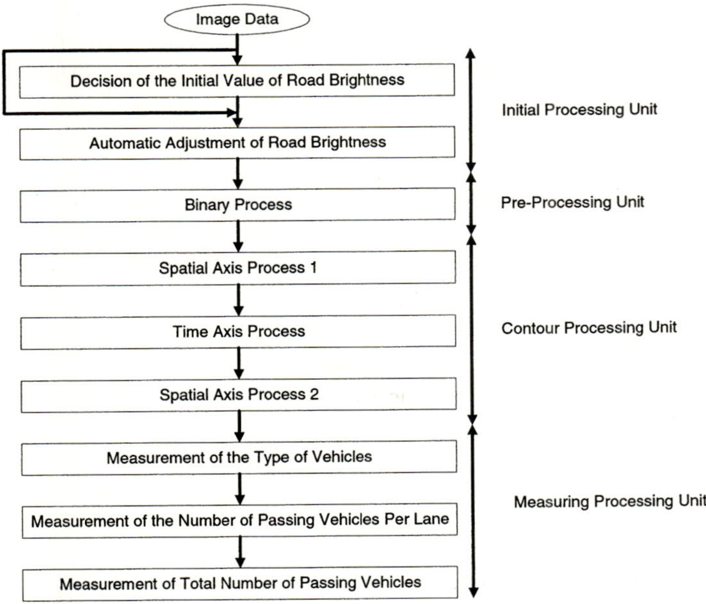


**Fig. 3.** Flow chart of measuring algorithm

## 3.2 The Measuring Algorithm

The flow chart of the measuring algorithm for the number of the passing vehicles per lane, the total number of passing vehicles and the type of vehicles is shown in Fig. 3. Each part of the flow chart is described below in detail.

### 3.2.1 Initial Processing Unit

*(1) Decision of the Initial Value of the Road Brightness*

For setting the initial value of the road, the value of brightness of the first frame is stored. If the value of brightness of the next frame is different from that of the first frame, the stored value is renewed. When the same brightness continues R times, the value is selected to be the value of road brightness at that time. The above processing is repeated for each sample point. When the values of the road brightness at all sample points are determined, the initial setting is completed. In the experiment, R is determined to reduce the time for setting the initial value and to use them for measurement more effectively. For initial trial, the parameter R is set to 5 empirically. Once the values of all sample points are set, this processing for image data is skipped and the automatic adjustment of road brightness is carried out as follows.

*(2) Automatic Adjustment of Road Brightness*

If the brightness of background (road) is changed for some reason, the correct processing of the measured images becomes impossible. The value of brightness of background changes not only by sudden change of weather condition but also with the passage of time. Therefore, we developed the algorithm such that background brightness can adapt automatically to the variations of the brightness of the background due to the environmental change.

### 3.2.2 Pre-Processing Unit

Pre-Processing unit is to detect the region where the brightness of sample point of a vehicle is different from that of road surface as a background. The task is carried out in the binary process. This is denoted by STEP 1 described below.

**STEP 1**

The value of brightness $I(n,t)$ at each sample point of the image is compared with the upper limit of background brightness $L_U(n,t)$ and the lower limit $L_L(n,t)$. Then the index $p(n,t)$ is obtained as follows.

$$p(n,t) = \begin{cases} 1, & \textit{if } I(n,t) < L_L \textit{ or } I(n,t) > L_U \\ 0, & \textit{otherwise} \end{cases} . \qquad (1)$$

where, $I(n,t)$ denotes the brightness at the time $t$ of $n$-th sample point and $t$ the interval of 1/15 sec. $L_U = X(I)+1$ and $L_L = X(I)-1$ are the upper limit and the lower limit of brightness of the road, respectively.

### 3.2.3 Contour Processing Unit

In the $p$ pattern "1" is assigned to the sample point of a vehicle, and "0" to the background sample point. The background samples are extracted from the background image by the binary processing of the pre-processing unit. In the process following problems can be arisen owing to electrical and optical noise.

① There can exists noise assigned to "0" inside vehicle region
② There can exists noise assigned to "1" inside background region
③ If the brightness of middle part between front part and back part of a large vehicle like cargo truck, trailer is similar that of the background, then in this case one vehicle may be recognized as two vehicles.

The contour processing unit solves these problems and produce contours. To obtain the contour, the algorithm carries out the spatial axis and time axis processing in the following.

*(1) Spatial Axis Processing 1*
Spatial Axis Processing 1 eliminates the noise assigned to "0" inside contour of vehicles. This is denoted by STEP 2 described below.

**STEP 2**
The noise being $p(n,t)=0$ at the spatial axis is removed:

If $p(n,t)$ is "0" successively not less than 2 times, then we set $P(n,t)=0$. Otherwise $P(n,t)=1$.

*(2) Time Axis Processing*
Time Axis Processing prevents recognition of a part of a vehicle as a separate vehicle. This is denoted as STEP 3 and the corresponding algorithm is described below:

**STEP 3**
From time sequence $P(n,t)$, the following index of presence $P^*(n,t)$ is obtained.

If $P(n,t-1)=0$ and $P(n,t)$ is successively "1" $\Delta_1$ times since $P(n,t-\Delta_1+1)$, then we set $P^*(n,t)=1$.
If $P(n,t-1)=1$ and $P(n,t)$ is successively "0" $\Delta_2$ times from $P(n,t-\Delta_2+1)$, then we set $P^*(n,t)=0$.

where, $\Delta_1$ and $\Delta_2$ are set to 3 and 5 respectively chosen from experiments

*(3) Spatial Axis Processing 2*
Spatial Axis Processing 2 eliminates the noise assigned to "1" in the background (road). This is denoted by STEP 4 and the algorithm is described below:

**STEP 4**
If $P^*(n,t)$ is "1" successively not less than 3 times in the spatial axis, then we set $P^{**}(n,t)=1$. Otherwise $P^{**}(n,t)=0$.

### 3.2.4 Measurement Processing Unit

Based on the previous processing, we obtain contours of the vehicles. From the contours, we measure the number of passing vehicles in each lane, the total number of passing vehicles and the type of vehicles. The measuring algorithm is described in the following.

*(1) Determination of the Type of Vehicles*

The type of a vehicle is determined by counting the number of sample points corresponding to the width of a contour. We can identify the type of vehicles more precisely by utilizing the width and length of a vehicle together. In this paper, we call small-size car, middle-size car and large-size car if the width of a vehicle is less than 1.7m , between 1.8m and 2.3m, and larger than 2.4m, respectively.

*(2) Measurement of the Number of Passing Vehicles*

The center line of a contour is detected in the following STEP 5. To measure the number of passing vehicles in a lane, first we determine the lane to which the contour belongs. This is done by simply checking the ordinal number of the sample point of a contour along the sample points line, since the sample points on the line are equally spaced. Once the lane is known, we can measure the number of passing vehicles per lane by counting the number of the first sample point on the center line of the contour belong to the lane of interest. Also we can measure the total number of passing vehicles by adding up the number of vehicles for 3 lanes.

**STEP 5**

It is assumed that from $t = \tau_1$ the pattern $P^{**}(n,t)$ begins to be "1".

i ) If $\sum_{t=\tau_1}^{\tau} P^{**}(n,t) \geq \sum_{t=\tau_1}^{\tau} P^{**}(n-1,\tau)$ , then we set $P_{RC}(n,\tau)=1$ . Otherwise $P_{RC}(n,\tau)=0$ .

ii ) If $\sum_{t=\tau_1}^{\tau} P^{**}(n,t) \geq \sum_{t=\tau_1}^{\tau} P^{**}(n+1,\tau)$ , then we set $P_{LC}(n,\tau)=1$ . Otherwise $P_{LC}(n,\tau)=0$ .

iii ) When $P^{**}(n,t)$ is successively "1" from $t=\tau-\Delta_3$ to $t=\tau$ , then we set $P_{RC}(n,\tau)=0$ and $P_{LC}(n,\tau)=0$ .

iv ) $P_C(n,t)$ is set by the logical AND of $P_{RC}(n,\tau)$ and $P_{LC}(n,\tau)$ .

## 4 Experimental Results

For illustration of the performance of the proposed algorithm, we carried out experiments. In the experiment, the total width of the three lanes was 1050cm and the number of sample points for three lanes was 120. Hence the interval between any two neighboring sample points is 8cm. We can determine the type of vehicles by counting the number of sample points corresponding to the width of the contour. The maximum error might be 16cm and can decrease by increasing of the number of the sample points on the line. Similarly we can measure the length of a vehicle by counting the number of sample points of the contour in the direction of vehicle's movement. Another method to measure the length of a vehicle is using the vehicle's speed. The speed of a vehicle can be calculated also by counting the number of sample points of the contour and by multiplying it to the frame speed.

In the experiment we measured the number of passing vehicles per lane and total number of passing vehicles for three lanes. For the case of a single lane, we tested the traffic data of 7 blocks. Each block contains 2250 frames (150 seconds) . For the three lanes, we measured 10 blocks, each block contains 1350 frames (90 seconds). The results are summarized in Table 1 and Table 2. The computer display of the traffic flow measuring system using real time dynamic image processing is displayed in Fig. 4. In this display, we selected the 350-th scan line from the top as the line of sample points.

**Table 1.** The result of experiments for one lane

| Blocks | 1 | 2 | 3 | 4 | 5 | 6 | 7 | 8 | 9 | 10 | Total |
|---|---|---|---|---|---|---|---|---|---|---|---|
| Observed number | 84 | 75 | 75 | 90 | 78 | 78 | 78 | 66 | 87 | 117 | 828 |
| Measured number | 78 | 75 | 78 | 90 | 78 | 78 | 78 | 63 | 87 | 117 | 822 |
| Error | -6 | | 3 | | | | | -3 | | | -6(12) |

**Table 2.** The result of experiments for 3 lanes

| Blocks | 1 | 2 | 3 | 4 | 5 | 6 | 7 | Total |
|---|---|---|---|---|---|---|---|---|
| Observed number | 33 | 39 | 39 | 69 | 51 | 36 | 36 | 303 |
| Measured number | 33 | 39 | 39 | 66 | 51 | 36 | 33 | 297 |
| Error | | | | -3 | | | -3 | -6 |

The error rate is 2% for a single lane and 1.4% for three lanes. In both cases, the results indicate excellent performance of the proposed algorithm. The error is caused from the fact that the vehicles having similar brightness to that of the road are eliminated by the contour processing unit.

## 5 Conclusion

In this paper, we have developed an automatic measuring system and its real-time image processing algorithm for traffic flow measurement. In the algorithm, the image of vehicles is digitized to obtain sample points and the brightness of each point. By comparing the brightness of the sample points and those of the road, we detected the presence of vehicles. Using smoothing techniques we obtain the contours of vehicles from the sampled image. The type of a vehicle is identified by counting the number of sample points corresponding to the width of the contour. We measure the number of passing vehicles by counting the number of the first sample points of the center line of the contour. The measuring error was within of 1~2% in our experiment. Velocity of each vehicle will be measured by computing time difference between a pair of sample points.

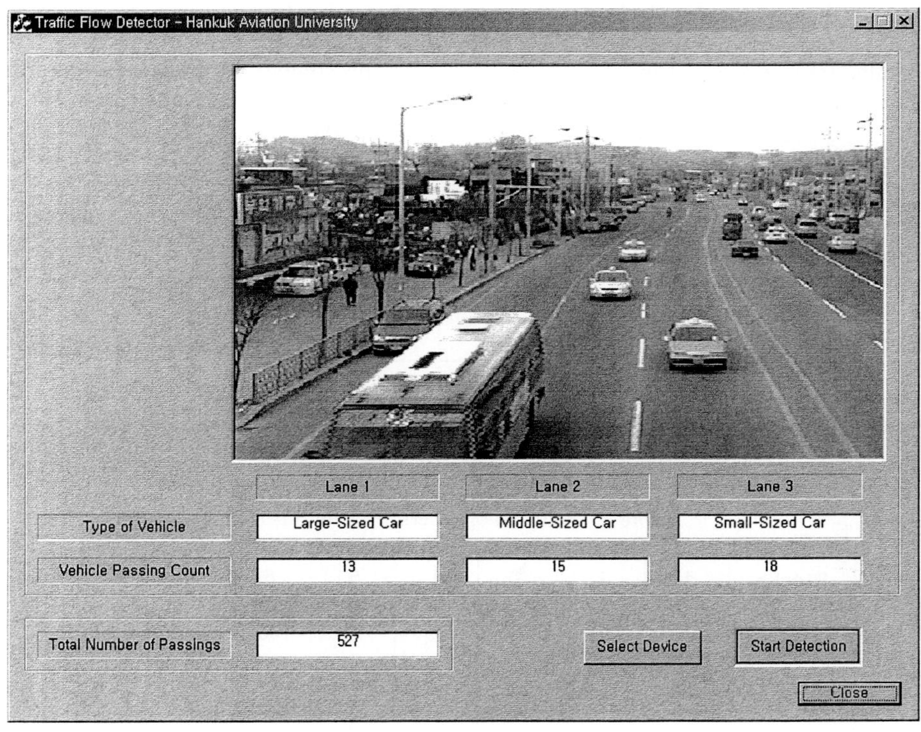


**Fig. 4.** Computer display of the traffic flow measuring system

## References

1. Gloyer, B., Aghajan, H. K., Siu, K. Y., Kailath, T.: Vehicle Detection and Tracking for Freeway Traffic Monitoring. IEE Record of the Twenty-Eighth Asilomar Conference on Signals, Systems and Computers. **2** (1994) 970-974
2. Cucchiara, R. and Piccardi, M.: Vehicle Detection under Day and Night Illumination. ISCSIIA99, (1999)
3. Fathy, M., Siyal, M. Y.: An Image Detection Technique Based on Morphological Edge Detection and Background Differencing for Real-Time Traffic Analysis. Pattern Recognition Letters. **16** (1995) 1321-1330

4. Ali, A. T., Dagless, E. L.: Computer Vision for Automatic Road Traffic Analysis. International Conference on Automation, Robotics and Computer Vision. (1990) 875-879
5. Malik, J.: A Machine Vision Based Surveillance System for California Roads. PATH Project MOU-83 Final Report. University of California Berkeley (1994)
6. Jung, Y. K., Ho, Y. S.: Robust Vehicle Detection and Tracking for Traffic Surveillance. Picture Coding Symposium'99. (1999) 227-230
7. Rao, B. S. Y., Durrant-Whyte, H. F. and Sheen, J. A.: A Fully Decentralized Multi-Sensor System for Tracking and Surveillance. The International Journal of Robotics Research. **12** (1993) 20-24
8. Dickinson, K. W., Waterfall, R. C.: Video Image Processing for Monitoring Road Traffic. IEE International Conference on Road Traffic Data Collection. (1984) 105-109
9. Koller, D., Weber, J., Huang, T., Malik, J., Ogasawara, G., Rao, B. and Russell, S.: Towards robust automatic traffic scene analysis in real-time. 12th IAPR International Conference on Pattern Recognition. **1** (1994) 126 -131
10. Fathy, M., Siyal, M. Y.: Real-Time Measurement of Traffic Queue Parameters by Using Image Processing Techniques. Fifth International Conference on Image Processing and Its Applications. (1995) 450-453
11. Soh, J., Chun B. T., Wang, M.: Analysis of Road Sequences for Vehicle Counting. IEEE International Conference on Systems, Man and Cybernetics. **1** (1995) 22-25
12. Hwang, Byong-Won, et al.: Measurement of Traffic Flow Using Real Time Processing of Moving Pictures. IEEE International Conference on Vehicular Technology (1982) 488-494
13. Hwang, Byong-Won, et al.: A Study on the Real Time Measurement of Vehicle Speed Using Dynamic Image Processing. 5th World Congress on Intelligent Transport Systems. (1998)
14. Hwang, Byong-Won, et al.: A Traffic Flow Measuring System Using a Solid-State Image Sensor. IEE International Conference on Road Traffic Data Collection. (1984)
15. Klein, L.A. and Kelly, M.R.: Detection Technology For IVHS, Vol. I, Final report No. FHWA-RD-95-100, FHA, DOT, McLean, Virginia. (1996)
16. EIS Inc.: RTMS User Manual, Issue 3.0, EIS Electronic Integrated Systems Inc., Toronto, Canada. (2002)

# Infrared Sensor Data Correction for Local Area Map Construction by a Mobile Robot

V. Koval[1], Volodymyr Turchenko[1], Anatoly Sachenko[1], J. A. Becerra[2], Richard J. Duro[2], and V. Golovko[3]

[1] Ternopil Academy of National Economy, Institute of Computer Information Technologies, 3 Peremoga Square, 46004, Ternopil, Ukraine, Phone +380 (352) 43-6038, Fax: +380 (352) 43-6354 (24 hrs),
vko_ukr@yahoo.com, http://www.tanet.edu.te.ua

[2] Universidade da Coruña, Escuela Politécnica Superior, Mendizabal s.n., 15403 Ferrol, Spain, Phone: (+34) 981 33 7400 (ext. 3281), Fax: (+34) 981 33 7410
richard@udc.es

[3] Vladimir Golovko, Brest Polytechnic Institute, Department of Computers and Mechanics, Moscowskaja 267, 224017 Brest, Republic of Belarus
gva@bstu.by, gva@brpi.unibel.by

**Abstract.** The construction of local area maps on the based on heterogeneous sensor readings is considered in this paper. The Infrared Sensor Data Correction method is presented for the construction of local area maps. This method displays lower calculation complexity and broader universality compared to existing methods and this is important for on-line robot activity. The simulation results showed the high accuracy of the method.

## 1 Introduction

The actuality of intelligent mobile robots, which can replace people in environments that are dangerous for their health is in permanent increase. The term autonomous robot refers to a technical system that can easily navigate in an environment and/or perform tasks through the control of its effectors without outside help [1], [2], [3]. The information about the state of the environment is a necessary component for mobile robot autonomy. As a rule deliberative mobile robots use global and local area maps (LAM), which conform an inherent part of their behavior control system. They permit representing the environment and navigating in it. LAM contain information limited by an abstract "W" dimension window centered in the position of the mobile robot [4], [5], [6].

The straight use of sensor readings is one of possible approaches to the perception of the environment for the construction of environment maps and a necessary condition for mobile robot autonomy. Sensors are devices with limited accuracy that are subject to noise. Therefore the practical problem is to obtain sufficiently exact parameters of environment in which the mobile robot operates [4], [7], [8], [9], [10], [11]. Sensor fusion techniques are one of the methods, which provide more accurate and comprehensive information about this environment. This general technique aims

P.W.H. Chung, C.J. Hinde, M. Ali (Eds.): IEA/AIE 2003, LNAI 2718, pp. 306–315, 2003.

to sum the advantages of each type of participating sensors and compensate their deficiencies [8], [12], [13].

One of the methods proposed for LAM construction permits defining a LAM in a radial coordinate system through the fusion of readings from infrared and ultrasound sensors [14], [15]. This method, however presents considerable computational complexity and is hard to implement in practice. At the same time, the operation of a mobile robot in real time demands the simplification these processing algorithms. This is the motivation of this article, to develop an advanced Infrared Sensor Data Correction that presents lower calculation complexity and higher universality when compared to existing methods.

## 2 Existing Approach for Local Area Map Construction

There are a lot of methods for environment map construction for mobile robots. One of such method presents an environment in polar coordinates, and characterizes the location of obstacles in terms of angles and linear distances to them. For example, a LAM is constructed with a radius of 2.4m from the mobile robot position and it characterizes obstacle locations in an angle range from 0 to 180 degrees in one degree steps [14]. The data from the ultrasonic sensors and infrared scanner are input information for this method. The mobile robot "Walter", which included seven ultrasonic sensors and an infrared scanner was used for the experiments.

The ultrasound sensors are located on the perimeter of the mobile robot (Fig. 1a) and characterized by a 45 Hz frequency, 10 m maximum detection linear distance to the obstacles and a 20 degree aperture angle of the beam. This kind of sensors allows to measure a distance to the obstacles very precisely but does not permit a precise measurement of the angle coordinates to the obstacle because of poor directionality, frequent misreadings and specular reflections [4], [7]. Each of the causes mentioned above leads to the measurement of an incorrect linear distance to the obstacle that can generate incorrect behaviors of the mobile robot.

The infrared scanner used by Walter is a "Leuze electronic" RS-180. The visible field for this infrared scanner goes from a radius of 0.3 to 2 m. The infrared scanner divides 180 degrees of the environment into 36 sectors (Fig. 1b). The available angular range of the infrared sensors is 5 degrees. The accuracy of the infrared scanner depends on different external factors and the types of obstacle surfaces where scanner beam is reflected [16]. The error in the determination of the linear distance to the obstacle by the infrared scanner is larger than using ultrasound sensors. Consequently, the objective of fusing ultrasound and infrared readings in the algorithm for LAM construction is the determination of linear and angle distances to the obstacles more accurately.

There are three main stages for LAM construction of mobile robot environment according to the existing method [14]:

1. LAM construction between ultrasound sensors 0, 1, 2 (Fig. 2a);
2. LAM construction between ultrasound sensors 0, 6 and 2, 3 (Fig. 2b);
3. LAM construction between ultrasound sensors 3, 4 and 5, 6 (Fig. 2c).

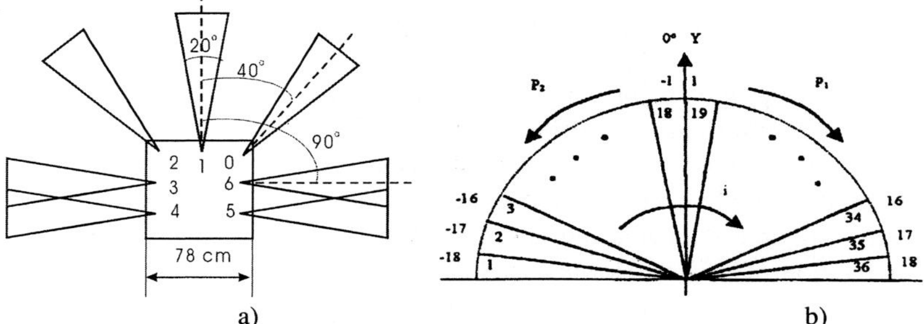


**Fig. 1.** Positions of (a) ultrasound sensors and (b) infrared sensors

Let us consider the process of LAM construction in stage 1 (Fig. 2). U(i) shows distance to the obstacle perceived by ultrasound sonar *i*, IR(p) shows the distance to the obstacle, perceived by the *-sector* of the infrared scanner. The angle direction of the infrared scanner is chosen in the middle of the sector. We now consider the case of the construction of the LAM between ultrasound sonars 1 and 0. The same approach is used for the construction of the LAM between sonars 1 and 2. The field of view of zero sonar cover 6...9 sectors of infrared scanner, and the field of view of first sonar cover -2…2 sectors of infrared scanner accordingly.

For the construction of the LAM in stage 1 it is necessary to execute 4 basic steps:

(i) to determine the infrared scanner sector covered by each ultrasonic sonar with minimum difference between the linear distance readings to the obstacle:

$$k_1 = \min_p \left| U(1) - IR(p) \right|, \quad p = \overline{-2...2}; \tag{1}$$

$$k_2 = \min_p \left| U(0) - IR(p) \right|, \quad p = \overline{6...9}. \tag{2}$$

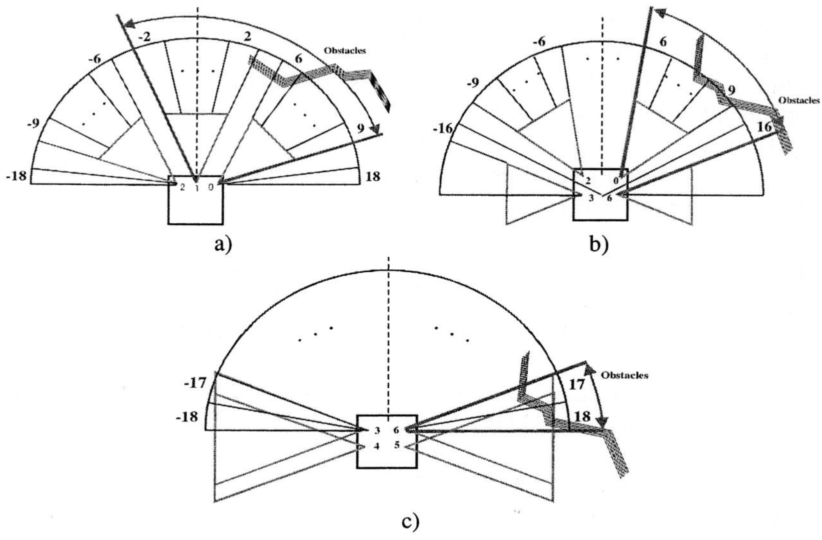


**Fig. 2.** Three steps of Robot map construction

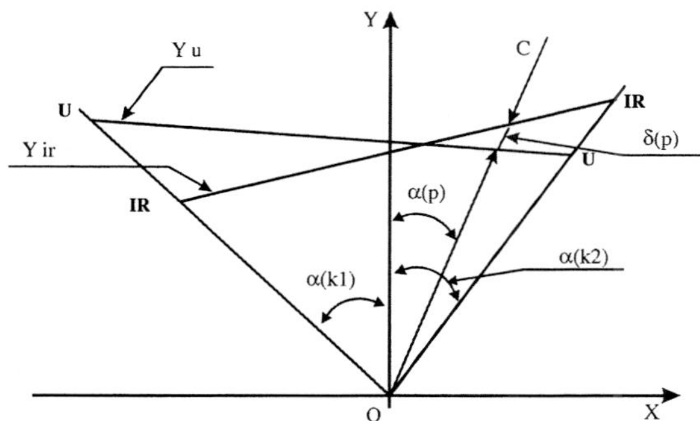


**Fig. 3**. Geometrical interpretation of local area map construction

Then sectors $k_1$ and $k_2$ uniquely determine the angle to the obstacle $\alpha(k_1)$ and $\alpha(k_2)$ (Fig. 3).

(ii) to provide an indication of the readings of infrared and ultrasound sensors according to directions $\alpha(k_1)$ and $\alpha(k_2)$ (points U and IR on lines $k_1$ and $k_2$ of figure 3). To build straight lines *Yu* and *Yir* between two points of infrared sectors and ultrasound sonar following directions $k_1$ and $k_2$:

$$Yu = f(Xu); \tag{3}$$

$$Yir = f(Xir); \tag{4}$$

(iii) to determine the coordinates of the points for each $p$ sector of the infrared scanner, for which $=[k_1...k_2]$, Such coordinates lie on the intersection of lines Yu and Yir with line OC characterizing the angular direction of the infrared sectors. After this one the distances between definite points are determined.

$$\delta(p) = b\sqrt{(X_u(p) - X_{ir}(p))^2 + (Y_u(p) - Y_{ir}(p))^2}\,,\; p = \overline{k1...k2}; \tag{5}$$

$$b = \begin{cases} 1, & if\ \sqrt{X_{ir}^2(p) + X_u^2(p)} < \sqrt{X_u^2(p) + X_{ir}^2(p)} \\ -1, & else \end{cases},\; p = \overline{k1...k2}. \tag{6}$$

(iv) to construct the LAM between ultrasonic sensors 0 and 1 by correcting the infrared scanner readings through value δ:

$$MAP1(p) = IR(p) + \delta(p), \quad p = \overline{k1...k2}. \tag{7}$$

If the ultrasonic sensor readings are more than 2.4m, they do not provide data corrections for the infrared scanner. As a result we receive a LAM between sensors 0 and 1. The same approach is used for LAM construction between sensors 1 and 2.

In the second stage, the LAM for mobile robot is constructed in the sector range between 6…16 and –6...-16 of the infrared scanner (Fig. 2) and divided on two steps:

(i) The distance δ is calculated only for direction *k2*, which displays the minimum difference between readings from ultrasound sensor 0 and readings from infrared sensors 6...9.

$$\delta(p)=b\sqrt{(X_u(p)-X_{ir}(p))^2+(Y_u(p)-Y_{ir}(p))^2},\ p=k2; \tag{8}$$

$$b=\begin{cases}1, & if\ \sqrt{X_{ir}^2(p)+X_u^2(p)}<\sqrt{X_u^2(p)+X_{ir}^2(p)} \\ -1, & else\end{cases},\ p=k2. \tag{9}$$

(ii) If the readings of ultrasound sensor 0 are larger than 2.4m then the correction of the infrared scanner values is not carried out. Otherwise the correction is performed for each sector of the infrared scanner covered by the ultrasound sensor.

$$\begin{cases}MAP1(p)=IR(p)+\delta(p), & p=\overline{k2..16},\quad if\ [IR(p)andU(p)]<2.4meter \\ MAP1(p)=IR(p), & p=\overline{k2..16},\quad else\end{cases} \tag{10}$$

The LAM between sectors 6...16 of the infrared scanner is constructed similar.

As a third stage, the LAM for the mobile robot is constructed in the sector range between 17…18 and –17…-18 of the infrared scanner (Fig. 2). For this stage it is necessary to execute the following steps:

(i) to fill sectors 17 and –17 using readings from sectors 6 and 3 of the ultrasound sensors without corrections

$$MAP1(17) = IR(17); \tag{11}$$

(ii) to calculate the average values of ultrasonic sensors 6, 5 and 3, 4 in sectors 18 and -18 of LAM

$$MAP1(18)=\frac{U(5)+U(6)}{2}. \tag{12}$$

After execution of the three stages described above it is possible to obtain a LAM divided into 36 sectors, which characterizes the distances to the obstacles. It is necessary to execute additional transformations in order to produce a more detailed LAM for the mobile robot and which consists of 180 sectors. These steps are:

1. to fill all the angles of sectors 18 and -18 one degree steps by linear readings perceived in these sectors:

$$\begin{cases}MAP(i)=MAP1(1), & for\quad i=\overline{0^\circ..5^\circ}; \\ MAP(i)=MAP1(36), & for\quad i=\overline{175^\circ..180^\circ};\end{cases} \tag{13}$$

2. to provide received points linked by the straight lines and calculate distances to such lines in one degree steps between sectors - 17 and 17 of the infrared scanner

$$MAP(i)=LINE[MAP1(p),MAP1(p+1)],\quad for\quad i\in[p,p+1],\quad p\in\overline{2..35}. \tag{14}$$

3. To carry out a bounding process of the LAM in a radius of 2.4 m

$$\begin{cases}MAP(i)=MAP(i), & if\quad MAP(i)<2.4\,meter,\quad i=\overline{1..180}; \\ MAP(i)=2.4\,meter, & if\quad MAP(i)\geq 2.4\,meter,\quad i=\overline{1..180}.\end{cases} \tag{15}$$

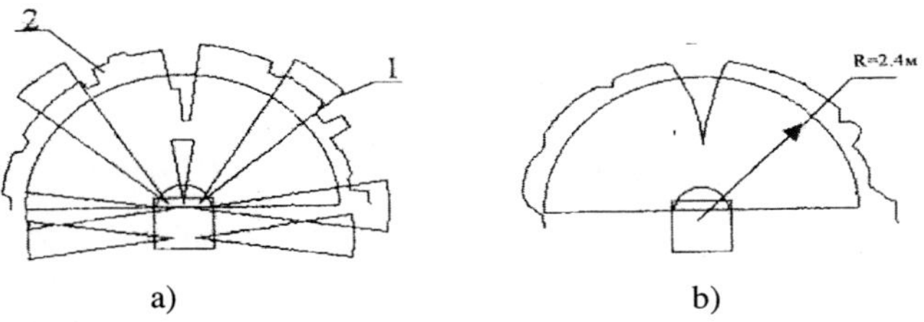


**Fig. 4.** Defining of the local area map: ). input data from ultrasound (1) and infrared (2) sensors; b). local map

As a result of these actions we obtain a LAM for the mobile robot in a range from 0 to 180 degrees in one degree steps (Fig. 4).

Thus, this approach to LAM construction is characterized by the complexity of the algorithm's implementation, taking into account the set of stages necessary. In addition, the sensors have fixed locations and therefore the software also has fixed properties and will not be able to construct LAMs correctly if the hardware configuration changes. The use of infrared scanner readings in sectors 18 and –18 are not effective and the determination of the distance to the obstacles by linearization is not very accurate. In this paper we propose an advanced approach that avoids these disadvantages for LAM mobile robot construction.

## 3 Advanced Approach to Infrared Sensor Data Correction for Local Area Map Construction

The first stage from Section II above was taken as a basis for the proposed Infrared Sensor Data Correction (ISDC) method for LAM construction. However the method includes one stage, which contains 4 steps for execution. As input information for the ISDC method we use the readings from infrared and ultrasonic sensors (Fig. 5). The result of the proposed method is the LAM constructed in polar coordinates from 0 to 360 degrees in one degree steps depending on the number of sensors located on a mobile robot.

Let us consider the ISDC method on the "Walter" mobile robot. It comprises the following steps:

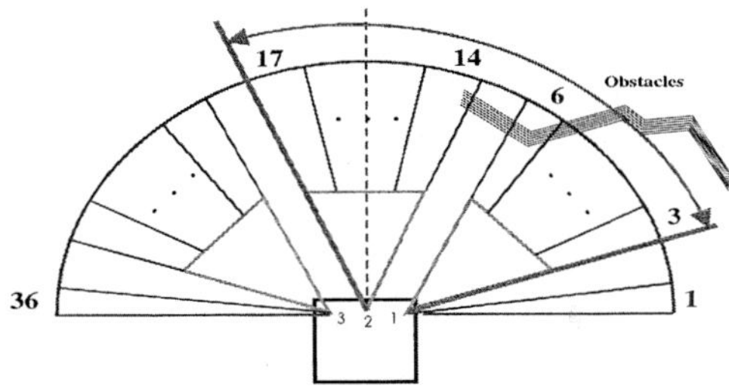


**Fig. 5**. Representation of Infrared Sensor Data Correction method

1. to determinate the sector of the infrared scanner covered by each ultrasonic sensor with minimum difference between the linear distance readings to the obstacle:

$$k_i = \min_p |U(i) - IR(p)|, \quad p \in i, \quad i = \overline{1..Size(U)}, \tag{16}$$

where $i$ – number of ultrasound sensors available to the mobile robot, p –sector of the infrared scanner;

2. to obtain the readings of the infrared and ultrasonic sensors in directions $\alpha(k_i)$ and $\alpha(k_{i+1})$ (points $U$ and $IR$ on the lines $k_i$ and $k_{i+1}$ of Fig. 6). To build straight lines $Yu$ and $Yir$ between two points of the infrared scanner and ultrasonic sensor according to directions $k_1$ and $k_2$

$$Yu = f(Xu); \tag{17}$$

$$Yir = f(Xir), \tag{18}$$

where Xir, Yir, Xus, Yus are the cartesian coordinates of the points of the infrared sectors and ultrasound sonar in directions $k_i$ and $k_{i+1}$ according to Fig. 6;

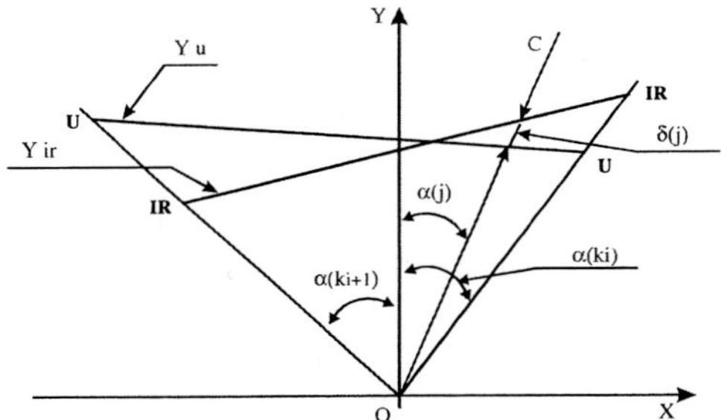


**Fig. 6.** Geometrical Interpretation of Local Area Map Construction according to ISDC Method

3. to determine the coordinates of the points for each sector $j$ of the infrared scanner where $j=[k_i...k_{i+1}]$. Such coordinates lie on the intersections of lines $Yu$ and $Yir$ with line OC that characterizes an angle direction of the infrared sectors in one degree steps. The calculated correction factor δ between defined points raises interpolation intervals between infrared sensor readings and provides a more detailed LAM of the mobile robot

$$\delta(j) = b\sqrt{(X_u(j) - X_{ir}(j))^2 + (Y_u(j) - Y_{ir}(j))^2}, \ j = \overline{k_i...k_{i+1}}, \ step = 1; \tag{19}$$

$$b = \begin{cases} 1, & if \ \sqrt{X_{ir}^2(j) + X_u^2(j)} < \sqrt{X_u^2(j) + X_{ir}^2(j)} \\ -1, & else \end{cases}, \ j = \overline{k_i...k_{i+1}}, \ step = 1. \tag{20}$$

4. to build a LAM in a range between 0 and 180 degrees. The main reason for this stage is to add correction value δ to infrared scanner readings $p$ between $k_1$ and $k_{Size(U)}$. Outside this range, infrared scanner readings should not be corrected

$$MAP(j) = \begin{cases} IR(p),\ j \in p,\ if\ \ j < k_1\ OR\ j > k_{Size(U)},\ p = \overline{1...Size(IR)} \\ IR(p) + \delta(j),\ p = \overline{k_i...k_{i+1}},\ i = \overline{1...(Size(U)-1)}, else \end{cases},\ j = \overline{0...180}. \quad (21)$$

5. to bound LAM to a certain radius, depending on the sensor parameters, that is the maximum distance an obstacle can be detected. For the mobile robot "Walter" the LAM is constructed with a radius of 2.4m

$$\begin{cases} MAP(j) = MAP(j), & if \quad MAP(j) < 2.4\ meter, \quad j = \overline{1...180}; \\ MAP(j) = 2.4\ meter, & if \quad MAP(j) \geq 2.4\ meter, \quad j = \overline{1...180}. \end{cases} \quad (22)$$

# 4 Simulation Results

The proposed ISDC method was simulated using software routines designed in Matlab 6.0 [17]. During simulation we considered a configuration of the mobile robot using an infrared scanner with 36 sectors and 5 ultrasonic sensors directed at points with 0, 50, 90, 130 and 180 degrees. The angle error of the infrared scanner is 5 degree per sector and 30 cm in the linear distances to the obstacles. The angle error of each ultrasonic sensor is 20 degrees and 10 cm into the linear distance to the obstacles. Each pixel is in accordance to the 1 cm on into the linear distance. All errors were specified as random uniformly distributed numbers.

The operating environment of the mobile robot was presented as a binary matrix (Fig. 7). The LAM constructed was presented in radial coordinates on Fig. 9a. Such LAM was constructed using the infrared sensor readings shown on Fig. 8a and the ultrasonic sensors readings shown on Fig. 8b. The relative errors of linear distances determination to the obstacles are presented on Fig. 9b. The maximal error of the linear distances determination to the obstacles by the offered method is 46.5% while prototype is 133.8%.

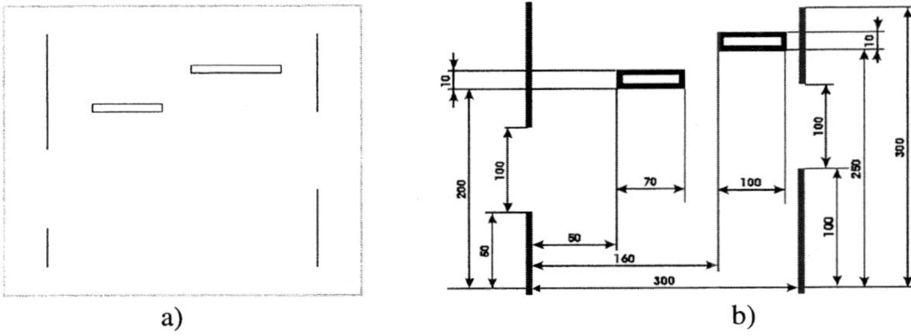


**Fig. 7.** Modeling the operating environment of mobile robot: ) presenting the operating environment as binary matrix; b) distance specifications of the operating environment

The simulation results have shown that the accuracy of the local area map thus constructed is 80% higher than the accuracy of the infrared scanner depending on the distance to the obstacles. It is also 20 % higher than the ultrasound sensors in terms of the angle to the obstacle. The algorithmic complexity of advanced method is 0.16 sec, while the time of LAM construction by the prototype is 0.22 sec, that is 42.1% and 57.9% of the total time for LAM construction by both approaches. Such results were obtained using the profiler techniques of designed routines in Matlab 6.0 without drawing of the diagrams on the PC with processor AMD Duron 700 MHz.

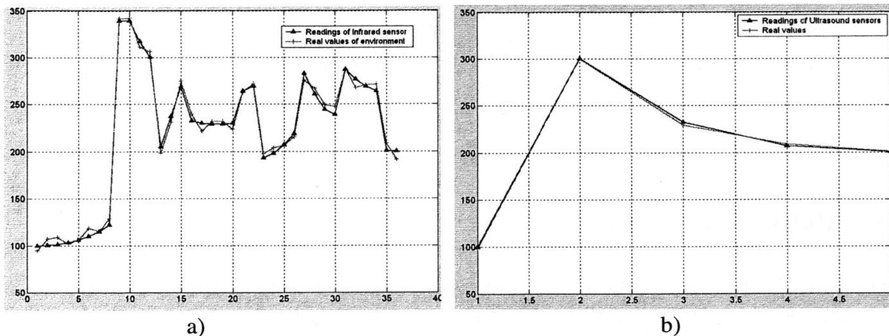


**Fig. 8.** Modeling of sensor readings of mobile robot: ) infrared sensor; b) ultrasound sensors.

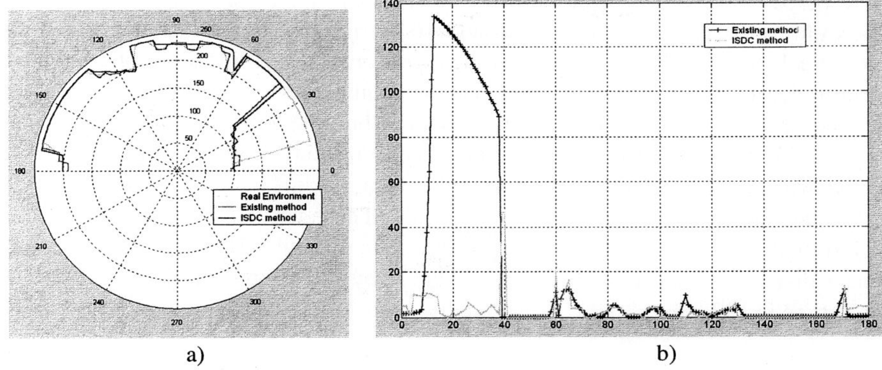


**Fig. 9.** Simulation results of ISDC method: a) constructed environment in polar coordinates; b) relative errors of constructed environment

# 5 Conclusions

In this paper we considered sensor fusion techniques for local area map construction in the control of mobile robot behavior. The method proposed, that is Infrared Sensor Data Correction, presents less computational complexity than existing methods, and is more universal in its application. In addition it has no strong dependence on the hardware of the mobile robot and therefore it can be easily updated to changing configurations of the mobile robot.

**Acknowledgements**

The authors are grateful for the support of the NATO Scientific Affairs Division within the International Project PST.CLG.978744, "Using Sensor Fusion and Neural Network Techniques for Robot Control".

## References

1. Popov E.P., Oismennyj G.V., The robotics bases, M: "High school", 1990, pp. 224
2. Dorst L., An Introduction to Robotics for the computer sciences, University of Amsterdam, 1993, pp.78
3. Durrant-Whyte H. F., Integration, Coordination and Control of Multi-sensor Robot Systems, Kluwer, Boston, MA, 1988.
4. Joris van Dam, Environment Modeling for Mobile Robots: Neural Learning for Sensor Fusion, Amsterdam: University van Amsterdam – Met lit. opg., 1998, pp.225
5. Barraquand J., Langlois B., Latombe J.C., Numerical potential field techniques for robot path planning, Report No. STAN CS 89 1285, Dept. of Computer Science, Stanford University, 1989
6. Besierre P., Dedieu E., Mazer E., Representing robot/environment interactions using probabilities: the beam in the beam experiment, From Perception to Action Conference, IEEE computer society press, Sept.1994
7. Borenstein J., Koren Y., Real-time obstacle avoidance for fast mobile robots, IEEE Transactions on Systems, Man, and Cybernetics, Vol. 19, No. 5, Sept./Oct. 1989, pp. 1179-1187
8. Mongi A. Abidi, Rafael C. Gonzalez, Data fusion in robotics and machine intelligence, Academic Press, Inc., 1992, pp.546.
9. Richard J. Duro, Jose Santos, Manuel Graña, Biologically inspired robot behavior engineering, Physica-Verlag, 2003, pp. 438
10. Poncela, E.J. Perez, A. Bandera, C. Urdiales, F. Sandoval, Efficient integration of metric and topological maps for directed exploration of unknown environments, Robotics and Autonomous Systems, No. 41 (2002), pp. 21–39
11. H. Maaref, C. Barret, Sensor-based navigation of a mobile robot in an indoor environment, Robotics and Autonomous Systems, No. 38 (2002) 1–18
12. Brooks R., Iyengar S., "Multi-sensor fusion: fundamentals and applications with software". Prentice-Hall PTR, 1998, 416p
13. J.L. Crowly, Y.Demazeau, Principles and techniques for sensor data fusion, Signal Processing, No. 32, 1993, pp. 5-27.
14. Golovko V.A., Neurointelligence: theory and application, BPI, Brest, 1999, 228 p.
15. Flynn A.M., Combining sonar and infrared sensors for mobile robot navigation, International journal of robotic research, Vol. 7, No. 6, 1988
16. G. Benet, F. Blanes, J.E. Simó, P. Pérez, Using infrared sensors for distance measurement in mobile robots, Robotics and Autonomous Systems, No. 40 (2002), pp. 255–266
17. Stephen J. Chapman, MATLAB Programming for Engineers, 2nd Edition, Brooks/Cole Publishing Company, 2002

# An Improved Compound Gradient Vector Based Neural Network On-Line Training Algorithm

Zaiping Chen[1,2], Chao Dong[1], Qiuqian Zhou[1], and Shujun Zhang[1]

[1] The Department of Automation Tianjin University of Technology, China
[2] Centre for Intelligent Systems and Complex Processes
Swinburne University of Technology, Australia
chenzaiping@yahoo.com.au

**Abstract.** An improved compound gradient vector based a fast convergent NN online training weight update scheme is proposed in this paper. The convergent analysis indicates that because the compound gradient vector is employed during the weight update, the convergent speed of the presented algorithm is faster than the back propagation (BP) algorithm. In this scheme an adaptive learning factor is introduced in which the global convergence is obtained, and the convergence procedure on plateau and flat bottom area can speed up. Some simulations have been conducted and the results demonstrate the satisfactory convergent performance and strong robustness are obtained using the improved compound gradient vector NN online learning scheme for real time control involving uncertainty parameter plant.

## 1 Introduction

In recent years, neural networks (NN) have attracted much attention for their potential to solve a number of difficult problems in various areas. These include areas such as dynamic modelling, pattern recognition and system control involving uncertainty parameters. The most common NN structure is the multiplayer feedforward NN, which is proved to be a universal approximator of non-linearity. Updating weights involve the minimization of a quadratic output error criterion. Normally the optimisation problem is usually handled using the BP algorithm in which the error evaluated at output layer is propagated back through the hidden layers. Several different BP algorithm improvement schemes have been presented in the literature [1] - [12]. The standard weight update formula of the BP algorithms can be written as below:

$$\Delta w(k) = \nabla_w E(k) + \alpha \Delta w(k-1) = -\eta \frac{\partial E(k)}{\partial w(k)} + \alpha \Delta w(k-1) \tag{1}$$

where $\nabla_w E(k)$ is the gradient of the cost function in weight space, $\eta$ is the so-called learning rate and $\alpha$ is the momentum factor. To speed up training and reduce convergence to local minima, several improving schemes have been investigated in [5],[8]-[10]. However most of these improvements are based on the use of heuristic factors to dynamically adapt the learning rate, which only leads to a slight convergence rate improvement [12]. A significant improvement is possible by using

P.W.H. Chung, C.J. Hinde, M. Ali (Eds.): IEA/AIE 2003, LNAI 2718, pp. 316–325, 2003.

various second order approaches such as Newton, conjugate gradient, or the Levenberg-Marquardt (LM) method [7],[10],[11]. The demand for memory to operate with large Jacobians and the necessity to invert large matrices are major disadvantages of the LM algorithm [12]. The rank of the matrix to be inverted is equal to the number of adjustable parameters in the system [12]. The large number of computations takes significant time and it is difficult to utilize these algorithms in real time control systems.

An improved, compound gradient vector based, fast convergent NN is proposed in this paper. This scheme overcomes the drawbacks of using heuristic factors and the large computation demands of other schemes. The convergent analysis indicates that because the compound gradient vector [13] is employed during the weight update, the convergent speed of the algorithm is faster than the standard BP algorithm. Further, the adaptive learning factor is introduced in which the global convergence is obtained and the convergence procedure on plateau regions can be speed up in this scheme. Some simulations have been conducted and the results demonstrate the satisfactory convergent performance and strong robustness obtained using the improved compound gradient vector NN online learning scheme, in real time control in a plant with uncertainty parameters.

## 2 The Compound Gradient Vector Based NN Online Training Algorithm

The choice of learning rate in the BP algorithm affects the performance of the weight update and thus the research about convergence of algorithm and learning rates has been seen as a hot spot. The standard BP weight updating formula (without momentum) can be rewritten as follow:

$$\Delta w(k) = -\eta \frac{\partial E(k)}{\partial w(k)} = \eta(-\frac{\partial E(k)}{\partial w(k)}) \tag{2}$$

The Eq. (2) can be written as following formation:

$$Y(k) = \eta U(k) \tag{3}$$

or

$$\frac{Y(k)}{U(k)} = \eta = D(k) \tag{4}$$

where

$$Y(k) = \Delta w(k) \tag{5}$$

$$U(k) = -\frac{\partial E(k)}{\partial w(k)} \tag{6}$$

If Eq. (4) is considered as the system description, $Y(k)$ and $U(k)$ represent the output and input of the system respectively, and $D(k)$ or $\eta$ is the system model the control strategy is involved with. Obviously, $D(k)$ has significant effects on the response under the system input $U(k)$. Therefore, from the view of system theory, it is the reason why the learning rate $\eta$ in the weight updating formula needs to be paid such attention.

Taking $\Delta w$ and $-\partial E/\partial w$ to be the output and input of the system respectively, the s-domain transfer function D(s) that consists of proportional, integral and differential components can be given as follow:

$$D(s)=k_p(1+\frac{k_i}{s}+\frac{k_d s}{1+\frac{k_d s}{N}}) \tag{7}$$

where $\frac{1}{1+\frac{k_d s}{N}}$ is a low-pass filter, which limits noise gain at high frequencies.

For the equivalent transform between the $z$-domain $D(z)$ and s-domain $D(s)$, the Tustin bilinear transform is used in $D(s)$ as below:

$$D(z)=k_p-\frac{a_1(z^{-1}+1)}{z^{-1}-1}-\frac{b_1(z^{-1}-1)}{b_2 z^{-1}+1} \tag{8}$$

where $a_1=\frac{1}{2}k_p k_i T$ , $b_1=\frac{2k_p k_d}{T(1+\frac{2k_d}{NT})}$, $b_2=\frac{1-\frac{2k_d}{NT}}{1+\frac{2k_d}{NT}}$

$$\frac{Y(z)}{U(z)}=k_p-\frac{a_1(z^{-1}+1)}{z^{-1}-1}-\frac{b_1(z^{-1}-1)}{b_2 z^{-1}+1} \tag{9}$$

$$Y(z)=\eta_1 U(z)+\eta_2 z^{-1}U(z)+\eta_3 z^{-2}U(z)+\alpha_1 z^{-1}Y(z)+\alpha_2 z^{-2}Y(z) \tag{10}$$

where $\eta_1=a_1+b_1+k_p$, $\eta_2=-k_p+k_p b_2+a_1+a_1 b_2-2b_1$, $\eta_3=a_1 b_2+b_1-k_p b_2$, $\alpha_1=1-b_2$, $\alpha_2=b_2$. the factor of $z^{-1}$ in the $z$-domain implies that the time-domain signal is delayed by one sample interval while the expression $z^{-2}$ indicates a delay of two cycles.

In Eq. (10) , the $z$-domain model can be converted into time-based equation as the follow:

$$Y(k)=-\eta_1 U(k)-\eta_2 U(k-1)-\eta_3 U(k-2)+\alpha_1 Y(k-1)+\alpha_2 Y(k-2) \tag{11}$$

Considering $Y(k)=\Delta w(k)$ and $U(k)=-(\partial E/\partial w)(k)$, equation (11) can be written as:

$$\Delta w(k)=\eta_1\frac{\partial E}{\partial w}(k)+\alpha_1\Delta w(k-1)-\eta_2\frac{\partial E}{\partial w}(k-1)+\alpha_2\Delta w(k-2)-\eta_3\frac{\partial E}{\partial w}(k-2) \tag{12}$$

The first two items on the right side of Eq. (12) are the weight updating formula with the momentum item of BP algorithm. The 3rd and 4th items are one order delay gradient training component. The last item in the Eq. (12) is the second order delay gradient training component without momentum item.

The BP algorithm approximates a local minimum of E and always converges when $\eta$ is chosen to meet the relation $\sup\|Q(w)\|\le\eta^{-1}<\infty$ in some bounded region where the relation $E(\boldsymbol{w}) \leq E(\boldsymbol{w}_0)$ holds[11]; $Q(w)$ denotes the Hessian matrix of $E$ with respect to the weight vector $\boldsymbol{w}$, and $\boldsymbol{w}_0$ denotes the initial weight vector. The behaviour of $E$ in the neighbourhood of a local minimum is determined by the eigensystem of the matrix $Q$. In the neural network implementation, the storage and computational requirements of the approximated Hessian for FNNs with several hundred weights make its use impractical. Thus, the learning rate is usually chosen according to the relation $0< \eta <1$ in such a way that successive steps in weight space do not overshoot the minimum of the error surface [3].

Using this restraining conditions, the training rates in this scheme can be derived. Assuming the sample interval $T$=0.01s and $k_d=T/2$, if the relation $200<k_i<400$ and $k_p<0.25$ are chosen, the condition mentioned above can be satisfied. It is important that the sample interval $T$ is associated with the choice of training rates so that this algorithm is adapted to its application to practical computer based control systems.

## 3 Analysis of the Weight Updating Convergent Speed

In the gradient descent search method, the relationship between the two successive step gradients is given as follows [14]:

$$[-\nabla E(w_k)]\cdot[-\nabla E(w_{k-1})]=0 \tag{13}$$

When the $k$th and ($k$-1)th time searches are carried out, $w_k$ and $w_{k-1}$ are the $k$th and ($k$-1)th step weight vectors. Eq. (13) shows that $\nabla E(w_k)$ is always orthogonal to $\nabla E(w_{k-1})$. Obviously, the search path is always tortuous with right angles in the conventional gradient descent technique and as a result the convergent speed is affected. From the Eq. (12), the relation can be rewritten as below:

$$\Delta w(k) = -\eta\frac{\partial \tilde{E}}{\partial w}(k) + \alpha_1 \Delta w(k-1) + \alpha_2 \Delta w(k-2) \tag{14}$$

Where

$$\eta\frac{\partial \tilde{E}}{\partial w} = \eta_1 \frac{\partial E}{\partial w}(k) + \eta_2 \frac{\partial E}{\partial w}(k-1) + \eta_3 \frac{\partial E}{\partial w}(k-2) \tag{15}$$

In Eq. (15), the $\eta(\partial\tilde{E}/\partial w)$ term can be considered as the compound effects of the $\eta_1(\partial E/\partial w)(k)$ , $\eta_2(\partial E/\partial w)(k-1)$ and $\eta_3(\partial E/\partial w)(k-2)$ three successive gradient vectors, and the $\eta(\partial\tilde{E}/\partial w)$ can be called a compound gradient vector. Considering the relationship between the successive step gradients, the compound gradient vector in the presented scheme is given in Fig.1.

Since the orthogonal directions between each successive step gradients, the gradient vectors $\eta_1(\partial E/\partial w)(k)$ and $\eta_2(\partial E/\partial w)(k-1)$ , and vectors $\eta_2(\partial E/\partial w)(k-1)$ and $\eta_3(\partial E/\partial w)(k-2)$ respectively are vertical to each other.

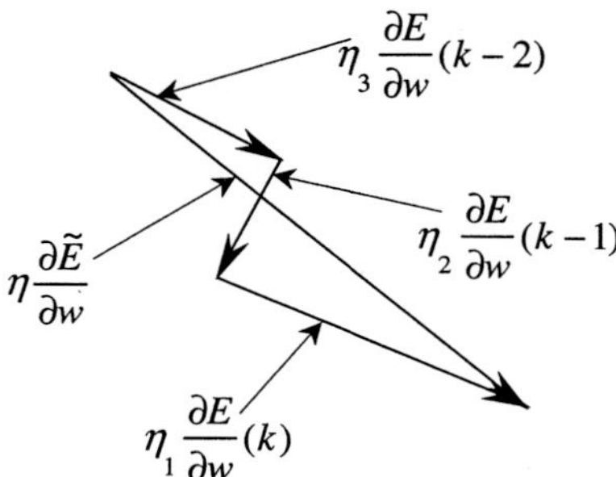


**Fig. 1.** Diagram of compound gradient vector

Fig. 1 shows that, because the compound gradient $\eta\partial\tilde{E}/\partial w$ is composed of the three vectors and the known information $(\partial E/\partial w)(k-1)$, $(\partial E/\partial w)(k-2)$ used in the update processes, it will result in faster descent speed compared to the standard BP algorithm. Therefore the convergence rate in the scheme could outperform that of standard BP algorithm.

## 4 Improved Compound Gradient Vector Algorithm (ICGVA)

Considering the error function is defined by:

$$E = \frac{1}{2}\sum(O_i - O_{di})^2 \tag{16}$$

where the outputs of neural networks are denoted by $O_i$ and the desired outputs are denoted by $O_{di}$. The gradient of error function in weight space $\frac{\partial E}{\partial W}$ can be defined by $\nabla_w E$.

From the analysis above, it can be seen that the speed of weight update of CGV algorithm based on the compound gradient vector could be superior to the standard BP algorithm speed. However the global convergence of the CGV algorithm can't be obtained during the procedures of the weight update. Thus it is necessary that the global convergence weight update algorithm should be investigated, in order to meet the practical control requirement for neural networks.

The weight update algorithm based on the compound gradient vector can be rewritten as:

$$\Delta w(k) = -\eta_1\frac{\partial E}{\partial w}(k) + \alpha_1\Delta w(k-1) - \eta_2\frac{\partial E}{\partial w}(k-1) + \alpha_2\Delta w(k-2) - \eta_3\frac{\partial E}{\partial w}(k-2) \tag{17}$$

Eq. (17) can be written as:

$$\Delta w(k) = -\eta\frac{\partial \tilde{E}}{\partial w}(k) + \alpha_1\Delta w(k-1) + \alpha_2\Delta w(k-2) \tag{18}$$

where

$$\eta\frac{\partial\tilde{E}}{\partial w}=\eta_1\frac{\partial E}{\partial w}(k)+\eta_2\frac{\partial E}{\partial w}(k-1)+\eta_3\frac{\partial E}{\partial w}(k-2) \tag{19}$$

Eq. (19) we rewrite

$$\eta\frac{\partial\tilde{E}}{\partial w}=\breve{\eta}(\breve{\eta}_1\frac{\partial E}{\partial w}(k)+\breve{\eta}_2\frac{\partial E}{\partial w}(k-1)+\breve{\eta}_3\frac{\partial E}{\partial w}(k-2)) \tag{20}$$

Here we choose

$$\breve{\eta}=\overline{\eta}\frac{E_k}{\left\|\nabla_w E_k\right\|^2} \tag{21}$$

as adaptive learning factor and Eq. (20) becomes

$$\breve{\eta}\frac{\partial\hat{E}}{\partial w}=\overline{\eta}\frac{E_k}{\left\|\nabla_w E_k\right\|^2}(\breve{\eta}_1\frac{\partial E}{\partial w}(k)+\breve{\eta}_2\frac{\partial E}{\partial w}(k-1)+\breve{\eta}_3\frac{\partial E}{\partial w}(k-2)) \tag{22}$$

Eq. (22) is called the Improved Compound Gradient Vector Algorithm (ICGVA).

From BP or Compound Gradient Vector Algorithm, it can be seen that when the updating weight procedures are trap as local mina or plateaus, $\nabla_w E\to 0$ will result in failure of the learning procedure. If the adaptive learning factor is introduced in the Improved Compound Gradient Vector Algorithm, $\breve{\eta}=\overline{\eta}E_k/\left\|\nabla_w E_k\right\|^2$ will not tend to zero when $\nabla_w E\to 0$. The learning rate $\breve{\eta}$ will automatically adjust the weight value update strength, according to the error function $E$ and $\nabla_w E$, the gradient of the error function in weight space, thus it can assure that updating weight procedures can't trap the system in a local minima or plateau area, and global convergence is obtained.

## 5 Simulation Results

Comparisons of proposed Improved Compound Gradient Vector Algorithm, CGV algorithm and standard BP algorithm are obtained by simulation. The simulation model of the plant is given as follow:

$$y_k=1.9849y_{k-1}-0.974y_{k-2}+0.502u_k+0.0005u_{k-1}-0.0487u_{k-2} \tag{23}$$

When the plant model parameter 1.9849 is changed to 1.968 and the poles of the controlled plant are changed from (-0.1001+*i*0.9526, -0.1001-*i*0.9526) to (–0.1001+*i*8.384, -0.1001- *i*8.384). Under the variation of parameters, the simulations with ICGVA, CGVA and BP algorithm are given in Fig.2-Fig.13 respectively.

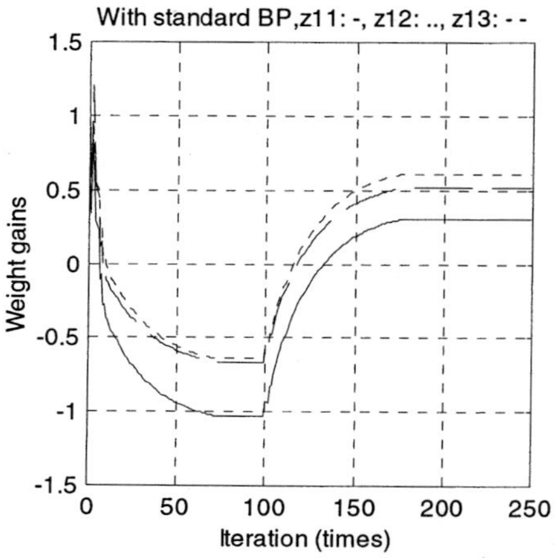


Fig.2. Some output layer weight learning processes with standard BP algorithm

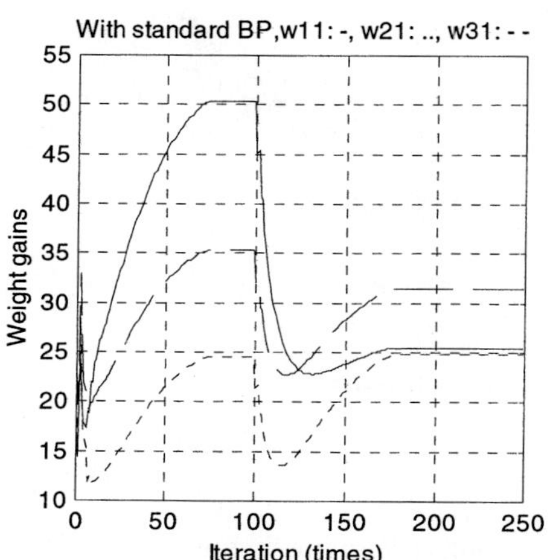


Fig.3. Some hidden layer weight learning processes with standard BP algorithm

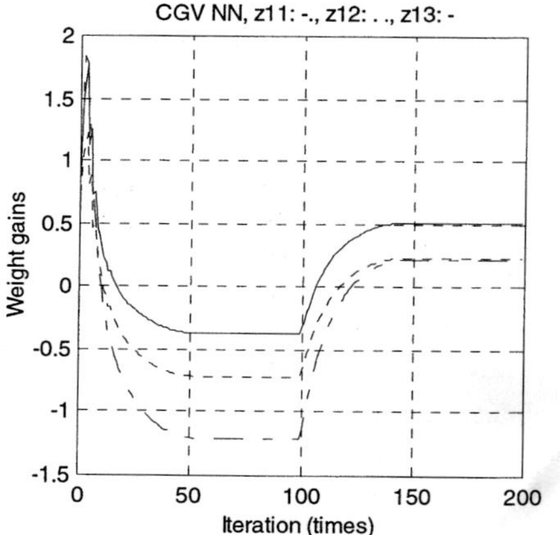


Fig.4. Some output layer weight learning processes with compound gradient vector algorithm

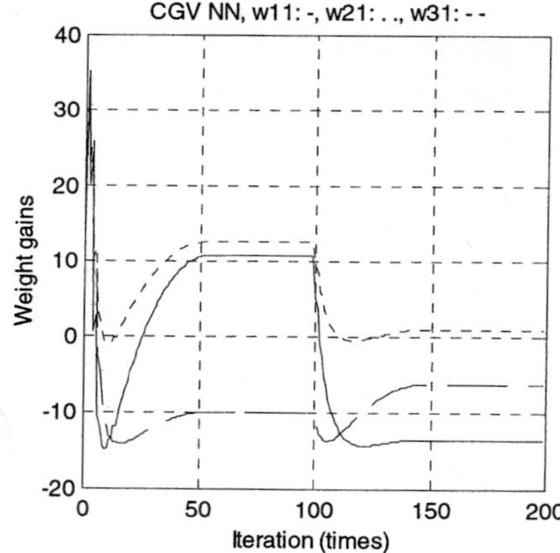


Fig.5. Some hidden layer weight learning processes with compound gradient vector algorithm

Due to the large range changes of plant pole positions, the learning of the standard BP algorithm is not yet complete until 180th iteration about 80 time iterations lasted, which can be seen in Fig.2 and Fig.3. The BP algorithm learning rate utilized in the simulation is as $\eta$=0.8. The online learning procedures of CGV NN algorithm are shown in Fig. 4 and Fig. 5. The updating weight procedures of ICGV NN algorithm are shown in Fig. 6 and Fig. 7. The contrasts of ICGV, CGV algorithm and standard BP algorithm, the convergence speed of ICGV NN online learning algorithm is much faster than BP algorithm, and the learning procedures can be finished only lasting about 10 time iterations using ICGV NN algorithm.

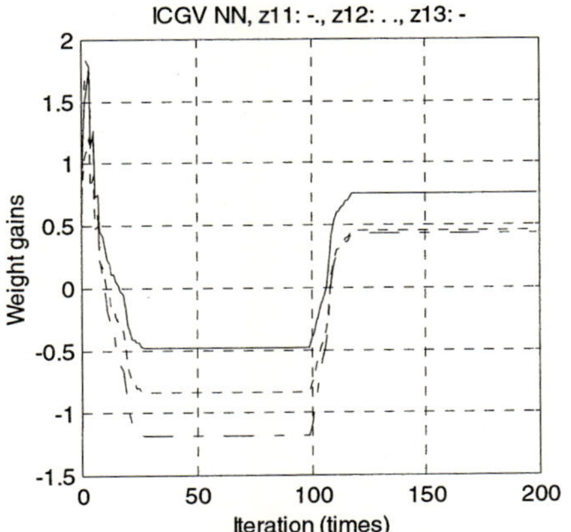


**Fig.6.** Some output layer weight learning processes with improved compound gradient vector algorithm

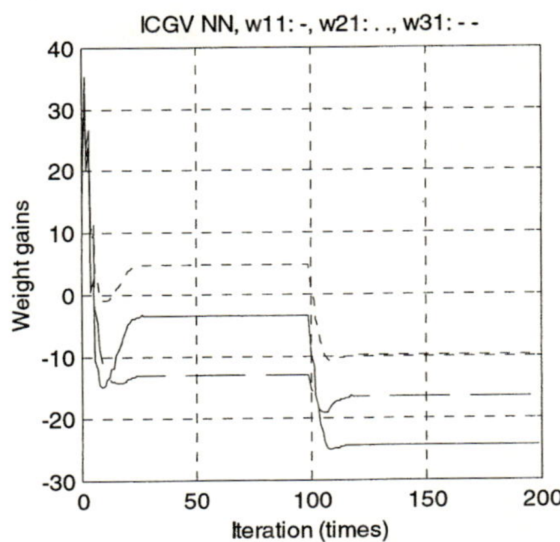


**Fig.7.** Some hidden layer weight learning processes with improved compound gradient vector algorithm

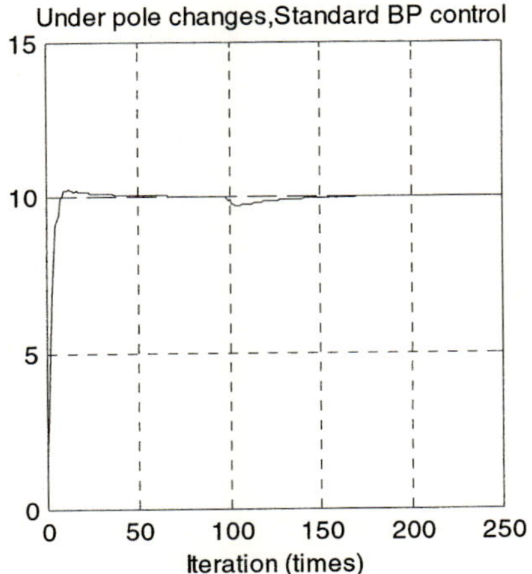


**Fig.8.** The system response with standard BP algorithm under pole changes

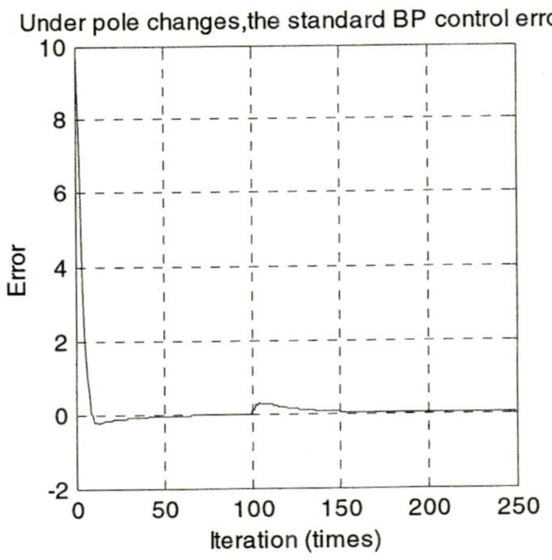


**Fig.9.** The system error with standard BP algorithm under pole changes

The outputs and the errors of systems with ICGV, CGV and standard BP algorithm are shown in Fig.8 - Fig.13 respectively. From these simulation results, it can be seen that very good dynamic behaviours are obtained by utilizing presented ICGV algorithm under the variations of parameter._

The parameters utilized in the compound gradient vector algorithm are as $T$=0.01, $K_i$=300, $K_d$ =0.005, initial value of $K_p$=0.2, $\beta_1$=0.01$K_p$, $\beta_2$=0.6. Thus, the initial values of learning rate and momentum item in the simulations [15] are $\eta_1$=0.6818, $\eta_2$=0.2, $\eta_3$=0.3, $\alpha_1$=0.01 and $\alpha_2$=0.0198 respectively.

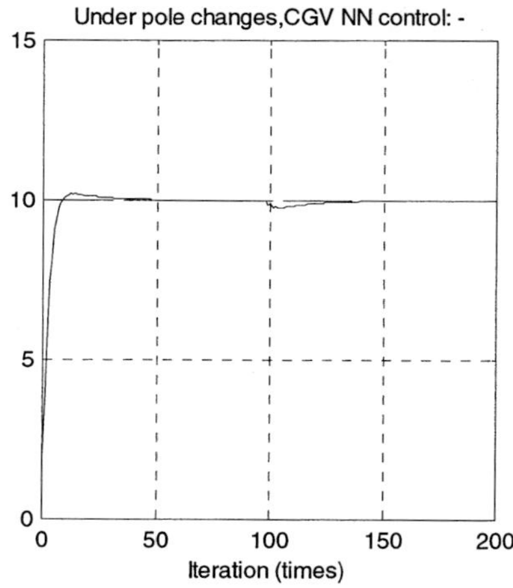


Fig.10. The system response with CGV algorithm under pole changes

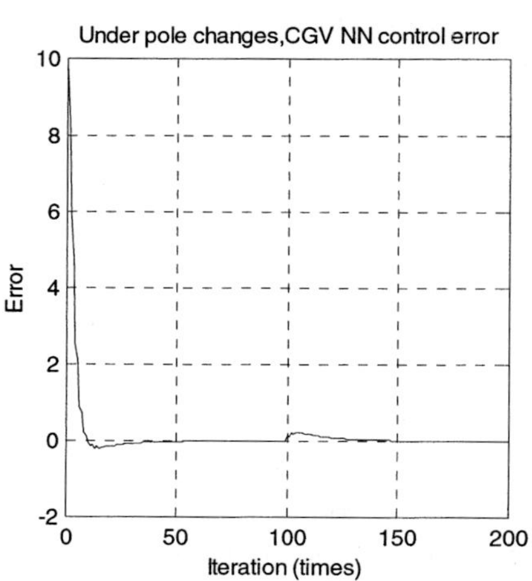


Fig.11. The system error with CGV algorithm under pole changes

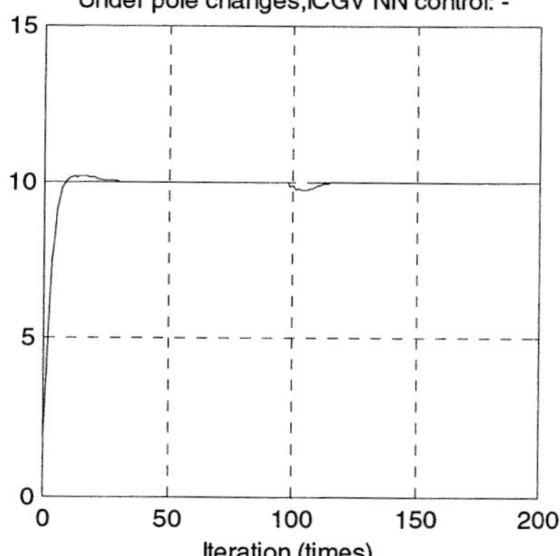


Fig.12. The system simulation with ICGV algorithm under pole changes

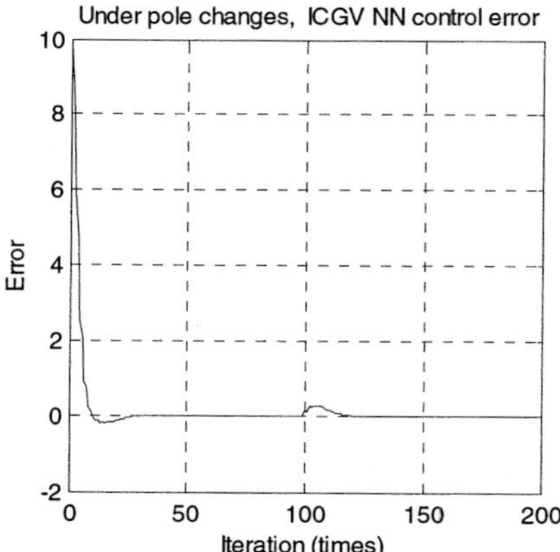


Fig.13. The system error with ICGV algorithm under pole changes

## 6 Conclusions

In this paper, an ICGVA has been proposed. A convergent analysis of the algorithm has been carried out and the results indicate that the convergent speed of presented ICGV algorithm is much faster than that of the standard BP algorithm, and the ICGVA can assure that updating weight procedures can't trap into local minima or plateau area. Various simulation results have been given and the strong robustness and ideal convergent performance are obtained by using ICGVA for real time control with uncertainty parameter systems.

**Acknowledgements**

The authors acknowledge with thanks the financial support by China Scholarship Council, Tianjin Natural Science Foundation under Grant 003800811, Tianjin Education Committee Key Discipline Grant. The authors wish to acknowledge contributions made to this paper by Dr. Gerard Murray and Professor Tim Hendtlass, the Director of the Centre for Intelligent Systems and Complex Processes, Swinburne University of Technology. The authors would also like to thank the anonymous reviewers for their helpful comments.

## References

1. Kuan Chung-Ming, Hornik Kurt: Convergence of Learning Algorithms with Constant Learning Rates. IEEE Transactions on Neural Networks, vol.2 (5, 1991) 484-489
2. Ngolediage J.E., Naguib R.N.G, Dlay S.S.: Fast Back-Propagation for Supervised Learning. Proceedings of 1993 Internatioanl Joint Conference on Neural Networks, (1993) 2591-2594
3. Maugoulas G.D., Vrahatis M.N., Androulakis G.S.: Effective Backpropagation Training with variable stepsize, Neural Networks, (1,1997) 69-82
4. Van der Smagt P.P.: Minimisation methods for Training Feedforward Neural networks, Neural Networks, (1, 1994) 1-11
5. Van Ooyen A., Nienhuis B.: Improving the convergence of the Back-Propagation Algorithm, Neural Networks, (3,1992) 465-471
6. Zhou G. Si J.: Advanced Neural Networks Training Algorithm with Reduced Complexity based on Jacobian Deficiency, IEEE Transactions on Neural Networks, (3,1998) 448-453
7. Hagan M.T., Menhaj M.B.: Training feedforward Neural Networks with the Marquardt Algorithm, IEEE Transactions on Neural Networks, (6, 1994) 989-993
8. Samad T.: Backpropagation Improvements based Heuristic Arguments, Proceedings of International joint Conference on Neural Networks, (1990) 565-568
9. Bello M. G.: Enhanced Training Algorithms, and Integrated Training/Architecture Selection for Multilayer Perceptron Networks, IEEE Transactions on Neural networks, (6,1992) 864-875
10. Shah S. Palmieri F.: MEKA-A Fast, Local Algorithm for Training Feedforward Neural Networks, Proceedings of international Joint Conference on neural Networks, (1990) 41-46
11. Parisi R., Di Claudio E. D., Orlandi G., Rao B. D.: A generalized Learning Paradigm Exploiting the Structure of Feedforward Neural Networks, IEEE Transactions on Neural networks, (6,1996) 1450-1459
12. Wilamowski Bogdan M.,Iqlikci Serdar, Kaynak Okyay, Onder Efe M.: An Algorithm for Fast Convergence in Training Neural Networks, IEEE Proceedings of International Joint Conference on Neural Networks, (2001) 1778-1782
13. Zaiping Chen, Jun Li, etc., A Neural Network Online Training Algorithm based on Compound Gradient Vector, LNAI, (2002), vol.2457
14. Xu Lina: Neural Networks Control. Harbin Industrial University Press, Harbin (1999) 123-124
15. Chen Zaiping, Du Taihang,: Control System Simulations and CAD. Tianjin University Press, Tianjin(2001)

# Document Clustering Based on Vector Quantization and Growing-Cell Structure

Zhong Su, Li Zhang, and Yue Pan

IBM China Research Lab. 2F, HaoHai Building, No. 7, 5th Street, ShangDi
Beijing 100085, P.R.China
{suzhong, lizhang, panyue}@cn.ibm.com

**Abstract.** In this paper, we proposed a new hybrid clustering algorithm based on Vector Quantization (VQ) and Growing-Cell Structure (GCS). The basic idea is using VQ to refine the GCS clustering results and thus to improve the clustering performance. Moreover, the output of the proposed clustering algorithm has a graph structure which is generated gradually during the incremental self-learning process. We evaluate the proposed method on real collections of text documents and the experimental results show that our method achieves better performance comparing with others.

## 1 Introduction

Clustering is an important document mining method and widely used in information retrieval systems. It is an unsupervised content analysis tool in text knowledge management. Much work has been done in this field (Rocchio, 1966; Voorhees, 1986; Fritzke, 1994). Several problems exist in real applications and will affect the performance of clustering algorithms. Firstly, because the cost of the document digitalization is continuously decreasing, the size of document digital database is increasing very fast. To handle the increasing number of documents, clustering algorithm has to solve the incremental problems besides its high efficiency in large data set. Secondly, in text based retrieval, document is always represented as a long vector in feature space. One keyword corresponds to a specific dimension in vector space and thus the feature space always has more than thousands of dimensions because the corpus size is always very huge. However, feature vector is often very sparse. It is caused by the limited corpus size of individual document. For example, in most cases, there are only several hundred dimensions of document feature having non-zero values. So, clustering algorithm should be very effective in super high dimensional and very sparse vector space.

To handle the problems described above, in this paper, we proposed a new hybrid document clustering methods. It is based on GCS (Fritzke, 1994) and VQ (Kohonen, 1995). GCS is a clustering algorithm with artificial neural network approach. It is developed from Self-Organizing Maps (SOM) (Kohonen 1982) and proposes a growing cell structures to produce distribution-preserving mappings. During the GCS

P.W.H. Chung, C.J. Hinde, M. Ali (Eds.): IEA/AIE 2003, LNAI 2718, pp. 326–336, 2003.

clustering progress, the number of clusters and the connections among them are dynamically assigned. New cells can be inserted and existent cells can be removed in order to adapt the output map to the distribution of the input vectors. Generally, GCS tries to preserve the original data distribution and maps such distribution into an undirected graph data structure. Each vertex in the graph represents a specific clustering center. The edge represents the correlation between the pair of vertices at both sides. GCS has following assumption on data distribution: the denser the data area is, the more vertices (clusters) and edges (correlations) are located.

GCS has a dynamic structure during the training process and it makes a big difference comparing with SOM. However, potentially, it also involves a significant weakness and such weakness will affect the clustering performance. The weakness is caused by insufficient training for each state of the dynamical structure. The structure is updated and for a certain state, only few training iterations occurs. To solve the insufficient training problem, we use VQ to tune the GCS clustering output. VQ is a common tool in data compression and is widely used in image, video and audio compression. VQ can be considered as a basic competitive learning network having one layer of input nodes and one layer of output nodes. In VQ, we assume there is a codebook which is defined by a set of M prototype vectors. An input belongs to cluster i if i is the index of the closest prototype (closest in the sense of the normal Euclidean distance). VQ updates only the winning prototype vector weights. This has the effect of dividing up and updating the input space into a Voronoi tessellation (Fritzke, 1994). In our algorithm, we use VQ to tune the clustering output from GCS. The GCS clustering output node weights are considered as the initial codebook of VQ. Then after several rounds of training, the new updated codebook of VQ will replace the GCS node weights. Such process can be considered as an additional training process on GCS clustering results and solve the insufficient training problems in GCS. According to the experimental results, the new hybrid clustering method achieves better performance than the original one.

This paper is organized as follows. Section 2 introduces related works. Section 3 describes the hybrid algorithm in detail. The experimental results are shown in section 4. The conclusion remarks will be given in the final section.

## 2 Related Works

Typical of the clustering work are the K-means clustering (Rocchio, 1966) and hierarchical agglomerative clustering (HAC) (Voorhees, 1986). K-means can be viewed as a greedy algorithm to partition the feature space into k clusters so as to minimize the sum of the square distances to the cluster centers. The biggest weakness of K-means algorithm is that it has to re-train from the very beginning in handling new inserted data. Moreover, K-means needs the pre-determined cluster number k. If the value of k has been changed, the classifier also needs to be trained again. In practical usage, the update of the cluster number and inserting new data into database could happen very frequently and it will cause huge cost using K-means. K-means has another weakness in algorithm design. It needs to assign values to initial k clusters.

Usually we use random value as the initial values. However, the quality of the outcome is usually dependent on the quality of the initial assignment. It will make the clustering results unstable and affect the performance.

HAC algorithms involve building a hierarchical classification of compounds in a dataset by a series of binary mergers. Initially, HAC creates N single-document clusters, where each document in database is considered as an independent cluster. In each stage, merge two clusters with greatest similarity. Then a binary cluster tree will be created. It is easy to explore the set of possible k-cluster values. A single "partition" (slice across the hierarchy) can then be taken at any level to give the desired number of clusters. To increase the efficiency of the algorithm, a modification is the frequent set algorithms that are designed to find sets of similar items in large collections (Agrawal et al, 1993). This algorithm has advantages to K-means. It has stable outputs and tree structured outputs. However, one big problem affects the wide use of this kind of algorithm. The output always “un-balanced”, which means in clustering results, most documents are clustered into very few clusters and the size of most of the clusters is very small.

In 1982, Kohonen proposed an unsupervised neural network architecture called Self Organizing Map (SOM) to mimic two-dimensional arrangements of neurons in the brain (Kohonen, 1982). The main idea of SOM is as follows. The spatial concentration of the network activity is on the neuron best tuned to the present input. The best matching neuron and its topological neighborhood will be modified so that it is closer to the input vector. Generally, a lower-dimensional output topological structure (usually two-dimensional) of a mapping can be generated from high-dimensional input signal spaces. SOM can be viewed as a clustering algorithm with topological outputs. Many people have tried SOM on document clustering and reported its effectiveness in different kind of data. SOM also has several weaknesses. Similar with K-means, SOM needs a predefined topology structure and cluster number. Moreover, during training, the topology structure and cluster number will not be changed. To improve SOM, in 1994, Fritzke (Fritzke, 1994) proposed a new unsupervised neural network architecture called GCS based on SOM. GCS has a dynamical structure during the training process and it makes a big progress comparing with SOM. In the next section, we will describe GCS in detail and propose our hybrid clustering algorithm.

## 3 Hybrid Clustering Method

As mentioned in introduction, to solve the insufficient training problem in GCS, we use VQ to tune the GCS clustering output. In the following sections, firstly, we will introduce GCS and VQ in detail. Then, the new updated algorithm will be presented.

SOM produces topology-preserving mapping; that is, the topology of the network and the number of clusters are fixed prior to the training of the network. Based on Kohonen SOM, Fritzke (1994) proposed growing cell structures to produce distribution-preserving mappings. The general principle of GCS is as follows.

- The number of clusters and the connections among them are dynamically assigned during the network training.

- Adaptation strength is constant over time.
- Only the best-matching cell and its neighborhood are adapted.
- Adaptation implies the increment of signal counter for the best-matching cell and the decrement in the remaining cells.
- New cells can be inserted and existent cells can be removed in order to adapt the output map to the distribution of the input vectors.

Denote the document collection as $D$. The feature vector $f_i$ of each document $d_i$ of $D$ has been extracted. Each node $n_j$ of GCS has its signal-counters $\tau_i$ and associate weight $w_i$. The nodes of GCS are connected in a triangular way. The map initially consists of only 3 nodes forming a triangle. During the training process, new nodes are added in areas receiving a high number of input signals. Nodes are added right within the map while adjusting the connections between nodes in order to keep the triangular connectivity. Some nodes may develop weight vectors that receive no or only few input signals. These nodes are deleted together with all connections being part of the corresponding triangle, which may lead to splitting up the network into several smaller subnets that continue to grow and split independently. In training process the signal-counter of the winning unit $c$ is increased by 1 whereas the signal-counter of a non-winning unit is decreased by a factor at every training cycle. The equations are shown as follows.

$$\tau_c(t+1) = \tau_c(t) + 1 \tag{1}$$

$$\tau_i(t+1) = \tau_i(t) - \alpha\tau_i(t); \forall i, i \neq c \tag{2}$$

This is due to the fact that we want to put more emphasis on units having been selected as winner recently. Following a certain number of training steps (i.e. after completion of a so-called 'organizational phase') the unit $q$ exhibiting the highest signal-counter is selected. A new node is added between unit $q$ and its neighborhood unit $r$ that differs the most concerning their respective weight vectors. The weight vector of the added new unit is initialized as the mean of the two neighboring units q and r.

$$w_{new} = \frac{1}{2}(w_q + w_r) \tag{3}$$

The signal-counters of all units in the neighborhood of the newly added unit are modified according to the decrease in size of their decision region $V$*( abbreviation of Voronoi tessellation )*. The signal-counter of the new unit can then be given as the sum of changes of its immediate neighbors' signal-counters.

$$\forall i \in N_{new} : \tau_i(t+1) = \tau_i(t) + \frac{V_i(t+1) - V_i(t)}{V_i(t)} \cdot \tau_i(t) \tag{4}$$

$$\tau_{new}(t+1) = -\sum_{i \in N_{new}} \frac{V_i(t+1) - V_i(t)}{V_i(t)} \cdot \tau_i(t) \tag{5}$$

where $V_i = \frac{1}{card(N_i)} \cdot (\sum_j \| w_i - w_j \|)$ with *card(N*$_i$*)* being the number of units in the neighborhood of unit *i. $N_i$ denotes the neighbors of node i.*

Deletion takes place when the signal-counter of some unit is below a given threshold. In this case, special care has to be taken not to violate the triangular structure of the network.

**GCS Training Process**

The following is a list of the training process of GCS.

1. select one input vector $f_i$, randomly from all possible inputs of $D$
2. calculate the state of each unit with respect to the selected input using the activation function
3. select the best-matching unit as winner
4. adapt weight vectors of the winner and the units in the neighborhood according to triangular structure
5. modify signal-counters
6. repeat steps 1 to 5 until an organizational phase is completed
7. grow new nodes in areas receiving many input signals initializing weight vectors and signal-counters accordingly, and delete nodes that receive no input signals mapped onto.
8. start next organizational phase

GCS has a dynamical structure during the training process. However, the updated topology structure also involves a significant weakness and it will affect the clustering performance according to our experiment results. The weakness is caused by insufficient training of each state of the dynamical structure. Considering the algorithm efficiency, an *organizational phase* in training can not be very long. Otherwise, the training time will be extended. Within the short organization phase, the weight of each node cannot be stabilized before the next *organizational phase* starts. To solve the insufficient training problem, we use VQ to tune the GCS clustering results. VQ (Kohonen, 1995) is a common tool in data compression and is widely used in image, video and audio compression. VQ can be considered as a basic competitive learning network having one layer of input nodes and one layer of output nodes. In VQ, we assume there is a codebook which is defined by a set of M prototype vectors. An input belongs to cluster *i* if *i* is the index of the closest prototype (closest in the sense of the normal Euclidean distance). VQ updates only the winning prototype vector weights. This has the effect of dividing up and updating the input space into a Voronoi tessellation. In our algorithm, we use VQ to tune the clustering results from GCS.

**VQ Training Process**

The following is the working flow of traditional VQ:

1. Choose the number of clusters $L$
2. Initialize the prototypes $w_1$,... $w_L$ ; one simple method for doing this is to randomly choose $L$ vectors from the input data.
3. Repeat until stopping criterion is satisfied:
   - Randomly pick an input $x$

- Determine the "winning" node k by finding the prototype vector that satisfies $|w_k - x| <= |w_i - x|$ ( for all $i$ )
- Update only the winning prototype weights according to $w_k(new) = w_k(old) + m(x - w_k(old))$, where $m$ is a constant value.

We use VQ to tune the GCS output. The tuning is only occurred on the weights of GCS nodes. It will not affect the topology structure. Also, we do several modifications on the original GCS and VQ algorithms. Firstly, we use zeros to initial the GCS map instead of random values. The random initial values will cause the output unstable. In other words, different training session on same dataset will have different outputs. So, we eliminate the randomize process in GCS initialization. Secondly, the parameter $m$ in updating the wining prototype of VQ will be decreased in each cycle of training. The purpose of VQ is to slightly tune the GCS clustering output. Using the decreasing parameter $m$ will make the tuning process converge to a stable status quickly.

**Hybrid Process**

1. Initial the GCS map with 3 nodes forming a triangle.
   - $w_1=w_2=w_3=0,\ \tau_1 = \tau_2 = \tau_3 = \frac{1}{3}$
2. Sequentially select one document feature $f_i$ from $D$
3. Do GCS training
4. Repeat Last 2 steps until the GCS stopping criterion is satisfied
   - Could stop at user predetermined cluster number
   - Could stop at the state where all patterns have been divided into different clusters. The patterns are provided by the user and they belong to different categories.
5. GCS has output M clusters with corresponding weights $w_i$ and topology structure.
6. Initial a VQ classifier
   - Cluster number is M
   - Initial the prototypes using the weights of GCS, $W_i(VQ) = W_i(GCS)$
7. Sequentially select the document from $D$ and do VQ training until stopping criterion is satisfied
   - The parameter $m$ in updating the wining prototype will be decreased in each cycle of training. In our experiment, $m(new\ training\ cycle) = m(old\ training) / 2$.
   - VQ training could stop after user pre-determined training cycle
8. Using the output VQ prototypes to update the weights of GCS
   - $W_i(GCS) = W_i(VQ)$
9. The final GCS output is the final clustering output.

The proposed training process is incremental because GCS training is an incremental process. For new inserted documents, we do not need to train the net again from the very beginning. Also, the update of clustering number is an incremental process. Update can be done based on the previous results.

## 4 Experiment Results

**Experiment Datasets**

Two testing data sets are used in our experiments. The first one is "*Reuters-21578*" [10]. The data was originally collected and labeled by Carnegie Group, Inc. and Reuters, Ltd. in the course of developing the CONSTRUE text categorization system. It contains 21,578 Reuters financial news. We selected 10,794 documents with human-labeled category information from the collection. Others are filtered out because they have no ground truth category information. The selected news collection belongs to 118 categories. The biggest category contains 3,964 documents and the smallest one contains only 1 document. The second data set is from the biggest web news portal in Chinese [11]. It contains 2,358 documents in 7 categories.

Using category information to evaluate the clustering results is more objective. It can reflect how far the generated clusters are from the real classification scheme. All document features have been normalized using TF/IDF (Term Frequency / Inverse Document Frequency) method (Salton 1988). *Reuters* dataset is clustered to 100 clusters and for *sina* dataset, 50 clusters are generated. Four clustering methods have been tried: K-Means, VQ, GCS and the Hybrid one.

**Evaluation Metrics**

Two evaluation methods are popularly used in clustering work. One is Shannon Entropy measure (Shannon 1948) which is widely used in information theory field. The other is F-Measure (Van Rijsbergen 1979) popularly used in Information Retrieval area. Both measures output a value to describe how good the clustering result is. For Shannon Entropy, the less it is, the better the clustering results are. For F-Measure, it is just the reverse, the bigger the F-Measure value is, the better the clustering results are. Suppose $N$ documents are clustered into $M$ clusters $C_1,\ldots,C_M$, where $C_i$ contains $N_i$ documents and $\sum_{i=1..M} N_i = N$. The documents belong to $K$ categories $S_1,\ldots S_k$. According to Shannon's theory, first we will calculate the class distribution $P_{i,j}$, the probability that a member of cluster $C_j$ belong to category $S_i$ : $P_{i,j} = \frac{|C_j \cap S_i|}{N_j}$. Then we can calculate the entropy of cluster j by: $E_j = -\sum p_{i,j} \log(p_{i,j})$. Finally, total entropy of clustering results is:

$$E = \sum(\frac{N_j E_j}{N}) \tag{6}$$

To define F-Measure, firstly we need to define *precision* and *recall.* For category *i* and cluster *j,*

$$\text{Precision}_{i,j} = \frac{|C_j \cap S_i|}{N_j}, \quad \text{Recall}_{i,j} = \frac{|C_j \cap S_i|}{|S_i|}$$

Then, the F-Measure for category $i$ and cluster $j$ is:

$$F_{i,j} = \frac{2 \cdot \text{Recall}_{i,j} \cdot \text{Precision}_{i,j}}{\text{Precision}_{i,j} + \text{Recall}_{i,j}}$$

The total F-Measure value can be calculated by following equation:

$$F = \sum_i (\max_j (F_{i,j}) \frac{N_i}{N}) \quad (7)$$

Shannon's entropy and F-Measure will output a specific value to evaluate the clustering results. Both values can describe how good the clustering results from the aspect of the entropy and the retrieval aspects are. However, they cannot describe the clustering results in detail mode. As a matter of fact, in this paper, besides the Shannon entropy and F-Measure, we present two additional evaluation metrics. They can illustrate the clustering results in details. One is *Macro Average of Uniform Clusters*; the other is *Micro Average of Uniform Documents*. Following are their definitions.

Firstly, we define *uniformity degree* for cluster as the following equation:

$$u(C_i) = \max_{j=1}^{k} (\frac{|C_i \cap S_j|}{N_i}) \quad (8)$$

Here is an example. Suppose 80 percentage of a cluster $c$ belongs to the same category, then *u(c)=0.8*. Such measure identifies the percentage of the biggest subset of the cluster where documents in the subset are from the same category. Then we define *Macro Average of Uniform Clusters* $U_1(\alpha)$ and *Micro Average of Uniform Documents* $U_2(\alpha)$.

$$U_1(\alpha) = \frac{m(\alpha)}{M} \quad (9)$$

where m(a) is the number of the clusters whose uniformity degree are no less than a.

$$U_2(\alpha) = \frac{\sum_{u(c_i) \geq \alpha} N_i}{N}, \quad (10)$$

$U_1(\alpha)$ tells the number of clusters whose *uniform degrees* are no less than $a$ and $U_2(\alpha)$ identifies how many documents of those clusters there are.

**Experiment Results**

**Table 1.** Comparing Entropy between different methods

| | K-Means | LVQ | GCS | Hybrid |
|---|---|---|---|---|
| *Sina* | 0.5714 | 0.8177 | 0.5444 | 0.5828 |
| *Reuters* | 0.3801 | 0.5615 | 0.3926 | 0.3934 |

**Table 2.** Comparing F-Measure between different methods

| | K-Means | LVQ | GCS | Hybrid |
|---|---|---|---|---|
| *Sina* | 0.3364 | 0.5027 | 0.3596 | 0.4795 |
| *Reuters* | 0.2770 | 0.3976 | 0.2852 | 0.3498 |

Table 1 and Table 2 show the performance comparison using Shannon Entropy and F-Measure defined in Equation 6 and 7. Results show that there is a big gap between these two evaluation measures. For example, Using Entropy, LVQ got the worst clustering results. However, if we use F-Measure, LVQ is the best. The huge difference is caused by evaluations from different aspects of data. However, in both tables, the Hybrid method achieves the performance very close to the best one. For example, in Entropy table, Hybrid method got 0.5828 and 0.3976 in two datasets comparing with the best one GCS's 0.5444 in Sina and *K-Means*'s 0.3801 in *Reuters*. In F-Measure table, the Hybrid method got the second best results and very close to the best results achieved by LVQ. Generally, the Hybrid method achieves best performance considering both evaluation measures.

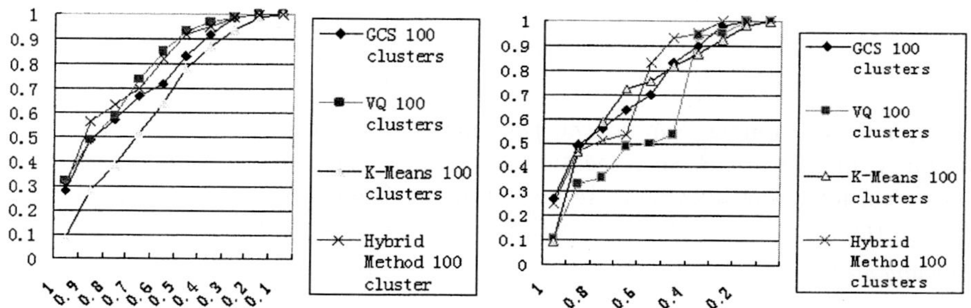


**Fig. 1.** Comparison $U_1$ (left) and $U_2$ (right) in *Reuters* dataset

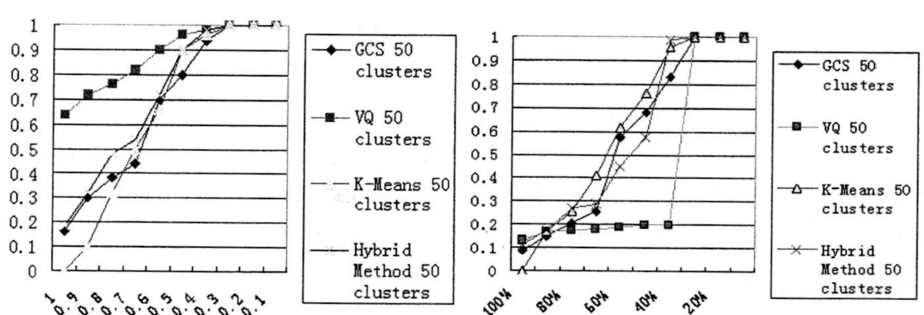


**Fig. 2.** Comparison $U_1$ (left) and $U_2$ (right) in *Sina* dataset

As we have emphasized in previous section, we proposed two measures to evaluate the clustering results in detail mode. Results are shown in Figure 1 and Figure 2 respectively. Horizontal axis represents different value of *a*, from 1 down to 0. From these two figures, we can draw the following conclusions:

1. Both GCS and Hybrid methods are stable under both evaluation metrics. However, K-Means and VQ are very un-stable. For example, in Reuters dataset, K-Means get good performance in $U_2$. However, it got poor values if we use $U_1$ to evaluate it. This phenomenon also appears in *Sina* dataset for VQ.
2. In both four figures, Hybrid methods get better performance than GCS.

Besides, by keeping the topology structure of GCS output, the hybrid algorithm identifies the relationship between clusters. This information will be very useful for further analysis of data. Figure 3 illustrate the topology structure of clustering results using Hybrid method in *Sina* dataset.

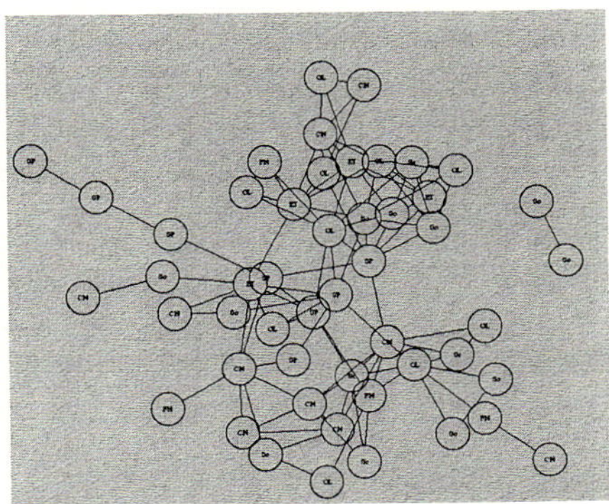

**Fig. 3.** Topology structure of clustering results using Hybrid method on *Sina* dataset.

## 5 Conclusions

In this paper, we proposed a new hybrid clustering algorithm based on Vector Quantization and Growing-Cell Structure. The basic idea is using VQ to refine the GCS clustering results to solve the insufficient training problem in GCS. According to the experiment results, the proposed method achieves better performance than others. By keeping the topology structure of GCS outputs, the clustering result has a graph structure to give the distribution of clusters in 2D space.

## References

1. Agrawal, R., Imielinski, T. and Swami, A., Mining associations between sets of items in massive databases. In Buneman, P., Jajodia, S. (eds). Proceedings of the ACM SIGMOD international conference on management of data, Washington DC, May 1993, pp 207-216
2. Fritzke, B., Growing cell structures - a self-organizing network for unsupervised and supervised learning. Neural Networks, 7(9):-1460, 1994.
3. Kohonen, T., Self-organized formation of topologically correct feature maps. Biological Cybernetics, pp 43:-69, 1982

4. Kohonen, T., Learning vector quantization. In M. Arbib, editor, The Handbook of Brain Theory and Neural Networks, pages 537--540. MIT Press, 1995.
5. Van Rijsbergen, C. J., Information Retrieval. 2nd edition, London, Butterworths, 1979.
6. Rocchio, J., Document Retrieval Systems – Optimization and Evaluation. PhD. Thesis, Harvard University, 1966.
7. Salton, G. and Buckley, C. Term-weighting approaches in automatic text retrieval. Information Processing and Management, 24:513-523. 1988
8. Shannon, C., E., A Mathematical Theory of Communication, Bell Syst. Tech. J., 27, 379-423, 623-656. 1948
9. Voorhees, E. M., Implementing agglomerative hierarchical clustering algorithms for use in document retrieval. Information Processing and Management, 22:465-476, 1986
10. http://www.daviddlewis.com/resources/testcollections/reuters21578/
11. http://www.sina.com

# Using a Modified Counter-Propagation Algorithm to Classify Conjoint Data

Hans Pierrot and Tim Hendtlass

Centre for Intelligent Systems and Complex Processes,
Swinburne University of Technology,
P.O.Box 218, Hawthorn Australia 3122.
hpierrot@swin.edu.au, thendtlass@swin.edu.au

**Abstract.** Conjoint data is data in which the classes abut but do not overlap. It is difficult to determine the boundary between the classes as there are no inherent clusters in conjoint data and as a result traditional classification methods, such as counter propagation networks, may under perform. This paper describes a modified counter propagation network that is able to refine the boundary definition and so perform better when classifying conjoint data. The efficiency with which it uses the network resources suggests that it is worthy of consideration for classifying all kinds of data.

## 1 Introduction

Data classification is a common task and artificial neural networks have shown success in achieving this task, see for example (Bishop 1997). A number of different specialist classification networks exist, they all attempt to position a number of reference neurons in the problem space so that examples can be categorised by assigning to them the category of the closest reference neuron. A number of algorithms for positioning the reference neurons and distance measures exist. Typically the number of reference neurons will exceed the number of user specified final categories, so that some consolidation output layer is required to map the subcategories represented by the reference neurons to the designated output categories.

Classification of data with clearly separate categories does not pose many challenges, however as the categories get closer and closer the classification performance typically degrades. Obviously categories that overlap will cause enormous difficulties. When the categories in the data abut but do not overlap (conjoint data) the definition of the inter category boundaries must be optimum to achieve good performance, a condition that conventional training algorithms have trouble achieving. This paper reports an investigation into an improved algorithm that can achieve optimal boundary definition.

In the rest of this communication first a commonly used version of a specialist classification network, the Counter-Propagation Artificial Neural Network, is described (Hecht-Nielsen 1987). After this a sample conjoint data set is introduced and the performance of the Counter-Propagation Network on this data is described, with particular emphasis on the origin of the errors exhibited. A modified algorithm is then introduced and the performance of this on the same data discussed.

P.W.H. Chung, C.J. Hinde, M. Ali (Eds.): IEA/AIE 2003, LNAI 2718, pp. 337–347, 2003.

### 1.1 The Counter-Propagation Artificial Neural Network (ANN)

Our Counter-propagation ANN is based on the NeuralWorks implementation (NeuralWare 1993) of the unidirectional version which in turn is based on the Moody Darken Radial Basis Function (RBF) network (Moody and Darken 1989) except that the output pattern units form a competitive layer. This means that the pattern unit with the largest transfer function outputs a one and the other units output a zero. An adaptive K-means algorithm (Selim and Ismail 1984) is used to implement the RBF layer and effectively implements a competitive Kohonen learning layer.

The algorithm first trains the RBF internal classification layer using the following algorithm.

1. Input an example.
2. If there are as yet no used neurons in the classification layer go to 6.
3. Calculate the similarity of the current input to the stored exemplar in each RBF neuron.
4. Find the most similar exemplar (in the neuron with the smallest difference output).
5. If the similarity is above a user specified threshold (e.g. 0.1) then go to 7, if not go to 6.
6. If there are unused neurons start a new exemplar in a new neuron and go to 1. If not go to 7.
7. Merge this example into the most similar exemplar then go to 1.

If the input consists of $N$ components $I_1$ to $I_N$ and $LR$ is the user specified learning rate then the merging process applies the following operation on each of the stored exemplar components $X_1$ to $X_N$. Exemplar component $X_j$ is updated as

$$X_{jNEW} = (1 - LR)X_{jOLD} + LR * I_j \tag{1}$$

After training for the desired number of examples, the width parameter for each RBF internal classification layer neuron is set to establish how much of the problem space, centred on the exemplar, is to be represented by that neuron.

Let the neuron $R$ whose $N$ components exemplars are $X_{R1}$ to $X_{RN}$ have the $P$ closest exemplars $C_1$ to $C_P$. Then the width parameter $W_R$ is given by

$$W_R = \sqrt{\frac{\sum_{i=1}^{P}\left(\sum_{j=1}^{N}(X_{Rj} - X_{Cij})^2\right)}{P}} \tag{2}$$

To calculate the output from the $R^{th}$ neuron, let the $N$ components of the input be $I_1$ to $I_N$. The internal activation of the $R^{th}$ neuron $I_R$ is given by:

$$I_R = \sqrt{\sum_{j=1}^{N}(I_j - X_{Rj})^2} \tag{3}$$

The final output from the $R^{th}$ neuron is given by:

$$O_R = \exp - \left( \frac{I_R}{W_R} \right)^2 \tag{4}$$

$O_R$ is a Gaussian shape whose width is governed by $W_R$. The peak output is one when the input equals the stored exemplar, but $W_R$ controls how fast the output drops off as the similarity decreases. The hidden layer representation is achieved by self-organisation alone, without user supplied mapping information. This is similar to a Kohonen internal classification layer.

Once the hidden layer has been trained the examples are again examined to determine how many instances of each category are represented by each neuron. The category that occurs most often becomes the output category for this neuron.

## 1.2 The Conjoint Data Used for These Experiments

The data used for these experiments (shown in Fig. 1) was obtained from the equation

$$y = Sin\left( \frac{\pi}{180} Mod\left( \frac{18}{17} Int\left( \frac{N * Freq}{360} 360 \right) + (N * Freq) \right), 360 \right).$$

For the first cycle *Freq* =1, for the second two *Freq*=2 and for the final three *Freq*=3. The value of *N* is in the range 0 to 1086.

A number of examples are derived from this list of Y values. Example N starts with entry N in the list and will consist of entries N, N+7, N+14, N+21, N+28, N+35 and N+42. Together these examples form the data set.

All the data examples were then normalised by adding two to all points and then dividing them with the middle or fourth point in each example thus ensuring that all values were positive and it was no longer possible to determine a top or bottom sequence from the value of the data points.

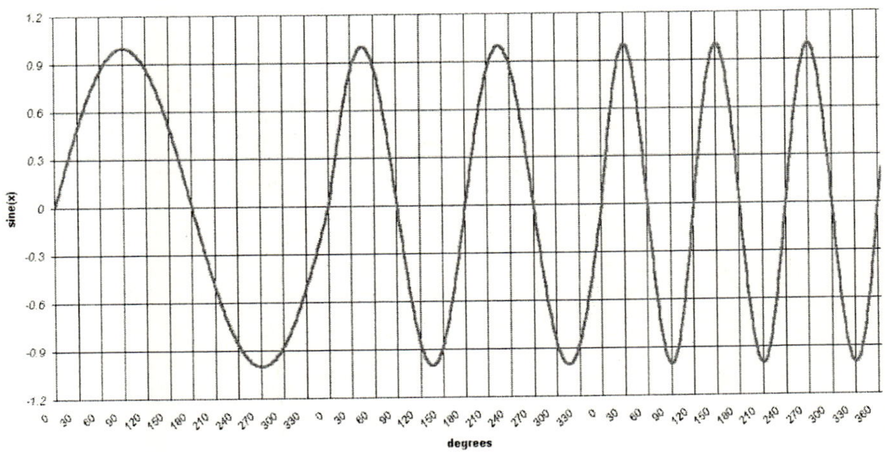


**Fig. 1.** A graphical representation of the conjoint data used in this work

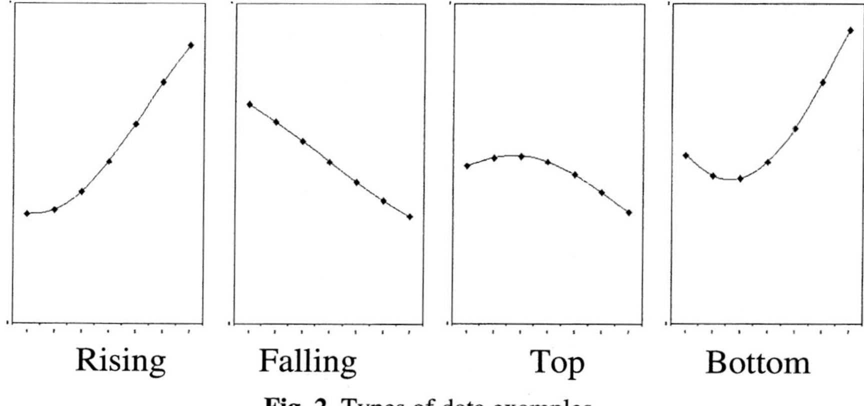


**Fig. 2.** Types of data examples

Each example could be classified into one of four classes, rising (each point higher than the previous point), falling (each point lower than the previous point), top (the end points are below one or more of the intermediate points) and bottom (the end points are higher than one or more of the intermediate points). Fig. 2 shows examples of these classifications.

The aim is to correctly classify each example, a task complicated by the fact that there may only be one point that distinguishes two classifications, for example a rising from a top.

A visual representation that can show all examples (and the boundaries between them) is desirable so that misclassification can be shown together with their proximity to the classification boundaries. This is achieved by plotting each example on a plane using the values of the end points to define the position.

Fig. 3 shows the result of plotting the normalised data this way; each frequency is clearly shown, as are the points as transitions are made between frequencies.

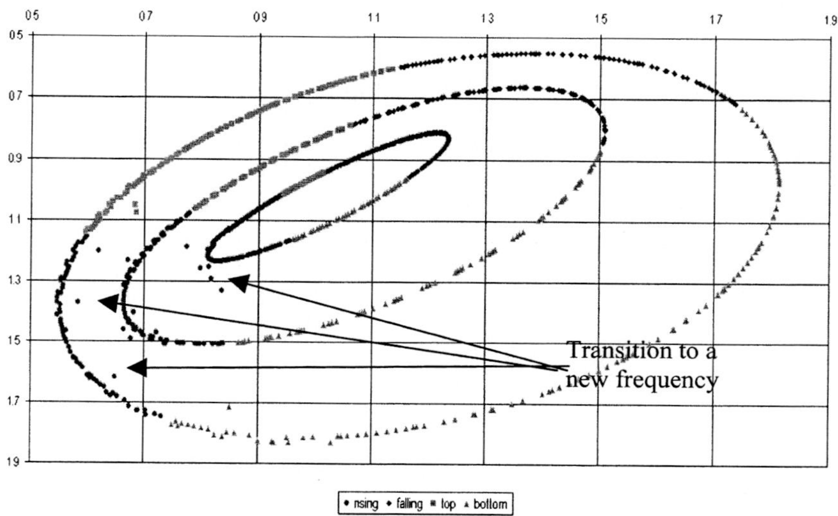


**Fig. 3.** The problem space after data normalisation

From the graph it can be seen that the different categories do not fall into obvious clusters. This is what causes the problem with the classification of the examples.

## 2 The Performance of the Conventional Counter Propagation Algorithm

The performance of a counter propagation network on this data is similar to that shown in Fig. 4. After a while the performance decreases with further training passes through the data. A closer inspection of two sections of the run, as circled in Fig. 4, is instructive. The first section early in the run showed a number of high success values while the second section, towards the end of the run, had appreciably fewer success values. Each section consisted of seven consecutive passes.

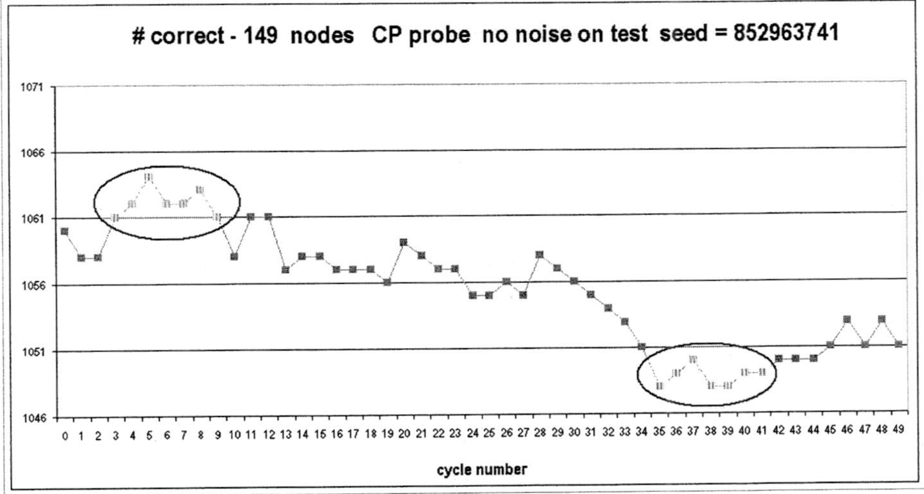


**Fig. 4.** Counter-Propagation performance before modification

Thirteen examples gave correct results in section one but gave incorrect results in section two while five examples gave incorrect results in section one but correct results in section two. There were two effects that caused an example to change its classification, both due to the way an example resolves to the locus of a neuron. Each neuron has a hyperspace around it; all points in this hyperspace are closer to this neuron than to any other neuron and are assigned the category associated with this neuron.

Effect one was that the centre of the hyperspace moved as training progressed. During training the closest, or winning, neuron is always moved towards the current example. This meant that as the centre is moved potentially different examples would resolve to that neuron.

Effect two was a change in the category assigned to the neuron, which was the category of the majority of training examples that resolved to this neuron. During training the mix of examples resolving to a neuron may change sufficiently so that the output category may change.

Our counter propagation network uses an unsupervised Radial Basis Function (RBF) layer in which there is no process to prevent examples of different categories resolving to the same hidden layer neuron. To combat this extra supervision or guiding needs to be added to the training algorithm to make it more effective with this type of data.

## 3 The Modified Algorithm

The modified algorithm needs to move the centre of the neurons that are causing the classification errors to better positions in hyperspace where they better delineate the boundary between different outcome zones, thus addressing effect one. It would also be desirable if neurons that match examples of different categories can also be moved so that they only match examples of a single category. This would address effect two.

1. The first modification only addresses the first effect and simply moves the neurons. After a number of conventional unsupervised training passes a special supervised pass, the shift pass, is performed. In this pass all neurons that are representing more than one class of example are identified. For each of these neurons the examples from the majority represented classification are identified. The neuron weight values that are a result of all the examples that are being represented are discarded and replaced by weight values found by averaging the weight values from the majority class examples that it now represents. This hopefully moves the neurons hypersphere centre away from the examples that belong to a different class and lets them resolve to another neuron of the correct class.
2. The second modification, the split pass, attempts to treat both effects. As well as carrying out the first modification as above, the minority class examples are used to position a new neuron whose weights are set to the average of the weight values from the minority class examples that this new neuron is now to represent.

The second modification addresses both of the effects that are causing the problems observed, but at the cost of increasing the number of neurons in the unsupervised Radial Basis Function layer.

## 4 Results

### 4.1 Using the Conventional Algorithm

Fig. 5 shows the whole problem space after one pass of all the examples. The closed points are the examples from the training data set while the open points show the loci of the neuron hyperspaces. The network resolves each example to the nearest neuron and uses it to determine the category to which the example resolves. The cross marks show where examples have been resolved to the incorrect category. These incorrectly resolved examples are all near category boundaries.

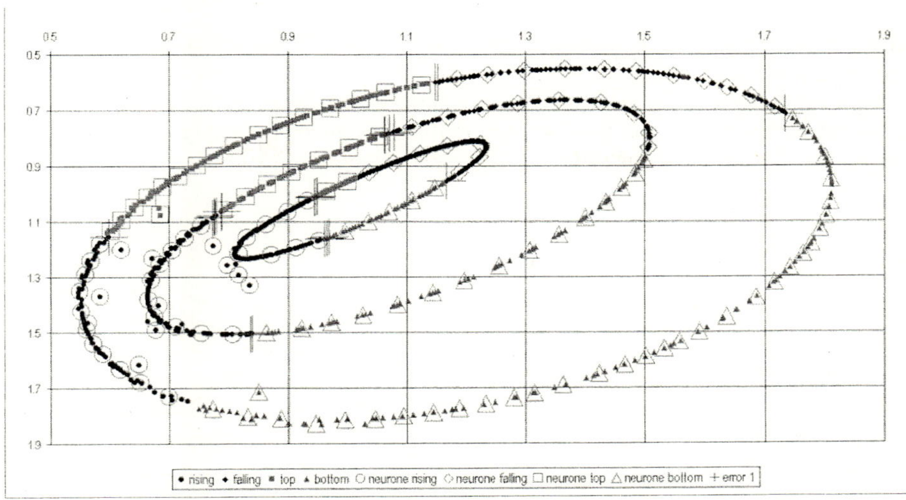


**Fig. 5.** Results after just one pass

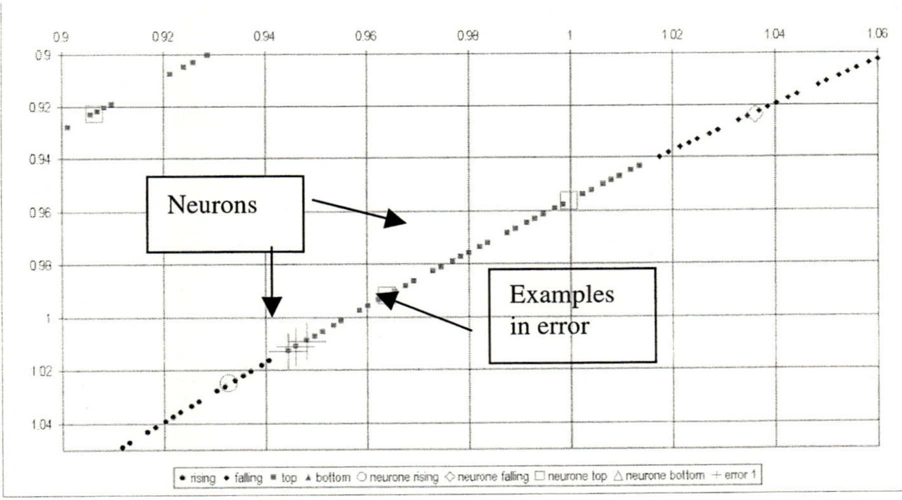


**Fig. 6.** Detail of problem space after one pass

Fig. 6 shows a detailed view of part of the problem space. Several neurons can be seen which classify rising and top sequences. Several of the top examples have been incorrectly classified as they are closer to the rising neuron than they are to the top neuron and are marked by plus signs.

Fig. 7 shows a detailed view of the problem space with the positions of neurons after both passes one and two. The + signs are the examples in error for pass one as seen in the previous figure. The X signs are the examples in error for pass two. All the neurons have moved position (as shown by he arrows) and as a result two new errors have appeared and none have been eliminated in the area shown. The extra errors occurred because the falling neuron moved further away from the category boundary than the top neuron.

After ten passes there are four errors visible in the detail view shown in Fig. 8. Again these are due to the neuron representing the incorrect category being closer than the next nearest neuron, which is the correct category.

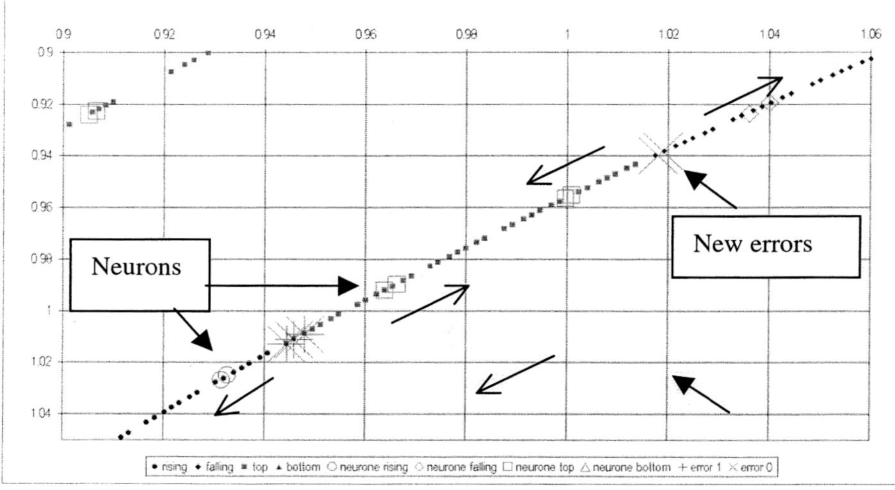


**Fig. 7.** Detail view showing transition from pass one to pass two

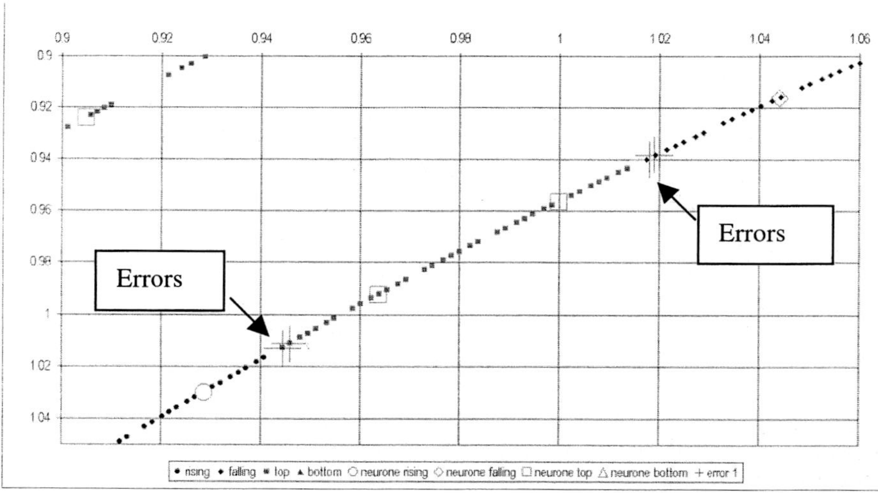


**Fig. 8.** Detail view after ten passes of the training data

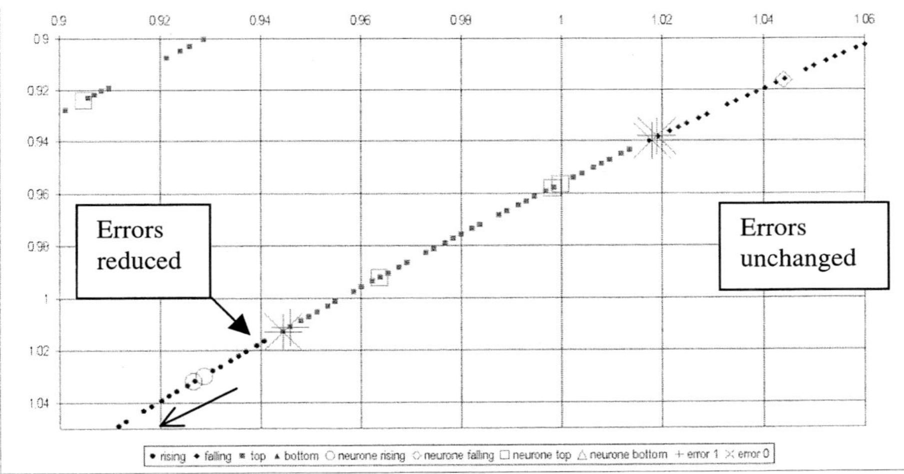


**Fig. 9.** Detail view after pass ten and shift pass

## 4.2 Using the Modified Algorithm

Fig. 9 shows what has happened as a result of a shift pass (as described in section 3) performed immediately following pass ten. In Fig. 9 two neurons that were representing two categories have been repositioned as a result of now only being required to represent their majority class. In one case this reduced the errors from two to one and in the other case had no effect. The + symbols mark the examples which were incorrectly classified before the shift pass and are the same as in the previous figure. The X symbols mark the examples that are incorrectly classified after the shift pass. The arrows show in what direction the neurons moved as a result of the shift pass.

Fig. 10 shows what has happened as a result of a split pass (as described in section 3) in the pass after pass ten. Now, as well as the shift operation, a new neuron is added to represent the minority class orphaned as a result of the shift operation. This has the effect, in the above figure, of removing all the existing errors but introducing new errors in the majority examples. This can occur because the new neuron is placed too close to the border between the two classes. This is normally corrected in later split passes. Therefore there are no examples marked with both a + symbol and an X symbol as occurred when only the shift of neurons took place. However more examples are marked with a cross in this particular instance. The arrows again show where neurons were shifted and two new neurons have also been introduced as annotated in Fig. 10.

The position of the shifted and new neurons have only been determined from a subset of examples and during subsequent conventional training further repositioning will occur as the effects of this special pass ripple through the entire RBF layer. It would be optimistic to assume that the positions derived in isolation as optimal for a few examples would be optimal in the context of the whole RBF layer. Hence further special shift or split passes may be periodically required as conventional training progresses.

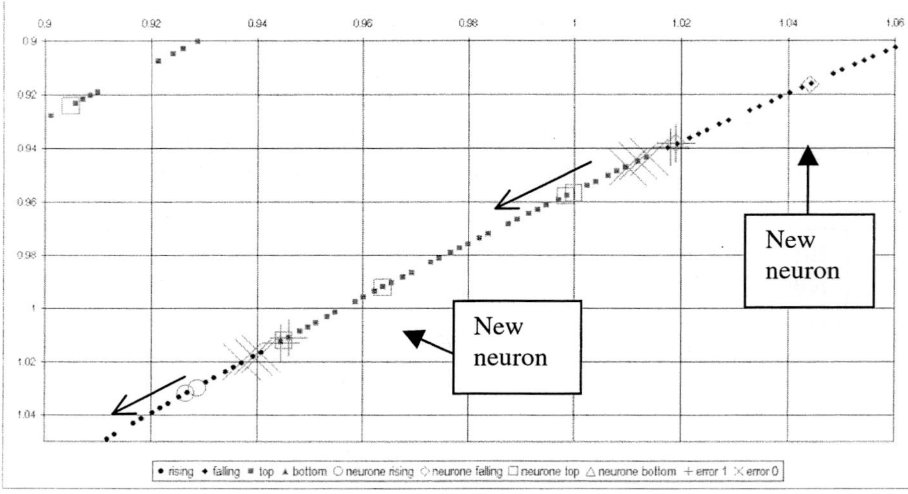


**Fig. 10.** Detailed view after pass ten and a split pass

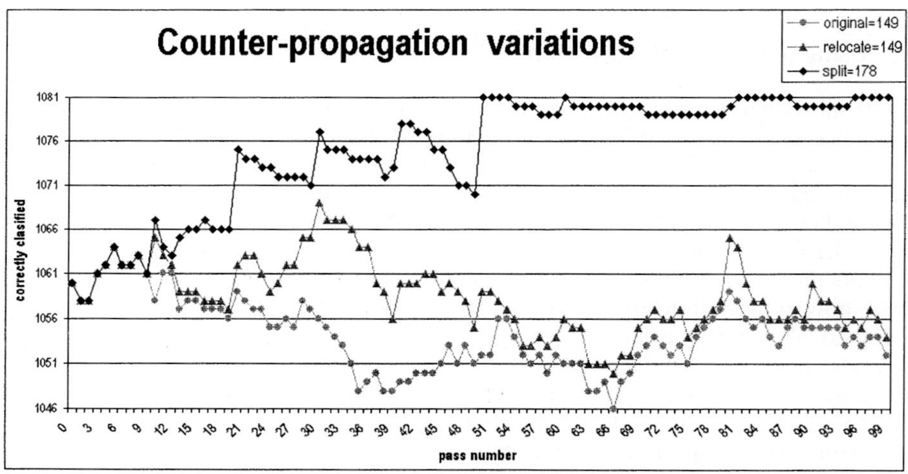


**Fig. 11.** A comparison of the different Counter-Propagation algorithms

## 4.3 Total Performance

Fig. 11 shows a comparison of how the different algorithms for Counter-Propagation performed. These runs all used the same training data, the same initialisation of the neurons and the starting point for the random number stream driving the basic neural network algorithm. The performance starts to diverge after the tenth pass when the modifications start to take effect. When used, shift or split passes were inserted after every ten conventional training passes. Initially the shift pass improves the results but then this does not appear to have any significant long-term effect so that by pass 100 the results are almost identical to the original algorithm. The split algorithm however does improve the results quite effectively at the cost of inserting additional neurons. As can be seen in the graph by the time we come to pass 50 the network has achieved an almost perfect score. The results degrade between the times that the split pass is invoked due to the whole RBF layer absorbing the effects of the split. Some performance noise can also be attributed to the examples being presented in a random order.

By the time the process reaches pass 100 the split pass algorithm has settled to a perfect answer on the training data and is using 178 neurons. This is in comparison to 149 neurons allocated by the original algorithm and the algorithm with the added shift pass.

## 5 Conclusion

In this paper the normal counter propagation training algorithm was modified by the addition of a supervised training pass after every ten normal training passes. The performance of the 'counter propagation with periodic split passes' algorithm with 178 neurons is better than a network with the same number of neurons trained by the conventional counter propagation algorithm alone owing to the more targeted placement of the neurons. The conventional algorithm when provided with 178 neurons was not actually able to make use of them all let alone place them where they were most needed.

The value ten is not critical, although the supervised passes should not occur so frequently that the whole RBF layer cannot absorb the effect before the next supervised training pass occurs. The efficiency with which it uses the network resources suggests that deliberately starting with an under resourced network (too few RBF neurons) and then adding carefully targeted extra ones is a strategy worthy of consideration for classifying all kinds of data.

## References


1. Bishop, Christopher M. Neural Networks: A Pattern Recognition Perspective.: Institute of Physics Publishing & Oxford University Press; 1997;(B6):(Fiesler, Emile and Beale, Russell editors. Handbook of Neural Computation. ISBN: 0 7503 0312 3.
2. Hecht-Nielsen, R. Counterpropagation Networks. Applied Optics. 1987; 26(23):4979-4984.
3. Moody, J. and Darken, C. J. Fast learning in networks of locally turned processing units. Neural Computation. 1989; 1:281-294.
4. NeuralWare. Neural Computing; A Technology Handbook for Professional II/PLUS and NeuralWorks Explorer. Pittsburgh, PA: NeuralWare; 1993.
5. Selim, Shokri Z. and Ismail, M. A. K-means-type algorithms: A generalized convergence theorem and characterization of local optimality. IEEE Transactions on Pattern Analysis and Machine Intelligence. 1984 Jan; 6(1):81-87.

# A Comparison of Corporate Failure Models in Australia: Hybrid Neural Networks, Logit Models and Discriminant Analysis

Juliana Yim and Heather Mitchell

School of Economics and Finance, RMIT University
239 Bourke Street, Victoria 3000 Australia
Juliana.Yim@ems.rmit.edu.au
Heather.Mitchell@rmit.edu.au

**Abstract.** This study investigated whether two artificial neural networks (ANNs), multilayer perceptron (MLP) and hybrid networks using statistical and ANN approaches, can outperform traditional statistical models for predicting corporate failures in Australia one year prior to the financial distress. The results suggest that hybrid neural networks outperform all other models. Therefore, hybrid neural network model is a very promising tool for failure prediction. This supports the conclusion that for shareholders, policymakers and others interested in early warning systems, hybrid networks would be useful.

## 1 Introduction

It is very important to control the number of firms that fail to guarantee sustainable economic growth [1]. Jinn *et al.* [2] suggest that the abnormal behaviour of firms should be used as leading indicators of financial crisis. As a consequence, researchers, shareholders and policymakers have demonstrated a great interest in investigating for the indicators of corporate distress to develop early warning systems and to take actions to prevent firm failure.

Prior studies indicate that researchers generally test and evaluate corporate financial distress models using two popular standard statistical techniques, logit [3, 4] and discriminant analysis [5, 6, 7]. There are few studies in Australia that investigate the power of statistical models for predicting firm failures [8, 9, 10]. However, logit, probit and discriminant analysis (DA) models require assumptions such as normality of the data and independence of the predictors. In particular DA assumes the covariance matrix for the failed and non-failed groups are the same. When the data do not satisfy these assumptions, both logit and DA provide non-optimal solutions [5, 3]. On the other hand, as a non-parametric and non-linear model, the artificial neural network (ANN) does not rely on these assumptions that are often adopted to make traditional statistical methods tractable. No study known to the authors has used ANN for predicting corporate failure in Australia.

P.W.H. Chung, C.J. Hinde, M. Ali (Eds.): IEA/AIE 2003, LNAI 2718, pp. 348–358, 2003.

Some work has been done using ANNs for markets outside Australia, most notably the USA. Most of the papers that have been published on the comparison of ANNs and statistical models for corporate failure prediction indicated that ANNs outperformed statistical models [11, 12]. One study presented findings that were contrary to those established by previous comparative studies. This was the study by Altman et al. [13], which compared ANN models with DA for Italian industrial firms using a large sample size. The results indicated that DA outperformed ANN models. The authors suggested integrating ANNs and the DA approach, because the performance of neural network might be improved by integrating it with statistical techniques.

There are few papers that discuss the integration between statistical models and ANN. Markham and Ragsdale [14], combined output estimated by DA with ANN to produce more accurate models. The results indicated that the hybrid network performed better than the DA and ANN used individually. Han *et al.* [15] was the first study that suggested hybrid neural networks for firm bankruptcy prediction. This work combined neural network models with other statistical or artificial intelligence models. Empirical results show that hybrid neural network models are very powerful for bankruptcy prediction. Therefore, according to most of the studies described above, neural networks have potential as a forecasting approach and its integration with other statistical techniques might improve its overall performance.

This study investigated whether an artificial neural network (ANN), the multilayer perceptron (MLP) and hybrid networks using statistical and ANN approaches, can outperform traditional statistical models for predicting corporate failures in Australia one year prior to the financial distress. The results suggest that hybrid neural networks outperform all other models. Therefore, hybrid neural network model is a very promising tool for failure prediction. This supports the conclusion that for those interested in early warning systems, hybrid networks would be useful.

This paper is organized as follows. Section 2 introduces the hybrid neural networks. Section 3 describes the data. Section 4 presents the results of estimated models. Section 5 presents an evaluation and comparison of neural network models, hybrid models and statistical models. Section 6 presents concluding comments.

## 2 Hybrid Neural Network Model

The ANN used in this study uses a multilayer perceptron network (MLP), trained by a gradient descent algorithm called backpropagation [16]. It is the most common type of formulation and is used for problems that involve supervised learning. This section introduces a methodology to be applied to create hybrid models. We will consider two different approaches to hybrid models. The first approach is to use the statistical models to select the variables to be used as inputs to the ANN. The second is to use output, such as an estimated probability, as an input to a neural net. We decided to combine ANN's and statistical models because ANN's have problem when dealing with large numbers of variables, the time taken for this selection and the possibility of overfitting. By combining statistical models with ANN's we can reduce the problems in the following ways:

- Using statistical models to preselect variables reduces the risk of overfitting and also reduces the time taken to select the model.

- Using output from a statistical model as input to a ANN efficiently condenses information.

To denote the various hybrid models we use the following system. Firstly, we call ANN models using the logit model and DA as pre-processors for selecting variables ANN-logit and ANN-DA, respectively. Secondly, we call ANN models using the probability of failure predicted by the logit model or DA as input into a network ANN-Plogit and ANN-PDA, respectively. Finally, we call ANN models using logit model and DA as pre-processors for selecting variables and the probability of failure predicted by the logit model or DA as input into a network ANN-logit-Plogit, ANN-logit-PDA, ANN-DA-PDA and ANN-DA-Plogit.

Next, following the formulation used by Markham and Ragsdale [14], we will describe how the DA, logit and ANN models might be integrated. The output from the neural network can be written as follows:

$$P(ANN) = f\,(x_1, x_2, \ldots, x_m) \qquad \textbf{(2.1)}$$

where P(ANN) is the probability estimated by the ANN and $x_1, x_2, \ldots, x_m$ are the inputs.

The output from the hybrid neural network ($ANN_H$) using both the inputs and probabilities estimated by DA or logit models as new inputs to the network can be written as follows:

$$P(ANN_H) = f_1\,[P(ANN), PDA)].$$

or

$$P(ANN_H) = f_2\,[(P(ANN), Plogit] \qquad \textbf{(2.2)}$$

where PDA, Plogit, P(ANN) and $P(ANN_H)$ are the probabilities estimated by DA, logit, ANN and $ANN_H$ models, respectively.

Using ANN to estimate P(ANN) and a second $ANN_H$ integrate these values with PDA or Plogit, as can be observed in (2.2). However, P(ANN) = f $(x_1, x_2, \ldots, x_m)$. Therefore, (2.2) might be written as follows,

$$P(ANN_H) = f_1\,(x_1, x_2, \ldots, x_m, PDA).$$

or

$$P(ANN_H) = f_2\,(x_1, x_2, \ldots, x_m, Plogit). \qquad \textbf{(2.3)}$$

## 3 The Description of the Data

The sample consists of a total of 100 Australian firms listed on the Australian Stock Exchange (ASX), 20 of which failed between 1996 and 2000[1]. The successful companies were matched by year with the failed companies by randomly selecting firms with same asset size and industry grouping. The sample consists of companies from all sectors and the information was obtained from the CD-Financial Analysis

[1] Values of ratios for each company can be obtained from the authors by request.

Publication 2001. Data used for the failed firm is from the last financial statement issued before the firm failed.

Table 3.1 lists 13 variables that comprise candidates for final variables of the failure prediction models. These variables are classified in five standard ratio categories, including profitability, growth, gearing, employee and liquidity. Table 1A of the appendix shows the descriptive statistics of the financial ratios. TheJarque-Bera statistics (JB) indicates that the most of the financial ratios are non-normal.

**Table 3.1.** List of Financial Ratios

| Category | Financial Ratio | Code |
|---|---|---|
| **Profitability** | OPABT Over Shareholders Funds | OSF |
| | OPABT Over Sales | OVS |
| | OPABT Over Total Assets | OTA |
| **Gearing** | Shareholders' Interest | SHI |
| | Debt / Equity | DEQ |
| | Working Capital / Total Assets | WCT |
| | Long Term Debt / Total Debt | LTD |
| **Liquidity** | Current Ratio (times) | CUR |
| | Quick Ratio (times) | QUR |
| | Debt / Gross Cash Flow (years) | DGC |
| | Trade Debtors Period (days) | TDP |
| **Growth** | Growth in Total Assets | GTA |
| **Employee** | Sales per Employee | SPE |

# 4 Empirical Investigation: Predicting Corporate Failures in Australia

## 4.1 Discriminant Analysis

This section analyses the ability of DA to predict corporate failures in Australia. The first part involves estimating the discriminant function and determining whether or not they are statistically significant. The second part evaluates the predictive accuracy of the discriminant function.

First we will estimate an optimum discriminant function and determine whether or not it is statistically significant. Several different models[2] were estimated and the best was found to contain three variables: OPBAT over shareholders' funds, OPBAT over total assets and growth in total assets. The stepwise[3] procedure is shown in the Table 4.1:

**Table 4.1.** The Stepwise Selection of the DA Model

| Step | Variable Selected | Min.D Squared Statistic | Exact F Statistic | Sig. |
|---|---|---|---|---|
| 1 | OPBAT/Shareholders' funds | 1.783 | 28.528 | 0.001 |
| 2 | OPBAT / Total Assets | 2.275 | 18.016 | 0.001 |
| 3 | Growth in Total Assets | 2.703 | 14.120 | 0.001 |

2 Estimated using the software package SPSS 10.0.

3 Full detail of all steps can be obtained from the authors by request.

The final discriminant function is:

$$Z= 0.358 - 0.007\ OSF - 0.059\ OTA - 0.005\ GTA$$

The main assumptions required by DA are that the predictors should have a normal distribution and the covariance matrices of the two group (failed and non-failed) should be equal. Based on the Jarque-Bera statistics in Table 1A of the appendix all the variables are non-normal. The assumption of equal covariance matrices is tested using Box's M test [17], which tests the equality of the determinants. The value of this statistic is M = 241.691, p-value = 0.000 using the F approximation, so the assumption of constant variance is not satisfied. This means that the tests of model adequacy which follow may not be reliable.

Next the canonical correlation is used because it is a measure of association between the groups formed by the dependent and given discriminant function. The discriminating function for the best model is significant and displays a canonical correlation of 0.553. One interprets this correlation by squaring it $(\text{canonical correlation})^2 = 0.31$, and concluding that 31% of the variance in the dependent variable can be accounted for by this model. The Wilk's lambda test is used for analyzing the significance of each discriminant function. The model produced a Wilk's lambda of 0.694, which indicates that the selected discriminant function is significant.

For this study, the critical cutting score is zero, so a firm is classified as non-failed if its discriminant score is negative and as failed if its discriminant score is positive. Table 4.2 lists the predicted status, the discriminant score and the probability of failure for misclassified firms. The overall success rate of the model was 84%. More specifically, the success rate of predicting failure was 75% and that of success, 86.3%.

**Table 4.2.** Probability of Failure[4] and Discriminant Score for Misclassified Firms

| ASX Code | Companies | Predicted Status | Z-Score | Prob. of failure |
|---|---|---|---|---|
| ACH | AUSTRALIAN CHEMICAL HOLDING LTD | Success | -0.20 | 0.24 |
| ELT | ELTIN LTD | Success | -0.12 | 0.27 |
| GKL | GOLDFIELDS KALGOORLIE LTD | Success | -0.65 | 0.13 |
| QIW | Q.I.W. RETAILER | Success | -0.44 | 0.48 |
| VPM | VANGUARD PETROLEUM NL | Success | -0.29 | 0.42 |
| ADM | AURIDIAM LTD | Failure | 0.55 | 0.52 |
| ANM | AUSTRALIAN MAGNESIUM CORPORATION LTD | Failure | 0.56 | 0.53 |
| ARC | AMALG RESOURCES NL | Failure | 0.92 | 0.67 |
| AUM | AUSTRALIAN MINING INVESTMENTS LTD | Failure | 1.53 | 0.85 |
| BLO | BLIGH OIL & MINERALS LTD | Failure | 0.87 | 0.65 |
| CNB | CANBERRA INVESTMENTS CORPORATION LTD | Failure | 0.53 | 0.52 |
| EMP | EMPEROR MINES LTD | Failure | 0.85 | 0.64 |
| EZY | EASYCALL INTERNATIONAL LTD | Failure | 1.14 | 0.74 |
| IHG | INTELLECT HOLDINGS LTD | Failure | 1.12 | 0.74 |
| MGM | MACQUARIE GOODMAN MANAGEMENT LTD | Failure | 0.49 | 0.51 |
| TEH | TECHNICHE LTD | Failure | 0.63 | 0.55 |

4 Values of probability of failure for each company can be obtained from the authors by request.

## 4.2 Logistic Regression

This section analyses the predictive ability of logistic regression for forecasting corporate failure in Australia. The probit model was also tried, but its results were not reported in this study. This is because its outputs were very similar to the ones estimated by logistic regression. Several different models[5] were estimated using maximum likelihood and the best used three financial ratios. These are OPBAT over shareholders' funds, working capital over total assets and growth in total assets, a growth ratio. The regression coefficients and significant variables at 5 percent error level are given in Table 4.3.

**Table 4.3.** The Final Logit Model

| Variable | Coefficient | Std. Error | z-Statistic | Prob. |
|---|---|---|---|---|
| OPBAT Over S'holders' Funds | -0.074896 | 0.026695 | -2.805606 | 0.0050 |
| Working Capital / Total Assets | -0.053755 | 0.019198 | -2.800074 | 0.0051 |
| Growth in total assets | -0.062556 | 0.022256 | -2.810818 | 0.0049 |

The final logistic function is:

$$\text{Pr (failure)}=\frac{1}{1+e^{-Z_i}}$$

where $Z_i = -0.074OFS - 0.053WTA - 0.062GTA$

The test statistic for the log likelihood ratio test is 84.24, which has the p-value = 0.000 ($\chi_3^2$), indicating that the model fits to the data. Also, the Hosmer and Lemeshow test [18] was used to compare the fitted expected values to the actual values by group. If these differences are large, we reject the model as providing an insufficient fit to the data. The Hosmer and Lemeshow goodness-of-fit test has a p-value of 0.55, which is greater than 0.05, implying that the model's estimates fit the data at an acceptable level.

For the logistic regression, the institutions were classified as failed if the probability of failure exceeds a cutoff point of 0.5. Table 4.4 shows probability of failure for misclassified firms. The overall success rate of the model was 90%. More specifically, the success rate of predicting failure was 80% and that of non-failure, 91.2%.

## 4.3 ANN Models

This section analyses the predictive ability of ANNs and hybrid ANNs for predicting Australian corporate failures. Two types of hybrid ANNs were considered. The first uses statistical models to preselect variables. The second uses the output from logit model and DA as input for an ANNs. Each network was trained for 20,000 iterations. The sigmoid function was the activation function specified in all neural networks, because it provided the best results. The number of hidden neurons in the hidden layer

[5] Estimated using the software package SPSS 10.0.

was selected experimentally based on the testing set performance of each neural network. Learning rates and momentum for each of the models were chosen experimentally. The final values chosen for each of the models are given in Table 2A of Appendix .

**Table 4.4.** Probability of Failure for Misclassified Firms

| ASX Code | Companies | Predicted Status | Prob. of failure |
|---|---|---|---|
| ACH | AUSTRALIAN CHEMICAL HOLDING LTD | Success | 0.11 |
| ELT | ELTIN LTD | Success | 0.27 |
| GKL | GOLDFIELDS KALGOORLIE LTD | Success | 0.06 |
| MDB | McDONALD BRUSHWARE LTD | Success | 0.49 |
| ADM | AURIDIAM LTD | Failure | 0.87 |
| ARC | AMALG RESOURCES NL | Failure | 0.64 |
| CNB | CANBERRA INVESTMENT CORPORATION LTD | Failure | 0.69 |
| EMP | EMPEROR MINES LTD | Failure | 0.62 |
| EZY | EASYCALL INTERNATIONAL LTD | Failure | 0.97 |
| IHG | INTELLECT HOLDINGS LTD | Failure | 0.59 |
| OLH | OLDFIELDS HOLDINGS LTD | Failure | 0.52 |

From all ANN models[6] tried, the best specification consisted of six variables in the input layer. The selected input variables were working capital over total assets, OPBAT over shareholders' fund, OPBAT over total assets, shareholders' interest, growth in total assets and quick ratio. Three neurons were selected in the hidden layer by experimentation and one neuron in the output layer. The overall success rate of the model was 91 %. More specifically, the success rate of predicting failure was 80% and that of non-failure, 94%. The companies were classified as failed if the probability exceeds a cutoff point of 0.5. Table 4.5 shows the probability of failure for misclassified.

**Table 4.5.** Probability of Failure for Misclassified Firms

| Code | Companies | Predicted Status | Prob. of Failure |
|---|---|---|---|
| ACH | AUSTRALIAN CHEMICAL HOLDING LTD | Success | 0.11 |
| AHY | AUSTRALIAN HYDROCARBONS LTD | Success | 0.35 |
| ELT | ELTIN LTD | Success | 0.19 |
| GKL | GOLDFIELDS KALGOORLIE LTD | Success | 0.02 |
| ADM | AURIDIAM LTD | Failure | 0.52 |
| ARC | AMALG RESOURCES NL | Failure | 0.74 |
| AUM | AUSTRALIAN MINING INVESTMENTS LTD | Failure | 0.54 |
| EMP | EMPEROR MINES LTD | Failure | 0.56 |
| EZY | EASYCALL INTERNATIONAL LTD | Failure | 0.69 |

When we compare the results from the DA, logit and ANN models we see that each technique misclassified different firms. So, each approach must be using the information in different ways. For that reason, the combination of statistical models and ANN may produce better results. The ANN models were combined with the best statistical models estimated in previous section to perform hybrid neural networks. Firstly, we used statistical models to pre-select the variables used in the ANNs. The

[6] Estimated using the software package Neuroshell 2.

ANN-logit and ANN-DA models used DA and logit models as pre-processors for selecting the appropriate input variables, which are then used, by the MLP networks. Secondly, the outputs from the statistical models were used as inputs into a network (ANN-Plogit and ANN-PDA). Finally, we combined the preselected variables from the statistical models and the output from the statistical models (ANN-logit-Plogit, ANN-logit-PDA and ANN-DA-PDA).

**Table 4.6.** Probability of Failure For Misclassified Firms

| Code | Companies | ANN-DA | ANN-PDA | ANN-DA-PDA | ANN-logit | ANN-Plogit | ANN-logit-Plogit | ANN-logit-PDA |
|---|---|---|---|---|---|---|---|---|
| ACH | AUSTRALIAN CHEMICAL HOLDING LTD | **0.15** | **0.02** | **0.08** | **0.13** | **0.10** | **0.11** | **0.02** |
| AHY | AUSTRALIAN HYDROCARBONS LTD | 0.51 | **0.21** | 0.51 | **0.29** | 0.55 | 0.66 | **0.24** |
| ELT | ELTIN LTD | **0.17** | **0.06** | **0.09** | **0.23** | **0.22** | **0.19** | **0.08** |
| GKL | GOLDFIELDS KALGOORLIE LTD | **0.08** | **0.01** | **0.05** | **0.09** | **0.10** | **0.09** | **0.01** |
| MDB | McDONALD BRUSHWARE LTD | 0.51 | 0.51 | 0.64 | **0.25** | 0.51 | 0.50 | 0.59 |
| QIW | Q.I.W. RETAILERS LTD | **0.33** | 0.51 | **0.32** | 0.51 | 0.57 | 0.63 | 0.52 |
| VPM | VANGUARD PETROLEUM NL | **0.28** | 0.51 | **0.22** | 0.51 | 0.52 | 0.56 | 0.51 |
| WHK | WHITTAKERS LTD | 0.51 | 0.51 | 0.57 | **0.29** | 0.51 | 0.55 | 0.57 |
| ADM | AURIDIAM LTD | 0.38 | 0.29 | 0.45 | 0.44 | **0.60** | **0.69** | **0.54** |
| ARC | AMALG RESOURCES NL | 0.49 | **0.79** | **0.54** | **0.51** | **0.53** | **0.58** | **0.71** |
| AUM | AUSTRALIAN MINING INVESTMENTS LTD | **0.64** | 0.47 | **0.68** | 0.21 | 0.18 | 0.10 | **0.72** |
| BLO | BLIGH OIL & MINERALS LTD | 0.47 | 0.25 | **0.54** | 0.16 | 0.13 | 0.13 | **0.52** |
| CNB | CANBERRA INVESTMENT CORPORATION LTD | 0.37 | 0.12 | 0.44 | 0.27 | **0.53** | **0.60** | 0.28 |
| EMP | EMPEROR MINES LTD | 0.47 | 0.39 | **0.57** | 0.33 | 0.47 | **0.55** | **0.64** |
| EZY | EASYCALL INTERNATIONAL LTD | **0.56** | **0.75** | **0.67** | **0.72** | **0.64** | **0.71** | **0.72** |
| IHG | INTELLECT HOLDINGS LTD | **0.56** | **0.54** | **0.69** | 0.25 | 0.47 | **0.52** | **0.63** |

The final topology chosen for each of the hybrid network, are given in Table 1A of Appendix. Table 4.6 indicates that he best hybrid model is the ANN-Plogit network. Figures in bold represent a misclassification and figures in italic represent failed companies. The overall success rate of the models was 94%. The success rate of predicting failure was 85% and that of non-failed, 96%.

## 5 Comparison of the Models

According to Table 5.1, the best statistical model was the logit model. The results from ANN were very similar to the statistical models. The performance of the ANN was improved when the hybridization with DA and logit models was considered. The best model was ANN-Plogit network. So, the results show that hybrid neural network model is very promising model for failure prediction.

The last step to complete this study is to test the prediction models using an independent holdout sample. Each prediction model was applied to an independent sample of 10 failed companies in 2001 and 2002 and 36 non-failed companies to test the validity of the model. The failed firms failed after the selection of the original sample. Table 5.1 indicates that the statistical models are superior to ANN for predicting failed firms correctly. The best model is ANN-logit-PDA network, 80% of failed firms and 94% of non-failed firms are correctly classified on the one statement prior failure. These holdout test results for the hybrid ANNs are very encouraging.

**Table 5.1.** Classification Accuracy from the Best Models

| BEST MODEL | In-sample | | Holdout sample | |
|---|---|---|---|---|
| | Non-failed firm correctly classified (%) | failed firms correctly classified (%) | Non-failed firm correctly classified (%) | failed firms correctly classified (%) |
| DA | 86 | 75 | 86 | 60 |
| Logit | 91 | 80 | 89 | 60 |
| ANN | 94 | 80 | 94 | 50 |
| ANN-DA | 98 | 75 | 92 | 50 |
| ANN-PDA | 96 | 80 | 94 | 50 |
| ANN-DA-PDA | 93 | 75 | 92 | 60 |
| ANN-logit | 98 | 70 | 94 | 50 |
| ANN-Plogit | 96 | 85 | 89 | 60 |
| ANN-logit-Plogit | 93 | 85 | 89 | 60 |
| ANN-logit-PDA | 91 | 80 | 94 | 80 |

## 6 Conclusions

This study investigated whether two artificial neural networks, multilayer perceptron and hybrid networks, can outperform traditional statistical models for predicting corporate failures in Australia one year prior to the financial distress. The results in-sample from the statistical models are similar to multilayer perceptron, but inferior to hybrid networks. The results holdout sample indicated that the hybrid network that combined ANN with DA and logit models presented a superior performance to all other models. Therefore, hybrid neural network model is very promising tool for failure prediction. Further, it has the additional advantage over the simple ANN of reducing the time required for selecting input variables. This supports the conclusion that for researchers, shareholders, policymakers and others interested in early warning systems, hybrid networks would be useful.

**Acknowledgements**

The authors wish to thank Michael McKenzie for some helpful comments.

## References

1. Warner, J.B., 'Bankruptcy costs: some evidence', *The Journal of Finance*, 32, 1997, 337-347.
2. Jinn, T. and J. H. Nam, 'Bankruptcy Prediction: Evidence from Korean Listed Companies during IMF Crisis', *Journal of International Financial Management and Accounting,* 11, 2000, 179-197.
3. Ohlson, J., 'Financial ratios and the probabilistic prediction of bankruptcy', *Journal of Accounting Research*, 18, 1980, 109-31.

4. Gentry, J. A., P. Newbold and D. T. Whitford, 'Classifying bankruptcy firms with funds flow components', *Journal of Accounting Research*, 1985, 146-160.
5. Altman, E., G.E. Pinches,and J.S Trieschmann, 'Discriminant analysis, classification results and financially distressed property-liability insurers', *Journal of Risk and Insurance*, 1977, 289-298.
6. Deakin, E.B, 'A discriminant analysis of predictors business failure', *Journal of Accounting Research*, Spring, 1972, 167-179.
7. Blum, M. P., 'Failing company discriminant analysis', *Journal of Accounting Research*, 12, 1974.
8. Castagna, A.D., and Z.P. Matolcsy, 'The prediction of corporate failure:testing the Australian experience', *Australian Journal of Management,* 1986.
9. Lincoln, M, 'An empirical study of the usefulness of accounting ratios to describe levels of insolvency risk', *Journal of Banking and Finance*, 7, 1984, 321.
10. Izan, H, 'Corporate Distress in Australia', *Journal of Banking and Finance*, 8, 1984, 303.
11. Odom, M. D. and R. Shard, 'A Neural Network Model for Bankruptcy Prediction', International Joint Conference on Neural Networks, San Diego, CA, 2, 1990, 163-67.
12. Coats, P. K and L. F. Fant, 'Recognizing financial distress patterns using neural network tool', *Financial Management* , 22, 1993, 142-155.
13. Altman E., G. Marco,. and F. Varetto, 'Corporate distress diagnosis: Comparisons using linear discriminant analysis and neural networks (the Italian experience)', *Journal of Banking and Finance*, 18, 1994, 505-529.
14. Markham, I. and C. Ragsdale, 'Combining neural networks and statistical predictions to solve the classification problem in discriminant analysis', *Decision Sciences*, 26, 1995, 229-241.
15. Han, I., Y. Kwon, and K. C. Lee, 'Hybrid neural network models for bankruptcy predictions', *Decision Support Systems*, 18, 1996, 63-72.
16. Rumelhart, D., J. McClelland and PDP Group, Parallel distributed processing. Exploration in the Microstructure of Cognition, .1: Foundation. Cambridge, Mass.: MIT Press, 1986.
17. Norusis, M. J, 'SPSS advanced statistics user's guide', SPSS, 1990.
18. Hosmer, D. W. and S. Lemeshow, 'Applied Logistic Regression', John Wiley & Sons, 1989.


# Appendix

**Table 1A.** The best ANN topologies

| Name | Model | Learning rate | Momentum |
|---|---|---|---|
| ANN | 6x3x1 | 0.5 | 0.7 |
| ANN-DA | 3x2x1 | 0.7 | 0.5 |
| ANN-PDA | 7x2x1 | 0.7 | 0.5 |
| ANN-DA-PDA | 4x1x1 | 0.7 | 0.5 |
| ANN-logit | 3x1x1 | 0.7 | 0.5 |
| ANN-Plogit | 7x2x1 | 0.5 | 0.5 |
| ANN-logit-Plogit | 4x2x1 | 0.7 | 0.5 |
| ANN-logit-PDA | 4x1x1 | 0.7 | 0.5 |

**Table 2A.** Descriptive Statistics

| Financial Ratios | Failed | | Non-failed | |
|---|---|---|---|---|
| | mean | J-B | mean | J-B |
| OSF | -48.78 | 122.47 | 16.77 | 272.25 |
| OVS | -10.29 | 10.29 | -267 | 19779 |
| OTA | -9.04 | 1.98 | 7.21 | 197.74 |
| SHI | 39.71 | 4.15 | 55.12 | 29.4 |
| DEQ | 160.79 | 208.72 | 59.72 | 15254 |
| WCT | 1.77 | 85.77 | 21.33 | 24.58 |
| LTD | 34.26 | 2.25 | 46.81 | 7.88 |
| CUR | 1.74 | 152.35 | 3.14 | 4146.57 |
| QUR | 1.33 | 170.13 | 2.41 | 4779.01 |
| DGC | -0.4 | 28.54 | 3.04 | 2925 |
| TDP | 34.79 | 254 | 44.77 | 228.3 |
| GTA | 885.14 | 44.91 | 648.76 | 16755 |
| SPE | -17.37 | 3.05 | 31.559 | 8.15 |

# An Ontology-Based Information Retrieval System

Péter Varga, Tamás Mészáros, Csaba Dezsényi, and Tadeusz P. Dobrowiecki

Department of Measurement and Information Systems, Budapest University of Technology and Economics (BUTE), Magyar tudósok körútja 2. H-1117 Budapest, Hungary
{pvarga, meszaros, dezsenyi, dobrowiecki}@mit.bme.hu

**Abstract.** Authors describe a general architecture and a prototype application for the concise storage and presentation of the information retrieved from a wide spectrum of information sources. The proposed architecture was influenced by particular challenges of knowledge intensive domain, mining the knowledge content of primarily unstructured textual information, demands for context driven, multi-faceted, up-to-date query and presentation of the required information, and by the intricacies of the Hungarian language, calling for special solutions to a number of linguistic problems.

## 1 Introduction

The Information and Knowledge Fusion international EUREKA project aims at the design and implementation of a new Intelligent Knowledge Warehousing environment, which would allow advanced knowledge management in various application domains (e.g. banking, legal information, education, health care, etc.) [1]. The developed IKF Framework implements this environment using information retrieval and extraction, various knowledge representation and information access methods. The IKF Framework is a generic, domain-independent architecture that can be used to build IKF Applications providing services in specific domains.

The Hungarian IKF project (IKF-H) concentrates on developing a financial advisory prototype application. In an earlier paper [3] we have already presented the general model of the problem along with a high level architecture and the key technologies to implement such a system. In order to build a successful information retrieval and integration application we have proposed a strong usage of background knowledge about the application domain. This paper presents the first results in developing a general methodology of how this background knowledge should be organized and used in the IKF Framework. We also present the architecture and operation of the IKF-H prototype application.

### 1.1 Overview of the IKF Architecture

At a properly abstracted level all of the application areas mentioned above can be conceptualised as an interaction of three information environments [3]. By the **Target Environment** we denote that fragment of the real world, where the targeted (monitored) objects (corporations, bank clients, business processes, etc.) do exist. The

P.W.H. Chung, C.J. Hinde, M. Ali (Eds.): IEA/AIE 2003, LNAI 2718, pp. 359–368, 2003.

**Information Cumulating Environment** comprises all forms and media, which cumulate information about the targets. In our case it is the Internet, various Intranet resources, corporation databases, published resources, financial experts' personal expertise and the like. Finally, the **Information Utilizing Environment** represents the users of information (e.g. the staff of a bank), at various level of management. Figure 1 shows the high level IKF architecture.

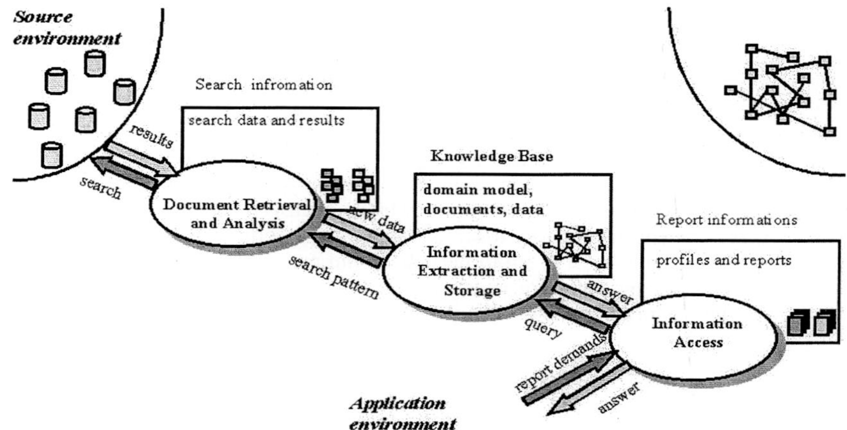


**Fig. 1.** The IKF high level architecture

## 2 The Role of Ontology in the IKF System

In order to surpass the performance of a typical information retrieval system (both in precision and recall), the process of a human information retrieval must be studied and, at least partially, followed. Even the shallowest analysis of the human performance shows that its advantage consists of two main factors: (1) the use of *linguistic competence* and (2) the benefits of *background knowledge*.

Since linguistics techniques are rapidly being added to implemented information retrieval systems, the construction, mapping and incorporation of background knowledge becomes the biggest challenge. This involves abandoning the solely index-based searching methods, and requires making use of some logical apparatus. This is one of the central designing goals of the IKF-H application.

The designer of any such information retrieval system has to face a complex problem: how to transform the background knowledge (which resides in humans) to terms of computer science that can lead to an implemented system. Although human knowledge, the nature of which is itself a huge philosophical problem, might be modelled with the use of intensional logic, but this would clearly lead to an almost unimplementable system burdened with theoretical problems. If a retrieval system is aiming at making use of background conceptual knowledge, its implementers must confine themselves to a less powerful logical apparatus. As it is well known, the use of ontologies can provide a solution to this paradox.

A suitable definition for ontology can be found in [9] [12] [13]: an *ontology* is a theory formulated in the less powerful language of the working system, which theory tries to cover those models of this language that, in some manner, correspond to the conceptualisation (which is an intensional system trying to account for the human background knowledge).

The crucial role of well-defined ontology has already been recognised. IEEE Computer Society pioneered a Standard Ontology Study Group [8]. A research group related to the IKF project is tackling the question of the meta-organisation of the ontological hierarchies [9], finally fairly recently a number of ontology based enterprise models has been developed [10] [11]. All these developments serve as a basis for the development of the suitable Hungarian enterprise ontology.

## 3 Building the IKF-H Ontology

The consideration of the specific requirements of an information retrieval system could gain several insights. First, a strict distinction must be drawn between conceptual knowledge and factual knowledge. Efforts to a design-time incorporation of the second would be a *petitio principi*, since this is the very information we want to retrieve. On the other hand, the conceptual knowledge must be included before the system starts working. As described above, this separated incorporation is to be done via ontologies.

Further insights emerge from the comparison with existing initiatives in the ontology research. Whilst one central function of ontologies nowadays is to ensure semantic agreement between communicating computer systems, IKF, in its primer form, does not involve communication with other systems, therefore possesses less need of a rigorously defined ontology.

After identifying these designing requirements the task of constructing the ontology could start. Unfortunately, the very first step of this process proves to be the most difficult, since it involves deciding what to include at the top-level. On one hand, it raises extremely difficult philosophical questions; on the other hand, it leads to a jungle of currently proposed top-level ontology standards. Making justice between them and creating the ideal top-level ontology would be a great challenge, but definitely not the most important task to solve in building an information retrieval system. Fortunately, such systems do not need an ideal and exact ontology of the world, since neither their input, nor their output is to be considered ideal or exact; but they may utilise an ontology to improve accuracy (just like humans do).

Even building a simple top-level ontology requires considering several possible world descriptions. In the following, we explain how the Aristotelian ontology[1] was adopted in theIKF-H system.

The backbone of the IKF-H ontology consists of several *concept hierarchies* based upon the generic-specific distinction (a graph theorist would call it a *forest*). The genus-concept is partitioned into several species-concepts, which stand in mutual exclusion (this is a kind of semantics of the graph-theory). It is important to state, that the bottom parts (the leafs) of a hierarchy are also concepts, not instances (every

[1] What we call Aristotelian ontology is the mainstream reception of his logical works. Apart from Aristotle's own works, it also rests upon authors like Porphyrios.

species and a genus concept stands in an *is-a* relation). These conceptual hierarchies provide an easily computable yet expressive basis of the ontology.

Of course, up to this point the concept of ontology proposed is not far from trivial. The main trick is the introduction of the system of categories. There is only a previously known, fixed number of concept-hierarchies (trees), each with a fixed meaning. (For example there are substances (roughly saying entities) with their own hierarchy, there are qualities (again with their own hierarchy), there are quantities and so on). For the purpose of a prototype-system, the original categories of Aristotle were adopted[2], but later it can be changed depending upon specific needs.

The notion of intercategorial relation is also introduced, i.e. a concept can involve constraints on a concept of an another category (i.e. natural substance involves colour). These relations are of logical nature (implication or exclusion, maybe of complex concepts). The fact, that the assignment of categories is done before designing the ontology, makes it possible to introduce implicit relations joining together the root concepts of each category. The intercategorial relations, then, are only refinements of these primordial relations. (This could help the ontology designer to sketch the possible intercategorial relations.) This concept of ontology results in a system that is capable of incorporating taxonomies as well as handling constraints that join together different taxonomies. It is also capable of coping with *partially known information,* since categories related to the unknown piece of information reduce in default to the category's ancestor concept.

In the following we describe the prototype IKF application and how the ontology was used in this system.

# 4 The Prototype IKF-H Application

In the framework of the Hungarian IKF project a prototype system is under development in order to implement and demonstrate theoretical ideas in a real-world application. This prototype system collects available information about Hungarian companies from the World Wide Web, and provides it in a concise and integrated way to end users in a bank to support their decision processes (e.g. loan management).

The prototype application contains the following main components

- Information Retrieval Subsystem,
- Document Analysis Subsystem,
- Knowledge Repository,
- Document Repository, and
- Search and Report Interface.

Documents retrieved by the Retrieval Subsystem are analysed and stored in the repositories. End users access the repositories via a search and report generation interface. In the following we give a closer look on the document retrieval and analysis.

---

[2] These are: substances (entities), quantities, qualities, relations (relational qualities), space (spatial qualities), time (temporal qualities), positions, states, actions and passions.

### 4.1 Information Retrieval in the IKF System

The Retrieval Subsystem automatically traverses the information sources, retrieves documents, and prepares them for information extraction. It works as an autonomous agent ], that receives its goals (in the form of document source URLs and search patterns) from the rest of the IKF system, and achieves them by collecting and analysing documents from the sources [2] information extraction methods [16]. Its internal structure and working mechanism is shown in Figure 2.

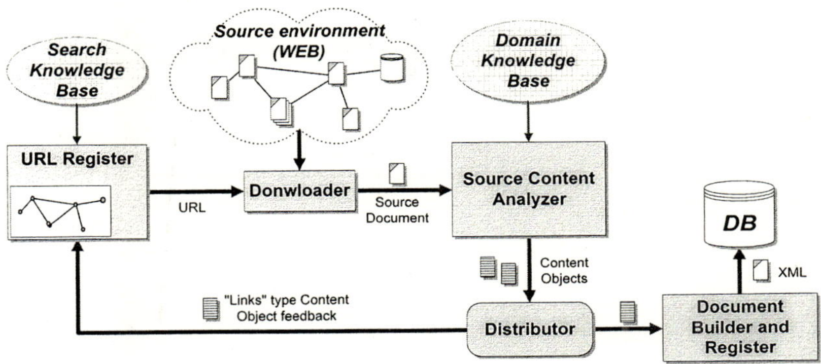


**Fig. 2.** Architecture of the document retrieval system

The Retrieval Subsystem works the following way. The URL register builds an internal model of the structure of the source environment [4]. With this, the agent has a general view of all the web places it visited or needs to be visited. The task of the Downloader module is to select the next URL, and to retrieve the document from the selected address, and build the so called **IKF Source Document**, which is the internal representation of the original source document in XML form.

The next step is to perform an initial analysis of the IKF Source Document. This is done by the **Source Content Analyser** that is responsible for recognizing the structure and main characteristics of the retrieved document.. It extracts so called **content objects**, that hold all the relevant information found in the original documents. These content objects are XML documents containing the extracted information in a structured form according to domain-specific type definitions. These definitions indicate the meaning of the content. For example, a common and simple content type is the list of links present in a document.

Typically, these content objects hold unstructured text between the tags, but these text fragments contain the information we want to extract. The Source Content Analyser also performs **textual analysis** on the content objects in order to describe them in more detail. This is based on indexing and information retrieval methods. The result is content descriptions attached to the content objects that help the deeper analysis of the retrieved texts.

Figure 3 shows an example of extracting information from articles of a news portal. The left side contains a sample picture of one article. It is embedded in a page that contains advertisements, menus, and other non-relevant information. On the right hand the resulting content object is shown. In this simple example the title, date, author, article-text and the citations (links) inside of the article text were extracted.

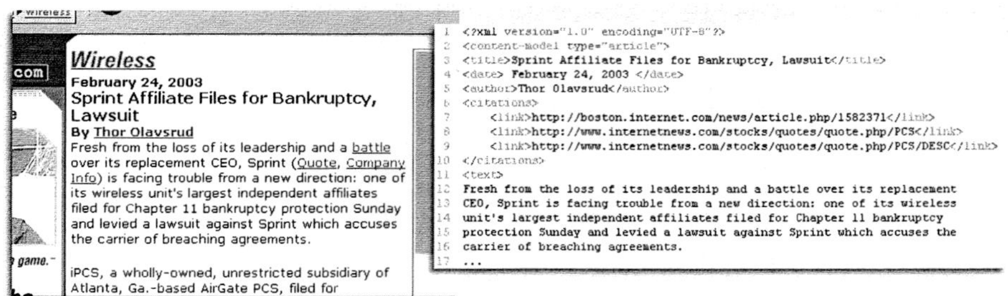


**Fig. 3.** Example for source document parsing

## 4.2 Document Analysis

The IKF Retrieval system performs only a shallow analysis of the source documents. Its main task is to transform them into XML structures (content objects) that help the further and deeper analysis. The final goal is to extract knowledge pieces from the IKF Documents that can be integrated into an IKF Application's knowledge repository.

In order to achieve this goal, the IKF Document Analysis module utilizes several analysis techniques. Based on the XML technology we created a general framework for document analysis. This general framework does not have any document processing capabilities by itself. It employs so called **document analysis plugins** (i.e. modules) in a dynamically configurable way to perform the analysis. These plugins share the same interface. Their inputs and outputs are IKF Documents, and they uniformly perform some kind of transformation upon them. Typically an analysis plugin creates or modifies an XML structure found in the IKF Document. There are several types of plugins, from a simple address, email, or phone number extractor, to the more complex grammatical analysis.

The most complex analysis plugin is the **linguistic analyser** [15]. It analyses the documents at several level: words, sentences and paragraphs. Its main goal is to build a grammatical construe that helps the knowledge extraction process. This is done in three steps: morphologic analysis, nominal phrase recognition, and verbal phrase recognition. The morphologic analysis identifies the words in the sentences and creates the morphologic representation of these words. Recognition of nominal and verbal phrases is based on a rule fitting mechanism. The nominal phrase rules refer to the morphologic information in the words, and the verbal phrase recognition is based on both morphologic and semantic information (based on the Hungarian Explanatory Dictionary).

The main aim of the creation of the grammatical construe is to enhance the effectiveness of the information extraction. This can be done in several ways. Noun constructions help in identifying objects and attaching attributes to them. It makes it possible to establish links between the analysed documents and the ontology) of the application area. Verbs and their complements help in recognizing relations between objects. They also allow the transformation of the information found in the documents into a standardized form suitable for knowledge representation and reasoning.

### 4.3 Application of the Ontology

There are several methods to utilise the potential of the ontology. Let us suppose that a powerful index-based search engine is available, along with a vast collection of documents (as it is in the IKF application). In a typical case the user wants to retrieve a relevant set of documents. In practice, the user defines relevance by supplying a list of words in a query. Typically, the user does not specify an extensive and precise list of words. There could be several reasons for it. Some of these extra words might seem trivial, some subtle; still they would significantly enhance the quality of the result. The simplest proof of this hypothesis is the monitoring of how a failed search query continues: by supplying a refined search term, i.e. more search terms.

This led to the idea that ontology should assist in *expanding the query*, i.e. in adding search terms that are implied by the background knowledge. When proposing new query terms based on background knowledge, a computed weight factor could be also assigned which estimates the relevance of the term. Disjunction constraints (and implications resulting in negations) could be also utilized via negative weight.

As it is implemented in the IKF prototype application, the query supplied by the user is also processed by the linguistic analyser. In order to achieve the query expanding functionality, the word stems are converted to concept names found in the ontology. It must be noted, that this relation is not a bijection, since a concept might have several names in natural language. (Although the current implementation treats the relation as a function, it is also theoretically possible that one name signifies several concepts).

After query words are converted into their conceptual counterparts, the essential function of this process could follow: the expansion of query terms (see Figure 4 on the next page). Given our structure of ontology this could be done in the following way: subsuming and superseding concepts (with a decreased weight factors) are also to added to the query list, and this process could be iterated up to some level (with respectively decreased weight factors). The intercategorial constraints also could be utilized via specifying those concepts from other categories, which are implied by these constraints.

A query containing several words is mapped onto list of concept names. This could be seen as complex concepts joined together by a conjunction, and therefore an equivalent simple concept could be also retrieved from the ontology. If such search fails, then it should be considered as a disjunctive complex concept in order for the process to continue. Another possibility is to apply the same process to the negated concept list (with negative value factors).

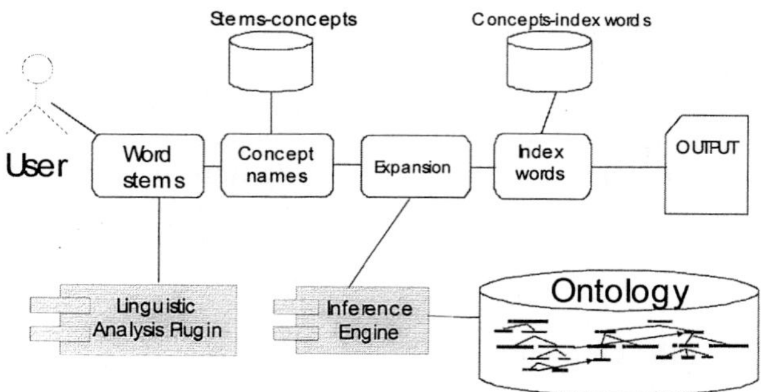


**Fig. 4.** The process of expanding a query

This step results in an another list of concepts, which again must be converted. The output of this conversion, however, will be utilized by an index-based search method so another mapping is also required, which relates concept names to index words. Again, this relation ought not to be a strict bijection and every index word could carry an extra weight multiplication factor. The resulting index word list serves as an input to the index-based search.

The advantages that can be gained from using ontologies depend on the content and structure of the whole ontology, but still can be illuminated by the following simple example. Suppose that a computer user is searching for information on so-called "exploit." Using a simple ontology depicted on the left side of Figure 5. the query could be supplemented with additional weighted terms (right side).

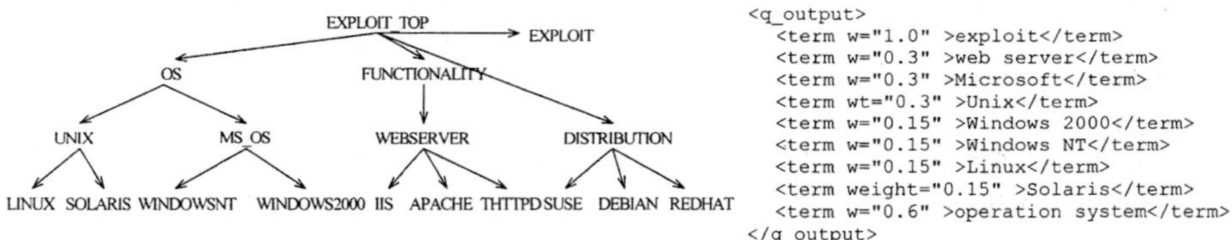


**Fig. 5.** An ontology fragment (only taxonomy shown) and the resulting query

For the sake of example a collection of 101 documents (approx. 1.2 MB) containing the word "exploit" was fetched from the Internet and loaded in the Document Repository. Each of these documents was manually classified into one of three categories: relevant, semi-relevant and irrelevant.

Using this example it can be seen that because of polysemity and different contexts of usage the simple index search using vector model delivered inadequate results, whilst the same search engine with the supplemented query performed much better (see Figure 6). It should be noted, that this technique results improves both on pinpointing specific results and eliminating irrelevant ones, which are fruitful advances factors from the viewpoint of further processing the results.

This example is only to illustrate the original idea of how index-based searching can profit from using ontologies. As mentioned above, in the IKF Application ontologies fulfill a more complex role: they assign weight factors to each term and are

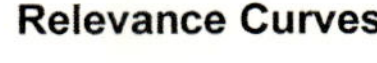


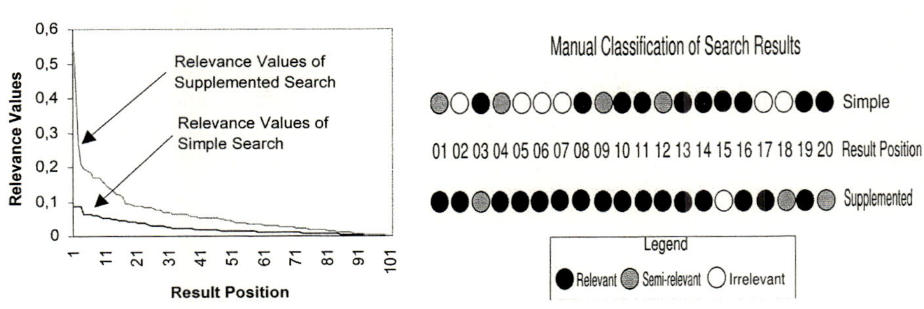


**Fig. 6.** Relevance Examination of the Two Results Sets

also responsible for the translation of linguistically analyzed natural language terms into terms of the index language.

The process of query completion described above is implemented in a prototype system, which proves its utility value (and was also used to produce the example above). For the sake of this implementation a *prototype ontology* was also developed (primarily concerning concepts related to business processes). In order to execute queries in the ontology, an implementation of a suitable logical apparatus must be selected. For the purpose of prototyping, the selected one was I. Horrock's FaCT (fast Classification of Terms) system [14]. The whole implementation was done in component-based Java with XML and CORBA interfaces.

Further improvements of this ontology-based functionality might make use of other levels of linguistic analysis, or might include reasoning with instances.

## 5 Summary

In this paper we have shown how the generic information and knowledge fusion architecture (envisioned within an international EUREKA cooperation) takes shape of a Hungarian language, financial domain specific application.

The key issue in progressing toward well functioning application is the development of a suitable domain ontology, as the basis for the interpretation and grounding of the knowledge extracted from short financial news. The identified practical and theoretical requirements led to the construction of an ontology with a structure conforming to human way of describing the world, yielding no extra implementation problems and still being theoretically well founded.

The developed prototype system autonomously retrieves documents from assumed information sources (e.g. web resources, here Hungarian electronic financial publications). Based upon the proposed structure of the ontology, functionality was designed and implemented, which expand queries by adding terms implied by the background (ontological) knowledge.

The system selects then an appropriate source content parser based on previously defined document and source models, and transforms the retrieved source content into XML structures (called content objects). Then, a document analysis module performs various text analysis tasks on content objects in order to extract information from the source documents. These tasks include also linguistic analysis with tools suited to the application language.

Although there is still much to be done with the prototype the lesson learned so far is the crucial role of the ontology to every of the system services and the dismaying fact that in the interpretation of the Hungarian language news widely used linguistic tools are not enough, and that the language calls for essentially heuristic approach.

## References


[1] EUREKA PROJECT "IKF - Information and Knowledge Fusion", March 2000.

[2] "The IKF architecture", IKF project report, August, 2002.

[3] T. Mészáros, Zs. Barczikay, F. Bodon, T. Dobrowiecki, Gy. Strausz, "Building an Information and Knowledge Fusion System", IEA/AIE-2001 The Fourteenth International IEA/AIE Conference, June 4-7, 2001, Budapest, Hungary

[4] S. Chakrabarti, et.al., "Mining the Web's Link Structure," IEEE Computer 32: 60-67, 1999

[5] J. M. Broadshaw, "Software Agents", The MIT Press, 1997

[6] John Sowa's web site devoted to knowlege representation and related topics of logic, ontology, and computer systems, http://www.bestweb.net/~sowa/direct/index.htm

[7] J. Sowa, "Knowledge Representation: Logical, Philosophical, and Computational Foundations," Brooks Cole Publishing Co., Pacific Grove, CA, 2000

[8] Standard Upper Ontology, IEEE Study Group, IEEE Computer Society, Standards Activity Board, June 2000, wysiwyg://634/http://ltsc.ieee.org/suo/index.html

[9] N. Guarino and Ch. Welty, "A Formal Ontology of Properties", LADSEB/CNR Technical Report 01/2000, http://www.ladseb.pd.cnr.it/infor/ontology/Papers/OntologyPapers.html

[10] M.S. Fox, J.F. Chionglo, and F.G. Fadel, "A Common-Sense Model of the Enterprise", Proceedings of the 2nd Industrial Engineering Research Conference, 1993, pp. 425-429, Norcross GA: Institute for Industrial Engineers

[11] US Taxonomies, US GAAP C&I Taxonomy 00-04-04

[12] N. Guarino, "Formal Ontology in Information Systems," In N.Guarino (ed.) Formal Ontology in Information Systems. Proceedings of FOIS'98, Trento, Italy, 6-8 June 1998. IOS Press, Amsterdam: 3-15.

[13] N. Guarino, and Giaretta, P. "Ontologies and Knowledge Bases: Towards a Terminological Clarification," In N. Mars (ed.) Towards Very Large Knowledge Bases: Knowledge Building and Knowledge Sharing. IOS Press, 1995, Amsterdam: 25-32.

[14] I. Horrocks. The FaCT system. In H. de Swart, editor, Automated Reasoning with Analytic Tableaux and Related Methods: International Conference Tableaux'98, number 1397 in Lecture Notes in Artificial Intelligence, pages 307-312. Springer-Verlag, Berlin, May 1998.

[15] B. Benkõ, Katona, T., and Varga, P. „Understanding Hungarian language texts for information extraction," Internal Report, Dept. of Measurement and Information Systems, Budapest University of Technology and Economics, 2002 (in Hungarian)

[16] Eikvil, L., "Information Extraction from World Wide Web - A Survey", Report No. 945, Norweigan Computing Center, July 1999.

# A Bidders Cooperation Support System for Agent-Based Electronic Commerce

Tokuro Matsuo and Takayuki Ito

Center of Knowledge Science, Japan Advanced Institute of Science and Technology, 1-1 Asahidai, Tatsunokuchi-machi, Nomi-gun, Ishikawa 923-1292, Japan,
{t-matsuo,itota}@jaist.ac.jp,
http://www.jaist.ac.jp/~{t-matsuo,itota}

**Abstract.** Internet is becoming an increasingly prosperous network for many types of commerce. Internet Auctions represent a particularly effective form of electronic commerce and have become a promising field for applying agent technologies. In many existing auction sites, some sellers deal in the same sort of goods or their imitations. Buyers bid for each item on sale. Buyers cannot always purchase goods at the lowest price because buyers compete, that is they do not cooperate with each other. Thus, buyers need to search hard to find items they can purchase. In this paper, we propose a bidders support system based on a mediated agent for auctions on the Internet. In our system, buyers can purchase goods at the lowest price by working in cooperation with each other. Each buyer selects an item based on his/her multi-attribute preferences. A mediated agent calculates the buyers' utilities, and determines the successful bidders. We consider an assumption of linear utility based on multi-attribute utility theory. The advantages of the bidder cooperation support system are as follows. (1) Each buyer can purchase an item at the lowest price. (2) The buyer's multi-attribute utilities are reflected. (3) The mechanism is robustness for buyer's anticipating. We conducted an experiment to investigate and compare buyers' utilities between existing auctions and our system. Our experiment shows that buyers utilities in our system are sufficiently higher than these in existing auctions.

## 1 Introduction

As the Internet develops, it has become an increasingly prosperous network for many types of commerce. Internet auctions have been a particularly effective form of electronic commerce [eBay]. Internet auctions have made rapid progress in recent years, and there have been many investigations into Internet auctions [Yokoo 00][Turban 00]. Internet auctions have been recognized as a promising field to apply agent technologies [Ito 01][Matsuo 02].

Substitute goods are sold on a large number of existing Internet auction sites. We define that good A is a substitute for good B as follows. Good A can be purchased in place of good B by buyers. Even if being the identical or substitute goods, some goods are bid on by buyers, while other goods are never bid on. On existing Internet auction sites, there are a lot of goods that receive no bids, thus, they remain unsold. Buyers cannot always purchase goods at a lower price because buyers compete, hence,

P.W.H. Chung, C.J. Hinde, M. Ali (Eds.): IEA/AIE 2003, LNAI 2718, pp. 369–378, 2003.

they do not cooperate with each other [Matsuo 03]. Thus, each buyer cannot purchase an item which satisfies his/her preference. Therefore, each buyer's preference is not effectively reflected. To solve the problems, we propose a bidder support system for multiple auctions based on the buyer's preference. Buyers cooperate with each other in our system. Buyers can purchase goods at the lowest price by making collusion. In our system, each buyer selects an item to purchase based on a good's multi-attribute. Here, we assume the multi-attribute utility theory, whereas when a buyer purchases a good, each buyer has multi-attribute preferences to select a good. Our system supports to form collusion for buyers based on multi-attribute utility theory.

There are some related work concerned with Internet auctions in electronic commerce. Yamamoto and Sycara proposed a stable and efficient buyer coalition formation scheme "GroupBuyAuction" for e-marketplaces; buyers form a group based on item categories [Yamamoto 01]. The group leader agent splits the group into sub groups (coalitions), selects a winning seller for each coalition, and calculates surplus the division among buyers. Li and Sycara proposed an algorithm for combinatorial coalition formation and payoff division in electronic commerce [Li 02]. They consider an e-market where each buyer places a bid on a combination of items with a reservation cost, and sellers offer price discounts for each item based on volumes. In general, coalition formation problems for multiple agents are NP-hard problems. When agents increase, solution spaces will be exponential huge. Leyton-Brown *et al.* proposed the $BiddingClub$. In the $BiddingClub$, buyers form collusion and purchase goods. In the $BiddingClub$, agents conduct a pre-auction. After the pre-auction, monetary transfers take place. However, the buyer's multi-attribute preferences are not reflected into trades in these researches. We propose a bidder support system for users to participate in multiple auctions based on buyers' multi-attribute preferences. Our system can realize that buyers can purchase goods at the lowest price, and the buyers' utilities are reflected effectively.

The rest of the paper is organized as follows. Section 2 describes the outline of our market. In Section 3, we show how our system supports cooperation support among buyers. In Section 4, we show an example of a user interface and present related work. Finally in Section 5, we provide some final remarks.

## 2 The *Cooperation Market*

### 2.1 Internet Auction

Internet auction is a remarkable and effective form of electronic commerce [Matsuo 02c]. In an auction called an English protocol, a bid (evaluation) value is presented and a bidder can increase a bid value freely until his/her reservation price [eBay][Yahoo]. Reservation price means the highest price a buyer will pay [Varian 00]. When the price of the good is higher than the buyer's reservation price, the buyer does not purchase it. When bidders no longer desire a change of value, the good is awarded to the highest bidder and the bid value is paid. Deadlines for participation are generally due to time and the bid price. First, start and end time are created, and participation closes at the end time. Bidding is closed at the predetermined time. Second, when the price that a seller can deal in is bidden by a buyer, the buyer can purchase the good at the price.

**Table 1.** Number of successful bids

| 11/2002 | Yahoo! Auctions | Bidders |
|---|---|---|
| Number of exhibitions | 3,180,000 | 580,000 |
| Number of successful bids | 827,000 | 43,000 |
| Rates of successful bids | 26% | 7.5% |

In existing auction sites, there are not high rates of successful trades. Table 1 shows the number of successful trades in Yahoo! Auctions and Bidders Auction [Yahoo][bidders]. In November, 2002 for Yahoo! Auctions, the number of goods on sale was 3,180,000 and the number of successful trades was 827,000. The average number of sales was about 26% of the total item sold [toukei]. At the Bidders Auction for the same period, the number of goods on sale was 580,000 and the number of successful trades was 43,000. The average number of sale was about 7.5% of the total number of items put up for auction.

It is clear from the above statistics that a lot of items unsold. We focus on these unsold goods.

### 2.2 An Outline of the *Cooperation Market*

Fig. 1 shows a bidding cooperation support system in the *Cooperation Market*. The system is built as CGI written in Perl. The user interface is written in JavaScript and Html.

We show an outline of trading in the *Cooperation Market*. First, substitute goods are registered in the market. Goods information includes details of the goods, such as color, shape, picture, and so on. A time limit for registration is decided based on number of goods. When the number of participants equals the number of goods, new buyers can not participate in the market.

## 3 A Cooperation Support System

### 3.1 Multi-attribute Utility Theory

We assume the multi-attribute utility theory. A buyer's preference is shown as a utility function. A utility function consists of multiple independent attributes based on MAUT ( Multi Attribute Utility Theory ) [Shintani 00][Keeney 76]. In general, MAUT handles problems for which outcomes are characterized by two or more attributes. For example, purchasing a new car requires consideration of the price, the shape, the color, the type, etc. In MAUT, for an alternative $C_i$, the attributes $X_1$, $X_2$, ..., $X_n$ exist, and their values are $x_1(C_i)$, $x_2(C_i)$, ...,$x_n(C_i)$. We can represent the utility $u(C_i)$ for the attribute $C_i$ as

$$U(C_i) = f(f_1(x_1(C_i)), ..., f_n(x_n(C_i))),$$

where $f$ is a certain function. We can select several options with respect to $f$, according to the application area. Based on the above utility, each agent has a preference, and according to von Neumann-Morgenstern, we define an agent's preference as follows:

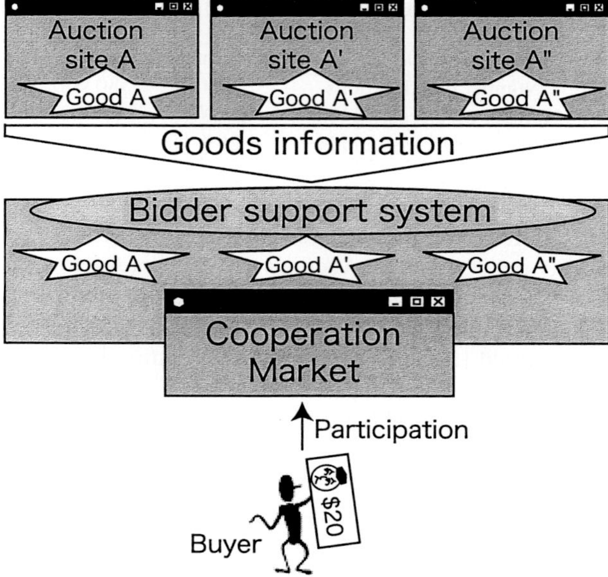


**Fig. 1.** The *Cooperation Market*

$C_i \succ C_j \iff u(C_i) > u(C_j)$ and $C_i \sim C_j \iff U(C_i) = U(C_j)$. Here, $C_i \succ C_j$ means that the agent prefers $C_i$ to $C_j$, whereas $C_i \sim C_j$ means that the agent has no preference for $C_i$ or $C_j$. A user's preference is quantified into a multi-attribute utility by using MAUT [Matsuo 02b].

### 3.2 Linear Utility

In this paper, it is assumed that an agent's utility function is quasi-linear for calculating buyer's utility. By the quasi-linear utility, if a buyer with the evaluation value b* buys one unit of a good at the paying price, p, we assume his or her utility is defined as b* - p. If a buyer cannot obtain a unit, we assume a utility of 0.

In our system, each buyer presents his/her reservation price. The reservation price is the maximum price buyer will pay. When buyer $i$'s reservation price $r_i$ is above the good price, the buyer can purchase it. We assume a linear utility based on multi-attribute utility. The buyer's utility is defined for good $i$ as follows:

$$U_i = u_i(x_1) + u_i(x_2) + ... + u_i(x_k) + ... + u_i(x_n)$$

Namely,

$$U_i = \sum_{k=1}^{n} u_i(x_k)$$

Here, $u_i(x_k)$ shows the utility for attribute $k$. $U_i$ is a good $i$'s utility which is the sum of multi-attribute utilities. We define multi-attribute utilities as a buyer's reservation price

**Table 2.** Buyer's reservation price

| Attributes | Specs | Price |
|---|---|---|
| CPU | 1 GHz | $180 |
| Hard disk | 50 Gb | $220 |
| Memory | 128 Mb | $35 |
| Accessories | | $65 |
| Sum Total | | $500 |

**Table 3.** Buyer's reservation price

| Attributes | Specs | Price |
|---|---|---|
| CPU | 1 GHz | $180 |
| Hard disk | 40 Gb | $180 |
| Memory | 256 Mb | $95 |
| Accessories | | $65 |
| Sum Total | | $520 |

for calculating the multi-attribute preferences. For example, we consider that buyer 1's reservation price is $500 for personal computer A. Except for the good's price, the personal computer A's multi-attribute and specifications are described as CPU (1 GHz), hard disk (50 Gb), memory (128 Mb), and accessories. While, buyer 1 evaluates that personal computer B's reservation price is $520. Except for the good's price, personal computer B's multi-attribute and its specifications are described as CPU (1 GHz), hard disk (40 Gb), memory (256 Mb), and accessories. The buyer's reservation price can be distributed as Table 2 and Table 3.

When the buyer must make a choice between computer A and computer B, the buyer focus on the goods' attributes. Here, a reservation price function is generalized as follows:

$$r_i = r_i(x_1) + r_i(x_2) + ... + r_i(x_k) + ... + r_i(x_n)$$

Namely,

$$r_i = \sum_{k=1}^{n} r_i(x_k)$$

$r_i$ is buyer 1's reservation price for good $i$. $r_i(x_k)$ means a multi-attribute reservation price for good $i$. We can compare a multi-attribute value and a reservation price. For example, a comparison of memory between personal computers A and B is $60. When buyer 1 purchased personal computer A for $480, the buyer's utility calculated $500 - $480 = $20.

### 3.3 Decision of Successful Bidders

In this section, we show concerned with the decision of successful bidders. A successful bidders are decided large order of their utilities. Each buyer's reservation price must be above the lowest price. The lowest price is submitted by a seller, namely, a seller hoping to make a deal above the lowest price. Here, we assume that each buyer does not bid based on a false evaluation value. Fig. 2 shows the trading of procedure in the *Cooperation Market*. First, buyers register and present reservation price (evaluation value) for each attribute. The multi-attribute reservation price is summed as the reservation price for the good. When a buyer's minimum evaluation value is less than the maximum price for any goods, the buyer can not participate in the *Cooperation Market*. Next, the total of the buyer's utilities are calculated, and a set of maximum utilities is decided. Finally, a mediated agent bids the minimum price at the deadline time, and the buyers wait until the deadline of the real auctions. If other potential buyers (side the *Cooperation*

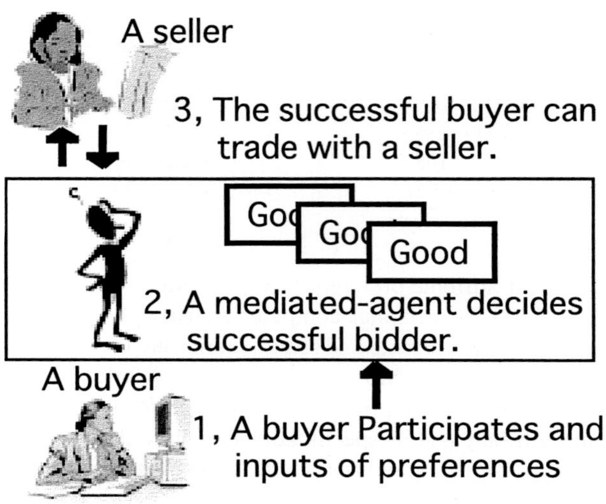


**Fig. 2.** An Outline of a Trade

*Market*) bids based on an evaluation value above reservation price a participant has bid, the participant can not purchase the good.

## 4 Experiment

We conducted an experiment to investigate and compare buyers' utilities between existing auctions and our system. Buyers' utilities are described as a difference between the total of reservation prices and the sum total payment. We assumed that all auctions are of the English auction type. The English auction has been adopted by Yahoo!, eBay, etc. We assume each buyer's evaluation value is a private value. Their values are given based on a uniform distribution. First, Fig. 3. shows the experimental result graphically indicating buyers' utilities in the existing auction systems as well as our own. The horizontal axis shows at what rates buyers compete. The vertical axis shows buyers' total utilities. We conducted 10 auctions for each setting and calculated the average. In the experiment, we assumed there were four buyers and four substitute goods. For each case, we compared the existing auctions with the cooperation support system. When our system was used, the buyers' total utilities were always higher than these in the existing auctions. When the rate at which buyers compete against each other is 10% (like Bidders Auction), the difference of buyers' utilities shows 46.3 - 20.1 = 26.2. When the rate at which buyers compete against each other is 25% (like Yahoo! Auctions) , the difference of buyers' utilities shows 34.3 - 23.1 = 11.2. When our system is compared with the existing auctions, an obvious difference appears in the buyers' total utilities. We insist that the average of buyers' utilities our system realizes is always larger than the average of buyers' utilities that the existing auctions realize.

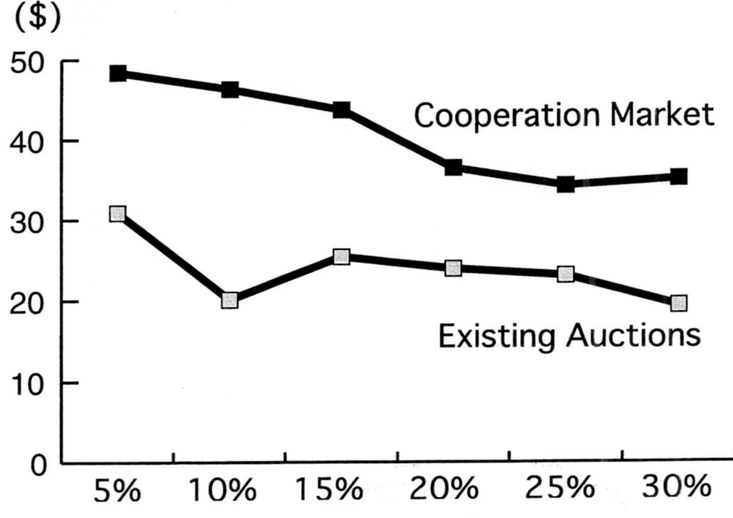


**Fig. 3.** An average of buyers' utilities

# 5 Discussion

## 5.1 User Interface Example

Fig. 4 shows an example of our user interface in *Cooperation Market*. A buyer selects the category of goods for a purchase. The number of participants and goods are displayed. Each buyer registers by the deadline. Each participant inputs his/her multi-preferences, and the buyer's order of preferences are determined.

## 5.2 Advantages of Our System

In existing Internet auctions, a lot of goods remain unsold. There is not a high rate of successful bid. We focus on what substitute goods are left on the shelf. In our system, buyers form collusion with each other. When a bidding ring is successful, each buyer can purchase a good at the lowest price. Thus, buyers preferences are reflected effectively. Our mechanism is robust against stealing the march, because our system handles substitute goods. Our system allocates a good to a buyer. After allocation, the buyer need not steal a march because the goods are substitute. Even if a buyer succeeds to steal the march, the buyer's utility is reduced.

## 5.3 Related Work

In this section, we present an overview of the work of others related to our study. AuctionBot [Wurman 98] is an auction server where users can create auctions to sell their items. In auctions, agents can bid according to a pre-defined protocol. AuctionBot provides an API for users to create agents. Kasbah [Chaves 96] provides a marketplace

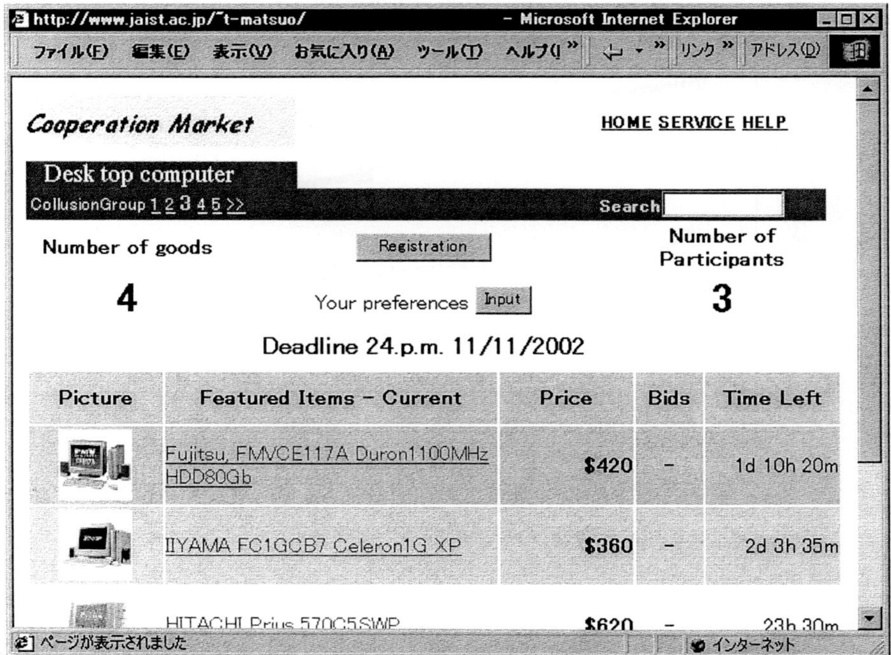


**Fig. 4.** An example of user interface

on the Web where users can create agents that buy and sell in the marketplace. On Kasbah, deals between agents are conducted based on a simple protocol. FishMarket [Rodriguez 97] provides an electronic auction site where users can encode several bidding strategies to their agents. Although FishMarket is an experimental system, several virtual tournaments have been conducted on it. Tete-A-Tete [Guttman 98] provides an electronic market where agents cooperatively negotiate with each other based on arguments. eMediator [Sandholm 99] is an electronic commerce server and consists mainly of eAuctionHouse and eCommitter. eAuctionHouse is a configurable auction place that supports many auction types, while eCommitter is a leveled commitment contract optimizer that can solve the Nash equilibrium thresholds. The above systems do not handle volume discount.

GroupBuyAuction [Yamamoto 01] is an agent-based electronic market on which agents automatically negotiate with each other on behalf of their users. In particular, in the GroupBuyAuction, buyer agents can form coalitions to buy goods at volume discount prices. The difference between our approach and that of GroupBuyAuction is the exchanging mechanism among seller agents. Li and Sycara considered an e-market where each buyer places a bid on a combination of items with a reservation cost, and sellers offer price discounts for each item based on volumes [Li 02]. By artificially dividing the reservation cost of each buyer among the items, optimal coalitions with respect to each item are constructed. These coalitions satisfy the complementarity of the items by reservation cost transfers, and induce the optimal solution. The *BiddingClub*

[Leyton-Brown 00] was proposed by Leyton-Brown, Shoham and Tennenholtz. In the *BiddingClub*, agents conduct a pre-auction. After the pre-auction, monetary transfers take place. The buyer's multi-attribute preferences were not referred to in these studies.

## 6 Conclusion

We proposed an agent-based *Cooperation Market* where buyers can form collusion based on their multi-attribute preferences. We focused on these unsold goods in existing Internet auction sites. In the *Cooperation Market*, substitute goods are dealt in, and buyers form collusion to purchase the goods at the best price available. In our system, each buyer can purchase goods at the lowest price, because each buyer engage in a form of collusion. Thus, a buyer's multi-attribute utilities are reflected effectively. In our experiments, the buyers' utilities in our system were higher than those in existing auction sites.

## References

[bidders] http://www.bidders.co.jp/

[eBay] http://pages.ebay.com/

[toukei] http://www16.big.or.jp/ shumaru/

[Yahoo] http://auctions.yahoo.co.jp/

[Chaves 96] Chavez A., and Maes P.: Kasbah: An agent marketplace for buying and selling goods, in Proceedings of the 1st International Conference and Exhibition on The Practical Application of Intelligent Agents and Multi-Agents (PAAM96), pp. 75-90, 1996.

[Guttman 98] Guttman R. H. and Maes P.: Agent-mediated integrative negotiation for retail electronic commerce, in Proceedings of the 2nd International Workshop on Cooperative Information Agents (CIA'98), 1998.

[Ito 01] Ito T., Shintani T.: Implementation Technologies for Multiagent Systems and Their Applications, Journal of the Japanese Society for Artificial Intelligence, Vol.16, No.4, pp. 469-475, 2001.

[Ito 98] Ito T. and Shintani T.: Utility Revision in a Java-based Group Decision Support System, In the Proceedings of the 5th Pacific Rim International Conferences on Artificial Intelligence (PRICAI'98) Workshop on Java-based Intelligent systems, 1998.

[Keeney 76] Keeney R.K. and Raiffa H.: Decisions with Multiple Objects, John Wiley and Sons, New York, 1976.

[Leyton-Brown 00] Leyton-Brown K., Shoham Y., Tennenholtz M.: Bidding Clubs: Institutionalized Collusion in Auction, in the proceeding of ACM Conference on Electronic Commerce (EC'00), pp. 253-259, 2000.

[Li 02] Li C., Sycara K.: Algorithms for Combinational Coalition Formation and Payoff Division in an Electronic Marketplace, in the proceedings of International Joint Conference on Autonomous Agents and Multi-agent Systems (AAMAS-2002), 2002.

[Matsuo 03] Matsuo T., Ito T.: A Bidder Group Support System to Participate in Multiple Auctions, in the proceedings of the 1st International Forum on Information and Computer Technology (IFICT 2003), pp.62-67, 2003.

[Matsuo 02] Matsuo T., Ito T.: A Decision Support System for Group Buying based on Buyers' Preferences in Electronic Commerce, in the proceedings of the Eleventh World Wide Web International Conference (WWW-2002), 2002.

[Matsuo 02b] Matsuo T., Ito T.: A Designate Bid Reverse Auction for Agent-based Electronic Commerce, in the proceeding of the International Conference on Industrial and Engineering Applications of Artificial Intelligence and Expert System (IEA/AIE-2002), Lecture Note in Artificial Intelligence 2358, pp. 460-469, 2002.

[Matsuo 02c] Matsuo T., Ito T.: Effects of Nomination in a Multiagent Reverse Auction, in the proceeding of the 6th World MultiConference on Systemics, Cybernetics and Informatics (SCI-2002), pp. 199-204, 2002.

[Rodriguez 97] Rodriguez J.A., Noriega P., Sierra C., and Padget J.: FM96.5: A Java-based Electronic Auction House, in Proceedings of the 2st International Conference and Exhibition on The Practical Application of Intelligent Agents and Multi-Agents (PAAM97), 1997.

[Sandholm 99] Sandholm T.: eMediator: A next generation electronic commerce server, in Proceedings of the Sixteenth National Conference on Artificial Intelligence (AAAI99) AAAI Press, pp. 923-924, 1999.

[Shintani 00] Shintani T., Ito T., Sycara K.: Multiple Negotiations among Agents for a Distributed Meeting Scheduler, in the proceeding of the Fourth International Conference on Multi Agent Systems (ICMAS-2000), pp. 435-436, 2000.

[Turban 00] Turban E., Lee J., King D., and Chung H. M.: Electronic Commerce: A Managerial Perspective, Pearson Education, 2000.

[Varian 00] Varian H. R.: Intermediate Microeconomics: A Modern Approach, 2nd ed., W. W. Norton & Company, 1990.

[Wurman 98] Wurman P.R., Wellman M.P., and Walsh W.E.: The Michigan internet auction-bot: A con.gurable auction server for human and software agents, in Proceedings of the 2nd International Conference on Autonomous Agents (Agents-98), 1998.

[Yamamoto 01] Yamamoto, J. and Sycara, K.: A Stable and Efficient Buyer Coalition Formation 40 Scheme for E-Marketplaces, in the proceedings of International Joint Conference on Autonomous Agents and Multi-agent Systems (AAMAS-2001), 2001.

[Yokoo 00] Makoto Yokoo: Internet Auctions: Theory and Application, Journal of the Japanese Society for Artificial Intelligence, Vol.15, No.3, pp. 404-415, 2000.

# SumTime-Turbine: A Knowledge-Based System to Communicate Gas Turbine Time-Series Data

Jin Yu, Ehud Reiter, Jim Hunter, and Somayajulu Sripada

Department of Computing Science
University of Aberdeen
Aberdeen, AB24 3UE, UK
{jyu, ereiter, jhunter, ssripada}@csd.abdn.ac.uk

**Abstract:** *SumTime-Turbine* produces textual summaries of archived time-series data from gas turbines. These summaries should help experts understand large data sets that cannot be visually presented in a single graphical display. *SumTime-Turbine* is based on pattern detection, knowledge-based temporal abstraction (KBTA), and natural language generation (NLG) technology. A prototype version of the system has been implemented and is currently being evaluated.

## 1 Introduction

In order to get the most out of gas turbines, *TIGER* [2] has been developed by Intelligent Application Ltd to continuously monitor and assess the condition of gas turbines. *TIGER* can collect and archive about 600 data points per second from more than 250 channels [1]. Since these archived data are potentially very valuable for supporting diagnosis, anomaly detection, and prediction, it's worthwhile to develop techniques and implement tools to help domain experts to mine these data. Currently, human examination of time series data is generally done either by direct inspection of the numerical values of the data (for small data sets), by graphical visualisation, or by statistical analyses. The volume of *TIGER* data is so huge that it's not feasible for domain engineers to go through the graphical displays looking for events of interest. A further possibility is the generation of textual summaries. So a knowledge-based system named *SumTime-Turbine* is being implemented to produce text summaries of these archived temporal data.

The value of *SumTime-Turbine* is that it could provide a good abstraction of the data in terms of event patterns and give a concise summary from these abstractions for engineers. So it could help engineers to formulate useful knowledge that is beneficial to fault detection and diagnosis in gas turbines.

The organisation of the remainder of this paper is as follows. Section 2 presents the architecture of *SumTime-Turbine*. Main functions and implementation of the prototype system of *SumTime-Turbine* are explained in Section 3. Evaluation methods on the system are introduced in Section 4. Section 5 compares our system with those of others and Section 6 gives future work in the prototype system.

P.W.H. Chung, C.J. Hinde, M. Ali (Eds.): IEA/AIE 2003, LNAI 2718, pp. 379–384, 2003.

## 2 Architecture of SumTime-Turbine

Based on knowledge acquisition sessions with human experts, we have discovered that the system should perform the tasks shown in Figure 1.

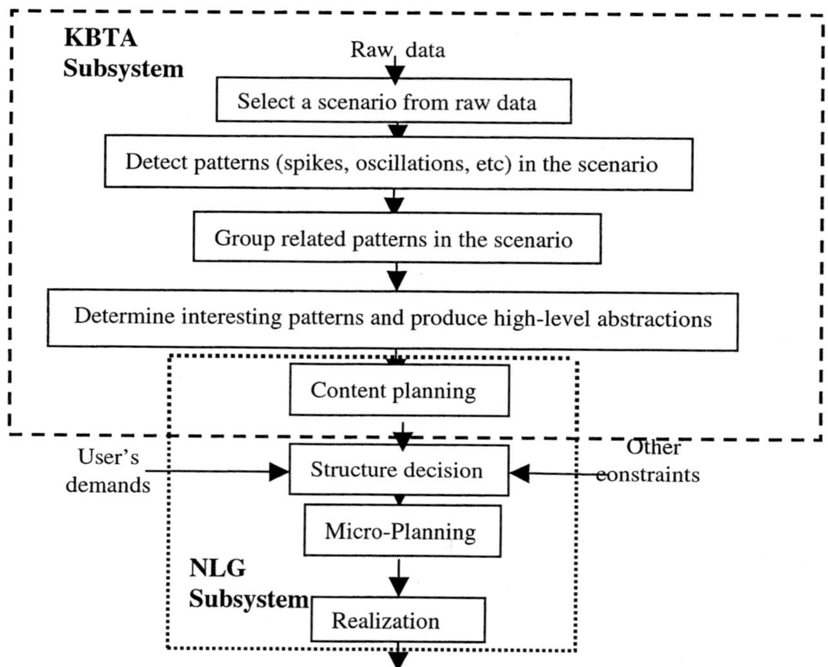


**Fig. 1.** Architecture of SumTime-Turbine

This KBS system could be implemented in two subsystems: KBTA and NLG, to carry out these tasks. These two subsystems form separate, reusable modules, which are connected through a content planning module (Fig. 1). The advantage of this architecture is that both the subsystems are reusable. At the same time, much information about natural language generation provided by the KBTA subsystem probably can be used for the reliable generation of summary in the NLG subsystem, thus improving the quality of contents, word usage, etc in the output summary.

## 3 Functions of the Prototype System of SumTime-Turbine

A prototype system of *SumTime-Turbine*, implemented based on the above architecture and techniques, includes eight analysis functions. (1) Primitive Pattern Recognition, (2) Primitive Pattern Description, (3) High Level Abstraction, (4) Summary, (5) Interesting Pattern Recognition, (6) Primitive Pattern Evaluation, (7) Interesting Pattern Evaluation, and (8) Summary Evaluation; plus two evaluation functions: (1) Non-Experts Marking Up Patterns, and (2) Experts Marking Up Patterns.

### 3.1 Primitive and Interesting Pattern Recognition

In the gas turbine domain, we have noticed that engineers are very interested in turbulence patterns that can be further classified into three primitive patterns: spikes, oscillations, and steps. Each of them has different special meanings for engineers when they investigate the raw data. A systematic method, including a turbulence-locator and a pattern-classifier, has been developed to automatically identify such patterns [8].

We have found that the process of primitive pattern recognition is domain-independent while that of determining which patterns are interesting is domain-dependent. Interesting pattern recognition applies domain knowledge to decide which primitive patterns are interesting. For example, in the gas turbine domain, spikes that occur simultaneously across all channels such as a set of spikes at 23:55:57 (Fig. 2) are interesting for domain engineers while small stand-alone spikes such as a spike at 23:59:02 in channel TNH (Fig. 2) are not interesting. In a sense, primitive patterns should include as many candidates for interesting patterns as possible.

### 3.2 Primitive Pattern Description

This function abstracts informatiton about patterns including: pattern names, start time of patterns, temporal length of patterns, size of patterns. Such information can be explained in linguistic format. The following is a linguistic description about primitive patterns occurring in channel FSGR in Figure 2.

Channel name: FSGR (Linguistic format)
Very big downward spike at 21:50:08, 21:51:36, 21:53:36, and 22:36:05.
Big erratic spike at 23:56:17.

### 3.3 High Level Abstraction

This function is mainly based on KBTA method [4] [5]. Currently it carries out vertical and horizontal aggregation. Vertical aggregation is based on simultaneous check and horizontal aggregation involves joining nearby patterns to form a main set of patterns. The following is the results of high level abstracton on the sample data set.

Vertical aggregation (Linguistic format)
Spikes in all channels at 21:49:49, 21:51:31, 21:53:17, 23:55:57
Mostly spikes with some steps in all channels at 22:35:02
Horizontal aggregation (Linguistic format)
Spikes in all channels at 21:49:49 and 23:55:57
Mostly spikes with some steps in all channels at 22:35:02,

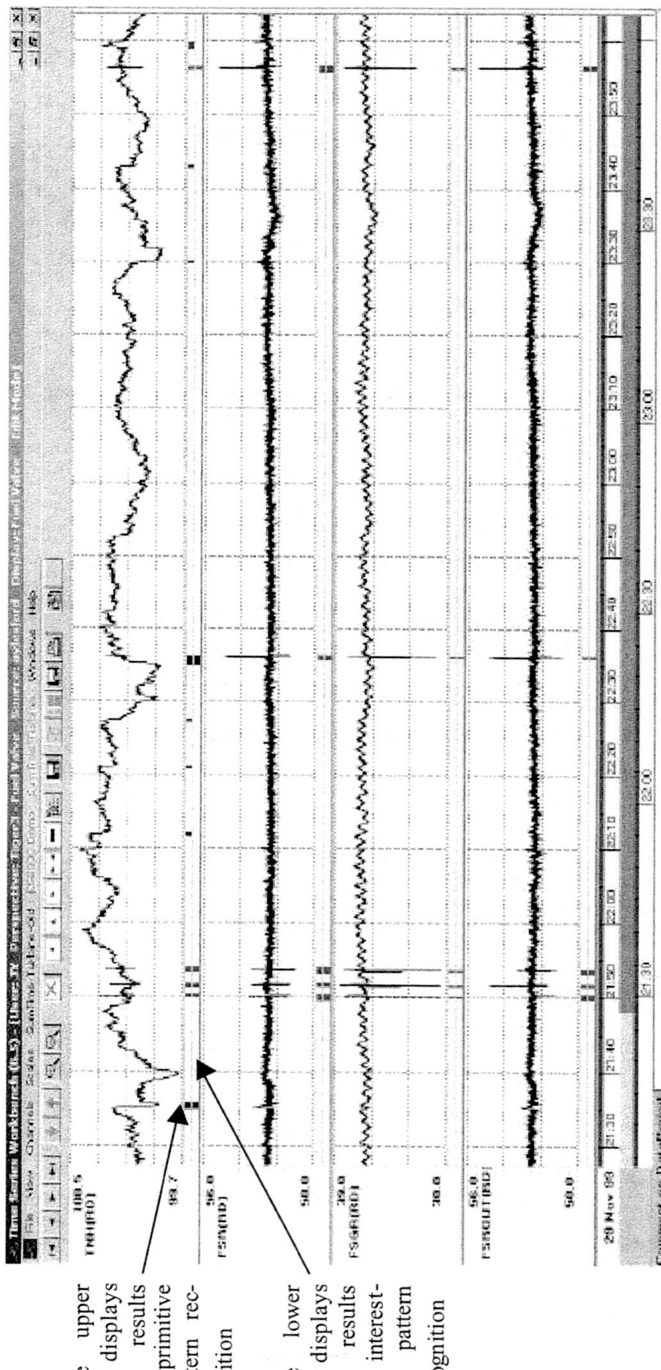


**Fig. 2.** Results of primitive and interesting pattern recognition produced by the sy stem

From the above results, we can see that 5 sets of simultaneous patterns are discovered in the sample data set after vertical aggregation. Horizontal aggregation reduces these to 3 main sets of simultaneous spikes because three sets of spikes at 21:49:49, 21:51:31, and 23:55:57, which are near each other, form one main set of spikes.

### 3.4 Summary

In this function, a summary with two parts is produced from different high-level abstractions. The first part gives the background knowledge about the current scenario and the other part describes interesting patterns in the scenario. The following is the summary produced by the prototype system on the sample temporal data set. We plan to use NLG technique [3] to improve the linguistic quality of the summary.

This scenario is about Fuel Valve subsystem which is being monitored by channels: TNH, FSR, FSGR, FSROUT, when the gas turbine is running in normal load state from 21:03:41.00 28 Nov 99 to 00:03:41 29 Nov 99.

During the time period, 3 main sets of spikes simultaneously occur in these channels. For example: Spikes in all channels at 21:49:49 and 23:55:57. Mostly spikes with some steps in all channels at 22:35:02.

Particularly, some large patterns occurred. For example: in channel TNH, a medium drop step at 21:35:04; in channel FSR, very big downward spike at 21:50:08, 21:51:36, 21:53:36; very big spikes with a medium rise step at 22:35:02 across all channels.

## 4 Evaluation of the Prototype System of SumTime-Turbine

The prototype system is being evaluated in two stages. The first stage is to evaluate primitive and interesting pattern recognition methods. The second stage is to evaluate the content of the output summary.

We have evaluated the pattern modules in randomly selected data sets from the *Tiger* data archive as described in [8]. The preliminary evaluation results are promising and we are extending the evaluation to more data sets

We have not yet evaluated output summary. Two possible methods have been proposed. One is let experts score summaries produced by *SumTime-Turbine*. Another is let experts write summaries about the same scenario and then compares the computer generated and human writers' summaries.

## 5 Related Work

There are a number of systems, which are related with summarised time-series data, of which are *RESUME*, *GoalGetter*, and *SumTime- Mousam*.

*RESUME* [4] uses KBTA method to create temporal abstractions from medical data. The KBTA framework provides the most comprehensive starting point for generating summaries of temporal data. However, it doesn't produce textual summaries.

*GoalGetter* [7] is a data-to-speech system, which generates Dutch spoken summaries of football matches. Its input data is teletext, while the input data of *SumTime-Turbine* is complex high-frequency multi-channel time-series data.

*SumTime-Mousam* [6] generates textual weather forecasts for the offshore oil rig applications by summarising time series data produced by numerical weather prediction (NWP) models. A major difference between the two systems is that *SumTime-Mousam* works with much sparse data (one point every three hours instead of one point second in *SumTime-Turbine*).

## 6 Future Work

Currently a working prototype system of *SumTime-Turbine* has been implemented. More functions are being developed and will be added into the system. For example, in KBTA subsystem, temporal pattern matching technique will be used to detect patterns suggested by domain experts. In NLG subsystem, micro planning and realisation will be improved in order to enhance the linguistic quality of text.

**Acknowledgements**

We are grateful to our collaborators at IA, especially Dr. Rob Milne and Dr. Jon Aylett, for their contributions to knowledge acquisition, and system implementation. This project is supported by the UK EPSRC under grant GR/M76881.

## References

1. R. Milne, L.T. Massuyes (1997), Model Based Aspects of the TIGER Gas Turbine Condition Monitoring System, LAAS Report, 97416, CAAS-CNRS, Toulouse France
2. R. Milne, L.T. Massuyes, T. Escobet (2000), TIGER with Model Based Diagnosis: Initial Deploymen, LAAS Report, 00553, CAAS-CNRS, Toulouse France
3. E. Reiter and R. Dale (2000), Building Natural Language Generation Systems, Cambridge University Press
4. Y. Shahar, M. A. Musen (1996), Knowledge-Based Temporal Abstraction in Clinical Domains, Artificial Intelligence in Medicine 1996 8(3): 267-298
5. Y. Shahar, M. Molina (1998) "Knowledge-Based Spatial temporal Linear Abstraction". Pattern Analysis and Applications 1(2): 91-104, 1998
6. S. G. Sripada, E. Reiter, J. Hunter, J. Yu (2002), Segmenting Time Series for Weather Forecasting. In Ann L. Macintosh, Richard Ellis, and Frans Coenen (Eds) Applications And Innovations in Intelligent Systems X, Springer, London, pages 193-206
7. M. Theune, E. Klabbers (2001), From Data to Speech: A General Approach, Natural Language Engineering 7(1): 47-86
8. J. Yu, J. Hunter, E. Reiter, and S. G. Sripada (2002), Recognising Visual Patterns to Communicate Time-Series Data in the gas turbine domain, In Ann L. Macintosh, Richard Ellis, and Frans Coenen (Eds) Applications And Innovations in Intelligent Systems X (Cambridge, U.K.), Springer, London, pages 105-118

# A Blackboard-Based Learning Intrusion Detection System: A New Approach

Mayukh Dass, James Cannady, and Walter D. Potter

Artificial Intelligence Center, University of Georgia,
Athens, Georgia – 30602-7415, U.S.A.,
dass@uga.edu, j.cannady@computer.org, potter@uga.edu

**Abstract.** Intrusion Detection is one of the crucial real-time problems in the field of computer networking. With the changing technology and the exponential growth of Internet traffic, it is becoming difficult for any existing intrusion detection system to offer a reliable service. From earlier research, we have found that there exists a behavioral pattern in the attacks that can be learned. That is why an Artificial Neural Network is so successful in detecting network intrusions. Still, this approach is not effective in a dynamic environment where changes take place frequently. This paper proposes a blackboard-based Learning Intrusion Detection System, which is controlled by autonomous agents and has an online learning capability. This feature enables the system to adapt itself with the changing environment and to perform better than present systems.

**Keywords:** Network Security, Intrusion Detection, Blackboard Architecture, Autonomous Agents, Artificial Neural Network.

## 1 Introduction

Intrusion Detection has been a hard problem from the early days of computer networking. This problem has become more prominent with the rapid increase in vulnerable Internet applications and automated attack scripts. Every year, business and industry loose a huge amount of revenue due to data manipulation caused by computer network intruders. According to the 2001, CSI/FBI Computer Crime and Security Survey, more than $35 million was lost per company due to unauthorized net access costing them an average of $357,160 per incident [1]. As a result, there has been an increasing requirement to effectively protect crucial business information with a reliable, robust and flexible intrusion detection system. There are many commercially available Intrusion Detection Systems (IDS), but unfortunately they are costly and of limited reliability. These systems are rule based and are unable to maintain their performance with the increasing complexity of the Internet. This has led to worldwide research interest In effective intrusion detection techniques with artificial intelligence [2], data mining [3] and statistical techniques [4]. From the works of Denning [4], we have found that there exists a behavioral pattern in attacks. Hence, Pattern Matching approaches [4] and Artificial Neural Networks [2, 7] have been very effective in detecting intrusions.

P.W.H. Chung, C.J. Hinde, M. Ali (Eds.): IEA/AIE 2003, LNAI 2718, pp. 385–390, 2003.

Using a blackboard architecture in an Intrusion Detection System is not a new approach. Works of Dasgupta [5] reveal an optimistic attempt to detecting intrusions with agents in a blackboard architecture. These agents exchange information among themselves through a discrete data path. There are also some approaches with autonomous agents as in [6] where the agents interact among themselves and exchange information to detect intrusions. There has not been any attempt in building a learning system. Researchers argue that Artificial Neural Networks (ANN) are learning systems, but they are very domain specific and cannot perform well in a dynamic environment unless they are trained dynamically. Works in [7] show effective approaches with ANN to intrusion detection. There have also been some approaches with Genetic Algorithms [8], but they failed to show the same level of performance as Artificial Neural Networks did.

This paper presents the description of a blackboard based three-tier autonomous agent architecture of a Learning Intrusion Detection System (LIDS), which is still under development. This system has a learning capability and can adapt to any computer network environment. It uses the classifying power of the ANN and the Genetic Algorithm to detect intrusions.

## 2 Intrusion Detection and Learning

Intrusion Detection can be defined as the identification of attempted or ongoing attacks on a computer system or network. Intrusion Detection can be differentiated into two categories [9]: anomaly detection and misuse detection. The former refers to the detection of abnormal behavior in the use of network services and computing resources. Misuse detection, on the other hand relies on the identification of well-defined attacks or vulnerabilities in network or computer software. Unfortunately, intrusions rarely follow an expected pattern. The increasing availability of attack tools, the rise in the number of exploitable system vulnerabilities, and the growing creativity of attackers mean that traditional intrusion detection approaches are inadequate.

Intrusion Detection Systems are also classified according to the network system area they audit. They can be Host Based or Network Based. A Host Based Intrusion Detection System can be defined as a security system that is capable of detecting inside abuses in a computer network. A Network Based Intrusion Detection System is capable of identifying abusive uses or attempts of unauthorized usage of the computer network from outside the system. Our work most closely resembles a Network Based Intrusion Detection System that uses computational intelligence techniques to dynamically detect intrusions.

Prior approaches to this problem used some form of rule-based analysis [10]. Rule-Based analysis relies on predefined rule-sets that are provided by an administrator, automatically created by the system, or both. Expert Systems are the most common form of rule-based intrusion detection approaches. Rule-based systems suffer from the inability to detect attack scenarios that may occur over an extended period of time. They also lack flexibility in the rule-to-audit record representation. Slight variations in the attack sequence may reduce the effectiveness of the system. There have been some optimistic attempts with genetic algorithms [8], data mining [3] and pattern recognition techniques [4] to develop a high performance IDS, but these techniques are still undergoing research.

Prior research [7] has demonstrated the ability to convert attack patterns into data vectors. This will allow ANN or any other pattern recognition technique to perform well. But, these approaches rely upon the training data and ultimately will fail because of the changing nature of the computer network. Our proposed architecture has another learning layer above these analysis techniques, which will regularly maintain and update the training data set of the ANN or any other machine learning technique.

Some examples of the more common types of malicious attacks in the network are:

- Denial-of-service Attack (DoS) - This is a particularly serious form of attack that has resulted in damage worth millions of dollars over the past few years. While a significant problem, DoS attacks are usually quite simple. They typically involve an attacker disabling or rendering inaccessible a network-based information resource.
- Guessing rlogin Attack - Here the intruder tries to guess the password that protects the computer network in order to gain access to it.
- Scanning Attacks - The intruder goes about scanning different ports of the victim's system to find some vulnerable points from where they can launch other attacks.

## 3 Blackboard and Proposed Architecture

The blackboard architecture is considered one of the most general and flexible knowledge system architectures for building decision-based applications. It is highly preferred over other alternatives due to its modularity, dynamic control, generality, concurrency, high design efficiency, robustness and ability in dealing with multiple knowledge sources. As a result, the blackboard-based architecture is considered a good solution in developing our proposed Intrusion Detection System. The proposed architecture will also include the use of Autonomous Agents that are software agents which perform certain security monitoring functions at a host. The agents are independently running entities whose performance is not affected by any other agents. These kinds of agents are very useful in network security because they run continuously, can resist subversion and have minimal overhead. They are also configurable, easily adaptable, scalable, dynamically reconfigurable and degrade gracefully. The proposed architecture consists of autonomous agents that are integrated in a blackboard-based architecture and placed in a tier form.

The use of blackboard techniques and autonomous agents [5] in detecting network intrusions is not a new concept. In [5] , Dasgupta described how a blackboard-based agent architecture helps in detecting intrusions. He developed a distributed blackboard architecture that is embedded among the agents. A manager agent controls the monitoring, decision and action agents. The unidirectional flow of information in the system has a major impact on the flexibility of the system. Weiss, in his work [11] suggested many approaches that can be utilized, but it all has the problem of adaptation. Our proposed system that is designed in a multi-tier format removes this inefficiency.

The proposed Learning Intrusion Detection System is shown below (Figure 1).

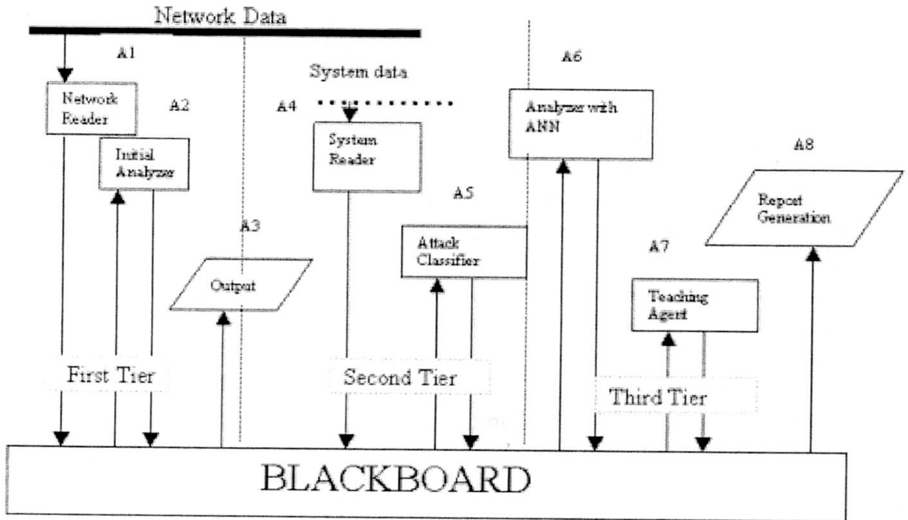


**Fig. 1.** Learning Intrusion Detection System Architecture

The system agents are divided into three tiers. Though they are autonomous agents, this tier bifurcation is done according to their contribution to the system. The first tier consists of all the autonomous agents required for the initial alert feature. A1 is the Network Reader. It collects network data with the help of a program called tcpdump. Tcpdump is a network utility tool that records network data in a specific format. The A1 autonomous agent collects network data in groups of 1000 data packets (network activity information) and pastes them on the blackboard. The second agent A2 is the initial analyzer. It calls a Rule-based classifier system that is written as a dll in C++. This classifier system analyzes the network data and checks whether there is any anomaly in the network data or not. The third agent is the display agent, A3, or the output agent. This is used to report the initial analysis to the user.

The second tier consists of all the agents that analyze system specific information. It consists of the System Reader (A4) that gathers system specific information on the protected system and posts it on the blackboard. These system data are very helpful in detecting the extent of damage caused by any attack.

The type of information gathered includes Available Network Bandwidth, CPU Usage, Network Packets/second, Memory usage, Number of connections, Connection attempts, Protocol, Source address to destination ports ratio (variety of ports accessed) and Packet length. There are many sub-class attacks that fall under one kind of attack. For example, a denial-of-service attack can be separated into a Ping Flood Attack, a UDP Packet Storm Attack, an FTP Brute Force Attack and so on. The fifth agent (A5) is the attack classifier that identifies different sub-classes of intrusions present in the network data. This agent sends the system information from the blackboard to a micro genetic algorithm based classifier that uses the multiple-fault diagnosis concept to perform the above function and posts its result back to the blackboard. The result states which kind of attack is present and what is its probability of presence in the dataset.

The third tier contains the autonomous agents that give full details of the attacks. The detail contains information about the data packets that are affected. A6 analyzes the information about the attacks and decides which type of ANN will be useful in further analysis of the data. The ANNs are in the form of dlls written in C++. If the analysis finds no attack in the dataset, the agent flags the dataset as it is a false positive alarm from the initial analyzing agent. The next agent is the teaching agent. This agent updates the rule set of A2 or the Initial Analyzer so that the A2 agent is capable of adapting to the changing environment. Ultimately, the Report Generation agent displays a complete report of the analysis to the user.

In a blackboard-based architecture, there is a requirement for an agent manager to control the activity of all the participating agents, but the notion of autonomous demands all the agents to work independently. Hence, we included a control pattern in the architecture of the agent. This pattern allows the last agent to look at the blackboard first and the first agent last in order to ensure that each agent gets a chance at least once to look at the blackboard in one process cycle. We have completed developing the Network Reader Agent (A1), the Initial Analyzer Agent (A2), the Attack Classifier Agent (A5) and the ANN Analyzer Agent (A6). We are using readily available DSSTools to create the blackboard environment. The Attack Classifier as discussed above is a Micro Genetic Algorithm (GA). This GA along with the ANN is in the form of dlls written in C++.

## 4 Future Work

In designing the proposed architecture we have tried to use the best AI techniques for the different knowledge-based problems. This hybrid approach should fulfill the deficiencies of other systems and the learning capability can also make it more efficient in a dynamic network environment. This paper tries to present a hybrid system using the agents-based architecture. While developing the system, vital information about intrusion detection was uncovered which needs further research. We have successfully developed an attack classifier with the Genetic Algorithm, which is capable of determining sub-classifications of attacks. This approach modelled after"multiple-fault diagnosis"is new and can be the subject of further research.

Though this system promises greater flexibility than most of the present Intrusion Detection Systems in a changing environment, we need to test it after the completion of its development. This work also helps in providing ideas in developing learning Intrusion Detection Systems.

## References

1. Raytheom, The Insider Threat, White Paper of SilentRunner, Inc. published in 01/09/02.
2. Lane, T and Brodley C E, Temporal Sequence Learning and Data Reduction for Anomaly Detection, In ACM Transaction on Information and System Security, Vol. 2, No. 3, August 1999.
3. Lee, W, Stolfo S and Mok K, Adaptive Intrusion Detection: A Data Mining Approach, In Artificial Intelligence Review, Kluwer Academic Publishers, 14(6): 533 - 567, December 2000.
4. Denning D E, An Intrusion-Detection Model, In IEEE Transaction on Software Engineering, Vol. Se-13, No. 2, February 1987, 222-232.
5. Dasgupta D., Gonzalez F., K. Yallapu, Gomez, J., Yarramsettii, R., Dunlap, G. and Greveas, M. , CIDS: An Agent-based Intrusion Detection System, In CS Technical Report No. CS-02-001., Feb, 2002.
6. Balasubramaniyan, J, Fernandez J O, Isacoff D, Spafford E. and Zamboni D, An Architecture for Intrusion Detection Using Autonomous Agents, In COAST Technical Report 98/5, Purdue University, June 1998.
7. Cannady, J., Artificial Neural Network of Misuse Detection, in the Proceedings of the 1998 National Information Systems Security Conference (NISSC'98) October 5-8 1998. Arlington, VA
8. Ludovic, ME, GASSATA, a Genetic Algorithm as an Alternative Tool for Security Trails Analysis, in the Proceedings of First International Symposium of Recent Advances in Intrusion Detection, 1998.
9. Anderson, D., Frivold, T. and Valdes, A Next-generation Intrusion Detection Expert System (NIDES): A Summary, SRI International Technical Report SRI-CSL-95-07, May, 1995.
10. Sebring, M., Shellhouse, E., Hanna, M. and Whitehurst, R., Expert Systems in Intrusion Detection: A Case Study, In Proceedings of the 11th National Computer Security Conference.1988.
11. Weiss S., Kulikowski C., Computer System That Learn, Morgan Kauffman, California, 1991.

# Developing a Goodness Criteria for Tide Predictions Based on Fuzzy Preference Ranking

Alexey L. Sadovski, Carl Steidley, Patrick Michaud, and Philippe Tissot

Department of Computing and Mathematical Sciences
Department of Physical and Life Sciences
Texas A&M University - Corpus Christi
6300 Ocean Dr. Corpus Christi, Texas 78412,
USA
steidley@falcon.tamucc.edu
http://www.cbi.tamucc.edu

**Abstract.** The paper deals with the developing of the tool to measure quality of predictions of water levels in estuaries and shallow waters of the Gulf of Mexico, when tide charts cannot provide reliable predictions. In future this goodness criteria of predictions will be applied to different regions.

## 1 Introduction

The goal of our on-going research is to develop effective and reliable tools for predicting water levels in the shallow waters of the Gulf of Mexico. Different methodologies for the prediction of water levels include: statistical models [1], harmonic analysis, numerical methods based on finite elements/finite differences, neural networks [2], etc. We have discussed a statistical based model of prediction (SMP) of tides and compared it with neural network predictions (NNP) [3]. Both of these approaches are under development at the Center for Coastal Studies in cooperation with the Department of Computing and Mathematical Sciences both of Texas A&M University-Corpus Christi (A&M-CC). Many stations of the Texas Coastal Ocean Observation Network (TCOON) located in the coastal waters of the Gulf of Mexico provide data for such predictions [4].

TCOON consists of approximately 50 data gathering stations located along the Texas Gulf coast from the Louisiana to Mexico borders. Data sampled at these stations include: precise water levels, wind speed and direction, atmospheric and water temperatures, barometric pressure, and water currents. The measurements collected at these stations are often used in legal proceedings such as littoral boundary determinations; therefore data are collected according to National Ocean Service standards. Some stations of TCOON collect parameters such as turbidity, salinity, and other water quality parameters. All data are transmitted back to A&M-CC at multiples of six minutes via line-of-sight packet radio, cellular phone, or GOES satellite, where they are then processed and stored in a real-time, web-enabled database. TCOON has been in operation since 1988.

There are several alternative methodologies for the prediction of water levels: statistical methods [2],[3], harmonic analysis, numerical methods based on finite

P.W.H. Chung, C.J. Hinde, M. Ali (Eds.): IEA/AIE 2003, LNAI 2718, pp. 391–401, 2003.

elements/finite differences, neural networks [5],[6[,[7],[8], etc. If two or more methods are developed for a particular location the performance of the models will likely vary depending on the conditions. Coastal users will be interested in the model which best predicts water levels for their particular field of interest but different users will have different priorities. Coastal populations and emergency management entities, worried about flooding, will favor models with good performance when the water levels are considerably higher than normal. Port authorities and other interests regulating navigation will be mostly interested in models performing well when the water levels are considerably lower than normal to avoid ship grounding.

In this paper, after a brief summary of our models, we present the development of aggregated criteria to evaluate the goodness of water level predictions in the Gulf of Mexico. While tide charts are generally the method of choice for the forecast of water levels there are limitations to their use.

Tide charts are mostly based on astronomical forcing or the influence on water levels of the respective motions of the earth, the moon, and the sun. There are locations around the world, including the Gulf of Mexico, where other factors such meteorological forcing often dominate tidal forcing [9] and limit significantly the application of tide charts. In such cases other models must be developed to forecast water levels.

The goal of this paper is to introduce a procedure to develop the unique "criteria of goodness" of prediction. This approach is based on the ratings methods of preference ranking developed by one of the authors [10].

## 2 Statistical Model

The general idea is to predict water levels for the next two hours by using a multi-regression model. Then step by step - using these predicted levels as the given levels - predict water level for 4, 6,...,48 hours. We have considered three different models for two-hour predictions, and two of these produced quite reliable predictions. The first of these models is a multi-regression model in which two-hour prediction is based on the levels of water, speeds and directions of wind for the previous 48 hours with a step of 2 hours. This model did not produce expected results, because R squared for such a prediction was less than 0.5.

The second approach is another multi-regression model in which two-hour predictions of water level are based on the levels of water during the previous 48 hours, using 2-hour steps. Here we now believe that information about weather (pressure, wind, temperature, etc.) is hidden in the previous levels of water. This model worked remarkably well: R squared for all stations was greater than 0.95. To make further predictions we used the previously determined levels of water. Such a step by step approach produced quite good predictions. Table 1 below presents statistical data for differences between predicted and real levels of water for 6, 12, 18, 24, 30, 36, 42, and 48 hours:

The third approach is based on linear multi-regression of the levels of water, first differences, and second differences for such levels for the previous 48 hours with the step equal to two hours. This approach produces the same quality of water level prediction as the second approach. These results are quite understandable, because in both cases we have to deal with linear combinations of previous water levels. The difference in these two models is as follows: third approach has between four (4) and eight (8) significant variables in a linear regression while in the second model of linear regression we use all twenty four (24) variables.

**Table 1.** Statistical characteristics of prediction errors (in meters)

| | Mean | Median | Std. Deviation | Min. range | Max. range |
|---|---|---|---|---|---|
| Error 6hr | 0.0124 | 0.0121 | 0.310 | -0.858 | 0.796 |
| Error 12hr | 0.0129 | 0.0117 | 0.105 | -0.421 | 0.442 |
| Error 18hr | 0.0155 | 0.0108 | 0.313 | -0.951 | 0.866 |
| Error 24hr | 0.00924 | 0.0023 | 0.177 | -0.580 | 0.622 |
| Error 30hr | 0.0176 | 0.0062 | 0.297 | -0.748 | 0.803 |
| Error 36hr | 0.0140 | 0.0198 | 0.184 | -0.653 | 0.641 |
| Error 42hr | 0.0156 | - 0.0034 | 0.293 | -0.746 | 0.828 |
| Error 48hr | 0.0265 | 0.0289 | 0.193 | -0.568 | 0.593 |

The statistical model may be useful as a means to fill gaps in the observed water level data. To fill gaps in water level data, we will use the following procedure. First, we will find backward and forward linear regressions for the predicted water levels, and then we will evaluate lost data as a linear combination of forward and backward predictions with weights proportional to the distances from the edges of the gap.

## 3 Factor Analysis

To determine why our regression models that do not include wind and atmospheric pressure data provide us with a much better prediction than the models that include such data, we performed a Factor Analysis. The analysis of the major components has shown that 5 factors explain 95% of variance for water levels. In deep water the first three components are periodical. In the shallow water the major component is not periodical, while the other components are periodical. Our conclusion is that the prime factor is weather. It is well known that the weather affects tides much more in shallow waters than in deep waters [1], [2]. Linear regression models for different locations have different coefficients for the same variables. This difference may be explained by the geography of the location where the data are collected.

## 4 ANN Modeling and Predictions

The application of Artificial Neural Networks (ANN) to a number of fields including environmental modeling started shortly after the development of the backpropagation algorithm by Rumelheart et al. [11]. During the past five to ten years ANNs have been successfully applied to a growing number of applications including coastal and riverine cases for forecasting physical or water quality parameters [5], [6], [7], [8], [9], the forecasting of flooding along rivers [12], [13] and the forecasting of water levels along the coasts of the Gulf of Mexico [12]. Back propagation neural networks use the repeated comparison between the output of an ANN and an associated set of target vectors to optimize the weights of the neurons and biases of the model. The learning process consists more specifically in backpropagating a function of the error through the network. The main advantages and key characteristics of ANNs for water level forecasting are their non-linear modeling capability, their generic modeling capacity, their robustness to noisy data, and their ability to deal with high dimensional data [14]. Forecasting water levels with ANNs consists of finding weights and biases by training the model using historical measurements. Our model's inputs consist of time series of previous water level and wind measurements as well as tidal data. All measurements and tidal forecasts for this work were extracted from the TCOON database. The typical structure of the neural networks used in this work consists of one hidden layer with one to a few neurons and one output layer consisting of one neuron when predicting individually each water level. The tidal forcing is included in the model by using water level differences between the measured and hindcasted water levels and the water levels predicted by the tide tables published by NOAA. The water level differences are then a direct function of the meteorological forcing. Finally the model predicts changes in water level differences rather than absolute water level differences. This methodology allows for a more direct relationship between short-term forcing and changes in water levels and also allows for the inclusion of long-term effects such as steric effects as part of the input to each short-term forecast. The models were tested with and without wind hindcasts. All the ANNs discussed in this work were trained using the Levenberg-Marquardt backpropagation algorithm and implemented within version 4.0 of the Matlab Neural Network Toolbox and the MATLAB 6.0 Release 12 computational environment [16] running on a Pentium PC.

## 5 The Problem

To address the different priorities of coastal users different criteria were developed mostly by the National Oceanographic and Atmospheric Administration (NOAA) [17] (see Table 2 below) to evaluate the quality of the predictions. The criteria listed reflect different concerns. The average error will address the possible bias of a model, the absolute error will give information on the overall accuracy of the model, and the standard deviation will give information on the variability of the forecasts. Other, more specialized, criteria such as the positive and negative outlier frequencies will be useful to characterize model performance for unusually high or low water level situations. It is clear that some forecasting methodologies will be better suited for some criteria and worse for others. For example, predictions based on Harmonic Analysis are very good when evaluated by the standard deviation criteria and not as good when using the absolute error criteria. The table below provides measurement tools frequently used for the quality of water level forecasts.

## 6 Rating Methods of Preference Ranking

The most effective method of solution is to find one unified (or aggregated) quality criteria G ( $v_1(x), \ldots, v_n(x)$) of a given set of different kinds of measurements.

Usually function G(·) depends on the preferences of decision-makers or it is based upon expert information. Let us consider some linear-weighted function as an integrated objective function (utility function):

$$G = \alpha_1 v_1(x) + \ldots + \alpha_n v_n(x).$$

The question is how to determine the weight coefficients. Using rating methods of preference ranking, we can ask decision-makers (expert, advisers, etc.) to present their preferences of objective functions $v_1(x), \ldots, v_n(x)$ in the form of ranking, or binary, or multi-comparisons, and find coefficients $\alpha k$ based on final consensus ranking .

Preference ranking is one of the methods used to solve so-called selection problems. Selection problems are very important for decision making in unique systems such as medical, environmental or ecological systems. Very often the right decision is based upon expert information. Below we deal with some approaches to the choice of the best variants, and its application to create unique criteria to make decisions. We also present axiomatic systems of rating methods of preference ranking. Results include the convergence of consensus ranking to the real ranking almost everywhere, and the inclusion of the consensus ranking into the Kemeny Median set [18]. Also we will show that all contemporary rating systems, (for instance those used by Sadovski in sports classifications [19]), are congruent in the sense of producing the same final preference ranking.

There are a few ways to solve the problem under consideration. The first one is to determine a Pareto set P = $\{P \,/\, \cap Q_k \subseteq P \subseteq Q_k\}$, but set P is too wide. The second method of the solution presented by Arrow [20] was based on a contradictory system of five axioms. The most useful result obtained by Kemeny, is the so-called Kemeny Median H= $\{K \,/\, \Sigma d(K, Q_k) = \min \Sigma d(P, Q_k)\}$, which can be determined by methods of integer programming. It is necessary to outline that the Kemeny Median satisfies four of Arrow's five axioms. Also, there is an inclusion $H \subseteq P$, the set H is still quite wide.

The methods presented in this paper have some advantages. First, there is a very simple numerical procedure. The second improvement is the possibility of using different forms of expert information such as preference ranking, binary and multi-comparison at the same time; this significantly differs from previous methods based on uniform types of expert information. The third advantage is that the result of this rating procedure is a unique preference ranking and not just some set of suitable alternatives such as a Pareto Set or a Kemeny Median. Similar results are true if some (or all) experts present information of their preferences in the form of fuzzy relationships.

As a result of such a procedure of preference ranking we can obtain ratings $r_1, \ldots, r_n$ for different criteria. Suppose that we have found such ratings $r_1 \geq r_2 \geq \ldots r_n$. Let the value of coefficient $\alpha_1$ to be equal to one, in this case using the structure of the rating procedure we can find other weight coefficients from the following relationship:

**Table 2.** Criteria for the evaluation of water level forecasts

| Variable | Expression | Explanation |
|---|---|---|
| Error | $e_i = p_i - r_i$ | The error $e_i$ is defined as the predicted value $p_i$ minus the observed value $r_i$ |
| Average Error | $\overline{E} = \frac{1}{N}\sum e_i$ | The average error with N the size of the time series |
| Absolute Error | $\lvert e_i\rvert = \lvert p_i - r_i\rvert$ | The absolute error is defined as the predicted value $p_i$ minus the observed value $r_i$: $e_i = p_i - r_i$ |
| Average Absolute Error | $\lvert\overline{E}\rvert = \frac{1}{N}\sum \lvert e_i\rvert$ | The average absolute error with N the size of the time series |
| RMSE – Root Mean Square Error | $E_{rms} = \sqrt{\frac{1}{N}\sum e_i^2}$ | |
| SD– Standard Deviation | $E_{std} = \sqrt{\frac{1}{N-1}\sum \left(e_i - \overline{e}\right)^2}$ | |
| RMSS– Root Mean Square Signal | $R_{rms} = \sqrt{\frac{1}{N}\sum r_i^2}$ | |
| Normalized RMS Error | $NE = E_{rms} / R_{rms}$ | |
| POF(X)– Positive Outlier Freq. | | Fraction (percentage) of errors that are greater than X |
| NOF(X) – Negative Outlier Freq. | | Fraction (percentage) of errors that are less than - X |
| MDPO(X) Max Duration of Positive Outlier | | A positive outlier event is two or more consecutive occurrences of an error greater then X. MDPO is the length (number of consecutive occurrences) of the longest event. |
| MDNO(X) Max Duration of Negative Outlier | | A negative outlier event is two or more consecutive occurrences of an error greater then X. MDNO is the length (number of consecutive occurrences) of the longest event. |

$$\frac{\alpha_1}{\alpha_i} = f\ (\Delta_{1i}), i = 1, \ldots, n,$$

Here $f$ and $\Delta_{ij}$ are defined by the system of axioms of preference ranking listed below. Such defined weight coefficients give us an opportunity to use additive integrated utility function as a criterion of goodness of a forecast:

$$G = \alpha_1 v_1(x) + \ldots + \alpha_n v_n(x).$$

Now let us consider the rating procedure a little bit more closely. Suppose there is some (maybe unknown to the decision-maker) order of different criteria (objects) $a_1$, ..., $a_n$ under consideration. Let us assume, that we have chosen some arbitrary scale, and each object has its own yet unknown value $r_0(a_i)$ in this chosen scale. The following is an axiom of existence:

**Axiom 1.** There is some order of given objects in any chosen scale.

Let us denote by $\Delta_{ij} = r_0(a_i) - r_0(a_j)$ the difference between real rating values. We believe that binary relationships given by experts satisfy

**Axiom 2.** The ratio $\dfrac{[number\ of\ preferences\ a_i \succ a_j]}{[number\ of\ preferences\ a_j \succ a_i]} = f\ (\Delta_{ij}),$

where function $f\ (\Delta)$ is a positive strictly increasing function such that $f(0)=1$.

This assumption shows the odds or fuzzy odds of preferences by experts, who are asked to rank or compare objects.

Let $r_i(0)$ $i = 1, \ldots, n$ be some arbitrary initial ratings, $r_i(k)$ is rating of an i-th object after k-th recalculation and $\Delta_{ij}\ (k) = r_i(k) - r_j(k)$.

The next statement gives the simple way to recalculate ratings of objects according the results of expert estimations.

**Axiom 3.**

$$r_i(k) = r_i(k-1) + q_{ij}(k)\, F\,(\Delta_{ij}(k-1)),$$

$$r_j(k) = r_j(k-1) + q_{ji}(k)\, F\,(\Delta_{ji}(k-1)),$$

where

$$q_{ij}(k) = \begin{cases} 1, if\ a_1 \succ a_j \\ 0, if\ a_i \_ a_j \\ -1, if\ a_j \succ a_i \end{cases}$$

and $F\ (\Delta)$ is nonnegative decreasing function.

In the case of fuzzy information coefficients $q$ are equal values of membership function

of a fuzzy binary relationships provided by experts respectively. For fuzzy relationships the formulas in axiom 3 should be change as follows:

$$r_i(k) = r_i(k-1) + q_{ij}(k)\,F(\Delta_{ij}(k-1)) + q_{ji}(k)\,F(\Delta_{ji}(k-1)),$$
$$r_j(k) = r_j(k-1) + q_{ji}(k)\,F(\Delta_{ji}(k-1)) + q_{ij}(k)\,F(\Delta_{ij}(k-1))$$

This means that an increase in rating value is proportional to a fuzzy preference and that its decrease is proportional to a fuzzy non-preference.

It is reasonable to assume that for large $\Delta_{ij}$ increasing of $r_i(k)$ should be small, if $a_i \succ a_j$, but decreasing should be large if $a_i \prec a_j$. This idea is very useful, for instance, in methods of teams or players classifications: it means that if a strong team or player ousts a weak one, then there is almost no increasing in the rating for the winner. However in the case of losing the game the higher rated team should lose many points. That is why we have the following two assumptions for function *F*:

**Axiom 4.** $$\lim_{\Delta \to \infty} F(\Delta) = 0$$

**Axiom 5.** $$\lim_{\Delta \to -\infty} F(\Delta) = L > 0$$

The following proposition establishes equivalency for all rating systems of preference ranking including rankings based on fuzzy information.

**Proposition 1.** For any initial ratings any method based on axioms 1 through 5 presents some preference ranking which is the same as a real unknown ranking with probability one in the space of realization, when $k \to \infty$.

Proposition 1 shows that all rating systems are equal. Indeed, we have just discussed the so called additive rating systems of preference ranking, but the same statements and ideas are correct for multiplicative rating methods in which

$$r_i(k) = r_i(k-1) * q_{ij}(k) * F(\Delta_{ij}(k-1)).$$

Considering the Ratings and Kemeny Median**.** Let us assume that experts present information about preferences in matrix form:

$$Q_k = (q_{ij}(k)),\ i,j = 1, \ldots, n,\ k = 1, \ldots, m.$$

For any two matrices of binary relations $Q_k$ and $Q_l$ distance between them may be defined in the following way:

$$d(Q_k, Q_l) = \frac{1}{2} \sum_{1}^{n} \sum_{1}^{n} I q_{ij}(k) - q_{ij}(l) I$$

If matrices $Q_k$ present preference ranking by experts then Kemeny median [18] is such a matrix $K$ that

$$\sum_{1}^{m} d(K, Q_k) = \min \sum_{1}^{m} d(P, Q_k)$$

The Kemeny median is really a set of such matrices $K$, and at the present moment it is considered the most useful consensus ranking, however the determination of this median involves the problem of integer programming with all the difficulties of such calculations. The following result establishes connection between Kemeny median and rating rankings:

**Proposition 2.** The consensus preference ranking obtained as a result of rating procedure belongs, with probability one, to the Kemeny Median set in the space of all realizations $\Omega$.

It is easily seen that rating methods are iterative procedures for determining the Kemeny Median. The proof of this theorem is based on fact that the Kemeny Median as well as a rating preference ranking satisfy four of the five Arrow axioms. Rating systems of preference ranking are very flexible. They provide an opportunity to work with different types of expert information such as binary and multi-comparison, ranking, etc. Moreover, there is a possibility to work with fuzzy information [21]. If, for instance, $\mu_{ij}$ is measure of belonging such that $a_i \succ a_j$, then it is enough to replace $q_{ij}$ by $\mu_{ij}$ in axiom 3 to use fuzzy relationship offered by experts. The last remark concerns the theorem of equivalency of rating systems, which holds also under conditions of fuzziness.

## 7 Conclusion

Obtaining such an aggregated criteria is very useful for the evaluation of the quality of predictions of tides, as well as for checking the quality of methods to fill gaps in the data collected by the Texas Coastal Ocean Observation Network (TCOON) [22].

The next step is the selection of expert scientists and representatives of port authorities with the goal of obtaining their real evaluation of the relative importance of different measurements.

The work presented in this paper is funded in part by the following federal and state agencies:

- National Aeronautic and Space Agency (NASA Grant #NCC5-517)
- Texas General Land Office

- National Oceanic and Atmospheric Administration (NOAA)
- Coastal Management Program (CMP).

The views expressed herein are those of the authors and do not necessarily reflect the views of NASA, TGLO, NOAA, CMP or any of their sub-agencies.

## References

[1]. Cox, D.T., Tissot P.E., and Michaud P. R., Water Level Observations and Short-Term Predictions Including Meteorological Events for the Entrance of Galveston Bay, Texas, Journal of Waterways, Port, Coastal, and Ocean Engineering, 128-1, 21-29, 2002.

[2]. Thomson Bosley K, and Hess, K.W., Comparison of Statistical and Model-Based Hindcasts of Subtidal Water Levels in Chesapeake Bay, Journal of Geophysical Research, v. 106, no C8, 16,869-16,885, 2001.

[3]. Sadovski, A. L. P. Tissot, P. Michaud, C. Steidley, Statistical and Neural Network Modeling and Predictions of Tides in the Shallow Waters of the Gulf of Mexico, Proceedings of 2002 WSEAS International Conference on System Science, Applied Mathematics & Computer Science and Power Engineering Systems, Rio de Janeiro, Brazil, October, 2002.

[4] Michaud, P., G. Jeffress, R. Dannelly, and C. Steidley 2001. Real Time Data Collection and the Texas Coastal Ocean Observation Network. *Proc. International Measurement and Control (InterMAC)*, Tokyo, Japan, in press.

[5] Mase, H., Sakamoto, M., and Sakai, T. 1995. Neural Network for Stability Analysis of Rubble-Mound Breakwaters. *Journal of Waterway, Port, Coastal, and Ocean Engineering*, 121 (6), ASCE, 294-299.

[6] Moatar F., Fessant, F., and Poirel, A. 1999. pH Modelling by Neural Networks. Application of Control and Validation Data Series in the Middle Loire River. *Ecological Modeling*, 120, 141-156.

[7] Recknagel, F., French, M., Harkonen, P., and Yabunaka, K-I. 1997. Artificial Neural Network Approach for Modeling and Prediction of Algal Blooms. *Ecological Modeling*, 96, 11-28.

[8] Tsai, C-P., and Lee, T-L. 1999. Back-Propagation Neural Network in Tidal-Level Forecasting. *Journal of Waterway, Port, Coastal, and Ocean Engineering*, 125(4),ASCE,195-202.

[9] Tissot P.E., Cox D.T., Michaud P. 2002. Neural Network Forecasting of Storm Surges along the Gulf of Mexico. *Proceedings of the Fourth International Symposium on Ocean Wave Measurement and Analysis (Waves `01)*, ASCE, 1535-1544.

[10]. Sadovski A.L, Multi-Objective Optimization and Decisions Based on Rating Methods of Preference Ranking, GMD FIRST, Germany, 1997.

[11] Rumelhart, D. E., Hinton, G. E., and Williams, R.J. 1986. Learning Representations by Back-Propagating Errors. *Nature*, 323, 533-534.

[12] Campolo, M., Andreussi, P., and Soldati, A. 1997. River Flood Forecasting with a Neural Network Model. *Water Resources Research*, 35 (4), 1191-1197.

[13] Kim, G., and Barros, A. 2001. Quantitative Flood Forecasting Using Multisensor Data and Neural Networks. *Journal of Hydrology*, 246, 45-62.

[14] Rumelhart, D. E., Durbin, R., Golden, R., and Chauvin, Y. 1995. Backpropagation: The Basic Theory. *Backpropagation: Theory, Architectures, and Applications*, Rumelhart, D.E., Chauvin, Y., eds, Lawrence Erlbaum Associates, Publishers, Hillsdale, 1-34.

[15] The MathWorks, Inc. 1998. *Neural Network Toolbox for use with Matlab 5.3/version 3*, The MathWorks, Natick, MA.

[16] Stearns, J., Tissot, P.E., Michaud, P., Colllins, W.G., and Patrick, A.R., "Comparison of MesoEta Wind Forecasts with TCOON Measurements along the Coast of Texas" Proceedings of the 19th AMS Conference on Weather Analysis and Forecasting/15th AMS Conference on Numerical Weather Prediction, 12-16 August 2002, San Antonio, Texas, accepted.

[17]. NOS Procedures for Developing and Implementing Operational Nowcast and forecast Systems for PORTS, National Oceanic and Atmospheric Administration, U.S. Department of Commerce, 1999

[18]. Kemeny, J., Snell J., *Mathematical Models in Social Sciences*, The MIT Press, 1972.

[19]. Sadovski L.E., Sadovski A.L., *Mathematics and Sports*, American Mathematical Society, RI, 1993.

[20]. Arrow K.J., Social Choice and Individual Values, Wiley&Sons, NY, 1963.

[21]. Sadovski A.L., Preference Ranking and Decisions Based on Fuzzy Expert Information, in "Advances in Fuzzy Systems and Evolutionary Computation", World Scientific Engineering Society Press, USA, 2001

[22]. Michaud, P., Jeffress, G. A., Dannelly, R. S., Steidley, C, Real-Time Data collection and the Texas Coastal Ocean Observation Network, Instrument Society of America, proceedings of Emerging Technologies Conference, Houston, Texas, 2001

# Debugging VHDL Designs Using Temporal Process Instances

Daniel Köb, Bernhard Peischl, and Franz Wotawa*

Technische Universität Graz, Institute for Software Technology (IST),
Inffeldgasse 16b/2, A-8010 Graz, Austria,
{dkoeb,peischl,wotawa}@ist.tu-graz.ac.at

**Abstract.** In this paper we outline the usage of model-based diagnosis for fault localization in VHDL-RTL designs. In contrast to previous research, our approach makes use of temporal aspects of a VHDL program. The facts that the conversion of the VHDL program to a logical representation can be done automatically, and that a standard model-based diagnosis engine can be used, make the approach easy to implement and use. In the first part of the paper, we show how a model can be used to compute diagnosis for a VHDL program. In the second part, we introduce a new logical model that allows the diagnosis engine to deal with temporal information directly by unfolding the circuit with respect to time, thereby employing temporal instances of VHDL processes.

**Keywords:** model-based diagnosis, software debugging, debugging of hardware designs

## 1 Introduction

The use of hardware-description languages, such as VHDL (very high speed integrated circuit hardware-description language) or Verilog has become state of the art in hardware design. Almost all companies are using some sort of hardware-description languages for this purpose. The design process starts with a specification that describes the desired properties on a very abstract level. Based on this specification the functionality is refined until an abstraction level is reached that allows the whole circuit to be simulated and tested. Ideally, the output of the design process is a program that describes the functionality and structure of the circuit and can automatically be synthesized into a gate level representation. This process allows for detecting and correcting faults in an early stage of the design cycle and thus may significantly decrease the overall design costs.

However, searching for faults in a design written in a hardware description language tends to be a very difficult and time consuming process, since complex designs reach dimensions of several 100.000 lines of code and may be written by a team of designers that are located at different physical locations. Automated

* Authors are listed in alphabetical order.

P.W.H. Chung, C.J. Hinde, M. Ali (Eds.): IEA/AIE 2003, LNAI 2718, pp. 402–415, 2003.

debugging tools that support fault localization and correction within hardware designs may thus provide considerable aid in decreasing the time to market and may contribute to the reduction of overall costs in today's fast paced economy.

There are several papers that deal with debugging VHDL programs. Friedrich and colleagues [4] and Wotawa [18] introduce the underlying techniques of VHDL-DIAG, a tool that supports designers in finding faulty statements in a VHDL program. The first version of VHDLDIAG makes use of underlying dependencies between signals and variables similar to program slicing [14, 15]. Further papers [16, 17, 19] extend the model by incorporating the VHDL semantics in the model. However, several aspects like handling the temporal behavior of a VHDL design were not captured by previous research.

In this paper we introduce a model of VHDL that captures the semantics of the language VHDL and the following two aspects. First, the model is closer to the VHDL semantics with respect to the treatment of processes and the computation of signal values over time. Second, the model handles the temporal behavior of VHDL by unfolding process executions over time. Hence, unlike previous models, our model introduces temporal aspects to diagnostic reasoning about VHDL programs. Other advantages of former models, retained here, include the integration into existing design environments comprising a VHDL compiler as well as a simulator and a waveform viewer that presents the output of the simulation run to the developer.

By applying model-based diagnosis [12, 2] to the domain of software debugging, VHDLDIAG provides considerable support in focusing the attention of the designer to parts of the program that may be responsible for the observed discrepancy. In contrast to other techniques such as program slicing [14, 15] or dependency analysis [9, 8] model-based diagnosis provides the advantage of a well founded theory and the existence of fast algorithms that are independent of the representation of the logical model. In [20] the relationship between program slicing and model-based debugging is explained in detail.

This article deals with the representation of the logical model and presents a typical scenario. A logical representation is introduced that allows the diagnosis engine to deal with temporal information by using temporal instances of the processes that are declared in the VHDL design.

The paper is organized as follows. In Section 2 the basic definitions of model-based diagnosis are reviewed. Model-based diagnosis is applied to the debugging of VHDL-RTL (register transfer level) designs by presenting an example in Section 3. Subsequently, in Section 4, we discuss ongoing research issues that investigate the utilization of process instances in order to take advantage of the temporal behavior of the signals. The paper is concluded in Section 5 by reviewing the main results.

## 2 Basic Definitions – Model-Based Diagnosis and Automated Debugging

To be self contained we briefly recapitulate the basic definitions of model-based diagnosis [12, 2] in this section. In model-based or more precisely consistency-based [10] diagnosis the logical model of a system and the specification of its intended behavior are used for the computation of diagnosis. Note that in contrast the abductive diagnosis (also see [10, 1]) we do not need the specification of the faulty behavior of a component. A precise definition of consistency-based and abductive diagnosis can be found in [1]. The paper also discusses the relationship between both approaches and suggests a unified framework.

In contrast to physical models, which are usually given as a set of differential equations, a logical model allows the derivation of facts from a given knowledge and the storage of the knowledge in an explicit fashion. Formally, a diagnosis system is a tuple $(SD, COMP)$ where $SD$ is a logical description of the structure of the system and the behavior of the components, and $COMP$ denotes the set of system components. Each component in $COMP$ is associated with so called component modes. When using model-based diagnoses for fault localization, the correct behavior for every component has to be specified. The corresponding mode that represents the correct behavior of component $C$ is referred to as $\neg AB(C)$ mode, whereas $AB(C)$ stands for a faulty component $C$. For example, in Figure 1 a system that consists of three inverters $inv_1$, $inv_2$, and $inv_3$ is outlined. The connections between the inverters are denoted by $s_1$, $s_2$, $s_3$, and $s_4$. The behavior of an inverter $inv_1$ can be formalized by the following Horn clauses:

$$\neg AB(inv_1) \wedge (in(inv_1) = false) \rightarrow (out(inv_1) = true)$$

$$\neg AB(inv_1) \wedge (in(inv_1) = true) \rightarrow (out(inv_1) = false)$$

$$\neg AB(inv_1) \wedge (out(inv_1) = false) \rightarrow (in(inv_1) = true)$$

$$\neg AB(inv_1) \wedge (out(inv_1) = true) \rightarrow (in(inv_1) = false)$$

The function *in* denotes the input ports of the component given as an argument and *out* correspondingly formalizes the output ports. In the case of the inverter presented above there is only one input and one output port but in general, when using more complex components, there may be several inputs as

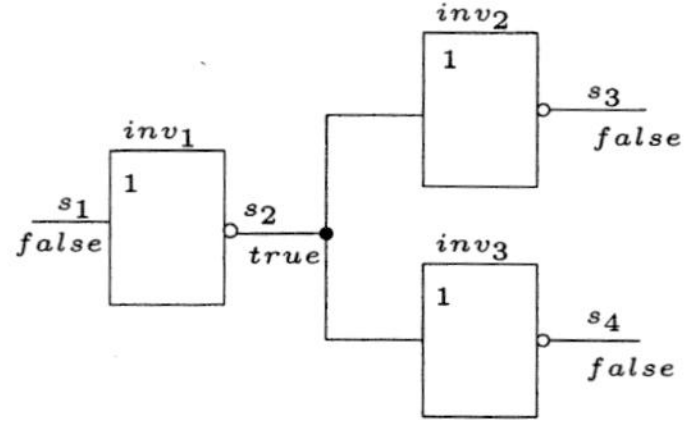


**Fig. 1.** The logical model of the circuit consists of components and connections.

well as outputs. In addition, the structure of the circuit can be expressed by the following logical sentence:

$$(val(s_1) = in(inv_1)) \wedge (val(s_2) = out(inv_1)) \wedge (val(s_2) = in(inv_2)) \wedge$$

$$(val(s_2) = in(inv_3)) \wedge (val(s_3) = out(inv_2)) \wedge (val(s_4) = out(inv_3))$$

The sentences presented above describe the behavior together with the structural knowledge and thus build up the system description $SD$ of the circuit. The function $val(s)$ simply denotes the value of the signal $s$. Furthermore, the set of components $COMP$ is given by $\{inv_1, inv_2, inv_3\}$.

The diagnosis system $(SD, COMP)$ together with a specification of the correct behavior $SPEC$ is referred to as diagnosis problem. In formal terms a diagnosis problem is a triple $(SD, COMP, SPEC)$ thereby $SPEC$ represents the intended behavior of the system that is also represented in the form of logical sentences.

For example, consider the specification $\{val(s_1) = false, val(s_3) = false, val(s_4) = true\}$ for the circuit given above. If all components are assumed to behave correct, that is $\neg AB(inv_1)$,$\neg AB(inv_2)$ and $\neg AB(inv_3)$ are considered true, then applying the value false to the input of the circuit contradicts the signal $s_4$, since according to the specification $val(s_4)$ has to be true.

In automated software debugging our interest is devoted to finding the cause of the observed misbehavior. This can be reached by defining diagnosis for a diagnosis problem $(SD, COMP, SPEC)$ as a set of mode assignments $\Delta$, mapping system components $C$ to their actual mode $m(C)$, such that the logical sentence $SD \cup SPEC \cup \{m(C) | m(C) \in \Delta\}$ does not lead to a contradiction.

Referring back to the example above, the mode assignments $\{\neg AB(inv_1), \neg AB(inv_2)\}$ and $\{\neg AB(inv_3)\}$ are minimal diagnosis[2]. Computing diagnosis can be done in a straightforward way by selecting a subset $\Delta$ of $COMP$ and a mode assignment for the components of $COMP$ in order to check if $\Delta$ fulfills the diagnosis definition. However, this procedure is rather inefficient and thus can hardly be used in a practical setting. Nevertheless, currently there are several algorithms [12, 2, 6, 5, 3, 13] available that compute diagnoses in a much faster and more efficient way.

## 3 Software Debugging of VHDL Designs

In Section 3.1, the most important constructs of VHDL are introduced. Afterwards, in Section 3.2, the component-connection model, which can be derived from the VHDL design automatically, is introduced and a typical debugging scenario is presented. This paper's main contribution towards model-based diagnosis of hardware designs is presented in Section 4. There the logical model is extended by unfolding the circuit in time. This allows the diagnosis engine to deal with temporal information of the signal values which is the new and main contribution of this paper to further advances in model-based diagnosis.

[2] The term minimal refers to a minimum with respect the subset relation, that is, no subset of a given diagnosis is itself a diagnosis.

### 3.1 An Introduction to VHDL

VHDL designs consist of entities, architectures, and statements, to mention the most important program constructs. Entities represent the physical parts or subdivisions of the circuit to be designed and architectures are used to describe the internal structure of an entity. In the common terminology of programming languages an entity corresponds to abstract data type and an architecture describes its implementation.

The behavior of an entity is described by its body that usually consists of several processes. A process itself is composed of statements, such as signal assignments or conditionals. Whenever at least one signal from the sensitivity-list of a process changes its value, the statements in the process are executed and the resulting changes to its output signals are propagated to other processes, possibly causing them to be executed in turn. Thus, the communication between processes is done by means of signals. The parallel execution of the processes of different entities, resulting in the simulated behavior of the hardware unit to be designed, is performed by executing the VHDL program and recording the signal changes.

An overview of the VHDL language features and a definition of syntax and semantics can be found in [7]. Furthermore, [11] provides an introduction into designing circuits with VHDL.

### 3.2 Debugging VHDL-RTL Programs

In this section the behavioral and structural model of a simple counter that is taken from [17] is outlined. The basic principles of the model were introduced by Wotawa [17, 19]. The underlying modeling principles are (except some changes) the same. The changes include the explicit handling of process sensitivity-lists which is a prerequisite for handling temporal instances. Moreover, the resulting model is closer to the VHDL semantics than models introduced previously. They are subsumed by the new model.

Figure 2 shows the VHDL program consisting of an entity *counter* and an architecture $BEHAV$. The counter is reseted by a positive value at the $RESET$ input and counts up every time a positive edge of the clock input $CLK$ is detected.

The signals $CLK$ and $RESET$ denote inputs whereas $O1$ and $O2$ are the outputs of the device. Two processes, *mem* and *comb_in*, are implementing the desired functionality. The communication between the processes is done by means of the signals $O1$, $O2$, $D1$, and $D2$. $D1$ and $D2$ are used to store future values of the counter. Whenever $CLK$ changes from false to true, the future values are transferred to $O1$ and $O2$ by process *mem* and new values are computed by process *comb_in*.

For software debugging, a model of the program that comprises the structural and behavioral part has to be found. The structural part can be obtained by viewing statements as diagnosis components and signals and variables as connections between them. Figure 3 lines out the structural part of the counter. The description of the behavior of the components remains to be introduced.

```
entity COUNTER is
end COUNTER;

architecture BEHAV of COUNTER is
  signal CLK, RESET : BIT ;
  signal O1, O2 : BIT ;
  signal D1,D2 : BIT ;
begin
  .
  :    -- VHDL code for test case stimulating CLK and RESET
  mem: process ( CLK, RESET )
  begin
    if RESET = '1' then
      O1 <= '0';
      O2 <= '0';
    else
    if CLK = '1' and CLK'EVENT then
        O1 <= D1;
        O2 <= D2;
    end if;
  end if;
  end process mem;

  comb_in : process ( O1, O2 )
    variable V: BIT;
  begin
    V := not(O1);
    D1 <= V;
    D2 <= not((O1 and O2) or (V and not(O2)));
  end process comb_in;
end BEHAV;
```

**Fig. 2.** The VHDL-RTL program specifying the counter

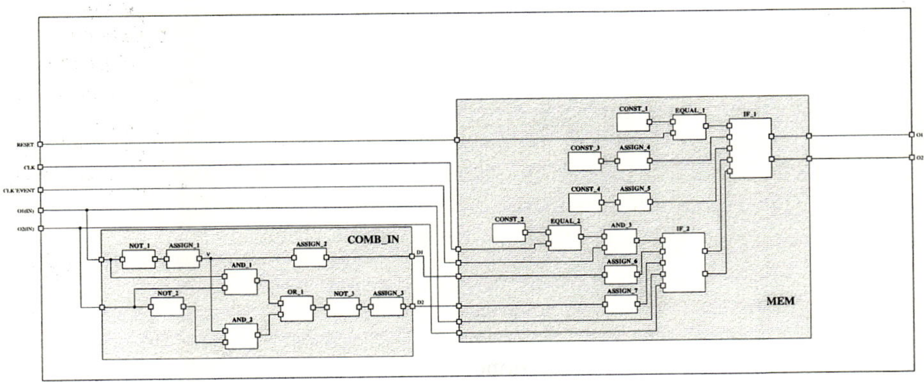


**Fig. 3.** The structure of the logical model of the counter program.

To simplify the presentation of the components' behavior the predicate calculus is used. However, the sentences presented below can easily be transformed into propositional Horn clause theory. In the following, the formalization of the behavior of the if-then-else statement and that of a process is outlined and the main ideas of the behavioral models are pointed out. However, the main principles can be applied to other VHDL constructs such as statements and expressions in a similar fashion.

The output of an if-then-else statement 'if' is determined by so called subblocks, that represent the statements in the if and the else branch, respectively. If the component works as expected, that is, $\neg AB(if)$ is assumed to be true, and the condition evaluates to true, the then-subblock, that is associated with the statements in the if branch, is transferred to the output. Otherwise the evaluated subblock that represents the else branch is assigned to the output. In formal terms this can be expressed as follows:

$$\forall x \in stmts_{then} \cdot \neg AB(if) \wedge cond(if) = true \rightarrow out(if, x) = in_{then}(if, x)$$

$$\forall x \in stmts_{else} \cdot \neg AB(if) \wedge cond(if) = false \rightarrow out(if, x) = in_{else}(if, x)$$

Thereby $stmts_{then}$ denotes the signal assignment-statements in the if-branch and $stmts_{else}$ represents the statements in the else-branch. The signal $out(if, x)$ denotes a single output $x$ of component 'if' whereas $out(if)$ denotes the set of outputs of the if component. This formalization requires that the same signals are assigned in the then and the else branch. If this is not the case in the considered if-statement, the branch that contains the smaller number of statements is extended by assignment-statements of the form $Z <= Z$ so that the same signals are assigned in both branches. The formal terms introduced above can be represented as depicted in Figure 4.

In the next step the formalization of a process statement is presented. A process $p$ is executed if at least one of the signals that occur in its sensitivity-list has changed its value immediately before. If this is the case, the values of the signals used as a target in the sequential statement part of $p$ are computed according to the VHDL semantics. This computation is formally represented by subblocks that become associated with the sequential statements of process $p$. Hence, the value of the signals are given by the values computed by the subblock that is connected to the input ports $in$. If none of the signals that occur on the sensitivity-list have changed its value, then the original input values before executing the sequential statement block are propagated to the output of the process component. Formally, this can be written as follows:

$$\forall y \in inputs(p) \cdot \exists x \in sensitivity - list(p) \cdot s(x, p) = true \rightarrow out(y, p) = in(y, p)$$

$$\forall y \in inputs(p) \cdot \forall x \in sensitivity - list(p) \cdot s(x, p) = false \rightarrow out(y, p) = def(y, p)$$

$$\forall y \cdot out(y, p) = def(y, p) \leftrightarrow out_{EVENT}(y, p) = false$$

In the sentences presented above, $inputs(p)$ denotes the set of inputs of the process $p$ and $sensitivity\_list(p)$ represents the sensitivity-list of the process $p$. The triggering input port $s(x, p)$ of process $p$ indicates whether or not signal $x$ has changed its value, i.e., $s(x, p)$ is set to true if $x$ has changed its value in the previous computation step. Thus, the sentences presented above formalize whether an event on at least one of the signals enumerated in the sensitivity-list of process $p$ occurs. If this is the case, the process is said to be triggered in the following. The signal value after executing the sequential statement $y$ is represented by $in(y, p)$ whereas the corresponding unmodified input of the process $p$ becomes represented in formal terms by $def(y, p)$. Moreover, additional

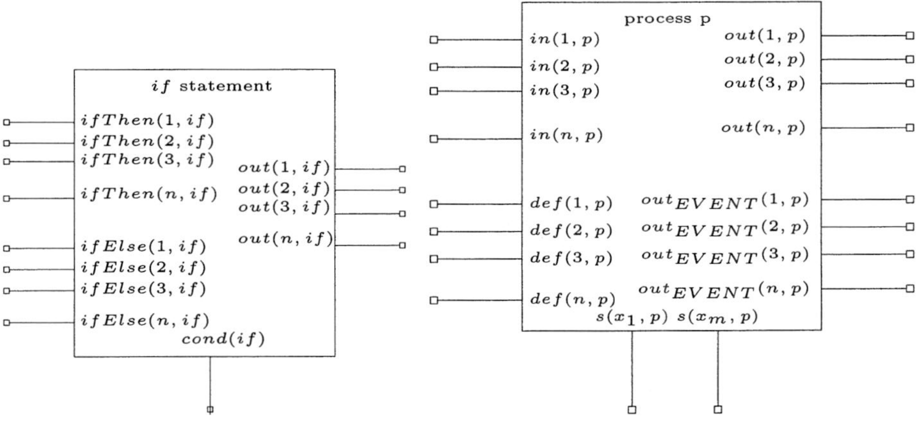


**Fig. 4.** The input and output ports of an if-then-else component.

**Fig. 5.** The input and output ports of the process component.

ports that provide information about whether an event has occurred on a specific signal are introduced. If an output $out(y,p)$ changes by virtue of executing process $p$, the corresponding event port $out_{EVENT}(y,p)$ is set to true. Figure 5 illustrates the process component and its ports graphically.

For the purpose of demonstration a bug is introduced into the program by replacing the or operator in line 27 (see Figure 2) by an and operator:

27. D2 <= **not**((O1 **and** O2) **and** (V **and** **not**(O2)));

The component-connection model of the buggy program is equal to the original one presented in Figure 2 except that the or component $OR_1$ is replaced by an and component. However, in the following it is assumed that both components have the same name, that is, $OR_1$. Table 1 lines out a part of the specification of the intended behavior of the counter.

By employing the system description that has been created by using the buggy program and the test case 7, it can be proved that the resulting set of sentences is inconsistent assuming that all components behave correct. This contradiction can be resolved by searching for faulty components, e.g., if component

**Table 1.** An abstract of the specification of the intended behavior of the counter.

| test | *RESET* | *CLK* | *CLK'EVENT* | *Q1(IN)* | *Q2(IN)* | *Q1* | *Q2* |
|---|---|---|---|---|---|---|---|
| 1 | '1' | '0' | true | '0' | '0' | '0' | '0' |
| 2 | '1' | '1' | true | '0' | '0' | '0' | '0' |
| ... | ... | ... | ... | ... | ... | ... | ... |
| 7 | '0' | '1' | true | '0' | '0' | '1' | '0' |
| 8 | '0' | '0' | true | '1' | '0' | '1' | '0' |
| 9 | '0' | '1' | true | '1' | '0' | '0' | '1' |
| ... | ... | ... | ... | ... | ... | ... | ... |
| 13 | '0' | '1' | true | '1' | '1' | '0' | '0' |
| ... | ... | ... | ... | ... | ... | ... | ... |

$IF_1$ is assumed to be faulty, then it can be proved that the resulting sentence is consistent. Thus $\{AB(IF_1)\}$ is a single diagnosis. By using the VHDLDIAG tool, in summary 12 minimal diagnosis can be obtained:
$\{AB(AND_1)\}, \{AB(OR_1)\}, \{AB(NOT_3)\}, \{AB(ASSIGN_3)\},$
$\{AB(ASSIGN_7)\}, \{AB(IF_2)\}, \{AB(CONST_2)\}, \{AB(EQUAL_2)\},$
$\{AB(AND_3)\}, \{AB(CONST_1)\}, \{AB(EQUAL_1)\}, \{AB(IF_1)\}.$

## 4 Using Temporal Instances for Modeling VHDL Designs

In the approach outlined above, diagnoses are computed by considering the input and the corresponding output signal values at a given point in time. If a discrepancy between the specified and the simulated output is observed, the component modes are assigned to components in a way that explains the observed misbehavior.

In this section the approach presented above is extended by adding temporal information thus taking the waveform of the signals into account. Rather than considering the signal values at a fixed moment in time, the signal changes that occur within a certain period of time are used in order to compute diagnoses. A straightforward approach towards taking into account the temporal behavior of the circuit is to employ some sort of temporal logic in order to perform the reasoning process. However, although today's diagnostic engines [2, 12] have reached a high level of maturity they are only capable of dealing with propositional logic. Thus we unfold the circuit with respect to the simulation time by using temporal instances of processes. In the following, the logical model that is employed when dealing with temporal instances is briefly introduced. Thereafter the encountered intricacies are discussed.

As outlined in Section 3.2, the VHDL design has to be converted to a component-connection model in order to apply model-based diagnosis. Figure 6 depicts the main idea of our approach by lining out a part of the structure of the component-connection model when using temporal process instances. The model is discussed informally in the following.

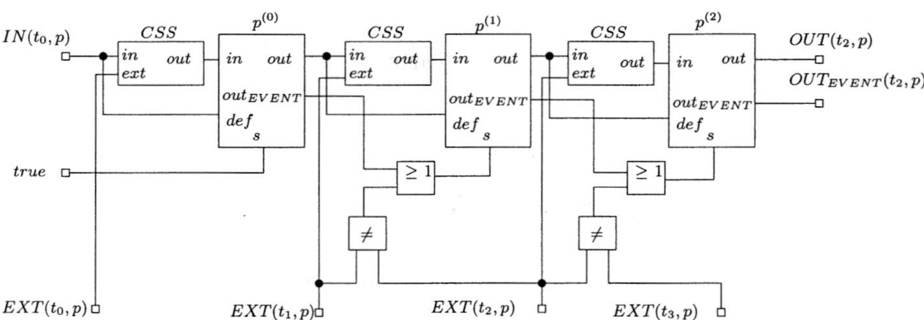


**Fig. 6.** The VHDL design is unfolded with respect to time by means of temporal instances.

For the ease of demonstration a separate component, denoted by $CSS$ in the figure, that represents the sequential statement part of a process is used. This component stands for the target signal values after executing the sequential statement part of a process and may also be influenced by signals that become modified by other processes than that under consideration. Such signals are referred to as external signals with respect to a specific process $p$. Considering a certain point in time $t$ the corresponding external signal values of process $p$ are denoted by $EXT(t,p)$ in the discussion given below.

By connecting the $OUT_{EVENT}$ port of a process instance $p^{(i-1)}$ to the input port $s(x,p^{(i)})$ of the process $p^{(i)}$, a chain of temporal process instances is created. Each instance of a process behaves according to the semantics of VHDL: The sequential statement part of a process instance $p^{(i)}$ is executed iff any signal that is enumerated within $p^{(i)}$'s sensitivity-list has changed. According to the behavior rules of a process given in Section 3.2, either the values at the *in* port or the values at the $def$ port are transferred to the *out* port of the process component. Note that in Figure 6, $s$ denotes a set of triggering inputs, namely $s = \{s(x,p) | x \in sensitivity\_list(p)\}$. Likewise, *out* , *in* and *ext* stand for the set of inputs, outputs and external signals of process $p$, respectively.

A process instance may either be triggered by an event that is a consequence of the preceeding instance or it may be triggered by means of an external signal[1]. In the first case the $out_{EVENT}$ port is responsible for propagating the signal events to the succeeding instances. Events on external signals are detected by directly comparing the value of the signals to their subsequent values. In the figure this is indicated by the component denoted by $\neq$. The or component below ensures that both an external event as well as an event from the preceeding temporal instance may trigger a process instance. According to the semantics of VHDL each process is triggered at the beginning of program execution, thus the first instance $p^{(0)}$ is tied to the logical value true.

For the computation of diagnoses the model has to be converted to a Horn clause theory. Thus, the number of process instances has to be known in advance. This is done by restricting the system in a way such that an upper bound on the number of process activations can be computed at time of model construction. In the following the restrictions as well as an upper bound for the number of processes is outlined.

The discussion is divided into three parts. First, the restrictions that are assumed for the purpose of our case study are explained. Afterwards, the number of process activations that may result from external signals is determined. In the last part the number of process instances that have to be forseen between subsequent external activations of a process instance is derived. The obtained results are afterwards used to deduce an upper bound of the total number of process activations.

In our case study we assumed that there are no cycles with respect to process activation. Thus, if a process $p$ activates a process $q$ then $q$ is not allowed to

[1] For instance, the clock signal is a typical example of an external signal that may be responsible for triggering a temporal instance of a process.

activate $p$. If process $p$ activates process $q$ and $q$ were allowed to activate process $p$ then the number of process activations in general would depend on the logic that is implemented within the processes $p$ and $q$. However, in the following we assume that such mutual activations do not occur at all.

The total number of process activations depends on the number of events that result from external signals within the considered period of time. To simplify the discussion, consider a clocked circuit. Every time the clock signal changes its value, a process may be triggered. Thus, the number of events that occur on the clock signal within the time span considered for diagnosis is an upper bound for the number of process activations caused by external signals.

Nevertheless, there may be additional process activations between subsequent external signals triggering the process. A VHDL design in general consists of several processes. A process $p$ may also be triggered since another process $q$ caused an event on a signal that is enumerated in the sensitivity-list of $p$. According to the assumptions with respect to process activations each process of a VHDL design that comprises $n$ processes in total can be activated by $n-1$ other processes. In addition, it becomes activated the first time by an external signal. Thus, a process becomes activated at most $n$ times between subsequent external activations. As a consequence, there is an upper bound for the total number of process activations that is given by the product of the number of external events that occur in the period of time taken into account and the number of processes in the VHDL design.

As indicated in Figure 6 the unfolded system is applied for the computation of diagnoses. However, the temporal instances of the process $p$ are handled completely independent, thus there may be a significant number of diagnoses since the number of components that may account for misbehavior has increased in comparison to the original model. Thus, before presenting the diagnoses to the user, the instances are mapped back to the components in the following way:

$$\varphi : \Delta^* \subseteq COMP^* \mapsto \Delta \subseteq COMP$$
$$\varphi(\Delta^*) = \{C_i | C_i^{(j)} \in \Delta^*\}$$

In the mapping given above $COMP^*$ denotes the instances of the components whereas $COMP$ refers directly to the components. In similar fashion, $\Delta^*$ stands for the diagnoses that are computed using temporal instances and $\Delta$ simply denotes the corresponding components. Moreover, $C_i^{(j)}$ denotes instance $j$ of component $C_i$.

For instance, by using our counter example and unfolding it over 4 process executions, thus considering 2 rising edges of the clock signal in order to compute diagnoses, we obtained 7 minimal diagnoses after mapping the temporal instances back to the components as described above. Moreover, the computation of all dual diagnoses resulted in 15 components that are possibly erroneous. In summary the diagnosis correspond to the statements 9, 11, 15, 22, 25, 27 and include the introduced bug. The statements 9, 11, 15, and 22 correspond to a process or a conditional statement. Only the diagnosis for statements 25 and 27 can be mapped back to functional faults, e.g., wrong operators, in the code.

This result indicates that the new approach can localize the statement that is responsible for the misbehavior. Moreover, because of the information at which point in time which statements must be assumed to behave faulty, the user gets more information in comparison to the previous model.

By unfolding the counter example over 12 process executions we observed that the erroneous component still is in the set of computed diagnoses. However, for the user of an automated debugging tool a fault diagnosis in the context of 6 rising edges of the clock signal may be less useful since tracing the overall effects caused by the (proposed) faulty component can become rather laborious. Hence, we believe that a fewer number of process executions may provide more meaningful results for a circuit designer.

Using the model outlined above several experiments have been conducted using small to medium sized VHDL designs. However, we observed that the computational effort for computing diagnoses increased dramatically since of two reasons: First, the number of Horn clauses that built up the new model has increased since of the growth in the number of components. Note that for every component a fixed number of rules is created to represent its behavior. Second, to take full advantage of the approach, all the higher order diagnosis , e.g., dual and triple diagnoses have to be computed. As a consequence, the computational effort increases dramatically.

However, as it is also the case when using the original model presented in Section 3.2, the faulty component always is detected. Furthermore, if a diagnosis that contains only instances of a single component is obtained, e.g., $\Delta^* = \{C_i^{(1)}, C_i^{(2)}, .., C_i^{(n)}\}$, this is a strong indication that component $C_i$ is indeed erroneous.

## 5 Conclusion and Forthcoming Research

In this paper we introduced a new model for debugging VHDL designs. This novel approach includes the explicit handling of signals in the sensitivity-list of a process and allows for considering temporal behavior of signals by employing temporal instances of a process to build up the logical model. Rather than only considering the values of the signals at a fixed moment in time the new approach allows the signal values to be observed during a certain period of time in order to compute diagnoses. Since today's diagnostic engines employ propositional logic, our approach unfolds the diagnosis problem with respect to time and thus is able to use a standard diagnosis engine. At the cost of increased computational effort the diagnoses that are obtained by using the proposed model always contain the faulty component. However, in several examples we were able to provide more accurate diagnoses. Further research should focus on getting out more information of the temporal instances, and should also deal with improving diagnosis performance by switching between different models and by making use of hierarchical diagnosis. For example, several temporal instances can be mapped back to a single diagnosis component if necessary.

**Acknowledgments**

The work was partially supported by the Austrian Science Fund (FWF) under project grant P15163-INF.

## References

1. Luca Console, Daniele Theseider Dupré, and Pietro Torasso. On the relationship between abduction and deduction. *Journal of Logic and Computation*, 1(5):661–690, 1991.
2. Johan de Kleer and Brian C. Williams. Diagnosing multiple faults. *Artificial Intelligence*, 32(1):97–130, 1987.
3. Yousri El Fattah and Rina Dechter. Diagnosing tree-decomposable circuits. In *Proceedings* $14^{th}$ *International Joint Conf. on Artificial Intelligence*, pages 1742 – 1748, 1995.
4. Gerhard Friedrich, Markus Stumptner, and Franz Wotawa. Model-based diagnosis of hardware designs. *Artificial Intelligence*, 111(2):3–39, July 1999.
5. Peter Fröhlich and Wolfgang Nejdl. A Static Model-Based Engine for Model-Based Reasoning. In *Proceedings* $15^{th}$ *International Joint Conf. on Artificial Intelligence*, Nagoya, Japan, August 1997.
6. Russell Greiner, Barbara A. Smith, and Ralph W. Wilkerson. A correction to the algorithm in Reiter's theory of diagnosis. *Artificial Intelligence*, 41(1):79–88, 1989.
7. IEEE. *IEEE Standard VHDL Language Reference Manual LRM Std 1076-1987*, 1988.
8. Daniel Jackson. Aspect: Detecting Bugs with Abstract Dependences. *ACM Transactions on Software Engineering and Methodology*, 4(2):109–145, April 1995.
9. Ron I. Kuper. Dependency-directed localization of software bugs. Technical Report AI-TR 1053, MIT AI Lab, May 1989.
10. Peter Lucas. Symbolic diagnosis and its formalisation. *The Knowldege Engineering Review*, 12(2):109–146, 1997.
11. Zainalabedin Navabi. *VHDL: Analysis and Modeling of Digital Systems.* McGraw-Hill, 1993.
12. Raymond Reiter. A theory of diagnosis from first principles. *Artificial Intelligence*, 32(1):57–95, 1987.
13. Markus Stumptner and Franz Wotawa. Diagnosing tree-structured systems. In *Proceedings of the Eighth International Workshop on Principles of Diagnosis*, Le Mont-Saint-Michel, France, 1997. Also appeared in IJCAI-97.
14. Mark Weiser. Programmers use slices when debugging. *Communications of the ACM*, 25(7):446–452, July 1982.
15. Mark Weiser. Program slicing. *IEEE Transactions on Software Engineering*, 10(4):352–357, July 1984.
16. Franz Wotawa. *Applying Model-Based Diagnosis to Software Debugging of Concurrent and Sequential Imperative Programming Languages.* PhD thesis, Technische Universität Wien, 1996.
17. Franz Wotawa. New Directions in Debugging Hardware Designs. In *Proceedings of the International Conference on Industrial and Engineering Applications of Artificial Intelligence and Expert Systems*, 1999. Springer, Lecture Notes in Artificial Intelligence 462 (LNAI 462).
18. Franz Wotawa. Debugging VHDL Designs using Model-Based Reasoning. *Artificial Intelligence in Engineering*, 14(4):331–351, 2000.

19. Franz Wotawa. Debugging Hardware Designs using a Value-Based Model. *Applied Intelligence*, 16(1):71–92, 2002.
20. Franz Wotawa. On the Relationship between Model-Based Debugging and Program Slicing. *Artificial Intelligence*, 135(1–2):124–143, 2002.

# Efficient Pattern Matching for Non-strongly Sequential Term Rewriting Systems

Nadia Nedjah and Luiza de Macedo Mourelle

Department of Systems Engineering and Computation, Faculty of Engineering,
State University of Rio de Janeiro,
Rio de Janeiro, Brazil
{nadia, ldmm}@eng.uerj.br
http://www.eng.uerj.br/~ldmm

**Abstract.** Pattern matching is a fundamental feature in many applications such as rule-based expert systems. Usually, patterns are pre-processed into a deterministic finite automaton. With ambiguous patterns a subject term may be an instance of more than one pattern and so a priority rule is usually engaged to select the matched pattern. The pre-processing of the patterns adds new patterns, which are instances of the original ones. When the original patterns are ambiguous, some of the instances supplied may be irrelevant. Their introduction causes unnecessary increase of space requirements. Furthermore, they slow down the matching process. Here, we devise a new pre-processing operation that identifies and avoids including such irrelevant instances and hence improves space and time requirements for the matching automaton and process.

## 1 Introduction

Pattern matching is an important operation in several applications such as functional, equational and logic programming [5], [17], theorem proving [4] and rule-based expert systems [3]. With ambiguous patterns, an input term may be an instance of more than one pattern. Usually, patterns are partially ordered using priorities. Notice that pattern matching techniques usually fall into two categories:

- *Root* matching techniques determine whether a given subject term is an instance of a pattern in a given set of patterns.
- *Complete* matching techniques determine whether the subject term contains a subterm (including the term itself) that is an instance of a pattern in the pattern set.

Thus, complete matching subsumes root matching and root matching may be used to implement complete matching (by a recursive descent into the subject term). Throughout this paper, we only deal with root matching.

Pattern matching automata have been studied for over a decade. It can be achieved as in lexical analysis by using a finite automaton [2], [7], [8], [11-16], [18]. Gräf [7] and Christian [2] construct deterministic matching automata for unambiguous patterns based on the left-to-right traversal order. In functional programming, Augustsson [1]

P.W.H. Chung, C.J. Hinde, M. Ali (Eds.): IEA/AIE 2003, LNAI 2718, pp. 416–425, 2003.

and Wadler [20] describe matching techniques that are also based on left-to right traversal of terms but allow prioritised overlapping patterns. Although these methods are economical in terms of space usage, they may re-examine symbols in the input term. In the worst case, they can degenerate to the naive method of checking the subject term against each pattern individually. In contrast, Christian's [2] and Gräf's [7] methods avoid symbol re-examination at the cost of increased space requirements. In order to avoid backtracking over symbols already examined, like Gräf's our method introduces new patterns. These correspond to overlaps in the scanned prefixes of original patterns. When patterns overlap, some of the added patterns may be irrelevant to the matching process. The method proposed here improves Gräf's in the sense that it introduces only a subset of the patterns that his methiod adds. This improves both space and time requirements as we will show later. Sekar [18] uses the notion of irrelevant patterns to compute traversal orders of pattern matching. His algorithm eliminates a pattern $\pi$ whenever a match for $\pi$ implies a match for a pattern of higher priority than $\pi$. In contrast with Sekar's method, we do not introduce irrelevant patterns at once. In this paper, we focus on avoiding the introduction of irrelevant patterns while constructing matching automata. This results in a more efficient pattern-matcher.

First, we recall from [11], [12] a method for generating a deterministic tree matching automaton for a given pattern set. Although the generated automaton is efficient since it avoids symbol re-examination, it may contain unnecessary branches. As we shall see, the main reason for this is the presence of ambiguous patterns with more general patterns having higher priority. Here, we modify that method so that only relevant patterns are added. A smaller and more efficient automaton is thereby obtained. We then back this claim using a set of miscellaneous benchmarks.

## 2 Preliminaries

In this section, we recall the notation and concepts that will be used in the rest of the paper. Symbols in a *term* are either function or variable symbols. The non-empty set of function symbols $F = \{a, b, f, g, ...\}$ is *ranked* i.e., every function symbol $f$ in $F$ has an *arity* which is the number of its arguments and is denoted $\#f$. A term is either a constant, a variable or has the form $ft_1 t_2 ... t_{\#f}$ where each $t_i$, $1 \leq i \leq \#f$, is itself a term. Terms are represented by their corresponding abstract tree. We abbreviate terms by removing the usual parentheses and commas. This is unambiguous in our examples since the function arities will be kept unchanged throughout, namely $\#f = 3$, $\#g = 1$, $\#a = \#b = 0$. Variable occurrences are replaced by $\omega$, a meta-symbol which is used since the actual symbols are irrelevant here. A term containing no variables is said to be a *ground* term. We generally assume that patterns are linear terms, i.e. each variable symbol can occur at most once in them. Pattern sets will be denoted by $L$ and patterns by $\pi_1$, $\pi_2$, ..., or simply by $\pi$. A term $t$ is said to be an *instance* of a (linear) pattern $\pi$ if $t$ can be obtained from $\pi$ by replacing the variables of $\pi$ by corresponding subterms of $t$. If term $t$ is an instance of pattern $\pi$ then we denote this by $t \lhd \pi$.

**Definition 1.** A *matching item* is a triple $r{:}\alpha\bullet\beta$ where $\alpha\beta$ is a term and $r$ is a *rule label*. The label identifies the origin of the term $\alpha\beta$ and hence, in a term rewriting system, the rewrite rule which has to be applied when $\alpha\beta$ is matched. The label is not written explicitly below except where necessary. The meta-symbol • is called the *matching dot*, $\alpha$ and $\beta$ are called the *prefix* and *suffix* respectively. A *final* matching item is one of the form $\alpha\bullet$.

Throughout this paper left-to-right traversal order is used. So the matching item $\bullet\beta$ represents the initial state prior to matching the pattern $\beta$. In general, the matching item $\alpha\bullet\beta$ denotes that the symbols in $\alpha$ have been matched and those in $\beta$ have not yet been recognised. Finally, the matching item $\alpha\bullet$ is reached on successfully matching the whole pattern $\alpha$.

**Definition 2.** A set of matching items in which all the items have the same prefix is called a *matching set.* A matching set in which all the items have an empty prefix is called an *initial* matching set whereas a matching set in which all the items have an empty suffix is called a *final* matching set.

**Definition 3.** For a set $L$ of pattern suffixes and any symbol $s$, let $L\backslash s$ denote the set of pattern suffixes obtained by removing the initial symbol $s$ from those members of $L$, which commence with $s$ and excluding the other members of $L$. Then, for $f \in F$ define $L_\omega$ and $L_f$ as follows, wherein $\omega^{\#f}$ denotes a string of $\#f$ symbols $\omega$ and $\varnothing$ is the empty set. The *closure* $\overline{L}$ of a pattern set $L$ is then defined recursively by Gräf [7] as follows:

$$L_\omega = L\backslash\omega$$

$$L_f = \begin{cases} L\backslash f \cup \omega^{\#f} L\backslash\omega & L\backslash f \neq \varnothing \\ \varnothing & L\backslash f = \varnothing \end{cases}$$

$$\overline{L} = \begin{cases} L & \text{if } L = \{\varepsilon\} \text{ or } L = \varnothing \\ \bigcup_{s \in F \cup \{\omega\}} s\overline{L_s} & \text{otherwise} \end{cases}$$

Roughly speaking, with two item suffixes of the form $f\alpha$ and $\omega\beta$ we always add the suffix $f\omega^{\#f}\beta$ in order to postpone by one more symbol the decision between these two patterns. Otherwise backtracking might be required to match $\omega\beta$ if input $f$ leads to failure to match $f\alpha$.

## 3 Tree Matching Automata

In this section, we briefly recall from [11] a practical method to construct a deterministic tree-matching automaton for a prioritised ambiguous pattern set. The pattern set $L$ is extended to its closure $\overline{L}$ while generating the matching automaton.

The automaton is represented by the 4-tuple $\langle S_0, S, Q, \delta\rangle$ where $S$ is the state set, $S_0 \in S$ is the initial state, $Q \subseteq S$ is the final state set and $\delta$ is the state transition function. The states are labelled by matching sets, which consist of original patterns whose prefixes match the current input prefix, together with extra instances of the patterns, which are added to avoid backtracking in reading the input. In particular, the matching set for $S_0$ contains the initial matching items formed from the original patterns and labelled by the rules associated with them. Transitions are considered according to the symbol at the *matching position*, i.e. that immediately after the matching dot. For each symbol $s \in F \cup \{\omega\}$ and state with matching set $M$, a new state with matching set $\delta(M,s)$ is derived using the composition of the functions *accept* and *close* defined in Figure 1.

$$accept(M, s) = \{r{:}\alpha s \bullet \beta \mid r{:}\alpha \bullet s\beta \in M\}$$
$$close(M) = M \cup \{r{:}\alpha \bullet f\omega^{\#f}\mu \mid r{:}\alpha \bullet \omega\mu \in M \text{ and } \exists\, q{:}\alpha \bullet f\lambda \in M \text{ for some suffix } \lambda,\ f \in F\}$$
$$\delta(M, s) = close(\, accept(M, s)\,)$$

**Fig. 1.** Previous Automata Transition Function

The items obtained by recognising the symbols in those patterns of $M$ where $s$ is the next symbol form the set *accept*($M$,$s$) which is called the *kernel* of $\delta(M,s)$. However, the set $\delta(M,s)$ may contain more items. The presence of two items $\alpha \bullet \omega\mu$ and $\alpha \bullet f\lambda$ in $M$ creates a non-deterministic situation since the variable $\omega$ could be matched by a term having $f$ as head symbol. The item $\alpha \bullet f\omega^{\#f}\mu$ is added to remove this non-determinism and avoid backtracking. The transition function thus implements simply the main step in the closure operation described by Gräf [6] and set out in the previous section. Hence the pattern set resulting from the automaton construction using the transition function of Figure 1 coincides with the closure operation of Definition 3. The item labels simply keep account of the originating pattern for when a successful match is achieved. As we deal here with root-matching, every faillure transition ends up in a single global *faillure state*.

Non-determinism is worst where the input can end up matching the whole of two different patterns. Then we need a priority rule to determine which pattern to select.

**Definition 4:** A pattern set $L$ is *ambiguous* if there is a ground term that is an instance of at least two distinct patterns in $L$. Otherwise, $L$ is *non-ambiguous*.

**Definition 5:** A *priority rule* is a partial ordering on patterns such that if $\pi_1$ and $\pi_2$ are distinct ambiguous patterns then either $\pi_1$ has *higher* priority than $\pi_2$ or $\pi_2$ has *higher* priority than $\pi_1$. In the latter case, we write $\pi_1 \prec \pi_2$.

When a final state is reached, if several patterns have been successfully matched, then the priority rule is engaged to select the one of highest priority. An example is the *textual* priority rule which is used in the majority of functional languages [1], [9], [10], [19]. Among the matched patterns, the rule chooses the pattern that appears first in the text. Whatever rule is used, we will apply the word *match* only to the pattern of highest priority, which is matched:

**Definition 6.** For a prioritised pattern set $L$ and pattern $\pi \in L$, the term $t$ is said to *match* $\pi$ *in* $L$ if, and only if, $t$ is an instance of $\pi$ but not instance of any other pattern in $L$ of higher priority than $\pi$.

**Example 1.** Let $L = \{1{:}fa\omega\omega, 2{:}f\omega aa, 3{:}f\omega ba, 4{:}fg\omega g\omega b\}$ be the pattern set where $\#f = 3$, $\#g = 1$ and $\#a = \#b = 0$, as throughout this paper. Assuming a textual priority rule, the matching automaton for $L$ is given in Figure 2. Transitions corresponding to failures are omitted. Each state is labelled with its matching set. In the construction process, each new item is associated with the rule from which it is directly derived and whose pattern it is known to match. So, an added item $\alpha\bullet f\omega^{\#f}\beta$ is associated with the same rule as is its parent $\alpha\bullet\omega\beta$. At the final nodes, whatever item is matched, the matching rule of highest priority is chosen. This rule may be different from the one inherited by the item at that node. When this happens, it indicates what we call *irrelevancy* in the next section. During pattern matching, a $\omega$-transition is only taken when there is no other available transition, which accepts the current symbol. The automaton can be used to drive pattern matching with any chosen term rewriting strategy.

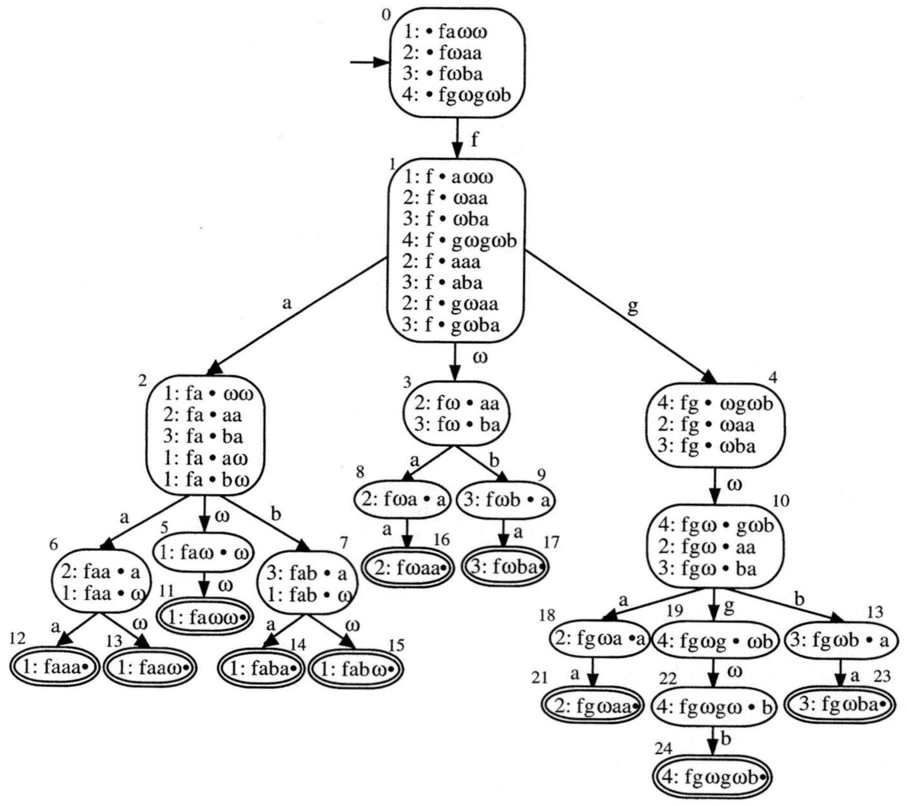


**Fig. 2.** Matching automaton for {1:faωω, 2:fωaa, 3:fωba, 4:fgωgωb}

## 4 Reduced Matching Automaton for Ambiguous Patterns

Now, we observe that the *close* function of Figure 1 may add more items than it need when the patterns are ambiguous. For example, in Figure 2 consider the items 2:*f*•*aaa* and 3:*f*•*aba* which *close* adds to state 1. Every term matching these items will instead be eventually associated with derivatives of the higher priority item 1:*f*•*aωω* also of state 1 and so the two items could have safely been omitted. We return to this example again after several definitions.

A *position* in a term is a path specification, which identifies a node in the abstract tree of the term. Positions are specified here using a list of positive integers. The empty list Λ denotes the position of the root of the abstract tree and the position $p.k$ ($k \geq 1$) denotes the root of the $k$th argument of the function symbol at position $p$. For a term $t$ and a position $p$ in this term, we denote by $t[p]$ the symbol at position $p$ in $t$.

**Definition 7.** A term $t$ is said to be *more general than a term t′ at the position p* if, and only if, the symbol $t[p]$ is $\omega$, $t'[p]$ is a function symbol and the prefixes of $t$ and $t'$ ending immediately before $p$ are the same. Without too much confusion, we hope, we will also say $t$ is *initially more general than t′* if $t$ is more general than $t'$ at the first position for which the symbols of $t$ and $t'$are different.

The function *close* adds new patterns to which the priority rule of the original rule set must be extended. The following definition enables us to associate a unique item amongst all those which pattern-match a given term: if there is a unique pattern-matched item whose rule has highest priority then that is chosen; otherwise, when there are several pattern-matched items associated with rules of maximal priority, those items must all derive from the same original pattern and we can select the initially most general. (Any other uniquely defined choice would also be acceptable, but this is the most convenient in what follows.)

**Definition 8.** Item $r{:}\alpha\bullet\beta$ has *higher priority* than item $r'{:}\alpha'\bullet\beta'$ if the original pattern of $r$ has higher priority than that of $r'$ or $r = r'$ and $\alpha\beta$ is initially more general than $\alpha'\beta'$. For a matching set $M$ and item $r{:}\alpha\bullet\beta \in M$, a term $t$ is said to *match* $r{:}\alpha\bullet\beta$ *in M* if, and only if, $t$ is an instance of $\alpha\beta$ but not an instance of any other item in $M$ of higher priority.

Although the pattern $\alpha\beta$ of the item $r{:}\alpha\bullet\beta$ will always match the pattern of rule $r$, it may match a pattern of higher priority. This could have been used in defining a priority rule on all terms and hence on items, but is computationally more expensive, and unnecessary here. It is now possible to determine which patterns are useful for *close* to include. Indeed, we can start by considering the usefulness of each pattern in the initial pattern set:

**Definition 9.** Suppose $L\cup\{\pi\}$ is a prioritised pattern set. Then $\pi$ is said to be *relevant for L* if there is a term that matches $\pi$ in $L\cup\{\pi\}$ in the sense of Definition 6. Otherwise, $\pi$ is *irrelevant for L*. Similarly, an item $\pi$ is *relevant for* (*the matching set*) *M* if there is a term that *deterministically* matches $\pi$ in $M\cup\{\pi\}$ in the sense of Definition 8.

Clearly, any term that matches an element of a pattern set, resp. item of a matching set, will still have that property even when an irrelevant pattern, resp. item, is removed. We can therefore immediately prune irrelevant patterns one by one from the initial pattern set until every remaining pattern is relevant to the remaining pattern set, and do the same for each matching set generated by *close*.

The function *close* of Figure 1 may certainly supply items that are irrelevant for subsequent matching. This may happen when the original pattern set contains ambiguous patterns with more general ones having lower priorities. For instance, in Example 1, the original patterns $fa\omega\omega$ and $f\omega aa$ are ambiguous $f\omega aa$ is more general than $fa\omega\omega$ at position 1 yet $fa\omega\omega$ has higher priority. The *close* function supplies the items $2{:}f\bullet aaa$, $3{:}f\bullet aba$ and two others to state 1. Then accepting symbol $a$ would yield a superset of $\{1{:}fa\bullet\omega\omega, 2{:}fa\bullet aa, 3{:}fa\bullet ba\}$. At this stage, based only on the item $fa\bullet\omega\omega$ a match for $fa\omega\omega$ can be announced and hence $fa\bullet aa$ and $fa\bullet ba$ are redundant, and indeed irrelevant under the definition above. Note also that the items $1{:}fa\bullet a\omega$ and $1{:}fa\bullet b\omega$ are similarly irrelevant for the matching set of state 2, in this case because the item $1{:}fa\bullet\omega\omega$ has higher priority due to its initially greater generality (at position 2).

Since the relevance of items may depend on the order in which items are added to a matching set $M$ to form *close*($M$), we need to be careful about re-defining *close* to exclude irrelevant items; the result may depend on this order. The new, improved function is *close*′ defined (non-uniquely) from the initial *close* by Figure 3. It seems best to consider items for inclusion using an ordering, which preserves decreasing priorities. So, highest priority items will be added first. This ensures that items already added to the partially created *close*′($M$) never subsequently become irrelevant.

$$\begin{aligned} close'(M) &= \text{any maximal subset } S \text{ of } close(M) \text{ such that} \\ &\quad \text{if } \pi \in close(M)\backslash S \text{ then } \pi \text{ is irrelevant for } S. \end{aligned}$$

**Fig. 3.** Closure function that supplies only relevant items

Finally, we consider a special case where the revised specification for *close* can be computed more easily. For this new definition, we assume that there is at least one function symbol in $F$ that does not occur in any original pattern. This definition is given in Figure 4 where the first line duplicates the conditions of the initial *close* and the subsequent lines add an extra condition to exclude some irrelevant items. Roughly speaking, this condition says that any potentially added item $\alpha\bullet f\omega^{\#f}\beta$ must contribute new terms, which are not already covered by patterns in $M$ with higher priority. However, in the general case when *close* is computed iteratively an added item may actually be covered by a previously added item, superseded by a subsequent item of higher priority or even covered by a number of more specific items.

$$\begin{aligned} close''(M) = M \cup \{\, r{:}\alpha\bullet f\omega^{\#f}\beta \mid\ & r{:}\alpha\bullet\omega\beta \in M \text{ and } \exists r', f, \beta'\,(r'{:}\alpha\bullet f\beta' \in M) \text{ and} \\ & \forall r''{:}\alpha\bullet f\beta'' \in M \ (\text{if } \ r{:}\alpha\bullet\omega\beta \prec r''{:}\alpha\bullet f\beta'' \\ & \text{then } \alpha f\omega^{\#f}\beta \ntrianglelefteq \alpha f\beta'' \text{ else } \beta \neq \omega..\omega\,) \quad \} \end{aligned}$$

**Fig. 4.** Intermediate closure function that may supply only relevant items

**Theorem.** Assuming that there is at least one function symbol which does not occur in any pattern, then all items supplied by the function *close*" are relevant.

**Proof.** We proceed by induction on matching sets. Assuming that all original patterns are relevant, then all items in the initial matching set are relevant. For the general case which unfolds in two subcases, let $M = \delta(N, s)$, $\alpha \bullet \beta \in M$ and $s \in F \cup \{\omega\}$:

1. When $\alpha \bullet \beta \in kernel\ (M)$, then it is clear that $\alpha \bullet \beta$ is relevant for $M$ as by induction hypothesis, the item $\alpha \bullet s\beta$ is relevant for the matching set $N$.

2. Suppose that $\alpha \bullet \beta = \alpha \bullet f\omega^{\#f}\beta' \notin kernel(M)$. Then there are some items $\alpha \bullet \omega\beta'$ and $\alpha \bullet f\beta''$ in $kernel(M)$. Depending on the priorities of these patterns, there are two cases to consider: first, assume that $\alpha \bullet f\beta'' \prec \alpha \bullet \omega\beta'$. Then when $\beta' \neq \omega..\omega$, the item $\alpha \bullet f\omega^{\#f}\beta'$ is always relevant for $M$ because it is needed to deterministically match either $\alpha \bullet f\beta'$ or $\alpha \bullet f\omega^{\#f}\beta'$. If $\beta'$ is a sequence of $\omega$s, the item $\alpha \bullet \beta = \alpha \bullet f\omega..\omega$ is not relevant for $M$ since a match for the item $\alpha \bullet \omega\beta'$ is already determined (at this matching set $M$); Now, suppose that $\alpha \bullet f\beta''_1, \ldots, \alpha \bullet f\beta''_n$ are all the items in $kernel(M)$ such that $\alpha\omega\beta' \prec \alpha \bullet f\beta''_i$, $1 \le i \le n$ and $\alpha \bullet \omega\beta'_1, \ldots, \alpha \bullet \omega\beta'_m$ are all the items in $kernel(M)$ such that $\alpha\omega\beta' \prec \alpha \bullet \omega\beta'_k$, $1 \le k \le m$. The *close*"function would add the item $j = \alpha \bullet f\omega^{\#f}\beta'$ if the term $t_j = \alpha f\omega^{\#f}\beta'$ were not an instance of any term $\alpha f\beta''_i$. We need to show that if $t_j$ is not an instance of any $\alpha f\beta''_i$ then there is a term $t$ that matches $t_j$ i.e., $t$ is an instance of $t_j$, $t$ is not an instance of any of the terms $\alpha f\beta''_i$ and $t$ is not an instance of any of the so far added items (by *close*"). Here, we need only to consider added items having an $f$ at the matching position of $M$ and higher priority than $\alpha \bullet \beta$, i.e., any item $\alpha \bullet f\omega^{\#f}\beta'_k$ already in $M$. Using the induction hypothesis, $\alpha\omega\beta'$ is not an instance of any of the terms $\alpha\omega\beta'_k$. So, $\alpha f\omega^{\#f}\beta'$ is not an instance of any of the terms $\alpha f\omega^{\#f}\beta'_k$.

Now we construct a term $t$ that matches $\alpha \bullet f\omega^{\#f}\beta'$. For this purpose, let $g$ be a function symbol that does not occur in any original pattern and $t$ the term obtained from $t_j$ by substituting all the $\omega$s by the term $g\omega^{\#g}$. The fact that $t_j$ is not an instance of any $\alpha f\beta''_i$ and $\alpha f\omega^{\#f}\beta'_k$ means that for each of these terms there is a position $p_i$, respectively $p_k$, such that $\alpha f\beta''_i[p_i]$, respectively $\alpha f\omega^{\#f}\beta'_k[p_k]$ is a function symbol and $\alpha f\beta''_i[p_i] \neq t_j[p_i]$, respectively $\alpha f\omega^{\#f}\beta'_k[p_k] \neq t_j[p_i]$. $t_j$ cannot have a function symbol at position $p_i$ and $p_k$ because $\alpha f\beta''_i$ and $\alpha\omega\beta'_k$ overlap with $\alpha\omega\beta$ and so are $\alpha f\beta''_i$ and $\alpha f\omega^{\#f}\beta'_k$ with $t_j$. Then $t_j[p_i]$ and $t_j[p_k]$ is an $\omega$symbol and so $t[p_i] = t[p_k] = g$. Hence, $t$ cannot be an instance of any of the terms $\alpha f\beta''_i$ or $\alpha f\omega^{\#f}\beta'_k$ because $g$ does not occur in any original pattern. ■

**Example 2.** Using any of the improved closure functions, the automaton corresponding to $L = \{1{:}fa\omega\omega, 2{:}f\omega aa, 3{:}f\omega ba, 4{:}fg\omega g\omega b\}$ is given in Figure 5. As usual, transitions corresponding to failure are omitted. Notice that for the same pattern set, the automaton of Figure 2 has six more states, namely states 6, 7, 12, 13, 14 and 15. Pattern matching for the terms *faaa* and *faba* using the automaton of Figure 2 requires four symbol examinations whereas by using the automaton of Figure 5 only two symbols need to be examined as ωs match any term. Thus, using the new function *close* in this example, not only does the automaton have fewer states but it also allows pattern matching to be performed more quickly.

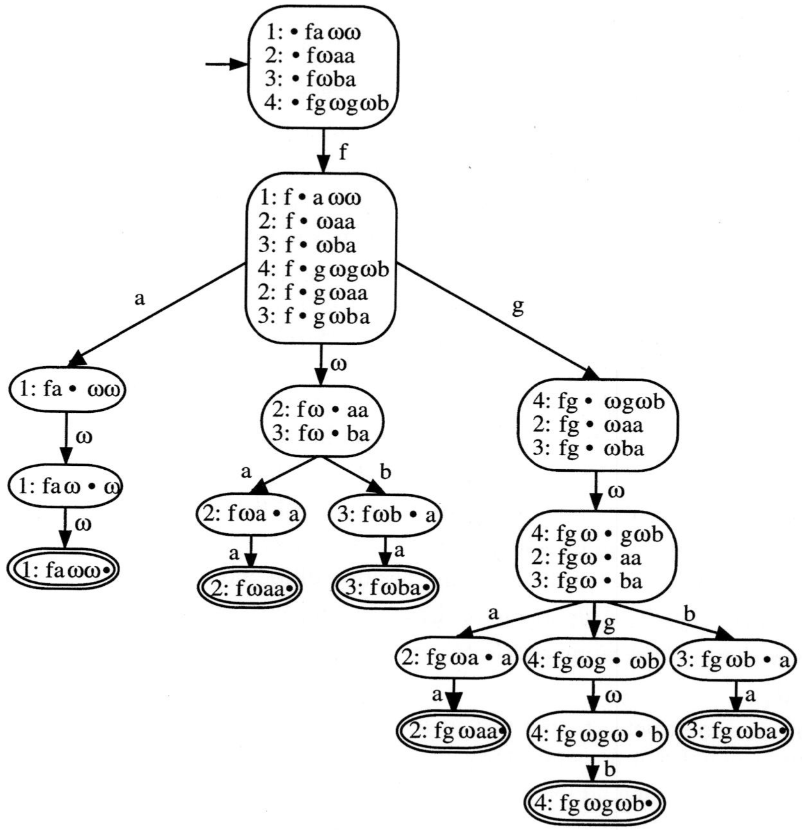


**Fig. 5.** Matching automaton using a revised function for close

## 5 Conclusion

In this paper, we began by recalling a practical method that compiles prioritised ambiguous patterns to a deterministic matching automaton. However, we showed that the obtained automaton include unnecessary branches when the patterns are ambiguous. In the main body of the paper, we identified those branches by considering relevant patterns and. By avoiding irrelevant patterns, we modified the method so that only necessary branches are included in the matching automaton. An example showed how the matching automaton obtained can improve both the space and time requirements.

## References


1. A. Augustsson, *A Compiler for lazy ML*, Proc. Conference on Lisp and Functional Programming, ACM, pp. 218-227, 1984.
2. J. Christian, *Flatterms, Discrimination nets and fast term rewriting*, Journal of Automated Reasoning, vol. 10, pp. 95-113, 1993.
3. D. Cooper and N. Wogrin, *Rule-based programming with OPS5*, Morgan Kaufmann, San Francisco, 1988.
4. N. Dershowitz and J.P. Jouannaud, *Rewrite systems*, Handbook of Theoretical Computer Science, vol. 2, chap. 6, Elsevier Science, 1990.
5. A.J. Field and P.G. Harrison, *Functional programming*, International Computer Science Series, 1988.
6. J.A Goguen and T. Winkler, *Introducing OBJ3*, Technical report SRI-CSL-88-9, Computer Science Laboratory, SRI International, 1998.
7. A. Gräf, *Left-to-right tree pattern matching*, Proc. Conference on Rewriting Techniques and Applications, Lecture Notes in Computer Science, vol. 488, pp. 323-334, 1991.
8. C.M. Hoffman and M.J. O'Donnell, *Pattern matching in trees*, Journal of ACM, vol. 29, n° 1, pp. 68-95, 1982.
9. P. Hudak and al., *Report on the programming language Haskell: a Non-Strict, Purely Functional Language*, Sigplan Notices, Section S, May 1992.
10. A. Laville, *Comparison of priority rules in pattern matching and term rewriting*, Journal of Symbolic Computation, n° 11, pp. 321-347, 1991.
11. N. Nedjah, C.D. Walter and S.E. Eldridge, *Optimal left-to-right pattern matching automata*, Proc. Conference on Algebraic and Logic Programming, Southampton, UK, Lecture Notes in Computer Science, M. Hanus, J. Heering and K. Meinke Eds., Springer-Verlag, vol. 1298, pp. 273-285, 1997.
12. N. Nedjah, *Postponing redex contractions in equational programs*, Proc. Symposium on Functional and Logic Programming, Kyoto, Japan, M. Sato and Y. Toyama Eds., World Scientific, pp. 40-60, 1998.
13. N. Nedjah, C.D. Walter and S.E. Eldridge, *Efficient automata-driven pattern matching for equational programs*, Software-Practice and Experience, vol. 29, n° 9, pp. 793-813, John Wiley, 1999.
14. N. Nedjah and L.M. Mourelle, *Dynamic deterministic pattern matching*, Proc. Computing: the Australasian Theory Symposium, Canberra, Australia, D.A. Wolfram Ed., Electronic Notes in Theretical Computer Science, Elsevier Science, vol. 31, 2000.
15. N. Nedjah and L.M. Mourelle, *Improving time, space and termination in term rewriting-based programming*, Proc. International Conference on Industrial & Engineering Applications of Artificial Intelligence & Expert Systems, Budapest, Hungary, Lecture Notes in Computer Science, L. Monostori, J. Váncsa and A. M. Ali Eds., Springer-Verlag, vol. 2070, pp. 880-890, June 2001.
16. N. Nedjah and L.M. Mourelle, *Optimal Adaptive Pattern-Matching*, Proc. International Conference on Industrial & Engineering Applications of Artificial Intelligence & Expert Systems, Cairn, Australia, Lecture Notes in Computer Science, T. Hendtlass and A. M. Ali Eds., Springer-Verlag, vol. 2358, pp. 768-779, June 2002.
17. M.J. O'Donnell, *Equational logic as programming language*, MIT Press, 1985.
18. R.C. Sekar, R. Ramesh and I.V. Ramakrishnan, *Adaptive pattern matching*, SIAM Journal, vol. 24, n° 5, pp. 1207-1234, 1995.
19. D.A. Turner, *Miranda: a Non strict functional language with polymorphic Types*, Proc. Conference on Lisp and Functional Languages, ACM, pp. 1-16, 1985.
20. P. Wadler, *Efficient compilation of pattern matching*, In "The Implementation of Functional Programming Languages", S. L. Peyton-Jones, Prentice-Hall International, pp. 78-103, 1987.

# A Policy Based Framework for Software Agents

Christos Stergiou and Geert Arys

Liverpool University, Dept. of Computer Science, Liverpool L69 7ZF,UK
c.stergiou@ieee.org,
geert.arys@chello.be

**Abstract.** In this paper we provide a policy based framework for managing and modelling agent social interaction. We specify and implement agent conversation patterns and protocols using an agent policy language. These patterns classify agent interaction, using a blend of communication protocols, security and management policies as well as Object Oriented software design principles. All services, including management services, interact with their agent clients using the same conversation patterns as defined in this paper. Any conversation begins with three steps: requesting a service, negotiating a conversation pattern, and establishing pattern roles. Role theory and reusable policy specifications regulate the way agents participate, providing a rich source of information for conversation management. Further, role theory is used to define agent roles and relationships, which are then described using the Agent Policy Language in terms of policies (i.e. obligations and authorisations). Policy based agents have the ability to interpret policies and assume roles for a certain interaction pattern dynamically. The methodology promotes platform independence and fits the needs of a modular, distributed environment; enabling services to use the powerful 'plug-and-play' concept. Co-operation patterns being more complex are built upon conversation patterns, but also describe the 'social' relationships between agents based on beliefs, desires and intentions.

## 1 Introduction

Research on agent communication languages has until very recently focussed on performative-level issues, such as the semantics of messages. Over the last few years, however, attention has shifted to the conversation/protocol level. Despite this shift of attention, comparatively little effort has been devoted to the problem of understanding how agents in an open society may *dynamically join* conversations, and understand the rules by which they are governed. In this paper, we address this problem. We have developed an *agent policy specification language*, (APSL), by means of which it is possible to specify the rules that govern agent conversations using XML. APSL allows conversations to be composed from each other. In addition, we have implemented a translator, which takes as input an APSL specification, and generates as output a set of rules for the Java-based Expert System Shell (JESS), so that JESS agents directly interpret APSL specifications; other translators are possible for other frameworks.

The remainder of this paper is structured as follows. We begin by introducing the notion of a *policy aware agent* and *polite agent* and outlining our complete framework. In section 3, we give the grammar of the APSL and its basic constructs,

P.W.H. Chung, C.J. Hinde, M. Ali (Eds.): IEA/AIE 2003, LNAI 2718, pp. 426–436, 2003.

including agent conversation patterns. In section 4 we present the UML diagram of our implementation. In section 5 we present our Agent Policy Management Framework, based on the JADE multi-agent platform and the JESS rule based language. We conclude in section 6 by discussing the overall advantages of our approach.

## 2 Policy Aware Agents – The BDI + OA Concept

A *policy aware agent* is an entity whose state is viewed as consisting of mental components such as beliefs, desires, intentions, capabilities (modelled as authorisations) and commitments (modelled as obligations). The agent-oriented approach can be recognised by the use of mental states for reasoning, analysing and controlling the software component. The BDI (Beliefs, Desires, Intentions) model is a well known and widely accepted agent oriented approach [5][6], and we adopt this model as the basis of our agent's internal decision making. But we enhance this decision making with *obligations* and *authorisations*, which constrain the way an agent can translate beliefs, desires and intentions into actions. Our basic approach is to use *authorisation policies* to define what actions an agent is permitted or forbidden to do with available resources and when interacting with peer agents. For example, in the case of itinerant agents visiting an agent platform, authorisation policies might specify the resources to be made available to incoming agents. Unique to our approach is that the same policy mechanisms are used to define the protocols, which must be followed by such foreign agents in order for them to negotiate access to resources controlled by local agents. Further, by using our methodology, we are able to specify and guide any conversation between agents.

Policies in our approach are formally defined using an experimental language inspired by Ponder [4]. They define the actions that agents are obliged to perform either periodically, in response to trigger events, or proactivity. The agent is responsible for ensuring that these constraints interact with its beliefs, desires and intentions at the reasoning stage, before acting towards its goals. Bratman[5] argues that intentions play a significant and distinct role in practical reasoning. He treats intentions as partial plans of action that the agent is committed to execute in order to fulfil its goals. Cohen and Levensque [6] formalise part of Bratman's theory according to which intentions are defined in terms of temporal sequences of an agent's beliefs and goals.

We extend the above notions by adding formalised constraints called *authorisations* and *obligations*, terms which arise in our case from object-oriented distributed systems management. These constraints are what an agent "**should (not) do**" as opposed to BDI intentions, which have in common the "**(not) want to do**" part. The following example illustrates our point. In most systems, it is a policy that when an agent "*wants to*" subscribe to an email list then the agent "*should*" send an email message with the message content: *subscribe*. In this obligation, one may distinguish two parts. The first part is the "want" part, coming from the classical BDI logic of the agent and constitutes part of its internal strategy. The second part is the "should" part and compels the agent to take an action in order to get subscribed. So, an agent with the intention to subscribe into the mailing list will have the constraint that it needs to send an email message in order to achieve its goal.

Our methodology is compatible with the BOID approach [8], which develops an architecture in order to study the conflicts between beliefs, obligations, intentions, and agent desires. However, our usage of the word 'obligation' is rather different. We use the system management interpretation of the term, in which an obligation is a formal rule, imposed by the system. In the BOID approach, an obligation is the constraint experienced by an individual agent.

### 2.1 Polite Agents – An "Honest" and "Social" Policy Aware Agent

The BOID framework mentioned above studies goal-oriented reasoning with constraints – we regard this as part of the *internal mechanism* of an agent. We focus instead on the use of policies to govern communication between agents, which constitutes part of the *external behaviour* of an agent. In our framework, we assume that an agent will obediently follow these externally defined rules. This indicates the definition of *politeness*: "behaving or speaking in a way that is correct for the social situation you are in". In the same way, our policy-aware agent is a polite agent when this agent follows all communication policies. We will show how entire protocols can be defined using policies, and how an agent can dynamically learn how to behave at a particular occasion. For instance, an agent may not be aware how an English auction works, but it can learn to participate by reading an XML policy file relating to the English auction.

Agent conversation patterns, as defined below, complete the picture. They are finer grained than protocols. In fact, protocols are conversation patterns that describe a complete inter-agent conversation. Conversation patterns describe the social rules that govern social interactions between agents in the same way that etiquette precepts describe the finesse of politeness in real life. Protocols can be composed from these patterns. The polite agent can adopt them, and plan actions according to them.

### 2.2 The Agent Policy Based Framework

We have developed an experimental framework within which to evaluate our ideas. The framework consists of three steps, as shown in Figure 1. The first step is to describe social behaviour using policies in an XML policy file. In step two, we parse the policy file: an abstract syntax tree template of the policies is produced, which is fed to the agent. The agent is responsible for obeying these policies. Thus the third step is the agent specific part. In our experiments we have developed a translator, which evaluates the applicability of the policies, and feeds them into a *rule generator*, which automatically generates rules for the JESS Java-based expert system shell (http://herzberg.ca.sandia.gov/jess/). The final output is thus a set of JESS 'policy' rules, which can be directly used by a JESS-capable agent. So, we start from an XML file and we end up with JESS policy rules containing the authorizations and obligations constituting the constraints an agent has. In our implementation, we also model an agent's BDI decision-making in terms of JESS rules: this makes it possible for BDI rules to relate to policies, obligations and the like. Both policy and BDI rules are merged and fed to the JESS inference engine. In this way, the Polite Agent can act (execute intentions) according to its Beliefs and Desires (internal strategy),

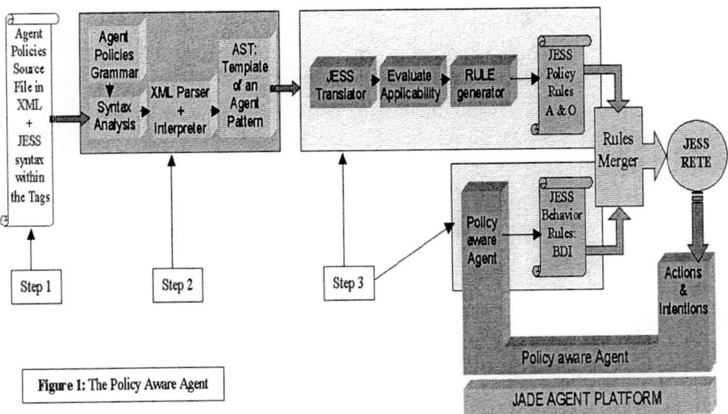


**Fig. 1.** The Policy Aware Agent

constrained by the obligations and authorisations. Normally, it is up to the agent to follow the "want" and "should" parts as it sees fit. As we model only a polite agent in our experimental framework, the obligations are always followed naively, so the rules merger just adds both sets of rules together, giving the highest priority to the policy rules. This means also that the actions, which result by firing its obligations rules, are translated directly into intentions. We will call them "should" type intentions from now on.

Currently there is neither a policy enforcement agent nor a police type agent to 'catch' the agents that do not adhere to the rules and laws of the system. It is up to the peer agent B to detect that the agent A with whom the contract holds does not follow the rules, and stop dealing with agent A. However, the expected actions are public knowledge described in a policy file and can be easily cross-checked, rendering it possible to implement a 'Police agent' to receive complaints and take actions against fraud and misconduct in a straightforward manner.

## 3 The Agent Policy Specification Language (APSL)

The core of our framework is the *Agent Policy Specification Language,* which was inspired by Ponder [4]. Ponder was developed and used for the policy-based management of Object Oriented distributed systems. It is a declarative language, offering flexibility, extensibility and adaptability to a wide range of management requirements. The APSL builds upon these advantages: it extends Ponder for specifying security, management *and communication* policies for distributed *agent* based systems. The grammar for APSL contains the FIPA specified agent based constructs as well as other interaction constructs. The language is a mixture of the following elements:

1. Basic Policies: *Obligations*, *Authorisations* and *Delegations*. (section 3.1)
2. Composite Policies: *Roles*, *Relationships*, *Groups* and *Domains* (section 3.2)
3. FIPA agent communication acts ( section 3.3)
4. *Conversation Patterns* and social *co-operation patterns* (sections 3.4)

### 3.1 APSL: Basic Agent Policies

*Management policies* are a normative specification of the obligations and authorisations of management actors towards their target managed agents. An agent must be able to dynamically change its policy knowledge base over time according to the evolution of the managed agent system (by making new 'contracts' with other agents) or according to changes in management strategy (e.g. from the administrator of the agent platform). We support the following policies for our agents:

*Obligation Policies*: specify the list of actions an agent must perform in response to an event.

*Authorisation Policies*: specify the list of actions that subjects are permitted or prohibited to perform to other Agents or their Environment. The language allows negative authorization policies, which explicitly forbid access or actions.

*Delegation Policies*: permit an Agent to grant privileges that they posses (due to an existing authorisation policy), to other agents called. Delegation Policies are of central importance for co-operation patterns, which are primarily used by an agent to establish contracts with another agent.

### 3.2 APSL: Composite Agent Policies

Basic policies are insufficient for structuring devolved control in the enterprise context (or agent society). We need to group them in relevant entities, so we use concepts developed in role theory [3] i.e., that managers are appointed to roles within the organisation, which define their rights and duties. Organisational goals, policies and procedures further determine their rights and duties within the departments, teams, and projects of which they are members. Software agents can then be dynamically assigned or removed from roles according to changes in the organisational structure. Furthermore, new tasks can be included or removed from role specifications, thus varying the repartition of responsibilities.

**Roles:** In the multi-agent systems literature, it is customary to define the concept of role in terms of the functionality or behaviour, within an organisational context, associated to some type or class of agents [7]. However, agent systems are frequently viewed as agent-societies in which each agent may take on a number of roles during their life-cycle, either at the same time or consecutively. We have investigated how policies can be used to specify these roles. We have used the concept of *role* to group policies that apply to a certain agent. This enables us to simplify the management of agent permissions (which we model using authorisation policies) and duties (which we model using obligation policies). For instance, agents can be assigned to or removed from roles dynamically without changing the policies contained in the *service role position*. In particular, the use of roles in services allows to group policies with the same subject. In short, a role is an abstract representation of an agent's function, service, or identification within a group. A role can be defined with respect to a relationship: a relationship is an aggregate of two or more roles, which describes the mutual dependence between agents.

**Relationships:** Managers appointed to roles do not work in isolation but interact and collaborate with each other in order to perform their tasks. We define the concept of a Relationship between roles to group the policies pertaining to the related roles or to shared resources. The relationship may also specify the interaction protocols between roles. The relationship needs at least 2 agents in order to exist. So, the relationship can have many agent-interactions, since the Relationship is defined between at least 2 agents, which communicate with each other.

**Groups:** A group is a set of Agents. An agent can be a member in several different groups at the same time, perhaps playing a different role (or roles) in each of them, and can move from one group to another dynamically. The **AgentGroup** has at least one relationship, which is special (i.e. a membership relationship). It is this relationship that links the Group to its members. For instance, an employment relationship links the company to its employees.

Code extract 1 represents part of the grammar definition of the Agent Policy Specification Language in XML. It contains some of the core elements such as the policy definition, roles and relationships.

```
<!ATTLIST policy id CDATA #REQUIRED>
<!ATTLIST policy compel (pos_authorisation |neg_authorisation |obligation |refrain) #REQUIRED>
<!ELEMENT when (#PCDATA)>                    <!-- uses a constraint -->
<!ELEMENT on (#PCDATA)>                      <!-- defines an event -->
<!ELEMENT action (#PCDATA)>
<!ELEMENT relationship ( (type | inst), (extends)*, (domain)?, (policy | role)* )>
<!ATTLIST relationship id CDATA #REQUIRED>
<!ATTLIST relationship conversationId CDATA #IMPLIED>
<!ELEMENT role ( (type | inst), (extends)*, (domain)?, (agent | policy | definition)* )>
<!ATTLIST role id CDATA #REQUIRED>
```

**Code Extract 1**: from the XML DTD of the APSL

### 3.3 APSL: FIPA Agent Communicative Acts

The FIPA agent communicative acts (http://www.fipa.org, document number: XC00037H) are the basic constructs of our APSL language. They describe all possible messages that can be passed between agents. These are part of the basic actions that an agent can perform.

### 3.4 APSL: Conversation Patterns & Co-operation Patterns

Conversation patterns [1] are the combination of the principles used by the KQML facilitators and those of the Object Oriented software design patterns. Basically, it is a technique we use for managing multi-agent dynamics which enables us to direct (or restrict) the way agents interact for as many situations as possible by proposing a set of generic roles that can be played. Thus, either very simple co-operation protocols or well-defined generic co-operation patterns are preferable according to our experience. They are a set of roles, with policies that define a "standard" conversation. Any agent that wishes to be able to participate in the pattern in any given role must implement the policies for that particular role.

We have defined a simple template for describing our agent-oriented conversation patterns. We use the following conventions concerning the role related policies: **A+** means “allowed to”, **A-** means “is not allowed to” and **O+** means “has the obligation to”.

**Subscription Conversation Pattern:** A very common pattern in agent communication is the subscription (see Pattern Template 1), which is used to build new relationships between service provider agents and its clients. In KQML, this is called the "subscription facilitator", and agent platforms like Jade offers a standard implementation for it.

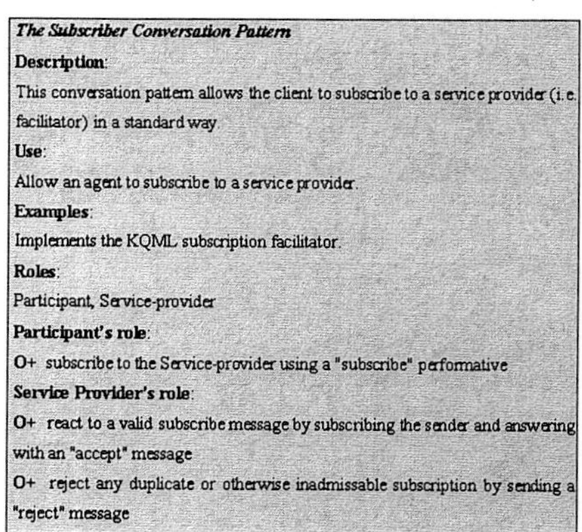

***The Subscriber Conversation Pattern***

**Description**:

This conversation pattern allows the client to subscribe to a service provider (i.e. facilitator) in a standard way.

**Use**:

Allow an agent to subscribe to a service provider.

**Examples**:

Implements the KQML subscription facilitator.

**Roles**:

Participant, Service-provider

**Participant's role**:

O+ subscribe to the Service-provider using a "subscribe" performative

**Service Provider's role**:

O+ react to a valid subscribe message by subscribing the sender and answering with an "accept" message

O+ reject any duplicate or otherwise inadmissable subscription by sending a "reject" message

**Pattern Template 1**: The Subscription conversation pattern

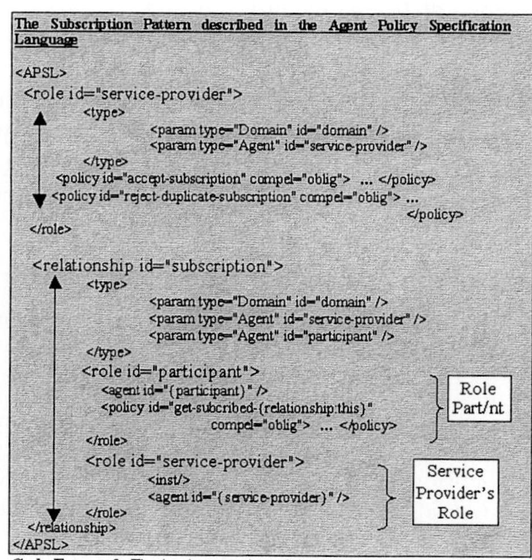

**The Subscription Pattern described in the Agent Policy Specification Language**

```
<APSL>
 <role id="service-provider">
        <type>
                <param type="Domain" id="domain" />
                <param type="Agent" id="service-provider" />
        </type>
        <policy id="accept-subscription" compel="oblig"> ... </policy>
        <policy id="reject-duplicate-subscription" compel="oblig"> ...
                                                          </policy>
 </role>

 <relationship id="subscription">
        <type>
                <param type="Domain" id="domain" />
                <param type="Agent" id="service-provider" />
                <param type="Agent" id="participant" />
        </type>
        <role id="participant">
                <agent id="{participant}" />
                <policy id="get-subcribed-{relationship:this}"
                        compel="oblig"> ... </policy>
        </role>
        <role id="service-provider">
                <inst/>
                <agent id="{service-provider}" />
        </role>
 </relationship>
</APSL>
```



**Code Extract 2**: The implementation of the Subscription conversation pattern in APSL

The partial code extract 2 shows the implementation of the subscription pattern in the Agent Policy Specification Language (APSL). Note that the inner policy definitions are omitted, so that the reader can see the structure clearly. The service-provider role must exist before a relation is formed, thus we define it outside the relationship. Then follows a relationship between the "service-provider" and the "Participant" at a particular "domain". This "domain" field may be used to refer to an Ontology.

Whenever an agent offers a service that requires an interchange of messages, the agent can "offer" one or more conversation patterns to his client. When they agree on a certain pattern to be used, they assume the roles and start the communication. These newly defined patterns describe the social interaction of an agent. An agent uses the pattern's definition to learn how to behave at a particular circumstance.

As a service, agent management uses conversation patterns on two levels: Firstly, the management modules can use the patterns to communicate with the other agents. In other words, it is the hook into the system they manage. Secondly, patterns contain extra information on how the communication between agents works. Management modules can use this to enforce policies, measure response time to obligation triggering events, agent visualisation, 'law' enforcement police agents and so on. In other words, any interaction between agents can be established in an infinite number of ways. In order to standardise some of them without constraining or limiting the capabilities of the software agent at all, we use a set of pre-defined software design patterns. This creates also a more visible system to manage.

*Conversation patterns* are limited to the description of the roles in terms of messaging concepts. *Co-operation patterns* [1] extend conversation patterns by including role specifications based on beliefs, desires and intentions. A co-operation pattern can thus include concepts as delegation of tasks and joining forces to reach a goal. The relationship the agents assume in the pattern follows one of the types of relationship defined in: control, peer, benevolence, dependency or ownership. In other words, they encapsulate also the 'social' relationship between roles. *Co-operation patterns* mimic human interaction behaviour. Therefore, the specific strengths of agents are used. Manager agents will now be able to measure a new aspect in agent interaction: quality of work delivered (how set goals are met and to what extent).

## 4 The UML of the Policy Based Agents

So far, we have defined the patterns using a concepts like 'role', 'relationship', and so on. The way these notions are linked to each other can be summarised in the UML figure which includes the vocabulary we use in our implementation.

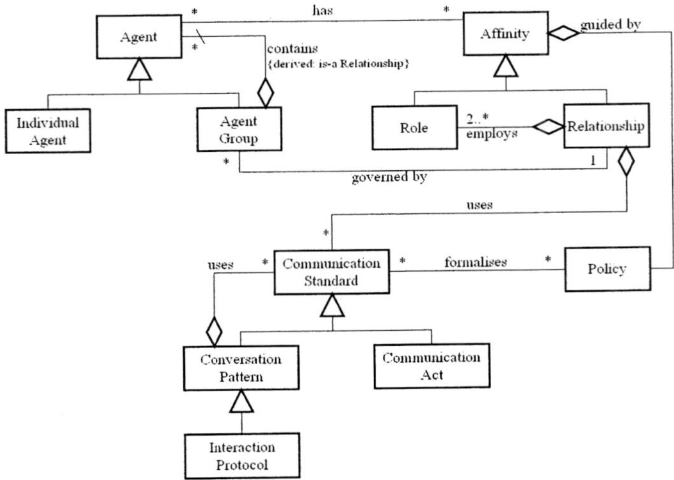


1. A **Role** is the part, which is played by the agent in the system.
2. A **Relationship** is mostly used to describe how two agents depended on each other, but it can also be used to describe merely a common origin. It needs at least two agents in order to exist, so at least two roles are needed to define it. We define a "Relationship" which represents a temporary or permanent connection between 2 agents where the focus is on the mutual dependencies of the roles
3. And, in this way, we reserve the **AgentGroup** for a real collection of Agents, which behaves as an independent agent with its own desires and goals (e.g. a company or a government). It has at least one Relationship, which is the membership relationship. It is the Relationship that describes the coherence of the Group.
4. The *Relationship* utilizes a number of Communication Standards (Politeness rules). In our model, no communication is possible without a relationship. Consider two agents just saying 'hello' to each other as having a brief 'encounter' relationship. However, saying 'hello' also follows politeness rules. Our model enables us to have communication protocols between more than two roles.

5. The **CommunicationStandard** can be a single **CommunicationAct** or a sequence of Communication Acts defining a Conversation Pattern. The **Interaction Protocol** is a **Conversation Pattern** that describes all rules governing of a valid conversation of a given type.

## 5 The Architecture of the Agent Policy Management Framework

As noted above, we have implemented our framework using the JADE platform. JADE (http://sharon.cselt.it/projects/jade/) is a FIPA compliant agent platform written in Java, which has three main components: AMS (Agent Management Service), DF (Directory Facilitator) and the ACC (Agent Communication Channel), which enables inter agent communication through the JADE Message Transport. The communication between these components and between other agents is done using message passing with a high level protocol that ensures delivery of messages (i.e. messages are not lost). The communication language used to represent messages in JADE is the FIPA-ACL (Agent Communication Language), which is an agent-worldwide accepted representation.

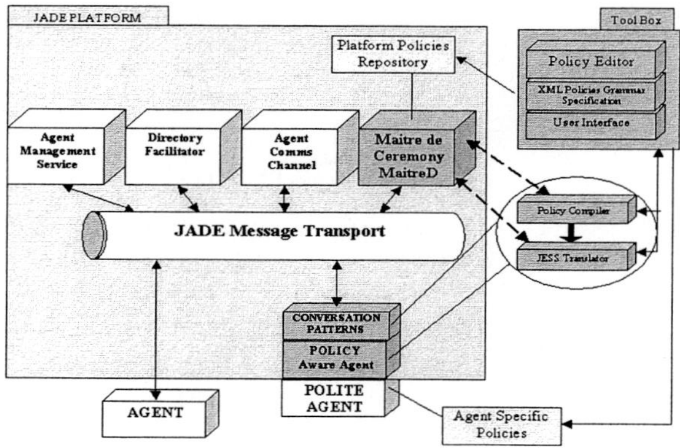


Our implementation does not interact directly with the core JADE components; instead it simply uses the Message Transport provided by JADE and interacts with ACL messages. There are two main advantages to this approach. First, we ensure loose coupling between our framework and JADE; second, we gain portability, in that the implementation-architecture is modular and runs with minimal modifications (only on the message passing part) on any other platform.

The extensions are indicated in blue in the JADE Platform Figure. Arrows show how messages travel through the system, while dashed arrows show logical interaction. We can think of the extensions as being a new layer defining a way in which various types of policies can be applied, either dynamically or statically to either enhance communication and/or cooperation. Further, it provides a valid framework in order to control and manage the interactions of agents. We can distinguish two different key applications:

*Agent conversations* are governed by the policies encapsulated in communication patterns written in a generalized XML format. One or more agents can dynamically agree on a specific interaction pattern without them having any prior knowledge of the rules. In other words, they can 'load' the politeness policies that are needed in order to take part in a conversation.

*Control, Security enforcement, monitoring and QoS:* pre-defined policy files in XML format could be used, which are the responsibility of an agent called the MaitreD, read it as “Maître des Cérémonies”, acting as a policy repository and possibly as a policy enforcer for various agent management services.

In our implementation we have created a class called “PoliteAgent” which extends the basic JADE “agent” class by keeping the same external interface of “Agent”. The “PoliteAgent” class provides all implementation for the framework, with the naïve-obedient approach to all policies. A client wanting to use this framework simply sub-classes PoliteAgent instead of Agent. Another component is the Toolbox, which comprises three logical sub-components: i) Policy Editor, ii) XML Policies Grammar Specifications and iii) a User Interface. The *policy editor* is used to generate the XML grammar based policy files, which may be stored either locally (directly uploaded at initialisation of the Polite Agent) or centrally by the MaitreD agent, depending on the functionality.

## 6 Conclusions

We believe that agents and agent societies will benefit from our policy based framework on many levels. Our policy based framework includes policies such as obligations and authorisations as well as organisational concepts such as roles, relationships and groups and conversation patterns & co-operation patterns that describe agent social interaction scenarios for a peer to peer agent interaction and on an agent to platform level (e.g. can be used for engineering agent management services).

In particular on the agent level a further advantage is obtained since in contrast to classical agent development in which intelligence logic of the agent is strongly coupled to the communications logic; in our policy based framework we have decoupled them completely. The communications (i.e. agent interaction) logic is described in the APSL in a separate policy file and each and every policy based agent can plug ‘n’ play it dynamically.

On the agent platform level management services can have common interfaces and be fully distributed by using the conversation and co-operation patterns that we have developed. Moreover, organisational concepts modelled through policies can be used to build various management services to control the agents on a society level, like in the real society life in which rules and laws indicate to us our priviledges and responsibilities (i.e. authorisations and obligations on the agent level).

At last but not the least interoperability with a non-agent platform is enhanced since one could also interact with any true agent platform available in the network, simply by adopting the conversation patterns.

## References

[1] C. Stergiou, G. Arys, "Implementing Agent Management Using Conversation Patterns and Role Theory", Springer Lecture Notes in AI 2070, June 2001.

[2] C. Stergiou, G. Arys, "A Policy based Framework for Agents: On the Specification of an Agent Policy Language including roles, Relationships, Conversation & Co-operation Patterns", Autonomous Agents 2003, Melbourne, Australia, July 2003.

[3] E.C. Lupu, "A Role-Based Framework for Distributed Systems Management". Ph.D. Thesis, University of London, July 1998.

[4] N.C. Damianou, "A Policy Framework for Management of Distributed Systems". Ph.D. Thesis, University of London, February 2002.

[5] M. E. Bratman. Intentions, "Plans and Practical Reason". Harvard University Press, Massachusetts, 1987.

[6] P.R. Cohen and H.J. Levensque. "Intention is choice with commitment". Artificial Intelligence, 42(3), 1990.

[7] J. Ferber, O. Gutknetch, "A meta-model for the analysis and organisations in multi-agent systems". In Y. Demazeau, editor, ICMAS'98, pages 128-135, IEEE press 1998.

[8] J. Broersen, M.Dastani, J. Hulstijn, z. Huang, L. Torre, "The BOID Architecture – Conflicts between Beliefs, Obligations, Intentions and Desires", In the conference proceedings of Autonomous Agents 2001, Montreal Canada.

# Intelligent Support for Solving Classification Differences in Statistical Information Integration

Catholijn M. Jonker[1] and Tim Verwaart[2]

[1] Department of Artificial Intelligence, Vrije Universiteit Amsterdam, De Boelelaan 1081a, 1081 HV Amsterdam
jonker@cs.vu.nl
[2] Agricultural Economics Research Institute LEI, Burg. Patijnlaan 19, 2585 BE den Haag
d.verwaart@lei.wag-ur.nl

**Abstract.** Integration of heterogeneous statistics is essential for political decision making on all levels. Like in intelligent information integration in general, the problem is to combine information from different autonomous sources, using different ontologies. However, in statistical information integration specific problems arise. This paper is focussed on the problem of differences in classification between sources and goal statistics. Comparison with existing information integration techniques leads to the conclusion that existing techniques can only be used if individual data underlying the statistics is accessible. This requirement is usually not met, due to protection of privacy and commercial interests. In this paper a formal approach and software tools are presented to support statistical information integration, based on a generic ontology for descriptive statistics, and heuristics that work independent of the domain of application. The heuristics were acquired from economic experts working in the field of European Common Fisheries Policy.

## 1 Introduction

Statistics are indispensable for political decision making. Economic, demographic and environmental statistics are used for monitoring social and physical processes and for measuring policy effectiveness. National governments usually have organised statistics services in order to fulfil their demand for decision support. In supranational organisations like the European Commission homogeneous statistics are often not available. Organizing supranational statistics is a time-consuming and precarious task. In many cases political decisions have to be made and processes have to be monitored long before homogeneous statistics can be available. Then heterogeneous statistics from a variety of independent sources must be integrated.

European Common Fisheries Policy (CFP) [1] is an example of a field where insufficient homogeneous statistics are available. Annually an economic report is prepared by a group of experts from the involved countries [2]. The statistics in this report integrate a broad variety of national and regional statistics. This task is performed in two annual workshops. In spring, the experts meet in order to agree on the contents of the report and to plan the data collection. Back home they collect the best available data. In the autumn workshop the data is integrated. Providing automated support for the integration process would make more time available for

P.W.H. Chung, C.J. Hinde, M. Ali (Eds.): IEA/AIE 2003, LNAI 2718, pp. 437–446, 2003.

economic analysis in the workshop, and improve the quality of the statistics because under pressure of time the experts sometimes make errors.

Over the past ten years much has been achieved in the field of intelligent information integration. Examples of approaches that support integration of quantitative data are SIMS [3], COIN [4], HERMES [5] and InfoSleuth [6]. None of these systems, however, supports integration of statistics by explicit mechanisms for mapping aggregated data from a particular classification to a target classification, as described in section 3. Most current research is focused on extending integration techniques from structured databases to semi-structured data on the web, as can be illustrated by Ariadne [7]. In integration of statistics, all general problems known from other areas of information integration occur, such as ontological and notational differences and differences in units of measurement and typology. In addition, specific problems in the integration of statistics are:

- differences in population, e.g., differences in threshold for inclusion of objects. For example, does a boat with engine power less than 20 hp count as a fishing vessel?
- differences in reported statistics, e.g., sum versus average.
- differences in classification, e.g. age classes bounded by 20, 35, 50 and 65 years vs. 15, 35 and 55 years; or length vs. gross register tonnage as vessel size indicator.

This paper concentrates on the fundamental problem of classification differences.

The specific problems of integration of statistics occur only if the underlying individual data sets are inaccessible. If all individual data would be accessible, available integration support systems like SIMS [3] could be applied and the integrated results could be aggregated to the desired level of specification. In many cases individual data is inaccessible for reasons of privacy or commercial protection. Therefore, dedicated methods have to be developed for integrating statistics.

One of the problems underlying statistics is that semantics of statistics are not included explicitly in the statistics itself, nor are they universally defined. The specific semantics of a statistic are often obtainable, but, in general, this is not a trivial process. Integration of several heterogeneous statistics requires the understanding of the semantics of each of the statistics, heuristic knowledge about the domain of application, and a general understanding of the discipline of statistics. Therefore, techniques for automated support for statistical information integration require the explicit use of heuristic knowledge and cannot be seen as a mere statistical problem and the implementation of a statistical technique. This heuristic knowledge must be acquired from human experts in the field.

In this paper a generic model is presented for resolving classification differences, applying domain heuristics. The model contains a generic ontology of descriptive statistics, and an explicit model of a specific method, the "weight matrix method". The approach exploits in a generic manner domain specific heuristic knowledge about relationships between statistical variables. As a result the approach and its software can be used on any domain, given arbitrary (domain specific) sources and heuristic knowledge. The approach has been implemented in a prototype.

In section 2 the problem addressed in this paper is elaborated. In section 3 the approach to solve classification differences is explained and motivated by the experience of human experts. The model is presented in section 4. Section 5 gives an example of the application of the model. The results are discussed in section 6.

## 2 Statistical Heterogeneity

In this section the concepts of homogeneity and heterogeneity are defined with respect to statistics, and classification difference is introduced as one of the causes of statistical heterogeneity.

A statistic is a non-empty set of values of one or more statistical variables, specified over zero, one or more dimensions. A statistical variable is a variable that describes an aggregated property of a population of objects or of one or more subclasses of a population. A subclass is a population subset, defined by the value of one or more variables. The classifying variables are referred to as dimensions of the statistic. An example of a statistic is a table describing total catch of fish (the statistical variable) per species per week (the dimensions) for the North-sea fishing fleet (the population).

A set of statistics is semantically homogenous, if

1. all objects represented in the population are subject to the same inclusion criteria,
2. all statistical variables that describe the same property have equivalent definitions,
3. all subclasses either overlap completely or do not overlap at all, and
4. all variables classifying for equivalent dimensions have equivalent definitions.

A set of statistics is called semantically heterogeneous if at least one condition for homogeneity is not satisfied. Following this definition, statistics are semantically heterogeneous if they differ in what they *intend* to describe. Differences in data collection process and data processing are excluded from the definition of semantic heterogeneity, although they may cause data inconsistency. These differences are excluded from the definition because they apply to the way statistics are produced, just like other causes of inconsistency (omissions, errors and fraud).

In order to integrate statistics that are heterogeneous only with respect to their dimensions, they have to be mapped from their original source classification to a common target classification. Two kinds of mappings are used in statistical information integration: individual and aggregated mappings. In the process of mapping data about individual objects, object identity is preserved: only attribute values are mapped to values of other attributes. For aggregated statistics object identity is not preserved in the mapping. The following example illustrates these issues. Assume that statistic S distinguishes between large and small vessels at class boundary 40 m, and statistic T also distinguishes between large and small vessels, but at class boundary 50 m. A 45 m vessel is classified "large" in S and "small" in T, but it remains the same vessel: it has the same identity in both S and T. The class of large vessels in S, however, is different from the class of large vessels in T, and comparing them requires information about some vessels that are called small in T.

## 3 Resolving Classification Differences

Classification differences can be solved by finding an appropriate matrix $W$ that relates the values of a statistical variable according to different classification:

$$WC=D \qquad (1)$$

where $C$ and $D$ are $n \times 1$ and $m \times 1$ matrices respectively, representing the values according to the respective classifications, and $W$ is an $m \times n$ matrix representing the relationship. If the statistical variable is the total value (sum) of a population variable for each class, matrix $W$ is a weight matrix representing the distribution of $C$ over the classification of $D$. In the remainder of this section the approach human experts take and a general recipe for the weight matrix method are described.

An interesting case is integration of data about Belgian fisheries. Two departments of the Belgian ministry of agriculture and fisheries published statistics on the aspects of fisheries they are responsible for: landings (amount of fish brought ashore) [9] and financial results [10] respectively. Both aspects are included and compared in the annual economic reports for the CFP. However, the two Belgian reports use different vessel classifications. The approach taken by human experts (fisheries economists) is to redistribute the total value of landings per class from [9] over the classification of [10]. To create a weight matrix, the experts used known fishing effort data, specified for the cross product of both classifications. So, fishing effort (in kWdays) is used as a proxy variable for value of landings (the term proxy is used in econometrics for a stand-in variable that is approximately proportional to an unobservable variable [11]).

The recipe for the weight matrix method, as given by the experts, is as follows:

1. Primary source determination:
   - Find the sources that contain the requested statistical variable (or a variable that can be transformed to it) for the requested population.
   - If a source exists of which the classification matches the requested classification, homogeneous data is available that can serve as goal table.
   - Else, select the most reliable source as primary source.
2. Weight source determination: if the request is not yet satisfied, find a source containing the source classification variable for the primary source, the goal classification variable, and a variable that can be used as proxy variable for the requested statistic.
3. Construct the weight matrix.
4. Multiply primary source with weight matrix to compute the goal statistic.

This recipe is applicable for transforming sum data. In order to transform other statistics, e.g. average data, the experts transform to sum data before applying the recipe. The latter transformation process is not in the scope of this paper. Steps 2 and 3 are the most complex. Step 2 requires proportionality models describing the trust that experts have in usability of variables as proxy for other variables. Step 3 entails aggregation of the proxy variable from individual data, according to the cross product of both classifications. These steps are further explained in the next section.

## 4 Statistical Support Model

In this section the process model for statistical support is introduced. The compositional development method DESIRE [12] was used to specify and implement the model. The model basically follows the steps of the weight matrix method as introduced in the previous section (see Figure 1). The model includes a statistical ontology that uses generic terms and relations common to statistics. First the ontology is introduced, and then the components of the process model are explained. The ontology elements occurring in this paper are:

```
relations:
goal_population: SN;
goal_variable: VAR;
goal_classification_variable: VAR;
source_classification_variable: VAR * C_DESCRIPTION;
goal_classification: VAR * C_DESCRIPTION;
gc_description: C_DESCRIPTION;
goal_type: TYPE;
goal_table: SN;
contains: SN * VAR;
source_aggregation_level: SN * AGRR_LEVEL;
describes_population: SN * POPULATION;
proportion_model: P_MODEL * TRUST
possible_sc_var_wrt: CLASSIFICATION * SN;
candidate_weight_source: SN;
possible_weight_tuple: VAR * SN * TRUST;
terms:
i_class(...) /* interval class */
class_var(...) /* population variable used in classification */
```

where SN is the sort of source names, VAR is the sort of statistical variables, population variables, and classifications. The sort TYPE describes the type of statistic (e.g., total, mean). Classification descriptions (e.g., list of intervals) belong to sort C_DESCRIPTION. Aggregation levels (individual, aggregated) are indicated by sort AGGR_LEVEL. POPULATION is the sort of individuals described by a statistical source. The sort of P_MODEL contains descriptions of proportionality models. The sort CLASSIFICATION is the sort consisting of objects built up out of a variable name and a C_DESCRIPTION. The sort TRUST indicates the confidence experts have in a model.

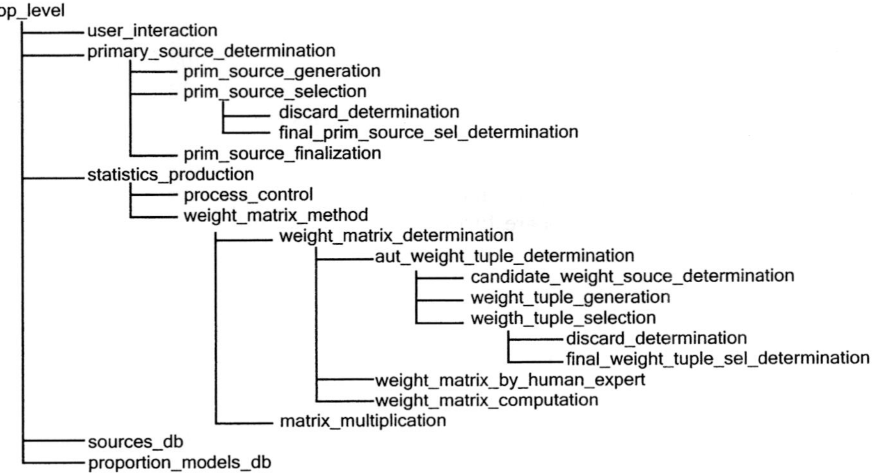


**Fig. 1.** Process Composition

Component user_interaction contains the interfaces necessary to obtain requests and to present results. It analyses the request in terms of goal population, goal variable, and goal classification. Components sources_db, and proportion_models_db refer to databases containing all available source descriptions (and links to XML documents containing their data) and proportionality models.

Component primary_source_determination corresponds to step 1 of the weight matrix method. Its task is to determine the primary source, containing the goal variable. It consists of three processes: generation (prim_source_generation), selection of the most reliable candidate (prim_source_selection), and collecting associated, necessary facts of the selected source (prim_source_finalization). Only the knowledge used in the generation component is described here.

```
if      goal_variable(G: P_VAR)
  and   goal_type(T: TYPE)
  and   goal_population(P: POPULATION)
  and   contains(S: SN, stat_var(T: TYPE, G: P_VAR))
  and   contains(S: SN, SC: CLASSIFICATION)
  and   describes_population(S: SN, P: POPULATION)
then    possible_sc_var_wrt (SC: CLASSIFICATION, S: SN);

/* optimal case: SN satisfies the request */
if      goal_classification_variable(X : P_VAR)
  and   gc_description(CD: C_DESCRIPTION)
  and   possible_sc_var_wrt
            (class_var(X: P_VAR,CD: C_DESCRIPTION), S: SN)
then    goal_table(S: SN);
```

The component statistics_production is set up to be extendable with more methods for production of statistics, e.g. transformations between sum and average. For the same reason the component process_control is included. In this paper, the focus is on component weight_matrix_method, which consists of weight_matrix_determination (steps 2 and 3 of Section 3.2) and matrix_multiplication (step 4).

The component weight_matrix_determination consists of weight_matrix_computation, aut_weight_tuple_determination, and wm_by_human_expert. If the automated construction of the weight matrix fails, a human expert can enter a matrix directly. The automated process starts with aut_weight_tuple_determination. That process is composed again (see Figure 1). The first step is to select candidate weight sources.

```
if      source_classification_variable(X: P_VAR)
  and   goal_classification_variable(Y: P_VAR)
  and   goal_population(P: POPULATION)
  and   contains(S: SN, X: P_VAR)
  and   contains(S: SN, Y: P_VAR)
  and   describes_population (S: SN, P: POPULATION)
then    candidate_weight_source(S: SN);
```

The next step is to select candidate proportionality models in order to obtain possible weight tuples (triples of proxy variable, weight source and trust):

```
if      goal_variable(G: P_VAR)
  and   proportion_model(input_output_vars
            (I: P_VAR, G: P_VAR), P: MODEL_PRECISION)
```

```
  and  candidate_weight_source(S: SN)
  and  contains(S: SN, I: P_VAR)
then   possible_weight_tuple(I: P_VAR, S: SN, P: TRUST);
```

From the triples, one is selected with the highest trust (a quality indication for the proportionalty, provided by experts). If this succeeds, a precursor of the weight matrix is computed using (XML) data from the weight source. The elements of the precursor are computed as sums of weight values by adding up the input values from the weight source for which the classification variable values match both the corresponding goal class and the corresponding source class. The matching criterion for interval classes is `lower_bound ≤ classification_variable_value < upper_bound`. For other types of classifications the criterion is semantic equivalence of strings.

The precursor $m$ x $n$ matrix $[w'_{ij}]$ is normalized by dividing each element by the sum of all elements matching the same goal class, in order to produce a weight $m$ x $n$ matrix $W$ $[w_{ij}]$:

$$w_{ij} = w'_{ij} / \sum_{i=1}^{m} w'_{ij} \qquad (2)$$

The next step in the process is extraction of (XML) data from the primary source to create the $n$ x 1 input data matrix $C$ obtained by taking the relevant vector from the primary source with respect to the source classification variable. The last step is the multiplication $WC$ to obtain the goal table.

The transformation method described in this section transforms sum data for one variable of one population. To create an integrated statistic, it has to be executed for every combination of goal population and goal variable in the request. Furthermore, the transformation of average to sum data (and reverse) may be required. The next section gives a detailed example for a simple transformation.

## 5 Example Transformation Process

Length is used as an indicator for ship size in German fisheries statistics. In Danish statistics, gross register tonnage is the common indicator for ship size. Suppose the following goal table is requested in order to compare German catch with Danish data:

Total catch of the German fleet in 2000, by gross register tonnage (GRT) class

| GRT class (tons) | total catch (tons) |
|---|---|
| 0-40 | ... |
| 40-400 | ... |
| 400 or more | ... |

Internally, this request is formulated as follows:

```
goal_population('German fleet 2000');
goal_variable(stat_var(total,'catch'));
goal_classification('GRT_class',
   [i_class('0-40', 0.0, 40.0),
```

```
    i_class('40-400', 40.0, 400.0),
    i_class('400 or more', 400, ANY)]);
```

No source is available that can provide this data. However, a primary source (the German "Fangstatistik") exists for total catch by ship length:

Total catch of the German fleet in 2000, by length class

| Length over all (m) | total catch (tons) |
|---|---|
| 0-10 | 6268 |
| 10-20 | 30223 |
| 20-50 | 54131 |
| 50 or more | 116594 |

The primary source description is as follows:

```
contains('total catch Germany 2000', class_var('LOA',
   [i_class("0-10", 0.0, 10.0),
    i_class("10-20", 10.0, 20.0),
    i_class("20-50", 20.0, 50.0),
    i_class("50 or more", 50.0, ANY)]));
contains('total catch Germany 2000',stat_var(total,'catch'));
source_aggregation_level
   ('total catch Germany 2000', aggregated);
describes_population
   ('total catch Germany 2000', 'German fleet 2000');
```

The following weight matrix is required in order to compute the goal table.

| | Length over all | | | |
|---|---|---|---|---|
| GRT | 0-10 | 10-20 | 20-50 | 50+ |
| 0-40 | ... | ... | ... | ... |
| 40-400 | ... | ... | ... | ... |
| 400+ | ... | ... | ... | ... |

In the databases, the German fleet register of 1998 is available, giving length over all and gross register tonnage for each ship. This satisfies the constraints for a candidate weight source: it contains source classification variable and goal classification variable, and describes a population similar to the goal population. The relevant description elements are:

```
contains('Fleet register Germany 1998', 'LOA');
contains('Fleet register Germany 1998', 'GRT');
source_aggregation_level
   ('Fleet register Germany 1998', individual);
describes_population
   ('Fleet register Germany 1998', 'German fleet 2000');
```

The source `'Fleet register Germany 1998'` is selected as a candidate weight source. Fisheries expert knowledge about proportionality between catch and engine power is formulated as follows:

```
proportion_model
  (input_output_vars ('engine power', 'catch'), 0.7);
```

The factor 0.7 indicates the confidence that experts have in using engine power as a proxy for catch; 0 would indicate complete distrust, 1 complete trust. This model matches a variable occurring in a candidate weight source with the goal variable. Combined with 'Fleet register Germany 1998' it is selected and the following precursor weight matrix is constructed. It contains total engine power per cell.

| | Length over all | | | |
|---|---|---|---|---|
| GRT | 0-10 | 10-20 | 20-50 | 50+ |
| 0-40 | 24251 | 54523 | 221 | 0 |
| 40-400 | 0 | 7893 | 39562 | 0 |
| 400+ | 0 | 0 | 0 | 28865 |

In this example data content is concentrated in part of the cells. This is generally the case in this type of integration process. This is exactly the reason why experts apply this method. The final result is in most cases rather insensitive for uncertainty in the proportionality model. The model uncertainty is usually propagated to the final result a relatively small amount of the data.

The normalized weight matrix $W$ is obtained by dividing cell values by column totals. Multiplication $WC$, where $C$ is the primary source data content, subsequently results in the goal table content:

Total catch of the German fleet in 2000, by GRT class

| GRT class (tons) | total catch (tons) |
|---|---|
| 0-40 | 32970 |
| 40-400 | 57653 |
| 400 or more | 116594 |

## 6 Discussion

This paper addresses the socio-economically relevant problem of statistical information integration for political decision making. The problem occurs in countless areas of application over all levels of government and management. From a research perspective this problem is close to the areas of intelligent information integration and statistics. From another perspective the problem can be seen as introducing statistics to the intelligent information integration, which introduces a number of specific problems.

Literature study reveals that the results of intelligent information integration do not cover the specific problems of statistical information integration. An exception is [8] in which an overall model was proposed, that is dedicated to the statistical integration process used to support the European Common Fisheries Policy. That model does not use either a generic ontology of statistics, or generic models of statistical methods. Furthermore, the problem of possible classification differences was solved in ad hoc manner for specific data sources.

Statistical techniques that are an obvious source of inspiration are not generally applicable. This is caused by the inaccessibility of data and by lack of domain specific statistical models. Formalisation of human expert knowledge did not solve these problems. However, the acquired heuristic knowledge did enable the formalisation and implementation of a model that is more generally applicable. The model uses heuristics for selecting primary sources, proportionality models, and weight matrices to overcome the classification differences of heterogeneous sources. The "weight matrix method" distilled from the expertise of humans in the field takes a central place in the model. The structure of the model is set up in such a way that it allows easy extension with other methods.

In the research reported in this paper, the focus was on heuristics and software support. From the examples that were studied, the weight matrix method appears to give reliable results. Current research is focused on extension of the system with statistical techniques to quantify the reliability of the results produced by the weight matrix method. Future research will create dedicated software for statistical techniques to further support integration of heterogeneous statistics.

## References


1. http://europa.eu.int/comm/fisheries/doc_et_publ/green1_en.htm.
2. Economic Performance of Selected European fishing Fleets, Annual report 2000, Concerted Action FAIR PL97-3541, ISBN 90-5242-624-4. LEI, Den Haag, 2000.
3. Arens Y., C.Y. Chee, C-N Hsu, C.A Knoblock: Retrieving and Integrating Data from Multiple Information Sources. International Journal on Intelligent and Cooperative Information Systems, 2, 1993.
4. Goh, C., S. Bressan, S. Madnick, M. Siegel: Context Interchange: New Features and Formalism for the Intelligent Integration of Information. MIT-Sloan Working Paper 3941, 1997.
5. Subrahmanian V.S., S. Adali, A. Brink, R. Emery, J.J. Lu, A. Rajput, T.J. Rogers, R.Ross, C. Ward: HERMES: Heterogeneous Reasoning and Mediator System. http://www.cs.umd.edu/projects/hermes/publications/postscripts/tois.ps, 1996.
6. Nodine, M., J. Fowler, T. Ksiezyk, B Perry, M. Taylor, A. Unruh: Active Information Gathering in InfoSleuth. International Journal on Cooperative Information Systems, 9, 2000.
7. Knoblock, C.A., S. Minton, J.L. Ambite, N. Ashish, I. Muslea, A.G. Philpot, S. Tejada: The Ariadne Approach to Web-based Information Integration. International Journal on Cooperative Information Systems, 10, 2001.
8. Klinkert, M., Treur, J., Verwaart, D.: Knowledge-Intensive Gathering and Integration of Statistical Information on European Fisheries. In: R. Loganantharaj, G. Palm and M. Ali (eds.), Proceedings IEA/AIE 2000. Lecture Notes in AI, vol. 1821, Springer Verlag, 2000.
9. Welvaert, M.: De Belgische zeevisserij – aanvoer en besomming. Ministerie van Landbouw – Bestuur der Economische Diensten – Dienst voor de zeevisserij, Brussels, 1993.
10. Uitkomsten van de Belgische zeevisserij 1993. Ministerie van Landbouw – Bestuur der Economische Diensten – Dienst voor de zeevisserij, Brussels, 1993.
11. Wooldridge, J.M.: Introductory Econometrics. South-Western College Publishing, 2000.
12. Brazier, F.M.T., C.M. Jonker, J. Treur, Principals of Compositional Multi-agent Systems Development. In: J. Cuena (ed.), Proceedings of the 15th IFIP WCC, Conference on Information Technology and Knowledge Systems, IT&KNOWS'98, IOS Press, 1998.

# Supporting Collaborative Product Design in an Agent Based Environment

Weidong Fang, Ming Xi Tang, and John Hamilton Frazer

Design Technology Research Centre, School of Design,
The Hong Kong Polytechnic University
{sdfang, sdtang, john.frazer}@polyu.edu.hk

**Abstract.** One of the problems in building collaborative and intelligent design systems is the difficulty in integrating Artificial Intelligence (AI) and Computer Supported Collaborative Work (CSCW) with design knowledge to generate results to the satisfaction of designers who often have high demands on aesthetics as well as scientific aspects of a supporting tool. In this paper, we present an open and flexible design computing architecture, which has the characteristics of both Client/Server (C/S) model and distributed model. Two collaboration processes (synchronous and asynchronous) are facilitated in this proposed architecture. For the design of agents, we propose a new model to deal with various types of knowledge sources, which have to be incorporated in the collaboration process. Versioning and locking mechanisms are implemented to support synchronous and asynchronous collaborations. Based on this architecture, a collaborative design environment has been implemented using the standard of Distributed Component Object Model (DCOM).

**Keywords**: Autonomous Agents, Collaborative Design, AI, DCOM, MAS

## 1 Introduction

As a new paradigm for analysing, designing, and implementing software systems, agent technology has brought us a lot of successful examples in recent years. In a Multi-Agent System (MAS) architecture, many intelligent agents, which are considered to be autonomous entities, can interact with each other. Such a framework makes it convenient for agents to share knowledge, communicate, and work collaboratively. Because the behaviour of the participants in a CSCW system are much similar to those of the agents in MAS, it is possible that we can make a CSCW system work more efficiently by developing it in accordance with the MAS architecture.

However, compared with general CSCW systems, a collaborative design system has many unique problems that have to be tackled, such as,

- Flexible, open, and reliable system architecture,
- Capability of supporting design in an evolutionary and generative process,
- Shared graphical user interfaces (GUI) with ease of control,

P.W.H. Chung, C.J. Hinde, M. Ali (Eds.): IEA/AIE 2003, LNAI 2718, pp. 447–460, 2003.

- Collaborative design communication languages and protocols, and
- Conflict resolution.

Thus if we adopt the MAS architecture mechanically in the development of collaborative systems, we may not get the expected result. Some key issues, such as an enhanced architecture, an agent model that facilitates design activities and collaboration techniques must be solved properly to meet the requirements of design process.

In our proposed architecture, we adopted two models for agents to exchange message and share knowledge. For those agents located on the same host, their communication mechanisms are blackboard-based, while for those located on different hosts the communication mechanisms are actor-based. To process different knowledge efficiently, we developed two components for retrieving and updating knowledge from and to the knowledge base respectively. There are two kinds of collaboration in our architecture. We employed "versioning" to deal with asynchronous collaboration and "locking" to deal with synchronous one. To make it more flexible and reusable, a collaborative design environment is implemented in accordance with Microsoft's DCOM paradigm.

This paper is organised as follows. Section 2 introduces our proposed architecture of a collaborative design environment. Section 3 describes agent-based design within this proposed architecture. Section 4 addresses how to support design collaboration. Section 5 shows the implementation of the design environment and Section 6 is the conclusion of this paper.

## 2 Architecture

In this section, we will first present a brief review of related works about MAS architecture, and then introduce our proposed model, the knowledge sharing mechanism and the agents to run on design workstations following this architecture.

### 2.1 Related Works

In recent multi-agent collaborative design systems, the agents, which communicate through a common framework, act as "experts" in that they represent the results produced by their encapsulated applications and present them to the design process. Currently these approaches offer an unobtrusive solution to communicating between large tools used in concurrent engineering design [7-10].

Cutkosky et al. [3] described the Palo Alto Collaborative Testbed (PACT), which integrated four legacy concurrent engineering systems into a common framework. It involved thirty-one agent-based systems arranged into a hierarchy around facilitators. The experiment demonstrated the potential of agent-based approach in facilitating knowledge sharing between heterogeneous systems. However, no clear results were presented on exporting an interface so that new design tools can be integrated.

Bento et al. [5] presented a reactive agent-based approach to design founded on an extended logic and object-oriented representation of design object descriptions. They utilised object reactivity to propagate design changes and constraints. But the collaboration only occurs between objects in a single design system.

## 2.2 MAS Model

While agent technologies, methods, and theories are currently contributing to diverse domains, two MAS models, i.e. the blackboard-based model and the actor-based one, have been proposed. In a blackboard-based model, a collection of intelligent agents gather around a blackboard, looking at pieces of information written on it, thinking about them, and adding their conclusions as they come. Some characteristics of a blackboard-based model can be highlighted as follows.

- All the agents can see all of the blackboards at a time, what they see is the current state of the solution,
- Any agent can write their conclusions on the blackboard at any time,
- The act of writing on the blackboard will not confuse any other agents as they work.

It is convenient in a blackboard-based model to share knowledge among agents. However, because all communications are in broadcasting mode, the collaboration efficiency of those agents located on different computers is not so good in this model. In an actor-based model, every agent is treated as an "actor". The computation is reactive and the actor processes a linear sequence of computations. An actor remains dormant until it receives signals. There are no local variables in basic actor models, and the agent communication is through the mail system. Because messages are not guaranteed to arrive in the order in which they are sent, real-time collaboration systems are seldom developed based on such a model.

According to their locations, agents in a collaborative design system fall into two classes: local agents and remote agents. A local agent helps a designer to obtain design results properly and quickly. In our architecture, a designer is assisted by an agent called 'design assistant', which accepts requests from and brings results to the designer. A design assistant collaborates with other agents located on the local host closely to complete a designer's request, and communicate with remote agents when necessary.

Because the communication among local agents is far heavier than those among remote agents, and there is no worry about network speed, we therefore set up a blackboard for local agents to share knowledge and exchange messages. The communication paradigm for remote agents is similar to that of actor-based MAS, except that the message delivery is synchronous, i.e. all the messages will arrive in the order in which they are sent.

### 2.3 Knowledge Sharing

So far, there are two prevalent models for the implementation of network based systems, i.e. the C/S model and distributed model. The traditional C/S model has obvious deficiency in dealing with point-to-point communication, which occurs frequently in a distributed collaboration environment. However, while a purely distributed model seems to fit with such an environment, it has many difficulties in task management and knowledge sharing. The Pros and Cons of these two models are compared with in Table 1.

**Table 1.** Comparisons between C/S model and distributed model

| Comparison | C/S | Distributed |
|---|---|---|
| Knowledge sharing | Easy | Difficult |
| Design management | Easy | Difficult |
| Agent distribution & update | Easy | Difficult |
| Agent searching | Easy | Difficult |
| Remote agent communication | Difficult | Easy |
| Agent migration | Difficult | Easy |

In our architecture, these two models are combined in order to meet the special requirements of design collaboration. Common knowledge which is shared by all design agents, together with other public data such as the registry of agents, the information on design projects and designers, etc., are located on servers, while task-related knowledge and other kinds of information are distributed over the network.

### 2.4 Agents on Design Workstations

In a client application, there is only one agent (the design assistant) that is responsible for interacting with the designer. However, there are many other agents behind the design assistant which work collaboratively to finish the requested operations issued by the design assistant. Fig. 1 shows the main agents in a client application and their relationships.

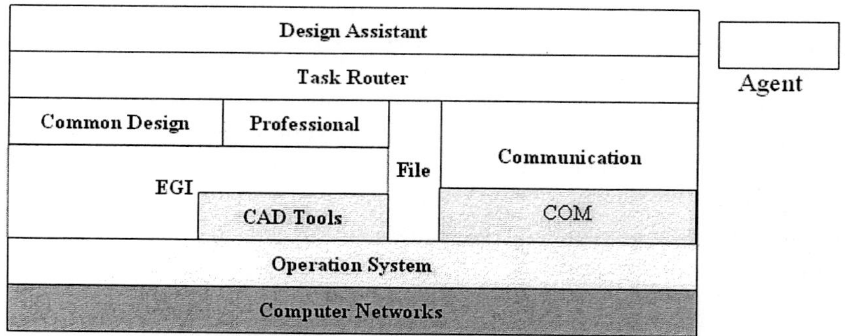


**Fig. 1.** Agents in a design workstation

The roles of those agents shown in Fig.1 are described below.

- *Design assistant agent* is the interface between the design collaboration platform and the designer. It provides a convenient interface for the designer to request for various assistances, and pass requests to the task router agent, which will then order corresponding agents to perform the requested tasks.
- *Task router agent* forwards the requests from the design assistant agent to their corresponding agents. It holds a register table where the information of all existing agents is stored. If the requested agent is not active, the task router will then wake it up.
- *Common design agents* perform basic design tasks such as drawing simple shapes (lines, circles, rectangles, cubes, etc), texture, lighting, rotating, zooming, and the like.
- *Professional agents* are domain-dependent and semi-autonomous agents, which help with the design of various products. Such agents are usually complex in terms of the required knowledge in special domains to design a product.
- *File agent* performs various file related tasks, such as backup, restore, search, graph format conversion, and so forth. Version control is one of its prominent features, which can keep different versions of a graph.
- *EGI agent* (or Enhanced Graphical Interface agent) provides a virtual graphical interface for the common design agents and professional agents. By interacting with the GDI provided by the operation system and/or the API provided by CAD tools, it is possible to choose the most efficient way to complete graph commands issued by the common design agents and professional agents.
- *Communication agent* performs communication tasks with other agents located on local or remote hosts. In our system, we designed a class to provide a full duplex communication interface by encapsulating WinSock.

The agents in design server are similar to those in a design workstation, except for that its core agent is the task router instead of design assistant as in design workstations.

## 3 Agent Design

As an intelligent and autonomous entity, an agent has its unique structure. Though a good model can make applications flexible, understandable, and reusable, the agent design should first meet the specific domain requirements, especially in knowledge management and learning.

### 3.1 Components of an Agent

To make the environment more flexible and robust, instead of retrieving and updating knowledge via a single module as designed in most agent applications, we developed

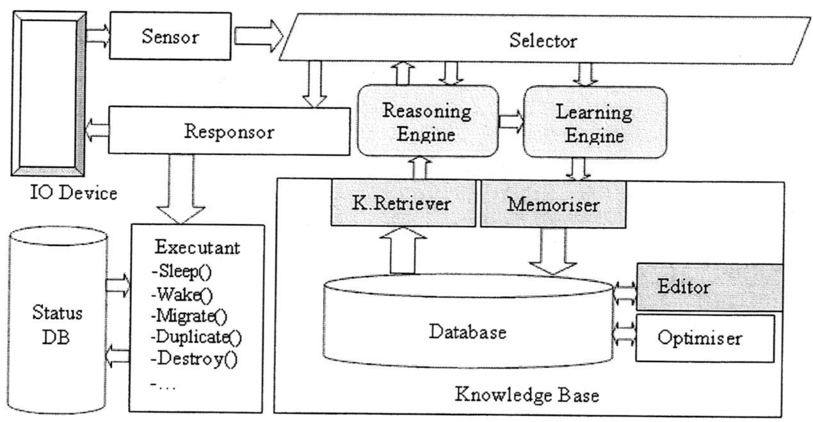


**Fig. 2.** Components in a general agent

knowledge retriever and memoriser to do these jobs respectively. The main components of a general agent are shown in Fig. 2.

The knowledge base is the core component of an agent. In addition to a database where knowledge is stored, it has a couple of components as described below. These components consist of a memoriser for adding new knowledge, a knowledge retriever for loading existing knowledge from the database, an editor for allowing the user to modify knowledge in a visual mode, and an optimiser for keeping the knowledge in the database consistent and for deleting knowledge when contradiction occurs.

The selector acts like a message router. It accepts messages from the sensor (a component for information collection and transfer) and, if the message is a piece of new knowledge, passes the message to a learning engine. If the piece of message it receives isn't a new one, it will pass the message along with the context of current environment to the reasoning engine.

Two engines, the reasoning engine and the learning engine, play important roles in an agent. The reasoning engine is a component capable of using a variety of analytical models, such as Bayesian inference, vector-space or belief networks to translate concepts within a document into a compact symbol, which then can be stored into any database. The learning engine is a component capable of autonomous acquisition and integration of knowledge. This capacity to learn from experience, analytical observations, and other means, makes it possible for an agent to continuously self-improve and thereby offer increased efficiency and effectiveness.

The 'responsor' receives instructions from the 'selector' and then it either shows some message to the outside or forward the instructions to the 'executant'. The 'executant' component is designed to perform routine actions of an agent, such as sleep, wake, migrate, duplicate, destroy, etc. It interacts with a status database where the private data of an agent is stored.

### 3.2 Knowledge Representation

Among various methods in knowledge representation, frame is a very popular one because it provides a powerful way for encoding information to support reasoning. A frame is a data structure, which is used to describe an object (an entity, event, concept, etc). It consists of an attribute value list (S, V). Each S is called a slot of the frame. The value V of a slot may be either a value or another frame. Frames can also be regarded as an extension to Semantic nets, while it's much more flexible and structured.

Generally, there in the design process are 3 kinds of knowledge, i.e. general design knowledge, domain related knowledge, and designer-specific knowledge. Though frame provides an efficient way to represent knowledge, on its own it doesn't support inheritance, which is an important relationship between objects. So we adopted a Hierarchical Frame Network (HFN) to represent these kinds of knowledge. An HFN is a tree each of whose nodes is a frame and for each child node the link to the parent node is an inheritance link. Following is a simple description of the HFN node.

```
<Frame> ::= <Head> <Slots>
<Head> ::= < Name>
<Name> ::= String
<Slots> ::= {<Slot>}
<Slot> ::= <Slot Name> <Slot Value>
<Slot Name> ::= String
<Slot Value> ::= Integer | Float | String | Frame
```

## 4 Supporting Collaborative Design

Collaboration mechanism is one of the most important issues to be addressed in all CSCW systems. The collaborative design platform introduced here aims to provide designers with a shared environment where they can work on the same project and one's actions can be perceived by others if necessary.

According to whether there are overlaps over the designers' working times on the same object, collaborations in design may work in two modes, i.e. synchronous mode and asynchronous mode (Fig. 3). Synchronous collaborations are usually more

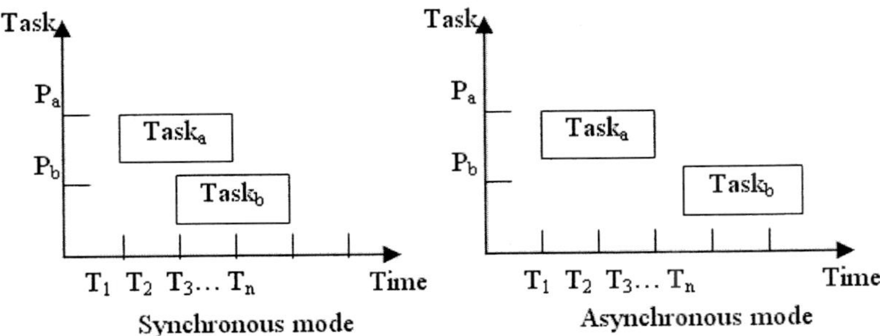


**Fig. 3.** Two working modes in design collaborations

difficult to deal with than asynchronous ones for their concurrent operations. Prevalent methods to implement synchronous collaborations include locking, token ring, central controller, conflict detection, storage control, operation conversion, etc [12].

In our architecture, we employ versioning to deal with asynchronous collaboration, and set up locks to prevent confliction.

### 4.1 Versioning

In such a method, the design environment is divided into 3 working domains:

- A private domain supports the design activities of one designer. It keeps the latest version of the owner's design results. All data stored in the designer's private environment is not accessible to other designers. The designer owning this space has all rights to read, write, modify, add and delete the design results in it.
- A group domain is designed to store design results from all designers in a group. A designer in a group can publish his/her design results into a group domain, so that other designers in the same group can view or test these results. A group leader is responsible for maintaining the information in this domain.
- The public domain contains all released design results from each group. The information here is visible to all designers of the whole environment. The design results stored here are promoted from group domains and cannot be modified by any individual designers.

Accordingly, design results are categorised into 3 versions, each with an associated working domain.

Released versions appear in the public domain. Usually these versions have been examined by their corresponding groups, so they are considered immutable, although they may be copied to any work spaces and give rise to new designs.

Working versions exist in the group domains. They are considered stable and cannot be modified by most designers, but can be updated by their owners. A working version can be promoted to released version after being tested by the whole group. They may be copied by any designer in the group to give rise to transient versions.

A transient version can be derived from any of the above versions or created from scratch. It belongs to the user who created it and it is stored in his or her private domain. Transient versions can be updated, deleted and promoted to the working versions. Table 2 shows the main characteristics of these versions.

### 4.2 Locks

During a design process, when a designer is applying a lock to an object, the system usually immediately gives him/her a temporary lock on the specified object. After that, the system will check whether it can give a formal lock to the applicant. Based on what an applicant holding a temporary lock can do before he or she receives a formal lock, we classify locks into three types, i.e. pessimistic locks, semi-optimistic locks and optimistic locks. The characteristics of these 3 types are summarised in Table 3.

**Table 2.** Principal characteristics of different versions

| Characteristics | Transient | Working | Released |
|---|---|---|---|
| Location | | | |
| Public domain | | | • |
| Group domain | | • | |
| Private domain | • | • | |
| Admissible operation | | | |
| Add | • | | |
| Delete | • | • | |

**Table 3.** Characteristics of different locks.

| Lock type | Right 1 | Right 2 |
|---|---|---|
| Pessimistic | × | × |
| Semi-optimistic | • | × |
| Optimistic | • | • |

*Right 1* – to work on the object before a formal lock is authorized
*Right 2* – to release the temporary lock before a formal lock is authorized

Although a pessimistic lock is the safest one among three locks, it needs the designer to wait for a long time for a formal lock. An optimistic lock usually gives the applicant a good responding speed. However, when a designer releases a temporary lock before a formal one comes, his or her modifications on the object will be abandoned. A semi-optimistic lock is a compromise between the other two locks, which means that the applicant can work on the requested object before he or she receives a formal lock, but he or she cannot release the temporary lock within this time. In our system, we have implemented all these 3 types, allowing the designer to choose the one he or she likes.

Because a large lock granularity usually results in longer waiting time, while a small one means a larger possibility in concurrency occurrence, it is very important to choose an appropriate lock granularity when employing locks to deal with synchronous collaborations. In our platform, designers can determine the size of the lock granularity by themselves, which makes the system more flexible.

## 5 Implementation

There are many ways in which collaboration systems are implemented, and the object-oriented method is the most frequently used one. In the implementation of an agent-based collaborative design environment, we adopted Microsoft's DCOM as the design paradigm. DCOM is an extension of the Component Object Model (COM), which defines how components and their clients interact. This interaction is defined such that the client and the component can connect without the need of any intermediary system component. DCOM makes it straightforward for components to communicate over networks or the Internet. Fig. 4 shows how a client agent requests services from other agents based on the DCOM paradigm.

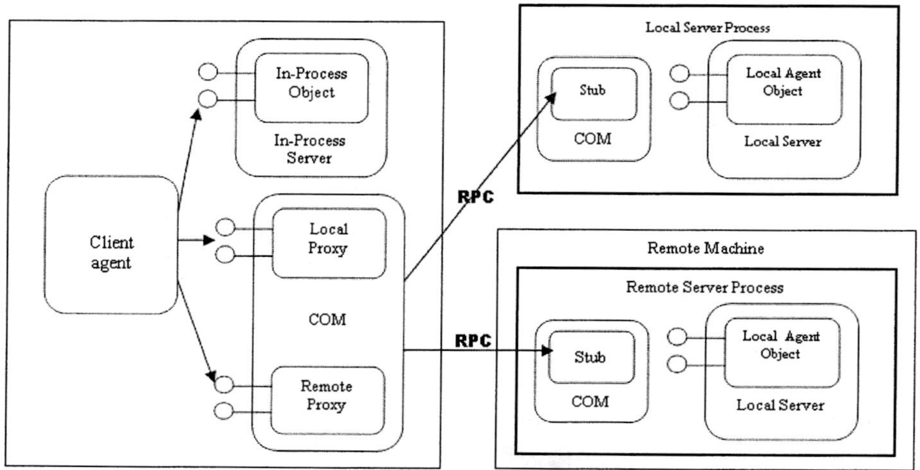


**Fig. 4.** How a client agent requests services from other agents

An interface is the way in which an agent exposes its functionality to the outside world. In COM, an interface is a table of pointers (like a C++ vtable) to functions implemented by the object. The table represents the interface, and the functions to which it points are the methods of that interface. Because all the agents in our collaborative design platform have a common set of behaviour, we defined an interface, called IAgent, as the parent interface for all agents (as shown below).

```
interface IAgent: public IUnknown
{
  private:
    ULONG m_ulAge;
    struct LOCATION m_locWhere;
    ...
  public :
    virtual HRESULT __stdcall Create() = 0;
    virtual HRESULT __stdcall Wake() = 0;
    virtual HRESULT __stdcall Sleep() = 0;
    virtual HRESULT __stdcall Ask(void **ppv) = 0;
    virtual HRESULT __stdcall Answer(void **ppv) = 0;
    virtual HRESULT __stdcall Duplicate(void **ppv) = 0;
    virtual HRESULT __stdcall Migrate(struct LOCATION *) = 0;
    ...
};
```

Based on the architecture and techniques described in previous sections, we have implemented a platform to support collaborative design over computer networks running TCP/IP. As described in section 4, there are two working modes in our collaborative design system, i.e. synchronous mode and asynchronous mode. For design actions in the asynchronous mode, every designer individually works on a transient version of his/her part and conflictions occur only when multi agents read/write knowledge base or design database simultaneously. By using database systems which support concurrent control, such as Microsoft SQL server, Oracle, Sybase, etc., such conflictions can be solved without much effort. Fig. 5 shows the main window of the client application where a designer can view others' design results stored in public or group domains while working in an asynchronous mode.

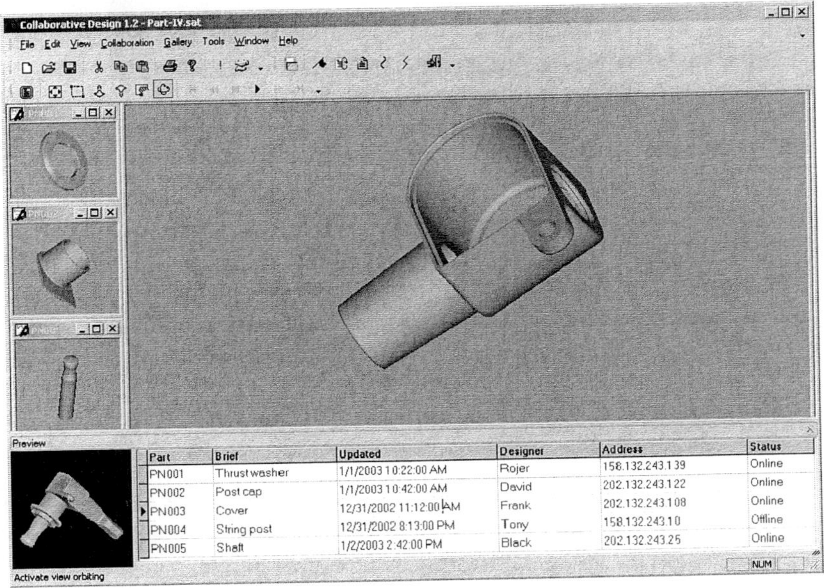


**Fig. 5.** A designer can view others' designs while working on his own

In the synchronous working mode, besides those occurring in the knowledge base and design database, much more conflictions will occur when designers work on an object at the same time. When the design assistant agent applies a lock onto a specific object, it fills a *Primitive* structure and transfers it to the coordinator agent, which in turn determines whether assign or reassign a lock to it. This structure is defined as follows.

```
typedef struct tagPrimitive
{
    WORD   wPrimType;
    DWORD  dwObjectID;
    WORD   wParamSize;
    PVOID  pParamBuffer;
} Primitive;
```

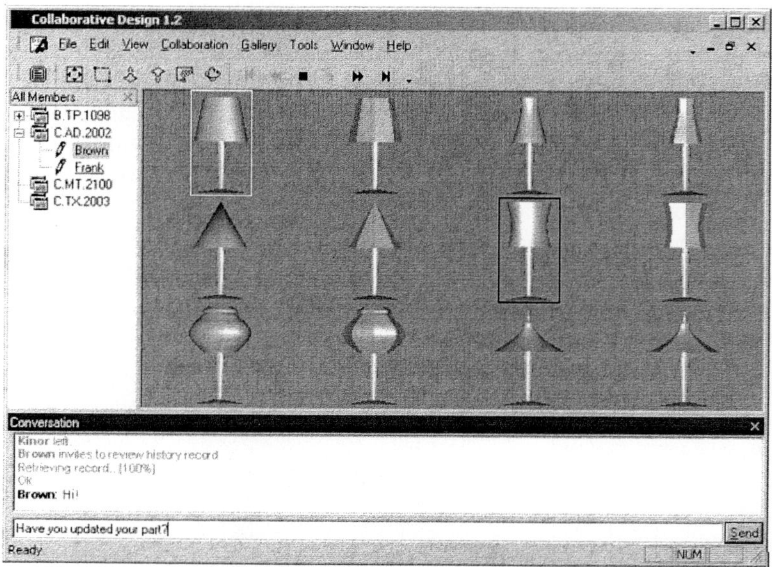


**Fig. 6.** Two designers picking out models

Fig. 6 shows two designers picking up a lamp model to be studied in detail from the design history which is maintained by an agent during the design process.

## 6 Conclusions

This paper addressed some key issues in supporting collaborative design in an agent based environment and introduced the techniques we developed or adopted in building a design collaboration platform, including the architecture, agent design, collaboration support and implementation techniques. Based on our proposed architecture and techniques, the implemented software is an open environment that supports design collaboration and is able to interoperate with several popular design systems such as Autodesk® Inventor, Auto CAD® and MicroStation®.

Future design systems will be globally distributed, Internet supported, cooperative and intelligent. To meet this requirement, the evolutionary design techniques are needed in a collaborative design environment with more powerful knowledge bases, effective machine learning techniques.

While CAD tools are becoming more powerful in terms of helping designers in dealing with graphics, they have little intelligence and ability in evolving designs. How to develop design systems that can evolve designs through agent-based learning is our current research focus, and we expect to develop the environment described in this paper into an intelligent design tool in the domain of product design.

**Acknowledgements**

This paper is supported by the research project BQ4.20 of The Hong Kong Polytechnic University. We would like to thank Dr Liu Hong for her help and support in writing this paper and implementing the design environment.

## References

1. Frazer, J. H. "Design Workstation on the Future". Proceedings of the Fourth International Conference of Computer-Aided Industrial Design and Conceptual Design (CAID & CD '2001), International Academic Publishers, Beijing, 2001;17-23.
2. Campbell M, Cagan J, Kotovsky K. Agentbased synthesis of electromechanical design configurations, 1998.
3. Cutkosky, M.R., Englemore, R.S., Fikes, R.E. Genesereth, M.R., Gruber, T.R., Mark, W.S., Tenenbaum, J.M., Weber, J.C.: PACT: An expriment in integraging concurrent engineering systems. IEEE Computer 26(1) (1993) 28-37
4. Whitehead, S. A complexity analysis of cooperative mechanisms in reinforcement learning.
5. Wellman, M.P.: A computational market model for distributed configuration design. AI EDAM 9 (1995) 125-133.
6. Tan, M. Multi-agent reinforcement learning: Independent vs. Cooperative agents. Multi Learning: Proc. of the Tenth International Conference, San Mateo, CA: Morgan Kaufmann, 1993.
7. Matthew I. C., Jonathan C. & Kenneth K. A-Design: An Agent-Based Approach to Conceptual Design in a Dynamic Environment. Research in Engineering Design, 1999; 11:172-192.
8. Lander, E. S., "Issues in Multiagent Design Systems", IEEE Expert, 1997; 12(2): 18-26.
9. Goldstein D., An agentbased architecture for concurrent engineering. Concurrent Engineering: Research and Applications 1994; 2:117-123.
10. Hong Liu & Zongkai Lin. A Cooperative Design Approach in MADS. Proceedings of the 4th International Conference on CSCW in Design (CSCWD'99), Compiegne, France, Sep.29-Oct.1, 1999; 297-303.
11. Fang Weidong, Liu Peiyu and Zhang Zhidong, The Computer Supported Cooperative OOT System, OOT China'99 & Tools Aisa'99, 1999, Nanjing P. R. China.
12. Fang Weidong, Liu Shuchang, Liu Peiyu and Xu Liancheng, Cooperative Work Model for Class Evolution, Computer Science, vol 25, 1998.5
13. Tomiyama, T. From general design theory to knowledge-intensive engineering. AIEDAM, 1994;8(4):319-333.
14. AAAI-91, 607-613,1991.
15. Grecu DL, Brown DC, Design agents that learn. AIEDAM, 1996; 10:149-150.
16. Jennings, N.R. Commitments and conventions: The foundation of coordination in multi-agent systems. The Knowledge Engineering Review, 1993; 8(3): 223-250.
17. Liu H., Zeng G. Zh. & Lin Z.K. An agent-oriented modelling approach. ACM Software Engineering Notes, 1998;23(3):87-92.
18. Tang, M. X. Knowledge-based design support and inductive learning. PhD Thesis, Department of Artificial Intelligence, University of Edinburgh, 1996.

19. Tang, M.X. A knowledge-based architecture for intelligent design support. The Knowledge Engineering Review, 1997;12(4):387-406.
20. Hong Liu, Tang M.X. & Frazer, J. H., Supporting Learning in a Shared Design Environment. International Journal of Advances in Engineering Software, Elsevier, 2001; 32(4): 285-293.
21. Frazer, J. H. Creative Design and the Generative Evolutionary Paradigm. In P. Bentley ed. Creativity and Design, 2000.
22. Chan K. H., Frazer J. H.and Tang M. X., 2000, Handling the evolution and hierarchy nature of designing in computer-based design support systems, in the proceedings of the third international conference on computer aided industrial design and conceptual design, 26-27th November, published by International Academic Publisher.
23. Durfee, E.H., Lesser, V.R. and Corkill, D.D. Trends in Cooperative Distributed Problem Solving. In: IEEE Transactions on Knowledge and Data Engineering, March 1989, KDE-1(1), pages 63-83.

# Fast Feature Selection by Means of Projections*

Roberto Ruiz, José C. Riquelme, and Jesús S. Aguilar-Ruiz

Departamento de Lenguajes y Sistemas, Universidad de Sevilla,
Avda. Reina Mercedes S/N. 41012 Sevilla, España,
{rruiz,riquelme,aguilar}@lsi.us.es

**Abstract.** The attribute selection techniques for supervised learning, used in the preprocessing phase to emphasize the most relevant attributes, allow making models of classification simpler and easy to understand. The algorithm (SOAP: Selection of Attributes by Projection) has some interesting characteristics: lower computational cost (O(m n log n) m attributes and n examples in the data set) with respect to other typical algorithms due to the absence of distance and statistical calculations; its applicability to any labelled data set, that is to say, it can contain continuous and discrete variables, with no need for transformation. The performance of SOAP is analyzed in two ways: percentage of reduction and classification. SOAP has been compared to CFS [4] and ReliefF [6]. The results are generated by C4.5 before and after the application of the algorithms.

## 1 Introduction

The data mining researchers, especially those dedicated to the study of algorithms that produce knowledge in some of the usual representations (decision lists, decision trees, association rules, etc.), usually make their tests on standard and accessible databases (most of them of small size). The purpose is to independently verify and validate the results of their algorithms. Nevertheless, these algorithms are modified to solve specific problems, for example real databases that contain much more information (number of examples) than standard databases used in training. To accomplish the final tests on these real databases with tens of attributes and thousands of examples is a task that takes a lot of time and memory size.

It is advisable to apply to the database preprocessing techniques to reduce the number of attributes or the number of examples in such a way as to decrease the computational time cost. These preprocessing techniques are fundamentally oriented to either of the next goals: feature selection (eliminating non-relevant attributes) and editing (reduction of the number of examples by eliminating some of them or calculating prototypes [1]). Our algorithm belongs to the first group.

* This work has been supported by the Spanish Research Agency CICYT under grant TIC2001-1143-C03-02.

P.W.H. Chung, C.J. Hinde, M. Ali (Eds.): IEA/AIE 2003, LNAI 2718, pp. 461–470, 2003.

In this paper we present a new method of attribute selection, called SOAP (Selection of Attributes by Projection), which has some important characteristics:

- Considerable reduction of the number of attributes.
- Lower computational time O(m n log n) than other algorithms.
- Absence of distance and statistical calculations: correlation, information gain, etc.
- Conservation of the error rates of the classification systems.

The hypothesis on which the heuristic is based is: "place the best attributes with the smallest number of label changes". The next section discusses related work. Section 3 describes the SOAP algorithm. Section 4 presents the results. Which deal with several databases from the UCI Repository [3]. The last section summarizes the findings.

## 2 Related Work

Algorithms that perform feature selection as a preprocessing step prior to learning can generally be placed into one of two broad categories: wrappers, Kohavi [7], which employs a statistical re-sampling technique (such as cross validation) using the actual target learning algorithm to estimate the accuracy of feature subsets. This approach has proved to be useful but is very slow to execute because the learning algorithm is called upon repeatedly. Another option called filter, operates independently of any learning algorithm. Undesirable features are filtered out of the data before induction begins. Filters use heuristics based on general the characteristics of the data to evaluate the merit of feature subsets. As a consequence, filter methods are generally much faster than wrapper methods, and, as such, are more practical for use on data of high dimensionality. FOCUS [2], LVF [14] use class consistency as an evaluation meter. One method for discretization called Chi2 [13]. Relief [6] works by randomly sampling an instance from the data, and then locating its nearest neighbour from the same and opposite class. Relief was originally defined for two-class problems and was later expanded as ReliefF [8] to handle noise and multi-class data sets, and RReliefF [12] handles regression problems. Other authors suggest Neuronal Networks for an attribute selector. In addition, learning procedures can be used to select attributes, like ID3 [10], FRINGE [9] and C4.5 [11]. Methods based on the correlation like CFS [4], etc.

## 3 SOAP: Selection of Attributes by Projection

### 3.1 Description

To describe the algorithm we will use the well-known data set IRIS, because of the easy interpretation of their two-dimensional projections.

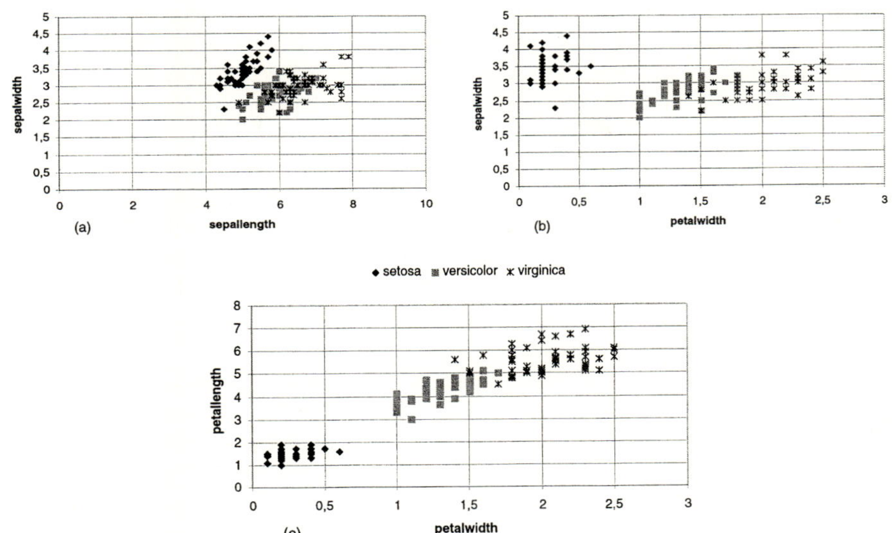


**Fig. 1.** Representation of Attributes (a) *Sepalwidth-Sepallength* and (b) *Sepalwidth-Petalwidth* (c) *Pepallength-Petalwidth*

Three projections of IRIS have been made in two-dimensional graphs. In Figure 1(a) it is possible to observe that if the projection of the examples is made on the abscissas or ordinate axis we can not obtain intervals where any class is a majority, only can be seen the intervals [4.3,4.8] of Sepallength for the Setosa class or [7.1,8.0] for Virginica. In Figure 1(b) for the Sepalwidth parameter in the ordinate axis clear intervals are not appraised either. Nevertheless, for the Petalwidth attribute is possible to appreciate some intervals where the class is unique: [0,0.6] for Setosa, [1.0,1.3] for Versicolor and [1.8,2.5] for Virginica. Finally in Figure 1(c), it is possible to appreciate the class divisions, which are almost clear in both attributes. This is because when projecting the examples on each attribute the number of label changes is minimum. For example, it is possible to verify that for Petallength the first label change takes place for value 3 (setosa to Versicolor), the second in 4.5 (Versicolor to Virginica). there are other changes later in 4.8, 4,9, 5,0 and the last one is in 5.1.

SOAP is based on this principle: to count the label changes, produced when crossing the projections of each example in each dimension. If the attributes are in ascending order according to the number of label changes, we will have a list that defines the priority of selection, from greater to smaller importance. SOAP presumes to eliminate the basic redundancy between attributes, that is to say, the attributes with interdependence have been eliminated. Finally, to choose the more advisable number of features, we define a reduction factor, RF, in order to take the subset from attributes formed by the first of the aforementioned list.

Before formally exposing the algorithm, we will explain with more details the main idea. We considered the situation depicted in Figure 1(b): the projection of the examples on the abscissas axis produces a ordered sequence of intervals (some of then can be a single point) which have assigned a single label or a set of them: [0,0.6] Se, [1.0,1.3] Ve, [1.4,1.4] Ve-Vi, [1.5,1.5] Ve-Vi, [1.6,1.6] Ve-Vi, [1.7,1.7] Ve-Vi, [1.8,1.8] Ve-Vi, [1.9,2.5] Vi. If we apply the same idea with the projection on the ordinate axis, we calculate the partitions of the ordered sequences: Ve, R, R, Ve, R, R, R, R, R, R, R, R, R, R, Se, R, Se, R, Se, where R is a combination of two or three labels. We can observe that we obtain almost one subsequence of the same value with different classes for each value from the ordered projection. That is to say, projections on the ordinate axis provide much less information that on the abscissas axis.

In the intervals with multiple labels we will consider the worst case, that being the maximum number of label changes possible for a same value.

The number of label changes obtained by the algorithm in the projection of each dimension is: Petalwidth 16, Petallength 19, Sepallenth 87 and Sepalwidth 120. In this way, we can achieve a ranking with the best attributes from the point of view of the classification. This result agrees with what is common knowledge in data mining, which states that the width and length of petals are more important than those related to sepals.

### 3.2 Definitions

**Definition 1:** Let the attribute $A_i$ be a continuous or discrete variable that takes values in $I_i = [min_i, max_i]$. Then, A is the attributes space defined as $A = I_1 \times I_2 \times \ldots \times I_m$, where $m$ is the number of attributes.

**Definition 2:** An *example* e $\in$ E is a tuple formed by the Cartesian product of the value sets of each attribute and the set C of labels. We define the operations *att* and *lab* to access the attribute and its label (or class): att: E x N $\rightarrow$ A and lab: E $\rightarrow$ C, where N is the set of natural numbers.

**Definition 3:** Let the *universe* U be a sequence of example from E. We will say that a database with n examples, each of them with m attributes and one class, forms a particular universe. Then U=<u[1],...,u[n]> and as the database is a sequence, the access to an example is achieved by means of its position. Likewise, the access to j-th attribute of the i-th example is made by att(u[i],j), and for identifying its label lab(u[i]).

**Definition 4:** An *ordered projected sequence* is a sequence formed by the projection of the universe onto the i-th attribute. This sequence is sorted out in ascending order and it contains the value of the projected attribute. For example, in Figure 1(c) for Petalwidth attribute we have 0.1,0.2,0.3,...

**Definition 5:** A partition in *constant subsequences* is the set of subsequences formed from the ordered projected sequence of an attribute in such a way as to maintain the projection order. All the examples belonging to a subsequence have the same class and every two consecutive subsequences are disjointed with respect to the class. For Petalwidth in Iris, we observe [0.1,0.6][1.0,1.3]..., subsequences with different class.

**Definition 6:** A *subsequence of the same value* is the sequence composed of the examples with identical value from the i-th attribute within the ordered projected sequence. This situation can be originated in continuous variables, and it will be the way to deal with the discrete variables. In Figure 1(c) for Petalwidth, we have [1] a subsequence of the same value, one, with the same label, and for value [1.5] we have a subsequence with different label.

### 3.3 Algorithm

The algorithm is very simple and fast, see Fig. 4. It has the capacity to operate with continuous and discrete variables as well as with databases which have two classes or multiple classes. In the ascending-order-task for each attribute, the QuickSort [5] algorithm is used. This algorithm is O(n log n), on average. Once ordered by an attribute, we can count the label changes throughout the ordered projected sequence. NumberChanges in Fig. 5, considers whether we deal with different values from an attribute, or with a subsequence of the same value (this situation can be originated in continuous and discrete variables). In the first case, it compares the present label with that of the following value. Whereas in the second case, where the subsequence is of the same value, it counts as many label changes as are possible (function ChangesSameValue).

The k first attribute which NLC (number of label changes) under NLClim will be selected. NLClim is calculated applying the follow equation:

$$NLC_{lim} = NLC_{min} + (NLC_{max} - NLC_{min}) * RF \tag{1}$$

RF: reduction factor.

*Main Algorithm*

```
Input: E training (N examples, M attributes)
Output: E reduced (N examples, K attributes)
  for each attribute i with i in {1..M}
      QuickSort(E,i)
      NLCi = NumberChanges(E,i)
  NLC Attribute Ranking
  Select the K first
```

*NumberChanges function*

```
Input: E training, i
Output: Number of Label Changes (NLC)
  for each example ej in E with j in {1..N}
      if att(u[j],i) in subsequence of the same value
          NLC += ChangesSameValue()
      else
          if lab(u[j]) <> lastLabel)
              NLC++
```

After applying QuickSort, we might have repeated values with the same or different class. For this reason, the algorithm firstly sorts by value and, in

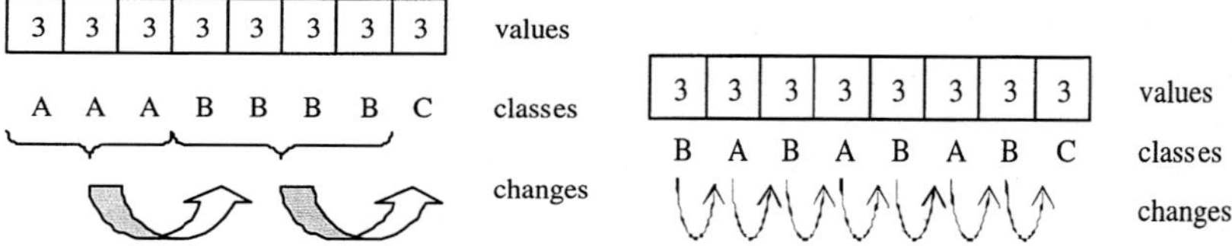


**Fig. 2.** Subsequence of the same value (a) two changes (b) seven changes

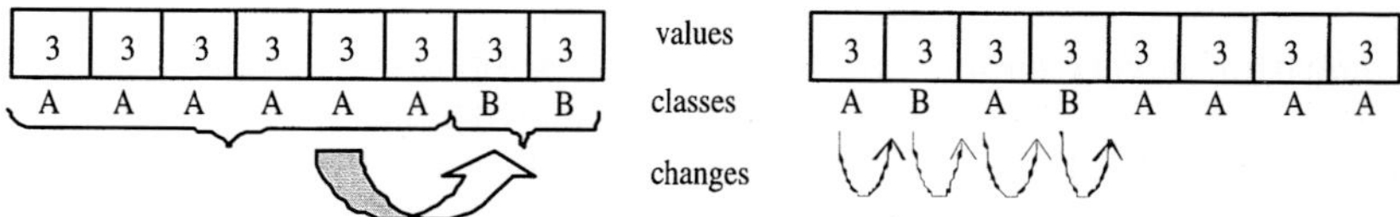


**Fig. 3.** Example

case of equality, it will look for the worst of the all possible cases (function ChangesSameValue).

We could find the situation as depicted in Figure 2(a). The examples sharing the same value for an attribute are ordered by class. The label changes obtained are two. The next execution of the algorithm may find another situation, with a different number of label changes. The solution to this problem consists of finding the worst case. The heuristic is applied to obtain the maximum number of label changes within the interval containing repeated values. In this way, the ChangesSameValue method would produce the output shown in Figure 2(b), seven changes. This can be obtained with low cost. It can be deduced counting the class' elements

In Figure 2(a) we can observe a subsequence of the same value with eight elements: three elements are class A, four class B and one C. Applying formula 2 there is no relative frequency greater than half of the elements. Then, the maximum number of label changes is nelem-1, seven. In Figure 2(b) we verify it.

From Figure 3 it can be seen that the function ChangesSameValue will return four label changes, because a relative frequency greater than nelem/2 exists (class A). Then, the result is (8-6)*2=4. In this way, we always will find the maximum number of label changes within the interval containing repeated values.

This algorithm allows working with discrete variables. We consider each projection of this attribute like a subsequence of the same value.

## 4 Experiments

In order to compare the effectiveness of SOAP as a feature selector for common machine learning algorithms, experiments were performed using sixteen standard data sets from the UCI repository [4]. The data sets and their characteristics are summarized in Table 3. The percentage of correct classification with C4.5, averaged over ten ten-fold cross-validation runs, were calculated for each algorithm-data set combination before and after feature selection by SOAP (RF 0.35), CFS and ReliefF (threshold 0.05). For each train-test split, the dimensionality was reduced by each feature selector before being passed to the learning algorithms. The same fold were used for each feature selector-learning scheme combination.

To perform the experiment with CFS and ReliefF we used the Weka[1] (Waikato Environment for Knowledge Analysis) implementation.

Table 1 shows the average number of features selected and the percentage of the original features retained. SOAP is a specially selective algorithm compared with CFS and RLF. If SOAP and CFS are compared, only in one dataset (labor) is the number of characteristics significantly greater than those selected by CFS. In six data sets there are no significant differences, and in nine, the number of features is significantly smaller than CFS. Compare to RLF, only in glass2 and diabetes, SOAP obtains more parameters in the reduction process (threshold 0.05 is not sufficient). It can be seen (by looking at the fourth column) that SOAP retained 23,7% of the attributes on average.

**Table 1.** Number of selected features and the percentage of the original features retained

| **Data** | | **Soap** | **CFS** | **RLF** |
|---|---|---|---|---|
| Set | Atts | Atts( %) | Atts( %) | Atts( %) |
| autos | 25 | 2.9(11.8) | 5.3(21.3) | 10.9( 43.7) |
| breast-c | 9 | 1.5(16.7) | 4.1(45.9) | 3.7( 41.6) |
| breast-w | 9 | 5.2(57.6) | 9.0(99.7) | 8.1( 89.4) |
| diabetes | 8 | 2.8(34.9) | 3.1(38.9) | 0.0( 0.0) |
| glass2 | 9 | 3.2(35.7) | 4.0(43.9) | 0.3( 3.6) |
| heart-c | 13 | 6.3(48.2) | 6.4(49.1) | 6.9( 53.4) |
| heart-stat | 13 | 5.4(41.8) | 6.3(48.2) | 6.3( 48.2) |
| hepatitis | 19 | 2.6(13.6) | 8.7(45.6) | 13.3( 70.0) |
| horse-c.OR. | 27 | 2.3( 8.6) | 2.0( 7.4) | 2.3( 8.6) |
| hypothyroid | 29 | 1.7( 5.7) | 1.0( 3.4) | 5.2( 18.0) |
| iris | 4 | 2.0(50.0) | 1.9(48.3) | 4.0(100.0) |
| labor | 16 | 4.3(27.0) | 3.3(20.8) | 8.8( 55.3) |
| lymph | 18 | 1.8( 9.9) | 8.9(49.2) | 11.8( 65.8) |
| sick | 29 | 1.0( 3.4) | 1.0( 3.4) | 7.1( 24.5) |
| sonar | 60 | 3.0( 5.0) | 17.8(29.7) | 3.9( 6.5) |
| vote | 16 | 1.6(10.0) | 1.0( 6.3) | 15.5( 96.9) |
| **Average** | 19.0 | 3.0(23.7) | 5.2(35.1) | 6.8( 45.3) |

Table 2 shows the results for attribute selection with C4.5 and compares the size (number of nodes) of the trees produced by each attribute selection scheme against the size of the trees produced by C4.5 with no attribute selection. Smaller trees are preferred as they are easier to interpret, but accuracy is generally degraded. The table shows how often each method performs significantly better

[1] http://www.cs.waikato.ac.nz/ ml

**Table 2.** Result of attribute selection with C4.5. Accuracy and size of trees. ∘ , • Statistically significant improvement or degradation (p=0.05)

| Data | | | Soap | | CFS | | RLF | |
|---|---|---|---|---|---|---|---|---|
| Set | Ac. | Size | Ac. | Size | Ac. | Size | Ac. | Size |
| autos | 82.54 | 63.32 | 73.37 • | 45.84 ∘ | 74.54 • | 55.66 ∘ | 74.15 • | 85.74 • |
| breast-c | 74.37 | 12.34 | 70.24 • | 6.61 ∘ | 72.90 | 18.94 • | 70.42 • | 11.31 |
| breast-w | 95.01 | 24.96 | 94.64 | 21.28 ∘ | 95.02 | 24.68 | 95.02 | 24.68 |
| diabetes | 74.64 | 42.06 | 74.14 | 7.78 ∘ | 74.36 | 14.68 ∘ | 65.10 • | 1.00 ∘ |
| glass2 | 78.71 | 24.00 | 78.96 | 14.88 ∘ | 79.82 | 14.06 ∘ | 53.50 • | 1.70 ∘ |
| heart-c | 76.83 | 43.87 | 77.06 | 34.02 ∘ | 77.16 | 29.35 ∘ | 79.60 ∘ | 28.72 ∘ |
| heart-stat | 78.11 | 34.58 | 80.67 ∘ | 19.50 ∘ | 80.63 ∘ | 23.84 ∘ | 82.33 ∘ | 14.78 ∘ |
| hepatitis | 78.97 | 17.06 | 80.19 | 5.62 ∘ | 81.68 ∘ | 8.68 ∘ | 80.45 | 11.26 ∘ |
| horse-c.OR. | 66.30 | 1.00 | 66.30 | 1.00 | 66.30 | 1.00 | 66.28 | 1.36 • |
| hypothyroid | 99.54 | 27.84 | 95.02 • | 4.30 ∘ | 96.64 • | 5.90 ∘ | 93.52 • | 12.52 ∘ |
| iris | 94.27 | 8.18 | 94.40 | 8.12 | 94.13 | 7.98 | 94.40 | 8.16 |
| labor | 80.70 | 6.93 | 78.25 | 3.76 ∘ | 80.35 | 6.44 | 80.00 | 5.88 ∘ |
| lymph | 77.36 | 28.05 | 72.84 • | 7.34 ∘ | 75.95 | 20.32 ∘ | 74.66 | 24.10 ∘ |
| sick | 98.66 | 49.02 | 93.88 • | 1.00 ∘ | 96.32 • | 5.00 ∘ | 93.88 • | 1.00 ∘ |
| sonar | 74.28 | 27.98 | 70.05 • | 7.00 ∘ | 74.38 | 28.18 | 70.19 • | 9.74 ∘ |
| vote | 96.53 | 10.64 | 95.63 • | 3.00 ∘ | 95.63 • | 3.00 ∘ | 96.53 | 10.64 |
| **Average** | 82.93 | 26.36 | 80.98 | 11.94 | 82.24 | 16.73 | 79.38 | 15.79 |

(denoted by ∘) or worse (denoted by •) than when performing no feature selection (column 2 and 3). Throughout we speak of results being significantly different if the difference is statistically at the 5% level according to a paired two-sided t test. Each pair of points consisting of the estimates obtained in one of the ten, ten-fold cross-validation runs, for before and after feature selection. For SOAP, feature selection degrades performance on seven datasets, improves on one and it is equal on eight. The reason for why the algorithm is not as accurate is the number of attribute selected, less than three feature. Five of these seven datasets obtain a percentage less than 10% of the original features. The results are similar to ReliefF and a little worse than those provided by CFS. Analyzing the datasets in which SOAP lost to CFS, we can observe breast-c, lymph and sonar, where the number of feature selected by SOAP is 25% of CFS (breast-c 4,1 to 1,5 with SOAP, lymph 8,9-1,8 and sonar 17,8-3). Nevertheless the accuracy reduction is small: breast-c 72,9 (CFS) to 70,24 with SOAP, lymph 75,95-72,84 and sonar 74,38-70,05.

It is interesting to compare the speed of the attribute selection techniques. We measured the time taken in milliseconds to select the final subset of attributes. SOAP is an algorithm with a very short computation time. The results shown in Table 3 confirm the expectations. SOAP takes 400 milliseconds[2] in reducing 16 datasets whereas CFS takes 853 seconds and RLF more than 3 minutes. In general, SOAP is faster than the other methods and it is independent of the classes

[2] This is a rough measure. Obtaining true cpu time from within a Java program is quite difficult.

**Table 3.** Data sets. Time in milliseconds

| | **Data** | | | **Soap** | **CFS** | **RLF** |
|---|---|---|---|---|---|---|
| Set | Instances | Atts | Classes | t-ms | t-ms | t-ms |
| autos | 205 | 25 | 7 | 15 | 50 | 403 |
| breast-c | 286 | 9 | 2 | 4 | 6 | 174 |
| breast-w | 699 | 9 | 2 | 6 | 35 | 1670 |
| diabetes | 768 | 8 | 2 | 6 | 39 | 1779 |
| glass2 | 163 | 9 | 2 | 2 | 9 | 96 |
| heart-c | 303 | 13 | 5 | 6 | 10 | 368 |
| heart-stat | 270 | 13 | 2 | 4 | 12 | 365 |
| hepatitis | 155 | 19 | 2 | 4 | 9 | 135 |
| horse-c.OR. | 368 | 27 | 2 | 16 | 43 | 941 |
| hypothyroid | 3772 | 29 | 4 | 180 | 281 | 94991 |
| iris | 150 | 4 | 3 | 3 | 3 | 44 |
| labor | 57 | 16 | 2 | 1 | 3 | 21 |
| lymph | 148 | 18 | 4 | 3 | 7 | 109 |
| sick | 3772 | 29 | 2 | 120 | 252 | 93539 |
| sonar | 208 | 60 | 2 | 21 | 90 | 920 |
| vote | 435 | 16 | 2 | 9 | 4 | 651 |
| **Sum** | | | | 400 | 853 | 196206 |

number. Also it is possible to be observed that ReliefF is affected very negatively by the number of instances in the dataset, it can be seen in "hypothyroid" and "sick". Eventhough these two datasets were eliminated, SOAP is more than 3 times faster than CFS, and more than 75 times than ReliefF.

Figure 4 summarizes the power of our algorithm, SOAP. It diminishes, in a significant percentage, the number of attributes, obtaining simple classification models, with a computational time lower than that of the other methods and with a similar average accuracy.

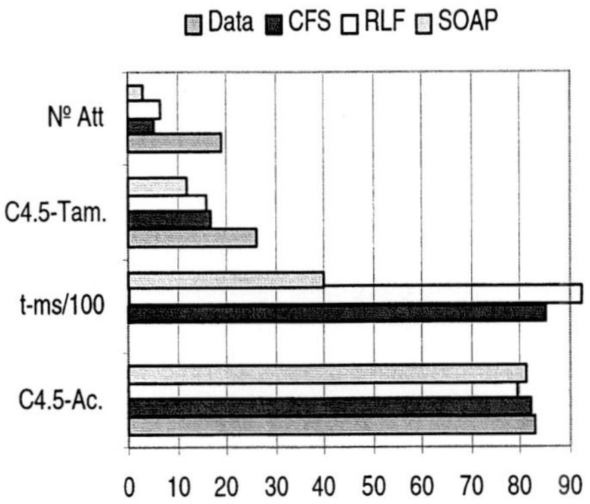


**Fig. 4.** Summary

## 5 Conclusions

In this paper we present a deterministic attribute selection algorithm. It is a very efficient and simple method used in the preprocessing phase A considerable reduction of the number of attributes is produced in comparison to other techniques. It does not need distance nor statistical calculations, which could be very costly in time (correlation, gain of information, etc.). The computational cost is lower than other methods O(m n log n).

## References

1. Aguilar-Ruiz, Jesús S., Riquelme, José C. and Toro, Miguel. Data Set Editing by Ordered Projection. Intelligent Data Analysis Journal. Vol. 5, nō5, pp. 1-13, IOS Press (2001).
2. Almuallim, H. and Dietterich, T.G. Learning boolean concepts in the presence of many irrelevant features. Artificial Intelligence, 69(1-2):279-305 (1994).
3. Blake, C. and Merz, E. K. UCI Repository of machine learning databases (1998).
4. Hall M.A. Correlation-based feature selection for machine learning. PhD thesis, Department of Computer Science, University of Waikato, Hamilton, New Zealand (1998).
5. Hoare, C. A. R. QuickSort. Computer Journal, 5(1):10-15 (1962).
6. Kira, K. and Rendell, L. A practical approach to feature selection. In Proceedings of the Ninth International Conference on Machine Learning. pp. 249-256, Morgan Kaufmann (1992).
7. Kohavi, R. and John, G. H. Wrappers for feature subset selection. Artificial Intelligence, 97, 273-324 (1997).
8. Kononenko, I. Estimating attibutes: Analisys and extensions of relief. In Proceedings of the Seventh European Conference on Machine Learning. pp. 171-182, Springer-Verlag (1994).
9. Pagallo, G. and Haussler, D. Boolean feature discovery in empirical learning. Machine Learning, 5, 71-99 (1990).
10. Quinlan, J. Induction of decision trees. Machine Learning, 1(1), 81-106 (1986).
11. Quinlan, J. C4.5: Programs for machine learning. Morgan Kaufmann (1993).
12. Robnik-Šikonja, M. And Kononenko, I. An adaption of relief for attribute estimation in regression. In Proceedings of the Fourteenth International Conference on Machine Learning. pp. 296-304, Morgan Kaufmann (1997).
13. Setiono, R., and Liu, H. Chi2: Feature selection and discretization of numeric attributes. In Proceedings of the Seventh IEEE International Conference on Tools with Artificial Intelligence (1995).
14. Setiono, R., and Liu, H. A probabilistic approach to feature selection-a filter solution. In Proceedings of International Conference on Machine Learning, 319-327 (1996).

# Hybrid Least-Squares Methods for Reinforcement Learning

Hailin Li and Cihan H. Dagli

Department of Engineering Management, Smart Engineering Systems Laboratory,
229 Engineering Management, University of Missouri-Rolla,
65409-0370 Rolla, MO, USA
{hl8p5, dagli}@umr.edu

**Abstract.** Model-free Least-Squares Policy Iteration (LSPI) method has been successfully used for control problems in the context of reinforcement learning. LSPI is a promising algorithm that uses linear approximator architecture to achieve policy optimization in the spirit of Q-learning. However it faces challenging issues in terms of the selection of basis functions and training sample. Inspired by orthogonal Least-Squares regression method for selecting the centers of RBF neural network, a new hybrid learning method for LSPI is proposed in this paper. The suggested method uses simulation as a tool to guide the "feature configuration" process. The results on the learning control of Cart-Pole system illustrate the effectiveness of the presented method.

## 1 Introduction

Similar to dynamic programming, reinforcement learning (RL) is concerned with rational decision-making process under uncertain environment. The goal of RL is to analyze how decisions ought to be made in the light of clear objectives so that agent can generate a series of actions to influence the evolution of a stochastic dynamic system. Compared with the classical dynamic programming algorithm, RL can handle the situation that no priori model information such as MDP state transition probability is available. This salient characteristic makes RL more flexible than dynamic programming. Much research work already has been done in this area. Among them the major development include the temporal-difference learning algorithm proposed by [1] and Q-learning introduced in the thesis [2].

The intractability of solutions to sequential decision problems in terms of the size of state-action space and the overwhelming requirement for computation stimulates the development of many approximation methods in machine learning area. In general, they can be classified into three main categories. Model approximation is the approach to replace complex system model using more tractable one. Policy approximation uses parameterized class of policies and optimizes the parameter values. Finally, most of RL algorithms fit into the value function approximation category. Instead of approximating policies, the objective here is to select a parameterization of value function and then try to compute parameters that can produce an accurate enough approximation to the optimal value function.

In principle, all kinds of approximators for nonlinear mapping can be used as the value function approximation architecture. Although feed-forward multi-layer

P.W.H. Chung, C.J. Hinde, M. Ali (Eds.): IEA/AIE 2003, LNAI 2718, pp. 471–480, 2003.

perceptron can provide excellent generalization ability, it is not always the choice for RL applications. As pointed out by [3]: RL algorithms focus on on-line learning so that there is no readily available training set. We require methods that are able to learn from incrementally on-line acquired data and handle non-stationary target functions. The key issue here is that minimizing MSE is not necessarily the most important goal because the thing we really care about is to find the acceptable policy. For this reason, linear function approximators can be the better alternatives as approximation architecture mainly due to their transparent structure.

Unlike the Neuro-dynamic programming methods that require long time off-line simulation and training, [4] introduced the linear Least-Squares algorithms for temporal difference learning (LSTD) and showed that LSTD can converge faster than conventional temporal difference learning methods in terms of the prediction ability. Unfortunately [5] pointed out that LSTD couldn't be used directly as part of a policy iteration algorithm in many cases. In order to extend the linear Least-Squares idea to control problem, [6] developed the model-free Least-Squares Q-learning (LSQ) and Least-Squares Policy Iteration (LSPI) algorithm. These algorithms produced good results on a variety of learning domains. The impressive aspects of LSPI include the effective sample data reusing, no approximate policy function needed and fast policy search speed if the "good" sample data set is selected. Similar to any linear approximator architecture, LSPI also face challenge about how to choose basis functions. In essence, such feature extraction process needs lot of prior intuition about the problem. Furthermore, LSPI algorithm is very sensitive with the distribution of training samples. It produces the key disadvantage for applications.

Today, Radial Basis Function Neural Network (RBF NN) is used commonly as linear parameterization architecture, which is characterized by weighted combinations of basis functions. [7] provides a systematic learning approach based on the orthogonal Least-Squares (OLS) method to solve center selection problem so that the newly added center maximizes the amount of energy of the desired network output. This OLS training strategy is very efficient way for producing size-controllable RBF NN.

Inspired by the LSPI and OLS training algorithm for RBF NN, a new hybrid learning method is proposed in this paper. Our effort is to produce the effective way to overcome the problem that LSPI algorithms face, that is, selection of feature functions and sample data. In such hybrid learning method, a typical linear approximator using Gaussian function for all features is used as approximation architecture and the LSQ algorithm is used in order to approximate Q value functions. The number of features and the center of features are selected using OLS training strategy based upon the training set generated by simulation. The proposed hybrid learning method is applied to the classical Cart-Pole system and the simulation results are presented to show the effectiveness of the method.

## 2 Least-Squares Methods for Q-learning

In this paper, the attention is restricted to the discrete-time dynamic system that the system evolution at time $t$, action takes on a state $x_t$ can be shown as:

$$x_{t+1} = f(x_t, a_t, w_t), \tag{1}$$

where $w_t$ is a disturbance and $a_t$ is a control decision generated by policy $\mu$. Each disturbance $w_t$ is independently sampled from some fixed distribution.

In most reinforcement learning systems, its underlying control problem is modeled as a Markov Decision Process (MDP). The MDP can be denoted by a quadruple $\{S, A, P, R\}$ where: $S$ is the state set, $A$ is the action set, $P$ is the state transition probability and $R$ denotes the reward function $g(x_t, a_t)$. The policy $\mu$ is a mapping $\mu : S \rightarrow \Pr(A)$, where $\Pr(A)$ is a probability distribution in the action space. Let $\{x_0, x_1, x_2, \ldots\}$ be a Markov chain. For each policy $\mu$, the value function $J^{\mu}$ is

$$J^{\mu}(x) = E\left[\sum_{t=0}^{\infty} \alpha^t g(x_t, \mu(x_t)) \middle| x_0 = x\right], \ \alpha \in [0,1) \ . \tag{2}$$

The state sequence is generated according to $x_0 = x$ and the system evolution (1).

Each $J^{\mu}(x)$ can be viewed as the assessment of long term rewards given that we start in state $x$ and control the system using a policy $\mu$. If the optimal value function $J^*$ is available, the generation of optimal action requires computing one expectation per element of the decision space. Q value function is introduced in order to avoid this computation, which is defined by

$$Q^*(x,a) = \underset{w}{E}\left[g(x,a) + \alpha J^*(f(x,a,w))\right] \ . \tag{3}$$

Therefore, the optimal actions can be obtained without the requirement for evaluating the system function. The exact Q-values for all $x-a$ pairs can be obtained by solving the Bellman equations (full backups):

$$Q^{\mu}(x_t, a_t) = \sum_{x_{t+1}} P(x_t, a_t, x_{t+1}) g(x_t, a_t, x_{t+1}) + \gamma \sum_{x_{t+1}} P(x_t, a_t, x_{t+1}) Q^{\mu}(x_{t+1}, \mu(x_{t+1})) \ . \tag{4}$$

Or, in matrix format:

$$Q^{\mu} = \Re + \gamma \mathrm{P}^{\mu} Q^{\mu} \ . \tag{5}$$

$\mathrm{P}^{\mu}(|S||A| \times |S||A|)$ denotes the transition probability from $(x_t, a_t)$ to $(x_{t+1}, \mu(x_{t+1}))$.

In the absence of the model of the MDP ($\Re$ and $\mathrm{P}^{\mu}$ are unknown), Q-learning algorithm use sample data $\{x_t, a_t, r_t, x_{t+1}\}$ generated by the interaction between agent and environment. $r_t$ is the immediate reward. The value of temporal difference $d_t$ and one-step Q-learning updated equation are as following:

$$d_t = g(x_t, a_t) + \alpha \max_{a_{t+1}} \hat{Q}(x_{t+1}, a_{t+1}) - \hat{Q}(x_t, a_t) \ . \tag{6}$$

$$\hat{Q}^{(t+1)}(x,a) = \hat{Q}^{(t)}(x,a) + \gamma d_t, \ \gamma \in (0,1] \ . \tag{7}$$

$\hat{Q}$ can be guaranteed to converge to $Q^*$ under necessary preconditions. As the case for controlled TD learning, it is often desirable to add exploration noise $\eta_t$.

Obviously Q value functions can be stored in tables of size $|S||A|$, but it is not always practical case for most real world application. The intractability of state-action spaces calls for value function approximation. The LSQ algorithm in [6] uses the parameterization of the linear form

$$\hat{Q}(x,a,w) = \sum_{k=1}^{K} w(k)\phi_k(x,a) = \phi(x,a)^T W , \tag{8}$$

where $\phi_1,...,\phi_k$ are "basis functions" generated through human intuition and trial-error process. $W = (w(1),...,w(K))'$ is a vector of scalar weights.

For a fixed policy $\mu$, $\Phi$ is $(|S||A| \times K)$ matrix and $K \ll |S||A|$. Then:

$$\hat{Q}^{\mu} = \Phi W^{\mu} . \tag{9}$$

If the model of MDP is available, the form of $\Phi$ and the expected reward $\Re$ are:

$$\Phi = \begin{bmatrix} \phi(x_1,a_1)^T \\ \cdots \\ \phi(x\ ,a\ )^T \\ \cdots \\ \phi(x_{|S|},a_{|A|})^T \end{bmatrix}, \text{ and } \Re = \begin{bmatrix} \sum_{x_{t+1}} P(x_1,a_1,x_{t+1})g(x_1,a_1,x_{t+1}) \\ \cdots \\ \sum_{x_{t+1}} P(x\ ,a\ ,x_{t+1})g(x\ ,a\ ,x_{t+1}) \\ \cdots \\ \sum_{x_{t+1}} P(x_{|S|},a_{|A|},x_{t+1})g(x_{|S|},a_{|A|},x_{t+1}) \end{bmatrix}. \tag{10}$$

For such situation, the policy $W^{\mu}$ can be computing directly using equation:

$$W^{\mu} = A^{-1}B , \tag{11}$$

where $A = \Phi^T(\Phi - \gamma P^{\mu}\Phi)$ and $B = \Phi^T \Re$.

Under the model-free circumstance, LSQ use the sample set collected from the MDP to construct approximator. If samples $\{(x_i^t,a_i^t,r_i^t,x_i^{t+1}) | i=1,2,...,L\}$ are "good" data set, LSQ algorithm can promise the convergence to the true $W^{\mu}$. For the fixed policy $\mu$, each sample $(x^t,a^t,r^t,x^{t+1})$ contributes to the construction of approximation ($A,B$ matrix) using following two equations.

$$\hat{A} \leftarrow \hat{A} + \phi(x^t,a^t)\left(\phi(x^t,a^t) - \gamma\phi(x^{t+1},\mu(x^{t+1}))\right)^T, \ \gamma \in (0,1] . \tag{12}$$

$$\hat{B} \leftarrow \hat{B} + \phi(x^t,a^t)r^t . \tag{13}$$

LSQ can learn state-action value functions of fixed policy effectively using the potentially controlled sample set so it is natural to extend this algorithm to policy iteration procedure, which is called LSPI algorithm [6]. Based upon the Q value function computed by LSQ, the next step optimal policy can be found simply using

$$\mu^{t+1}(x) = \arg\max_{a} \overset{\wedge}{Q}^{\mu^t}(x,a) = \arg\max_{a} \phi(x,a)^T W^{\mu^t} \quad . \tag{14}$$

The greedy policy is represented by the parameter $W^{\mu^t}$ and can be determined on demand for any given state. Clearly, the policy improvement procedure of LSPI can be achieved without model knowledge and explicit representation for policy.

## 3 Simulation and OLS Regression for RBF NN Training

Although it is reasonable to extend LSQ to control problems directly [8], failures are likely happen for many applications mainly due to the significant bias for value approximation in the early steps. LSPI integrate LSQ with policy iteration idea to solve learning control problems and produce more robust solution. But the question still remains for the selection of basis functions for LSQ and "good" sample data set.

The training samples of LSQ are collected from controllable "random episodes" starting from the very beginning. The better sample data are, the faster approximation will converge to true value. Simulation is powerful data generation tool for traditional neural network training, especially for the situation that system is hard to model but easy to simulate. Simulation can also tend to implicitly indicate the features of the system in terms of the state visiting frequency. This characteristic may help us to understand the potential useful system trajectories.

Orthogonal Least-Squares (OLS) algorithm introduced by [7] for training an RBF network is a systematic learning approach for solving center selection problem so that the newly added center always maximizes the amount of energy of the desired network output. For the RBF NN that has a single output, the network mapping can be viewed as a regression model of the form:

$$\begin{bmatrix} y(1) \\ y(2) \\ \dots \\ y(M) \end{bmatrix} = \begin{bmatrix} h(x_1,c_1,\sigma_1) & h(x_1,c_2,\sigma_2) & \dots & h(x_1,c_K,\sigma_K) \\ h(x_2,c_1,\sigma_1) & h(x_2,c_2,\sigma_2) & \dots & h(x_2,c_K,\sigma_K) \\ \dots & \dots & \dots & \dots \\ h(x_M,c_1,\sigma_1) & h(x_M,c_2,\sigma_2) & \dots & h(x_M,c_K,\sigma_K) \end{bmatrix} \begin{bmatrix} w_1 \\ w_2 \\ \dots \\ w_K \end{bmatrix} + \begin{bmatrix} e_1 \\ e_2 \\ \dots \\ e_M \end{bmatrix} . \tag{15}$$

Or, in matrix format: $Y = \mathrm{H}W + \mathrm{E}$ . The actual output of RBF NN is

$$\overset{\wedge}{y} = \mathrm{H}\overset{\wedge}{W} = [\mathrm{h}_1, \ \mathrm{h}_2, \ \dots \ \mathrm{h}_K]\overset{\wedge}{W} \ . \tag{16}$$

The centers of RBF NN are chosen from the input data set, which include $M$ candidates. We summarize the algorithm in [7] that performs the systematic selection of $K < M$ centers so that the size of RBF can be reduced significantly and the center of each basis function can be chosen by the order of their importance.

Step 1 $j = 1$ , For $1 \le i \le M$ ,

$$b_1^{(i)} = \mathrm{h}_i \text{, and } [err]_1^i = \frac{\left(b_1^{(i)T} Y\right)^2}{b_1^{(i)T} b_1^{(i)} \cdot Y^T Y} \ . \tag{17}$$

Search

$$[err]_1^{i_1} = \max\left\{[err]_1^i , 1 \le i \le M\right\} . \quad \textbf{(18)}$$

Select

$$b_1 = \mathrm{h}_{i_1} \text{ , and center } c_1 = c_{i_1} . \quad \textbf{(19)}$$

Step 2 $j \ge 2$, For $1 \le i \le M$ , $i \ne i_1, i \ne i_2, ..., i \ne i_{j-1}$ ,

$$a_{pj}^i = \frac{b_p^T \mathrm{h}_i}{b_p^T b_p} , \ 1 \le p \le j-1 . \quad \textbf{(20)}$$

Let

$$b_j^i = \mathrm{h}_i - \sum_{p=1}^{j-1} a_{pj}^i b_p \text{ , and } [err]_j^i = \frac{\left(b_j^{(i)T} Y\right)^2}{b_j^{(i)T} b_j^{(i)} \cdot Y^T Y} . \quad \textbf{(21)}$$

Search

$$[err]_j^{i_j} = \max\left\{[err]_j^i , 1 \le i \le M, i \ne i_1, i \ne i_2, ..., i \ne i_{j-1}\right\} . \quad \textbf{(22)}$$

Select

$$b_j = b_j^{i_j} \text{ , center } c_j = c_{i_j} . \quad \textbf{(23)}$$

Step 3 Repeat step 2. The algorithm is stopped at step $N$ when $1 - \sum_{p=1}^{N} [err]_p \le \rho$ . $0 \le \rho \le 1$ is tolerance value defined by user.

## 4 Hybrid Learning Method for LSPI

Motivated by the simplicity of model-free approximate policy iteration algorithm and the effectiveness of OLS regression method for selecting the centers of RBF NN among input data set, a new hybrid learning method for LSPI is proposed in this paper. The pre-learning process is added in order to set up necessary parameters of LSPI. Such "feature configuration" procedure using OLS regression provides a systematic way to select centers of basis functions for parameterization of linear form. It also guides the selection of sample data for LSPI. As mentioned before, simulation is powerful tool not only in neural network community but also for "on-line" reinforcement learning methods. Unlike the situation of those neural network applications, there are no readily available training sets that can be used to configure the feature of system in the RL context. For proposed hybrid learning method, simulation and classical one-step Q-learning running for limited steps are used in "feature configuration" procedure to roughly evaluate the state-action value functions under given policies. Although it will create analytical difficulties, this is probably the only way to extract the system characteristic under model-free circumstance.

Following is a brief description for complete hybrid learning algorithm.

It is assumed that the problem can be formulated as kind of finite MDP. The simulation for model-free system starts from a random state following the greedy policy produced by preliminary Q-learning and generates a series of observable time-sequence sample set $\Gamma:\left\{\left(x_i^t, a_i^t, r_i^t, x_i^{t+1}\right)\middle| i=1,2,\dots,L\right\}$, where $x_i \in S$, and $a_i \in A$. The total possible action types of $a \in A$ are $N$.

Step 1. Initialize the table representation for complete Q value set, $Q\left(x_{|S|}, a_{|A|}\right)=0$.

Step 2. While the stop criterion is not satisfied (this step will be terminated far before the classic Q-learning algorithm converge to true value), the approximate state-action values $Q(x \in \Gamma, a \in \Gamma)$ are calculated using one-step Q-learning algorithm according to equation (6) and (7). Simulation will follow the greedy policy. Now, the strong exploration ability is preferred so noise $\eta_t$ is likely to take comparatively big value.

Step 3. Generate $N$ input-output training data set $\left\{(X_d \leftrightarrow Y_d)\middle| d=1,2,\dots N\right\}$ from simulation set $\Gamma$ for center selection. Here, $X_d:\left\{(x \in \Gamma, a_d \in \Gamma)\right\}$ and $Y_d: Q(X_d)$.

Step 4. Using OLS regression algorithm described at section 3 to select $N$ kinds of centers set for LSQ's basis functions from $N$ training set. Each selected centers set will be used to approximate the value functions for corresponding action type.

Step 5. Refine simulation sample set $\Gamma$. It is reasonable to remove obviously useless samples base upon rough Q-values at step 2 so that the bias will likely be decreased.

Now we set up the parameters for LSPI as following:

$k_d | d=1,2,\dots N$: Centers of basis functions for state-action$_{(d|d=1,2\dots N)}$ space.

$\phi$: Using Gaussian function as LSQ basis function.

$\Gamma$: Training sample set for LSQ.

Step 6. Let $W_0=0$, $W^{\mu}=W_0$ and $W^{\mu'}=W^{\mu}$: Initial policy

Do

Get sample data from $\Gamma$ (Add/remove/maintain samples).

$\mu=\mu'$, That is, $W^{\mu}=W^{\mu'}$.

$\mu'=LSQ(\Gamma, k, \phi, W^{\mu})$, Using equation (11), (12) and (13) to compute $W^{\mu'}$.

While $(\mu \neq \mu')$, which means $\left\|W^{\mu'}-W^{\mu}\right\|>\varepsilon$

The new insight of the above hybrid learning approach is the "feature configuration" process in which simulation is used as a tool to produce the collection of samples for LSQ and OLS center selection algorithm is used to generate the basis functions for LSQ algorithm and guide the selection for "good" samples. The effectiveness of the proposed method will be illustrated in the classical Cart-Pole problem.

## 5 Results in the Cart-Pole System

Cart-Pole dynamic system is a classical pole-balancing environment. The objective of the problem is to exert a sequence of forces upon the cart's center of mass so that the pole is balanced for as long as possible and the cart does not hit the end of the track. For the RL controller, the dynamics of this system is assumed to be unknown. But in our simulation case following dynamics described by [9] is used for the system.

$$\ddot{\theta}_t = \frac{g\sin\theta_t + \cos\theta_t\left[\dfrac{-F_t - m_p l \dot{\theta}_t^2 \sin\theta_t + \mu_c \operatorname{sgn}\left(\dot{x}_t\right)}{m_c + m_p}\right] - \dfrac{\mu_p \dot{\theta}_t}{m_p l}}{l\left[\dfrac{4}{3} - \dfrac{m_p \cos^2\theta_t}{m_c + m_p}\right]}, \tag{24}$$

$$\ddot{x}_t = \frac{F_t + m_p l\left[\dot{\theta}_t^2 \sin\theta_t - \ddot{\theta}_t \cos\theta_t\right] - \mu_c \operatorname{sgn}\left(\dot{x}_t\right)}{m_c + m_p}. \tag{25}$$

In the above equations, the parameters $x_t, \dot{x}_t, \theta_t, \dot{\theta}_t, m_c, m_p, \mu_c, \mu_p, l, F_t$ are the horizontal position of the cart relative to the track, the horizontal velocity of the cart, the angle between the pole and vertical, clockwise being positive, the angular velocity of the pole, the mass of the cart (1.0), mass of the pole (0.1), coefficient of friction of cart on track, coefficient of friction of pivot, the distance from center of mass of pole to the pivot (0.5), and the force exerted on the cart's center of mass at time $t$, respectively. The sample rate for system simulation and applying control force are the same: 50 Hz. There are 2 possible action types here: $A = \{-10, +10\}$ but the actual force to the system is noisy $F_t = (a_t + \eta_t)$, where $a_t \in A$ and noise $\eta_t$ follows uniformly distribution. The state at time $t$ is specified by variables $\left\{x_t, \dot{x}_t, \theta_t, \dot{\theta}_t\right\}$ and the continuous state space is separated to 163 discrete states. The external reinforcement signal (reward) is defined as:

$$r_t = \begin{cases} 0, & \text{if -0.21 radians} < \theta_t < 0.21 \text{ radians and -2.4m} < x_t < 2.4\text{m} \\ -1, & \text{otherwise.} \end{cases} \tag{26}$$

The results are shown in following two figures. Simulation starts from a random state and follows rough policy learned from preliminary one-step Q-learning. The selected state-action centers for basis functions are plotted in figure 1. Orthogonal Least-Squares center selection algorithm is applied to two input-output training data sets generated by simulation. A set of 70 Gaussian functions (35 for each action type) over one dimension state space is generated automatically without human involvement to approximate the state-action value functions. The selection result is also used to refine the sample set $\Gamma$ for LSQ, which means we are likely to remove the data far away from the selected centers. Figure 2 illustrates the performance of controller learned by proposed hybrid Least-Squares methods. The Y-axis number shows the log function value for successful balancing time at each training episode. After only about 350 training episodes, the method returns the policy under which system-balancing period already exceeds 5000 seconds (250000 steps). Such convergence speed is much faster than traditional Q-learning and almost the same as the pure LSPI with pretty human selected basis functions and training sample set. Obviously the new hybrid method for LSPI is more smart and robust.

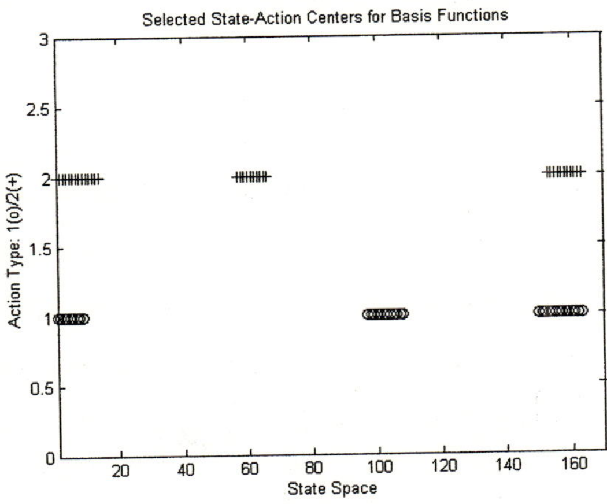


**Fig. 1.** Result on center selection in state-action space

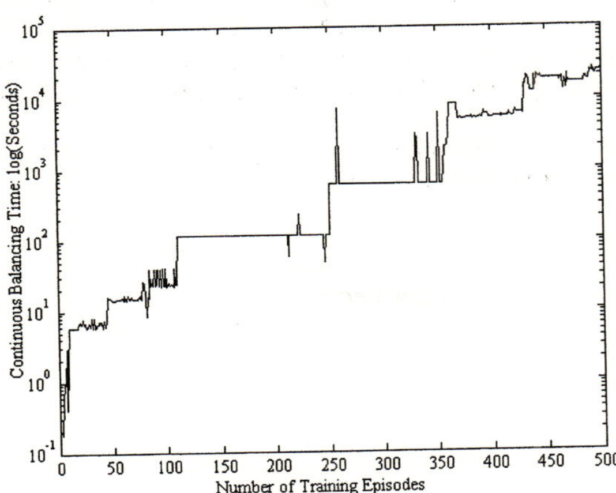


**Fig. 2.** Training result using hybrid Least-Squares method

## 6 Conclusions

A novel hybrid learning method is proposed in this paper to solve reinforcement learning control problems. This method combines Least-Squares policy iteration algorithm with orthogonal Least-Squares regression strategy for selecting feature centers automatically. Simulation is introduced as a tool to generate rough representation for feature so that the construction of training sample set for model-free Least-Squares Q-learning is guided. Results in the Cart-Pole system demonstrate the effectiveness of the proposed hybrid Least-Squares learning method. Other applications of this method are now in progress.

## References

1. R.S.Sutton.: Learning to Predict by the Methods of Temporal Difference. Machine Learning, Vol.3, No.1 (1988) 9-44
2. C.J.C.H.Watkins.: Learning From Delayed Rewards. PhD thesis, Cambridge University, Cambridge, UK (1989)
3. R.S.Sutton, A.Barto.: Reinforcement Learning: An Introduction. MIT Press, Cambridge, MA (1998)
4. Steven J.Bradtke, A.Barto.: Linear Least-Squares Algorithms for Temporal Difference Learning. Machine Learning. 22(1/2/3) (1996) 33-57
5. Daphne Koller, Ronald Parr.: Policy Iteration for factored MDPs. Proceedings of the 16th Conference on Uncertainty in Artificial Intelligence (UAI-00), Morgan Kaufmann. (2000) 326-334
6. Michail Lagoudakis, Ronald Parr.: Model Free Least Squares Policy Iteration. Proceedings of the 14th Neural Information Processing Systems (NIPS-14), Vancouver, Canada. December (2001)
7. S.Chen, C.F.Cowan, P.M.Grant.: Orthogonal Least Squares Algorithm for Radial Basis Function Networks, IEEE Transactions on Neural Networks, vol.21. (1990) 2513-39
8. Michail Lagoudakis, Michael L.Littman.: Algorithm Selection Using Reinforcement Learning. Proceedings of the 7th International Conference on Machine Learning. San Francisco, CA (2000) 511-518
9. R.S.Sutton.: Temporal Aspects of Credit Assignment in Reinforcement Learning. PhD thesis, University of Massachusetts (1984)

# HMM/ANN System for Vietnamese Continuous Digit Recognition

Dang Ngoc Duc[1], John-Paul Hosom[2], and Luong Chi Mai[3]

[1] Alcatel NSV,
Vietnam Post and Telecommunication,
124 Hoang Quoc Viet St., Hanoi, Vietnam,
dang-ngoc.duc@hn.vnn.vn

[2] Center for Spoken Language Understanding (CSLU-OGI),
Oregon Graduate Institute (OGI),
20000 N.W. Walker Rd., Beaverton, OR, 97006 USA, hosom@ece.ogi.edu

[3] Institute of Information Technology,
National Center for Science and Technology of Vietnam,
Hoang Quoc Viet St., Hanoi, Vietnam,
lcmai@ioit.ncst.ac.vn

**Abstract.** The study of a system for Vietnamese continuous digit recognition is described. The CSLU Toolkit was used to develop and implement hybrid HMM/ANN recognition systems. Experiments were done with a corpus of 442 sentences with 2340 words, which were extracted from two telephone-speech corpora: "22 Language v1.2" and "Multi-Language Telephone Speech v1.2". In our experiments, a context-dependent phoneme recognizer has achieved better recognition performance than a context-dependent demi-syllable recognizer and a context-independent phoneme recognizer. Among feature sets applied to the context-dependent phoneme recognizer, the set of 12 PLP features with CMS, energy and corresponding delta values has achieved the best recognition result (96.83% word accuracy and 87.67% sentence correct).

## 1 Introduction

Automatic speech recognition (ASR) is one branch of the field of artificial intelligence, dealing with automatic knowledge acquisition, models of human language, (acoustic) pattern recognition, and adaptation. Despite decades of research in ASR, acceptable "real-world" performance on even simple tasks remains, in some cases, elusive. In this paper, we describe research on the recognition of Vietnamese digits (the numbers zero through nine) spoken over the telephone channel without deliberate pauses between each word. Despite the small vocabulary size, this task is considered challenging because (a) the telephone channel has a severe impact on ASR performance and (b) statistical models of the frequency of word combinations that improve performance on other tasks can not be applied to digit recognition. The task is then necessarily focused on pattern recognition in a noisy environment.

P.W.H. Chung, C.J. Hinde, M. Ali (Eds.): IEA/AIE 2003, LNAI 2718, pp. 481–486, 2003.

The purpose of the work reported here is to apply language-independent ASR techniques to the recognition of Vietnamese digits, to investigate the effect of different types of phonetic units on recognition performance, and to evaluate feature sets used in classification. High accuracy on the digits task will enable better automatic spoken-word acquisition, and might provide new techniques in pattern recognition that can be applied to fields other than speech recognition. (For example, techniques used in handwriting recognition are very similar to those in speech recognition.)

The CSLU Toolkit [[4]] was used in this work to carry out two experiments. In the first experiment, we compared the recognition performance of three recognizers based on three different basic speech units: context-dependent demi-syllables, context-independent phonemes and context-dependent phonemes. In the second experiment, we studied the effects of different feature sets to find the most suitable feature set for Vietnamese digit recognition.

## 2 Basic Phonetic Structure of Vietnamese

Vietnamese is a monosyllable tonal language. Each Vietnamese syllable may be considered a combination of Initial, Final and Tone components. The Initial component is always a consonant, or it may be omitted in some syllables. There are 21 Initials in Vietnamese. There are 155 Final components in Vietnamese [[1]] and the Final may be decomposed into Onset, Nucleus and Coda. The Onset and Coda are optional and may not exist in a syllable. The Nucleus consists of a vowel or a diphthong, and the Coda is a consonant or a semi-vowel. There is 1 Onset, 16 Nuclei and 8 Codas in Vietnamese.

The Tone is a super-segment and contains all parts of a syllable. There are six distinct tones in Vietnamese, and they can affect word meaning; six different tones applied to a syllable can result in six distinct words.

The Initial, Tone, Onset, Nucleus and Coda may be combined together to make a syllable; however not all combinations are possible. There are a total of 18958 pronounceable distinct syllables in Vietnamese [[1]].

## 3 Corpus

The corpus used in this work for training, developing and testing our recognizers consists of 442 sentences with 2340 words. It was extracted from two corpora from the Center for Spoken Language Understanding (CSLU): "22 Language v1.2", and "Multi-Language Telephone Speech v1.2".

Each sentence of the corpus consists of a number of digits in Vietnamese from 0 to 9. The sentences were recorded from 208 speakers (78 females and 130 males), who recited their telephone numbers, street addresses, ZIP codes or other numeric information over the telephone network in a natural speaking manner. The data were collected from different environments and may contain a noticeable amount of noise and other "real-life" aspects such as breath, glottalization, and music. The corpus was digitized at an 8000 Hz sampling rate with

A/D conversion precision of 8 bits. All the sentences in the corpus have been time-aligned and transcribed at the phonetic level.

## 4 Experiment

### 4.1 Recognition System

The recognizers in this work were trained, developed and tested by the use of the CSLU Speech Toolkit [[5]], which is freely downloaded for research purposes from the OGI Web site. The hybrid HMM/ANN architecture, in which the phonetic likelihoods are estimated using a neural network, was chosen for all of our experiments. The document [[4]] was used as a guide for carrying our experiments.

Three-fifths of the data was randomly chosen for the training set, another one-fifth of the data was used for the development set, and the other one-fifth was used for the test set. The same data was used for all experiments.

The feature vectors were computed from the hand-labeled training data for each 10ms frame. The feature set contains features of the frame to be classified and features of frames at -60, -30, 30 and 60ms relative to the given frame.

The feature vectors were used for training a three-layer feed-forward neural network with an error back-propagation procedure. The neural network has 200 hidden nodes. The number of input nodes depends on the number of features (130 or 195 nodes); the number of output nodes depends on the number of categories of each recognizer. The training was adjusted by negative penalty modification as described in [[8]]. The training was done for 30 iterations.

The development set was used for evaluating the trained networks to find the best iteration. The best neural network was used for "forward-backward" (FB) training to improve the recognition results.

In the "forward-backward" (FB) training, the training strategy proposed by Yan et al. [[6]] was applied. In this method, the targets used to train the neural network are derived from posterior state occupation probabilities. The forward-backward re-estimation algorithm was used to regenerate the targets for training sentences. The neural network trained with hand-labeled data was used for the initial neural network. Unlike other hybrid systems, this hybrid HMM/ANN used within-phone model transitions. The training was finished after doing "forward-backward" training two times and the best FB2 recognizer was found for testing.

### 4.2 Experiment 1

In this experiment, we compared the recognition performance of three systems, based on different basic speech units: context-dependent demi-syllables, context-independent phonemes and context-dependent phonemes.

The first recognizer was a context-dependent demi-syllable recognizer. The Initial was defined as right dependent to take into account co-articulation effects from the first vowel in Final on Initial. The Final was split into 3 categories. The list of Initials and Finals in this recognizer is described in Table 1.

**Table 1.** Acoustic units for demi-syllable and phoneme recognition systems

| English | Vietnamese | Initial-Final | phoneme |
|---|---|---|---|
| zero | khoong | /kh/ /oong/ | /kh/ /oo/ /ng/ |
| one | mootj | /m/ /oot/ | /m/ /oo/ /te/ |
| two | hai | /h/ /ai/ | /h/ /a/ /i/ |
| three | ba | /b/ /a/ | /b/ /a/ |
| four | boons | /b/ /oon/ | /b/ /oo/ /n/ |
| five | nawm | /n/ /awm/ | /n/ /aw/ m/ |
| six | saus | /s/ /au/ | /s/ /a/ /u/ |
| seven | baayr | /b/ /aai/ | /b/ /aa/ /i/ |
| eight | tams | /t/ /am/ | /uc/ /t/ /a/ m/ |
| nine | chins | /ch/ /in/ | /uc/ /ch/ /i/ n/ |

The second recognizer in this experiment was a context-independent phoneme recognizer. Each phoneme was defined as one part. A list of phonemes is provided in Table 1, in which the unvoiced closure /uc/ is inserted in front of the unvoiced stops.

The last recognizer used in this experiment was based on context-dependent phonemes. Each phoneme was divided into one, two or three parts. The vowels were split in three parts, and all stops were defined as one part because they are very short.

The same grammar was used for all three recognizers. This grammar allows any digit to follow any other digit with equal probability, and each digit may be separated by either silence or "garbage" [[3]]. All three recognizers for this experiment were trained, developed and tested using the same feature set: 12 MFCC coefficients with cepstral mean subtraction, plus energy and their delta (D) values.

### 4.3 Experiment 2

In this second experiment, we applied different feature sets to our context-dependent phoneme recognizer. The 13 PLP coefficients (PLPC13) and 13 MFCC coefficients (MFCC13) were computed with one of two pre-processing techniques: RASTA (RelAtive SpecTrAl) or CMS (Cepstral Mean Subtraction). The delta-delta (D2, or acceleration) values were also added to the feature set. The motivation of this experiment was to study the influence of feature extraction on recognition performance.

## 5 Results

Table 2 shows the results of Experiment 1. Table 3 shows the results of Experiment 2. In the Experiment 1, the context-dependent phoneme recognizer has better performance in comparison with the context-independent phoneme recognizer, demonstrating the effectiveness of context-dependent modeling. The

**Table 2.** Recognition performance of three recognizers: context-dependent demi-syllable, context-independent phoneme and context-dependent phoneme. " WA " indicates word-level accuracy (in percent), and " SC " indicates sentence-level correct (in percent)

| basic speech unit | set | WA | SC |
|---|---|---|---|
| context-dependent demi-syllable | dev | 93.80 | 79.22 |
| | test | 93.02 | 79.45 |
| context-independent phoneme | dev | 92.99 | 76.62 |
| | test | 90.48 | 73.97 |
| context-dependent phoneme | dev | 95.69 | 81.82 |
| | test | 96.19 | 87.67 |

**Table 3.** Recognition performance of the context-dependent phoneme recognizer with eight different feature sets

| basic speech unit | set | WA | SC |
|---|---|---|---|
| mfcc13(cms)+D | dev | 95.69 | 81.82 |
| | test | 96.19 | 87.67 |
| mfcc13(rasta)+D | dev | 93.80 | 77.92 |
| | test | 92.38 | 72.60 |
| plpc13(cms)+D | dev | 96.23 | 84.42 |
| | test | 96.83 | 87.67 |
| plpc13(rasta)+D | dev | 92.99 | 75.32 |
| | test | 94.60 | 80.82 |
| mfcc13(cms)+D+D2 | dev | 96.50 | 87.01 |
| | test | 95.87 | 86.30 |
| mfcc13(rasta)+D+D2 | dev | 95.15 | 81.82 |
| | test | 93.02 | 75.34 |
| plpc13(cms)+D+D2 | dev | 96.50 | 85.71 |
| | test | 96.83 | 87.67 |
| plpc13(rasta)+D+D2 | dev | 92.99 | 74.03 |
| | test | 94.29 | 76.71 |

context-dependent phoneme recognizer has better recognition accuracy than the context-dependent demi-syllable recognizer, showing that the basic phonetic unit suitable for continuous digit recognition is the context-dependent phoneme.

In the Experiment 2, the context-dependent phoneme recognizer with PLP13 (CMS) plus delta values achieves the best result with 96.83% word accuracy and 87.67% sentence correct. The experiment also demonstrates that the addition of D2 in the feature set does not improve significantly the performance of the recognizers.

## 6 Conclusions

In this paper, we have presented our study on continuous digit recognition for Vietnamese over the telephone line. The results show that context-dependent demi-syllable recognition has lower accuracy in comparison with our context-dependent phoneme recognizer. The context-dependent phoneme recognizer has better recognition results in comparison with the context-independent phoneme recognizer. Thus, context-dependent phonetic units are better suited to continuous Vietnamese digit recognition. Furthermore, this investigation of the type of sub-word units points to the need to carefully choose the basic units of classification. We also found in our experiments that among the feature sets used in context-dependent phoneme recognizers, the feature set with 12 PLP coefficients with CMS, plus energy and their delta values achieves the best result. In comparison with continuous digit recognition over the telephone for English (using a much larger number of speakers for training) [[3]], our system has comparable performance: 96.83% word accuracy and 87.67% sentence correct.

In future research, more experiments with larger amounts of data need to be conducted to further confirm our findings. Also, experiments are planned to include information on pitch contours to further improve accuracy.

## References


1. Vu K. B., Trieu T.T.H, Bui D.B: "Am tiet tieng Viet kha nang hinh thanh va thuc te ung dung". Proc. of conference in IT, Institute of IT, 2001.
2. Jim J.W, Li D., Jacky C: "Modeling context-dependent phonetic units in a continuous speech recognition system for Mandarin Chinese". Proceeding of ICSLP '96.
3. Hosom, J.P., Cole, R.A, and Cosi, P.: "Improvements in Neural-Network Training and Search Techniques for Continuous Digit Recognition." Australian Journal of Intelligent Information Processing Systems (AJIIPS), vol. 5, no. 4 (Summer 1998), pp. 277-284.
4. Hosom, J. P., Cosi, P. and Cole, R., Fanty, M., Schalkwyk, J., Yan, Y. and Wei, W.: "Training Neural Networks for Speech Recognition" http://cslu.cse.ogi.edu/tutordemos/ nnet_training/tutorial.
5. http://cslu.cse.ogi.edu/toolkit.
6. Y., Fanty, M and Cole, R.: "Speech Recognition Using Neural Networks with Forward-Backward Probability Generated Targets", In Proceedings ICSDDP97, April 1997, Vol. 4.
7. Lander. T.: "CSLU Labeling Guide". Center for Spoken Language Understanding, Oregon Graduate Institute. 1997.
8. Wei, W and Van Vuuren, S.: "Improved Neural Network Training of Inter-Word Context Units for Connected Digit Recognition". In Proceedings of International Conference on Acoustic Speech and Signal Processing (ICASSP '98), Seattle, Washington, May 1998, Vol. 1, pp. 497-500.

# UMAS Learning Requirement for Controlling Network Resources

Abdullah Gani, Nasser Abouzakhar, and Gordon Manson

Centre for Mobile Communication Research (C4MCR)
Dept of Computer Science
The University of Sheffield
Regent Court, 211 Portobello St, Sheffield S1 4DP
United Kingdom
agani@ieee.org, n.abouzakhar@dcs.shef.ac.uk,
g.manson@dcs.shef.ac.uk

**Abstract.** This paper presents an intelligent User Manager Agent System (UMAS) which has capability of making management decisions for balancing the network load with the users' requests for accessing network resources. A conventional users' request for accessing network resources depends on the rigid rules setting and it can affect the overall performance of network services. UMAS provides additional measure in controlling the network services availability and responsiveness. In providing a different level of services to users, UMAS is required to perform an appropriate learning activity that can furnish an input for a decision of time allocation for a single session. This paper demonstrates the use of Neuro Fuzzy Logic for performing the learning that will be integrated into the UMAS.

## 1 Introduction

The term of learning was originally used to describe the process of human learning and always be associated with the knowledge capturing through understanding and applying it for changing the behaviour towards desirable outcomes. Pavlov and Skinner's theory on learning that based on experiments were conducted on animal in order to understand animal learns. However, it is believed that a sequential type-operating machine of computer can be 'taught' like in Pavlov's experiment where dogs were used as a subject. Soft computing as a domain provides a foundation for artificial intelligence techniques to be further explored and integrated into a 'thinkable' machine.

In order to achieve a 'thinkable' machine that can be used to solve many real-world problems, learning for machine needs to be defined and all the requirements are identified and provided. Educationists like Weiss and Bloom believe that learning is a process of applying the captured knowledge towards desirable behavioural outcomes. Hence, learning must be associated with behaviour changes, knowledge acquisition and memory storage. These three fundamental elements must be a basis for any learning to be applied to.

In the next section, the learning concept will be presented, followed by the UMAS description that outlines the functions of UMAS has.

P.W.H. Chung, C.J. Hinde, M. Ali (Eds.): IEA/AIE 2003, LNAI 2718, pp. 487–494, 2003.

## 2 Learning Definitions

One of the main features for the UMAS to be distinctive from a conventional program is the ability of learning. Semantically learning is a process of acquiring knowledge for the desired behavioural outcomes. This only can be achieved if a 'learner' has some degrees of reasoning in which knowledge is used for comparison and logic computation. However, for an agent of the UMAS to do the learning it means that it is capable of making a correct decision upon users' requests for network resources. Given a program, P, and some input x, a normal program would produce the same result, y. P(x) = y for every request. In the case of agents in the UMAS, the program can alter its initial state, q, so that the decision is made on the account of several knowledge domain and accordingly. Thus, P(x|q) = y, where y is the result of applying program, P, to input, x , given the initial state, q [1].

Bigus [1] states several forms of learning that can take place. The most common learning that obviously takes place is a rote learning, in which an example is given and agent copies the example and exactly reproduces the behaviour. In the case of UMAS, the agent will produce the result of the training data. For example, simulation results are presented to an agent to generate a new situation and later use the presented results for responding to a new situation occurrence. Another form of learning is parameter or weighted adjustment. In this type, important factors are known but the weight of their impacts on final result is unknown. This is a basis for neural network learning. Induction is a process of learning by example in which extraction of important characteristics of the problem is carried out for generalizing an input.

Another type of learning is clustering, chunking or abstraction of knowledge. It is about detecting a common pattern and generalise to a new situation. By chunking ten cases into one more general case, storage and searching time can be improved. Clustering looks at high-dimensional data and has similarity that bases on some criterion [1].

## 3 Learning Paradigms

Learning can be perceived from different perspectives. The definition of learning is directly influenced by the perspective. It has a direct relationship. Another perspective for defining the learning is called a machine learning (ML). According to this perspective, it has at least three major paradigms of learning – supervised, unsupervised and reinforcement. In a supervised learning, agent is trained by showing it the examples of the problem states or attributes along with the desired output or action. Agent will make prediction and if differs from the desired output, the agent will adjust or adapt the input to produce the correct output. This process is repeated several times until the agent makes accurate classifications or predictions. Learning of this type requires historical data from databases, sensor logs, trace logs as a training and example data and learning algorithms that normally used are back propagation neural network and decision tree.

The second paradigm is unsupervised learning in which agents need to recognise similarities between inputs or to identify the features in the input data. Data that is presented to the agents is partitioned into groups by clustering or segmenting. The process of clustering or segmenting continues until the same data is placed in the same group. Common attributes of the data are extracted and technique that normally used is Kohonen Map. Finally, the third paradigm is reinforcement learning that is used when explicit input/output pairs of training data are not available. Reinforcement learning also is used when there is a sequence of inputs and the desired output is only known after the specific sequence occurs. The process of identifying the relationship between a series of input values and a later output values is called temporal credit assignment. It is the most realistic learning even though taking longer time and less efficient.

The UMAS will use the Machine Learning (ML) approach of acquiring knowledge for learning purposes.

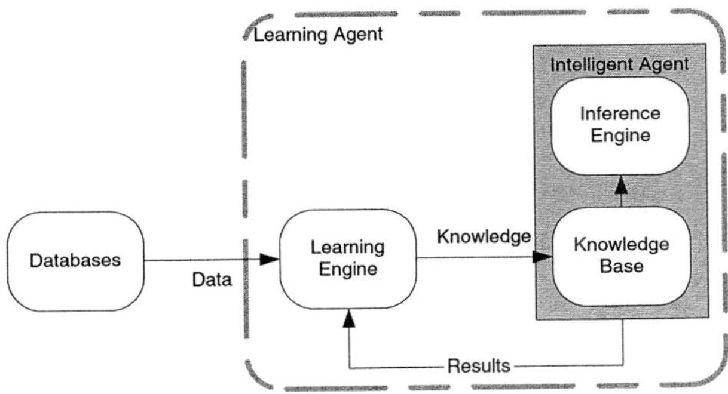


**Fig. 1.** Overview of the General Machine Learning Approach

There are a number of learning algorithms and each has a specific suitability for different kind of learning. UMAS will perform the learning activities upon the data that was collected on three parameters – policy, profile and network states [2].

## 4 UMAS Description

Generically, UMAS is an interface between users and networks for the purpose of controlling network resources that are requested by users. Figure 2 shows a high level diagram of UMAS with the example of network resources. The Router and server are examples of network resources that are critical in the use of network applications.

Based on three sets of data, UMAS determines the access time for a specific session of a particular user. This measure is needed so that network resources particularly bandwidth can be allocated for only legitimate purposes. For example, if a number of users accessing network resources are relatively small compared to available resources, the least critical applications are allowed to be accessed. However, if the number of users increased, then the least critical application of the session will be discarded from the network.

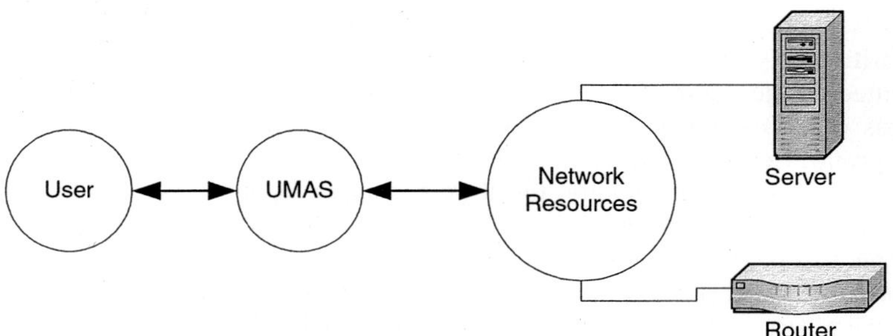


**Fig. 2.** High Level Diagram of UMAS

When a user logs in to the network, the UMAS will read the profile file of the user and use the knowledge base of the network. A system administrator creates a Profile file and it contains a collection of user settings such as desktop attributes and allowed network connections. A Knowledge base is a repository for learned knowledge of the use of network elements such as router, bandwidth, servers and applications. This knowledge is critical in the process of granting access to the network application request because it helps the UMAS to decide the best option for a network to be utilised for a particular session. The decision making process for determining a session period will be updated periodically at the interval time of 100 ms., which is believed to be sufficient for establishing communication between UMAS with other network objects.

The UMAS consists of several agents that each is assigned with a specific task. Figure 3 illustrates the components of the UMAS in which each component has a specific task to be performed and governed by the manager that resides in the UMAS.

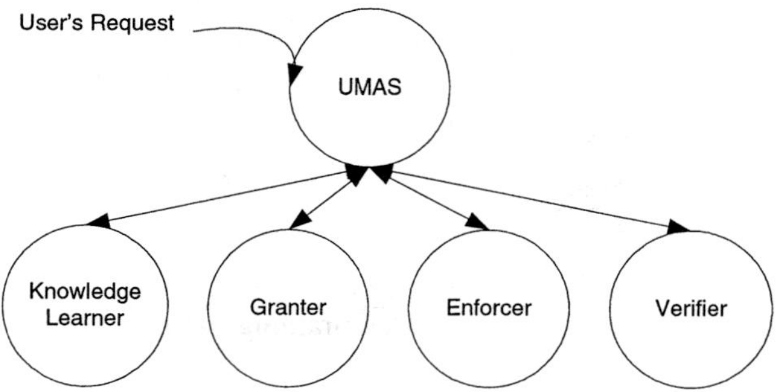


**Fig. 3.** UMAS components

The Knowledge Learner is responsible for capturing a set of variables and these are stored in the repository for future retrieval. When a request has been received by the UMAS for accessing a particular application, it needs to be processed with the consideration of network resource availability and the criticality of the application to the organisation's objectives. The UMAS will forward the message of request to the Granter for a decision whether to approve or otherwise. In deciding on the request, the Granter relies on information about the users that are currently logging in to the network and the network resource usage in order to determine if a potential approval will be detrimental to the performance of the network. The Granter will use Fuzzy set data supplied by the Knowledge Learner for computing the time that practically can be allocated for the session. The decision taken by the Granter then will be forwarded to the UMAS for execution.

The component of Enforcer is responsible for executing the decision by communicating with the routers to inform them of changing packet priority. At the same time, the Granter will set the clock on and start counting. However, the Granter needs to inform the Verifier as well because it is responsible for verifying the decision by checking the user profile with the server. If the allocated time is 'correct' then the user can have such application to be accessed otherwise a new computation of time will be asked. Of course, the UMAS needs to be informed about any decision taken by both the Granter and the Verifier, as it needs to inform the user too [3]

## 5 UMAS Learning

The UMAS adopts the supervised learning notion in which training data is supplied to the Granter for deciding the allocation of time. However, the size of the training data sets are relatively large and contain a number of sets, the learning processes are conducted in stages. This is due to the dependency of learning input to the previous learning outcomes. A unit of processor handles a particular set of training data and the outcomes are used for a next learning process.

The goal of UMAS learning is to minimise the error rate of the time allocation decision by the Granter. This can be achieved by training the data through a number of attempts. The smaller value of the error rate, the better it would. The learning will base on the following Neuro diagram.

Figure 4 shows only two inputs for the training data that will be used. This is because the limitation of ANFIS to do the learning.

## 6 UMAS Learning Simulation

The simulation has been conducted using Matlab ver 5.3. The purpose of simulation was to establish rules with minimum error rate that will be integrated into the UMAS learning mechanisms. In order this, the training data that was collected using Windump and Windows Network Monitor tools was converted into numeric format before being put into use. This is because ANFIS, the learning algorithm of neuro fuzzy logic can only accept numeric representations and limited input [4][5][6]. For that reason, the simulation was based on two set of inputs – application criticality and user priority. Both inputs were given a similar scale of 1 – 10. A smaller number for application criticality denotes the higher criticality it was.

Figure 5 illustrates the rules that have been automatically created by the ANFIS, which shows the allocated time is 100% if the application criticality and user priority are high. On the other hand, the allocated time drops substantially if both inputs are decreasing. However, because of the criticality is given higher weighting, any changes in the values significantly affect the outcome of the allocated time.

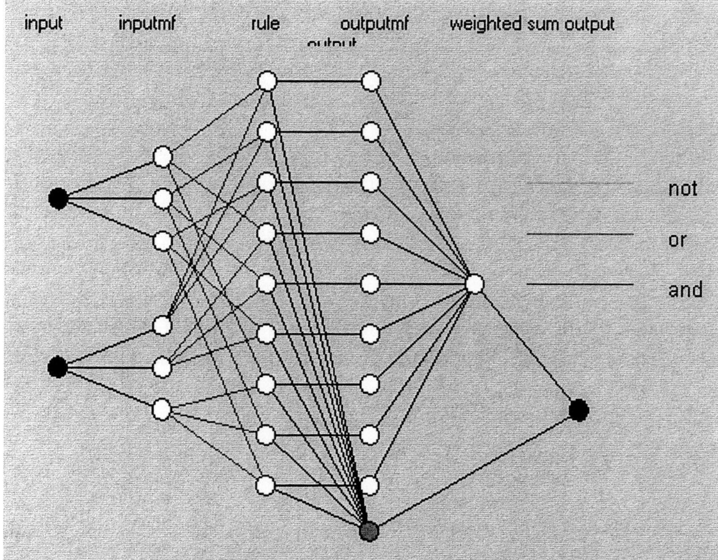


**Fig. 4.** Neuro diagram

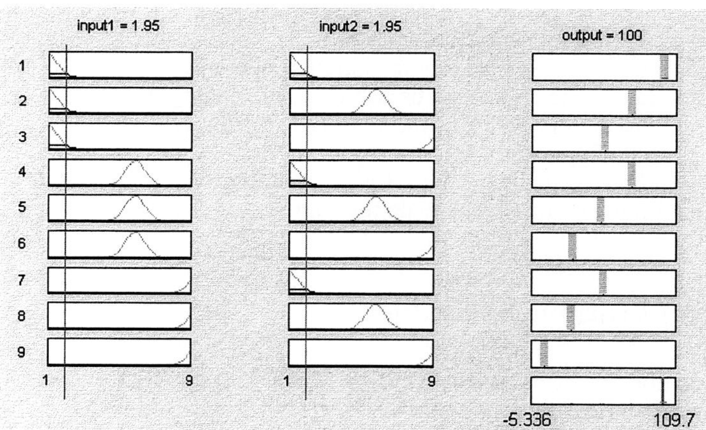


**Fig. 5.** Generated rules

Figure 6 is the results of the simulation in which clearly shown that all data were distributed into three clusters – high, medium and low. Most the data were scattered in the medium interval and with minimum error rate. The results of simulation indicate that learning had taken place in which error was 0.0000158

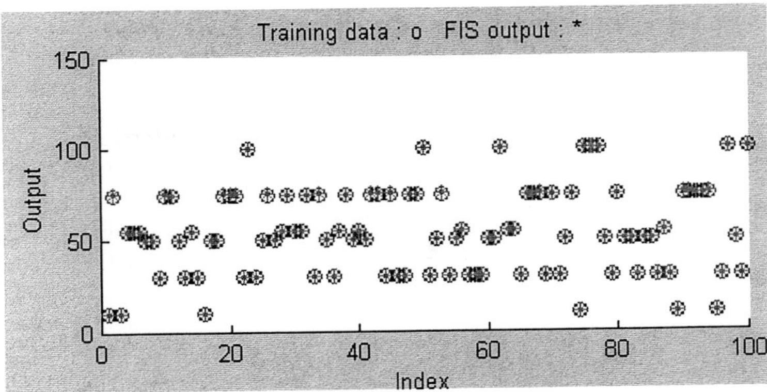


**Fig. 6.** Results of the simulation

## 7 Conclusion

The undertaken simulation had generated a set of rules with minimum error rate that can be integrated into the UMAS agents' development. In addition, the outcome of the simulation can be used for the Granter to decide the best allocation of session time for a user.

The UMAS will have the capability of making decisions intelligently based on the current situation of the network and the user's roles through the undertaken learning. This will enable the network resources to be allocated for achieving the main aims of network establishment and the organisation's goals. At the same time, users can receive appropriate levels of network services, in term of application availability and satisfied network responsiveness. As the UMAS has learning capability, the Knowledge Base will be gradually getting larger and this will lead to higher intelligence of the UMAS [7].

The idea of UMAS can be extended into other network management activities such as traffic management, Quality of Service and as a 'teacher' for training an agent that is newly introduced to the network.

## References


1. J.P. Bigus, Jennifer Bigus, Constructing Intelligent Agents Using Java, 2nd.ed. John Wiley, 2001.
2. L.L.Peterson and B.S.Davie, Computer Networks – A System Approach. Morgan Kaufmann, 2000.
3. Abdullah Gani, et.al., "The Roles of Intelligent User Manager Agent for Controlling an Access to Network Resources," presented at 3rd Annual PostGraduate Symposium The Convergence of Telecommunications, Networking and Broadcasting, John Moore Univ., Liverpool, UK, 2002.

4. Michael Knapik and Jay Johnson, Developing Intelligent Agents for Distributed Systems, Exploring Architecture, Technologies, and Applications, 1998, McGraw-Hill.
5. Eral Cox, The Fuzzy Systems Handbook, A Practitioner's Guide to Building, Using, and Manipulating Fuzzy Systems, Second Edition, 1999, AP Professional.
6. Adrian A. Hopgood, Intelligent Systems for Engineers and Scientists, Second Edition, 2001, CRC Press LLC.
7. V. R. B. Rudi Studer, Dieter Fensel, "Knowledge Engineering : Principles and methods," Data and Knowledge Engineering, vol. 25, pp. 161-197, 1998.

# Dialogue Management in an Automatic Meteorological Information System

Luis Villarejo, Núria Castell, and Javier Hernando

TALP Research Center, Universitat Politècnica de Catalunya, Campus Nord – A0, Jordi Girona 1-3, 08034 Barcelona, Spain,
{luisv, castell, javier}@talp.upc.es

**Abstract.** In this paper we present a real automatic meteorological information system that, not only provides friendly voice access to real-time data coming from automatic sensors, but also establishes an automatic warning service on the weather. It aims to extend the availability, personalization and friendliness of the meteorological information by means of a reusable easy-to-use friendly oral natural language interface. This interface takes advantage of the improvements in speech processing, dialogue handling and the great growth of mobile telephony. After the description of the functionalities of the system and its architecture, we present in detail the features of the dialogue manager. The main goals we have considered are: to provide the right information, to design a friendly interface, and to help the user never getting lost during the dialogue.

**Keywords:** intelligent interfaces, natural language and speech processing.

## 1 Introduction

Meteorological information has long been provided by television and radio as weather reports scheduled at a fixed timetable giving impersonal information. Nowadays there are telephonic systems that offer this information but in an unnatural way. Usually these systems offer some menus operated via the telephone keyboard and a very limited vocabulary. These features condemn the system to failure in the real world due to a lack of naturalness and fluency in the dialogue. This kind of systems usually provide da ta more general and updated less frequently than desired.

The interest and research on interactive speech systems has increased in the last years due to the extended use of telephone information systems. We should mention the TRINDI[1] (Task-Oriented Instructional Dialogue) project, which focuses in generic technology for the creation of a dialogue movement engine. Nowadays there are systems that offer a good level of interaction during the information exchange. Some examples are the following: ARISE[2] (Automatic Railway Information Systems for Europe), TRAINS[3], and BASURDE[4] (Spontaneous Speech Dialogue System in a Semantically Restricted Domain), all of them about railway information, and ATIS[5] (Air Travel Information

P.W.H. Chung, C.J. Hinde, M. Ali (Eds.): IEA/AIE 2003, LNAI 2718, pp. 495–504, 2003.

System), about flights. Only few systems are designed to offer meteorological information in a user-friendly way. A reference work in this field is the JUPITER[6] project.

The system described here provides personalized real-time data, in the Catalan language, on a set of meteorological conditions on each place of the Catalan geography through an easy-to-use natural language interface. It also provides an alarm and warning system, based on the same interface, that keeps the user informed on the variables of his/her interest whenever they occur. The whole system has been constructed on the basis of VoiceXML (the voice standard promoted by the World Wide Web Consortium), specifically the voice framework and the dialogue manager. By building a voice framework based on VoiceXML, the dialogue manager becomes independent not only of the voice technology but also of the application logic. The development of this system has been promoted by the Catalan government, aTTemps project, and it is actually running.

In this paper we start by presenting, in section 2, the services offered by the system and its meteorological data source, the Catalan Meteorological Service. In section 3, the system architecture is presented and a brief description on how the system works is done. After that, the issues related to the dialogue manager are discussed in section 4. Section 5 introduces the speech processing. In section 6 the evaluation of the system is discussed. At the end of the document, section 7, we present the conclusions and further work.

## 2 The Catalan Meteorological Service and aTTemps

The information offered by the system is collected by the *Servei Meteorològic Català* (SMC)[7] from four different sources:

1) The *Xarxa Meteorològica* (XMET, Meteorological Net) and the *Xarxa de Vigilància i Previsió de la Contaminació Atmosfèrica* (XVPCA, Atmosferic Pollution's Surveillance and Forecasting Net) nets consists of ninety one automatic meteorological ground stations, scattered over the Catalan geography. These stations are constantly acquiring information on different variables, such as temperature or direction and force of the wind, in order to supply measures of each of them every half an hour (via satellite or modem) to the meteorological centre.
2) The *Xarxa d'Instruments Oceanogràfics i Meteorològics* (XIOM, Meteorological and Oceanographic Instruments Net) net consists of four automatic meteorological buoys, scattered over the Catalan coast. These buoys are constantly acquiring information on maritime variables, such as the sea disturbances, the ground swell and the height of the waves, to supply measures of each of them every sixty minutes (via radio) to the meteorological centre.
3) The rain forecast which provides information, updated twice per day, on the rain's intensity and areas for the next thirty six hours.
4) The weather alarms which provide information, updated every half an hour, on risk situations such as hailstorms, danger of floods, avalanches or risk of fires.

### 2.1 aTTemps Services

As we stated in the Introduction section, the system developed under the aT-Temps project can be used in two ways, depending on the user needs:

1) Asking for immediate information: The user needs to know some meteorological variables or the rain forecast. The system initiates a dialogue to get the desired variable and the location of interest in order to provide the information.
2) Asking for activation/deactivation of a warning. The user needs to be notified (with an SMS or a voice message) on the weather conditions either when some meteorological conditions occur or just at a concrete time of the day. The system initiates the dialogue and saves the user warning profile in its database.

In all cases the user can ask for information not only in all the Catalan municipalities (949), but also in larger areas (regions, mountains, natural parks, etc), other spots which have a particular tourist interest (airport, etc), and popular abbreviations of names. In addition, if the system does not have information from the requested place, information from the closest place (climatologically speaking) will be provided.

### 2.2 aTTemps Dialogue Example

Here we will show a typical dialogue, translated from Catalan, in order to give an idea of the basic interaction between the user and the system.

*System*: Welcome to the ATTEMPS meteorological warning and information system. You can always say help, correction, repetition or exit. From which Catalan place do you want information, or do you want to establish a warning?
*User*: I am interested in Barcelona, please.
*System*: From Badalona, which information do you need?
*User*: I want to correct, not from Badalona.
*System*: From which Catalan place do you want information?
*User*: I want to know the weather right now in Barcelona.
*System*: From Barcelona, which information do you need?
*User*: I need the temperature, please.
*System*: In the last measure at 14:30h, in the meteorological station of Barcelona, the temperature was 20 degrees. Do you need any other information?
*User*: No, that was all. Thanks.
*System*: Thanks for calling. Good bye.

## 3 System Architecture

The system is made up of four main blocks , as can be seen in Figure 1, which correspond with: 1)the VoiceXML framework, which integrates the speech processing and the telephony hardware, 2)the VoiceXML dialogue manager (made

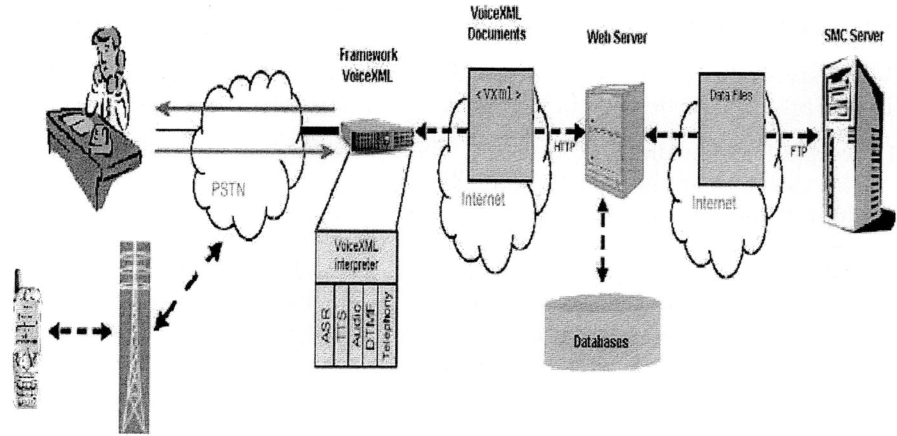


**Fig. 1.** System architecture

up of documents and the application logic both in the web server), which integrates the dialogue control and the language generation, 3)the system databases and 4)the data acquisition module, which provides the real-time meteorological contents by accessing the SMC server. In order to understand later sections, a short overview of all modules (excluding the one of the dialogue manager that is going to be explained in detail in section 4) is done in this section. A more detailed overview of this system can be found in[14].

The VoiceXML framework is made up on the basis of the OpenVXI 2.0[8] from SpeechWorks[9]. An specific development has been done in order to integrate the Dialogic[10] components for telephony purposes and the Ibervox[11] (cf. section 5) components for speech processing purposes.

The databases module is composed of two main databases which store the two kinds of information that the system must maintain: the meteorological data and the user's profiles for warnings. The first one (referred from now as meteorological database) is stored in a relational database which is updated constantly by the data acquisition module. While the second one (referred from now as user database) is stored in a LDAP (Lightweight Directory Access Protocol) database in order to optimize searches. This database is updated every time that a user activates or deactivates a warning message.

The data acquisition module consists of a process that acquires, every half an hour, the meteorological data in real time from the SMC databases and updates the local meteorological database. This process guarantees that we get the new data as soon as there is in the remote database.

The system works as follows:

1) The framework waits for a telephone call.
2) When a call is received, the root VoiceXML document of the dialogue manager is executed by the framework.

3) This execution causes the reproduction of the welcome message (by means of the voice technology integrated in the framework) that gives a little notion about how to interact with the system.
4) Then the system asks to the user about which information he/she wishes.
5) The grammars that should pick up the user's answer are loaded.
6) When the user answers, his/her reply is given back to the document. Once the reply is received, the execution of the document can go on.
7) Depending on the user needs, the dialogue manager will ask another question to the user or will do a request on the server to get data from the database.

7.1) In that last case, the query is sent to the database interface and the result is picked up and used, in the server, to build a document with dynamic content that will be sent to the framework for execution.

8) Once all user requested data has been collected, the system provides the meteorological information (contained in the dynamically generated document) to the user in natural language or takes record of the warning profile for that user.

## 4 The Dialogue Manager Module

The main goals of the dialogue manager are: to provide the right information in the minimum time, to be a friendly oral natural language interface that facilitates as much as possible the interaction with the user, and to guide the user in order to avoid situations where he/she would be lost. Setting up the dialogue manager strategy we have to take into account several factors including the dialogue flow, the confirmation policy, the amount of data per turn, the helping features and the language generation.

### 4.1 Dialogue Flow

The dialogue is made up of turns in which typically a question, as clear as possible, is made to the user guiding him/her to the kind of answer expected by the system in each turn. Once the user has answered, the system processes the input and initiates the next turn that can contain another question or a message to the user. As it is seen, the automatic system takes the initiative guiding the dialogue, but it lets the user to answer with a great range of syntactic possibilities. And what is not less important: lets the user to interrupt the system at any time in order to ask for help or repetition or even to answer a question before it is finished. This last property, called 'barge-in', strengthens the fluency, naturalness and speed of the dialogue by shortening turns when a mistake is done or when the system faces an expert user who knows what the system is going to say, just listening to the beginning of the message. Taking into account all this factors, the flowchart of the dialogue was designed in order to improve naturalness, as can be seen in Figure 2.

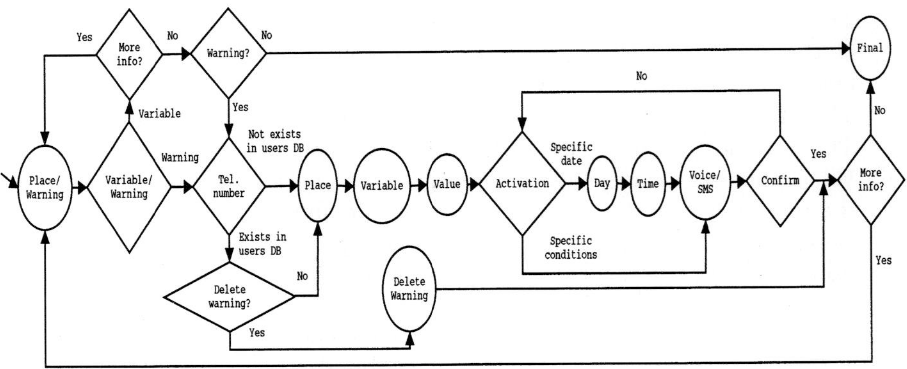


**Fig. 2.** Dialogue flow

### 4.2 Confirmation Policy

Every utterance got from the user must be confirmed in order to be sure that the system successfully understood what the user was saying. This is done by means of two different confirmation policies: explicit and implicit. Explicit confirmations are used to confirm either critical information or a big set of data by means of a direct question to the user, asking him/her whether the last information acquired was correct or not. Implicit confirmations can be used to confirm every data got from the user, the data appear by means of a short sentence at the beginning of the next question and thus without penalizing the fluency of the dialogue with an extra question. In this work we mixed both policies, using implicit confirmations as a general rule, while explicit confirmations were used to confirm critical information or the final step of a whole process. Giving as a result not only an efficient and effective interface, but also a natural dialogue flow between the human and the system.

### 4.3 Amount of Data per Turn

The amount of data captured by the system in one turn is closely related, on the one hand, to the user's predisposition and naturalness in giving more than one data in the same turn, and on the other hand, to the complexity of the task associated with each turn. We kept the balance between both aspects by recognizing more than one data only in turns that did not involve a high complexity task, like the one of getting the temperatures between the user wants to be notified, but isolating hard tasks, such as the one that gets the municipality, in order to improve its recognition success.

### 4.4 Helping Features

The helping features have been focused on two points. Firstly, a set of Catalan key words/expressions, as can be seen in Table 1, has been defined in order to

**Table 1.** Catalan key words/expressions

| Key word or expression (Translated to English) | What the user needs | What the system does when detects the situation |
|---|---|---|
| "I need help", "Help"... | Help | Throws a helping message |
| "Could you repeat?", "Repeat"... | Repetition | Throws the last message |
| "I want to correct", "Correction"... | Correction | Asks for the last value given |
| "Bye", "Exit"... | Exit | Throws a farewell message and finishes the dialogue |

help the user to interact with the system. This key words can be accessed by saying the exact word or just an expression containing a key word (e.g. "Help", "Help me, please", "I need some help"). Secondly, an automatically adaptable helping message policy has been set up. During the preliminary evaluation of the system, we detected that the users missed more messages telling them what they could do in every moment. However, repeating in each turn helping information involves penalizing the fluency of the dialogue because we could substantially increase the time spent in most dialogues. So we decided to take an intermediate solution. At the beginning, the system provides an initial message where welcomes the user, introduces itself and notices the user about the key words/expressions and its use: *"Welcome to the Catalan government meteorological warning and information system. You can always say help, correction, repetition or exit"*. During the dialogue, an automatically adaptable help service only provides help when the system detects the user did not understand something or has problems to continue with the dialogue. This help service is activated when one of the following three different situations is detected: the user keeps quiet, the user says something that is not understood by the system, or the user explicitly asks for help.

### 4.5 Language Generation

The language generation has been done using templates that are dynamically filled with the adequate data to originate the final messages reproduced to the user. An example of template is "In the meteorological station of [place] the [variable] at [hour] is [value] [measure]" which, once filled, can result for instance in *"In the meteorological station of Blanes the temperature at 8:30 is 20 degrees"*.

However, in order to introduce variability and more naturalness in the system's answer, the history of the dialogue and a set of different templates with the same meaning is kept. So in each turn of the dialogue the system gives its answers using different templates for the same kind of information. In addition, the system is ready to include a complete text generation module [13] designed for aTTemps, and based on linguistic components.

### 4.6 Implementation

Structurally the dialogue has been built by means of a set of VoiceXML dialogue documents, stored in a web server, that contained each one a differentiated part of the dialogue. For example, the initial document gives the welcome message, gets the first utterances from the user and invokes the document containing the part of the dialogue that fits the user needs.

As we stated before, we decided to make the development of the dialogue manager as independent as possible from the managing of the speech technology in order to clarify the dialogue manager, and also to build a dialogue independent platform that can be easily reused by dialogue managers for other domains than the meteorological one. So we built a framework for dialogue managers and the dialogue manager itself based on the VoiceXML language, enabling telephony applications to be developed in an open-standards based environment.

## 5 The Speech Processing

The recognition of the user utterance is based on non-stochastic grammars. These grammars have been developed following the Augmented Bacus-Naur Form (ABNF) that is used to specify languages, protocols and text formats. The ABNF grammar format uses special characters to define grammar expressions in a text string: such as '$' for non-terminal symbols, '[ ]' for optional values and '{ }' for return values. All grammars have been designed in order to give the user as much flexibility as possible.

Ibervox[11] has been used as the text to speech and speech recognition engine in Catalan for this system. The recognition system uses non-stochastic grammars and filling words. A confidence recognition measure is provided when the recognition has been done.

## 6 Evaluation

Two evaluations were done while developing the system in order to accomplish three general objectives: to assess the effectiveness of the user-machine communication, to evaluate the global performance of the system, and to identify the possible lacks of the system that may have kept unnoticed to the people involved in the project. These evaluations became a part of the development process that helped to improve the system having into account the user opinion.

Each evaluation consisted in giving user satisfaction surveys to the users, who answered filling a form on a web site. We decided to carry out an opinion poll letting two different groups of users interact with the system and polling them afterwards in order to determine which were the lacks of the system. The first group was made up of colleagues not involved directly in this work; and the second one, with general public. In the web site, the users were asked to specify the degree in which they agree (from 1 for "completely disagree" to 6 for "completely agree") with 14 statements about the system. The form was divided into two parts: a mandatory one, with 6 statements; and an optional one, with 8 more statements. These statements were oriented to determine whether the speech recognition and the text-to-speech component were working properly, the flow of the dialogue and the behaviour of the system were natural and predictable, the user knew in every moment the actions that he/she could take, the help provided was useful, the repair strategy was useful and easy, and which were the parts of the dialogue where the user had a higher difficulty to success. In this preliminary evaluation we obtained an average of 3.68 and 3.43 (over 6)for each evaluation group. These results are good enough taking into account that have been obtained while developing the system.

## 7 Conclusions and Future Work

We have described a working automatic information system that provides two different services: on one hand, to obtain information about real time and personalized meteorological data, and on the other hand, to manage a meteorological warning service. Both services are accessed through a natural language interface, in Catalan, and help is provided when needed.

The main advantages of the architecture of our system are: it separates the dialogue control, not only from the managing of the voice technology but also from the application logic, it provides a portable dialogue manager among different voice technologies, it provides an easily changeable interface, and it provides a portable voice framework among different domains application. All this occurs as a result of the VoiceXML standard based design and its architecture that clearly encapsulates every functional area in an independent component.

The performance of our system, already running, is acceptable but, of course there are some points that can be improved. Firstly, the grammars can be enriched to recognize a greater range of utterances from the user. Secondly, the system messages and the grammars can be translated to other languages in order to incorporate speech tools in other languages satisfying tourists needs. And finally, the text generation module[13] should be included to introduce more naturalness in the system answer.

### Acknowledgements

This work has been supported by the Catalan Secretary for the Information Society and by the Spanish Government (TIC2000-1735-C02-01). This project has been developed in collaboration with the Catalan Meteorological Service, Mensatec and ATLAS (Applied Technology on Language and Speech S.L.) companies, and the Phonetic Group of the Department of Filología Española at the Autonomous University of Barcelona. We would also like to thank J. Padrell for his advices, and A. Febrer and A. Abad for his help in the early steps of the project.

## References

1. TRINDI project: http://www.linglink.lu/le/projects/trindi.
2. Lamel, L., Rosset, S., Gauvain, J.L., Bennacef, S.: "The Limsi Arise System for Train Travel Information", in Proceedings of ICASSP'99(1999).
3. Allen, J.F., Miller, B.W., Ringger, E.K., Sikorski, T.: "A Robust System for Natural Spoken Dialogue", in Proceedings of ACL'96(1996).
4. Álvarez, J., Arranz, V., Castell, N., Civit, M.:"Linguistic and Logical Tools for an Advanced Interactive Speech System in Spanish", in Proceedings of IEA/AIE 2001, LNAI 2070, 2001.
5. Cohen, M., Rivlin, Z., Bratt, H.: "Speech Recognition in the ATIS Domain Using Multiple Knowledge Sources", in Proceedings of ICASSP'99(1999).
6. Zue, V., Seneff, S., Glass, J.R., Polifroni, J., Pao, C., Hazen, T.J., Hetherington, L.: "Jupiter: A Telephone-Based Conversational Interface for Weather Information", IEEE Transactions on Speech and Audio Processing, vol. 8, nō 1, pp. 85-96, 2000.
7. Servei Meteorològic Català http://smc.gencat.es.
8. Eberman, B., Carter, J., Meyer, D., Goddeau, D.: "Building VoiceXML Browsers with OpenVXI", 2002. http://www2002.org/CDROM/refereed/260/index.html
9. SpeechWorks, provider of over-the-telephone automated speech recognition solutions. http://www.speechworks.com.
10. Dialogic, supplier of computer telephony products. http://www.dialogic.com
11. Ibervox from Atlas-CTI. http://www.atlas-cti.com/es/ibervoxasr.htm
12. Villarejo Muñoz, L.: "Gestor de diálogo de un sistema de información meteorológica", in Spanish, Master Thesis in Informatics Engineering, FIB, 2002.
13. García Zorrilla, P. "Sistema d'accés en llenguatge natural a informació meteorològica", in Spanish, Master Thesis in Informatics Engineering, FIB, 2002.
14. J.Hernando, J. Padrell, A. Bonafonte, N. Castell, J.B. Mariño, C. Nadeu, J.A. R. Fonollosa, H. Rodríguez, A. Abad, L. Villarejo: "aTTemps: A Meteorological Information Service through the Telephone Network", Internal Report, UPC, 2002.

# Agent-Based Implementation on Intelligent Instruments

Richard Dapoigny, Eric Benoit, and Laurent Foulloy

Laboratoire d'Informatique, Systèmes, Traitement de l'Information et de la Connaissance,
University of Savoie, BP 806, 74016 ANNECY Cedex
{richard.dapoigny, eric.benoit, laurent.foulloy}@univ-savoie.fr
http://www.listic.univ-savoie.fr/

**Abstract.** The use of agent to infer actions from domain specific knowledge has proved to be a successful approach. In this paper, we implement an agent-based system extracting knowledge from ontology-based databases that are embedded in intelligent instruments. As the ontology produces static information on the environment, the emerging behavior results from dependence relations between this information and the functional role of each instrument. Agents are organized in two processing agents. The first of them allows dynamic inference on data meaning. In the second agent, knowledge analysis leads to establish dependence relationships between the basic components of the instruments (i.e., variables and services) and to fire remote modes and external services. In such a way, the local model of the intelligent instrument is dynamically extended with capabilities of any other instrument.

## 1 Introduction

Both technological advances in the areas of industrial networks and micro-controller capabilities encourage the design of systems composed of smart components which are either sensing their environment or acting upon it [1][2]. Their fundamental property is the inclusion of an active processing element which encapsulates a number of functionalities, known as external services, and that are accessible through a network interface via perceptual channels. With their ability to spontaneously interact with each other, the intelligent instruments enable a modular system architecture in which smart autonomous components co-operate to control physical processes. The instrument modeling achieve a predictable behavior even in the case of missing resources. Therefore, to exploit the full advantages of this system model, a higher level view is required, with the notion of operating modes [3]. As reported in previous work [4], industrial entities are good candidates for agenthood. The present work proposes an implementation of an agent model for cooperative Intelligent Instruments. Each instrument has its own user-defined data set, and a first challenge is to automatically identify and associate variables that represent the same entity. This task is achieved with an information agent. Based on dynamic knowledge extracted from other instruments, other agents are responsible to establish dependence relationships between the basic components of the instruments (i.e., variables and services) and to fire automatically remote modes and external services. In addition, the agent implementation must satisfy low-cost and low-memory constraints. Above these assumptions, agents interoperate with other agents and information databases

P.W.H. Chung, C.J. Hinde, M. Ali (Eds.): IEA/AIE 2003, LNAI 2718, pp. 505–515, 2003.

whereas the reactive aspect relies on triggering by events. In section 2, we describe the knowledge representation in the intelligent instruments modeling. Section 3 describes a new architecture of agents for modeling and designing Industrial Measurement and control System. Section 4 gives the impact of the agent behavior on an example. Conclusion and future works follow in section 5 and 6.

# 2 Knowledge Representation in Intelligent Instruments

## 2.1 Basic Modeling

Intelligent instruments are based on the service concept [5]. It represents either the instrument functionalities from the user point of view, or a simple goal from a DAI framework. At a lower level, each instrument service is defined as a set of internal services [6] where a causal dependence is achieved with events. In each service, the internal services are linked through an ordered graph that behave like a plan in the DAI framework. Services are organized into subsets called USOM (USer Operating Modes) in which a given service can be started iff the current active mode includes this service. This property prevents requiring services when they cannot be available.

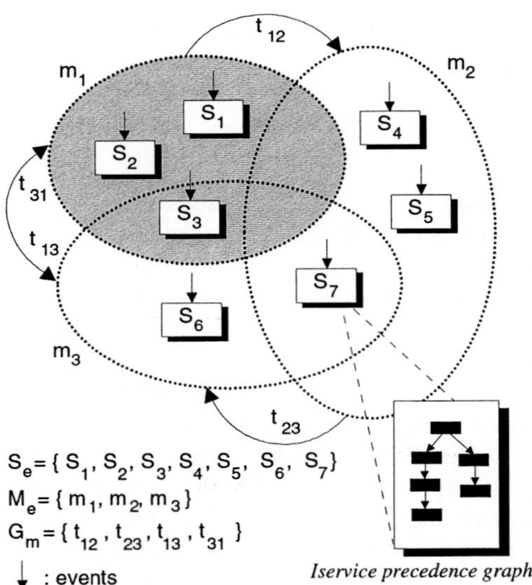


**Fig. 1.** The external USOM viewpoint

The dynamic behavior is achieved with external events, and as a consequence, if an external service and an external event are related, then the occurrence of the event activates this service. Therefore, in the service based approach, an instrument can be externally defined by the tuple $<S_e, E, M_e, G_m>$, where $S_e$ represents the set of external services, *E*, the set of events, $M_e$, the set of external modes and $G_m$, the transition graph between USOM. Classical examples of external modes are *configuration* and *measurement* modes. Note that either external instruments or user can only operate on elements of that tuple (not on internal elements). Figure 1 describes an overview of the basic Intelligent Instrument modeling. In the iservice precedence graph, the events are responsible of the selection process that decides which portion of the path to use. While events are all of the same type, different entities can manipulate them. For example, services are fired on events originated by users (or agents) while internal services are fired on events occurring when internal services end or when any variable is received.

## 2.2 The System Ontology

The basic modeling is limited, due to a complex state-transition graph in the case of n instruments interacting through a network[1]. As there is no corresponding terminology between instruments, some incoherence may arise in the distributed knowledge. To solve these problems, a formalization of knowledge via ontologies is proposed. It serves as a basis for a multi-agent implementation in which agents extract only relevant knowledge from other instruments. With this property, both the network bandwidth usage and response-time are minimized. In the run-time process, agents operate on explicit knowledge about potential services. The possibility of modifying the knowledge during run-time is implemented in two levels, a data level where agents try to establish data associations based on each data semantic content, and a functional level where agents must be able to fire remote services using dependence relations between services. Both external and internal services exchange and act upon variables. Thus, the agent model will be centered on the variable conceptualization while the agent mechanism relies on variable association that is related both to identity and dependence concepts. Therefore, any variable describing a part of a physical process is related both to extensional and intensional part of information. The intensional part expresses the physical quantity as detailed in Physical Ontologies [7], while the extensional part is derived from top-level ontologies such as Mereology and Topology [7], [8]. Engineering knowledge is organized in an ontology that represents in an explicit way physical and structural aspects of the physical system in interaction with the instruments. The System ontology results from a Mereo-Topology centered both on concepts of physical quantity and System individual. The mereology of system components[2] describes the physical system structure, via a *part_of* decomposition into smaller components. The topological relationship allows components to be linked together via connections. that indicate the path for physical interactions between components. The physical information is derived from standard ontology [9] with definitions such as physical quantity and physical dimension Explicit assumptions about the system decomposition are made and then, their correctness are verified. As a result, a machine understandable database is produced at compile-time in the form of a tree-like structure [10].

[1]In this case, the global graph is the product of n individual graphs

[2] examples are step motor, stator, rotor, axis, sample holder

# 3 Agent Implementation

In the measurement/control context, each instrument is responsible of producing some measurement variable or consuming variables that are issued from other instruments. Therefore, we define three instrument types, a sensor type, an actuator type and a calculator type. The sensor type can produce a measurement variable representing a physical quantity $p_1$ and can eventually consume an external one representing the physical quantity $p_2$ if the measurement of $p_1$ prior requires the measurement of $p_2$. The actuator type consumes one or more external variables and the calculator type both consumes and produces variables. The calculator type is an essential resource due to an insufficient memory space in the instruments[3]. The framework that is presented here, concerns the instrument modeling part associated to agent paradigm. It is important to point out that the global representation of the physical environment is built in order to provide an initial local representation of the physical environment for each instrument. This is a part of the agent work to supplement that representation with dynamic knowledge according to the instrument environment evolution.

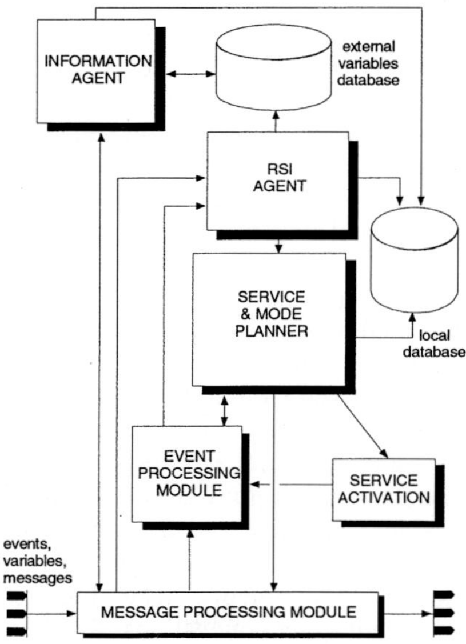


**Fig. 2.** Agent functional model

The proposed model (see figure 2) can be divided in two active parts, a low level agent or information agent that is responsible of external variable processing and a high level agent or RSI agent[4] which is concerned with conditional remote service activation under certain conditions. These process agents require a service model with service specifications such as trigger/stop events, service description, planning (scheduling and exception handling) and execution including monitoring, initiation and stopping of events. The following subsections will develop these aspects.

[3] i.e., intensive computing like fuzzy analysis

[4] Remote Service Invocation

### 3.1 The Information Agent

Each instrument can handle exported and imported variables. The variables we are dealing with are attached to a physical process. In that framework, two ore more instruments can read the same variable, but only one instrument is able to produce a given variable. Let *V(k)*, the set of all variables that belong to instrument *k*. Then, let $V_e$(k) and $V_i$(k) be the respective sets of exported and imported variables. Thus, if we call $V_d$(k), the dynamic external knowledge in instrument *k*, we assume that :

$$V_d(k) = \bigcup_{i \neq k} V_e(i) \quad \textbf{(1)}$$

The information agent is designed to support the instrument on finding data in the distributed system and it must know where to look for this data. The information agent is concerned with two tasks as detailed on figure 3. Each instrument starts the first task at the beginning of its life cycle while the second task performs identification of variables during process execution. Concerning the first task, each information agent acts in two steps in order to achieve dynamic knowledge of external variables. First, each time a new instrument comes in line, its information agent sends a request TYPE_VAR_BROADCAST that broadcasts the new database to other agents. In a second step, each concerned agent replies (TYPE_ACK_BROADCAST) with its own database[5] thus the local database is updated with all the external variables from other instruments. This simple process ensures that each instrument is dynamically aware of all external variables on the network.

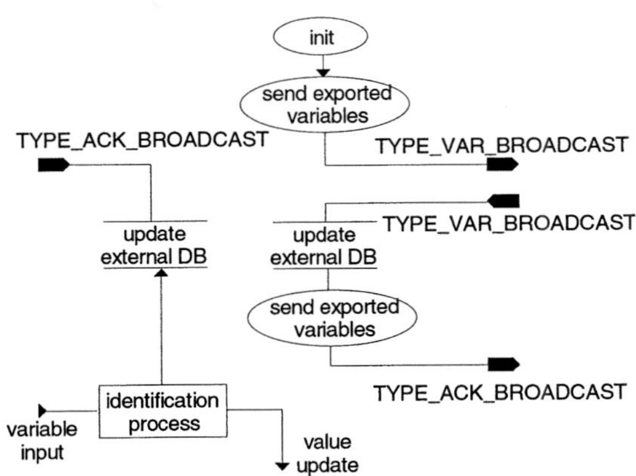


**Fig. 3.** The information agent functional diagram

The second task of the information agent is the identification process that uses field comparisons between local variables database and external database. This process leads to the following consequence. A local variable and a remote external one are said to be conceptually identical iff their physical quantities or their role (intensional part) and their individual features (extensional part) are identical. Each incoming variable is dynamically linked to a remote one via the external database. This mechanism is kept necessary because each external variable is described with a local

[5] if it has no exported variables, it sends a default acknowledge

number on a given instrument. For example, if the variable labeled *x*, with number 2 on instrument 1 is the same as variable *Distance* with number 1 on instrument 4 they must be linked in the database of each instrument. In such a way, the variable naming process is independent from the identification process. The low-level agent achieves dynamic knowledge discovery, and the designer only needs to handle local variables for each instrument.

### 3.2 The RSI Agent

The RSI situated agent is automatically required when a new service begins. Its main objectives are to find dependency relations between variables, and if they exist, it sends a request to find the concerned instrument via the destination RSI agent. The latter sends an acknowledgement with the contextual information (i.e., the right mode, the service involved to consume or produce dependant variables and the relevant iservice to start). Then, the contextual information is added to the dependency table for later service invocation. With these information, the RSI agent tries to switch the concerned instrument in the available mode, and if it successes, it selects the right iservice based on decision rules and then, it starts it. According to the results obtained, an acknowledgement is sent. Based on local knowledge, the RSI agent uses semantic information to send a request to other agents. Obviously, each agent behaves either like a server or like a client.

**Knowledge Formalization.** The knowledge representation model relies on the notion of variable and its attributes. It is also based on the assumption that services are mapped onto the System ontology and as a service produces or consumes variables, these variables are conceptually both associated to the connections (i.e. energy path) between system individuals and the system individuals themselves. Any exchanged variable will be represented as a pair :

$$v = <a, c> \tag{2}$$

where $a$ denotes a set of variable attributes and $c$, the concept represented by the variable. The set of attributes used in this model is defined as the tuple :

$$a = < label, type, value > \tag{3}$$

and the concept, by the pair :

$$c = < p, s > \tag{4}$$

where $p$ denotes the physical quantity, i.e. the intensional part of the concept, and $s$ the system individual (i.e., the extensional part) resulting from the System ontology. As already stated, two variables issued from any instrument related to the same environment are identical iff they have the same intensional part and the same extensional part.

$$\forall\ v_1(k), v_2(j), (p_1=p_2) \wedge (s_1=s_2) \Rightarrow v_1(k)= v_2(j) \tag{5}$$

A dependency table issued from the ontological analysis at compile-time defines for each instrument $k$, a set of connectors, each of them being represented by the tuple :

$$X_i(k) = < s_i^s, s_i^d, p_i > \tag{6}$$

where $s_i^s$ and $s_i^d$ are respectively associated with the system individuals source and destination, and $p_i$, the physical quantity exchanged between this source and this destination. In other words, these connectors denote the energy path between individual system parts of the physical environment. As the pair $<s, p>$ is assumed to be unique, there are no situations where two actuators produce the same pair. Using an inferential process, it is possible when facing an application, to determine whether a measurement service producing a variable $v_1$ on a given instrument, requires or not some other service on another instrument producing or consuming a variable $v_2$ dependent on $v_1$. For this, the RSI agent must request for the target agent of a remote instrument that has either an input variable or an output variable using the pair $<s^s, p>$ extracted from the dependency table. We define an instrument with the pair :

$$I = <n, type>,$$

Where $n$ is the instrument identifier and *type*, the target instrument type that can be an actuator (0), a sensor (1) or a calculator (2). Assuming that the current instrument is related to the system individual $s^0$, the agent try to find in the dependency table if it exists a pair having $s^0$ as destination individual.

$$\exists X_i / (s_i^d = s^0) \rightarrow c_i = <s_i^s, p_i> \quad \textbf{(7)}$$

For an actuator, the inferential process is expressed by :

$$\exists j, j \neq k \rightarrow (v_{imp}(j) = <a, s_i^s, p_i>) \wedge (I = <j, 0>) \quad \textbf{(8)}$$

And for a sensor-type instrument :

$$\exists j, j \neq k \rightarrow (v_{exp}(j) = <a, s_i^s, p_i>) \wedge (I = <j, 1>) \quad \textbf{(9)}$$

One or more instruments may satisfy the above rules. In the last case, the actuator will be given a higher priority. After this step, the remote service is identified, but this information is not sufficient. As previously stated (see section 2), a given iservice can be available in several services. Therefore, additional information is required to solve that decision process, i.e. which service and which event must be active. That information is precisely related to the constraints. Most often, constraints are expressed either as limits on physical quantities, or as a graph that represents all the available transitions between different functional modes [11]. As constraints relative to the instrument functional modes are taken into account by the switching mode mechanism, we limit the model to the case where service constraints affect only the physical quantity attached to the variables produced or consumed by that service. Basically, a given service on instrument $k$ can be seen as the following pair :

$$S(k) = <g, c_t> \quad \textbf{(10)}$$

Where $g$ is associated to the elementary goal of the service and $c_t$ represents the constraint attached to the activation of that service that can be expressed by the tuple :

$$c_t = <type/role, expression, ievent> \quad \textbf{(11)}$$

The first field describes either a physical quantity (a maximum distance, a limit workload ...) or a property concerning variables (for example, the precision of a measure), the expression represents the evaluation of any mathematical expression or a symbolic value, the ievent fields is related to the corresponding value. Thus, when remote information (instrument, mode and service) is extracted from another instrument, the local instrument examines the constraints attached to each possible remote service and compares it to the current service constraint. If their fields type/role and expression coincide, then that service is selected with the correct imode and ievent.

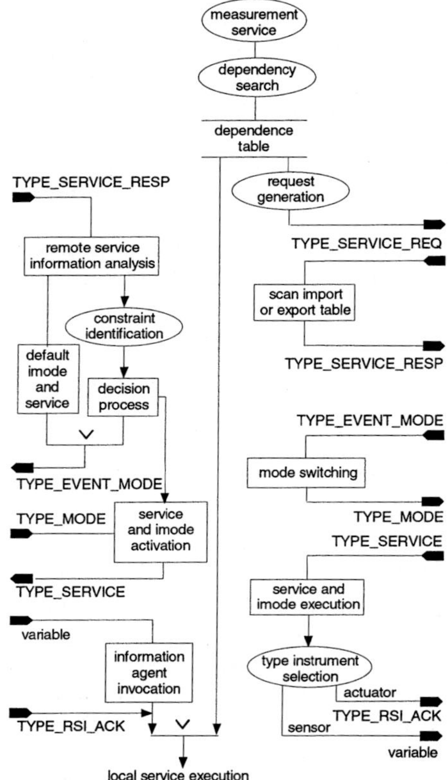


**Fig. 4.** The RSI agent functional diagram

## Implementation

Such as the classical model used in most agent architectures [12], the agent-based USOM model relies on goals, plans and knowledge base modules, with the following equivalences in the instrument modeling. Any service corresponds to an elementary goal, a single iservice sequence can be associated to a plan and the imodes express all the possible plans for a given instrument. Knowledge bases are relative to variables, services, iservices and their attributes. On the programming level, an event-based interaction model has been adopted (see figure 4). Agents inter-operate asynchronously with other agents through a well-defined message passing mechanism (messages input and output are on both sides on figure 4). Messages are divided in three types, messages, events and variables. Communication channels between certain actuators and specialized sensors are able to capture actuator effects on the environment. In that case, an actuator variable is related to a sensor whose measurement operation depends on the actuator activation. This fact is related to the basic hypothesis of the model, i.e., there must exist an energy path relating the different instruments through the physical environment. The starting point of the RSI agent is any measurement service activation in a given instrument. If there are no dependencies, the local service is achieved, but in case of dependencies, the actions described on figure 4 are performed. We can see that, if the service invocation concerns a variable production (the requester and the destination are both sensors), then the information agent is required during the variable reception. The RSI agent presents many benefits. First, no functional description of other instruments is needed, from the instrument viewpoint. It solves the perceptual aliasing problem [13], in the sense of the RSI agent can discriminate between two situations where the sensor information is not sufficient. It enhances autonomy of the whole measurement system by establishing dynamic relationship between services on different instruments. Finally, it enables data fusion among different agents operating in the same environment.

# 4 Application Example

In a simple example, two intelligent instruments are communicating through a CAN network. to supply automatic color analysis of samples. The physical system consists of two parts, one describing the step-motor, and another one, the sample holder.

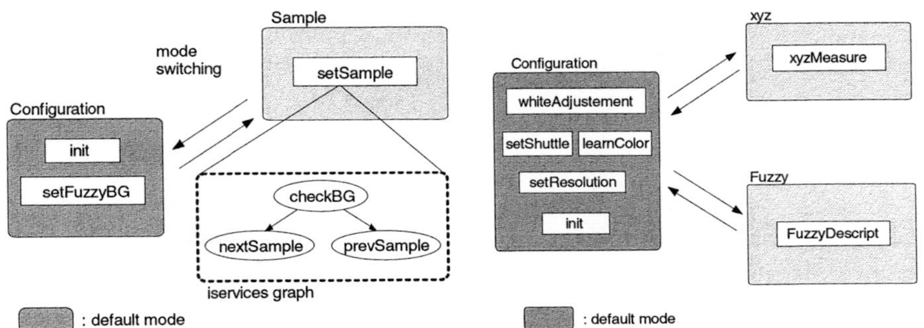


**Fig. 7**. Step motor and spectrometer external services.

The spectrometer instrument can perform a conventional measurement of xyz chromaticity coordinates or a fuzzy description of the color. When the user activates the *Sample* mode, a new value of *sampleNumber* initiates the *fuzzydescript* service via the RSI agents cooperation. On the step_motor, the RSI agent takes benefits of the dependence table : $X_2$ = < "sample_holder", "step_motor", color >. The pair < "step_motor", "color" > extracts the service *fuzzyDescript* on the spectrometer. As there are no constraints for this service, the RSI agent of the step_motor switches the mode to Fuzzy on the spectrometer, and then initiates the *fuzzyDescript* service. The *fuzzyDescript* mode invocation, starts first the RSI agent that finds in the spectrometer dependence table : $X_2$ = < "step_motor", "sample_holder", number >. Then looking for the pair < "sample_holder", number >, it extracts the *setSample* service on the step_motor instrument database. Constraint on the color property selects the right iservice in the *setSample* service and the next sample moves in front of the spectrometer. Finally, the end of the *setSample* service synchronizes the measurement in *fuzzyDescript*.

## 5 Related Works

In [14], the authors have developed an agent-based supervision system involving smart instruments, but the major burden is shifted on personal computers, the micro-controllers only dealing with quick reactive decisions. Our system performs decentralized intelligence at the instrument level. One of the most important difficulties of this work was to both satisfy the low-memory constraint and to maximize the instrument capabilities such as autonomy, database size, representation of the environment and service potentialities. Other agent-based applications structures in the area of industrial measurement systems derive from the function-block standard model [15]. The IEC-1499 Function Block specifications uses an explicit event driven model and provides for both data-flow and finite-state automata-based control. This emerging standard has been extended to agent-based control in manufacturing process [16]. In a few words, that model describes an application through a network in which nodes are basic or composite Function Blocks, arcs represent data and connections are events. Execution of the operations specified in the algorithm part of the Function Block, is triggered by events. This model is essentially suited for purely reactive applications and there are no functions that implement semantic knowledge about the environment. This last point is the major contribution of this work that gives full intelligent behavior based on ontological tools.

## 6 Conclusion

In this paper, we have addressed the problem of dynamic access to external services in the context of Intelligent Instruments without global control. Unlike the Intelligent Manufacturing Systems, where methods are based on control code updating whenever there are changes in control relationship, this method is based on dynamic access to external resources (variables, services) through ontologic description of physical relationship between the physical components attached to each instrument. The agent implementation on intelligent instruments derive intelligent behavior from concept attributes and relations between them, allow integration of symbolic measurement techniques, support modularity and transparence of service access and supply reconfigurability of exported variable database within a given environment. In addition, it maximizes the ratio engineering knowledge/network communications. The major limitation to this work comes from hardware constraints due to micro-controllers limited capabilities. Moreover, the distributed intelligent agent-based approach provides a viable alternative to other functional models. The current work marries solutions issued from three distinct domains, automation, measurement science and distributed artificial intelligence. The system is also coherent due to conceptual choice for variable attributes and the initial checking choice for ontological commitments. Further work will attempt to deal with temporal aspects that have some impact on information availability.

## References

[1] Object Management Group, Smart Transducer Interface, OMG Document, orbos/2000-12-13, Dec. 2000

[2] H. Kopetz, M. Holzmann, W. Elmenreich, A Universal Smart Transducer Interface : TTP/A, Int. Journal of Computer System Science & Engineering, 16 (2), March 2001

[3] M. Staroswiecki, M. Bayart, Models and languages for the interoperability of smart Instruments, Automatica, 1996, 32 (6), 859-873

[4] S. Bussmann, N.R. Jennings & M. Wooldridge, On the identification of Agents in the design of Production Control systems, AOSE, 2000, 141-162

[5] E. Benoit, L. Foulloy, J. Tailland, InOMs model : a service-based approach to intelligent instrument design, 5th World Conf. On Systemics, Cybernetics and Informatics, 22-25 july 2001, Orlando (Fa)

[6] E. Benoit, L. Foulloy, J. Tailland, Automatic Smart sensors Generation based on InOMs, Proc. of the 16th IMEKO World Congress, Vienna (AU), 25-28 sept. 200, 9, 335-340

[7] W.N. Borst, J.M. Akkermans, A. Pos & J.L. Top, The PhysSys Ontology for physical systems, 9th Int. Workshop on Qualitative Reasoning, 16-19 May 1995, 11-21

[8] P. Salustri, "Function Modelling for an Integrated Framework : A progress Report", Procs. of FLAIRS'98, D. Cook, Eds., 1998, AAAI, pp 339-343

[9] T.R. Gruber, G.R. Olsen, An ontology for Engineering Mathematics, 4th Int. Conf. on Principles of Knowledge Representation and Reasoning, Bonn, 1994

[10] R. Dapoigny, E. Benoit, L. Foulloy, Ontology Implementation for Knowledge Representation in Intelligent Instruments, Proc. of the 2th IEEE Int. Symp. on Signal Processing and Information Technology (dec. 2002), 17-21

[11] A. Bouras, M. Staroswiecki, How can Intelligent Instruments interoperate in an Application Framework? A mechanism for taking into account operating constraints, IFAC SICICA'97, Annecy (France), June 1997, 465-472

[12] D. Kinny, M. Georgeff and A. Rao, A Methodology and Modeling techniques for Systems of BDI Agents, in W. Van de Velde & J.W. Perram Eds., Springer Verlag, Procs. Of the 7th European Workshop on Modeling Autonomous Agents in a MultiAgent World, Berlin 1996, (1038), 56-71

[13] S.D. Whitehead and D.H. Ballard, Learning to perceive and act by trial and error, Machine Learning, 1991, (7), 45-83

[14] N. Flix & Al., Generic control/command distributed system : Application to the supervision of moving stage sets in theaters, European Journal of Control, (8), 1, 2002

[15] IEC TC, Function Blocks for Industrial Process Measurement and Control Systems, Part. 1 : Architecture, 1998, IEC-TC65/WG6 Committee Draft

[16] B. Zhou, L. Wang and D.H. Norrie, Design of distributed Real-time Control Agents for Intelligent Manufacturing Systems, 2nd Int. Workshop on Intelligent Manufacturing Systems, Sept. 1999, Leuven (BE), 237-244

# Granules and Reasoning Based on Granular Computing

Qing Liu

Department of Computer Science, Nanchang University, Nanchang 330029

**Abstract.** This paper discusses the granules and granular computing. The granule of decision rules is defined. The inclusion and closeness degree between granules are also defined. A new reasoning model is proposed. The reasoning model may be used in reasoning of expert systems. Granule is thought as a pair $(\varphi, d(\varphi))$, it is the both logic and set theory. Where $\varphi$ may be a formula in rough logic or in classical logic or in any non-standard logic, $d(\varphi)$ is the interpretation domain of formula $\varphi$, The pair $(\varphi, d(\varphi))$ is called an elementary granule. Finally, the validity and feasibility of the reasoning model are illustrated with real examples. Related theorems and its proofs are discussed.

**Keywords:** Elementary Granule, Granular Computing,Reasoning Model, Inclusion and Closeness.

## 1 Introduction

Reasoning methods are usually classified three classes: deductive, inductive and common sense reasoning. Deductive methods are generally based on axioms and deductive rules, which is used in classical logic or in approximate reasoning of non-standard logic, being a reasoning based on axiomatization or hypothesis precondition. The logicians and the most of natural scientists are interesting in the reasoning; Inductive reasoning relies on data and inductive rules, which is used in natural science, being a reasoning based on statistics and experience of experts or experimental data; whereas common sense reasoning depends on common knowledge and common sense evident inference from the knowledge, which is used in human science, this is a reasoning to meet almost everywhere people's debates in every day life.

In this paper, a granular reasoning model is proposed, which is a reasoning of searching goal based on granular computing in artificial intelligence. Moreover, we discuss also the resolution reasoning, and global theory is collapsed into local and local theories are amalgamated into global for solving-problem. Although the collapsing and amalgamating reasoning is only primary or ordinary, but providing a generalized ways for solving-problem in artificial intelligence.

## 2 Operation Rules of Granules

Let $\varphi \to \psi$ be a decision rule on $DT = (U, A, C, D)$, where $U$ is a nonempty finite set of objects, $A$ is nonempty finite set of attributes, which is divided into

P.W.H. Chung, C.J. Hinde, M. Ali (Eds.): IEA/AIE 2003, LNAI 2718, pp. 516–526, 2003.

condition attribute set $C$ and decision attribute set $D$, and $C \cap D = \emptyset$. $\varphi$ and $\psi$ are the formulas in rough logic defined on $DT$. $\varphi$ is called a condition and $\psi$ is called a decision. The decision rule is denoted by $(\varphi, \psi)$. The granulation is written by $(((\varphi, d(\varphi)), (\psi, d(\psi)))$[1,2,3,4,5,6]. For example, in decision table 1 of neighborhood values, $DT = (\{1,2,3,4,5,6\}, \{a,b,c\} \cup \{d\})$, where $n(i)$ is a neighborhood value of attributes with respect to object on $N$[5]. Thus, the granulation corresponding to $a_{n(5)} \wedge b_{n(4)} \rightarrow d_{n(1)}$ is $((a_{n(5)} \wedge b_{n(4)}, \{1\}), (d_{n(1)}, \{1,4,6\}))$, where $\varphi$ is $a_{n(5)} \wedge b_{n(4)}$, $\psi$ is $d_{n(1)}$.

**Decision Table 1.** $DT = (U, A \cup \{d\})$

| N \ A | a | b | c | d |
|---|---|---|---|---|
| 1 | n(5) | n(4) | n(0) | n(1) |
| 2 | n(3) | n(4) | n(0) | n(0) |
| 3 | n(3) | n(4) | n(0) | n(2) |
| 4 | n(0) | n(2) | n(0) | n(1) |
| 5 | n(3) | n(2) | n(1) | n(2) |
| 6 | n(5) | n(2) | n(0) | n(1) |

Let $IS = (U, A)$ be an information system, $(a, v)$ or $a_v$ is a descriptor defined on $IS$[2,3,5,8]. $(a_v, d(a_v))$ is defined a $G - atom$[5,8], which is also called as an elementary granule on $IS$, where $G$ is an abbreviation of granular; $(\varphi, d(\varphi))$ denotes a logical combination of form $(a_v, d(a_v))$. If $\varphi$ is false then the granule $(\varphi, d(\varphi))$ is thought false on $IS$, namely $d(\varphi) = \emptyset$; while $d(\varphi) = U$, $\varphi$ is thought true in $IS$, the granule $(\varphi, d(\varphi))$ is also true on $IS$; By $\emptyset \subseteq (\varphi) \subseteq U$, $\varphi$ is thought satisfiable on $IS$, namely $(\varphi, d(\varphi))$ is thought satisfiable on $IS$.

For any $\varphi \in RL_{IS}$ where $RL_{IS}$ is an abbreviation symbol of Rough Logic defined on $IS$, and the granules of lower and upper approximations of formula $\varphi$ with respect to subset $B \subseteq A$ is $(B_*\varphi,\ B_*(d(\varphi)))$ and $(B^*\varphi,\ B^*(d(\varphi)))$ respectively, which are also an elementary granule. Thus, each rough logical formula $\varphi \in RL_{IS}$ can be transformed into an elementary granule, and interpretation domains corresponding to them can be computed by union, intersection and complement. The following lists the granular computing corresponding with rough logical formula $\varphi \in RL_{IS}$[5,6,7,8].

**Definition 1.** Let $\forall \varphi,\ \psi \in RL_{IS}$, The logical operations of them with respect to $\sim$, $\vee$ and $\wedge$ equal to the operations of interpretation domains in granules $(\varphi, d(\varphi))$ and $(\psi, d(\psi))$ with respect to $-$, $\cup$ and $\cap$ respectively.

(1) $\models_{IS} \sim \varphi$ iff $\models_{IS} (U - d(\varphi))) \neq \emptyset$;
(2) $\models_{IS} \varphi \vee \psi$ iff $\models_{IS} d(\varphi) \cup d(\psi) \neq \emptyset$;
(3) $\models_{IS} \varphi \cap \psi$ iff $\models_{IS} d(\varphi) \cap d(\psi) \neq \emptyset$.

We note that an information granule is a binary pair consisting of a logical formula $\varphi$ and its interpretation domain $d(\varphi)$, written by $(S(\varphi), d(\varphi))$ formally, where $S(\varphi)$ is called granular syntax of $\varphi$, $d(\varphi)$ is called granular semantics set of $\varphi$, or to call interpretation domain of $\varphi$; For example, an elementary conjunction of $\varphi$ on $IS$ is denoted by $CNF_B(x)$, where $x \in U$, $B \subseteq A$ is a subset of attribute set $A$. If let $B = \{a, b\}$, $\varphi = CNF_B(x) = a_1 \wedge b_1$, then the elementary granule of $\varphi$ is denoted by $(\varphi, d(\varphi)) = (a_1 \wedge b_1, d(a_1 \wedge b_1)) = (a_1 \wedge b_1, d(a_1) \cap d(b_1))$.

**Definition 2.** Let $G = (\varphi, d(\varphi))$ and $G' = (\varphi', d(\varphi'))$ be two G-formulas, the operations of them with respect to connectives $\sim$ (*negative*), $\oplus$(*or*), $\otimes$(*and*), $\odot$(*implicit*) and $\ominus$(*equivalent*) in the G-language[1] are defined as follows:

(1) $\sim (\varphi, d(\varphi)) = (\sim \varphi, U - d(\varphi))$;
(2) $(\varphi, d(\varphi)) \otimes (\varphi', d(\varphi')) = (\varphi \wedge \varphi', d(\varphi \cap d(\varphi'))$;
(3) $(\varphi, d(\varphi)) \oplus (\varphi', d(\varphi')) = (\varphi \oplus \varphi', d(\varphi) \cup d(\varphi'))$;
(4) $(\varphi, d(\varphi)) \odot (\varphi', d(\varphi')) = (\varphi \rightarrow \varphi', d(\varphi) \subseteq d(\varphi') \vee (d_*(\varphi) \subseteq d_*(\varphi') \wedge d^*(\varphi) \subseteq d^*(\varphi'))$;
(5) $(\varphi, d(\varphi)) \ominus (\varphi', d(\varphi')) = (\varphi \leftrightarrow \varphi', (d(\varphi) \subseteq d(\varphi') \wedge d(\varphi') \subseteq d(\varphi)) \vee ((d_*(\varphi) \subseteq d_*(\varphi') \wedge d_*(\varphi') \subseteq d_*(\varphi)) \wedge (d^*(\varphi) \subseteq d^*(\varphi') \wedge d^*(\varphi') \subseteq d^*(\varphi))))$.

We see that the calculus of granules in the language are the operations of pairs called granule. Because the binary pair is an entirety consisting of both syntax and semantics, hence the binary pair is both logic and set theory. So we can use both logical method and set theory method in approximate reasoning or other uncertainty reasoning. The reasoning will be used to searching reasoning in artificial intelligence and deductive reasoning in rough logic.

## 3 A Searching Reasoning in AI

After introducing granule and its computing in the above, we can do the approximate reasoning. Hence we define following concepts.

**Definition 3 (degree inclusion and closeness).** Let $G = (\varphi, d(\varphi))$ and $G' = (\varphi', d(\varphi'))$ be two Granules[2,3], the degree inclusion and closeness of them are defined as follows respectively:

(1) $G$ is included in $G'$ in degree at least $p$, denoted by $V_p(G, G')$, where $p \in [0, 1]$. Formally,

$$V_p(G, G') = \begin{cases} Card(G \otimes G')/Card(G) & for \quad G \neq \emptyset \\ 1 & for \quad Otherwise \end{cases}$$

where $\otimes$ is a symbol of granular operations. For given positive real number $p \in [0, 1]$, if $V(G, G') \geq p$, then the relation of $G$ included in $G'$ in degree at least $p$ is thought to be an extraction or a satisfaction;
(2) $G$ closes to $G'$ in degree at least $p$ , namely closeness relation $Cl_p(G, G')$ is denoted by $V_p(G, G') \wedge V_p(G', G)$. Formally, having $Cl_p(G, G')$ iff $V_p(G, G') \wedge V_p(G', G)$.

**Proposition 1.** $\vdash (\varphi \to \psi, d(\varphi \to \psi))$ is derivable iff $\vdash \varphi \to \psi$ is derivable and $d(\varphi) \subseteq d(\psi)$ is held

**Proposition 2.** $\forall \varphi, \psi \in RL_{IS}$, then

(1) $d(a_v) = \{x \in U : a(x) = v \in V\}$, where $V$ is the set of attribute values, $d$ is a symbol of interpretation domain function of common logical formulas;
(2) $(\sim \varphi, d(\sim \varphi) = U - (\varphi, d(\varphi))$;
(3) $(\varphi \vee \psi, d(\varphi \vee \psi)) = (\varphi, d(\varphi)) \oplus (\psi, d(\psi))$;
(4) $(\varphi \wedge \psi, d(\varphi \wedge \psi)) = (\varphi, d(\varphi)) \otimes (\psi, d(\psi))$;
(5) $((\forall x)\varphi(x), d(\varphi)) = (\varphi(e_1) \wedge \ldots \wedge \varphi(e_n), d(\varphi (e_1) \wedge \ldots \wedge \varphi(e_n))) = (\varphi(e_1), d(\varphi(e_1))) \otimes \ldots \otimes (\varphi(e_n), d(\varphi(e_n)))$.

Aassuming here that universe $U$ of all objects is finite. In the fact, $IS$ is finite. And for $\forall x \in VAR$, $u_r \in VAL$, there exists an entity $e_i \in U$, such that $u_r(x) = e_i$, $i = 1, \ldots, n$, where $u_r$ is an assigned symbol to object variable[5,6,7]. The formulas with connectives $\to$ and $\leftrightarrow$ can be substituted by $\sim$ and $\vee$ or $\wedge$.

**Proposition 3.** Let $G = ((\varphi, d(\varphi)), (\psi, d(\psi)))$ and $G' = ((\varphi', d(\varphi')), (\psi', d(\psi')))$ be two granulations. They are close in degree at least $p$ in $IS$, written by $Cl_p(G, G')$, then having

(1) $Cl_p(d(\varphi), d(\varphi'))$;
(2) $Cl_p(d(\psi) - d(\varphi), d(\psi') - d(\varphi'))$;
(3) $Cl_p(U - d(\varphi), U - d(\varphi'))$.

**Proposition 4.** If $G = ((\varphi, d(\varphi)), (\psi, d(\psi)))$ and $G' = ((\varphi', d(\varphi')), (\psi', d(\psi')))$ are the granulations defined by decision rules and $Cl_p((\varphi, d(\varphi)), (\varphi', d(\varphi'))$, then having $Cl_p((\psi, d(\psi)), (\psi', d(\psi')))$.

This proposition will be an important criterion for search reasoning in Artificial Intelligence. The search reasoning is finished in rule base of expert systems. The rule base of tradition is a set of rules form as $\varphi_1 \to \psi_1, \ldots, \varphi_i \to \psi_i, \ldots, \varphi_n \to \psi_n$. The granulations corresponding with them are the form $((\varphi_1, d(\varphi_1)), (\psi_1, d(\psi_1))), \ldots, ((\varphi_i, d(\varphi_i)), (\psi_i, d(\psi_i))), \ldots, ((\varphi_n, d(\varphi_n)), (\psi_n, d(\psi_n)))$ respectively. The set of the granulations is the granulation base of form $((\varphi_i, d(\varphi_i), (\psi_i, d(\psi_i)))$, where $i = 1, 2, \ldots, n$. Thus, the inference in rule base of tradition is transformed into a reasoning in granulation base. Namely, what to do is the matching between the granule $(\varphi,\ d(\varphi))$ of gathering in situation and condition granule $(\varphi_i,\ d(\varphi_i))$ of a granulation in granulation base. If $Cl_p((\varphi, d(\varphi)), (\varphi_i, d(\varphi_i)))$ is held then the decision $(\psi_i, d(\psi_i))$ of granulation $((\varphi_i, d(\varphi_i)), (\psi_i, d(\psi_i)))$ is chosen. Following is the procedure of inference:

(1) Gathering a group data to have contact with goal of searching;
(2) The group data is denoted by a rough logical formula $\varphi$, it is constructed as an elementary granule $(\varphi,\ d(\varphi))$ on $IS$;

(3) Computing the closeness degree $p_i$ between the granule and condition granule $(\varphi_i,\ d(\varphi_i))$ of each granulation $((\varphi_i,\ d(\varphi_i)),\ (\psi_i,\ d(\psi_i)))$ in granulation base, and if $p_i \geq p$, then $\{p_i\} \cup List$, where $p$ is a given threshold and $List$ is a table of storing closeness degree $p_i$. Until the end of matching with each granulation in the granulation base. That is,
For (i=1; eof (f); i++)
{$\mathrm{p}_i$=V(G, $\mathrm{G}_i$); $\mathrm{p}_i$'=V($\mathrm{G}_i$, G); $\mathrm{p}_i$"=min($\mathrm{p}_i$, $\mathrm{p}_i$');
if ($\mathrm{p}_i$" ≥ p) List={$\mathrm{p}_i$"} ∪ List;
}* f is a file of granulation base, p is a given threshold, List is a table of storing closeness degree of satisfying*\;
(4) $\mathrm{p}_i$=max$(\mathrm{List})_i$.

Therefore, the goal is the decision granule $((\psi_i,\ \mathrm{d}(\psi_i))$ of the granulation $((\varphi_i,\ \mathrm{d}(\varphi_i)),\ (\psi_i,\ \mathrm{d}(\psi_i)))$ corresponding to the closeness degree $\mathrm{p}_i$. If maximal $\mathrm{p}_i$ is one more, such as $\{p_{i_1}, \ldots, p_{i_j}, \ldots, p_{i_m}\}$, then $i_j = min\{i_1, \ldots, i_j, \ldots, i_m\}$, namely the decision part $(\psi_{i_j}, d(\psi_{i_j}))$ of the most former granulation $((\varphi_{i_j}, d(\varphi_{i_j})), (\psi_{i_j}, d(\psi_{i_j})))$ corresponding to the close degree $p_{i_j}$ is one of our needful goals.

## 4 Resolution Reasoning Based on Granular Computing

The Reasoning is called as G-resolution method, where $G$ is an abbreviation of granular. It is similar from the resolution of clauses in classical logic. Since the conjunction of two elementary granules of complement literals in granular theory is false or rough false, which equals to exactly to the intersection of interpretation domains of two complement literals to be empty or closing to empty with a rough degree.

**Definition 4.** Let $\forall\varphi \in RL_{IS}$, if there is not free individual variable in $(\varphi, d(\varphi))$, then the $(\varphi, d(\varphi))$ is called as a ground granule $(\varphi, d(\varphi))$.

**Theorem 1.** $(\varphi, d(\varphi))$ corresponding to any $\varphi \in RL_{IS}$ can be transformed equivalently into G-clause form $(C_1, d(C_1)) \otimes \ldots \otimes (C_n, d(C_n))$, where each $(C_i, d(C_i))$ is an elementary granule and a set of form $(a, d(a))$, $(a, B_*(a))$, $(a, B^*(a))$, or negation of them or union of them is also an elementary granule.

**Definition 5.** Let $C_1$ and $C_2$) be two G-clauses called granule, where $C_1$: $(C_1', d(C_1')) \oplus (a, d(a))$ and $C_2$: $(C_2', d(C_2')) \oplus (b, d(b))$ are ground G-clauses via joint valuation[5], then resolvent of $C_1$ and $C_2$, $GR(C_1, C_2)$ is defined as follows:

(1) If the ground G-atom $(a, d(a))$ occurring in $C_1$ and $(b, d(b))$ occurring in $C_2$ respectively is a complement literal pair[6,7,8], then resolvent of $C_1$ and $C_2$ , $GR(C_1, C_2)$:

$$\frac{\begin{array}{c} C_1 : (C_1', d(C_1')) \oplus (a, d(a)) \\ C_2 : (C_2', d(C_2')) \oplus (b, d(b)) \end{array}}{C : (C_1', d(C_1')) \oplus (C_2', d(C_2')).}$$

If $(a, d(a))$ or $(b, d(b))$ is not definable, but granules of the lower and upper approximations, $(B_*a, B_*(d(a)))$ and $(B^*a, B^*(d(a)))$ are definable, and one of granules of the lower and upper approximations is complement with other in the G-clauses, such as $(b, d(b))$ is the complement literal pair with $(B_*a, B_*(d(a)))$ or $(B^*a, B^*(d(a)))$, then resolvent of $C_1$ and $C_2$ , $GR(C_1, C_2)$:

$$\frac{\begin{array}{c} C_1 : (C'_1, d(C'_1)) \oplus (B_*a, B_*(d(a)) \\ C2 : \quad (C'_2, d(C'_2)) \oplus (b, d(b)) \end{array}}{C : (C'1, d(C'1)) \oplus (C'_2, d(C'_2)).}$$

Or

$$\frac{\begin{array}{c} C_1 : (C'_1, d(C'_1)) \oplus (B^*a, B^*(d(a)) \\ C_2 : \quad (C'_2, d(C'_2)) \oplus (b, d(b)) \end{array}}{C : (C'_1, d(C'_1)) \oplus (C'_2, d(C'_2)).}$$

**Table 2.** Information System

| N \\$A$ | a | b | c | d | e |
|---|---|---|---|---|---|
| 1 | 5 | 4 | 0 | 1 | 0 |
| 2 | 3 | 4 | 0 | 2 | 1 |
| 3 | 3 | 4 | 0 | 2 | 2 |
| 4 | 0 | 2 | 0 | 1 | 2 |
| 5 | 3 | 2 | 1 | 2 | 2 |
| 6 | 5 | 2 | 1 | 1 | 2 |

**For example,** Let $IS = (U, A)$ be an information system, as following table 2 shows. It can be constructed a system of granular language from the table by the way defined in [4, 6, 8, 9]. We extract a formula from $RL_{IS}$:

$$\varphi(a_5, b_2, b_4, c_0, \sim e_0) = (a_5 \vee b_4) \wedge b_2 \wedge (c_0 \vee \sim e_0) \tag{1}$$

(1) may be written by following $G - \varphi$:

$$G - \varphi(a_5, b_2, b_4, c_0, \sim e_0) =$$
$$((a_5, d(a_5)) \vee (b_4, d(b_4))) \wedge (b_2, d(b_2)) \wedge ((c_0, d(c_0)) \vee (\sim e_0, d(\sim e_0))) \tag{2}$$

By theorem 1, this is G-clause form, where each intersection item is a G-clause. By definition 2, the ground G-clause form of $G - \varphi$ follows as

$$G - \varphi(a_5, b_2, b_4, c_0, \sim e_0) = ((a_5, \{1, 6\}) \vee (b_4, \{1, 2, 3\})) \wedge (b_2, 4, 5, 6) \wedge$$
$$((c_0, 1, 2, 3, 4) \vee (\sim e_0, \{2, 3, 4, 5\})) \tag{3}$$

Where each item is a ground G-clause. Obviously, $(a_5,\{1, 6\})$ and $(\sim e_0,\{2,3,4,5\})$ is a complement ground literal pair[1,7]. So, the resolvent of $C_1$: $(a_5, \{1, 6\}) \vee$

$(b_4, \{1,2,3\})$ and $C_2$: $(c_0, \{1,2,3,4\}) \vee (\sim e_0, \{2,3,4,5\})$, $GR(C_1, C_2)$:

$$\begin{array}{rl} C_1: & (a_5,\{1,6\}) \vee (b_4,\{1,2,3\}) \\ C_2: & (c_0,\{1,2,3,4\}) \vee (\sim e_0,\{2,3,4,5\} \\ \hline C: & (b_4,\{1,2,3\}) \vee (c_0,\{1,2,3,4\}) \end{array}$$

Hence, (3) have

$$(b_4, \{1,2,3\}) \oplus (c_0, \{1,2,3,4\}) \otimes (b_2, \{4,5,6\}) \tag{4}$$

Suppose again that we extract a formula from $RL_{IS}$ as follows:

$$\varphi(a_0, a_3, a_5, b_2, c_0, e_2) = (\sim a_3 \vee e_2) \wedge (\sim a_0 \vee b_2) \wedge (a_5 \vee e_2) \wedge c_0 \tag{5}$$

The $G - \varphi$ corresponding to it as follows

$$\begin{aligned} & G - \varphi(a_0, a_3, a_5, b_2, c_0, e_2) = \\ & \quad ((\sim a_3, d(\sim a_3)) \oplus (e_2, d(e_2))) \otimes (((\sim a_0, d(\sim a_0)) \oplus \\ & \quad (b_2, d(b_2))) \otimes ((a_5, d(a_5)) \oplus (e_2, d(e-2))) \otimes (c_0, d(c_0)) \end{aligned} \tag{6}$$

First item $(e_2, d(e_2))$ in (6) is indefinable with respect to $B = \{a\}$, namely, $G-\varphi$ is not observable with respect to $B$ in $(e_2, d(e_2))$[4]. Hence, we will observe it in observable granules of lower and upper approximations, $(B_*e_2, B_*(d(e_2)))$ and $(B^*e_2, B^*(d(e_2)))$. Thus by (6) we have a ground G-clause form as follows:

$$\begin{aligned} & G - \varphi(a_0, a_3, a_5, b_2, c_0, B_*e_2, B_*e_2) = \\ & \quad ((\sim a_3, \{1,4,6\}) \oplus (B_*e_2, \{4\})) \otimes ((\sim a_3, \{1,4,6\}) \oplus (B^*e_2, \{2,3,4,5\})) \otimes \\ & \quad ((\sim a_0, \{1,2,3,5,6\}) \oplus (b_2, \{4,5,6\}) \otimes ((a_5, \{1,6\}) \oplus (e_2, \{3,4,5\})) \otimes \\ & \quad (c_0, \{1,2,3,4\}) \end{aligned} \tag{7}$$

There exists a complement ground G-literal pair in ground G-clause $C_1 : (\sim a_3, \{1,4,6\}) \oplus (B_*e_2, \{4\}))$ and $C_3 : (\sim a_0, \{1,2,3,5,6\}) \oplus (b_2, \{4,5,6\})$, so the resolvent of $C_1$ and $C_3$, $GR(C_1, C_3)$:

$$\begin{array}{rl} C_1: & (\sim a_3,\{1,4,6\}) \oplus (B_*e_2,\{4\})) \\ C_3: & (\sim_0,\{1,2,3,5,6\}) \oplus (b_2,\{4,5,6\}) \\ \hline C: & (\sim a_3,\{1,4,6\}) \oplus (b_2,\{4,5,6\}) \end{array}$$

To have $GR(C_1, C_3)$:

$$C : (\sim a_3, \{1,4,6\}) \oplus (b_2, \{4,5,6\}) \tag{8}$$

Similarly, there exists a complement ground literal pair in ground G-clauses $C_2 : (\sim a_3, \{1,4,6\}) \oplus (B^*e_2, \{2,3,4,5\})$ and $C_4 : (a_5, \{1,6\}) \oplus (e_2, \{3,4,5\})$, so the resolvent of $C_2$ and $C_4$ , $GR(C_2, C_4)$:

$$\begin{array}{rl} C_2: & (\sim a_3,\{1,4,6\}) \oplus (B^*e_2,\{2,3,4,5\}) \\ C_4: & (a_5,\{1,6\}) \oplus (e_2,\{3,4,5\}) \\ \hline C: & (\sim a_3,\{1,4,6\}) \oplus (e_2,\{3,4,5\}) \end{array}$$

To have $GR(C_2, C_4)$:

$$C : (\sim a_3, \{1,4,6\}) \oplus (e_2, \{3,4,5\}) \tag{9}$$

(8) and (9) is merged together, to have following form

$$\begin{aligned} G - \varphi(a_3, b_2, c_0, e_2) &= GR(C_1, C_3) \otimes GR(C_2, C_4) \otimes (c_0, \{1,2,3,4\}) \\ &= ((\sim a_3, \{1,4,6\}) \oplus (b_2, \{4,5,6\})) \otimes \\ &\quad ((\sim a_3, \{1,4,6\}) \oplus (e_2, \{3,4,5\})) \otimes (c_0, \{1,2,3,4\}) \end{aligned}$$

The above can be simplified as follows:

$$\begin{aligned} G - \varphi(a_3, b_2, c_0, e_2) = ((\sim a_3, \{1,4,6\}) \oplus ((b_2, \{4,5,6\}) \otimes \\ (e_2, \{3,4,5\}))) \otimes (c_0, \{1,2,3,4\}) \end{aligned} \tag{10}$$

**Theorem 2.** Let $\triangle$ be a set of G-clauses, if there is a deduction of G-resolution G-clause $C$ from $\triangle$, then $\triangle$ implies logically $C$.

**Proof:** It is finished by simple induction on length of the resolution deduction. For the deduction, we need only to show that any given resolution step is sound. Suppose that $C_1$ and $C_2$ are arbitrary two G-clauses from G-clause form in step $i$, $C_1$: $C_1' \oplus (a, d(a))$, $C_2$: $C_2' \oplus (b, d(b))$, where $C_1'$ and $C_2'$ are still G-clause.

Assuming that $C_1$ and $C_2$ are two correct G-clauses in step $i$. $(a, d(a))$ and $(b, d(b))$ is a complement G-literal pair in step $i$, hence $(a, d(a))$ and $(b, d(b))$ is resolved to produce a resolvent $GR(C_1, C_2)$, to be a new G-clause $C : C_1' \oplus C_2'$. Now proving that $C$ is also a correct G-clause. By definition 5, we discuss in following several cases:

- (*i*) Two G-clauses to join in resolution are $C_1$ and $C_2$ , If there are the complement G-literal $(a, \emptyset)$ in $C_1$ and $(b, U)$ in $C_2$ respectively, then $C_1'$ is a correct G-clause, so the new G-clause $C : C_1' \oplus C_2'$ is correct; If there are $(b, \emptyset)$ in $C_2$ and $(a, U)$ in $C_1$ respectively, then $C_2'$ is correct, so $C : C_1' \oplus C_2'$ is a correct new G-clause;
- (*ii*) Two G-clauses to join in resolution are $C_1$ and $C_2$ , a complement G-literal pair $(a, \emptyset_R)$ and $(b, U_R)$ or $(b, U)$ is in $C_1$ and $C_2$ respectively , then $C_1'$ is a rough correct G-clause, hence $C : C_1' \oplus C_2'$ is a rough correct G-clause, Vice versa;
- (*iii*) Two G-clauses to join in resolution are $C_1$ and $C_2$ , the complement G-literal pair $(a, U - \emptyset)$ and $(b, U - \emptyset)$ is in $C_1$ and $C_2$ respectively, where $U - \emptyset$ is undecidable then $C_1'$ and $C_2'$ are a correct or undecidable G-clause, hence $C : C_1' \oplus C_2'$ is correct or undecidable.

As a general rule, one of the complement G-literal pair could be $(B_* a, B_*(a))$ or $(B^* a, B^*(a))$; since the extract of resolution step $i$ could be arbitrary, the proof of G-resolution deduction is finished.

## 5 Decomposition of Granulation and Amalgamating of Granules

In this section, we discuss decomposition of the granulation and the composing of granules. The purpose here is to propose an idea of constructing simple sub-formulas, up to predicates out of more complex ones. We resolve the sub-formulas or predicates to be easy, and the answers among sub-formulas or predicates are easily translated, recruited and enlightened each other. And then the answers can be amalgamated the answer of original global formula via granular computing. The following is a real example , which we are developing "Diagnosis Software System of Blood Flowing Dynamic Theory".

**For example,** Let the data set of gathering in clinic for the patient, $P = \{WangHon, Male, 65, 3.5\}$, where Wang Hon is name, Male is sex, 65 is age and 3.5 is clinical testing data via testing instrument. The patient $P$ can be diagnosed the degree of his(her) blood viscosity by this system, namely the constructed formula $\varphi = name_{WangHon} \wedge Sex_{male} \wedge Age_65 \wedge TV_{3.5}$ can be resolved. We collapse this formula into various sub-formulas or predicates and to resolve the answers for these sub-formulas or predicates according to the algorithm in system[9]. And then we amalgamate the answers, to have an answer of global formula. Possessive steps are as following:

1. Computing average value $AV$ and standard deviation $SD$ of Normal People Reference Value Interval by rough-fuzzy and fuzzy-rough set approach. Let $[a, b]$ be a interval. An indiscernbility relation $R$ is defined on the interval, namely $\forall x_1, x_2 \in [a, b]$, $x_1 \quad R \quad x_2$ iff $\mid x_1 - x_2 \mid \leq 0.618$, the transitivity of $R$ is defined on $[j * 0.618, 1 + j * 0.618] \subseteq [a, b]$, $j = 0, 1, \ldots$.Thus the interval is divided by $R$, until $a + n * 0.618 > b$, where n is the total of small intervals. 0.618 here is chosen from "Gold Cut" in Chinese ancient mathematics. And Professor Luogen Hua, famous Chinese mathematician in the world used also the data in his book "Methods for Plan as a Whole"(in Chinese). Which is called best choosing point on $[0, 1]$, to be also a fuzzy concept, and defining an indiscernibility relation by it. The partition on $[a, b]$ is also called granulating. We compute the average value and standard deviation by following formulas for the interval $[a, b]$ via granulating,

$$AV = (a + \sum_{j=1}^{n-2}(a + j * 0.618) + b)/n \tag{1}$$

and

$$SD = sqrt(\sum_{j=0}^{n-1}((a + j * 0.618) - AV)^2/n) \tag{2}$$

where $sqrt$ is a functional symbol of square root. And to compute the index value corresponding to the clinical testing data $TV$, namely

$$IV = \begin{cases} (TV - AV)/SD & for \quad TV > a \\ (-TV + AV)/SD & for \quad TV \leq a \end{cases} \tag{3}$$

where $TV$ is the clinic testing blood viscosity data via testing instrument. a is the lower bound corresponding to the interval.

Formula $\varphi$ is collapsed into sub-formulas, that is, predicates $P_1 = name_{Wang-H}$, $P_2 = Sex_{male}$, $P_3 = Age_{65}$ and $P_4 = TV_{3.5}$. The granules corresponding to them are $G_1 = (P_1, d(P_1))$, $G_2 = (P_2, d(P_2))$, $G_3 = (P_3, d(P_3))$ and $G_4 = (P_4, d(P_4))$ respectively. The granulation corresponding to $\varphi$ is written as $G = (\varphi, d(\varphi))$, so $G = G_1 \otimes G_2 \otimes G_3 \otimes G_4$, this creates a framework from global to local, contrarily amalgamating into global from locals. The granule corresponding with sub-formula $P_2$ is $G_2 = (sex_{male}, d(sex_{male}))$ according to theories in the system of developing. Hence, male's normal people reference value interval $[4.42, 4.79]$ is chosen[9], which is granulated by rough-fuzzy, fuzzy-rough set approach. To have the average value and the standard deviation of interval $[4.42, 4.79]$ is $AV_2 = 4.70$ and $SD_2 = 0.28$ respectively.

2. Computing index value $IV$ of $TV_{3.5}$ by (3) above and granule corresponding to $P_4$. Having $IV_2 = -3.74$.

3. Computing level of index value $IV$ by the rules in the system[9], having $level_2 = -5$.

4. Diagnosing the degree of blood viscosity for the patient by the levels. The degree computed is -3.22 by the experience of experts offering in the system[9]. Which belong to blood lower-viscosity syndrome.

In the example, collapsing global formula into local sub-formulas or predicates, which is easy. But amalgamation of various local granules seems not clean. In the fact, sub-formulas resolving is translated, recruited and enlightened each other in the steps. Solving of name $P_1$ and age $P_3$ is described in searching for case history base, namely the degree of blood viscosity is added or subtracted a correct value according to case history and age of the patient. Hence, the procedure for solving-problem in the system of our developing is a reasoning of the collapsing and amalgamating.

## 6 Conclusion

Structure of G-formulas is both logic and set theory, so operations of the formulas may use the both operation symbols $\sim$, $\vee$ and $\wedge$ in logic and operation symbols $\sim$, $\cup$ and $\cap$ in set theory. Here we discuss a method of extracting relative decision by computing closeness degree between gathering granule and conditional granule of each granulation in granulation base of expert systems. We always extract the decision of the granulation of greater closeness degree, so the reasoning may solve the conflict problems occurring in reasoning procedure better. Collapsing and amalgamating methods based on granular computing have a special fashion in reasoning, namely we may use both logical method and set theory method in reasoning. Based on granular computing, the reasoning of G-resolution can also be used in the machine theorem proving. We are perfecting the "Diagnosis System of Blood Flowing Dynamic Theory" , so that the system can be used to various solving-problem in artificial intelligence. In fact,This is an expert system in medicine based on the reasoning of granular computing, which is tried to use in the clinic of the hospital.

**Acknowledgements**

This study is supported by the State Natural Science Fund (#60173054) and Natural Science Fund of Jiangxi province. The author gratefully acknowledges the support of K.C.Wang Education Foundation, Hong Kong.

## References

1. Q.Liu, Granular Language and Its Deductive Reasoning, Communications of Institute of Information and Computing Machinery, Vol. 5, No. 2, Taiwan, May, 2002, 63-66.
2. A.Skowron, Toward Intelligent Systems: Calculi of Information Granules, Proceedings of International Workshop on Rough Set Theory and Granular Computing (RSTGC- 2001). Bulleting of International Rough Set Society, Vol.5, No.1/2, May.20-22,2001, 9-30.
3. A.Skowron and J.Stepaniuk, Extracting Patterns Using Information Granules, Proceedings of International workshop on Rough Set Theory and Granular Computing (RSTGC-2001), Bulleting of International Rough Set Society, Vol.5, No.1/2, May 20-22,2001, 135-142.
4. T.Y.Lin and Q.Liu, First-Order Rough Logic I: Approximate Reasoning Via Rough Sets, Fundamenta Informaticae, Vol.27, No.2-3, Aug.1996, 137-154.
5. Q. Liu, Neighborhood Logic and Its Data Reasoning in Information Table of Neighborhood Values, Chinese Journal of Computers, Vol.24, No.4, 2001,4,405-410.
6. Q,Liu, The OI-Resolution of Operator Rough Logic, LNAI 1424, Springer, June 22-26,1998, 432-435.
7. Q. Liu, Rough Sets and Rough Reasoning (in Chinese), Academic Pub.,BeiJing, 2001.
8. Q.Liu and S.H.Liu, Rough Logic and Its Applications in Data Mining, Journal of Software (in Chinese), Vol.12, No.3,2001.3, 415-419.
9. Q.Liu, F.Jiang and D.Y.Deng, "Design and Implement for the Diagnosis System of Blood Flowing Dynamic Theory on Blood Viscosity Syndrome Based on Granular Computing ", appear in LNAI, Springer, May 26-29,2003.

# A Comparison of the Effectiveness of Neural and Wavelet Networks for Insurer Credit Rating Based on Publicly Available Financial Data

Martyn Prigmore and J. Allen Long

South Bank University, Computing, Information Systems and Mathematics
103 Borough Road, London, SE1 0AA, UK
{prigmoms, longjaa}@sbu.ac.uk

**Abstract.** We apply neural and wavelet network architectures to publicly available financial data to match the credit ratings of insurance companies. The main aim is to assess whether wavelet networks are likely to provide sufficiently improved results to justify further work. We consider three aspects when comparing the networks: complexity, predictive accuracy and prediction confidence.

## 1 Introduction

Assessing the credit worthiness of a company is a key service provided both to that company and to investors. Several international companies provide credit rating services; for example, Standard and Poor's and Moody's. In this paper we concentrate on Standard and Poor's letter based Insurer Financial Enhancement Rating. This system assigns a rating, from AAA, 'extremely strong', down to CC, 'currently highly vulnerable' [8]. Ratings AA to CC may be modified by a '+' or '-', although we do not include this variation in our analysis. Ratings BBB and above are classed as good investments; 'investment grade'. Ratings BB and below "are regarded as having significant speculative characteristics" [8]; these are 'non-investment grade'. Ratings are based upon information provided both by the company being rated and from other reputable sources. However the rating mechanism relies on the judgement of financial analysts whose knowledge of the insurance market and the past performance of individual companies will inform their decisions.

Since companies pay to have their credit worthiness assessed, credit ratings tend to be commissioned at intervals of six months or more. A company's credit worthiness can change significantly between rating exercises, so it is desirable to have some means to provide interim assessments of credit worthiness. The use of computer based analyses seems a sensible approach to providing these interim assessments. The complexity of the problem has meant that direct, mathematical analyses are intractable. However, an empirical approach, analysing the effectiveness of a variety of classification techniques, is feasible. The effectiveness of tree structured classifiers, linear discriminant analysis, memory based reasoning, and various forms of neural network have been investigated in [7] and [2]. In this paper we continue this work,

P.W.H. Chung, C.J. Hinde, M. Ali (Eds.): IEA/AIE 2003, LNAI 2718, pp. 527–536, 2003.

investigating the relative effectiveness and computational complexity of standard neural networks and wavelet networks. Specifically, we begin an investigation of the interplay between three factors: the accuracy of predictions; the confidence with which the prediction is made; and the complexity of the network making the prediction.

The wavelet network was introduced by Qinghua Zhang and Albert Benveniste in [10] as an alternative to feed-forward neural networks for approximating non-linear functions. Since then the wavelet network has been developed for parametric modelling [3] non-parametric regression estimation [11], [6] and forecasting futures trading [9]. Wavelet networks are universal approximators in the same sense as are neural networks. They also use non-linear transformations of input data. It is this last property that is of interest in classification problems. The idea is to use a non-linear transformation to cast a problem into a higher dimensional space, and thereby increase the separation of the input vectors. Ideally the transformation should produce a transformed data set that is linearly separable. Our aim here is to introduce a simple modification of the wavelet network to exploit the non-linear transformation property, making the approach more suitable for classification problems.

Initial tests on generating a wavelet network indicated that with five attributes the wavelet network included over 30 000 distinct wavelets; this illustrates the difficulty of analysing high dimension problems. Thus our experiments use a small subset of the available data to compare the relative effectiveness of neural and wavelet networks for the credit rating classification problem. Details of the comparison methodology are given below. With only a small subset of attributes it seemed sensible to attempt only to classify companies into investment grade (BBB or above) and non-investment grade (BB or below). If these experiments proved successful then further work, seeking to utilise all available attributes and all eight categories, would be justified.

## 2 Data

The data set includes credit ratings and publicly available financial data on 533 insurance companies. 391 are investment grade and 142 non-investment grade companies. Table 1 shows the distribution of companies across the ratings.

**Table 1** Distribution of companies across credit ratings

| Rating | Frequency |
|---|---|
| AAA | 0 |
| AA | 18 |
| A | 110 |
| BBB | 263 |
| BB | 88 |
| B | 50 |
| CCC | 4 |
| CC | 0 |

**Table 2** Data attributes

| No | Attribute name |
|---|---|
| 1 | Country |
| 2 | Company Name |
| 3 | Account date |
| 4 | Current rating |
| 5 | Bonds+Stocks+Shares / Adj Sh Funds |
| 6 | Combined Ratio |
| 7 | Commission/W Exp / Net Prem Written |
| 8 | Gross Premiums |
| 9 | Gross Prems / Adj Sh Funds |
| 10 | Insurance Debts / Adj Sh Funds |
| 11 | Insurance Debts / Total Assets |
| 12 | Liabilities / Liquid Assets |
| 13 | Loss+Fun+Oth Tech Rsrvs / Adj Sh Funds |
| 14 | Loss+Fun+Oth Tech Rsrvs / Net Prem Written |
| 15 | Net Losses Incurred / Net Prem Earned |
| 16 | Net Prems / Adj Sh Funds |
| 17 | Net Prems / Gross Prems |
| 18 | Overall Operating Ratio |
| 19 | Tech Res / Liquid Assets |
| 20 | Tech Rsrvs / Adj Sh Funds |
| 21 | Tech Rsrvs / Net Prem Written |
| 22 | Tech Rsrvs + Adj Sh Funds / Net Prem Written |
| 23 | U/W Profit / Net Invest Income |

Table 2 lists the available attributes.

## 3 Algorithms

In this section we describe the neural network and wavelet network algorithms used in the experiments.

### 3.1 Neural Network

Neural networks are a well established tool for the analysis of financial and business data. Previous work on predicting company credit ratings using neural networks by one of the authors was noted above. The properties of these networks are well known (see e.g. [5] or [1]) and acceptable implementations are available from commercial vendors. The neural networks in this study were implemented using NeuroShell2 Release 4.0 from Ward Systems Inc.

The neural network architecture chosen was a three layer, fully connected back propagation network. Details of the structure of the networks are given below.

### 3.2 Wavelet Network

We give a brief summary of the wavelet transform and wavelet networks, referring the reader to [4] and [10] for a more detailed exposition. A wavelet function is a function $f : \mathrm{R}^d \to \mathrm{R}$ that is localised, in the sense that it is zero everywhere except within a region known as its *support*. (In fact, it need not be zero outside its support, it is sufficient that it is rapidly vanishing.) It can be shown that for such an $f$, the countable family of functions

$$\mathrm{F}[a,b] = \{ f[\boldsymbol{m},n](\boldsymbol{x}) = a^{-0.5dn} f(a^{-n}\boldsymbol{x} - b\boldsymbol{m}) : n \in \mathrm{Z}, \boldsymbol{m} \in \mathrm{Z}^d \}$$

forms a wavelet frame (vector variables are indicated by **bold** type); all the functions are translated and dilated versions of the single wavelet $f = f[\mathbf{0},0]$ called the mother wavelet. Any square integrable function can be approximated to any desired degree of accuracy by a linear combination of functions in $\mathrm{F}[a,b]$. The parameters $a$ and $b$ define the dilation and translation step sizes respectively and satisfy $a > 1$ and $b > 0$.

The basic wavelet network consists of an input layer, a single hidden layer of neurons and a single output neuron. The neurons in the hidden layer have activation functions taken from some wavelet frame. The output neuron is a linear combiner. The network is fully connected, however the connections between the input layer and the hidden layer of neurons do not have any weights. Only the connections between the hidden layer and the single output neuron are weighted. These weights may be determined using the LMS algorithm.

Since the wavelet frame is infinite, we must first identify a suitable finite subset of wavelets. The initial choice uses information from the training data set: we select those wavelets whose support contains one of the training inputs. Since the training set is finite, so is this *truncated wavelet frame*. It may be used to construct the wavelet network, however it is often very large. [10] and [11] suggest algorithms for thinning the truncated frame further.

This brief description highlights the main features of wavelet networks as they are used for function estimation. First, the training input vectors are used to provide an initial guess as to which wavelets are required to estimate the function. These wavelets are used as the activation functions of neurons in the hidden layer of a fully connected network; the wavelet layer. Next, each training input vector is passed to each neuron in the *wavelet layer*. The output of the neuron is multiplied by some weight and passed to the single neuron in the output layer. Here, the weighted outputs are summed. By the universal approximation property of the wavelet frame, there should be some combination of weights that provides the expected value for the given input vector, to the desired degree of accuracy. The least mean squares algorithm is used to identify these weights.

As noted, our aim in this paper is to introduce a simple modification of the wavelet network architecture for use in classification problems. Rather than passing the weighted outputs of the wavelet layer to a linear combiner, they are used as the input vector to a standard neural network. The idea is that the wavelet layer casts the classification problem into a higher dimensional space, where the standard neural network has a better chance of separating the inputs. We also suggest an alternative method for thinning down the truncated wavelet frame. We construct our wavelet network as follows:

Step1 – Define the truncated wavelet frame. Identify those wavelets in F[a,b] which contain one or more of the training input vectors; let $\{f_1, \ldots, f_w\}$ be the truncated wavelet frame.

Step 2 – Thin the truncated wavelet frame. The output of the wavelet network is a linear combination of the outputs of the individual wavelets. Thus, if a given wavelet can be written as a linear combination of the other wavelets, we can remove it from the frame. This is the key to thinning the truncated wavelet frame. For each wavelet $f_1, \ldots, f_w$ and for training input vectors $\boldsymbol{x}_1, \ldots \boldsymbol{x}_N$ calculate the wavelet output vector:

$$\boldsymbol{v}_i = (f_i(\boldsymbol{x}_1), \ldots f_i(\boldsymbol{x}_N))$$

Provided the training data accurately describes the problem space we may eliminate those wavelets $f_i$ whose corresponding wavelet output vector, $\boldsymbol{v}_i$, can be written as a linear combination of the other wavelet output vectors.

At this point our approach differs from [11]. There, an orthonormal subset of the set $\{ \boldsymbol{v}_1, \ldots \boldsymbol{v}_w \}$ is identified and the corresponding wavelets used to form the thinned truncated wavelet frame. A simpler solution is to write the wavelet output vectors as rows of a matrix, say

$$A = [a_{ij}] = [f_1(\boldsymbol{x}_j)]$$

Using simple matrix row operations (interchanging two rows, multiplying a row by a scalar or adding two rows) we reduce this matrix to echelon form. We may now thin the truncated frame by removing those wavelets whose corresponding row in the echelon matrix consists wholly of zeroes. Let the thinned truncated wavelet frame be $\{f_1, \ldots, f_M\}$.

Step 3 – Transform the training input data. For each training input vector $\boldsymbol{x}_1, \ldots \boldsymbol{x}_N$ calculate the transformed input vector:

$$\boldsymbol{u}_i = (f_1(\boldsymbol{x}_i), \ldots f_M(\boldsymbol{x}_i))$$

This transformed input vector represents the outputs of the neurons in the wavelet layer. Thus, our "wavelet network" is actually just a standard neural network, but with the input vectors pre-processed through the wavelet transform.

Step 4 – Train the neural network. Use the set $\{ \boldsymbol{u}_1, \ldots, \boldsymbol{u}_N\}$ as the training inputs for a neural network. The expected output for each $\boldsymbol{u}_i$ will be the same as the expected output for $\boldsymbol{x}_i$.

## 4 Experiments

Here, we explain the methodology adopted, and describe the various experiments.

## 4.1 Methodology

To allow a fair comparison of the two architectures we sought to minimise differences due to data input. We identified a training set of 383 samples, test set of 100 samples and validation set of 50 samples in advance, using the same sets for both the wavelet and neural networks. Note that the imbalance between the number of investment grade and non-investment grade companies in the original sample was reflected in these three data sets.

The un-transformed training data was used to create a neural network trained using the back-propagation algorithm. The learning rate, momentum and number of hidden neurons were chosen to suit the four dimensional input data set. Next, a second neural network with the same learning rate, momentum and number of hidden neurons was created, this time using the transformed data - the output of the wavelet layer - as its input. As the transformed data has a higher dimension, the number of hidden neurons in the second network is not optimal. Thus two further networks were constructed. The third network took as inputs the transformed data. Learning rate, momentum and number of hidden neurons were chosen to suit this higher dimensional input. Finally the un-transformed data was used to create a neural network with the same learning rate, momentum and number of hidden neurons as the third. In this last case the number of hidden neurons is rather high compared to the input dimension.

All four networks were evaluated using the appropriate validation set. In evaluating the performance of the networks we measured both the predictive accuracy and the confidence of the prediction. We classify the output of the neural network as follows:

**Table 3** Classification of network outputs

| Output Range | Rating |
|---|---|
| x = 0.00, ..., 0.40 | confident non-investment grade |
| x = 0.41 ..., 0.50 | tentative non-investment grade |
| x = 0.51 ..., 0.59 | tentative investment grade |
| x = 0.60, ..., 1.00 | confident investment grade |

Given expected output *d* and actual output *x* we have the following possibilities:

**Table 4** Evaluation of network outputs

| Description | Expected | Actual |
|---|---|---|
| correct confident non-investment grade | d = 0 | x = 0.00,..., 0.40 |
| correct tentative non-investment grade | d = 0 | x = 0.41,..., 0.50 |
| incorrect tentative investment grade | d = 0 | x = 0.51,..., 0.59 |
| incorrect confident investment grade | d = 0 | x = 0.60,..., 1.00 |
| incorrect confident non-investment grade | d = 1 | x = 0.00,..., 0.40 |
| incorrect tentative non-investment grade | d = 1 | x = 0.41, ..., 0.50 |
| correct tentative investment grade | d = 1 | x = 0.51,..., 0.59 |
| correct confident investment grade | d = 1 | x = 0.60,..., 1.00 |

By analysing both the confidence and accuracy of the prediction we can gain some insight into the relative performance of the two types of network.

## 4.2 Experimental Results

The above methodology was used to run two experiments, taking a different subset of the available attributes for each, though using the same training, test and validation data sets. Both experiments began with the wavelet frame F[2,3].

### 4.2.1 Experiment 1

The following four attributes were selected:

Gross Prems / Adj Sh Funds
Insurance Debts / Total Assets
Liabilities / Liquid Assets
Net Losses Incurred/Net Prem Earned

The truncated wavelet frame was generated at scale levels n = -5, ..., 5. In fact, fewer scale levels would have been sufficient, as some scale levels were not represented in the thinned truncated wavelet frame. The truncated wavelet frame consisted of 6576 wavelets, the thinned wavelet frame of 34. The network parameters for the first pair of neural and wavelet networks, 1NN1 and 1WN1 respectively, were:

Learning rate = 0.05
Momentum = 0.5
Hidden neurons = 22

For the second pair of networks, 1NN2 and 1WN2, the parameters were:

Learning rate = 0.05
Momentum = 0.5
Hidden neurons = 37

The following table describes the results of this experiment, showing the number of validation samples that fall into each of the eight categories described above.

**Table 5** Results Of Experiment 1

| | 1NN1 | 1WN1 | 1NN2 | 1WN2 |
|---|---|---|---|---|
| correct confident non-investment grade | 2 | 4 | 4 | 6 |
| correct tentative non-investment grade | 2 | 4 | 1 | 2 |
| incorrect tentative investment grade | 0 | 0 | 1 | 2 |
| incorrect confident investment grade | 10 | 6 | 8 | 4 |
| incorrect confident non-investment grade | 1 | 2 | 0 | 2 |
| incorrect tentative non-investment grade | 0 | 1 | 0 | 0 |
| correct tentative investment grade | 1 | 1 | 0 | 0 |
| correct confident investment grade | 34 | 32 | 36 | 34 |

#### 4.2.2 Experiment 2

The following four attributes were selected:

Bonds+Stocks+Shares / Adj Sh Funds
Gross Prems / Adj Sh Funds
Insurance Debts / Adj Sh Funds
U/W Profit / Net Invest Income

The truncated wavelet frame was generated at scale levels n = -5, ..., 5. The truncated wavelet frame consisted of 10103 wavelets, the thinned wavelet frame of 23. The network parameters for the first pair of neural and wavelet networks, 2NN1 and 2WN1 respectively, were as follows:

Learning rate = 0.05
Momentum = 0.5
Hidden neurons = 15

The network parameters for the second pair of neural and wavelet networks, 2NN2 and 2WN2 respectively, were as follows:

Learning rate = 0.05
Momentum = 0.5
Hidden neurons = 24

The following table describes the results of this experiment, showing the number of validation samples that fall into each of the eight categories described above.

**Table 6** Results of Experiment 2

| | 2NN1 | 2WN1 | 2NN2 | 2WN2 |
|---|---|---|---|---|
| correct confident non-investment grade | 7 | 11 | 7 | 11 |
| correct tentative non-investment grade | 3 | 0 | 3 | 2 |
| incorrect tentative investment grade | 1 | 2 | 1 | 0 |
| incorrect confident investment grade | 3 | 1 | 3 | 1 |
| incorrect confident non-investment grade | 3 | 7 | 3 | 4 |
| incorrect tentative non-investment grade | 2 | 3 | 2 | 3 |
| correct tentative investment grade | 8 | 0 | 8 | 4 |
| correct confident investment grade | 23 | 26 | 23 | 25 |

## 5 Conclusions and Further Work

The following table summarises the predictive accuracy of the eight networks for identifying non-investment grade companies, investment grade companies and the overall accuracy of their predictions.

**Table 7** Predictive accuracy of the networks

| | Correctly classified Non-investment Grade | Correctly classified Investment Grade | Overall Correct Classification |
|---|---|---|---|
| 1NN1 | 29% | 97% | 78% |
| 1WN1 | 57% | 92% | 82% |
| 1NN2 | 36% | 100% | 82% |
| 1WN2 | 57% | 94% | 84% |
| 2NN1 | 71% | 86% | 82% |
| 2WN1 | 79% | 72% | 74% |
| 2NN2 | 71% | 86% | 82% |
| 2WN2 | 93% | 81% | 84% |

In Experiment 1, the plain neural networks 1NN1 and 1NN2 are particularly poor at identifying non-investment grade companies. The better performance of the wavelet networks 1WN1 and 1WN2 in this aspect is encouraging. It suggests that the wavelet transform is helping to separate the investment grade and non-investment grade companies. The good performance of all the networks in identifying investment grade companies may be partly due to a bias towards this classification. This would be reasonable, given the preponderance of investment grade companies in the original data set. The networks in Experiment 2 show a more rounded performance, though again the wavelet networks are consistently better at classifying the non-investment grade companies, with 2WN2 having the best overall performance.

Regarding prediction confidence, in Experiment 1 there were few tentative predictions, and a clear problem with non-investment grade companies being classified as investment grade. This may be due to the choice of attributes, or lower representation of non-investment grade companies in the original data set. However, it is notable that the wavelet networks are much less likely to make such an incorrect confident classification. Experiment 2 has a slightly different profile, with roughly the same number of incorrect confident predictions from all four networks. However, here we see that the wavelet networks make consistently fewer tentative predictions.

These results indicate that using the wavelet transform to pre-process the data can improve both the confidence and accuracy of the predictions made by the neural network. This suggests that the non-linear wavelet transform does, as hoped, increase the separation of the input vectors. For 2WN1 this increased prediction confidence is offset by decreased predictive accuracy as compared to 2NN1. 2WN2 indicates that by increasing the complexity of the network (more hidden neurons) we can retain some of the increased prediction confidence of 2WN1 and match the predictive accuracy of 2NN1. Thus our experimental results illustrate nicely the interplay between these three factors.

Although these results are encouraging additional work is required before the utility of wavelet networks for company credit rating is established. First, additional preliminary experiments using alternative small subsets of the attributes listed in Section 2 above need to be completed. If the results from these further experiments are encouraging then research into improving the algorithms used to construct the wavelet network would be justified. In particular, a more sophisticated approach to the thinning of the truncated wavelet frame is needed. One important topic for research is to identify which wavelets are the "best" discriminants and ensure that these are included in the thinned truncated frame.

## References


1. Bose, N. K. & Liang, P. Neural network fundamentals with graphs, algorithms and applications McGraw-Hill, Singapore (1996)
2. Bursteinas, B. & Long, J. A. Tree structured classifiers, interconnected data and predictive accuracy Intelligent Data Analysis, 2000. 4(1): p.397-410.
3. Colla, V., Reyneri, L. M. & Sgarbi, M. Neuro-wavelet parametric modelling in IJCNN 2000 - Proceedings of the IEEE-INNS-ENNS International Joint Conference on Neural Networks, Vol4 (2000)
4. Daubechies, I. Ten lectures on wavelets CBMS-NSF regional series in applied mathematics (1992)
5. Haykin, S Neural networks - a comprehensive foundation 2nd ed, Prentice Hall, New Jersey USA (1999)
6. Holmes, C.C. & Mallick, B. K. Bayesian wavelet networks for nonparametric regression in IEEE Transactions on Neural Networks, Vol 11 No. 1, January 2000
7. Long, J.A. & Raudys, A. Modelling company credit ratings using a number of classification techniques (2000)
8. Standard & Poor's Insurer financial enhancement rating, (2001) [Internet] http://www.standardandpoors.com/ResourceCenter/RatingsDefinitions.html
9. Zhang, B-L., Coggins, R., Jabri, M. A., Dersch, D. & Flower, B. Multiresolution forecasting for futures trading using wavelet decomposition in IEEE Transactions on Neural Networks, Vol. 12 No. 4, July 2001
10. Zhang, Q. & Benveniste, A. Wavelet networks in IEEE Transactions on Neural Networks, Vol. 3 No. 6, November 1992
11. Zhang, Q. Using wavelet networks in non-parametric estimation in IEEE Transactions on Neural Networks, Vol. 8 No. 2 March 1997

# A New System Based on the Use of Neural Networks and Database for Monitoring Coal Combustion Efficiency

Karim Ouazzane and Kamel Zerzour

London Metropolitan University
Department of Computing and Communication Technology
{k.ouazzane,k.zerzour}@londonmet.ac.uk

**Abstract.** Monitoring the combustion process for electricity generation using coal as a primary resource is of a major concern to the pertinent industries, power generation companies in particular. The carbon content of fly ash is indicative of the combustion efficiency. The determination of this parameter is useful to characterise the efficiency of coal burning furnaces. Traditional methods such as Thermogrametric Analysis (TGA) and Loss on Ignition which are based on ash collection and subsequent analysis, proved to be tediously difficult, time consuming and costly. Thus, a need for a new technology was inevitable and needed to monitor the process in a more efficient method yielding a better exploitation of the resources at a lower cost. The main aim of this work is to introduce a new automated system which can be bolted onto a furnace and work online. The system consists of three main components, namely, a laser instrument for signal acquisition, a neural network tool for training, learning and simulation, and a database system for storage and retrieval. The components have been designed, adapted and tuned for knowledge acquisition of this multidimensional problem. The system has been tested for a range of coal ashes and proved to be efficient.

## 1 Introduction

It is anticipated that coal will remain the major source of energy for electricity generation in the foreseeable future. Therefore monitoring the efficiency of coal is of crucial importance. In particular the carbon content in fly ash which is indicative of the furnace efficiency need to be measured accurately. The other elemental component of fly ash are silicon, aluminium, iron, calcium and magnesium. The concentrations of the different elements are dependent on the type of coal and need to be determined. Traditionally fly ash carbon content is determined by various techniques such as thermal gravimetric analysis, loss on ignition, infrared emission spectrometry. Those techniques are all based on empirical and intrusive method which causes a significant disturbance, and require collection of fly ash samples followed by subsequent analysis. Also, the process is time consuming, costly and sometimes producing less efficient data. Therefore, this problem needs a new technology to resolve difficulties and obstacles at power enterprises level. The prospect of integrating the above process in one automated system is of a great interest to the relevant industry and will make a big impact in terms of improving the process, yielding a better exploitation of the energy and resources. The aim of this

P.W.H. Chung, C.J. Hinde, M. Ali (Eds.): IEA/AIE 2003, LNAI 2718, pp. 537–544, 2003.

work is the presentation of a new automated system which can significantly reduce the cost and speed up the process without affecting the data accuracy.

## 2 Traditional Methods and Process Control

Traditional methods of measuring the carbon content in ash from the combustion process, include Thermogravimetric Analysis (TGA), Loss on Ignition and burn out in a furnace followed by measurement of the $CO_2$ evolved [1]. The process for the above techniques requires a collection of fly ash from the furnace which is tediously difficult, and subsequently analysed using an expensive and sensitive instrument. Extreme care should be taken during analysis and operations and the ambient temperature must be appropriate and maintained. The process consists of four long steps, each of those requires data collection for the determination of carbon in ash. The analysis of ash coal would take up to one week provided the calibration is carried out properly. Table 1 describes results over a range of coal ash analysis performed at Powergen (UK power station) using TGA. The time scale of the overall process is also shown. It is evident that the technique is awkward, expensive and time consuming. Therefore a need of a new technology for improving the process in the relevant industries is essential for a better exploitation of coal resources yielding an efficient electricity generation for domestics and others use. A new automated system has been developed to resolve difficulties and obstacles caused by traditional methods which are widely used for ash coal process engineering in general.

**Table 1.** Traditional Method

| Ash Coals | %C/TGA | Samples | Duration | Overall cost |
|---|---|---|---|---|
| BET96042 | 4.9 | 3 | 2 Weeks | £ 5.000 |
| ELC99011 | 9.1 | 2 | 1 Week | £ 3.000 |
| LAC98062 | 9.2 | 1 | 1 Week | £ 3.000 |
| FOR98062 | 10.1 | 1 | 1 Week | £ 3.000 |
| ATC98062 | 12.1 | 2 | 1 Week | £ 3.000 |
| KNP98092 | 12.6 | 1 | 1 Week | £ 3.000 |
| ELC97050 | 13.1 | 1 | 1 Week | £ 3.000 |
| LAJ98062 | 16.4 | 3 | 2 Weeks | £ 5.000 |
| | | | | £25.000 |

## 3 The New Automated System

To overcome the above incovenience, a new automated system has been developed. Fig. 1 illustrates the architecture of the new system. The system is integrated and consists of a laser instrument, a neural network tool and a database repository. Details about each component's description will be highlighted below.

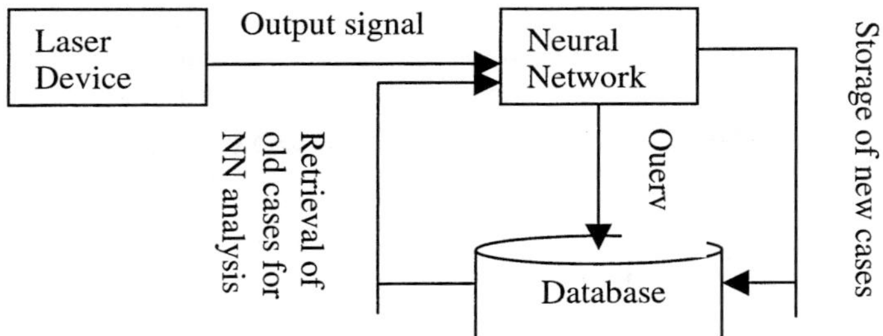


**Fig. 1.** The New System's Architecture

### 3.1 The Instrument

Fig. 2 shows the measurement process carried out by the laser instrument [2]. This process measures the combustion efficiency quantified by the carbon in ash. The instrument shines a laser beam in the test space inside a furnace. As individual coal ash particle passes through, the laser light is scattered resulting in a new frequency. This frequency is proportional to the percentage of carbon in ash. The backward signal is collected by a collecting lenses and subsequently the frequency is quantified. The frequency is fed to the neural network tool along with predetermined percentage of minerals which are coal's others components.

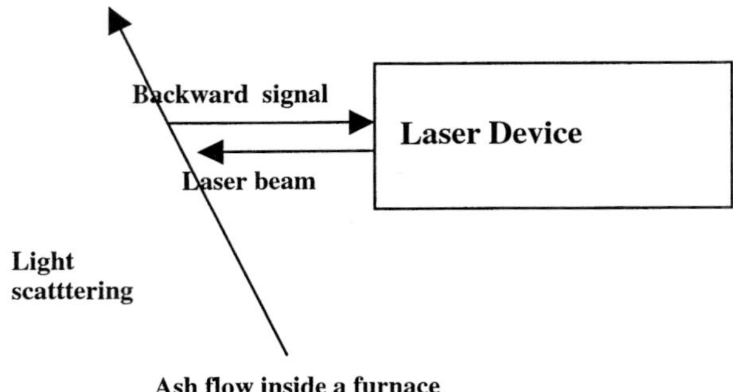


**Fig. 2.** Process measurement using the instrument

### 3.2 Neural Networks

Of the various neural network models only General Regression Neural Network (GRNN) which is based on the radial basis function (which has its origin in techniques used for exact interpolation between data points in multidimensional spaces), has been investigated in this paper. The facilities of the neural network toolbox of the Matlab software have been used in the computation. The interpolation with radial basis functions presented in this paper have been made with a Matlab function, which has as many hidden neurons as there are input output pairs. This causes the interpolation function to make exact mapping. It is similar to the radial basis network but has a slightly different second layer. For more details on the topology see Ouazzane et al. [3] .The question is how does this network behave following an input *p* through the network to the output . If we present an input vector to such a network, each neuron in the radial basis layer will output a value according to how close the input vector is to each neuron's weight vector. Thus, radial basis neurons with weight vectors quite different from the input p will have outputs near zero. These small outputs will have only a negligible effect on the linear output neurons. In contrast a radial basis neurons with a weight vectors **IW** (Input Weight) close to the input vector *p* will produce a value near 1. If a neuron has an output of 1 its output weight in the second layer pass their values to the linear neurons in the second layer.

In this particular application we are dealing with a supervised learning, where the input vectors include {P, Fe, Al, Si, Ca, Mg, Ti, K} and the target being carbon in ash {C}. P is the frequency measured online by the instrument and the rest of the above elements are respectively, iron, aliminium, silicon, calcium, magnisium, titanium and potasium. Those elements were measured at Powergen environment. The neural network results were achieved within a maximum training periods (epochs) of 1000. The network was trained with 50 of the 63 ashes, the remaining 13 being aside for validation. Detailed information about the ashes components from previous cases is stored in a database repository along with the equivalent frequencies. The information is retrieved in a form of query to the database, performed by the neural network system, for training and learning process. The input for the neural network has two paths.

Path1: input from the laser device and proximate analysis and take the form:
$[P_n$ , $FeO_{2\,n,}$ Aln , Sin , Can ,Mgn , Tin , Kn ] n stands for new values.
Path2: input of the previous successful cases stored in the database and takes the following form:
$[C_1\ \ C_2\ \ C_3\ \ C_4\ \ C_5\ \ C_6 \ldots\ldots\ldots\ldots C_{m}]$
Where for instance,
$C_1= f\ (P_1, Fe_{1,}\ Al_1, Si_1, Ca_1, Mg_1, Ti_1, K_1)$

### 3.3 The Database Repository

The database component is intended to provide an efficient storage, indexing and retrieval of previous information about the process determining coal efficiency in electricity generation.

The kind of information that needs to be stored and retrieved from the database include:

1. Coal: coal type and coal country of origin
2. Ash: where the ash originates from (coal), the frequency {P} quantified by the LASER instrument and a set of chemical components that make up the ash (Al, K, Na, Mg, etc).
3. Ash components: Fe, Al, Si, Ca, Mg, Ti, Ba, Na, K, P, Mn and S.These elements are found in most of the ashes with varying quantities.

Tables and instances needed for the relational database are shown below:

Coal Table

| *CoalType* | *CoalOrigin* |
|---|---|
| CT1 | Germany |
| CT2 | Chile |
| CT3 | France |

Ash Table

| *AshId* | *CoalType* | *Frequency* | *%C from TGA* |
|---|---|---|---|
| BET96042 | CT1 | 20 | 4.90% |
| ELC990111 | CT2 | 23 | 9.10% |
| LAC980624 | CT3 | 17 | 9.20% |
| FOR98062 | CT4 | 23 | 10.10% |

Per-Ash-Component Table

| *AshId* | *CompType* | *Percentage* |
|---|---|---|
| BET96042 | Fe | 13.70% |
| ELC990111 | Al | 28% |
| LAC980624 | Si | 46.40% |
| FOR98062 | Ca | 1.30% |

Component Table

| *Type* |
|---|
| Fe |
| Al |
| Si |
| Ca |

## 4 Description of the Process Cycle

The aim of the process is to determine the efficiency of coal burning in generating energy. Fig.3 illustrates the process cycle.

Ash components and their percentages are determined at PowerGen laboratories.

1. The target %C for the Neural Network training is measured using TGA.
2. Frequency {P} is determined experimentally using the Laser instrument.
3. Taking the ash components' percentages and the frequency {P} as inputs and C% as target, the Neural Net produces a carbon content estimate for the ash in question.
4. Initially the Neural Net is trained with the aid of a set of experimental data that is already stored in the database.
5. Each time the Net outputs a (valid) result; it is stored in the database along with other information, i.e. ash components' percentages and frequency {P}, along with coal information such as the type of the coal and its origin.

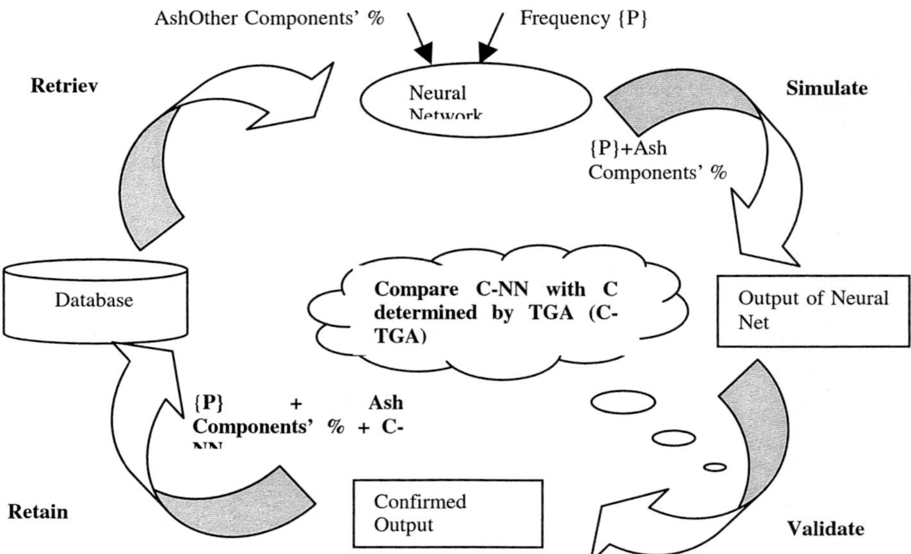


**Fig. 3.** Simulation of the Neural Networks in Collaboration with the Database and the Laser Instrument

## 5 Test and Performance of the New System

The whole system was bolted onto a furnace and aligned for testing at Powergen environment. Powergen supplied samples from four different coals together with their proximate analysis (mineral contents) which are needed as an input to the neural network system. This is shown in table 2.

**Table 2.** Coal Mineral Components(%)

| Coals | Fe | Al | Si | Ca | Mg | Ti | K |
|---|---|---|---|---|---|---|---|
| LAC | 7.1 | 25.8 | 52.6 | 3.6 | 1.1 | 1.2 | 1.1 |
| FOR | 3.7 | 28 | 45.7 | 6.9 | 2.2 | 1.5 | 0.6 |
| ELC | 6.8 | 22.3 | 51.1 | 3.2 | 1.6 | 1.0 | 1.7 |
| LAJ | 6.1 | 21.7 | 50.9 | 2.8 | 0.7 | 1.0 | 1.5 |

The process starts when the instrument picks up particles. The signal is processed and subsequently a frequency is calculated and then fed into the neural network as a second input. The neural network learns and trains using values retrieved from previous successful cases stored in the database, before making simulation for new cases. A set of 13 different ashes, which are 4 samples of LAJ type, 4 samples of ELC type, 4 samples of FOR type and one sample of LAC type, were investigated as part of the validation of the new system. Validation was carried out against values from TGA method performed at laboratory environment. The result is shown in Table 3. Note that NAS denotes new automated system. The new system worked continuously with its integrated components, and no major problem was identified during the process. From the results illustrated in Table 3 it is shown that the new system offers quality result as the carbon content could be determined to within ± 0.05% accuracy, regardless of coal type. The desired results were achieved in 8 hours using a system that costs less than £ 2,000 which is significantly important for the relevant industries. The graphical representation on validation is displayed in Fig. 4.

**Table 3.** Validation of the New System

| Ash coals | %C (TGA) | Time (TGA) | %C (NAS) | Time (NAS) |
|---|---|---|---|---|
| LAJ | 12.8 | 2 days | 12.6 | 35 min |
| LAJ | 2.20 | 2 days | 2.10 | 30 min |
| LAJ | 8.30 | 3 days | 8.30 | 30 min |
| LAJ | 7.10 | 3 days | 7.30 | 35 min |
| ELC | 12.6 | 3 days | 12.7 | 45 min |
| ELC | 9.50 | 3 days | 9.20 | 50 min |
| ELC | 9.30 | 2 days | 9.00 | 60 min |
| ELC | 10.3 | 3 days | 9.50 | 60 min |
| FOR | 9.90 | 2 days | 9.40 | 50 min |
| FOR | 4.50 | 3 days | 4.70 | 45 min |
| FOR | 1.80 | 3 days | 1.90 | 50 min |
| FOR | 3.80 | 3 days | 4.00 | 45 min |
| c | 7.60 | 3 days | 7.80 | 45 min |

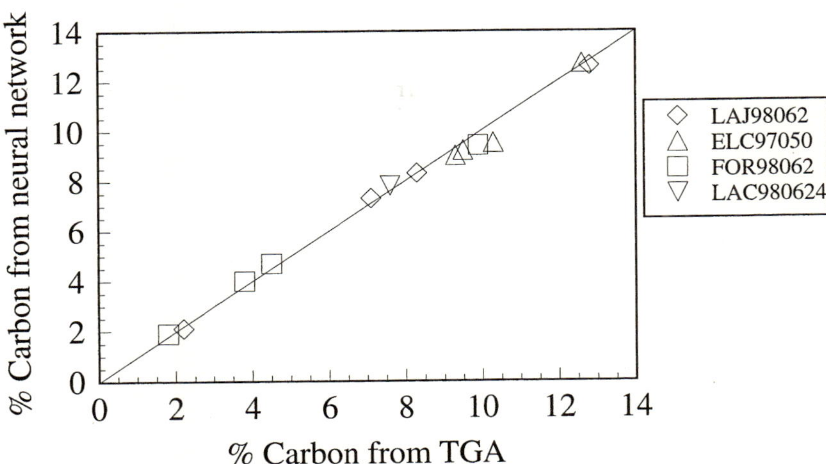


**Fig. 4** Comparison between TGA results and neural network simulation of carbon in ash percentage

## 6 Conclusions

A new integrated system for monitoring power efficiency has been introduced. The system, consisting of a Laser instrument, neural network system and database repository, has been tested for a range of coal ashes, and proved to be efficient, reliable and cheap. The system has been validated against data fron TGA method and found to be highly accurate. The savings in terms of cost and time achieved using the new system are not the only benefit. The system can be further explored where the resulting database could be shared for use in different applications and even uploaded on the Internet to be exploited by other organisations. This will certainly financially benefit the system holder.

## References

[1] Brown, R.C, 1991, Method and apparatus of measuring unburned carbon in fly-ash, US Patent N 506955.

[2] Ouazzane, A.K, Zerzour, K and Marir, F, 2002, Neural network technique to improve carbon content, WSEA Press, pp. 85-92.

# Application of Artificial Neural Network for Identification of Parameters of a Constitutive Law for Soils

Alessio Nardin[1], Bernhard Schrefler[1], and Marek Lefik[2]

[1] Department of Structural and Transportation Engineering - University of Padua, Italy via Marzolo 9, 35131 Padua, Italy nardin@caronte.dic.unipd.it

[2] Chair of Mechanics of Materials - Technical University of Lódz, Poland Al. Politechniki 6; 93-590,ŁLódz, Poland

**Abstract.** A common problem of excavation machinery based on mechanical actions is the unknown interaction of the cutting tools with geological settings. This interaction determines for different soils a different wear and consequently different economical costs for the excavation. We apply a strategy for soil modelling which is based on discretization of the continuum with rigid disks and suitable contact models and concentrate at contact level the real mechanical behaviour of the soil. In order to carry out the proposed strategy a "macro" and a "micro" level are established. In this paper an application of Artificial Neural Network (ANN) for identification of the parameters of the contact constitutive law is shown. The ANN is first trained using the theoretical results obtained from the developed numerical model. Results of some numerical tests concerning the choice of the proper topology of ANN, the best training set and the sensitivity of the identified parameters are shown.

## 1 Introduction

A common problem of excavation machinery based on mechanical actions is the unknown interaction of the cutting tools with various types of rock and more in general with geological settings. The problem is very important for the industry. In fact the interaction of the cutting tools with different soils determines a different wear and consequently different economical costs for the excavation. Due to the involved non-linearities, the numerical analysis of such phenomena is very complex. The classical continuum approach for soil modelling, in fact, presents several drawbacks, especially when large strains and crack propagation take place. To simplify the non-linear aspects some authors proposed to model the soil as a collection of spheres [1], [2].

Here we apply a strategy for soil modelling which is based on discretization of the soil with rigid disks and suitable contact models. The basic idea is to concentrate at contact level the real mechanical behaviour of the soil. The goal is achieved by extending the general concept of contact as an unilateral constraint condition, through a suitable constitutive law. For this purpose constitutive laws have been implemented in the node-to-segment contact formulation within the framework of the penalty method [3]. In this case the penalty parameter is not simply a constant based on

P.W.H. Chung, C.J. Hinde, M. Ali (Eds.): IEA/AIE 2003, LNAI 2718, pp. 545–554, 2003.

numerical necessities (e.g. to avoid ill conditioning of the stiffness matrix), but it is transformed into a non-linear function through the constitutive law itself. In order to carry out the proposed strategy a "macro" and a "micro" level are established: in the micromechanical model the mutual contact interaction between two disks is studied. In the macromechanical model the behaviour of a random array of disks is described in the framework of the finite element method. This modelling approach requires that, by linking the micro and macro levels, the most relevant parameters of the micromechanical model, which are the unknowns, have to be tuned to obtain a macroscopic behaviour similar to that of experimental data.

Due to the fact that this material model is becoming more and more complex to reproduce as closely as possible the observed experimental behaviour, we need several parameters to characterize the constitutive law. In this paper an application of Artificial Neural Network (ANN) for parameter identification of the constitutive law is shown. The overall aim consists in predicting the parameters of the micromechanical model as consequence of the real soil behaviour. The ANN is first trained using the theoretical results obtained from the developed numerical model: a large set of curves is calculated for this purpose by varying at random the values of the most important micromechanical parameters. We have to match the measured macroscopic behaviour, hence we have to pass through equivalent stresses and strains, defined on the packing of disks. Results of several numerical experiments concerning the choice of the proper topology of ANN, the best training set and the sensitivity of the identified parameters are presented. In the following we summarize first basic considerations of contact constitutive laws. After this we describe the ANN procedure for parameter identification. Finally the identification of some soils is performed.

## 2 The Micromechanical Model

We start from the representation of the continuum as an assembly of cylindrical rigid discrete elements (disks). In this strategy the reproduction of material properties is obtained trough a suitable contact law between the disks. The contact law is based on the classical concepts of elasto-plasticity theories, with suitable modifications. Usually, the contact law relates the contact force acting between two disks to their relative displacement. Within the FE framework the continuum deformation is modelled with classical displacement-based finite elements. Each element is able to capture the mechanical behaviour, in terms of strains and stresses by postprocessing the primary variable solution, i.e. the displacement field. In our strategy the displacement of a control volume results from the overlapping of the disks. The equivalent mechanical answer is then governed by the contact law, which transforms the classical error of a penalty contact formulation into the required displacement field. With this respect it has to be underlined that:

- the contact formulation deals with nodal forces and relative displacements;
- the contact force is the resultant of the contact stresses on the contact area associated to each contact node;
- the contact constitutive law is suitably tuned to get the equivalent global answer, still in terms of forces and displacements;
- from the above values a mean equivalent strain and stress field can be recovered for the control volume.

In the following we refer to these last two quantities. An analogous equivalence can be defined also for the tensile behaviour, using a cohesive contact law.

As previously stated, the model is based on the elasto-plastic relationships established for both normal and tangential direction

$$\sigma_i(F_i)=E_i\cdot\left(\varepsilon_i(g_i)-\varepsilon^{p}{}_i\left(g^{p}{}_i\right)\right) \qquad i=n,t \tag{1}$$

where $\sigma$ is the normal or tangential stress, $\varepsilon$ is the total strain, $\varepsilon^p$ is the plastic component of the total strain, $F$ is the contact force, $g$ is the total relative displacement between two disks, $g^p$ is the plastic component of the relative displacement, $n, t$ are the normal and tangential directions; $E$ are the elastic parameters, which characterize the elastic properties of the soil.

The yield function is defined for the normal stress-strain relation and for the tangential one. A general non-linear yield criterion has been formulated as follows

$$f(\sigma_i,\alpha_i)=\mid\sigma_i\mid-[\sigma_Y+H(\alpha_i)], \qquad i=n,t \tag{2}$$

where $H(\alpha)$ is the expression of plastic strain and is written as function of the softening or hardening parameter, $\alpha:[0,T]\rightarrow\Re_+$, $\sigma_Y$ is the limit of the elastic range. By changing these parameters we can define different shapes of the yield locus and simulate different soil behaviours.

The plastic strain increment, in normal and tangential direction, can be completely described for any admissible state of stress $\sigma_i\in E_\sigma$ by

$$\dot{\varepsilon}_i^p=\gamma_i\cdot sign(\sigma_i), \quad E_\sigma=\left\{(\sigma_i,\alpha_i)\in\Re\times\Re_+ \,\middle|\, f(\sigma_i,\alpha_i)\leq 0\right\}, \qquad i=n,t \tag{3}$$

where $\dot{\varepsilon}:[0,T]\rightarrow\Re$ is the time derivative of the plastic strain (normal or tangential), $T$ is the time parameter, $\gamma\geq 0$ is the absolute value of the slip rate and its variation is calculated trough the consistency parameter $\Delta\gamma$ and $E_\sigma$ is the domain of the admissible stresses. The adopted evolution equations for $\alpha$ in the normal and in the tangential contact law are

$$\dot{\alpha}_n=\left|\dot{\varepsilon}_n^p\right|, \qquad \dot{\alpha}_t=\left|\dot{\varepsilon}_t^p\right| \tag{4}$$

Dependence of the tangential force on the normal one is expressed by the application of a multi-parameter failure criterion. In this criterion the slip between two surfaces of a continuum is assumed to occurs when the shear stress, $\tau$, on any plane at a point in the soil material reaches a critical value, which depends non-linearly upon the normal stress in the same plane. In the numerical implementation at each step the value of the normal force is fixed and a yield surface is used to establish the elastic range of the tangential force, as shown in Figure 1.

The basic concept of the strength criterion is that the shear strength of a rock-like material is made up of two parts varying with the normal applied stress: an elastic "cohesive" part and a frictional plastic part. The shear strength can be written as follows:

$$\tau=E_t(\sigma_n)\cdot(\varepsilon_t-\varepsilon_t^p)-\left(n(\sigma_n)+H(\alpha)\right) \tag{5}$$

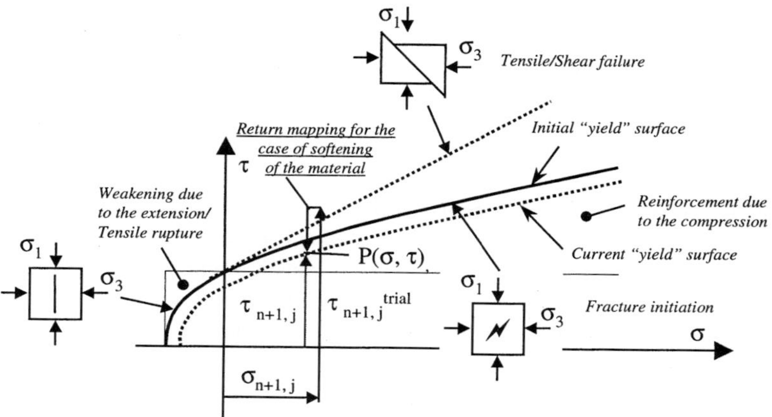


**Fig. 1.** Sketch of the 2D yield surface for the contact constitutive law.

where $\tau$ is the tangential critical stress; $\sigma_n$ is the applied normal stress; $\varepsilon_t$ and $\varepsilon_t^p$ are respectively the total and the plastic tangential strain, $H$ is a non-linear function of plasticity which correspond to those described in the equation (2), and $\alpha$ is obtained from the second of equations (4). The plastic softening (or hardening) frictional behaviour starts when the value of $\tau$ exceeds the limit flow, which is a function of the normal applied stress: $n(\sigma_n)$ delimits the flow range and it is expressed as

$$n(\sigma_n) = \eta \cdot (\sigma_n + c) \tag{6}$$

where $\eta$ and $c$ are material parameters which represent the contributes respectively of the frictional and cohesive behaviour of the material. The parameter $E_t$ characterizes the real shear modulus of the material. Equation (6) allows to model the experimentally observed increase of shear strength with increasing normal applied stress: this is a characteristic behaviour of a wide range of soils.

# 3 ANN Application for Parameter Identification

Artificial neural networks represent a qualified tool for solving complex inverse problems in computational mechanics. An overview of some relevant applications is given in [4], [5]. As stated in the introduction, our goal consists in predicting the values of the parameters of the micromechanical model starting from the real behaviour of the soil. To apply this numerical procedure it is necessary to have:

-1. A numerical and/or mathematical model which will be able to describe the studied physical phenomenon

-2. A sufficiently large set of observations (i.e. experimental tests, numerical simulations, etc...) which statistically reproduces the real or modelled phenomenon.

Regarding the first point, in this work we consider the soil discretization strategy previously stated (see § 2). A series of tests were carried out with some rock like materials (i.e. tuff, marble, andesite, etc…) using the constitutive law with the following plastic function

$$H(\alpha_i) = b_1\alpha_i^2 + b_2\alpha_i + b_3 \tag{7}$$

Initially four parameters will be identified: $E_n$, $b_1$, $b_2$, $b_3$. All tests are performed to define the proper ANN topology, to choose the minimal training set and to study the sensitivity of the identified parameters. Afterwards, we employ this tuned ANN to identify a larger number of parameters.

As shown in [6] the chosen mathematical model presents a set of parameters $s$ that, in our case, represents some important physical characteristics for defining the behaviour of the material. The set of parameters $s$ is obviously linked with a set of $S$ real values. For some parameters this link is direct, i.e. the elastic modulus and the shear modulus. For others, such as the parameters of the plastic function, there is an indirect transition through the macromechanical behaviour because they do not have a real physical meaning. The unknowns, true values of these parameters form a set $S$. The parameter identification correlates these sets by minimizing the error between the predicted and real behaviour. This is done through one of optimization procedures such as the least squares formulation and/or others, including statistical concepts.

The mathematical model involves a trial set $s$ which generates, as input data for the ANN, a set of values $t_p$. This set $t_p$ corresponds, to the experimental data set $t_{exp}$. The set $t_p$ can represent a graphical curve of important characteristics of the material (i.e. stress-strain curve) or a series of characteristic points of these curves. The couples of points determine the set $p = p(u_i, f_j)$ of sampling points, where $i = 1,\ldots,I$, $j = 1,\ldots,J$ and the number of sampling point is $m = IJ$. Starting from these assumptions, the performance of the ANN model can be measured by the following expression

$$\text{find } s^0 \text{ such that: } \forall s \left\| t_{p^0}(u_i, f_j) - t_{exp}(u_i, f_j) \right\| < \left\| t_p(u, f_j) - t_{exp}(u, f_j) \right\| \tag{8}$$

We consider an ordinary Euclidean norm in $m$ dimensional vector space: the task of the described model is to find $s^0$ that define the best fit according to equation (8).

Using the ANN, two main general approaches are available. The first, which is proper also of other identification techniques, consists in the direct solution of equation (8) as a minimization problem [4]. The second one, which is used in this work, deals with the construction of an additional operator $\Im$. This operator transforms the set of all trial data into a set of possible parameter values available for the specific model. In this way it is possible to attribute to each trial input set the value of the parameters that are used to its definition in the framework of the model. This procedure permits, for instance, to define the real set of parameters $s^0$ as an image of the experimental graphs. The relation that links, trough $\Im$, $s^0$ to the Cartesian graphical representation of the model characteristics is

$$\Im : \;\; \rightarrow R_S \;\; \Im(t_p) = s \quad thus \quad \Im(t_{exp}) = s^0 \tag{9}$$

$\Sigma$ is here a set of all possible curves generated by the model. If this operator exists, it can be approximated by ANN with sigmoidal transfer function. Moreover, if the mapping $\Im$ is continuous the ANN can be used as its universal approximator. In our work we used as input data set the points of the curve that describes the macroscopical behaviour of the material. The parameter values of the micromechanical model are calculated through ANN: this approach permits to link directly the micromechanical and macromechanical models. Finally the proposed algorithm can be divided in two principal tasks as follows

1) network activity in training mode
   - at input layer there is the representation of the data set of characteristic trial results obtained with different trying parameters;
   - at output layer there are values of the trying parameters;
   - the learning of the network stops when the training quality is achieved.
2) network activity in recall mode (for trained network)
   - at input layer there is the representation of the data set of experimental data;
   - at output layer the results are interpreted as the set of identified parameters.

## 4 Procedure of Numerical Identification and Sampling of Input Data Preparation

In this work we have adopted a Multi Layer Perceptron (MLP) neural network. This type of network is widely used and organizes its nodes (or neurons) in layers. Usually these layers can be divided in three main categories: input layer, hidden layer and output layer. The practical application of the presented method is made up of the following steps:

1) generation of trial data set through the identified model;
2) training of the developed multi-layer ANN;
3) presentation of the experimental graph at the input of the trained network to get as output the best approximation of the actual values of the soil parameters.

The simulation and training of the neural network has been performed using the Qnet2000 and SNNS codes (back propagation net generators). As previously explained, to train the network a rich sample set is required. Each set constitutes the input data for the identification parameter of the function.

The simulation of experimental tests reproduces the uniaxial compression and traction tests performed by S. Okubo and K. Fukui [8]. Through modified finite element code FEAP [7], the real specimen was discretized with different regular packing of disks (325 or 1250) as shown in Fig.2. The local stresses and strains are obtained in this case through a scaling law.

The soil specimen is reproduced according to actual size ($\phi = 25\,mm$, $h = 50\,mm$) and material characteristics. The plastic deformation is generated by the polynomial function of equation (7).

The ANN application to the identification predicts first the following target parameters: the elastic modulus $E_n$ and the plastic function parameters: $b_1, b_2, b_3$. With these parameters it is possible define the behaviour of some soils and rocks through the stress-strain curve such as to obtain a numerical curve comparable to the experimental one with a limited error range. An additional parameter considered is then $\sigma_t$. For a comparison of the quality of different topology of neural networks during training, Qnet2000 provides an error measure denoted by RMS. This error

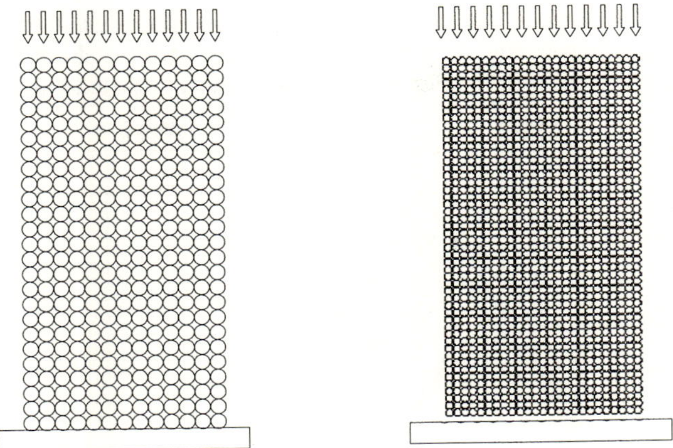

**Fig. 2.** Discretization of the specimen with 325 and 1250 rigid disks.

defines the convergence of training procedure at each step by computing the difference between the network response and the training target.

## 5 Applications

As previously stated, we have generated several stress-strain curves with the numerical model. These curves can be treated as the characteristics of any defined soil. Each curve is obtained starting from the real curve of the material and changing the value of the characteristic parameters: the concentration of all curves near to the real one permits a faster learning procedure. For this reason the parameters differ from the starting ones in the range given by a "quasi-Gauss" function which determines a distribution of the frequency values as depicted in Fig. 3. In all results shown in the sequel the maximum deviation of the initial value amounts to ± 25%.

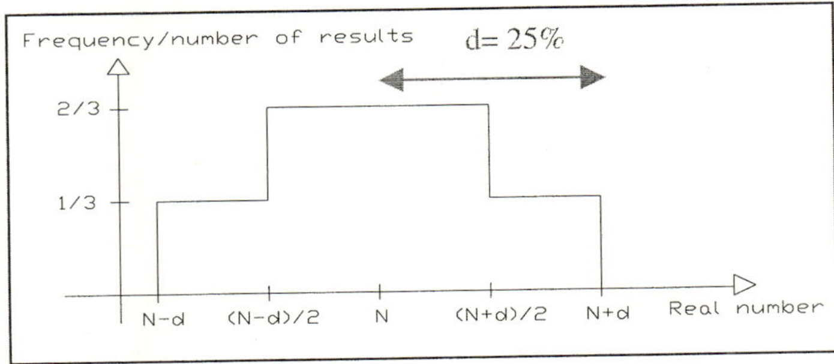


**Fig. 3.** "Quasi- Gauss" frequency function of the changed values of the micromechanical parameters

For all tested materials more than 150 training curves were created. Each curve has been described by a sufficient number of characteristic points, which have to capture the shape of the real curve. Only these "fictitious" curves are used for the neural network training as shown in Fig. 4. Some of the training patterns should be set apart as test patterns in order to check the degree of learning during the teaching process.

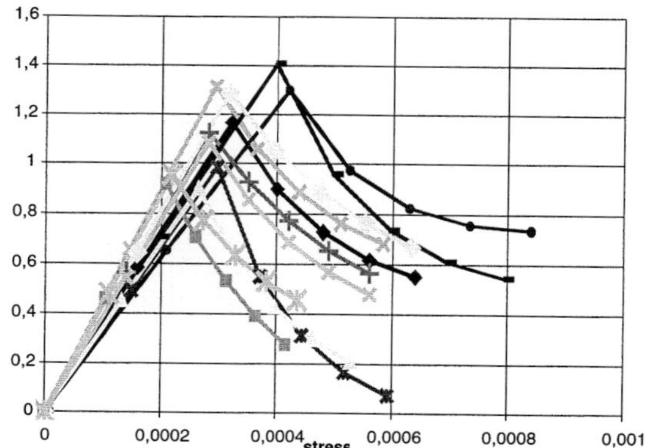


**Fig. 4.** Some samples of the neural network learning set for Japanese tuff in traction.

The starting parameters for the teaching are the following: learn rate coefficient = 0.001; momentum factor = 0.8. In order to keep a smooth course of the error decrease, the learn rate was changed gradually to its final values 0.0001-0.00005. However, to accelerate the training process, momentum factor was increased gradually to 1.

The first performed test is the uniaxial traction of the Japanese tuff. At the beginning the four parameters $E_n$, $b_1$, $b_2$, $b_3$ were changed. Subsequently also the yield stress, $\sigma_t$, (i.e. peak stress of the curve) has been varied, see Tables 1 and 2. As previously stated, these parameters have been changed in a random way. The identification abilities of the trained networks were checked using, as input data points, the couples of Cartesian coordinates of the real curve. The outputs of the networks also are shown in Tables 1 and 2.

**Table 1.** Identification of four parameters for Japanese tuff in traction.

| Parameter | Target data | Network output |
|---|---|---|
| $E_n$ | 87600 | 8.7555e+04 |
| $b_1$ | 8.64E+08 | 8.6238e+08 |
| $b_2$ | -48000 | -47870.79297 |
| $b_3$ | 0.0 | 0.0 |

**Table 2.** Identification of five parameters for Japanese tuff in traction.

| Parameter | Target data | Network output |
|---|---|---|
| $E_n$ | 87600 | 8.7626e+04 |
| $\sigma_t$ | 1.17 | 1.17080 |
| $b_1$ | 864000000 | 8.6826e+08 |
| $b_2$ | -48000 | -48144.62109 |
| $b_3$ | 0.0 | o.0 |

In Fig. 5 we show the curves generated by the identified parameters through the model for tuff in compression. We have used two different training data sets: in the first one the peak point of the curves is always included (pink curve, Qnet real 1), in the second one the points of the curve are randomly chosen (green curve, Qnet real 3).

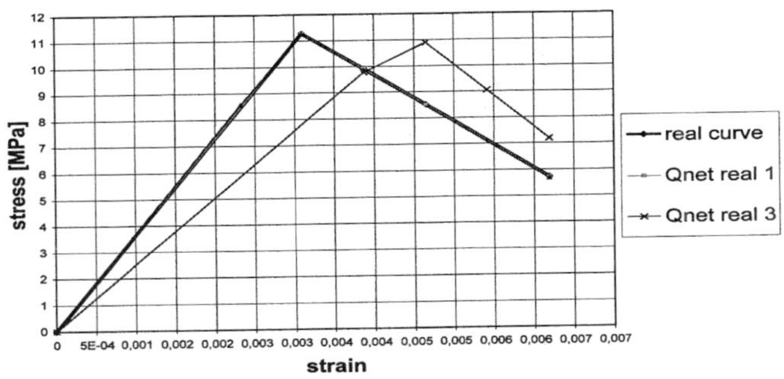


**Fig. 5.** Uniaxial compression for Japanese tuff: Comparison between the curves obtained from different ANN and the real one.

Finally, the results obtained for marble in uniaxial compression are shown. We compare in Fig. 6 the curves obtained from the identified parameters through the model. Also in this case we have adopted two training sets of data: in the first some random characteristic points of the curve are defined (pink curve, ANN 1), in the second one we adopt a regular constant step of increment of imposed displacement (black curve, ANN 2). The results show that the parameter identification is strongly dependent on the way with which we define the curve in the numerical test (i.e. the input data set).

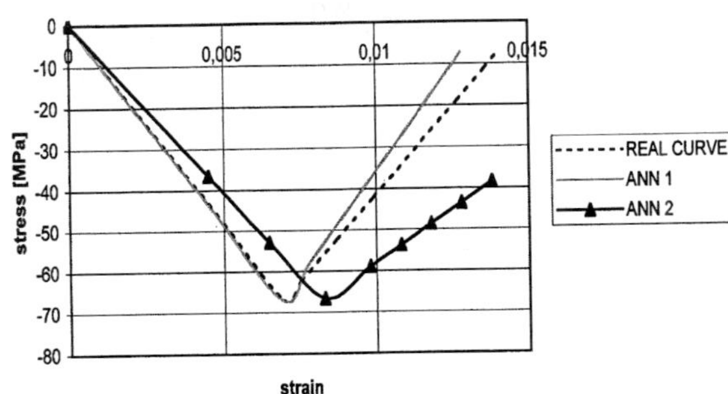


**Fig. 6.** Uniaxial compression for marble: comparison between real and ANN obtained curve.

## 6 Conclusions

An application of artificial neural network for parameter identification of a constitutive law has been presented. The ANN was trained using the theoretical results obtained from the developed macro and micro-mechanical numerical model.

Results of some numerical experiments concerning the choice of the proper topology of ANN, the best training set definition and the sensitivity of the identified parameters are shown. We have trained different networks with different input data sets for two materials with a regular packing of disks were used. The results show that the definition of input data set influences the learning procedure of the network.

**Acknowledgment**

Support of E.U. (project GRD1-1999-10330 "CUTTER") is gratefully acknowledged.

## References

1. Emeriault F. Cambou B. Micromechanical modeling of anisotropic non-linear elasticity of granular medium. Int. J. Solids Structures, Vol 33, No. 18, pp. 2591-2607 (1996).
2. Cundall P.A., Strack D.L. A discrete numerical model for granular assemblies, Géotechnique, 29, 47-65, 1979.
3. Zavarise G., Wriggers P., Stein E., Schrefler B. "Real Contact Mechanism and Finite Element Formulation- a Coupled Thermomechanical Approach". Int. Jour. For Numerical Meth. in Eng. Vol 35 pgg. 767-785 (1992).
4. Pincus A. Approximation theory of the MLP model in neural networks. Acta Numerica. (1999). pp. 143-195.
5. Huber N. Tsakmakis Ch. A neural network tool for identifying the material parameters of a finite deformation viscoplasticity model with static recovery. Comp. Meth. Appl. Mech. Engr. 191 (2001) pp. 353-384.
6. Lefik M., Gawin D. Application of neural networks for the identification of function describing heat and mass sources intensity during hardening of fresh concrete. ECCM-2001 Creacow Poland.
7. G. Zavarise, A. Nardin, B.A. Schrefler. Discrete methods for soil modeling. Nafems "Conference and Users' Meeting 2002". (3-4 Ottobre 2002 Bergamo (Italy).
8. Okubo S., Fukui K.: Complete Stress_Strain Curves for Various Rock Types in Uniaxial Tension, Int. J. Rock Mech. Min. Sci. & Geomech. Abstr. Vol 33. N° 6 . pp 549-556.(1996).

# Visualising the Internal Components of Networks

Clinton Woodward and Gerard Murray

Centre for Intelligent Systems and Complex Processes
School of Biophysical Sciences and Electrical Engineering
Swinburne University of Technology, Australia
cjw@swin.edu.au, gmurray@swin.edu.au

**Abstract.** Feed forward artificial neural networks (FFANN), trained by supervision, are useful modelling tools. Data models are developed by statistical regression of some measure of error in network performance over the period of training. The success of training can only be gauged after the testing phase. Valuable information concerning how a network develops a representative model, the act of modelling, is lost as only the final weight state of the network, the model, is considered relevant. A group of visualisation techniques are presented that allows network performance to be studied in real time, from any output perspective of any network component during the training phase. Although confined to data subsets with a two-dimensional input vector, these techniques offer fast functional elucidation in image form, without computational expense or exhaustive mathematical analysis.

## 1 Introduction

FFANNs are generally applied in one of two ways. In the first instance, the relationship between the input vector and the output of the network remains obscured. A relationship exists but it is implied and cannot be easily established. The network output is the transformed weighted sum of the inputs and to calculate this, the inputs must be encoded with the weight metric. Given this, all that is of interest is that the network was trained to a desired tolerance, tested with data that was not included in the training set and perhaps validated with yet another subset of the data. This is typically labelled the "black box" approach. Inputs are presented to the network where some "black box" transform is applied and an output results.

The second instance of FFANN application is more involved then the train-test-use approach. Here, the model that the fully trained network represents is of interest, but of equal or greater importance is the understanding of the modelling process and the relationships established through this process between the inputs and the output. Such understanding always comes at very high computational expense given that the inputs are further convoluted as they are fed forward through successive hidden layers.

A number of different approaches have been developed that allow the user to relate the structure of the artificial neural network (ANN) to the way in which it functions. Fundamental to this is some means of extracting and interpreting the internal representations generated by the network.

Rule extraction [1,2] from fully trained networks is an algorithmic approach but to get a concise or minimal set of symbolic rules network structure must be changed to

P.W.H. Chung, C.J. Hinde, M. Ali (Eds.): IEA/AIE 2003, LNAI 2718, pp. 555–564, 2003.

remove redundant connections or units [3]. Network rationalisation requires pruning algorithms that are time consuming [3] because they are iterative. Often the rules generated require further analysis to be fully understood.

Weight state clustering, contribution analysis and sensitivity analysis find patterns in the effect different input dimensions have on the output of processing units in subsequent layers of the network. These methods are input specific and cannot infer anything about the global properties of the network [4].

Hyperplane analysis is a technique that generates visual representations of the hyperplanes associated with artificial neurons in a network. Global properties of the network can be described by this method [4].

A way to obtain exact representations and not approximations is to analyse the decision regions in input space [4]. The output of the network defines the partitioning of input space into regions. Unlike the network, decision regions directly map the input vector to the output without the intermediate mappings to any hidden layers. Representations are exact and decision regions can be visually inspected.

The emphasis in all of these methods is the model. A model, in the form of an approximated function, is constructed and then methodically broken up to infer network properties.

The authors contend that the modelling process is as important as the model and suggest a methodology that provides real time access to the output characteristics of any network component, or the network, itself without disrupting the interdependence of one network component upon another. Both local and global properties of the network, although qualitative in nature, can be perceived in the context of the network's parametric state and no more information processing is required other than that of the feed forward cycle itself.

Visual representation of this information allows the exploitation of the human eye and visual cortex for fast recognition of relevant patterns and transient features.

## 2 Methodology

The general methodology used to represent the ANN output is not unique, but the application of this technique to constituent components of a network, and in particular weighted values, is particularly novel and can be generically applied to ANN research. Below we discuss the method of sampling, the use of colour scales, data point representation, 3D representation, sampling considerations and other extensions of the technique.

### 2.1 Sampling Process

The work presented here has used a limited ANN system of two inputs although the technique can be extended to N inputs. A single output is typical and commonly used, however many outputs can be presented in parallel. Of special note is a network with three outputs that can be mapped to red, green and blue (RGB) components of colour and works particularly well with exclusive output classes.

With the simple network case of two inputs and one output, we present the system with a series of input vectors that will provide an even sampling of points across the normal range of input values. For each input vector the network generates a response and we record the output value generated. These recorded values are then presented visually as either a bitmap image where each pixel location corresponds to a sample vector and pixel colour correlates to the recorded value, or alternatively the value can be used as a height component (z) of a three dimensional (3D) point where the sample vector is used for the (x) and (y) components.

## 2.2 Colour Scale Utilisation

A conversion is made from the numerical recorded value to a corresponding colour. For the examples given in this paper we are limited to grey-scale representations where low values are represented by black scaling up to high values represented by white. Additionally we utilise transitions in chrominance, also known as pseudo colour scales, to accentuate the visual impression of features of interest, but unfortunately we cannot present these in this work. Sensibly, researchers need to be aware of potential problems with pseudo colour representation in that human visual sensitivity to chrominance change can misrepresent the true importance of features.

Positively however, one particularly useful pseudo colour scale we have implemented shows "banded" regions of unique colour to represent acceptable error levels around the normalised output values (typically logic "high" and "low"). From this pseudo colour representation we can quickly identify points or regions of the network output space that are not within acceptable error tolerances.

## 2.3 Data Point Representation

Data point sets used for training and testing of the system can be overlayed on any visual display. Function based training can also be represented by sampling the function and displaying the sampled points as a representative example. Although important to visualise the data points a network is being trained or tested on, a large number of data points will obscure the sampled network output. Additionally the display of many points can be computationally expensive, depending on the implementation techniques used, so the ability to selectively display or hide data points is useful.

## 2.4 Representation of a 3D Surface

A 3D surface can be created by triangulation between neighbouring sample points. The term "surface" is used because the output values from a network are a continuous function although we are only taking discrete samples to represent this. When creating a 3D surface, we are assuming that our sampling points are representative of the features in the output surface but this depends on the sampling quality.

It is sometimes visually useful to change the display of a 3D surface from a solid surface back to single points or the lines of the triangulated mesh to better examine features. A friendly visual user-interface tool that allows easy rotation and scaling is particularly useful. Further the addition of pseudo colour mapping to height allows for better recognition of features observed from an equivalent "flat" bitmap representation (an example of this is shown in figure 2).

### 2.5 Sampling Resolution Considerations

The changing nature of feature complexity for a network output means that a suitable sample vector resolution can be a dynamic property. If the sampling vectors chosen are spaced too far apart with respect to changing features of the output surface, aliasing errors (or quantisation) in the representation will result. Conversely, if the sampling vector resolution is increased, the computation time required to sample the response of the network increases exponentially. Additionally, the more complex the architecture of the ANN the greater the computational expense involved in generating responses for each individual input vector.

For practical reasons it is best if the sampling resolution can be adjusted dynamically so that an acceptable compromise between computational time and suitable sampling resolution can be achieved. Later we discuss "real-time" visual sampling and the computation requirement is also a consideration for selecting a sample resolution value.

### 2.6 Internal Component Inspection

To extend the visual inspection of a network, the response of the system can also be measured at any exterior (output node) or internal point. Examples of internal points include hidden node activation values, weighted summation (input activation) within hidden nodes, current weight values and weighted input values.

Because of the combinatorial nature of internal network components, the representation of a single isolated internal component contains limited quantitative value. Rather it is the qualitative aspects of internal components, when displayed with other relevant internal components, which are of qualitative value. This removes the requirement for assigning singular numerical data significance and allows for feature-based qualities to be observed instead.

### 2.7 Multimap View

As the visual features extracted from internal components are of more benefit when observed in comparison to other internal components, and in particular the internal components on the equivalent hierarchical level, we commonly present responses from internal components in a form we call a multimap view. This is a reasonably logical organisation of all inspected internal and external system components organised in a hierarchical manner based on the network architecture information.

For example, we represent two input nodes by simple circles located at the bottom of the map, while the response of the output nodes, represented as small bitmaps, are displayed at the top. In between we represent all inspected internal components as a series of bitmaps with equivalent hierarchical levels on the same horizontal level. Individual bitmaps are kept to a minimal size to reduce the computation cost involved in sampling and translating the many potential recorded values into the visual form.

Once displayed, the multimap view can be saved as a single bitmap image for easy reference.

An additional consideration when displaying samples of the internal components is that the range of values possible from each type of component can be different. The internal activation values or weighted input values can be very large, while the output from a Tanh activation function is nicely limited to ±1. How to represent these values, and whether to scale or simply limit values for the representation, has to be considered. We tend to use a consistent scale range for all internal component values (and limit large values), rather than scaling for each type of component, so that a comparison between elements of similar values is easily possible. Inspection of particular architectures may benefit from different scaling strategies.

Typically we do not display data points on top of every bitmap in the multimap view. This can easily be done and may assist in identifying component contributions to the system output, but given that the multimap view only displays small bitmaps, all but the smallest data sets would obscure each individual bitmap.

Various colour scales can be used for the multimap view, however some colour scales are not suitable for internal components. For example the "banded" pseudo colour scale described previously is only suitable for the output layer as the banded regions do not correlate to values used by internal components.

To investigate the contrasting or contributing influences of various internal components, extra investigative maps can be added to the normal maps of the multimap view (see figure 4). For example we have created additional layers that display the current output map with the influence of one internal component removed or subtracted from the result. Building on this, the difference between the complete output map and the subtracted output map show the internal components contribution to the complete output.

## 2.8 3D Map Surface / Hierarchical Tree View

While the representation of an internal component response value in the multimap view allows an overview of the contribution of all components, examining in detail the output of single component is best achieved with the 3D map representation.

We have implemented an interface that allows a user to select a single component from a tree hierarchy of the network components (based on the same information used for the multimap view) and then view, rotate, scale, etc. a representation of that component's response values as a 3D surface. As for each single 3D output surface, various parameters for sample resolution, pseudo colour height mapping, and surface rendering are all available and adjustable.

## 2.9 Real-Time and Time Dependent Visual Representations

A natural progression from the inspection techniques developed so far is to allow for the inspection of a network system in transit from one state of weight values to a new set based on a training algorithm such as back-propagation. These visual images could be observed in real time as they are generated, saved as images and observed sequentially at a later time, or the images combined and converted into a convenient movie format for playback. The images used could be simple small bitmaps of the output surface, large and detailed bitmaps of the output surface, multimap views or bitmap version of 3D output views.

In the exhaustive and complete sense we could represent a new visual output representation for every new weight or set of weight values. This provides for some very interesting information regarding the training changes that a system experiences, but for more than trivial network systems, it becomes extremely computationally expensive and usually generates more information than is practically useful from the perspective of temporal validity.

## 2.10 Sample Event Determination

Instead of exhaustive sampling after every training cycle there are several alternative approaches that can be used to sample. We use the term "sample event determination" to describe the process used to decide when to automatically sample a network system.

The general factor that influences sample event determination is the detail required for experimentation juxta positioned with the computational cost of sampling. Exhaustive sampling that halts training while it samples will slow the system by orders of magnitude. The first approach to minimise this expense is to sub-sample based on training events such as after a required number of examples have been shown to the network, when an epoch has occurred (and the network weights have actually changed), after a complete pass of the entire training data, or at longer intervals of several complete data set passes. These sub-sampling event intervals can be linked quite nicely with interesting training events.

Another approach is the sparse "snap-shot" technique whereby key events such as the number of data points correctly modelled or the level of system error are used to signify that a sample event should occur. These events are also typically of interest as significant stages in the training progress.

So far we have discussed strongly coupled sample events where training is halted while the network is sampled. If the use of visualisation is as a quick inspection of progress or there is a strong desire not to impede progress of the training algorithm, separate "thread" techniques can be used for both the training algorithm and the visualisation sampling. This requires careful consideration of threading methodologies and data access, but in simple terms the visualisation thread should require minimum restrictive access to a main training thread.

Briefly, one threading technique used involves the replication of only the weight values into a separate equivalent network structure that can be used for sampling. The actual replication can be done by the main training thread quickly, requiring less computational operations than full sampling, while the longer process of sample input presentation and sampling for each point required to build a map or sample takes place in the separate visualisation thread. The topic of effective threading strategies is complex and interesting, however any more detail is beyond the scope of this paper.

Our implementations typically make use of small low-resolution bitmap samples that operate in a separate thread and occur at a frequency determined by the number of passes through the entire data set that a training algorithm has performed. Because of the low-resolution samples we extrapolate the bitmap images to a larger bitmap area. Although this results in large areas of aliased information, it provides enough information about the systems training progress, in a bitmap size large enough to see effectively, while keep computational expense low.

### 2.11 Recording and Recreating System State

When investigating the effect of parameter adjustment, and in particular dynamic training parameters, visual techniques and tools as described above can assist in several ways. Firstly they provide an understanding, through observation, of training stage dynamics and the current system status. Secondly they can be used to perform parallel comparisons of equivalent systems with different training parameters. Thirdly they can be used to visually indicate qualitative stages of training, such as premature convergence and resource exhaustion, although these can sometimes be extremely subjective qualities.

Although not strictly related to visualisation techniques, if the implemented ANN system allows for the recording and recreation of the ANN, its parameters and its weight values, an investigation can be constructed that uses different training parameters for each of the identified stages or where changes in parameters are triggered by recognition of such stages. Additionally, the ability to record and recreate network architecture and its complete weighted state is an excellent validation methodology for new architectures and training or modelling paradigms.

## 3 Results / Examples

Figures 1-4 show various visual representation of information about a simple 2-3-4-1 MLP network (2 inputs, 2 hidden layers of 3 and 4 nodes respectively and one output node), trained on a synthetic nine point Boolean dataset designed to encourage interesting folds of network output surface.

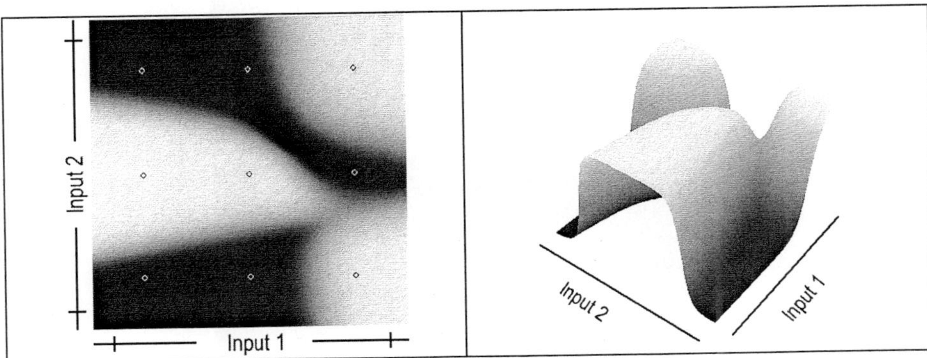


**Figure 1**. Sampled response from output node of a MLP network displayed as a bitmap image with values represented as greyscale colours. Data points are shown as small coloured circles where colour matches value.

**Fig. 2**. Same sample data represented as 3D surface. Note that in this case response values have been represented by both a height component and a corresponding greyscale colour to enhance presentation.

Figures 1 and 2 present the same response information but in the form of a greyscale bitmap and 3D surface respectively. In figure 4 we see the multimap view displaying internal component responses as well as a smaller version of the network output. Hidden layers are numbered with respect to the feed forward convention. Note that figure 4 immediately provides more information than is available from figure 3.

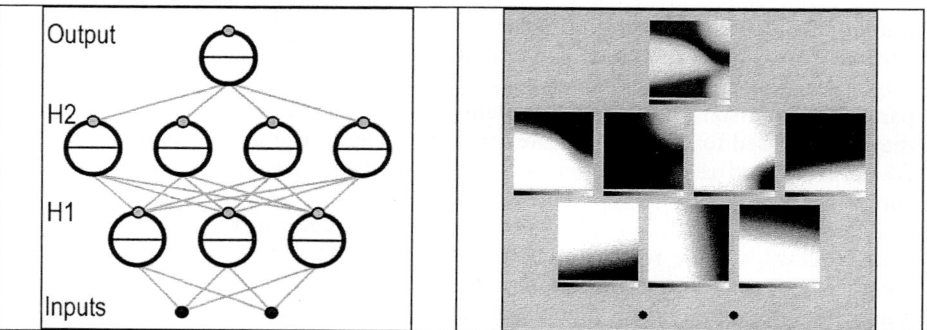


**Fig. 3**. MLP architecture used for figures 1,2 & 4. Note the multimap structure relationship in figure 4.

**Fig. 4**. Multimap view with each small bitmap corresponding to the response of a component – in this case the network nodes.

The ramp and hill data set [5] presents a difficult and interesting problem for artificial neural network modelling systems. Our research has successfully applied micro-net architectures to this data [6]. Figure 5 shows the output bitmap created from the sampled micro-net, while figure 6 is the original ramp and hill training data represented as a 3D contour plot for comparison with the 3D surface created from the micro-net sampled response.

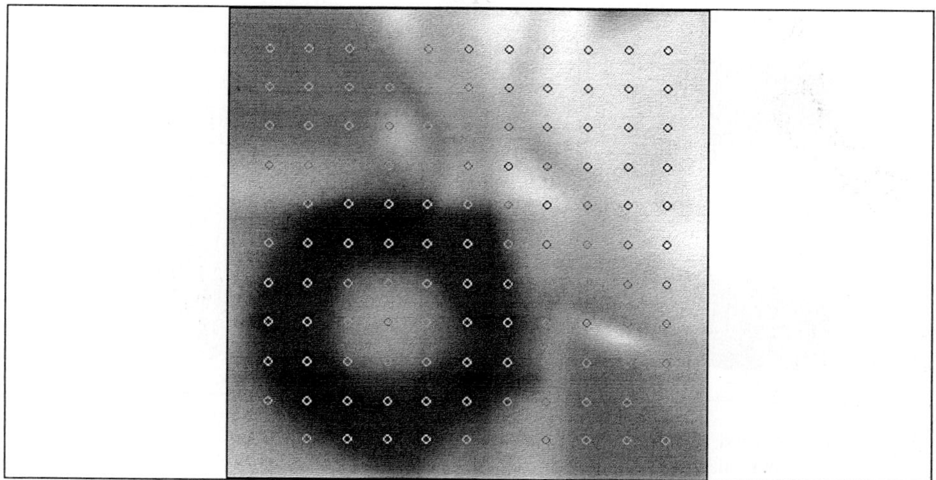

**Fig. 5.** Plannar view of the sampled output from a micro-net that has modelled the ramp and hill data.

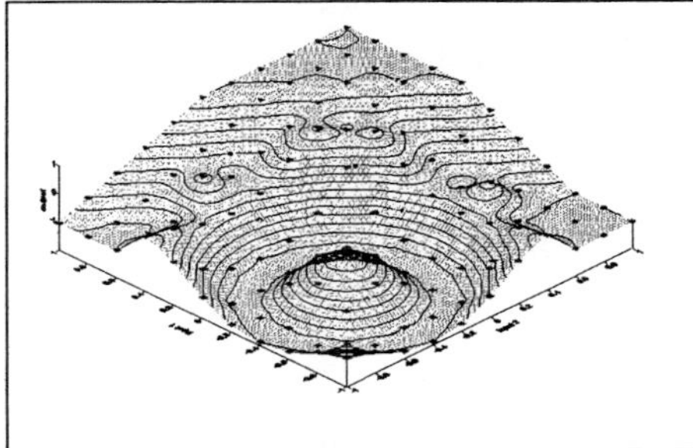

**Fig. 6** Ramp and hill data set as a contour plot showing the distribution of points.

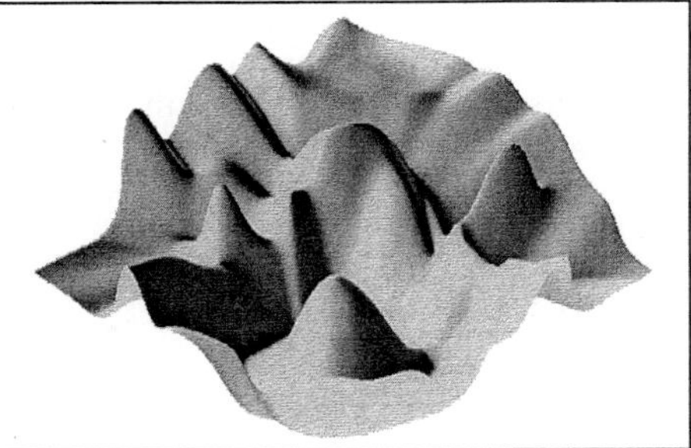

**Fig. 7.** 3D surface plot of the sampled output response (also shown in figure 5). Note the feature similarities to figure 6.

A multimap view of the internal components used by the micro-net architecture (not included in this communication) to model the ramp and hill data is interesting in that it illustrates how the system has decomposed the problem space into smaller regions and then applied component resources to model specific features of the data. Visual insights, provided by real-time sampling, into the dynamic effects of training paradigms have been an invaluable part of the micro-net development.

## 4 Discussion

The requirement of a two input system is normally a major limitation of visualisation techniques. However, even though using a limited input system, these techniques provide important modelling and training paradigm insights that can be applied by the researcher to higher dimensional input systems. Several applications of these visualisation techniques have provided interesting qualitative information (results not present here) and are worth noting. For example comparing the effect of architectural differences with similar training paradigms, or equivalent architectures with varying training parameters. Similarly, when applied to different networks types such as pi-sigma or sigma-pi, these techniques demonstrate immediate differences in functionality and training.

It is possible to extend or apply the techniques described here in several ways. Observed qualitative properties of internal components could be used as modifiers for credit assignment or error quantities. Using input winnowing techniques, or by constraining select inputs and sampling across two remaining inputs, visualisation can be successfully applied to higher input systems.

One interesting extension to this visual technique is a three input system where each sample vector point would be represented by a volumetric pixel (voxel) using transparency and pseudo colour mapping as an indication of sampled values. Effective navigation of such a volumetric representation is an interesting consideration.

We observe that bitmap and wire-frame surface representations of network component responses provide insight into the convergent state of the network and the continued viability of training. Real-time visual sampling represents not only the static network state but also the dynamic changes experienced by the system during training. These techniques use existing information from the network system and do not try to constrain or modify the system, as other visual or investigative techniques do, to extract useful information.

## 5 Conclusion

The methodology suggested has been applied to the analysis of a number of data sets, both synthetic and real. It has proven to be invaluable especially in the elucidation of the behaviour of new network architectures and training paradigms. Application of these techniques may be of use to other investigators interested in understanding both temporal and persistent component contributions with in a network. The techniques may also be useful for the analysis of different ANN architectures and training paradigms outside the scope of conventional ANN's.

### Acknowledgments

The authors gratefully acknowledge all the members of the Centre for Intelligent Systems and Complex Processes for their support and encouragement during this research.

## References

1. Andrews, R., Diederich, J. and Tickle, A.B., A survey and critique of techniques for extracting rules from Trained artificial neural networks, *Knowledge-Based Systems*, **8**, (1995), 373-389.
2. Duch, W., Adamczak, R., Grabczewski, K., Ishikawa, M. and Ueda, H., Extraction of crisp logical rules using constrained backpropagation networks, *Proceedings of the international Conference of the European Symposium on Artificial Neural Networks*, (1997), 109-114.
3. Setiono, R. and Leow, W.K., FERNN: A algorithm for fast extraction of rules from neural networks, *Applied Intelligence*, **12**, *nos.* 1-2, (2000), 15-25.
4. Melnik, Ofer and Pollack, Jordan. Exact representations from feed-forward networks, *Technical Report* CS-99-205, Volen Center for Complex Processes, Brandeis University; (1999), 1-33.
5. McNames, J., Innovations in Local Modeling for Time Series Prediction, *PhD Thesis*, Stanford University (1999).
6. Murray, G. and Hendtlass, T., Enhanced Artificial Neurons for Network Applications, *Proceedings of the 14$^{th}$., International Conference on Industrial and Engineering Applications of Artificial Intelligence and Expert Systems*, Hungary, (2001).

# Bayesian Web Document Classification through Optimizing Association Word

Su Jeong Ko[1], Jun Hyeog Choi[2], and Jung Hyun Lee[1]

[1] School of Computer Science & Engineering, Inha University
Yong_hyen dong , Namgu, Inchon, Korea
sujung@nlsun.inha.ac.kr, jhlee@inha.ac.kr

[2] Division of Computer Science, Kimpo College
San 14-1, Ponae-ri, Wolgot-myun
Kimpo, Kyonggi-do, Korea
jhchoi@kimpo.ac.kr

**Abstract.** Previous Bayesian document classification has a problem because it does not reflect semantic relation accurately in expressing characteristic of document. In order to resolve this problem, this paper suggests Bayesian document classification method through mining and refining of association word. Apriori algorithm extracts characteristic of test document in form of association words that reflects semantic relation and it mines association words from learning documents. If association word from learning documents is mined only with Apriori algorithm, inappropriate association word is included within them. Accordingly it has disadvantage of lack of accuracy in document classification. In order to complement the disadvantage, we adopt method to refine association words through use of genetic algorithm. Naïve Bayes classifier classifies test documents based on refined association words.

## 1 Introduction

Previous study of automatic classification of document includes use of probability [9,14], use of statistics[5] and use of vector similarity[11]. Among them, document classification through Bayesian probability is effective method[10,13]. Since document classification through use of simple Naïve Bayes classifier[12] extracts all words appeared in document, it is hard to reflect characteristic of document accurately. Mistaken classification caused by this reduces accuracy of classification. Because of this, Bayesian document classification method[8] that uses TF•IDF to make it more accurate was suggested. Suggested method extracts characteristic of document through use of TF•IDF from document. It also gives weight to characteristic extracted from document and so mistaken classification caused by noises is reduced more than simple Naïve Bayes classifier. However, since characteristic of extracted document does not reflect semantic relation, it could not resolve the problem of mistaken classification caused by ambiguity of word.

P.W.H. Chung, C.J. Hinde, M. Ali (Eds.): IEA/AIE 2003, LNAI 2718, pp. 565–574, 2003.

In order to resolve this problem, this paper suggests Bayesian document classification method through mining and refining of association word. In suggested method, Apriori algorithm extracts characteristic of test document in the form of association word that reflects semantic relation between words. Since it resolves problem of mistaken classification caused by ambiguity it makes document classification more accurate. In addition, Apriori algorithm mines association words from learning documents. Then genetic algorithm[6] refines association words to reduce classification errors caused by noises. Naïve Bayes learning gives probability to refined association words and Naïve Bayes classifier classifies test document whose characteristic was extracted in the form of association word.

## 2 Previous Naïve Bayes Classifier

As for Simple Naïve Bayes classifier, if characteristic of test document (D) is $\{n_1,n_2,\ldots,n_k,..,n_m\}$, it classifies the document into one class among {class1, class2,..,classID,..,classN} according to Equation (1).

$$class = \arg\max_{classID=1}^{N} P(classID)\prod_{k=1}^{m} P(n_k|classID) \quad (1)$$

In Equation (1), P(classID) is the probability that it is classified as classID and $P(n_k|classID)$ is an probability that $n_k$ is within classID. Each word of $\{n_1,n_2,\ldots,n_k,..,n_m\}$ is assumed to be independent regardless of context. Probability of $P(n_k|classID)$ on each word based on assumption of independence can be obtained through adoption of Equation (2).

$$p(w_k \mid classID) = \frac{numk_{classID}+1}{num_{classID}+|Voc|} \quad (2)$$

In Euation (2), $num_{classID}$ is a total number of words within classID and $numk_{classID}$ is frequency of appearance of word $w_k$ in classID and |Voc| is a total number of words of classID.

Naïve Bayes classifier through use of TF•IDF makes morphological analysis of document to extract characteristic of document and extracts only nouns from its outcome. TF•IDF[4] of all extracted nouns can be obtained through Equation (3).

$$W_{nk} = f_{nk} \bullet [\log_2 \frac{n}{DF} + 1] \quad (3)$$

In Equation (3), $fn_k$ is relative frequency of word $n_k$ against all words within the document and n is the number of study documents and DF is the number of learning documents where word $n_k$ appeared. If characteristic of test document(D) is $\{n_1,n_2,\ldots,n_k,..,n_m\}$, Naïve Bayes classifier classifies test document(D) into one class among {class1,class2,..,classID,..,classN} according to Equation (4).

$$class = \arg\max_{classID=1}^{N} P(classID)\prod_{k=1}^{m} W_{nk} P(n_k|classID) \quad (4)$$

# 3 Bayesian Web Document Classification through Mining and Refining of Association Word

This chapter explains Bayesian web document classification through mining and refining of association word.

## 3.1 Mining and Refining of Association Word

This paper expresses the document as association word. Apriori algorithm[1,2] extracts association rule between words through data mining. In order to extract the most proper association word, confidence should be fixed at not less than 85% and support not more than 25%[6]. Table 1 is an example of association words in game class.

**Table 1.** Association words in game class

| |
|---|
| (1)game&organization&athlete&match&sports&participation=>selection |
| (2)domestic&newest&technology&installation=>development |
| (3)game&participation&popularity&user&access=>event |
| ... |
| (18)game&provision&illustration=>explanation |

Genetic algorithm extracts important association word by using gene, chromosome and population. Gene indicates association word extracted through mining technique and expressed as bit of 0 and 1. Chromosome expresses each web document and it consists of group of genes expressed in bits. Population is the whole documents. Genetic algorithm refines association words through initialization, fitness calculation, recomposition, selection, crossover, mutation, fitness evaluation. In initialization stage, collected documents are defined as chromosome and expressed as gene. To do this, we extract nouns from selected ten documents through such process as morphological analysis. In Table 2, we show these nouns.

**Table 2.** Extracted nouns from web documents in population

| Document | Nouns |
|---|---|
| Doc1 | organization, page, genesis, rule, image, ... |
| Doc2 | participation, wedding, athlete, couple, . .. |
| Doc3 | individual match, reorganization, game, ... |
| .... | ... |
| Doc10 | individual match, sports, group match, .. |

If nouns included into association word in Table 1 exist in nouns in Table 2, gene for constituting document becomes 1. If it does not exist gene becomes 0. Through this initialization, each document is expressed as a gene as shown in Table 3.

**Table 3.** Expressing web document as chromosome

| Document | Chromosome(the first generation) |
|---|---|
| Doc1 | 1011000000000100000 |
| Doc2 | 0010000000000001001 |
| Doc3 | 1010111101000001111 |
| ... | ... |
| Doc10 | 1010110100000000010 |

This paper calculates fitness to find out whether selected document is proper for use in class. To do this, we use Jaccard method[3] of Equation (5). In Equation (5), #(doc*n* *U* doc*m*) indicates the sum of the number of genes having the value of 1 in chromosome that represents doc*n* and the number of genes having the value of 1 in chromosome that represents doc*m*. #(doc*n* • doc*m*) indicates the number of genes having the value of 1 at same bit in chromosome that represents doc*n* and chromosome that represents doc*m*.

$$\text{Fitness}(\text{doc}n,\text{doc}m)=\#(\text{doc}n \bullet \text{doc}m)/\#(\text{doc}n \cup \text{doc}m) \tag{5}$$

In recomposition stage, Equation (6) for adjusting fitness is used. Equation (6) calculates ratio of fitness (Fitness[class,doc]) of each document against total fitness of all documents that belong to class. According to this, fitness is readjusted and saved in Fitness-s[class,doc].

$$Fitness\_s[class,doc]=\frac{Fitness[class,doc]}{\sum_{doc=1}^{t} Fitness[class,doc]} \tag{6}$$

In selection stage, select document subject to crossover based on recomposed fitness. In that case, doc3, doc4, doc5, doc6, doc8 are highly likely to be selected as parent chromosome because they have higher recomposed fitness than the others. In crossover stage, selected documents are subject to crossover. This paper uses 1-point crossover method, which is to select one point randomly and to exchange subsequent genes with genes of other documents. Pc is probability that crossover is conducted on selected document. This paper has used 0.9 crossover probability. In mutation stage, a bit is changed into another value according to given probability. Mutation rate is probability that genes of chromosome change into another value. This paper designates 0.01 as mutation rate.

In evaluation stage, whether to continue evolution is decided. In this paper, if average fitness is smaller than 1 when fitness critical value is set as 1, evolution repeats from recomposition stage. Table 4 demonstrates chromosome from the first generation to the last generation, the eighth, and average fitness of each generation.

As in Table 4, while evolution proceeds average fitness has increased, and in the eighth generation where average fitness becomes 1, evolution has been concluded. Association word that represents gene of 1 in chromosome of the eighth generation is adopted and association word that represents gene of 0 is removed. Accordingly, if association word that represents gene of 0 among game class association words in Table 3 is removed, game class of association word knowledge base is optimized.

**Table 4.** The chromosome evolution

| Generation | Chromosome | Fitness | Average Fitness |
|---|---|---|---|
| 1 | doc1:101100000000100000<br>doc2:001000000000001001<br>... | Doc1:0.277170<br>Doc2:0.275670<br>... | 0.517669 |
| 8 | doc1:101011110100001111<br>doc2:101011110100001111<br>...<br>doc10:101011110100001111 | 1<br>1<br>...<br>1 | 1.00000 |

## 3.2 Naïve Bayes Classifier Based on Optimized Association Word Knowledge Base

Naïve Bayes classifier can classify documents through learning phase and classification phase. The learning phase gives probability to association word mined from learning document by Apriori and genetic algorithm. Equation (7) is used to give probability to association word $(w_{k1}\&w_{k2}\ldots\&w_{k(r-1)}{=}{>}w_{kr})$ within *classID*. In this paper, probability of association word $(w_{k1}\&w_{k2}\ldots\&w_{k(r-1)}{=}{>}w_{kr})$ within *classID* is expressed as $P((w_{k1}\&w_{k2}\ldots\&w_{k(r-1)}{=}{>}w_{kr})\,|classID)$. In that case, n is the total number of mined association word and $n_k$ is number of association word that corresponds with association word $(w_{k1}\&w_{k2}\ldots\&w_{k(r-1)}{=}{>}w_{kr})$ in class. *ClassID* is label of class, and |AW| is total number of association words within all classes.

$$P((w_{k1}\ \&\ w_{k2}\ \cdots\ \&\ w_{k(r-1)}\ {=}{>}\ w_{kr})\,|classID\ ) = \frac{n_k + 1}{n + |AW|} \tag{7}$$

In probability granting phase, outcome of accumulation is applied to Equation (7) and probability is granted to association word. Through this process, probability is added to association word in class. Table 5 is the outcome of adding probability to association word in game class of Table 1 according to Equation (7). AW indicates association word in class and OAW means optimized association word in class.

**Table 5.** Granting probability to association word of game class

| Association words in Table 1 | $n_k$ | n | \|AW\|(\|OAW\|) | AW | OAW |
|---|---|---|---|---|---|
| (1)game&organization&match&sports=>selection | 23 | 25 | 231(161) | 0.09375 | 0.129032 |
| (2)domestic&newest&technology=>development | 2 | 5 | 231(161) | 0.0127 | Delete |
| (3)game&participation&popularity&user=>event | 25 | 28 | 231(161) | 0.100386 | 0.137566 |
| .. | . | . | . | . | . |
| (18)game&provision&illustration=>explanation | 21 | 26 | 231(161) | 0.085603 | 0.117647 |

In classification phase, Naïve Bayes classifier can divide test document by class using association word knowledge base where probability is given. Apriori algorithm extracts characteristic in the form of association word from test document as described in Section 3.1. If characteristic of test document(D) is $\{d(w_{11}\&w_{12}\ldots\&w_{1(r-1)}{=}{>}w_{1r}), d(w_{21}\&w_{22}\ldots\&w_{2(r-1)}{=}{>}w_{2r}),\ldots,d(w_{k1}\&w_{k2}\ldots\&w_{k(r-1)}{=}{>}w_{kr}),..,d(w_{m1}\&w_{m2}\ldots\&w_{m(r-1)}{=}{>}w_{mr})\}$, Naïve Bayes classifier classifies test document by class using Equation (8).

"d" of $d(w_{k1}\&w_{k2}...\&w_{k(r-1)}{=>}w_{kr})$ indicates association word extracted from test document.

$$class = \underset{classID=1}{\overset{N}{\arg\max}} P(classID) \prod_{k=1}^{m} P(d(w_{k1} \& w_{k2} ... \& w_{k(r-1)} => w_{kr}) | classID) \quad (8)$$

In Equation (8), class where document(D) is to be classified is *class* and total number of classes is N. $P(d(w_{k1}\&w_{k2}...\&w_{k(r-1)}{=>}w_{kr})|classID)$ is probability according to Equation (7) and P(classID) is probability that it is classified as classID.

# 4 An Example of Bayesian Web Document Classification

This chapter describes how to classify document based on method proposed in this paper. Learning document has been manually classified into eight classes of computer science. Eight classes is label of {game, graphic, news and media, semiconductor, security, Internet, electronic publishing, hardware} and it is expressed as {class1,class2,,,,classN}. Fig. 1 is Korean web document for Naïve Bayes to classify. Since Korean web document of Fig. 1 is homepage to promote game player, it should be classified as class 1 of game class. Web document of Fig. 1 is English translation of Korean web document.

<body>
Neojio pocket. Neojio pocket that has been loved for image of small size and reasonable price was reborn as smaller and cheaper impression(Korean insang). SNK's Neojio pocket color that has never looked large and heavy came to us again as surprisingly small and light impression(Korean insang). In particular, upgraded soft attracts more users. Many consumers positively respond to the new product. Price hike is to provide better service. But there will be no more price increase(Korean insang) in the future. Please contact us for more information on price.
</body>

**Fig. 1.** Web document that appeared in URL

Table 6 shows examples of how Naïve Bayes classifier classifies document of Fig. 1 through mining and refining of association word and previous methods in Chapter 2. Since simple Naïve Bayes classifier extracts assumed words from all nouns of Fig. 1, many noises are intervened by class. For example, "question" is not an important word in the document but it reduces accuracy of document classification because each of class3, class8 generates assumed result and it is applied to Equation (1). Since Naïve Bayes classifier cannot tell what "impression" (Korean insang) in Table 6 means between "increase of price" ((Korean insang) of price) and "impression of image"((Korean insang) of image), they are translated as the same word despite that they have different meaning. Because of this, simple Naïve Bayes classifier makes a mistake of classifying web document of Fig. 1 as class 2. Naïve Bayes classifier using TF•IDF calculates TF•IDF on words by adopting Equation (3) to words extracted as a result of morphological analysis. Naïve Bayes classifier designates TF•IDF as weight and classifies document by using Equation (4). Since Naïve Bayes classifier using TF•IDF only adopts words with high weight as subject word, it reduces error in document classification due to words with low weight but ambiguity of word reduces accuracy of document classification as shown in the example of

**Table 6.** Example of classifying document

<table>
<tr><th>Naïve Bayes classifier</th><th>Method of extracting characteristic</th><th>Characteristic of document</th><th>Value assumption Equation</th><th>Probability of characteristic</th><th>Classific ation Equation</th><th>class</th></tr>
<tr><td>Simple</td><td>All nouns extracted as a result of morphological analysis</td><td>Game<br>Purchase<br>Appearance(Korean Insang)<br>Question</td><td>Equation (2)</td><td>P(game |class1)=0.02121)<br>P(purchase |class1)=0.00072)<br>P(purchase |class8)=0.00092)<br>P(appearance|class2)=0.00211)<br>P(question|class3)=0.00564</td><td>Equation (1)</td><td>class2</td></tr>
<tr><td>TF.IDF</td><td>Phase 1: calculate TF.IDF by using Equation (3) .Phase 2: align words in order of ranking and adopt only word of higher ranking</td><td>impression (0.890452)<br>image(0.397963)<br>price(0.216647)<br>background(0.135783)<br>pocket(0.132654)</td><td>Equation (2)</td><td>P(impression |class1)=0.00891<br>P(impression |class2)=0.0127)<br>P(improve|class8)=0.00901<br>P(image |class2)=0.0201)<br>P(price |class1)=0.00031</td><td>Equation (4)</td><td>class2</td></tr>
<tr><td>Apriori</td><td>Apriori algorithm</td><td>image&impression =>pocket,<br>game&soft =>version<br>price &increase &service =>provision,<br>image &increase(Korean insang) ->game</td><td>Application of Equation (7) to Mined association word</td><td>P(image&improve =>image |class2)=0.012<br>P(game&soft =>version |class1)= 0.096154<br>P(price &increase =>service |class1)= 0.100775</td><td>Equation (8)</td><td>class1</td></tr>
<tr><td>Apriori-Genetic</td><td>Apriori algorithm</td><td>image &impress ->pocket,<br>game &soft =>version<br>price &increase &service =>provision<br>image &increase(Korean insang) ->game</td><td>Application of Equation (7) to mined and refined association word</td><td>P(image&iimprove =>figure |class2)=0.120<br>P(game &soft =>version |class1)= 0.1315789<br>P(price &increase =>service |class1)= 0.138297</td><td>Equation (8)</td><td>class1</td></tr>
</table>

simple Naïve Bayes. Therefore, it causes an error of being classified into class 2 of graphic class.

Naïve Bayes classifier using mining of association word extracts subject word in the form of association word. Since Naïve Bayes classifier extracts characteristic of document in the form of association word, it reduces errors in classification due to ambiguity. For example, association word of "image & impression(Korean insang)" is classified into class 2 of graphic class and "price & increase(Korean insang)" is classified into class 1 of game class and so it does not cause any confusion in meaning. And web document is classified into class1 of game class. But since association words of "price & increase & service" appear not only in class 1 but also in class8, noise occurs in classification. Naïve Bayes algorithm using mining and refining of association word has correctly classified web document as class 1 by removing confusion in meaning of words and was able to get rid of noises because association words of "price & increase & service" did not appear in class 8.

## 5 Performance Evaluation

In order to evaluate performance of Bayesian document classification using mining and refining association word(Bayesian-OAWKB) suggested in this paper, it was compared with Bayesian-document categorization using mining association word(Bayesian-AWKB), simple Bayesian document categorization(Bayesian),

Bayesian document categorization using TF•IDF(Bayesian-TF•IDF). In order to evaluate, we use documents described in Chapter 4. In order to evaluate classification performance, partition table shown in Table 7 is made on document classified by class[7].

**Table 7.** 2 X 2-partition table

| Partition 2 \ Partition 1 | | Partition 1 | |
|---|---|---|---|
| | | YES | NO |
| Partition 2 | YES | a | b |
| | NO | c | d |

F-measure of Equation (9) is used to measure classification. In the Equation (9), P indicates accuracy and R means recall and in that case, the higher F-measure the better classification. Beta indicates relative weight of recall against accuracy and if it is 1.0, weight of accuracy and recall is the same.

$$F\_measure = \frac{(\beta^2 + 1)PR}{\beta^2 P + R} \quad P = \frac{a}{a+b} 100\,\% \quad R = \frac{a}{a+c} 100\,\% \tag{9}$$

In this experiment, beta was designated as 1.0 to analysis result of classification, and different results of F-measure according to change in value of beta from 0.5 to 1.4 were observed. Fig. 2 indicates result of analysis after application of accuracy and recall to Equation (9).

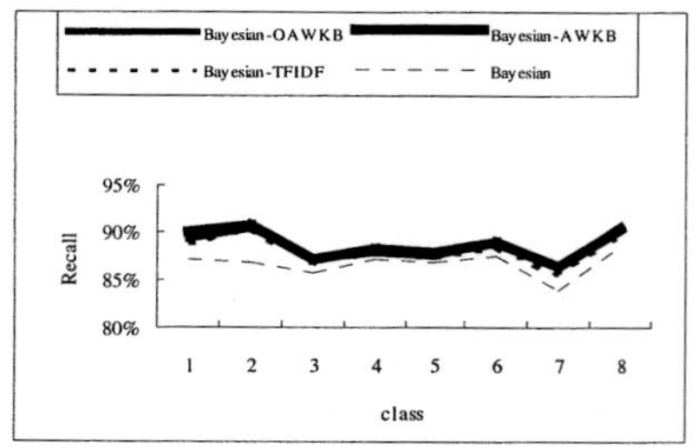


(a) Recall of document classification

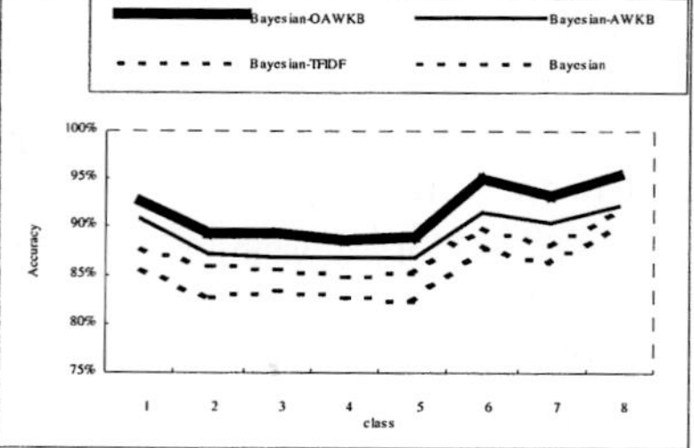


(b) Accuracy of document classification

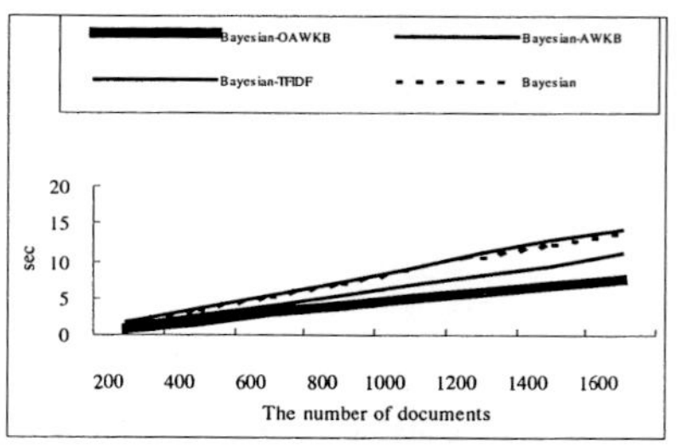


(c) Document Classification Speed

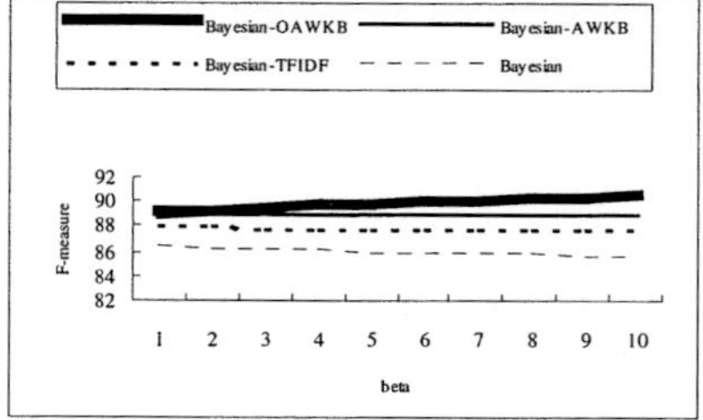


(d) F-measure of document classification

**Fig. 1.** The performance of document classification

In Fig. 2(a), recall according to Bayesian-OAWKB is 88.12 and it 0.22% lower in performance than Bayesian-AWKB, and it is 0.30% and 1.90% higher than Bayesian-TF•IDF and Bayesian respectively. Fig. 2(b) shows that accuracy according to Bayesian-OAWKB is 89.64 and it is 2.53% higher than Bayesian-AWKB and it is 4.12% and 6.36% higher than Bayesian-TFIDF and Bayesian, respectively. Fig. 2(c) indicates speed of classification of 1600 documents. Bayesian-OAWKB is the fastest 7.72sec followed by 10.95sec of Bayesian-AWKB, 14.4sec of Bayesian-TFIDF and 13.9sec of Bayesian. In terms of speed, Bayesian-OAWKB and Bayesian-AWKB are excellent in comparison with others and remainder records similar speed. Fig. 2(d) indicates analyzed performance of F-measure according to change of beta value from 0.5 to 1.4. Bayesian-OAWKB represents a rising curve as beta value increases and so it records better performance in terms of accuracy than recall. But in Bayesian-AWKB and Bayesian-TF•IDF, change of beta value hardly affects F-measure value and so it has similar level of performance in terms of recall and accuracy. However, in Bayesian, it has a bit higher performance in terms of recall than accuracy. On average, if beta is 1.0, Bayesian-OAWKB has 1.13% higher performance than Bayesian-AWKB and 2.18% Bayesian-TF•IDF and 4.11% Bayesian.

## 6 Conclusion

In order to resolve problems that previous Bayesian document classification methods have, this paper has suggested Bayesian document classification using mining and refining of association word. The method that this paper has suggested has two advantages. First, it has refined association words so that Naïve Bayes classifier effects accurate and speedy classification of document. Second, it removes confusion in meaning by expressing characteristic of test document in the form of association word. In order to evaluate performance of Bayesian method using mining and refining of association word, it was compared with previous Bayesian methods. As a result, the method using mining and refining association word had 1.13% higher performance than method using association word mining and 2.18% higher than method using TF•IDF method and 4.11% than simple method.

## References

[1] R. Agrawal and R. Srikant, "Fast Algorithms for Mining Association Rules," Proceedings of the 20th VLDB Conference, Santiago, Chile, 1994.

[2] R. Agrawal and T. Imielinski and A. Swami, "Mining association rules between sets of items in large databases," In Proceedings of the 1993 ACM SIGMOD Conference, Washington DC, USA, 1993.

[3] H. Chen, Y. Chung, M. Ramsey, C. Yang, P. Ma, J. Yen, "Intelligent Spider for Internet Searching," *Proceedings of the 30th Annual Hawaii International Conference on System Sciences - Volume IV*, pp. 178-188, 1997.

[4] W. Frakes and R. Baeza-Yates, information Retrieval, Prentice Hall, 1992.

[5] T. Joachims, "A probabilistic analysis of the Rocchio algorithm with TFIDF for text categorization," ICML-97, 1997.

[6] S. J. Ko and J. H. Lee, "Feature Selection using Association Word Mining for Classification," In Proceedings of DEXA2001, LNCS2113, 2001.

[7] V. Hatzivassiloglou and K. McKeown, "Towards the automatic identification of adjectival scales: Clustering adjectives according to meaning," Proceedings of the 31st Annual Meeting of the ACL, pp. 172-182, 1993.

[8] Introduction to Rainbow URL:http://www.cs.cmu.edu/afs/cs/project/theo-11/www/naïve-bayes.html.

[9] D. D. Lewis, "Naive (Bayes) at forty: The Independence Assumption in Information Retrieval," In European Conference on Machine Learning, 1998.

[10] Y. H. Li and A. K. Jain, "Classification of Text Documents," The Computer Journal, Vol. 41, No. 8, 1998.

[11] M. E. Maron, "Automatic indexing : An experimental inquiry," Journal of the Association for Computing Machinery, 8:404-417, 1961.

[12] T. Michael, *Maching Learning*, McGraw-Hill, pp. 154-200, 1997.

[13] A. McCallum and K. Nigram, "A Comparison of Event Models for Naive Bayes Text Classification," AAAI-98 Workshop on Learning for Text Categorization, 1998.

[14] J. McMahon and F. Smith, "Improving statistical language model performance with automatically generated word hierarchies," Computational Linguistics, Vol. 22, No. 2, 1995.

[15] D. Mladenic, "Feature subset selection in text-learning," Proceedings of the 10th European Conference on Machine Learning, pp. 95-100, 1998.

[16] Cognitive Science Laboratory, Princeton University, "WordNet - a Lexical Database for English," http://www.cogsci.princeton.edu/~wn/.

# The Use of a Supervised $k$-Means Algorithm on Real-Valued Data with Applications in Health

Sami H. Al-Harbi and Vic J. Rayward-Smith

School of Information Systems, University of East Anglia,
Norwich, NR4 7TJ, United Kingdom,
{shh,vjrs}@sys.uea.ac.uk

**Abstract.** $k$-means is traditionally viewed as an unsupervised algorithm for the clustering of a heterogeneous population into a number of more homogeneous groups of objects. However, it is not necessarily guaranteed to group the same types (classes) of objects together. In such cases, some supervision is needed to partition objects which have the same class label into one cluster. This paper demonstrates how the popular $k$-means clustering algorithm can be profitably modified to be used as a classifier algorithm. The output field itself cannot be used in the clustering but it is used in developing a suitable metric defined on other fields. The proposed algorithm combines Simulated Annealing and the modified $k$-means algorithm. We also apply the proposed algorithm to real data sets, which result in improvements in confidence when compared to C4.5.

## 1 Introduction

Classification, often referred to as supervised learning, is one of the core topics in data mining, and involves the prediction of the classes of unclassified instances with the help of a given set of classified examples. An example of such classification might be classifying a group of animals into fish, birds and mammals. The primary characteristic of classification is that the different classes are well-defined. A training set, which consists of previous labelled examples, is available. The labelling defines the class of the object and is often referred to as the output field.

On the other hand, clustering, in general, differs from classification in that it does not depend upon a predefined set of classes. It operates on a set of objects that must be grouped according to some notion of similarity. So, similarity is fundamental to the definition of a cluster, and the measure of similarity between two objects drawn from the same feature space is essential to most clustering algorithms.

In a metric space, the similarity between two objects is modelled with a distance function that satisfies the triangle inequality. It gives a numerical value to the notion of closeness between two objects in a high-dimensional space.

**Definition 1.** *Let $\mathcal{M}$ be a non-empty space and for each $x, y \in \mathcal{M}$ let $\delta(x, y)$ be a real number satisfying*

P.W.H. Chung, C.J. Hinde, M. Ali (Eds.): IEA/AIE 2003, LNAI 2718, pp. 575–581, 2003.

- $\delta(x, y) = 0$ *if and only if* $x = y$;
- $\delta(x, y) = \delta(y, x)$ *for each* $x, y \in \mathcal{M}$;
- $\delta(y, z) \leq \delta(y, x) + \delta(x, z)$ *for each* $x, y$ *and* $z \in \mathcal{M}$.

*Then* $\delta$ *is called a metric or distance on* $\mathcal{M}$; *and* $\mathcal{M}$, *together with* $\delta$, *is called a metric space* $(\mathcal{M}, \delta)$. *The objects of the set* $\mathcal{M}$ *are also called the points of the metric space* $(\mathcal{M}, \delta)$.

More details of metric spaces can be found, for example, in [3].

Supervised clustering is similar to that of learning from examples, i.e. we aim to generate a classification technique from a given set of examples. However, rather than delivering a rule or tree technique, we deliver a clustering so that each cluster has a strong tendency to have the same output. Any new case assigned to the same cluster can also be assumed to have that output, and thus belong to the same class as the majority of objects in that cluster. The output field itself is used to aid and bias the building of a suitable metric defined on the other fields.

In this paper, we introduce a new technique, used to partition the objects that have the same label into one cluster. The algorithm, called supervised $k$-means, is an extension of the well known $k$-means algorithm.

In the next section, we briefly review the $k$-means algorithm and its important properties. Section 3 discusses the use of weighted metrics. In section 4, we present the proposed algorithm. Section 5 shows experimental results and section 6 summarizes our research.

## 2 $k$-Means Algorithm

The $k$-means algorithm is a method commonly used to automatically partition a data set into $k$ groups. It depends upon the notion of a centroid where the centroid is defined as follows.

**Definition 2.** *Given any set of points,* $C$, *in a metric space* $\mathcal{M}$, *a point* $\hat{c} \in \mathcal{M}$ *is called a centroid if*

$$\sum_{x \in C} \delta(\hat{c}, x) \text{ is minimized.} \tag{1}$$

Note that the centroid $\hat{c}$ is not necessary an element of $C$.

MacQueen [8] has built the $k$-means algorithm upon the following four basic operations.

1. Selection of a random initial $k$ clusters, $C_i$, $1 \leq i \leq k$ and the computation of the centroid of each cluster, $\hat{c}_i$.
2. Measuring the distance between an object and the centroid of each cluster.
3. Re-assigning an object to its nearest centroid.
4. Adjusting the centroid of the cluster from which an object has been removed, and the one to which that object has been reassigned.

Steps (2) to (4) are repeatedly performed in the algorithm until the algorithm converges. The $k$-means algorithm has the following important properties [5, 6].

a) In its basic form, it works only on numeric values.
b) It uses the Euclidean metric and hence the centroid of $C$ is the mean of the points in $C$.
c) It is efficient in processing large data sets. The computational complexity of the algorithm is $O(nkt)$, where $n$ is the total number of objects, $k$ is the number of clusters and $t$ is the number of iterations. In clustering large data sets, the $k$-means algorithm is much faster than the hierarchical clustering algorithms, whose general computational complexity is $O(n^2)$.
d) It terminates at a local optimum.

Unlike the $k$-means algorithm, the supervised clustering requires a weighted metric, and as the number of classes is predetermined, then the value of $k$ is known. These will be presented in more depth in the following sections.

## 3 Weighted Metrics

When measuring the distances between fields, it may be necessary to assign greater significance to one field over another. To achieve this, weights can be introduced.

**Definition 3.** *$\mathbb{R}_+$ is the set of positive real numbers, $\mathbb{R}_+ = \{x \in \mathbb{R} | \, x \geq 0\}$.*

**Definition 4.** *Let $\mathcal{M} = \mathbb{R}^n$, $w \in \mathbb{R}^n_+$ be a positive weight vector, and for $x, y \in \mathcal{M}$, define*

$$\delta_w(x, y) = \sqrt{\sum_{i=1}^{n} w_i (x_i - y_i)^2} \quad \textit{where } n \in \mathcal{N}. \tag{2}$$

*Then $\delta_w$ is called a weighted Euclidean metric.*

**Theorem 1.** *Given any set of points, $C$, in the weighted Euclidean space, the value of $\hat{\mathbf{c}}$ is the mean of $x$ in $C$, i.e. $\hat{\mathbf{c}} = \sum_{\mathbf{x} \in C} \mathbf{x} / |\, C \,|$.*

*Proof.* Let $\hat{\mathbf{c}} = (y_1, y_2, \ldots, y_n)$, and $\mathbf{w} = (w_1, w_2, \ldots, w_n)$ be two points such that $f(\mathbf{x}) = \sum_{\mathbf{x} \in C} \sqrt{\sum_{i=1}^{n} w_i \, (x_i - y_i)^2}$ is minimized.

Now

$$\frac{\partial f(\mathbf{x})}{\partial y_j} = \sum_{\mathbf{x} \in C} \frac{-2 w_j (x_j - y_j)}{2 \sqrt{\sum_{i=1}^{n} w_i \, (x_i - y_i)^2}}$$

$$\frac{\partial f(\mathbf{x})}{\partial y_j} = 0 \Leftrightarrow \sum_{\mathbf{x} \in C} -w_j (x_j - y_j) = 0$$

$$\Leftrightarrow y_j = \sum_{\mathbf{x} \in C} \frac{x_j}{|C|} \text{ for } j = 1, \ldots, n.$$

□

The above theorem shows that using the weighted Euclidean metric does not unduly effect the $k$-means paradigm and its efficiency to cluster large data sets.

The weighted metric estimates the distance between any two objects that belong to the same class. Different approaches for measuring weights, $w_i$, have been proposed in the literature. The first approach measures the weights based on an intuitive judgement of what is important [4]. In other words, the investigator gives weights to fields based on his understanding of the data. A second approach uses some statistical techniques such as *Information Gain* [1].

Alternatively, choosing the appropriate set of weights can be seen as an optimization problem that can be addressed with any heuristic technique. In the proposed algorithm we use Simulated Annealing [9] to determine the appropriate set of weights for the clustering task. The objective is to maximize the confidence of the partitions generated by the $k$-means algorithm.

## 4 Supervised $k$-Means Algorithm

The supervised $k$-means algorithm combines Simulated Annealing and $k$-means. The algorithm iteratively creates clusters attempting to cluster together records which have the same class label. The fitness of a set of weights is obtained by first running the $k$-means algorithm with the corresponding weighted Euclidean metric. After clustering, each member of a cluster may be compared to its class label.

Thus, each record, $r$, is assigned to a cluster, $\mathcal{C}(r)$. The output field of the record is denoted by class($r$), and for each cluster, $\mathcal{C}$, there is an associated output taken to be the most common output of records assigned to that cluster; we denote this output as class($\mathcal{C}$). The fitness of the weights is then

$$|\{r \mid class(r) = class(\mathcal{C}_r)\}|. \quad (3)$$

Simulated Annealing is used to find the weights which maximise this fitness. The confidence of the clustering can then be determined by calculating the percentage of correctly classified objects with respect to the total number of objects in the data set. Moreover, the value of $k$ is set to be the number of distinct class values.

In summary, the supervised $k$-means algorithm requires the following steps:

1. Prepare the pre-classified database (including removing missing values and transforming categorical data).
2. Initially assign each field with a random weight.
3. Run the $k$-means algorithm using the weighted metric with the selected weights and compute the fitness.
4. Improve the weight of each field by using Simulated Annealing, based on the feedback of step 3.
5. Repeat steps 3 and 4 until local optimal weights are found.

Once the supervised $k$-means algorithm is completed, we can test the classification using the test data set.

## 5 Experiments and Results

To illustrate the performance of the proposed technique, breast cancer and Pima Indians diabetes data sets were taken from the UCI repository. The results were then compared with C4.5 classification techniques.

The Breast Cancer data set was originally collected by Dr. William Wolberg of Wisconsin University [11]. The number of cases is 699, and each case involves 10 attributes plus the class attribute. Each attribute contains integer values varying from 1 to 10.

As the first field is the sample code, it was removed from the test. Moreover, 16 of the 699 cases contained missing values, therefore they were also removed. Then the data set was randomly split into two parts, a training data set (of 479 records), and a test data set (of 204 records).

After applying C4.5 (which is supported by Data Lamp V2 [7]), a 92.90% confidence on the training data set, and a 95.59% confidence on the test data set were obtained. However, by using supervised $k$-means with the added optimal weights obtained from Simulated Annealing, it was possible to increase the confidence further on the training and test data sets to 98.0% and 97.0% respectively. Table 1 shows the optimal set of weights for the fields of the breast cancer data set.

**Table 1.** Weights of fields

| No. | Filed | Weight |
|---|---|---|
| 1. | Clump-Thick | 47.2 |
| 2. | Unif-of-Cell Size | 139.2 |
| 3. | Unif-of-Cell Shape | 31.1 |
| 4. | Marginal Adhesion | 15.3 |
| 5. | Single Epithelial Cell Size | 26.1 |
| 6. | Bare Nuclei | 153.8 |
| 7. | Bland Chromatin | 54.7 |
| 8. | Normal Nucleoli | 101.6 |
| 9 . | Mitoses | 22.2 |

In such applications (e.g health applications), the user needs to be sure that all cases of the most important classes are classified properly and the algorithm does not incorrectly classify a single case. Consequently, the algorithm was run again to target just the malignant cases, i.e. the fitness function was $|\{r \mid class(r) = class(C_r)\ \&\ class(r) = \text{malignant}\}|$. The Simulated Annealing algorithm searched for the appropriate weights to assist the $k$-means algorithm in classifying all the malignant cases into one cluster. The algorithm succeeded in increasing the confidence of this cluster to 100.0% on both the training and test data sets.

Table 2 shows the set of optimal weights for the fields. Naturally, when the confidence of one particular class increased, the confidence of the other classes

**Table 2.** Revised weights of fields

| No. | Filed | Weight |
|---|---|---|
| 1. | Clump-Thick | 10 |
| 2. | Unif-of-Cell Size | 1 |
| 3. | Unif-of-Cell Shape | 9 |
| 4. | Marginal Adhesion | 0 |
| 5. | Single Epithelial Cell Size | 0.3 |
| 6. | Bare Nuclei | 50 |
| 7. | Bland Chromatin | 0.1 |
| 8. | Normal Nucleoli | 40 |
| 9 . | Mitoses | 2 |

decreased (which, in our experiment, was the benign class). Therefore, the user should be clear about the target of his/her experiments, be it for general confidence or specific confidence.

The Pima Indians diabetes data set was originally collected by National Institute of Diabetes [10]. The number of cases is 768, and each case involves 8 attributes plus the class attribute. Unlike breast cancer data set, the data set involves continuous values with no missing records. Moreover, the data set was randomly split into two parts, a training data set (of 512 records), and a test data set (of 256 records).

After applying C4.5, a 76.4% confidence on the training data set, and a 74.2% confidence on the test data set were obtained. However, by using supervised $k$-means with the added optimal weights obtained from the Simulated Annealing, it was possible to increase the confidence further on the training and test data sets to 77.8% and 76.3% respectively. Table 3 shows the optimal set of weights for the fields of the diabetes data set.

The Simulated Annealing algorithm uses a geometric cooling scheme with initial temperature 1 and multiplier $\alpha = 0.99$. The temperature was decreased every 100 iterations until it was below 0.005. This is similar to that used in [2].

**Table 3.** Weights of fields

| No. | Filed | Weight |
|---|---|---|
| 1. | No-of-Pregnant | 16 |
| 2. | Plasma glucose | 773 |
| 3. | Blood pressure | 169 |
| 4. | Triceps skin-fold | 173 |
| 5. | 2-Hour serum insulin | 249 |
| 6. | Body mass index | 723 |
| 7. | Diabetes pedigree function | 277 |
| 8. | Age | 247 |

## 6 Conclusions and Future Work

The $k$-means algorithm has been developed and adapted to be used as a classifier, and this has been done by combining it with Simulated Annealing. This iterative process involves using Simulated Annealing to find the near optimal weights for the fields, and using the $k$-means algorithm to generate clusters, using the corresponding weighted Euclidean metric. From this process, the confidence may be computed. This may be repeated until a near optimal confidence has been obtained.

Some points, however, need careful consideration. Firstly, arriving at the correct weights is vital, and various techniques for determining the neighbourhood are possible. Determining the best option merits further work. In practice, it may be advisable to try different methods in order to obtain good solutions.

Secondly, the distribution of class labels within the data sets may be important, and therefore balancing may be advisable. This may be done beforehand by careful data cleansing in order to avoid one class label dominating the others.

The initial results of these investigations are promising and the prospects of more successful analyses are good. Current research involves using techniques to transform categorical data into numerical data, so supervised $k$-means can be efficiently and effectively applied to databases which contain mixed data.

## References


1. Ayan, N. F.: Using Information Gain as Feature Weight. 8th Turkish Symposium on Artificial Intelligence and Neural Networks. (1999)
2. Brittain, D.: Optimisation of the Telecommunication Access Network. Bristol, UK: Univer sity of Bristol (1999)
3. Copson, E. T.: Metric Spaces. Cambridge University Press (1968)
4. Everitt, B.: Cluster Analysis. Social Science Research Council (1974)
5. Hartigan, J.: Clustering Algorithms. John Wiley and Sons Inc (1975)
6. Huang, Z.: Clustering Large Data Sets with Mixed Numberic and Categorical Values. Proceedings of The First Pacific-Asia Conference on Knowledge Discovery and Data Mining (1997)
7. Lanner Group Inc.: Data Lamp Version 2.02: Technology for knowing. http://www.lanner.com.
8. MacQueen, J.:Some methods for classification and analysis of multivariate observations. Proceeding of the 5th Berkeley Symposium. (1967) 281–297
9. Rayward-Smith V. J., Osman I. H., Reeves C. R. and Smith G. D.: Modern Heuristic Search Methods. John Wiley and Sons Ltd. (1996)
10. Sigillito V.:National Instituite of Diabetes and Digestive and Kidney Diseases. http://www.icu.uci.edu/pub/machine-learning-data-bases. UCI repository of machine learining databases.
11. William H. Wolberg and O.L. Mangasarian.:pattern separation for medical diagnosis applied to breast cytology. http://www.icu.uci.edu/pub/machine-learning-databases. UCI repository of machine learining databases.

# SymCure: A Model-Based Approach for Fault Management with Causal Directed Graphs

Ravi Kapadia

Gensym Corporation, 1776 Yorktown Ste 830, Houston TX 77056, USA
rkapadia@gensym.com

**Abstract.** SymCure is an object-oriented graphical model-based fault management methodology that integrates automated and interactive fault diagnosis, testing, recovery, and impact prediction. SymCure allows domain experts to define class level fault models over generic events that are represented in the form of causal directed graphs. At run time, SymCure combines these generic fault models with incoming events and a specific domain representation, which describes a particular system configuration and relations among specific components, to diagnose root causes for abnormal system behavior. This methodology can be used for fault management in domains as diverse as enterprise wide communications and manufacturing processes. This paper describes SymCure's architecture, its diagnostic knowledge representation, fault management procedures, and discusses its contributions.

## 1 Introduction

Fault management plays a vital role across a broad spectrum of commercial and industrial applications, ranging from service level management and telecommunications network management in the Information Technology (IT) world, to abnormal condition management in manufacturing, chemical, oil and gas industries. The size and complexity of these applications often necessitates automated expert system support for fault management. A small number of root cause problems in IT communication networks often result in a large number of messages and alarms that cannot be handled by human operators in real time. Failure to identify and repair the root cause problems results in increased system downtime and poor service levels. Abnormal conditions in manufacturing and processing plants may result in unplanned shutdowns, equipment damage, safety hazards, reduced productivity, and poor quality products. The US National Institute of Standards and Technology (NIST) estimates that in the absence of adequate fault management, billions of dollars are spent in addressing the problems caused by equipment failure, degradation, process drift, and operator overload [1].

Fault management across these industries shares some common goals, such as improving application availability and utilization, reducing operator overload, and minimizing operation costs. In order to achieve these goals, it is necessary to develop fault management tools with the following capabilities.

P.W.H. Chung, C.J. Hinde, M. Ali (Eds.): IEA/AIE 2003, LNAI 2718, pp. 582–591, 2003.

1. *Symptom monitoring*. Symptoms are manifestations of underlying root causes and must be monitored to detect the occurrence of problems as soon as they happen.
2. *Diagnosis* identifies the root causes of known symptoms. (Diagnosis is also often referred to as fault isolation.) Some studies have shown that 80% of the fault management effort is spent in identifying root causes after the manifestation of symptoms [2].
3. *Correlation* is the process of recognizing and organizing groups of events that are causally related to each other - usually such events share one or more root causes - for diagnostic inference and presentation to system operators.
4. *Prediction*. Early prediction of the impacts of underlying root causes before the effects are manifested is critical for proactive maintenance, safety, and optimal system utilization.
5. *Testing*. In large systems, it is impractical and sometimes impossible to monitor every variable. Instead key observable variables are monitored to generate symptom events. Diagnostic inference typically identifies a set of suspected root causes. Additional variables can then be examined by running associated tests to complete the diagnosis process.
6. *Automated recovery*. Identifying and automating recovery procedures allows for growth in equipment, processes, and services, without increasing the supervisory burden on system operators.
7. *Notification*. Operators must be notified of the presence of root causes and their potential impacts. Raw alarms, which can overload an operator with redundant information, must be replaced with concise diagnostic summaries of root causes and their impacts.
8. *Postmortem*. Information from the diagnostic problem solving is fed back to the fault management system for historic record keeping and proactive fault management in the future.

SymCure (derived from "Symptom Cure") is a tool that addresses a number of fault management functions, including diagnosis, correlation, prediction, testing, automated recovery and notification. It provides a powerful object oriented model-based framework to specify diagnosis knowledge in the form of a persistent, generic (i.e., class-level), graphical, fault propagation model library. It performs diagnosis and prediction by combining the fault propagation models with specific domain information and incoming events at run time. It detects and resolves multiple system failures, and notifies the results of its diagnostic reasoning to external systems using messages and other suitable means. SymCure's methodology is domain independent and it has been used for fault management in diverse applications across different industries, including abnormal condition management for heaters and service management for enterprise wide software systems[1].

This document describes the key elements of SymCure's architecture (Section 2), which includes diagnostic knowledge and diagnostic reasoning. Diagnostic knowledge is represented by a combination of fault models and fault management procedures (Section 3). Fault management algorithms use this knowledge to correlate events, hypothesize and verify root causes, predict impacts, and fix problems at run

---

[1] SymCure is the diagnostic reasoning engine for Gensym Corporation's Integrity and Optegrity products [3], which are directed towards fault management in the IT infrastructure and manufacturing process worlds, respectively.

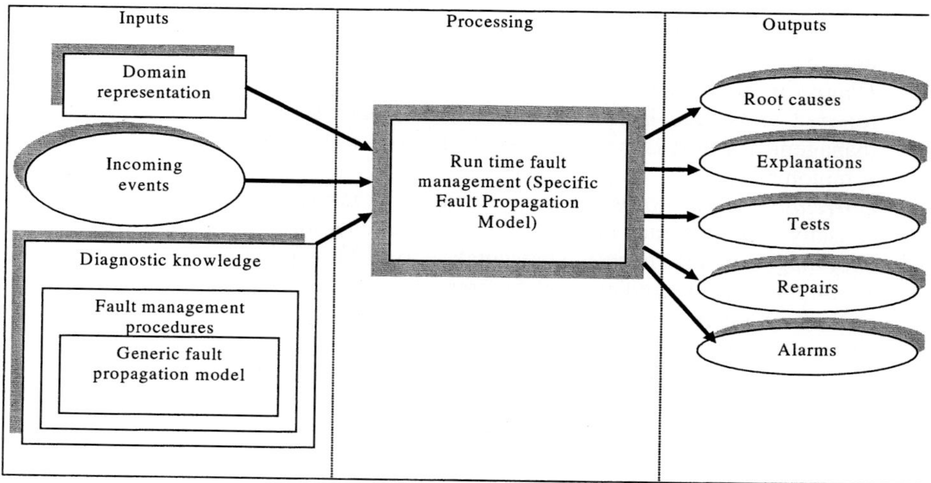


**Fig. 1.** Architecture of SymCure

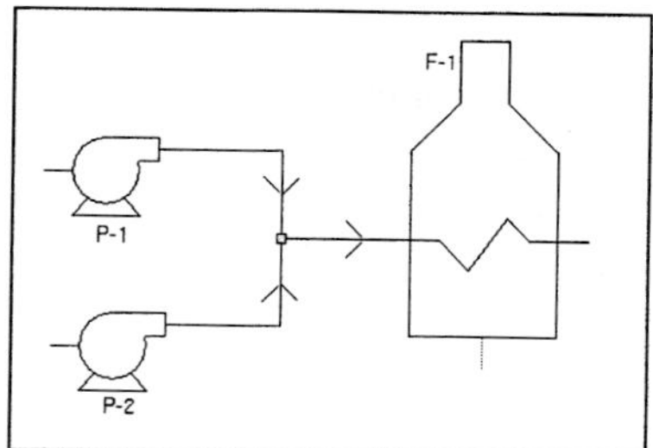


**Fig. 2.** Sample domain representation

time (Section 4). The document concludes with a discussion of our contributions towards the development of intelligent fault management systems (Section 5).

## 2 Architecture

Fig. 1 shows the input, processing, and output elements of a SymCure application.

*Domain representation* is a graphical object oriented representation of the domain objects that are being managed by SymCure. It includes class definitions for domain objects[2], their specific instances (i.e., the managed domain objects), and relationships between these instances, including connectivity (e.g., one object is connected upstream of another) and containment (i.e., one object is contained inside another). Fig. 2 shows the managed objects and their connections for a heating system. In this example, a furnace F-1 is connected downstream of two pumps P-1 and P-2.

[2] Integrity and Optegrity [3] contain a library of class definitions, icons, palettes, and behaviors that can be used to quickly create and configure a domain representation.

The *incoming events* stream includes both symptoms that indicate the presence of problems and test results that validate or rule out suspected events. Symptoms are manifestations of underlying root causes on domain objects. They are detected by external procedures that monitor, aggregate, filter and analyze numerical data, sensor readings, network management traps, signals, and other forms of raw data to generate events for SymCure[3]. SymCure responds to the stream of incoming events with the following actions:

1. Diagnose the root causes of the incoming event stream.
2. Predict the impact of the root causes on other events.
3. Report the results of diagnosis and impact prediction to system operators.
4. Initiate any tests required to verify the occurrence of suspected root causes.
5. Initiate recovery actions to repair the target object of the root causes.

*Diagnostic knowledge* comprises of generic fault models that are used to reach diagnostic conclusions and procedures that verify and respond to these conclusions. Section 3 describes SymCure's representation of diagnostic knowledge.

*Processing:* At run time in response to incoming events, SymCure instantiates generic models for a specific domain representation by constructing a specific fault model. It uses the specific fault model for diagnosis, correlation, impact prediction, and to select and execute tests and repair actions. Section 4 describes SymCure's run time fault management process in detail.

*Outputs*: SymCure generates root causes, alarms, and explanations, and proposes tests and repair actions to resolve and recover from faults. Events can be configured to send notifications to operators. SymCure sends requests for tests and repair actions to a rudimentary workflow management component, which schedules and executes them.

## 3 Diagnostic Knowledge

A key challenge for knowledge-based fault management expert systems is to develop powerful knowledge representation schemes that permit human experts to specify their domain knowledge. When there is sufficient understanding of failure modes of system components and their effects on the behavior of the system, diagnostic reasoning for fault management is based on fault models (e.g., [2], [4], [5], [6]). Alternative diagnosis techniques often described as consistency based methods (e.g., [7], [8]) use models of "normal" behavior, where diagnostic reasoning focuses on identifying causes for discrepancies between the normal behavior predicted by the model, and the aberrant behavior manifested by the device. Fault models can be far more abstract than models of normal behavior, and are therefore easier to construct. For example, fault models can easily capture causal relations such as "if an IP card fails, the device cannot communicate", and "if a pump fails, flow stops", without requiring detailed models that simulate normal behavior. Causal fault models capture paths of causal interactions between root causes (i.e., faults) and their effects (i.e., symptoms). Diagnosing root causes from known symptoms is achieved by tracing upstream along the causal pathways from the symptoms to the faults. Predicting the impact of root causes is performed by propagating downstream from causes to effects.

---

[3] Integrity and Optegrity [3] provide a combination of generic and domain specific tools to generate SymCure events from raw data.

SymCure integrates two kinds of diagnostic knowledge for fault management.

Fault propagation knowledge uses Generic Fault Propagation Models (GFPMs) that capture fault propagation knowledge in the form of causal relations among events defined over generic classes. This knowledge is used for diagnosis, correlation, and impact prediction.

Procedural knowledge supplements the fault models by specifying processes for responding to diagnostic conclusions and predictions. It includes test mechanisms for resolving suspected root causes and repair actions for recovering from identified, predicted, and suspected failures.

A GFPM for a class of domain objects defines the propagation of failures within its instances and to instances of other classes via generic domain relationships (e.g., Fig. 3. shows a GFPM for a generic furnace). Events may represent observable symptoms, alarms that are used to alert operators of potential problems, underlying failures (i.e., root causes), or may be introduced simply for modeling convenience. GFPMs are intended to be independent of any specific collection of domain objects and relationships actually present at any particular site. Thus the diagnosis knowledge can be made impervious to changes in system topology and operating modes and GFPMs can be reused across different applications. GFPMs can be inherited from parent classes in a class hierarchy in accordance with Object Oriented Programming principles. They can be developed from "first principles" models, expert knowledge, or Failure Mode Effects Analysis (FMEA) results.

GFPMs are stored in containers called *diagram folders*. Typically, there is one diagram folder for each domain object class definition, but generic events for a class definition may be distributed across different diagram folders. Propagation from an event in one folder to an event in another folder is achieved by *event views*, which act as bridges among different diagram folders.

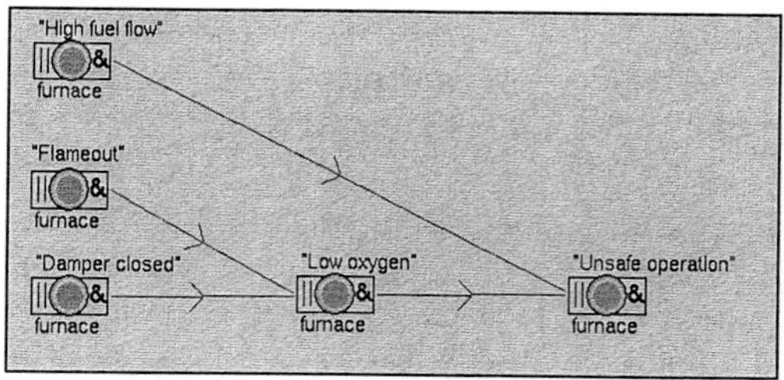


**Fig. 3.** Generic Fault Propagation Model for furnace

SymCure supports two types of fault management procedures which supplement GFPMs.

1. Tests are used to verify the occurrence of an underlying event.
2. Repair actions are used to recover from failures.

Fault management procedures have a set of associated actions that may be applied to the managed system. The actions may be automated, or may simply be a request to an operator, or a combination of the two. Such actions include "pinging" an IP address to test for network connectivity, extracting a data point from a database, and even sending a repair technician to a remote site to conduct manual tests and repairs. Upon completion, a test action must return a result (true or false) to SymCure.

The specification for a fault management procedure has three parts:

1. An attribute specification that includes its name, its target domain object, the conditions for activating the procedure, and the resources, costs, and information necessary for scheduling the procedure.
2. A relation linking it to an event in the GFPM (the procedure is invoked in response to suitable state changes of an underlying event).
3. A procedural specification (written in any computer programming language) that lays down the sequence of actions that must be performed to obtain the result for a test or to fix a problem.

SymCure provides a graphical user interface to create, configure, and compile GFPMs, and to create tests and repair actions, configure them, and relate them to generic events.

Figs. 3 and 4 show sample fault propagation models for a furnace and a pump, respectively. A *generic event*, represented by a node in the GFPM, applies to a class of objects. It is uniquely identified by a combination of its name (e.g., "Pump overload") and its target class (e.g., pump)[4]. A directed edge between two events specifies a *causal relation* (the direction of the edge specifies the direction of causality). In Fig. 4 the event "Pump overload" causes the event "High temperature" on any pump. An edge may also specify a propagation relation between instances of the target class of the cause and the target class of the event. For example, consider the causal relation between the event "Pump overload" on any pump and the event view "High fuel flow" on cdg-domain-object. (Cdg-domain-object is the parent class for all target objects.) The view acts as a bridge to a corresponding event defined in Fig. 3. The propagation relation "connected-upstream" on the edge specifies that "High fuel flow" on any domain object is caused by "Pump overload" on any pump that is connected upstream of the domain object.

"Test pump overload" and "Repair pump overload" are a generic test and a generic repair action, respectively. Both are associated with the generic event "Pump overload". (These associations are not depicted in the figure to avoid clutter.) "Test pump overload" may be run whenever it is suspected that "Pump overload" may have occurred for any instance of a pump. The test may involve extracting a sensor reading from a database or perhaps scheduling a visit by an operator to the pump to do a manual check. "Reset pump" may be executed whenever it is detected that "Pump overload" has occurred for any instance of a pump. This may be achieved simply by sending a control command to the pump or perhaps by ordering the operator to manually twist a knob on the device.

Causal propagation may be characterized by the logical relationships between a target event and the set of events that can cause the target to occur. Traditional causal modeling approaches (e.g., [2], [4], [5], [6]) use one or both of the following forms of causal propagation: *disjunctive* propagation (in which a target event is true if any one of the events in its set of causes is true — this is often referred to as OR logic) and conjunctive propagation (in which the target event is true if every one of the events in its set of causes is true — this is often called AND logic). These forms of propagation are unsuitable for a variety of real world applications that require more subtle reasoning. For instance, an event may be true only if a certain fraction of its causes are true, e.g., internet service providers often have a number of backup servers

[4] In this document, whenever the target of an event is obvious, we refer to the event by its name only.

and internet service degradation may occur only when over a certain fraction of the servers go out of service. Noisy operating environments can mask the symptoms of a root cause causing misdiagnoses, unless the fault model can capture this behavior. Causal propagation may depend on the state of the system (e.g., propagation through a switch may depend on its position – ON or OFF) in addition to the causes of the event. SymCure overcomes a number of problems encountered in traditional causal modeling methodologies by providing for a wide range of causal propagation logic to fit many real world diagnostic situations that arise from incomplete models, uncertain propagation, and context dependent failure propagation. Further discussion of SymCure's propagation logic is beyond the scope of this paper; a detailed description is provided elsewhere [9].

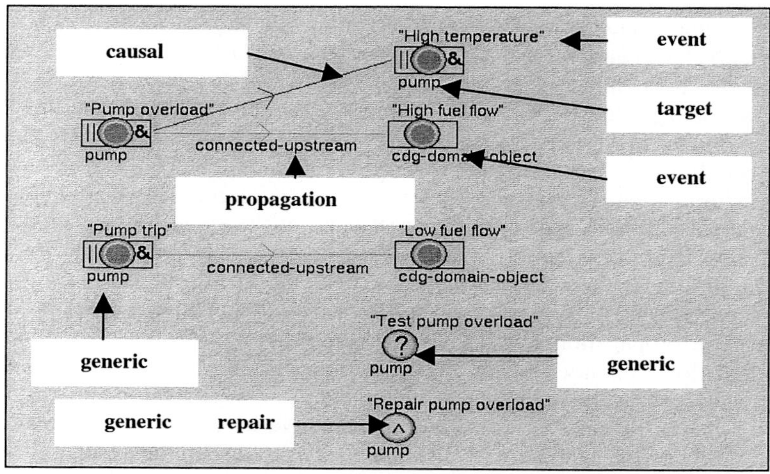


**Fig. 4.** Generic fault model for pump

# 4 Run Time Fault Management

SymCure's fault management algorithms respond to incoming symptoms by hypothesizing and identifying root causes, predicting their impacts, running tests and repair actions, and notifying operators. At the heart of fault management is a causal model constructed from the generic fault propagation models and specific domain objects. Diagnosing root causes from known symptoms is achieved by tracing upstream along the causal pathways from the symptoms to the faults. Predicting the impact of root causes is performed by propagating downstream from causes to effects.

SymCure combines the generic fault models with the domain representation and builds focused Specific Fault Propagation Models (SFPMs) to investigate observed symptoms. Using the SFPMs, SymCure recognizes that a group of events are correlated to each other, identifies suspect faults that could have caused the symptoms, and selects and executes tests and repair actions to resolve the problems. The SFPM describes causal interactions among events within and across the specific domain objects. It also captures the current state of the diagnostic process and can be used to generate explanations for symptoms, diagnostic conclusions, and tests and repair actions. For the sake of efficiency, in response to an incoming event SymCure builds the minimal set of specific events upstream of the event to diagnose possible causes and downstream of the event to predict impacts.

Like generic fault models, SFPMs are also represented as causal directed graphs. A specific event, represented by a node in an SFPM, is a statement about a specific target object and is uniquely identified by the combination of its name and target object. An event in an SFPM can have the following values:

1. true, i.e., the event is known to have occurred;
2. false, i.e., the event is known to not have occurred;
3. unknown, i.e., it is not known whether the event has occurred; or
4. suspect, i.e., it is suspected that the event may be true.

SymCure uses heuristic best first search to propagate event values for an SFPM. At a very high level, starting from an incoming event, the logic for propagating event values in an SFPM from an incoming event is as follows.

**for** any event *e* when its value changes **do**
propagate the value of the event upstream to all *Causes* (where *Causes* = all causes of *e*);
propagate value of the event downstream to *Effects* (where *Effects* = all effects of *Causes* + *e*);
**end for**

The time complexity of the propagation algorithm is linear in the number of events and edges of the SFPM. The maximum number of events in an SFPM is bound by product of the number of managed domain objects and the size of the largest generic fault model. In practice, since SymCure constructs only the events that are correlated to incoming symptoms, the actual size of an SFPM is usually a small subset of the maximum possible size.

Fig. 5 shows the SFPM created by combining the domain representation of Fig. 2, the generic fault models of Figs. 3 and 4, and the symptom "High fuel flow" on F-1. A *root cause* event in an SFPM is an event that is not caused by any other event (e.g., "Pump overload" on P-1) while a *symptom* (e.g., "High fuel flow" on F-1) is an event that is caused either directly or indirectly by a combination of one or more root cause events. In this example, SymCure initially treats "Pump overload" on both P-1 and P-2 as suspect and executes "Test pump overload" for each suspected event, which leads to the identification of "Pump overload" on P-1 as a root cause.

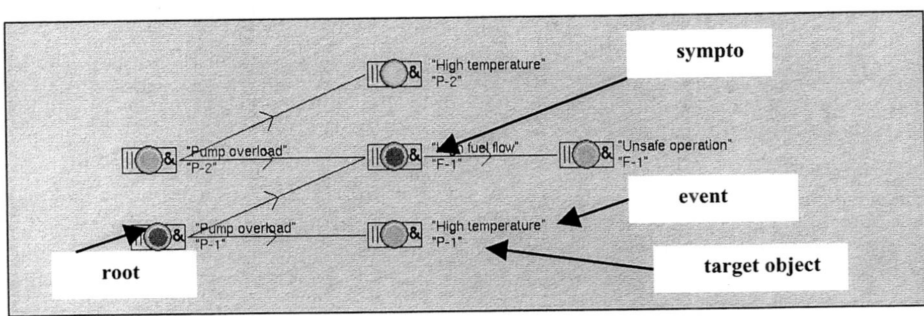


**Fig. 5.** Specific Fault Propagation Model (SFPM)

SymCure is able to reason over relations among different objects and across different GFPMs to build an SFPM. Thus, SymCure can correlate a symptom on F-1 to its potential causes on P-1 and P-2. Note that it only builds the events relevant to the diagnosis for "High fuel flow", ignoring "Pump trip", "Low oxygen" and other events that are not required for diagnosing the causes of the incoming event.

Adding new equipment, reconnecting or removing existing equipment does not affect SymCure's generic fault models. In response to dynamic domain object changes, if an SFPM exists as a result of an ongoing diagnosis, SymCure can dynamically update it by adding or deleting the necessary events and edges.

## 5 Discussion

SymCure is an object-oriented, graphical, model-based fault management methodology that performs automated and interactive fault diagnosis, testing, recovery, and impact prediction. It has been implemented in G2, Gensym Corporation's graphical object-oriented platform for building expert system applications. It has been used for fault management in diverse applications including offshore drilling platforms [9], heating systems [10], and enterprise wide software systems [11]. This section discusses SymCure's strengths, limitations, and lessons we've learned from applying the technology to real world problems.

Diagnosis is essentially an iterative process that generates hypotheses in response to incoming symptoms and refines the hypotheses by obtaining additional information (through tests and additional symptoms). SymCure integrates test and repair management with fault diagnosis which allows the fault management system to optimally obtain additional information to identify and repair root causes. Unlike diagnosis techniques that implicitly assume that there is a single point of failure (e.g., [5]), SymCure can handle multiple simultaneous failures and situations where new faults overlap with existing ones. Complex systems are often composed of a large number of interconnected and interrelated components. While a problem may originate on one component, often it is manifested on some other related component. SymCure's specific fault models are built at the system-level, which permits it to diagnose root causes and predict events that propagate across components. SymCure's fault management methodology is scalable for large complex systems because it employs an efficient diagnosis algorithm with linear complexity, and "management by exception" to only instantiate a localized specific model at run time when incoming events indicate the existence of a problem. SymCure overcomes the problems encountered in traditional causal modeling methodologies by providing for a wide range of causal propagation logic to fit a number of real world diagnostic situations that arise from incomplete models, uncertain propagation, and context dependent failure propagation.

Like any knowledge based reasoning system, the accuracy of SymCure's diagnostic inference is constrained by the correctness of the underlying fault models and the availability of instrumentation to observe symptoms and perform tests to resolve diagnostic candidates. Obviously, SymCure cannot handle faults that are not part of the fault models but it can identify novel combinations of known faults. Because SymCure processes an event as soon as it is received, diagnostic results are susceptible to the order of incoming events. In theory, this can cause problems over short time spans if the values of observed events are inconsistent (because of propagation delays, noise, and faulty sensors). In practice, this has not been a significant issue. SymCure allows domain experts to represent events in their terminology at an arbitrary level of abstraction suitable to their application. However, the burden of detecting the occurrence of an event is placed on external monitoring mechanisms, which may require sophisticated filtering and aggregation techniques. SymCure does not explicitly model propagation delays or the likelihoods (i.e., probabilities) of events.

Not surprisingly, our greatest challenge in building SymCure applications has been in acquiring fault models. The bulk of this effort is in getting domain experts to specify their diagnostic knowledge in terms of causal fault models rather than inverse causality rules of the form "if this symptom, then conclude that fault". (We believe that causal fault models are better suited to bi-directional fault management than rule based approaches, which require separate sets of rules for diagnosis and impact prediction that may interfere with other leading to circular conclusions [12]. Furthermore, as the size of the rule base increases, it becomes increasingly difficult to maintain consistency.) Building reusable applications requires constructing fault models in a manner such that they are completely independent of system topologies. Like good software engineering practice, this requires a lot of discipline on the part of the application developer and is easier said than done.

## References


1. Siegel, D.: Abnormal Condition Management: Minimizing Process Disruptions and Sustaining Performance through Expert Systems Technology. In: Natl. Petroleum Refiners Assn. 2001 Comp. Conf., Dallas, USA (2001)
2. Stanley, G., Vaidhyanathan, R.: A Generic Fault Propagation Modeling Approach to On-line Diagnosis and Event Correlation. In: Proc. of the 3rd IFAC Workshop on On-line Fault Detection and Supervision in the Chemical Process Industries, Solaize, France (1998)
3. Integrity SymCure Developer's Guide. Version 3.6 Rev 0. Gensym Corporation (2002)
4. Porcheron, M., Ricard, B.: Model-based diagnosis for reactor coolant pumps of EDF nuclear power plants. In: Proc. of the 10th Intl. Conf. IEA/AIE 97, Atlanta, USA (1997) 411-420
5. Kliger, S., Yemeni, S., Yemeni, Y., Ohsie, D., Stolfo, S.: A Coding Approach to Event Correlation. In: Proc. of the 4th Intl. Symp. on Integrated Network Management (1995)
6. Finch, F., Oyeleye, O., Kramer, M.: A robust event-oriented methodology for diagnosis of dynamic process systems. Comp. and Chem. Engg. 14 (12) 1379 (1990)
7. Biswas, G., Kapadia, R., Yu, X.: Combined Qualitative-Quantitative Diagnosis of Continuous valued Systems. IEEE Sys. Man, and Cybernetics. Vol 27, No. 2 (1997) 167-185
8. Hamscher, W., Console, L., de Kleer, J. (eds.): Readings in Model-based Diagnosis. Morgan Kaufman (1992)
9. Kapadia, R.: Causal modeling for fault management with SymCure. Gensym Corporation Technical Report (2003)
10. Noureldin, H., Ruveta, F.: Using Expert System and Object Technology for Abnormal Condition Management. BIAS 2002 Intl. Conf. Milan Italy (2002)
11. Warpenburg, M., Stanley, G., Vaidhyanathan, R.: PATROL ROOT CAUSE ANALYSIS: A New Standard for Event Automation in an Enterprise Computing Environment. Gensym Corporation Technical Report (1999)
12. Rich, E., Knight, K.: Artificial Intelligence. 2nd ed. McGraw-Hill (1991)

# Efficient Initial Solution to Extremal Optimization Algorithm for Weighted MAXSAT Problem

Mohamed El-bachir Menai[1] and Mohamed Batouche[2]

[1] Computer Science Department, Tebessa University, 12000 Tebessa, Algeria, bmenai@wissal.dz

[2] LIRE Laboratory, Computer Science Department, Mentouri University, Constantine, Algeria, batouche@wissal.dz

**Abstract.** Stochastic local search algorithms are proved to be one of the most effective approach for computing approximate solutions of hard combinatorial problems. Most of them are based on a typical randomness related to uniform distributions for generating initial solutions. Particularly, Extremal Optimization is a recent meta-heuristic proposed for finding high quality solutions to hard optimization problems. In this paper, we introduce an algorithm based on another distribution, known as the Bose-Einstein distribution in quantum physics, which provides a new stochastic initialization scheme to an Extremal Optimization procedure. The resulting algorithm is proposed for the approximated solution to an instance of the weighted maximum satisfiability problem (MAXSAT). We examine its effectiveness by computational experiments on a large set of test instances and compare it with other existing meta-heuristic methods. Our results are remarkable and show that this approach is appropriate for this class of problems.

## 1 Introduction

The satisfiability problem (SAT) in propositional logic is known to be $NP$-complete ($NP$ denotes the set of all decision problems solvable by a non deterministic polynomial time algorithm) [7] and requires algorithms of exponential time complexity to solve in the worst case: Given a propositional formula, decide whether it has a model. Many problems in artificial intelligence, mathematical logic, computer aided design and databases can be formulated as SAT. The maximum satisfiability problem (MAXSAT) is an extension of SAT and consists of satisfying the maximum number of clauses of the propositional formula. It is known to be $NP$-hard (optimization problem that has a related $NP$-complete decision version problem) even when each clause contains exactly two literals (MAX2SAT). Since finding an exact solution to this problem requires exponential time, approximation algorithms to find near optimal solutions in polynomial time, appear to be viable. Developing efficient algorithms and heuristics for

P.W.H. Chung, C.J. Hinde, M. Ali (Eds.): IEA/AIE 2003, LNAI 2718, pp. 592–603, 2003.

MAXSAT can lead to general approaches for solving combinatorial optimization problems.

The present work is encouraged by the recent remarkable results obtained by Boettcher and Percus [5], [6] with their new meta-heuristic method called *Extremal Optimization (EO)* on graph partitioning problem. Furthermore, its application to handle unweighted MAXSAT problem instances [17] showed that this method improves significantly previous results obtained with *Simulated Annealing* [14] and *Tabu Search* [10], [11] methods on a bed test of random unweighted MAX3SAT and MAX4SAT instances. In addition, several MAXSAT studies have shown that providing interesting start-up assignments to a local search algorithm can improve its performance.

In the GRASP procedure [19] each iteration consists of a construction phase which provides a start-up assignments to a local search phase. The GRASP solution for MAXSAT is generally significantly better than that obtained from a random starting point [19].

Boettcher and Percus [6] have enhanced the convergence of EO for the partitioning of geometric graphs by using a clustering algorithm which separates initially the graph into domains. They indicate that EO can perform extremely better when using a *clever* start-up routine.

Szedmak [25] has applied the Bose-Einstein distribution, well known in quantum physics, rather than the uniform one to generate initial solutions for a hill climbing heuristic. The experimental results obtained on unweighted MAXSAT problem instances from the DIMACS repository, prove its efficiency according to a heuristic introduced by Johnson [13].

In this paper, we introduce an algorithm based on the Bose-Einstein distribution which provides a new stochastic initialization scheme to an Extremal Optimization procedure and compare it to the more frequently used methods like WSAT, Simulated Annealing and Tabu Search on an appropriate test set of MAXSAT instances. Finally, we present experimental results which demonstrate the superiority of this new approach with respect to alternative methods on the same benchmark.

## 2 Local Search for MAXSAT

Let $X = \{x_1, x_2, ..., x_n\}$ be a set of Boolean variables. The set of literals over $X$ is $L = \{x, \overline{x} \mid x \in X\}$. A clause $C$ on $X$ is a disjunction of literals. A clause form or CNF is a conjunction of clauses. An assignment of Boolean variables is a substitution of these variables by a vector $v \in \{0,1\}^n$. A clause is satisfied by an assignment if the value of the clause equals 1, otherwise the clause is unsatisfied. A weighted formula is a pair $WF = \{CF, W\}$ where $CF = (C_i)_{i \leq m}$ is a clause form and $W = (w_i)_{i \leq m} \in N^m$ is an integer vector; for each $i \leq m$, $w_i$ is the weight of the clause $C_i$. An assignment $v \in \{0,1\}^n$ determines a weight value at the weighted formula $WF$ as:

$$wc(CF, W, v) = \sum_{c_i(v)=1} w_i \tag{1}$$

The MAXSAT problem asks to determine an assignment $v_0 \in \{0,1\}^n$ that maximizes the sum of the weights of satisfied clauses:

$$wc(CF, W, v_0) = Max\{wc(CF, w, v) \mid v \in \{0,1\}^n\} \tag{2}$$

MAX$k$SAT is the subset of MAXSAT instances in which each clause has exactly $k$ literals. If each weight is equal to one, we call the resulting problem unweighted MAXSAT, otherwise we speak of weighted MAXSAT or simply MAXSAT.

While finding an exact solution to MAXSAT problem is $NP$-hard, local search has become an important general purpose method for solving satisfiability problems: It starts with a random initial solution and tries to improve it by moving to neighbouring solutions. It can be trapped in local poor minima or *plateaux*, it requires therefore a strategy to escape from these local minima and to guide the search toward good solutions. Different strategies can be cited: Simulated Annealing [14], [24], Tabu Search [10], [11], Ant Colony Optimization [8] and Reactive Search [3]. Although, the list of competitive heuristics is not exhaustive.

In the literature, effective local search algorithms to solve MAXSAT have been proposed. The most popular one is for sure GSAT (for G*reedy* SAT*isfiability*) [21], [22] defined initially for SAT and applied next to MAXSAT. It works as follows: It starts with an initial random assignment and, at each iteration, flips the variable which decreases the number of the most unsatisfied clauses. It is not a pure hill climbing algorithm as it accepts also moves which either produce the same objective function value or increase it. The process is repeated until a maximum number of non-improving moves is reached. Different *noise* strategies to escape from basins of attraction are added to GSAT. Its variants like WSAT [23], Novelty and R-Novelty [16] were generalized to handle weighted MAXSAT problems.

In the Tabu Search method [10], [11], a list of forbidden moves *tabu list* is used to avoid the search process revisiting the previously found solutions. MAXSAT problem was one of its first applications [12], but GSAT seemed to outperform its best results. Different history-based heuristics have been proposed to intensify and diversify the search into previously unexplored regions of the search space with collecting information from the previous phase. HSAT [9] introduces a tie-breaking rule into GSAT so that if more moves produce the same best results, the preferred move is the one that has been applied for the longest period. HSAT can be considered as a version of Tabu Search [15] and the results obtained on some MAXSAT benchmark tasks present a better performance with respect to WSAT.

Simulated Annealing (SA) is a method inspired by natural systems [14], [24]. It emulates the behaviour of frustrated physical systems in thermal equilibrium: A state of minimum energy may be attained by cooling the system slowly according to a temperature schedule. SA local search algorithm moves through the space configurations according to the Metropolis algorithm [18] driving the system to equilibrium dynamics. Selman *et al.* [23] affirm that they were unable to find a cooling schedule that outperformed GSAT.

## 3 Extremal Optimization Method

Extremal Optimization (EO) is a recently introduced meta-heuristic [4] for hard optimization problems. It was inspired by the Bak-Sneppen model [2] which was proposed to describe the self-organization phenomenon in the biological evolution of species. In this model, species $x_i$ have an associated value $\lambda_i \in [0,1]$ called *fitness* and a selection process against the extremely bad ones is applied. At each iteration, the specie having the smallest fitness value is selected for a random update which impacts obviously the fitness of interconnected species. After a sufficient number of steps, the system reaches a highly correlated state known as *self-organized criticality* [1] in which all species have reached a fitness of optimal adaptation.

A general modification of EO [4], [5] noted $\tau$-EO, consists to rank all variables from rank $k=1$ for the worst fitness to rank $k=n$ for the best fitness $\lambda_k$. For a given value of $\tau$, a power-law probability distribution over the rank order $k$ is considered:

$$P(k) \propto k^{-\tau}, \ (1 \leq k \leq n) \tag{3}$$

At each update, select a rank $k$ according to $P(k)$ and update the state of the variable $x_k$. The worst variable (with rank 1) will be chosen most frequently, while the best ones (with higher ranks) will sometimes be updated. In this way, a bias against worst variables is maintained and no rank gets completely excluded. The search process performance depends on the value of the parameter $\tau$. For $\tau = 0$, the algorithm becomes a random walk through the search space. While for too large values of $\tau$, only a small number of variables with bad fitness would be chosen at each iteration and, in this way, the process tends to a deterministic local search. Boettcher and Percus [6] have established a relation between $\tau$, run time $t$ and $n$ the number of variables of the system to estimate the optimal value of $\tau$. Let $t = An$ where $A$ is a constant $(1 \ll A \ll n)$, then:

$$\tau \sim 1 + \frac{\ln(A/\ln(n))}{\ln(n)}, \ (n \longrightarrow \infty) \tag{4}$$

At this optimal value, the best fitness variables are not completely excluded from the selection process and hence, more space configurations can be reached so that greatest performance can be obtained.

## 4 Bose-Einstein Extremal Optimization Algorithm (BE-EO)

### 4.1 Bose-Einstein Distribution

Commonly used methods for MAXSAT problems generate initial assignments randomly over the set of variables that appear in clauses. These variables get their values separately with the same uniform distribution. So, the number of variables with value 1 and those with value 0 in all generated assignments are around the same average. If the optimal assignment contains a very different number from this average, the generated initial assignments will be far away from the optimal one and thus, it will be hard to find this optimum. It turns out that a probability distribution which guarantees that an arbitrary proportion of 1s and 0s will appear in an initial assignment set, can improve the performance of the search algorithm. Szedmak [25] proved that only the Bose-Einstein distribution satisfies the previous condition. He demonstrated its effectiveness by showing that the Hamming distance between the optimal and the initial assignments set, is reduced when the initial assignments are generated by this distribution rather than the uniform one. For the binary case, the Bose-Einstein distribution can be outlined as follows [25]: Let $V = \{1, ..., n\}$ be a base set for a given $n$, $X = \{x_1, x_2, ..., x_n\}$ be a set of Boolean variables and $p_X$ be the probability distribution of $X$ in the space $\{0,1\}^n$. For a subset $S$ of $V$, let $X[S] = \sum_{i \in S} x_i$ be the number of the variables of $X$ equal to 1 in $S$. We are looking for a distribution such that $X[S]$ is uniformly distributed on $\{0, ..., |S|\}$ for all subsets $S$ of $V$:

$$\forall k \in \{0, ..., |S|\}, \forall S \subseteq V, \quad P(X[S] = k) = \frac{1}{|S| + 1}, \tag{5}$$

The Bose-Einstein distribution satisfies the Eqn.5 and it is defined by [20]:

$$\forall X \in \{0,1\}^n, \quad p_X = \frac{1}{(n+1)\binom{n}{X[V]}} \tag{6}$$

Its conditional probability is given by:

$$p(x_j = 1) = \frac{X[S] + 1}{(j-1) + 2} \quad \text{where } S = \{1, ..., (j-1)\} \tag{7}$$

### 4.2 BE-EO Algorithm

Let us consider a MAXSAT problem instance of $n$ Boolean variables and $m$ weighted clauses $WF = \{CF, W\}$ where $CF = (C_j)_{j \leq m}$ and $W = (w_j)_{j \leq m} \in N^m$. Let $v$ be the current assignment. For each variable $x_i$, the fitness $\lambda_i$ is defined as the fraction of satisfied clauses weights sum in which that variable appears by the total weights sum:

$$\lambda_i = \frac{\sum_{x_i \in C_j \text{ and } C_j(v)=1} w_j}{\sum_{k=1}^{m} w_k} \tag{8}$$

The cost function $CS(v)$ is the total cost contributions of each variable $x_i$. To maximize the sum of the weights of satisfied clauses, we have to minimize $CS(v)$. Hence,

$$CS(v) = -\sum_{i=1}^{n} \lambda_i \tag{9}$$

The procedure BE-EO for MAXSAT is briefly summarized as follows:

**Procedure** BE-EO_MAXSAT
**Input** *WeightedCl*, *Tho*, *Sample*, *MaxSteps*.
**Output**: *Vbest*, CS(*Vbest*), *UnsatCl*, *WeightUnsat*.
*Vbest*:= Random_BE_Assignment (variables that appear in *WeightedCl*).
*TotalWeight*:= sum of *WeightedCl* weights.
for l:=1 to *Sample* do
    *V*:= Random_BE_Assignment (variables that appear in *WeightedCl*).
    *UnsatCl*:= set of clauses not satisfied by *V*.
    *WeightUnsat*:= sum of *UnsatCl* weights.
    for k:=1 to *MaxSteps* do
        if *V* satisfies *WeightedCl* then return (*V*, *TotalWeight*).
        Evaluate $\lambda_i$ for each variable $x_i$ in *WeightedCl* w.r.t. Eqn.8.
        Rank all variables $x_i$ w.r.t. $\lambda_i$ from the worst to the best.
        Select a rank $j$ with probability $P(j) \propto j^{-Tho}$.
        *Vc*:= *V* in which the value of $x_j$ is flipped.
        if CS(*Vc*)
$<$
CS(*Vbest*) then *Vbest*:= *Vc*.
        *V*:=*Vc*.
        Update (*UnsatCl*, *WeightUnsat*).
    endfor
endfor

Given an initial Bose-Einstein assignment $V$ generated randomly by the function Random_BE_Assignment. A fixed number of tries *MaxSteps* is executed. Each step in the search process corresponds to flipping the value assigned to a variable according to EO strategy. The best current assignment *Vbest* is related to the current maximum total weights of satisfied clauses. The unsatisfied clauses set *UnsatCl* and their weights sum *WeightUnsat* are then updated. This process is repeated as necessary up to *Sample* times, the size of Bose-Einstein sample of initial assignments.

## 5 Experimental Results

We now report on our experiment results obtained with a version of the procedures EO and BE-EO. The programs were coded in C language and their behaviours were investigated through experiments performed on a PC Pentium III (256 MB memory, 450 MHz) and conducted both on random weighted and unweighted MAXSAT instances.

### 5.1 Problem Instances

The test suite was dedicated to several hard instances: (1) random unweighted MAX3SAT, MAX4SAT, MAXSAT instances, (2) random weighted MAXSAT instances. For random unweighted MAX3SAT and MAX4SAT the instances considered are respectively $(100, 500)$, $(100, 700)$, $(300, 1500)$, $(300, 2000)$, $(500, 5000)$

and (100, 700), (300, 1500), (300, 3000). For each couple $(n, m)$ of $n$ variables and $m$ clauses, 10 instances were generated. The generator of these random instances is available at the web site `http://www.cs.cornell.edu/home/selman/sat/sat-package.tar`. In addition, we tested 10 random unweighted MAXSAT instances of $n = 1000$ and $m = 11050$, which are available at `http://www-or.amp.i.kyoto-u.ac.jp/~yagiura/sat/`. Results were also discussed on 10 random weighted MAXSAT instances of $n = 1000$ and $m = 11050$ where clause weights are integers uniformly distributed between 1 and 1000, and available at the same web site. Yagiura and Ibaraki [26] observed that no satisfying assignments usually exist for such instances. We finally tested 17 random instances (identified by `jnh1-jnh19`) of $n = 100$ and $m = 850$ where clause weights are chosen randomly from [1, 1000]. These instances have been obtained from `http://www.research.att.com/~mgcr/data/maxsat.tar.gz`. We ran our experiments on these instances so that our results could be readily compared with those of alternative methods.

### 5.2 Effect of Parameter $\tau$

Our first set of experiments involves the numerical investigation of the optimal value for $\tau$ and its impact on the performance of BE-EO. The procedure BE-EO_MAXSAT is run 10 times for each instance where *MaxSteps* is fixed to $5n$ and *Sample* to $100n$. In EO algorithm, *MaxSteps* is fixed to $1000n$ and it is run 10 times for each instance. We note that all algorithms have been run with additional iterations, but they have not produced significantly better results. Figures 1-3 illustrate the average error in % of a solution from the upper bound $\sum_{i=1}^{m} w_i$ while varying $\tau$ between 0.5 and 1.7. Let $wc(CF, W, v_0)$ be given by

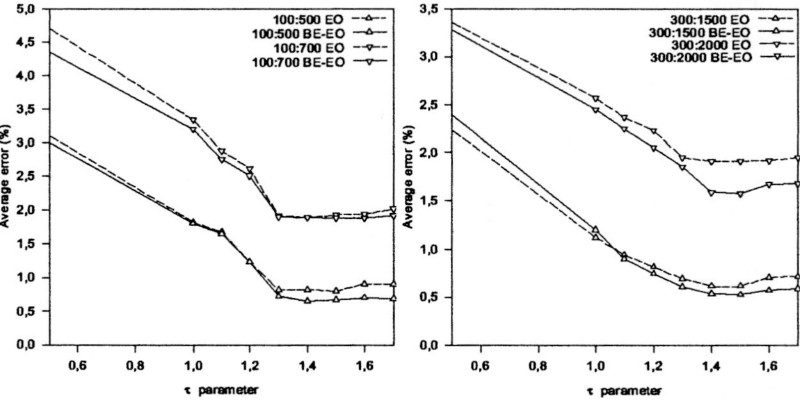


**Fig. 1.** Effect of parameter $\tau$ of EO and BE-EO for random unweighted MAX3SAT instances of (*left graph*) $n = 100$, $m = 500, 700$; (*right graph*) $n = 300, m = 1500, 2000$

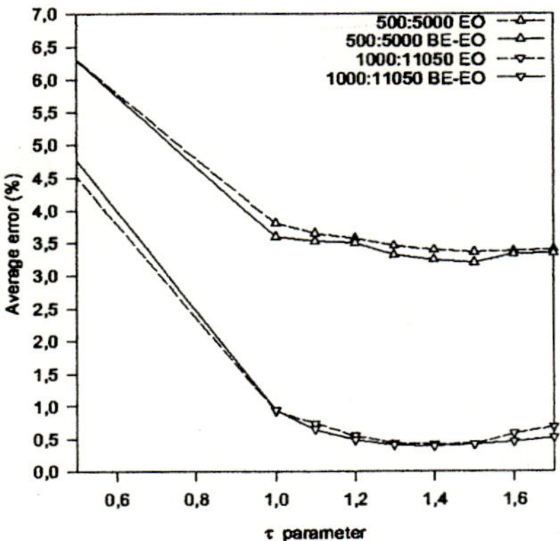


**Fig. 2.** Effect of parameter $\tau$ of EO and BE-EO for random unweighted MAX3SAT instances of $n = 500$, $m = 5000$ and random unweighted MAXSAT instances of $n = 1000$, $m = 11050$

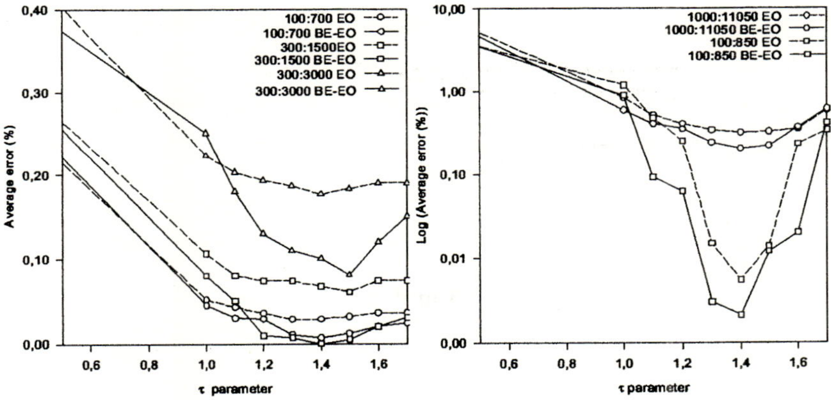


**Fig. 3.** Effect of parameter $\tau$ of EO and BE-EO for (*left graph*) random unweighted MAX4SAT instances of $n = 100, 300$ and $m = 700, 1500, 3000$; (*right graph*) random weighted MAXSAT instances of $n = 1000, m = 11050$ and $n = 100, m = 850$

Eqn.2, then:

$$error\,(\%) = \left(1 - \frac{wc\,(CF, W, v_0)}{\sum_{i=1}^{m} w_i}\right) \times 100 \tag{10}$$

Results of both procedures show that the optimal values for $\tau$ are similar for all random instances ranging from 1.3 to 1.5. Comparable values of parameter $\tau$ have been obtained on instances of graph partitioning problem [6]. We can notice that for $n = 100$, the optimal value of $\tau$ is, in average, from 1.3 to 1.4 while for the other values ($n =$ 300, 500, 1000) it is between 1.4 and 1.5.

### 5.3 Comparisons

For comparison purposes we examine the performance of BE-EO with that of EO, GSAT, WSAT, SA and SAMD. We refer to results obtained in a previous comparative study executed on SA, SAMD and alternative methods for unweighted MAX3SAT and MAX4SAT instances [12], [23]. GSAT and WSAT codes are taken from the web site `http://www.cs.cornell.edu/home/selman/sat/sat-package.tar`. We experimented with GSAT and WSAT for unweighted instances where the default parameters were used as suggested in the authors implementation ($p = 0.5$, $MAXFLIPS = 10000$) [23]. In the weighted MAXSAT case, we compare our results to those obtained by Yagiura and Ibaraki [26] with MAXSAT versions of GSAT and WSAT on the same instances. Tables 1, 2 and 3 compare the average error in % (Eqn. 10) of BE-EO with those of considered methods on instances of respectively unweighted MAX3SAT, unweighted MAX4SAT, unweighted MAXSAT of $n = 1000$ and $m = 11050$, weighted MAXSAT of $n = 1000$ and $m = 11050$, and weighted MAXSAT of $n = 100$ and $m = 850$. The data for the first two lines of Tables 1 and 2 are derived from those obtained by Hansen and Jaumard [12] and Selman *et al.* [23], and converted from average number of unsatisfied clauses to average error (%). The

**Table 1.** Average error for random unweighted MAX3SAT instances

| Variables ($n$) | 100 | 100 | 300 | 300 | 500 |
|---|---|---|---|---|---|
| Clauses ($m$) | 500 | 700 | 1500 | 2000 | 5000 |
| SA | 1.6400 | 2.5857 | 2.0000 | 2.9000 | 4.5280 |
| SAMD | 1.0200 | 2.1000 | 1.0200 | 1.9500 | 3.6560 |
| GSAT | 0.5560 | 1.9143 | 0.5507 | 1.5970 | 3.2788 |
| WSAT ($p = 0.5$) | 0.5520 | 1.9143 | 0.5413 | 1.6140 | 3.3400 |
| EO | 1.2800 | 2.1857 | 0.8067 | 2.3100 | 3.5020 |
| $\tau$-EO | 0.8200 | 1.8857 | 0.6133 | 1.9100 | 3.3620 |
| | ($\tau = 1.4$) | ($\tau = 1.4$) | ($\tau = 1.5$) | ($\tau = 1.5$) | ($\tau = 1.5$) |
| BE-EO | 0.6520 | 1.8810 | 0.5467 | 1.5750 | 3.2024 |
| | ($\tau = 1.4$) | ($\tau = 1.4$) | ($\tau = 1.5$) | ($\tau = 1.5$) | ($\tau = 1.5$) |

**Table 2.** Average error for random unweighted MAX4SAT instances

| Variables ($n$) | 100 | 300 | 300 |
|---|---|---|---|
| Clauses ($m$) | 700 | 1500 | 3000 |
| SA | 0.0429 | 0.0667 | 0.4767 |
| SAMD | 0.0143 | 0.0867 | 0.3133 |
| GSAT | 0 | 0 | 0.1687 |
| WSAT ($p = 0.5$) | 0 | 0 | 0.1573 |
| EO | 0.0429 | 0.0800 | 0.2400 |
| $\tau$-EO | 0.0286 | 0.0667 | 0.1767 |
| | ($\tau = 1.3$) | ($\tau = 1.5$) | ($\tau = 1.4$) |
| BE-EO | 0.0071 | 0 | 0.0800 |
| | ($\tau = 1.4$) | ($\tau = 1.5$) | ($\tau = 1.4$) |

**Table 3.** Average error for random unweighted and weighted MAXSAT instances

| | Unweighted | | Weighted | | Weighted | |
|---|---|---|---|---|---|---|
| Variables ($n$) | 1000 | | 1000 | | 100 | |
| Clauses ($m$) | 11050 | | 11050 | | 850 | |
| | Error (%) | Iterations | Error (%) | Iterations | Error (%) | Iterations |
| GSAT | 0.5484 | 5000000 | 0.7348 | 15000 | 0.4890 | 2000 |
| WSAT | 0.4525 ($p = 0.5$) | 25000000 | 0.2733 ($p = 0.2$) | 100000 | 0.0099 ($p = 0.5$) | 12264 |
| EO | 0.5311 | 1000000 | 0.3156 | 100000 | 0.0151 | 10000 |
| $\tau$-EO ($\tau = 1.4$) | 0.0286 | 1000000 | 0.2544 | 100000 | 0.0054 | 10000 |
| BE-EO ($\tau = 1.4$) | 0.0071 | 100000 | 0.2024 | 100000 | 0.0021 | 10000 |

first two lines of Table 3 are from the results of Yagiura and Ibaraki [26], they represent both average error (%) and the related total number of iterations on a workstation Sun Ultra 2 Model 2300 (1 GB memory, 300 MHz).

The results show that $\tau$-EO significantly improves upon the results obtained with SA and SAMD while they trail those of GSAT and WSAT. In Table 1, we can observe that WSAT with $p = 0.5$ gives the best results for $(100, 500)$, $(300, 1500)$ instances and BE-EO gives the best ones for $(100, 700)$, $(300, 2000)$, $(500, 5000)$ instances. In Table 2, the best results for instance of $(100, 700)$ are obtained with WSAT ($p = 0.5$), while BE-EO gives the best ones for instance of $(300, 3000)$. As can be seen in Table 3, all the best results are obtained by the procedure BE-EO which significantly outperforms GSAT, WSAT and $\tau$-EO.

We can observe that the overall best performance is given by BE-EO. It is at least as good as WSAT for each type of instances and generally it provides better results. The BE-EO high quality solution can have the following explanations. Firstly, MAXSAT search spaces are known to hold too many local minima and the large fluctuations of EO allow search process to explore many of these local minima without loosing well-adapted portions of a solution. Secondly, it is difficult to construct an initial assignment near an optimal one but the Bose-Einstein distribution samples an initial assignments set more efficient than that provided with the usual uniform distribution. Hence, combining EO with this distribution may guarantee that the resulting algorithm efficiently seeks out the region of the fitness landscape containing the global optimum.

## 6 Conclusion

In this paper, we examined experimentally the effectiveness of sampling initial solutions set to Extremal Optimization search process with the Bose-Einstein distribution. EO is a simple and powerful method to find high quality solutions to hard optimization problems and Bose-Einstein distribution has proved to generate more efficient initial solutions for searching than uniform distribution. A new algorithm called BE-EO has been proposed to approximate solution of weighted MAXSAT problem instances and computational tests were conducted on both random weighted and unweighted instances. The results provide experimental evidence that this approach is efficient for this class of problems and demonstrate generally its superiority with respect to Simulated Annealing, Tabu Search, GSAT, WSAT and $\tau$-EO heuristic methods. The solution quality achieved by this procedure is due both to the flexibility of EO process to explore more space configurations and to the ability of Bose-Einstein distribution to generate efficient initial assignments so that the number of searching steps needed to reach an optimum is reduced. Furthermore, this new method requires few control parameters, is easy to implement and test, therefore providing motivation to adapt it for solving various classes of $NP$-hard optimization problems.

## References


1. Bak, P., Tang, C., Wiesenfeld, K.: Self-organized Criticality: An Explanation of $1/f$-noise. Physical Review Letters, V86 N23. (1987) 5211-5214
2. Bak, P., Sneppen, K.: Punctuated Equilibrium and Criticality in a Simple Model of Evolution. Physical Review letters, 59. (1993) 381-384
3. Battiti, R., Protasi, M.: Reactive Search, a History-Sensitive Heuristic for MAX-SAT. ACM Journal of Experimental Algorithmics, Vol. 2, Paper 2 (1997)
4. Boettcher, S., Percus, A.G.: Nature's Way of Optimizing. Elsevier Science, Artificial Intelligence, 119. (2000) 275-286
5. Boettcher, S., Percus, A.G.: Optimization with Extremal Dynamics. Physical Review Letters, V86 N23. (2001a) 5211-5214
6. Boettcher, S., Percus, A.G.: Extremal Optimization for Graph Partitioning. Physical Review E, V64 026114. (2001b) 1-13
7. Cook, S. A.: The Complexity of Theorem Proving Procedures. Proceedings of the 3rd Annual ACM Symposium of the Theory of Computation. (1971) 263-268
8. Dorigo, M., Maniezzo, V., Colorni, A.: The Ant System: Optimization by a Colony of Cooperating Agents. IEEE Transactions on Systems, Man, and Cybernetics-Part B, Vol. 26, N1. (1996) 1-13
9. Gent, I.P., Walsh, T.: Towards an Understanding of Hill-Climbing Procedures for SAT. Proceedings of the 11th National Conference on Artificial Intelligence. (1993) 28-33
10. Glover, F.: Tabu Search: Part I. ORSA Journal on Computing 1 (3). (1989a) 190-206
11. Glover, F.: Tabu Search: Part II. ORSA Journal on Computing 2 (1). (1989a) +32
12. Hansen, P., Jaumard, B.: Algorithms for the Maximum Satisfiability Problems. Computing, 44. (1990) 279-303
13. Johnson, D.: Approximation Algorithms for Combinatorial Problems. Journal of Computer and System Sciences, 9. (1974) 256-278
14. Kirkpatrick, S., Gelatt, C.D., Vecchi, P.M.: Optimization by Simulated Annealing. Science, 220. (1983) 671-680
15. Mazure, B., Sais, L., Gregoire, E.: Tabu Search for SAT. Proceedings of the 14th National Conference on Artificial Intelligence and 9th Innovative Applications of Artificial Intelligence Conference. (1997) 281-285
16. McAllester, D., Selman, B., Kautz, H.A.: Evidence for Invariants in Local Search. Proceedings of AAAI'92. MIT Press (1997) 321-326

17. Menai, M.B., Batouche, M.: Extremal Optimization for MAXSAT. Proceedings of the International Conference on Artificial Intelligence (IC-AI'02), Las Vegas, USA. 954-958
18. Metropolis, N., Rosenbluth, A.W., Rosenbluth, M.N., Teller, A.H., Teller, E.: Equation of state calculations by fast computing machines. Journal of Chemical Physics, 21. (1953) 1087-1092
19. Resende, M.G.C., Pitsoulis, L.S., Pardalos, P.M.: Approximate Solution of Weighted MAX-SAT Problems using GRASP. In Satisfiability Problem: Theory and Applications, Vol. 35 of DIMACS Series in Discrete Mathematics and Theoretical Computer Science (American Mathematical Society, 1997). (1997) 393-405
20. Ross, M. S.: Introduction to Probability Models. Academic Press, New York. (2000) 137-141
21. Selman, B., Kautz, H.A.: An Empirical Study of Greedy Local Search for Satisfiability Testing. Proceedings of the 11th National Conference on Artificial Intelligence. (1993a) 46-51
22. Selman, B., Kautz, H.A.: Domain Independent Extensions to GSAT: Solving Large Structured Satisfiability Problems. Proceedings of the 13th International Joint Conference on Artificial Intelligence. (1993b) 290-295
23. Selman, B., Kautz, H.A., Cohen B.: Noise Strategies for Improving Local Search. Proceedings of the 12th National Conference on Artificial Intelligence. (1994) 337-343
24. Spears, W. M.: Simulated Annealing for Hard Satisfiability Problems. In D.S. Johnson and M.A. Trick (eds.), Cliques, Coloring and Satisfiability: Second DIMACS Implementation Challenge, Vol. 26 of DIMACS Series in Discrete Mathematics and Theoretical Computer Science (American Mathematical Society, 1996). (1996) 553-558
25. Szedmak, S.: How to Find More Efficient Initial Solution for Searching ? RUTCOR Research Report, 49-2001, Rutgers Center for Operations Research, Rutgers University. (2001)
26. Yagiura, M., Ibaraki, T.: Efficient 2 and 3-Flip Neighborhood Search Algorithms for the MAX SAT: Experimental Evaluation. Journal of Heuristics, 7. (2001) 423-442

# Adaptive Resource Location in a Peer-to-Peer Network

Michael Iles and Dwight Deugo

Carleton University, Ottawa, Ontario Canada, K1S 5B6
miles@magma.ca
deugo@scs.carleton.ca

**Abstract.** Flooding broadcast networks have proven themselves capable of meeting most major criteria for successful peer-to-peer networks, but they have one major shortcoming: an inefficient resource discovery mechanism that has difficulty scaling. We develop a 'meta-protocol' for flooding broadcast networks that is expressive enough to describe a range of existing and deployed flooding broadcast network protocols. We then describe how to apply genetic programming to obtain specific network protocols from this meta-protocol that are optimized for various specific network scenarios.

## 1 Introduction

The decentralized network—a network in which machines interact with each other as relative equals instead of in a master and slave relationship—was a common paradigm in the early days of networking, as the widely-distributed Internet took form to link pre-existing computing centers on equal footings. As the Internet evolved and traffic rose, however, a fairly static web of dedicated communication servers took over the job of routing packets and the majority of machines were pushed to the fringes. The underlying communications infrastructure remains, but increasing connection speeds and the rising power of desktop machines has brought a resurgence of interest in decentralized, or peer-to-peer networks.

Decentralized networks and peer-to-peer networks in general have recently drawn tremendous interest from both the academic communities and the general public. The potential for such networks is great: fault tolerance, storage, content distribution, anonymity, public naming mechanisms, individual publishing, distributed cost, censorship-resistance, and resource discovery are some of the abilities touted.

Among the many extant and proposed types of peer-to-per networks, the broad category of flooding broadcast networks has generated by far the most popular interest. The combined size of the flooding broadcast Gnutella and FastTrack (KaZaA) networks ranges into the millions of peers. There are other viable peer-to-peer alternatives—most notably the distributed hashing systems [3] but flooding broadcast networks [4],[9] have demonstrated their utility and robustness in many real-world scenarios.

Flooding broadcast networks have proven themselves capable of meeting most major criteria for successful peer-to-peer networks (principally decentralized administration and robustness to peer transience and failure), but they have one major shortcoming: an inefficient resource discovery mechanism that has difficulty scaling. There is no obvious solution to the decentralized resource discovery problem: the

P.W.H. Chung, C.J. Hinde, M. Ali (Eds.): IEA/AIE 2003, LNAI 2718, pp. 604–613, 2003.

number of neighbors a peer should maintain, how it should choose those neighbors, how it should keep from becoming overloaded with traffic, and how varying bandwidths and search scopes should be accommodated are all open for debate. A wide range of protocols to achieve resource discovery in flooding broadcast peer-to peer networks have sprung up, with no clear winner among them.

All of the flooding broadcast protocols currently in use have one attribute in common: they are hand-crafted heuristics. In other words, they are a human designer's best guess at how peers in a decentralized network should interact.

In this paper, we describe the use of genetic programming, a machine learning technique, to remove some of the human bias from this search for heuristics. We show that this approach is capable of producing optimal flooding broadcast network protocols[1] for arbitrary network scenarios.

Our contributions are twofold. First, we develop a 'meta-protocol' for flooding broadcast networks that is expressive enough to describe a range of existing and deployed flooding broadcast network protocols, and then describe how genetic programming is a viable method to obtain specific network protocols from this meta-protocol that are optimized for various specific network scenarios.

In section 2, we briefly discuss techniques that have been employed to solve the resource discovery problem in both centralized and decentralized networks, and hashing systems. Section 3 develops the general flooding broadcast network protocol and describes the network model and genetic programming mechanisms employed in the simulated peer-to-peer network. Section 4 presents an overview of our experimental results obtained from our simulations. Section 5 summarizes.

## 2 Background

There are a wide variety of strategies for achieving resource discovery in decentralized networks. Centralized or decentralized indices are an obvious solution but pose scalability and single-point-of-failure problems. Distributed hashing systems use highly structured networks to achieve very efficient searching, but do not deal well with highly transient peers and do not allow for flexible searching. Flooding broadcast networks provide infinitely flexible searches and allow for transient nodes, but are limited by a simplistic and inefficient propagation mechanism. These factors are summarized in Table 1.

The two most promising approaches to organizing a peer-to-peer network then are flooding broadcast networks and distributed hashing systems. Distributed hashing systems, despite their great promise, are complicated and untested in the real world and currently exist only within the realm of academic research. On the other hand, flooding broadcast networks (including Gnutella and FastTrack/KaZaA) comprise the vast majority of deployed peer-to-peer networks, and despite their scaling difficulties are approaching the participation levels of the original Napster. We have chosen, therefore, to build on this base in an attempt to improve on current resource discovery strategies in flooding broadcast networks.

---

[1] The term protocol is used in this thesis not in the narrow computer science sense of a wire protocol, but in the broader sense of an earthquake protocol or diplomatic protocol: a set of rules to be followed in specific situations.

**Table 1.** A comparison and ranking of the approaches presented in this chapter. The variable $n$ refers to the number of nodes in the network, and $n_{hosts}$ refers to the number of nodes hosting the distributed index

| | Centralized Indices | Decentralized Indices | Flooding Broadcast Networks | Distributed Hashing Systems |
|---|---|---|---|---|
| scalability | poor | good | poor | good |
| flexible searching | yes | yes | yes | no |
| single point of failure | yes | yes | no | no |
| distributed cost | no | somewhat | yes | yes |
| peers queried | 1 | 1 | $O(n)$ | $O(\log n)$ |
| peers affected by addition or removal of resource | 1 | $n_{hosts}$ | 1 | $O(\log n)$ |
| robustness to host failure | poor | average | excellent | good |
| bounded search completion | yes | yes | no | yes |

Although numerous augmentations and modifications have been proposed since its inception, the original Gnutella protocol [5] can be though of as one of the simplest (possibly to the point of naiveté) peer-to-peer protocols in that all nodes are considered equal in the network and no adaptive modifications to the network topology are attempted. Texar's s-peer [11] and Sun's JXTA [10] protocols are functionally identical in terms of network construction and message routing.

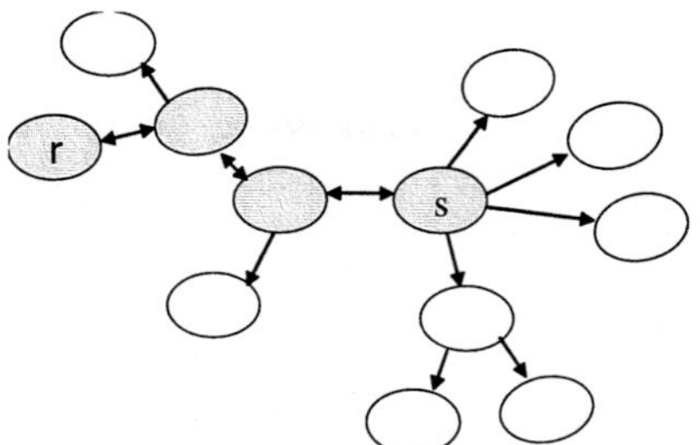


**Fig. 1.** A Broadcast Message and a Response

The Gnutella protocol gives rise to a decentralized network where each node interacts only with its neighboring nodes. A node joins the network by obtaining the address of any other node currently in the network, and then broadcasts an advertisement of its presence to other nodes which respond in turn with their own addresses. Each node aims to maintain a fixed number of connections, typically seven. A node will re-broadcast messages it receives to the rest of its neighbors, so broadcasts propagate outwards in breadth-first fashion subject to a maximum depth. (This depth, or *time-to-live*, is typically seven.) Each node remembers the neighbor it received a broadcast message from, so when a node responds to a request that response is routed back to the original sender based on each node's memory of the path the original broadcast message took. This behavior is illustrated in figure 1, which shows the outward propagation of the message broadcast by node *s* and the reverse path traced by node *r*'s response.

Since flooding broadcast networks are widely deployed and effective but suffer in general from inefficient resource-discovery techniques, we combine flooding broadcast networks and genetic programming together to develop a meta-protocol to describe a broad class of flooding broadcast network protocols, and to locate the best and new protocols to use under given constraints.

## 3 Approach

We wanted to develop a flooding broadcast meta-protocol (FBMP) capable of describing a wide range of possible flooding broadcast network protocols, and to show that genetic programming is a viable method for deriving specific network protocols from this meta-protocol that are optimized for specific network scenarios. Achieving these goals would give a flooding broadcast network the ability to adapt to and optimize itself for arbitrary traffic patterns.

In this pursuit, we first describe the idealized simulated peer-to-peer network in which both the Gnutella protocol and the FBMP will be implemented. Next we describe the FBMP itself. The aim of this meta-protocol is to provide a specification mechanism that is general enough to allow the Gnutella, s-peer and FastTrack/KaZaA protocols and a subset of the JXTA protocols to be expressed. Finally, we explain how genetic programming will be used to derive new flooding broadcast network protocols from the FBMP that are optimized for specific network scenarios. This can be thought of as a search for optimal protocols through the protocol-space described by the FBMP. The end result will be a system that is able to search for new flooding broadcast network protocols that satisfy certain criteria, and to evaluate these new protocols against the existing Gnutella protocol.

### 3.1 The Simulation

The simulated peer-to-peer network models a flooding broadcast overlay network. This follows the lead [1] of virtually all recent peer-to-peer research in adopting the use of an overlay network using the Internet as the underlying communication mechanism.

The targeting of the Internet implies that the performance distribution of the machines participating in the peer-to-peer network will follow that of the Internet. Studies have shown that such a distribution on the Internet generally follows a power-law relationship. This in turn implies that the majority of machines participating in such a network are of a relatively low power. This conclusion is borne out by the observed participants in widely deployed peer-to-peer networks such as Napster, Gnutella and FastTrack, which are overwhelmingly populated by end-user machines whose bandwidth bottleneck is in the 'last hop' to their machine over a dial-up or home broadband link.

The physical model includes the peers, the backbone, and the connections being maintained between the peers. The corresponding logical model includes a logical connection requiring a bandwidth allotment from each of the two peers it connects, so its effective bandwidth is constrained by the lower of the two allotments available to it.

Upon joining the network, a peer broadcasts an advertisement of its presence and begins receiving replies to this broadcast informing it of the presence of other peers. As well, the peer begins working its way through its predetermined list of searches to perform. It maintains a fixed number of concurrent active searches at all times, and allots each search a window of time to receive responses before it begins the next search. Each peer also has a predetermined list of resources that it possesses, and it responds affirmatively to any queries that it receives for those resources. All peers co-operate with their neighbors by forwarding any broadcast and routed traffic that they receive from them. Each peer maintains a collection of statistics for every other peer in the network that it is aware of. Information in this collection is gathered by examining messages that are passed through the peer, through interactions with neighboring peers, and through responses to messages that the peer itself has broadcast. These statistics include, for example, the shortest number of hops that messages have taken between two peers, and the number of successful responses to search queries that another peer has provided. This historical information is maintained using a sliding window of fixed size to ensure that it is always relevant.

The simulation follows a discrete-event model [2], which has two attributes that are desirable in this context. The first is that the simulation operates independently of processor speed, which is important when simulating a large number of individual machines on one processor. The second is that it allows the end of the simulation to be easily detected. A negative attribute of search in a flooding broadcast network is that there is no definitive end to a given query: the querying peer has no knowledge of whether or not its query is continuing to reach new peers. In a discrete-event simulation the end of the network run is clearly established when there are no further messages to process anywhere in the network.

The purpose of the simulation is to allow different network protocols to be compared based on the performance of the network under their control, and these statistics allow such comparisons to be made.

The simulation allows the network to be governed by one of two network protocols: the Gnutella protocol or an instance of the FBMP, described in the next section.

### 3.2 The Flooding Broadcast Meta-protocol

The purpose of the FBMP is to provide a general specification mechanism that allows a wide range of specific flooding broadcast network protocols to be expressed. The range of the meta-protocol presented here encompasses the Gnutella protocol, the s-peer protocol, the FastTrack/KaZaA protocol, and a subset of the JXTA protocol.

The aim of specifying such a meta-protocol is to allow a search mechanism to explore the protocol space that these protocols exist in and to arrive at specific protocols that are optimal for specific network scenarios. This section describes the construction of the meta-protocol.

These degrees of freedom are achieved by representing each instance of the metaprotocol with two expressions. The CONN expression is evaluated to specify the number of connections for that peer to maintain, and the RANK expression is then evaluated for each existing or potential connection. The connections are ordered based on the rating the RANK expression gives them, and the top-ranked ones are used to fill the quota specified by the CONN expression.

Both expressions make use of the standard operators multiply, protdivide (protected divide, where divide-by-zero returns 1), add, subtract and random0to1 (which returns a random number between 0 and 1). The RANK expressions can also use if (which returns its second or third arguments depending on whether its first argument is positive or negative) and greater (which returns 1 or -1 depending on whether its first argument is greater than its second argument).

Both expressions also draw from a set of terminals representing information that the peer is able to gather locally from its observations of its immediate neighbours and of the traffic it has received. The terminals available to a CONN expression as follows: *numberOfNeighbours* (The number of connections the peer currently has); *averageMaxQueueSize* (The average over all of the peer's connections of the maximum number of queued messages each connection has experienced); *maxQueueSize* (The maximum queue size of any connection the peer has); *nodeBandwidth* (The overall bandwidth for a peer, in kilobits per second); *maxSocketBandwidth* (The maximum bandwidth, in kilobits per second, of any connection the peer has had); *totalTraffic* (The total amount of traffic, in bits, that the peer has processed); *currentConnectionLimit* (The current connection limit. This is set initially to a fixed value and is then modified by subsequent evaluations of the CONN expression.)

The terminals available to a RANK expression as follows: *distance* (The shortest known distance, in hops, to the given peer); *isNeighbour* (This is -1 or 1 depending on whether a connection exists between this peer and the given peer); *numberOfResources* (The number of resources the other peer possesses. A new peer joining the network broadcasts this information, and existing peers respond with the number of resources they possess); *searchHits* (The number of search query responses the other peer has provided); *timedOutSearchHits* (The number of search query responses returned after this peer had expired the search); *broadcastTrafficGenerated* (The amount of broadcast traffic (in bits) the other peer has generated); *totalTraffic* (If a connection exists between the two peers then this is the total amount of traffic (in bits) that the peer has passed on; otherwise it is 0. originator For connected peers, this is -1 or 1 depending on whether this peer or the other peer originated the connection. Otherwise, it is 0); bandwidth (The current bandwidth, in kilobits per second, of the connection between the two peers, or 0 if they are not connected); *queueSize* (The current number of messages queued on the connection, or 0 if they are not connected); *maxQueueSize* (The maximum number of messages queued on the connection, or 0 if they aren't connected); *minBandwidth* (The minimum bandwidth of the connection, in kilobits per second, or 0 if there is no connection); maxBandwidth (The maximum bandwidth of the connection, in kilobits per second, or 0 if there is no connection); *lengthOfConnection* (The length of time, in milliseconds, that the peers have been connected, or 0 if they are not connected); *minResponsiveness* (The minimum round-trip time, in milliseconds, messages between the two peers); *maxResponsiveness* (The maximum round-trip time, in milliseconds, of messages between the two peers.)

Two sample protocols for Gnutella and s-peer using this FBMP are shown in figure 2. The FBMP gives rise to a huge space of possible flooding broadcast network protocols. To search for worthwhile protocols within this space, we employ the genetic programming approach described in the following section.

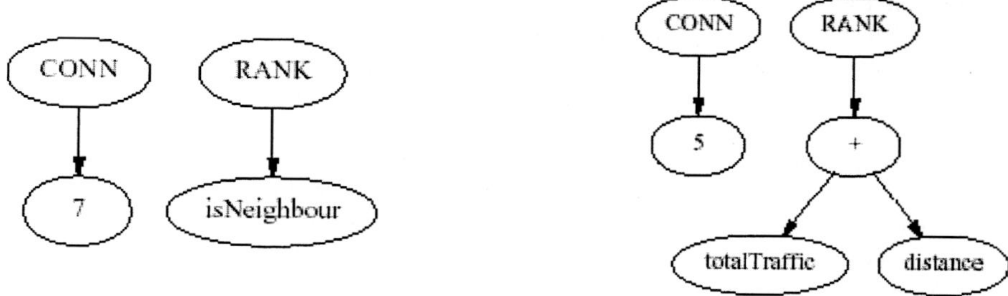


**Fig. 2.** The 7-neighbour Gnutella protocol (left) and the s-peer protocol as expression trees

### 3.3 Genetic Programming

We have so far developed the FBMP which allows us to describe a broad class of arbitrary flooding broadcast network protocols, and a simulated peer-to-peer network in which these protocols can be implemented and tested. Genetic programming [6] provides the final link: the automatic generation of new protocols from the FBMP.

$$fitness = searches_{successful} + 0.5searches_{timed\text{-}out}$$

**Fig. 3.** Fitness Function

The genetic programming search for new protocols proceeds as follows. The CONN and RANK expressions and their set of terminals and operators provide the vocabulary, and the expressions are manipulated with the given crossover and mutation operators. Each new protocol (represented by a pair of CONN and RANK expressions) generated by the genetic programming engine is evaluated in the simulated peer-to-peer network by applying it to the same set of peers, searches and resources as each of the other protocols, and then establishing its fitness relative to all the other protocols by ranking it according to the resulting number of successful searches.

The fitness function used to achieve this ranking is fundamental to all the genetic programming results obtained, and its choice is not taken lightly. To the best of our knowledge there are no other studies using genetic programming to derive new peer-to-peer network protocols, so we have no prior work to inform our choice of fitness function.

The actual fitness function used is given in figure 3, where $searches_{successful}$ is the number of successful search responses received within the five second window following the search request, and $searches_{timedOut}$ is the number of successful search responses received outside of this window. A higher score is better. Any number of other fitness functions are possible, and a different fitness function applied to the same network scenarios would likely give rise to an entirely different set of network protocols. The fitness function is held constant so that the only variable affecting the evolved network protocols is the specific network scenario that the protocols arise from.

The experimental results presented the next section were obtained using a modified form of the freely-available lil-gp genetic programming package from the University of Michigan [8].

## 4 Results

To establish the viability of using genetic programming to search for new flooding broadcast network protocols, the simulated peer-to-peer network described in the previous section was used to generate optimal protocols from the FBMP for a variety of specific network scenarios. The scenarios are intended to be a representative sampling of realistic peer interactions and traffic flows in a typical peer-to-peer network. The scenarios include such variations as differing peer bandwidths to simulate the discrepancies between dialup and broadband users, and differing 'resource pools' to simulate peers seeking and providing disjoint sets of resources. The scenarios cover a broad range of differing peer bandwidths and types of traffic, but are not exhaustive; any number of additional scenarios could be created and would likely give rise to new optimal network.

A breakdown of these scenarios is given in table 2. Each peer in the network has a fixed maximum bandwidth. These bandwidths correspond roughly to the real world as follows: a 56k modem connection is roughly 40 kbps, a home broadband connection is roughly 800 kbps, and a T1 line is roughly 12000 kbps. Each peer also has a fixed set of resources that it possesses, and a fixed set of searches that it performs. These resources are drawn from a pool of resources shared by other peers. The 'Resource Pools' property refers to the number of distinct pools that the peers' resources are drawn from. In Scenario A, for example, all peers draw from the same set of resources. In Scenario B, each draws exclusively from one of the two pools of resources.

**Table 2.** Breakdown of Scenarios

| | A | B | C | D | E | F |
|---|---|---|---|---|---|---|
| Sub-scenarios | 7 | 7 | 5 | 1 | 1 | 1 |
| Peers | 30 | 30 | 30 | 30 | 30 | 30 |
| Peer Bandwidths(kbps) | 40-500 | 40-500 | 40/800 | 200/600 | 40/800/12000 | 200 |
| Resource Pools | 1 | 2 | 1-5 | 1 | 1 | 2 |
| Resources per Peer | 50 | 50 | 50 | 50 | 50 | 50 |
| Searches per Peer | 200 | 200 | 200 | 200 | 200 | 200 |

Figure 4 shows the results from one of the experiments from scenario A. Each scenario was re-run a number of times with the two different protocols in place. In the case of the Gnutella protocol, the results presented are the average of 20 runs. For the FBMP results, the 'fittest' evolved protocol is presented. In all cases the FBMP runs were re-done either two or three times, and in all cases but one they converged to the same result.

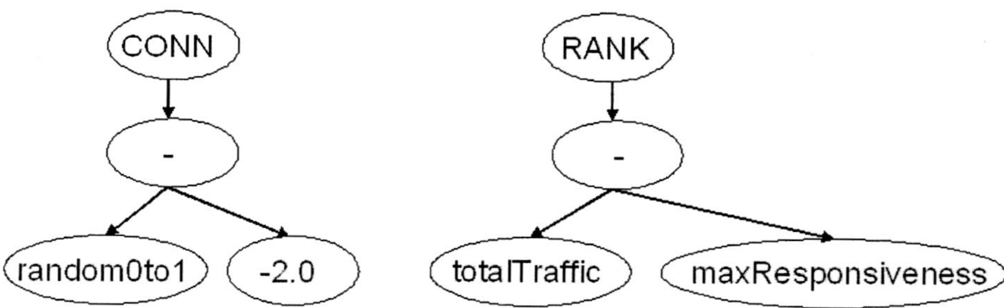


**Fig. 4.** Scenario A-1 evolved protocol expressions. The totalTraffic term favors existing neighbours, but new connections are ranked with -maxResponsiveness which favors other close connections

The full set of experiments can be found in [7]. From our experiments, we have made the following observations:

- The Gnutella protocol exhibits two distinct behaviors characterized by search times that differ by an order of magnitude: coherent and efficient operation when the peers' bandwidth is sufficient, and chaotic, inefficient operation when the peers are bandwidth-constrained.
- The Gnutella protocol arose numerous times as an optimal FBMP protocol. This leads us to conclude that when the Gnutella protocol is working efficiently, it is often optimal.
- The Gnutella protocol is not able to take advantage of disparities between peer bandwidths.
- The Gnutella protocol on its own results in networks with high small worldfactors.
- The 'optimal' node degree utilized by the evolved FBMP protocols varies proportionally with the bandwidth of the peers.
- In homogeneous networks where all peers were drawing from the same resource pools, two distinct FBMP protocols arose: in the low-bandwidth cases that resulted in chaotic Gnutella behavior, we see the adoption of a low node degree, 'short-circuiting' protocol similar to the s-peer protocol that explicitly creates non-small-world networks. In the high- bandwidth cases, we see the emergence of the Gnutella protocol itself as optimal.
- Resource-pool separation strategies and other dynamic protocols are penalized by the Gnutella protocol's inability to handle unroutable messages, although in many cases they are still optimal despite this penalty.
- Supernode strategies are also very effective, and are characterized by protocols that vary the connection limit of the peer proportionally with the bandwidth available to the peer and inverse-proportionally to the average or maximum size of the queues on the peer's connections. This allows peers to take advantage of high bandwidths, and employs a 'throttling' feedback mechanism to shed connections if a peer becomes overloaded.
- The Gnutella protocol is optimal in scenarios in which the peers are not bandwidth constrained and the resources being sought are fairly homogeneous.

We conclude by noting that in all cases the search times achieved by the evolved FBMP protocols are very reasonable (they are mostly within the five-second timeout window), even in the cases where the Gnutella protocol is highly inefficient.

## 5 Conclusion

From our work, we have seen the effectiveness of the Gnutella protocol in two ways: by direct simulation of the protocol we have seen that six connections per node is optimal, rather than the widely-used heuristic of seven connections per node; and, we have received further validation through genetic programming where we see that the Gnutella protocol often arose independently as an optimal network protocol.

We have seen that genetic programming is an effective search technique for exploring the given space of Gnutella-like protocols, and that protocols exist in this space that result in more numerous resource locations than the Gnutella protocol itself.

We concluded by suggesting that genetic programming could be used to tailor a network protocol to a given scenario and provide adaptability and context-awareness to individual nodes in a network.

## References


1. David G. Andersen, Hari Balakrishnan, M. Frans Kaashoek, and Robert Morris. The case for resilient overlay networks. In Proc. of the 8th Annual Workshop on Hot Topics in Operating Systems (HotOS-VIII), May 2001.
2. Jerry Banks, Barry Nelson, and John Carson. Discrete-Event System Simulation. Prentice Hall, 1995.
3. F. Dabek, E. Brunskill, M. F. Kaashoek, D. Karger, R. Morris, I. Stoica, and H. Balakrishnan. Building peer-to-peer systems with chord, a distributed lookup service. In Proceedings of the 8th Workshop on Hot Topics in Operating Systems (HotOS), Schloss Elmau, Germany, May 2001. IEEE Computer Society.
4. Clip2. The Gnutella protocol specification v0.4. 2002, http://www.clip2.com/GnutellaProtocol04.pdf.
5. Mihajlo A. Jovanovic, Fred S. Annexstein, and Kenneth A. Berman. Scalability issues in large peer-to-peer networks: A case study of Gnutella. University of Cincinnati Technical Report 2001, 2001, http://www.ececs.uc.edu/mjovanov/Research/paper.html.
6. John R. Koza. Genetic Programming: On the programming of computers by means of natural selection. MIT Press, 1992.
7. Michael Iles, ADAPTIVE RESOURCE LOCATION IN APEER-TO-PEER NETWORK. Master's Thesis, Carleton University, Ottawa, Canada, 2002.
8. Bill Punch and Douglas Zongker. The lil-gp genetic programming system. Available as http://garage.cps.msu.edu/software/lil-gp/lilgpindex.html, 1998.
9. M. Ripeanu, I. Foster, and A. Iamnitchi. Mapping the gnutella network: Properties of large-scale peer-to-peer systems and implications for system design. IEEE Internet Computing Journal, 6(1), January/February 2002.
10. Sun. http://www.jxta.org, 2002.
11. Texar. http://www.texar.com, 2002.

# Computing Lower Bound for MAX-CSP Problems

Hachemi Bannaceur and Aomar Osmani

Laboratoire LIPN-CNRS UMR7030,
Avenue Jean-Baptiste Clément, F-93430 Villetaneuse,
{ao,bennaceu}@lipn.univ-paris13.fr

**Abstract.** The inefficiency of the branch and bound method for solving Constraint Optimization Problems is due in most cases to the poor quality of the lower bound used by this method. Many works have been proposed to improve the quality of this bound. In this, paper we investigate a set of lower bounds by considering two criteria: the quality and the computing cost. We study different ways to compute the parameters of the parametric lower bound and we propose heuristics for searching the parameters maximizing the parametric lower bound. Computational experiments performed over randomly generated problems show the advantages of our new branch and bound scheme.

## 1 Introduction

The constraint satisfaction problem (CSP) consists in assigning values to variables which are subject to a set of constraints. A solution of a CSP is a total assignment satisfying every constraint. When the CSP does not admit a solution, we are interested in finding an assignment satisfying as many constraints as possible. The maximal constraint satisfaction problem (Max-CSP) consists in finding a total assignment satisfying the maximum number of constraints. This problem occurs in many concrete applications. Max-CSP is a NP-hard problem and generally is more difficult to solve than the CSP problem. The basic complete method for solving this problem was designed by Freuder and Wallace [14]. The efficiency of their branch and bound method strongly depends on the quality of the bounds computed at each node of the search. Many improvements have been brought to this method, using different kinds of variable and value ordering heuristics and constraint satisfaction tools such as directional arc-consistency, arc-consistency [4], and forward checking technique [13].

Most of the works developed for improving the basic method focused on the computation of a good lower bound of the minimum number of unsatisfied constraints. Wallace [13] has proposed the use of the directional arc-consistency with forward checking to improve the quality of the lower bound used in the basic method. This method was enhanced by [7, 4, 6].

The approach proposed in [1] provides a mathematical formalism of the lower bounds based on the arc consistency count, and have proposed a parametric lower bound of the minimum number of unsatisfied constraints. In this paper,

P.W.H. Chung, C.J. Hinde, M. Ali (Eds.): IEA/AIE 2003, LNAI 2718, pp. 614–624, 2003.

we investigate a set of lower bounds which can derive from this parametric bound by considering two criteria: the quality and the computing cost of these lower bounds. For this, we study different ways to compute the parameters of the parametric lower bound and we propose heuristics for searching the parameters maximizing the value of this bound.

This paper is organized as follows. Section 2 provides some results on Max-CSP. Section 3 describes different lower bounds derived from the parametric lower bound and heuristics to compute the parameters leading to a good quality of this bound. Section 4 is devoted to experimental results.

## 2 Preliminaries

### 2.1 CSP Formalism

Constraint Satisfaction Problems ($CSP_s$) involve the assignment of values to variables which are subject to a set of constraints. Formally, a binary CSP is defined by a quadruplet (X,D,C,R) [8] where: $X$ is a set of n variables $\{X_1, X_2, \ldots, X_n\}$, $D$ is a set of n domains $\{D_1, D_2, ..., D_n\}$ where each $D_i$ is a set of $d_i$ possible values for $X_i$, $C$ is a set of $m$ constraints in which a constraint $C_{ij}$ involves variables $X_i$ and $X_j$ and is defined by a relation $R_{ij}$, and $R$ is a set of m relations, where $R_{ij}$ is a subset of the Cartesian product $D_i \times D_j$.

The predicate $R_{ij}(v_r, v_s)$ holds if the pair $(v_r, v_s)$ belongs to $R_{ij}$. For the problems which are of our interest here, we will require that: $(v_r, v_s) \in R_{ij} \Rightarrow (v_s, v_r) \in R_{ji}$

A solution of the CSP is a total assignment satisfying each of the constraints. In some cases the CSP may be over-constrained, and thus admits no such solution. We are then interested in finding a total assignment satisfying as many constraints as possible. This problem is usually referred as Max-CSP.

### 2.2 Finding Parameters for Lower Bound

We consider in our work, the MAX-CSP formulated as a quadratic 0-1 minimization problem

$$(Q): \begin{cases} min\ q(x) = \sum_{i=1}^{n} \sum_{\substack{j:j>i \\ R_{ij}\in R}} \sum_{r=1}^{d_i} \sum_{s:(v_r,v_s)\notin R_{ij}} x_{ir}x_{js} \\ \left.\begin{array}{l} s.t. \sum_{r=1}^{d_i} x_{ir} = 1 \quad i = 1, \ldots, n \\ x_{ir} \in \{0,1\} \quad i = 1, \ldots, n, \ r = 1, \ldots, d_i \end{array}\right\} (*) \end{cases}$$

Using this formulation, the parametric lower bound is expressed as a minimum number of unsatisfied constraints. This bound is given by the following formula:

$$\sum_{i=1}^{n} \min_{1\le r\le d_i} \sum_{\substack{j:j\neq i \\ R_{ij}\in R}} w_{ij} P_{irj} \ where\ P_{irj} = \begin{cases} 1\ if v_r\ of\ X_i\ has\ no\ support\ in\ D_j, \\ 0\ otherwise. \end{cases}$$

This section presents a study for determining good parameters for the parametric lower bound and gives a generalization of this bound when the weights are assigned to pairs of values of each constraint. Indeed, for determining the best parameters of the lower bound we must solve the following max-min linear program (PL):

$$\begin{cases} \max \left( \sum_{i=1}^{n} \min_{1 \le r \le d_i} (\sum_{\substack{j:j \ne i \\ R_{ij} \in R}} w_{ij} P_{irj}) \right) \\ s.t.\ 0 \le w_{ij} \le 1\ and\ w_{ij} + w_{ji} = 1 \quad for\ i,j = 1,\dots,n\ j \ne i \end{cases}$$

**Example.** Let us consider the following over-constrained CSP, and compute the parametric lower bound with different weights. The CSP $P$ contains 4 variables $X_1, X_2, X_3, X_4$. The domains of these variables are $D_1 = D_2 = D_3 = D_4 = \{1,2\}$, the constraints are defined by the following relations: $R_{12} = \{(2,1),(2,2)\}, R_{13} = \{(1,1)\}, R_{23} = \{(1,1)\}, R_{24} = \{(2,2)\}, R_{34} = \{(1,1),(2,1),(2,2)\}, R_{14} = \emptyset$. The minimum number of unsatisfied constraints is $v(P) = 3$.

The corresponding max-min linear program (PL) can be written as follows:

$$\max_{0 \le w_{ij} \le 1:\ 1 \le i < j \le 4} \begin{pmatrix} \min(w_{12} + w_{14}, w_{13} + w_{14}), \min(1 - w_{12} + w_{24}, w_{23}) + \\ \min(0, 1 - w_{13} + 1 - w_{23}) + \min(1 - w_{14} + 1 - w_{24}, 1 - w_{14}) \end{pmatrix}$$

We first compute the lower bound using directional arc consistency (DAC), assume for instance that the variable ordering is $X_1, X_2, X_3, X_4$. Then, $w_{12} = w_{13} = w_{14} = w_{23} = w_{24} = w_{34} = 1$, and the value of PL for these values is:

$$\min(2,2) + min(1,1) + min(0,0) + min(0,0) = 3$$

Thus the DAC lower bound is 3. The case where $w_{ij} = w_{ji} = 1/2$ $(1 \le i < j \le 4)$ which corresponds to the arc consistency (AC) lower bound is 2. When $w_{ij} = 2/3$ and $w_{ji} = 1/3$, the lower bound will be 3. In the first and last cases the optimum lower bound is reached.

These tree cases show that the quality of the lower bound depends on the values of $w_{ij}$. The best lower bound corresponds obviously to the optimal solution of PL. But, unfortunately, the solving of PL is NP-hard. In the next section, we propose two heuristics for determining a solution of PL.

## 3 Methods for Solving PL

We propose two simple heuristics for solving (PL), the first combines arc consistency and directional arc consistency (DAC-IC), the second is based on linear programming techniques (LP).

### 3.1 DAC-AC Heuristic

The heuristic combines arc consistency and directional arc consistency: the domain of weights will be $\{1, 0, 1/2\}$.

If we consider two variables $X_i$ and $X_j$, $w_{ij} = 1$ when there exists at least one arc consistent value in $D_j$ and all the values of $D_i$ are arc inconsistent. Intuitively, the arc inconsistency counts are affected to the values of $D_i$ ($w_{ij} = 1$) in order to increase the minimum number of inconsistencies over the values of $D_i$, since the minimum number of arc inconsistencies over the values of $D_j$ is 0 ($w_{ji} = 0$). For all other cases, the value of $w_{ij}$ is 1/2.

*DAC-AC Algorithm*

```
Input: X,R
Output: w
Begin
  For each relation Rij do
    For each value vr of Xi do
      If vr of Xi has no support in Dj then
        count(Xi,vr)= count(Xi,vr)+1;
    endFor
    For each value vs of Xj do
      If vs of Xj has no support in Di then
         count(Xj,vs)= count(Xj,vs)+1;
    endFor
  endFor
  For each Xi do min(i) = min(count (Xi,vr))
    For each Rij do
      If min(i) > 0 and min(j)=0 then
        wij=1; wji=0;
      else wij=1/2; wji=1/2;
    endFor
  endFor
end
```

**Example:** Let us consider the previous example: $count(X1, 1) = 2, count(X1, 2) = 2, count(X2, 1) = 1, count(X2, 2) = 1, count(X3, 1) = 0, count(X3, 2) = 2, count(X4, 2) = 1, count(X4, 1) = 2$ The application of DAC-AC algorithm gives the following result:

$$\begin{cases} w_{13} = w_{23} = w_{43} = 1, \quad w_{12} = w_{21} = 1/2, \\ w_{14} = w_{41} = 1/2, \quad w_{24} = w_{42} = 1/2. \end{cases}$$

In this example, the PL value is 2,5. Since the number of unsatisfied constraints is integer then we deduce that the lower bound is 3. Using the DAC-AC heuristic, the optimum is reached for this example.

The DAC-AC heuristic complexity is $O(md^2)$. First, we compute the arc inconsistency count for each value, this operation needs $O(md^2)$ consistency checks. Then, using the minimum arc inconsistency count of each variable we determine the weights $w_{ij}$ and $w_{ji}$ for each constraint.

### 3.2 Linear Programming Heuristic

This heuristic builds a set of continuous linear programs (LP) with variables in [0,1]. We denote $v(P)$ the optimal value of P, where P is an optimization problem.

The linear program (RLP(i)) built at a steep $i$ of the LP heuristic is a continuous relaxation of the Max-Min linear program (PL): $(\forall i)\ v(RLP(i)) \leq v(PL)$ and

$$(\forall i)(\forall j)(i < j),\ v(RLP(i)) \leq v(RLP(j)).$$

The linear program RLP of the last steep is a lower bound of the minimum number of unsatisfied constraints. We show below on the previous example how the relaxation RLP(i) is built. In this example, we have to solve the following problem:

$$\max_{0 \leq w_{ij} \leq 1:\ 1 \leq i < j \leq 4} \begin{pmatrix} \min\left(w_{12} + w_{14}, w_{13} + w_{14}\right), \min\left(1 - w_{12} + w_{24}, w_{23}\right) + \\ \min\left(0, 1 - w_{13} + 1 - w_{23}\right) + \min\left(1 - w_{14} + 1 - w_{24}, 1 - w_{14}\right) \end{pmatrix}$$

For $X_3$ the minimum is 0. Assume that: for $X_1$ the minimum is $w_{12} + w_{14}$, for $X_2$ the minimum is $w_{23}$ and for $X_4$ the minimum is $1 - w_{14} + 1 - w_{24}$, then we must have the linear constraints:

$$\begin{cases} w_{12} + w_{14} \leq w_{13} + w_{14} \\ w_{23} \leq 1 - w_{12} + w_{24} \\ 1 - w_{14} + 1 - w_{24} \leq 1 - w_{14} \end{cases}$$

Under these assumptions, the value of linear program PL is equal to the value of the relaxation RLP defined as follows:

$$Max\ (w_{12} + w_{14} + w_{23} + 1 - w_{14} + 1 - w_{24})$$

$$s.t. \begin{cases} w_{12} + w_{14} \leq w_{13} + w_{14} \\ w_{23} \leq 1 - w_{12} + w_{24} \\ 1 - w_{14} + 1 - w_{24} \leq 1 - w_{14} \\ O \leq w_{ij} \leq 1, \end{cases}$$

which can be rewritten as: $2 + Max\ (w_{12} + w_{23} - w_{24})$

$$s.t. \begin{cases} w_{12} - w_{13} \leq 0 \\ w_{23} + w_{12} - w_{24} \leq 1 \\ -w_{24} \leq -1 \\ O \leq w_{ij} \leq 1 \end{cases}$$

Note that $v(RLP) \leq v(LP)$, and we can built an exponential number (in $O(d^n)$) of RLP relaxations. The LP heuristic makes a local search by exploring a subset of these RLP relaxations, and each visited RLP relaxation may be solved using a linear programming technique as the simplex, interior points methods [10]. Note that in the previous example, the value of RLP is 3, which is the minimum number of unsatisfied constraints.

Many strategies can be applied for building at each step i, RLP(i): one strategy consists on defining the first relaxation problem RLP(1) by setting in the objective function the terms having the greatest constant and the maximum number of variables with positive coefficients. RLP(i) can be built from RLP(i-1) by replacing the optimal solution of RLP(i-1) in each term of the PL problem.

The terms having the greatest values will be used to build the objective function of RLP(i).
The LP heuristic can be stopped, for instance, when two successive relaxations have the same optimal value.

**Example.** In the previous example, this strategy leads to choose:

For $X_3$ the minimum is 0. For $X_1$ the minimum can be $w_{12}+w_{14}$ or $w_{13}+w_{14}$, for $X_2$ the minimum is $1-w_{12}+w_{24}$ and for $X_4$ the minimum is $1-w_{14}+1-w_{24}$.

Then RLP(1) will be:

$$Max\ (w_{13}+w_{14}+1-w_{12}+w_{24}+2-w_{14}-w_{24})$$

$$s.t. \begin{cases} w_{13}+w_{14} \leq w_{12}+w_{14} \\ 1-w_{12}+w_{24} \leq w_{23} \\ 1-w_{14}+1-w_{24} \leq 1-w_{14} \\ O \leq w_{ij} \leq 1, \end{cases}$$

which can be rewritten as: $3+Max\ (w_{13}-w_{12})$

$$s.t. \begin{cases} w_{13}-w_{12} \leq 0 \\ -w_{23}-w_{12}+w_{24} \leq -1 \\ -w_{24} \leq -1 \\ O \leq w_{ij} \leq 1 \end{cases}$$

The value of RLP(1) is 3, the optimum is reached for:$w_{12}=w_{13}=w_{24}=w_{23}=1$

RLP(2) can be built by reporting the optimal solution of RLP(1) in each term of PL. Then, for $X_1$ we obtain $1+w_{14}$ and $1+w_{14}$. So, either $w_{12}+w_{14}$ or $w_{13}+w_{14}$ will be used to built the objective function of RLP(2). For $X_2$ we obtain 1 and 1, and for $X_4$ we obtain also the same result. Since the optimal solution is reached with RLP(1), RLP(2) does not improve the value of RLP(1).

## 4 Enhancement of the Parametric Lower Bound

In the parametric lower bound, the weights are assigned to constraints; we will show in this section that different weights can be assigned to the pairs of values of the same constraint. Indeed, $q(x)$ can be written as follows:

$$q(x)=\sum_{i=1}^{n}\sum_{\substack{j:j>i\\R_{ij}\in R}}\sum_{r=1}^{d_i}\sum_{s:(v_r,v_s)\notin R_{ij}} w_{irjs}x_{ir}+w_{jsir}x_{js}$$

where $0 \leq w_{irjs}, w_{jsir} \leq 1$ *and* $w_{irjs}+w_{jsir}=1$

$$q(x)=\sum_{i=1}^{n}\sum_{\substack{j:j\neq i\\R_{ij}\in R}}\sum_{r=1}^{d_i}\sum_{s:(v_r,v_s)\notin R_{ij}} w_{irjs}x_{ir}x_{js}$$

where $0 \leq w_{irjs} \leq 1$ *and* $w_{irjs} + w_{jsir} = 1$ By factorizing by the left side variables, we obtain:

$$q(x) = \sum_{i=1}^{n} \sum_{r=1}^{d_i} x_{ir} \sum_{\substack{j:j \neq i \\ R_{ij} \in R}} \sum_{s:(v_r,v_s) \notin R_{ij}} w_{irjs} x_{js}$$

Let $v(Q)$ denotes the optimal value of $(Q)$; $v(Q) = q(x^*)$ where $x^*$ is an optimal solution of $(Q)$.

$$v(Q) \geq \min \left\{ \sum_{i=1}^{n} \sum_{r=1}^{d_i} x_{ir} \underbrace{(min \sum_{\substack{j:j \neq i \\ R_{ij} \in R}} w_{irjs} \sum_{s:(v_r,v_s) \notin R_{ij}} x_{js}) \quad s.t. \ (*)}_{P_{ir}} \right\}$$

$$v(Q) \geq \left\{ \sum_{i=1}^{n} \underbrace{min \sum_{r=1}^{d_i} x_{ir} P_{ir} \quad s.t. \ (*)}_{T_i} \right\} \ and \ \sum_{i=1}^{n} T_i \ is \ the \ GLB \ lower \ bound.$$

By attributing a weight to each pair of values of each relation, the quality of the parametric lower bound can be improved. But, due to its computing cost, we believe that its use in a branch and bound algorithm may be not efficient.

## 5 Experimental Results

In this section, we evaluate the practice use of the DAC-AC algorithm in the set of random binary CSPs benchmarks proposed by Larrosa et al. [6]. Each problem class is characterized by four parameters: $< N; K; C; T >$, where: $N$ is the number of variables, $D$ is the domain cardinality (all variables have the same domain), $C$ is the number of constraints (graph connectivity), $T$ is the number of no-goods at each constraint, defined as the number of tuples not allowed. In the implemented algorithm, $T$ varies from $T_{min}$ (minimum no-goods for each constraint) to $T_{max}$ (maximum no-goods for each constraint).

For each $T$, an a priori, number of instances are randomly generated following the five parameter. Each problem is generated by randomly picking C constraints out of $C_n^2$ total possible constraints, and picking T no-goods out of $D^2$ maximum possible for each constraint.

Results given by our algorithm are compared with an efficient algorithm for solving MaxCSP: MRDAC as proposed and implemented by Larrosa and all. [6].

The first class of our experiments, presented in this paper, was performed with the same instances tested by Larrosa and all. These instances are:
$< 5, 15, 10 \ to \ 25, 100 >$, $< 5, 20, 10 \ to \ 25, 100 >$, $< 5, 25, 10 \ to \ 25, 100 >$, $< 10, 10, 50 \ to \ 100, 45 >$, $< 10, 15, 50 \ to \ 100, 50 >$, $< 10, 25, 50 \ to \ 100, 37 >$.

For comparison, we have tested MRDAC algorithm as implemented by Larrosa with C language, using a highly optimized code. DAC-AC algorithm is implemented in C++ language. Both codes are compiled and executed using LINUX system and 1GH CPU machine. The following figures show the performance measure regarding time execution, consistency checks, and number of visited nodes for each algorithm.

Figure 1 shows the time execution of both algorithms. The first remark is that MRDAC algorithm and DAC-AC algorithm have the same performance with simple problems and some times MRDAC is better with simple problems. But the DAC-AC algorithm became better for hard problems.

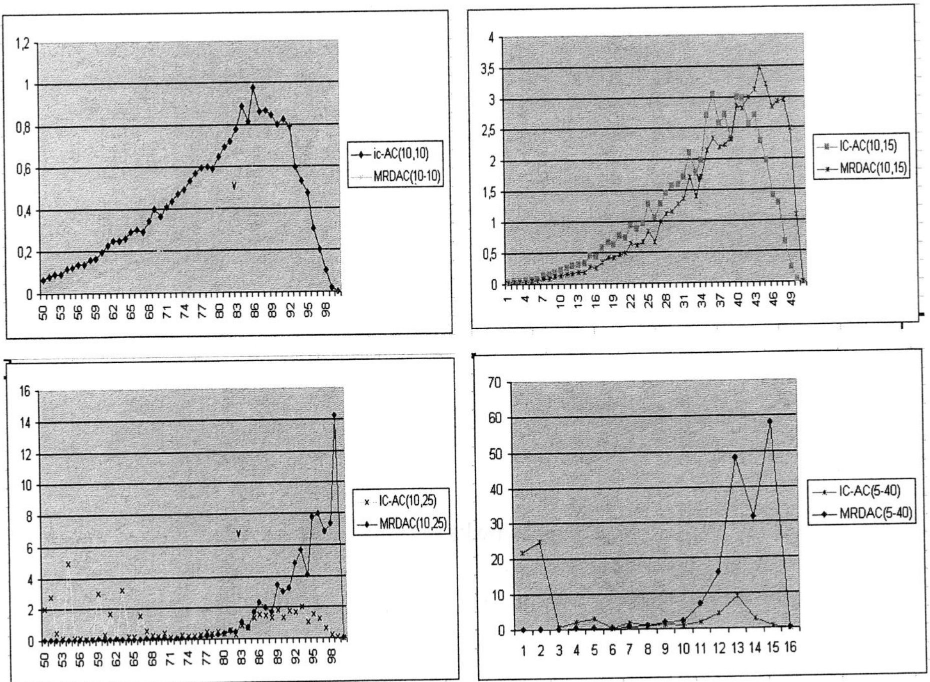


**Fig. 1.** Time execution for DAC-AC and MRDAC algorithms (X-axis: problems size, Y-axis =time execution).

In figure 2 and in figure 3 we observe that DAC-AC algorithm visits less nodes and does less checks than MRDAC algorithm. The gain is more important for hard problems. It's means that, DAC-AC heuristic contributes to compute a good lower bound and the quality of lower bound increase with the hardness the problem. This experiment result encourage us to propose the second formal LP heuristic presented in section 3.2. But we observe some times chaotic behavior of the DAC-AC for simple problems (see figure 3.e). This observation is done only for few cases, it's mean that for some soft constrained problems, the number

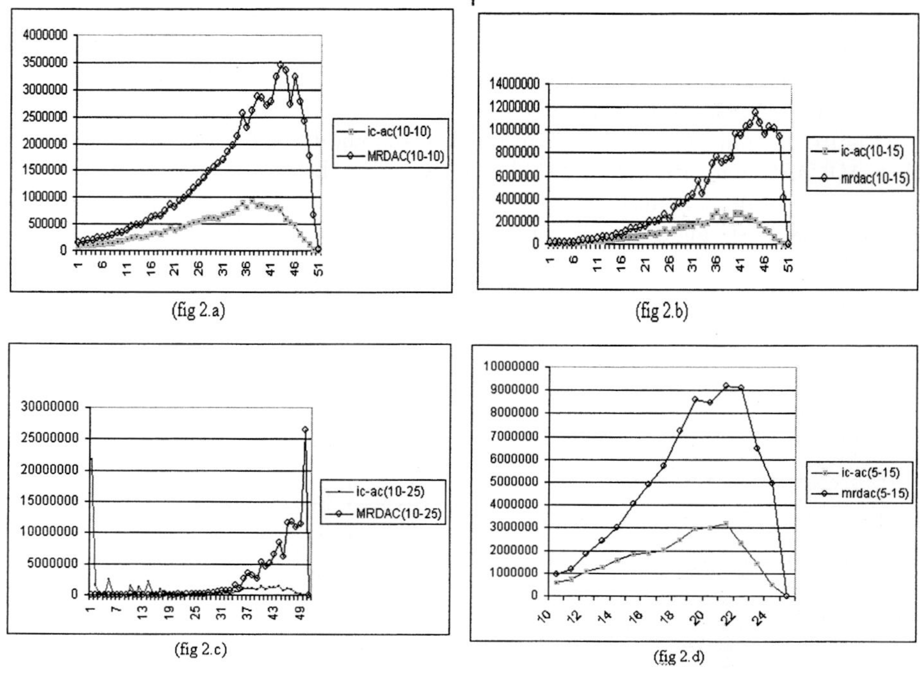


**Fig. 2.** Checks number for DAC-AC algorithm and for MRDAC algorithm(X-axis: problems size, Y-axis =checks number).

of visited nodes depends on the initial configuration because in the cases the contribution of $w_{ij}$ are not significant.

Several intermediate heuristics are tested. The main idea is to find a better distribution of penalties for variables and for values according to partial inconsistency. From this observation, we have proposed the second heuristic based on the transformation of the problem of finding the maximal lower bound the MaxCSP problem to the PL problem as presented in the section 3.2.

## 6 Conclusion

We have studied the parametric lower bound for MaxCSP and shown that the weight can affect the quality of this bound. We have proposed two heuristics to determine these weights: one combines directional arc consistency and arc consistency, the other is based on linear programming techniques.

We have used the first heuristic in a branch and bound algorithm and comparing it with an efficient method for solving MaxCSP. The experiments results show the advantages of our approach.

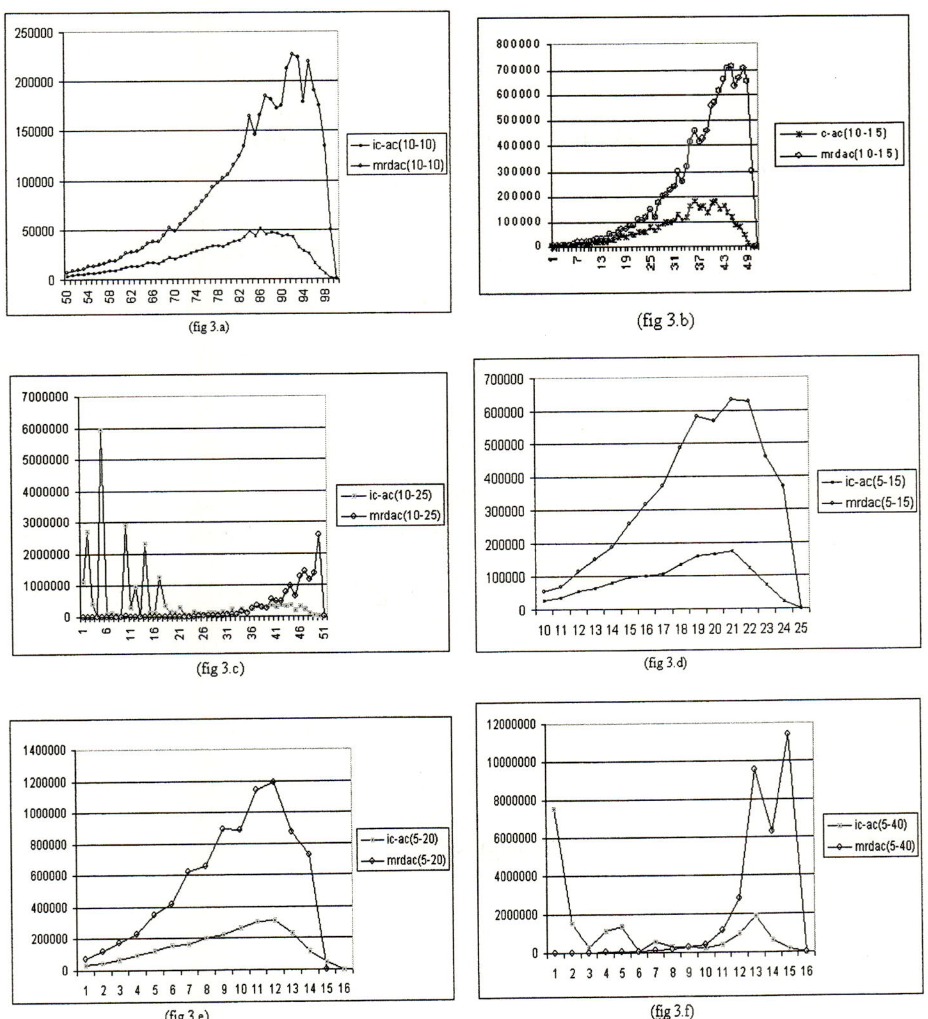


**Fig. 3.** visited nodes number for DAC-AC algorithm and for MRDAC algorithm (X-axis: problems size,Y-axis =number ofvisited nodes).

## References

1. M.S. Affane and H. Bennaceur,'A weighted arc consistency technique for max-CSP', in Proc. of the 13th ECAI, pp. 209–213, 1998.
2. [1] E. C. Freuder and R. J. Wallace, 'Partial Constraint Satisfaction', Artificial Intelligence, 58, 21–70, (1992).
3. P. Hubbe and E.C. Freuder, 'An Efficient Cross-Product Representation of the Constraint Satisfaction Problem Search Space', in Proc. of the 10th National Conferenceon Artificial Intelligence (AAAI92), pp. 421–427, (1992).

4. J. Larrosa and P. Meseguer,'Exploiting the Use of DAC in MAXCSP', in Proc. of the 2nd International Conference on Principle and Practice of Constraint Programming (CP96, LNCS 1118), pp. 308–322, Cambridge, MA, USA, (1996). bibitemLarrosa:01 R. Dechter and Kalev Kask and J. Larrosa,'A General Scheme for Multiple Lower Bound Computation in Constraint Optimization', in Proc. of the 2nd International Conference on Principle and Practice of Constraint Programming (CP01, LNCS 2239), pp. 346–360, 2001.
5. J. Larrosa and P. Meseguer, 'Phase Transition in MAXCSP', in Proc. of the 12th European Conference on Artificial Intelligence (ECAI96), pp. 190–194, Budapest, Hungary, (1996).
6. J. Larrosa and P. Meseguer and T. Schiex, 'Maintaining reversible DAC for MAXCSP', in Artificial Intelligence, 107(1):149–163 (1999).
7. P. Meseguer and J. Larrosa, 'Constraint Satisfaction as Global Optimization', in Proc. of the 14th International Joint Conference on Artificial Intelligence (IJCAI95), pp. 579–584, Montr'eal, CANADA, (1995).
8. U. Montanari, 'Networks of Constraints: Fundamental Properties and Applications to Picture Processing', Inform. Sci., 7 n2, 95–132, (1974).
9. P.M. Pardalos, F. Rendl, and H. Wolkowicz, 'The Quadratic Assignment Problem: A Survey and Recent Developments', in DIMACS Series in Discrete Mathematics and Theoretical Computer Science, (1994).
10. Neuhauser, Wolsey, 'Integer and Combinatorial Optimization',Wiley ed.,(1988).
11. M. Wallace, in Proc. of the Third International Conference on the Practical Application of Constraint Technology (PACT97), London, UK, (1997).
12. R.J. Wallace, 'Directed Arc Consistency Preprocessing', in Proc. of the ECAI94 Workshop on constraint Processing (LNCS 923), pp. 121–137, (1994).
13. R.J. Wallace, 'Enhancements of Branch and Bound Methods for the Maximal Constraint Satisfaction Problem', in Proc. of the 13th National Conference on Artificial Intelligence (AAAI96), pp. 188–195, Portland, OR, USA, (1996).
14. Wallace, R.: 1995, 'Directed Arc Consistency Preprocessing'. In: M. Meyer (ed.): Selected papers from the ECAI94 Workshop on Constraint Processing, No. 923 in LNCS. Berlin: Springer, pp. 121–137.

# Efficient Pre-processing for Large Window-Based Modular Exponentiation Using Genetic Algorithms

Nadia Nedjah and Luiza de Macedo Mourelle

Department of Systems Engineering and Computation, Faculty of Engineering,
State University of Rio de Janeiro,
Rio de Janeiro, Brazil
{nadia, ldmm}@eng.uerj.br
http://www.eng.uerj.br/~ldmm

**Abstract.** Modular exponentiation is a cornerstone operation to several public-key cryptosystems. It is performed using successive modular multiplications. This operation is time consuming for large operands, which is always the case in cryptography. For software or hardware fast cryptosystems, one needs thus reducing the total number of modular multiplication required. Existing methods attempt to reduce this number by partitioning the exponent in constant or variable size windows. However, these window methods require some pre-computations, which themselves consist of modular exponentiations. In this paper, we exploit genetic algorithms to evolving an optimal addition sequence that allows one to perform the pre-computations in window methods with a minimal number of modular multiplications. Hence we improve the efficiency of modular exponentiation. We compare the evolved addition sequences with those obtained using Brun's algorithm.

## 1 Introduction

Public-key cryptographic systems (such as the RSA encryption scheme [6], [12]) often involve raising large elements of some groups fields (such as GF($2^n$) or elliptic curves [9]) to large powers. The performance and practicality of such cryptosystems is primarily determined by the implementation efficiency of the modular exponentiation. As the operands (the plain text of a message or the cipher (possibly a partially ciphered) are usually large (i.e. 1024 bits or more), and in order to improve time requirements of the encryption/decryption operations, it is essential to attempt to minimise the number of modular multiplications performed.

A simple procedure to compute $C = T^E \bmod M$ based on the paper-and-pencil method is described in Algorithm 1. This method requires $E-1$ modular multiplications. It computes all powers of $T$: $T \to T^2 \to T^3 \to \ldots \to T^{E-1} \to T^E$.

**Algorithm 1.** *simpleExponentiationMethod*(T, M, E)

```
    C = T;
    for i = 1 to E-1 do
       C = (C × T) mod M;
    return C
end algorithm.
```

P.W.H. Chung, C.J. Hinde, M. Ali (Eds.): IEA/AIE 2003, LNAI 2718, pp. 625–635, 2003.

The computation of exponentiations using Algorithm 1 is very inefficient. The problem of yielding the power of a number using a minimal number of multiplications is *NP*-hard [5], [10]. There are several efficient algorithms that perform exponentiation with a nearly minimal number of modular multiplications, such that the window based methods. However, these methods need some pre-computations that if not performed efficiently can deteriorate the algorithm overall performance. The pre-computations are themselves an ensemble of exponentiations and so it is also *NP*-hard to perform them optimally. In this paper, we concentrate on this problem and engineer a new way to do the necessary pre-computations very efficiently. We do so using evolutionary computation. We compare our results with those obtained using the Brun's algorithm [1].

Evolutionary algorithms are computer-based solving systems, which use evolutionary computational models as key element in their design and implementation. A variety of evolutionary algorithms have been proposed. The most popular ones are *genetic algorithms* [4]. They have a conceptual base of simulating the evolution of individual structures via the Darwinian natural selection process. The process depends on the adherence of the individual structures as defined by its environment to the problem pre-determined constraints. Genetic algorithms are well suited to provide an efficient solution of *NP*-hard problems [3].

This paper will be organised as follows: in Section 2, we present the window methods; in Section 3, we define the concepts of addition chains and sequences and how they can be used to improve the pre-computations in window methods; in Section 4, we give an overview on genetic algorithms concepts; in Section 5, we explain how these concepts can be used to compute a minimal addition chain to perform efficiently pre-computations in the window methods. In Section 6, we present some useful results.

## 2 Window Methods

Generally speaking, the window methods for exponentiation [5] may be thought of as a three major step procedure: *(i)* partitioning in $k$-bits windows the binary representation of the exponent $E$; *(ii)* pre-computing the powers in each window one by one, *(iii)* iterating the squaring of the partial result $k$ times to shift it over, and then multiplying it by the power in the next window when if window is different from 0.

There are several partitioning strategies. The window size may be constant or variable. For the $m$-ary methods, the window size is constant and the windows are next to each other. On the other hand, for the sliding window methods the window size may be of variable length. It is clear that zero-windows, i.e. those that contain only zeros, do not introduce any extra computation. So a good strategy for the sliding window methods is one that attempts to maximise the number of zero-windows. The details of $m$-ary methods are exposed in Section 2.1 while those related to sliding constant-size window methods are given in Section 2.2. In Section 2.3, we introduce the adaptive variable-size window methods.

### 2.1 *M*-ary Methods

The *m*-ary methods [3] scans the digits of $E$ form the less significant to the most significant digit and groups them into partitions of equal length $\log_2 m$, where $m$ is a power of two. Note that 1-ary methods coincides with the square-and-multiply well-known exponentiation methods.

In general, the exponent $E$ is partitioned into $p$ partitions, each one containing $l = \log_2 m$ successive digits. The ordered set of the partition of $E$ will be denoted by $\wp(E)$. If the last partition has less digits than $\log_2 m$, then the exponent is expanded to the left with at most $\log_2 m - 1$ zeros. The *m*-ary algorithm is described in Algorithm 2, wherein $V_i$ denotes the decimal value of partition $P_i$.

**Algorithm 2.** *m-aryMethod*(T, M, E)

```
    Partition E into p l-digits partitions;
    for i = 2 to m   Compute T^i mod M;     (*)
    C = T^(V_(p-1)) mod M;
    for i = p-2 downto 0
       C = C^(2^l) mod M;
       if V_i≠0 then C = C×T^(V_i) mod M;
    return C;
end algorithm.
```

### 2.2 Sliding Window Methods

For the sliding window methods the window size may be of variable length and hence the partitioning may be performed so that the number of zero-windows is as large as possible, thus reducing the number of modular multiplication necessary in the squaring and multiplication phases. Furthermore, as all possible partitions have to start (i.e. in the right side) with digit 1, the pre-processing step needs to be performed for odd values only. The sliding method algorithm is presented in Algorithm 3, wherein $d$ denotes the number of digits in the largest possible partition and $L_i$ the length of partition $P_i$.

### 2.3 Adaptive Window Methods

In adaptive methods [7] the computation depends on the input data, such as the exponent $E$. *M*-ary methods and window methods pre-compute powers of all possible partitions, not taking into account that the partitions of the actual exponent may or may not include all possible partitions. Thus, the number of modular multiplications in the pre-processing step can be reduced if partitions of $E$ do not contain all possible ones.

**Algorithm 3.** *slidingWindowMethod*(T, M, E)

```
Partition E using the given strategy;
for i = 2 to 2^d -1 step 2 Compute T^i mod M;     (*)
C = T^(P_(p-1)) mod M;
for i = p-2 downto 0
      C = C^(2^(L_i)) mod M;
      if V_i≠0 then C = C×T^(V_i) mod M;
return C;
end algorithm.
```

Let $\wp(E)$ be the list of partitions obtained from the binary representation of $E$. Assume that the list of partition is non-redundant and ordered according to the ascending decimal value of the partitions contained in the expansion of $E$. As before let $p$ be the number of the partition of $E$ and recall that $V_i$ and $L_i$ are the decimal value and the number of digits of partition $P_i$. The generic algorithm for describing the computation of $T^E$ mod $M$ using the window methods is given in Algorithm 4.

**Algorithm 4.** *AdaptiveWindowMethod*(T, M, E)

```
Partition E using the given strategy;
for each partition in ℘(E) Compute T^(V_i) mod M;     (*)
C = T^(V_(b-1)) mod M;
for i = p-2 downto 0
   C = C^(2^(L_i)) mod M;
   if V_i ≠ 0 then C = C×T^(V_i) mod M;
return C;
end algorithm.
```

In Algorithm 2 and Algorithm 3, it is clear how to perform the pre-computation indicated in line (*). For instance, let $E$ = 1011001101111000. The pre-processing step of the 4-ary method needs 14 modular multiplications ($T \rightarrow T \times T = T^2 \rightarrow T \times T^2 = T^3 \rightarrow \ldots \rightarrow T \times T^{14} = T^{15}$) and that of the maximum 4-digit sliding window method needs only 8 modular multiplications ($T \rightarrow T \times T = T^2 \rightarrow T \times T^2 = T^3 \rightarrow T^3 \times T^2 = T^5 \rightarrow T^5 \times T^2 = T^7 \rightarrow \ldots \rightarrow T^{13} \times T^2 = T^{15}$). However the adaptive 4-ary method would partition the exponent as $E$ = 1011/0011/0111/1000 and hence needs to pre-compute the powers $T^3$, $T^7$, $T^8$ and $T^{11}$ while the method maximum 4-digit sliding window method would partition the exponent as $E$ = 1/0/11/00/11/0/1111/000 and therefore needs to pre-compute the powers $T^3$ and $T^{15}$. The pre-computation of the powers needed by the adaptive 4-digit sliding window method may be done using 6 modular multiplications $T \rightarrow T \times T = T^2 \rightarrow T \times T^2 = T^3 \rightarrow T^2 \times T^2 = T^4 \rightarrow T^3 \times T^4 = T^7 \rightarrow T^7 \times T = T^8 \rightarrow T^8 \times T^3 = T^{11}$ while the pre-computation of those powers necessary to apply the adaptive sliding window may be accomplished using 5 modular multiplications $T \rightarrow T \times T = T^2 \rightarrow T \times T^2 = T^3 \rightarrow T^2 \times T^3 = T^5 \rightarrow T^5 \times T^5 = T^{10} \rightarrow T^5 \times T^{10} = T^{15}$. Note that Algorithm 4 does not suggest how to compute the powers (*) needed to use the adaptive window methods. Finding the best way to compute them is a $NP$-hard problem [4], [7].

## 3 Addition Chains and Addition Sequences

An *addition chain* of length $l$ for an positive integer $N$ is a list of positive integers $(a_0, a_1, a_2, ..., a_l)$ such that $a_0 = 1$, $a_l = N$ and $a_k = a_i + a_j$, $0 \le i \le j < k \le l$. Finding a minimal addition chain for a given positive integer is an *NP*-hard problem. It is clear that a short addition chain for exponent $E$ gives a fast algorithm to compute $T^E \bmod M$ as we have if $a_k = a_i + a_j$ then $T^{a_k} = T^{a_i} \times T^{a_j}$. The adaptive window methods described earlier use a near optimal addition chain to compute $T^E \bmod M$. However these methods do not prescribe how to perform the pre-processing step (lines 1 and 2 of Algorithm 4). We now show how to perform this step with minimal number of modular multiplications.

### 3.1 Addition Sequences

There is a generalisation of the concept of addition chains, which can be used to formalise the problem of finding a minimal sequence of powers that should be computed in the pre-processing step of the adaptive window method.

An *addition sequence* for the list of positive integers $V_1, V_2, \ldots, V_p$ such that $V_1 < V_2 < \ldots < V_p$ is an addition chain for integer $V_p$, which includes all the remaining integers $V_1, V_2, \ldots, V_p$ of the list. The length of an addition sequence is the numbers of integers that constitute the chain. An addition sequence for a list of positive integers $V_1, V_2, \ldots, V_p$ will be denoted by $\mathcal{S}(V_1, V_2, \ldots, V_p)$.

Hence, to optimise the number of modular multiplications needed in the pre-processing step of the adaptive window methods for computing $T^E \bmod M$, we need to find an addition sequence of minimal length (or simply minimal addition sequence) for the values of the partitions included in the non-redundant ordered list $\wp(E)$. This is an *NP*-hard problem and we use genetic algorithm to solve it. Our method showed to be very effective for large window size. General principles of genetic algorithms are explained in the next section.

### 3.2 Brun's Algorithm

Now we describe briefly, Brun's algorithm [1] to compute relatively short addition sequences. The algorithm is a generalisation of the continued fraction algorithm [1]. Assume that we need to compute the addition sequence $\mathcal{S}(V_1, V_1, \ldots, V_p)$. Let $Q = \left\lfloor {V_p}/{V_{p-1}} \right\rfloor$ and let $\mathcal{B}(Q)$ be the addition chain for $Q$ using the binary method (i.e. Algorithm 2 with $l = 1$). Let $R = V_p - Q \times V_{p-1}$. By induction we can construct an addition sequence $\mathcal{S}(V_1, V_2, \ldots, R, \ldots, V_{p-1})$. Then obtain:

$$\mathcal{S}(V_1, V_2, \ldots, V_p) = \mathcal{S}(V_1, V_2, \ldots, R, \ldots, V_{p-1}) \cup V_{p-1} \times \mathcal{B}(Q) \backslash \{1\} \cup \{V_p\}$$

The Brun's addition sequence for 47, 117, 343 is (1, 2, 4, 6, 8, 15, 17, 30, 47, 94, 109, 117, 234, 343). This addition sequence allows us to perform the pre-computation step with 13 modular multiplications.

# 4 Principles of Genetic Algorithms

Genetic algorithms maintain a *population* of *individuals* that evolve according to *selection* rules and other *genetic operators*, such as *mutation* and *recombination*. Each individual receives a measure of *fitness*. *Selection* focuses on individuals, which shows high fitness. *Mutation* and *crossover* provide general heuristics that simulate the *recombination* process. Those operators attempt to perturb the characteristics of the parent individuals as to generate *distinct* offspring individuals.

Genetic algorithms are implemented through the following generic algorithm described by Algorithm 5, wherein parameters *ps*, *f* and *gn* are the population size, the fitness of the expected individual and the number of generation allowed respectively.

**Algorithm 5.** `GA(ps, f, gn):individual;`
```
 generation  = 0;
 population  = initialPopulation();
 fitness = evaluate(population);
 do
    parents    = select(population);
    population= reproduce(parents);
    fitness    = evaluate(population);
    generation= generation + 1;
 while(fitness[i]<f, ∀ i∈population)& (generation< gn);
 return fittestIndividual(population);
end algorithm.
```

In Algorithm 5, function *intialPopulation* returns a valid random set of individuals that compose the population of the first generation, function *evaluate* returns the fitness of a given population. Function *select* chooses according to some criterion that privileges fitter individuals, the individuals that will be used to generate the population of the next generation and function *reproduction* implements the crossover and mutation process to yield the new population.

# 5 Application to Addition Sequence Minimisation Problem

It is perfectly clear that the shorter the addition sequence is, the faster Algorithm 4. The addition sequence minimisation problem consists of finding a sequence of numbers that constitutes an addition sequence for a given ordered list of $n$ positive integers, say $V_i$ for $0 \le i \le n\text{-}1$. The addition sequence should be of a minimal length. This is an *NP*-complete problem. We propose a novel idea based on genetic algorithm to solve this minimisation problem.

## 5.1 Individual Encoding

Encoding of individuals is one of the implementation decisions one has to make in order to use genetic algorithms. It very depends on the nature of the problem to be solved. There are several representations that have been used with success [8], [11]

In our implementation, an individual represents an addition sequence. We use the *binary encoding* wherein 1 means that the entry number is a member of the addition sequence and 0 otherwise. For instance, let $V_1 = 3$, $V_2 = 7$ and $V_3 = 11$, be the list of positive integers for which we wish to yield an addition sequence. The encoding of Fig. 1 represents the valid addition sequence (1, 2, **3**, 4, **7**, 9, **11**):

| *1* | *2* | ***3*** | *4* | *5* | *6* | ***7*** | *8* | *9* | *10* | ***11*** |
|---|---|---|---|---|---|---|---|---|---|---|
| 1 | 1 | **1** | 1 | 0 | 0 | **1** | 0 | 1 | 0 | **1** |

**Fig. 1.** Addition sequence encoding

### 5.2 The Individual Reproduction

Besides the parameters, which represent the population size, the fitness of the expected result and the maximum number of generation allowed, the genetic algorithm has several other parameters, which can be adjust by the user so that the result is up to his or her expectation. The selection is performed using some *selection probabilities* and the reproduction, as it is subdivided into crossover and mutation processes, depends on the kind of crossover and the mutation rate and degree to be used.

Given the parents populations, the reproduction proceeds using replacement as a reproduction scheme, i.e. offspring replace their parents in the next generation. Obtaining offspring that share some traits with their corresponding parents is performed by the *crossover* function. There are several *types* of crossover schemes [8]. The newly obtained population can then suffer some mutation, i.e. some of the individuals of some of the genes. The crossover type, the number of individuals that should be mutated and how far these individuals should be altered are set up during the initialisation process of the genetic algorithm.

There are many ways how to perform crossover and these may depend on the individual encoding used [8]. We present crossover techniques used with binary, permutation and value representations. *Single-point crossover* consists of choosing randomly one *crossover point*, then, the part of the bit or integer sequence from beginning of offspring till the crossover point is copied from one parent, the rest is copied from the second parent. *Double-points crossover* consists of selecting randomly two *crossover points*, the part of the bit or integer sequence from beginning of offspring to the first crossover point is copied from one parent, the part from the first to the second crossover point is copied from the second parent and the rest is copied from the first parent. *Uniform crossover* copies integers randomly from the first or from the second parent. Finally, *arithmetic crossover* consists of applying some arithmetic operation to yield a new offspring.

The single point and two points crossover use randomly selected crossover points to allow variation in the generated offspring and to avoid premature convergence on a local optimum [2], [8]. In our implementation, we tested single-point and double-point crossover techniques.

Mutation consists of changing some genes of some individuals of the current population. The number of individuals that should be mutated is given by the parameter *mutation rate* while the parameter *mutation degree* states how many genes of a selected individual should be altered. The mutation parameters have to be chosen carefully as if mutation occurs very often then the genetic algorithm would in fact change to *random search* [2]. When mutation takes place, a number of genes are randomised and mutated: when the gene is 1 then it becomes 0 and vice-versa. The parameter *md* indicates the number of gene to be mutated.

### 5.3 The Fitness Evaluation

This step of the genetic algorithm allows us to classify the individuals of a population so that fitter individuals are selected more often to contribute in the constitution of a new population. The fitness evaluation of addition sequence is performed with respect to two aspects: *(i)* how much a given addition sequence adheres to the Definition 1, i.e. how many members of the addition sequence cannot be obtained summing up two previous members of the sequence; *(ii)* how far the addition sequence is reduced, i.e. what is the length of the addition chain. Algorithm 7 describes the evaluation of fitness used in our genetic algorithm.

For a valid addition sequence, the fitness function returns its length, which is smaller than the last integer $V_n$. The evolutionary process attempts to minimise the number of ones in a valid addition sequence and so minimise the corresponding length. Individuals with fitness larger or equal to $V_n$ are invalid addition chains. The constant *large penalty* should be larger than $V_n$. With well-chosen parameters, the genetic algorithm deals only with valid addition sequences.

**Algorithm 7.** `int evaluate(individual s)`

```
int fitness = 0;
   for i = 2 to n-1 do
      if s[i] == 1 then
         fitness = fitness + 1;
         if ∄j,k| 1≤j,k≤i & i==j+k & s[j]==s[k]==1 then
             fitness = fitness + largePenalty;
      else   if i == Vi then fitness = fitness + largePenalty;
   return fitness;
end algorithm.
```

## 6 Implementation Results

In applications of genetic algorithms to a practical problem, it is difficult to predict a priori what combination of settings will produce the best result for the problem in a relatively short time. The settings consist of the population size, the crossover type, the mutation rate and the mutation degree. We investigated the impact of different values of these parameters in order to choose the more adequate ones to use. We found out that the ideal parameters are: a population of at most 50 individuals; the double-points crossover; a mutation rate between 0.4 and 0.7 and a mutation degree of about 1% of the value of the last value in sequence $V_p$.

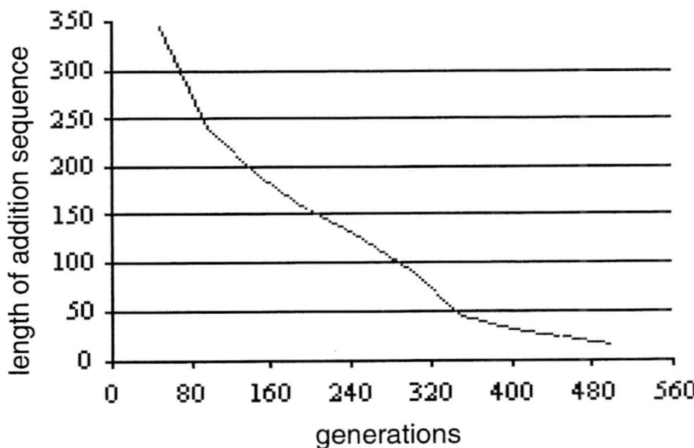


**Fig. 3.** The convergence curve of the genetic algorithm evolving $\mathcal{S}(47, 117, 343)$

The curve of Fig. 3 shows the progress made in the first 500 generations of an execution to obtain $\mathcal{S}(47, 117, 343)$. The settings used are: a 100 individual per population, double-points crossover, a mutation rate of 0.645 and a mutation degree of 3.

The Brun's algorithm [1] yields (1, 2, 4, 6, 8, 15, 17, 30, <u>47</u>, 94, 109, <u>117</u>, 234, <u>343</u>) and the genetic algorithm yield the same addition sequence as well as (1, 2, 4, 8, 11, 18, 36, <u>47</u>, 55, 91, 109, <u>117</u>, 226, <u>343</u>). Both addition sequences have the same length. They allow performing the pre-computation step with 13 multiplications.

Finding the best addition sequence is impractical. However, we can find near-optimal ones. Our genetic algorithm always finds addition sequences far shorter than those used by the *m*-ary method independently of the value of *m* and by the sliding windows independently of the partition strategy used, and as short as the addition sequence yield by the Brun's algorithm. Table 1 shows some examples for $\mathcal{S}(5, 9, 23)$, $\mathcal{S}$ (9, 27, 55) and $\mathcal{S}(5, 7, 95)$. For bigger $V_p$ i.e. of 500 bits or more, however, the genetic algorithm yields shorter addition sequences than those obtained using Brun's algorithm as it graphically shown in Fig. 4.

## 7 Conclusions

In this paper, we presented an application of genetic algorithms to minimisation of addition sequences. We first explained how individuals are encoded. Then we described the necessary algorithmic solution. Then we presented some empirical observations about the performance of the genetic algorithm implementation.

This application of genetic algorithms to the minimisation problem proved to be very useful and effective technique. Shorter addition sequences compared with those obtained by the *m*-ary methods, those obtained for the sliding window methods as well as those obtained using Brun's algorithm (see Table 1 of the previous section) can be obtained with a little computational effort. A comparison of the performance of the *m*-ary, sliding window and the Brun's method vs. the genetic algorithm is shown in Fig. 4. Our method showed to be very effective when the window size is large and so the powers for which the addition sequence is required are big, as it is shown in Fig. 4. A satisfactory addition sequence can be obtained in a 0.1 seconds to 4 minutes using a Pentium III with a 256 MB of RAM and depending on the size of the last $V_p$.

**Table 1.** The addition sequences yield for $\mathcal{S}(5, 9, 23)$, $\mathcal{S}(9, 27, 55)$ and $\mathcal{S}(5, 7, 95)$

| $V_i$ | *Method* | *Addition sequence* | *#Mult* |
|---|---|---|---|
| 5, 9, 23 | 5-ary | (1, 2, 3, 4, 5, 6, 7, 8, 9, …, 22, 23, …, 30, 31) | 30 |
| | 5-window | (1, 2, 3, 5, 7, 9, 11, …, 31) | 16 |
| | Brun's | (1, 2, 4, 5, 9, 18, 23) | 6 |
| | Genetic algorithm | (1, 2, 4, 5, 9, 18, 23) | 6 |
| | | (1, 2, 4, 5, 9, 14, 23) | 6 |
| 9, 27, 55 | 6-ary | (1, 2, 3, …, 8, 9, …, 26, 27, …, 54, 55, …, 63 ) | 62 |
| | 6-window | (1, 2, 3, …, 7, 9, …, 25, 27, …, 53, 55, …, 63) | 31 |
| | Brun's | (1, 2, 3, 6, 9, 18, 27, 54, 55) | 8 |
| | Genetic algorithm | (1, 2, 4, 8, 9, 18, 27, 28, 55) | 8 |
| | | (1, 2, 3, 6, 9, 18, 27, 54, 55) | 8 |
| 5, 7, 95 | 7-ary | (1, 2, 3, 4, 5, 6, 7, …, 95) | 94 |
| | 7-window | (1, 2, 3, 5, 7, …, 95) | 43 |
| | Brun's | (1, 2, 4, 5, 7, 14, 21, 42, 84, 91, 95) | 10 |
| | Genetic algorithm | (1, 2, 3, 5, 7, 10, 20, 30, 35, 65, 95) | 10 |
| | | (1, 2, 4, 5, 7, 14, 21, 42, 84, 91, 95) | 10 |

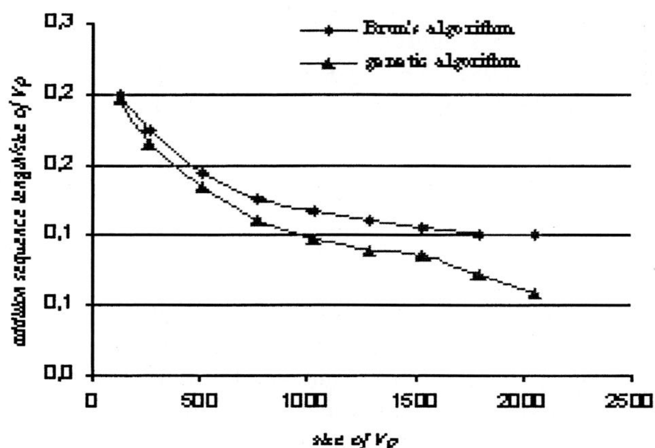


**Fig. 3.** Ratio for the addition sequences yield by the GA vs. Brun's methods.

## References


1. Begeron, R. Berstel, J, Brlek, S. and Duboc, C., *Addition chains using continued fractions*, Journal of Algorithms, no. 10, pp. 403-412, 1989.
2. DeJong, K. and Spears, W.M., *An analysis of the interacting roles of the population size and crossover type in genetic algorithms*, In Parallel problem solving from nature, pp. 38-47, Springer-Verlag, 1990.
3. DeJong, K. and Spears, W.M., *Using genetic algorithms to solve NP-complete problems*, Proceedings of the Third International Conference on Genetic Algorithms, pp. 124-132, Morgan Kaufmann, 1989.
4. Haupt, R.L. and Haupt, S.E., *Practical genetic algorithms*, John Wiley and Sons, New York, 1998.
5. Knuth, D.E., *The Art of Programming: Seminumerical Algorithms*, vol. 2. Reading, MA: Addison_Wesley, Second edition, 1981.
6. Koç, Ç.K., *High-speed RSA Implementation*, Technical report, RSA Laboratories, Redwood City, califirnia, USA, November 1994.
7. Kunihiro, N. and Yamamoto, H., *New methods for generating short addition chain*, IEICE Transactions, vol. E83-A, no. 1, pp. 60-67, January 2000.
8. Michalewics, Z., *Genetic algorithms + data structures = evolution program*, Springer-Verlag, USA, third edition, 1996.
9. Menezes, A.J., *Elliptic curve public key cryptosystems*, Kluwer Academic, 1993.
10. Nedjah, N. and Mourelle, L.M., *Minimal addition chains using genetic algorithms*, Proceedings of the Fifteenth International Conference on Industrial & Engineering Applications of Artificial Intelligence & Expert Systems, Cairns, Australia, (to appear in Lecture Notes in Computer Science, Springer-Verlag), 2002.
11. Neves, J., Rocha, M., Rodrigues, Biscaia, M. and Alves, J., *Adaptive strategies and the design evolutionary applications*, Proceedings of the Genetic and the Design of Evolutionary Computation Conference, Orlando, Florida, USA, 1999.
12. Rivest, R.L., Shamir, A. and Adleman, L., *A method for obtaining digital signature and public-key cryptosystems*, Communication of ACM, vol. 21, no.2, pp. 120-126, 1978.

# Improving Genetic Algorithms' Efficiency Using Intelligent Fitness Functions

Jason Cooper and Chris Hinde

Department of Computer Science, Loughborough University, Loughborough LE11 3TU, UK,
j.l.cooper@lboro.ac.uk, c.j.hinde@lboro.ac.uk

**Abstract.** Genetic Algorithms are an effective way to solve optimisation problems. If the fitness test takes a long time to perform then the Genetic Algorithm may take a long time to execute. Using conventional fitness functions Approximately a third of the time may be spent testing individuals that have already been tested. Intelligent Fitness Functions can be applied to improve the efficiency of the Genetic Algorithm by reducing repeated tests. Three types of Intelligent Fitness Functions are introduced and compared against a standard fitness function The Intelligent Fitness Functions are shown to be more efficient.

**Keywords:** Genetic Algorithms

## 1 Introduction

Genetic Algorithms (GA) [5] are based on Darwin's theory of evolution [2]. They were invented in the 1950s, some of the early papers being by Fraser [3,4] and Bremermann [1]. Later on work by Holland[6–9] popularised genetic algorithms and Holland's work is often cited as the origins of Genetic Algorithms. A GA consists of a population of individuals, each individual represents a possible set of parameters for the algorithm. Each individual is tested and assigned a level of fitness depending on how well they solve the problem. The fitness levels are then used to decide which individuals should be used to produce the next generation. The better the fitness of an individual the more likely they are to produce the next population.

The next generation is produced using two genetic operators after selecting the parents. Parents are selected based on their fitness level. The higher their fitness the more likely they are to be chosen as parents. The first operator is crossover where two individuals swap part of their genes. The second is mutation where an part of an individuals genes are changed. The combination of these operators with parent selection and a fitness function enables the GA to evolve better solutions.

P.W.H. Chung, C.J. Hinde, M. Ali (Eds.): IEA/AIE 2003, LNAI 2718, pp. 636–643, 2003.

## 2 Need for Efficiency

In a GA the majority of the time maybe spent fitness testing the individuals. If a fitness test for an individual takes 1 minute to run then a fitness test of 6000 individuals will take approximately 4 days and 4 hours.

One method which may increase the number of generations that are produced is to reduce the population size. Slow fitness functions associated with small population sizes can lead to problems with premature convergence and lack in diversity of the population.

A test of 6000 individuals does not mean that 6000 locations in the search space have been examined. Individuals with the same genomes keep appearing. The graph shown in figure 2 shows how many fitness test have been performed against how many unique tests have been performed (how much of the search space has been searched). The graph shown in figure 2 is the results of running a GA on the test problem and the parameters described in section 4.

The graph in figure 2 shows that on hard problems it is easy for a GA to spend a third of its time fitness testing individuals it has already tested before. This is not an obvious result considering that in the example the size of the search space is $2^{40}$ so the chances of randomly duplicating an individual are very small. The reason that there are so many duplicates produced in the GA is because they are not randomly created each time. The next generation is based on the previous generation which was based on the one before. It is this fact that directs the search of the GA but it is also this that causes individuals to appear multiple times.

The graph in figure 2 shows that if the fitness test takes 1 minute to test an individual then the GA would have wasted approximately one and a half days. In the case of a fitness test that was evolving transmission strategies for sending data over a network a simple fitness test could take a week or more. The GA would have wasted over 38 years of time. To make the GA more efficient it needs to reduce the number of fitness tests it is repeating.

If a fitness test takes a long time to run it may be possible to use an approximation for the fitness test which will take less time to test an individual but not give accurate results. A survey of approximations was produced by Yaochu Jin [10]. Rasheed, Ni and Vattam [11] have used approximations to speed up the run time of GA's. Unfortunately there are problems that have no known approximations that might be used; real world network transmissions is just one of them.

## 3 Intelligent Fitness Functions Concept

The standard fitness function in a GA takes an individual as the parameters for an algorithm and evaluates the result. The better the result the better the fitness. Intelligent fitness functions have memory; they can calculate an individuals fitness based on the information stored from previous evaluations. There are two types of memory that an intelligent fitness function can use :

- Short Term Memory
- Long Term Memory

The short term memory is cleared at the start of each new generation and so can only store information about the current generation. The long term memory never gets cleared, but is not able to store every piece of information about previous generations. The fitness function needs to decide what to keep and what to overwrite as it has a limited memory.

An example of the use of short term memory is to check whether an individual is a duplicate of one encountered earlier in the current generation. If it is it returns a low fitness level to stop premature convergence and to increase the diversity of the population.

An example of long term memory to store copies of the best few individuals so far with their fitness. Then when it is asked to fitness test an individual it checks to see if it has tested it before and if it has it simply returns the fitness level it had last time it tested it. This will reduce the number of tests that are performed multiple times by the GA.

## 4 Test Problem

The problem that is used to test the intelligent fitness functions is one that has been designed as hard for a GA to solve. An individuals is mapped into and array, $i$, which consists of "dim" eight bit integers. The array is then used to calculate the distance from a point $C$, coordinates $c_k$, using equation 1. The result of equation 1 is then used in equation 2 to calculate a fitness value for the individual.

$$dist = \sqrt{\sum_{k=1}^{dim} (i_k - c_k)^2} \quad (1)$$

$$Fitness = \cos\left(2 * \pi * \frac{dist}{rad} * amp * \left(2^{-\frac{dist}{ahl}}\right) + height * \left(2^{-\frac{dist}{hhl}}\right)\right) \quad (2)$$

The default values used for the tests were the following
$dim = Number\ of\ Dimensions = 5$
$rad = radius = 50$
$height = 10.0$
$amp = amplitude = 5$
$hhl = height\ half\ life = 200$
$ahl = amplitude\ half\ life = 200$

## 5 The Fitness Functions

### 5.1 Standard Fitness Function

The standard fitness function is a normal GA's fitness function that calculates the fitness of each individual in the current generation.

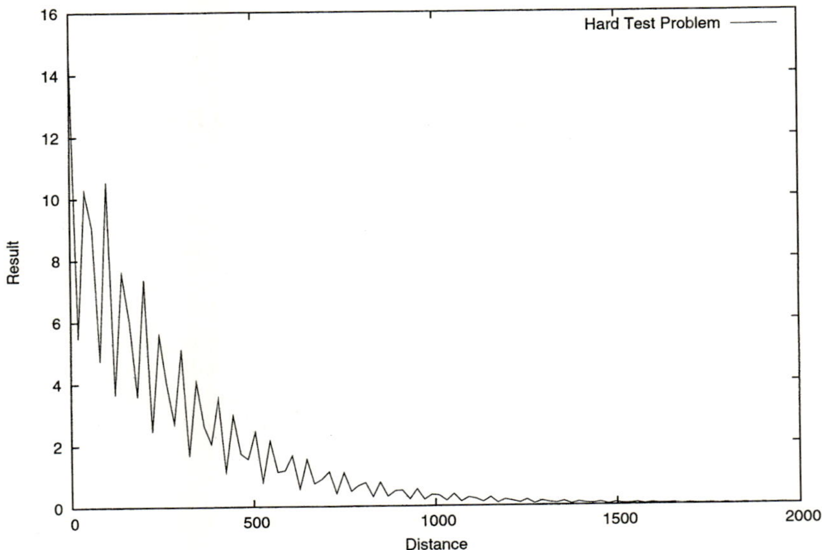


**Fig. 1.** A graph of the hard test problem with one dimension

### 5.2 Intelligent Fitness Function

Three intelligent fitness functions were tested. One had a short term memory which was used to discover if the current individual being tested has already been tested in this generation. If it has then the individual was given a fitness value of 0.

One had a long term memory which was used to discover if it had a record of testing the individual in a previous generation. If the individual has been tested before then the fitness value in memory for that individual is used. If there is no record found then it tests the individual and if it does well enough it stores it in the long term memory for later reference.

The final intelligent fitness function had both a long term memory and a short term memory. The short term memory had precedence over the long term memory.

## 6 Result

All the standard fitness function and the intelligent fitness function reached the same level of fitness at the same number of generations.

On graphs in figures 2 to 11 the closer the two lines the more efficient the GA. The graph shown in figure 2 shows the efficiency of the standard fitness function. The graph shown in figure 3 shows the efficiency of the Intelligent fitness function with short term memory. The graph shown in figures 4, 6, 8 and 10 shows the efficiency of the intelligent fitness function with long term memory of sizes 100,

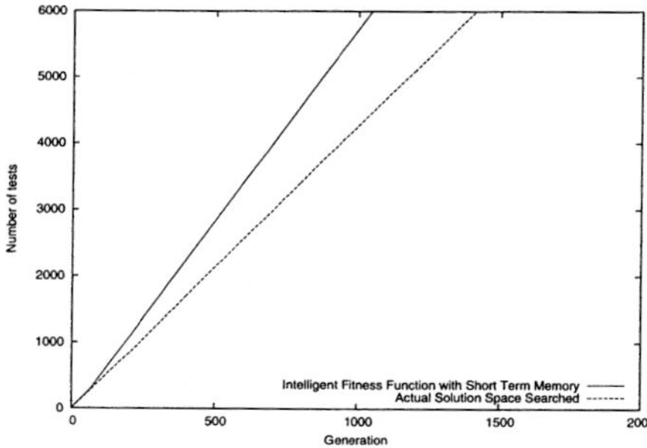


**Fig. 2.** Fitness tests performed and solution space searched when run over 10000 generations, with a population size of 6, a genome length of 40

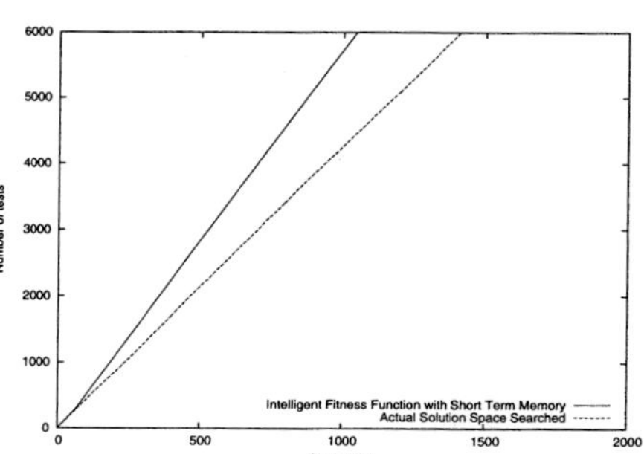


**Fig. 3.** Fitness tests performed and solution space searched when run over 10000 generations, with a population size of 6, a genome length of 40 with a short term memory

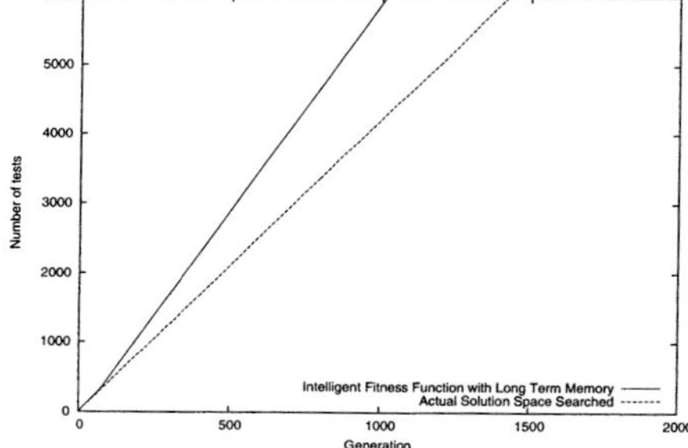


**Fig. 4.** Fitness tests performed and solution space searched when run over 10000 generations, with a population size of 6, a genome length of 40 with a long term memory of 100 individuals

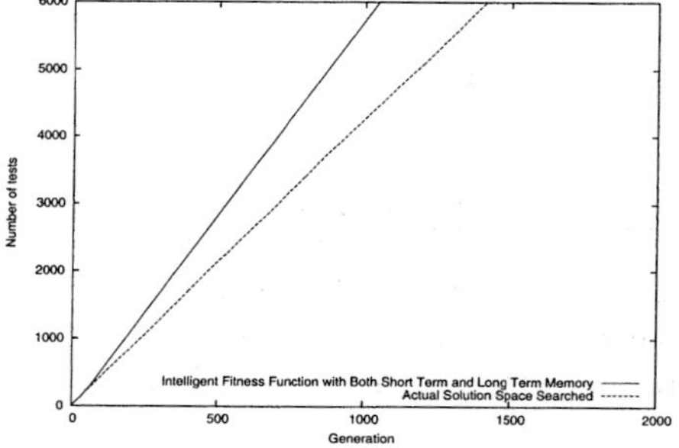


**Fig. 5.** Fitness tests performed and solution space searched when run over 10000 generations, with a population size of 6, a genome length of 40 with a short term memory and a long term memory of 100 individuals

500, 1000 and 2000 individuals. The graph shown in figures 5, 7, 9 and 11 shows the efficiency of the intelligent fitness function with short term memory and long term memory of sizes 100, 500, 1000 and 2000 individuals.

The graph in figure 2 shows that approximately one third of tests carried out by a standard fitness function fitness have already been carried out previously by it.

The graph in figure 3 shows that an intelligent fitness function with short term memory can evolve more generations in the same number of fitness tests as a standard fitness function.

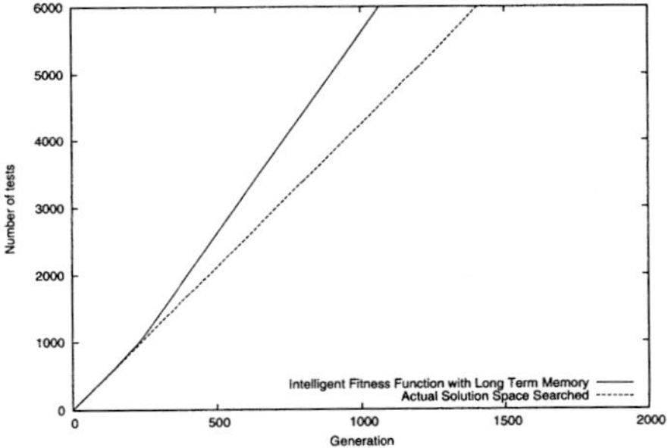


**Fig. 6.** Fitness tests performed and solution space searched when run over 10000 generations, with a population size of 6, a genome length of 40 with a long term memory of 500 individuals



**Fig. 7.** Fitness tests performed and solution space searched when run over 10000 generations, with a population size of 6, a genome length of 40 with a short term memory and a long term memory of 500 individuals

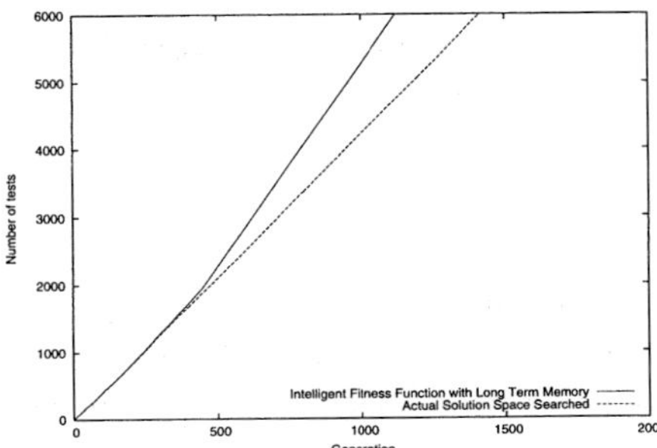


**Fig. 8.** Fitness tests performed and solution space searched when run over 10000 generations, with a population size of 6, a genome length of 40 with a long term memory of 1000 individuals

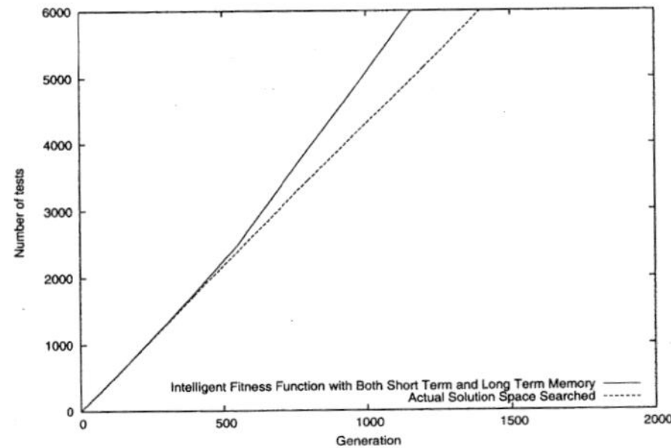


**Fig. 9.** Fitness tests performed and solution space searched when run over 10000 generations, with a population size of 6, a genome length of 40 with a short term memory and a long term memory of 1000 individuals

Figure 4 shows that a small long term memory enables the GA to evolve for a more generations than a standard fitness function over the same number of fitness tests performed.

The graph in figure 5 shows that an intelligent fitness function with a short term memory and a small long term memory is almost the same as one with just a short term memory.

The graphs in figures 6, 8 and 10 shows that as the size of the long term memory is increased the efficiency of the GA is also increased.

The graphs in figures 7, 9 and 11 shows that as the size of the long term memory is increased in an intelligent fitness function, with long term memory

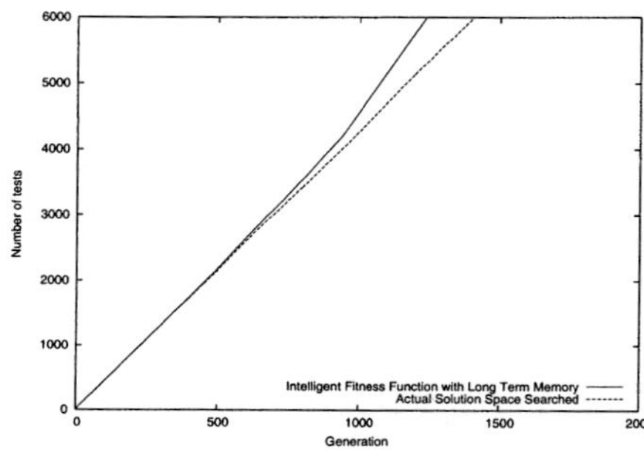


**Fig. 10.** Fitness tests performed and solution space searched when run over 10000 generations, with a population size of 6, a genome length of 40 with a long term memory of 2000 individuals

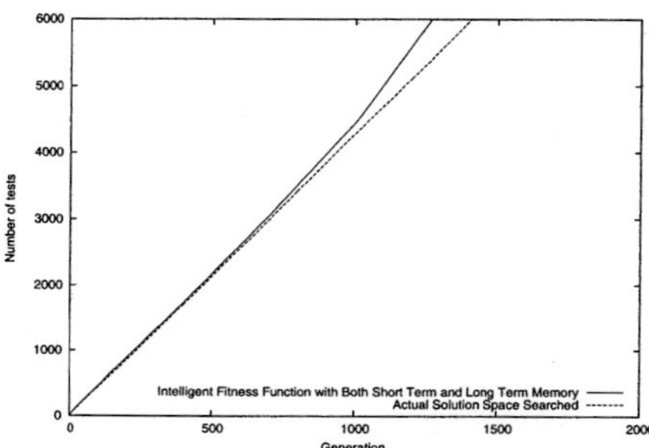


**Fig. 11.** Fitness tests performed and solution space searched when run over 10000 generations, with a population size of 6, a genome length of 40 with a short term memory and a long term memory of 2000 individuals

and short term memory, then the efficiency of the GA increases better than in an intelligent fitness function with just long term memory.

## 7 Conclusion

When using a GA which has a fitness function which takes a long length of time to run the GA's efficiency can be improved by the use of intelligent fitness functions. The use of a short term memory on its own in an intelligent fitness function makes a small difference to a GA's efficiency. The effect on a GA by an intelligent fitness function with long term memory increases as the size of the long term memory increases. When an intelligent fitness function has both long term memory and short term memory then the efficiency of the GA is increased more than using either of the memories on their own.

### Acknowledgements

The authors of this paper would like to acknowledge the support of Nortel Networks, both financially and intellectually.

## References

1. Bremermann H.J. (1962). Optimization through evolution and recombination. in [12]. pp. 93-106.
2. Darwin, C. The Origin Of Species. Oxford University Press, Walton Street, Oxford. OX2 6DP, UK. Based on: On The Origin Of Species by Means of Natural Selection, or the Preservation of Favoured Races in the Struggle for Life. Second Edition, London 1859. First Published 24 Nov 1859.

3. Fraser A.S. (1957a). Simulation of Genetic Systems by Automatic Digital Computers 1, Introduction. Australian J. of Biol.Sci., Vol. 10, pp. 484-491.
4. Fraser A.S. (1957b). Simulation of Genetic Systems by Automatic Digital Computers 2, Effects of Linkage on Rate of Advance under Selection. Australian J. of Biol.Sci., Vol. 10, pp. 492-499.
5. Goldberg D.E., 1989, Genetic Algorithms in Search, Optimization, and Machine Learning. ISBN 0-201-15767-5.
6. Holland, J. H. Adaption in Natural and Artificial Systems. A Bradford Book, The MIT Press. ISBN 0-262-08213-6.
7. Holland J.H. (1973). Genetic Algorithms and the Optimal Allocation of Trials. In SIAM Journal on Computing, 2(2):88-105, June.
8. Holland J.H. (1975). Adaption in Natural and Artificial Systems. MIT Press.
9. Holland J.H. (1992). Adaption in Natural and Artificial Systems. MIT Press, Second Edition.
10. Yaochu Jin. Fitness Approximation in Evolutionary Computation - A Survey. Approximation and Learning In Evolutionary Computation Workshop, GECCO 2002. Pg 3 – 4.
11. Khaled Rasheed, Xiao Ni, Swaroop Vattam. Comparison of Methods for Using Reduced Models to Speed Up Design Optimization. Approximation and Learning In Evolutionary Computation Workshop, GECCO 2002. Pg 17 – 20.
12. Yovits M.C., Jacobi G.T. & Goldstein G.D. (1962). Self Organizing Systems. Spartan Books, Washington D.C.

# Clustering Hoax Fire Calls Using Evolutionary Computation Technology

Lili Yang[1], Michael Gell[1], Christian W. Dawson[2], and Martin R. Brown[3]

[1] School of Computing and Technology, University of Derby, UK
{L.Yang, M.Gell}@Derby.ac.uk
[2] Computer Science Department, Loughborough University, Loughborough, UK
C.W.Dawson1@Lboro.ac.uk
[3] Department of Computing, University of Central Lancashire, Lancashire, UK
martinbrown@uclan.ac.uk

**Abstract.** Hoax fire calls put an unnecessary burden on service resources and endanger life by making personnel and appliances unavailable for genuine incidents. Identifying the higher risk areas of hoax fire calls will be helpful in reducing the hoax calls In this paper, the hoax caller is located by a 6-figure map reference with two lead letters. A GA based evolutionary computation technology is proposed and applied to cluster the hoax calls into several groups according to their locations. The number of clusters is fixed at each GA run, and it is incremented by 1 for each iteration until the desired fitness (quality of the clustering partition) is achieved. The novel fitness function allows each cluster geographically covering a similar size of the areas and avoids empty clusters occur. The algorithm is then applied to the identification of higher risk areas of hoax fire calls. A spatial visualization is also used to display the clustering results in which three higher risk areas are clearly identified.

## 1 Instruction

Every year, hoax fire calls account for some 5% of all emergency calls received, and produce great losses, not only in wasting money and putting an unnecessary burden on service resources, but also endangering life by making personnel and appliances unavailable for genuine incidents, disturbing road traffic, and increasing environment noise. The majority of hoax fire calls are made from public pay phones by children and some adults. Previous research provides strong evidence that hoax fire calls are spatially concentrated and associated with deprivation. The hoax fire calls have been categorised as social problems and are often clustered in areas with crime, unemployment and poor physical environment.

One of the objectives of the Derbyshire Fire & Rescue Service in next three years is to reduce hoax fire calls by 10% each year within Derbyshire. One promising way to reduce the hoax calls is to implement a system to cluster the hoax fire calls database, identify the higher risk areas, and cooperate with community education and police stations in these higher risk areas.

A generic description of the clustering objectives is to maximize homogeneity within each cluster while maximizing heterogeneity among clusters [1]. Data

P.W.H. Chung, C.J. Hinde, M. Ali (Eds.): IEA/AIE 2003, LNAI 2718, pp. 644–652, 2003.

clustering identifies the sparse and the crowded places, and hence discovers the overall distribution patterns of the data set. There exists a rich literature on clustering methods. The most frequently used clustering method is the k-means method, which identifies a certain number of groups of similar objects; it may be used in a combination with the nearest-neighbour rules, which classifies any new object in the group most similar to it. Alternatively, systems based on statistical classification methods, such as AutoClass, which uses a Bayesian classification method, have been used with reported success for clustering real world databases. Basically, there are three kinds of clustering techniques: overlapping, hierarchical and partitioning. Identification of higher risk areas of hoax calls deals with the partitioning approach, which assigns each hoax fire call (object) to exactly one cluster.

Formally, let us consider a set of N hoax fire calls $X=\{X_1, X_2,\ldots,X_n\}$ to be clustered, where each $X_i$ is an attribute vector. The hoax calls must be clustered into non-overlapping groups $C = \{C_1, C_2,\ldots, C_k\}$ where k is the number of clusters, such that:

$$C_1 \cup C_2 \cup \cdots \cup C_k = X \tag{1}$$

$$C_i \neq \Phi, \quad and \quad C_i \cap C_j = \Phi \quad for \quad i \neq j \tag{2}$$

$$C_i \neq \Phi, \quad and \quad C_i \cap C_j = \Phi \quad for \quad i \neq j \tag{3}$$

where $\Phi$ is an empty set.

The problem with finding an optimal solution to the partition of N data into k classes is NP-complete. Genetic algorithms are widely believed to be effective on NP-complete global optimisation problems and they can provide good sub-optimal solutions in reasonable time. Therefore, the application of genetic algorithms in clustering optimisation problems can be very effective and efficient. A genetic algorithm-based clustering technique, called GA-clustering, was proposed by Maulik and Bandyopadhyay[2] to search for appropriate cluster centres in the feature space such that a similarity metric of the resulting clusters is optimised. In the case where the distances between elements are metric and both the number of attributes and the number of clusters are large, Franti et. al. [3] showed the genetic algorithms give high quality clustering, but at the expense of long running time. Even though there are many characteristics of genetic algorithms which qualify them to be a robust search procedure for clustering problem, still there are some drawbacks, for example, genetic algorithms are not well suited to perform a finely tuned search. Therefore combining local search and clustering techniques with genetic algorithms has been tried by some researchers [4]. Usually, considering the problem of clustering m objects into c clusters, the objects are presented by points in an n-dimensional Euclidean space, the objective is to classify these m points into c clusters such that the distance between points within a cluster and its centre is minimized. Jiang and Dema [5] compared the performance of this idea with that of the k-means and simulated annealing algorithms and showed that this idea is better than the well-known k-means and simulated annealing algorithms.

In this work we adopted the above n-dimensional Euclidean space idea [5], [6], but the hoax fire calls in a database are partitioned using a modified genetic algorithm - an iterative GA. After achieved clustering, the number of hoax fire calls and their centre location for each cluster are displayed using spatial visualization technology (3-D surface). Three higher risk areas are clearly identified based on the clustering results.

## 2 Hoax Fire Calls Database

Derbyshire Fire & Rescue Service provided details of all hoax fire calls logged on their computer dispatch system during 1999. In total 1101 records were in this database. Each hoax call had the following key attributes:

- Unique incident number
- Map reference
- Time, date and day
- Address
- Station area
- Risk category
- Hoax caller telephone number

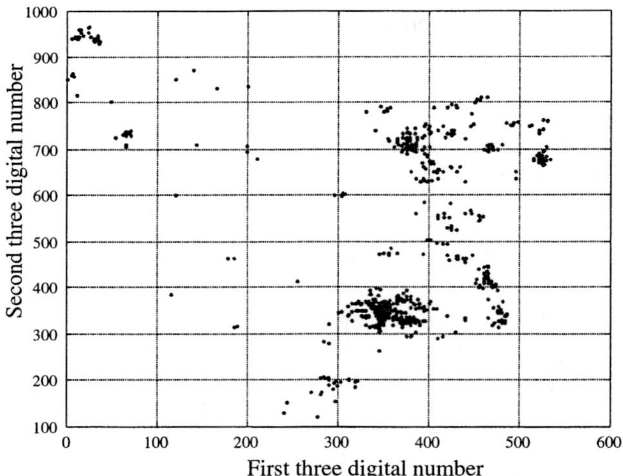


**Fig. 1.** The hoax fire call distribution

The map reference is a 6-figure grid reference with two lead letters, for example SK385695, and is used to locate a particular place on a map. The two letters are used to identify a 100-kilometre grid square. Great Britain is covered by a number of such squares. First three digital numbers (385 in above example) express the coordinate in the easting, and second three digital numbers (695) the coordinate in the northing, from the south west corner. The majority of hoax calls were located to a precision of around one hundred metres by using the map reference. Hoax fire calls referenced by the pair of location coordinates, can be easily mapped as a "dot map" shown in Fig. 1. Since all hoax fire calls in the database are located in a same 100-kilometre grid square, the two lead letters in the map references are ignored in this study.

## 3 Clustering Hoax Fire Calls Using an Iterative GA

In order to identify higher risk areas, hoax fire calls in the database are partitioned into several groups based on their diversity such as a spatial distribution. Assuming the size of the area that each group covers is similar. Then the larger the number of hoax fire calls in a group is, the higher the risk is in the area. There are many methods, which can be used for data clustering. The method used here is to describe a clustering as a set of guide points in the data space to be investigated. The task of clustering a database is then changed to search a set of suitable guide points.

Genetic algorithms provide a good mechanism to find the guide points. Genetic algorithms are a simulation of a simplified process of evolution. The fundamental object of data used by a GA is referred to as a chromosome. A number of chromosomes exist simultaneously in a population. The GA transforms one population into a succeeding population using operators that are analogous to the biological operators of reproduction, cross-over, and mutation. A measure of the quality of each chromosome, analogous to the fitness of a biological organism in an environment and typically provided by an optimisation objective, is evaluated and used to probabilistically select chromosomes to serve as parents. With an increasing number of generations, the overall fitness of the population increases and the diversity represented in the population decreases.

We employ k guide points $P_1$, $P_2$, ... $P_k$ and choose the string consisting of the coordinates of all guide points as a chromosome. The co-ordinate of the guide point $P_i$ $_{(i=1, 2, ..k)}$ is denoted as ($X_{pi}$, $Y_{pi}$). The map reference of the guide points is made of $X_{pi}$ as the first three digital numbers and $Y_{pi}$ as the second three digital numbers. The chromosome is expressed as an integer string with a length of 2k (the double of the number of the guide points) as below:

$$X_{p1}Y_{p1}X_{p2}Y_{p2}\cdots X_{pk}Y_{pk}$$

The size of population of a generation consists of a number of chromosomes (50 in this study). In the initial stage, all guide points will be selected randomly, so GA will start with several chromosomes that describe a number of random solutions to the clustering problem. The average distance of the points in the sample space to the closest guide point is chosen as a fitness function as below. A set of guide points will give a better clustering if the average distance of all the points to the closest guide point is minimal.

Taking the number of empty clusters into consideration, the fitness function includes a term to penalize degenerate solution, similar to the works by Hall et al. [7] and Meng et al. [8]. Any value of the fitness function is scaled with a penalty factor. This penalty factor is represented by 1 plus the number of the empty clusters E divided by the total number of clusters *k*.

$$f_{fitness} = \frac{1}{N}\sum_{i=1}^{N} \min_{j=1}^{k}((X_i - X_{pj})^2 + (Y_i - Y_{pj})^2)^{1/2}(1 + E/k) \qquad (4)$$

In the above fitness function, the points, i.e. locations of hoax calls, in the sample space is denoted as $(X_i, Y_i)_{i=1, ..., N}$. N is the number of the hoax calls in the database

(N=1101 in this study). $X_i$ is the first three digital numbers, and $Y_i$ is the second three digital numbers in the map reference.

It has been declared in the beginning of this section: if the size of the area that each cluster covers is similar, then the larger the number of hoax fire calls in a group is, the higher the risk is in the area. Obviously, the fitness function shown in Equation (4) does not produce a similar covering area for all the clusters. A further penalty item is required for this particular purpose. This mean square error (MSE) of the average distance of all the clusters is selected as below.

$$MSE = \frac{\sum_{j=1}^{k} (D_j - \overline{D})^2}{k} \tag{5}$$

where $D_j$ is the average distance of the points in the cluster j to the centre of this cluster (i.e. the guide point of the cluster j),

and $\overline{D} = \frac{\sum_{j=1}^{k} D_j}{k}$

It can be seen that if all the clusters cover a same size of the area the MSE item is equal to zero, otherwise this penalty item has a greater value. Adding this penalty item into Equation (4) the final fitness function is obtained as shown in Equation (6).

$$f_{fitness} = \frac{1}{N} \sum_{i=1}^{N} \min_{j=1}^{k} ((X_i - X_{pj})^2 + (Y_i - Y_{pj})^2)^{1/2} (1 + E / k + MSE) \tag{6}$$

The desired value of the fitness is the radius of the area preset for each cluster. The trial and error method can be used for the selection of the desired value. For the sake of simplicity, we use one quarter of a ward as the area preset for each cluster while selecting the desired value.

Since there is not any pre-knowledge about the number of guide points available an iterative GA is proposed here. As shown in Fig. 2, the number of clusters, i.e. the number of guide points, is initialised as 2. In each iteration the GA is terminated by the maximum number of generations (100 in the study) or the fitness value if the desired value is achieved. If the desired fitness value is not achieved by the termination of the GA the number of guide points k increments by 1, the next iteration starts and the GA is invoked again. The procedure repeats until the desired fitness value is achieved. The obvious advantage of using the above procedure is that no pre-knowledge about the number of clusters is required. Fig. 3 shows the best fitness value for each iteration during the clustering process.

Fig. 4 shows the clustering results of the hoax fire call database using the above iterative GA. The hoax fire calls are partitioned into 5 clusters. Table 1 shows the guide point and the number of hoax fire calls in each cluster. Table 1 and Fig. 4 shows that clusters 1 and 2 are the higher risk areas, clusters 3, 4 and 5 are the lower risk areas. In order to reduce hoax fire call initiating community education initiatives should be made for the higher risk areas, such as visits to schools and warning notices in kiosks giving the maximum penalty for giving a false call.

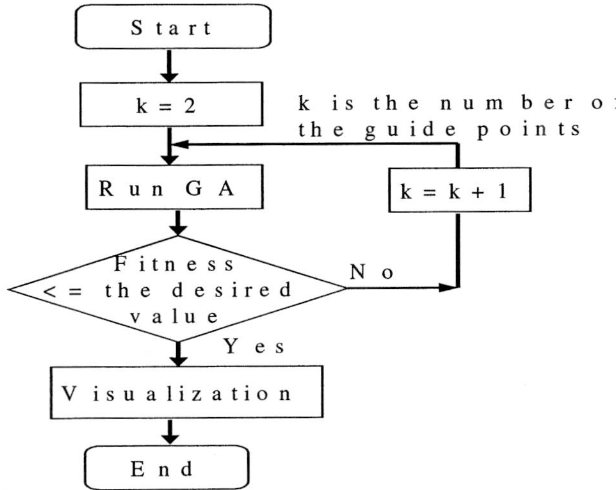


**Fig. 2.** Auto-clustering using an iterative GA

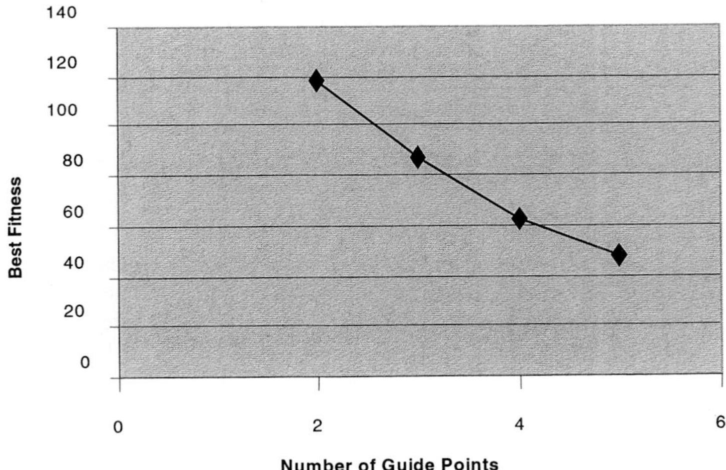


**Fig. 3.** Best fitness values for each iteration

**Table 1.** Guide points and the number of hoax fire calls in each group

| Group | 1 | 2 | 3 | 4 | 5 |
|---|---|---|---|---|---|
| Number of hoax calls | 692 | 281 | 15 | 84 | 29 |
| Guide point-x | 388 | 450 | 272 | 3 | 282 |
| Guide point-y | 375 | 680 | 549 | 901 | 109 |

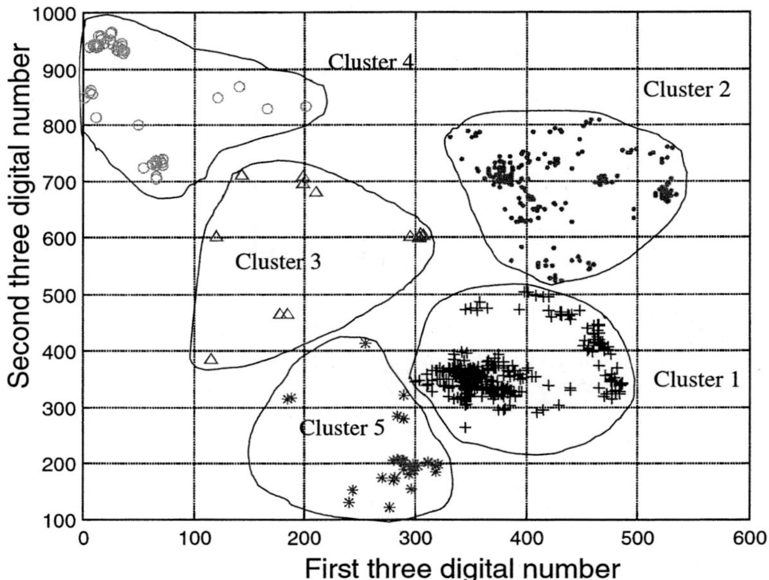


**Fig. 4.** The clustering of the hoax fire calls

# 4 Identification of Higher Risk Areas Using Spatial Visualization

Visualization has been developed primarily to help people extract ideas from masses of multidimensional data. Such visual data exploration technologies have not yet been heavily used in fire incident analysis, but are being applied elsewhere in, for example, climatology and meteorology. On the other hand, the widespread availability of various commercial software such as GIS [9] and MatLab [10] coupled with the wealth of point data in digital form, has led to a demand for visualization to represent and analyse such data.

This dot map as shown in Fig. 1 and Fig 4 can give a reasonable impression of variations in the number of hoax fire calls in each cluster. Table 1 can clearly show the higher risk areas but no any geographical information is included. Therefore, Fig. 4 and Table 1 must be considered together in order to identify the higher risk areas and their locations. 3-D surface provides an efficient way to carry out this integration.

Suppose that the number of hoax calls in each clsuter is located at the guide point (centre point) of the group. As shown in Fig. 5, given that the number is a spatially continuous variable, it is possible to transform the dot map of points into a continuous number surface. The surface can be rotated in different angles and viewed. For example, the result shown in Fig. 5 can be viewed from the back. The peaks around each cluster in the surfaces is clearly shown in the 3D surfaces.

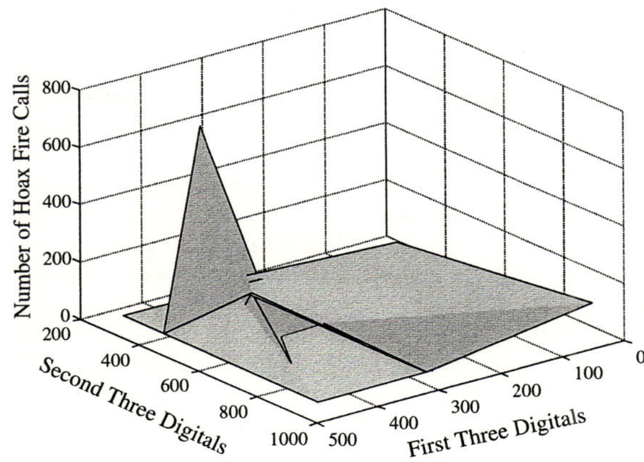


**Fig. 5.** Visualized higher risk areas of hoax fire calls from the front view

## 5 Conclusions

Many researches have been done in the clustering using GA. Few can be found in fire incidents, especially in monitoring and reducing hoax fire calls. The above results suggest that it is feasible and worthwhile to use GA to cluster the hoax fire calls referenced by the map reference and to identify the higher risk areas by creating a dot map of the clustering of hoax calls and surfaces that, in general sense, serve as maps of the spatial variation in number of hoax calls. The methodology is sufficiently general as to be applicable in a range of situations, such as accidental fire incidents, and malicious fire incidents in domestic areas. There are two scientific contributions in this study. First is to automatically identify the higher risk areas using an iterative GA and a proper fitness function which can avoid empty clusters occurrence and allow all the clusters covering a similar size of the area. Second is to visualize the clustering results, which is more helpful than purely displaying the spatial distribution of the hoax calls.

There are some limitations in this study. The iterative approach for clustering proposed seems quite sensitive to the choice of the desired fitness value. Some general principle to guide the setting of this important parameter is required. Using the spatial visualization will be difficult when the number of features goes up. If it is the case, the principal component analysis (PCA) can be used to extract the main features and reduce the dimension of the data. Furthermore, it would be more useful to try to predict whether or not a given call is a hoax fire call, which suggests a classification task for our future research.

## References


1. Hruschka, E.R., Ebecken, N.F.F.: Credit approval by a clustering genetic algorithm. In Data Mining II edited by N. Ebeken and C.A. Brebbia. Wit press. (2000) 403-412
2. Maulik, U., Bandyopadhyay, S.: Genetic algorithm-based clustering technique. Pattern Recognition, Vol. 33. (2000) 1455-1465
3. Franti, P., Kivijarvi, J., Kaukoranta, T., and Nevalainen, O.: Genetic algorithms for large-scale clustering problems. Computer Journal, Vol. 40. (1997) 547-554
4. Areibi, S.: The effect of clustering and local search on genetic algorithms. In: John, R., Birkenhead, R. (eds.): Advances in Soft Computing. Workshop 99 on Recent Advances in Soft Computing. (1999) 172-177
5. Jiang, T.Z., DeMa, S.: Cluster analysis using genetic algorithms. ICSP'96 –1996 3$^{rd}$ International Conference on Signal Processing, Proceeding, I&II. (1996) 1277-1279
6. Adriaans, P., Zantinge, D.: Data mining. Addison-wesley longman limited. (1996) 72-78
7. Hall, L.O., Ozyurt, I.B., & Bezdek, J.C., Clustering with a genetically optimised approach, IEEE Transactions on Evolutionary Computation, 3(2), (1999) 103-112
8. Meng, L., Wu, Q.H., & Yong, Z.Z., A faster genetic clustering algorithm, Lecture Notes in Computer Science, 1803, (2000) 22-33
9. Hearnshaw, H.M., Unwin D.J.: Visualization in Geographical Information Systems. Jonn Wiley & Sons Ltd. (1994) 65-75
10. The MATH WORK Inc.: Using MATLAB Graphics, MA 01760-1500, (1996) 3-32- 3_34

# Packet Transmission Optimisation Using Genetic Algorithms

Mark Withall, Chris Hinde, Roger Stone, and Jason Cooper

Department of Computer Science, Loughborough University,
Loughborough, Leics. LE11 3TU, United Kingdom,
{m.s.withall2,c.j.hinde,r.g.stone,j.l.cooper}@lboro.ac.uk

**Abstract.** A Genetic Algorithm (GA) is used to optimise the parameters for a sequence of packets sent over the Internet. Only the parameters that a client machine can change are used and the fitness is based on the delay time returned by the Traceroute program. The GA performance is compared to a fixed packet size with no priority used to assess the status of the network. The GA generally performed to the same level as the control settings but in some cases significant improvements were made.

**Keywords.** Internet Applications, Genetic Algorithms, Adaptive Control

## 1 Introduction

Various work has been done on using heuristic and adaptive techniques, such as Genetic Algorithms (GA), to solve networking problems (see for example [4, 6, 14]). The main focus of this work has been on areas such as network topology design, routing table construction and performance analysis. Most of these areas involve having some form of control or access to large areas of the network. This work looks at what performance increase, if any, can be gained from the perspective of a single client machine on the Internet, without having any external effect on the network other than the packets sent.

The aims of the experiments were to find good parameters for a sequence of packet transmissions to optimise the time taken to send 10,000 bytes of data (experiment 1) and minimise the delay of the slowest packet (experiment 2), over the Internet. The parameters being varied were the packet size, and hence the number of packets, and the priority settings of the packets. The optimisation was performed using a Genetic Algorithm[9] and was compared to a control setting, to monitor the state of the network, of the maximum packet size and no priority settings.

## 2 Genetic Algorithms

Genetic Algorithms (GA) began in the 1950s, some of the early papers being by Fraser [7, 8] and Bremermann [1]. Later on work by Holland[10–12] popularised

P.W.H. Chung, C.J. Hinde, M. Ali (Eds.): IEA/AIE 2003, LNAI 2718, pp. 653–661, 2003.

genetic algorithms and Holland's work is often cited as the origins of Genetic Algorithms. GAs are based on Darwin and Wallace's theories of *Natural Selection*[5, 18] and Gregor Mendel's theory of *Genetic Inheritance*[15]. A GA takes a population of possible solutions to a given problem (individuals), evaluates these solutions based on some criteria (fitness) and then genetically recombines the solutions based on the fitness of the individuals (using genetic operators) in the population to form a new generation of the population. This process is repeated until some termination criterion is met. Figure 1 gives the basic flow diagram for a GA.

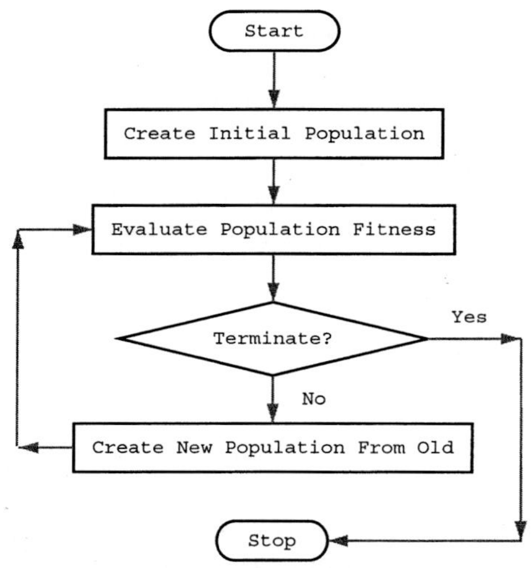


**Fig. 1.** Flow diagram for the basic Genetic Algorithm

### 2.1 Representation

The way that the individuals are represented (genome) can have a great effect on the performance of the GA. Traditionally, GA individuals are represented as binary strings, however, any representation that is appropriate for the problem can be used.

### 2.2 Initial Population

The initial population of a GA is important as it specifies the gene values which the GA has to work with. This gene pool can then be expanded using mutation as the GA runs. It is usual to start with a randomly generated population.

### 2.3 Fitness Evaluation

The fitness evaluation, for the GA, determines how good an individual from a population is at solving a given problem. The fitness is traditionally given as some integer or real number value, where the higher the value the greater the fitness. The fitness value is used to select parents for the reproduction stage of the algorithm.

### 2.4 Reproduction

Parent selection is used to determine which individuals from a population will be used to create the next generation of individuals. Genetic operators are used to manipulate the genes of the selected parents to create new individuals for the next generation. There are two main genetic operators: *crossover* and *mutation*.

**Crossover:** This consists of combining the genes from two or more parent individuals to create a new individual. This can take the form of picking a random point on the genome and using the genes before this point from one parent and those after from the other. Multiple points can be chosen and used in the same way. At the most extreme, a decision can be made for every gene for which parent to take it from.

**Mutation:** This consists of changing one or more genes in the individual to a new random value.

### 2.5 Termination Conditions

The two main methods of terminating a GA are to pre-specify a number of generations to run the algorithm for or to run until a member of the population reaches a specific fitness level.

### 2.6 Variables

Both the population size and the probability of a mutation can be instantiated with different values. The values set can greatly affect the performance of the GA.

## 3 Experimental Procedure

The following subsections describe the particular GA being used for the experiments. The first subsection describes the representation being used for the individuals in the population. The second subsection describes the method of fitness evaluation for the individuals in each experiment. The third subsection describes the genetic manipulation operators being used and other parameters for the GA. Finally, the hardware and software used for testing is summarised.

### 3.1 Problem Representation

There are two parameters being varied in this experiment: the packet size and the priority. As two parameters would be too few to be usefully varied, the values are represented in binary. The packet size is represented as an 11-bit value (0–2047), however, the packet size is restricted to being between 500 and 1460 bytes in length, plus a 40 byte header. If the packet size is less than 500 it is rounded up and if greater than 1460 it is rounded down. The priority is represented as an 8-bit value which directly maps to the 8 bits for priority in the packet header, shown in Figure 2. Therefore, the representation of each individual is a 19-bit binary string which means there are 524288 possible settings being searched through, although some will be functionally the same.

```
---------------------------
| DS Codepoint | Unused   |  DS Field
|    (6 bits)  | (2 bits) |
---------------------------

Bits 0-2 define class Bits 3-5 define relative priority with class
```

[Format from http://www.itec.uni-klu.ac.at/~hellwagn/RN-QoS/rn2-kap5-DiffServ.pdf]

**Fig. 2.** The DiffServ priority octet

### 3.2 Fitness Evaluation

The fitness evaluation for the GA was conducted by recording the delay time for each packet of a 10,000 byte message being sent over the Internet. For experiment 1, the total time taken (sum of packet delays) to send the 10,000 bytes was used as the fitness value. For experiment 2, the time taken (delay) for the slowest packet was used as the fitness value. The data was sent to an IP address in Japan, as the path was quite a slow one. The source and destination IP addresses are given in Figure 3. To test the effectiveness of a transmission strategy takes a week or two. The method used here will not tell us the effectiveness of the individual except at the time of the test. The reason for using this method is that it is quicker and that it will show if there are improvements to be made at times. If it shows that there are times where the GA performs better than the control then it would be worth running a GA using a partial fitness function [2] to evolve transmission strategies.

The data was sent using the Traceroute program with the following command line switches:

```
traceroute -q 1 -n -S 28 -t <priority> <address> <packetsize>
```

The `-q` switch specifies how many packets to send, the `-n` switch keeps output concise, the `-S` switch specifies only to print the information for the destination address and not intermediate servers and the `-t` switch specifies the priority.

The shorter the time, for both experiments, the better. This value is inverted and normalised so that the higher the value the fitter the individual, for easier selection at the reproduction stage.

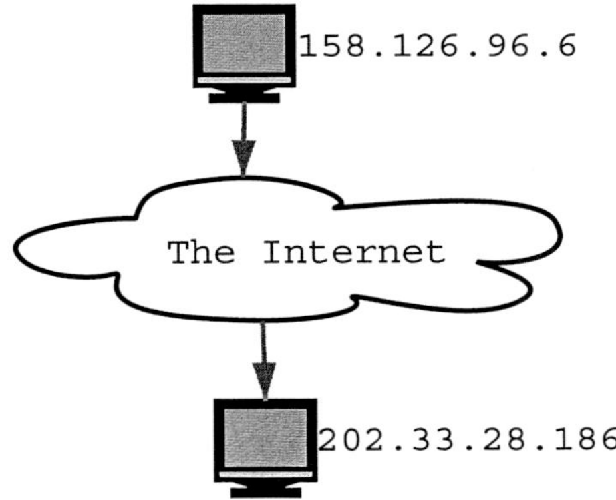


**Fig. 3.** Source and destination addresses used for the experiment

In addition to the GA tests, a control was run with no priority and a packet size of 1500 bytes (including header). This control was run once for every individual in the population i.e. ten individual runs and ten control runs.

### 3.3 Genetic Operators and Parameters

The GA uses two types of genetic operator. The first is a crossover operator, where two parents are chosen and some genes from one parent and some from the other are used to create the new individual. The crossover is uniform i.e. performed at every point in the genome[16]. The second genetic operator is mutation, where one gene value is randomly changed to a new random value. All new individuals are created by the crossover of two parent individuals with some probability of mutation in the new individual.

The population size used for the experiment was 10 individuals and the mutation rate was a probability of 1 gene in 100. The population was initialised randomly.

### 3.4 Hardware and Software

The GA was written in Perl version 5.6.1[17] and used Traceroute version 6.0 GOLD. The experiments were run on a Sun Sparc 4 with a Debian Linux operating system. The machine was connected to the Internet over a 10Mb/s switched LAN and to the SuperJanet network.

## 4 Results

The following sections give the results for the two experiments. The aim of experiment 1 was to minimise the total delay to send 10,000 bytes of data over the Internet and the aim of experiment 2 was to minimise the delay for the slowest packet in the same transmission.

### 4.1 Experiment 1

The graph in Figure 4 shows the best control at each generation against the best evolved individual at each generation.

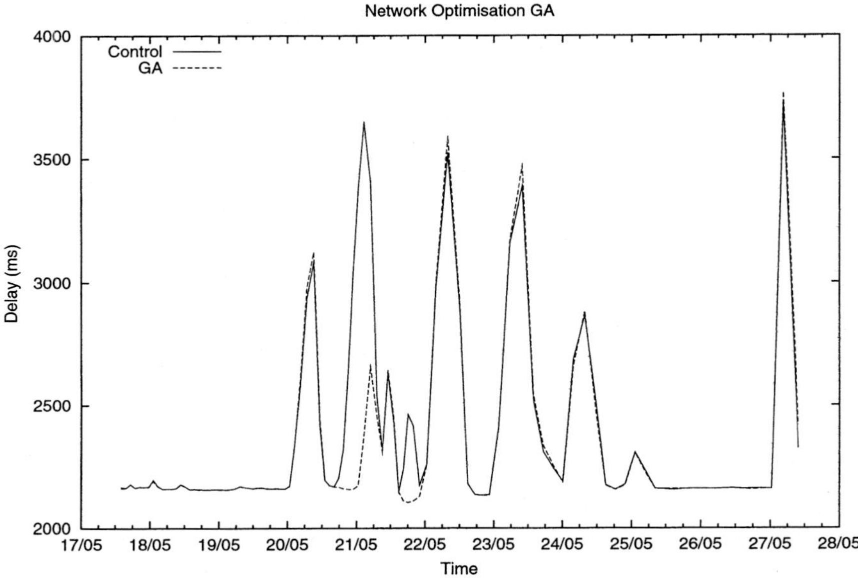


**Fig. 4.** Delay against time for the best control and best GA solution, at each generation, for experiment 1

For most of the experiment, the best GA individual and the best control performance are virtually identical. The GA quickly learns that the largest packet sizes perform best. There are two main occasions where the GA performs significantly better than the control. These occur at around generation 3000 (~00:00 21/05) and generation 4440 (~18:00 21/05). The priority settings at these points are generally 199 (class 6, priority 1) and 207 (class 6, priority 3) in the first instance and 227 (class 7, priority 0) and 243 (class 7, priority 4) in the second. The result seems logical as the higher priority classes would be likely to receive better service. However, it is uncertain why the GA can not maintain this performance.

### 4.2 Experiment 2

The graph in Figure 5 shows the best control at each generation against the best evolved individual at each generation.

The results for experiment 2 are quite different to those in experiment 1. The GA in most cases manages to keep up with the performance of the control when

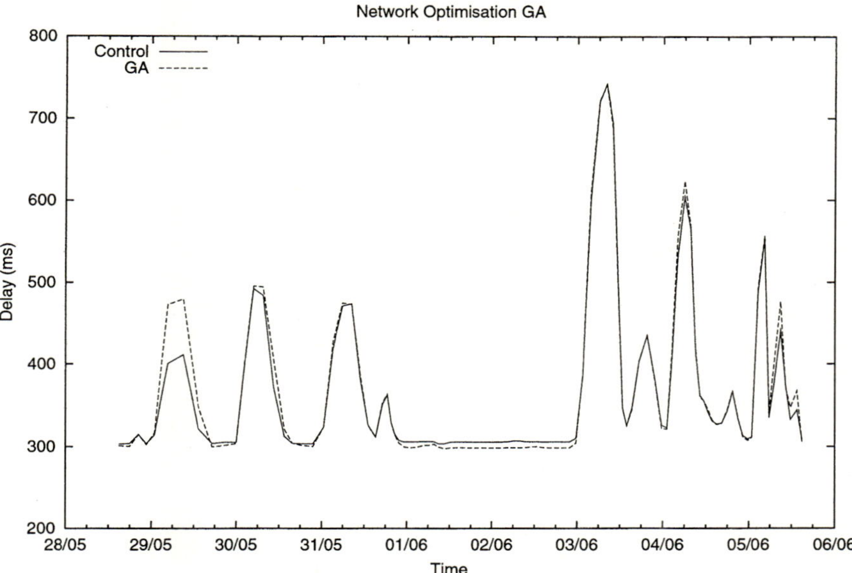


**Fig. 5.** Delay against time for the best control and the best GA solution, at each generation, for experiment 2

the network is busy but when the network is quiet it can outperform the control. The results show that the GA uses a large packet size when the network is busy. This seems reasonable as sending less packets decreases the chance that one of them will be held up in the congestion. When the network was quiet, the GA used a small packet size. This gives enough of a performance improvement to beat the control with a fixed maximum packet size when there is less chance of a packet being held up in traffic. The priority settings being used in the three main areas of improved performance were 33 (class 1, priority 0, at ~20:00 29/05), 120 (class 3, priority 6, at ~19:00 30/05) and 123 (class 3, priority 6, at ~00:00 02/06). It seems as if the main performance improvement for the GA in this situation is caused by the decrease in packet size rather than the priority setting.

## 5 Summary and Conclusions

For experiment 1, the GA performed, in general, at the same level as the control settings. However, for two periods the GA showed a significant improvement over the control by using high priority classes. Unfortunately, this performance could not be maintained. For experiment 2, the GA performed well during the periods of low network congestion but only to the level of the control settings or worse during high congestion periods.

In conclusion, the GA managed to adapt to different conditions on the network, and different fitness requirements, quite well but was inconsistent in its ability to outperform the control settings' performance. Although external factors play the major role in determining transmission delays the experiments have shown that some improvements can be made from the perspective of an individual machine. Further work is required to find if any consistent improvements can be obtained over a simple fixed parameter setting.

Alternative approaches to the problem include a *Nested Evolution Strategy*, which has been shown to be good at many adaptive problems. *Genetic Programming* could be used to produce a parameter control program to adjust the packet settings based on the performance of previous packets sent (and perhaps even other known facts about the network being used). This approach would probably be an improvement of the simple GA, which is just reacting blindly to the changing conditions of the network without memory of previous network changes. The disadvantage to this approach is that a reasonable complete fitness evaluation would take about a week per individual (or even more) and therefore it would take a very long time to evolve good solutions.

Partial fitness functions [2] is a promising approach which uses an individuals fitness combined with the age of the individual, this allows the fitness testing to continue to completion but also uses early results to permit promising individuals to breed. A study using evaluations of over a week shows that the most effective policy depends on the destination and route taken. For example, priority settings on one route which produce good transmission times fail to replicate across a range of routes but do replicate across limited sets of routes. This indicates that the optimum strategy depends on the destination and route chosen [3].

**Acknowledgements**

Thanks to Nortel for their support, both intellectual and financial, during the project.

## References

1. Bremermann H.J. (1962). *Optimization through evolution and recombination.* in [19]. pp. 93-106.
2. Cooper J.L. & Hinde C.J. (2003). *Improving the performance of Genetic Algorithms Using Partial Fitness Functions.* Submitted to GECCO 2003.
3. Cooper J.L. Withall M.S. Hinde C.J. & Stone R.G. (2003). *Investigation into the effects of varying the parameters of packets travelling across the Internet.* Loughborough University Department of Computer Science Internal Report no. 1070.
4. Corne D. Smith G. & Oates M. (2000). Telecommunications Optimization: Heuristic and Adaptive Techniques. John Wiley and Sons Ltd.
5. Darwin C. (1996). The Origin of Species. Oxford University Press. First published 1859.
6. Di Caro G. & Dorigo M. (1998). *AntNet: Distributed Stigmergetic Control for Communications Networks.* In Journal of Artificial Intelligence Research, 9:317-365.

7. Fraser A.S. (1957a). Simulation of Genetic Systems by Automatic Digital Computers 1, Introduction. Australian J. of Biol.Sci., Vol. 10, pp. 484-491.
8. Fraser A.S. (1957b). Simulation of Genetic Systems by Automatic Digital Computers 2, Effects of Linkage on Rate of Advance under Selection. Australian J. of Biol.Sci., Vol. 10, pp. 492-499.
9. Goldberg D.E. (1989). Genetic Algorithms in Search Optimization and Machine Learning. Addison-Wesley Publishing Co. Inc.
10. Holland J.H. (1973). *Genetic Algorithms and the Optimal Allocation of Trials.* In SIAM Journal on Computing, 2(2):88-105, June.
11. Holland J.H. (1975). Adaption in Natural and Artificial Systems. MIT Press.
12. Holland J.H. (1992). Adaption in Natural and Artificial Systems. MIT Press, Second Edition.
13. Langdon W.B.,(2002). Proceedings of the Genetic and Evolutionary Computation Conference 2002,Morgan Kaufmann.
14. Liang S. Zincir-Heywood A.N. & Heywood M.I. (2002). *Intelligent Packets for Dynamic Network Routing using Distributed Genetic Algorithm.* In [13]. pp. 88-96.
15. Mendel G. (1865). Experiments in Plant Hybridization.
16. Syswerda G. (1989). *Uniform Crossover in Genetic Algorithms.* In Schaffer D., editor, Proceedings of the Third International Conference on Genetic Algorithms, 2-9. Morgan Kaufmann.
17. Wall L. Christiansen T. & Schwartz R.L. (1996). Programming Perl. O'Reilly & Associates, Inc., Second Edition.
18. Wallace A.R. (1858). *On the Tendency of Varieties to Depart Indefinitely From the Original Type.* In Journal of the Proceedings of the Linnean Society: Zoology 3(9):53-62.
19. Yovits M.C., Jacobi G.T. & Goldstein G.D. (1962). *Self Organizing Systems.* Spartan Books, Washuington D.C.

# Design and Implementation of Personality of Humanoids in Human Humanoid Non-verbal Interaction*

Hiroshi G. Okuno[1,2], Kazuhiro Nakadai[2], and Hiroaki Kitano[2,3]

[1] Graduate School of Informatics, Kyoto University, Kyoto 606-8501 Japan,
okuno@i.kyoto-u.ac.jp, http://winnie.kuis.kyoto-u.ac.jp/~okuno/
[2] Kitano Symbiotic Systems Project, ERATO,
National Institute of Advanced Industrial Science and Technology,
M-31, 6-31-15 Jingumae, Shibuya, Tokyo 150-0001 Japan,
{nakadai,kitano}@symbio.jst.go.jp
http://www.symbio.jst.go.jp/SIG/
[3] Sony Computer Science Laboratories, Inc., Shinagawa, Tokyo

**Abstract.** Controlling robot behaviors becomes more important recently as active perception for robot, in particular active audition in addition to active vision, has made remarkable progress. We are studying how to create social humanoids that perform actions empowered by real-time audio-visual tracking of multiple talkers. In this paper, we present *personality* as a means of controlling non-verbal behaviors. It consists of two dimensions, dominance vs. submissiveness and friendliness vs. hostility, based on the Interpersonal Theory in psychology. The upper-torso humanoid *SIG* equipped with real-time audio-visual multiple-talker tracking system is used as a testbed for social interaction. As a companion robot, with friendly personality, it turns toward a new sound source in order to show its attention, while with hostile personality, it turns away from a new sound source. As a receptionist robot with dominant personality, it focuses its attention on the current customer, while with submissive personality, its attention to the current customer is interrupted by a new one.

## 1 Introduction

Social interaction is essential for humanoid robots, because they are getting more common in social and home environments, such as a pet robot in a living room, a service robot at office, or a robot serving people at a party [4]. Social skills of such robots require robust complex perceptual abilities; for example, it identifies people in the room, pays attention to their voice and looks at them to identify, and associates voice and visual images. Intelligent behavior of social interaction should emerge from rich channels of input sensors; vision, audition, tactile, and others.

Perception of various kinds of sensory inputs should be *active* in the sense that we hear and see things and events that are important to us as individuals, not sound waves or light rays [7]. In other words, selective attention of sensors represented as looking

* This research was partially supported by the Ministry of Education, Culture, Sports, Science and Technology, Grant-in-Aid for Informatics, No.14019051, and Informatics Research Center for Development of Knowledge Society Infrastructure (COE program of MEXT, Japan)

P.W.H. Chung, C.J. Hinde, M. Ali (Eds.): IEA/AIE 2003, LNAI 2718, pp. 662–673, 2003.

versus seeing or listening versus hearing plays an important role in social interaction. Other important factors in social interaction are recognition and synthesis of emotion in face expression and voice tones [2, 3].

*Selectivity* and *capacity limitation* are two main factors in attention control [19]. A humanoid does some perception intentionally based on selectivity [23]. It also has some limitation in the number of sensors or processing capabilities, and thus only a limited number of sensory information is processed. Since selectivity and capacity limitation are the flip side of the same coin, only selectivity is argued in this paper. Selective attention of auditory processing called the *cocktail party effect* was reported by Cherry in 1953 [6]. At a crowded party, one can attend to one conversation and then change to another one. But the questions are to what one pays one's attention and how one changes one's attention.

*Personality* in selective attention consists in answers of these questions. Reeves and Nass use the *Five-Factor Model* in analyzing the personality of media including software agents [20]. The *big five* dimensions of personality are *Dominance/Submissiveness*, *Friendliness*, *Conscientiousness*, *Emotional Stability*, and *Openness*. Although these five dimensions generally define an human's basic personality, they are not appropriate to define humanoid's one, because the latter three dimensions cannot be applied to current capabilities of current humanoids.

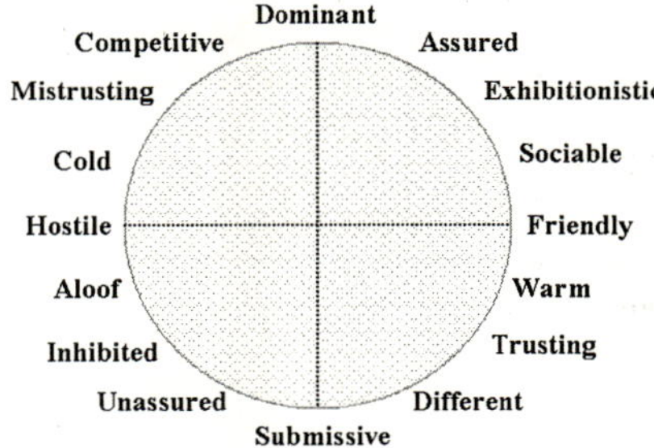


**Fig. 1.** Interpersonal Circumplex: variation of personality

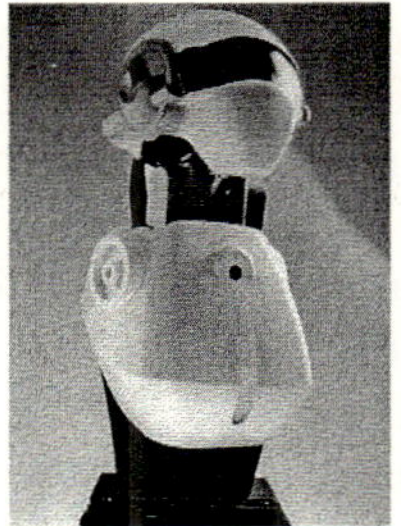

**Fig. 2.** *SIG* the Humanoid

We use the *Interpersonal Theory* instead for defining personality in selective attention. It deals with people's characteristic interaction patterns, as is shown in Figure 1, varying along the *Dominance/Submissiveness* and *Friendness/Hostility*. The variation is represented by the *interpersonal circumplex*, which is a circular model of the interpersonal domain of personality [11].

Physically embodied agents, or humanoid robots have no explicit personality as far as we know. Usually personality is emphasized in language generation, whether verbal or textual. Although the most important human communication means is language, non-verbal sensori-motor based behavior is non-the-less important. In this paper, we use personality to define attention control and report some observations of non-verbal interactions between humanoid and human.

### 1.1 Related Work

Personality for software agents are studied extensively. Bates and his group propose *believable agents* that can express emotion clearly in appropriately timed manner [1]. Cassell developed conversational agents that integrate face and gesture [5]. She also argues that implementation of conversational agents should be based on actual study of human-human interaction. Hayes-Roth organizes the Virtual Theater project, which studies the creation of intelligent, automated characters that can act either in well-defined stories or in improvisational environments [8].

Personality for robots are also investigated to widen communication channels in human-robot interaction, although some works mention personality explicitly.

Miwa *et al* have developed human-like head robots and implements personality to attain smooth and effective communication with human [13]. In their system, personality consists of the sensing personality and expression personality. The sensing personality determines how a stimulus works for a robot's mental state. Seven emotions were mapped out in the 3D mental space based on the *Five Factor Model*. Once the robot determines its emotion, it expresses its emotion based on the expression personality, which is represented by a matrix. They realized six kinds of personality in their robot.

Not a few works mention foucus of attention. Ono *et al.* use the robot called *Robovie* to make common attention between human and robot by using gestures [18]. Breazeal incorporates the capabilities of recognition and synthesis of emotion in face expression and voice tones into the robot called *Kismet* [2, 3]. Waldherr *et al.* makes the robot called *AMELLA* that can recognize pose and motion gestures [21]. Matsusaka *et al.* built the robot called *Hadaly* that can localize the talker as well as recognize speeches by speech-recognition system so that it can interact with multiple people [12]. Nakadai *et al* developed *real-time* auditory and visual multiple-tracking system for the upper-torso humanoid called *SIG* [14]. They extended the system to attain in-face interaction by incorporating *auditory fovea* that is the azimuth dependency in resolution of sound source localization [17].

Usually personality is emphasized in language generation, whether verbal or not. Although the most important human communication means is language, non-verbal sensori-motor based behavior is non-the-less important. In this paper, we use personality to define focus-of-attention control and report some observations of non-verbal interactions between humanoid and human.

## 2 Humanoid Hardware

As a testbed of integration of perceptual information to control motor of high degree of freedom (DOF), we designed a humanoid robot (hereafter, referred as *SIG*) with the following components:

- 4 DOFs of body driven by 4 DC motors — Each DC motor has a potentiometer to measure the direction.
- A pair of CCD cameras of Sony EVI-G20 for stereo vision input.
- Two pairs of omni-directional microphones (Sony ECM-77S). One pair of microphones are installed at the ear position of the head to collect sounds from the external

world. Each microphone is shielded by the cover to prevent from capturing internal noises. The other pair of microphones is to collect sounds within a cover.

- A cover of the body (Figure 2) reduces sounds to be emitted to external environments, which is expected to reduce the complexity of sound processing.
  This cover, made of FRP, is designed by our professional designer for making human robot interaction smoother as well [16].

## 3 Perceptual Systems in Real-Time Multiple-Talker Tracking

The real-time multiple-talker tracking system is designed based on the client/server model (Figure 3). Each server or client executes the following logical modules:

1. Audition client extracts auditory events by pitch extraction, sound source separation and localization, and sends those events to Association.
2. Vision client uses a pair of cameras, extracts visual events by face extraction, identification and localization, and then sends visual events to Association.
3. Motor client generates PWM (Pulse Width Modulation) signals to DC motors and sends motor events to Association.
4. Association module groups various events into a stream and maintains association and deassociation between streams.
5. Attention module selects some stream on which it should focus its attention and makes a plan of motor control.
6. Dialog client communicates with people according to its attention by speech synthesis and speech recognition. We use "Julian" automatic speech recognition system [10].

The status of each modules is displayed on each node. SIG server displays the radar chart of objects and the stream chart. Motion client displays the radar chart of the body

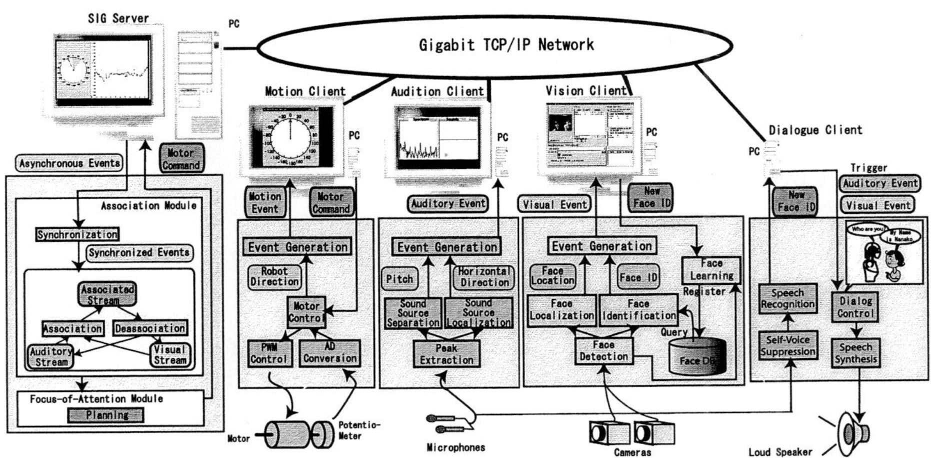


**Fig. 3.** Hierarchical architecture of real-time audio and visual tracking system

direction. Audition client displays the spectrogram of input sound and pitch (frequency) vs sound source direction chart. Vision client displays the image of the camera and the status of face identification and tracking.

To attain real-time tracking, the above modules are physically distributed to five Linux nodes connected by TCP/IP over Gigabit Ethernet TCP/IP network and run asynchronously. The system is implemented by distributed processing of five nodes with Pentium-IV 1.8 GHz. Each node serves Vision, Audition, Motion and Dialogue clients, and SIG server. The whole system upgrades the real-time multiple-talker tracking system [14] by introducing stereo vision systems, adding more nodes and Gigabit Ethernet and realizes social interaction system by designing association and attention control modules.

### 3.1 Active Audition Module

To localize sound sources with two microphones, first a set of peaks are extracted for left and right channels, respectively. Then, the same or similar peaks of left and right channels are identified as a pair and each pair is used to calculate interaural phase difference (IPD) and interaural intensity difference (IID). IPD is calculated from frequencies of less than 1500 Hz, while IID is from frequency of more than 1500 Hz.

Since auditory and visual tracking involves motor movements, which cause motor and mechanical noises, audition should suppress or at least reduce such noises. In human robot interaction, when a robot is talking, it should suppress its own speeches. Nakadai *et al* presented the *active audition* for humanoids to improve sound source tracking by integrating audition, vision, and motor controls [15]. We also use their heuristics to reduce internal burst noises caused by motor movements.

From IPD and IID, the epipolar geometry is used to obtain the direction of sound source [15]. The key ideas of their real-time active audition system are twofold; one is to exploit the property of the harmonic structure (fundamental frequency, $F0$, and its overtones) to find a more accurate pair of peaks in left and right channels. The other is to search the sound source direction by combining the belief factors of IPD and IID based on Dempster-Shafer theory.

Finally, audition module sends an auditory event consisting of pitch ($F0$) and a list of 20-best direction ($\theta$) with reliability for each harmonics.

### 3.2 Face Recognition and Identification Module

Vision extracts lengthwise objects such as persons from a disparity map to localize them by using a pair of cameras. First a disparity map is generated by an intensity based area-correlation technique. This is processed in real-time on a PC by a recursive correlation technique and optimization peculiar to Intel architecture [9].

In addition, left and right images are calibrated by affine transformation in advance. An object is extracted from a 2-D disparity map by assuming that a human body is lengthwise. A 2-D disparity map is defined by

$$DM_{2D} = \{D(i,j)|i = 1,2,\cdots W, j = 1,2,\cdots H\} \quad (1)$$

where $W$ and $H$ are width and height, respectively and $D$ is a disparity value.

As a first step to extract lengthwise objects, the median of $DM_{2D}$ along the direction of height shown as Eq. (2) is extracted.

$$D_l(i) = Median(D(i,j)). \tag{2}$$

A 1-D disparity map $DM_{1D}$ as a sequence of $D_l(i)$ is created.

$$DM_{1D} = \{D_l(i)|i = 1, 2, \cdots W\} \tag{3}$$

Next, a lengthwise object such as a human body is extracted by segmentation of a region with similar disparity in $DM_{1D}$. This achieves robust body extraction so that only the torso can be extracted when the human extends his arm. Then, for object localization, epipolar geometry is applied to the center of gravity of the extracted region. Finally, vision module sends a visual event consisting of a list of 5-best Face ID (Name) with its reliability and position (distance $r$, azimuth $\theta$ and elevation $\phi$) for each face.

### 3.3 Stream Formation and Association

Association synchronizes the results (events) given by other modules. It forms an auditory, visual or associated stream by their proximity. Events are stored in the short-term memory only for 2 seconds. Synchronization process runs with the delay of 200 msec, which is the largest delay of the system, that is, vision module.

An auditory event is connected to the nearest auditory stream within $\pm 10°$ and with common or harmonic pitch. A visual event is connected to the nearest visual stream within 40 cm and with common face ID. In either case, if there are plural candidates, the most reliable one is selected. If any appropriate stream is found, such an event becomes a new stream. In case that no event is connected to an existing stream, such a stream remains alive for up to 500 msec. After 500 msec of keep-alive state, the stream terminates.

An auditory and a visual streams are associated if their direction difference is within $\pm 10°$ and this situation continues for more than 50% of the 1 sec period. If either auditory or visual event has not been found for more than 3 sec, such an associated stream is deassociated and only existing auditory or visual stream remains. If the auditory and visual direction difference has been more than 30° for 3 sec, such an associated stream is deassociated to two separate streams.

## 4 Attention System with Personality

Attention control focuses on one of auditory, visual, or associated streams. This selective attention is basically performed at two level, that is personaly and task. To define personality, the interpersonal circumplex of the Interpersonal Theory is used. With its two mutually independent axes, dominant and friendly, variations of personality are *Dominant, Assured, Exhibitionistic, Sociable, Friendly, Warm, Trustaing, Different, Submissive, Unassured, Inhibited, Aloof, Hostile, Cold, Mistrusting*, and *Competitive* (Figure 1) [11].

Since these variations are represented as a circle (circumplex), each variation of personality is represented as a point, $(r, \theta)$, inside the interpersonal circumplex, where $0 \leq r \leq 1$ and $0 \leq \theta \leq 2\pi$. Therefore, the value of *Friendly/Hostile* axis and that of *Dominant/Submissive* axis are represented as $r\cos\theta$ and $r\sin\theta$, respectively. Each variation occupies a pie of $\pi/8$. For example, *Friendly* is specified as a pie section of $-\frac{\pi}{16} \sim \frac{\pi}{16}$, and *Dominant* as that of $\frac{3\pi}{16} \sim \frac{5\pi}{16}$.

To what the system attend is called "*interested*". The total amount of interest in the system keeps the same and a newly focused stream takes all the amount of interest in winner-take-all competition between streams. attention control module selects the stream of the largest interest. Three mental factors are defined.

1. interest in a new stream — When a new stream is generated, the stream gets interest according to its status, auditory, visual or associated. The initial value of interest for a new stream is given at the streeam generation.
2. decay of interest — The interest of a focused stream is reduced at the rate of $e^{-kT}$ every minute, where $k$ is $\{1.5$ - "the value of *Dominant/Submissive*"$\}$/3. The lost interest is distributed to other streams.
3. decay of belief — Disappeared stream still remains in the system, because a unseen talker resumes to talk after a short time of silence. If disappeared stream is deleted immediately, the continuity of stream is difficult to maintain. In this paper, the constant value is used for the decay factor of belief.

The initial value of interest for a new stream is determined by what kind of interaction the robot will attend. For task-oriented manner, an associated stream has the highest initial value, while for socially-oriented manner, any new stream has the equal oooportunity.

Task-oriented attention control forces Attention to behave according to a specific script. For example, a receptionist robot should focus on the user for whom an associated stream is generated. Therefore, the initial values of interest for auditory, visual and associated stream are 1, 1 and 2, respectively, in this paper. The essence of assignment is that the value for associated streams is highest.

Socially-oriented attention control forces Attention to show the interest of the robot. As an example of socially-oriented control, we implement a companion robot. It should pay attention to a new auditory or visual event, and thus all initial values of interest for any kind stream is the same, say 1 in this paper.

## 5 Experiments and Observation

Experiments was done with a small room in a normal residential apartment. The width, length and height of the room of experiment is about 3 m, 3 m, and 2 m, respectively. The room has 6 down-lights embedded on the ceiling. Two kinds of experiments are conducted in this section.

### 5.1 Task-Oriented Interaction: *SIG* as a Receptionist Robot

One scenario to evaluate the above control is specified as follows: (1) A known participant comes to the receptionist robot. His face has been registered in the face database. (2) He says Hello to *SIG*. (3) *SIG* replies "Hello. You are XXX-san, aren't you?" (4) He says "yes". (5) *SIG* says "XXX-san, Welcome to the party. Please enter the room.".

Figure 4 depicts two snapshots of this script. Figure 4 a) shows the initial state. The loud speaker on the stand is the mouth of *SIG*'s. When a participant comes to the receptionist, but *SIG* has not noticed him yet, because he is out of *SIG*'s sight. When he speaks to *SIG*, Audition generates an auditory event with sound source direction, and sends it to Association, which creates an auditory stream. This stream triggers Attention to make a plan that *SIG* should turn to him, and *SIG* does it (Figure 4 b)).

This experiment demonstrates *SIG*'s two interesting behaviors. One is voice-triggered tracking, and the other is that *SIG* does not pay attention to its own speech. As a receptionist robot, once an association is established, *SIG* keeps its face fixed to the direction of the talker of the associated stream. Therefore, even when *SIG* utters via a loud speaker on the left, *SIG* does not pay an attention to the sound source, that is, its own speech.

Another script is that a hostile *SIG* turns away from an associated stream. In Figure 5, when a participant says "Hello" to *SIG*, *SIG* turns away from him. The way of turn away depends on the absolute value of the *Friendly/Hostile* axis.

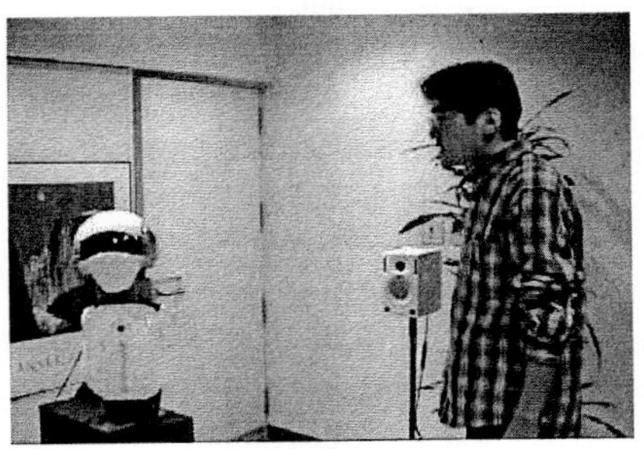

a) When a participant comes and says "Hello", *SIG* turns toward him.

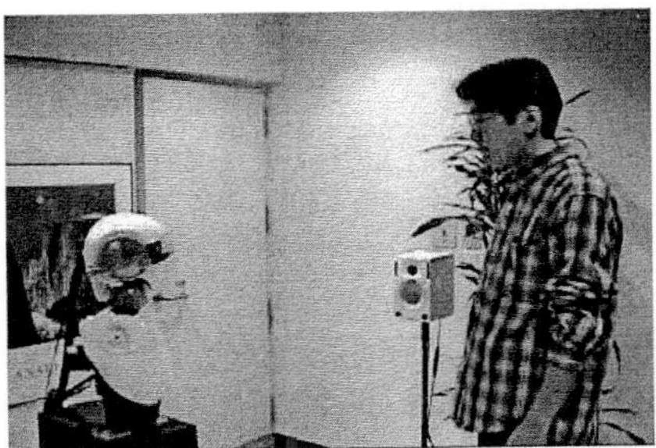

b) *SIG* asks his name and he introduces himself to it.

**Fig. 4.** Task-oriented Control of Friendly *SIG*

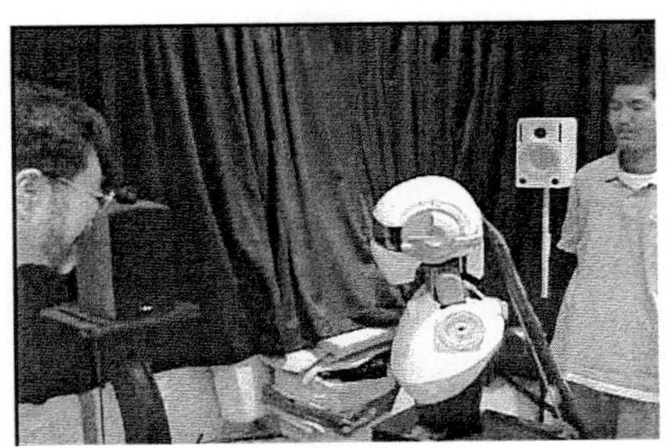

a) A participant says "Hello".

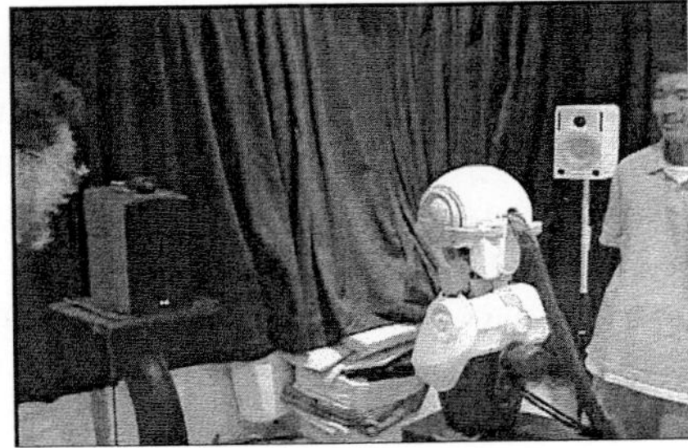

b) *SIG* turns away from him.

**Fig. 5.** Task-oriented Control of Hostile *SIG*

### 5.2 Socially-Orineted Interaction: *SIG* as a Companion Robot

When four talkers actually talks spontaneously in attendance of *SIG*, *SIG* tracks some talker and then changes focus-of-attention to others. The observed behavior is evaluated by checking the internal states of *SIG*; that is, auditory and visual localization shown in the radar chart, auditory, visual, and associated streams shown in the stream chart, and peak extraction as shown in Figure 6 a)∼b).

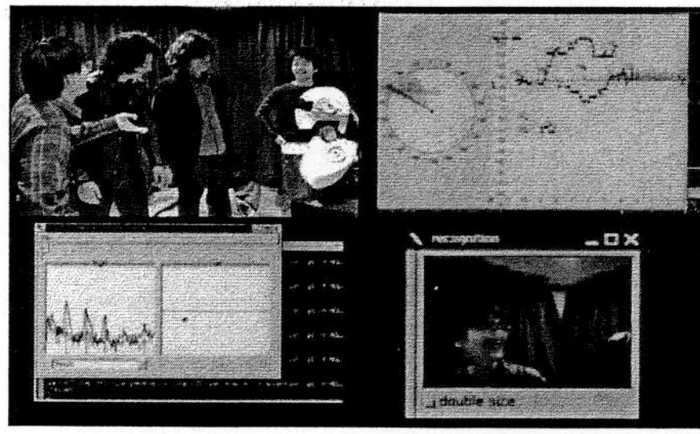

a) The leftmost man says "Hello" and SIG is tracking him.

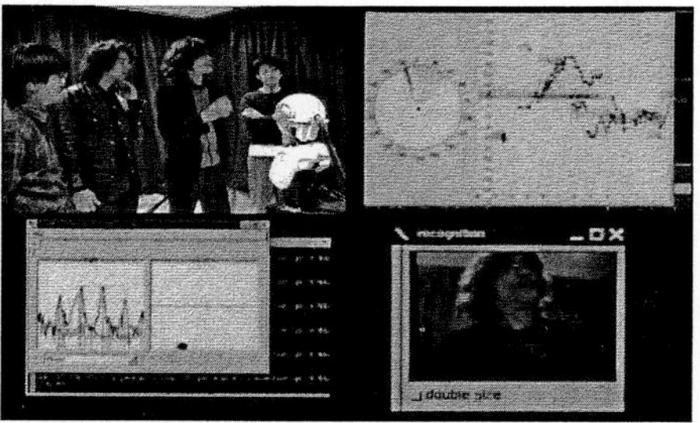

b) The second right man says "Hello" and SIG turns toward him.

**Fig. 6.** Temporal sequence of snapshots for a companion robot: scene (upper-left), radar and sequence chart (upper-right), spectrogram and pitch-vs-direction chart (lower-left), and face-tracking chart (lower-right).

The top-right image consists of the radar chart (left) and the stream chart (right) updated in real-time. The former shows the environment recognized by *SIG* at the moment of the snapshot. A pink sector indicates a visual field of *SIG*. Because of using the absolute coordinate, the pink sector rotates as *SIG* turns. A green point with a label is the direction and the face ID of a visual stream. A blue sector is the direction of an auditory stream. Green, blue and red lines indicate the direction of visual, auditory and associated stream, respectively. Blue and green *thin* lines indicate auditory and visual streams, respectively. Blue, green and red *thick* lines indicate associated streams with only auditory, only visual, and both information, respectively.

The bottom-left image shows the auditory viewer consisting of the power spectrum and auditory event viewer. The latter shows an auditory event as a filled circle with its pitch in X axis and its direction in Y axis.

The bottom-right image shows the visual viewer captured by the *SIG*'s left eye. A detected face is displayed with a red rectangle. The top-left image in each snapshot shows the scene of this experiment recorded by a video camera.

The temporal sequence of *SIG*'s recognition and actions shows that the design of companion robot works well and pays its attention to a new talker. The current system has attained a passive companion. To design and develop an active companion may be important future work.

### 5.3 Observation: *SIG* as a Non-verbal Eliza

As socially-oriented attention control, interesting human behaviors are observed. The mechanism of associating auditory and visual streams and that of socially-oriented attention control are explained in advance to the user.

1. Some people walk around talking with their hand convering *SIG*'s eyes in order to confirm the performance of auditory tracking.
2. Some people creep on the floor with talking in order to confirm the performacne of auditory tracking.
3. Some people play hide-and-seek games with *SIG*.
4. Some people play sounds from a pair of loud speakers with changing the balance control of pre-amplifier in order to confirm the performance of auditory tracking.
5. Whe one person reads loud a book and then another person starts to read loud a book, *SIG* with *Dominant* personality turns its head to the second talker for a short time and then is back to the first talker and keeps its attention on him/her. On the contrary, *SIG* with *Submissive* personality often turns its head to each talker. In either case, the value of $r$ is set to 1.

Above observations remind us of Eliza [22], although *SIG* does not say anything except a receptionist robot. When the user says something to *SIG*, it turns to him/her, which invites the participation of the user into interaction. *SIG* also invites exploration of the principles of its functioning, that is, the user is drawn in to see how *SIG* will respond to variations in behavior. Since *SIG* takes only passive behaviors, it does not arouse higher expectations of verisimilitude that it can deliver on.

Needless to say, there are lots of work remaining to validate the proposed approach for personality of artifacts. We are currently working to incorporate active social interaction by developing the capability of listneing to simultaneous speeches.

## 6 Conclusions

In this paper, we demonstrate that auditory and visual multiple-talker tracking subsystem can improve social aspects of human robot interaction. Although a simple scheme of behavior is implemented, human robot interaction is drastically improved by real-time multiple-talker tracking system. We can pleasantly spend an hour with *SIG* as a companion robot even if its behavior is quite passive.

Since the Interpersonal Theory research community provides software for analysing circumplex correlation matrices, we have plan to gather the data of user interaction to evaluate whether the presented architecture of selective attention based on personality realizes the target variation of personality. This persuit may lead to a general theory of personality for software agents and humanoid robots.

**Acknowledgments**

We thank our former colleagues of Symbiotic Intelligence Group, Kitano Symbiotic Systems Project for their discussions, and Prof. Tatsuya Kawahara of Kyoto University for his supports in using "Julius" automatic speech recognition system.

## References


1. Bates, J. The role of emotion in believable agents. *Comm. of the ACM 37*, 7 (1994), 122–125.
2. Breazeal, C., and Scassellati, B. A context-dependent attention system for a social robot. In *Proceedings of 16th International Joint Conference on Atificial Intelligence (IJCAI-1999)*, pp. 1146–1151.
3. Breazeal, C. Emotive qualities in robot speech. In *Proceedings of IEEE/RSJ International Conference on Intelligent Robots and Systems (IROS-2001)*, IEEE, pp. 1389–1394.
4. Brooks, R. A., Breazeal, C., Irie, R., Kemp, C. C., Marjanovic, M., Scassellati, B., and Williamson, M. M. Alternative essences of intelligence. In *Proceedings of 15th National Conference on Artificial Intelligence (AAAI-1998)*, pp. 961–968.
5. Cassell, J. More than just another pretty face: Embodied conversational interface agents. *Comm. of the ACM 43*, 4 (2000), 70–78.
6. Cherry, E. C. Some experiments on the recognition of speech, with one and with two ears. *Journal of Acoustic Society of America 25* (1953), 975–979.
7. Handel, S. *Listening*. The MIT Press, MA., 1989.
8. Hayes-Roth, B., Ball, G., Lisetti, C., Picard, R., and Stern, A. Affect and emotion in the user interface. In *Proceedings of 1998 International Conference on Intelligent User Interfaces* (1998), ACM, pp. 91–96.
9. Kagami, S., Okada, K., Inaba, M., and Inoue, H. Real-time 3d optical flow generation system. In *Proc. of International Conference on Multisensor Fusion and Integration for Intelligent Systems (MFI-1999)*, pp. 237–242.
10. Kawahara, T., Lee, A., Kobayashi, T., Takeda, K., Minematsu, N., Itou, K., Ito, A., Yamamoto, M., Yamada, A., Utsuro, T., and Shikano, K. Japanese dictation toolkit – 1997 version –. *Journal of Acoustic Society Japan (E) 20*, 3 (1999), 233–239.
11. Kiesler, D. The 1982 interpersonal circle: A taxonomy for complementarity in human transactions. *Psychological Review 90* (1993), 185–214.
12. Matsusaka, Y., Tojo, T., Kuota, S., Furukawa, K., Tamiya, D., Hayata, K., Nakano, Y., and Kobayashi, T. Multi-person conversation via multi-modal interface — a robot who communicates with multi-user. In *Proceedings of 6th European Conference on Speech Communication Technology (EUROSPEECH-1999)*, ESCA, pp. 1723–1726.
13. Miwa, H., Takanishi, A., and Takanobu, H. Experimental study on robot personality for humanoid head robot. In *Proceedings of 2001 IEEE/RSJ International Conference on Intelligent Robots and Systems (IROS 2001)*, IEEE, pp. 1183–1188.
14. Nakadai, K., Hidai, K., Mizoguchi, H., Okuno, H. G., and Kitano, H. Real-time auditory and visual multiple-object tracking for robots. In *Proceedings of 17th International Joint Conference on Artificial Intelligence (IJCAI-2001)*, IJCAI, pp. 1425–1432.
15. Nakadai, K., Lourens, T., Okuno, H. G., and Kitano, H. Active audition for humanoid. In *Proc. of 17th National Conference on Artificial Intelligence (AAAI-2000)*, AAAI, pp. 832–839.
16. Nakadai, K., Matsui, T., Okuno, H. G., and Kitano, H. Active audition system and humanoid exterior design. In *Proceedings of IEEE/RAS International Conference on Intelligent Robots and Systems (IROS 2000)*, IEEE, pp. 1453–1461.
17. Nakadai, K., Okuno, H. G., and Kitano, H. Exploiting auditory fovea in humanoid-human interaction. In *Proceedings of 18th National Conference on Artificial Intelligence (AAAI-2002)*, AAAI, pp. 431–438.
18. Ono, T., Imai, M., and Ishiguro, H. A model of embodied communications with gestures between humans and robots. In *Proceedings of Twenty-third Annual Meeting of the Cognitive Science Society (CogSci2001)*, AAAI, pp. 732–737.
19. Pashler, H. *The Psychology of Attention*. The MIT Press, MA., 1997.

20. Reeves, B., and Nass, C. *The Media Equation: How People Treat Computers, Television, and New Media Like Real People and Places*. Cambridge University Press, Cambridge, UK, 1996.
21. Waldherr, S., Thrun, S., Romero, R., and Margaritis, D. Template-based recoginition of pose and motion gestures on a mobile robot. In *Proceedings of 15th National Conference on Artificial Intelligence (AAAI-1998)*, AAAI, pp. 977–982.
22. Weizenbaum, J. Eliza – a computer program for the study of natural language communication between man and machine. *Communications of the ACM 9*, 1 (1966), 36–45.
23. Wolfe, J., Cave, K. R., and Franzel, S. Guided search: An alternative to the feature integration model for visual search. *Journal of Experimental Psychology: Human Perception and Performance 15*, 3 (1989), 419–433.

# Improving the Predictive Power of AdaBoost: A Case Study in Classifying Borrowers

Natthaphan Boonyanunta[1,2] and Panlop Zeephongsekul[1]

[1] Department of Mathematics and Statistics, RMIT University, Melbourne, Australia
panlopz@rmit.edu.au
[2] Experian Asia Pacific, Melbourne, Australia
natthaphan.boonyanunta@au.experian.com,

**Abstract.** Boosting is one of the recent major developments in classification methods. The technique works by creating different versions of a classifier using an adaptive resampling procedure and then combining these classifiers using weighted voting. In this paper, several modifications of the original version of boosting, the AdaBoost algorithm introduced by Y. Freund and R.E. Schapire in 1996, will be explained. These will be shown to substantially improve the predictive power of the original version. In the first modification, weighted error estimation in AdaBoost is replaced by unweighted error estimation and this is designed to reduce the impact of observations that possess large weight. In the second modification, only a selection of base classifiers, i.e. those that contribute significantly to predictive power of the boosting model, will be included in the final model. In addition to these two modifications, we will also utilise different classification techniques as base classifiers in order to product a final boosting model. Applying these proposed modifications to three data sets from the banking industry provides results which indicate a significant and substantial improvement in predictive power over the original AdaBoost algorithm.

## 1 Introduction

Boosting is one of several well known methods which is used to improve the predictive power of a classification technique. The idea of boosting was first proposed in the computational learning literature in 1990 [1]. In its generic form, boosting refers to a procedure which is capable of producing a very accurate classification rule by combing rather weak base classifiers [2]. One of the most well known boosting algorithm currently in use is the so called AdaBoost, which was introduced by Freund and Schapire in 1996 [3]. In AdaBoost, a classification algorithm is sequentially developed using reweighted versions of the original training data and the final classification model is obtained by taking a weighted majority vote of the sequence of classifiers thus produced [4]. Recent researches have shown that boosting significantly improved the performance of a classification technique on both simulated and real data sets ([3],[4],[5]).

The algorithm underlying AdaBoost will be discussed in Section 2. Although this is well known and widely disseminated in the literature, we have included it because a detailed description of the procedures will aid the reader in understanding how the

P.W.H. Chung, C.J. Hinde, M. Ali (Eds.): IEA/AIE 2003, LNAI 2718, pp. 674–685, 2003.

modifications we are proposing fit into the original scheme. We then apply AdaBoost to our data sets using classification trees as base classifiers. Contrary to our expectation, the results obtained were disappointing. This then provided us with the impetus to modify the AdaBoost algorithm in the following sections with the objective to improve its predictive power.

In Section 3, we introduce a simple modification of the AdaBoost algorithm in which weighted error estimation at each step of the boosting process is replaced by unweighted error estimation. The empirical results obtained clearly shows that this modification improves the predictive power of the original AdaBoost.

A second modification to AdaBoost is introduced in Section 4. Here, we select only some highly predictive classifiers out of all base classifiers produced by AdaBoost and use these in the final boosting model. This modification involves a reordering of base classifiers in order to differentiate between the highly predictive classifiers from the less predictive ones and then remove the ones that do not contribute to the over all predictive power of the boosting model. The empirical results again show that improvement in predictive power can be achieved using this approach.

To the best of our knowledge, past researches use only a single classification technique to develop base classifiers for a boosting model. Since each technique has its own characteristic approach in searching for patterns in a data set, it is likely that by combining different classification techniques using boosting algorithm, we would expect that further improvement in predictive power will be achieved. A motivation behind this approach is also based on the study of Krogh and Vedelsby [6] and Webb [7] which concluded that increase in disagreements of predictions by committee members without affecting their individual error rates can increase the predictive power of an ensemble. Since employing different classification techniques in a boosting model would tend to increase the disparity between base classifiers in their predictions, we would expect further improvement in the performances to be achieved if the conclusion of the aforementioned studies is valid. In this paper, logistic regression, multilayered neural networks with backpropagation learning algorithm and classification tree are used as base classifiers.

## 2 AdaBoost Algorithm

Assume we have training data $(x_1, y_1), (x_2, y_2) \ldots, (x_N, y_N)$ where $x_i$ is vector of input values and $y_i$ = +1 or -1. Boosting begins by assigning equal resampling weight, i.e. resampling probability, to all observations in the training data. At step m in a boosting process, the new training data set is generated by bootstrap sampling from the original training data set using resampling weight $w_i^{(m)}$. After the classifier based on this resampled training data set is developed, it is then applied to the original training data set in order to obtain the classification error which is used to update the sampling weight in the next step, i.e. $w_i^{(m+1)}$. At the end of M steps, the base classifiers are combined using weighted voting. The number of steps in a boosting process, i.e. M, is predetermined by the model developer. The boosting algorithm is summarised in the following steps.

- Start with weights $w_i^{(1)} = 1/N, \quad i = 1,2,\ldots,N$
- Repeat for m = 1,2,3,…,M;

  a) Fit the classifier $f_m(x) \in \{-1,1\}$ using weight $w_i^{(m)}$ on the training data

  b) Let $d_i$ = 1 if the ith case is classified incorrectly, otherwise zero. Then compute error $E_m$ where

$$E_m = \sum_{i=1}^{N} w_i^{(m)} d_i \,. \tag{1}$$

  c) Update weight of step m+1 by

$$w_i^{(m+1)} = w_i^{(m)} \beta_m^{d_i} \Big/ \sum_{i=1}^{N} w_i^{(m)} \beta_m^{d_i} \text{, where } \beta_m = (1 - E_m)/E_m \tag{2}$$

- After M steps, the $f_1(x),\ldots,f_m(x)$ are combined using weighted voting with $f_m$ having weight of $\log(\beta_m)$, i.e. the algorithm outputs

$$F(x) = sign\left(\sum_{m=1}^{M} \log(\beta_m) f_m(x)\right). \tag{3}$$

We applied the above AdaBoost algorithm to our data sets taken from the banking industry and used classification trees [8] as base classifiers. The number of base classifiers in the boosting model was set at 30. Before summarising the results that were obtained, we briefly provide a detailed description of our data sets used in this study, i.e. data set 1, 2 and 3.

Data sets 1 & 2 contain account information and financial transaction information of existing borrowers with their subsequent credit performance information. These two data sets contain 7,600 and 7,000 observations respectively. Half of each data set is the information on good credit risk borrowers and the remainder are the information on the poor credit risk borrowers. Our objective was to predict future performance of existing borrowers using their current account and financial transaction information. This classification problem is widely known in banking industry as *behavioural scoring* [9]. Data set 3 contains application information and performance information of 6,200 home loan borrowers. Half of the data set is the information on the borrowers who repay their loan in advance by more than 6 months and the remainder on borrowers who do not repay their loan in advance. For this data set, our objective was to predict the likelihood of the borrowers repaying their loan in advance by more than 6 months.

We partitioned each data set into 3 subsets: training, validation and test set. Training data set was used to develop the initial classifier. However, a classifier developed using only training data set tends to over-fit the data and performs poorly on unseen data. Validation data set was therefore required to estimate some parameters of the model in order to reduce the incidence of overfitting. For example, a classification tree is developed using the training data set and then pruned by validation data set. Lastly, the predictive power of a classification model is assessed using the test data set.

In this study, 60% of data is used for training, 20% for validation and the remaining 20% for testing. We note that the total number of cases in Data Set 1 & 2 and 3 are 7,600, 7000 and 6200 respectively. In Figure 1 below, the predictive power of AdaBoost applied to our three data sets are displayed.

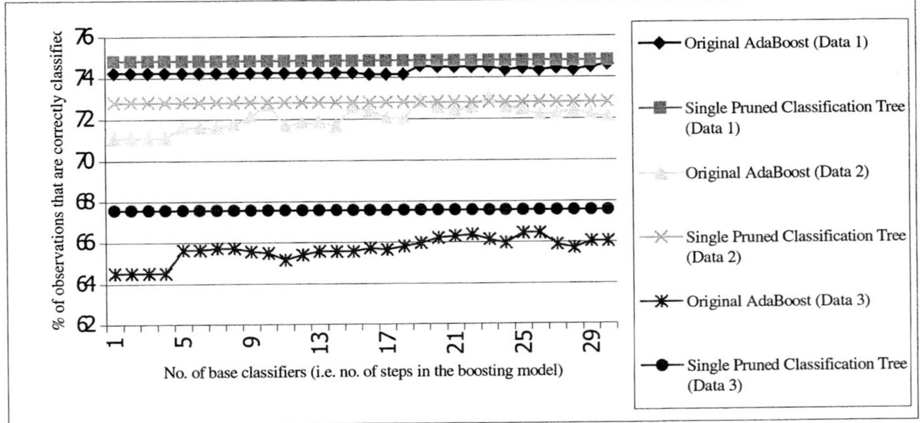


**Fig. 1.** Predictive power of AdaBoost using classifier tree as base classifiers compared with the predictive power of a single pruned classification tree on data set 1,2,3

Performances of AdaBoost on these data sets are somewhat below expectation. After running boosting for 30 steps, their predictive power on the test data sets are no better than those of single prune classification trees. Although, the results show that the predictive powers on test data sets tend to improve as the number of base classifiers increases. Nevertheless, the rate of improvement is very small and shows a steady decline as more base classifiers are used.

In the next two figures, we display the values of $\beta_m$ and $E_m$ for boosting step m = 1,2,…,30 using our data sets. Notice that $E_m$ increases very rapidly after a few steps and reaches a plateau of around 0.5 for the duration of the process. This is also mirrored in the rapid decline of $\beta_m$ reaching 1 after a very few steps. One of the reasons given for the success of AdaBoost in boosting the predictive power of a relatively weak learner at each step is its ability to learn from errors made in the previous steps. This is achieved through the addition of a base classifier developed using resampled cases that contains a large proportion of misclassified cases from the previous steps. Since during step m, the weights are updated through $\beta_m$ and these weights determine the cases selected at step m+1, the rapid decline to 1 of $\beta_m$ means that no further improvement in the predictive power will be forthcoming as new classifiers are added to the existing ones. This explains the poor performances of AdaBoost on our data sets.

The following Figure 2 and 3 show the value of error and $\beta_m$ at each step of the boosting processes.

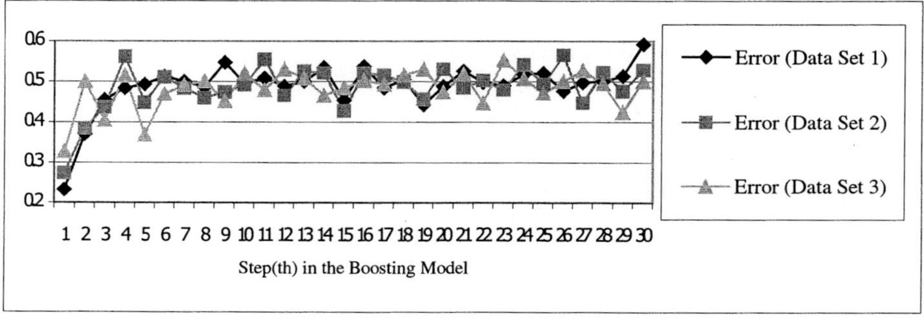


**Fig. 2.** Misclassification error at each boosting step

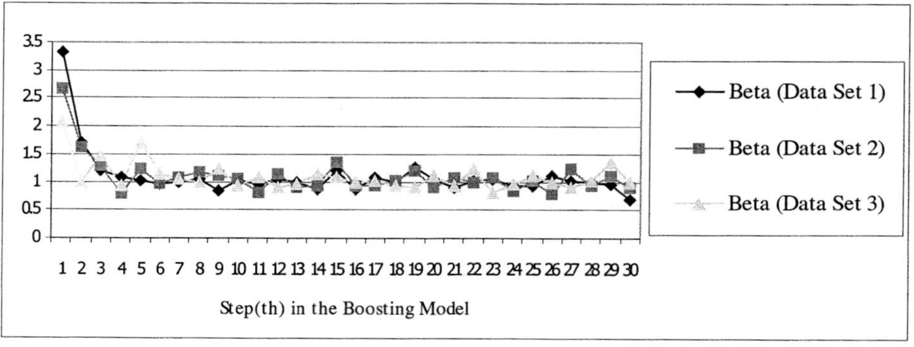


**Fig. 3.** Value of Beta $(\beta_m)$ at each boosting step

## 3 Unweighted Error Boosting

In this section, we look at the performances of AdaBoost after weighted error in step (b) of the algorithm is replaced by unweighted error. Specifically, at each step m of the algorithm, we use the uniformly weighted error

$$E_m = \sum_{i=1}^{N} w_i^{(1)} d_i = \frac{1}{N} \sum_{i=1}^{N} d_i \,. \tag{4}$$

I.e. the error at each step is calculated based on an uniform selection of the cases. This estimation of error will have the effect of reducing the impact of cases that are frequently misclassified and therefore heavily weighted during the resampling process. It is precisely these frequently misclassified cases that contribute to the sharp increase in error at each stage resulting in a decline in the value of $\beta_m$ which led to the poor performance of AdaBoost.

We apply unweighted error estimation to develop a boosting model consisting of 30 classification trees. Figure 4 below shows the results obtained using this approach.

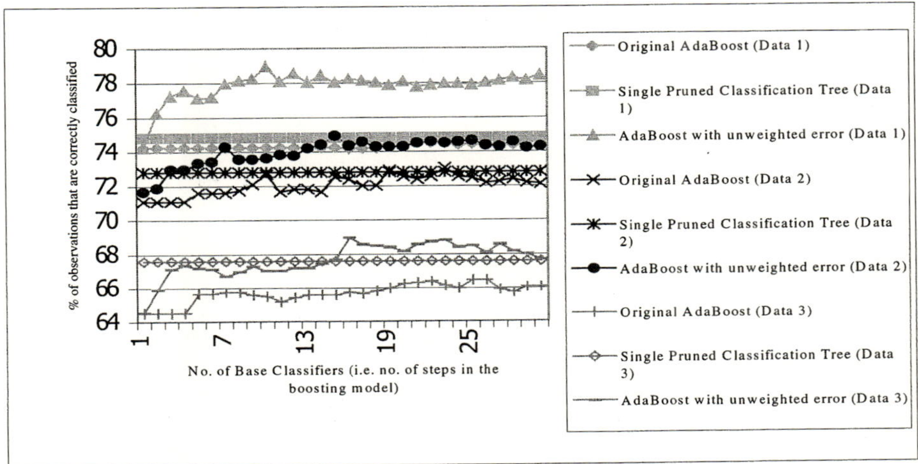


**Fig. 4.** Predictive power of AdaBoost compared with the predictive power of Unweighted Error AdaBoost on data set 1,2,3

Comparing this figure with Figure 1, it is clear that a significant improvement in predictive power has been achieved using unweighted error estimation. The predictive power on test data sets are improved approximately by 4%, 2% and 2% for Data Set 1,2 and 3 respectively. Note that further improvement in predictive power can be achieved by using less than 30 base classifiers for all data sets. For example, using only 17 base classifiers on data set 3 results in around 1% improvement in predictive power over that of using 30 base classifiers. The results obtained also shows that the predictive power increases rapidly initially, then the rate of improvement steadily decline as more base classifiers are added. This relationship is similar to results obtained by Schapire et. al. [10] and Webb [7].

In figure 5 below, we plot the values of $\beta_m$ for Data Set 1 using this modification of AdaBoost and compare them with those values obtained using the original AdaBoost. Similar results were obtained using the other two data sets. Notice how the values of $\beta_m$ for the modified AdaBoost stay above 1 and does not rapidly drop to 1 as exhibited by the original AdaBoost. The effect of this is to increase sampling weights of misclassified cases so that these have an elevated chance of being selected to form the classifier in the next stage. Since boosting works by learning from past errors, this process therefore certainly lead to an improvement in predictive power of the final model.

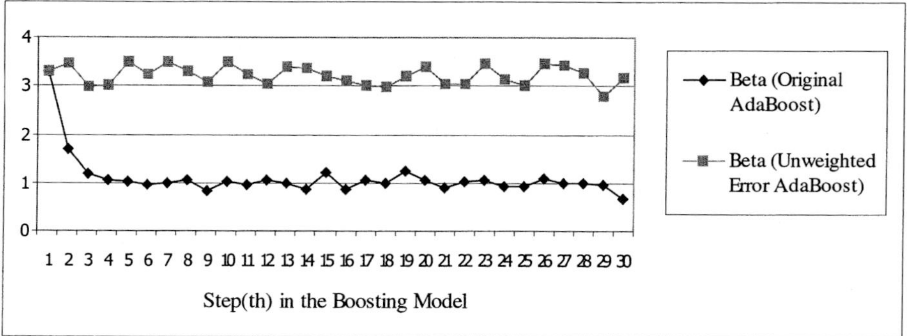


**Fig. 5.** Values of beta $\beta_m$ on data set 1

# 4 Reordering of Base Classifiers

In this section, we introduce another approach which will be shown to improve the predictive power of the original AdaBoost algorithm. It is based on the assumption that in order to obtain the most predictive boosting model, all base classifiers developed by the original AdaBoost algorithm may not have to be included in the final boosting model. By using only some selected base classifiers in the final model, a boosting model with a superior predictive power may be obtained.

The main idea of this approach is to group highly predictive base classifiers together to allow them to be combined without any interference from less predictive base classifiers. This approach involves two steps. Firstly, we reorder all the base classifiers in the final model according to their predictive power. Since a highly predictive classifier would tend to have low classification error rate ($E_m$) and hence a large coefficient $\log(\beta_m)$, the classifiers are reordered according to these coefficients. Secondly, we identify the optimum number of base classifiers for the final boosting model. This can be done by observing the trend of improvement in predictive power on the validation data set as more base classifiers are added according to reordering scheme. Each base classifier is included in the final boosting model as long as it contributes to an improvement in predictive power. We note that using more than optimum number of base classifiers will result in no significant improvement in predictive power of the final model.

As an example illustrating the above method, suppose we have developed a boosting model using 5 base classifiers with the result

$$F(x) = sign(0.4f_1(x) + 0.9f_2(x) + 1.1f_3(x) + 0.6f_4(x) + 1.2f_5(x))$$

In the classifier reordering approach, the order in which the base classifiers are added follow the following sequence:

$$f_5(x) \rightarrow f_3(x) \rightarrow f_2(x) \rightarrow f_4(x) \rightarrow f_1(x)$$

Once all the base classifiers have been reordered, we apply this reordered model to the validation data set and then plot the graph of predictive power versus the number of base classifiers. We then determine the optimum number of base classifiers in the final boosting as the point where there will be no significant improvement in the predictive power regardless of how many more base classifiers are added.

Next, we apply our 'reordering of base classifiers' approach to our data sets. The results obtained are shown in the Figure 6.

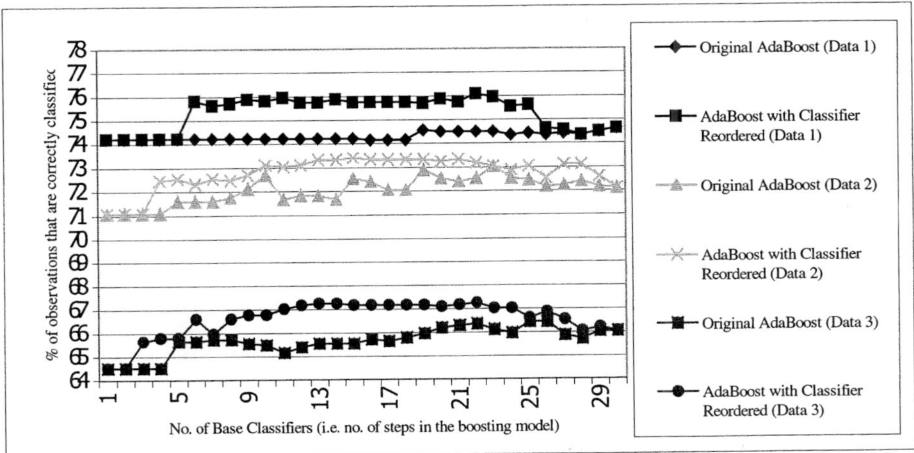


**Fig. 6.** Predictive power of the original AdaBoost when the 'Base Classifier Reordering' was applied.

The obtained results indicate that the predictive power of AdaBoost improves after the 'reordering of base classifier' approach was applied. The improvement in the predictive power is significant in almost all steps in the boosting model on all data sets. According to the graphical plot showing the relationship between the number of base classifiers and predictive power of boosting models displayed in Figures 6, we need only 6, 15, 13 base classifiers in the boosting models for the optimum predictive power on data set 1, 2 and 3 respectively. Using more than 6, 15, 13 base classifiers results in either no significant improvement or even a slight deterioration in the predictive power.

It is important to note that by adopting this approach, we have removed a large number of base classifiers that do not contribute to the improvement the overall predictive power of a boosting model. By combining only highly predictive base classifiers, Figure 6 shows that the performances achieved are even better than those without using 'reordering of base classifiers'.

## 5 Combining Different Classification Techniques in Boosting

In this section we explore the consequences of combining different classification techniques in boosting rather than just using a single technique. The reason for combining different technique is due mainly to the fact that since each technique has its own unique approach in searching for pattern in a data set, combining different techniques should lead to more cases being correctly classified thus leading to a final model which has a higher predictive power. Two approaches are proposed to determine which technique is to be deployed to produce a base classifier at each boosting step. Based on the empirical results discussed in Section 3, we will continue to use unweighted error estimation in developing a base classifier in order to improve the efficiency of the final boosting model.

For both approaches, a selection of n classification techniques will be used to develop the final boosting model. We will assume M = kn where k is a positive integer greater than 1. The following steps describe the first approach.

- At step m = 1
  1. apply n techniques to develop n base classifiers;
  2. run n base classifiers on training data to obtain predictive power of each classifier;
  3. select the best performing classifier which will be used at this step.
- At step m+1, m = 1,2,3,…,n
  1. apply the techniques which have not been selected in the previous steps, i.e. step 1,2,3,…,m, to develop base classifiers;
  2. run classifiers on training data to obtain predictive power of each classifier;
  3. select the best performing technique to be used at this step.
- The sequence of techniques used in the first n steps is repeated in the next n steps and so on (k times) until m = M.

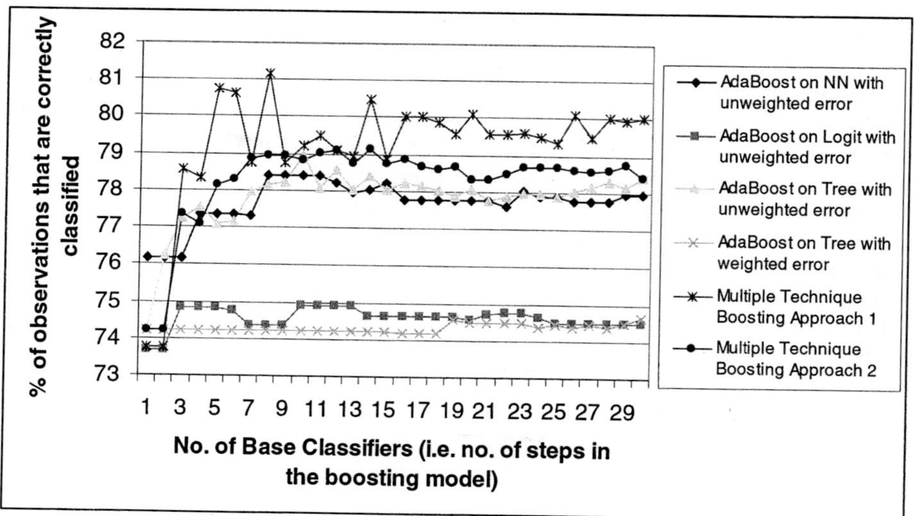


**Fig. 7.** Predictive power of multiple technique boosting models compared to other approaches on data set 1.

Note that this approach allows all techniques to have an equal chance of being involved in developing the final boosting model. The second approach differs from the first one only in the first stage of step m+1 which is replaced by

- At step m+1, m = 1,2,3,...,n
  1. apply the techniques which have not been selected in the previous step, i.e. step m to develop base classifiers;

Notice that there is less constraint placed on the selection of classifier to be used at each stage in the second approach than in the first. The main reason behind this approach is based on the fact that since resampled data at step m+1 will usually contain a large proportion of cases that are misclassified at step m, therefore the technique that has already been selected at step m should not be used again in the next step. Other classification techniques are likely to perform better on this resampled data.

We applied the above approaches to our data sets and compared the predictive power of the final models with the boosting models using only a single technique. Neural Networks, Logistic Regression and classification tree were used. We again set the number of boosting steps at M=30. The results are displayed in the figures below.

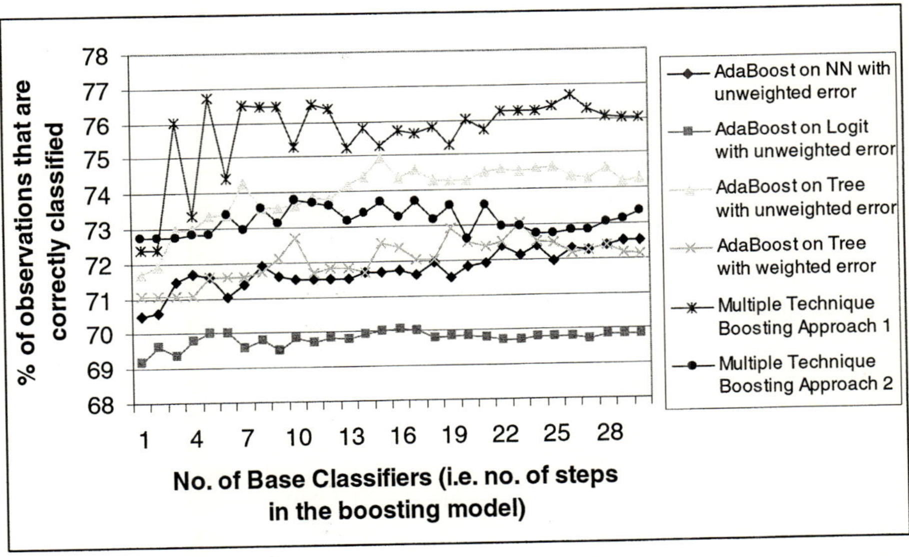


**Fig. 8.** Predictive power of multiple technique boosting models on data set 2.

For all data sets, our empirical results show that boosting approaches that use several classification techniques can improve the performances of the models which only use a single technique. This is especially true for data set 1 where both approaches produce boosting models which outperform models using only a single technique to produce the base classifiers. For data set 2, the first multiple technique boosting approach significantly outperforms the second approach and all single technique boosting models. For data set 3, the result is different: the first multiple technique boosting performs poorly whereas the second approach performed relatively well. The second approach outperform other techniques when the number of steps exceed 24. The reason for this anomaly is unclear to us but could be due to the different structure of data pattern contains in data set 3 to those contain in data set 1 and 2. Nevertheless and most importantly, either one or both of boosting model where multiple techniques are employed can outperform all single technique boosting on all three data sets.

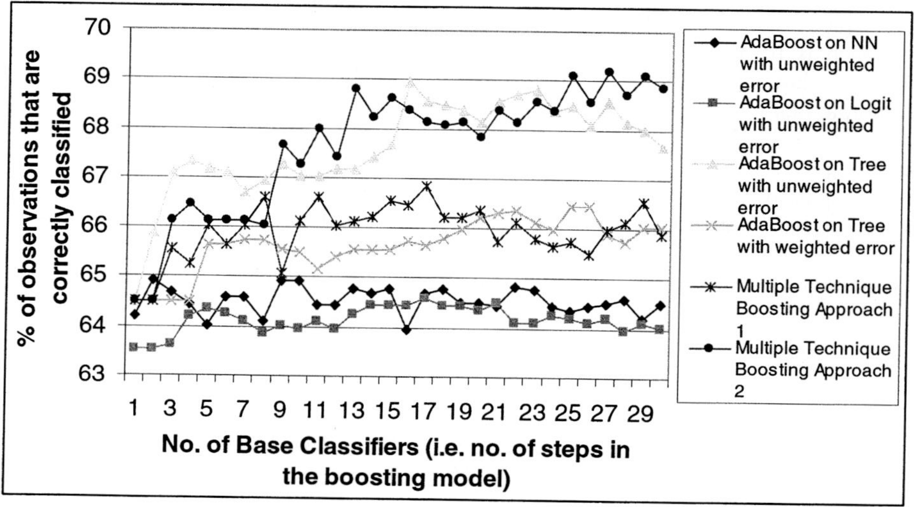


**Fig. 9.** Predictive power of multiple technique boosting models on data set 3.

## 6 Conclusion

In this paper, several variations of the original AdaBoost algorithm are proposed and developed. These modifications involve using unweighted error estimation, the reordering of base classifiers and combining different classification techniques to develop a boosting model. When applied to real data sets, these have shown to significantly improve the predictive power of original AdaBoost on our real data sets.

From the empirical results obtained by applying 'reordering base classifiers' approach, we could divide boosting process into 2 separate processes. The first process involves the improvement of each individual base classifier based on the misclassification in the previous steps. The second process involves the selection and combination of these base classifiers into the final boosting model. Our results indicate that it is not necessary to incorporate all base classifiers which were developed by AdaBoost algorithm into the final model. Using only some selected base classifiers may results in a higher predictive power achieved as shown in this study.

Finally, as AdaBoost was developed to improve the classification process in learning theory, it will be interesting to see whether the modification proposed in this paper can be applied to other forms of boosting which are given in Friedman [4] and have applications to general pattern recognition problem.

## References


1. Schapire, R. E.: The strength of weak learnability. Machine Learning **5** (1990) 197-227
2. Freund, Y.,Schapire, R.: A decision-theoretic generalization of on-line learning and an application to boosting. *J. Comput. System Sci.* **55** (1997) 119-139
3. Freund, Y., Schapire, R.: Experiment with a new boosting algorithm. In Machine Learning: Proceedings of the Thirteenth International Conferences (L. Saitta, ed.). Morgan Kaufmann, San Francisco (1996) pp 148-156
4. Friedman, J., Hastie, T., Tibshirani, R.: Additive Logistic Regression: A Statistical View of Boosting. The Annals of Statistics **28(2)** (2000) 337-407
5. Breiman, L.: Arcing Classifiers. The Annals of Statistics **26(3)** (1998) 801-849
6. Krogh, A., Vedelsby, J.: Neural network ensembles, cross validation, and active learning. Tesauro, G., Touretzky, D., Leen, T. (Eds.), Advances in Neural Information Processing Systems, Vol. 7. MIT Press, Boston, MA (1995)
7. Webb, G. I.: MultiBoosting: A Technique for Combining Boosting and Wagging. Machine Learning. **40** (2000) 159-196
8. Breiman, L., Friedman, J. H., Olshen, R. A., Stone, C. J.: Classification and Regression Trees. Wadsworth Internation Group, Belmont, CA (1984)
9. Thomas, L. C.: A survey of credit and behavioural scoring: forecasting finance risk of lending to consumers. International Journal of Forecasting **16** (2000) 149-172
10. Schapire, R., Freund, Y., Bartlett, P. , Lee, W. S.: Boosting the margin: A new explanation for effectiveness of voting methods. The Annals of Statistics. **26** (1998) 1651-1686

# Proposition of the Quality Measure for the Probabilistic Decision Support System

Michal Wozniak

Chair of Systems and Computer Networks, Wroclaw University of Technology, Wybrzeze Wyspianskiego 27, 50-370 Wroclaw, Poland
wozniak@zssk.pwr.wroc.pl

**Abstract.** Paper deals with the knowledge acquisition process. For the decision support systems type we consider we can get the rules from different sources (experts). Each rule has not logical interpretation, but probabilistic one. Proposed method of the knowledge quality management modifies the probabilities given by expert on the basis of their qualities.

## 1 Introduction

Machine learning is the attractive approach for building decision support systems[7]. For this type of software, the quality of the knowledge base plays the key-role. In many cases we can meet following problems:

- the experts can not formulate the rules for decision problem, because they might not have the knowledge needed to develop effective algorithms, but we can get the learning data and experts only classify each record to the correct class,
- the knowledge given by experts is uncompleted or qualities of experts (knowledge sources) are different for each of them.

For the first problem machine learning algorithms can give us the set of rules on the base on the learning set, but we have to answer following question:

1. Who made the object description? (Can we trust the operator?)
2. Who did confirm the diagnosis and what was the quality of the expert?

In the second problem we get the rules from different experts and their qualities are different. The paper deals with problem where only the qualities of experts are important. This problems was described for the induction learning [1,2,6]. The following paper concerns on rules qualities for the probabilistic reasoning.

The content of the work is as follow: Section 2 introduces necessary background and provides the probabilistic decision problem statement. Next section presents the form of rule for the probabilistic expert systems and proposes the rule-based algorithm. Section 4 defines statistical confidence measure of the knowledge and shows how modify the knowledge base according to confidence measure of rules. Section 5 presents the interpretation of proposed measure for the estimation process based on the typical statistical model. The last section concluded the paper.

P.W.H. Chung, C.J. Hinde, M. Ali (Eds.): IEA/AIE 2003, LNAI 2718, pp. 686–691, 2003.

## 2 Decision Problem Statement

Among the different concepts and methods of using "uncertain" information in pattern recognition, an attractive from the theoretical point of view and efficient approach is through the Bayes decision theory. This approach consists of assumption [4] that the feature vector $x=(x^{(1)},x^{(2)},...,x^{(d)})$ (describing the object being under recognition) and number of class $j\in\{1,2...,M\}$ (the object belonged to) are the realization of the pair of the random variables $X$, $J$. For example in medical diagnosis $X$ describes the result of patient examinations and $J$ denotes the patient state. Random variable $J$ is described by the prior probability $p_j$, where

$$p_j = P(J = j), \tag{1}$$

$X$ has probability density function

$$f(X = x|J = j) = f_j(x) \tag{2}$$

for each $j$ which is named conditional density function. These parameters can be used to enumerating *posterior* probability according to Bayes formulae:

$$p(j|x) = p_j f_j(x) \bigg/ \sum_{k=1}^{M} p_j f_j(x). \tag{3}$$

The formalisation of the recognition in the case under consideration implies the setting of a optimal Bayes decision algorithm $\Psi(x)$, which minimizes probability of misclassification for 0-1 loss function[3]:

$$\Psi(x) = i \text{ if } p(i|x) = \max_{k\in\{1,...,M\}} p(k|x). \tag{4}$$

In the real situation the *prior* probabilities and the conditional density functions are usually unknown, but we can use the rules and/or the learning set for the constructing decision algorithms.

## 3 Rule-Based Decision Algorithm

The wide numbers of the machine learning algorithms can generate the decision rules. This form of learning information is the most popular form for the logical decision support systems. For systems we consider the rules given by experts have rather the statistical interpretation than logical one.

### 3.1 Available Learning Information

The form of rule for the probabilistic decision support system[5] is usually as follow

`if A then B with the probability` $\beta$,

where $\beta$ is interpreted as the estimator of the *posterior* probability $(\beta = P(B|A))$.

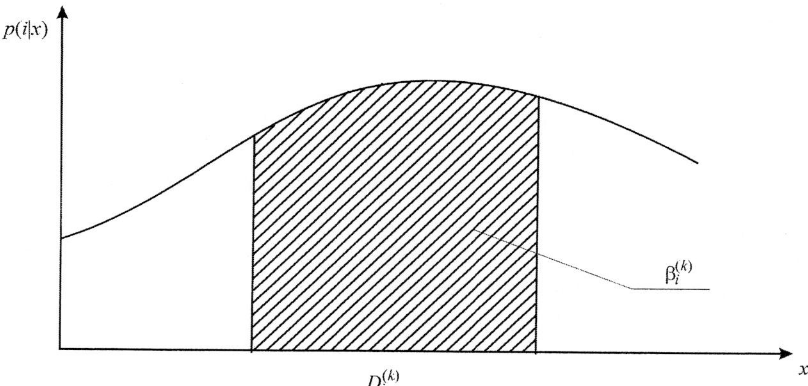


**Fig. 1.** Graphical interpretation of the *posterior* probability estimator given by the expert rule

More precisely, in the case of the human knowledge acquisition process, experts are not disposed to formulate the exact value of the $\beta$, but he (or she) rather prefers to give the interval for its value

$$\underline{\beta} \leq \beta \leq \overline{\beta}.$$

The analysis of different practical examples leads to the following forms of rule $r_i^{(k)}$:

IF $x \in D_i^{(k)}$ `THEN state of object is` $i$ `WITH posterior probability` $\beta_i^{(k)}$ `grater than` $\underline{\beta}_i^{(k)}$ `and less than` $\overline{\beta}_i^{(k)}$.

Where

$$\beta_j^{(k)} = \int_{D_i^{(k)}} p(i|x)dx. \tag{5}$$

The graphical interpretation of the *posterior* probability estimator for the decision area given by rule is depicted on Fig.1.

### 3.2 The Rule-Based Decision Algorithm

For that form of knowledge we can formulate the decision algorithm $\Psi_R(x)$ which point at class $i$ if $\hat{p}(i|x)$ (the *posterior* probability estimator obtained from the rule set) has the biggest value for this class. The knowledge about probabilities given by expert estimates the average *posterior* probability for the whole rule decision area. As we see for decision making we are interested in the exact value of probability for given observation. A rule, for logical knowledge representation, witch small decision area can be overfitting the learning set. For our proposition the estimator is more precise if rule decision region will be smaller and differences between upper and lower bound of the probability given by expert will be smaller.

For the problem under consideration definition of the relation "more specific" between the probabilistic rules pointed at the same classes is very useful.

Definition

Rule $r_i^{(k)}$ is "more specific" than rule $r_i^{(l)}$ if

$$\left(\overline{\beta}_i^{(k)} - \underline{\beta}_i^{(k)}\right)\left( \int_{D_i^{(k)}} dx \Big/ \int_X dx \right) < \left(\overline{\beta}_i^{(l)} - \underline{\beta}_i^{(l)}\right)\left( \int_{D_i^{(l)}} dx \Big/ \int_X dx \right). \tag{6}$$

Hence the proposition of the *posterior* probability estimator $\hat{p}(i|x)$ is as follow.
From subset of rules $R_i(x) = \left\{ r_i^{(k)} : x \in D_i^{(k)} \right\}$ choose the "most specific" rule $r_i^{(m)}$.

$$\hat{p}(i|k) = \left(\overline{\beta}_i^{(m)} - \underline{\beta}_i^{(m)}\right) \Big/ \int_{D_i^{(m)}} dx. \tag{7}$$

## 4 The Confidence Measure of the Rule

### 4.1 Definition

This estimator $\hat{p}(i|x)$ is obtained under the following assumption:

1. learning set is noise free (or expert tell us true),
2. target concept contained in the set of class number $\{1, \ldots, M\}$,
3. the prior probabilities of classes are unknown,

We consider decision under the first assumption given by the following formulae:

$$P(\text{If A then B with probability } \beta) = 1.$$

During the expert system designing process the rules are obtained from different source and the sources have the different confidence. For the knowledge given by experts we can not assume that expert tell us true or/and if the rule set is generated by the machine learning algorithms we can not assume the learning set is noise free. Therefore we postulate that we have not to trust all the getting information or the believe on it only with the $\gamma$ factor, proposed as the confidence measure. It can be formulated as

$$P(\text{If A then B with probability } \beta) = \gamma \leq 1.$$

Lets as $\gamma_i^{(k)}$ denote the value of the *confidence measure of rule* $r_i^{(k)}$.

### 4.2 Using Confidence Measure for Rule Base Modification

We defined confidence measure. Now, lets us propose how use this measure for the modification the set of rules. We propose the following procedure, which should be started after the acquisition process:

```
for i:=1 to M:
        for each rule pointed at class i r_i^(k) :
```
$\overline{\beta}_i^{(k)} = 1-\left(1-\overline{\beta}_i^{(k)}\right)\gamma_i^{(k)}$ ; $\underline{\beta}_i^{(k)} = \underline{\beta}_i^{(k)}\ \gamma_i^{(k)}$ ;
```
        end.
end.
```

## 5 Statistical Estimation of the *Posterior* Probabilities and Their Confidence Measure

The presented method is also typical for the statistical estimation of $\beta$, where we assume the significant level[11]. The significant level can be interpreted as the confidence measure. Each rule gives the index of the class. If the feature vector value belongs to the decision area given by the rule, the decision depends on the previous state and on the applied therapy. While constructing the artificial rule set, we have to define somehow the decision areas for the new rule set. For example we can want to obtain for each rule *posterior* probability estimator, which is not less than a fixed value or in the practice we can use the one of very well known machine learning algorithms like AQ,CN2 [7]. For each of the given intervals $k$ we have to obtain the estimator of the *posterior* probability.

We use the following statistical model [10]:

- the learning set is selected randomly from a population and there exists two class of points: marked (point at the class $i \in \{1, ..., M\}$) and unmarked (point at the class $l$, where $l \in \{1, ..., M\}$ and $l \neq i$ ),

1. - the expected value for the population is $p$,
2. - the best estimator of $p$ is $\hat{p} = m/n$, where $n$ means the sample size and $m$ - the number of the marked elements.

For the fixed significance level $\alpha$
we obtain

$$P\left( m/n - \mu_\alpha \sqrt{\frac{m/n\,(1-m/n)}{n}} < p < m/n + \mu_\alpha \sqrt{\frac{m/n\,(1-m/n)}{n}} \right) \leq 1-\alpha\,, \tag{8}$$

where $\mu_\alpha$ denotes the value of the $t$-distribution on $n$-1 degrees of freedom and for the significance level $\alpha$ (for $n \leq 100$) or is the value of normal standardized N(0, 1) distribution for the significance level $\alpha$ (for $n > 100$).

In this case we get rule $r_i^{(k)}$, for which confidence measure of rule $\gamma_i^{(k)} = 1-\alpha$ is given by the following equation

$$\underline{\beta}_i^{(k)} = m/n - \mu_\alpha \sqrt{\frac{m/n\,(1-m/n)}{n}} \quad \text{and} \quad \overline{\beta}_i^{(k)} = m/n + \mu_\alpha \sqrt{\frac{m/n\,(1-m/n)}{n}}\,. \tag{9}$$

## 6 Conclusion

The presented idea of confidence management can be used for the fusion of rules from different sources. From the theoretical and practical point of view only Dempster's rule of combination [9] can produces unified rules on base on the set of rules (for the same decision area) obtained from different experts. We have shown how rules from different expert could be mixed for classical probabilistic decision systems. The proposed quality measure can be also applied to the decision support systems based on the logical "if-then" set of rules. It could be used in case of the contradiction detected in the set of rules. Then we propose to remove rule by rule according to their value of confidence measure until contradiction is detected.

Let us present future works under the concept of the information quality:

1. developing the method how to judge the expert quality (now we propose arbitrary judgment),
2. applying proposed method to the real medical decision problems,
3. performing simulation experiments on computer generated data to estimate the dependencies between the size of the decision area and the data quality versus correctness of classification.

## References


1. Bruha I., Quality of Decision Rules: Definition and Classification Schemes for Multiple Rules [in] Nakhaeizadeh G., Taylor C.C. [eds], *Machine Learning and Statistic*, John Wiley and Sons, 1997.
2. Dean P., Famili A., Comparative Performance of Rule Quality Measures in an Inductive Systems, *Applied Intelligence*, no 7, 1997.
3. Devijver P. A., Kittler J., *Pattern Recognition: A Statistical Approach*, Prentice Hall, London 1982.
4. Duda R.O., Hart P.E., *Pattern Classification and Scene Analysis*, John Wiley and Sons, New York, 1973
5. Giakoumakis E., Papakonstantiou G., Skordalakis E., Rule-based systems and pattern recognition, *Pattern Recognition Letters*, No 5, 1987.
6. Gur-Ali O., Wallance W.A., Induction of rules subject to a quality constraint: probabilistic inductive learning, *IEEE Transaction on Knowledge and Data Engeineering*, vol. 5, no 3, 1993.
7. Mitchell T., *Machine Learning*, McGraw Hill, 1997.
8. Pearl J., *Probabilistic Reasoning in Intelligent Systems: Networks of Plausible Inference*, Morgan Kaufmann Pub. Inc., San Francisco, California, 1991.
9. Pearl J., Bayesian and Belief-Functions Formalisms for Evidential Reasoning: A Conceptual Analysis [in] Schafer G., Pearl J., [red.] *Readings in Uncertain Reasoning,* Morgan Kaufmann Publ., Inc., San Mateo, California.
10. Sachs L., *Applied Statistic. A Handbook of Techniques*, Springer-Verlag, New York Berlin Heideberg Tokyo, 1984.
11. Wozniak M., Blinowska A., Unification of the information as the way of recognition the controlled Markov chains, *Proc. of the Congress on Information Processing and Management of Uncertainty in Knowledge Based Systems,* Granada, Spain 1996.

# Using Local Information to Guide Ant Based Search

Simon Kaegi and Tony White

School of Computer Science, Carleton University
1125 Colonel By Drive
Ottawa, Ontario, Canada K1S 5B6
{skaegi, arpwhite}@scs.carleton.ca

**Abstract.** Marco Dorigo et al. used Ant System (AS) to explore the Symmetric Traveling Salesman Problem and found that the use of a small number of elitist ants can improve algorithm performance. The elitist ants take advantage of global knowledge of the best tour found to date and reinforce this tour with pheromone in order to focus future searches more effectively. This paper discusses an alternative approach where only local information is used to reinforce good tours thereby enhancing the ability of the algorithm for multiprocessor or network implementation. In the model proposed, the ants are endowed with a memory of their best tour to date. The ants then reinforce this "local best tour" with pheromone during an iteration to mimic the search focusing of the elitist ants. Results are compared with Ant System.

## 1 Introduction

Ant algorithms represent a relatively new heuristic search technique that has been successfully applied to solving NP hard problems [1]. Perhaps not surprisingly ant algorithms are biologically inspired from the behavior of colonies of real ants, and in particular how they forage for food. One of the main ideas behind this approach is that the ants can communicate with one another wholly through indirect means by making modifications to the pheromone level in their immediate environment.

Ant Colony Optimization (ACO) is the so-called meta-heuristic for ant algorithms applied to optimization problems and as these are the problems we're generally working with we tend to use the terms interchangeably.

The Traveling Salesman Problem (TSP) is an NP hard problem addressed by the optimization community having been studied extensively and been the target of considerable research [6]. There are two classes of TSP problem: symmetric TSP, and asymmetric TSP (ATSP). The difference is that whereas with symmetric TSP the distance between two cities is the same regardless of the direction you travel, with asymmetric TSP this is not necessarily the case. Ant Colony Optimization has been successfully applied to both classes of TSP with good results. The earliest implementation, Ant System, was just applied to the symmetric TSP problem initially and as this paper presents a proposed improvement to Ant System this is where we will focus our efforts.

While the ant foraging behaviour on which the Ant System is based has no central control or global information on which to draw, the use of global best information in the Elitest form of the Ant System represents a significant departure from the purely

P.W.H. Chung, C.J. Hinde, M. Ali (Eds.): IEA/AIE 2003, LNAI 2718, pp. 692–701, 2003.

distributed nature of ant-based foraging. Use of global information presents a barrier to a fully distributed implementation of Ant System algorithms in a live network. This observation motivates the fully distributed algorithm – the Ant System Local Best Tour – described in this paper.

The next section provides further detail of the algorithm introduced above. The Local Best Tour (LBT) algorithm is then introduced and the experimental setup for its evaluation described. An analysis section follows, and the paper concludes with an evaluation of the algorithm with proposals for further experimentation and improvement.

## 2 Ant System (AS)

As mentioned, Ant System was the earliest implementation of Ant Colony Optimization and was applied to the symmetric Traveling Salesman Problem. A brief description of the algorithm follows. For a comprehensive description of the algorithm see [1], [2], [3], or [6].

### 2.1 Algorithm

Expanding upon the algorithm above, an ACO consists of two main sections: *initialization* and a *main loop*. The main loop runs for a user-defined number of iterations. These are described below:

*Initialization*

- Any Initial parameters are loaded.
- Each of the roads is set with an initial pheromone value.
- Each ant is individually placed on a random city.

***Main Loop Begins***

*Construct Solution*

- Each ant constructs a tour by successively applying the probabilistic choice function and randomly selecting a city it has not yet visited until each city has been visited exactly once.

$$p_{ij}^{k}(t) = \frac{[\tau_{ij}(t)]^{\alpha} \cdot [\eta_{ij}]^{\beta}}{\sum_{l \in N_i^k} [\tau_{il}(t)]^{\alpha} \cdot [\eta_{il}]^{\beta}}$$

- The probabilistic function, $p_{ij}^{k}(t)$, is designed to favour the selection of a road that has a high pheromone value, $\tau$, and high visibility value, $\eta$, which is given by: $1/d_{ij}$, where $d_{ij}$ is the distance to the city. The pheromone linearity, $\alpha$, and visibility linearity, $\beta$, are parameters used to tune the relative importance of pheromone and road length in selecting the next city.

*Apply Local Search*

- Not used in Ant System, but is used in several variations of the TSP problem where 2-opt or 3-opt local optimizers 0 are used.

*Best Tour check*

- For each ant, calculate the length of the ant's tour and compare to the best tour's length. If there is an improvement update it.

*Update Trails*

- Evaporate a fixed proportion of the pheromone on each road.
- For each ant perform the "ant-cycle" [1] pheromone update.
- Reinforce the best tour with a set number of "elitist ants" performing the "ant-cycle" pheromone update.

***Main Loop Ends***

*Output*

- The best tour found is returned as the output of the problem.

### 2.2 Discussion

Ant System in general has been identified as having several good properties related to directed exploration of the problem space with out getting trapped in local minima [1]. The initial form of AS did not make use of elitist ants and did not direct the search as well as it might. This observation was confirmed in our experimentation.

The addition of elitist ants was found to improve ant capabilities for finding better tours in fewer iterations of the algorithm, by highlighting the best tour. However, by using elitist ants to reinforce the best tour the algorithm is now taking advantage of global data and there is the additional problem of deciding on precisely how many elitist ants to use. If one uses too many elitist ants the simulation can easily become trapped in local minima [1], [3].

There have been a number of improvements to the original Ant System algorithm. They have generally focused on two main areas of improvement [6]. First, they more strongly exploit the globally best solution found. Second, they make use of a fast local search algorithm like 2-opt, 3-opt, or the Lin-Kernighan heuristic to improve the solutions found by the ants.

The algorithm improvements to Ant System have produced some of the highest quality solutions when applied to the TSP and other NP hard problems [1].

As described in section 2.1, retrofitting AS with a local search facility would be straightforward. The area of improvement proposed in this paper is to explore an alternative to using the globally best tour (GBT) to reinforce and focus on good areas of the search space. The Local Best Tour algorithm is described in the next section.

## 3 Local Best Tour (LBT)

The use of an elitist ant in Ant System exposes the need for a global observer to watch over the problem and identify what the best tour found to date is on a per iteration basis. The idea behind the design of Local Best Tour is specifically to avoid this notion of a global observer. Instead, each individual ant keeps track of the best tour it has found to date and uses it in place of the elitist ant tour to reinforce tour goodness.

It is as if the scale of the problem has been brought down to the ant level and each ant is running its individual copy of the Ant System algorithm using a single elitist ant. Remarkably, the ants work together effectively even if indirectly and the net effect is very similar to that of using the pheromone search focusing of the elitist ant approach.

### 3.1 Algorithm

The algorithm used is identical to that described for Ant System with the replacement of the elitist ant step with the ant's local best tour step. Referring, once again, to the algorithm described in section 2.1 with the following changes made:

Where the elitist ant step was:

- Reinforce the best tour with a set number of "elitist ants" performing the "ant-cycle" pheromone update.

For Local Best Tour we now do the following:

- For each ant perform the "ant-cycle" pheromone update using its local best tour.

The rest of the Ant System algorithm is unchanged, including the newly explored tour's "ant-cycle" pheromone update.

### 3.2 Experimentation and Results

For the purposes of demonstrating Local Best Search we constructed an Ant System simulation and applied it to a series of TSP Problems from the TSPLIB95 collection [5]. Although not the only problem studied – "eil76" and "kro101" were also studied -- the data presented in this paper comes from running the simulation against the symmetric TSP problem "eil51", a problem for which the optimal tour is known. This problem is a 51-city problem set up in a 2 dimensional Euclidean plane. The weight assigned to each road comes from the linear distance separating each pair of cities.

The simulation created for this paper was able to emulate the behavior of the original Ant System, Ant System with elitist ants, and finally Ant System using the local best tour approach proposed in this paper. These three approaches were tested thoroughly to examine their relative performance on "eil51."

#### 3.2.1 Parameters and Settings

Ant System requires you to make a number of parameter selections. In his original work on Ant System Marco Dorigo did work to tune and find appropriate values for a number of these parameters [3]. The values Dorigo found that do not depend on the size of the problem were used for this simulation.

- Pheromone Linearity ($\alpha$) = 1
- Visibility Linearity ($\beta$) = 5
- Pheromone Decay Rate ($\rho$) = 0.5
- Initial Pheromone ($\tau_0$) = $10^{-6}$

For those parameters that depend on the size of the problem our simulation made an effort to select good values based on knowledge of the problem and number of cities. Recent work [4] on improved algorithm parameters was unavailable to us when developing the LBT algorithm. We intend to explore the performance of the new parameters settings and will report the results in a future research paper.

The Pheromone additive constant (Q) was eliminated altogether as a parameter by replacing it with the global best tour (GBT) length in the case of standard Ant System and the local best tour (LBT) length for the approach in this paper. We justify this decision by noting that Dorigo found that differences in the value of Q only weakly affected the performance of the algorithm and a value within an order of magnitude of the optimal tour length was acceptable. This means that the pheromone addition on an edge becomes:

$\frac{L_{best}}{L_{ant}}$ For a normal "ant-cycle" pheromone update

$\frac{L_{best}}{L_{best}} = 1$ For an elitist or LBT "ant-cycle" pheromone update

The key factor in the pheromone update is that it remains inversely proportional to the length of the tour and this still holds with our approach. The ants now are not tied to a particular value of Q in the event of a change in the number of cities in the problem. We consider the removal of a user-defined parameter another attractive feature of the LBT algorithm.

For the number of ants (m) we simply set this equal to the number of cities, as this seems to be a reasonable selection according to the current literature [1], [3], [6].

For the number of elitist ants we tried various values dependant on the size of the problem and eventually settled on a value of $1/6^{th}$ of the number of cities. This value worked well for the relatively low number of cities we used in our simulation but for larger problems this value might need to be tuned. The current literature is unclear on the best value of the number of elitest ants to be used.

With the LBT AS approach, all ants perform the LBT "ant-cycle" update so subsequently the number of elitist ants is not needed. This paper does indicate the notion of an LBT constant that allows tuning of the LBT pheromone update rate as a possible improvement. This, however, this is not explored in the experimental results of this paper and subsequently the LBT constant is not varied and simply set to 1.

### 3.2.2 Results

Overall, the results of the simulation showed considerable promise for the Local Best Tour approach. Table 1 shows a comparison of the results for the three Ant System approaches explored on the eil51 TSP problem after 100, 500, and 2000 iterations respectively. The results shown are the average best tour lengths and the overall best tour lengths after 100 runs.

**Table 1.** Ant System Results for eil51

| | 100 iterations | | | 500 iterations | | | 2000 iterations | | |
|---|---|---|---|---|---|---|---|---|---|
| | **Best Tour** | **Avg. Tour** | **Std. Dev.** | **Best Tour** | **Avg. Tour** | **Std. Dev.** | **Avg. Tour** | **Aver age** | **Std. Dev.** |
| LBT AS | 437 | **442.4** | 5.23 | 430 | **433.4** | **2.91** | **428** | **429.4** | 1.35 |
| Elitist AS | **430** | 443.4 | 6.77 | **429** | 438 | 4.29 | **428** | 429.9 | **1.20** |
| AS | 443 | 451.5 | **4.67** | 438 | 445.1 | 5.99 | **428** | 441.4 | 8.34 |

After 100 iterations we see that the LBT AS algorithm is producing a slightly better average result than the Elitist algorithm. On the other hand, the Elitist AS algorithm has over the course of the 100 runs been able to produce the best result. The standard deviations shown are all relatively high here however, the original AS algorithm despite showing relatively poor results has the lowest standard deviation.

After 500 iterations the LBT AS algorithm has increased its lead for producing the best average results. Again, the Elitist AS produced the single best result although its best tour average was a fair bit worse than that of LBT AS. The standard deviation of the LBT AS is now substantially lower than the other two algorithms.

After 2000 iterations all of the algorithms found a best tour of length 428. The optimal tour length for this problem is actually 426 and so, unfortunately, none of the approaches were successful in finding it. This is however, in line with previous findings [1], [2]. That being said, the LBT Ant System was very effective and, in fact, had the best average results. Both the Elitist AS and LBT AS had relatively good, and really quite similar, results over the extended experiment. Although the original AS also tied the other approaches and managed to find a path of length 428, its average and standard deviation were both quite high relative to the other two Ant Systems.

Overall, the result for LBT AS show that it is at least in a similar class as the Elitist AS approach. The classical AS algorithm does not really manage to keep up and certainly requires many more iterations to achieve a similar performance for the final output best tour length.

## 4 Analysis

### 4.1 Best Tour Analysis

As has been shown in the Results section, LBT AS is competitive with the Elitist AS approach. In this section we take a comparative look at the evolution of the best tour in all three systems and then look at the evolution of the best tour found per iteration.

In Figure 1, we see can see the key difference between the Elitist AS approach and LBT AS. Whereas Elitist AS quickly finds a few good results, holds steady and then improves in relatively large pronounced steps, LBT AS improves more gradually at the beginning but continues improvements at a steadier rate. In fact, if one looks closely at the graph one can see that even the classical AS system has found a better result during the early stages of the simulation compared to LBT AS. However, by about iteration 75, LBT AS has overtaken the other two approaches and continues to gradually make improvements until the end of the simulation.

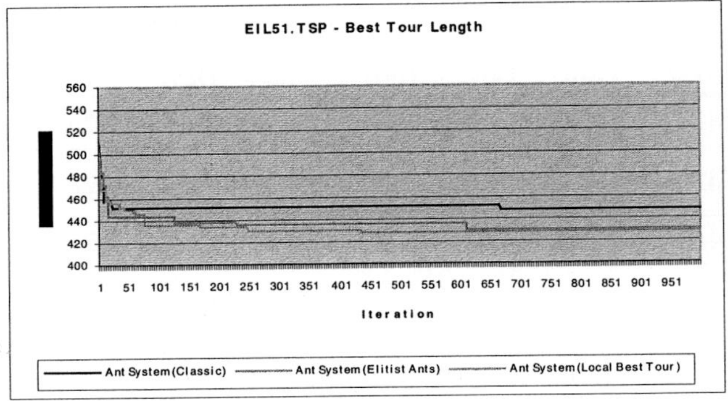


**Fig. 1.** Evolution of Best Tour Length

Overall, LBT AS's behavior could be described as slower but steadier. It takes slightly longer at the beginning to focus pheromone on good tours but after it has, it improves more frequently and steadily and on average will overtake the other two approaches given enough time. We have confirmed this hypothesis by experimentation with the eil76 and kro101 TSP problem datasets.

In Figure 2 we can see the distribution of best tours is more tightly focused with a smaller deviation for LBT AS compared to the other two systems. In addition, on average the LBT AS best tour space is much closer to the optimal solution.

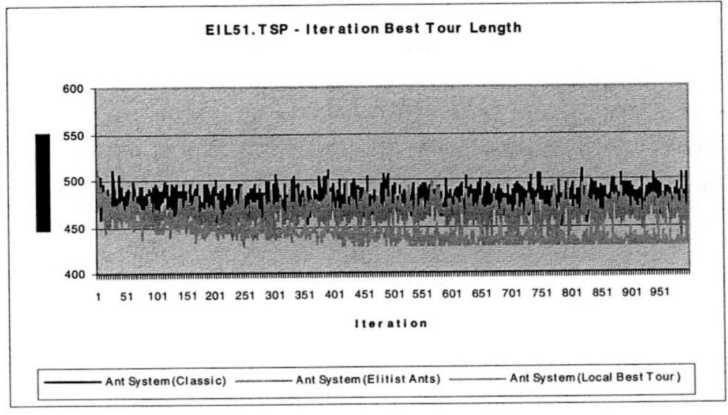


**Fig. 2.** Best Tour Length for Individual Iterations

As mentioned earlier none of the Ant Systems were able to find the optimal tour length for this problem. Judging from the flattening of the LBT AS graph line there looks to be a very real danger that the algorithm is caught in a local minimum. However, there is still a significant deviation in the best tour per iteration results. Later in this paper we look at ways to improve the algorithm and safeguard against this behaviour.

### 4.2 Average Tour Analysis

In the Best Tour Analysis we saw that the LBT AS algorithm tends to gradually improve in many small steps. With our analysis of the average tour we want to confirm that the relatively high deviation of ant algorithms is working in the average case meaning that we are continuing to explore the problem space effectively. In this section we look at the average tour length per iteration to see if we can identify any behavioural trends.

In Figure 3 we see a very similar situation to that of the Best Tour Length per Iteration. The LBT AS algorithm is on average exploring much closer to the optimal solution. Perhaps more importantly, the LBT AS graph trend line is behaving very similarly in terms of its deviation to that of the other two systems. This suggests that the LBT AS system is working as expected and is in fact searching in a better-focused fashion closer to the optimal solution. Referring back to Figure 2, one striking observation with LBT is the point in the experiment at which the best tour typically emerges; 900 iterations versus well over a 1000 for the elitest ant algorithm and in excess of 1500 iterations for the basic AS algorithm.

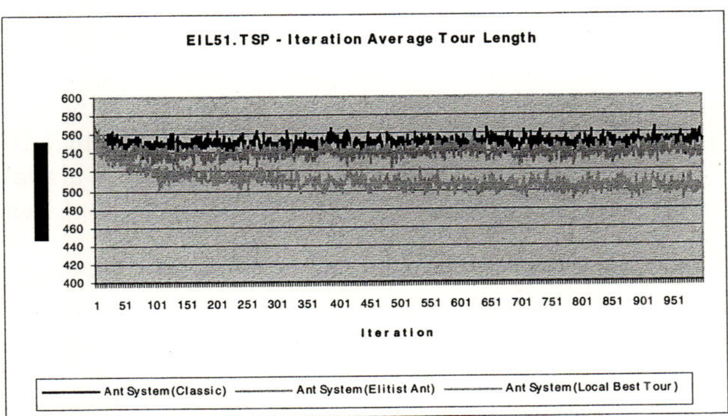


**Fig. 3.** Average Tour Length for Individual Iterations

### 4.3 Evolution of the Local Best Tour

The Local Best Tour approach is certainly very similar to the notion of elitist ants; only it is applied at the local level instead of at the global level. In this section we look at the evolution of the global worst, average, and best LBT of the ants.

From Figure 4 we can see that over time both the average and worst LBTs approach the value of global best tour. It is clear that the longer the simulation runs the closer the LBT "ant-cycle" pheromone update resembles that of an elitist ant's update scheme. However, as noted in the previous section, the number of iterations required by the LBT algorithm is considerably smaller than that required for the elitest ant algorithm.

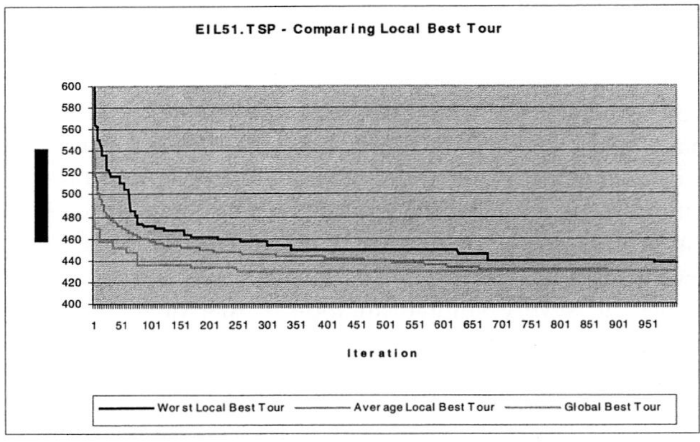


**Fig. 4.** Evolution of the Local Best Tour

# 5 Conclusions

Through the results and analysis shown in this paper, Local Best Tour has proven to be a reasonable alternative to the use of the globally best tour for focusing ant search through pheromone reinforcement. In particular, the results show that the LBT Ant System algorithm has excellent average performance characteristics. By removing the need for the global information required for an elitest ant algorithm, we have improved the ease with which a parallel or live network implementation can be achieved.

Analysis of the best tour construction process shows that LBT AS, while initially converging more slowly than Elitist AS, is very consistent at incrementally building a better tour and on average will match or overtake the Elitist approach early in the search of the problem space.

Average and best iteration tour analysis has shown that LBT AS shares the same variability characteristics of the original Ant System that make it resistant to getting stuck in local minima. Furthermore, LBT AS is very effective at focusing its search efforts in the region of the optimal solution.

Finally, LBT AS follows in the notion that the use of best tours to better focus an ant's search is an effective optimization. As hypothesized, the emergent behaviour of a set of autonomous LBT ants is to, in effect, become elitist ants over time.

This paper has demonstrated that an ACO algorithm using only local information can be applied to the TSP without compromising performance. While exhaustive experimentation has yet to be completed, the early results are promising and appear to support a hypothesis that LBT is competitive with, or superior to, AS with elitest ants.

## References

1. Bonabeau E., Dorigo M., and Theraulaz G. Swarm Intelligence From Natural to Artificial Systems. Oxford University Press, New York NY, 1999.
2. Dorigo M. & L.M. Gambardella. Ant Colony System: A Cooperative Learning Approach to the Traveling Salesman Problem. IEEE Transactions on Evolutionary Computation, 1(1):53-66. ftp://iridia.ulb.ac.be/pub/mdorigo/journals/IJ.16-TEC97.US.pdf
3. Dorigo M., V. Maniezzo & A. Colorni. The Ant System: Optimization by a Colony of Cooperating Agents. IEEE Transactions on Systems, Man, and Cybernetics-Part B, 26(1):29-41. ftp://iridia.ulb.ac.be/pub/mdorigo/journals/IJ.10-SMC96.pdf
4. Pilat M. and White T., Using Genetic Algorithms to optimize ACS-TSP. In Proceedings of the 3rd International Workshop on Ant Algorithms, Brussels, Belgium. 2002.
5. Reinelt G. TSPLIB I A Traveling Salesman Problem Library. ORSA Journal on Computing, 3:376-384, 1991. http://www.iwr.uni-heidelberg.de/groups/comopt/software/TSPLIB95/
6. Stützle T. and Dorigo M. ACO Algorithms for the Traveling Salesman Problem. In K. Miettinen, M. Makela, P. Neittaanmaki, J. Periaux, editors, Evolutionary Algorithms in Engineering and Computer Science, Wiley, 1999.

# The Generalised Method for Solving Problems of the DEDS Control Synthesis*

František Čapkovič

Institute of Informatics, Slovak Academy of Sciences,
Dúbravská cesta 9, 845 07 Bratislava, Slovak Republic,
Frantisek.Capkovic@savba.sk, utrrcapk@savba.sk,
http://www.savba.sk/~utrrcapk/capkhome.htm

**Abstract.** The method represents a generalisation of the author's method presented recently. It extends the validity of the original method to the wider class of discrete-event dynamic systems (DEDS) to be controlled. Both the original method and the innovated one are suitable for DEDS able to be described by ordinary Petri nets (OPN). The earlier method can be successfully used only in case of the DEDS described by the special class of OPN - so called state machines (SM). The method proposed here can be used in case of DEDS described by the bounded OPN. While SM have special restrictions on their structure the bounded OPN have no structural restrictions. Namely, SM are OPN with transitions having only the single input place and the single output place. Thus, the validity of the method is extended because the class of bounded OPN is undoubtedly many times wider than the class of OPN represented by SM. Both the original method and the proposed one can alternatively utilize ordinary directed graphs (ODG) or bipartite directed graphs (BDG).

## 1 Introduction

he DEDS control synthesis is important area of control theory. Solving the related problems can be complicated. Petri nets (PN) are often used for DEDS modelling, analysis and control synthesis - see e.g. [10, 12]. Usually, PN places represent DEDS subsystem activities and PN transitions express discrete events occurring in DEDS. Approaches based on OPN allow us to use methods of linear algebra for DEDS modelling as well as for the DEDS control synthesis. However, in spite of this fact there exists no general method for the control synthesis of DEDS modelled by OPN.

The author has published in [2–4] the method suitable for SM - the special class of OPN - where each transition has only one input place and only one output place. The control synthesis method utilizing directed graphs (DG) was developed there for such a kind of DEDS. The improved method for SM control synthesis was published recently in [5]. BDG described e.g. by Diestel in [9] were used there. Thus, finding the control vectors was simpler and more comfortable.

* Partially supported by the Slovak Grant Agency for Science (VEGA) under grant # 2/3130/23

P.W.H. Chung, C.J. Hinde, M. Ali (Eds.): IEA/AIE 2003, LNAI 2718, pp. 702–711, 2003.

This paper is devoted to the control synthesis of DEDS described by bounded OPN. Such a class of OPN is far wider in comparison with the class of OPN represented by SM. Before describing the new approach it is necessary to mention the principle of the original one. We emphasize that in this paper the term vector means by definition the column vector.

## 2 The Principle of the Original Method

SM are understood here to be the special ODG with the OPN places being the ODG nodes and the OPN transitions being fixed to the ODG edges. In addition to this the nodes are marked in order to express dynamics development. The SM reachability tree (RT) was developed in [1] as follows

$$\mathbf{x}(k+1) = \mathbf{\Delta}_k.\mathbf{x}(k)\ , \quad k = 0, ..., N \tag{1}$$

where $k$ is the discrete step (the level of the tree); $\mathbf{x}(k) = (\sigma_{p_1}^{(k)}(\gamma), ..., \sigma_{p_n}^{(k)}(\gamma))^T$, $k = 0, ..., N$ is the $n$-dimensional state vector in the step $k$; $\sigma_{p_i}^{(k)}(\gamma)$, $i = 1, ..., n$ is the state of the elementary place $p_i$ in the step $k$; it depends on actual enabling its input transitions and $\gamma$ symbolizes this dependency; $\mathbf{\Delta}_k = \{\delta_{ij}^{(k)}\}_{n \times n}$, $\delta_{ij}^{(k)} = \gamma_{t_{p_i|p_j}}^{(k)}$, $i = 1, ..., n$, $j = 1, ..., n$ is the functional matrix where $\gamma_{t_{p_i|p_j}}^{(k)} \in \{0, 1\}$ is the transition function of the PN transition fixed on the edge oriented from $p_j$ to $p_i$.

To avoid problems with computer handling $\mathbf{\Delta}_k$ two simple approaches to control synthesis were proposed. The first of them published in [2–4] is based on ODG and the second one presented in [5] is based on BDG.

### 2.1 The ODG-Based Approach

It operates with the matrix $\mathbf{\Delta}$ being the transpose of the adjacency matrix of the ODG representing the SM. The idea is very simple. To obtain feasible trajectories from a given initial state $\mathbf{x}_0$ to a prescribed terminal state $\mathbf{x}_t$ a special intersection of both the straight-lined RT (SLRT) and the backtracking RT (BTRT) is performed. The SLBT is developed from $\mathbf{x}_0$ towards $\mathbf{x}_t$ as follows

$$\{\mathbf{x}_1\} = \mathbf{\Delta}.\mathbf{x}_0 \tag{2}$$

$$\{\mathbf{x}_2\} = \mathbf{\Delta}.\{\mathbf{x}_1\} = \mathbf{\Delta}.(\mathbf{\Delta}.\mathbf{x}_0) = \mathbf{\Delta}^2.\mathbf{x}_0 \tag{3}$$

$$\dots \qquad \dots \qquad \dots$$

$$\{\mathbf{x}_N\} = \mathbf{\Delta}.\{\mathbf{x}_{N-1}\} = \mathbf{\Delta}^N.\mathbf{x}_0 \tag{4}$$

where $\mathbf{x}_N = \mathbf{x}_t$. In general, $\{\mathbf{x}_j\}$ is an aggregate all of the states that are reachable from the previous states. According to graph theory $N \leq (n-1)$. The BTRT is developed from the $\mathbf{x}_t$ towards $\mathbf{x}_0$, however, it contains the paths oriented towards the terminal state. It is the following

$$\{\mathbf{x}_{N-1}\} = \mathbf{\Delta}^T.\mathbf{x}_N \tag{5}$$

$$\{\mathbf{x}_{N-2}\} = \mathbf{\Delta}^T.\{\mathbf{x}_{N-1}\} = (\mathbf{\Delta}^T)^2.\mathbf{x}_N \tag{6}$$

$$\dots \quad \dots \quad \dots$$

$$\{\mathbf{x}_0\} = \mathbf{\Delta}^T.\{\mathbf{x}_1\} = (\mathbf{\Delta}^T)^N.\mathbf{x}_N \tag{7}$$

Here, $\{\mathbf{x}_j\}$ is an aggregate all of the states from which the next states are reachable. It is clear that $\mathbf{x}_0 \neq \{\mathbf{x}_0\}$ and $\mathbf{x}_N \neq \{\mathbf{x}_N\}$. It is the consequence of the fact that in general, $\mathbf{\Delta}.\mathbf{\Delta}^T \neq \mathbf{I_n}$ as well as $\mathbf{\Delta}^T.\mathbf{\Delta} \neq \mathbf{I}_n$ ($\mathbf{I}_n$ is $(n \times n)$ identity matrix). The intersection of the trees is made as follows

$$\mathbf{M}_1 = (\mathbf{x}_0, {}^1\{\mathbf{x}_1\}, \dots, {}^1\{\mathbf{x}_{N-1}\}, {}^1\{\mathbf{x}_N\}) \tag{8}$$

$$\mathbf{M}_2 = ({}^2\{\mathbf{x}_0\}, {}^2\{\mathbf{x}_1\}, \dots, {}^2\{\mathbf{x}_{N-1}\}, \mathbf{x}_N) \tag{9}$$

$$\mathbf{M} = \mathbf{M}_1 \cap \mathbf{M}_2 \tag{10}$$

$$\mathbf{M} = (\mathbf{x}_0, \{\mathbf{x}_1\}, \dots, \{\mathbf{x}_{N-1}\}, \mathbf{x}_N) \tag{11}$$

where the matrices $\mathbf{M}_1$, $\mathbf{M}_2$ represent, respectively, the SLRT and the BTRT. The special intersection both of the trees is performed by means of the column-to-column intersection both of the matrices. Thus, $\{\mathbf{x}_i\} = \min({}^1\{\mathbf{x}_i\}, {}^2\{\mathbf{x}_i\})$, $i = 0, \dots, N$ with ${}^1\{\mathbf{x}_0\} = \mathbf{x}_0$, ${}^2\{\mathbf{x}_N\} = \mathbf{x}_N$.

### 2.2 The BDG-Based Approach

The OPN in general (SM as well) can be understood to be BDG. Let $S = \{P, T\}$ is the set of BDG nodes where $P$ is the set of PN places and $T$ is the set of PN transitions. Let $\Delta$ is the set $S \times S$ of BDG edges. Thus, the occurrence of the edges can be expressed by the $((n+m) \times (n+m))$ matrix

$$\mathbf{\Delta} = \begin{pmatrix} \emptyset_{n\times n} & \mathbf{G}^T \\ \mathbf{F}^T & \emptyset_{m\times m} \end{pmatrix} \tag{12}$$

where $\emptyset_{i\times j}$ in general is the $(i \times j)$ zero matrix; $\mathbf{G}$ is the $(m \times n)$ incidence matrix expressing $T \times P$; $\mathbf{F}$ is the $(n \times m)$ incidence matrix representing $P \times T$. Hence, BDG can be understood to be DG and (1) turns to

$$\{\mathbf{s}_{k+1}\} = \mathbf{\Delta}.\{\mathbf{s}_k\}\ ,\ k = 0, 1, \dots, 2N-1 \tag{13}$$

with $\mathbf{s}_k$ being the augmented $(n + m)$-dimensional vector defined as follows

$$\{\mathbf{s}_k\} = \begin{cases} (\{\mathbf{x}_{k/2}\}^T, \emptyset_m^T)^T & \text{if } k = 0, 2, 4, \dots, 2N-2 \\ (\emptyset_n^T, \{\mathbf{u}_{(k-1)/2)}\}^T)^T & \text{if } k = 1, 3, 5, \dots, 2N-1 \end{cases} \tag{14}$$

where $\emptyset_j$ in general is the j-dimensional zero vector; $\mathbf{x}_{k/2} = \mathbf{G}^T.\mathbf{u}_{(k-2)/2}$, $k = 2, 4, \dots, 2N-2$; $\mathbf{u}_{(k-1)/2} = \mathbf{F}^T.\mathbf{x}_{(k-1)/2}$, $k = 1, 3, 5, \dots, 2N-1$.

Now, the ODG-based approach could be applied. However, because of the special block form of both the matrix $\mathbf{\Delta}$ and the vector $\mathbf{s}_k$ we can alternate step-by-step two procedures with dimensionalities $n$, $m$, respectively. In such a way two matrices **X** and **U** with dimensionalities $(n \times (N+1))$, $(m \times N)$, respectively, are obtained instead of the matrix **M**. They are the following

$$\mathbf{X} = (\mathbf{x}_0, \{\mathbf{x}_1\}, \ldots, \{\mathbf{x}_{N-1}\}, \mathbf{x}_N) \tag{15}$$

$$\mathbf{U} = (\{\mathbf{u}_0\}, \{\mathbf{u}_1\}, \ldots, \{\mathbf{u}_{N-1}\}) \tag{16}$$

More details about the BDG-based approach can be found in [5].

## 3 The Suggestion of the New Approach

The class of DEDS able to be described by SM is too narrow. At present parallel processes increasingly assert themself in practice. Therefore, the main aim of this paper is to extend the validity of the above method (in both of its forms - based on ODG and BDG) to the wider class of OPN - to the bounded OPN with general structure. The idea of the proposed approach consists in the fact that RT of OPN can be undestood to be the SM. Hence, the procedure of extending the applicability of the above method to the bounded OPN is the following

1. setting a given initial state vector $\mathbf{x}_0$ of the OPN places to be the root node
2. computing the *quasi-functional* adjacency matrix of the RT developed from the root node as well as the reachable state vectors representing the RT leaves (terminal nodes); $\mathbf{x}_0$ and the reachable states create feasible states
3. understanding the RT to be the special ODG mentioned above. However, here the ODG nodes represent entire state vectors during the system dynamics development (while in the earlier ODG-based method mentioned above the nodes were only the states of the elementary OPN places).
4. creating RG in two steps: (i) mutual connecting the RT leaves occurring repeatedly (i.e. having the same name) into one node; (ii) connecting the obtained node with the nonterminal RT node with the same name
5. understanding the RG to be SM
6. utilizing one of the methods mentioned above

To quantify the approach the following items are necessary: the mathematical model of OPN, and the algorithm for enumerating the RT and RG parameters (the *quasi-functional* adjacency matrix and the feasible states).

### 3.1 The Mathematical Model of OPN

To deal with the control synthesis problem automatically let us describe OPN mathematically. The simple mathematical model is the following

$$\mathbf{x}_{k+1} = \mathbf{x}_k + \mathbf{B}.\mathbf{u}_k \quad , \quad k = 0, N \tag{17}$$

$$\mathbf{B} = \mathbf{G}^T - \mathbf{F} \tag{18}$$

$$\mathbf{F}.\mathbf{u}_k \leq \mathbf{x}_k \tag{19}$$

where $k$ is the discrete step of the dynamics development; $\mathbf{x}_k = (\sigma_{p_1}^k, ..., \sigma_{p_n}^k)^T$ is the $n$-dimensional state vector of DEDS in the step $k$; $\sigma_{p_i}^k \in \{0, c_{p_i}\}$, $i = 1, ..., n$

express the states of the DEDS elementary subprocesses or operations - 0 (passivity) or $0 < \sigma_{p_i} \leq c_{p_i}$ (activity); $c_{p_i}$ is the capacity of the DEDS subprocess $p_i$ as to its activities; $\mathbf{u}_k = (\gamma_{t_1}^k, ..., \gamma_{t_m}^k)^T$ is the $m$-dimensional control vector of the system in the step $k$; its components $\gamma_{t_j}^k \in \{0,1\}$, $j = 1, ..., m$ represent occurring of the DEDS elementary discrete events (e.g. starting or ending the elementary subprocesses or their activities, failures, etc. - 1 (presence) or 0 (absence) of the corresponding discrete event; $\mathbf{B}$, $\mathbf{F}$, $\mathbf{G}$ are structural matrices of constant elements; $\mathbf{F} = \{f_{ij}\}_{n \times m}$, $f_{ij} \in \{0, M_{f_{ij}}\}$, $i = 1, ..., n$ , $j = 1, ..., m$ expresses the causal relations among the states of the DEDS (in the role of causes) and the discrete events occuring during the DEDS operation (in the role of consequences) - 0 (nonexistence), $M_{f_{ij}} > 0$ (existence and multiplicity) of the corresponding causal relations; $\mathbf{G} = \{g_{ij}\}_{m \times n}$, $g_{ij} \in \{0, M_{g_{ij}}\}$, $i = 1, ..., m$, $j = 1, ..., n$ expresses very analogically the causal relations among the discrete events (causes) and the DEDS states (consequences); because $\mathbf{F}$ and $\mathbf{G}$ are the arcs incidence matrices the matrix $\mathbf{B}$ is given by means of them according to (18); $(.)^T$ symbolizes the matrix or vector transposition.

### 3.2 The Algorithm Generating RT

There exists the relatively simple algorithm for generating RT of OPN with general structure. It is verbally described in [12] and formally expressed in details by many other authors. We need the parameters of RT - the functional adjacency matrix and feasible states. A simple computer realization of the algorithm in the form of the MATLAB procedure was developed by the Czech research group in [8]. It fully satisfies our needs. The inputs of the procedure are $\mathbf{x}_0$, $\mathbf{F}$, $\mathbf{G}$ and their dimensionalities $n$, $m$. The procedure yields on its output the $(n_{RT} \times n_{RT})$-dimensional matrix $\mathbf{A}_{RT}$ and the $(n \times n_{RT})$-dimensional matrix $\mathbf{X}_{reach}$. $\mathbf{A}_{RT}$ represents the adjacency matrix of the RT in the *quasi-functional* form. Its elements $a_{i,j}^{RT}$, $i = 1, ..., n_{RT}$, $j = 1, ..., n_{RT}$ are either equal to 0 (when there exists no oriented arc connecting the RT nodes $i$, $j$) or they have the form of the positive integer denoting the ordinal number of the transition through which the oriented arc passes from the RT node $i$ to the RT node $j$. The integer $n_{RT}$ denotes the number of feasible states (i.e. $\mathbf{x}_0$ and all of the states reachable from $\mathbf{x}_0$). The feasible states are given as the columns of the matrix $\mathbf{X}_{reach}$. It is necessary to say that $\mathbf{A}_{RG} = \mathbf{A}_{RT}$. The procedure is the following

```
Xreach=x0
Art=[0]
[n,m]=size(F);
B=Gt-F
i=0
while i < size(Xreach,2)
        i=i+1;
        for k=1:m
            x(k)=all(Xreach(:,i) >= F(:,k));
        end
        findx=find(x)
        for k=1:size(findx,2)
```

```
            bb = Xreach(:,i)+B(:,findx(k));
            matrix=[];
            for j=1:size(Xreach,2)
                matrix=[matrix,bb];
            end;
            v=all(matrix == Xreach);
            j=find(v);
            if any(v)
                Art(i,j)= findx(k);
            else
                Xreach=[Xreach,bb];
                Art(size(Art,1)+1,size(Art,2)+1)=0;
                Art(i,size(Art,2))=findx(k);
            end;
        end;
Xreach;
Art;
end
```

The following functions are used in the MATLAB procedure: *any(v)* returning 1 if any of the elements of the vector **v** are non-zero, *all(v)* returning 1 if all of the elements of the vector **v** are non-zero, and $j$ = *find(v)* returning the indices of the vector **v** that are non-zero. In addition to this the function *size* is utilized. When their operand is a matrix **M** with the dimensinality $(n \times m)$ the command $d$ = *size(M)* returns the two-element row vector $\mathbf{d} = (n, m)$ containing the number of rows and columns of the matrix **M**. When the second operand - the scalar *dim* - is added, then the command $x$ = *size(M,dim)* returns the length $x$ of the dimension specified by the scalar *dim*. When *dim* = *1* it returns the number of rows ($x = n$), when *dim* = *2* it returns the number of columns ($x = m$) of the matrix **M**.

To utilize the matrix $\mathbf{A}_{RT}$ in the control synthesis algorithm its elements must be modified. The modification consists in the replacement of the positive integers by the integer 1. In such a way we obtain the (0, 1)-matrix expressing the classical numerical adjacency matrix **A**. Putting $\mathbf{\Delta} = \mathbf{A}^T$ the ODG-based approach can be utilized without any problem.

### 3.3 The Modification of the BDG-Based Approach

The above described BDG-based approach handles matrices **F**, **G** as well as the OPN transitions. However, the new approach do not know them. Thus, after enumerating the matrix $\mathbf{A}_{RT}$ we have to disassamble this matrix into the matrices $\mathbf{F}_{RG}$, and $\mathbf{G}_{RG}$. In addition to this the original OPN transitions can occur more then once among the elements of $\mathbf{A}_{RT}$. Consequently, some confusions could occur. To avoid these it is necessary to rename the original OPN transitions in order to obtain fictive transitions that occure only once. The number of them is $T_r$ being the global number of the elements of $\mathbf{A}_{RT}$. The renaming is performed raw-by-raw so that the nonzero elements are replaced by integers - ordinal numbers starting from 1 and finishing at $T_r$. Thus, the auxiliary matrix $\mathbf{A}_{T_r}$ is obtained. The dissassambling of the matrix $\mathbf{A}_{T_r}$ into the incidence matrices $\mathbf{F}_{RG}$ and $\mathbf{G}_{RG}$ is given as follows. For $i = 1, ..., n_{RT}$, $j = 1, ..., n_{RT}$ if $A_{RT}(i,j) \neq 0$ and $A_{T_r}(i,j) \neq 0$ we set $T_{rTt}(A_{RT}(i,j), A_{T_r}(i,j)) = 1$, $F_{RG}(i, A_{T_r}(i,j)) = 1$, $G_{RG}(A_{T_r}(i,j), j) = 1$ else we set the elements of the matrices to be equal to 0. Here, $\mathbf{T}_{rTt}$ is the transformation matrix between the original set of transitions and the fictive one. Hence, $\mathbf{U} = \mathbf{T}_{rT_t}.\mathbf{U}^*$ where the matrix $\mathbf{U}^*$ yields the control strategies (16) computed by means of the set of the fictive transitions.

### 3.4 The Illustrative Example

Consider the simple case of DEDS having the OPN-based model with general structure (even with multiplicity of the oriented arcs) given in [11]. The OPN-based model is presented on the left in Fig. 1. We can see that $n = 5$, $m = 3$, $\mathbf{x}_0 = (2, 0, 1, 0)^T$ and the structural matrices are the following

$$\mathbf{F} = \begin{pmatrix} 2 & 0 & 0 \\ 0 & 1 & 0 \\ 0 & 0 & 1 \\ 0 & 2 & 0 \end{pmatrix} \mathbf{G} = \begin{pmatrix} 0 & 1 & 1 & 0 \\ 1 & 0 & 0 & 0 \\ 1 & 0 & 0 & 2 \end{pmatrix} \mathbf{B} = \begin{pmatrix} -2 & 1 & 1 \\ 1 & -1 & 0 \\ 1 & 0 & -1 \\ 0 & -2 & 2 \end{pmatrix}$$

Utilizing the above MATLAB procedure we obtain parameters of the corresponding RT placed on the right in Fig. 1. The RT edges are given by the elements of $\mathbf{A}_{RT}$ while the feasible states are expressed by the columns of the matrix $\mathbf{X}_{reach}$.

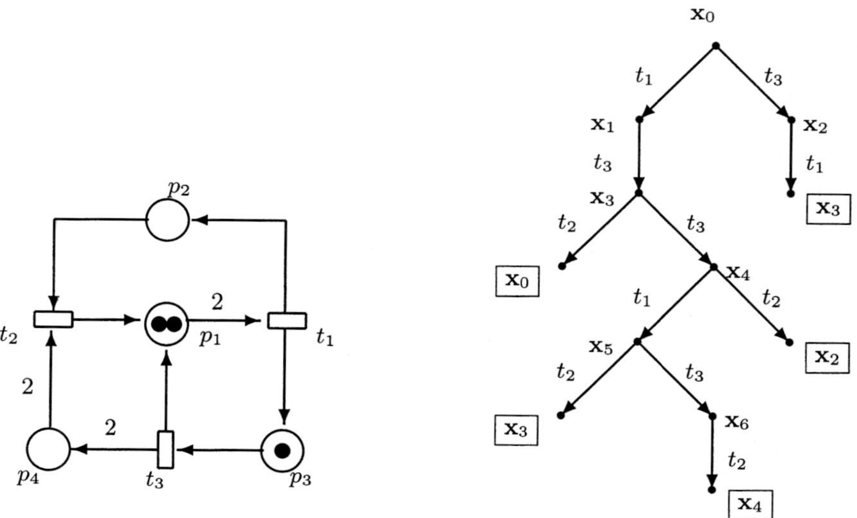


**Fig. 1.** The OPN-based representation of the DEDS (on the left) and the corresponding reachability tree (on the right)

They represent the vectors $\mathbf{x}_0, \mathbf{x}_1, ..., \mathbf{x}_6$.

$$\mathbf{A}_{RT} = \begin{pmatrix} 0 & 1 & 3 & 0 & 0 & 0 & 0 \\ 0 & 0 & 0 & 3 & 0 & 0 & 0 \\ 0 & 0 & 0 & 1 & 0 & 0 & 0 \\ 2 & 0 & 0 & 0 & 3 & 0 & 0 \\ 0 & 0 & 2 & 0 & 0 & 1 & 0 \\ 0 & 0 & 0 & 2 & 0 & 0 & 3 \\ 0 & 0 & 0 & 0 & 2 & 0 & 0 \end{pmatrix} \quad \mathbf{X}_{reach} = \begin{pmatrix} 2 & 0 & 3 & 1 & 2 & 0 & 1 \\ 0 & 1 & 0 & 1 & 1 & 2 & 2 \\ 1 & 2 & 0 & 1 & 0 & 1 & 0 \\ 0 & 0 & 2 & 2 & 4 & 4 & 6 \end{pmatrix}$$

To use the ODG-based approach the matrix $\mathbf{\Delta} = \mathbf{A}^T$ is sufficient ($\mathbf{A}$ is given below). However, for using the BDG-based approach the renamed set of the transitions is needed (their number is $T_r = 11$ in this case). Thus, the transformation matrix $\mathbf{T}_{rTt}$ is enumerated by means of $\mathbf{A}_{RT}$ and the auxiliary matrix $\mathbf{A}_{T_r}$ constructed on the base of $\mathbf{A}_{RT}$. Hence, the matrices $\mathbf{F}_{RG}$, $\mathbf{G}_{RG}$ are computed. All of the matrices in question are the following

$$\mathbf{A} = \begin{pmatrix} 0 & 1 & 1 & 0 & 0 & 0 & 0 \\ 0 & 0 & 0 & 1 & 0 & 0 & 0 \\ 0 & 0 & 0 & 1 & 0 & 0 & 0 \\ 1 & 0 & 0 & 0 & 1 & 0 & 0 \\ 0 & 0 & 1 & 0 & 0 & 1 & 0 \\ 0 & 0 & 0 & 1 & 0 & 0 & 1 \\ 0 & 0 & 0 & 0 & 1 & 0 & 0 \end{pmatrix} \quad \mathbf{A}_{T_r} = \begin{pmatrix} 0 & 1 & 2 & 0 & 0 & 0 & 0 \\ 0 & 0 & 0 & 3 & 0 & 0 & 0 \\ 0 & 0 & 0 & 4 & 0 & 0 & 0 \\ 5 & 0 & 0 & 0 & 6 & 0 & 0 \\ 0 & 0 & 7 & 0 & 0 & 8 & 0 \\ 0 & 0 & 0 & 9 & 0 & 0 & 10 \\ 0 & 0 & 0 & 0 & 11 & 0 & 0 \end{pmatrix} \quad \mathbf{T}_{rTt}^T = \begin{pmatrix} 1 & 0 & 0 \\ 0 & 0 & 1 \\ 0 & 0 & 1 \\ 1 & 0 & 0 \\ 0 & 1 & 0 \\ 0 & 0 & 1 \\ 0 & 1 & 0 \\ 1 & 0 & 0 \\ 0 & 1 & 0 \\ 0 & 0 & 1 \\ 0 & 1 & 0 \end{pmatrix}$$

$$\mathbf{F}_{RG} = \begin{pmatrix} 1&1&0&0&0&0&0&0&0&0&0 \\ 0&0&1&0&0&0&0&0&0&0&0 \\ 0&0&0&1&0&0&0&0&0&0&0 \\ 0&0&0&0&1&1&0&0&0&0&0 \\ 0&0&0&0&0&0&1&1&0&0&0 \\ 0&0&0&0&0&0&0&0&1&1&0 \\ 0&0&0&0&0&0&0&0&0&0&1 \end{pmatrix} \quad \mathbf{G}_{RG}^T = \begin{pmatrix} 0&0&0&0&1&0&0&0&0&0&0 \\ 1&0&0&0&0&0&0&0&0&0&0 \\ 0&1&0&0&0&0&1&0&0&0&0 \\ 0&0&1&1&0&0&0&0&1&0&0 \\ 0&0&0&0&0&1&0&0&0&1&0 \\ 0&0&0&0&0&0&0&1&0&0&0 \\ 0&0&0&0&0&0&0&0&0&0&1 \end{pmatrix}$$

In case when $\mathbf{x}_t = \mathbf{x}_6 = (1, 2, 0, 6)^T$ is chosen to be the terminal state the ODG-based method of the DEDS control synthesis yields the solution (20) of the state trajectories. Its graphical expression is on the left in Fig. 2. When the BDG-based method is used the solution of the state trajectories is the same like that in the ODG-based method. The solution of the control trajectories is given by (**??**) and graphically expressed on the right in Fig. 2.

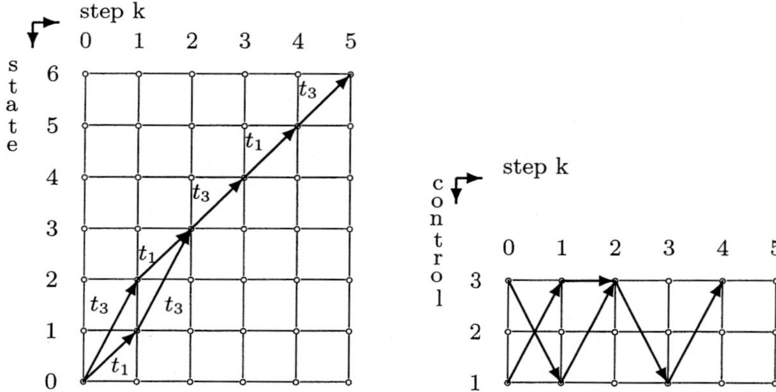


**Fig. 2.** The solution of the state trajectories (on the left) and the control trajectories (on the right)

$$\mathbf{X}_1 = \begin{pmatrix} 1&0&0&2&0&0\\ 0&1&0&0&2&0\\ 0&1&0&0&4&0\\ 0&0&2&0&0&8\\ 0&0&0&2&0&0\\ 0&0&0&0&2&0\\ 0&0&0&0&0&2 \end{pmatrix} \mathbf{X}_2 = \begin{pmatrix} 2&0&0&0&0&0\\ 0&1&0&0&0&0\\ 0&1&0&0&0&0\\ 0&0&1&0&0&0\\ 3&0&0&1&0&0\\ 0&2&0&0&1&0\\ 0&0&1&0&0&1 \end{pmatrix} \mathbf{X} = \begin{pmatrix} 1&0&0&0&0&0\\ 0&1&0&0&0&0\\ 0&1&0&0&0&0\\ 0&0&1&0&0&0\\ 0&0&0&1&0&0\\ 0&0&0&0&1&0\\ 0&0&0&0&0&1 \end{pmatrix} \quad (20)$$

$$\mathbf{U}_1^* = \begin{pmatrix} 1&0&0&2&0\\ 1&0&0&2&0\\ 0&1&0&0&2\\ 0&1&0&0&4\\ 0&0&2&0&0\\ 0&0&2&0&0\\ 0&0&0&2&0\\ 0&0&0&2&0\\ 0&0&0&0&2\\ 0&0&0&0&2\\ 0&0&0&0&0 \end{pmatrix} \mathbf{U}_2^* = \begin{pmatrix} 1&0&0&0&0\\ 1&0&0&0&0\\ 0&1&0&0&0\\ 0&1&0&0&0\\ 0&0&0&0&0\\ 0&0&1&0&0\\ 1&0&0&0&0\\ 2&0&0&1&0\\ 0&1&0&0&0\\ 0&1&0&0&1\\ 0&0&1&0&0 \end{pmatrix} \mathbf{U}^* = \begin{pmatrix} 1&0&0&0&0\\ 1&0&0&0&0\\ 0&1&0&0&0\\ 0&1&0&0&0\\ 0&0&0&0&0\\ 0&0&1&0&0\\ 0&0&0&0&0\\ 0&0&0&1&0\\ 0&0&0&0&0\\ 0&0&0&0&1\\ 0&0&0&0&0 \end{pmatrix} \quad (21)$$

$$\mathbf{U} = \mathbf{T}_{rTt}.\mathbf{U}^* = \begin{pmatrix} 1&1&0&1&0\\ 0&0&0&0&0\\ 1&1&1&0&1 \end{pmatrix}$$

## 4 Conclusions

The presented approach seems to be powerful and very useful for the bounded OPN. In the ODG-based form it yields the state trajectories from $\mathbf{x}_0$ to $\mathbf{x}_t$. Its BDG-based form offers also the control trajectories in addition to the state ones.

Another problem is how to choose the most suitable trajectory when control task specifications are prescribed. Because for DEDS they are usually given in nonanalytical terms a suitable representation of knowledge is necessary. The author's works [6, 7, 13] are interested in the knowledge-based control. It should be very useful to apply the knowledge-based approach at the choice of the most suitable control trajectory. It is the interesting challenge for the future research.

## References


1. Čapkovič, F.: Automated Solving of DEDS Control Problems. In: El-Dessouki, A., Imam, I., Kodratoff, Y., Ali, M. (eds.): Multiple Approaches to Intelligent Systems. Lecture Notes in Computer Science, Vol. 1611. Springer-Verlag, Berlin Heidelberg New York (1999) 735–746
2. Čapkovič, F.: Intelligent Control of Discrete Event Dynamic Systems. In: Koussoulas, N.T., Groumpos, P.P., Polycarpou, M. (eds.): Proc. of IEEE International Symposium on Intelligent Control. IEEE Press, Patras, Greece (2000) 109–114.
3. Čapkovič, F.: Modelling and Control of Discrete Event Dynamic Systems. BRICS Report Series, RS-00-26. University of Aarhus, Denmark (2000) 58 p.
4. Čapkovič, F.: A Solution of DEDS Control Synthesis Problems. In: Kozák, Š., Huba, M. (eds.): Control System Design. Proceedings of IFAC Conference. Pergamon, Elsevier Science. Oxford, UK (2000) 343–348.
5. Čapkovič, F.: An Approach to the Control Synthesis of State Machines. In: Trappl, R. (ed.): Cybernetics and Systems. Proceedings of 16th European Meeting on Cybernetics and Systems Research, Vol. 1. Austrian Society for Cybernetics Studies, Vienna, Austria (2002) 81–86.
6. Čapkovič, F.: Knowledge-Based Control Synthesis of Discrete Event Dynamic Systems. In: Tzafestas, S.G. (ed.): Advances in Manugacturing. Decision, Control and Information Technology. Chapter 19. Springer-Verlag, London (1998) 195–206.
7. Čapkovič, F., Čapkovič, P.: Intelligent Control Synthesis of Manufacturing Systems. In: Monostori, L., Vancza, J., Ali, M. (eds.): Engineering of Intelligent Systems. Lecture Notes in Computer Sciences, Vol. 2070. Springer-Verlag, Berlin Heidelberg New York (2001) 767–776.
8. CzechResGr.: http://dce.felk.cvut.cz/cak/Research/index_Research.htm
9. Diestel, R.: Graph Theory. Springer-Verlag, New York (1997)
10. Holloway, L., Krogh, B., Giuia, A.: A Survey of Petri Net Methods for Controlled Discrete Event Systems. Discrete Event Dynamic Systems: Theory and Applications **7** (1997) 151–180.
11. Pastor, E., Cortadella, J., Pena, M.A.: Structural Methods to Improve the Symbolic Analysis of Petri Nets. In: Donatelli, S., Kleijn, J. (eds.): Application and Theory of Petri Nets 1999. Lecture Notes in Computer Sciences, Vol. 1639. Springer-Verlag, Berlin Heidelberg New York (1999) 26–45
12. Peterson, J.L.: Petri Net Theory and Modeling the Systems. Prentice Hall, New York (1981)
13. Tzafestas, S.G., Čapkovič, F.: Petri Net-Based Approach to Synthesis of Intelligent Control for DEDS. In: Tzafestas, S.G. (ed.): Computer Assisted Management and Control of Manufacturing Systems, Chapter 12. Springer-Verlag, Berlin Heidelberg New York (1997) 325–351

# Nurse Rostering Using Constraint Programming and Meta-level Reasoning*

Gary Yat Chung Wong[1] and Hon Wai Chun[2]

[1] City University of Hong Kong , Department of Electronic Engineering , Tat Chee Avenue, Kowloon, Hong Kong SAR
ycwong@ee.cityu.edu.hk

[2] City University of Hong Kong, Department of Computer Science, Tat Chee Avenue, Kowloon, Hong Kong SAR
andy.chun@cityu.edu.hk

**Abstract.** Constraint programming techniques have been widely used in many different types of applications. However for NP-hard problems, such as scheduling, resources allocation, etc, basic constraint programming techniques may not be enough solve efficiently. This paper describes a design and implementation of a simplified nurse rostering system using constraint programming and automatic implied constraint generation by meta-level reasoning. The nurse rostering system requires generating a weekly timetable by assigning work shifts to nurse. Although the problem set is simplified, the search is difficult because it involves more than hundred constraints with a search space of about $3.74 \times 10^{50}$. Using only traditional constraint programming techniques, even in addition with popular heuristics, no timetable can be generated in reasonable time. To improve the search, we propose to use automatic implied constraint generation by meta-level reasoning. Several solvable and non-solvable problem instances were tested. With our approach, these instances can be solved or identified as non-solvable within one second.

## 1 Introduction

In this paper, we present a design and implementation of a simplified nurse rostering system. The task is to generate a weekly timetable, involving 12 nurses with four shifts including three work shifts and a day off shift. Timetable generated should satisfy three sets of constraints, which are daily, weekly and shift pattern constraints. Although the problem set is simplified, the generation of timetable is difficult because there are *more than a hundred* different constraints involved and the search space is $4^{(7\times12)}$ (i.e. about $3.74 \times 10^{50}$), which is of course *extremely huge*.

Because of flexibility in modeling and ease of search method extension, constraint programming is used as the core of this nurse rostering system [2], [10], [19]. As the complexity of this nurse rostering problem is high, using traditional constraint

* The work described in this paper was substantially supported by a grant from the Research Grants Council of the Hong Kong Special Administrative Region, China (Project No. 9040517, CityU 1109/00E). This work was also partially supported by a grant from City University of Hong Kong (Project No. 7001286).

P.W.H. Chung, C.J. Hinde, M. Ali (Eds.): IEA/AIE 2003, LNAI 2718, pp. 712–721, 2003.

programming techniques alone will not find a solution that can satisfy all constraints in reasonable time (over 12 hours). No solution can be found even with the use of popular heuristics, such as Fail First Principle (FFP) and Most Constrained First (MCF) [16], etc. To reduce the search time, we propose to use automatic implied constraint generation by meta-level reasoning. It is a process executed before conventional constraint programming search starts. It automatically generates a set of implied constraints for the problem and reduces unnecessary trials in searching by further pruning the search tree. Besides, it may also be able to discover non-solvable problem before search starts. On the contrary, conventional constraint programming cannot identify non-solvable instance until the whole search space is examined. Several problem instances were tested. With our approach, we were able to solve these instances or discover that there is no solution within only *one second*.

In the following Sections, we first describe some background research related to this topic. In Section 3, the detail of the nurse rostering problem is described. In Section 4, we explain how our approach solves this problem. Finally this paper closes with statistical results of different test cases and conclusion.

## 2 Background

Constraint Programming is proposed to solve different kinds of industrial applications [2], including nurse rostering [1], [10], [19], because of the ease in modeling and a set of well-developed tool in searching. In this Section, we describe the background of constraint programming and also different approaches developed for nurse rostering.

Constraint Programming (CP) [9], [16] techniques can be used to solve problems after they are modeled as Constraint Satisfaction Problems (CSP). A CSP [11] consists of *a set of variable*, each of them is associated with *finite domain of possible values*, and a *set of constraints*, which restrict the combination of value that associated variables can take. And the goal in CSP solving is to find a *consistent assignment* of values to the set of variables so that all constraints can be satisfied *simultaneously*. As modeling only involves variables and constraints, many real world problems can be modeled directly. Research in Constraint Programming can be divided into three categories; they are search methods, problem reduction and ordering heuristics [9], [16]. Several *search methods* have developed such as generate-and-test, backtrack search and backjumping [16], etc. However, considering the efficiency and ease of implementation backtrack search is generally used. *Problem reduction* prunes search space dynamically when state of CSP is modified, different arc-consistency maintenance methods [12], [14], [17] are developed. Higher-level of consistency maintenance [16] is also studied; however, as the computation complexity is high, arc-consistency and some domain reduction technique for n-ary constraints are usually used instead. *Ordering heuristics* included variable and value ordering. According to probability and graph theory [4], a set of generic ordering heuristics are developed, such as Minimal-Width Ordering (MWO) [5], Minimal-Conflict First (MCF) [16], Fail First Principle (FFP) [16], MWO/FFP Hybrid [20], etc. Most constraint programming tools are equipped with basic set of search methods, problem reduction routines and ordering heuristics, such as ILOG Solver [6], JSolver [3], etc. These techniques are efficient in solving some problems, but for complicated problems, such as Nurse Rostering example in this paper, solution cannot be obtained within reasonable time. Therefore, additional techniques are usually needed.

In the following, different approaches in solving nurse rostering problem are studied. They are grouped into three categories, which are Mathematical approach [13], [15], [18] Evolutionary Algorithm [7], [8] and Constraint Programming [1], [10], [19]. Mathematical approach involves mathematical modeling of problem and applies operations research to solve the problem [13], [18], but this approach is inflexible. Although domain specific heuristics and algorithms [15] can be used to improve the flexibility, the modeling and implementation cost is high and not generic. In addition, successful algorithms and heuristics in a particular scenario may not perform well in other problem domains (mentioned in [1]). Evolutionary Algorithm represents possible solutions by chromosomes, and tries to find feasible solution by genetic operations such as crossover and mutation. In order to reduce complexity, constraints are coded in chromosomes [8], or search based on history [7]. Thus these lead to inflexibility in constraint modeling and cannot guarantee to find solution even without time limitation. In addition, same as mathematical approaches, it is not generic. And the last approach is Constraint Programming. In terms of modeling flexibility and ease of extending search methods, it is an adequate approach used to model and solve real world problems [2], [10], [19]. As mentioned before, rich set of basic constraint programming tools has already been well developed. However for complicated problems, it may suffer from long computation time in traversing the search tree. Therefore, Cheng [1] used redundant modeling to speed up constraint propagation to improve search speed. Experiments are done to confirm the efficiency of the approach. However, the extra modeling used becomes the disadvantage of this approach.

In our approach, we adopt constraint programming as the core of scheduling system, different from redundant modeling, additional constraints are not created by human, instead meta-level reasoning is used to generate implied constraint automatically. Different from traditional constraint programming research, it is neither a new search method nor ordering heuristic, but considers relationships between constraints in order to discover implicit limitation of the problem, preventing unnecessary tries and speed up the search. This approach is potentially become a new research direction in constraint programming. Detail will be explained in Section 4.

## 3 Nurse Rostering Problem

This Section describes the simplified nurse rostering problem. Although it is simplified, it contains all the basic elements in a practical nurse rostering system. In addition, this sample problem is not solvable with conventional constraint programming techniques (with ordering heuristics such as MWO, FFP, MWO/FFP hybrid, etc) in reasonable time and memory. In the following, the detail of rostering problem and modeling will be described.

In this nurse rostering problem, there are twelve nurses working three different shifts. The three shifts are Morning Shift (A), Afternoon Shift (P) and Overnight Shift (N) and the symbol (DO) represents a Day Off. The goal is to assign duty shifts and day off to each nurse in a week with three main types of constraint; Daily Constraints, Weekly Constraints and Shift Pattern Constraints.

*Daily Constraints* (vertical constraints) define the manpower needed in a particular shift for each day. In this paper, we have six different instances of daily constraints requirement for testing (see Test Cases Results in Section 5).

*Weekly Constraints* (horizontal constraints) define the expected work for each nurse within a week. There are three weekly constraints (used in all six instances):

- Each nurse should get at least one day off
- Each nurse should work at least one overnight shift
- Each nurse can work at most four morning shifts

*Shift Pattern Constraints* define legal or desirable shift assignment sequences for a nurse. There is one shift pattern constraint (also used in all test cases):

- After working an overnight shift, the nurse should be given a day off or should continue to work another overnight shift.

In problem modeling, shift assignment for a nurse in a particular day is modeled by constraint variable, and the domain of each variable is 0 to 3, which represents DO, A, P & N respectively. Besides, cardinality constraint is used to model both daily and weekly constraints. i.e. *Cardinality Equals to* (*CardEq*) model daily constraint. *Cardinality Greater than or Equals to* (*CardGE*) and *Cardinality Less than or Equals to* (*CardLE*) model weekly constraint:

*Daily constraints:*
*C1:* *CardEq*(A,daily_requirement) : (Vertical, total 7, Mon-Sun)
*C2:* *CardEq*(P,daily_requirement) : (Vertical, total 7, Mon-Sun)
*C3:* *CardEq*(N,daily_requirement) : (Vertical, total 7, Mon-Sun)
*Weekly constraints:*
*C4:* *CardGE*(N,1) : (Horizontal, total 12 nurses)
*C5:* *CardGE*(DO,1) : (Horizontal, total 12 nurses)
*C6:* *CardLE*(A,4) : (Horizontal, total 12 nurses)

To simplify explanation, constraints are grouped and labeled with *C1* to *C6*. For example, daily morning shift constraints are labeled as *C1*. In table point of view, *C1* is vertical constraint, and there are 7 *C1* constraints in a week (Similar for *C2* and *C3*). Weekly constraints are posted on each nurse (horizontal constraints). For example, *C4* defines the overnight shift requirement for each nurse, and therefore there are 12 *C4* constraints in a weekly timetable. *C5* and *C6* define requirement of day off and morning shift respectively. Same as *C4*, there are 12 *C5* and *C6* constraints in a weekly timetable. Fig. 1 below shows a successful generated timetable by given daily and weekly constraint C1 to C6, which also satisfy shift pattern constraints. To model shift patterns, it is straightforward to make use of conditional constraints. For example: *If* ($Tom_{mon}=N$), *then* ($Tom_{tue}=N$ *or* $Tom_{tue}=DO$). Of course, shift pattern constraints should cover the whole table for all nurses, not only for Tom and not only on Monday or Tuesday. Although it is straightforward to model shift pattern by if... then... constraints, to make it easier to consider relationships with other constraints, we define a new shift pattern constraint type to model it directly.

The newly defined *Shift Pattern constraint* consists of two set of compound labels, which are **key compound label** and *element compound label*. Key compound label is a set of condition label (i.e. If statement), and when all condition labels in key compound label are satisfied, element compound label (i.e. then statement) should be instantiated. Fig. 2 below shows the first 8 of 14 possible shift pattern constraints *for each nurse* according to shift pattern constraints.

| Name | S | M | T | W | T | F | S | A | P | N |
|---|---|---|---|---|---|---|---|---|---|---|
| *John* | DO | A | N | N | *DO* | A | DO | 2 | 0 | 2 |
| *Kate* | DO | A | N | N | *DO* | A | A | 3 | 0 | 2 |
| *Tom* | A | N | *DO* | A | A | A | P | 4 | 1 | 1 |
| *Susan* | A | N | *DO* | A | A | A | P | 4 | 1 | 1 |
| *Jan* | N | *DO* | A | A | A | A | P | 4 | 1 | 1 |
| *Nancy* | N | *DO* | A | A | A | P | A | 4 | 1 | 1 |
| *Linda* | *DO* | A | A | A | A | P | N | 4 | 1 | 1 |
| *David* | *DO* | A | A | A | P | P | N | 3 | 2 | 1 |
| *Jerry* | A | A | A | P | P | N | *DO* | 3 | 2 | 1 |
| *Amy* | P | P | P | P | P | N | *DO* | 0 | 5 | 1 |
| *Mary* | P | P | P | P | N | *DO* | A | 1 | 4 | 1 |
| *Bill* | P | P | P | P | N | *DO* | A | 1 | 4 | 1 |
| C1: *A* | 3 | 5 | 5 | 6 | 5 | 5 | 4 | | | |
| C2: *P* | 3 | 3 | 3 | 4 | 3 | 3 | 3 | | | |
| C3: *N* | 2 | 2 | 2 | 2 | 2 | 2 | 2 | | | |

**Fig. 1.** Example: A successful generated timetable

| | Sun | Mon | Tue | Wed | Thr | Fri | Sat |
|---|---|---|---|---|---|---|---|
| 1 | N | *N* | } After working an overnight shift, the nurse should be given a day off or continue to work another overnight shift. | | | | |
| 2 | N | *DO* | | | | | |
| 3 | | N | *N* | | | | |
| 4 | | N | *DO* | | | | |
| 5 | | | N | *N* | | | |
| 6 | | | N | *DO* | | | |
| 7 | | | | N | *N* | | |
| 8 | | | | N | *DO* | | |
| .. | | | | | ... | ... | |

**Fig. 2.** Possible shift patterns for each nurse (8 of 12)

For each nurse, there are 7 shift pattern requirements to cover shift pattern requirement in a week and each shift pattern can be modeled by 2 newly defined shift pattern constraints (e.g. first two pattern in figure above). Therefore we have 14 shift pattern constraints for each nurse in a week. With this modeling method, meta-level reasoning can be done more directly and will be explained in next Section.

## 4 Meta-level Reasoning

This Section describes the detail of meta-level reasoning for implied constraint generation. Meta-level reasoning is a process that considers relationship among constraints to discover implicit limitation of the problem, preventing unnecessary tries and speeding up the search. Note that, meta-level reasoning is done on constraint level. In other words, it is domain independent and this technique can also be used on other problem domains. In this Section, we focus on constraints used in nurse rostering problem and explain how our approach works.

As mentioned in last Section, this nurse rostering problem contains cardinality constraints and newly defined shift pattern constraints. In the following, we explain how meta-level reasoning generates implied constraints by considering constraints of same and different type. In other words, we analyze "relationships between shift pattern constraints", "relationships between cardinality constraints", and also "relationships between cardinality constraints and shift pattern constraints".

## 4.1 Relationships between Shift Pattern Constraints

According to hypothetical syllogism in statement calculus, we know that, "If X⇒Y and Y⇒Z, then X⇒Z". Apply this to relationships between shift pattern constraints, we know that: If element compound label of a shift pattern constraint is subset of another shift pattern constraint's key compound label, then they can be combined to form new shift pattern constraints. Following are 2 examples:

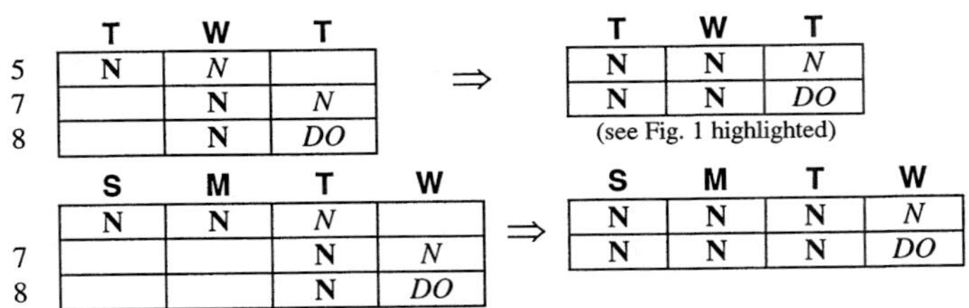

**Fig. 3.** Relationship between shift pattern constraints

The first example in Fig. 3 above shows how *pattern 5*, *7* and *8* (use labeling in Fig. 2.) are used to generate two new patterns. In this case, pattern 5 is removed after new patterns generated, because its element compound label is combined with *pattern 7* and *8*. Note that *pattern 7* and *8* remain after new pattern generated. And the new generated patterns can be used to generate new patterns again.

As seen from the example above, relationships between shift pattern constraints can be used to generate new shift pattern constraints. And newly generated shift pattern constraints can also be used to further generate more shift pattern constraints recursively with other patterns.

| | Sun | Mon | Tue | Wed | Thr | Fri | Sat |
|---|---|---|---|---|---|---|---|
| **Pattern 1** | N | *DO* | | | | | |
| ***new 1*** | N | N | *DO* | | | | |
| ***new 2*** | N | N | N | *DO* | | | |
| ***new 3*** | N | N | N | N | *DO* | | |
| ***new 4*** | N | N | N | N | N | *DO* | |
| ***new 5*** | N | N | N | N | N | N | *DO* |

**Fig. 4.** Pattern 1 and new patterns generated with respect to Pattern 1

The table above shows the set of new patterns generated by *Pattern 1* (labeled in Fig. 2) with other patterns in Fig. 2. Note that besides of *Pattern 1*, *Pattern 3, 5, 7* also satisfy the condition of generate new patterns (i.e. pattern's element is subset of some other pattern's key). And their new patterns are similar to above, but shifted.

### 4.2 Relationships between Cardinality Constraints

It is more complicated to find relationship between cardinality constraints compare with shift pattern constraints because there are different type of cardinality constraints, such as *CardEq*, *CardGE*, *CardLE*, etc. And they can have different constrained value; *A*, *P*, *N* and *DO*. Besides, we can consider cardinality constraints associated to same set of variable, intersect set of variable (only a subset of variables is common), or disjoint set of variables. To consider all the relationship, number of combination of 57 cardinality constraints in this problem is extremely huge (Equation 1) and impossible to do so. Therefore we have to select useful constraint relationship for reasoning. And we choose *disjoint* and *same set* relationship for analysis.

$$\text{Number of combination} = \sum_{i=2}^{57} C_i^{57} \qquad \text{— (Equation 1)}$$

**CASE 1:** In grouping of *disjoint sets* of cardinality constraints, we further reduce the number of combination by only grouping constraints of "*same type* and with *same constrained value*" because it is more meaningful for reasoning. Therefore, by grouping daily requirement from Monday to Sunday, we can obtain the number of A, P and N shift needed *in a week* (i.e. *in whole timetable*). As see the example below:

| | | S | M | T | W | T | F | S | | For whole table |
|---|---|---|---|---|---|---|---|---|---|---|
| C1: | A | 3 | 5 | 5 | 6 | 5 | 5 | 4 | ⇒ | *CardEq(A, 33)* |
| C2: | P | 3 | 3 | 3 | 4 | 3 | 3 | 3 | ⇒ | *CardEq(P, 22)* |
| C3: | N | 2 | 2 | 2 | 2 | 2 | 2 | 2 | ⇒ | *CardEq(N, 14)* |

**Fig. 5.** Constraint generated by grouping C1 to C3 (group of vertical constraints)

Similarly, by grouping weekly constraint, another set of requirement on N, DO and A shift can be obtained (see Fig. below).

| Weekly | | For whole table |
|---|---|---|
| 12 nurses x C4: CardGE(N,1) | ⇒ | *CardGE(N, 12)* |
| 12 nurses x C5: CardGE(DO,1) | ⇒ | *CardGE(DO, 12)* |
| 12 nurses x C6: CardLE(A,4) | ⇒ | *CardLE(A, 48)* |

**Fig. 6.** Constraint generated by grouping C4 to C6 (group of horizontal constraints)

**CASE 2:** To group constraints of "*same set, same constraint type and different constrained value*", we can discover limitations on other values. Apply this to our nurse rostering problem, daily requirement on *A*, *P* and *N* shift can be used to find the day off requirement. Following is an example that extends Fig. 5 daily requirements. As there are 12 nurses, therefore sum of each column should be 12, and the day off requirement can be obtained as below:

| | S | M | T | W | T | F | S | | For whole table |
|---|---|---|---|---|---|---|---|---|---|
| A | 3 | 5 | 5 | 6 | 5 | 5 | 4 | ⇒ | *CardEq(A, 33)* |
| P | 3 | 3 | 3 | 4 | 3 | 3 | 3 | ⇒ | *CardEq(P, 22)* |
| N | 2 | 2 | 2 | 2 | 2 | 2 | 2 | ⇒ | *CardEq(N, 14)* |
| DO | 4 | 2 | 2 | 0 | 2 | 2 | 3 | ⇒ | *CardEq(DO, 15)* |

**Fig. 7.** Day Off requirement generated

In the example above we discover that there should be **no** day off on Wednesday. However, in conventional constraint programming, it is possible to assign day off on Wednesday since there is no constraint restricting the assignment explicitly, so it may cause serious backtrack. Therefore the implied constraints generated can help in reduce search space and improve the search.

For weekly constraints, as number of overnight shift and day off must be greater than or equals to one (*CardGE*), it implies that number of morning and afternoon shift per week should be less than 5 (7 days - at least 1 night shift - at least 1 day off) and number of overnight shift and day off should be less than 6, i.e. *CardLe* constraints generated and this holds for each nurse.

**CASE 3:** Grouping *same set* of cardinality constraints of *different type but same constrained value* (for example: *CardEq(14,N)* in Fig. 5 and *CardGE(12,N)* in Fig. 6) seems to be redundant, since there is only one constraints useful (in this example, *CardEq(14,N)*). However, as *CardGE(12,N)* is generated by 12 *CardGE(N,1)* weekly constraints, the limitation of *CardEq(14,N)* can propagate to the 12 *CardGE(1,N)* and generate *twelve new weekly constraints, CardLE(3,N)*, because only 2 extra *N* (14–12) can be added for each nurse in a week.

Besides, the analysis result may tighten *dynamically* when the state of problem is changing. For example, if there is a nurse already assigned with 3 overnight shifts in a week, than other nurse should work only one overnight shift a week (because 3 + 11 x 1 = 14), i.e. new generated weekly constraint of other nurses are tighten from *CardLe(3,N)* to *CardEq(1,N)* and this situation is also handled in our implementation.

### 4.3 Relationships between Cardinality Constraint and Shift Pattern Constraints

When considering relationship between cardinality constraints and shift pattern constraints, we can view shift pattern constraints as compound labels and cardinality constraints are responsible to check if the set of compound labels are feasible or not. If there exists infeasible pattern, it should be removed. For example, according to example in case 3 above, the number of night shift is less than or equal to 3 a week, therefore the last three patterns, *new 3,4* and *5* in Fig. 4 can be removed. Besides, in Case 2 above, *CardEq(DO,0)* constraint is generated on Wednesday, therefore the pattern, *new 2* in Fig. 4 can also be removed.

As shown above, we have gone through different ways to generate redundant constraints automatically. Note that when there are new constraints generated, they are put into constraint analysis for redundant constraint generation iteratively until no more constraints can be generated.

Above paragraphs explained how constraints relationships considered to generate new useful implied constraints and demonstrate by nurse rostering example. As process is done on constraint level, therefore it is domain independent. Although shift pattern constraint is re-modeled by a pattern constraint, this constraint can be reused consider as a compound label. Pattern can be found in other constraint type such as "or constraint", "equal constraint", etc. In this nurse rostering problem, pattern is selected by *CardEq* constraint to fill into the timetable before traditional search starts (see Fig. 1 highlighted). *CardEq* constraint is used because it has higher chance to instantiate correct compound label. This approach can also used in other problem domain, but more study is needed on constraint priority and pattern ordering.

## 5 Test Case Results

There are 6 test cases, which have different set of daily constraints but same weekly requirement and shift pattern constraints. By use of meta-level reasoning, solution can be found for the first 5 test cases and report the last test case is non-solvable within *one second* (see statistical result** in Fig. 9). In conventional constraint programming, problem cannot be identify as non-solvable until the whole search space is checked, which is extremely time consuming. However our approach is able to determine the case is non-solvable before search starts. To explain how it can be achieved, some constraints generated by meta-level reasoning are listed in the table below.

| | S | M | T | W | T | F | S | | For whole table |
|---|---|---|---|---|---|---|---|---|---|
| **A** | 4 | 4 | 4 | 4 | 4 | 4 | 4 | ⇒ | *CardEq(A, 28)* |
| **P** | 5 | 5 | 5 | 5 | 5 | 5 | 5 | ⇒ | *CardEq(P, 35)* |
| **N** | 1 | 1 | 1 | 1 | 1 | 1 | 1 | ⇒ | *CardEq(N, 7)* |

**Fig. 8.** Test case 6 daily requirements and some constraints generated

Compare the overnight shift requirement in generated above and overnight shift requirement in Fig. 6 (generated by weekly constraints), conflict is found, because CardEq(N,7) and CardGE(N,12) cannot be satisfied simultaneously. Therefore, we able to discover no solution before search.

Although this is a simplified nurse rostering problem, our approach has great improvement on traditional constraint programming, since this problem cannot be solved by traditional constraint programming, even with generic heuristics.

| | *Case 1* | *Case 2* | *Case 3* | *Case 4* | *Case 5* | *Case 6* |
|---|---|---|---|---|---|---|
| *# of fail* | 0 | 0 | 0 | 0 | 0 | - |
| *# of choice pt.* | 81 | 85 | 54 | 78 | 78 | - |
| *Elapse time* | 0.33 sec | 0.39 sec | 0.66 sec | 0.61 sec | 0.49 sec | - |

**Fig. 9.** Statistic of test cases

## 6 Conclusion

This paper presented the design and implementation of a nurse rostering system using constraint programming and meta-level reasoning. With meta-level reasoning, implied constraints are automatically generated to help to solve NP-hard nurse rostering problems that were not solvable before conventional techniques in reasonable time. There are two main contributions in our work. For constraint programming, we provide an alternative research direction – to explore relationships among constraints – meta-level reasoning. This technique can further prune the search space and speed up the search. In addition, our conflict detection technique between existing and generated implied constraints may discover there is *no solution* even before search. In conventional constraint programming, *non-solvable* problems can only be discovered after traversing the whole search tree. From an application point of

** Our scheduler is implemented by JSolver [3], and run on a Pentium III (700MHz) machine.

view, the nurse rostering problems that cannot be solved with conventional constraint programming can now be solved within *one second*. Besides, for some instances, our approach may able to discover non-solvable problems before search.

A future direction of development is to design more reasoning methods for different kinds of constraints relationships, so that this technique can apply on problems of different domains.

## References


1. B.M.W. Cheng, J.H.M. Lee and J.C.K. Wu, "A Nurse Rostering System Using Constraint Programming and Redundant Modeling," *IEEE Transactions on Information Technology in Biomedicine*, 1, pp. 44-54, 1997
2. H.W. Chun, "A methodology for object-oriented constraint programming," *in Proc. 4th Asia-Pacific Software Engineering and International Computer Science Conf.*, 1997
3. H.W. Chun, "Constraint Programming in Java with JSolver", in *Proceedings of the First International Conference and Exhibition on The Practical Application of Constraint Technologies and Logic Programming*, London, April 1999.
4. R. Dechter and J. Pearl, "Network-Based Heuristics for Constraint-Satisfaction Problems," In *Search in Artificial Intelligence,* eds. L. Kanal and V. Kumar, Springer-Verlag, 1988.
5. E. Freuder, "Backtrack-Free and Backtrack-Bounded Search," in *Search in Artificial Intelligence,* eds. L. Kanal and V. Kumar, pp. 343–369, New York: Springer-Verlag, 1988.
6. http://www.ilog.com/
7. A. Jan, M. Yamamoto, A. Ohuchi, "Evolutionary algorithms for nurse scheduling problem," *in Proc. Evolutionary Computation*, vol. 1, pp. 196-203, 2000
8. H. Kawanaka, K. Yamamoto, T. Yoshikawa, T. Shinogi, S. Tsuruoka, "Genetic algorithm with the constraints for nurse scheduling problem," *in Proc. Evolutionary Computation*, vol. 2, pp. 1123-1130, 2001
9. V. Kumar, "Algorithms for constraint satisfaction problems: A survey," *AI Magazine*, vol. 13, no. 1, pp. 32-44, 1992.
10. J.M. Lazaro, P. Aristondo, "Using SOLVER for nurse scheduling," *in Proc. ILOG SOLVER & ILOG SCHEDULE First Int. Users' Conf.*, July 1995.
11. A.K. Mackworth, "Consistency in networks of relations," *Artificial Intelligence*, 8, no. 1, pp. 99–118, 1977.
12. A.K. Mackworth and E.C. Freuder, "The complexity of some polynomial network consistency algorithms for constraint satisfaction problems," *Artificial Intelligence*, 25, pp. 65-74, 1985.
13. H.E. Miller, "Nurse scheduling using mathematical programming," *Oper. Res.*, vol. 24, no. 8, pp. 857-870, 1976
14. R. Mohr and T.C. Henderson, "Arc and path consistency revised," *Artificial Intelligence*, 28, pages 225-233, 1986.
15. I. Ozkarahan, J. Bailey, "Goal programming model subsystem of a flexible nurse scheduling support system," *IIE Trans.*, vol. 20, no. 3, pp. 306-316, 1988
16. E.P.K. Tsang, "Foundations of Constraint Satisfaction," *Academic Press*, 1993.
17. P. Van Hentenryck, Y. Deville, and C.M. Teng, "A generic arc-consistency algorithm and its specializations," *Artificial Intelligence*, 57, pages 291-321, 1992.
18. D.M. Warner, "Scheduling nursing personnel according to nursing preference: A mathematical programming approach," *Oper. Res.*, vol. 24, no. 8, pp. 842-856, 1976
19. G. Weil, K. Heus, P. Francois, and M. Poujade, "Constraint programming for nurse scheduling," *IEEE Eng. Med. Biol.*, vol. 14, no. 4, pp. 417–422, July/Aug. 1995.
20. G.Y.C. Wong and A.H.W. Chun "CP Heuristics: MWO/FFP Hybrid and Relaxed FFP," In *Proc. of the 4th Systemics, Informatics and Cybernetics*, Orlando, July 2000.

# An Application of Genetic Algorithm to Hierarchical Configuration of ATM Internetworking Domain with a Special Constraint for Scalable Broadcasting

Dohoon Kim

School of Business, Kyung Hee University
1-bunji Hoegi-dong, Dongdaemoon-gu
Seoul 130-701, Korea
dyohaan@khu.ac.kr
http://kbiz.khu.ac.kr/dhkim

**Abstract.** Presented is a Genetic Algorithm(GA) for dynamic partitioning of an ATM internetworking domain such as LANE(LAN Emulation) that provides guaranteed quality of service for mid-size campus or enterprise networks. There are few researches on the efficient LANE network operations to deal with scalability issues arising from multi-media broadcasting, limiting its potential in multimedia applications. To cope with the scalability issue here, proposed is a decision model named LANE Partitioning Problem(LPP) which aims at partitioning the entire LANE network into multiple virtual LANs. We also demonstrate with some experiments that compared with the current rule-of-thumb practice, the suggested LPP decision model and GA-based solution method significantly enhances performance, thereby providing good scalability in a large internetworking environment such as ATM LANE and mobile ATM LAN.

## 1 Introduction

With the demand for real time multimedia services growing, many technologies that provide QoS(Quality of Service) through legacy LAN systems have been introduced. For example, LANE(LAN Emulation) is one of the most representative solutions that employ ATM signaling and target campus or small enterprise networks. However, some scalability issues arise when distributing broadcast traffic generated by legacy LAN applications over LANE network. To cope with the scalability issues, an entire LANE network domain is usually divided into multiple areas called ELAN(Emulated LAN) which sets a limit of broadcast transmission. The inter-ELAN broadcast traffic needs additional modifications to be properly treated at the upper layers(e.g., IP layer), thereby increasing process overhead at the equipments, and degrading the service performance. As a result, partitioning a LANE network affects the overall performance of the network. However, there have been few researches to suggest guidelines for the ELAN configuration conducted so far.

P.W.H. Chung, C.J. Hinde, M. Ali (Eds.): IEA/AIE 2003, LNAI 2718, pp. 722–733, 2003.

In this study, we introduce operational issues for LANE network performance and provide a framework for efficient ELAN configuration and management. Focusing on broadcast traffic management, we suggest a decision model to partition a LANE network and a real-time automatic solution engine to configure logical ELANs, which are at the core of the framework. The next section presents an overview of LANE network and ELAN operations followed by a decision model to configure optimal ELANs for dealing with scalability issues. Provided are a solution method based on GA(Genetic Algorithm) and experiment results on a real campus network with some implications regarding LANE network operations.

## 2 ATM Internetworking Architecture and Scalability Issues

We describe the ATM-based LAN internetworking systems with focusing on the LANE architecture which works on the client-server basis. Firstly, the hosts on ATM networks emulate MAC(Media Access Control) layer protocols of traditional LANs. LEC(LAN Emulation Client), working as a client in the middle of legacy LANs and a ATM network, transforms LAN frames into ATM cells and vice versa. There are three kinds of servers: LES(LAN Emulation Server), BUS(Broadcast and Unknown Server), and LECS(LAN Emulated Configuration Server). LES translates between MAC address and ATM address on behalf of all the entities in the ATM network. LES responds to the clients with address resolution results so that sender(e.g., LEC) can establish data direct VCC(Virtual Channel Connection) with recipient(e.g., another LEC). For the transmission of broadcast traffic generated from ethernet or Novell SAP, BUS acts as a hub. LEC forwards its broadcast data to the BUS via multicast-send VCC, and BUS in turn, via its multicast-forward VCCs, sends the broadcast data to all the LEC under its control. LECS is responsible for assigning LECs to a certain pair of LES and BUS, thereby partitioning the entire set of LECs into groups called ELANs(Emulated LANs). LECS also manages dynamic membership of LECs in alignment with changes in traffic pattern over the LANE network.

The most advantageous feature of the LANE solution lies at the backward compatibility or transparency that all the legacy applications used in the existing LAN systems are directly applicable to the LANE architecture without major modification. This merit stems from inter-operations among different layers such as MAC of legacy LANs, ATM, and IP, while incurring additional costs of increased operational complexity, the overhead of address translation, in particular. Moreover, because of the hub-spoke transport structure when delivering broadcast traffic, the capacity of BUS sets a limit on the volume of broadcast traffic that can be processed during a unit time. This limit comes to be a practical factor that restricts the number of LECs under the control of a single BUS. Considering the operational overhead at LECs and a BUS, the possible overload at a LEC can be another factor to restrict the number of LECs covered by a BUS. Accordingly, when broadcast storm([6]) happens during a very short period of time, the overload at LECs and BUS can cause a serious performance degradation of the entire LANE network. These problems constitute the major sources of the scalability issues in the LANE network.

To alleviate the scalability problems arising in a large campus or enterprise LANE network, employed is a hierarchical configuration of the LANE network, where the entire LANE network is partitioned into groups of LECs. Each group is working as if it were a virtual LAN, so-called ELAN. As a result, a prospective hierarchical configuration and management module at LECS will organize and coordinate ELANs. An ELAN is composed of BUS, LES, and LECs, where seamless cooperation of all the entities makes intra-ELAN traffic seemingly work as if it were delivered in a LAN. However, inter-ELAN traffic should go through much more complex operations to be delivered via intermediary equipments like routers; that is, a sender(LEC) forwards data to its corresponding LES which has an intermediary device and relays the data to another LES in a different ELAN based on the upper layer routing protocol.

Since an ELAN is a logical group of LECs regardless of their physical connections, its configuration is flexible and easily changed by re-arranging database at LECS. Accordingly, at the heart of materializing this strength is the LECS with an efficient engine for the decisions on matching LECs and servers based on topological information and/or administrative policies. This flexible operational feature has great potentials which hardly can be seen in the case of expanding ordinary LANs.

Though a badly arranged ELAN with too many LECs is prone to failure due to broadcast storm, there have been few researches and practical guidelines regarding this critical decision issue directly linked with the LANE service quality. In this study, we introduce a decision framework for ELAN configuration and propose an efficient scheme to ease the loads of LESs and BUSs, which are the major performance bottlenecks. In particular, our model aims at effective management of dynamically changing broadcast traffic since upon partitioning a LANE network, broadcasting has far more effects on the network performance than unicasting.

## 3 LANE Partition Problem

### 3.1 Criteria of LANE Partition Problem (LPP)

In light of the backward compatibility, broadcast applications in a LANE network are basically the same as those for the current legacy LANs. For example, file sharing and multimedia interactive games using IPX and NETBEUI generate the most typical broadcast traffic in a LANE network. In hierarchical LANE networks, two LECs belonging to different ELANs require another upper layer protocols like IPoA(IP over ATM) and MPoA(Multi-Protocol over ATM) to perform re-treatment for broadcast traffic between them. Thus, they are likely to incur additional complexity and delay, thereby delivering inferior service quality to LEC pairs in the same ELAN. Here, a pair of LECs who belong to different ELANs and demand broadcast transmission will be called a cut-pair, and the broadcast demand for a cut-pair will be called re-treatment demand. Another assumption here is that the total cost incurred from re-treatment for a cut-pair is proportional to the size of re-treatment demand. Accordingly, the objective of LANE Partition Problem(LPP) to build efficient ELAN con-

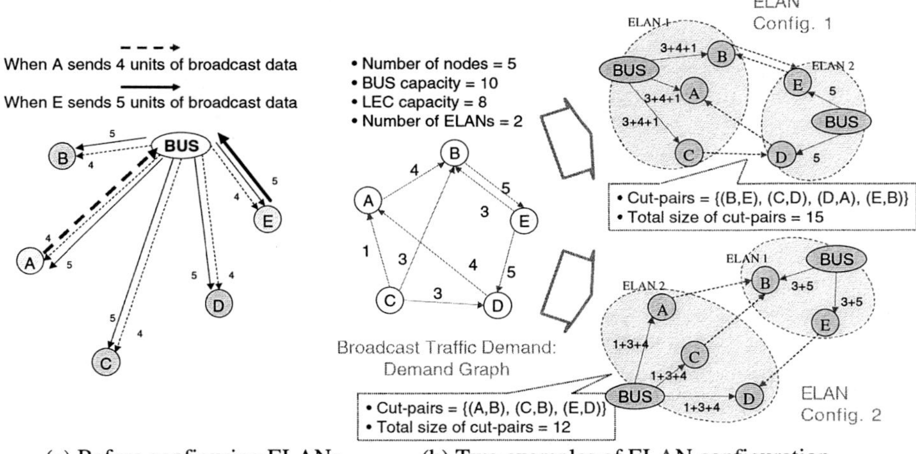


(a) Before configuring ELANs (b) Two examples of ELAN configuration

**Fig. 1.** 5 nodes(LECs) in figure (a) are to be clustered into two groups(ELANs) as in figure (b). The number beside an arc represents the broadcasting demand between LECs, which means the number of required VCs between the source LEC and BUS to transmit broadcast data. Similarly, the BUS and LEC capacities are measured by the number of VCs that can be processed in unit time interval. For example, the broadcast traffic from LEC A to LEC B demands 4 VCs in unit time interval; first, this data will be delivered to BUS, then broadcasted to all the LECs in the same ELAN. Figure (b) shows two alternative configurations where all the capacity constraints for BUS and LEC are met. However, the first alternative should retreat 15 units of traffic with 4 cut-pairs, whereas the second alternative is to handle 12 units of re-treatment with 3 cut-pairs. Re-treatment demands should trigger far more complex operations such as MPOA; otherwise, they cannot be served at all. In either case, the re-treatment demand causes degradation in service quality and/or additional operation overhead on entire network. Thus, with LPP alternative 2 is preferred to alternative 1

figurations is to minimize the total amount of re-treatment demand caused by cut-pairs.

### 3.2 LPP Formulation and Decision Model

Suppose that we know broadcast traffic pattern(demand) during a certain unit time interval for all the pairs of LECs in a LANE network. Given also are (1) $C_B$: the upper bound on the broadcast traffic amount that a BUS is capable of processing and carrying out during a unit time, (2) $C_L$: the upper bound on the broadcast traffic amount that a LEC can accommodate during a unit time, (3) $k$: the maximum number of ELANs to be configured. These parameters are easily calculated from the specs and the numbers of each equipment. A feasible solution to LPP will be a collection of LEC clusters which partition the entire LANE network and meet the constraints (1)-(3). The objective of LPP is to find a feasible partition that results in the minimum sum of re-treatment demands.

The LPP decision problem can be identified as a generalized Graph Partitioning Problem(GPP). Firstly, defined is a so-called demand network $G = (V, E)$ which represents the current broadcast demand pattern over the LANE network. In this network, $V$ means the set of nodes, each of which represents a LEC(i.e., $v \in V$), and $E$ stands for the set of directional arcs(simply arcs), $\{(u, v) \mid u, v \in V\}$ where $(u, v)$ expresses broadcast traffic from LEC $u$ to LEC $v$. We associate an integer number called arc weight $d_{uv}$ with each arc $(u, v)$, which represents the size of broadcast demand from $u$ to $v$. A valid node partition $\{V_1, V_2, \ldots, V_k\}$ is a complete collection of disjoint node subsets(that is, $V_p \cap V_q = \varnothing$ for any $p \neq q$ and $\cup_j V_j = V$), each of which meets constraints (1) and (2) and is allowed to be an empty set. An arc $(u, v)$ is said to belong to an arc-cut if $u \in V_p$ and $v \in V_q$ $(p \neq q)$. The size of an arc-cut is defined as the sum of weights of arcs which belong to the arc-cut. Then, it is easy to see that the arc-cut size equals to the sum of all the re-treatment demands in cut-pairs. Accordingly, finding a set of node clusters that partitions the given $G = (V, E)$ into a valid node partition whose arc-cut size is minimum turns out to be the same as finding an optimal solution to LPP. In sum, the following is the LPP model defined as a generalized GPP with given $k$ and an index set $K=\{1, 2, \ldots, k\}$.

$$\text{Minimize}_{\{V_1,\cdots,V_k\}} \quad \sum_{u \in V_i} \sum_{v \in V_j, j \neq i} d_{uv}$$

$$\text{Subject to} \quad |V_i| \times \sum_{e \in E_i} d_e \leq C_B, \ \forall i \in K \qquad (1')$$

$$\sum_{e \in E_i} d_e \leq C_L, \ \forall i \in K \qquad (2')$$

Here, $E_i$ means a subset of $E$, where $e=(u, v) \in E_i$ implies that both $u$ and $v$ belong to the same subset $V_i$(i.e., $E_i=\{e=(i, j) \in E \mid i, j \in V_i\}$). Note that the amount of broadcast traffic to be processed at a BUS during a unit time equals to the node cluster size $|V_i|$(the number of nodes in the cluster $V_i$) multiplied by the sum of weights of arcs in the same $E_i$. Then the constraint (1′) says that this product should not exceed the upper bound on the BUS capacity, $C_B$. Subsequently, the maximum amount of broadcast traffic to be processed at a LEC in $V_i$ during an unit time interval equals to the sum of weights of arcs in the same $E_i$, and should be kept smaller than $C_L$, the capacity upper bound for LEC, which the constraint (2′) implies. Upon looking at Capacitated GPP(CGPP) which has the same objective function and the constraint (2′), LPP is now identified as a generalized CGPP where the constraint (1′) is added to CGPP. Furthermore, the following proposition points out that LPP is no less difficult than CGPP.

**Proposition 1.** LPP is a NP-hard problem.
Proof) Setting the parameter $C_B$ in (1′) at sufficiently large number makes LPP directly applicable to CGPP. This implies that LPP includes NP-hard CGPP as a special case, which completes the proof. **Q.E.D**

# 4 Solution Method and Experiment

## 4.1 Solution Method Based on Genetic Algorithm

There have been lots of efficient solution methods including exact algorithms for GPP with fixed number of clusters(i.e., $k$ in this article) proposed so far([4], [9]). Moreover, for CGPP with additional capacity constraint on the node cluster(refer to the constraint (2) or (2′)), we have not only many exact algorithms based on branch-and-cut method but also various heuristics([5]). However, few solution methods have been reported with the generalized CGPP defined in the section 3.2 since the constraint (1) or (1′) has not been popular. Addition of valid inequalities for the constraint (1′) together with efficient separation algorithms makes an exact algorithm for CGPP extended to be applied for the proposed LPP model which is the generalized CGPP([10]).

However, since we are focusing on dynamic configuration of ELANs along with real-time changes in broadcast traffic pattern, we need a fast solution method so that it can support real-time ELAN management engine at LECS. Suggested here is a Genetic Algorithm(GA) which is known to generate good feasible solutions within reasonable time so that LECS can make dynamic adjustment in real time with this solution method([1]). Our experiment results in 4.2 indicate that the proposed GA is fast enough to be used in dynamical network configuration environment.

GA is an iterative procedure that tends to find an optimal or near optimal solutions from a pool of candidate solutions. The GA employed here to solve LPP starts with a chromosome encoding mechanism to represent a feasible solution for LPP. After generating an initial population, offspring is produced as the result of crossover between two randomly selected chromosomes from the population. The offspring mutates with a certain chance. All chromosomes are then evaluated by a fitness function, and selection process is followed. The greater fitness value a chromosome reveals, the higher opportunity it is given. This completes one cycle of a generation, and a new generation is again developed until some stopping criteria are met. In the next section, we introduce the design elements for the GA in detail, followed by experiment results in section 4.2.

**Chromosome Representation:** Here, a chromosome is a bit string of size $n$, the number of nodes(LECs). Employed is a group-number representation method to encode a feasible solution into a string as shown below.

$(v_1, v_2, \ldots, v_n)$, $v_j \in \{1, \ldots, k\}$ for all $j = 1, \ldots, n$ and $k$ is the max. number of clusters

Here, $(v_1, v_2, \ldots, v_n)$ corresponds to a feasible solution and gene $v_j$ takes value $p(\leq k)$ if the $j^{th}$ LEC node belongs to $p^{th}$ ELAN(cluster). For example, when with $n$=5 and $k$=2, nodes {1, 2} and {3, 4, 5} belong to cluster 1 and 2, respectively, this feasible solution is represented as (1,1,2,2,2).

**Evaluation and Selection:** First note that it is fairly easy to find cut-pairs through simple inspection of a chromosome, which also makes inter-ELAN traffic calculation easy. We employ the objective function in LPP model as the evaluation function(or fitness function) for our GA. Furthermore, elitism selection is adapted as the selection criteria. That is, the smaller total amount of re-treatment traffic a chromosome has, the more evaluation score the chromosome is given. Thus, employed is a roulette wheel method which gives a chromosome selection probability based on its evaluation score. This selection procedure is known to be quite steady a measure to guarantee the convergence toward an optimal solution([3], [7]). We also adjust GA control parameters in evaluation and selection steps to prevent GA from early converging into an inferior solution and to keep superior chromosomes developing from generation to generation.

**Basic GA Operators:** For crossover operations, employed is a modified structural crossover since structural crossover is known to be more efficient than other crossover operators like one-point crossover([7]). Structural crossover can also handle the number of clusters(here, $k$), which is not an easy feature to be implemented with other crossover operators. However, since the structural crossover operation may result in clusters that violate the constraint (1′) and/or (2′), we should check the validity of outcomes from the crossover operation and make some modification if necessary. Structural crossover makes it much easier to check feasibility and repair infeasible candidate chromosomes than other crossover operators. More detailed descriptions regarding the operators and modifications can be found in [10].

Furthermore, some mutation operators such as reciprocal exchange, insertion, and displacement will be used to expand the search space hoping to find another good solution structure different from what we already have. However, since mutation may produce invalid chromosome violating some constraints, required are check and repair processes similar to the crossover case. Detailed procedures are also found in [10]. With continual operations of crossover and mutation together with selection procedure, the optimal or near optimal chromosomes are expected to be bubble up.

**Other GA Parameters:** A population of size $P/2$ is initially created so that the condition for reproduction process is well prepared. After the first crossover and mutation operations, the population size grows up to $P$ and a half of the population is selected for possible replacement by new chromosomes at the next reproduction process, which will complete new one generation.

We also control other GA control parameters such as the number of generations, population size, crossover/mutation ratios, etc., to examine their impact on the algorithm performance and convergence speed. Employed stopping rule is to stop the process when the GA finds no further improvement over the last $m$ generations within a given number of maximum generations.

### 4.2 Experiment Results

**Experiment Design and Data:** We first applied our LPP model and solution method to a real campus network with 37 LECs. The following data is based on the real data from this network but a little bit modified for confidentiality reasons. Broadcast traffic demand between two LECs is defined as the required number of VCs since at least one VC should be set-up for the transmission. Similarly, the maximum number of VCs that can be established and maintained during a unit time defines the capacity of LEC($C_L$) or BUS($C_B$) according to an usual convention in the equipment vendor industry([12], [15]). The current operation of the LANE network ends up with 9 ELANs by a series of trial-and-error efforts. In the experiment, we will evaluate this rule-of-thumb and provide better solutions with the proposed LPP model.

Our solution method found optimal solutions in all the small size pilot tests where demand networks have about 10 nodes. Furthermore, in every pilot test, the proposed GA found the optimal solutions in a very short period of time, far before reaching the maximum number of generations($g$) of 300 with $m$=30. Based on the results from these prior experiments, $g$ was set at 100, 200, and 300 while the size of population was 50 and 100. Each combination of these GA parameters is expected to produce at least near optimal solutions within a reasonable period of time under the stopping rule defined as above. Lastly, the results from the pilot tests indicated that the convergence speed and the performance of the GA seemed to be insensitive to some GA control parameters such as the crossover/mutation ratios and the number of generations. Thus, these ratios will be fixed at 50% and 10%, respectively, according to [1] and [7].

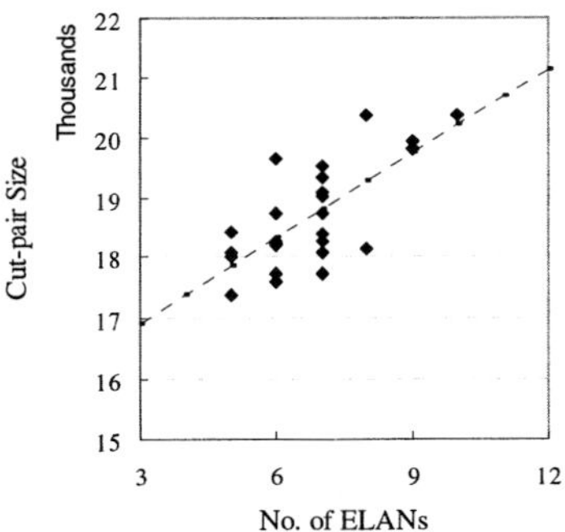


**Fig. 2.** Trade-off Relation between the Number of ELANs and Re-treatment Size

**Experiment Results:** In order to conduct sensitivity analysis to see the impact that the facility capacity has on the ELAN configuration, we ranked product specifications (with $C_L$=5,000 and $C_B$=65,000 as bases) and conducted experiments on each combination of them. With the currently available product specifications, in particular, we compared three kinds of broadcasting traffic pattern: type I for dense mode where many pairs of broadcasting traffic are to be uniformly generated, type II for sparse mode where broadcasting traffic is sparsely generated in a uniform fashion, and type III for hub-spoke mode where broadcasting traffic is unevenly generated and concentrated to some specific nodes. The following discussion is confined only to the cases where $g$(the maximum number of generations) and $P$(the population size) are set at 300 and 100, respectively. For each combination of two parameters $C_B$ and $C_L$, we repeated the GA 10 times to attain reliable computational results. Then, we collected the minimum cost solution in each set of 10 candidates as the best solution for the parameter combination. Basic statistics compiled from the experiments are as follows.

The coefficient of variations from each experiment ranges over 1.1%-3.2%. Moreover, at every parameter combination, the difference between the biggest best value and the smallest best value of the objective function was below 3% on average, and 6 out of 25 combinations conducted on the type I(dense mode) demand graph resulted in no gap between the biggest and the smallest; so, this case is deemed to found optimal solutions. These indicators show that all the instances converged to optimal or near optimal solutions before reaching $g$. Furthermore, every real network experiments were solved in 5 seconds with ordinary personal computers and converged to a single good solution. These facts also imply that the proposed model and solution method can secure enough time for the actual network to dynamically adapt to some changes in broadcasting traffic since network reconfiguration usually takes place every five to ten minutes or so in practice.

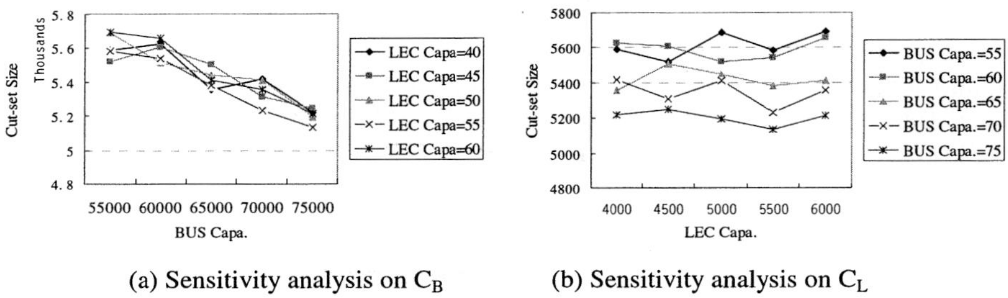


(a) Sensitivity analysis on $C_B$ (b) Sensitivity analysis on $C_L$

**Fig. 3.** Figure (a) and (b) depict the effect on the network performance(i.e., the size of retreated traffic) by individually changing the BUS capacity and LEC capacity, respectively with the other parameter fixed at various levels. Though the results came from the type III demand, similar patterns were observed with other types of demand

Figure 3 describes a clear positive relationship between the (near) optimal number of clusters(ELANs) and the (near) optimal cost(the amount of re-treatment). The experiment results with three types of typical traffic patterns show that the optimal number of ELANs is 7, which is smaller than that of the current operations while minimizing both the number of cut-pairs and the amount of re-treatment traffic. That is, with all the traffic patterns I, II, and III, the proposed LANE partition scheme with GA consistently outperforms the current rule-of-thumb. In particular, the amount of traffic that should be re-treated(i.e., the re-treatment size, or the arc-cut size) was reduced by 10.22%, 11.81%, and 7.40%, respectively. As easily expected, the degree of improvement was the least in case of the type III demand(hub-spoke mode), and the best result was attained at the $2^{nd}$ type of demand pattern(sparse mode). In sum, the optimal ELAN configuration suggested from the experiment not only reduces operational complexity but also improves the overall service performance.

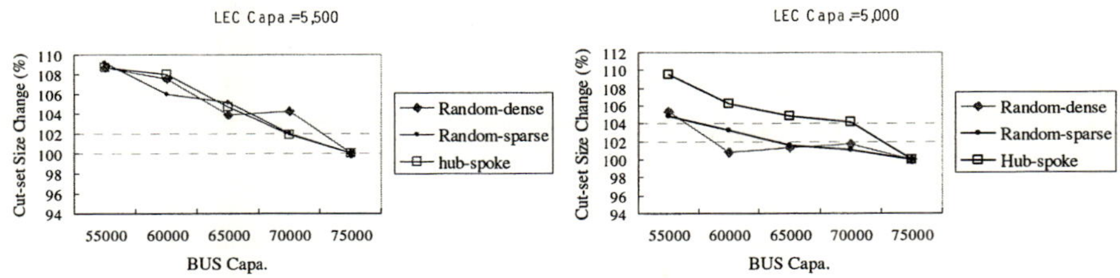


(a) Sensitivity analysis of the BUS capacity($C_B$) to different types of demand

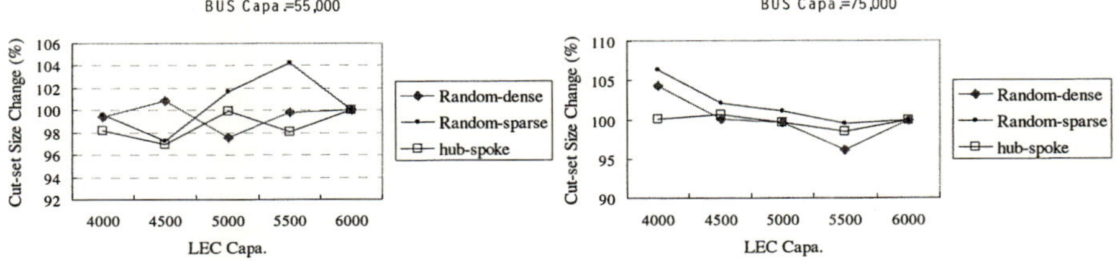


(b) Sensitivity analysis of the LEC capacity($C_L$) to different types of demand

**Fig. 4.** Depicted are the effects on the network performance with respect to the demand types at some fixed BUS and LEC capacities($C_B$ and $C_L$). Once again, the network performance is improving significantly as $C_B$ increases in (a) than both cases of increase of $C_L$ in (b)

Figure 4 also depicts the experiment results according to the changes in parameters $C_L$(LEC capacity) and $C_B$(BUS capacity). As seen in this figure, both optimal number of ELANs and the amount of re-treatment traffic are much more sensitive to BUS capacity than to LEC capacity. That is, as $C_B$ increases, we see a clear trend that the size of re-treatment traffic decreases at every level of $C_L$((a) in figure 3); the changes in $C_L$ does not show a comparable trend((b) in figure 3). This observation suggests that network administrators should pay more attention to determination of BUS capacity than to that of LEC capacity. Further analysis summarized in figure 4 could reveal some facts on the inter-relationship between these two facilities. This sort of costs and benefits comparison regarding the investment in LEC and BUS facilities will present meaningful insights to network administrators.

## 5 Concluding Remarks

This research explored optimal way to configure a clustered LANE network which has been introduced to employ ATM technology for addressing backward compatibility when expanding the legacy LANs. To improve network performance under the scalability restriction, in particular, LANE Partition Problem(LPP) was identified and analyzed along with the decision model and Genetic Algorithm(GA). From network administrators' point of view, partitioning LANE network into multiple ELANs aims at minimizing the burden of re-treatment of broadcast services at the upper layers. Here, LPP is formulated as an extended generalized Capacitated Graph Partition

Problem(CGPP) with an additional technical constraint unique to ATM network configuration for broadcasting. Furthermore, since GA has been well developed as a solution method to GPP(e.g., [1]), we refined GA to develop a solution method that fits the LPP model. Lastly, presented are experiment results of the proposed model and solution method applied to a real campus LANE network.

Experiment led to finding a much better ELAN configuration than the current ELAN configuration, which allows for less complicated operations with fewer ELANs, thereby reducing the size of re-treatment traffic. Furthermore, impact of design parameters such as BUS capacity and LEC capacity on the network management was analyzed. The analysis result indicates that BUS capacity($C_B$) has bigger impact on the optimal configuration of ELAN than LEC capacity($C_L$), implying the need to pay more attention to selection and deployment of BUS equipment.

We conclude the paper by discussing other prospective applications where the concepts and techniques presented here might be applied. The LPP model could be the basis on which to develop extended real-time network operations models incorporating various policy factors required in LANE and MPOA architectures. The model can also serve as an engine prototype running at a server(e.g., LECS) responsible for network management to be leveraged in supporting and automating network administrators' decision process. Finally, LPP has potential to be extended to any other internetworking environment where connection-oriented style broadcasting exists under a scalability condition: for example, the mobile ATM LAN configuration studies as in [3] and [8]. These prospective extensions are currently under investigation.

## References


1. Bui, T.N. and Moon, B.R.: Genetic Algorithm and Graph Partitioning, IEEE Trans. on Computers, Vol. 45, No. 7 (1996) 841–855
2. Chen, X. and Tantiprasut, D.T.: A Virtual Topology Management Protocol for ATM LAN Emulation, Bell Labs Technical Journal, Spring (1997) 132–150
3. Cheng, S.T., Chen, C.M., and Lin, J.W.: Optimal Location Assignment of Wireless Access Switches in a Mobile ATM Network, Proceedings of High Performance Computing in the Asia-Pacific Region, Vol. 1, (2000) 58–60
4. Chopra, S. and Rao, M.R.: The Partitioning Problem, Math. Programming, Vol. 59 (1993)
5. Ferreira, C.E. et al.: The Node Capacitated Graph Partitioning Problem: a Computational Study, Math. Programming, Vol. 81 (1998)
6. Finn, N. and Mason, T.: ATM LAN Emulation, IEEE Comm. Magazine, June (1996)
7. Haupt, R.L. and Haupt, S.E.: Practical Genetic Algorithms, John Wiley and Sons (1998)
8. Huang, N.F., Wang, Y.T., Li, B., and Liu, T.L.: Mobility Management of Interconnected Virtual LANs over ATM Networks, Proceedings of IEEE GLOBECOM (1996) 1156–1161
9. Johnson, E.L., Mehrotra, A., and Nemhauser, G.L.: Min-cut Clustering, Math. Programming, Vol. 62 (1993)
10. Kim, D.: Exact Algorithms and Meta-heuristics for General Graph Partition Problem with Special Capacity Constraints: with an Application to Hierarchical LANE Network Design and Operations," Technical Notes (in Korean), August (2002)
11. McDysan, D. and Spohn, D.: ATM Theory and Application, McGraw-Hill (1998)

12. Parker, J. et al.: Customer-Implemented Networking Campus Solution, Redbooks, available at http://www.redbooks.ibm.com (2001)
13. LAN Emulation Over ATM v1.0 Specification, The ATM Forum, #af-lane-0021.0000, February (1997)
14. LAN Emulation Over ATM ver.2-LUNI Specification, The ATM Forum, #af-lane-0084.000, July (1997)
15. Networking Requirements for Campus ATM Design, Cisco Documentations, available at http://www.cisco.com/warp/public (2001)

# Faster Speaker Enrollment for Speaker Verification Systems Based on MLPs by Using Discriminative Cohort Speakers Method

Tae-Seung Lee, Sung-Won Choi, Won-Hyuck Choi, Hyeong-Taek Park, Sang-Seok Lim, and Byong-Won Hwang

Hankuk Aviation University, School of Electronics, Telecommunication and Computer Engineering, Seoul, Korea
{tslee, swchoi, whchoi, htpark, sslim, bwhwang}@mail.hangkong.ac.kr

**Abstract.** Speaker verification system has been currently recognized as an efficient security facility due to its cheapness and convenient usability. This system has to achieve fast enrollment and verification in order to make a willing acceptance to users, as well as low error rate. For accomplishing such low error rate, multilayer perceptrons (MLPs) are expected to be a good recognition method among various pattern recognition methods for speaker verification. MLPs process speaker verifications in modest speed even with a low-capable hardware because they share their internal weights between all recognizing models. On the other hand, considerable speaker enrolling delay is made mainly due to the large population of background speakers for low verification error, since the increasing number of the background speakers prolongs the learning times of MLPs. To solve this problem, this paper proposes an approach to reduce the number of background speakers needed to learn MLPs by selecting only the background speakers nearby to an enrolling speaker. An experiment is conducted using an MLP-based speaker verification system and Korean speech database. The result of the experiment shows efficient improvement of 23.5% in speaker enrolling time.

## 1 Introduction

While we are living in the era that the various information devices such as computers, PDAs, and cellular phones are utilized widely, the means to protect private information come to be taken into consideration seriously. A biometric protection technology can be used to inhibit from accessing such information devices due to its great usability as well as good security performance itself. The major biometrics includes fingerprint, iris, face shape, and voice. Among them, the voice has advantages in that we can employ it easily and the processing cost is inexpensive relatively to other biometrics. So the various researches to attempt to adopt this technique to biometric-based security system are rigorously in progress [1].

The biometric technique using voice is called speaker recognition. The speaker recognition is divided into two areas. One is the speaker identification that enrolls plural speakers for system and classifies a test voice into one of the enrolled speakers, and the other is the speaker verification that verifies the identity of a test voice, by comparing it

P.W.H. Chung, C.J. Hinde, M. Ali (Eds.): IEA/AIE 2003, LNAI 2718, pp. 734–743, 2003.

with the claimed identity that has been enrolled for system beforehand. Out of the two approaches, the study of speaker verification is being conducted more widely and actively. It is because speaker verification targets any speakers and speaker identification system can be constructed by combining several speaker verification systems [2].

Individual speakers are recognized by using pattern recognition paradigm. The pattern recognition is divided into parametric-based recognition and nonparametric-based recognition in large. In parametric-based recognition, the models in a problem are represented by the mathematical function assumed priorly and parameters of the function are determined from the data of each model. As compared with this, nonparametric-based recognition determines model functions directly from their own data. When the presumed function type represents models properly, the parametric-based recognition shows a good recognition result. On the other hand, when learning capacity of recognizer are sufficient, the nonparametric-based recognition can perform more precise recognitions in that it needs not to presume any precise model function. The representative method is the maximum likelihood estimation (MLE) for parametric-based recognition and artificial neural networks for nonparametric recognition [3].

As an implementation for the artificial neural networks, multilayer perceptrons (MLPs) have advantages in recognition rate and operation speed, and these are obtained without having to presume any model function [4]. An MLP's internal parameters determine which class a test pattern belongs to and the parameters are shared with the whole models to be recognized. Thus, learning is conducted to reach objectives that the whole output errors are minimized. Such learning that utilizes inter-model correlation information marks lower error rates than the general parametric-based learning in which parameters of a function are searched to represent only each model as seen in the MLE. Although there are such methods that utilize inter-model correlation information to learn models in parametric-based recognition [5], MLPs represent the information by sharing parameters with the whole models and show more efficiency in parameter usage. And, the number of parameters required can be decreased because of the parameter sharing. If the number of internal parameters is low, the time required to recognize models is short and the memory amount to store the parameters is low. MLPs are tried to apply to many pattern recognition problems to benefit from such efficiencies [6].

In verifying speakers, speakers of three types are required: a customer, an enrolled speaker and background speakers. A customer's verification score is measured for an enrolled speaker claimed by the customer and in the measurement background speakers are needed to implement comparative measurements between the enrolled speaker and the background speakers. If the score is higher than a preset threshold, the customer is accepted as the same speaker to the enrolled speaker and rejected otherwise. In error rate evaluation, the customer speaker is classified into the true speaker who is the same speaker to the claimed speaker and the imposter who is not. The error rates of speaker verification system are measured in the false reject rate (FRR) that the system decides mistakenly the true speaker as an imposter, and the false accept rate (FAR) vice versa. But, it is common to measure the error rates in the equal error rate (EER) that a threshold is adjusted so that FRR and FAR have the same value for learning data set. Although the EER is commonly used, the FAR has more significance because acceptance for imposters is a critical defect to security systems.

To mark a low error rate, the precise decision must be made by comparing the likelihood of a customer to an enrolled speaker with the ones to the background speakers who are as similar as possible to the enrolled speaker, and determining which part the customer belongs to. However, it is impossible to know who will be a customer before he or she requests a verification test. So, many background speakers should be reserved so that the precise decision can be made whoever requests the verification of his or her claiming identity [7]. Unfortunately, it is evident that the amount of the computation needed to conduct a verification process increases along with the increasing number of background speakers.

Speaker verification system requires real-time speaker enrollment performance as well as real-time verification performance when user usability is considered. For speaker verification system to be used in daily life, it is necessary to consider a very rapid verification since the system must be used frequently. In addition to it, the user convenience criterion for a speaker verification system evaluates not only rapid verifications but also fast enrollments of speakers. Most users will want to use verification services just after enrolling him or herself for system. If they have to wait for a long time for the first usage, they may quit their enrolling process.

The real-time enrollment is also considered importantly when adaptation is implemented. The voices of the same speaker can be changed due to senility, disease or any time-relevant factors. To resolve such variability, many speaker verification algorithms introduce adaptation using the recent voices of the enrolled speaker to update their vocal characteristics [8], [9], [10]. The fast enrollment is serious even in this case because adaptation can be considered as refinement of earlier enrollment.

In this paper, an efficient method is proposed to shorten the speaker enrollment time of MLP-based speaker verification systems by introducing the cohort speakers method used in the existing parametric-based systems and reducing the number of background speakers needed to learn MLPs with enrolling speakers. This method has the feature that it shortens the speaker enrollment time but does not corrupt the fast speaker verification performance of MLPs at a cost of shortening the enrollment time unlike the original cohort speakers method, as well as does not damage the original verification error rate performance of the system.

## 2 Discriminative Cohort Speakers Method

The fundamental difference in enrolling speed between the existing parametric-based verification methods and MLPs lies in whether the information about background speakers can be obtained before enrolling a speaker. In the parametric-based verification based on the cohort speakers method, the likelihood parameters of background speakers are calculated beforehand. Below equation expresses the cohort speakers method [2], [7]:

$$L(\mathbf{X}) = \frac{p(\mathbf{X} \mid S_C)}{\sum\limits_{S_{Cohort},\, S_{Cohort} \neq S_C} p(\mathbf{X} \mid S_{Cohort})}. \tag{1}$$

where, $\mathbf{X}$ is the speech of a customer, $S_C$ the enrolled speaker of the identity claimed by the customer, $S_{Cohort}$ the cohort speakers adjacent to the enrolled speaker, $L$ the likelihood ratio function of the customer to the enrolled speaker and cohort speakers. The larger the number of background speakers is, the lower error rate the system achieves is [7]. In this method, the calculation required to learn an enrolling speaker occurs from just two processes: one is to determine the likelihood parameters of the enrolling speaker and the other to select the background speakers similar to the enrolling speaker by evaluating likelihoods to the enrolling speaker from the predetermined background speakers' parameters. This encourages a relatively short enrollment time of parametric-based verification. In contrast to it, the previous MLP-based speaker verifications have not been able to obtain the information of background speakers beforehand. The MLP learns models only in comparative mode [4]. So the entire background speakers are necessary for an MLP to learn an enrolling speaker. But if abundant background speakers are provided to achieve a very low verification error, it is indispensable for the MLP to take a long learning time.

To speedup the speaker enrollment time of MLPs, it is required to get the information for background speakers before enrolling a speaker. Thus, this paper adopts the cohort speakers method from parametric-based verification into MLP-based speaker verification. The original cohort speakers method selects background speakers to be compared with a customer at enrollment process so as to shorten the time necessary to verify the identity claimed by the customer at verification process. Unlike this, the reason that MLP-based speaker verification selects background speakers at enrollment process is to reduce the number of background speakers needed for comparative learning of an enrolling speaker.

The prospect to reduce background speakers in MLP-based speaker verification arises from the contiguity between learning models. That is, in MLP learning, a model's learning is cooperated only with its geometrically contiguous models. When an enrolling speaker is given into background speaker crowd for its learning, an MLP's decision boundary to learn the difference between the enrolling speaker and the background speakers is affected only by the background speakers adjacent to the enrolling speaker. This occurrence is depicted in Fig. 1(a). In this figure, the background speakers who do not face directly the enrolling speaker contribute hardly to learning of the enrolling speaker. However, a real speech pattern would have more dimensions than 2-dimension like in the figure, so the percentage of the background speakers not completely facing to enrolling speaker will not be so high. But, if a great number of background speakers are reserved to obtain very low verification error, the percentage of such background speakers does increase and the number of background speakers needed to learn decision boundary can be shortened.

The process to select the background speakers similar to an enrolling speaker in the cohort speakers method is implemented like this:

$$S_{Cohort} = Sel_{1,N,I}(Sort_{Dec}(P(\mathbf{X} \mid S_{BG}))), \quad S_{BG} = \{S_i \mid 1 \le i \le I\}. \tag{2}$$

where $\mathbf{X}$ is the speech of enrolling speaker, $S_{BG}$ the background speakers set of which population is $I$ , $Sort_{Dec}$ the function which sorts given value set in descending manner, $Sel_{1,N,I}$ the function which selects background speakers from 0 to $N$ -th element in the background speaker set, $S_{Cohort}$ the set of selected background speakers. The same process is conducted in MLP-based speaker verification proposed by this paper as follows:

$$S_{Cohort} = Sel_{1,N,I}(Sort_{Dec}(M_{MLP}(S_{BG} \mid \mathbf{X}))), \quad S_{BG} = \{S_i \mid 1 \le i \le I\}. \tag{3}$$

where, $M_{MLP}$ is the MLP function which evaluates likelihoods for each background speaker to given $\mathbf{X}$ .

In this paper, MLPs to calculate $M_{MLP}$ are called MLP-I and MLPs to learn an enrolling speaker using the background speakers selected by MLP-I are called MLP-II. And the speaker verification method based on MLPs and such background speaker selection is called Discriminative Cohort Speakers method. While MLP-Is are learned before enrollments using background speakers' data, MLP-IIs are learned at the time of enrolling speakers. It should be noted that although an MLP-II has one output node since it discriminates the current pattern input just into the enrolled speaker and the background speaker group, an MLP-I has $I$ output nodes since it has to evaluate the likelihoods of all background speakers. And, unlike parametric-based method of Eqn. 1, MLP-II learns a mapping function to transfer input patterns to output model likelihoods and it is by the finally settled decision boundary fabricated by the MLP's internal weights [6]. So it is not required to involve the same background speakers required at enrollment in verification calculation again and it leads to retain the inherently fast verification speed of MLPs. Fig. 1(b) describes the idea how the DCS selects background speakers and uses them to learn an enrolling speaker.

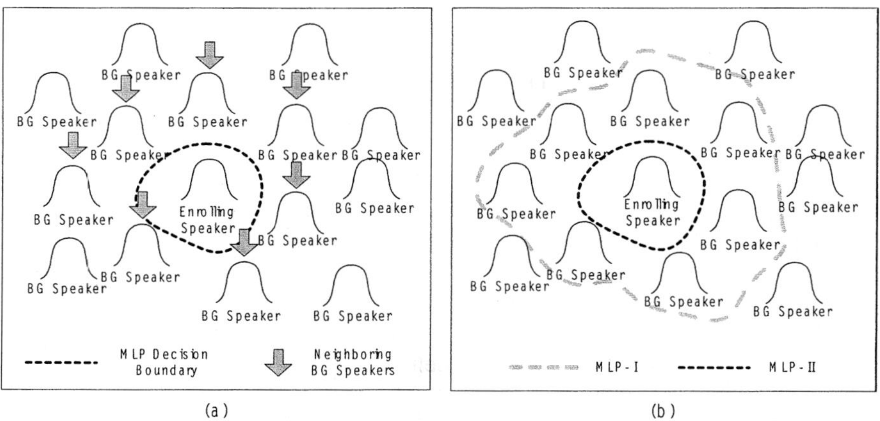


**Fig. 1.** (a) Relationship of MLP learning of decision boundary to background speakers, (b) Function of the DCS using MLP-I and MLP-II

## 3 Experiment

This paper implements an MLP-based speaker verification system and experiments the system using a speech database to prove the effect of the DCS proposed in the previous section. Because this system is based on continuants, which have the limited number of phonemes, it might adapt itself easily to any of text-mode, i.e. text-dependent, text-independent and text-prompt mode [2]. In this paper, the text-dependent mode is adopted for easy implementation, in which enrolling text should be the same to verifying text. The experiment compares the DCS with the online mode error backpropagation (EBP) algorithm [16] and measures enrolling time improvement of the DCS to the online mode EBP.

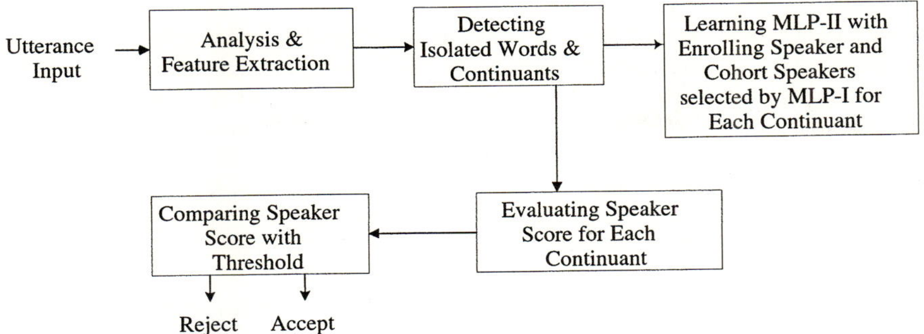


**Fig. 2.** The process flow of the MLP-based speaker verification system

### 3.1 System Implemented

The speaker verification system extracts isolated words from input utterances, classifies the isolated words into nine Korean continuants (/a/, /e/, /ə/, /o/, /u/, / /, /i/, /l/, nasals) stream, learns an enrolling speaker using MLP-I and MLP-II for each continuant, and calculates identity scores of customers. The procedures performed in this system are outlined in Fig. 2 and each procedure is described in the following:

(1) Analysis & Feature Extraction [11]
The utterance input sampled in 16bit and 16kHz is divided into 30ms frames overlapped every 10ms. 16 Mel-scaled filter bank coefficients are extracted from each frame and are used to detect isolated words and continuants. To remove the effect of utterance loudness from the entire spectrum envelope, the average of the coefficients from 0 to 1kHz is subtracted from all the coefficients and the coefficients are adjusted for the average of the whole coefficients to be 0. 50 Mel-scaled filter bank coefficients that are especially linear scaled from 0 to 3kHz are extracted from each frame and are used for speaker verification. This scaling adopts another study result that more information about speakers concentrates on the second formant [12]. To remove the effect of utterance loudness from the entire spectrum envelope, the average of the coefficients from 0 to 1kHz is subtracted from all the coefficients and the coefficients are adjusted for the average of the whole coefficients to be 0.

(2) Detecting Isolated Words & Continuants
Isolated words and continuants are detected using another MLP learned to detect all the continuants and silence in speaker-independent mode.

(3) Learning MLP-II with Enrolling Speaker for Each Continuant
For each continuant, the continuants detected from the isolated words are input to corresponding MLP-I and outputs of the MLP-I are averaged. Then the N best background speakers are selected. An MLP-II learns enrolling speaker with the N best background speakers.

(4) Evaluating Speaker Score for Each Continuant

For each continuant, the continuants detected from the isolated words are input to corresponding MLP-I, the outputs of the MLP-I are averaged and the N best background speakers are selected. When the selected background speakers include at least one speaker selected in the step (3), the outputs of MLP-II are averaged for each continuant. Then the averages of all continuants are averaged as well. If there are no background speakers selected in the step (3) for at least one continuant, the customer is rejected.

(5) Comparing Speaker Score with Threshold

The final reject/accept decision is made by comparing predefined threshold with the average of the step (4)

Since this speaker verification system uses the continuants as speaker recognition unit, the underlying densities show mono-modal distributions [13]. So it is enough for both MLP-I and MLP-II to have two layers structure that includes one hidden layer [14], [15]. And since the number of models for MLP-II to learn is 2, MLP-II can learn the models using only one output node and two hidden nodes. MLP-I consists of 10 hidden nodes and 29 output nodes, and nine MLP-Is are provided for all nine continuants.

### 3.2 Speech Database

The speech data used in this experiment are the recording of connected four digits spoken by 40 Korean male and female speakers, in which the digits are Arabic numerals each corresponding to /goN/, /il/, /i/, /sam/, /sa/, /o/, /yug/, /cil/, /pal/, /gu/ in Korean pronunciation. Each of the speakers utters total 35 words of different digit strings four times, and the utterances are recorded in 16kHz sampling and 16bit resolution. Three of the four utterances are used for enrolling utterances, and the other is used for verifying utterance. When enrolling speaker is learned, 29 Korean male and female speakers except for above 40 speakers are used.

### 3.3 Experiment Model

In the experiment, MLP-IIs to enroll a speaker are set up as follows [4]:

- MLPs are learned with the online mode EBP algorithm.
- Input patterns are normalized to the range from -1.0 to +1.0.
- The objective of output node, i.e. training target, is +0.9 for enrolling speaker and -0.9 for background speakers to obtain faster EBP learning speed.
- Speech patterns of two models are presented in alternative manner during learning. In most cases, the numbers of patterns for the two models are not the same. So the patterns of the model having fewer patterns are repetitively presented until all the patterns of the model having more patterns are once presented, completing one learning epoch.

- Considering the case being fallen in a local minimum, the maximum number of learning epochs is limited to 1000 times.
- The learning goal is such that averaged squared error energy is below 0.01, provided that change rate of this value is below 0.01 to prevent premature learning stop.

Each of the 40 speakers is regarded as both enrolling speaker and true speaker, and the other 39 speakers as imposters alternatively. As a result, for each speaker 35 times tests are performed as true speaker and 1,560 times as imposter tests. As a whole the experiment performed 1,400 trials as true speaker tests and 54,600 trials as imposter tests.

The experiment is conducted on an AMD 1.4GHz machine. In the experiment result, the error rate designates the EER, the number of learning patterns the total number of patterns used to enroll a speaker and the learning time the overall time taken to learn these patterns. Values of the error rate, the number of learning patterns and the learning time are the averages for three-time tests each with the same MLP learning condition.

### 3.4 Results and Analysis

In this experiment, measurements are recorded as the number of background speakers in cohort for the DCS is decreased by every 3 speakers. The experiment results are presented in Fig. 3 and 4. In the figures, it is shown that the learning speed improves near-linearly as the number of speakers in cohort decreases. However, the improvement is meaningful above 20 background speakers in cohort because the error rate does not increase at only those numbers. In the numbers, the maximum improvement rate of enrolling speed is recorded as 23.5%. It is noted that error rate is increased rapidly when the number of speakers in cohort is less than 14. This might be because the background speakers set used in this experiment consist of 15 males and 14 females. That is, it can be understood that the numbers below 14 mean the effective deceasing of the number of the same sex speakers to an enrolling speaker and this leads to the increasing error rate due to the deficiency of the background speakers directly contiguous to the enrolling speaker. It should be finally noted that in the numbers of cohort speakers 23 and 20, the verification errors are lower than one

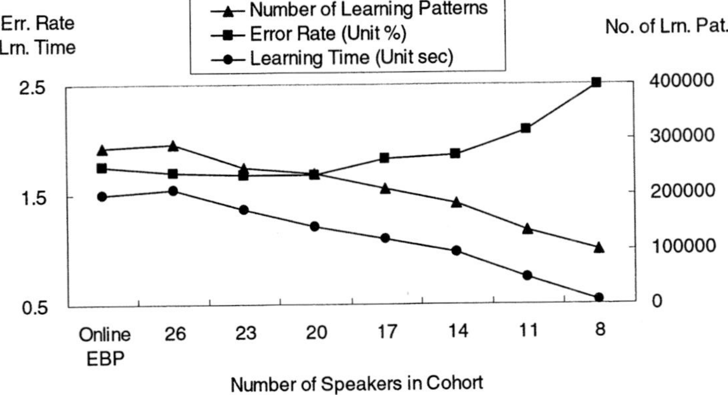


**Fig. 3.** Experiment result with the online EBP and the DCS

of the online EBP. This result can be inferred from that when the number of the cohort speakers decreases, the opportunity for learning cohort speakers increases due to the alternative model learning characteristic of MLPs. That is, too many cohort speakers lead to excess learning of enrolling speaker and shifting the decision boundary inappropriately to the areas of the cohort speakers. As a result, the online EBP to have full background speakers presents higher error rate than the DCS.

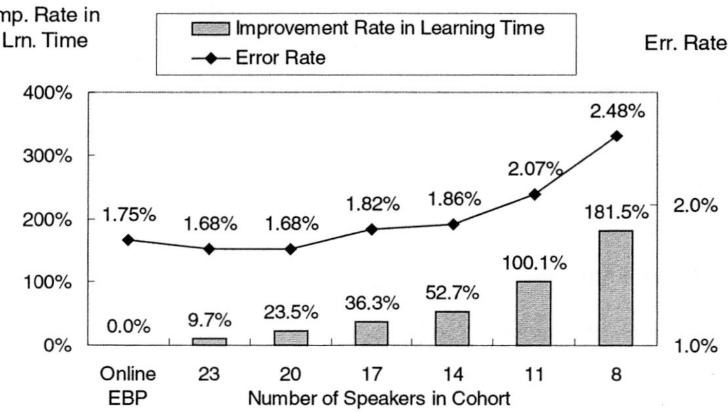


**Fig. 4.** Improvement rate changes in learning time with the DCS

## 4 Conclusion

The result of Fig. 4 proves that the DCS method achieves the goal to enhance the speaker enrollment speed of MLP-based speaker verification systems. In spite of several advantages that MLPs present against other pattern recognition methods, MLP-based speaker verification systems suffer from slow enrollment speed caused by large background speaker population to acquire a good verification rate. To cope with this problem, this paper attempted to introduce the cohort speakers method into the systems and reduce the number of background speakers required to enroll speakers and devised the DCS method. The experiment was conducted to use the speaker verification system based on MLPs and continuants and speech database. The result of the experiment assures that practical improvement can be achieved without increasing verification error rate. It is expected that if the number of background speakers is larger than that of this experiment and the DCS is cooperated with a faster MLP learning algorithm like [16], more improvement rate can be obtained.

## References


1. Li, Q. et al.: Recent Advancements in Automatic Speaker Authentication. IEEE Robotics & Automation Magazine. **6** (1999) 24-34
2. Furui, S.: An Overview of Speaker Recognition Technology. In: Lee, C. H. (eds.): Automatic Speech and Speaker Recognition. Kluwer Academic Publishers, Massachusetts (1996)
3. Duda, R. O., Hart, P. E., Stork, D. G.: Pattern Classification. Wiley-Interscience, New York (2001)
4. Bengio, Y.: Neural Networks for Speech and Sequence Recognition. International Thomson Computer Press, London (1995)
5. Normandin, Y.: Maximum Mutual Information Estimation of Hidden Markov Models. In: Lee, C. H. (eds.): Automatic Speech and Speaker Recognition. Kluwer Academic Publishers, Massachusetts (1996)
6. Haykin, S.: Neural Networks, 2nd edn. Prentice Hall, New Jersey (1999)
7. Rosenberg, A. E., Parthasarathy, S.: Speaker Background Models for Connected Digit Password Speaker Verification. IEEE International Conference on Acoustics, Speech, and Signal Processing. **1** (1996) 81-84
8. Matsui, T., Aikawa, K.: Robust Model for Speaker Verification against Session-Dependent Utterance Variation. IEEE International Conference on Acoustics, Speech and Signal Processing. **1** (1998) 117–120
9. Mistretta, W., Farrell, K.: Model Adaptation Methods for Speaker Verification. IEEE International Conference on Acoustics, Speech and Signal Processing. **1** (1998) 113–116
10. Matsui, T., Furui, S.: Speaker Adaptation of Tied-Mixture-Based Phoneme Models for Text-Prompted Speaker Recognition. IEEE International Conference on Acoustics, Speech and Signal Processing. **1** (1994) 125-128
11. Becchetti, C., Ricotti, L. P.: Speech Recognition. John Wiley & Sons, New York (1999)
12. Cristea, P. and Valsan, Z.: New Cepstrum Frequency Scale for Neural Network Speaker Verification. IEEE International Conference on Electronics, Circuits and Systems. **3** (1999) 1573-1576
13. Savic, M., Sorensen, J.: Phoneme Based Speaker Verification. IEEE International Conference on Acoustics, Speech, and Signal Processing. **2** (1992) 165-168
14. Lippmann, R. P.: An Introduction to Computing with Neural Nets. IEEE Acoustics, Speech, and Signal Processing Magazine. **4** (1987) 4-22
15. Delacretaz, D. P., Hennebert, J.: Text-Prompted Speaker Verification Experiments with Phoneme Specific MLPs. IEEE International Conference on Acoustics, Speech, and Signal Processing. **2** (1998) 777-780
16. Lee, T. S. et al.: A Method on Improvement of the Online Mode Error Backpropagation Algorithm for Pattern Recognition. Lecture Notes in Artificial Intelligence, Vol. 2417. Springer-Verlag, (2002) 275-284

# Improving the Multi-stack Decoding Algorithm in a Segment-Based Speech Recognizer

Gábor Gosztolya and András Kocsor

Research Group on Artificial Intelligence of the Hungarian Academy of Sciences and University of Szeged, H-6720 Szeged, Aradi vértanúk tere 1., Hungary,
ghosty@rgai.inf.u-szeged.hu, kocsor@inf.u-szeged.hu

**Abstract.** During automatic speech recognition selecting the best hypothesis over a combinatorially huge hypothesis space is a very hard task, so selecting fast and efficient heuristics is a reasonable strategy. In this paper a general purpose heuristic, the multi-stack decoding method, was refined in several ways. For comparison, these improved methods were tested along with the well-known Viterbi beam search algorithm on a Hungarian number recognition task where the aim was to minimize the scanned hypothesis elements during the search process. The test showed that our method runs 6 times faster than the basic multi-stack decoding method, and 9 times faster than the Viterbi beam search method.

**Keywords.** search methods, segmental speech model, speech recognition, multi-stack decoding, Viterbi beam search.

In the last two decades the performance of speech recognition has greatly improved. With the growth of computational power, the same algorithms are computed faster, and this also makes further refinements possible, which may result in a more accurate recognition system. However the more complex the approach, the bigger the hypothesis space might be. The search over the hypothesis space is a vital issue because there are usually millions of hypotheses, and most of them have very low probabilities. This is why the search methods remain an important issue in speech recognition even today.

The multi-stack decoding method [3] is a well-known search algorithm with a generally good performance. However, we sought to improve it by constructing a faster method which recognized the same amount of test words. Although we tested the improvements on Hungarian numbers, all of these strategies can be used for other languages and utterances as well. The tests were performed within the framework of our segment-based speech recognition system called the OASIS Speech Laboratory [5], [7].

The structure of the paper is as follows. First we briefly discuss the fundamentals of speech recognition, then compare the frame-based and segment-based approaches. Next we explain the standard multi-stack decoding method and the Viterbi algorithm, and our improvements on the former. The final part of the paper discusses the experiments, the effectiveness of each improvement, and the results we obtained in practice.

P.W.H. Chung, C.J. Hinde, M. Ali (Eds.): IEA/AIE 2003, LNAI 2718, pp. 744–749, 2003.

## 1 Frame-Based vs. Segment-Based Speech Recognition

In the following the speech signal $A$ will be treated as a chronologically increasing series of the form $a_1 a_2 \dots a_t$, while the set of possible phoneme-sequences (words) will be denoted by $W$. The task is to find the word $\hat{w} \in W$ defined by

$$\hat{w} = arg \max_{w \in W} P(w|A) = arg \max_{w \in W} \frac{P(A|w) \cdot P(w)}{P(A)} = arg \max_{w \in W} P(A|w) \cdot P(w),$$

where $P(w)$ is known as the *language model.* If we optimize $P(w|A)$ directly, we are using a discriminative method, while if we use Bayes' theorem and omit $P(A)$ as we did in the formula above the approach is generative. The speech recognition process can be frame-based or segment-based, depending on whether the model incorporates frame-based or segment-based features [4].

*Frame-based speech recognition.* In speech theory a widely-used model is Hidden Markov Modelling (HMM), which is a frame-based generative method. HMM models speech as a collection of states which are connected by transitions. Each state associates an output observation with an output probability, and each transition has an associated transition probability. Here, the feature vectors are the output observations. The output probability models the acoustic constraints, while the transition probability between HMM states models duration constraints. For further details on HMM see [6].

*Segment-based speech recognition.* In this less commonly used approach we assume for a word $w = o_1 \dots o_l$ that a phoneme $o_i$ is based on $A_i = a_j a_{j+1} \dots a_{j+r-1}$ (an $r$-long segment of $A$, where $A = A_1 \dots A_n$). With this $A_i$ segment first long-term features are extracted, then a *phoneme classifier* is used to identify the most probable phoneme covered by the underlying segment. In our framework Artificial Neural Networks (*ANN)* are employed, but the way the classifier actually works is of no concern to us here. We further assume that $P(w|A) = \prod_i P(o_i|A) = \prod_i P(o_i|A_i)$, i.e. that the phonemes are independent. In order to determine $P(o_i|A_i)$, we need to know the exact values of the $A_i$s. This is a hard task, and because automated segmentation cannot be done reliably, the method will make many segment bound hypotheses. So we must include this segmentation $S$ (which determines $A_1 \dots A_n$) in our formulae:

$$P(w|A) = \sum_S P(w, S|A) = \sum_S P(w|S, A) \cdot P(S|A) \approx \max_S P(w|S, A) \cdot P(S|A)$$

For a given $S$, both $P(w|S, A)$ and $P(S|A)$ can be readily calculated using a classifier. The former is computed via a phoneme classifier, while the latter leads to a two-class classification problem with classes called "phoneme" and "anti-phoneme" [1], [7].

## 2 The Search through the Hypothesis Space

In this section we will build the hypothesis space by using the segment-based approach, but in a frame-based system an equivalent hypothesis space would appear. In the following instead of a probability $p$ we will use the cost $c = \log p$. The hypothesis space is a subset of a Cartesian product space of two spaces. The first space consists of phoneme sequences, while the second consists of segmentations. An array $T_n = [t_0, t_1, \ldots, t_n]$ is called a *segmentation* if $0 = t_0 < t_1 < \cdots < t_n = t$ holds, which defines $n$ neighboring $[t_i, t_{i+1}]$ intervals. We also require that every phoneme fit into some overlapping interval $[t_i, t_q]$ $(i, q \in \{0, \ldots, n\}, 0 \leq i < q \leq n)$, i.e. the former $A_i$ speech segment here is referred by its start and end times. Given a set of words $W$, we use $Pref_k(W)$ to denote the k-long prefixes of all the words in $W$ having at least $k$ phonemes. Let $T_n^k = \{[t_{i_0}, t_{i_1}, \ldots, t_{i_k}] : 0 = i_0 < i_1 < \cdots < i_k \leq n\}$ be the set of sub-segmentations over $T_n$ with $k$ connected intervals. Now we will define the hypothesis space recursively by constructing a search tree containing all the hypothesis elements as its nodes. We will denote the root of the tree (the initial hypothesis) by $h_0 = (\emptyset, [t_0])$, and $Pref_1(W) \times T_n^1$ will contain the first-level nodes. For a $(o_1 o_2 \ldots o_j, [t_{i_0}, \ldots, t_{i_j}])$ leaf we link all $(o_1 o_2 \ldots o_j, [t_{i_0}, \ldots, t_{i_j}, t_{i_{j+1}}]) \in Pref_{j+1}(W) \times T_n^{j+1}$ nodes. We are looking for a leaf with the lowest cost.

If a hypothesis is discarded because of its high cost (i.e. we do not scan its descendants), we say that it was *pruned.* A *stack* is a structure for keeping hypotheses in. Moreover, we use limited size stacks in the multi-stack decoding algorithm: if there are too many hypotheses in a stack, we prune the ones with the highest cost. Extending a hypothesis $(o_1 o_2 \ldots o_j, [t_{i_0}, \ldots, t_{i_j}])$ having a cost $c$ with a phoneme $v$ and a time instance $t_{i_{j+1}}$ will result in the hypothesis $(o_1 o_2 \ldots o_j v, [t_{i_0}, \ldots, t_{i_j}, t_{i_{j+1}}])$, which has a cost of $c$ together with the cost of $v$ in the interval $[t_{i_j}, t_{i_{j+1}}]$.

*Multi-stack decoding method.* In this algorithm we assign a separate stack for each time instance $t_i$ and store the hypotheses in the stack according to their end times. In the first step we place $h_0$ into the stack associated with the first time instance then, advancing in time, we pop each hypothesis in turn from the given stack, extend them in every possible way, and put the new hypotheses into the stack belonging to their new end time [3]. Algorithm 1 in Appendix shows the pseudocode for multi-stack decoding.

*Viterbi beam search.* This algorithm differs only in one feature from the multi-stack decoding approach: instead of keeping the $n$ best hypotheses, a variable $T$ called the *beam width* is employed. For each time instance $t$ we calculate $D_{min}$, i.e. the lowest cost of the hypotheses with the end time $t$, and prune all hypotheses whose cost $D$ falls outside $D_{min} + T$ [2].

## 3 How Might Multi-stack Decoding Be Bettered?

When calculating the optimal stack size for multi-stack decoding, it is readily seen that this optimum will be the one with the smallest value where no best-scoring hypothesis is discarded. But this approach obviously has one major drawback: most of the time bad scoring hypotheses will be evaluated owing to the constant stack size. If we could find a way of estimating the required stack size associated with each time instance, the performance of the method would be significantly improved.

*i*) One possibility is to combine multi-stack decoding with a Viterbi beam search. At each time instance we keep only the n best-scoring hypotheses, and also discard those which are not close to the peak (thus the cost will be higher than $D_{min} + T$). Here the beam width can also be determined empirically.

*ii*) Another approach is based on the observation that, the later the time instance, the smaller the required stack. We attempted a simple solution for this: the stack size at time $t_i$ will be $s \cdot m^i$, where $0 < m < 1$ and $s$ is the size of the first stack. Of course $m$ should be close to 1, otherwise the stacks would soon be far too small for safe use.

*iii*) Another technique is a well-known modification of stacks. It can easily happen that there are two or more hypotheses which have the same phoneme-sequence and the same end times (it may be that some earlier phoneme bound is at a different time instance). In this case it is sufficient to retain only the most probable ones. Surprisingly, a simpler version of it worked better: we allowed the stacks to store more of these "same" hypotheses, but when extending a hypothesis in the stack, we popped it and then compared its phoneme sequence with the previously popped one (when there was one). The current hypothesis is extended only when the phoneme sequences differ.

*iv*) Yet another approach for improving the method comes from the observation that we need big stacks only at those segment bounds where they exactly correspond to phoneme bounds. So if we could estimate at a given time instance what the probability is of this being a bound, we could then reduce the size of the hypothesis space we need to scan. We trained an ANN for this task (on derivative-like features) where its output was treated as a probability $p$. Then a statistical investigation was carried out to find a function that approximates the necessary stack size based on this $p$. First, we recognized a set of test words using a standard multi-stack decoding algorithm with a large stack. Then we examined the path which led to the winning hypothesis, and noted the required stack size and the segment bound probability $p$ for each phoneme. The result represented as a stacksize–probability diagram was used to obtain a proper fitting curve estimating the required stack size. It can be readily shown that most of the higher stack sizes are associated with a high value of $p$, so the stack size can indeed be estimated by this probability. This observation was confirmed by the test results.

*v*) The last suggested improvement is based on our observation that the minimum size of a stack depends as well on the number of hypotheses the earlier stacks hold. The size of a new stack was estimated by the previous ones using preliminary statistics. But this type of prediction is only of value if other improvements were initially applied and stack-size reduction was achieved beforehand.

**Table 1.** Summary of the best performances of all the method combinations used.

| Method combinations | total ANN calls | avg. ANN calls |
|---|---|---|
| Viterbi beam search | *5,469,132* | *17,529.26* |
| multi-stack decoding | *3,754,456* | *12,033.51* |
| multi-stack + *i* | 2,263,738 | 7,255.57 |
| multi-stack + *ii* | 3,701,035 | 11,862.29 |
| multi-stack + *iii* | **1,555,747** | **4,986.36** |
| multi-stack + *iv* | 3,283,114 | 10,522.80 |
| multi-stack + *v* | — | — |
| multi-stack + *iii* + *i* | **888,445** | **2,847.58** |
| multi-stack + *iii* + *ii* | 1,409,434 | 4,517.41 |
| multi-stack + *iii* + *iv* | 1,280,783 | 4,105.07 |
| multi-stack + *iii* + *v* | — | — |
| multi-stack + *iii* + *i* + *ii* | 861,253 | 2,760.42 |
| multi-stack + *iii* + *i* + *iv* | **728,702** | **2,335.58** |
| multi-stack + *iii* + *i* + *v* | 808,635 | 2,591.77 |
| multi-stack + *iii* + *i* + *iv* + *ii* | 722,902 | 2,316.99 |
| multi-stack + *iii* + *i* + *iv* + *v* | **678,709** | **2,175.34** |
| multi-stack + *iii* + *i* + *iv* + *v* + *ii* | **677,309** | **2,170.86** |

## 4 Results and Conclusion

We had six speakers who uttered 26 numbers, each one twice, giving a total of 312 occurrences. We expected the methods to score the same results, which they did, although with different parameters even for each grouping. We monitored the methods by the number of hypothesis elements scanned: the lower the number, the better the method. We employed sequential forward selection: first we checked all improvements separately with their best parameters, then we chose the best and checked all the others combined with it, and so on. For comparison we also performed a standard Viterbi beam search test.

It is quite surprising that improvement *iii* produced the best results. After that, improvement *i* (the Viterbi beam search) reduced the search space the most, followed by improvement *iv* (with the segment bound probability). It can be seen that all improvements enhanced the performance of the recognition in every case; the best result was obtained by using all of them together. But we also suggest partial combinations such as combination *iii* + *i* + *iv* + *v* or *iii* + *i* + *iv*, having found that further extensions did not greatly better the performance.

Overall we conclude that, on examining the test results, it is apparent that we can indeed marry the multi-stack decoding and Viterbi beam search methods without any loss of accuracy, and with a marked improvement in performance. Further significant search space reductions were also possible, so our new combination ran some 6 times faster than the multi-stack decoding method, and some 9 times faster than the Viterbi beam search method.

## 5 Appendix

The multi-stack decoding pseudocode described by Algorithm 1. "$\leftarrow$" means that a variable is assigned a value; "$\Leftarrow$" means pushing a hypothesis into a stack. $Stack[t_i]$ means a stack belonging to the $t_i$ time instance. A $H(t,p,w)$ hypothesis is a triplet of time, cost and a phoneme-sequence. *Extending* a hypothesis $H(t,c,w)$ with a phoneme $v$ and a time $t_i$ results in a hypothesis $H'(t{+}t_i, c', wv)$, where $c' = c + c_i$, $c_i$ being the cost of $v$ in the interval $[t, t_i]$. We denote the maximal length of a phoneme by $maxlength$.

**Algorithm 1** Multi-stack decoding algorithm

```
Stack[t_0] ⇐ h_0(t_0, 0, "")
for i = 0...n do
  while not empty(Stack[t_i]) do
    H(t, c, w) ← top(Stack[t_i])
    if t_i = t_max then
      return H
    end if
    for l = i + 1 ··· i + maxlength do
      for all {v | wv ∈ Pref_{1+length of w}} do
        H'(t_l, c', w') ← extend H with v
        Stack[t_l] ⇐ H'
      end for
    end for
  end while
end for
```

## References


1. J. Glass, J. Chang, M. McCandless, *A Probabilistic Framework for Features-Based Speech Recognition,* Proceedings of International Conference on Spoken Language Processing, Philadelphia, PA, pp. 2277-2280, 1996.
2. P.E. Hart, N.J. Nilsson and B. Raphael, *Correction to "A Formal Basis for the Heuristic Determination of Minimum Cost Paths",* SIGART Newsletter, No. 37, pp. 28-29, 1972.
3. X. Huang, A. Acero, H.-W. Hon, *Spoken Language Processing,* Prentice Hall PTR, 2001.
4. F. Jelinek, *Statistical Methods for Speech Recognition,* The MIT Press, 1997.
5. A. Kocsor, L. Tóth and A. Kuba Jr., *An Overview of the Oasis Speech Recognition Project,* Proceedings of ICAI '99, Eger-Noszvaj, Hungary, 1999.
6. L.Rabiner and B.-H. Juang *Fundamentals of Speech Recognition* Prentice Hall, 1993.
7. L. Tóth, A. Kocsor and K. Kovács, A Discriminative Segmental Speech Model and its Application to Hungarian Number Recognition, *Text, Speech and Dialogue, 2000.*

# A Parallel Approach to Row-Based VLSI Layout Using Stochastic Hill-Climbing*

Matthew Newton[1], Ondrej Sýkora[1], Mark Withall[1], and Imrich Vrt'o[2]

[1] Department of Computer Science, Loughborough University,
Loughborough, Leics. LE11 3TU, United Kingdom,
{m.c.newton,o.sykora,m.s.withall2}@lboo.ac.uk http://parc.lboro.ac.uk/
[2] Department of Informatics, Institute of Mathematics, Slovak Academy of Sciences,
841 04 Bratislava, Slovak Republic,
imrich@ifi.savba.sk

**Abstract.** Parallel algorithms based on stochastic hill-climbing and parallel algorithms based on simple elements of a genetic algorithm for the one-sided bipartite crossing number problem, used in row-based VLSI layout, were investigated. These algorithms were run on a PVM cluster. The experiments show that the parallel approach does not bring faster computation but it does, however, much more importantly, bring a better quality solution to the problem, i.e. it generates drawings with lower numbers of pairwise edge crossings.

**Keywords.** Genetic Algorithms, Distributed Problem Solving, Heuristic Search

## 1 Introduction

Graph drawing addresses the problem of finding a layout of a graph that satisfies given aesthetic and readability objectives. One of the basic problems with the drawing of bipartite graphs is that of two layer automatic drawing where two vertex partitions are put in distinct points on two parallel lines and edges are drawn as straight line segments (see Figure 1). This type of drawing is the basic building block used for drawing hierarchical graphs[4, 10] or producing row-based VLSI layouts[12]. Probably the most important objective is minimisation of the number of edge crossings in the drawing, as the aesthetic and readability of graph drawings depend on the number of edge crossings (see [11]), and VLSI layouts containing less crossings are more easily realisable and consequently cheaper. Figures 1 and 2 show a bipartition of a 3x3 mesh, firstly with the vertices placed in random positions and secondly with the minimum number of edge crossings. There are two basic variants of the problem: the one-sided and two-sided crossing minimisation problems. In the one-sided problem the vertices of one part of the

* Research of the first two and last authors was supported by the EPSRC grant GR/R37395/01. Research of the second and the last authors was supported by the Slovak Scientific Grant Agency grant No. 2/3164/23.

P.W.H. Chung, C.J. Hinde, M. Ali (Eds.): IEA/AIE 2003, LNAI 2718, pp. 750–758, 2003.

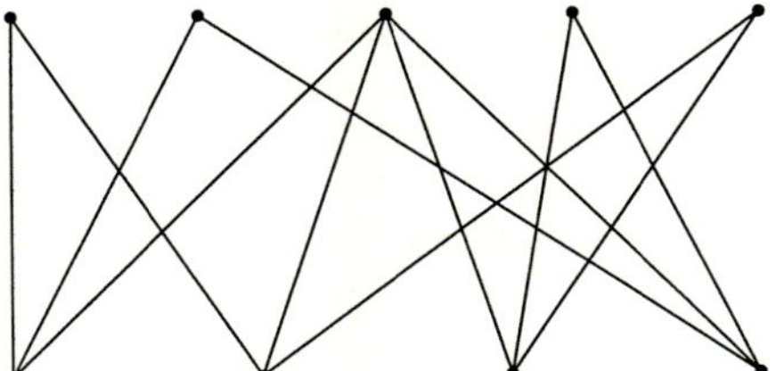

**Fig. 1.** Bipartition of a 3x3 mesh

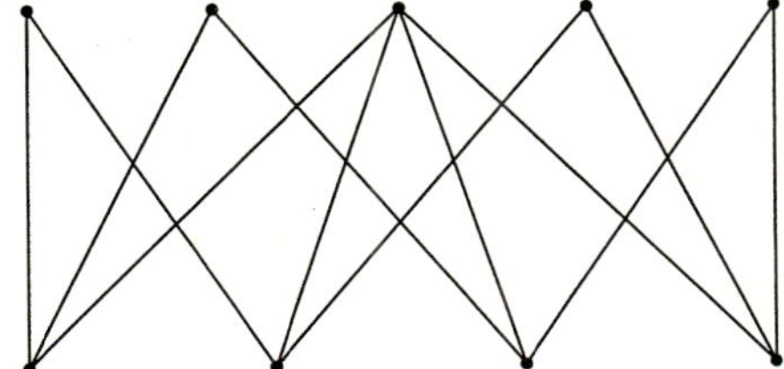

**Fig. 2.** Optimal drawing of a 3x3 mesh bipartition

bipartite graph are placed in fixed positions on one line (known as the fixed side) and the positions of the vertices of the other part, on the other line (known as the free side), are found so that the number of pairwise edge crossings is minimised. As both problems are NP-hard[5, 7], a lot of different methods—heuristics and approximation algorithms—to solve the problem have been designed (see, for example, [1, 3]).

Parallel computing has been a valuable tool for improving running time and enlarging feasible sizes of problems, and it has become an important economic and strategic issue. This paper focuses on the parallel implementation of genetic algorithms and stochastic hill-climbing for one-sided bipartite graph drawing. In comparison with the best sequential one-sided methods penalty minimization and sifting (see [3]), the presented heuristics are slower but they produce much higher quality results. The experiments show that better results are achieved than penalty minimization and sifting with the sequential version of the algorithm but using parallel (cluster) computing makes it possible to improve the quality of the solution in a significant way.

## 2 Notation

Let $G = (V, E), V = V_0 \cup V_1$ be a bipartite graph with vertex partitions $V_0$ and $V_1$. A *bipartite drawing* of $G$ is obtained by placing the vertices of $V_0$ and $V_1$ into distinct points on two horizontal lines, $y_0, y_1$ respectively, and drawing each edge with one straight line segment. It is assumed that $y_0$ is the line $y = 0$ and $y_1$ is the line $y = 1$.

Any bipartite drawing of $G$ is identified by two permutations $\pi_0$ and $\pi_1$ of the vertices on $y_0$ and $y_1$ respectively. It is assumed that the permutation $\pi_1$ is fixed. The problem of the one-sided bipartite drawing of $G$ is the problem of finding a permutation $\pi_0$ that minimises the number of pairwise edge crossings in the corresponding bipartite drawing.

Let $bcr(G, \pi_0, \pi_1)$ denote the total number of crossings in the bipartite drawing represented by the permutations $\pi_0$ and $\pi_1$. The *bipartite crossing number* of $G$ related to the fixed permutation $\pi_1$, denoted by $bcr(G, \pi_1)$, is the minimum number of crossings over all $\pi_0$. Clearly, $bcr(G, \pi_1) = \min_{\pi_0} bcr(G, \pi_0, \pi_1)$.

## 3 Stochastic Hill-Climbing for Bipartite Crossings

The space of orderings of the free side for the one-sided bipartite drawing problem can be represented by all permutations of $\{0, 1, 2, \ldots, n-1\}$, where $n$ is the number of vertices on the free side. To find a solution of the one-sided bipartite drawing problem means to search this space for a permutation providing the minimum number of crossings. To move across the space it is possible to use some steps (local or non-local). The new visited permutation can be evaluated and then accepted if it fulfils a condition (e.g. it has a lower or equal number of crossings). Searching is then continued from the new accepted permutation. If the new permutation was not accepted, the old permutation is used. A natural local step is vertex swapping which actually corresponds to transposition in permutations. The space of permutations with vertex swapping used for generating a new candidate for a solution can be represented by the so called complete transposition graph $CT_n = (V, E)$. The graph has $n!$ nodes labelled by all distinct permutations of the numbers from $\{0, 1, 2, \ldots, n-1\}$ and two vertices of $CT_n$ are adjacent if the corresponding permutations can be obtained from each other by a transposition of two elements. The transposition graph belongs to the class of Caley graphs[6], and its diameter is $n - 1$. To search the space for a solution, a genetic algorithm approach was used in [8]. The typical structure of a genetic algorithm is shown in Algorithm 1.

**Algorithm 1** Typical structure of a Genetic Algorithm

```
t ← 0
create the initial population P(0)
evaluate P(0)
while not termination-condition do
    t ← t + 1
    select individuals to be reproduced
    recombine {apply genetic operations to create new population P(t)}
    evaluate P(t)
end while
```

To create a concrete genetic algorithm it is necessary to fix some of the parameters of the above general scheme. It is necessary to define crossover (usually a binary operation) and mutation, and the way that the candidates for parents and mutation are chosen. Then the initial population should be chosen. In general, genetic algorithms provide better results than other, simpler, heuristics, the main problem being long computation time. To avoid it, it is possible to simplify the procedure by, for example, removing crossover, simplifying mutation and using a simple evaluation function. Very good results were achieved, better than the best heuristics in this area—sifting[9] and penalty minimization[3]—by mutation reduced to swapping two randomly chosen vertices and by applying hill-climbing using a differential fitness function (only the changed edges were checked), see Algorithm 2. This approach has not been applied before.

**Algorithm 2** Stochastic Hill-Climbing Bipartite Drawing (SHBD)

```
while not termination-condition do
   randomly choose two vertices
   swap their positions
   evaluate the crossing number of the new permutation
   if the crossing number decreases or is the same then
      take the new permutation
   else
      return to the previous permutation
   end if
end while
```

The termination condition can be defined by the number of iterations, the number of iterations that have passed since the last swap that gave an improvement to the crossing number (the number of stagnations) or a required crossing number can be given for the algorithm to achieve. From experimental observation, a run time of $O(f(n))$, where $f(n)$ appears to be at most a cubic function of the number of vertices, seems to be a good approximation.

## 4 Parallel Algorithms

Parallel computing has been a valuable tool for improving running time and enlarging feasible sizes of problems and it has become a key economic and strategic issue. Strong efforts are put into developing standards for parallel programming environments, such as PVM (Parallel Virtual Machine), MPI (Message Passing Interface), BSP (Bulk Synchronous Parallel) and HARNESS. Among these, one of the most common is currently PVM (see `http://www.csm.ornl.gov/pvm/`), although the situation is changing rapidly (see for example [2]). Algorithm 3 shows the general scheme of the parallel genetic algorithm used.

In the above approach, crossover, if any, is realised in the master. The mutation operator can be applied in parallel on every new permutation, or when stagnation has occurred. A parallel stochastic hill-climbing approach was used where the master randomly generates permutations that are sent to the slaves. A mutation of acyclic shift by $\lfloor in/p \rfloor$ positions is applied there. The mutations will generate permutations that are at least at distance $\lfloor n/2 \rfloor$ from each other because a permutation in the worst case can contain at most $\lfloor n/2 \rfloor$ cycles. This means that the mutations ensure a good distribution of starting positions over the space of permutations (which is probably the reason why the algorithms produce such good results). A slave finishes processing after some predefined number of runs of the procedure SHBD or after some predefined number of stagnations (where there has been no change of the best permutation). As soon as the slave halts, it sends the resulting permutation to the master and the master chooses the best one from all permutations sent by the slaves and halts.

The approach gave better results than sequential SHBD in a shorter time (see Figures 3, 4 and 5), which is not too surprising. The method of parallel SHBD

**Algorithm 3** General Parallel Genetic Algorithm

**MASTER** :

initialisation and start slave processes
load $G$ and generate randomly a permutation of the free side
send $G$ and the generated permutation to all slaves
generate a population
**while** not termination-condition **do**
  receive a permutation from a slave
  send back a permutation randomly chosen (or select according to a crossover procedure) from the current population
  **if** new permutation is better than or equal to the worst current permutation **then**
    include the received permutation in the current population
  **end if**
**end while**

**THE i-TH SLAVE** :

receive $G$ from the master
**repeat**
  receive a permutation from the master
  shift the permutation by $\lfloor (i * n)/p \rfloor$ {with (co-operative) stochastic hill-climbing, only shift once at the beginning}
  apply "Stochastic Hill-Climbing Bipartite Drawing"
  send the resulting permutation to master
**until** condition

was improved by introducing co-operation of slaves, by means of the master working as follows: the master resends a new permutation to the slave from which it has just received a message. It can either be the best or randomly chosen from those maintained as a current population, or it may be created by a crossover operation. In the experiments a crossover operation which would make improvements to the current population could not be found, so it was decided not to use one.

Mutation was used to further improve the co-operative parallel stochastic hill-climbing. This method took much more time but improvements to the crossing number over the previous parallel SHBD were observed.

## 5 Experimental Procedure

The parallel algorithms were implemented in C, running on 46 Sun ULTRA-sparc 5 workstations running Solaris 7. These were connected with 100Mb/s Ethernet via 3Com SuperStack II baseline 10/100 24 port switches. The algorithms were compiled with GNU C compiler version 2.95.2. PVM was used for the parallel communication and was configured as five parallel computers, each with 9 processors; one master and eight slaves. Another computer ran a job control system that was written in Perl to keep experiments running on the five machines.

The parallel and sequential algorithms, graph generators and the graphs used in the experiments are available from `http://parc.lboro.ac.uk/`.

### 5.1 Graph Test Sets

Two main types of graph where used in the experiment. Specific classes of graph, such as meshes, cycles, complete binary trees and caterpillars, were used to test the algorithm so that specific target crossing numbers were available. Randomly generated graphs were used as the main test to find out how the algorithm performs for more general types of graph.

**Standard Graphs.** Several standard graphs were used as benchmarks in the experiments. These graphs were generated so that the fixed side in the drawing was in its optimal ordering, while the free side permutation was generated randomly. The time for the algorithm to reach the known crossing number was measured. Complete binary trees (an $n$-level complete binary tree has a bipartite crossing number $\left(\frac{n}{3} - \frac{11}{9}\right) 2^n + \frac{2}{9}\left(-1\right)^n + 2$, see [13]), cycles (with a bipartite crossing number $\frac{n}{2} - 1$, if there are $n$ vertices in the cycle) and caterpillars (without crossings in the optimal drawing) have been used to test if the algorithms are working correctly. Rectangular meshes, $3 \times n$, (with a bipartite crossing number equal to $5n - 6$, see [14]) have been used as a more challenging problem than cycles.

**Random Graphs.** The random graphs used were generated based on edge density. The generator took two arguments, $n$ (the number of vertices) and $p \in [0..100]$ (the percentage chance that an edge will exist between two vertices). The general graphs were generated with sizes $n \in [100, 200, 300, \ldots, 1000]$ and densities of 10%, 1% and 0.1%. The minimum crossing number was not known so the fixed side could not be placed optimally.

### 5.2 Test Runs

The standard graphs were generated with sizes $n \in [100, 200, 300, \ldots, 1000]$ and were run on the algorithms to find out how well they performed against a known solution. It was possible to see that the parallel stochastic hill-climbing method was slightly faster in reaching the known crossing number than the co-operative stochastic hill-climbing algorithm.

Each one of the generated random graphs was initially run on the parallel stochastic hill-climbing algorithm. As the exact crossing number was not known, for each of the graphs, they were run for 3 minutes each and then stopped. The crossing number that they had then reached and the time taken to reach that number were recorded. Each of the algorithms was run 10 times and the average time and crossing number were calculated.

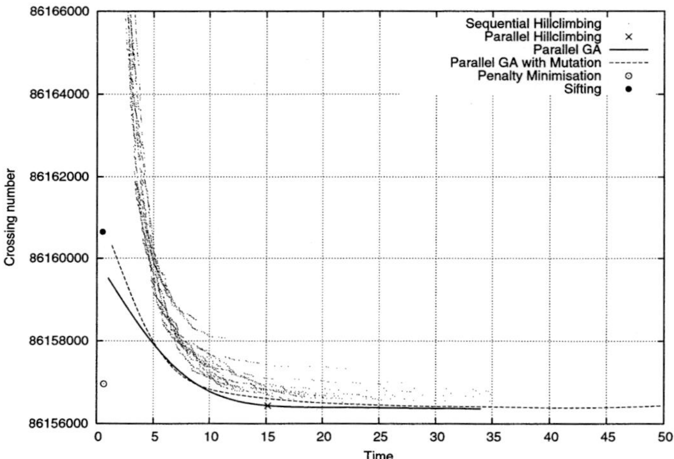


**Fig. 3.** Random graph, $n = 500$, $p = 10\%$

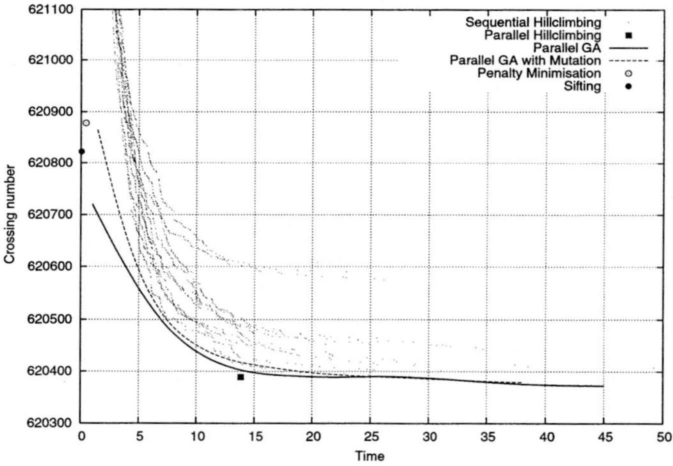


**Fig. 4.** Random graph, $n = 500$, $p = 1\%$

The graphs were then run on the parallel system running the co-operative stochastic hill-climbing algorithm, first without mutation and then with. A sequential hill-climbing version was also run for each of the machines. All experiments were, again, run 10 times each. The graphs in Figures 3, 4 and 5 show the comparisons between the four results for random graphs where $n = 500$. The results from the sequential stochastic hill-climbing algorithm have been shown in full due to the large diversity of the data.

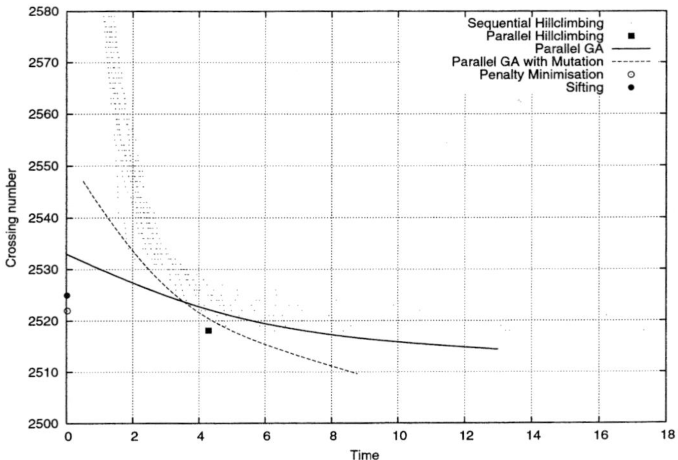


**Fig. 5.** Random graph, $n = 500$, $p = 0.1\%$

# 6 Summary and Conclusions

The experiments were run for several different classes of graph using parallel stochastic hill-climbing and parallel genetic algorithms. For the results it follows that the parallel SHBD algorithms can be used to find better solutions to the one-sided bipartite drawing problem, used in row-based VLSI layout, than the best available sequential heuristics such as penalty minimization and sifting. In addition, the SHBD can run much faster than a standard black-box algorithm due to the ability to implement a differential fitness evaluation. If co-operative stochastic hill-climbing is used, especially with mutation, the crossing number can be further improved (as compared to the results of the other parallel algorithms) at the expense of time.

# References


1. O. Bastert, C. Matuszewski. (2001). *Layered drawings of digraphs*, In: Drawing Graphs, Methods and Models (eds. M. Kaufmann, D. Wagner), Lecture Notes in Computer Science **2025**, Springer Verlag, 87–118.
2. J. Dongarra, G.A. Geist, J.A. Kohl, P.M. Papadopoulos, S. Scott, V. Sunderam. *HARNESS: Heterogeneous Adaptable Reconfigurable Networked Systems.* `http://www.csm.ornl.gov/harness/`.
3. C. Demetrescu., I. Finocchi. (2001). *Removing cycles for minimizing crossings.* J. Experimental Algorithmics. To appear.
4. G. Di Battista, P. Eades, R. Tamassia, I.G. Tollis. (1999). *Graph Drawing: Algorithms for Visualization of Graphs.* Prentice Hall.
5. P. Eades, N. Wormald. (1994). *Edge crossings in drawings of bipartite graphs*, Algorithmica, **11** 379–403.

6. J.A. Gallian. (1989). *A survey: recent results, conjectures and open problems in labelling graphs*, J. Graph Theory **13** 491–504.
7. M.R. Garey, D.S. Johnson. (1983). *Crossing number is* NP-*complete*, SIAM J. Algebraic Discrete Meth., **4** 312–316.
8. E. Mäkinen, M. Sieranta. (1994). *Genetic algorithms for drawing bipartite graphs*, International J. Computer Mathematics **53** 157–166.
9. C. Matuszewski, R. Schönfeld, P. Molitor. (1999). *Using sifting for k−layer straightline crossing minimization,* in: Proc. 7th International Symposium on Graph Drawing (GD'99), LNCS 1731, 217–224.
10. P. Mutzel. (2001). *Optimization in leveled graphs.* In: M. Pardalos, C.A. Floudas (eds.): Encyclopedia of Optimization. Kluwer, Dordrecht.
11. H. Purchase. (1998). *Which aesthetic has the greatest effect on human understanding?*, in Proc. Symposium on Graph Drawing, GD'97, Lecture Notes in Comput. Sci., 1353, Springer Verlag, Berlin, 248–261.
12. M. Sarrafzadeh, C.K. Wong. (1996). *An Introduction to VLSI Physical Design*, McGraw Hill, New York, NY.
13. F. Shahrokhi, O. Sýkora, L.A. Székely, I. Vrťo. (1998). *On bipartite crossings, largest biplanar subgraphs, and the linear arrangement problem*, in Proc. Workshop on Algorithms and Data Structures, WADS'97, Lecture Notes in Comput. Sci. 1272, Springer-Verlag, Berlin, 55–68.
14. F. Shahrokhi, O. Sýkora, L.A. Székely, I. Vrťo. (2000). *A new lower bound for the bipartite crossing number with algorithmic applications*, Theoretical Computer Science **245** 281–294.

# An Optimal Coalition Formation among Buyer Agents Based on a Genetic Algorithm


Masaki Hyodo, Tokuro Matsuo, and Takayuki Ito

Center for Knowledge Science, Japan Advanced Institute of Science and Technology, 1-1 Asahidai, Tatsunokuchi-machi, Nomi-gun, Ishikawa 923-1292, Japan,
{m-hyoudo,t-matsuo,itota}@jaist.ac.jp,
http://www.jaist.ac.jp/~{m-hyoudo,t-matsuo,itota}



**Abstract.** Group buying is a form of electronic commerce that is growing quickly. There are many group buying sites on the Internet. Group buying is a commercial transaction in which the unit price of goods changes with the number of buyers, and a buyer can purchase goods at a low price if many buyers participate in group buying. There are several group-buying sites that are selling similar (or the same) goods. Buyers are often distributed among these group-buying sites non-optimally. If we can optimally allocate buyers to several group buying sites, all buyers can buy a good at a lower price. possible that a participant can purchase the target or the simThe aim of this paper is to solve this optimal allocation problem by a Genetic Algorithm. Our method can effectively avoid the growth of fatal genes. In experiments, we compared our method with an exhaustive search algorithm and a brute search algorithm. The experimental results show that our algorithm can optimally allocate buyers in an efficient time.



**Keywords:** Genetic Algorithms, Internet Applications, Group Buying, Electronic Commerce.


## 1 Introduction

Recently, Electronic Commerce has become a popular channel for purchasing goods on the Internet. Group buying [bidders] [rakuten] is a noteworthy form of commerce. In group buying, the unit price of goods is decided based on the number of buyers, and a buyer can purchase goods at a low price if a sufficient number of buyers participate in group buying.

There are many group buying sites on the Internet, and they have different discount rates for each others. Also, they have limitations of the number of goods to sell. Therefore, there can be a huge number of possible allocations of buyers. Thus, for buyers, it is important to find an optimal allocation of buyers in group buying sites. We call this the optimal buyer allocation problem [Matsuo 02]. The optimal buyer allocation problem in group buying is an NP-hard problem, since the solution space exponentially increases due to the unspecified number of people who can participate. Therefore, searching for an optimal distribution by an exhaustive search is not practical because it takes too much time. It is necessary to instantaneously present a solution by a deadline. A genetic algorithm (GA) can calculates optimal solutions or semi-optimal solutions in real time.


P.W.H. Chung, C.J. Hinde, M. Ali (Eds.): IEA/AIE 2003, LNAI 2718, pp. 759–767, 2003.

The purpose of this paper is to show the characteristics of the optimal allocation of buyers and to solve the problem by using a search algorithm based on GA [Varian 90]. GAs have an advantage in that the algorithm does not depend on the problem.

The rest of this paper is organized as follows. Section 2 explains group buying and the optimal allocation problem. In section 3, we show the algorithm based on GA for the optimal allocation of buyers. In section 4, we show experiments. In section 5, we discuss the features of the problem space and related works. Finally in section 6, we provide some concluding remarks.

## 2 Outline of Group Buying

In group buying, sellers prepare a range and quantity of goods to deal in, and buyers purchase goods at a low price by cooperating with each other. Sellers have the opportunity to dispose of a large stock, and buyers benefit since they can purchase goods at a discount price.

One advantage of group buying is that buyers can form coalitions and buy goods at a discount price. Buyers can announce the number of participants who declare a demand for each good at a certain point. Sellers prepare a large stock of goods and show the unit price for each quantity of goods. Table 1 shows an example of a table that shows unit prices for the number of goods. For example, one good is sold for \$50 and a set of three goods is sold for \$48. If three buyers cooperatively make a group, they can purchase the good at a \$2 discount. If seven buyers cooperatively make a group, they can purchase the good at a \$12 discount. Buyers can decide to purchase the good by the information stated in discount tables.

**Table 1.** An Example of a Discount Rate Table for Group Buying

| number of goods | unit price |
|---|---|
| 1-2 | \$50 |
| 3-4 | \$48 |
| 5-6 | \$45 |
| 7-8 | \$38 |

Recently, many group buying sites have been selling similar or the same goods. It is important for buyers to decide when and when to purchase the desired good. Also, it is often difficult for buyers to gather for purchasing a good since they distributed on the Internet. If buyers are gathered in a group and then they are allocated optimally to distributed group-buying sites, they can purchase goods at an optimal price, i.e., the lowest price.

We focus on a situation in which several sellers are selling substitute goods. Since buyers can purchase whichever goods they want, they can purchase at a low price by being integrated into any other group. Fig. 1 shows an example of group buying based on substitute goods. The good A, the good B, and the good C are same-category goods. There is no difference among these goods for participants.

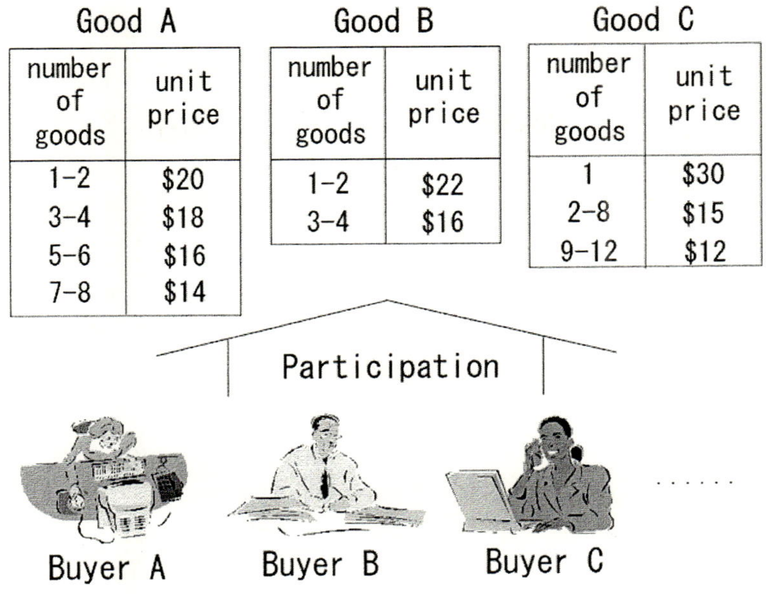


**Fig. 1.** Group Buying based on Substitute Goods

Sellers submit a discount rate for each good to the host (system administrator). Buyers show the reservation price to the host. The reservation price is the highest amount of money that a buyer can pay.

A unit price of one good is \$50. When the number of buyers is between two and five, the unit price of the good becomes \$40, i.e., they can purchase the good at a \$10 discount. When the number of buyers is six, the unit price is \$30, and they can purchase the good at a \$20 discount. Suppose there is a buyer A who tries to purchase this good. The reservation price of buyer A is \$35. When that the price of the good is higher than the reservation price, buyer A does not purchase the good. If five buyers have already made a group, buyer A can purchase the good at the price of \$30 if buyer A participates. In this paper, we assume a quasi-liner utility. The utility of buyer A is \$5 because the reservation price is \$35. If the number of participants purchasing this good is only four, the unit price is \$40. Buyer A does not participate in the group because the unit price is higher than reservation price. Fig. 3 shows an example of rate table and an example of reservation price.

We represent the number of buyers as $n$, the buyer $i$'s reservation price as $i_{MAX}$, and the unit price of a good as $i_{pay}$. The sum of utilities, $S$, is presented as follows.

$$S = \sum_{i=1}^{n} (i_{MAX} - i_{pay})$$

A coalition in which the unit price of a good is higher than the reservation price for one buyer is called an invalid solution. On a other hand, a coalition in which a reservation

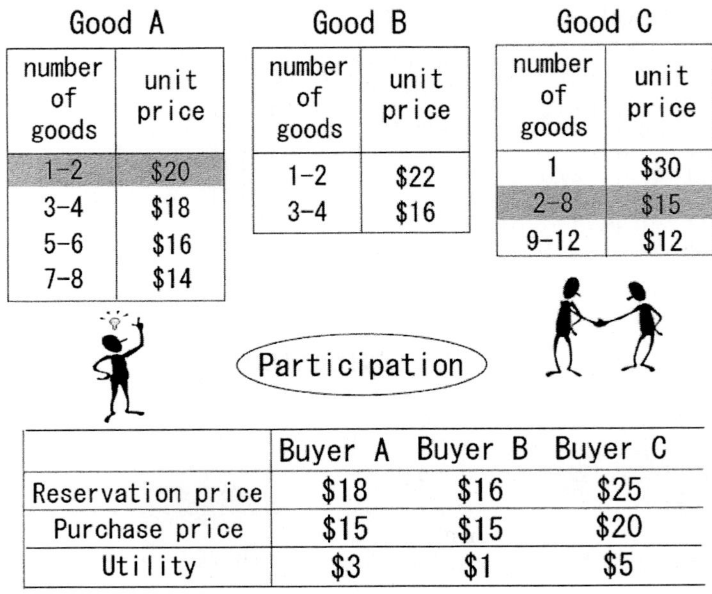


**Fig. 2.** An Example of Rate Table and Example of Reservation Price

| | Buyer 1 | Buyer 2 | Buyer 3 | ······ | Buyer n |
|---|---|---|---|---|---|
| The Gene | Good A | Good B | Good C | ······ | Good B |

**Fig. 3.** The Definition of Gene

price is higher than the unit prices of goods for all buyers is called a possible solution. A coalition in which the utility is the largest in the group of possible answers is called an optimal solution.

This problem can be widely applied to other optimal problems involving volume discount.

## 3 Optimal Allocation Algorithm Based on a GA

### 3.1 Coding

It is section, we describe a problem representation based on GA. By representing the problem with genes, we can express the allocated goods for buyers, the unit price of goods, and the buyer's utilities at once. The value of a coalition can be evaluated when all buyers are assigned goods. Thus, we represent a good. Fig. 3 shows an example of a gene. In this example, good A is assigned to buyer 1.

In this problem, we describe fatal genes. An optimal allocation has the two following constraints.

1) The number of goods is finite. Thus, a buyer cannot purchase a good if a certain seller does not have enough goods.

2) A Buyer cannot purchase the good if the unit price is higher than his reservation price.

A coalitions that satisfies those constraints is called a possible solution. Also the genes are called possible genes. A coalitions that does not satisfy those constraints is called an invalid solution, and the genes that do not satisfy the constraints are called invalid genes.

In this problem, fatal genes may occupy most of the answer space according to. However, general, the evaluation value of the fatal genes is zero in a GA. Thus, if there are many fatal genes in the group, it is quit difficult to obtain an optimal solution. In GA, we first assign numerical values to each element (gene locus) in a gene at random, and we call this operation of assigning "first selection." Therefore, in our algorithm, we first select genes that satisfy constraint (1). While constraint (1) can be satisfied relatively easy, it is hard to satisfy constrain (2) at the first stage.

Here, describe the evaluation method for this problem. All buyers have reservation prices, and a transaction is not conducted when the unit price is higher than the reservation price. The reservation price must be higher than the unit price for dealing to occur. If we employ constraint (2) directly as an evaluation method for a gene, there can be many fatal genes, since constraint (2) is a relatively strong constraint. Thus, through selection, crossover, and mutation in the GA, a gene is evaluated by the total price. Consequently, genes that have a small evaluation value can be viewed as good solutions. By evaluating a gene based on its total price, even if the gene violates the strong constraint (2), the gene can survive to the next generation. We call coalition (1) a superior solution. Also, a gene the represents a superior solution is called a superior gene.

### 3.2 Controlling Crossover of a Fatal Gene

Crossover is a very characteristic operation. However, if one-point crossover is carried out, this operation produces many fatal genes and decreases the efficiency of searching. Thus, we propose a crossover method (in Fig. 4). In the first place, this method determines whether to carry out crossover based on probability. When it determines that crossover should be carried out, two genes are operated by one-point crossover at all crossover points and them pooled. The two superior genes are selected from the pooled genes at random and survive to the next generation. Thus, even in the worst case, at minimum the pool-based genes can survive to the next generation. The advantage of this method is that fatal gene does cannot survive to the next generation.

## 4 Experiments

We conducted experiments to present the effectiveness of our improved algorithm. The brute search is a kind of hill climbing search. In the experiments, we compared our GA-based method with an exhaustive search algorithm and a brute search algorithm.

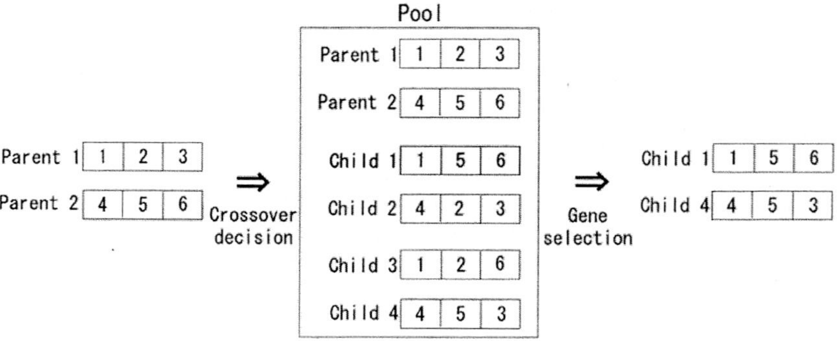


**Fig. 4.** The Outline of our crossover method

The brute search tries to select the lowest priced good at any branching point. When an allocation is obtained, it finishes searching. In the experiments, we applied our method to the two problems shown in Table 2 and Table 3. These tables show discount rates, and Table 4 shows the buyer's reservation price. The size of the search space is 9,765,625, since the number of tables is five and the number of buyers is ten. It is not determined whether either of the problems has a correct answer. Our method is parameters include a population size of 100, a crossover rate of 0.5, a mutation rate of 0.01, and a generation count of 200. The experimental environment has been written in the C++ language and executed on a Celeron/1GHz/128MB computer running Windows XP.

Table 5 and Table 6 show the results of calculations using the GA, an exhaustive search, and the brute search algorithm.

**Table 2.** Discount Rates (Problem 1)

| Good A | | Good B | | Good C | | Good D | | Good E | |
|---|---|---|---|---|---|---|---|---|---|
| number of goods | unit price | number of goods | unit price | number of goods | unit price | number of goods | unit price | number of goods | unit price |
| 1 | 2,000 | 1-2 | 1,800 | 1 | 2,000 | 1-3 | 1,520 | 1 | 2,000 |
| 2 | 1,900 | 3 | 1,310 | 2 | 1,320 | 4-5 | 1,440 | 2-3 | 1,600 |
| 3 | 1,450 | | | | | 6 | 1,330 | 4-5 | 1,500 |

**Table 3.** Discount Rates (Problem 2)

| Good A | | Good B | | Good C | | Good D | | Good E | |
|---|---|---|---|---|---|---|---|---|---|
| number of goods | unit price | number of goods | unit price | number of goods | unit price | number of goods | unit price | number of goods | unit price |
| 1-4 | 1,700 | 1 | 2,000 | 1-4 | 2,000 | 1-3 | 1,520 | 1 | 2,000 |
| 5 | 1,310 | 2 | 1,900 | 5 | 1,350 | 4-5 | 1,400 | 2-3 | 1,600 |
| | | 3 | 1,450 | | | 6 | 1,300 | 4-5 | 1,500 |

**Table 4.** Reservation Prices of Buyers

| Buyer | Reservation price | Buyer | Reservation price |
|---|---|---|---|
| Buyer A | 1,700 | Buyer F | 1,800 |
| Buyer B | 1,650 | Buyer G | 1,680 |
| Buyer C | 1,310 | Buyer H | 1,900 |
| Buyer D | 1,550 | Buyer I | 1,780 |
| Buyer E | 1,720 | Buyer J | 1,380 |

**Table 5.** Results: Total Utilities

| | GA | Exhaustive search | Brute search |
|---|---|---|---|
| Problem 1 | 2,900 | 2,900 | 2,900 |
| Problem 2 | 3,170 | 3,170 | no answer |

**Table 6.** Results: CPU time

| GA | Exhaustive search | Brute search |
|---|---|---|
| 1.38 sec | 6.76 sec | 0.01 sec |

**Table 7.** Results: Optimal Solutions and Possible Solutions in 100 problems

| | Problem 1 | Problem 2 |
|---|---|---|
| Optimal solutions | 23 | 4 |
| Possible solutions | 91 | 24 |

Table 5 shows the best solutions achieved by each algorithm. The optimal solution is found by an exhaustive search algorithm and our GA, since these problems are NP-hard. However, the brute search algorithm failed to find a possible solution in problem 2. Namely, the brute search is not flexible in terms of types of handling different problems. From the above results, we can say that the brute search algorithm is not suitable for a commercial transaction system on the Internet.

Table 6 shows the CPU time for each algorithm. The brute search can achieve an optimal solution in the shortest time among these searching algorithms. However, as shown in Table 5, in some cases the brute algorithm cannot achieve optimal solutions or an optimal solution. If we use the exhaustive search algorithm, we can exactly achieve an optimal solution, however, this takes a long time. For commercial transaction on the Internet, we need to find a suitable solution, i.e., an optimal or semi-optimal solution, in real time. Namely, the exhaustive search is not an effective method. Our GA can find an optimal solution in real time. Also, even if our GA fails to find an optimal solution, it can find a possible solution.

Table 7 shows the number of optimal solutions by using our the GA in our system. Our GA could find a possible solution at a probability of 91% in problem 1. Furthermore, at a probability of 23%, the GA could find optimal solutions.

Our GA easily to find a possible solution by increasing the size of the population and/or the number of generations.

## 5 Discussion

### 5.1 Solution Space

Group buying consists of multiple buyers and sellers. However, when the sellers do not sell sufficient number of goods, some buyers cannot purchase goods. Thus, when the prices of goods are higher than buyers' reservation prices, some trades are not successful. Therefore, the number of goods and the buyers' reservation price are the main constraints for trading. The candidate space of a solution in the entire solution space is restricted by those constraints.

In our experiment, there are 9,765,625 possible combinations of problems 1 and 2. However, there is a small number of solutions that satisfy the constraints (1) and (2). The number of solutions is 16,121 in problem 1 and 2,718 in problem 2. The optimal and possible solutions comprise only 0.17% in problem 1 and 0.03% in problem 2.

In our algorithm, the group of genes in the first selection is decided based on uniform distribution in the search space. However, finding optimal and possible solutions is difficult since most of the genes in the first selection become fatal genes due to the constrains. To solve this problem, we considered methods for constraints 1 and 2 as explained in section 3. First, we can easily create possible genes in the first selection by considering how many items are selling. For example, if there are only three item A, then we assign item A to three buyers, i.e., elements in a gene. Second, we employ total payments as an evaluation value instead of total utilities. This reduces the number of fatal gene, and facilitates convergence to optimal and possible solutions.

### 5.2 Related Works

Sen et al. [Sen 00] have proposed a GA-based search algorithm for optimal coalition structures. They used *Order Based Genetic Algorithm (OBGA)*. Although the *OBGA* has no performance guarantee, they insist that it surpasses existing deterministic algorithms. The difference between our approach and their approach can lies in how they are applied to Group Buying. Since the unit price of a good are changes based on the number of agents in a coalition, the problem is more complicated than Sen et al.'s problem.

Matsumoto et al. [Matsumoto 97] proposed a hybrid genetic algorithm to solve constraint satisfaction problems with an algorithm based on the min-conflicts heuristic. They solved the CSPs by a hybrid method that combined a GA with min-conflicts hill-climbing (MCHC). They showed that their proposed method generally provides better efficiency than either the GA or the naive randomly researching MHCH. The difference between our approach and their approach is the achievement of having improved the GA itself.

*GroupBuyAuction*, which was proposed by Yamamoto et al. [Yamamoto 01] is an agent-based electronic market in which agents automatically negotiate with each other on behalf of their users. In particular, the buyer agents can form coalitions to buy goods at a volume discount price. The difference between our approach and that of *GroupBuyAuction* is that we employ an improved GA method while they do not employ GAs.

Leyton-Brown et al. [Leyton-Brown 00] proposed the *BiddingClub*, where agents conduct a pre-auction. After the pre-auction, monetary transfers take place.

## 6 Conclusions

In this paper, we proposed a method of goods allocation by using a Genetic Algorithm. The advantages of using a GA are described as follows.

(1) We can solve problems that the brute search cannot solve.

(2) We can find an appropriate solution in an efficient time that the exhaustive search cannot find in such short time.

The buyers coalition problem has many constraints, and the solution space is not large. Therefore, it is a difficult problem for which to find an optimal/semi-optimal solution. To solve these problems, we proposed a GA method that has the following improvements. The group of first selection is formed by the genes that satisfy the constraints of 1) described above. In order to avoid to increasing the number of fatal genes, we proposed the following crossover method among genes. First, our method determines whether to carry out crossover based on probability. When it determines that crossover should be carried out, the genes in a pool of genes are operated by one-point crossover at all crossover point and stored in the pool of genes together with the genes already based there. By using the above method, the two superior genes are precisely selected from the pooled genes and can survive to the next generation. The above method can effectively reduce the number of fatal genes in searching for solutions. Experiments demonstrated that our method can more effectively find optimal solutions and possible solutions than an exhaustive search algorithm.

Future work includes a real-time searching mechanism for cases where the numbers of buyers, sellers, and items change dynamically.

## References

[bidders] http://www.bidders.co.jp/

[rakuten] http://www.rakuten.co.jp/groupbuy/

[Varian 90] Varian, H. R.: Intermediate Microeconomics: A Modern Approach, 2nd ed. W. W. Norton & Company, 1990.

[Matsuo 02] Matsuo, T. and Ito, T.:A Decision Support System for Group Buying based on Buyer's Preferences in Electronic Commerce,in the proceedings of the Eleventh World Wide Web International Conference(WWW-2002),2002.

[Leyton-Brown 00] Layton-Brown, K., Shoham Y. and Tennenholtz, M.:Bidding Club: Institutionalized Collusion in Auction, in the proceeding of ACM Conference on Electronic Commerce(EC'00), pp253-259, 2000.

[Yamamoto 01] Yamamoto, J. and Sycara, K.:A Stable and Efficient Buyer Coalition Formation Scheme for E-Marketplaces, presented at the Fifth International Conference on Autonomous Agents (Agents 2001) in Montreal Canada, May 28-June 1, 2001.

[Sen 00] Sen, S. and Dutta, S.:Searching for optimal coalition structures, in Proceedings of the Fourth International Conference on Multiagent Systems (pages 286–292), held between July 7–12, 2000 in Boston, MA.

[Matsumoto 97] Matsumoto, M., Kanoh, H. and Nishihara, S:Solving Constraint Satisfaction Problems by Hybrid Genetic Algorithms Based on Min-conflicts Heuristic, ,pages 962-969,May 1997.(in Japanese).

# Application of Cepstrum Algorithms for Speech Recognition

Anwar Al-Shrouf[1], Raed Abu Zitar[2], Ammer Al-Khayri[2], and Mohmmed Abu Arqub[3]

[1] Al-Kharj Technical College, Saudi Arabia
[2] College of Information Technology, Philadelphia University, Jordan
rzitar@philadelphia.edu.jo
[3] Dept. of Computer Science, Petra Private University, Amman, Jordan

**Abstract.** This paper proposes a novel method for speech recognition. This is method based on the calculation of correlation coefficients of cepestrum by linear prediction (LP). The results of the method is compared with other methods. The real cepstrum is used to separate/estimate the spectral content of the speech from its pitch frequencies. Some notes regarding the efficiency of the processors used in the simulations are also concluded.

## 1 Introduction

Many methods are used for analysis and recognition of speech signal in both time and frequency domain. The aim of this paper is to use the cepestrum method for speech recognition. Cepstrum makes it possible to extract information about the signal energy, the pulse response of the speaker's throat, and the frequency of vibration of the vocal cords. With the use of cepstrum, models of words (Dynamic Time Warping), syllabus, and phrases (Hidden Markov Models) can be generated. Libraries of these models, through comparison with the cepstral model of a word being recognized, help to recognize similarity of a model with a word known to the recognition system, and consequently help to classify it properly[1][2].

The most popular approach for comparing two signals is the correlation coefficient. However, the correlation coefficient doesn't serve as a good tool in many cases, especially, in voice recognition. This is due to the fact that almost the voice signal is accompanied by noise each time it is captured. Moreover, the same person may say the same word (voice signal) each time differently and with distinct intonations. The capturing process may play a role in producing out of phase signals with negatively affects the outcome of the correlation function. Out of phase signals will be present if the capturing process is incapable of detecting the starting moment of the speech. Actually, we are dealing with such kind of signals.

This study involves four methods for recognition, and these methods themselves are based on four tools. These tools are the correlation coefficients method, cepstrum only method, Fast Fourier Transform (FFT), and finally the linear prediction (LP)

P.W.H. Chung, C.J. Hinde, M. Ali (Eds.): IEA/AIE 2003, LNAI 2718, pp. 768–778, 2003.

with cepstrum [3] method. Each of the four methods uses one tool or a combination of tools. The main focus is on the robustness of the cepstrum method.

Correlation method simply uses the correlation function to compare two signals x, y to determine whether they are highly correlated or not ; i. e, same signal or not. The cepstrum only method computes the cepstrum of the two signals being compared. In the FFT method, the FFT of both signals is calculated and then we compute the correlation between FFT outputs. The three mentioned methods are Time-consuming irrespective of whether they are effective or not. The hardware implementation of these methods may be possible if real-time factors are excluded.

The fourth method comes to remedy this negative aspect of time-consumption. In this method, the linear prediction of both input signals is computed. The order of linear prediction is 15; i.e., the output of the LP stage is a series of 15 coefficients. Having two series of LP coefficients, one for each signal, the cepstrum tool is next used as a second processing stage. The outcome of the cepstrum stage represents an input to a third stage where a correlation function is invoked to compute the similarity between the inputs.

## 1.1 The Cepstrum

Let us consider a sequence {x (n)} having a z-transform X (z). We assume that {x (n)} is a stable sequence so that X (z) converges on the unit circle. The complex cepstrum of the sequence {x(n)} is defined as the sequence $\{c_x(n)\}$, which is the inverse z-transform of $C_x(z)$, where

$$C_x(z) = \ln X(z) \tag{1}$$

The complex cepstrum exists if $C_x(z)$ converges in the annular region r1< |z|<r2, where 0<r1<1 and r2>1. Within this region of convergence, $C_x(z)$ can be represented by the Laurent series

$$C_x(z) = \ln X(z) = \sum_{n=-\infty}^{\infty} c_x(n)\, z^{-1} \tag{2}$$

where

$$c_x(n) = \frac{1}{j2\Pi} \oint_c \ln X(z)\, z^{n-1} dz \tag{3}$$

c is the contour about the origin and lies within the region of convergence. Clearly, if $C_x(z)$ can be represented as in (1), the complex cepstrum sequence $\{c_x(n)\}$ is stable. Furthermore, if the complex cepstrum exist, $C_x(z)$ converges on the unit circle and hence we have

$$C_x(\omega) = \ln X(\omega) = \sum_{n=-\infty}^{\infty} c_x(n)\, e^{-j\omega n} \tag{4}$$

where $\{c_x(n)\}$ is the sequence obtained from the inverse Fourier transform of $\ln X(w)$, that is,

$$c_x(n) = \frac{1}{2\Pi} \int_{-\Pi}^{\Pi} \ln X(\omega)\, e^{j\omega n} d\omega \tag{5}$$

if we express X(w) in terms of magnitude and phase, say

$$X(\omega) = |X(\omega)| e^{j\theta(\omega)} \tag{6}$$

then

$$\ln X(\omega) = \ln|X(\omega)| + j\theta(\omega) \tag{7}$$

by substituting (7) in (5), we obtain the complex cepstrum in the form

$$c_x(n) = \frac{1}{2\Pi} \int_{-\Pi}^{\Pi} [\ln|X(\omega)| + j\theta(\omega)]\, e^{j\omega n} d\omega \tag{8}$$

We can separate the inverse Fourier transform in (8) into the inverse Fourier transform of $\ln|X(\omega)|$ and $\theta(\omega)$:

$$c_m(n) = \frac{1}{2\Pi} \int_{-\Pi}^{\Pi} \ln|X(\omega)| e^{j\omega n} d\omega \tag{9}$$

$$c_\theta(n) = \frac{1}{2\Pi} \int_{-\Pi}^{\Pi} \theta(\omega) e^{j\omega n} d\omega \tag{10}$$

In some applications, such as speech signal processing, only the component $c_m(n)$ is computed and the phase is ignored. The real cepstrum is used to separate/estimate the spectral content of the speech from its pitch frequencies[4],[5].

## 1.2 Cepstral Coefficients in Speech Recognition

Up to now, cepstrum has been the best parameter describing the speech signal. First of all, the unwanted elements such as pitch period, which conveys information characterizing the speaker, can be removed from the signal. Pitch period is the parameter, defining the frequency of vibration of vocal cords of the speaker and it is the unrepeatable element, so the information about it in the speech recognition is highly unwelcome.

There are only 15-20 significant cepstral coefficients. The remaining coefficients, together with pitch period are removed by cutting off this part of the signal (cepstrum can be treated as a signal in real time). Signal still contains the elements characteristic for the speaker, even by the cutting off the cepstrum of excitatory impulse. These elements are encoded mainly by the low order coefficients, and that is why it is suggested in this case to employ weighting by the means of the function, which has its maximum in the point where the medium order coefficients appear. The most popular way to determine cepstrum by using a Fourier transform, is not suitable to be employed on signal processors, because calculating of the signal spectrum, following logarithm of inverse Fourier transform is not effective. Cepstrum can be calculated much easier directly from the samples of the incoming signal by applying the algorithm of the linear predictive coding. As a result we receive LPC coefficients, which can be transformed into cepstral coefficients by the use of simple recursive algorithms. There are two way how to effectively calculate LPC coefficients, which are described in next section.

## 2 Linear Predictive Coding with Durbin and Burg Algorithm

In speech analysis spectral content of a frame of speech is often modeled by an autoregressive (AR) process [6](an all pole filter) so that the random process $x(n)$ excited by an white noise sequence $v(n)$ is obtained from

$$H(z) = \frac{1}{A(z)} \quad (11) \qquad \text{or} \qquad \sum_{n=0}^{M} a(k)x(n-k) = v(n) \quad (12)$$

In order to obtain the tap weights $a_k$ of the AR, the Yule-Walker equation could be solved,

RW=r

this is the same equation as the Wiener-Hopf equation

$RW_f$=r

that need to be solved for the forward linear prediction (LP). This is why linear prediction is often used to estimate the spectrum of speech. The linear prediction coefficients (LPC) are then the poles of the AR process.

In LP the next sample in the sequence are being predicted from a linear combination of the past $M$ samples, where p is the order of the predictor. A forward linear predictor consists of a linear transversal filter with $M$ tap weights, , and tap inputs

$$\hat{x}(n) = \sum_{n=1}^{M} a(k)x(n-k) \quad (13)$$

Where a(k) is k-*th* coefficients of prediction filter, and $p$ (shown next) is the prediction filter order.

The difference between the original signal and predicted one is called prediction error signal e(n):

$$e(n) = x(n) - \hat{x}(n) = x(n) - \sum_{n=1}^{M} a(k)x(n-k) \tag{14}$$

The mean square value of the error signal is:

$$e^2(n) = [x(n) - \hat{x}(n)]^2 \tag{15}$$

Consider the minimization of the $e^2(n)$:

$$\min[e^2(n)] = \min[x(n) - \hat{x}(n)]^2 \tag{16}$$

Such that by performing this minimization we will obtain the set of coefficients, a(1),a(2),…,a(M) which are optimal in the mean square sense. Thus taking expected value:

$$E[e^2(n)] = E[x(n) - \hat{x}(n)]^2 \tag{17}$$

and rewriting in vector notation, equation (3.1) becomes

$$\hat{x}(n) = X^T A = A^T X \tag{18}$$

where

$$X = \begin{bmatrix} x(n-1) \\ x(n-2) \\ . \\ . \\ . \\ x(n-M) \end{bmatrix} \tag{19}$$

is a vector of past data and

$$A^T = [a(1), a(2), ..., a(M)] \tag{20}$$

the coefficient vector. Thus equation (17) now becomes

$$E[e^2(n)] = E[x^2(n)] - 2E[x(n)X^T]A + A^T E[X X^T]A \tag{21}$$

By defining

$$r = E[x(n)X] = E\begin{bmatrix} x(n)x(n-1) \\ x(n)x(n-2) \\ . \\ . \\ . \\ x(n)x(n-p+1) \\ x(n)x(n-p) \end{bmatrix} = \begin{bmatrix} R(1) \\ R(2) \\ . \\ . \\ . \\ R(p-1) \\ R(p) \end{bmatrix} \tag{22}$$

Which can be seen to be an autocorrelation vector, and

$$R = \mathrm{E}[X\ \mathrm{X}^{\mathrm{T}}] = \begin{bmatrix} R(0) & R(1) & \cdots & R(p-1) \\ R(1) & R(0) & \cdots & R(p-2) \\ . & . & & . \\ . & . & & . \\ . & . & & . \\ R(p-2) & R(p-1) & \cdots & R(1) \\ R(p-1) & R(p-2) & \cdots & R(0) \end{bmatrix} \tag{23}$$

which an autocorrelation matrix we can rewrite equation (21) as:

$$\mathrm{E}[\mathrm{e}^2(\mathrm{n})] = \mathrm{E}[\mathrm{x}^2(\mathrm{n})] - 2\mathrm{r}^{\mathrm{T}}\mathrm{A} + \mathrm{A}^{\mathrm{T}}\mathrm{RA} \tag{24}$$

which can be seen to be a quadratic function in the coefficient vector **A**. Taking the gradient of equation (24) with respect to **A**:

$$\nabla = -2\mathrm{r} + 2\mathrm{RA} \tag{25}$$

We obtain a minimal error of prediction when gradient is equal to zero. After this we obtain normal equation, that can be written in the matrix form:

$$\mathrm{RA} = \mathrm{r} \tag{26}$$

R[k,i ]=E[x[n-i ]x[n-k]] (k=1,2,…,M column index, i = 1,2,…,M row index and n=1,2,…,M is a number of sample in actual matrix) is the symmetrical matrix of theoretical coefficients of auto-correlation of the signal x[n], vector A contains the coefficients of the filter, and Rp[k]=E[x[n]x[n-k]] is the vector of the theoretical coefficients of the auto-correlation of the signal x[n]. Normal equation (16) obtained with the use of Durbin's algorithm have the shape:

$$\begin{bmatrix} \mathrm{R}(0) & \mathrm{R}(1) & \mathrm{R}(p-2) & \mathrm{R}(p-1) \\ \mathrm{R}(1) & \mathrm{R}(0) & \mathrm{R}(p-1) & \mathrm{R}(p-2) \\ & & & \\ \mathrm{R}(p-2) & \mathrm{R}(p-1) & \mathrm{R}(0) & \mathrm{R}(1) \\ \mathrm{R}(p-1) & \mathrm{R}(p-2) & \mathrm{R}(1) & \mathrm{R}(0) \end{bmatrix} \begin{bmatrix} a(1) \\ a(2) \\ \\ a(p-1) \\ a(p) \end{bmatrix} = \begin{bmatrix} \mathrm{R}(1) \\ \mathrm{R}(2) \\ \\ \mathrm{R}(p-1) \\ \mathrm{R}(p) \end{bmatrix} \tag{27}$$

In order to introduce fast algorithms solving a system of normal equations, an augmented system of equations containing information about the energy of the prediction error, must be obtained [7]. It is done by multiplying both sides of (14) by x[n-k] (k=0,1,…,M) and using the mean value operator.

$$E[e(n)x(n-k)] = E[x(n-k)(\ x(n) - \hat{x}(n) = x(n) - \sum_{k=1}^{M} a(k)x(n-k)\ )] \tag{28}$$

the above equation can be written in matrix form as:

$$\begin{bmatrix} R(0) & R(1) & R(M-1) & R(M) \\ R(1) & R(0) & R(M-2) & R(M-1) \\ & & & \\ R(M-1) & R(M-2) & R(0) & R(1) \\ R(M) & R(M-1) & R(1) & R(0) \end{bmatrix} \begin{bmatrix} a(0) \\ a(1) \\ \\ a(M-1) \\ a(M) \end{bmatrix} = \begin{bmatrix} E_{min} \\ 0 \\ \\ 0 \\ 0 \end{bmatrix}$$

we obtained a Yule-Walker equations where $E_{min}$ is the minimal energy of prediction error and a(0)=1. We obtain the filter coefficients from (17) (this gives coefficients a[k]) and (19) (we obtain the value of the minimal energy of prediction). Because of the fact that auto correlation matrix is a *Toeplitz* [8] one a fast algorithms can be applied to solve the equation (27). The most effective method which give the solution of the M- order and all less orders from k=1 to M is a *Levinson's Durbin's* recursion that combines coefficients of different order filters:

a[k]=a [k] +a[m]a [m-k],

where k=1,2,…,m-1 and m=1,2,…,M (29)

and

$$E_o = R(0)$$

$$k_i = -[R(i) + \sum_{j=1}^{i-1} a_j^{i-1} R(i-j)] \Big/ E_{i-1}$$

$$a_i^i = k_i$$

$$a_j^i = a_j^{i-1} + k_i a_{j-1}^{i-1} \qquad j = 1,2,...,i-1$$

$$E_i = {(1 - k_i^2)} \Big/ {E_{i-1}}$$

where:

$E_i$: energy of prediction error signal for i-th order

$a_i^i = k_i$ : the last coefficient of order i and is called the reflection coefficient (also known as partial correlation coefficient).

The most important advantages of the above describe recursive method is that:

1. Calculating the optimal coefficients of the m-th order filter we can obtain the optimal coefficients for the all less orders i=1,2...M-1.

2. Reflection coefficients $\mathbf{k}_i$ can be calculated directly from the samples of speech signal.

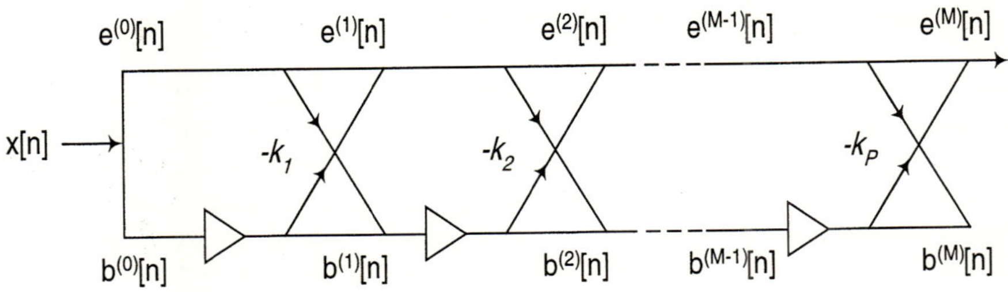


**Fig. 1.** Realization of predictor using Lattice structure

The reflection coefficients $\mathbf{k}_i$ determine a lattice filter (Figure1), while coefficients a[k] determine a transversal filter structure. In this algorithm the sum of square forward and backward prediction $E\{e^2(n)+ b^{2(}n)\}$ is minimized instead of the forward prediction error $E\{e^2(n)\}$. Now the recursive equation for $\mathbf{k}_i$ has the form:

$$k_i = \frac{2\sum_{n=1}^{N}[e^{(i-1)}(n)\, b^{(i-1)}(n-1)]}{\sum_{n=1}^{N}(e^{(i-1)}(n))^2 + (b^{(i-1)}(n))^2} \tag{30}$$

The most important advantage of this algorithm is, that values of coefficients k[m] are from the interval <-1:1> what gives a possibility to use fixed point signal processors, which will be our future job.

Results of simulations of both algorithms in MATLAB environment showed lower sensitivity of Burg's algorithm to the shape of weight window and high numerical precision comparing to *Durbin's* algorithm as well as to FFT cepstrum. Additionally, *Burg's* algorithm calculated reflection coefficients directly from signal samples. This justifies why this algorithm was chosen in this work. The cepstral coefficients were recalculated from LPC coefficients by simple recursive algorithm described in [9] and [10]:

$$c_i = \begin{cases} a_i - \sum_{j=1}^{i-1} \frac{i-j}{i} c_{i-j} a_j & 1 \leq i \leq M \\ -\sum_{j=1}^{M} \frac{i-j}{i} c_{i-j} a_j & i > M \end{cases} \tag{31}$$

## 3 Discussions of Experimental Results

The material for this study has been acquired from different sources. Recognition tests were made on same words spoken by different persons, on different words and on similar words spoken by the same person. Table(1) lists some excerpts of the spoken words and the results of each method. As an example of same word spoken by different persons is found in the first row of Table (1), namely, the word "sound", the third and the last rows present an example of two dissimilar spoken words. Similar spoken words appear in the fourth row. There we have the words: "sound" and "mouse". These words share the same principal phoneme /ou/. This corresponds to great similarity in frequency spectra of the two words. This fact is quite evident in the result of the FFT method (Table(1): row#4, column#3). In such a case, the FFT is unreliable and the robustness of the cepstrum algorithm reveals the fact that these two words are completely different.

In the case where two spoken words are the same, the output of the cepstrum algorithm is high (almost > 0.9). Briefly, Table(1) exhibits the response of each of the explored methods to test data.

**Table 1.** Responses for each of the explored methods

| ρ(x,y) | ρ(Cep(x,y)) | ρ(FFT(x),FFT(y)) | ρ(Cep(LP(x)), Cep(LP(y))) |
|---|---|---|---|
| X = "sound" | y = "sound" | | |
| 0.005 | 0.876 | 0.75 | 0.991 |
| X = "back" | y = "back" | | |
| -0.005 | 0.828 | 0.609 | 0.994 |
| X = "mouse" | y = "new" | | |
| 0.004 | 0.722 | 0.382 | -0.287 |
| X = "sound" | y = "mouse" | | |
| 0.000 | 0.768 | 0.690 | -0.247 |
| X = "sound" | y = "input" | | |
| -0.002 | 0.703 | 0.476 | 0.670 |

## 4 Conclusions

Cepstrum has been the best parameter describing the speech signal. First of all, the unwanted elements such as pitch period, which conveys information characterizing the speaker, can be removed from the signal. Pitch period is the parameter, defining the frequency of vibration of vocal cords of the speaker and it is the unrepeatable element, so the information about it in the speech recognition is highly unwelcome. The most important advantage of the proposed algorithm is that it could be implemented using fixed point signal processor [11]. On the base of the above mentioned results, it can be stated cepstrum has been the best parameter describing the speech signal. First of all, the unwanted elements such as pitch period, which conveys information characterizing the speaker, can be removed from the signal.

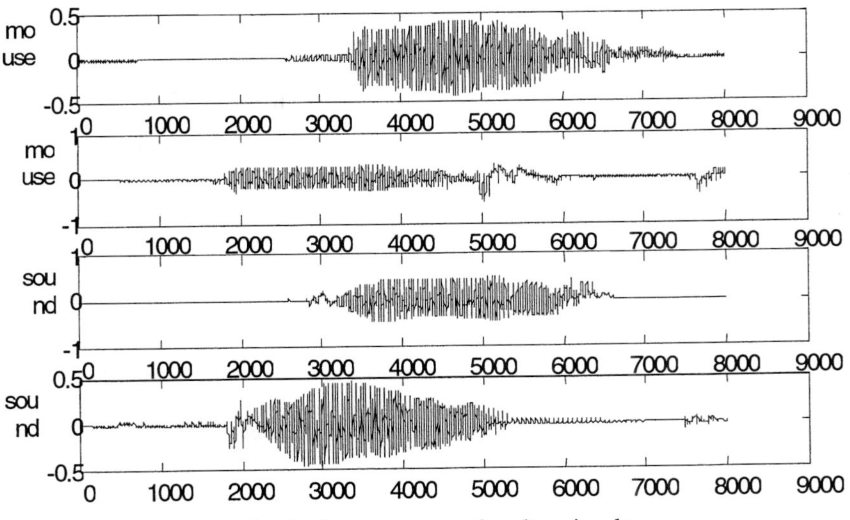


**Fig. 2.** Some excerpts of spoken signals

Moreover, we can say that the algorithms calculating cepstrum by means of the linear prediction can be implemented on a signal processor of medium calculating energy. The processor that we chose is able to do the required calculations in real time. The program that realizes the Burg algorithm and recursion calculating cepstrum from LPC coefficients takes approximately 60% of the energy of the processor, assuming that the frequency of sampling is 8kHz [12]. After simulation of the processors it was ascertained, that the accuracy of LPC calculations of the coefficients for the minimal amplitude was not sufficient and that it is caused by the loss of accuracy of multiplication and accumulation of the block of 128 samples of the signal. The possibilities of making calculations on TMS320C50 processor are limited to shifting the accumulator 6 bites to the right, and what follows it, the loss of accuracy. One of the solutions can be the application of the floating point arithmetic, for which the processor is prepared. In this case, however, energy is reduced to 1/3. Limiting for this case the order of LPC coefficients from 12 to 7 (the minimal useful order) makes it possible to calculate more accurately the magnitude of cepstrum and the minimal amplitude of the signal. There is a danger then, that this will not be enough time to calculate the delta cepstrum. The determination of cepstrum and its first derivative is on the border of processors possibilities. It is still possible to resign the second derivative of cepstrum or to shift its calculations to the other block of a recognition system. The other possible solution is the use of a processor of similar calculating energy, but with a better bit resolution and possibility of rounding results after the multiplication and the accumulation of 128 signal samples. For these requirements we can use Motorola 56000 family. These processors work with 24 bits resolution and posses 56 bits accumulator with the possibility of multiplication and accumulation of 256 signal samples without loss of accuracy during the calculations, and the rounding after that.

## References

1. Deller, J.R. Proakis, J. GHansen, . J.H.L. : *Discrete-Time Processing of Speech Signals* , Macmillan Publishing Comp. , New York, (1993).
2. Proakis J.G. and Manoalakis, D. G. :*Digital signal processing*. New Jersy, NJ: Prentice-Hall, (1996).
3. Makhoul, J. : Linear prediction: A tutorial review , *Proc. IEEE*, Vol.63, (1975). 561-580.
4. Bell, C.G. Fujisaki, H. .Heinz, J.M Stevens, K.N. and House, A.S. : Reduction of speech spectra by analysis-by-synthesis techniques, *J. Accost. Soc. Amer.*, Vol. 33, (1961). 1725-1736.
5. Kay, S.M. and Marple, S.L. : Spectrum analysis- A modern perspective , *Proc. IEEE*, Vol. 69, (1981) 1380-1419.
6. Martn, R. J. :Autoregression and cepectrum-domain filtering : *Signal processing* , Vol 76, (1999), 93-97.
7. Tourneret, J. Y. and Lacaze, B. : On the statistics of estimated reflection and cepstrum coefficients of an autoregressive process , *Signal processing* , Vol. 43, (1995), 253-267.
8. Heinig, G. Jankowski, . P. and Rost , K : Fast inversion algorithms of Toeplitz-plu-Hankel matrices, *Number. Math*, Vol. 52, 665-682.
9. Byrnes, C. I Enqvist, P. and Lindquist, A. : Cepstral coefficients, covariance lags, and pole-zero models for finite data strings", *Signal processing*, Vol. 49, (2001), 677-693.
10. Gadzow, J.A. : Spectral estimation: an over-determined rational model equation approach, P*roc . IEEE,* Vol.70, (1982), 907-939.
11. Ribeiro, M.I. Zerubia, J. Moura, J.M.F. and Alengrin, G : Comparison of two ARMA estimators, *in Proc.IEEE Int. conf. Accost.., Speech, Signal Process.*, Vol. 4, (1989), 2186-2189.
12. Stoica P. and Moses, R.: *Introduction to Spectral Analysis*. Englewood Cliffs, NJ: prentice-Hall, (1997).

# Maintaining Global Consistency of Temporal Constraints in a Dynamic Environment

Malek Mouhoub

Department of Computer Science, University of Regina, 3737 Waskana Parkway, Regina SK, Canada, S4S 0A2, mouhoubm@cs.uregina.ca

**Abstract.** Computational problems from many different application areas can be seen as constraint satisfaction problems (CSPs). For example, the problems of scheduling a collection of tasks, or interpreting a visual image, or laying out a silicon chip, can all be seen in this way. Solving a CSP consists of finding an assignment of values to variables such that all the constraints are satisfied. If such assignment (called solution to a CSP) is found, we said that the CSP is globally consistent.
Our aim in this paper is to maintain the global consistency of a constraint satisfaction problem involving temporal constraints during constraint restriction i.e. anytime a new constraint is added. This problem is of practical relevance since it is often required to check whether a solution to a CSP continues to be a solution when a new constraint is added and if not, whether a new solution satisfying the old and new constraints can be found.
The method that we will present here is based on constraint propagation and checks whether the existence of a solution is maintained anytime a new constraint is added. The new constraint is then accepted if the consistency of the problem is maintained and it is rejected otherwise. Experimental tests performed on randomly generated temporal constraint problems demonstrate the efficiency of our method to deal, in a dynamic environment, with large size problems.

**Keywords:** Temporal Reasoning, Constraint Satisfaction, Planning and Scheduling.

## 1 Introduction

In any constraint satisfaction problem (CSP) there is a collection of variables which all have to be assigned values from their discrete domains, subject to specified constraints. Because of the importance of these problems in so many different fields, a wide variety of techniques and programming languages from artificial intelligence, operations research and discrete mathematics are being developed to tackle problems of this kind. An important issue when dealing with a constraint satisfaction problem in the real world is the ability of maintaining the consistency of the problem in a dynamic environment in the case of a constraint restriction. Indeed this change may affect the solution already obtained with the old constraints. In the past decade several algorithms based on constraint

P.W.H. Chung, C.J. Hinde, M. Ali (Eds.): IEA/AIE 2003, LNAI 2718, pp. 779–788, 2003.

propagation have been proposed to enforce a particular case of local consistency, called arc consistency (or 2-consistency), in a dynamic environment. Our goal in this paper is to maintain the global consistency, in a dynamic environment, of a constraint satisfaction problem involving qualitative and quantitative temporal constraints. This is of practical relevance since it is often required to check whether a solution to a CSP involving temporal constraints continues to be a solution when a new constraint is added and if not, whether a new solution satisfying the old and new constraints can be found. In scheduling problems, for example, a solution corresponding to an ordering of tasks to be processed can no longer be consistent if a given machine becomes unavailable. We have then to look for another solution (ordering of tasks) satisfying the old constraints and taking into account the new information.

An important issue when reasoning on temporal information is the efficient handling of both the qualitative and the metric aspects of time. Indeed, the separation between the two aspects does not exist in the real world. In our daily life activities, for example, we combine the two type of information to describe different situations. This motivated us to develop the model TemPro[1] based on the interval algebra to express numeric and symbolic time information in terms of qualitative and quantitative temporal constraints. More precisely, TemPro translates an application involving temporal information into a binary Constraint Satisfaction Problem[1] where constraints are temporal relations. We call it Temporal Constraint Satisfaction Problem (TCSP)[2]. Managing temporal information consists then of maintaining the consistency of the related TCSP using constraint satisfaction techniques. Local consistency is enforced by applying the arc consistency for numeric constraints and the path consistency for symbolic relations. Global consistency is then obtained by using a backtrack search algorithm to look for a possible solution. Note that for some TCSPs local consistency implies global consistency[3].

In a previous work [4] we have proposed an adaptation of the new AC-3 algorithm [5, 6] used to maintain the arc consistency of numeric constraints in a dynamic environment. Our dynamic arc consistency algorithm offers a better compromise between time and space costs than those algorithms proposed in the literature [7–9] in both the restriction and relaxation of constraints.

In order to check for the global consistency of a TCSP in a dynamic environment, we have adapted the local consistency techniques and backtrack search used to solve TCSPs in order to handle the addition of constraints in an efficient way. Experimental tests on randomly generated TCSPs show the efficiency of our method to deal with large size temporal constraint problems in a dynamic environment.

---

[1] A binary CSP involves a list of variables defined on finite domains of values and a list of binary relations between variables.

[2] Note that this name and the corresponding acronym was used in [2]. A comparison of the approach proposed in this later paper and our model TemPro is described in [1].

The rest of the paper is organized as follows: in the next section, we will present through an example, the different components of the model TemPro. The method for maintaining the global consistency of TCSPs in a dynamic environment is then presented in section 3. Section 4 is dedicated to the experimental evaluation on randomly generated TCSPs of the method we propose. Concluding remarks and possible perspectives of our work are then presented in section 5.

## 2 Knowledge Representation

**Example 1:** Consider the following typical temporal reasoning problem[3]:

1. *John, Mary and Wendy* **separately** *rode to the soccer game.*
2. *It takes John* **30 minutes**, *Mary* **20 minutes** *and Wendy* **50 minutes** *to get to the soccer game.*
3. *John either* **started or arrived** *just as Mary* **started**.
4. *John left home* **between 7:00 and 7:10**.
5. *Mary arrived at work* **between 7:55 and 8:00**.
6. *Wendy left home* **between 7:00 and 7:10**.
7. *John's trip* **overlapped** *the soccer game.*
8. *Mary's trip took place* **during** *the game or else the game took place* **during** *her trip.*
9. *The soccer game* **starts** *at* **7:30** *and* **lasts 105 minutes**.

The above story includes numeric and qualitative information (words in boldface). There are four main events: John, Mary and Wendy are going to the soccer game respectively and the soccer game itself. Some numeric constraints specify the duration of the different events, e.g. *20 minutes is the duration of Mary's event.* Other numeric constraints describe the temporal windows in which the different events occur. And finally, symbolic constraints state the relative positions between events e.g. *John's trip overlapped the soccer game.*

Given this kind of information, one important task is to represent and reason about such knowledge and answer queries such as: "is the above problem consistent?", "what are the possible times at which Wendy arrived at the soccer game?", ... etc.

To reach this goal, and using an extension of the Allen algebra[10] to handle numeric constraints, our model TemPro transforms a temporal problem involving numeric and symbolic information into a temporal constraint satisfaction problem (TCSP) including a set of events $\{EV_1, \ldots, EV_n\}$, each defined on a discrete domain standing for the set of possible occurrences (time intervals) in which the corresponding event can hold; and a set of binary constraints, each representing a qualitative disjunctive relation between a pair of events and thus restricting the values that the events can simultaneously take. A disjunctive relation involves one or more Allen primitives.

---

[3] This problem is basically taken from an example presented by Ligozat, Guesgen and Anger at the tutorial: Tractability in Qualitative Spatial and Temporal Reasoning, IJCAI'01. We have added numeric constraints for the purpose of our work.

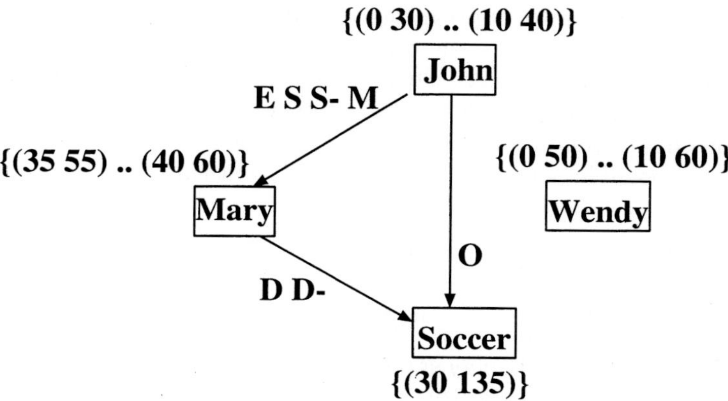


**Fig. 1.** A Temporal Constraint Satisfaction Problem.

**Table 1.** Allen primitives

| Relation | Symbol | Inverse | Meaning |
|---|---|---|---|
| X precedes Y | $P$ | $P^{\smile}$ | XXX YYY |
| X equals Y | $E$ | $E$ | XXX<br>YYY |
| X meets Y | $M$ | $M^{\smile}$ | XXXYYY |
| X overlaps Y | $O$ | $O^{\smile}$ | XXXX<br>YYYY |
| X during y | $D$ | $D^{\smile}$ | XXX<br>YYYYYY |
| X starts Y | $S$ | $S^{\smile}$ | XXX<br>YYYYY |
| X finishes Y | $F$ | $F^{\smile}$ | XXX<br>YYYYY |

Figure 1 shows the transformation of the temporal reasoning problem, we presented before, into a TCSP using the model TemPro. Information about the relative position between each pair of events is converted to a disjunction of Allen primitives. Indeed, Allen[10] has proposed 13 basic relations between time intervals: starts (S), during (D), meets (M), overlaps (O), finishes (F), precedes (P), their converses and the relation equals (E) (see table 1 for the definition of the 13 Allen primitives). For example, the information "John either started or arrived just as Mary started" is translated as follows: John $(S \vee M)$ Mary . The domain of each event corresponding to the set of possible occurrences (we call it SOPO) that each event can take is generated given its earliest start time, latest end time and duration.

## 3 Dynamic Maintenance of Global Consistency

Before we present the resolution method for maintaining the global consistency of temporal constraints in a dynamic environment let us introduce the notion of dynamic TCSPs.

### 3.1 Dynamic TCSPs

A dynamic temporal constraint satisfaction problem (DTCSP) is a sequence of static TCSPs: $TCSP_0, \ldots, TCSP_i, TCSP_{i+1}, \ldots, TCSP_n$ each resulting from a change in the preceding one imposed by the "outside world". This change corresponds to a constraint restriction or relaxation. More precisely, $TCSP_{i+1}$ is obtained by performing a restriction or a relaxation on $TCSP_i$. We consider that $TCSP_0$ (initial TCSP) has an empty set of constraints. In this paper we will focus only on constraint restrictions. A restriction can be obtained by removing one or more Allen primitives from a given constraint. A particular case is when the initial constraint is equal to the disjunction of the 13 primitives (we call it the universal relation $I$) which means that the constraint does not exist (there is no information about the relation between the two involved events). In this particular case, removing one or more Allen primitives from the universal relation is equivalent to adding a new constraint.

### 3.2 The Resolution Method

Given that we start from a consistent TCSP, the goal of the resolution method we present here consists of maintaining the global consistency (existence of a solution) anytime a new constraint is added (constraint restriction).

The pseudo-code of the resolution method is presented in figure 2. Anytime a new constraint is added (disjunction of some Allen primitives), the method works as follows:

1. Compute the intersection of the new constraint with the corresponding constraint in the consistent graph.
   **If** the result of the intersection is not an empty relation **then**
   (a) Replace the current constraint of the graph by the result of the intersection.
   (b) **If** the new constraint is inconsistent with the current solution **then**
      i. Perform the numeric → symbolic conversion for the updated constraint. If the symbolic relation becomes empty then the new constraint cannot be added.
      ii. Perform dynamic path consistency ($DPC$) in order to propagate the update of the constraint to the rest of the graph. If the resulting graph is not path consistent then the new constraint cannot be added.
      iii. Run again the numeric → symbolic conversion on the constraints updated after path consistency.

```
Function Restrict(i,j)
  t ← new_constraint ⋂ C_ij, updated_list ← {(i, j)}
  if (t = ∅) then
      return "Constraint cannot be added"
  else
    C_ij ← t
    if ¬ConsistentWithCurrentSol(updated_list) then
      if ¬NumSymb(updated_list) then
        return "Constraint cannot be added"
      if ¬DPC(updated_list) then
        return "Constraint cannot be added"
      if ¬NumSymb(updated_list) then
        return "Constraint cannot be added"
      if ¬DAC(updated_list) then
        return "Constraint cannot be added"
      if ¬DSearch(updated_list) then
        return "Constraint cannot be added"
```

```
Function DAC(updated_list)
    Q ← updated_list
    AC ← true
      (list initialized to the constraints updated after PC)
    While Q ≠ Nil Do
      Q ← Q − {(x, y)}
      if Revise(x, y) then
        if Dom(x) ≠ ∅ then
          Q ← Q ∪ {(k, x) | (k, x) ∈ R ∧ k ≠ y}
        else
          return AC ← false
```

```
Function Revise(x, y)
  REVISE ← false
  For each interval a ∈ SOPO_x Do
    If ¬compatible(a, b) for each interval b ∈ SOPO_y Then
      remove a from SOPO_x
      Revise ← true
```

```
Function DPC(updated_list)
  PC ← false
  L ← updated_list
  while (L ≠ ∅) do
    select and delete an (x, y) from L
    for k ← 1 to n, k ≠ x and k ≠ y do
      t ← C_xk ⋂ C_xy ⊗ C_yk
      if (t ≠ C_xk) then
        C_xk ← t
        C_kx ← INVERSE(t)
        L ← L ∪ {(x, k)}
        updated_list ← updated_list ∪ {(x, k)}
      t ← C_ky ∩ C_kx ⊗ C_xy
      if (t ≠ C_ky) then
        C_yk ← INVERSE(t)
        L ← L ∪ {(k, y)}
        updated_list ← updated_list ∪ {(y, k)}
```

**Fig. 2.** Dynamic Consistency Algorithm

iv. Perform dynamic arc consistency (*DAC*) starting with the updated constraints. If the new graph is not arc consistent then the new constraint cannot be added.

v. Perform the backtrack search algorithm in order to look for a new solution to the problem. The backtrack search will start here from the point (resume point) it stopped in the previous search when it succeeded to find a complete assignment satisfying all the constraints. This way the part of the search space already explored in the previous searches will be avoided. The search will explore the rest of the search space. If a solution is found then the point where the backtrack search stopped is saved as new resume point and the new solution is returned. Otherwise the graph is inconsistent (when adding the new constraint). The new constraint cannot be added.

**Else** the new constraint cannot be added otherwise it will violate the consistency of the graph.

*DPC* it the path consistency algorithm PC-2[11] we have modified in order to start with a list of specific constraints (instead of all the constraints of the problem). *DAC* is the new arc consistency algorithm AC-3[5, 6] we have adapted for temporal constraints in a dynamic environment. A detailed description of *DAC* can be found in [4]. Note that, although path consistency is more expensive than arc consistency, the advantage of applying path consistency before arc consistency is to reduce the size of the qualitative relations which will considerably reduce the number of consistency checks required later by the arc consistency algorithm. However, if arc consistency is applied first, it will not help the path consistency algorithm as this latter rely only on qualitative relations.

**Example 2:** The top right graph of figure 3 is the consistent TCSP obtained after performing our resolution method to the constraints of example 1 . Note that the constraint $M^{\smile} \vee O^{\smile} \vee P^{\smile}$ between the soccer game and Wendy is an implicit constraint deduced after the numeric $\rightarrow$ symbolic conversion and the path consistency phases (same for the constraint between John and Wendy, and the constraint between Mary and Wendy). The numeric solution obtained is:

$$\{John : (5, 35), Mary : (35, 55), Soccer : (30, 135), Wendy : (0, 50)\}.$$

Let us assume now that we have the following constraint restrictions:

1. John either **started or arrived** just as Wendy **started.**
2. Mary and Wendy **arrived together but started at different times.**
3. Wendy **arrived** just as the soccer game **started.**

Figure 3 shows the application of our resolution method when adding each of the above first two constraints.

The first operation corresponds to the addition of the relation $S \vee S^{\smile} \vee M \vee E$ between John and Wendy. The intersection of this relation with the current

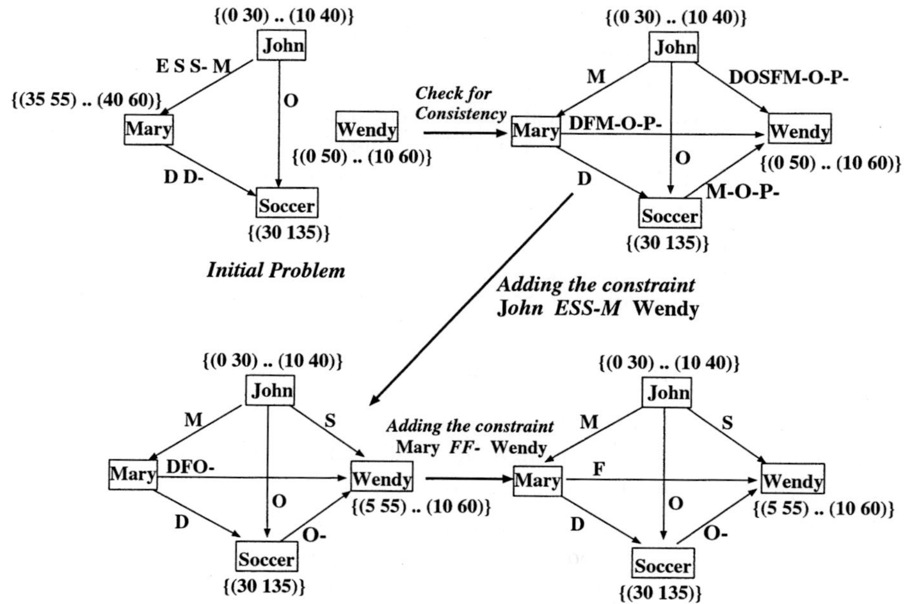


**Fig. 3.** Maintaining the global consistency of a TCSP

constraint between the two events will lead to the relation $S$. After applying the dynamic arc, path consistency and backtrack search the new solution obtained is:

$$\{John : (5,35), Mary : (35,55), Soccer : (30,135), Wendy : (5,55)\}.$$

The second operation corresponds to the addition of the relation $F \vee F^{\smile}$ between Mary and Wendy. The intersection of this relation with the current constraint between the two events will lead to the relation $F$. The relation $F$ does not conflict with the global solution obtained so far. Thus the consistency of the graph is maintained.

The third operation corresponds to the addition of the relation $P$ between Wendy and the soccer game. The intersection of this relation with the current constraint between the two events will lead to an empty relation. Thus, this third constraint cannot be added.

## 4 Experimentation

In order to evaluate the performance of the resolution method we propose we have performed experimental tests on randomly generated DTCSPs. The criteria used to evaluate the resolution algorithm is the running time needed to maintain the global consistency of the DTCSP. The experiments are performed on a SUN

SPARC Ultra 5 station. All the procedures are coded in C/C++. Each DTCSP is randomly generated as follows:

- Randomly generate $N$ temporal windows (SOPOs) corresponding to $N$ variables,
- and a list of $C$ temporal relations (disjunction of Allen primitives).

The resolution algorithm will then process the list of temporal relations in an incremental way. For each constraint the algorithm will check for the global consistency of the resulting temporal problem. If the problem is still consistent then the constraint is added otherwise the constraint is avoided.

Table 2 presents the results of tests performed on DTCSPs defined by the number of variables $N$ and the number of constraints $C$. The third and fourth columns indicate respectively the running time in seconds needed by the resolution method we propose (that we call incremental method) and the CSP-based method for solving TCSPs in a static environment [1]. As we can easily see, the new method we propose is much faster because anytime a constraint is added, it does not perform the backtrack search from the beginning at each time (as it is the case of the static method) but from the point (resume point) it stopped in the previous search where it succeeded to find a complete assignment satisfying all the constraints.

**Table 2.** Comparative tests on randomly generated DTCSPs.

| N | C | incremental method | static method |
|---|---|---|---|
| 20 | 95 | 0.10 | 1.47 |
| 40 | 390 | 0.35 | 14.25 |
| 60 | 885 | 1.02 | 89.90 |
| 80 | 1580 | 2.58 | 360.89 |
| 100 | 2475 | 6.10 | 1454.51 |
| 200 | 9950 | 28 | > 2 days |

## 5 Conclusion and Future Work

In this paper we have presented a method for maintaining in a dynamic environment the global consistency of a temporal constraint satisfaction problem. The method is of interest for any application where qualitative and numeric temporal information should be managed in an evolutive environment. This can be the case of real world applications such as reactive scheduling and planning where any new information corresponding to a constraint restriction should be handled in an efficient way.

One perspective of our work is to handle the relaxation of constraints during the backtrack search phase. For example, suppose that during the backtrack search process a given constraint is removed. Thus, the values removed previously because of this constraint should be put back in the search space. In this case, the assignment of the variables already instantiated should be reconsidered and the domains of the current and future variables (no assigned variables) should be updated.

## References


1. Mouhoub, M., Charpillet, F., Haton, J.: Experimental Analysis of Numeric and Symbolic Constraint Satisfaction Techniques for Temporal Reasoning. Constraints: An International Journal **2** (1998) 151–164, Kluwer Academic Publishers
2. Dechter, R., Meiri, I., Pearl, J.: Temporal constraint networks. Artificial Intelligence **49** (1991) 61–95
3. Meiri, I.: Combining qualitative and quantitative constraints in temporal reasoning. Artificial Intelligence **87** (1996) 343–385
4. Mouhoub, M., Yip, J.: Dynamic CSPs for Interval-based Temporal Reasoning. In: Fifteenth International Conference on Industrial and Engineering Applications of Artificial Intelligence and Expert Systems (IEA/AIE-2002), Cairns, Australia (2002) To appear.
5. Zhang, Y., Yap, R.H.C.: Making ac-3 an optimal algorithm. In: Seventeenth International Joint Conference on Artificial Intelligence (IJCAI'01), Seattle, WA (2001) 316–321
6. Bessière, C., Régin, J.C.: Refining the basic constraint propagation algorithm. In: Seventeenth International Joint Conference on Artificial Intelligence (IJCAI'01), Seattle, WA (2001) 309–315
7. Bessière, C.: Arc-consistency in dynamic constraint satisfaction problems. In: AAAI'91, Anaheim, CA (1991) 221–226
8. Debruyne, R.: Les algorithmes d'arc-consistance dans les csp dynamiques. Revue d'Intelligence Artificielle **9** (1995) 239–267
9. Neuveu, B., Berlandier", P.: Maintaining Arc Consistency through Constraint Retraction. In: ICTAI'94. (1994) 426–431
10. Allen, J.: Maintaining knowledge about temporal intervals. CACM **26** (1983) 832–843
11. van Beek, P., Manchak, D.W.: The design and experimental analysis of algorithms for temporal reasoning. Journal of Artificial Intelligence Research **4** (1996) 1–18

# Towards a Practical Argumentative Reasoning with Qualitative Spatial Databases*

José A. Alonso-Jiménez, Joaquín Borrego-Díaz, Antonia M. Chávez-González, Miguel A. Gutiérrez-Naranjo, and Jorge D. Navarro-Marín

Dept. of Computer Science and Artificial Intelligence – University of Sevilla,
{jalonso,jborrego,tchavez,magutier}@us.es

**Abstract.** Classical database management can be flawed if the Knowledge database is built within a complex Knowledge Domain. We must then deal with inconsistencies and, in general, with anomalies of several types. In this paper we study computational and cognitive problems in dealing qualitative spatial databases.

**Keywords:** Knowledge Management and Processing, Spatial Reasoning.

## 1 Introduction

Spatio-temporal representation and reasoning are topics that have attracted quite a lot of interest in AI. Since the spatial notions used by the humans are intrinsically qualitative, the reasoning about spatial entities, their properties and the relationship among them, are central aspects in several intelligent systems. But the problem is far to be solved in general. The spatial reasoning is more complex than the temporal one. The higher dimension of the things is not the unique problem. The topology is, in qualitative terms, hard to represent by formalisms with amenable calculus. The semantic of these representations offers incomplete support to our daily reasoning (the *poverty conjecture*: there is no purely qualitative, general purpose kinematics). Different ontologies have been proposed, but they are not of general purpose.

Among them, the theory called *Region Connection Calculus* (hereafter referred as RCC), developed by Randell, Cui and Cohn [4] have been extensively studied in AI [11], and in the field of Geographic Information Systems (GIS) [2]. A common deficiency of the theories representing topological knowledge, is that either the full theory is computationally unacceptable or they fail to meet basic desiderata for these logics [9]. For constraint satisfaction problems there are algorithms to work with the relational sublanguage, and tractable subsets of the calculus RCC-8 (a relational sublogic of RCC) have been found [11]. The intractability of the full theory is mainly due to the complexity of its models (topological spaces with separation properties [7]). We propose a practical approach (using an automated theorem prover) to investigate the verification

* Work partially supported by the MCyT project TIC 2000-1368-C03-0 and the project TIC-137 of the *Plan Andaluz de Investigación*

P.W.H. Chung, C.J. Hinde, M. Ali (Eds.): IEA/AIE 2003, LNAI 2718, pp. 789–798, 2003.

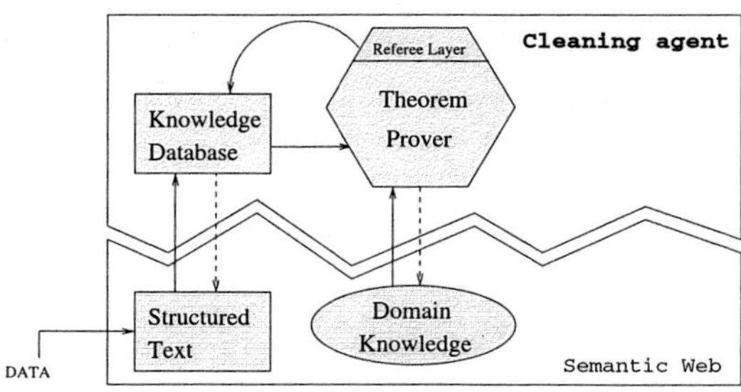


**Fig. 1.** Cleaning service process

problem of knowledge bases (KB) written in the language of RCC. In general, due to the complexity of the theories involved, the knowledge base may be inconsistent, although the environment was *well represented* by the relational part of the database. For a proper understanding of our framework, it is important to point out the following characteristics of the problem:

- The knowledge database is never completed (the user will write new facts in the future). Thus the difficulties begin with the future introduction of data.
- The *intensional theory* of the database is not clausal. Thus, is highly possible that Reiter's axiomatization of database theory [12] becomes inconsistent. Nevertheless, the self database represents a real spatial configuration.
- The knowledge base does not contain facts about all the relationships of the RCC language. It seems natural that only facts on primary relationships appear (we have selected for our experiment the relations `Connect`, `Overlaps` and `Part-of`, that one can consider as the *primary* relationships).

The preceding characteristics are important in order to classify the anomalies. The first one may produce inconsistencies that the user can repair, but the second one is a logical inconsistency and it is hard to solve. Thus, we have to reason with inconsistent knowledge. The last one implies that the (logic-based) deduction of new knowledge must replace to solving methods for CSP.

Our problem is only an interesting example of the more general problem of cleaning incomplete databases in the Semantic Web: the *cleaning agent* must detect anomalies in knowledge bases written by the user (in structured text), and associated to a complex ontology (see Fig. 1). A methodological approach to the cleaning problem was shown in [1] (where a cleaning cycle to the agent was proposed). It is necessary to point out that it is not our aim to find inconsistencies in the domain knowledge. In [6] it is shown an application of an automated theorem prover (the SNARK system) to provide a declarative semantics for languages for the Semantic Web, by translating first the forms from the semantic markup languages to first-order logic in order to apply the theorem prover to find inconsistencies. Our problem is not exactly that. We assume that the domain knowledge (the RCC theory and eventually the composition table for the relations of figure 3) is consistent, and that it is highly possible that RCC jointly with the database becomes inconsistent. However, in one of the experiments the theorem prover found an error in the composition table for the RCC-8 shown in [4]. Our problem has also another interesting aspect: the data inserted have not any spatial indexing.

## 2 The Theory of RCC

The Region Connection Calculus is a topological approach to qualitative spatial representation and reasoning where the *spatial entities* are non-empty regular sets[1] (a good introduction to the theory is [4]). The primary relation between such regions is the connection relation $\mathtt{C}(\mathtt{x},\mathtt{y})$, which is interpreted as *"the closures of* x *and* y *intersect"*. The axioms of RCC are two basic axioms on C, $\mathtt{A}_1 := \forall \mathtt{x}[\mathtt{C}(\mathtt{x},\mathtt{x})]$ and $\mathtt{A}_2 := \forall \mathtt{x},\mathtt{y}[\mathtt{C}(\mathtt{x},\mathtt{y}) \to \mathtt{C}(\mathtt{y},\mathtt{x})]$, plus several axioms/definitions on the main spatial relationships (see Fig. 2).

| | | |
|---|---|---|
| $\mathtt{A}_{\mathtt{DC}}$ : | $\mathtt{DC}(\mathtt{x},\mathtt{y}) \leftrightarrow \neg\mathtt{C}(\mathtt{x},\mathtt{y})$ | (x is disconnect from y) |
| $\mathtt{A}_{\mathtt{P}}$ : | $\mathtt{P}(\mathtt{x},\mathtt{y}) \leftrightarrow \forall \mathtt{z}[\mathtt{C}(\mathtt{z},\mathtt{x}) \to \mathtt{C}(\mathtt{z},\mathtt{y})]$ | (x is part of y) |
| $\mathtt{A}_{\mathtt{PP}}$ : | $\mathtt{PP}(\mathtt{x},\mathtt{y}) \leftrightarrow \mathtt{P}(\mathtt{x},\mathtt{y}) \wedge \neg\mathtt{P}(\mathtt{y},\mathtt{x})$ | (x is proper part of y) |
| $\mathtt{A}_{\mathtt{EQ}}$ : | $\mathtt{EQ}(\mathtt{x},\mathtt{y}) \leftrightarrow \mathtt{P}(\mathtt{x},\mathtt{y}) \wedge \mathtt{P}(\mathtt{y},\mathtt{x})$ | (x is identical with y) |
| $\mathtt{A}_{\mathtt{O}}$ : | $\mathtt{O}(\mathtt{x},\mathtt{y}) \leftrightarrow \exists \mathtt{z}[\mathtt{P}(\mathtt{z},\mathtt{x}) \wedge \mathtt{P}(\mathtt{z},\mathtt{y})]$ | (x overlaps y) |
| $\mathtt{A}_{\mathtt{DR}}$ : | $\mathtt{DR}(\mathtt{x},\mathtt{y}) \leftrightarrow \neg\mathtt{O}(\mathtt{x},\mathtt{y})$ | (x is discrete from y) |
| $\mathtt{A}_{\mathtt{PO}}$ : | $\mathtt{PO}(\mathtt{x},\mathtt{y}) \leftrightarrow \mathtt{O}(\mathtt{x},\mathtt{y}) \wedge \neg\mathtt{P}(\mathtt{x},\mathtt{y}) \wedge \neg\mathtt{P}(\mathtt{y},\mathtt{x})$ | (x partially overlaps y) |
| $\mathtt{A}_{\mathtt{EC}}$ : | $\mathtt{EC}(\mathtt{x},\mathtt{y}) \leftrightarrow \mathtt{C}(\mathtt{x},\mathtt{y}) \wedge \neg\mathtt{O}(\mathtt{x},\mathtt{y})$ | (x externally connected to y) |
| $\mathtt{A}_{\mathtt{TPP}}$ : | $\mathtt{TPP}(\mathtt{x},\mathtt{y}) \leftrightarrow \mathtt{PP}(\mathtt{x},\mathtt{y}) \wedge \exists \mathtt{z}[\mathtt{EC}(\mathtt{z},\mathtt{x}) \wedge \mathtt{EC}(\mathtt{z},\mathtt{y})]$ | (x tangential prop. part of y) |
| $\mathtt{A}_{\mathtt{NTPP}}$ : | $\mathtt{NTPP}(\mathtt{x},\mathtt{y}) \leftrightarrow \mathtt{PP}(\mathtt{x},\mathtt{y}) \wedge \neg\exists \mathtt{z}[\mathtt{EC}(\mathtt{z},\mathtt{x}) \wedge \mathtt{EC}(\mathtt{z},\mathtt{y})]$ | (x non-tang. prop. part of y) |

**Fig. 2.** Axioms of RCC

The eight jointly exhaustive and pairwise disjoint relations shown in Fig. 3 form the relational calculus RCC-8, that has been deeply studied by J. Renz and B. Nebel [11]. In that work CSP problems on RCC-8 are classified in terms of (un)tractability. These problems are, in some cases, tractable, but the relational language can be too weak for some applications. The consistency/entailment problems in the full theory RCC have a complex behaviour. If we consider topological models, the problem is computationally unacceptable. The restriction to *nice* regions of $\mathbb{R}^2$ is also hard to compute [8].

The problem of a good representation of a model by a knowledge base arises. Concretely, we must consider three classes of models: the class of all models (according to the classical definition from first order logic), the class of the topological models, and $\mathbb{R}^n$ where the constants are interpreted as the regular sets under study (*the intended model*). Formally,

[1] A set $x$ of a topological space is regular if it agrees with the interior of its closure.

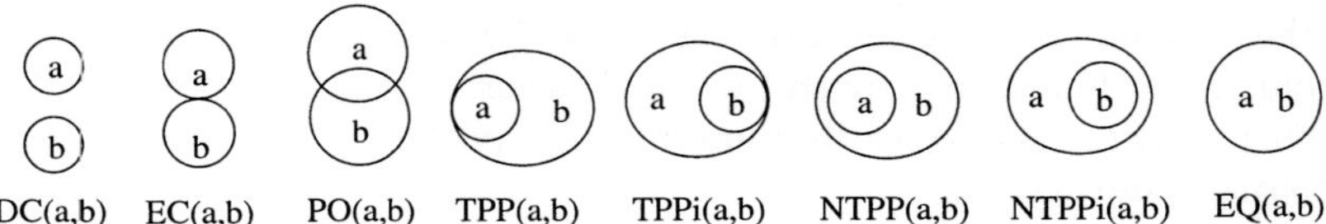


**Fig. 3.** The eight basic relations of RCC-8

**Definition 1.** *Let $\Omega$ be a topological space, and* X *be a finite set of constants. A structure $\Theta$ is called a* topological model *on $\Omega$ if it has the form*

$$\langle \mathcal{R}(\Omega)_{/\sim}, \mathtt{C}_{\Theta}, \{\mathtt{a}_{\Theta} \ : \mathtt{a} \in \mathtt{X}\}\rangle$$

*where $\mathcal{R}(\Omega)$ is the class of nonempty regular sets, $\sim$ is the equivalence relation* "the closures agree"[2], *$\mathtt{C}_\Theta$ is the intended interpretation of* C *and whenever* $\mathtt{a} \in \mathtt{X}$, $\mathtt{a}_\Theta \in \mathcal{R}(\Omega)_{/\sim}$.

Every structure is expanded to one in the full language of RCC, by the natural interpretation of the other relationships [7]: If $\Omega$ is a nontrivial connected $T_3$-space, the natural expansion of any topological structure on $\Omega$ to the full language is a model of RCC.

## 3 Towards an Automated Argumentative Reasoning

The logic-based argument theory is a formalism to reason with inconsistent knowledge [5]. An *argument* in $T$ is a pair $\langle \Pi, \phi\rangle$ where $\Pi \subseteq T$ and $\Pi \vdash \phi$. The argumentative structure of K is an hierarchy of arguments which offers a method to obtain useful knowledge from $T$ with certain properties. Also, it provides a method to estimate the robustness of an argument via *argument trees* [3]. However, this approach can not be directly applied on huge databases (it needs, for example, to find all maximally consistent subsets of the database). The problem can be solved in practice by adapting the notion of *argument* to an automated theorem prover. For this work we choose OTTER [10], a resolution-based automated theorem prover. Since it is not our aim to describe the methodology we need to work with the theorem prover, we simply assume that the system works in autonomous mode, a powerful feature of OTTER.

**Definition 2.**

1. *An* O*-argument (an argument for OTTER) is a pair $\langle \Pi, \phi\rangle$ such that $\Pi$ is the set of axioms from the OTTER's refutation of $\{\neg\phi\}$ (that we write $\Pi \vdash^{\mathtt{O}} \phi$).*
2. *If $\langle \Pi, \phi\rangle$ is an* O*-argument, the length of $\langle \Pi, \phi\rangle$, denoted as $len(\langle \Pi, \phi\rangle)$, is the length of the refutation of $\Pi \cup \{\neg\phi\}$ by OTTER.*

[2] The relation is necessary because of the extensionality of P given in the axiom $\mathtt{A_P}$. With this relation, the mereological relation EQ agree with the equality.

The argumentative structure can not be directly translated, because of the consistency notion[3]. By example, the argument class $\mathtt{A}\exists(\mathtt{K})$ may be adapted: $\mathtt{A}^{\mathtt{O}}\exists(\mathtt{K}) = \{\langle \Pi, \phi \rangle \ : \ \Pi \text{ is consistent and } \Pi \vdash^{\mathtt{O}} \phi\}$.

## 4 Anomalies in Complex Knowledge Bases

From now on, we will consider fix a topological model $\Theta$, the spatial model with we will work, and K a database representation of $\Theta$ (that is, K is a set of ground atomic formulae such that $\Theta \models \mathtt{K}$). To simplify we assume that the model satisfies the unique names axiom. Three theories describe the model: the formalization of Reiter's database theory $\mathtt{T_{DB}(K)}$, the theory $\mathtt{RCC(K)}$, whose axioms are those of K plus RCC, and $\mathtt{RCC(T_{DB}(K))}$. The three theories has a common language, $\mathtt{L_K}$. The following is an intuitive ontology of the anomalies in RCC-databases suggested by the experiments:

A1: The contradictions of the base due to the bad implementation of the data (e.g. absence of some knowledge)

A2: The anomalies due to the inconsistency of the model: the theorem prover derives from the database the existence of regions which do not have a name (possibly because they have not been introduced by the user yet). This anomaly may also be due to the *Skolem's noise*, produced when we work with the domain closure axioms but the domain knowledge is not clausal.

A3: Disjunctive answers (a logical deficiency).

A4: Inconsistency in the Knowledge Domain.

As we remarked, the anomalies come from several sources: the set may be inconsistent with the Domain Knowledge due to formal inconsistencies produced by wrong data, the database is not complete with respect to a basic predicate (the user will continue introducing data), etc. In Fig. 4 the most simple problem is shown. The system shows arguments with the Skolem function of the clausal form of $\mathtt{A_O}$ to questions as *"give us a region which is part of* a*"*.

If the spatial regions used in a GIS are semialgebraic sets, Skolem functions can be semi-algebraically defined [13]. In the practice, the spatial interpretation may be thought as a partial function. In the case of RCC, Skolem functions come from axioms $\mathtt{A_P}, \mathtt{A_O}, \mathtt{A_{TPP}}$ and $\mathtt{A_{NTPP}}$. It is possible to give a spatial interpretation of such functions. For example, the Skolem function for $\mathtt{A_O}$, $\mathtt{f_O(x,y)}$ gives the intersection region of x and y, if $\mathtt{O(x,y)}$. This idea allows one to eliminate useless results by a partial axiomatization of the intersection (see Fig.6).

## 5 Consistent Databases and Arguments

**Definition 3.** *Let $\Theta$ be a topological model. The* graph *of $\Theta$, denoted by $\Theta_G$, is the substructure of $\Theta$ whose elements are the interpretation of the constants.*

[3] An associated automated model finder, MACE, may be considered for a complete description.

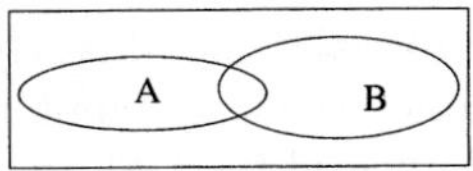


```
Database                                     OTTER's proof
-------------------------------------------------------------------
all x (x=A|x=B).                             1[] x=x.
A!=B.                                        5[] x!=A|y!=B|O(x,y).
all x y (x=A&y=B|x=B&y=A|x=A&y=A|            14[] P($f1(x,y),x)| -O(x,y).
         x=B&y=B -> O(x,y)).                 16[] -P(x,A)|$Ans(x).
all x y (x=A& y=B|x=B& y=A|x=A&y=A|          27[hyper,5,1,1]O(A,B).
         x=B&y=B -> C(x,y)).                 65[hyper,14,27]P($f1(A,B),A).
all x y ((exists z (P(z,x)&P(z,y)))<->O(x,y)).66[binary,65.1,16.1]
all x (P(x,A)->$Ans(x)).                         $Ans($f1(A,B)).
```

**Fig. 4.** A simple anomaly and an O-argument

**Definition 4.** *Let* K *be a set of formulas.*

- *The* world *of* K*, denoted by* W(K)*, is the set of the interpretations in* $\Theta$ *of the constants in the language of* $L_K$.
- *Consider an interpretation of the Skolem functions of the clausal form of* RCC*. The* cognitive neighborhood *of* K*,* $\Gamma$(K)*, is the least substructure of the expansion of* $\Theta$ *to the clausal language of* RCC*, containing* W(K).

It seems that the consistency of an argument depends only on its cognitive neighborhood. It is true for arguments with enough *credibility.*

**Definition 5.** *An* undercut *of* $\langle \Pi_1, \phi\rangle$ *is an argument* $\langle \Pi, \neg(\phi_1 \wedge \cdots \wedge \phi_n)\rangle$ *where* $\{\phi_1, \ldots, \phi_n\} \subseteq \Pi_1$*. The undercut is called* local *if* $\Gamma(\Pi) \subseteq \Gamma(\Pi_1)$.

**Definition 6.** $\langle \Pi, \alpha\rangle$ *is more conservative than* $\langle \Pi', \beta\rangle$ *if* $\Pi \subseteq \Pi'$ *and* $\beta \vdash^{\mathtt{O}} \alpha$.

**Definition 7.** *Let* T *be a theory, and* $\phi$ *a formula of the clausal language of* T.

- *A clause has* Skolem's noise *if it has occurrences of Skolem function symbols.*
- *The* degree of credibility *of an argument* $\langle \Pi, \phi\rangle$ *is*

$$gr(\langle \Pi, \phi\rangle) = \frac{len(\langle \Pi, \phi\rangle) - |\{\eta \in Proof^{\mathtt{O}}(\Pi, \phi) \;:\; \eta \text{ has Skolem's noise}\}|}{len(\langle \Pi, \phi\rangle)}$$

The degree of credibility estimates the robustness of the argument according to the use of Skolem functions in the proof, functions which become *ghost* regions (the credibility degree of the argument shown in Fig. 4 is 4/7).

**Theorem 1.** *Let* $\langle \Pi, \phi\rangle$ *be an* O*-argument of* RCC(K)*. If* $gr(\langle \Pi, \phi\rangle) = 1$ *then* $\langle \Pi, \phi\rangle \in \mathtt{A}^{\mathtt{O}}\exists(\mathtt{RCC(K)})$ *and* $\Gamma(\Pi) \models \Pi + \phi$.

**Corollary 1.** *If* $gr(\langle \Pi, \phi\rangle) = gr(\langle \Pi', \phi'\rangle) = 1$ *and the first argument is an undercutting argument of the second one, then*

- $\Gamma(\Pi) \nsubseteq \Gamma(\Pi')$ *(thus there is not local undercutting argument with degree of credibility 1).*
- *If* $\langle \Pi, \phi \rangle$ *is a canonical undercut, that is* $\phi \equiv \neg(\phi_1 \wedge \cdots \wedge \phi_n)$ *with* $\phi_i \in \Pi'$, *then* $\Gamma(\Pi') \subsetneq \Gamma(\Pi)$.

The preceding corollary relates undercutting arguments and spatial configurations, and it may be useful to estimate the size of *argument trees* [3].

**Definition 8.** *Let* K *be a knowledge database (a set of ground atomic formulae) for* $\Theta$. *The base* K

- *is* C-complete *if whenever* $\mathtt{a}, \mathtt{b} \in \mathrm{L_K}$, *if* $\Theta \models \mathtt{C(a,b)}$, *then* $\mathtt{C(a,b)} \in \mathtt{K}$.
- *is* extensional *for* P *if whenever* $\mathtt{a}, \mathtt{b} \in \mathrm{L_K}$

$$\mathtt{P(a,b)} \notin \mathtt{K} \quad \Longrightarrow \quad \exists \mathtt{c} \in \mathrm{L_K}\, [\mathtt{C(c,a)} \in \mathtt{K} \wedge \mathtt{C(c,b)} \notin \mathtt{K}]$$

- *is* refined *if whenever* $\mathtt{a}, \mathtt{b} \in \mathrm{L_K}$

$$\Theta \models \mathtt{O(a,b)} \quad \Longrightarrow \quad \exists \mathtt{c} \in \mathrm{L_K}\, [\{\mathtt{P(c,a)}, \mathtt{P(c,b)}\} \subseteq \mathtt{K}] \quad \Longrightarrow \quad \mathtt{O(a,b)} \in \mathtt{K}$$

- recognizes frontiers *if whenever* $\mathtt{a}, \mathtt{b} \in \mathrm{L_K}$ *such that* $\Theta \models \mathtt{P(a,b)}$

$$\Theta \models \mathtt{TPP(a,b)} \Longrightarrow \exists \mathtt{c} \in \mathrm{L_K} [\{\mathtt{C(c,a)}, \mathtt{C(c,b)}\} \subseteq \mathtt{K} \wedge \{\mathtt{O(c,a)}, \mathtt{O(c,b)}\} \cap \mathtt{K} = \emptyset]$$

The preceding definition shows a practical interpretation in some KB of the RCC-relationships. In fact, we have the following theorem.

**Theorem 2.** *If* K *has the above four properties, then* $\Theta_G \restriction_{\mathtt{W(K)}} \models \mathtt{RCC(K)}$.

An useful parameter on $\Theta_G$ is the *compactness level.*

**Definition 9.** *The* compactness level *of* $\Theta$ *is the least* $n > 0$ *such that the intersection of any set of regions of* $\Theta_G$ *is equal to the intersection of* $n$ *regions of the set.*

In general, a database is not refined. Notice that when a database K is refined, the Skolem function $\mathtt{f_O}$ is interpretable within W(K). Thus, we can add to the database a set of axioms with basic properties of such function, and $\mathtt{f_O}$ can be *syntactically defined* in K, and simplified by compactness level, if possible. If it is not refined, the partial definition is also useful (see table 1).

## 6 Experiments

We now report experiments with a spatial database on the relationships among three types of regions: counties, districts, and available maps on Andalucía, a Spanish autonomous region. The system works on a database built with the relationships of connection (`Connect`), nonempty-intersection ( `Overlaps`), and part-of (`Part-of`). Thus there exists hidden information, knowledge with respect to other topological relations among regions, not explicit in the database,

**Table 1.** Experiment without and with ($^+$) axiomatization of the compactness level

`P(x,Jaen) -> $Ans(x)`

| Exp. | CPU time (sec.) | generated clauses | results | (A1) | (A2) | (A3) |
|---|---|---|---|---|---|---|
| (R1) | 54.21 | 175 | 1 | 0 | 0 | 0 |
| (R1)$^+$ | 55,20 | 180 | 1 | 0 | 0 | 0 |
| (R2) | 59 | 671 | 25 | 102 | 1 | 0 |
| (R2)$^+$ | 60,26 | 677 | 25 | 0 | 2 | 0 |
| (R3) | 316 | 19,812 | 232 | 0 | 5 | 1 |
| (R3)$^+$ | 320 | 31,855 | 287 | 0 | 5 | 1 |
| (R4) | 54.79 | 570 | 1 | 0 | 1 | 0 |
| (R4)$^+$ | 55.6 | 575 | 1 | 0 | 1 | 0 |

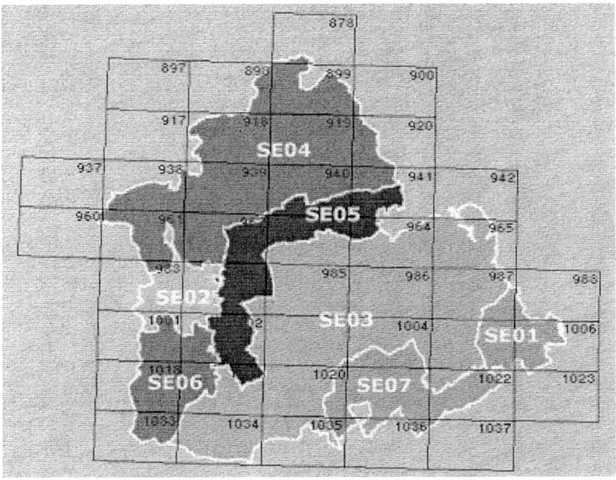


$K = \{\langle \texttt{Connect}: \texttt{SE04}, \texttt{SE05}\rangle, \langle \texttt{Connect}: \texttt{SE04}, \texttt{Map}-941\rangle,$
$\langle \texttt{Overlaps}: \texttt{Map}-920, \texttt{SE04}\rangle, \langle \texttt{Part}-\texttt{of}: \texttt{SE04}, \texttt{SEVILLA}\rangle \cdots\}$

**Fig. 5.** Partial view of the autonomous region and some facts from the database

that the theorem prover might derive (and, eventually, add to the database). The graph of $\Theta$ is formed by 260 regions, approximately, for which we have a database with 34000 facts (included the first-order formalization of databases, but the number can be reduced using some features of the theorem prover). This database has been made by hand, and it might have mistakes. It produces 40242 clauses (the processing takes 6.5 seconds). It has been used OTTER 3.2 on a computer with two Pentium III (800 Mhz) processors and 256 Mb RAM, running with Red Hat Linux operating system 7.0.

The database is C-complete but it is not refined. Thus, it is highly possible that the theorem prover detects anomalies of type (A2). It recognize accidentally the frontiers, its compactness level is 2, and it can be axiomatized and incorporated to the theory if we use the (partial) spatial interpretation of the Skolem

$$\texttt{Int}(x,x) = x \qquad \texttt{P}(x,y) \rightarrow \texttt{Int}(x,y) = x$$
$$\texttt{O}(x,y) \rightarrow \texttt{Int}(x,y) = \texttt{Int}(y,x)$$
$$\texttt{O}(y,z) \wedge \texttt{O}(x,\texttt{Int}(y,z)) \rightarrow \texttt{Int}(x,\texttt{Int}(y,z)) = \texttt{Int}(\texttt{Int}(x,y),z)$$
$$\texttt{O}(y,z) \wedge \texttt{O}(x,\texttt{Int}(y,z)) \rightarrow \left\{ \begin{array}{l} \texttt{Int}(x,\texttt{Int}(y,z)) = \texttt{Int}(y,z) \vee \\ \texttt{Int}(x,\texttt{Int}(y,z)) = \texttt{Int}(x,y) \vee \\ \texttt{Int}(x,\texttt{Int}(y,z)) = \texttt{Int}(x,z) \end{array} \right\}$$

**Fig. 6.** An axiomatization of $\texttt{f}_\texttt{O}$ (as `Int`) when the compactness level is 2

**Table 2.** Statistics for a complex question

`PP(x, Huelva) -> $Ans(x)`

| Exp. | CPU time (sec.) | generated clauses | results | (A1) | (A2) | (A3) | (A4) |
|---|---|---|---|---|---|---|---|
| (R1) | 2395.31 | 195,222 | 1 | 113 | 0 | 0 | 0 |
| (R2) | 2400 | 201,797 | 8 | 113 | 0 | 0 | 0 |
| (R3) | 2514.46 | 287,088 | 14 | 117 | 0 | 1 | 0 |
| (R4) | 54.15 | 286 | 0 | 1 | 0 | 0 | 0 |

**Table 3.** Statistics of an experiment when the composition table of [4] produces errors

`EC(x, Sevilla) -> $Ans(x):`

| CPU time (sec.) | generated clauses | results | (A1) | (A2) | (A3) | (A4) |
|---|---|---|---|---|---|---|
| 3845 | 11,673,078 | 25 | 113 | 0 | 6 | 72 |

function as *partial intersection* (see Fig. 6). Likewise, the higher compactness levels can be axiomatized.

We selected the predicates `Part-of, Proper-part, Externally-connect` as targets of the experiments. Several results are in tables 1, 2 and 3. `(R1)` shows the statistics for the first correct answer to the question, `(R2)` for 5 seconds later, `(R3)` for the first useless result and `(R4)` for the first error found.

It is not our aim to use the theorem prover as a simple database programming language. The idea is to ask complex questions which are unsolvable by constraint satisfaction algorithms or simple SQL commands. The questions are driven to obtain knowledge on spatial relationships not explicit in the database (as `Proper-part` or boolean combination of complex spatial relations). Some of the questions require an excessive CPU time. Surprisingly, the time cost is justified: the theorem prover *thought* all the time on the database and it found many errors of the type (A1), errors which may to be unacceptable. The degree of credibility allows to temporally accept some arguments. The number of useless argument can be significatively reduced by the spatial interpretation of $\texttt{f}_\texttt{O}$ (see table 1). As we remarked earlier, OTTER found an error in the composition table of RCC of [4] (type (A4)) working on a complex question (see table 3).

## 7 Conclusions and Future Work

We have focused on practical paraconsistent reasoning with qualitative spatial databases using logic-based argumentative reasoning. The problem is an example of *cleaning* databases within complex domain knowledge, which is a promising field of applications in the Semantic Web. This analysis supports —in a case study— a methodology for the computer-aided cleaning of complex databases [1]. A spatial meaning of some relationships between arguments has been shown. The next challenge is to model the robustness of an argument estimating the *number of arguments for or against* a particular argument by topological parameters on the graph of the model that it will be useful when we work with a vast amount of spatial information.

## References

1. J. A. Alonso-Jiménez, J. Borrego–Díaz, A. M. Chávez-González, M. A. Gutiérrez-Naranjo and J. D. Navarro-Marín. A Methodology for the Computer–Aided Cleaning of Complex Knowledge Databases. 28th Annual Conference of the IEEE Industrial Electronics Society (2002).
2. B. Bennett. The application of Qualitative Spatial Reasoning to GIS. In R.J: Abrahart (ed.) Proceedings of the First International Conference on GeoComputation, 44-47, Leeds, (1996).
3. P. Besnard, A. Hunter: A logic-based theory of deductive arguments. Artificial Intelligence 128(1-2):203-235 (2001)
4. A. G. Cohn, B. Bennett, J. M. Gooday and N. M. Gotts. Representing and Reasoning with Qualitative Spatial Relations about Regions. In O. Stock (ed.) Temporal and spatial reasoning. Kluwer (1997).
5. M. Elvang-Goransson and A. Hunter. Argumentative logics: Reasoning from classically inconsistent information. Data and Knowledge Engineering 16:125-145 (1995).
6. R. Fikes, D. L. McGuinness, and R. Waldinger. A First-Order Logic Semantics for Semantic Web Markup Languages. Tech. Rep. n. KSL-01-01. Knowledge Systems Laboratory, Stanford University (2002).
7. N. Gotts. An Axiomatic Approach to Topology for Spatial Information Systems. Tech. Rep. n. 96.24. School of Computer Studies. University of Leeds (1996).
8. M. Grigni, D. Papadias, and C. Papadimitriou. Topological inference. In C. Mellish (ed.) Proceedings of the 14th International Joint Conference on Artificial Intelligence (IJCAI), (1):901-906. Morgan Kaufmann (1995).
9. O. Lemon and I. Pratt: Complete Logics for Qualitative Spatial Reasoning. Journal of Visual Languages and Computing 9:5-21 (1998).
10. W. McCune. OTTER's user manual. Argonne National Laboratory (1994). `http://www-unix.mcs.anl.gov/AR/otter/`
11. J. Renz, B. Nebel. On the Complexity of Qualitative Spatial Reasoning: A Maximal Tractable Fragment of the Region Connection Calculus. Artificial Intelligence 108(1-2): 69-123 (1999).
12. R. Reiter. Towards a Logical Reconstruction of Relational Database Theory. in M.L. Brodie, J.L. Mylopoulos and J.W. Schmidt (eds.) On Conceptual Modelling, pp. 191-233. Springer, N.Y. (1982).
13. L. P. D. van den Dries. Tame Topology and O-minimal Structures. Cambridge U. Press (1998).

# The Object Event Calculus and Temporal Geographic Information Systems

Thomas M. Schmidt[1], Frederick E. Petry[2], and Roy Ladner[2]

[1] dr_thomas_m_schmidt@yahoo.com
[2] Naval Research Laboratory
Mapping, Charting and Geodesy
Stennis Space Center, MS 39529 USA
(rladner,fpetry)@nrlssc.navy.mil

**Abstract.** In our approach, the Event Calculus is used to provide a formalism that avoids the question of object timestamping by not applying time to objects. Rather, temporal behavior is reflected in events, which bring about changes in objects. Previous applications of the Event Calculus in databases are considered. An extension of the formalism to a fully bitemporal model is demonstrated. These extensions and the Object Event Calculus (OEC) form a framework for approaching temporal issues in object-oriented systems. Practical application issues as well as formal theory are described.
Current GISes will support areal calculations on geographic objects, and can also describe topological relations between them. However, they lack the ability to extrapolate from historical data. The sufficiency of the temporal GIS model to support inventory, updates, quality control and display is demonstrated. Follow-up and further extensions and areas of exploration are presented at the conclusion.

**Keywords:** Event Calculus, Temporal GIS, spatiotemporal data, temporal object model

## Introduction

Geographical Information Systems (GIS) are repositories of data that relate directly to the physical world. Like conventional databases, they are responsible for storing thematic data about objects in the world. In addition to this role, GISes store spatial data and must implement functions to display the features of the data stored. GISes must also manage relations among topological features.

A detraction of GISes as models of the world is the lack of a temporal component. Real-world processes take place on a timeline extending into the past and branching into the future, and these processes interact with spatial data. Gail Langran's *Time in Geographical Information Systems* [1] offers the first comprehensive survey of the field that has subsequently become known as the study of spatiotemporal data. Previous approaches included cadastral databases, i.e. those that need to maintain an

P.W.H. Chung, C.J. Hinde, M. Ali (Eds.): IEA/AIE 2003, LNAI 2718, pp. 799–813, 2003.

inventory of every owner of a particular piece of property going back to the establishment of the property recording system [2].

There are, however, a number of issues to address before any Temporal GIS (TGIS) can be realized. The proper modeling of time and capture of the information necessary to reflect accurately the state of the world and the state of the database is a complex problem. There are numerous temporal models, with most referencing or basing themselves on Allen's notion of temporal intervals. [3,4]. We also need to consider what underlying database engines can best support GIS queries.

Introduction to temporal database basic concepts is provided in [5,6]. The first comprehensive survey of the field in book format was Tansel's[7]. Advances since 1993 are explicated in [8], showing the increasing interest in non-relational temporal modeling.

Some basic temporal concepts are necessary to an understanding of this enterprise. Databases may be atemporal, that is, lacking explicit systematic support for temporality, as the original relational model was. They may track the change of the real world; this model of time is called valid time (or world time) and a database that supports it is an historical database. Databases may track transaction time (or system time) and support histories of objects as changed in the database. Such databases are rollback databases. Finally, databases that combine support for transaction and valid time are termed bitemporal. Current usage in temporal database research refers to temporal where bitemporal is meant.

Early attempts to apply temporal concepts in an object-oriented database model are discussed in [7]. Käfer [9] proposes a temporal extension to an object model. Other noteworthy temporal object models are found in [10,11,12]. Worboys [12] is different from these temporal object models in that his object model is event based, and he has applied it in the spatiotemporal arena [13,14].

The concepts discussed in [5,6] demonstrate the early focus in temporal database research on timestamping data. Other researchers have taken a different approach, focusing on time not as an attribute of data but of events that change data. Kowalski and Sergot [17] first proposed the Event Calculus as a way of talking about time in logic programming. Kowalski later demonstrated the use of the Event Calculus in database updates [18], a topic well covered for deductive databases by Sripada [19]. Worboys [13,14,15,20] and Peuquet [21] take an event-based approach to spatiotemporal data without using the formalism of the Event Calculus.

Kesim and Sergot [22] combine the Event Calculus with an object-oriented approach. Their Object-based Event Calculus (OEC) extends the Event Calculus with the ability to track objects with changes over time. However, their proposal offers only an historical approach.

The purpose of this paper is to propose extending the OEC to a bitemporal construction. This will allow an object-oriented temporal database to support queries both about the history of the modeled world and what was believed about the world at different points in time. In the first section, we discuss temporal logic and temporal databases in greater depth. We next describe the Event Calculus, and its extension to the Object Event Calculus. We propose our extension to the OEC for bitemporality, and then describe the uses of temporal data in support of GIS applications. Finally, we provide some advantages and limitations of the approach, and directions for further research.

## Temporal Logic and Databases

Logic has long formed a framework for understanding databases. If one considers the database as a series of assertions about the world at a series of times, then each state of the database directly correlates to a fact in the predicate logic. The sequence of changes (transactions) in the database likewise correspond to the insertions and deletions of facts in a predicate logic system.

Temporal modal logic represents time by means of modal operators (e.g., Past(Owns(Fred, Plot1)), Future(ISBlue(Sky)). It is an extension to classical logic that provides the logic of possibilities. It provides the ability to completely model the state of the world, regardless of event occurrence (e.g. if we discover that Fran also owned Plot1, we can add fact Past(Owns(Fran, Plot1)) ). (see [23] for a discussion of temporal logic representations)

Temporal modal logic does, however, possess a number of disadvantages. For example, because states are context sensitive, a context change can require a complex revision to the entire database (as noted particularly in [19] and [17], known as the frame problem). In addition, explicit references to time are difficult to implement. Proof procedures are less efficient than proof procedures for classical logic.

Allen's Temporal Logic [3] was developed as a method to better implement time in logic. Allen defines the following basic terminology:

> Facts: truths that represent states of a process, collected on a discrete or continuous basis;
> Events: "happenings" that modify the state of the world; considered instantaneous;
> Processes: "groupings" of events that modify the state of the world;
> Transitions/Mutations: characterize changes in objects caused by events or processes;
> Causation: the coupling of facts, events and processes.

Hajnicz [23] has expanded this list to include:

> Actions: Events put in motion by a mover;
> Strategies: planning of future actions.

Temporal intervals are at the core of the system. Intervals are fundamental and at base not further subdividable. Events occur in one temporal interval. Allen focuses acutely on the relationships between intervals, and defines seven basic relationships that can hold between intervals. (The diagram is taken from [3])

| Relation | Symbol | Symbol for Inverse Relation | Pictorial Example |
|---|---|---|---|
| X before Y | < | > | XXX YYY |
| X equal Y | = | = | XXX<br>YYY |
| X meets Y | m | mi | XXXYYY |
| **X overlaps Y** | o | oi | XXX<br>YYY |
| X during Y | d | di | XXX<br>YYYYYY |
| X starts Y | s | si | XXX<br>YYYYY |
| X finishes Y | f | fi | XXX<br>YYYYY |

Numerous scholars have proposed extensions to Allen's temporal logic. Some examples include Fuzzy Temporal Logic (really before, just after) for use in flexible querying [24], and Cobb's use of the temporal relationships in the spatial domain to help define topological relationships among spatial features in a GIS. [25]

The Situational calculus (see, e.g. [26]) was developed to expand upon the ideas first raised in the temporal modal logic. Here, global states are explicit parameters of time-varying relationships. Events are state transitions, with the predicate Holds associating relationship and state (e.g. Holds(Possess(Bob, Book1), S0)). Only one event of a given type may occur in a given state.

The combination of an event type and a state constitutes an event token. Preconditions of events can be expressed as integrity constraints on the states. Because states are named by means of previous states, updates using Happens must be in order (e.g. Happens(give(Bob Book1 John) S0), Happens(give(John Book1 Mary) S1) ).

The situational calculus has the advantage that implicit relationships are automatically updated. In addition, updates have semantic structure; they relate successive states. Initiation and termination of relationships is accomplished through event descriptions, not through explicit entry of facts into the fact base. The situational calculus shows a number of disadvantages as well. For instance, because of the use of global states, events need to be totally ordered; an event out of order will not be able to refer to the proper state to update it. Because of this ordering, it is not possible to assimilate new information about the past or make a correction to a previous event.

The implementation of time in relational databases is an ongoing process, from pioneering work developed from the logic arena to the recent TSQL2 and SQL3 standards. Understanding of time in databases requires a grasp of a number of concepts that have been generally accepted (see especially the consensus glossary in [5,6]).

When we talk about time in databases, we mean a system that can be linear, branching (linear in the past with multiple paths in the future) or cyclic. Time can be continuous, analogous to the real numbers, dense (analogous to, e.g. the rational numbers) or discrete. Time can be aggregated into temporal sets, intervals and periods, which are sets of intervals. Finally, time may be absolute (July 1, 1997) or relative (two weeks from now).

The building blocks of any time system are the elements that make up the time line. All systems present some image of a time line, which may or may not branch or have cyclic loops. On these time lines, we define an **Instant** as a time point on an underlying time axis. Likewise, a **Time Interval (TI)** is the time between two instants. We now come to understand the most important temporal object, according to Snodgrass, the **Chronon**. This is a non-decomposable TI of some fixed minimal duration. It can be multi-dimensional; for example, it can be the minimal period of time in both the historic and transactional sense. Any activity in a temporal database is understood to take place during the duration of at least one chronon.

As an example of multi-dimensional intervals, consider the two following definitions. A **Spatiotemporal Interval** is a region in n-space where one axis is spatial and all others are temporal. A **Spatiotemporal Element** is a finite union of these. Similar to this but lacking an explicit spatial component is the **Bitemporal Interval**, a region in two-space of valid time and transaction time (defined below).

Two more basic concepts of the temporal relational model can cause problems for those using other approaches. Most significantly, the **Event** is an instantaneous fact, i.e. something occurring at an instant. Finally, we can understand a **Temporal Element** as a finite union of n-dimensional TI's.

Thus, when we speak of **Valid Time**, (also known as historical time) we are describing when a fact becomes true in the modeled reality, while **Transaction Time** keeps track of when a fact is recorded in a database. Databases that support both time types are known as **Bitemporal** databases. A database can implement time using **User-defined Time**, which is an uninterpreted attribute domain of date and time, e.g. "birth day". Nevertheless, to implement temporality in a database, users must use some **Temporal Data Type** (a time representation specifically designed to meet the needs of users, with the same query-level support as DATE) with which they may **Timestamp** some object, (e.g. attribute value or tuple), and thus associate a time value associated with it.

We are now ready to approach the concepts in a **Temporal Database**. Using these definitions, the following four database models are commonly described. **Snapshot databases** are the conventional relational database, with flat table structures. **Historical databases** are databases whose underlying relation tracks valid-time; they are meant to track changes to object in the world. Rollback databases are databases whose underlying relation tracks transaction-time, and store every transaction in the database system. Bitemporal databases are databases whose underlying model is bitemporal, and thus a composite of transaction and valid time.

Models for integration of temporal data into the object-oriented arena have received attention recently (see [10] for a more complete recent survey). OODAPLEX, an object-oriented extension to the DAPLEX model, has been extended to support temporal data [7]. Story and Worboys have attempted to detail a class structure for supporting time on a system-wide basis in an object-oriented system. [12]

In contrast to the timestamping approach, several researchers have pursued an event-based approach to time in databases. Peuquet [21] builds a raster-based GIS storing events as changes to a base state. Claramunt [27] applies events in a vector-based GIS, while Worboys [12] adopts the view of change to databases occurring entirely through events without other update mechanisms. All event-based approaches build in some way on the Event Calculus, developed from the Situational Calculus by Kowalski and Sergot[17]

## The Event Calculus

The situational calculus was designed as a logical programming construct to allow for hypothetical planning based on logic programs augmented with a temporal logic. Situational calculus as a formalism, however, did not allow narrative approaches to time, e.g. what happened, when and what caused certain events to occur.

Kowalski's Event Calculus [17] is a formalism that extends logical reasoning about time to allow for narrative construction. Facts do not become evident in a database or logical system until engendered by events. Events, at least in original formalization, are fundamental and unchangeable; once an event is entered into a logical construct, it can have its resulting conclusions overridden by subsequent events, but it remains as part of the reasoning environment.

Event descriptions are used to describe the existence as well as the beginning and end of time periods. Time periods are determined by relationships which hold during time periods, and the events which can initiate and/or terminate these periods. One event can determine numerous time periods; for example, the event "Alice sold the farm to Bob" (event E1) necessarily defines two time periods: before(E1,has(Alice, Farm)), with has(Alice, Farm) the relationship, defines the time period terminated by event E1; after(E1, has(Bob, Farm)) defines the time period initiated by event E1.

The atom Holds(R1,TP1) means that the relationship R1 holds in the time period TP1. The atom Holds(R1, before(E1,R1)) means that the relationship R1 holds in the period before event E1. Were the term after(E1,R1), then we would know that relationship R1 holds after event E1.

Let us now review the formal axioms for the event calculus, as defined in [17] and refined in [19]. For discussion purposes, we will assume that events whose index is lower occur before events whose index is higher; thus, event E35 occurs before event E76.

Let E1 be an event where Alice sells a farm to Bob. Let event E3 be an event where Bob sells the farm to Charlie. In order for Alice to sell a farm to Bob, she must first possess it; for Bob to sell it to Charlie at event E3 he must possess it for some time before event E3. Event E1 terminates the time period in which Alice owns the farm, and initiates the time period in which Bob owns it. Event E3 terminates the time period of Bob's possession, and initiates the time period of Charlie's possession. Stated formally:

**Terminates(e,r) → Holds(r, before(e,r))**
**Initiates(e,r) → Holds(r, after(e,r))**

We now know four distinct time periods, defined by the two events we know about: before(E1, has(Alice, Farm)); after(E1, has(Bob, Farm)); before(E3, has(Bob, Farm)); after(E3, has(Charlie, Farm)). We do not know if after(E1, has(Bob, Farm)) is terminated by E3, we only know that it cannot be in force after E3.

We now discuss a method of describing the start and end of time periods. When we use the atom End(p, e) we mean that time period p has its end with event e. The atom Start(p, e) denotes that the time period p has its start with event e. From this we describe two axioms:

**Start(after(e,r), e)**
**End(before(e,r), e)**

Logically reasoning from these axioms, it is possible to conclude that the period after(E1,has(Bob, Farm)) is started by event E1. The period before(E1, has(Alice, Farm)) is ended by the event E1.

We now specify when a time period is the same. We do not know if the time period after(E1, has(Bob, Farm)) is the same as the time period before(E3, has(Bob, Farm)). We can use the atom Same(t1, t2) to mean that time periods t1 and t2 are identical.

**Same(after($e^i$, r), before($e^n$, r)) → Start(before($e^n$, r), $e^{i)}$**
**Same(after($e^i$, r), before($e^n$, r)) → End(after($e^i$, r), $e^{n)}$**

Using these two axioms, we can state that the period after(E1, has(Bob, Farm)) is terminated by event E3, provided that after(E1, has(Bob, Farm)) and before(E3, has(Bob, Farm)) are the same.

Negation by failure means that the failure to demonstrate a fact from the predicates present in the system means that the fact is proved false; this is an example of the closed-world assumption. Here, because we cannot prove from the predicates that Bob did not possess the farm, we can state that he did. We can state this formally as:

**Same(after($e^i$, r), before($e^n$, r)) ← Holds(r, after($e^i$, r)),**
**Holds(r, before($e^n$, r)),**
**$i < n$,**
**NOT Clipped($e^i$, r, $e^n$)**

The predicate Clipped($e^i$, r, $e^n$) means that relationship r, which is initiated by $e^i$ and terminated by $e^n$, is not a continuous relationship between $e^i$ and $e^n$. When an event clips a relationship, it means that it instantiates a relationship that is exclusive with a relationship that was known to exist before (or after, if the event terminates a relationship) the event. For instance, if Bob received the farm at event E1, and Bob sold the farm to Charlie at event E5, and event E3 initiates the time period before(E3, has(Dave, Farm)), we know that the relationship in event E3 implies that some event before E3 (presumably E2) terminated the relationship has(Bob, Farm) and some event after E2 and before E5 initiated the relationship has(Bob, Farm); relationship has(Bob, Farm) is clipped between E1 and E5 (in our example, again, presumably by E2). A relationship is always exclusive with itself, and a relationship r1 is exclusive with r2 if and only if it is incompatible with r2; e.g. has(Bob, Farm) is incompatible with has(Alice, Farm). Clipped in axiomatic form is:

$$\begin{aligned} &\mathbf{Clipped}(e^i, r^i, e^n) \leftarrow \mathbf{Holds}(r^j, \mathbf{after}(e^j, r^j)),\\ &\qquad \mathbf{Exclusive}(r^i, r^j),\\ &\qquad e^i < e^j\\ &\qquad e^j < e^n\\ &\mathbf{Clipped}(e^i, r^i, e^n) \leftarrow \mathbf{Holds}(r^j, \mathbf{before}(e^j, r^j)),\\ &\qquad \mathbf{Exclusive}(r^i, r^j),\\ &\qquad e^i < e^j,\\ &\qquad e^j < e^n \end{aligned}$$

From our initial example, we have the time period before(E1, has(Alice, Farm)) and before(E3, has(Bob, Farm)). There is an unknown event that brings about two mutually exclusive relationships. We can try to reason about this incomplete information. Use the function startpoint to return the event that generates the start point of a time period, and the function endpoint to return the event that generates the end point of a time period. Then:

$$\begin{aligned} &[\mathbf{Start}(\mathbf{before}(e^j, r^j), \mathbf{startpoint}(\mathbf{before}(e^j, r^j)))\\ &\mathbf{and}\\ &e^i <= \mathbf{startpoint}(\mathbf{before}(e^j,r^j))] \quad \leftarrow \quad \mathbf{Holds}(r^i, \mathbf{before}(e^i, r^i)),\\ &\qquad \mathbf{Holds}(r^j, \mathbf{before}(e^j, r^j)), \qquad \mathbf{Exclusive}(r^i, r^j),\\ &\qquad e^i < e^j,\\ &\qquad \mathbf{NOT\ Clipped}(e^i, r^j, e^j) \end{aligned}$$

Now consider the time periods after(E1, has(Alice, Farm)) and after(E5, has(Alice, Farm)). In the first case, the terminating event that caused Alice to lose the farm and regain it at event E5 is unknown; in the second case, the end of the period after(E1, has(Alice, Farm)) is unknown. The following axiom formalizes this notion:

$$\begin{aligned} &[\mathbf{End}(\mathbf{after}(e^i, r^i), \mathbf{endpoint}(\mathbf{after}(e^i, r^i)))\\ &\mathbf{and}\\ &\mathbf{endpoint}(\mathbf{after}(e^i, r^i))] =< e^j \leftarrow \quad \mathbf{Holds}(r^i, \mathbf{before}(e^i, r^i)),\\ &\qquad \mathbf{Holds}(r^j, \mathbf{before}(e^j, r^j)), \qquad \mathbf{Exclusive}(r^i, r^j),\\ &\qquad e^i < e^j,\\ &\qquad \mathbf{NOT\ Clipped}(e^i, r^j, e^j) \end{aligned}$$

The final uncertainty case we examine is the situation where the end of one time period and the beginning of another time period are unknown. We can infer events that cause the situation to change. For example, after(E1, has(Alice, Farm)) and before(E3, has(Bob, Farm)) are incompatible. We can state this more formally and generally as:

**[endpoint(after($e^i$, $r^i$)) <= startpoint(before($e^j$, $r^j$))**
**and Start(before($e^j$, $r^j$), startpoint(before($e^j$, $r^j$)))**
**and End(after($e^i$, $r^i$), endpoint(after($e^i$, $r^i$)))]** $\leftarrow$
**Holds($r^i$, before($e^i$, $r^i$)),**
**Holds($r^j$, before($e^j$, $r^j$)),**
**Incompatible($r^i$, $r^j$),**
**$e^i < e^j$,**
**NOT Clipped($e^i$, $r^j$, $e^j$)**

Now that we have formal axioms for determining if a relationship holds for a certain time period, we wish to describe if a relationship holds at any given time point. The following four axioms allow us to do so.

**HoldsAt(r,t)** $\leftarrow$ **Holds(r,p),**
**In(t,p)**

In other words, a relationship holds at a time t is it holds for a period p, and the time t is in period p. We define in as follows:

**In($t^j$,p)** $\leftarrow$ **Start(p, $e^i$), End(p,$e^k$),**
**Time($e^i$, $t^i$), Time($e^k$, $t^k$),**
**$t^i < t^j$,**
**$t^j < t^k$**
**In($t^j$,p)** $\leftarrow$ **Start(p, $e^i$),**
**Time($e^i$, $t^i$),**
**$t^i < t^j$,**
**NOT EXIST $e^k$ End(p, $e^k$)**
**In($t^j$,p)** $\leftarrow$ **End(p, $e^k$),**
**Time($e^k$, $t^k$),**
**$t^j < t^k$,**
**NOT EXIST $e^i$ Start(p, $e^i$)**

These are the 16 basic axioms of the Event Calculus as initially described by Kowalski and Sergot. As Sripada notes “the Event Calculus formalizes a treatment of valid time in historical databases.” [19] Provision is not made in the original Event Calculus for revisions to events, and so it cannot accommodate a bitemporal database.

## The Object Event Calculus

Kesim and Sergot [22] have described a partial extension of the Event Calculus to the object-oriented domain. Their model is incomplete in that it does not treat time symmetrically into past and future, and also fails to properly account for bitemporality. The OEC is designed by [KeSe] as an historical database.

As in the Event Calculus, an event initiates a period of time during which some property is true about an object, be it an attribute of the object or simply object existence. The predicate initiates is defined as **initiates(Event, Object, Attribute, Value)**. For example, the act of selling a farm to Bob from Alice initiates a period in which Bob owns the farm: initiates(buys(bob, farm), bob, ownsfarm, true). Its counterpart terminates has the same variable list: **terminates(Event, Object, Attribute, Value)**. In addition to the creation of facts in the database via initiates, OEC provides a method for keeping a journal of events: **happens(Event, Ts)**. Using happens and initiates, it is possible to determine the value of an object at a specific point in time with the holds_at predicate.

```
holds_at(Obj, Attr, Val, T) ←
        happens(Ev, Ts), Ts <= T,
        initiates(Ev, Obj, Attr, Val),
        not broken(Obj, Attr, Val, Ts, T)

broken(Obj, Attr, Val, Ts, T) ←
        happens(Ev*, T*),
        Ts < T* <= T,
        terminates(Ev*, Obj, Attr, Val)
```

Thus the query holds_at(bob, ownsfarm, Val, Jan 30 1999 11:00:00) returns the value true for the variable in the query. Holds_for calculates time periods in like fashion. It is defined as:

```
holds_for(Obj, Attr, Val, Ts-Te) ←
        happens(Ev, Ts),
        initiates(Ev, Obj, Attr, Val),
        terminated(Obj, Attr, Val, Ts, Te)

terminated(Obj, Attr, Val, Ts, Te) ←
        happens(Ev, Te), Ts < Te,
        terminates(Ev, Obj, Attr, Val),
        not broken(Obj, Attr, Val, Ts, Te)
```

To allow for states to persist when there is no terminating event, the holds_for predicate also can be defined with **not terminated_later**(Obj, Attr, Val, Ts) replacing the terminated clause. Terminated_later is defined as:

```
terminated_later(Obj, Attr, Val, Ts) ←
        happens(Ev, Te), Ts < Te,
        terminates(Ev, Obj, Attr, Val)
```

OEC creates objects by assigning them to a chosen class and then specifying that object's initial state. To determine if an object exists, the instance_of class membership describes a time-varying relationship: if the object is an instance_of a class at a particular time, then the object exists. To specify which events assign objects to new classes, Kesim and Sergot define a new predicate, **assigns.** This is defined as **assigns(Event, Object, Class)** and has a counterpart for object destruction. This is **destroys(Event, Object)** and it is used to delete objects from the system.

Note that the Event Calculus' need to talk about time in relation to events, and events creating the timeline, has been superceded by the Timestamping of events via the happens() predicate. We can now refer to time independently of events in relation to the ordinal years. Thus, while we preserve the ability to refer to time periods in terms of before and after, we can more generally refer to the timeline established by the granularity of time with which we have chosen to stamp events.

## Extending the OEC for Bitemporality

Because events in the OEC must be stored in the order that they occur in the real world, the database modeled, while tracking historical time, actually follows the implementation of a transaction-time temporal model. Recall that a transaction-time model cannot store events (transactions) in any order other than the system timestamp order; this is the order in which the database receives the transactions and any other is inconceivable. Indeed, as Kesim and Sergot [19] note, "if valid times and transaction times are distinguished but are exactly correlated, then [their model] can be seen as a 'degenerate bitemporal' database."

Kesim and Sergot implicitly implement a distinction between transaction-time and valid-time events. They note that they "have introduced two separate sets of predicates, one for dealing with change in internal state of objects and one for creation/deletion of objects." They do this because they "want to emphasize the conceptual difference between changes in an object's state … and changes to class membership." What they have really done is delineate the need to define predicates for maintenance of real-world objects (the changes in objects' state) and for maintenance of database objects (object creation/destruction, event revision).

Kesim and Sergot do face the problem of correct description of the world. What if an event that alters or creates an object has been recorded incorrectly? The database will always reflect the most recent understanding of the event. This is done by storing events in a "journal"; because events are objects in the OEC, this journal must be a database of event objects. Because revisions to knowledge about the real world are permitted, the database of event objects is permitted to be updated to reflect new information. The new event object supercedes the old event object and completely replaces it; neither the event that changed the event object, nor the prior version of the event object is retained.

We do not actually need separate predicates for real-world and database events, however. We can extend the real-world OEC predicates to apply to the "world" of the journal. Thus creation of an event that changes a real world object will result in at least one invocation of the assigns() predicate, to create the event object that changes the real-world object. If the event being added to the journal also creates a real-world object, the assigns predicate is again used to create it.

The journal of events described is, again, simply a collection of objects. Changes to these objects, and changes to the database itself, are, as Sripada noted, meta-events

[17]. Sripada proposes the revises(E', E) predicate to reflect revisions to events. The revises() predicate, while claimed of use by Sripada in an historical database, in fact implements a type of rollback database. We thus adopt it for use in the OEC, restricting the domain of objects upon which the predicate operates to the database of event objects, the journal.

We need to describe when revision to previous objects occurs. happens(Ev, Ts) relates an event's occurrence to the timeline we have chosen for our implementation. Likewise, we define **happens_t(Ev, Ts)** as a predicate, to timestamp the occurrence of transaction-time events.

When we examine the question of a revision to an event object, we will again assign an event object with the assigns predicate. Now we will also specify the object revised and the revisions to the object; this requires the use of the revises() predicate we adopted from Sripada. Since the event to be changed is an object, the revision event also initiates and terminates attribute values about certain objects, in this case already extant events.

We have now created a construct that allows a fully bitemporal view of the world. Since we timestamp events and meta-events, we can determine along two time axes the state of the world. We can now answer the following types of questions: What was the state of the world on Jan 1 2000? What did we believe was the state of the world on Jan 5 2000? On Jan 5 2000, what did we believe was the state of the world on Jan 1 2000? What changed about the world, and our belief about the world, between Jan 1 and Jan 10 2000?

## Applicability to Temporal GIS

Langran offers the following six justifications for a temporal GIS:

Inventory: a temporal GIS should be able to store the most complete possible description of the study area;

Analysis: since atemporal databases do not store changes, they provide no facility to examine processes that cause changes to features in the GIS;

Scheduling: a temporal GIS should allow for the user to set intervention points in the system;

Display: a temporal GIS should allow better displays of time-series data like the growth rings of a city like Chicago;

Updates: rather than distribute an entirely new copy of the database, a temporal GIS could send only the updates;

Quality Control: a temporal GIS could store the lineage of each item in it, allowing for better management of accuracy in data.

In addition to these six proposed by Langran, a temporal GIS should assist with at least two other issues:

Conflation: the process of combining two maps from different sources;
Uncertainty: it is not simple to represent uncertain and incomplete information correctly in current GISes.

Without the ability to answer questions in all eight of the areas outlined above, a GIS cannot be considered complete. The construction of a proper temporal GIS (TGIS) will require that functionality in the TGIS support each of these eight requirements. In supporting these requirements, the TGIS will need to offer a proper representation for time in the GIS. Likewise, the TGIS should support the thematic and spatial data in a storage structure that appropriately matches the needs of both of these types of data, just like any non-temporal GIS.

The OEC approach allows the underlying database to support each of Langran's requirements. Recording and storing all changes to objects allows for thorough inventory control. Distributing only the event objects that change the database will reduce the volume of data transmitted in, say, a CORBA over IIOP environment. Finally, as discussed in reference to the Event Calculus, we have a mechanism for reasoning about uncertain information.

## Conclusion

The bitemporal OEC displays the advantages of all event-based temporal models: mainly, time is not an inherent attribute of objects, but an attribute of events that occur at specific points or over specific periods. As an extension to the OEC, it allows for full modeling of temporal information about objects in the real world and the database. Because temporal support maintains a more complete history of the world, information that was previously destroyed on updates is preserved. This is advantageous in a wide range of applications, with particular focus on GISes.

The chief limitations of temporal approaches are in the volume of data needed to be stored, and the overhead in data retrieval. Several articles in [8] discuss optimization strategies for temporal queries. Revisions in a logic-based approach like the Event Calculus must necessarily require regeneration of all subsequent conclusions. This overhead has led most researchers to limit the ability to revise existing events. Query optimization techniques for deductive databases, like those presented by Nussbaum in [28] can allow the addition of event revisions.

Further work in the bitemporal OEC is suggested herein. We are pursuing an implementation in Java with persistent storage supplied by Objectstore. We intend to use this model to support a Temporal GIS.

Other applications include systems that need to combine reasoning abilities with persistent data storage. Production and rule-based systems can benefit from an event-oriented approach, as they will be able to determine not only courses of action, but the reasons why previous courses of action have been undertaken.

Finally, as a competing model to the timestamping paradigm for temporal databases, the OEC can supply the underlying engine where proposals call for a temporal database.

**Acknowledgements**

We would like to thank the Naval Research Laboratory's Base Program, Program Element No. 0602435N for sponsoring this research.

## References

[1] Langran, Gail. *Time in Geographic Information Systems,* Bristol, PA: Taylor and Francis, 1992.

[2] Basoglu, U. "The Efficient Hierarchical Data Structure for the US Historical Boundary File," *Harvard Papers on Geographical Information Systems,* 4: 1978.

[3] Allen, J. "Maintaining Knowledge about Temporal Intervals," *CACM* November 1983: 832.

[4] Allen, J., "Towards a general theory of action and time," *Artificial Intelligence* V.23 #2, pp. 123-54

[5] Jensen, C., Clifford, J., Elmasri, R., Gadia, S., et al., "A consensus glossary of temporal database concepts," *SIGMOD Record* V. 23, #1

[6] Jensen, C.S.; et al. "The consensus glossary of temporal database concepts-February 1998 version," in [8].

[7] Tansel, Abdullah Uz. *Temporal Databases: Theory, Design and Implementation.* New York: Benjamin/Cummings, 1993.

[8] Etzion, O.; Jajodia, S.; Sripada, S. *Temporal Databases: Research and Practice.* Berlin: Springer-Verlag; 1998.

[9] Käfer, W., Ritter, N., Schöning, H., "Support for Temporal Data by Complex Objects", *Proceedings of the 16th VLDB Conference*, Brisbane, Australia. New York: Springer-Verlag, 1991.

[10] Bertino, E., Ferrari, E. and Guerrini, G. "A Formal Temporal Object-Oriented Data Model," *International Conference on Extending Database Technology,* Avignon, 1996.

[11] Su SYW; Hyun SJ; Chen HHM. "Temporal Association Algebra - A Mathematical Foundation for Processing Object-Oriented Temporal Databases," *IEEE Transactions on Knowledge and Data Engineering* 1998, Vol 10, Iss 3.

[12] Story, P., and Worboys, M. "An object-oriented model of time," *Technical Report TR95-03.* Keele, Staffordshire, UK: Department of Computer Science, Keele University.

[13] Worboys, M. "A Unified Model for Spatial and Temporal Information," *The Computer Journal,* 37: 1, 1994.

[14] Worboys, M. "Object-Oriented Approaches to Geo-Referenced Information," *International Journal of Geographical Information Systems,* 8: 4, 1994.

[15] Worboys, M. "A Generic Model for Spatio-Bitemporal Geographic Information," in [16], pp 25-39.

[16] Egenhofer, M. and Golledge, R. *Spatial and Temporal Reasoning in Geographic Information Systems.* New York: Oxford University Press; 1998.

[17] Kowalski, R., and Sergot, M. "A Logic-Based Calculus of Events," *New Generation Computing,* 4: 1, 1986.

[18] Kowalski, R. "Database Updates in the Event Calculus," *Journal of Logic Programming,* 12, 121-146, 1992.

[19] Sripada, S. *Temporal Reasoning in Deductive Databases.* Doctoral Dissertation, University of London, 1991.

[20] Worboys, M., Hearnshaw, H., and Maguire, D., "Object-Oriented Data Modelling for Spatial Databases", *International Journal of Geographical Information Systems*, Vol. 4, No. 4, 1994.

[21] Peuquet, D. "An Event-Based Spatiotemporal Model for Temporal Analysis of Geographical Data," *International Journal of Geographical Information Systems,* 9: 1, 1995.

[22] Kesim, F., and Sergot, M. "A Logic Programming Framework for Modelling Temporal Objects," *IEEE Transactions on Knowledge and Data Engineering*, 8:5 1996, 724-741.

[23] Hajnicz, Elzbieta. *Time Structures: Formal Description and Algorithmic Representation.* New York: Springer, 1996.

[24] Bose, P, Connan, F, and Rocacher, D "Flexible Querying and Temporal Databases", 1997

[25] Cobb, M., Ph.D. thesis, Tulane University, 1995.

[26] Kowalski, R., and Sadri, F. "The Situational Calculus and Event Calculus Compared," *Proceedings of the International Symposium on Logic Programming*, pp. 539-553, 1994.

[27] Claramunt, C., and Theriault, M. "Managing Time in GIS: An Event-Oriented Approach," *Recent Advances in Temporal Databases,* Clifford, 1995.

[28] Nussbaum, M. *Building a Deductive Database.* Norwood, NJ: Ablex Publishing Corporation; 1992.

# Author Index

# Lecture Notes in Artificial Intelligence (LNAI)

Vol. 2475: J.J. Alpigini, J.F. Peters, A. Skowron, N. Zhong (Eds.), Rough Sets and Current Trends in Computing. Proceedings, 2002. XV, 640 pages. 2002.

Vol. 2479: M. Jarke, J. Koehler, G. Lakemeyer (Eds.), KI 2002: Advances in Artificial Intelligence. Proceedings, 2002. XIII, 327 pages. 2002.

Vol. 2484: P. Adriaans, H. Fernau, M. van Zaanen (Eds.), Grammatical Inference: Algorithms and Applications. Proceedings, 2002. IX, 315 pages. 2002.

Vol. 2499: S.D. Richardson (Ed.), Machine Translation: From Research to Real Users. Proceedings, 2002. XXI, 254 pages. 2002.

Vol. 2504: M.T. Escrig, F. Toledo, E. Golobardes (Eds.), Topics in Artificial Intelligence. Proceedings 2002. XI, 432 pages. 2002.

Vol. 2507: G. Bittencourt, G.L. Ramalho (Eds.), Advances in Artificial Intelligence. Proceedings, 2002. XIII, 418 pages. 2002.

Vol. 2514: M. Baaz, A. Voronkov (Eds.), Logic for Programming, Artificial Intelligence, and Reasoning. Proceedings 2002. XIII, 465 pages. 2002.

Vol. 2522: T. Andreasen, A. Motro, H. Christiansen, H. Legind Larsen (Eds.), Flexible Query Answering. Proceedings 2002. XI, 386 pages. 2002.

Vol. 2527: F.J. Garijo, J.C. Riquelme, M. Toro (Eds.), Advances in Artificial Intelligence – IBERAMIA 2002. Proceedings 2002. XVIII, 955 pages. 2002.

Vol. 2531: J. Padget, O. Shehory, D. Parkes, N. Sadeh, W.E. Walsh (Eds.), Agent-Mediated Electronic Commerce IV. Proceedings, 2002. XVII, 341 pages. 2002.

Vol. 2533: N. Cesa-Bianchi, M. Numao, R. Reischuk (Eds.), Algorithmic Learning Theory. Proceedings 2002. XI, 415 pages. 2002.

Vol. 2541: T. Barkowsky, Mental Representation and Processing of Geographic Knowledge. X, 174 pages. 2002.

Vol. 2543: O. Bartenstein, U. Geske, M. Hannebauer, O. Yoshie (Eds.), Web Knowledge Management and Decision Support. Proceedings, 2001. X, 307 pages. 2003.

Vol. 2554: M. Beetz, Plan-Based Control of Robotic Agents. XI, 191 pages. 2002.

Vol. 2557: B. McKay, J. Slaney (Eds.), AI 2002: Advances in Artificial Intelligence. Proceedings 2002. XV, 730 pages. 2002.

Vol. 2560: S. Goronzy, Robust Adaptation to Non-Native Accents in Automatic Speech Recognition. Proceedings, 2002. XI, 144 pages. 2002.

Vol. 2569: D. Gollmann, G. Karjoth, M. Waidner (Eds.), Computer Security – ESORICS 2002. Proceedings, 2002. XIII, 648 pages. 2002.

Vol. 2577: P. Petta, R. Tolksdorf, F. Zambonelli (Eds.), Engineering Societies in the Agents World III. Proceedings, 2002. X, 285 pages. 2003.

Vol. 2581: J.S. Sichman, F. Bousquet, P. Davidsson (Eds.), Multi-Agent-Based Simulation II. Proceedings, 2002. X, 195 pages. 2003.

Vol. 2583: S. Matwin, C. Sammut (Eds.), Inductive Logic Programming. Proceedings, 2002. X, 351 pages. 2003.

Vol. 2586: M. Klusch, S. Bergamaschi, P. Edwards, P. Petta (Eds.), Intelligent Information Agents. VI, 275 pages. 2003.

Vol. 2592: R. Kowalczyk, J.P. Müller, H. Tianfield, R. Unland (Eds.), Agent Technologies, Infrastructures, Tools, and Applications for E-Services. Proceedings, 2002. XVII, 371 pages. 2003.

Vol. 2600: S. Mendelson, A.J. Smola, Advanced Lectures on Machine Learning. Proceedings, 2002. IX, 259 pages. 2003.

Vol. 2627: B. O'Sullivan (Ed.), Recent Advances in Constraints. Proceedings, 2002. X, 201 pages. 2003.

Vol. 2631: R. Falcone, S. Barber, L. Korba, M. Singh (Eds.), Trust, Reputation, and Security: Theories and Practice. Proceedings, 2002. X, 235 pages. 2003.

Vol. 2636: E. Alonso, D, Kudenko, D. Kazakov (Eds.), Adaptive Agents and Multi-Agent Systems. XIV, 323 pages. 2003.

Vol. 2637: K.-Y. Whang, J. Jeon, K. Shim, J. Srivastava (Eds.), Advances in Knowledge Discovery and Data Mining. Proceedings, 2003. XVIII, 610 pages. 2003.

Vol. 2639: G. Wang, Q. Liu, Y. Yao, A. Skowron (Eds.), Rough Sets, Fuzzy Sets, Data Mining, and Granular Computing. Proceedings, 2003. XVII, 741 pages. 2003.

Vol. 2645: M.A. Wimmer (Ed.), Knowledge Management in Electronic Government. Proceedings, 2003. XI, 320 pages. 2003.

Vol. 2650: M.-P. Huget (Ed.), Communication in Multiagent Systems. VIII, 323 pages. 2003.

Vol. 2663: E. Menasalvas, J. Segovia, P.S. Szczepaniak (Eds.), Advances in Web Intelligence. Proceedings, 2003. XII, 350 pages. 2003.

Vol. 2671: Y. Xiang, B. Chaib-draa (Eds.), Advances in Artificial Intelligence. Proceedings, 2003. XIV, 642 pages. 2003.

Vol. 2680: P. Blackburn, C. Ghidini, R.M. Turner, F. Giunchiglia (Eds.), Modeling and Using Context. Proceedings, 2003. XII, 525 pages. 2003.

Vol. 2685: C. Freksa, W. Brauer, C. Habel, K.F. Wender (Eds.), Spatial Cognition III. X, 415 pages. 2003.

Vol. 2689: K.D. Ashley, D.G. Bridge (Eds.), Case-Based Reasoning Research and Development. Proceedings, 2003. XV, 734 pages. 2003.

Vol. 2691: V. Mařík, J. Müller, M. Pěchouček (Eds.), Multi-Agent Systems and Applications III. Proceedings, 2003. XIV, 660 pages. 2003.

Vol. 2702: P. Brusilovsky, A. Corbett, F. de Rosis (Eds.), User Modeling 2003. Proceedings, 2003. XIV, 436 pages. 2003.

Vol. 2718: P. W. H. Chung, C. Hinde, M. Ali (Eds.), Developments in Applied Artificial Intelligence. Proceedings, 2003. XIV, 817 pages. 2003.

Vol. 2721: N.J. Mamede, J. Baptista, I. Trancoso, M. das Graças Volpe Nunes (Eds.), Computational Processing of the Portuguese Language. Proceedings, 2003. XIV, 268 pages. 2003.

# Lecture Notes in Computer Science

Vol. 2660: P.M.A. Sloot, D. Abramson, A.V. Bogdanov, J.J. Dongarra, A.Y. Zomaya, Y.E. Gorbachev (Eds.), Computational Science – ICCS 2003. Proceedings, Part IV. 2003. LVI, 1161 pages. 2003.

Vol. 2663: E. Menasalvas, J. Segovia, P.S. Szczepaniak (Eds.), Advances in Web Intelligence. Proceedings, 2003. XII, 350 pages. 2003. (Subseries LNAI).

Vol. 2665: H. Chen, R. Miranda, D.D. Zeng, C. Demchak, J. Schroeder, T. Madhusudan (Eds.), Intelligence and Security Informatics. Proceedings, 2003. XIV, 392 pages. 2003.

Vol. 2667: V. Kumar, M.L. Gavrilova, C.J.K. Tan, P. L'Ecuyer (Eds.), Computational Science and Its Applications – ICCSA 2003. Proceedings, Part I. 2003. XXXIV, 1060 pages. 2003.

Vol. 2668: V. Kumar, M.L. Gavrilova, C.J.K. Tan, P. L'Ecuyer (Eds.), Computational Science and Its Applications – ICCSA 2003. Proceedings, Part II. 2003. XXXIV, 942 pages. 2003.

Vol. 2669: V. Kumar, M.L. Gavrilova, C.J.K. Tan, P. L'Ecuyer (Eds.), Computational Science and Its Applications – ICCSA 2003. Proceedings, Part III. 2003. XXXIV, 948 pages. 2003.

Vol. 2670: R. Peña, T. Arts (Eds.), Implementation of Functional Languages. Proceedings, 2002. X, 249 pages. 2003.

Vol. 2671: Y. Xiang, B. Chaib-draa (Eds.), Advances in Artificial Intelligence. Proceedings, 2003. XIV, 642 pages. 2003. (Subseries LNAI).

Vol. 2672: M. Endler, D. Schmidt (Eds.), Middleware 2003. Proceedings, 2003. XIII, 513 pages. 2003.

Vol. 2673: N. Ayache, H. Delingette (Eds.), Surgery Simulation and Soft Tissue Modeling. Proceedings, 2003. XII, 386 pages. 2003.

Vol. 2674: I.E. Magnin, J. Montagnat, P. Clarysse, J. Nenonen, T. Katila (Eds.), Functional Imaging and Modeling of the Heart. Proceedings, 2003. XI, 308 pages. 2003.

Vol. 2675: M. Marchesi, G. Succi (Eds.), Extreme Programming and Agile Processes in Software Engineering. Proceedings, 2003. XV, 464 pages. 2003.

Vol. 2676: R. Baeza-Yates, E. Chávez, M. Crochemore (Eds.), Combinatorial Pattern Matching. Proceedings, 2003. XI, 403 pages. 2003.

Vol. 2678: W. van der Aalst, A. ter Hofstede, M. Weske (Eds.), Business Process Management. Proceedings, 2003. XI, 391 pages. 2003.

Vol. 2679: W. van der Aalst, E. Best (Eds.), Applications and Theory of Petri Nets 2003. Proceedings, 2003. XI, 508 pages. 2003.

Vol. 2680: P. Blackburn, C. Ghidini, R.M. Turner, F. Giunchiglia (Eds.), Modeling and Using Context. Proceedings, 2003. XII, 525 pages. 2003. (Subseries LNAI).

Vol. 2681: J. Eder, M. Missikoff (Eds.), Advanced Information Systems Engineering. Proceedings, 2003. XV, 740 pages. 2003.

Vol. 2685: C. Freksa, W. Brauer, C. Habel, K.F. Wender (Eds.), Spatial Cognition III. X, 415 pages. 2003. (Subseries LNAI).

Vol. 2686: J. Mira, J.R. Álvarez (Eds.), Computational Methods in Neural Modeling. Proceedings, Part I. 2003. XXVII, 764 pages. 2003.

Vol. 2687: J. Mira, J.R. Álvarez (Eds.), Artificial Neural Nets Problem Solving Methods. Proceedings, Part II. 2003. XXVII, 820 pages. 2003.

Vol. 2688: J. Kittler, M.S. Nixon (Eds.), Audio- and Video-Based Biometric Person Authentication. Proceedings, 2003. XVII, 978 pages. 2003.

Vol. 2689: K.D. Ashley, D.G. Bridge (Eds.), Case-Based Reasoning Research and Development. Proceedings, 2003. XV, 734 pages. 2003. (Subseries LNAI).

Vol. 2691: V. Mařík, J. Müller, M. Pěchouček (Eds.), Multi-Agent Systems and Applications III. Proceedings, 2003. XIV, 660 pages. 2003. (Subseries LNAI).

Vol. 2692: P. Nixon, S. Terzis (Eds.), Trust Management. Proceedings, 2003. X, 349 pages. 2003.

Vol. 2694: R. Cousot (Ed.), Static Analysis. Proceedings, 2003. XIV, 505 pages. 2003.

Vol. 2695: L.D. Griffin, M. Lillholm (Eds.), Scale Space Methods in Computer Vision. Proceedings, 2003. XII, 816 pages. 2003.

Vol. 2701: M. Hofmann (Ed.), Typed Lambda Calculi and Applications. Proceedings, 2003. VIII, 317 pages. 2003.

Vol. 2702: P. Brusilovsky, A. Corbett, F. de Rosis (Eds.), User Modeling 2003. Proceedings, 2003. XIV, 436 pages. 2003. (Subseries LNAI).

Vol. 2704: S.-T. Huang, T. Herman (Eds.), Self-Stabilizing Systems. Proceedings, 2003. X, 215 pages. 2003.

Vol. 2706: R. Nieuwenhuis (Ed.), Rewriting Techniques and Applications. Proceedings, 2003. XI, 515 pages. 2003.

Vol. 2707: K. Jeffay, I. Stoica, K. Wehrle (Eds.), Quality of Service – IWQoS 2003. Proceedings, 2003. XI, 517 pages. 2003.

Vol. 2709: T. Windeatt, F. Roli (Eds.), Multiple Classifier Systems. Proceedings, 2003. X, 406 pages. 2003.

Vol. 2710: Z. Ésik, Z, Fülöp (Eds.), Developments in Language Theory. Proceedings, 2003. XI, 437 pages. 2003.

Vol. 2713: C.-W. Chung, C.-K. Kim, W. Kim, T.-W. Ling, K.-H. Song (Eds.), Web and Communication Technologies and Internet-Related Social Issues – HSI 2003. Proceedings, 2003. XXII, 773 pages. 2003.

Vol. 2714: O. Kaynak, E. Alpaydin, E. Oja, L. Xu (Eds.), Artificial Neural Networks and Neural Information Processing – ICANN/ICONIP 2003. Proceedings, 2003. XXII, 1188 pages. 2003.

Vol. 2716: M.J. Voss (Ed.), OpenMP Shared Memory Parallel Programming. Proceedings, 2003. VIII, 271 pages. 2003.

Vol. 2718: P. W. H. Chung, C. Hinde, M. Ali (Eds.), Developments in Applied Artificial Intelligence. Proceedings, 2003. XIV, 817 pages. 2003. (Subseries LNAI).

Vol. 2721: N.J. Mamede, J. Baptista, I. Trancoso, M. das Graças Volpe Nunes (Eds.), Computational Processing of the Portuguese Language. Proceedings, 2003. XIV, 268 pages. 2003. (Subseries LNAI).